The Editor

JEFFREY N. Cox is Professor of English and of Comparative Literature and Humanities and Associate Vice Chancellor for Faculty Affairs at the University of Colorado at Boulder. He is the author of *Poetry and Politics in the Cockney School: Shelley, Keats, Hunt, and Their Circle* and *In the Shadows of Romance: Romantic Tragic Drama in Germany, England, and France*. His edited books include *The Broadview Anthology of Romantic Drama* (co-edited with Michael Gamer), *Slavery, Abolition, and Emancipation in the British Romantic Period*, Volume 5: *The Drama, New Historical Literary Study* (co-edited with Larry Reynolds), and *Seven Gothic Dramas, 1789–1825*.

W. W. NORTON & COMPANY, INC.
Also Publishes

A NORTON CRITICAL EDITION

KEATS'S POETRY
AND PROSE

AUTHORITATIVE TEXTS
CRITICISM

Selected and Edited by

JEFFREY N. COX
UNIVERSITY OF COLORADO AT BOULDER

W • W • **NORTON & COMPANY** • New York • London

W. W. Norton & Company has been independent since its founding in 1923, when William Warder Norton and Mary D. Herter Norton first published lectures delivered at the People's Institute, the adult education division of New York City's Cooper Union. The Nortons soon expanded their program beyond the Institute, publishing books by celebrated academics from America and abroad. By mid-century, the two major pillars of Norton's publishing program—trade books and college texts—were firmly established. In the 1950s, the Norton family transferred control of the company to its employees, and today—with a staff of four hundred and a comparable number of trade, college, and professional titles published each year—W. W. Norton & Company stands as the largest and oldest publishing house owned wholly by its employees.

The text of this book is composed in Fairfield Medium
with the display set in Bernhard Modern.
Book design by Antonina Krass.
Composition by Binghamton Valley Composition.
Manufacturing by the Courier Companies—Westford division.
Production manager: Benjamin Reynolds.

Library of Congress Cataloging-in-Publication Data

Keats's poetry and prose : authoritative texts, criticism / selected and edited by
Jeffrey N. Cox. — 1st ed.
p. cm.— (A Norton critical edition)
Includes bibliographical references.

ISBN: 978-0-393-92491-6 (pbk.)

1. Keats, John, 1795–1821—Criticism, Textual.   2. English literature—Criticism,
Textual.   I. Cox, Jeffrey N.
PR4837.K43 2009
821'.7—dc22

2008023910

W. W. Norton & Company, Inc., 500 Fifth Avenue,
New York, NY 10110-0017
wwnorton.com

W. W. Norton & Company Ltd., Castle House,
75/76 Wells Street, London W1T 3QT

2 3 4 5 6 7 8 9 0

Contents

The Texts of Keats's Poetry and Prose

Criticism

Introduction

John Keats is one of the most beloved poets in the English language. His "Ode to a Nightingale" and "Ode on a Grecian Urn" are among the rather small body of poems known to almost everyone. His engaging letters with their rapid movement of thought and sharp insights perhaps receive more attention than any other poet's correspondence. His short life has been the subject of a series of brilliant biographies, as the story of the young poetic genius cut down at an early age and of the lover unable to act upon his love has continued to move even readers not familiar with most of his verse. He has in many ways become the model of the poet, or at least the "romantic" poet: tragically young, intensely introspective, brooding on love and death, writing snatches of verse as he listens, alone, to the song of the nightingale.

This is not the Keats that his contemporaries would have recognized, nor the Keats that is found within recent criticism of his poetry. While we most often admire his odes and other short lyrics, he was known at the time as the poet of the long romance, *Endymion*, and he provided pride of place to his narrative poems in his final volume, *Lamia, Isabella, The Eve of St. Agnes, and Other Poems*, where the odes are simply other poems. Far from being a poet of solitude and isolation, he was fully engaged in the poetic and political debates of his day, from his early "On Peace" and "To Lord Byron" to his late *Jealousies*, where he satirizes both the Prince Regent and contemporary poets such as Southey. He was firmly identified with the circle of radical poets and intellectuals that gathered in London around Leigh Hunt and that included the Shelleys, William Hazlitt, Charles Lamb, William Godwin, John Hamilton Reynolds, Horace Smith, the painter Robert Benjamin Haydon, and the musician Vincent Novello. This was the circle that came to be attacked as the "Cockney School," vilified for its poetics, its politics, its eroticism, and its religious views. As Z., the pseudonym of John Lockhart writing in the conservative *Blackwood's Edinburgh Journal*, would say in one of the notorious "Cockney School" attacks, "Keats belongs to the Cockney School of Politics, as well as the Cockney School of Poetry."

Recent scholarship, at least since Jerome McGann's "Keats and the Historical Method in Literary Criticism" (1979) and the 1986 special issue of *Studies in Romanticism* edited by Susan Wolfson, has sought to place Keats back into the arenas of aesthetic, cultural, social, and political debate that surrounded him. We have come to understand Keats's verse more fully within the contexts provided by the new historicism, by feminist and ecological studies, by the examination of empire and global culture. The critical essays included in this volume, while in the first instance providing strong readings of particular poems, help re-engage Keats's poetry with the world he inherited and helped make, showing how he experimented with poetry and thought in ways that still matter. These essays demonstrate the range and strength of contemporary scholarship on Keats.

This Norton Critical Edition seeks to return Keats to his cultural moment by tracking his emergence as a public poet. The edition is anchored by the work Keats offered to the public as he sought to establish himself as a new poetic voice in post-Napoleonic England. To that end, the three volumes published by Keats in his lifetime—*Poems* of 1817, *Endymion* of 1818, and *Lamia, Isabella, the Eve of St. Agnes, and Other Poems* of 1820—are presented in their entirety, with the volumes' poems placed in the order of their publication rather than of their composition. This enables the reader to encounter Keats's poetry as he intended the public to experience it. In order for the reader to see how these volumes arise out of Keats's lived life, out of his work on other poems, and out of the context provided by reviews of his work, other material is arranged in relation to these three volumes, with other material published by Keats and reviews of his work being arranged by their publication date and with unpublished poems and letters being arranged by date of composition. As explained more fully in "A Note on the Text," Keats's poetry has been edited from first print versions (with attention to the manuscript tradition behind those printings), so that the reader can see how his poetry entered into the public domain, but it is arranged by composition date, so that the reader can more easily study Keats's process of selection as he presents himself to the public during his lifetime. One goal of this Norton Critical Edition is to present as much of Keats's poetry as possible, outside the collaboration on the play, *Otho the Great*, with a good selection of his letters; another is to present various avenues through which to explore Keats's work.

Each of Keats's printed volumes is preceded by a headnote that describes the composition, publication, and structure of the volume. For the 1820 volume, additional headnotes have been provided for the most studied poems, and headnotes have been provided for some other key poems. For other poems, the first note provides composition and publication information. While I have not been able to present all the textual research that lies behind the presentation of these poems, these notes do provide information about the first publication of the poem and about relevant manuscripts lying behind that publication. In a few cases (i.e., "La Belle Dame Sans Merci"), two differing versions have been provided in their entirety, enabling the student to explore both the complexity of the individual poems and the processes by which editorial decisions about poems are made. Headnotes and first notes provide relevant source information, important contexts, and, in some cases, suggestions for critical readings. Annotations of the poems provide the student with the information necessary to appreciate and to understand these poems, given the fact that Keats was deeply engaged with literary tradition and with contemporary culture: literary and historical allusions and sources are indicated, unusual words and terms are glossed, and relevant material from other writings by Keats and his circle are provided; in some cases, where the version of the poem presented differs from those most likely familiar to the scholar, variants from manuscript versions are provided. The letters have received heavier annotation as the range of historical and personal reference is particularly dense. Where I have adopted information from another editor—Rollins, Allott, or Cook—I have so indicated, but I have not provided page numbers, as the reader can locate the note at the same point in another edition. Abbreviations in the notes refer to the list of abbreviations at the front of the edition. A chronology of Keats's life appears at the back of the volume, along with a selected bibliography of scholarship on Keats.

While Keats's poetry was attacked when it first appeared, it rapidly gained adherents and has long been the subject of distinguished scholarship and criticism. Recent criticism has shown how vital Keats's poetry and the scholarly tradition that has grown up around it still are. This Norton Critical Edition does not seek to present a particular "new Keats," but instead hopes to provide students and scholars the opportunity to experience Keats anew for themselves.

A Note on the Text

Keats has been exceptionally well served by the collectors and editors of his poetry and letters, from friends such as Charles Armitage Brown and Richard Woodhouse through Richard Monckton Milnes and Harry Buxton Forman to H. W. Garrod, Hyder Edward Rollins, Miriam Allott, and Jack Stillinger. Rollins's edition of Keats's letters (as well as his work on the Keats circle) is a model of its kind, and his accomplishments in editing and annotating Keats's correspondence have been supplemented by the work of Robert Gittings and Grant Scott. Stillinger's edition of the poetry, together with his *The Text of Keats's Poems*, is a monumental work of scholarship, providing a complete account of Keats's texts and their transmission; notwithstanding the fact that Stillinger's own ideas on editing have evolved, his work is the starting point for any modern edition of Keats's poetry. Editing Keats is a particularly precarious act of balancing on the shoulders of giants. Still, I have departed from these distinguished scholars on a number of small issues as I have re-edited Keats's poems and letters from their print and holograph or transcript sources (with the transcripts by Keats's friends being particularly important to our understanding of his texts).

The Poems

Stillinger has provided us with the best possible re-creation of Keats's final intentions for his poetry; following in most cases the printed versions of poems published in Keats's lifetime, he works through the holograph and transcript histories to rediscover what is the latest, authoritative version of the unpublished work. My goal has been different: to present Keats as he entered into the public realm. I might simply, then, have provided Keats's poetry in its first print version and in the order of its publication. While I have sympathies with such an approach, I have in fact adopted a hybridized approach to presenting Keats's texts. I have taken the first print editions as my copytext. For those poems published in Keats's lifetime, I have accepted the print versions as they appeared (with the few exceptions indicated below) as indicating how Keats wanted to see his poems before the public. With the three volumes that Keats saw into print, this is the practice of other editors, but I have also, for example, trusted versions of Keats's poems that appeared during his lifetime in the *Examiner*, edited by his close friend Leigh Hunt, where other editors have not. For those poems published after Keats's death, I felt another procedure was called for. First print versions obviously provide the Keats that came to be known to the general public, rather than the Keats that existed in a private manuscript or for his close circle of readers, but the errors that have entered into these versions of the poems are of a nature that would hinder the reading and appreciation of Keats's poetry. As a result, for the posthumous verse, I have begun with the first print edition, but I have worked back along the manuscript line leading to that print version, as described by Stillinger in *The Text of Keats's Poems*, to correct obvious errors that arose in transmission. That does not mean that I have necessarily returned to Keats's latest version of a poem, if that version was not the ultimate source of the printed text; I have corrected the first print edition against the manuscript line behind it, and that sometimes leads back to a Keats holograph and sometimes to a transcription by someone working within his circle: it does not always lead to a text that editors would see as embodying earliest or latest authorial intentions. The headnote or first note to each poem indicates the sources of my text. Where I have adopted a substantive print reading in opposition to a key Keats holograph or to a reading established by Stillinger, and thus most familiar to students and scholars of Keats, I have indicated the alternative reading in a note when I believe it would be useful to the student; similarly, where I have rejected a substantive reading in the first print text, I have in most cases provided that reading. In a few cases, such as "La Belle Dame Sans Merci," where scholars have made strong arguments for rival texts, I have included two versions. My hope is that the reader will be able to see in what form Keats's poetry entered the public realm but also understand how the posthumous verse arose out of the extant manuscripts, holographs and transcriptions. I should note that while I adopt a model of editing that differs from that of Stillinger, I still could not have done this edition without the benefit of the work he has done.

The following decisions have been made silently:

1. Obvious printer's errors have been corrected.

2. In the case of punctuation, erratic in Keats's manuscripts, I have begun with the print texts, accepting most punctuation of those poems printed in Keats's lifetime. In the case of posthumous poems, I have begun with the print version and checked it against the manuscript tradition leading to that version; I have substituted punctuation from a relevant manuscript when it makes a passage clearer or when it contributes to rhetorical expressiveness. Except in the case of obvious errors, all punctuation originates in a print text or a manuscript.

3. Keats's capitalization in his manuscripts does not follow a clear pattern, though he at times seems to conform to conventions of his day that would have used capitalization for rhetorical emphasis. I have accepted all capitalizations in versions of his poems printed during his lifetime (including initial words capitalized in their entirety). For posthumous poems, I have accepted capitalizations in print texts if they coincide with one of the main manuscripts behind that printed version. I have dropped capitals that exist only in a print text or in a manuscript.

4. I have adopted the pattern of lineation from the print texts except in cases where manuscript versions provide indentation patterns that make a poem easier to read. Print titles have also been kept, with the first-line titles used in other editions included in the table of contents and index.

5. In a few cases, Keats adopted the contemporary practice of placing quotation marks before every line of a long speech (or quoted passage in the letters). I have not followed this practice in the letters.

I have also not presented the poetry in either strict compositional order or simply by date of publication. This Norton Critical Edition is organized, first, around the three volumes that Keats published during his life as he sought to establish himself as a poet; additional print materials during his life—other poems printed during Keats's lifetime, his review of Kean's acting, reviews of Keats's poems—are arranged by their date of publication, but posthumous works and Keats's letters are ordered by their date of composition (except that *The Fall of Hyperion* has been placed after the print version of *Hyperion*). My hope is that the reader can thus understand how Keats created himself as a poet on the literary scene of post-Napoleonic England as the work he published is embedded within poems he chose not to publish, letters that reveal what he was doing or thinking about as he wrote his verses, and reviews that might have influenced his path as a writer.

The Letters

The letters are edited from Keats's holographs or from transcripts where no holograph is extant. Editing Keats's letters presented one particular problem. As noted above, Rollins did a superb job in editing Keats's letters, and I have leaned heavily, for example, on his annotations. However, in transcribing the letters anew, I became convinced that Rollins read marks at the end of grammatical units, which might be dashes, commas, or periods, consistently as dashes, even when another interpretation of the mark was possible; this plethora of dashes has produced the forward rushing, almost stream-of-consciousness style we are familiar with, that gives us a sense of immediacy, intimacy, and sincerity—that is, that gives us sense of a conventional "romantic" writer. Grant Scott, in his recent edition of selected letters from Keats (the introduction from which is included in this Norton Critical Edition, below, pp. 555–63), has decided to modernize or regularize Keats's letters so as to make them more accessible to the student. There is a great appeal in this approach, but I have, again, adopted a middle ground.

I have re-edited the letters from their manuscripts (though I have found few places to quibble with Rollins in the transcription of words). I have kept Keats's erratic spelling (which is often suggestive) except where the error is trivial or obscures the sense; one does not want to overcorrect the spelling and thus lose an example of Keats's punning or other word play. I have sought to follow his punctuation, but in the case of the marks that end what could be full sentences I have relied upon context to determine whether to read this as a dash or a period: the most obvious case is that I have used a period where the next word is capitalized to begin a new sentence. Keats also seems to me to use the end of lines or pages as if they supplied hard punctuation; quotation marks at times also seem to supply a close to a sentence. In these cases, I have supplied a period. In many cases where a Keats holograph and a transcript both exist, the transcript confirms that a nineteenth-century reader of these letters followed a similar practice for locating hard punctuation in the letters. Other editions have also tended to ignore page breaks unless there is an obvious new paragraph on the new page, but Keats often seems to change thought as he begins a new page; in those cases, I have supplied a paragraph break.

Abbreviations

1848	*Life, Letters, and Literary Remains, of John Keats*, ed. Richard Monckton Milnes, 2 vols. (London: E. Moxon, 1848)
1867	*Life and Letters of John Keats*, ed. Richard Monckton Milnes, (London: E. Moxon, 1867)
1876	*The Poetical Works of John Keats*, ed. Lord Houghton [R. M. Milnes] (London: Bell, 1876)
Allott	*The Poems of John Keats*, ed. Miriam Allott (Harlow: Longman, 1970)
ALS	Autograph Letter, Signed
Aske	Martin Aske, *Keats and Hellenism: An Essay* (Cambridge: Cambridge University Press, 1985)
Barnard	John Barnard, *John Keats* (Cambridge: Cambridge University Press, 1987)
Bate	Walter Jackson Bate, *John Keats* (Cambridge, MA: Harvard University Press, 1963)
Bennett	Andrew Bennett, *Keats, Narrative and Audience: The Posthumous Life of Writing* (Cambridge: Cambridge University Press, 1994)
Bush	Douglas Bush, *Selected Poems and Letters of John Keats* (Boston: Houghton Mifflin, 1959)
Colvin	Sidney Colvin, *John Keats: His Life and Poetry, His Friends, Critics, and After-Fame* (London: Macmillan, 1917)
Cook	*John Keats*, ed. Elizabeth Cook (New York and Oxford: Oxford University Press, 1990)
Cox	Jeffrey N. Cox, *Poetry and Politics in the Cockney School: Keats, Shelley, Hunt and their Circle* (Cambridge: Cambridge University Press, 1998)
de Selincourt	*The Poems: John Keats*, ed. E. de Selincourt (1905; rev. ed., London: Methuen, 1926)
Dickstein	Morris Dickstein, *Keats and His Poetry: A Study in Development.* (Chicago: University of Chicago Press, 1971)
E	Woodhouse's annotated copy of *Endymion*, held at the Berg Collection of English and American Literature, The New York Public Library, Astor, Lenox and Tilden Foundations; *The Manuscripts of the Younger Romantics: John Keats*, vol. 3: *Endymion (1818): A Facsimile of Richard Woodhouse's Annotated Copy in the Berg Collection*, ed. Jack Stillinger (New York and London: Garland Publishing, 1985).
ELH	*English Literary History*
Forman 1883	*The Poetical Works and Other Writings of John Keats*, ed. H. Buxton Forman, 4 vols. (London: Reeves and Turner, 1883)

Forman 1884   *The Poetical Works of John Keats Given from His Own Editions and Other Authentic Sources and Collated with Many Manuscripts*, ed. H. Buxton Forman (London: Reeves and Turner, 1884)

Forman 1898   *The Poetical Works and Other Writings of John Keats*, ed. H. Buxton Forman, 6th ed. (London: Reeves and Turner, 1898)

Forman 1901   *The Complete Works of John Keats*, ed. H. Buxton Forman, 5 vols. (Glasgow: Gowers & Gray, 1901)

Forman 1906   *Poetical Works of John Keats*, Oxford Standard Authors Edition, ed. H. Buxton Forman (Oxford: Oxford University Press, 1906)

Garrod   *Poetical Works of John Keats*. Ed. H. W. Garrod. 2nd ed. (Oxford: Oxford University Press, 1958)

Gillham   *John Keats: Poems of 1820 and The Fall of Hyperion*, ed. D. G. Gillham (London: Collins Publishers, 1969)

Gittings   Robert Gittings, *John Keats* (Boston: Little, Brown and Co., 1968)

Gittings 1954   Robert Gittings, *John Keats: The Living Year* (London: Heineman, 1954)

Gittings, *Letters*   *The Letters of John Keats*, ed. Robert Gittings (Oxford: Oxford University Press, 1970)

Hampstead Keats   *The Poetical Works and Other Writings of John Keats*. The Hampstead Keats. Ed. H. Buxton Forman; rev. Maurice Buxton Forman. 8 vols. New York: Charles Scribner's Sons, 1938–39. Rpt. New York: Phaeton Press, 1970.

HBF   Harry Buxton Forman

Haydon, *Diary*   *The Diary of Benjamin Robert Haydon*, ed. Willard Bissell Pope, 5 vols. (Cambridge, MA: Harvard University Press, 1960–63)

Jack   Ian Jack, *Keats and the Mirror of Art* (Oxford: Clarendon Press, 1967)

Jeffrey transcript   Transcripts by John Jeffrey of letters of John Keats, Harvard MS Keats 3.9

JKPMH   *John Keats: Poetry Manuscripts at Harvard: A Facsimile Edition*, ed. Jack Stillinger (Cambridge: Harvard University Press, 1990)

KC   *The Keats Circle: Letters and Papers 1816–1878*, ed. Hyder Edward Rollins, 2 vols. (Cambridge: Harvard University Press, 1948)

KCH   *Keats: The Critical Heritage*, ed. G. M. Matthews (New York: Barnes and Noble, 1971)

KH   *Keats and History*, ed. Nicholas Roe (Cambridge: Cambridge University Press, 1994)

KSJ   *Keats-Shelley Journal*

Kucich   Greg Kucich, *Keats, Shelley, and Romantic Spenserianism*. University Park: Pennsylvania State University Press, 1991

L   *The Letters of John Keats, 1814–1821*, ed. Hyder E. Rollins, 2 vols. (Cambridge: Harvard University Press, 1958)

Lemprière	John Lemprière, *Classical Dictionary* (1788)
Levinson	Marjorie Levinson, *Keats's Life of Allegory: The Origins of a Style* (New York: Basil Blackwell, 1988)
LMA	London Metropolitan Archives, City of London
Lowell	Amy Lowell, *John Keats*, 2 vols. (Boston: Houghton Mifflin, 1925)
McGann	Jerome J. McGann, "Keats and the Historical Method in Literary Criticism" (1979), reprinted in *The Beauty of Inflections: Literary Investigations in Historical Method & Theory* (Oxford: Clarendon Press, 1985), pp. 9–65
Motion	Andrew Motion, *Keats* (New York: Farrar, Straus and Giroux, 1997)
MYR: JK	*The Manuscripts of the Younger Romantics: John Keats*, ed. Jack Stillinger; General Editor Donald H. Reiman, 7 vols. (New York: Garland Press, 1985–88): vol. 1: *Poems 1817: A Facsimile of Woodhouse's Annotated Copy*; vol. 2: *Endymion: A Facsimile of the Revised Holograph Manuscript*; vol. 3: *Endymion (1818): A Facsimile of Woodhouse's Annotated Copy*; vol. 4: *Poems, Transcripts, Letters, Etc.: Facsimiles of Woodhouse's Scrapbook Materials in the Pierpont Morgan Library*; vol. 5: *Manuscript Poems in the British Library: Facsimiles of the "Hyperion" Holograph and George Keats's Notebook of Holographs and Transcripts*; vol. 6: *The Woodhouse Poetry Transcripts at Harvard: A Facsimile of the W² Notebook, with Description and Contents of the W¹ Notebook*; vol. 7: *The Charles Brown Poetry Transcripts at Harvard: Facsimiles including the Fair Copy of Otho the Great*
N&Q	*Notes and Queries*
OED	*Oxford English Dictionary*
PDSN	*Plymouth, Devonport, and Stonehouse News*
PDWJ	*The Plymouth and Devonport Weekly Journal*
PMLA	*Publications of the Modern Language Association*
Recollections	Charles Cowden Clarke and Mary Cowden Clarke, *Recollections of Writers* (London: Low, Marston, Searle & Rivington; New York: Charles Scribner's Sons, 1878)
Ricks	Christopher Ricks, *Keats and Embarrassment* (London: Oxford University Press, 1976)
Roe	Nicholas Roe, *John Keats and the Culture of Dissent* (Oxford: Clarendon Press, 1997)
Roe, *Fiery Heart*	Nicholas Roe, *Fiery Heart: The First Life of Leigh Hunt* (London: Pimlico, 2005)
SEL	*Studies in English Literature*
Shelley's Poetry and Prose	*Shelley's Poetry and Prose*, 2nd ed., ed. Donald H. Reiman and Neil Fraistat (New York: Norton, 2002)
SiR	*Studies in Romanticism*
Sperry	Stuart M. Sperry, *Keats the Poet* (Princeton: Princeton University Press, 1973)
Stillinger	*The Poems of John Keats*, ed. Jack Stillinger (Cambridge: Harvard University Press, 1978)

Stillinger 1971	Jack Stillinger, *"The Hoodwinking of Madeline" and Other Essays on Keats's Poems* (Urbana: University of Illinois Press, 1971)
Stillinger 1974	Jack Stillinger, *The Texts of Keats's Poems* (Cambridge: Harvard University Press, 1974)
SWLH	*The Selected Works of Leigh Hunt*, General Editors: Robert Morrison and Michael Eberle-Sinatra; Volume Editors: Jeffrey N. Cox, Greg Kucich, Charles Mahoney, and John Strachan, 6 vols. (London: Pickering and Chatto, 2003)
TLS	*Times Literary Supplement*
W¹	Commonplace book of transcripts of poems, mainly by Keats, compiled by Richard Woodhouse; Harvard MS Keats 3.1
W²	Commonplace book of transcripts of poems and other texts, mainly by Keats, compiled by Richard Woodhouse; Harvard MS Keats 3.2
W³	Scrapbook of poetry and letter manuscripts and transcripts of poems and other texts, mainly by Keats, compiled by Richard Woodhouse; Pierpont Morgan Library manuscript MA 215
Watkins	Daniel P. Watkins, *Keats's Poetry and the Politics of the Imagination* (Madison, N.J.: Fairleigh Dickinson University Press, 1989)
Wolfson	Susan Wolfson, *The Questioning Presence: Wordsworth, Keats, and the Interrogative Mode in Romantic Poetry* (Ithaca: Cornell University Press, 1986)
Woodhouse 1817	Richard Woodhouse's interleaved and annotated copy of Keats's *Poems* (1817); Huntington Library MS 151852
Woodhouse's letter-book	Commonplace book of transcripts of letters of Keats and others, compiled by Richard Woodhouse; Harvard MS Keats 3.3
Works	William Hazlitt, *The Complete Works of William Hazlitt*, ed. P. P. Howe, 21 vols. (London: J. M. Dent and Sons, 1930–34)

Acknowledgments

This edition draws upon the work of many hands. It owes a debt to the line of excellent editors of Keats, best represented in our day by Jack Stillinger, who has been generous with his help. Neil Fraistat, the co-editor of the Norton Critical Edition of Shelley, provided key advice at crucial moments and much-appreciated support throughout the project. I have relied upon the work of the fine scholars represented in the bibliography, consulted with a large number of colleagues, and received help from a wide variety of romanticists and other humanists whose number might be represented by such colleagues and friends as Alan Bewell, Christopher Braider, Julie Carlson, Margaret Ezell, Tim Fulford, Michael Gamer, Marilyn Gaull, Jill Heydt-Stevenson, Jennifer Jones, Theresa Kelley, Peter Knox, Greg Kucich, Beth Lau, Mark Lussier, Michael Macovski, Tilar Mazzeo, Anne Mellor, Jeffrey Robinson, Nick Roe, Chuck Rzepka, Charles Snodgrass, John Stevenson, Daniel White, and Paul Youngquist. I have learned a great deal from the work of Susan Wolfson, but her edition of Keats appeared too late in my project for me to draw upon it. I very much appreciate the great assistance I received from Carol Bemis and Rivka Genesen at Norton. At the University of Colorado, I want to thank Paula Anderson and Melanie Evans for their help, and I had the assistance of an incredible group of graduate students. Marc Cameron, Emily Fawcett, Jennifer Jahner, Peter Remien, and Katarzyna Rutkowski helped with proofreading. Scott Hagele, John Leffel, and Michele Speitz provided essential aid in a number of different ways. I owe a particular debt of gratitude to Terry Robinson and Dana Van Kooy, who have been involved at every stage of this project and whose cheerful assistance has helped keep me sane. Many thanks to the distinguished scholars whose essays are among the critical selections at the back of this book; thanks as well to their original publishers or other copyright holders (as indicated in the source note to each essay) for permission to publish their work.

This edition is based upon a re-examination of the manuscripts, transcripts, and first print appearances of Keats's poems and letters. Libraries, collections, and other institutions who have supplied either assistance or permission to draw upon their materials include Harvard's Houghton Library; the Keats House, Hampstead, and the London Metropolitan Archive, City of London; the Morgan Library; the Berg Collection of English and American Literature of the New York Public Library (Astor, Lenox and Tilden Foundations); the British Library; the Robert H. Taylor Collection, Manuscripts Division, Department of Rare Books and Special Collections, Princeton University Library (with materials published with permission of the Princeton University Library); the Huntington Library; Yale's Beinecke Library; the Bodleian Library; the Carl H. Pforzheimer Collection of Shelley and His Circle at the New York Public Library; the Humanities Research Center at the University of Texas; the Historical Society of Pennsylvania; Dumbarton Oaks; the Victoria and Albert Museum; the Wisbech and Fenland Museum; William Andrews Clarke Memorial Library; Bristol Central Library; Plymouth Central Library; Texas Christian University; Haverford College; Trinity College, Cambridge; and the University of Colorado.

More personal thanks are due to Julia, Emma, and Claire, who had to tolerate hearing about Keats manuscripts for three years, and Amy, who made me promise never to do this again.

The Texts of
KEATS'S POETRY AND PROSE

Before *Poems* (1817)

On Peace[1]

Oh Peace! and dost thou with thy presence bless
  The dwellings of this war-surrounded Isle;
Soothing with placid brow our late distress,
  Making the triple kingdom[2] brightly smile?
Joyful I hail thy presence; and I hail   5
  The sweet companions that await on thee;
Complete my joy—let not my first wish fail,
  Let the sweet mountain nymph[3] thy favorite be,
With England's happiness proclaim Europa's liberty.
Oh Europe, let not sceptred tyrants see   10
  That thou must shelter in thy former state;
Keep thy chains burst,[4] and boldly say thou art free;
  Give thy Kings law—leave not uncurbed the great;[5]
So with the honors[6] past thou'lt win thy happier fate.

Lines Written on 29 May, the Anniversary of Charles's Restoration, on Hearing the Bells Ringing[1]

Infatuate Britons, will you still proclaim
His memory, your direst, foulest shame?
    Nor patriots revere?
Ah! when I hear each traitorous lying bell,

1. Keats probably wrote this poem sometime after Napoleon's first abdication on April 11, 1814, and his subsequent departure for Elba. Allott points out that the poem, in its call for liberation rather than reaction at the close of the Napoleonic wars, adopts a stance similar to that taken by Hunt in the *Examiner* during the days following Napoleon's fall; the poem is also part of the large body of poems on Napoleon's abdication that includes Byron's "Ode to Napoleon Bonaparte" (1814), Hunt's "Ode for the Spring of 1814" (*Examiner*, April 17, 1814), and Reynolds's *An Ode* (1815). This is an irregular Shakespearean sonnet (abab cdcd ddedee) whereas Keats mainly composed Petrarchan sonnets at this stage in his career. The poem was first published by Ernest de Selincourt in *N&Q*, February 4, 1905, p. 82; text from de Selincourt with emendations from W³, f. 65 (*MYR: JK*, 4: 237).
2. The "Isle" of Great Britain composed of England, Scotland, and Wales.
3. Echo of Milton's "L'Allegro," l. 36: "The Mountain Nymph, sweet Liberty."
4. Perhaps invoking Rousseau's famous dictum from *The Social Contract* (1762), "Man is born free; and everywhere he is in chains."
5. This line is unfinished in the three extant transcripts; "the great" is Woodhouse's sensible penciled conclusion in W³, though a note opposite the transcript suggests that Woodhouse's source had "their state."
6. Stillinger emends this to "horrors" (also preferred by Forman according to a note in W³), which would recall the horrors of war now past rather than the possibly ironic "honors" bestowed in the past on tyrants who will now be curbed by law.
1. Written in 1814 or 1815, following either Napoleon's abdication in April 1814 or during the Hundred Days, though Gittings, p. 42, suggests it was written at the time of Louis XVIII's restoration. It was first published in Lowell (1: 66); text from Lowell with emendations from W³, f. 70 (*MYR: JK*, 4: 243).

'Tis gallant Sydney's, Russell's, Vane's sad knell,[2]   5
That pains my wounded ear.

[Fill for me a brimming bowl][1]

What wondrous beauty! From this Moment I efface from my Mind all
Women.

Terence's *Eunuch*. Act 2. Sc. 4

Fill for me a brimming bowl,
And let me in it drown my soul:
But put therein some drug designed
To banish woman from my mind:
For I want not the stream inspiring   5
That fills the mind with fond desiring;[2]
But I want as deep a draught
As e'er from Lethe's waves was quaft,[3]
From my despairing heart to charm
The image of the fairest form   10
That e'er my reveling eyes beheld,
That e'er my wandering fancy spell'd.

In vain!—Away I cannot chace
The melting softness of that face,
The beaminess[4] of those bright eyes,   15
That breast—earth's only paradise.

My sight will never more be blest,
For all I see has lost its zest;
Nor with delight can I explore
The classic page, the[5] Muse's lore.   20

Had she but known how beat my heart,
And with one smile reliev'd its smart,

2. Algernon Sidney (1623–1683), Lord William Russell (1639–1683), known as "the patriot," and Sir
Henry Vane (1613–1662) were heroes and martyrs for the Whigs and the Reformers, with Sidney
and Russell being executed for their involvement in the Rye House Plot and Vane being executed
on charges of treason. Keats seeks to replace the Stuart "martyr" Charles I with those who died for
opposing his descendants. Shelley would make a similar move in his unfinished *Charles I*; for a typical Huntian attack upon the Stuart memory, see his parallel between the Prince Regent and the
two Charleses in the *Examiner*, August 21, 1808, pp. 529–31; *SWLH*, 1: 69–73, esp. 70-1.
1. Written August 1814 after Keats had a "casual sight" of a woman at Vauxhall (W², f. 221v); "When
I have fears that I may cease to be" and "Life's sea hath been five years at its slow ebb" (pp. 118, 124,
below) refer to the same occasion. Allott suggests the influence of Byron's "To a Beautiful Quaker"
(1807), another poem on a chance encounter, and of the octosyllabic couplets of Milton's "L'Allegro" and "Il Penseroso." First published by Ernest de Selincourt in *N&Q*, February 4, 1905, p. 81.
Stillinger (1974, pp. 95–98) argues there are three authoritative states of the poem: Keats's fair copy
at the Morgan Library in W³, f. 66 (*MYR: JK*, 4: 219–20), Woodhouse's W³ transcripts with variants
from a lost MS (Stillinger's W³x, f. 64, *MYR: JK* 4: 244; and W³y, f. 65, *MYR: JK*, 4: 235–36), and
the uncorrected W³x which best represents a lost version in Mary Frogley's album, the ultimate
source for the *N&Q* version. In 1974, Stillinger preferred the W³x version, but in his 1978 edition he
followed the Morgan fair copy (FC). Text from *N&Q* with emendations from W³x; epigraph and paragraph breaks from the Morgan fair copy, with some variants from that version indicated in the notes.
2. FC has "That heats the Sense with lewd desiring."
3. Lethe is a river in Hades; its waters erase the memories of those about to be reborn. Allott suggests
an echo in ll. 7–8 of Thomas Moore's version (1800) of Anacreon's Ode 62.1–2: "Fill me, boy, as
deep a draught, / As e'er was fill'd, as e'er was quaff'd."
4. This is the reading of W³x; *N&Q* has "happiness."
5. *N&Q* reads this as "or."

I should have felt a sweet relief,
I should have felt "the joy of grief."[6]
Yet as a Tuscan mid the snow   25
Of Lapland thinks on sweet Arno,[7]
Even so for ever shall she be[8]
The Halo of my Memory.

Sonnet[1]

As from the darkening gloom a silver dove
    Upsoars, and darts into the eastern light,[2]
    On pinions[3] that nought moves but pure delight;
So fled thy soul into the realms above,
Regions of peace and everlasting love;   5
    Where happy spirits, crown'd with circlets bright
    Of starry beam, and gloriously bedight,[4]
Taste the high joy none but the blest can prove.
There thou or joinest the immortal quire[5]
    In melodies that even heaven fair   10
Fill with superior bliss, or, at desire
    Of the omnipotent Father, cleavest the air,[6]
On holy message sent—What pleasure's[7] higher?
    Wherefore does any grief our joy impair?

Sonnet.
To Lord Byron[1]

Byron! how sweetly sad thy melody!
    Attuning still the soul to tenderness,
    As if soft Pity, with unusual stress,
Had touched her plaintive lute; and thou, being by,

6. Quoted from Thomas Campbell's *Pleasures of Hope* (1799), 1.182: "And teach impassioned souls the joy of grief."
7. A river that flows through Florence in Tuscany. *Lapland*: largely inside the Arctic Circle, a vast region comprised of portions of Norway, Sweden, Finland, and Russia.
8. This is the reading of *N&Q* and W³x; the FC lacks "Even."
1. While dated 1816 in extant MSS, this poem was most likely written in December 1814: a shorthand note by Woodhouse (now in W³, f. 65v; *MYR: JK*, 4: 238) indicates that Keats told him "he had written it on the death of his grandmother, about four days afterward," and his grandmother was buried on December 19, 1814. First published in 1876, p. 58; text from 1876 with emendations from W², f. 8r (*MYR: JK*, 6: 1).
2. Allott suggests an echo in ll. 1–2 of Mary Tighe's *Psyche* (1811), 3.st. 30: "Meantime the dove had soared above their reach . . . Conspicuous mid the gloom its silver plumage shone."
3. Wings.
4. Arrayed, clothed.
5. Archaic form of "choir."
6. 1876 corrects the meter: "O' the omnipotent Father, cleav'st the air."
7. As Stillinger notes, the "pleasure's" from 1876 and in W² may be an archaic form of the plural "pleasures" from W³, so there may simply be a spelling difference between the transcripts as opposed to a variation from a plural to a contraction of "pleasure is."
1. Written December 1814, this poem reflects Keats's early delight in Byron during the noble poet's first fame, also indicated by the fact that as a medical student, Keats "used to go with his neck nearly bare á lá Byron" (Henry Stephens to G. F. Mathew, March 1848, *KC*, 2: 211). For Keats's reading of Byron, see Lau, *Keats's Reading of the Romantic Poets* (University of Michigan Press, 1991), pp. 115–46; for Byron's influence on Keats, see Duncan Wu, "Keats and Byron: A Reassessment," *The Byron Journal* 24 (1996): 12–23. First published in 1848, 1: 13; text from 1848 with emendations and title from W², f. 217r (*MYR: JK*, 6: 407).

Hadst caught the tones, nor suffered them to die.   5
  O'ershading sorrow doth not make thee less
  Delightful: thou thy griefs dost dress[2]
With a bright halo, shining beamily,
As when a cloud a[3] golden moon doth veil,
  Its sides are tinged with a resplendent glow,   10
Through the dark robe oft amber rays prevail,
  And like fair veins in sable marble flow;
Still warble, dying swan! still tell the tale,
  The enchanting tale, the tale of pleasing woe.

Sonnet.
To Chatterton.[1]

Oh Chatterton! how very sad thy fate!
  Dear child of sorrow! Son of misery!
  How soon the film of death obscured that eye,
Whence Genius wildly[2] flashed, and high debate!
How soon that voice, majestic and elate,   5
  Melted in dying murmurs![3] Oh! how nigh
  Was night to thy fair morning! Thou didst die
A half-blown flower[4] which cold blasts amate.[5]
But this is past: thou art among the stars
  Of highest Heaven; to the rolling spheres   10
Thou sweetly singest: nought thy hymning mars
  Above the ingrate world and human fears.
On earth the good man base detraction bars
  From thy fair name, and waters it with tears!

ODE TO APOLLO.[1]

I.

IN thy western halls of gold
  When thou sittest in thy state,
Bards, that erst sublimely told

2. Forman emends the line to "dost ever dress" (Hampstead Keats, 4: 14n.) to complete the meter; Garrod (p. 477n.) offers "thy thorny griefs."
3. 1848 has "the."
1. Written in 1815, this sonnet reflects Keats's admiration for Thomas Chatterton (1752–1770), the author of pseudo-medieval poems he published as the work of a fifteenth-century monk named Rowley. Chatterton committed suicide at the age of seventeen and became an emblem of the inspired artist destroyed by an unsympathetic world (see Coleridge, "Monody on the Death of Chatterton" [1796]; Wordsworth, "Resolution and Independence" [1807, ll. 43–49]). Keats would dedicate *Endymion* to him; in a letter of September 1819, he wrote, "The purest English . . . is Chatterton's" (*L*, 2: 212). See Beth Lau, "Protest, 'Nativism,' and Impersonation in the Works of Chatterton and Keats," *Studies in Romanticism* 42 (Winter 2003): 519–39. First published in 1848, 1: 12–13; text from 1848 with emendations from unidentified transcript in W³, f. 88r (*MYR: JK*, 4: 307) and title from W².
2. 1848 misreads as "mildly."
3. 1848 misreads as "numbers."
4. 1848 misreads as "flow'ret."
5. "Affright—Spenser" [W³ note]; 1848 cites Chaucer.
1. Written in February 1815, this is an early celebration of great poetry that, as Allott notes, imitates Hunt's *Feast of the Poets* (1811; rpt. 1814) and Gray's *The Progress of Poetry* (1757). Apollo, the god of the sun, appears here as the patron god of poets. First published in 1848, 2: 252–54; text from 1848 with emendations from W³, fol. 70 (*MYR: JK*, 4: 239–43).

Heroic deeds, and sung of fate,
  With fervour seize their adamantine[2] lyres,   5
Whose chords are solid rays, and twinkle radiant fires.

II.

There Homer with his nervous[3] arms
  Strikes the twanging harp of war,
  And even the western splendour warms,
    While the trumpets sound afar;   10
  But, what creates the most intense surprise,
His soul looks out through renovated eyes.

III.

Then, through thy Temple wide, melodious swells
  The sweet majestic tone of Maro's[4] lyre;
  The soul delighted on each accent dwells,—   15
    Enraptured dwells,—not daring to respire,
The while he tells of grief around a funeral pyre.

IV.

'Tis awful silence then again:
  Expectant stand the spheres;
  Breathless the laurell'd peers;   20
  Nor move, till ends the lofty strain,
  Nor move till Milton's tuneful thunders cease,
And leave once more the ravish'd heavens in peace.

V.

Thou biddest Shakspeare wave his hand,
  And quickly forward spring   25
  The Passions—a terrific band—
    And each vibrates the string
  That with its tyrant temper best accords,
While from their Master's lips pour forth the inspiring words.

VI.

A silver trumpet Spenser blows,   30
  And, as its martial notes to silence flee,
  From a virgin chorus flows
    A hymn in praise of spotless Chastity.[5]
'Tis still!—Wild warblings from the Æolian lyre[6]
Enchantment softly breathe, and tremblingly expire.   35

2. Hard, diamondlike.
3. Vigorous, sinewy.
4. Virgil (Publius Virgilius Maro) (70–19 B.C.E.), author of the *Eclogues*, the *Georgics*, and here the *Aeneid*, which includes the story of Aeneas and Dido, who dies by self-immolation (perhaps the "funeral pyre" of l. 17, though Allot suggests the burial of Misenus). Keats translated the *Aeneid* while at Enfield.
5. See *The Faerie Queene*, Book 3, "Contayning the Legend of Britomartis. Or of Chastitie."
6. The Aeolian harp is a stringed instrument that produces sounds when the wind passes over it. See Coleridge's "Effusion XXXV" (1796) / "The Eolian Harp" (1817).

VII.

Next, thy Tasso's ardent numbers[7]
  Float along the pleased air,
Calling youth from idle slumbers,
  Rousing them from pleasure's lair:—
Then o'er the strings his fingers gently move,   40
And melt the soul to pity and to love.

VIII.

But when *Thou* joinest with the Nine,[8]
  And all the powers of song combine,
    We listen here on earth:
  The dying tones that fill the air,   45
  And charm the ear of evening fair,
From thee, great God of Bards, receive their heavenly birth.

[Give me women, wine and snuff][1]

Give me women, wine and snuff
Until I cry out "hold, enough!"
You may do so sans objection
Till the day of resurrection;
For bless my beard they aye shall be   5
My beloved Trinity.

Sonnet[1]

OH! how I love, on a fair summer's eve,
  When streams of light pour down the golden west,
  And on the balmy zephyrs[2] tranquil rest
The silver clouds, far—far away to leave
All meaner thoughts, and take a sweet reprieve   5
  From little cares:—to find, with easy quest,
  A fragrant wild, with Nature's beauty drest,

---

7. Verses. Torquato Tasso (1544–1595), an Italian Renaissance poet whose *Jerusalem Delivered* (1575; 1580) exerted a strong influence on English literature and on romantic writers such as Byron and Goethe. Keats had read the poem in Fairfax's translation of 1600.
8. The nine muses.
1. Written in late 1815 or early 1816, while Keats was a medical student at Guy's Hospital, on the cover of a lecture notebook belonging to Keats's fellow student and friend, Henry Stephens (Trinity College, Cambridge, Cullum autograph collection, Cullum N 83/2); Stephens later (March? 1847) wrote to George Felton Mathew that this was the last remaining example of "many lines" Keats had "scribbled" on "my Syllabus of Chemical Lectures" (*KC*, 2: 210). On Keats's medical training, see Hermione de Almeida, *Romantic Medicine and Keats* (Oxford, 1991) and Roe (1997), pp. 160–81. First published in H. B. Forman's one-volume *Poetical Works of John Keats* (1884), p. 558; text from Forman's edition.
1. Written in 1816, perhaps in the summer, this sonnet draws on a standard Keatsian equation between natural bowers and books, here poetry and "patriotic lore" (l. 9). First published as sonnet I in 1848, 2: 287; text from 1848 with emendations from W², f. 9r (*MYR: JK*, 6: 3), which supplies the title.
2. The west wind.

And there into delight my soul deceive.
There warm my breast with patriotic lore,
     Musing on Milton's fate—on Sydney's bier—[3]
     Till their stern forms before my mind arise:
Perhaps on the[4] wing of Poesy upsoar,—
     Full often dropping a delicious tear,
     When some melodious sorrow spells mine eyes.

                                        10

Letter to C. C. Clarke, October 9, 1816[1]

                                  Wednesday Oct[r] 9th—
My dear Sir,

     The busy time has just gone by, and I can now devote any time you may mention to the pleasure of seeing M[r] Hunt[2]—'t will be an Era in my existence—I am anxious too to see the Author of the Sonnet to the Sun,[3] for it is no mean gratification to become acquainted with Men who in their admiration of Poetry do not jumble together Shakspeare and Darwin[4]—I have coppied out a sheet or two of Verses which I composed some time ago, and find so much to blame in them that the best ^worst^ part will go into the fire—those to G. Mathew[5] I will suffer to meet the eye of M[r] H. notwithstanding that the Muse is so frequently mentioned. I here sinned in the face of Heaven even while remembering what, I think, Horace says, "never presume to make a God appear but for an Action worthy of a God.[6] From a few Words of yours when last I saw you, I have no doubt but that you have something in your Portfolio which I should by rights see. I will put you in Mind of it. Although the Borough is a beastly place in dirt, turnings and windings; yet No 8 Dean Street[7] is not difficult

---

3. Reference to Milton's involvement in the English Civil War and Sydney's death for resisting the Stuarts (see p. 4, n. 2).
4. 1848 drops "the" to regularize the meter.
1. Written as Keats, finishing his medical studies, entered into London literary life. Charles Cowden Clarke (1787–1877) was the son of Keats's schoolmaster at Enfield School who became a friend and an important influence on his early literary tastes. Text from ALS in the Ferdinand Julius Dreer Collection, Coll. 175, English Poets, Historical Society of Pennsylvania.
2. Leigh Hunt (1784–1859), poet, editor of the key liberal weekly the *Examiner*, and a political martyr for reformers after he was imprisoned for lampooning the Prince Regent. Keats entered into Hunt's circle after the two poets met, sometime before the end of October.
3. Probably the publisher Charles Ollier (1788–1859) whose "Sonnet on Sunset" was copied into Clarke's commonplace book (the portfolio Keats soon mentions) in August 1813. Clarke himself has been suggested as the author, since he did write an "irregular effusion" to the sunset (perhaps in 1805) that he copied into his commonplace book on June 26, 1813, and later published in his *Carmina Minima* (1859). Another possibility is Horace Smith (1779–1849), writer, humorist, and another member of Hunt's circle, who published a sonnet "To the Setting Sun" in his *Amarynthus, the Nympholept* (1821) volume. For the argument that a sonnet contest among these three was involved, see Joan Coldwell, "Charles Cowden Clarke's Commonplace Book and Its Relationship to Keats," *KSJ* 10 (Winter 1961), p. 90; see also John Barnard, "Charles Cowden Clarke's 'Cockney' Commonplace Book," in *KH*, pp. 65–87.
4. Erasmus Darwin (1731–1802), physician, evolutionary theorist, and poet whose *The Botanic Garden* (1791), bringing together his *Loves of the Plants* and *The Economy of Vegetation*, offered popular poetic expositions of the Linnaean system, of an eroticized nature, and of evolution (influencing his grandson, Charles Darwin).
5. Keats's verse epistle (see below, pp. 40–42) to George Felton Mathew, Keats's early friend and center of a poetic circle; see headnote, p. 17.
6. Horace (65–8 B.C.E.), *Arts Poetica*, l. 191. M. B. Forman, *The Letters of John Keats* (4th ed. 1952), cites Roscommon's translation of 1709: "Never presume to make a God appear, / But for a Business worthy of a God."
7. Keats's lodging at No. 8 Dean Street was near Guy's Hospital; Dean Street, now buried under London Bridge Station, connected St. Thomas Street and Tooley Street.

to find; and if you would run the Gauntlet over London Bridge, take the first turning to the left and then the first to the right and moreover knock at my door which is nearly opposite a Meeting,[8] you would do one a Charity which as St Paul saith is the father of all the Virtues[9]—At all events let me hear from you soon—I say at all events not excepting the Gout in your fingers—

Your's sincerely
John Keats—

GEORGE FELTON MATHEW

To A Poetical Friend[1]

O thou who delightest in fanciful song,
And tellest strange tales of the elf and the fay;[2]
Of giants tyrannic, whose talismans strong
Have power to charm gentle damsels astray;

Of courteous knights-errant, and high-mettled steeds;   5
Of forests enchanted, and marvellous streams;—
Of bridges, and castles, and desperate deeds;
And all the bright fictions of fanciful dreams:—

Of captures, and rescues, and wonderful loves;
Of blisses abounding in dark leafy bowers;—   10
Of murmuring music in shadowy groves,
And beauty reclined on her pillow of flowers:—

O where did thine infancy open its eyes?
And who was the nurse that attended thy spring?—
For sure thou'rt exotic to these frigid skies,   15
So splendid the song that thou lovest to sing.

Perhaps thou hast traversed the glorious East;
And like the warm breath of its sun, and its gales,
That wander 'mid gardens of flowers to feast,
Are tinctured with every rich sweet that prevails?   20

O no !—for a Shakspeare—a Milton are ours!
And who e'er sung sweeter, or stronger than they?
As thine is, I ween[3] was the spring of *their* powers;
Like theirs, is the cast of thine earlier lay.

It is not the climate, or scenery round,   20
It was not the nurse that attended thy Youth;

---

8. There was a Baptist chapel on the west side of Dean Street, between Nos. 28 and 29.
9. 1 Corinthians 13.13.
1. Mathew's celebration of Keats. Text from the *European Magazine* (October 1816).
2. Fairy.
3. Suppose, imagine (archaic).

That gave thee those blisses which richly abound
In magical numbers to charm, and to soothe.

O no !—'tis the Queen of those regions of air—
The gay fields of Fancy—thy spirit has blest;   30
She cherish'd thy childhood with fostering care,
And nurtur'd her boy with the milk of her breast.

She tended thee ere thou couldst wander alone,
And cheer'd thy wild walks amidst terror and dread;—
She sung thee to sleep with a song of her own,   35
And laid thy young limbs on her flowery bed.

She gave thee those pinions[4] with which thou delightest
Sublime o'er her boundless dominions to rove;
The tongue too she gave thee with which thou invitest
Each ear to thy stories of wonder and love.   40

And when evening shall free thee from Nature's decays,[5]
And release thee from Study's severest control,
Oh warm thee in Fancy's enlivening rays,
And wash the dark spots of disease from thy soul.

And let not the spirit of Poesy sleep;   45
Of Fairies and Genii continue to tell—
Nor suffer the innocent deer's timid leap
To fright the wild bee from her flowery bell.

LEIGH HUNT

YOUNG POETS[1]

IN sitting down to this subject, we happen to be restricted by time to a much
shorter notice than we could wish; but we mean to take it up again shortly.
Many of our readers however have perhaps observed for themselves, that
there has been a new school[2] of poetry rising of late, which promises to
extinguish the French one, that has prevailed among us since the time of
Charles the 2d. It began with something excessive, like most revolutions,
but this gradually wore away; and an evident aspiration after real nature
and original fancy remained, which called to mind the finer times of the
English muse. In fact it is wrong to call it a new school, and still more so

---

4. Wings.
5. "Alluding to his medical character.—G. F. M." [Mathew's note].
1. Written as Hunt came to know Keats and Shelley, this is perhaps Hunt's most famous review. He
   announces the arrival on the literary scene of those two "young poets" along with John Hamilton
   Reynolds. He also proclaims the formation of the "Cockney School" *avant la lettre*, with this piece
   on a new school of poetry in part provoking the attacks on the "Cockney School" that would begin
   the next Fall in *Blackwood's Edinburgh Review* (see pp. 272–76, below). Hunt's account of the history of English Poetry as it moves from the eighteenth century dominated by a "French" school to a
   poetry of nature and imagination inaugurated by the "Lake Poets" parallels Keats's argument in
   "Sleep and Poetry" (see p. 63). Text from the *Examiner*, IX, December 1, 1816, pp. 761–62 (*SWLH*,
   2: 72–75).
2. The so-called Lake School of Wordsworth, Coleridge, and Southey.

to represent it as one of innovation, it's only object being to restore the same love of Nature, and of *thinking* instead of mere *talking*, which formerly rendered us real poets, and not merely versifying wits, and beadrollers of couplets.

We have delighted to see the departure of the old school acknowledged in the number of the *Edinburgh Review*[3] just published,—a candour the more generous and spirited, inasmuch as that work has hitherto been the greatest surviving ornament of the same school in prose and criticism, as it is now destined, we trust, to be still the leader in the new.

We also felt the same delight at the third canto of Lord Byron's *Child Harolde*,[4] in which, to our conceptions at least, he has fairly renounced a certain leaven of the French style, and taken his place where we've always said he would be found,—among the poets who have a real feeling for numbers, and who go directly to Nature for inspiration. But more of this poem in our next.*[5]

The object of the present article is merely to notice three young writers, who appear to us to promise a considerable addition of strength to the new school. Of the first who came before us, we have, it is true, yet seen only one or two specimens, and these were no sooner sent to us than we unfortunately mislaid them;[6] but we shall procure what has been published, and if the rest answer to what we have seen, we shall have no hesitation in announcing him for a very striking and original thinker. His name is PERCY BYSSHE SHELLEY, and he is the author of a poetical work entitled *Alastor, or the Spirit of Solitude*.

The next with whose name we became acquainted, was JOHN HENRY REYNOLDS;[7] author of a tale called *Safie*,[8] written, we believe, in imitation of Lord Byron, and more lately of a small set of poems published by Taylor and Hessey,[9] the principal of which is called the *Naiad*. It opens thus:—

> The gold sun went into the west,
> And soft airs sang him to his rest;
> And yellow leaves all loose and dry,
> Play'd on the branches listlessly:
> The sky wax'd palely blue; and high
> A cloud seem'd touch'd upon the sky—

3. See a review of Byron's poetry and particularly *Childe Harold III* in the *Edinburgh Review*, 54, (December 1816), pp. 277–310, esp. p. 278.
4. The third canto of *Childe Harold's Pilgrimage* was published in November of 1816; Hunt refers to what has been seen by many as the Wordsworthian (via Shelley but also and earlier Hunt) touches to the canto.
5. *By the way, we are authorized to mention, that the person in Cheapside who announces some new publications by his Lordship, and says he has given five hundred guineas for them, has no warrant whatsoever for so stating. We are sorry to hurt the man's sale, as far as some other booksellers are concerned, who are just as money-getting and impudent in different ways; but truth must be told of one, as it will also be told of others.—(Since writing this note, we find the business noticed in Chancery, and of the *verses* quoted, which will certainly satisfy the public that the Noble Poet was not the author) [Hunt's note]. On November 15, 1816, the bookseller J. Johnston of Cheapside claimed to have purchased the copyright of some of Byron's poems for £500. Murray, Byron's publisher, who was bringing out *Childe Harold III* at this time, disputed the claim.
6. Hunt would finally publish "Hymn to Intellectual Beauty" in the *Examiner*, X, January 19, 1817, p. 41, over Shelley's name rather than his pseudonym of "Elfin Knight."
7. Hunt gets John *Hamilton* Reynolds's name wrong.
8. *Safie, An Eastern Tale* (1814).
9. John Taylor (1781–1864) and James Augustus Hessey (1785–1870) founded a publishing house together in 1806; members of the circle that included Hunt, Keats, and Shelley, they would, in addition to publishing Reynolds's *Naiad* and his later *Peter Bell* (1819), print works by Keats, Elizabeth Kent, Hazlitt, Jane and Ann Taylor, Coleridge, Landor, Carlyle, and De Quincey; they later published the *London Magazine*.

A spot of cloud,—blue, thin, and still,
And silence bask'd on vale and hill.
    'Twas autumn-tide,—the eve was sweet,
        As mortal eye hath e'er beholden;
    The grass look'd warm with sunny heat,—
    Perchance some fairy's glowing feet
        Had lightly touch'd—and left it golden:
A flower or two were shining yet;
The star of the daisy had not yet set,—
It shone from the turf to greet the air,
Which tenderly came breathing there:
And in a brook which lov'd to fret
    O'er yellow sand and pebble blue,
    The lily of the silvery hue
All freshly dwelt, with white leaves wet.
Away the sparkling water play'd,
    Through bending grass, and blessed flower;
    Light, and delight seem'd all its dower:
Away in merriment it stray'd—
    Singing, and bearing, hour after hour,
Pale, lovely splendour to the shade.[1]

We shall give another extract or two in a future number. The author's style is too artificial, though he is evidently an admirer of Mr. Wordsworth. Like all young poets too, properly so called, his love of detail is too over-wrought and indiscriminate; but still he is a young poet, and only wants still closer attention to things as opposed to the seduction of words, to realize all that he promises. His nature seems very true and amiable.

The last of these young aspirants whom we have met with, and who promise to help the new school revive Nature and

"To put of a spirit of youth in every thing,"—[2]

is, we believe, the youngest of them all, and just of age. His name is JOHN KEATS. He has not yet published any thing except in a newspaper; but a set of his manuscripts was handed us the other day, and fairly surprised us with the truth of their ambition, and ardent grappling with Nature. In the fol-lowing Sonnet there is one incorrect rhyme, which might easily be altered, but which shall serve in the mean time as a peace-offering to the rhyming critics. The rest of the composition, with the exception of a little vagueness in calling the regions of poetry "the realms of gold," we do not hesitate to pronounce excellent, especially the last six lines. The word *swims* is com-plete; and the whole conclusion is equally powerful and quiet:—

ON FIRST LOOKING INTO CHAPMAN'S HOMER.

MUCH have I travel'd in the realms of Gold,
    And many goodly States and Kingdoms seen;
    Round many western Islands have I been,
Which Bards in fealty to Apollo hold;

1. Hunt quotes pp. 1–27 of Reynolds's "The Naiad" in *The Naiad: A Tale with Other Poems* (London: Taylor and Hessey, 1816).
2. Hunt adapts l. 3 of Shakespeare's Sonnet 98: "Hath put a spirit of youth in every thing."

But of one wide expanse had I been told,
    That deep-brow'd Homer ruled as his demesne;
    Yet could I never judge what men could mean,
Till I heard CHAPMAN speak out loud and bold.
Then felt I like some watcher of the skies,
    When a new planet swims into his ken;
Or like stout CORTEZ, when with eagle eyes
    He stared at the Pacific,— and all his men
Looked at each other with a wild surmise,—
    Silent, upon a peak in Darien.[3]

Oct. 1816.   JOHN KEATS.

We have spoken with less scruple of these poetical promises, because we really are not in the habit of lavishing praises and announcements, and because we have no fear of any pettier vanity on the part of young men, who promise to understand human nature so well.

Sonnet.
Written in disgust of vulgar superstition[1]

THE church bells toll a melancholy round,
    Calling the people to some other prayers,
    Some other gloominess, more dreadful cares,
More heark'ning to the sermon's horrid sound.
Surely the mind of man is closely bound   5
    In some black spell;[2] seeing that each one tears
    Himself from fireside joys, and Lydian airs,[3]
And converse high of those with glory crown'd.
Still, still they toll, and I should feel a damp,
    A chill as from a tomb, did I not know   10
That they are dying like an outburnt lamp;
    That 'tis their sighing, wailing ere they go
    Into oblivion—that fresh flowers will grow,
And many glories of immortal stamp.

3. Keats's sonnet would be included in a slightly different form in *Poems* (see pp. 54–55, below).
1. This sonnet was probably written on December 22, 1816, a Sunday, though perhaps on December 24, 1816 (Tom Keats's transcript has "Sunday Evening Decʳ 24 1816" and the closest Sunday was the 22); in any event, this poem, which Bush, *John Keats* (1966), p. 35, called "unwontedly anti-Christian," was penned either on the Sabbath or on Christmas eve. Tom Keats indicated on his transcript that the poem was "Written in 15 minutes," suggesting it was written as part of one of Hunt's sonnet contests, perhaps with Hunt penning "To Percy Shelley, on the Degrading Notions of Deity" published in *Foliage* (1818) (see Stillinger, p. 426 and Cox, p. 66, 110–12). The poem expresses Keats's long-time skepticism about organized religion and his delight in a pagan alternative. First published in 1876, pp. 58–59; text from 1876 with emendations from Keats's draft (Harvard MS Keats 2.10; *JKPMH*, p. 45) and Tom Keats's transcript (Harvard MS Keats 3.5, p. 19), which supplies the title.
2. 1876 has "To some blind spell."
3. Echo of Milton's "L'Allegro," ll. 135–36: "And ever against eating cares / Lap me in soft *Lydian* Aires."

Sonnet.[1]

After dark vapors have oppress'd our plains
  For a long dreary season, comes a day
  Born of the gentle SOUTH, and clears away
From the sick heavens all unseemly stains,
The anxious Month, relieving of[2] its pains,   5
  Takes as a long lost right the feel of MAY;
  The eyelids with the passing coolness play
Like Rose leaves with the drip of Summer rains.

The[3] calmest thoughts come round us; as of leaves
  Budding—fruit ripening in stillness—Autumn Suns   10
Smiling at Eve upon the quiet sheaves—
  Sweet SAPPHO's Cheek—a smiling[4] infant's breath—
The gradual Sand that through an hour-glass runs—
A woodland Rivulet—a Poet's death.[5]

1. Written on January 31, 1817, this sonnet was first published over Keats's initials in Hunt's *Examiner* for February 23, 1817, p. 124; text from the *Examiner* with some variants noted from W², f. 18r (*MYR: JK*, 6: 13).
2. W² has "from."
3. W² has "And."
4. W² has "sleeping." Sappho (b. mid-seventh century B.C.E.), Greek poetess from Lesbos.
5. Keats may be thinking of Chatterton here (see "Sonnet. To Chatterton," p. 6); in W², opposite f. 18, Keats's publisher John Taylor suggests the death of Alexander Pope.

Poems (1817)

Keats's first volume of poetry, issued simply as *Poems* in early March 1817, was printed by Charles Richards and published in a run of 500 or 750 copies by Charles and James Ollier, who had been members of Leigh Hunt's circle since 1811; they also published Hunt's *Foliage* (1818), *Poetical Works* (1819), and *Literary Pocket-Books*; Mary Shelley's *History of a Six Weeks' Tour* (1817); Hazlitt's *Characters of Shakespeare's Plays* (1817); and most of Percy Shelley's mature works from *Laon and Cythna/The Revolt of Islam* (1818) to *Hellas* (1822). Keats's volume was advertised in the *Morning Chronicle* and the *Times*, with Shelley apparently paying for the advertisements. *Poems* did not sell well, the Olliers terminated their arrangement with Keats, and the stocks were transferred to Taylor and Hessey, who still had the book for sale in 1824.

Keats's volume included thirty-one poems, opening with a dedication to Leigh Hunt and offering four sections marked by half-titles, "Poems," "Epistles," "Sonnets," and the closing "Sleep and Poetry." Beneath a motto, below, from Spenser's *Muiopotmos*, ll. 209–10 was a portrait usually identified as Spenser but probably intended to be Shakespeare (Stuart Sperry, "Richard Woodhouse's Interleaved and Annotated Copy of Keats's *Poems* (1817)," *Literary Monographs*, 1 [Madison: University of Wisconsin Press, 1967], pp. 120–21). On the verso page opposite the opening of "I stood tiptoe" was a note in square brackets: "THE Short Pieces in the middle of the Book, as well as some of the Sonnets, were written at an earlier period than the rest of the Poems." The poems were written between 1814 (the "Imitation of Spenser," probably from that year, was identified by Brown as Keats's "earliest attempt") and February 1817, when Keats composed the dedication at the time the proof sheets were brought to him at Hunt's house from the printer.

The volume reflects the interests of two literary groups of which Keats had been a part. In the last half of 1815, Keats had been introduced by his brother George into the circle around George Felton Mathew and his cousins, Caroline (*KC,* 2: 189–91) and Anne Mathew (on the Mathew circle, see Bate, pp. 51–58; Ward, pp. 42–43; Gittings, pp. 45–46; Motion, pp. 70–72; and Roe, "John Keats and George Felton Mathew: Poetics, Politics, and the *European Magazine*," *Keats-Shelley Journal* 49 [2000]: 31–46). The circle delighted in "little domestic concerts and dances" (*KC,* 2: 185) and in fashionable verse, ranging from the Gothic and the Byronic to Mary Tighe's *Psyche* and Wieland's *Oberon* (in Sotheby's translation). They kept a manuscript book, "The Garland: consisting of Poetical Extracts both ancient and modern," into which various members of the circle would copy poems (see Edmund Blunden, "Keats's Friend Mathew," *English* 1 [1936]: 46–55). Keats's poems from this period included in his

1817 volume are "To some Ladies" (addressed to Anne and Caroline), "On Receiving a Curious Shell and a Copy of Verses from the Same Ladies" (addressed to George), "O Solitude," and "To George Felton Mathew." "Woman! when I behold thee flippant, vain" may have come from this period and was certainly praised by Mathew in his review of *Poems* (*European Magazine* 71 [May 1817], pp. 434–37). Another piece, "O come, dearest Emma! the rose is full blown," written for Emma Mathew, would not be published until 1883 by Forman. By the time of Mathew's review of Keats, the friendship had foundered, perhaps over Keats's alliance with Hunt which Mathew criticized; Mathew would later draw a contrast between Keats as a member of "the skeptical and republican school" and himself as a believer in "the institutions of my country . . . harmonizing on the one hand with the Theocracy of heaven, and on the other with the paternal rule at home" (*KC,* 2: 185–86). Keats's note about his early poems also seems an attempt to distance himself from the tastes of Mathew and his group.

Keats had certainly left Mathew's conservative coterie behind by the fall of 1816 when he was introduced to Hunt by their mutual friend Charles Cowden Clarke (see letter of October 9, 1816, above, pp. 9–10). Hunt— editor of the important weekly Sunday paper, the *Examiner*, author of the controversial *Story of Rimini*, and martyr for the Reformist intelligentsia after his imprisonment for libeling the Prince Regent—was at the center of a brilliant circle that came to include such figures as Percy and Mary Shelley, Benjamin Robert Haydon, William Hazlitt, William Godwin, Vincent Novello, Horace Smith, John Hamilton Reynolds, and Charles Lamb. Keats's poems were read and appreciated by members of the circle, and he first became a public poet through Hunt's *Examiner*: his first published poem appeared there, he was first reviewed there, and Hunt published a large selection of Keats's verse between their meeting and the publication of Keats's volume. Keats insistently marks *Poems* as arising within the Hunt circle, with its dedication to Hunt, with the epigraph of its opening long poem coming from Hunt's *Rimini*, and with various poems naming Hunt or revealing his influence, including the closing "Sleep and Poetry," which celebrates the sociability of the Hunt household. The poems repeatedly invoke their occasional and social nature, as one can see in the dating of two of the sonnets and all the epistles and in the titles of such sonnets as "Written on the day that Mr. Leigh Hunt left Prison," "To a Friend who sent me some Roses," "On leaving some Friends at an early Hour," and most famously "On first looking into Chapman's Homer." The poems praise the value of society and sociality, as in the close of the opening sonnet to George Keats: "But what, without the social thought of thee, / Would be the wonders of the sky and sea?" "On the Grasshopper and Cricket" arose immediately out of the social life of the group, being the product of a sonnet contest with Hunt in which the poets wrote a poem on a common topic within fifteen minutes.

The three epistles, written as letters to Mathew, Clarke, and George Keats, are literally social documents, verse correspondence to friends and family. In these conversation poems, Keats confronts his doubts about his abilities as a poet and finds some resolution to his concerns in communing with others: in praising the poetry of Mathew, in imagining his brother reading his poetry, or in remembering moments with Clarke when they shared a love of music or poetry. The volume's opening and closing poems are longer investigations of the social, poetical, and ultimately political vision of these poems. "I stood tip-toe upon a little hill" offers a Cockney reworking of Wordsworth's treatment of myth in the fourth book of *The Excursion* to argue for the social and erotic as a response to the "despondency" of Wordsworth's Solitary from *The Excursion* (1814) and the "egotistical sublime" of Wordsworth himself. "Sleep and Poetry" is an appeal for inspiration, an outline of Keats's poetic project, and a sketch of poetic history. The project—that poetry "should be a friend / To sooth the cares, and lift the thoughts of man" (ll. 246–47)—is akin to Hunt's, who prefaced his *Foliage* volume with "Cursory Observations on Poetry and Cheerfulness." Keats offers a Cockney version of the Virgillian progress from pastoral through didactic poetry to the epic in his desire to overwhelm himself in poetry so that he can create erotic pastorals and then a poetry infused with a tragic vision (ll. 96–125). The history of poetry, with its celebration of earlier English poetry, its attack upon the "French" school, and its praise of Hunt and Wordsworth echoes Hunt's comments in his "Young Poets" review (pp. 11–14) and Hazlitt's attack on the heroic couplet (*Examiner*, August 20, 1815, p. 542). The poem closes upon a celebration of the sociability of the Hunt household, its "brotherhood, / And friendliness, the nurse of mutual good" (ll. 317–18). Keats finds inspiration in Hunt's books, the music that fills the house, the prints, bust, and portraits that decorated it— and in Hunt's much ridiculed sonnet contests: "The hearty grasp that sends a pleasant sonnet / Into the brain ere one can think upon it; / The silence when some rhymes are coming out; / And when they're come, the very pleasant rout" (ll. 319–22). If many poems in the volume seem concerned with Keats discovering himself as a poet, this final poem suggests he finds his voice within the chorus of the Hunt circle.

The volume received six reviews (see selection below, pp. 73–75, 90–98), including positive notices by Keats's friend, John Hamilton Reynolds, (*Champion*, March 9, 1817, pp. 78–81) and Hunt (*Examiner*, X, June 1, 1817, p. 345; July 6, 1817, pp. 428–29; and July 13, 1817, pp. 443–44). George Felton Mathew's review (*European Magazine* 71 [May 1817], pp. 434–37) reflected the cooling of his friendship with Keats. Josiah Conder in a not unsympathetic review (*Eclectic Review* n.s. 8 [September 1817], pp. 267–75) already complains about Keats's debt to Hunt, while an anonymous review in the *Edinburgh Magazine, and Literary Miscellany* (*Scots Magazine* 1 [October 1817], pp. 254–57) notes the "vivacious, smart, witty, changeful, sparkling, and learned" style he shares with Hunt and Hazlitt while decrying "the uncleannesses of this school." As Clarke later summed up the response:

> The first volume of Keats's minor muse was launched amid the cheers and fond anticipations of his circle . . . Alas! the book might have emerged in Timbuctoo with far stronger chance of fame and approbation . . . The whole community, as if by compact, seemed determined to know nothing about it. The word had been passed that its author was a Radical; and in those days of "Bible-Crown-and-Constitution" supremacy, he might have had better chance of success had he been an Anti-Jacobin. (*Recollections*, p. 140)

Modern criticism on the volume includes chapters in Aske (pp. 38–52), Barnard (pp. 15–34), Bennet (pp. 61–72), Cox (pp. 82–122), Dickstein (pp. 26–52), Jack (pp. 117–42), Levinson (pp. 227–54), Sperry (pp. 72–89), and Wolfson (pp. 206–26); John Kandl, "Private Lyrics in the Public Sphere: Leigh Hunt's *Examiner* and the Construction of a Public 'John Keats,'" *KSJ* 44 (1995): 84–101; William Keach, "Cockney Couplets: Keats and the Politics of Style," *Studies in Romanticism* 25 (Summer 1986): 182–96; and Jack Stillinger, "The Order of Poems in Keats's First Volume" (in 1971), pp. 1–13. For an overview of this volume and *Endymion* in their cultural context, see Roe's essay included in this Norton Critical Edition (pp. 573–83).

The text is that of *Poems* (1817). Woodhouse's interleaved and annotated copy of the volume (Huntington Library MS 151852; *MYR: JK* 1) provides useful information. Extant manuscripts in Keats's hand are indicated in the first note to each poem.

> "What more felicity can fall to creature,
> "Than to enjoy delight with liberty."
>
>   *Fate of the Butterfly.*—SPENSER

DEDICATION.
TO LEIGH HUNT, ESQ.[1]

GLORY and loveliness have passed away;[2]
    For if we wander out in early morn,
    No wreathed incense do we see upborne
Into the east, to meet the smiling day:
No crowd of nymphs soft voic'd and young, and gay,   5
    In woven baskets bringing ears of corn,
    Roses, and pinks, and violets, to adorn
The shrine of Flora[3] in her early May.
But there are left delights as high as these,
    And I shall ever bless my destiny,   10
That in a time, when under pleasant trees
Pan[4] is no longer sought, I feel a free
A leafy luxury, seeing I could please
    With these poor offerings, a man like thee.

1. Written in late February 1817, this dedication was penned by Keats as—"in the buzz of mixed conversation" of friends—he finished reading the proofs of *Poems* (see Clarke, *KC*, 2: 150; *Recollections*, pp. 137–38). The dedicatory poem not only signaled his aesthetic and personal debt to Leigh Hunt but also signed him on as a member of Hunt's circle, soon to be referred to by *Blackwood's* as the "Cockney School" of poetry and politics and often criticized for its "pagan" or "epicurean" proclivities. For Hunt, see above, p. 18
2. Echo perhaps of Wordsworth's "Intimations Ode," l. 18: "there hath past away a glory from the earth."
3. As Lemprière notes, the Roman goddess of flowers and gardens; "Some suppose that she was originally a common courtesan, who left to the Romans the immense riches which she had acquired by prostitution and lasciviousness, in remembrance of which a yearly festival was instituted in her honour."
4. A satyr, with horns and the lower body of a goat, Pan was the god of shepherds and the countryside. Keats pairs him with Flora of l. 8 to evoke the realm of "Flora, and old Pan" in "Sleep and Poetry" (l. 102). In "I stood tip-toe upon a little hill" (ll. 157–62), Keats recalls the story of Pan's attempted rape of the nymph Syrinx, who was transformed into a reed from which Pan then made his "pan-pipe."

[I stood tip-toe upon a little hill][1]

"Places of nestling green for Poets made."

STORY OF RIMINI.[2]

I STOOD tip-toe upon a little hill,[3]
The air was cooling, and so very still,
That the sweet buds which with a modest pride
Pull droopingly, in slanting curve aside,
Their scantly leaved, and finely tapering stems,   5
Had not yet lost those starry diadems
Caught from the early sobbing of the morn.[4]
The clouds were pure and white as flocks new shorn,
And fresh from the clear brook; sweetly they slept
On the blue fields of heaven, and then there crept   10
A little noiseless noise among the leaves,
Born of the very sigh that silence heaves:
For not the faintest motion could be seen
Of all the shades that slanted o'er the green.
There was wide wand'ring for the greediest eye,   15
To peer about upon variety;
Far round the horizon's crystal air to skim,
And trace the dwindled edgings of its brim;
To picture out the quaint, and curious bending
Of a fresh woodland alley, never ending;   20
Or by the bowery clefts, and leafy shelves,
Guess where the jaunty streams refresh themselves.
I gazed awhile, and felt as light, and free
As though the fanning wings of Mercury[5]
Had played upon my heels: I was light-hearted,   25
And many pleasures to my vision started;

1. Completed in December 1816 (and perhaps begun the previous summer), this untitled poem was placed first in Keats's volume of 1817; Keats referred to it in a letter of December 17, 1816, to Clarke as "Endymion" (*L*, 1: 121), but it was printed without a title on a page labeled "POEMS." Often seen as a locodescriptive poem meditating on the relationship between nature and poetry, it might further be read as a celebration of pleasure, from that found in the "posey" (l. 27) of flowers gathered in the first half of the poem to that found in the "poesy" of the second half 's treatment of myth. Keats's handling of myth draws on Wordsworth's account in Book 4 of *The Excursion* as was noted by early reviewers such as G. F. Mathew: "The principal conception of his first poem is the same as that of a contemporary author, Mr Wordsworth, and presumes that the most ancient poets, who are the inventors of the Heathen Mythology, imagined those fables chiefly by the personification of many appearances in nature; just as the astronomers of Egypt gave name and figure to many of our constellations, and as the late Dr Darwin ingeniously illustrated the science of Botany in a poem called 'the Loves of the Plants.'" (*European Magazine* 71 [May 1817], p. 435; see also Hunt in the *Examiner*, June 1, July 6 and 13, 1817, esp. p. 429). On the poem, see Marjorie Norris, "Phenomenology and Process: Perception in Keats's 'I Stood Tip-Toe,'" *KSJ* 25 (1976): 430–54; Levinson, pp. 235–43, and Cox, pp. 104–122. For what has survived of Keats's draft of the poem, see Garrod, pp. lxxiv–lxxxviii, and Stillinger (1974), pp. 122–23; the fair copy is at Harvard (Harvard MS Keats 2.9; *JKPMH*, pp. 33–43).
2. Hunt's *Story of Rimini* (1816). Canto 3: 430; Keats may also echo Hunt's poem at l. 21. Together with the dedicatory poem to Hunt, this opening allusion to Hunt's controversial retelling of the Paolo and Francesca story clearly allied Keats with Hunt. Like Hunt, Keats is experimenting with ways of opening up rhymed couplets.
3. Perhaps an ironic echo of Wordsworth's *Excursion*, 4: 112–13: "when, stationed on top / Of some huge hill."
4. Morning dew.
5. The Roman name for Hermes, messenger to the gods, conductor of souls into the underworld, and patron of travelers, shepherds, orators, and merchants but also thieves and pickpockets. Jupiter gave him a winged cap (*petasus*) and wings for his heels (*talaria*); he exchanged the lyre, which he invented, with Apollo for the *caduceus*, a wand with wings and intertwined serpents.

So I straightway began to pluck a posey
Of luxuries bright, milky, soft and rosy.

A bush of May flowers with the bees about them;
Ah, sure no tasteful nook would be without them;   30
And let a lush laburnum[6] oversweep them,
And let long grass grow round the roots to keep them
Moist, cool and green; and shade the violets,
That they may bind the moss in leafy nets.

A filbert hedge with wild briar overtwined,   35
And clumps of woodbine taking the soft wind
Upon their summer thrones; there too should be
The frequent chequer of a youngling tree,[7]
That with a score of light green brethren shoots
From the quaint mossiness of aged roots: 40
Round which is heard a spring-head of clear waters
Babbling so wildly of its lovely daughters
The spreading blue bells: it may haply mourn
That such fair clusters should be rudely torn
From their fresh beds, and scattered thoughtlessly   45
By infant hands, left on the path to die.

Open afresh your round of starry folds,
Ye ardent marigolds!
Dry up the moisture from your golden lids,
For great Apollo[8] bids   50
That in these days your praises should be sung
On many harps, which he has lately strung;
And when again your dewiness he kisses,
Tell him, I have you in my world of blisses:
So haply when I rove in some far vale,   55
His mighty voice may come upon the gale.

Here are sweet peas, on tip-toe for a flight:
With wings of gentle flush o'er delicate white,
And taper fingers catching at all things,
To bind them all about with tiny rings.   60

Linger awhile upon some bending planks[9]
That lean against a streamlet's rushy banks,
And watch intently Nature's gentle doings:
They will be found softer than ring-dove's cooings.
How silent comes the water round that bend;   65
Not the minutest whisper does it send
To the o'erhanging sallows:[1] blades of grass

6. Woodhouse (*1817*, opposite p. 3) offers "Deep coloured" for "lush"; *laburnum*: an ornamental (though poisonous) tree with bright yellow flowers often used for Easter decorations.
7. Pattern of light and shadow cast by the tree limbs.
8. See p. 6, n. 1.
9. Lines 61–106 were not in Keats's original draft (see Garrod, pp. lxxxiv–lxxxviii). Clarke (*Recollections*, pp. 138–39) indicated they were a reminiscence of Edmonton, which Keats left in October 1815; Ward (pp. 420–21) argues they were written when Keats was at Margate, August–September 1816.
1. Willows.

Slowly across the chequer'd shadows pass.
Why, you might read two sonnets, ere they reach
To where the hurrying freshnesses aye preach   70
A natural sermon o'er their pebbly beds;[2]
Where swarms of minnows show their little heads,
Staying their wavy bodies 'gainst the streams,
To taste the luxury of sunny beams
Temper'd with coolness. How they ever wrestle   75
With their own sweet delight, and ever nestle
Their silver bellies on the pebbly sand.
If you but scantily hold out the hand,
That very instant not one will remain;
But turn your eye, and they are there again.   80
The ripples seem right glad to reach those cresses,
And cool themselves among the em'rald tresses;
The while they cool themselves, they freshness give,
And moisture, that the bowery green may live:
So keeping up an interchange of favours,   85
Like good men in the truth of their behaviours.
Sometimes goldfinches one by one will drop
From low hung branches; little space they stop;
But sip, and twitter, and their feathers sleek;
Then off at once, as in a wanton freak: 90
Or perhaps, to show their black, and golden wings,
Pausing upon their yellow flutterings.
Were I in such a place, I sure should pray
That nought less sweet, might call my thoughts away,
Than the soft rustle of a maiden's gown   95
Fanning away the dandelion's down;
Than the light music of her nimble toes
Patting against the sorrel as she goes.
How she would start, and blush, thus to be caught
Playing in all her innocence of thought.   100
O let me lead her gently o'er the brook,
Watch her half-smiling lips, and downward look;
O let me for one moment touch her wrist;
Let me one moment to her breathing list;
And as she leaves me may she often turn   105
Her fair eyes looking through her locks aubùrne.

What next? A tuft of evening primroses,
O'er which the mind may hover till it dozes;
O'er which it well might take a pleasant sleep,
But that 'tis ever startled by the leap   110
Of buds into ripe flowers; or by the flitting
Of diverse moths, that aye their rest are quitting;
Or by the moon lifting her silver rim
Above a cloud, and with a gradual swim
Coming into the blue with all her light.   115
    O Maker of sweet poets,[3] dear delight

2. Echo of Shakespeare's *As You Like It*, 2. 2. 16–17: "tongues in trees, books in the running brook, / Sermons in stone."
3. The moon; see ll. 181–242 and *Endymion*.

Of this fair world, and all its gentle livers;
Spangler of clouds, halo of crystal rivers,
Mingler with leaves, and dew and tumbling streams,
Closer of lovely eyes to lovely dreams,   120
Lover of loneliness, and wandering,
Of upcast eye, and tender pondering!4
Thee must I praise above all other glories
That smile us on to tell delightful stories.
For what has made the sage or poet write   125
But the fair paradise of Nature's light?
In the calm grandeur of a sober line,
We see the waving of the mountain pine;
And when a tale is beautifully staid,
We feel the safety of a hawthorn glade: 130
When it is moving on luxurious wings,
The soul is lost in pleasant smotherings:
Fair dewy roses brush against our faces,
And flowering laurels spring from diamond vases;
O'er head we see the jasmine and sweet briar,   135
And bloomy grapes laughing from green attire;
While at our feet, the voice of crystal bubbles
Charms us at once away from all our troubles:
So that we feel uplifted from the world,
Walking upon the white clouds wreath'd and curl'd.   140
So felt he, who first told, how Psyche went
On the smooth wind to realms of wonderment;5
What Psyche felt, and Love, when their full lips
First touch'd; what amorous, and fondling nips
They gave each other's cheeks; with all their sighs,   145
And how they kist each other's tremulous eyes:
The silver lamp,—the ravishment,—the wonder—
The darkness,—loneliness,—the fearful thunder;
Their woes gone by, and both to heaven upflown,
To bow for gratitude before Jove's throne.   150
So did he feel, who pull'd the boughs aside,
That we might look into a forest wide,
To catch a glimpse of Fawns, and Dryades6
Coming with softest rustle through the trees;

4. The draft (Scottish National Portrait Gallery; transcription in *TLS*, July 17, 1937, p. 528) adds these cancelled lines: "Smiler on Lovers when they smile on thee / Thee must I place among these Pleasures / Thee must I praise above all other things / That give our thought a pair of little wings."
5. For his account of myth in ll. 141–242, Keats draws on Wordsworth's *Excursion*, 4: 718–62, 847–87, perhaps through the mediation of Hazlitt's review of Wordsworth's poem in the *Examiner* (August 21 and 28, 1814) and perhaps in concert with other retellings of myth by the Hunt circle, including Hunt's own "Bacchus and Ariadne" and "Hero and Leander." Keats offers four myths, the first and fourth of joyous erotic unions and the middle two of frustrated, self-involved love. He first (ll. 141–50) takes up the story of the erotic coupling of the immortal Cupid or Eros, the god of love, and the mortal Psyche (meaning both "soul" and "butterfly" in Greek) to which he would return in his "Ode to Psyche" (see pp. 463–65). Cupid visits Psyche in the dark of l. 148 until she, fearing her lover was a monster, hid the lamp of l. 147 to view him while asleep; when a drop of oil burns one of Cupid's wings, he flees, and Psyche only wins back his love through a series of trials, at the end of which the king of the gods, Jupiter or Jove (l. 150), unites them and deifies Psyche, thus the "latest born . . . Of all Olympus' faded hierarchy" ("Ode to Psyche," ll. 24–25). Keats would have known this story from classical sources including Apuleius (whom Woodhouse *1817* opposite p. 8 identifies as "he who first told" the tale in l. 141), Spenser (*Faerie Queene*, 3.6.50), and Mary Tighe's *Psyche* (1811).
6. Wood-nymphs. *Fawns*: satyrs with the legs, feet, and ears of goats.

And garlands woven of flowers wild, and sweet,   155
Upheld on ivory wrists, or sporting feet:
Telling us how fair, trembling Syrinx fled
Arcadian Pan, with such a fearful dread.[7]
Poor nymph,—poor Pan,—how he did weep to find,
Nought but a lovely sighing of the wind   160
Along the reedy stream; a half heard strain,
Full of sweet desolation—balmy pain.

What first inspired a bard of old to sing
Narcissus pining o'er the untainted spring?[8]
In some delicious ramble, he had found   165
A little space, with boughs all woven round;
And in the midst of all, a clearer pool
Than e'er reflected in its pleasant cool,
The blue sky here, and there, serenely peeping
Through tendril wreaths fantastically creeping.   170
And on the bank a lonely flower he spied,
A meek and forlorn flower, with naught of pride,
Drooping its beauty o'er the watery clearness,
To woo its own sad image into nearness:
Deaf to light Zephyrus[9] it would not move;   175
But still would seem to droop, to pine, to love.
So while the Poet stood in this sweet spot,
Some fainter gleamings o'er his fancy shot;
Nor was it long ere he had told the tale
Of young Narcissus, and sad Echo's bale.   180

Where had he been, from whose warm head out-flew
That sweetest of all songs, that ever new,
That aye refreshing, pure deliciousness,
Coming ever to bless
The wanderer by moonlight? to him bringing   185
Shapes from the invisible world, unearthly singing
From out the middle air, from flowery nests,
And from the pillowy silkiness that rests
Full in the speculation of the stars.
Ah! surely he had burst our mortal bars;   190
Into some wond'rous region he had gone,
To search for thee, divine Endymion![1]

He was a Poet, sure a lover too,
Who stood on Latmus' top, what time there blew

---

7. Keats retells (ll. 151–62) the story of Pan and Syrinx found in Ovid's *Metamorphoses* 1: 689–712 (the
   "he" in l. 151 is Ovid according to Woodhouse, *1817*, p. 9), and in Wordsworth's *Excursion* 4: 871–87.
   Pan chases the reluctant nymph Syrinx who asks her father, the River Ladon, to transform her into a
   reed; Pan is said to have created his pan pipe from the reeds, as art replaces his lost love.
8. Keats takes up (ll. 163–80) the story of Narcissus and Echo which he could have found in Ovid's
   Metamorphoses 3: 339–510. Narcissus falls in love with his own reflected image and is transformed
   into a flower when he dies languishing beside the water. Echo, whom Juno punished by reducing
   her speech to answering others, pined away over her unreturned love for Narcissus.
9. The west wind.
1. Keats's final myth (ll. 181–242) is that of Endymion and Cynthia/Diana/Phoebe, which he would
   have known from Ovid's *Metamorphoses* and Michael Drayton's *The Man in the Moone* (1606) and
   which would be the subject of his longest poem (see *Endymion*). Cynthia, the goddess of the moon,
   fell in love with Endymion, a shepherd, when she spied him naked "on Latmus' top" (l. 194).

Soft breezes from the myrtle vale below;   195
And brought in faintness solemn, sweet, and slow
A hymn from Dian's temple; while upswelling,
The incense went to her own starry dwelling.
But though her face was clear as infant's eyes,
Though she stood smiling o'er the sacrifice,   200
The Poet wept at her so piteous fate,
Wept that such beauty should be desolate:
So in fine wrath some golden sounds he won,
And gave meek Cynthia her Endymion.

Queen of the wide air; thou most lovely queen   205
Of all the brightness that mine eyes have seen!
As thou exceedest all things in thy shine,
So every tale, does this sweet tale of thine.
O for three words of honey, that I might
Tell but one wonder of thy bridal night!   210

Where distant ships do seem to show their keels,
Phœbus² awhile delayed his mighty wheels,
And turned to smile upon thy bashful eyes,
Ere he his unseen pomp would solemnize.
The evening weather was so bright, and clear,   215
That men of health were of unusual cheer;
Stepping like Homer at the trumpet's call,
Or young Apollo on the pedestal:³
And lovely women were as fair and warm,
As Venus⁴ looking sideways in alarm.   220
The breezes were ethereal, and pure,
And crept through half closed lattices to cure
The languid sick; it cool'd their fever'd sleep,
And soothed them into slumbers full and deep.
Soon they awoke clear eyed: nor burnt with thirsting,   225
Nor with hot fingers, nor with temples bursting:
And springing up, they met the wond'ring sight
Of their dear friends, nigh foolish with delight;
Who feel their arms, and breasts, and kiss and stare,
And on their placid foreheads part the hair.⁵   230
Young men, and maidens at each other gaz'd
With hands held back, and motionless, amaz'd
To see the brightness in each other's eyes;
And so they stood, fill'd with a sweet surprise,
Until their tongues were loos'd in poesy.   235
Therefore no lover did of anguish die:
But the soft numbers, in that moment spoken,
Made silken ties, that never may be broken.
Cynthia! I cannot tell the greater blisses,
That follow'd thine, and thy dear shepherd's kisses: 240

2. Apollo, Diana's brother and god of the sun.
3. The statue of the Apollo Belvedere, at the time one of the most famous pieces of classical sculpture, which Allott notes Keats would have known in Spence's *Polymetis* (1747), plate 11.
4. Aphrodite, the goddess of love, mother of Cupid.
5. Allott suggests that these lines may recall Keats's medical training walking the wards at St.
   Thomas's Hospital.

Was there a Poet born?—but now no more,
My wand'ring spirit must no further soar.—

SPECIMEN
OF AN
INDUCTION TO A POEM. [1]

Lo! I must tell a tale of chivalry;
For large white plumes are dancing in mine eye.
Not like the formal crest of latter days:
But bending in a thousand graceful ways;
So graceful, that it seems no mortal hand,   5
Or e'en the touch of Archimago's wand, [2]
Could charm them into such an attitude.
We must think rather, that in playful mood,
Some mountain breeze had turned its chief delight,
To show this wonder of its gentle might.   10
Lo! I must tell a tale of chivalry;
For while I muse, the lance points slantingly
Athwart the morning air: some lady sweet,
Who cannot feel for cold her tender feet,
From the worn top of some old battlement   15
Hails it with tears, her stout defender sent:
And from her own pure self no joy dissembling,
Wraps round her ample robe with happy trembling.
Sometimes, when the good Knight his rest would take,
It is reflected, clearly, in a lake,   20
With the young ashen boughs, 'gainst which it rests,
And th' half seen mossiness of linnets' nests. [3]
Ah! shall I ever tell its cruelty,
When the fire flashes from a warrior's eye,
And his tremendous hand is grasping it,   25
And his dark brow for very wrath is knit?
Or when his spirit, with more calm intent,
Leaps to the honors of a tournament,
And makes the gazers round about the ring
Stare at the grandeur of the balancing?   30
No, no! this is far off:—then how shall I
Revive the dying tones of minstrelsy,
Which linger yet about lone gothic arches,
In dark green ivy, and among wild larches? [4]
How sing the splendour of the revelries,   35
When butts of wine are drunk off to the lees? [5]

1. This poem announcing Keats's desire to write a romance was probably written in the spring of 1816 after the February publication of Hunt's *Story of Rimini*, which influenced Keats's poem, for example, in its use of participial nouns ("trembling," l. 18) and adverbs formed from present participles ("slantingly," l.12). The poem to which this is an "induction" is presumably "Calidore," which follows in *Poems*; the two poems are presented as parts of one work in Tom Keats's copybook (Harvard MS Keats 3.5, p. 1).
2. The magician, known for fashioning false images, in Spenser's *Faerie Queene*, 1.2.
3. A linnet is a common Old World finch.
4. A larch is a kind of pine tree.
5. Dregs.

And that bright lance, against the fretted wall,
Beneath the shade of stately banneral,[6]
Is slung with shining cuirass,[7] sword, and shield,
Where ye may see a spur in bloody field?[8]   40
Light-footed damsels move with gentle paces
Round the wide hall, and show their happy faces;
Or stand in courtly talk by fives and sevens:
Like those fair stars that twinkle in the heavens.
Yet must I tell a tale of chivalry: 45
Or wherefore comes that steed[9] so proudly by?
Wherefore more proudly does the gentle knight
Rein in the swelling of his ample might?
Spenser![1] thy brows are arched, open, kind,
And come like a clear sun-rise to my mind;   50
And always does my heart with pleasure dance,
When I think on thy noble countenance:
Where never yet was ought more earthly seen
Than the pure freshness of thy laurels green.
Therefore, great bard, I not so fearfully   55
Call on thy gentle spirit to hover nigh
My daring steps: or if thy tender care,
Thus startled unaware,
Be jealous that the foot of other wight[2]
Should madly follow that bright path of light   60
Trac'd by thy lov'd Libertas;[3] he will speak,
And tell thee that my prayer is very meek;
That I will follow with due reverence,
And start with awe at mine own strange pretence.
Him thou wilt hear; so I will rest in hope   65
To see wide plains, fair trees and lawny slope:
The morn, the eve, the light, the shade, the flowers:
Clear streams, smooth lakes, and overlooking towers.

CALIDORE.
A Fragment.[1]

YOUNG Calidore is paddling o'er the lake;[2]
His healthful spirit eager and awake
To feel the beauty of a silent eve,

---

6. Standard or pennon. Allott offers *The Faerie Queene*, 6.7.26: "Knightly bannerall."
7. A piece of armor consisting of a breastplate and backplate buckled together.
8. The shield displays an emblem of a spur on a field gules or red background.
9. *Poems* has "knight," but it is altered to "steed" in Tom Keats's copybook, several of Keats's presentation copies, and modern editions.
1. Edmund Spenser (c. 1552–1599), major poet of the Elizabethan period whose *Faerie Queene* (1590–96) was one of Keats's favorite poems. On Keats's debt to Spenser, see Kucich (1991).
2. Person, creature.
3. Keats's poetic name for Leigh Hunt, bestowed in honor of his imprisonment on the charge of committing seditious libel against the Prince Regent.
1. Probably written in the spring of 1816 after the February publication of Hunt's *Story of Rimini* and at the same time as the preceding poem. The protagonist's name is taken from Spenser's "The Legend of Sir Calidore, or, of Courtesie," *The Faerie Queene*, Book 6. As Allott notes, Hunt's influence is seen in the use of adjectives derived from present participles (i.e., "lingeringly" in l. 5), of abstract nouns ending in "ness" (i.e., "clearness" in l. 7), and of adjectives ending in "y" formed from verbs and nouns (i.e., "shadowy" in l. 10 and "bowery" in l. 26).
2. Allott cites the opening line of Spenser's *Faerie Queene*: "A Gentle Knight was pricking on the plaine."

Which seem'd full loath this happy world to leave;
The light dwelt o'er the scene so lingeringly.   5
He bares his forehead to the cool blue sky,
And smiles at the far clearness all around,
Until his heart is well nigh over wound,
And turns for calmness to the pleasant green
Of easy slopes, and shadowy trees that lean   10
So elegantly o'er the waters' brim
And show their blossoms trim.
Scarce can his clear and nimble eye-sight follow
The freaks, and dartings of the black-wing'd swallow,
Delighting much, to see it half at rest,   15
Dip so refreshingly its wings, and breast
'Gainst the smooth surface, and to mark anon,
The widening circles into nothing gone.

And now the sharp keel of his little boat
Comes up with ripple, and with easy float,   20
And glides into a bed of water lillies:
Broad leav'd are they and their white canopies
Are upward turn'd to catch the heavens' dew.
Near to a little island's point they grew;
Whence Calidore might have the goodliest view   25
Of this sweet spot of earth. The bowery shore
Went off in gentle windings to the hoar
And light blue mountains: but no breathing man
With a warm heart, and eye prepared to scan
Nature's clear beauty, could pass lightly by   30
Objects that look'd out so invitingly
On either side. These, gentle Calidore
Greeted, as he had known them long before.

The sidelong view of swelling leafiness,
Which the glad setting sun in gold doth dress;   35
Whence ever and anon the jay outsprings,
And scales upon the beauty of its wings.

The lonely turret, shatter'd, and outworn,
Stands venerably proud; too proud to mourn
Its long lost grandeur: fir trees grow around,   40
Aye dropping their hard fruit upon the ground.

The little chapel with the cross above
Upholding wreaths of ivy; the white dove,
That on the windows spreads his[3] feathers light,
And seems from purple clouds to wing its flight.   45

Green tufted islands casting their soft shades
Across the lake; sequester'd leafy glades,
That through the dimness of their twilight show
Large dock leaves, spiral foxgloves, or the glow

---

3. Tom Keats's transcript (Harvard MS Keats 3.5, p. 3) has "window . . . its."

Of the wild cat's eyes,[4] or the silvery stems   50
Of delicate birch trees, or long grass which hems
A little brook. The youth had long been viewing
These pleasant things, and heaven was bedewing
The mountain flowers, when his glad senses caught
A trumpet's silver voice. Ah! it was fraught   55
With many joys for him: the warder's ken[5]
Had found white coursers[6] prancing in the glen:
Friends very dear to him he soon will see;
So pushes off his boat most eagerly,
And soon upon the lake he skims along,   60
Deaf to the nightingale's first under-song;
Nor minds he the white swans that dream so sweetly:
His spirit flies before him so completely.

And now he turns a jutting point of land,
Whence may be seen the castle gloomy, and grand: 65
Nor will a bee buzz round two swelling peaches,
Before the point of his light shallop[7] reaches
Those marble steps that through the water dip:
Now over them he goes with hasty trip,
And scarcely stays to ope the folding doors: 70
Anon he leaps along the oaken floors
Of halls and corridors.

Delicious sounds! those little bright-eyed things
That float about the air on azure wings,
Had been less heartfelt by him than the clang   75
Of clattering hoofs; into the court he sprang,
Just as two noble steeds, and palfreys[8] twain,
Were slanting out their necks with loosened rein;
While from beneath the threat'ning portcullis[9]
They brought their happy burthens. What a kiss,   80
What gentle squeeze he gave each lady's hand!
How tremblingly their delicate ancles spann'd!
Into how sweet a trance his soul was gone,
While whisperings of affection
Made him delay to let their tender feet   85
Come to the earth; with an incline so sweet
From their low palfreys o'er his neck they bent:
And whether there were tears of languishment,
Or that the evening dew had pearl'd their tresses,
He feels a moisture on his cheek, and blesses   90
With lips that tremble, and with glistening eye
All the soft luxury
That nestled in his arms. A dimpled hand,
Fair as some wonder out of fairy land,

4. Speedwells or forget-me-nots; *dock*: a coarse, weedy herb; *foxgloves*: also herbs, that rise like spires.
5. Knowledge or skill, here primarily sight; warder: a soldier on watch in a castle.
6. Swift, spirited horses; chargers.
7. Light boat. This word, which appears again in *Endymion* 1: 423, might have been suggested by Shelley's *Alastor* (February 1816), l. 299, "A little shallop floating near the shore."
8. Light easy-gaited horses, not war-horses and often chosen for women riders.
9. An iron grate hung over the gateway of a fortified place that is lowered to prevent entry.

Hung from his shoulder like the drooping flowers
Of whitest Cassia,[1] fresh from summer showers:
And this he fondled with his happy cheek
As if for joy he would no further seek;
When the kind voice of good Sir Clerimond
Came to his ear, like something from beyond   100
His present being: so he gently drew
His warm arms, thrilling now with pulses new,
From their sweet thrall, and forward gently bending,
Thank'd heaven that his joy was never ending;
While 'gainst his forehead he devoutly press'd   105
A hand heaven made to succour the distress'd;
A hand that from the world's bleak promontory
Had lifted Calidore for deeds of glory.

Amid the pages, and the torches' glare,
There stood a knight, patting the flowing hair   110
Of his proud horse's mane: he was withal
A man of elegance, and stature tall:
So that the waving of his plumes would be
High as the berries of a wild ash tree,
Or as the winged cap of Mercury.[2]   115
His armour was so dexterously wrought
In shape, that sure no living man had thought
It hard, and heavy steel: but that indeed
It was some glorious form, some splendid weed,[3]
In which a spirit new come from the skies   120
Might live, and show itself to human eyes.
'Tis the far-fam'd, the brave Sir Gondibert,[4]
Said the good man to Calidore alert;
While the young warrior with a step of grace
Came up,—a courtly smile upon his face,   125
And mailed[5] hand held out, ready to greet
The large-eyed wonder, and ambitious heat
Of the aspiring boy; who as he led
Those smiling ladies, often turned his head
To admire the visor arched so gracefully   130
Over a knightly brow; while they went by
The lamps that from the high-roof'd hall were pendent,
And gave the steel a shining quite transcendent.

Soon in a pleasant chamber they are seated;
The sweet-lipp'd ladies have already greeted   135
All the green leaves that round the window clamber,
To show their purple stars, and bells of amber.
Sir Gondibert has doff'd his shining steel,
Gladdening in the free, and airy feel
Of a light mantle; and while Clerimond   140
Is looking round about him with a fond,

1. Honeysuckle.
2. See p. 21, n. 5.
3. Dress, clothing.
4. A name borrowed from Sir William Davenant's epic *Gondibert* (1651).
5. Armored; mail is a kind of armor made of metal links.

And placid eye, young Calidore is burning
To hear of knightly deeds, and gallant spurning
Of all unworthiness; and how the strong of arm
Kept off dismay, and terror, and alarm   145
From lovely woman: while brimful of this,
He gave each damsel's hand so warm a kiss,
And had such manly ardour in his eye,
That each at other look'd half staringly;
And then their features started into smiles   150
Sweet as blue heavens o'er enchanted isles.

Softly the breezes from the forest came,
Softly they blew aside the taper's flame;
Clear was the song from Philomel's[6] far bower;
Grateful the incense from the lime-tree flower;   155
Mysterious, wild, the far heard trumpet's tone;
Lovely the moon in ether, all alone:
Sweet too the converse of these happy mortals,
As that of busy spirits when the portals
Are closing in the west; or that soft humming   160
We hear around when Hesperus[7] is coming.
Sweet be their sleep. * * * * * * * * *

TO
SOME LADIES.[1]

WHAT though while the wonders of nature exploring,
    I cannot your light, mazy footsteps attend;
Nor listen to accents that, almost adoring,
    Bless Cynthia's face,[2] the enthusiast's friend:

Yet over the steep, whence the mountain stream rushes,   5
    With you, kindest friends, in idea I muse;[3]
Mark the clear tumbling crystal, its passionate gushes,
    Its spray that the wild flower kindly bedews.

Why linger you so, the wild labyrinth strolling?
    Why breathless, unable your bliss to declare?   10
Ah! you list to the nightingale's tender condoling,
    Responsive to sylphs,[4] in the moon beamy air.

6. A nightingale's. Philomel was raped by Tereus, her brother-in-law, who then cut out her tongue to
keep her from revealing his crime. She, however, managed to tell her story to her sister Procne
through weaving a tapestry. In revenge, Procne served Tereus their son for dinner. As he was about
to stab her, she was transformed into a swallow and Philomel into a nightingale.
7. The planet Venus after sunset is named for Hesperus, who disappeared after ascending Mount
Atlas to make observations of the stars.
1. Written in the summer of 1815 in response to a gift of a seashell from Caroline and Anne Mathew
who had vacationed at the seashore with their cousin, George Felton Mathew, the leader of a circle
of which Keats was a part at the time (see headnote, p. 17). Allott notes that the meter and style are
an imitation of Tom Moore's early poems. Keats may have taken the idea of joining his friends' journey through nature only in his imagination from Coleridge's "This Lime-Tree Bower My Prison,"
which he seems to echo in "Calidore" (ll. 154–55) and "To one who has long in city pent" (l. 1).
There is a holograph fair copy entitled "To the Misses M_" at Texas Christian University Library.
2. The moon; see p. 25, n. 1.
3. *Poems* has "rove" but the rhyme requires "muse" from the fair copy.
4. In Paracelsus, elemental beings inhabiting the air.

'Tis morn, and the flowers with dew are yet drooping,
    I see you are treading the verge of the sea:
And now! ah, I see it—you just now are stooping   15
    To pick up the keep-sake intended for me.

If a cherub, on pinions[5] of silver descending,
    Had brought me a gem from the fret-work of heaven;
And, smiles with his star-cheering voice sweetly blending,
    The blessings of Tighe[6] had melodiously given;   20

It had not created a warmer emotion
    Than the present, fair nymphs, I was blest with from you,
Than the shell, from the bright golden sands of the ocean
    Which the emerald waves at your feet gladly threw.

For, indeed, 'tis a sweet and peculiar pleasure,   25
    (And blissful is he who such happiness finds,)
To possess but a span of the hour of leisure,
    In elegant, pure, and aerial minds.

On receiving a curious Shell, and a Copy of Verses, from the same Ladies.[1]

HAST THOU from the caves of Golconda,[2] a gem
    Pure as the ice-drop that froze on the mountain?
Bright as the humming-bird's green diadem,
    When it flutters in sun-beams that shine through a fountain?

Hast thou a goblet for dark sparkling wine?   5
    That goblet right heavy, and massy, and gold?
And splendidly mark'd with the story divine
    Of Armida the fair, and Rinaldo the bold?[3]

Hast thou a steed with a mane richly flowing?
    Hast thou a sword that thine enemy's smart is?   10
Hast thou a trumpet rich melodies blowing?
    And wear'st thou the shield of the fam'd Britomartis?[4]

---

5. Wings.
6. Mary Tighe (1772–1810), Anglo-Irish poet, best known for *Psyche, or, The Legend of Love* (1805), which was admired by Tom Moore and Keats (*L*, 2: 18); see E. V. Weller, *Keats and Mary Tighe* (1928).
1. Written in the summer of 1815 for George Felton Mathew, the cousin of the Mathew sisters of the preceding poem, Keats's friend, and here, Eric, a knight. As is indicated in George Keats's transcript (in the Keats-Wylie Scrapbook at Harvard, MS Keats 3.4, f. 36r), which provides the title "Written on receiving a Copy of Tom Moore's 'Golden Chain,' and a most beautiful Dome shaped Shell from a Lady," the verses are Tom Moore's "The Wreath and the Chain," published in his *Epistles, Odes, and Other Poems* (1806). There is a holograph fair copy at Harvard (MS Keats 2.1; *JKPMH*, p. 3).
2. A sultanate in India, renamed Hyderabad, once an important source of diamonds, including perhaps the Hope Diamond. Allott cites Thomson's *The Seasons* (1730), *Summer*, ll. 870–71: "Deep in the bowels of the pitying earth / Golconda's gems . . . ."
3. Rinaldo: one of the heroes of Tasso's *Gerusalemme Liberata* (1581); *Armida*: his Saracen paramour. Keats read the poem in Fairfax's translation (1600) (*KC*, 1: 253).
4. Chaste warrior heroine of Spenser's *Faerie Queene*, Book 3.

What is it that hangs from thy shoulder, so brave,
   Embroidered with many a spring peering flower?
Is it a scarf that thy fair lady gave?   15
   And hastest thou now to that fair lady's bower?

Ah! courteous Sir Knight, with large joy thou art crown'd;
   Full many the glories that brighten thy youth!
I will tell thee my blisses, which richly abound
   In magical powers to bless, and to sooth.   20

On this scroll[5] thou seest written in characters fair
   A sun-beamy tale of a wreath, and a chain;
And, warrior, it nurtures the property rare
   Of charming my mind from the trammels[6] of pain.

This canopy mark: 'tis the work of a fay;[7]   25
   Beneath its rich shade did King Oberon languish,
When lovely Titania was far, far away,
   And cruelly left him to sorrow, and anguish.

There, oft would he bring from his soft sighing lute
   Wild strains to which, spell-bound, the nightingales listened; 30
The wondering spirits of heaven were mute,
   And tears 'mong the dewdrops of morning oft glistened.

In this little dome,[8] all those melodies strange,
   Soft, plaintive, and melting, for ever will sigh;
Nor e'er will the notes from their tenderness change; 35
   Nor e'er will the music of Oberon die.

So, when I am in a voluptuous vein,
   I pillow my head on the sweets of the rose,
And list to the tale of the wreath, and the chain,
   Till its echoes depart; then I sink to repose.   40

Adieu, valiant Eric! with joy thou art crown'd;
   Full many the glories that brighten thy youth,
I too have my blisses, which richly abound
   In magical powers, to bless and to sooth.

TO****[1]

HADST thou liv'd in days of old,
O what wonders had been told

---

5. Moore's poem (see above, n. 1).
6. Literally, fishing nets, and figuratively, anything that confines, restrains, fetters, or shackles.
7. A fairy. Oberon and Titania are king and queen of the fairies in Shakespeare's *A Midsummer Night's Dream*; Allott, however, suggests Keats refers here to William Sotheby's translation (1798) of Wieland's *Oberon* (1780) which focuses on Oberon's anguish over his separation from Titania.
8. The shell of the title.
1. As Woodhouse indicates (*1817*, p. 36), this poem was written on or before February 14, 1816, as a valentine from George Keats to Mary Frogley, Woodhouse's cousin; the poem was revised for publication. There is a revised holograph fair copy at the Wisbech and Fenland Museum (Townshend MS Collection 2003.35.170.2).

Of thy lively countenance,
And thy humid eyes that dance
In the midst of their own brightness;   5
In the very fane of lightness.
Over which thine eyebrows, leaning,
Picture out each lovely meaning:
In a dainty bend they lie,
Like to streaks across the sky,   10
Or the feathers from a crow,
Fallen on a bed of snow.
Of thy dark hair that extends
Into many graceful bends:
As the leaves of Hellebore²   15
Turn to whence they sprung before.
And behind each ample curl
Peeps the richness of a pearl.
Downward too flows many a tress
With a glossy waviness;   20
Full, and round like globes³ that rise
From the censer to the skies
Through sunny air. Add too, the sweetness
Of thy honied voice; the neatness
Of thine ankle lightly turn'd: 25
With those beauties, scarce discern'd,
Kept with such sweet privacy,
That they seldom meet the eye
Of the little loves⁴ that fly
Round about with eager pry.   30
Saving when, with freshening lave,
Thou dipp'st them in the taintless wave;
Like twin water lillies, born
In the coolness of the morn.
O, if thou hadst breathed then,   35
Now the Muses had been ten.⁵
Couldst thou wish for lineage higher
Than twin sister of Thalia?⁶
At least for ever, evermore,
Will I call the Graces four.   40

Hadst thou liv'd when chivalry
Lifted up her lance on high,
Tell me what thou wouldst have been?
Ah! I see the silver sheen
Of thy broidered, floating vest   45

2. "Name given by the ancients to certain plants having poisonous and medicinal properties, and esp. reputed as specifics for mental disease" (OED); in botany, name given to a class of plants common in English gardens, including the Christmas Rose; *fane*, above: temple.
3. Woodhouse (*1817*, opposite p. 37) glosses this as "smoke" from the incense burned in the censer of the next line; Allott offers Spenser's "Colin Clout's Come Home Againe," ll. 608–11.
4. Putti or winged cherubs; Allott suggests Spenser's *Epithalamion* (1595), ll. 357–59, with its "hundred little winged loves" that "fly" "about your bed."
5. Rather than the traditional nine; it is a common Renaissance conceit to praise a woman by adding her to the muses.
6. Often the muse of comic poetry, but also and here the Grace who presides over festivals; the addressee is made the fourth grace (l. 40), when traditionally there are three.

Cov'ring half thine ivory breast;
Which, O heavens! I should see,
But that cruel destiny
Has placed a golden cuirass[7] there;
Keeping secret what is fair.[8]   50
Like sunbeams in a cloudlet nested
Thy locks in knightly casque[9] are rested:
O'er which bend four milky plumes
Like the gentle lilly's blooms
Springing from a costly vase.   55
See with what a stately pace
Comes thine alabaster steed;
Servant of heroic deed!
O'er his loins, his trappings glow
Like the northern lights on snow.   60
Mount his back! thy sword unsheath!
Sign of the enchanter's death;
Bane of every wicked spell;
Silencer of dragon's yell.
Alas! thou this wilt never do: 65
Thou art an enchantress too,
And wilt surely never spill
Blood of those whose eyes can kill.[1]

TO
HOPE.[1]

WHEN by my solitary hearth I sit,
    And hateful thoughts enwrap my soul in gloom;
When no fair dreams before my "mind's eye" flit,[2]
    And the bare heath of life presents no bloom;
        Sweet Hope, ethereal balm upon me shed,   5
        And wave thy silver pinions[3] o'er my head.

Whene'er I wander, at the fall of night,
    Where woven boughs shut out the moon's bright ray,
Should sad Despondency my musings fright,

7. See p. 28, n. 7.
8. Keats appears to compare Mary to Spenser's Britomart (see p. 33, n. 4).
9. Helmet.
1. Woodhouse's transcript (in W³, original W², f. 5r; *MYR: JK*, 4: 233) adds from the original valentine: "Ah me! Whither shall I flee? / Thou has metamorphosed me! / Do not let me sigh and pine, / 'Prythee, be my Valentine!'"
1. Written in February 1815, "To Hope" is often taken to reflect Keats's gloomy spirits at the time following the break-up of the Keats home upon the death of his grandmother in December 1814; Keats was living with the surgeon, Thomas Hammond, as an apprentice, while his sister lived with their guardian Richard Abbey, for whom the two other Keats brothers were working. However, as the closing stanzas suggest, Keats wants to connect personal despair with national woes; while he probably would not have known yet of Napoleon's escape from Elba on February 26, 1815, he may have been concerned about civil liberties in the aftermath of the Napoleonic wars. The poem also explores a Huntian response of "Cheerfulness" to the "Despondency" of Wordsworth's Solitary from *The Excursion* (1814). The first two stanzas of a holograph fair copy, apparently in private hands, can be found *KSJ* 1 (1952): following p. 60.
2. Echo of *Hamlet*, 1.2.184: "In my mind's eye, Horatio."
3. See p. 5, n. 3.

And frown, to drive fair Cheerfulness away,   10
  Peep with the moon-beams through the leafy roof,
And keep that fiend Despondence far aloof.

Should Disappointment, parent of Despair,
  Strive for her son to seize my careless heart;
When, like a cloud, he sits upon the air,   15
  Preparing on his spell-bound prey to dart:
    Chace him away, sweet Hope, with visage bright,
    And fright him as the morning frightens night!

Whene'er the fate of those I hold most dear
  Tells to my fearful breast a tale of sorrow,   20
O bright-eyed Hope, my morbid fancy cheer;
  Let me awhile thy sweetest comforts borrow:
    Thy heaven-born radiance around me shed,
    And wave thy silver pinions o'er my head!

Should e'er unhappy love my bosom pain,   25
  From cruel parents, or relentless fair;
O let me think it is not quite in vain
  To sigh out sonnets to the midnight air!
    Sweet Hope, ethereal balm upon me shed,
    And wave thy silver pinions o'er my head!   30

In the long vista of the years to roll,
  Let me not see our country's honour fade:
O let me see our land retain her soul,
  Her pride, her freedom; and not freedom's shade.
    From thy bright eyes unusual brightness shed—   35
    Beneath thy pinions canopy my head!

Let me not see the patriot's high bequest,
  Great Liberty! how great in plain attire!
With the base purple of a court oppress'd,
  Bowing her head, and ready to expire: 40
    But let me see thee stoop from heaven on wings
    That fill the skies with silver glitterings!

And as, in sparkling majesty, a star
  Gilds the bright summit of some gloomy cloud;
Brightening the half veil'd face of heaven afar: 45
  So, when dark thoughts my boding spirit shroud,
    Sweet Hope, celestial influence round me shed,
    Waving thy silver pinions o'er my head.

February, 1815.

IMITATION OF SPENSER.[1]

* * * * * * *

Now Morning from her orient chamber came,
And her first footsteps touch'd a verdant hill;
Crowning its lawny crest with amber flame,
Silv'ring the untainted gushes of its rill;
Which, pure from mossy beds, did down distill,   5
And after parting beds of simple flowers,
By many streams a little lake did fill,
Which round its marge reflected woven bowers,[2]
And, in its middle space, a sky that never lowers.

There the king-fisher saw his plumage bright   10
Vieing with fish of brilliant dye below;
Whose silken fins, and golden scales'[3] light
Cast upward, through the waves, a ruby glow:
There saw the swan his neck of arched snow,
And oar'd himself along with majesty;   15
Sparkled his jetty[4] eyes; his feet did show
Beneath the waves like Afric's ebony,
And on his back a fay[5] reclined voluptuously.

Ah! could I tell the wonders of an isle
That in that fairest lake had placed been,   20
I could e'en Dido of her grief beguile;[6]
Or rob from aged Lear his bitter teen:[7]
For sure so fair a place was never seen,
Of all that ever charm'd romantic eye:
It seem'd an emerald in the silver sheen   25
Of the bright waters; or as when on high,
Through clouds of fleecy white, laughs the cœrulean[8] sky.

And all around it dipp'd luxuriously
Slopings of verdure through the glossy[9] tide,
Which, as it were in gentle amity,   30

1. Probably composed in early 1814, this is the first known poem by Keats; Brown (KC, 2:55–56) tells us that both Keats and his brothers indicated he was first inspired to write while reading Spenser's *The Faerie Queen*. Keats would not return to the Spenserian stanza until *The Eve of St. Agnes*. We see here already the contrast between romance and tragedy (cf. ll. 21–22) that Keats later developed in "Sleep and Poetry" among other poems. The asterisks at the beginning and end probably mark the fragmentary nature of the poem.
2. Keats often draws on the imagery of Spenser's Bower of Bliss, *Faerie Queen*, 2.12; *marge*: archaism for "margin," here shoreline.
3. Stillinger, following Tom Keats's transcript (Harvard MS Keats 3.5, p. 12), changes this to "scalès," dropping the possessive and making "light" an adjective.
4. Black.
5. See p. 10, n. 2.
6. See Virgil's *Aeneid*, Books 1–4, for the tale of Dido's love for Aeneas and her suicide when he deserts her to continue his epic journey to found Rome; Clarke (*Recollections*, p. 124) indicates that Keats translated a large portion of the epic while at school.
7. Archaic word for grief; Keats is probably thinking of Lear's grief at the death of his daughter Cordelia at the close of Shakespeare's play.
8. "Of the colour of the cloudless sky, pure deep blue, azure" (OED).
9. Stillinger, following Tom Keats's transcript, changes this to "glassy."

Rippled delighted up the flowery side;
As if to glean the ruddy tears, it tried,
Which fell profusely from the rose-tree stem!
Haply it was the workings of its pride,
In strife to throw upon the shore a gem   35
Outvieing all the buds in Flora's[1] diadem.

* * * * * * *

[Woman! when I behold thee flippant, vain][1]

WOMAN! when I behold thee flippant, vain,
  Inconstant, childish, proud, and full of fancies;
  Without that modest softening that enhances
The downcast eye, repentant of the pain
That its mild light creates to heal again: 5
  E'en then, elate, my spirit leaps, and prances,
  E'en then my soul with exultation dances
For that to love, so long, I've dormant lain:
But when I see thee meek, and kind, and tender,
  Heavens! how desperately do I adore[2]   10
Thy winning graces;—to be thy defender
  I hotly burn—to be a Calidore—
A very Red Cross Knight—a stout Leander[3]—
  Might I be loved by thee like these of yore.

Light feet, dark violet eyes, and parted hair;   15
  Soft dimpled hands, white neck, and creamy breast,
  Are things on which the dazzled senses rest
Till the fond, fixed eyes, forget they stare.
From such fine pictures, heavens! I cannot dare
  To turn my admiration, though unpossess'd   20
  They be of what is worthy,—though not drest
In lovely modesty, and virtues rare.
Yet these I leave as thoughtless as a lark;
  These lures I straight forget,—e'en ere I dine,
Or thrice my palate moisten: but when I mark   25
  Such charms with mild intelligences shine,
My ear is open like a greedy shark,
  To catch the tunings of a voice divine.

Ah! who can e'er forget so fair a being?
Who can forget her half retiring sweets?   30

---

1. See p. 20, n. 3.
1. The composition date of this poem, untitled in *Poems,* is unknown, but Bate (p. 40n.) and Ward
   (p. 418, n. 14) believe it was written in 1815 during Keats's involvement with G. F. Mathew who
   praised the poem in his *European Magazine* review of the volume. The untitled stanzas are Petrarchan sonnets, which has led some to print them as separate poems. Woodhouse wrote (*1817,* in
   shorthand opposite p. 49 for ll. 31–32), "When K had written these lines he burst into tears over-
   powered by the tenderness of his own imagination (conceptions)."
2. Woodhouse (*1817,* p. 47) offers "perdite amo" ("I love desperately") from Catullus 45.3.
3. *Leander,* the subject of a later poem by Hunt, died swimming across the Hellespont to reach his
   beloved Hero. *Calidore:* the hero of Spenser's *Faerie Queene,* Book 6, and of Keats's poem of that
   title (see, p. 28–32). *Red Cross Knight:* the hero of the first book of the *Faerie Queene.*

God! she is like a milk-white lamb that bleats
For man's protection. Surely the All-seeing,
Who joys to see us with his gifts agreeing,
Will never give him pinions,[4] who intreats
Such innocence to ruin,—who vilely cheats   35
A dove-like bosom. In truth there is no freeing
One's thoughts from such a beauty; when I hear
A lay that once I saw her hand awake,
Her form seems floating palpable, and near;
Had I e'er seen her from an arbour take   40
A dewy flower, oft would that hand appear,
And o'er my eyes the trembling moisture shake.

EPISTLES.[1]

TO
GEORGE FELTON MATHEW.[2]

SWEET are the pleasures that to verse belong,
And doubly sweet a brotherhood in song;
Nor can remembrance, Mathew! bring to view
A fate more pleasing, a delight more true
Than that in which the brother Poets[3] joy'd,   5
Who with combined powers, their wit employ'd
To raise a trophy to the drama's muses.
The thought of this great partnership diffuses
Over the genius loving heart, a feeling
Of all that's high, and great, and good, and healing.   10

Too partial friend! fain would I follow thee
Past each horizon of fine poesy;
Fain would I echo back each pleasant note
As o'er Sicilian seas, clear anthems float
'Mong the light skimming gondolas far parted,   15
Just when the sun his farewell beam has darted:
But 'tis impossible; far different cares[4]

---

4. Give wings; admit into heaven.
1. This marks the second section of Keats's *Poems*; Keats provides an epigraph on p. 51:

> "Among the rest a shepheard (though but young
> "Yet hartned to his pipe) with all the skill
> "His few yeeres could, began to fit his quill."
>   Britannia's Pastorals.—BROWNE."

Keats quotes William Browne's *Britannia's Pastorals* II (1616), Song 3, ll. 748–50. Keats's epistles, private letters made public, can be usefully compared to Hunt's seven epistles in *Foliage* (1818; originally appearing in the *Examiner*) and to Tom Moore's volumes of "intercepted" letters.
2. Written in November 1815, this epistle was sent as a verse letter (*L*, 1: 100–103) to George Felton Mathew as thanks for his "To a Poetical Friend" (*European Magazine*, October 1816: 365; see p. 10–11), where Keats is compared to Shakespeare and Milton (ll. 21–24). For Mathew's comments on the poem, see *KC*, 2: 181, 186–88.
3. Francis Beaumont (1584–1616) and John Fletcher (1579–1625), who collaborated on some fifteen plays; these "brother Poets" are a model for the "brotherhood of song" (l. 2) Keats imagines as sharing with Mathew.
4. McGann (1985, pp. 26–31), Allott, and ultimately Mathew (*KC*, 2: 186) suggest that the poem contrasts Keats's preoccupation with his medical training, "walking the hospitals," as Mathew puts it, with Mathew's freedom to write.

Beckon me sternly from soft "Lydian airs,"[5]
And hold my faculties so long in thrall,
That I am oft in doubt whether at all   20
I shall again see Phœbus in the morning:
Or flush'd Aurora in the roseate dawning!
Or a white Naiad in a rippling stream;
Or a rapt seraph[6] in a moonlight beam;
Or again witness what with thee I've seen,   25
The dew by fairy feet swept from the green,
After a night of some quaint jubilee
Which every elf and fay had come to see:[7]
When bright processions took their airy march
Beneath the curved moon's triumphal arch.   30

But might I now each passing moment give
To the coy muse, with me she would not live
In this dark city, nor would condescend
'Mid contradictions her delights to lend.
Should e'er the fine-eyed maid to me be kind,   35
Ah! surely it must be whene'er I find
Some flowery spot, sequester'd, wild, romantic,
That often must have seen a poet frantic;
Where oaks, that erst the Druid[8] knew, are growing,
And flowers, the glory of one day, are blowing;   40
Where the dark-leav'd laburnum's drooping clusters
Reflect athwart the stream their yellow lustres,
And intertwined the cassia's[9] arms unite,
With its own drooping buds, but very white.
Where on one side are covert branches hung,   45
'Mong which the nightingales have always sung
In leafy quiet: where to pry, aloof,
Atween the pillars of the sylvan roof,
Would be to find where violet beds were nestling,
And where the bee with cowslip bells was wrestling.   50
There must be too a ruin dark, and gloomy,
To say "joy not too much in all that's bloomy."[1]

Yet this is vain—O Mathew lend thy aid
To find a place where I may greet the maid—
Where we may soft humanity put on,   55
And sit, and rhyme and think on Chatterton;[2]
And that warm-hearted Shakspeare sent to meet him
Four laurell'd spirits, heaven-ward to intreat him.
With reverence would we speak of all the sages

---

5. Milton, "L'Allegro," ll. 135–36.
6. An angel of the highest rank, also known as a the seraphim. For *Phoebus* Apollo, see p. 6, n. 1;
   Aurora: the goddess of the dawn; *Naiad*: a water nymph.
7. Echo of Mathew's "To a Poetical Friend," ll. 1–2: "O Thou who delightest in fanciful song, / And
   tellest strange tales of the elf and the fay" (for "fay," see p. 10, n. 2).
8. Priest of the ancient Celts often seen in the poetry of the period as a philosophical bard of nature.
9. See p. 31, n. 1; *laburnum's*: see p. 22, n. 6.
1. Gittings (p. 57) sees this as an echoing complement to Mathew's "Written in Time of Sickness"
   included in his circle's miscellany *The Garland* : "The ruin'd monastery, the waving woods, / All
   show more gloomy in the doubtful light." Keats contrasts the beauties of nature experienced with
   Mathew with his own life "In this dark city" (l. 33).
2. See Keats's sonnet to Chatterton, p. 6, n. 1.

Who have left streaks of light athwart their ages: 60
And thou shouldst moralize on Milton's blindness,
And mourn the fearful dearth of human kindness
To those who strove with the bright golden wing
Of genius, to flap away each sting
Thrown by the pitiless world. We next could tell   65
Of those who in the cause of freedom fell:
Of our own Alfred, of Helvetian Tell;
Of him whose name to ev'ry heart's a solace,
High-minded and unbending William Wallace.[3]
While to the rugged north our musing turns   70
We well might drop a tear for him, and Burns.[4]

Felton! without incitements such as these,
How vain for me the niggard Muse to tease:
For thee, she will thy every dwelling grace,
And make "a sun-shine in a shady place:"[5]   75
For thou wast once a flowret blooming wild,
Close to the source, bright, pure, and undefil'd,
Whence gush the streams of song:[6] in happy hour
Came chaste Diana from her shady bower,
Just as the sun was from the east uprising;   80
And, as for him some gift she was devising,
Beheld thee, pluck'd thee, cast thee in the stream
To meet her glorious brother's greeting beam.
I marvel much that thou hast never told
How, from a flower, into a fish of gold   85
Apollo chang'd thee; how thou next didst seem
A black-eyed swan upon the widening stream;
And when thou first didst in that mirror trace
The placid features of a human face:
That thou hast never told thy travels strange,   90
And all the wonders of the mazy range
O'er pebbly crystal, and o'er golden sands;
Kissing thy daily food from Naiad's pearly hands.

November, 1815.

3. Scottish patriot (1272?–1305) involved in the resistance to English rule at the time of Edward I.
   Alfred the Great (849–99), King of Wessex (871–99), noted for governmental reforms and the
   revival of letters; he was seen as a model king, a benefactor of the people and author of key English liberties such as trial by jury. William *Tell*, the legendary liberator of the Swiss (thus Helvetian) from Austrian oppression, was the subject of a play by Schiller in 1804.
4. Robert Burns (1759–1796), Scots poet, whose 1786 *Poems, Chiefly in the Scottish Dialect* was an
   immediate success; contending with fame and political pressures after the French Revolution, he
   continued to write complex, highly sophisticated poetry that spoke for the rights of the common
   man. Keats offers here an international cast of freedom fighters from the Swiss William Tell to the
   Anglo-Saxon Alfred, from Milton the republican to Wallace the warrior against England.
5. Spenser, *Faerie Queene*, 1.3.4: "And made a sunshine in the shadie place."
6. Helicon, the springs of the Muses. Mathew goes through a series of Ovidian transformations that
   take him from the wellspring of song to Diana, goddess of the moon and Keats's "Maker of Sweet
   Poets" (see "I stood tip-toe," l. 116), to her brother Apollo, the god of poetry, before he becomes a
   swan, with its famous song, and then a human poet.

TO
MY BROTHER GEORGE.[1]

FULL many a dreary hour have I past,
My brain bewilder'd, and my mind o'ercast
With heaviness; in seasons when I've thought
No spherey strains[2] by me could e'er be caught
From the blue dome, though I to dimness gaze   5
On the far depth where sheeted lightning plays;
Or, on the wavy grass outstretch'd supinely,
Pry 'mong the stars, to strive to think divinely:
That I should never hear Apollo's song,
Though feathery clouds were floating all along   10
The purple west, and, two bright streaks between,
The golden lyre itself were dimly seen:
That the still murmur of the honey bee
Would never teach a rural song to me:
That the bright glance from beauty's eyelids slanting   15
Would never make a lay of mine enchanting,
Or warm my breast with ardour to unfold
Some tale of love and arms in time of old.

But there are times, when those that love the bay,[3]
Fly from all sorrowing far, far away;   20
A sudden glow comes on them, nought they see
In water, earth, or air, but poesy.
It has been said, dear George, and true I hold it,
(For knightly Spenser to Libertas[4] told it,)
That when a Poet is in such a trance,[5]   25
In air he sees white coursers paw, and prance,
Bestridden of gay knights, in gay apparel,
Who at each other tilt in playful quarrel,
And what we, ignorantly, sheet-lightning call,
Is the swift opening of their wide portal,   30
When the bright warder[6] blows his trumpet clear,
Whose tones reach nought on earth but Poet's ear.
When these enchanted portals open wide,
And through the light the horsemen swiftly glide,
The Poet's eye can reach those golden halls,   35
And view the glory of their festivals:
Their ladies fair, that in the distance seem
Fit for the silv'ring of a seraph's[7] dream;
Their rich brimm'd goblets, that incessant run
Like the bright spots that move about the sun;   40
And, when upheld, the wine from each bright jar

---

1. Composed while Keats was at Margate in August 1816, this poem was sent as a verse letter, which
   he indicated "may be kept for a fair Coppy" (Harvard MS Keats 1.1; *L*, 1: 109).
2. Music of the spheres. He goes on to worry if he will near the song of Apollo, the god of poetry, or
   write pastoral poetry ("a rural song") or romance ("tale of love and arms").
3. The laurel crown awarded to a poet.
4. See p. 28, n. 3.
5. See "Sleep and Poetry," esp. ll. 125ff.
6. A soldier on watch in the castle.
7. See p. 41, n. 6.

Pours with the lustre of a falling star.
Yet further off, are dimly seen their bowers,
Of which, no mortal eye can reach the flowers;
And 'tis right just, for well Apollo knows   45
'Twould make the Poet quarrel with the rose.
All that's reveal'd from that far seat of blisses,
Is, the clear fountains' interchanging kisses,
As gracefully descending, light and thin,
Like silver streaks across a dolphin's fin,   50
When he upswimmeth from the coral caves,
And sports with half his tail above the waves.

These wonders strange he sees, and many more,
Whose head is pregnant with poetic lore.
Should he upon an evening ramble fare   55
With forehead to the soothing breezes bare,
Would he naught see but the dark, silent blue
With all its diamonds trembling through and through?
Or the coy moon, when in the waviness
Of whitest clouds she does her beauty dress,   60
And staidly paces higher up, and higher,
Like a sweet nun in holy-day attire?
Ah, yes! much more would start into his sight—
The revelries, and mysteries of night:
And should I ever see them, I will tell you   65
Such tales as needs must with amazement spell[8] you.

These are the living pleasures of the bard:
But richer far posterity's award.
What does he murmur with his latest breath,
While his proud eye looks through the film of death?   70
"What though I leave this dull, and earthly mould,
"Yet shall my spirit lofty converse hold
"With after times.—The patriot shall feel
"My stern alarum, and unsheath his steel;
"Or, in the senate thunder out my numbers   75
"To startle princes from their easy slumbers.
"The sage will mingle with each moral theme
"My happy thoughts sententious; he will teem
"With lofty periods when my verses fire him,
"And then I'll stoop from heaven to inspire him.   80
"Lays have I left of such a dear delight
"That maids will sing them on their bridal night.
"Gay villagers, upon a morn of May,
"When they have tired their gentle limbs with play,
"And form'd a snowy circle on the grass,   85
"And plac'd in midst of all that lovely lass
"Who chosen is their queen,—with her fine head
"Crowned with flowers purple, white, and red:
"For there the lily, and the musk-rose, sighing,
"Are emblems true of hapless lovers dying: 90

8. Enchant.

"Between her breasts, that never yet felt trouble,
"A bunch of violets full blown, and double,
"Serenely sleep:—she from a casket takes
"A little book,—and then a joy awakes
"About each youthful heart,—with stifled cries,   95
"And rubbing of white hands, and sparkling eyes:
"For she's to read a tale of hopes, and fears;
"One that I foster'd in my youthful years:
"The pearls, that on each glist'ning circlet sleep,
"Gush ever and anon with silent creep,   100
"Lured by the innocent dimples. To sweet rest
"Shall the dear babe, upon its mother's breast,
"Be lull'd with songs of mine. Fair world, adieu!
"Thy dales, and hills, are fading from my view:
"Swiftly I mount, upon wide spreading pinions,[9]   105
"Far from the narrow bounds of thy dominions.
"Full joy I feel, while thus I cleave the air,
"That my soft verse will charm thy daughters fair,
"And warm thy sons!"[1] Ah, my dear friend and brother,
Could I, at once, my mad ambition smother,   110
For tasting joys like these, sure I should be
Happier, and dearer to society.
At times, 'tis true, I've felt relief from pain
When some bright thought has darted through my brain:
Through all that day I've felt a greater pleasure   115
Than if I'd brought to light a hidden treasure.
As to my sonnets, though none else should heed them,
I feel delighted, still, that you should read them.
Of late, too, I have had much calm enjoyment,
Stretch'd on the grass at my best lov'd employment   120
Of scribbling lines for you. These things I thought
While, in my face, the freshest breeze I caught.
E'en now I'm pillow'd on a bed of flowers
That crowns a lofty clift,[2] which proudly towers
Above the ocean-waves. The stalks, and blades,   125
Chequer my tablet with their quivering shades.
On one side is a field of drooping oats,
Through which the poppies show their scarlet coats;
So pert and useless, that they bring to mind
The scarlet coats that pester human-kind.[3]   130
And on the other side, outspread, is seen
Ocean's blue mantle streak'd with purple, and green.
Now 'tis I see a canvass'd ship, and now
Mark the bright silver curling round her prow.
I see the lark down-dropping to his nest,   135

9. See p. 5, n. 3.
1. In this passage, Keats, after having described the poet's imaginative experience (ll. 25–66), tracks
   the social impact of poetry on the "patriot" (ll. 73–76), the "sage" (ll. 77–80), and lovers (ll.
   81–109).
2. Keats wrote of these closing lines in Isabella Towers's copy of *Poems*, "Written on the cliff at Margate" (Garrod); Keats creates what Hunt would call a "Now," as in the one Hunt and Keats later
   wrote together, below pp. 510–13.
3. On Keats's sense that red-coated soldiers stationed in the countryside mar the landscape, see his
   letter to Reynolds of April 17, 18, 1817, p. 78.

And the broad winged sea-gull never at rest;
For when no more he spreads his feathers free,
His breast is dancing on the restless sea.
Now I direct my eyes into the west,
Which at this moment is in sunbeams drest: 140
Why westward[4] turn? 'Twas but to say adieu!
'Twas but to kiss my hand, dear George, to you!

August, 1816.

TO
CHARLES COWDEN CLARKE.[1]

Oft have you seen a swan superbly frowning,
And with proud breast his own white shadow crowning;
He slants his neck beneath the waters bright
So silently, it seems a beam of light
Come from the galaxy: anon he sports,—   5
With outspread wings the Naiad Zephyr courts,[2]
Or ruffles all the surface of the lake
In striving from its crystal face to take
Some diamond water drops, and them to treasure
In milky nest, and sip them off at leisure.   10
But not a moment can he there insure them,
Nor to such downy rest can he allure them;
For down they rush as though they would be free,
And drop like hours into eternity.
Just like that bird am I in loss of time,   15
Whene'er I venture on the stream of rhyme;
With shatter'd boat, oar snapt, and canvass rent,
I slowly sail, scarce knowing my intent;
Still scooping up the water with my fingers,
In which a trembling diamond never lingers.   20

By this, friend Charles, you may full plainly see
Why I have never penn'd a line to thee:
Because my thoughts were never free, and clear,
And little fit to please a classic ear;
Because my wine was of too poor a savour   25
For one whose palate gladdens in the flavour
Of sparkling Helicon:[3]—small good it were
To take him to a desert rude, and bare,
Who had on Baiæ's shore reclin'd at ease,
While Tasso's[4] page was floating in a breeze   30

---

4. Toward London and George.
1. Written in September 1816 while Keats was at Margate, this couplet poem was sent as a verse letter (*L,* 1: 109–13). Charles Cowden Clarke (1787–1877) was the son of the headmaster at Keats's
   school at Enfield and a teacher and friend to Keats, introducing him to Hunt's *Examiner* and later
   to Hunt himself and encouraging his love of literature. There is a holograph fair copy at the Huntington Library (HM 11903).
2. The swan opens its wings to the Zephyr, or the west wind, here imagined as a naiad or water nymph.
3. The mountain where the Hippocrene, the spring sacred to the muses, flows.
4. Torquato Tasso (1544–1595), who was brought up in Naples (thus "Baiæ's shore" or the Bay of
   Naples), was a Renaissance Italian poet whose masterpiece was *Jerusalem Delivered*; Armida (l. 31)
   is that poem's heroine.

That gave soft music from Armida's bowers,
Mingled with fragrance from her rarest flowers:
Small good to one who had by Mulla's stream
Fondled the maidens with the breasts of cream;
Who had beheld Belphœbe in a brook,   35
And lovely Una in a leafy nook,
And Archimago[5] leaning o'er his book:
Who had of all that's sweet tasted, and seen,
From silv'ry ripple, up to beauty's queen;
From the sequester'd haunts of gay Titania,[6]   40
To the blue dwelling of divine Urania:[7]
One, who, of late, had ta'en sweet forest walks
With him who elegantly chats, and talks—
The wrong'd Libertas,[8]—who has told you stories
Of laurel chaplets, and Apollo's glories;   45
Of troops chivalrous prancing through a city,
And tearful ladies made for love, and pity:
With many else which I have never known.
Thus have I thought; and days on days have flown
Slowly, or rapidly—unwilling still   50
For you to try my dull, unlearned quill.
Nor should I now, but that I've known you long;
That you first taught me all the sweets of song:
The grand, the sweet, the terse, the free, the fine;
What swell'd with pathos, and what right divine: 55
Spenserian vowels that elope with ease,
And float along like birds o'er summer seas;
Miltonian storms, and more, Miltonian tenderness;
Michael in arms, and more, meek Eve's fair slenderness.[9]
Who read for me the sonnet swelling loudly   60
Up to its climax and then dying proudly?
Who found for me the grandeur of the ode,
Growing, like Atlas,[1] stronger from its load?
Who let me taste that more than cordial dram,
The sharp, the rapier-pointed epigram?   65
Shew'd me that epic was of all the king,
Round, vast, and spanning all like Saturn's ring?
You too upheld the veil from Clio's[2] beauty,
And pointed out the patriot's stern duty;
The might of Alfred, and the shaft of Tell;   70
The hand of Brutus, that so grandly fell
Upon a tyrant's head.[3] Ah! had I never seen,

5. The hypocritical enchanter in Spenser's *Faerie Queene*, Books 1 and 2; *Mulla*: river near Spenser's home in Kilcolman, Ireland; *Belphœbe*: chaste huntress in his *Faerie* Queene; *Una*: character from the *Faerie Queene* who embodies the singleness of true religion. In line 34, Keats seems to echo Spenser's *Epithalamion*, 1. 175: "Her brest like to a bowle of creame uncrudded."
6. The queen of the fairies in Shakespeare's *A Midsummer Night's Dream*.
7. The muse of astronomy, named by Milton as his muse in Book 7 of *Paradise Lost*.
8. See p. 28, n. 3; in lines 46–47, Keats appears to allude to Hunt's *Story of Rimini*, 1:147ff.
9. The archangel Michael and Eve are characters in Milton's *Paradise Lost*. In this section, Keats thanks Clarke for introducing him to a wide range of poetry from the pithy epigram to the epic.
1. A Titan who fought the Olympians and who, as Mount Atlas, was said to bear the heavens on his shoulders.
2. The muse of history.
3. Marcus Junius Brutus (c. 85–42 B.C.E.) became an emblem of the resistance to tyranny as a result of his involvement in the assassination of Julius Caesar in 44 B.C.E. For *Alfred* and *Tell*, see p. 42, n. 3. As in his epistle to his brother George, Keats celebrates both poets and heroes of liberty.

Or known your kindness, what might I have been?
What my enjoyments in my youthful years,
Bereft of all that now my life endears?   75
And can I e'er these benefits forget?
And can I e'er repay the friendly debt?
No, doubly no;—yet should these rhymings please,
I shall roll on the grass with two-fold ease:
For I have long time been my fancy feeding   80
With hopes that you would one day think the reading
Of my rough verses not an hour misspent;
Should it e'er be so, what a rich content!
Some weeks have pass'd since last I saw the spires
In lucent Thames reflected:—warm desires   85
To see the sun o'er peep the eastern dimness,
And morning shadows streaking into slimness
Across the lawny fields, and pebbly water;
To mark the time as they grow broad, and shorter;
To feel the air that plays about the hills,   90
And sips its freshness from the little rills;
To see high, golden corn wave in the light
When Cynthia[4] smiles upon a summer's night,
And peers among the cloudlet's jet and white,
As though she were reclining in a bed   95
Of bean blossoms, in heaven freshly shed.[5]
No sooner had I stepp'd into these pleasures
Than I began to think of rhymes and measures:
The air that floated by me seem'd to say
"Write! thou wilt never have a better day."   100
And so I did. When many lines I'd written,
Though with their grace I was not oversmitten,
Yet, as my hand was warm, I thought I'd better
Trust to my feelings, and write you a letter.
Such an attempt required an inspiration   105
Of a peculiar sort,—a consummation;—
Which, had I felt, these scribblings might have been
Verses from which the soul would never wean:
But many days have past since last my heart
Was warm'd luxuriously by divine Mozart;   110
By Arne delighted, or by Handel madden'd;
Or by the song of Erin[6] pierc'd and sadden'd:
What time you were before the music sitting,
And the rich notes to each sensation fitting.
Since I have walk'd with you through shady lanes   115

4. See p. 25, n. 1.
5. Allott finds the comparison of the clouds to bean blossoms as having the "flavour of direct observation," but ll. 92–96 might also echo Coleridge's "Aeolian Harp" (published as "Effusion XXXV"
in *Poems on Various Occasions* [1796]): "watch the clouds, that late were rich with light, / Slow-
saddening round, and mark the star of eve / Serenely brilliant . . . / Shine opposite! How exquisite
the scents / Snatch'd from you bean-field!" (ll. 6–10).
6. Probably Thomas Moore's *Irish Melodies* (1808–1834). Wolfgang Amadeus *Mozart* (1756–1791), Austrian composer and one of the greatest composers of all time, whose works, including *Don Giovanni*
(1787), were admired by the Hunt circle (see *L*, 1: 395). Thomas *Arne* (1710–1778), English composer
of operas and theater music whose works include "Rule Britannia!," settings for Shakespeare's songs,
and music for Milton's *Comus*. Georg Friedrich *Handel* (1685–1759), German composer who worked
in England after 1710 and whose compositions include his oratorio *Messiah*, *L'Allegro*, and the *Ode
for St. Cecilia's Day*. Clarke was known as a fine pianist.

That freshly terminate in open plains,
And revel'd in a chat that ceased not
When at night-fall among your books we got:
No, nor when supper came, nor after that,—
Nor when reluctantly I took my hat;   120
No, nor till cordially you shook my hand
Mid-way between our homes:—your accents bland
Still sounded in my ears, when I no more
Could hear your footsteps touch the grav'ly floor.
Sometimes I lost them, and then found again;   125
You chang'd the footpath for the grassy plain.
In those still moments I have wish'd you joys
That well you know to honour:—"Life's very toys
"With him," said I, "will take a pleasant charm;
"It cannot be that ought will work him harm."   130
These thoughts now come o'er me with all their might:—
Again I shake your hand,—friend Charles, good night.

September, 1816.

SONNETS.[1]

I.

TO MY BROTHER GEORGE.[2]

MANY the wonders I this day have seen:
  The sun, when first he kist away the tears[3]
  That fill'd the eyes of morn;—the laurel'd peers[4]
Who from the feathery gold[5] of evening lean;—
The ocean with its vastness, its blue green,   5
  Its ships, its rocks, its caves, its hopes, its fears,—
  Its voice mysterious, which whoso hears
Must think on what will be, and what has been.
E'en now, dear George, while this for you I write,
  Cynthia[6] is from her silken curtains peeping   10
So scantly, that it seems her bridal night,
  And she her half-discover'd revels keeping.
But what, without the social thought of thee,
Would be the wonders of the sky and sea?[7]

1. The section heading for the next seventeen poems. On Keats's experiments with the sonnet form, see Lawrence John Zillman, *Keats and the Sonnet Tradition: A Critical and Comparative Study* (1939; rpt. New York: Octagon Books, 1970) and Helen Vendler, "John Keats: Perfecting the Sonnet," in *Coming of Age as a Poet: Milton, Keats, Eliot, Plath* (Cambridge: Harvard University Press, 2003), pp. 41–79.
2. Written at Margate in August 1816, this is the first of seventeen Petrarchan sonnets printed in the "Sonnets" section of *Poems*; some, like the current poem, have titles, all are numbered. There are two holograph MSS at Harvard (MS Keats 2.2, 2.3; *JKPMH*, pp. 9, 11).
3. Dew.
4. Woodhouse (*1817*, opposite p. 79) offers "The poets," as a gloss, then "*the Poets* in heaven," on the basis of Keats's "Ode to Apollo," l. 20. In this sequence of natural objects, it seems more likely that Keats means some sort of tree.
5. Perhaps an echo of Shelley's *Queen Mab* (1813), 2:16: "far clouds of feathery gold."
6. See p. 25, n. 1.
7. Cook cites *L*, I: 242 (March 13, 1818): "Scenery is fine—but human nature is finer." Also compare the close of Shelley's "Mont Blanc" (1817): "And what were thou, and earth, and stars, and sea, / If to the human mind's imaginings / Silence and solitude were vacancy?" (ll. 142–44).

II.
TO * * * * * *[1]

HAD I a man's fair form, then might my sighs
    Be echoed swiftly through that ivory shell
    Thine ear, and find thy gentle heart; so well
Would passion arm me for the enterprize:
But ah! I am no knight whose foeman dies;   5
    No cuirass[2] glistens on my bosom's swell;
    I am no happy shepherd of the dell
Whose lips have trembled with a maiden's eyes.
Yet must I dote upon thee,—call thee sweet,
    Sweeter by far than Hybla's[3] honied roses   10
    When steep'd in dew rich to intoxication.
Ah! I will taste that dew, for me 'tis meet,
    And when the moon her pallid face discloses,
    I'll gather some by spells, and incantation.

III.
Written on the day that Mr. Leigh Hunt
left Prison.[1]

WHAT though, for showing truth to flatter'd state,
    Kind Hunt was shut in prison, yet has he,
    In his immortal spirit, been as free
As the sky-searching lark, and as elate.
Minion of grandeur! think you he did wait?   5
    Think you he nought but prison walls did see,
    Till, so unwilling, thou unturn'dst the key?
Ah, no! far happier, nobler was his fate!
In Spenser's halls he strayed, and bowers fair,
    Culling enchanted flowers; and he flew   10
With daring Milton through the fields of air:[2]
    To regions of his own his genius true
Took happy flights. Who shall his fame impair
    When thou art dead, and all thy wretched crew?[3]

1. Written in 1815 or 1816; Gittings and Allott, following Woodhouse's note about Keats writing three valentines in commenting on "Hadst thou live'd in days of old" (W[2] f. 222v), suggest this is another valentine, perhaps to Mary Frogley for February 1816. Readings have tended to follow Woodhouse's biographical note, "The author has an idea that the diminutiveness of his size makes him contemptible, and that no woman can like a man of small stature" (1817, shorthand note opposite p. 80). The poem contrasts the poet with the heroes of romance (ll. 5–6) and pastoral lovers (ll. 7–8).
2. See p. 28, n. 7.
3. A mountain in Sicily, famous for its flowers, bees, and honey; Hunt would much later (1847) write his A Jar of Honey from Mount Hybla.
1. Written on February 2, 1815, the day Hunt was released from prison after serving two years for libeling the Prince Regent in his famous attack, "The Prince on St. Patrick's Day" (Examiner, March 22, 1812: 177–80; SWLH 1: 215–21). Keats gave the poem to Clarke, who had introduced Keats to the Examiner, who would later introduce Keats to Hunt, and who was at that moment going to see Hunt. Woodhouse did not agree with the sentiment of the poem, writing (1817, opposite p. 81) that Hunt's "punishment was deserved—he appeared determined to persist in his abuse until it sho[d] be noticed."
2. Hunt expressed his delight in Spenser and Milton in his Feast of the Poets (1811; rev. 1814).
3. See Satan's "horrid crew" in Milton's Paradise Lost 1.51.

IV.
[How many bards gild the lapses of time][1]

How many bards gild the lapses of time!
  A few of them have ever been the food
  Of my delighted fancy,—I could brood
Over their beauties, earthly, or sublime:
And often, when I sit me down to rhyme,   5
  These will in throngs before my mind intrude:
  But no confusion, no disturbance rude
Do they occasion; 'tis a pleasing chime.
So the unnumber'd sounds that evening store;
  The songs of birds—the whisp'ring of the leaves—   10
The voice of waters—the great bell that heaves
  With solemn sound,—and thousand others more,
That distance of recognizance bereaves,[2]
  Make pleasing music, and not wild uproar.

V.
To a Friend who sent me some Roses.[1]

As late I rambled in the happy fields,
  What time the sky-lark shakes the tremulous dew
  From his lush clover covert;—when anew
Adventurous knights take up their dinted shields:
I saw the sweetest flower wild nature yields,   5
  A fresh-blown musk-rose; 'twas the first that threw
  Its sweets upon the summer: graceful it grew
As is the wand that queen Titania[2] wields.
And, as I feasted on its fragrancy,
  I thought the garden-rose it far excell'd: 10
But when, O Wells! thy roses came to me
  My sense with their deliciousness was spell'd:
Soft voices had they, that with tender plea
  Whisper'd of peace, and truth, and friendliness unquell'd.

1. Date of composition unknown, but generally thought to be written in 1816. Clarke indicates (*Rec-ollections*, pp. 132–33) that this was one of the poems he showed to Hunt and Horace Smith in October 1816.
2. Woodhouse (*1817*, opposite p. 82) glosses this line, "which distance prevents from being distinctly recognized." Horace Smith admired the last six lines, and this line in particular, exclaiming, according to Clarke (*Recollections*, pp. 132–33), "What a well-condensed expression for one so young!"
1. This sonnet is dated in Tom Keats's transcript at Harvard (MS Keats 3.5, p. 20) as having been written on June 29, 1816. The friend is Charles Wells (1800?–1879), a school friend of Tom Keats and attached to the Hunt circle, being particularly close to Hazlitt; Wells published *Stories After Nature* (1822), reflecting the group's interest in Italian stories, and *Joseph and his Brethren* (1824), a dramatic poem. The roses may have been sent to end a quarrel (see KC, 2: 115). Keats and Wells later fell out over a joke the latter played on Tom (see L, 1: 84, 192n, and 2: 82, 90–91). There is a holograph fair copy at the Morgan Library (MA 214.1).
2. See p. 34, n. 7.

VI.
To G. A. W.[1]

NYMPH of the downward smile, and sidelong glance,[2]
  In what diviner moments of the day
  Art thou most lovely? When gone far astray
Into the labyrinths of sweet utterance?
Or when serenely wand'ring in a trance   5
  Of sober thought? Or when starting away,
  With careless robe, to meet the morning ray,
Thou spar'st the flowers in thy mazy dance?
Haply 'tis when thy ruby lips part sweetly,
  And so remain, because thou listenest: 10
But thou to please wert nurtured so completely
  That I can never tell what mood is best.
I shall as soon pronounce which grace more neatly
  Trips it before Apollo[3] than the rest.

VII.
[O Solitude! if I must with thee dwell][1]

O SOLITUDE! if I must with thee dwell,
  Let it not be among the jumbled heap
  Of murky buildings; climb with me the steep,—
Nature's observatory[2]—whence the dell,
Its flowery slopes, its river's crystal swell,   5
  May seem a span; let me thy vigils keep
  'Mongst boughs pavillion'd, where the deer's swift leap
Startles the wild bee from the fox-glove[3] bell.
But though I'll gladly trace these scenes with thee,
  Yet the sweet converse of an innocent mind,[4]   10
  Whose words are images of thoughts refin'd,
Is my soul's pleasure; and it sure must be
Almost the highest bliss of human-kind,
  When to thy haunts two kindred spirits[5] flee.

1. Written December 1816 (so dated in Tom Keats's transcript at Harvard, MS Keats 3.5, p. 21), this sonnet was composed, according to Woodhouse (*1817*, shorthand note opposite p. 84), "by the author at the request of his brother George to be sent by the latter to Miss Georgiana Ann Wylie [c. 1797–1879], the lady to whom G. K. was afterward married." There is a holograph fair copy at Harvard (MS Keats 3.4, f. 31v; *JKPMH*, p. 23).
2. Allott cites Thomson's *The Seasons* (1730), "Summer," l. 1280: "In sidelong glances from her downcast eye."
3. See p. 6, n. 1.
1. Written in 1815 or 1816 (many date it in October or November 1815 as Keats found himself in a new urban environment when he began his medical studies), this sonnet was Keats's first poem to appear in print; Hunt published it as "To Solitude" in the *Examiner*, May 5, 1816, p. 282, though he had not yet met Keats. There is a holograph fair copy in the Morgan Library W[3], f. 83v (*MYR: JK*, 4: 222), and another (the Lyte-Philpotts-Bromley Martin MS) at the William Andrews Clark Memorial Library, UCLA (MS K256M1 [1816]).
2. Perhaps an allusion to Wordsworth's *Excursion*, Book 4, where Wordsworth imagines various pagan celebrations of nature, including the Chaldeans' "observations natural" (l. 708).
3. See p. 30, n. 4. Lines 7–8 are close to George Felton Mathew's "To a Poetical Friend" (above, pp. 10–11), ll. 47–48: "Nor suffer the innocent deer's timid leap / To fright the wild bee from her flowery bell."
4. For "But . . . Yet," the *Examiner* version has "Ah! Fain would I frequent such scenes with thee; / But."
5. Middleton Murray (1930, pp. 1–6) and others have argued that this reference is to Keats and Mathew, based on the idea that Mathew echoes Keats's ll. 7–8 in his "To a Poetical Friend" (see n. 3 above). Gittings (p. 53) argues that the reference is to the Mathew sisters.

VIII.
TO MY BROTHERS.[1]

SMALL, busy flames play through the fresh laid coals,
    And their faint cracklings o'er our silence creep
    Like whispers of the household gods[2] that keep
A gentle empire o'er fraternal souls.
And while, for rhymes, I search around the poles,   5
    Your eyes are fix'd, as in poetic sleep,
    Upon the lore so voluble and deep,
That aye at fall of night our care condoles.[3]
This is your birth-day Tom, and I rejoice
    That thus it passes smoothly, quietly.   10
Many such eves of gently whisp'ring noise
    May we together pass, and calmly try
What are this world's true joys,—ere the great voice,[4]
    From its fair face, shall bid our spirits fly.

November 18, 1816.

IX.
[Keen, fitful gusts are whisp'ring here and there][1]

KEEN, fitful gusts are whisp'ring here and there
    Among the bushes half leafless, and dry;
    The stars look very cold about the sky,
And I have many miles on foot to fare.[2]
Yet feel I little of the cool bleak air,   5
    Or of the dead leaves rustling drearily,
    Or of those silver lamps that burn on high,
Or of the distance from home's pleasant lair:
For I am brimfull of the friendliness
    That in a little cottage I have found;   10
Of fair-hair'd Milton's eloquent distress,
    And all his love for gentle Lycid drown'd;[3]
Of lovely Laura in her light green dress,
    And faithful Petrarch gloriously crown'd.[4]

1. This sonnet was written on November 18, 1816, to celebrate Tom Keats's seventeenth birthday. Allott notes the stylistic similarities to Hunt's "Quiet Evenings. To Thomas Barnes, Esq." and "To T. M. Alsager" (1815). There is a holograph draft of ll. 1–8 and two fair copies, all at Harvard (MS Keats 2.2, 2.5, 2.6; *JKPMH*, pp. 15, 17, 19).
2. Lares and Penates, Roman gods of hearth, home, and family.
3. The "lore" "condoles" "our care"; reading and poetry sooth our worries.
4. Allott offers "God (or perhaps death)" for "great voice." Perhaps, with the classical allusion to household gods and the "whisp'ring noise," there is an echo of Wordsworth's sonnet "Composed By the Side of Grasmere Lake" (1807): "But list! a voice is near; / Great Pan himself low-whispering through the reeds" (ll. 11–12).
1. Keats wrote this sonnet in October or November 1816 after a visit to Hunt's cottage in the Vale of Health, Hampstead, "very shortly after [Keats's] installation in [Hunt's] cottage," according to Clarke (*Recollections*, p. 134). Keats and Hunt had first met in October (see p. 18).
2. Hampstead was about five miles from Keats's lodgings in London.
3. Milton's *Lycidas* commemorates the death of "gentle Lycid," his friend Edward King, who drowned on August 10, 1637.
4. Francesco Petrarca (1304–1374), Italian Renaissance poet and humanist who celebrated his beloved "Laura" in his sequence of sonnets and other poems. Hunt had a portrait of the two lovers in his cottage. Cook points out the pun between Laura's name and Petrarch's laurel crown.

X.

[To one who has been long in city pent][1]

To one who has been long in city pent,[2]
  'Tis very sweet to look into the fair
  And open face of heaven,—to breathe a prayer
Full in the smile of the blue firmament.
Who is more happy, when, with heart's[3] content,   5
  Fatigued he sinks into some pleasant lair
  Of wavy grass, and reads a debonair
And gentle tale of love and languishment?
Returning home at evening, with an ear
  Catching the notes of Philomel,[4]—an eye   10
Watching the sailing cloudlet's bright career,
  He mourns that day so soon has glided by:
E'en like the passage of an angel's tear
That falls through the clear ether silently.

XI.

On first looking into Chapman's Homer.[1]

MUCH have I travell'd in the realms of gold,   ] *New World*
  And many goodly states and kingdoms seen; |
  Round many western islands have I been |
Which bards in fealty to Apollo hold.[2]   ]
Oft of one wide expanse had I been told   5
  That deep-brow'd Homer ruled as his demesne;[3]
  Yet did I never breathe its pure serene[4]
Till I heard Chapman speak out loud and bold:

1. Written "in the Fields—June 1816," according to Georgiana Wylie's transcript (Harvard MS Keats 3.4, f. 5r). Allott notes the similarities to Hunt's sonnets on Hampstead published in the *Examiner* (1813–15) and gathered in *Foliage* (1818).
2. See Milton, *Paradise Lost*, 9.445: "As one who long in populous City Pent"; Coleridge, "To the Nightingale" (1796), l. 2: "Bards in city garret pent"; and "This Lime-Tree Bower my Prison" (1800; 1810), ll. 28–30: "thou . . . In the great City pent."
3. The reading of MSS by George and Tom Keats (Harvard Keats MS 3.4, f.32v and 3.5, p. 24); 1817 has "hearts."
4. See p. 32, n. 6.
1. Written in October 1816 and first published in Hunt's "Young Poets" essay in the *Examiner*, December 1, 1816: 761–62 (see that version, pp. 13–14, where the date is supplied), this is the most admired of Keats's early poems. Upon reading it, Hunt shared it with Godwin and Hazlitt, praised it in his review, and later celebrated it in his *Lord Byron and Some of his Contemporaries* (1828; pp. 248–49). Keats had rapidly composed it after an evening with Clarke, reading George Chapman's translation of Homer (1614) in a folio owned by their friend Thomas Alsager, a financial writer for the *Times* and later its editor. Their admiration for Chapman (1559?–1634) was shared by Hunt, Lamb, and Godwin, whose *Lives of Edward and John Philips, Nephews and Pupils of Milton. Including Various Particulars of the Literary and Political History of Their Times* (1815) offers (pp. 241–42) an account of translation that could stand as a defense of Keats's often criticized approach to Homer through Chapman. Clarke (*Recollections*, pp. 128–30) remembers that they read through the " 'famousest' passages, as we had scrappily known them in Pope's version," with Keats giving "one of his delighted stares" on hearing the line "The sea had soak'd his heart through" from the account of Odysseus's shipwreck (*Odyssey* V); Clarke reports, "when I came down to breakfast the next morning, I found upon my table a letter with no other enclosure than his famous sonnet . . . . We had parted . . . at day-spring, yet he contrived that I should receive the poem from a distance of, may be, two miles by ten o'clock." For an account of the controversies surrounding the close of the poem and a strong contextual reading, see Charles Rzepka, " 'Cortez—or Balboa, or Somebody Like That': Form, Fact, and Forgetting in Keats's 'Chapman's Homer' Sonnet," *K-SJ* 51 (2002): 35–75. See Marjorie Levinson's reading, included here (below, pp. 552–55). There are two holograph MSS., one at Harvard (MS Keats 2.4; *JKPMH*, p. 13) and the other at the Morgan (MA 214.2).

Then felt I like some watcher of the skies
  When a new planet swims into his ken;[5]   10
Or like stout Cortez when with eagle eyes
  He star'd at the Pacific—and all his men
Look'd at each other with a wild surmise—
  Silent, upon a peak in Darien.[6]

[handwritten margin notes: "very imperialistic pt. of view"; "mistaken Balboa for Cortez"]

XII.
On leaving some Friends at an early Hour.[1]

GIVE me a golden pen, and let me lean
  On heap'd up flowers, in regions clear, and far;
Bring me a tablet whiter than a star,
Or hand of hymning angel, when 'tis seen
The silver strings of heavenly harp atween: 5
And let there glide by many a pearly car,
  Pink robes, and wavy hair, and diamond jar,
And half discovered wings, and glances keen.
The while let music wander round my ears,
  And as it reaches each delicious ending,   10
    Let me write down a line of glorious tone,
And full of many wonders of the spheres:
  For what a height my spirit is contending!
'Tis not content so soon to be alone.

XIII.
ADDRESSED TO HAYDON.[1]

HIGHMINDEDNESS, a jealousy for good,
  A loving-kindness for the great man's fame,

---

2. Poets are feudal vassals of Apollo as god of poetry.
3. Dominion.
4. A clear, bright sky.
5. Usually taken to refer to F. W. Herschel's discovery of Uranus (March 13, 1781), described in J. Bonnycastle's *Introduction to Astronomy* which Keats owned. Roe (pp. 35–37) suggests that Keats may be recalling an exercise at Enfield School, where he met Clarke, in which students created a "living orrery" or moving model of the solar system.
6. Keats's images of the exploration and conquest of the New World come from his schoolboy reading of William Robertson's *History of America* (1777), with Robertson, for example, describing the isthmus of Darien as "not above sixty miles in breadth; but this neck of land, which binds together the continents of North and South America, is strengthened by a chain of lofty mountains, stretching through its whole extent" (1: 286). Critics from Tennyson on have noted that it was Balboa, not Cortez, who was the first European to see the Pacific coast of the isthmus, but Rzepka (see n. 1), in recounting that critical history, argues that Keats's choice is "well informed and deliberate."
1. This sonnet was written in October or November 1816, as Keats became part of Hunt's circle. Woodhouse's incomplete shorthand note (*1817*, p. 90) for "friends" reads "(Reynolds Hunt and   )" in a hackney coach." The third friend is probably Clarke. There is a holograph draft at the Morgan Library (MA 658).
1. This sonnet praising Keats's friend Benjamin Robert Haydon was written in 1816, perhaps as a response to Wordsworth's "To B. R. Haydon," published in the *Champion* (February 4, 1816) and the *Examiner* (March 31, 1816). Hunt published a poem to Haydon in the *Examiner* (October 20, 1816), and Reynolds would write "To Haydon" in response to Keats's sonnet. Benjamin Robert Haydon (1786–1846), a historical painter known at the time for such works as *Dentatus* and *The Judgment of Solomon*, was a member of Hunt's circle with whom Keats became close friends. In 1816, he was working on his *Christ's Entry into Jerusalem* into which he would work portraits of Keats, Wordsworth, Lamb, and Hazlitt, and he was active in the controversy over the aesthetic value of the Elgin Marbles, sculptures from the Parthenon shipped from Athens to England by Lord Elgin (ll. 9–12; and see below pp. 72–73).

Dwells here and there with people of no name,
In noisome alley, and in pathless wood:
And where we think the truth least understood,   5
Oft may be found a "singleness of aim,"[2]
That ought to frighten into hooded shame
A money mong'ring, pitiable brood.[3]
How glorious this affection for the cause
Of stedfast genius, toiling gallantly!   10
What when a stout unbending champion awes
Envy, and Malice to their native sty?
Unnumber'd souls breathe out a still applause,
Proud to behold him in his country's eye.

XIV.
ADDRESSED TO THE SAME.[1]

GREAT spirits now on earth are sojourning;
He of the cloud, the cataract, the lake,
Who on Helvellyn's summit, wide awake,
Catches his freshness from Archangel's wing:[2]
He of the rose, the violet, the spring,   5
The social smile, the chain for Freedom's sake:[3]
And lo!—whose stedfastness would never take
A meaner sound than Raphael's whispering.[4]
And other spirits there are standing apart
Upon the forehead of the age to come;   10
These, these will give the world another heart,
And other pulses. Hear ye not the hum
Of mighty workings?[5]——
Listen awhile ye nations, and be dumb.

2. Keats quotes Wordsworth's "Character of the happy warrior" (1807), l. 40.
3. A sentiment in keeping with Hunt's frequent attacks upon "money-getting" in the *Examiner* and perhaps with the opening attack upon "getting and spending" in Wordsworth's sonnet, "The world is too much with us" (1807).
1. Written November 20, 1816, this sonnet was sent in a letter to Haydon (see *L*, 1: 117; also 118–19 for a copy apparently intended for Wordsworth). Keats had spent the evening of the 19th in Haydon's studio, where the painter did a profile sketch of the poet. A month later, Haydon sent the poem to Wordsworth who found it of "good promise" (*The Letters of William and Dorothy Wordsworth: The Later Years*, rev. Mary Moorman and Alan Hill [Oxford: Oxford University Press, 1970], 3: 361). There are three holograph fair copies at Harvard, the first two in letters to Haydon and the third a fair copy (MS Keats 1.3, 1.4, 2.7; *JKPMH*, p. 21).
2. As Woodhouse notes (*1817*, opposite p. 92), "Wordsworth, who resides near Mount Helvellyn in Cumberland"; Helvellyn is the highest peak in the Lake District.
3. As Woodhouse notes (*1817*, opposite p. 92), Hunt, celebrated here for his sociability, his poetry, and his imprisonment for libeling the Prince Regent.
4. As Woodhouse notes (*1817*, opposite p. 92), "Haydon, the painter"; Hunt would also celebrate Haydon as the successor to the great Italian Renaissance painter Raphael (1483–1520) in his "To Benjamin Robert Haydon. Written in a blank leaf of his Copy of Vasari's Lives of the Painters" (*Examiner*, October 20, 1816).
5. The manuscript sent to Haydon has the full line, "Workings in a distant Mart"; Keats adopted the daring ("I glory in it," he wrote Haydon) ellipsis at Haydon's suggestion.

XV.
On the Grasshopper and Cricket.[1]

THE poetry of earth is never dead:[2]
  When all the birds are faint with the hot sun,
  And hide in cooling trees, a voice will run
From hedge to hedge about the new-mown mead;
That is the Grasshopper's—he takes the lead   5
  In summer luxury,—he has never done
  With his delights; for when tired out with fun
He rests at ease beneath some pleasant weed.
The poetry of earth is ceasing never:
  On a lone winter evening, when the frost   10
  Has wrought a silence,[3] from the stove there shrills
The Cricket's song, in warmth increasing ever,
  And seems to one in drowsiness half lost,
    The Grasshopper's among some grassy hills.

December 30, 1816.

XVI.
TO KOSCIUSKO.[1]

GOOD Kosciusko, thy great name alone
  Is a full harvest whence to reap high feeling;
  It comes upon us like the glorious pealing
Of the wide spheres—an everlasting tone.
And now it tells me, that in worlds unknown,   5
  The names of heroes, burst from clouds concealing,
  Are changed[2] to harmonies, for ever stealing
Through cloudless blue, and round each silver throne.
It tells me too, that on a happy day,
  When some good spirit walks upon the earth,   10
  Thy name with Alfred's,[3] and the great of yore
Gently commingling, gives tremendous birth

---

1. This poem was written on December 30, 1816, during one of Hunt's sonnet contests. Woodhouse notes (*1817*, opposite p. 93), "The author & Leigh Hunt challenged each other to write a sonnet in a Quarter of an hour.—The Grasshopper & Cricket' was the subject.—Both performed the task within the time allotted." Hunt's poem was first published (along with a reprint of Keats's) in the *Examiner* for September 21, 1817 (see p. 90). For other contest poems, see "Written in Disgust of Vulgar Superstition" (p. 14), "On Receiving a Laurel Crown" (pp. 69–70), and "To the Nile" (pp. 124–25). There is a fair copy in the Forster Collection (Forster MS 316), Victoria and Albert Museum.
2. Clarke (*Recollections*, p. 135) records Hunt's comment, "Such a prosperous opening."
3. Clarke (*Recollections*, p. 136) records Hunt's comment, "Ah! that's perfect! Bravo Keats!"
1. This sonnet was written in December 1816, as indicated when first printed in the *Examiner*, February 16, 1817, p. 107. Thaddeus Kosciusko (1746–1817), Polish general and national hero, fought in the American Revolution before returning to Poland to join the struggle for his nation's independence against Russia. He led an uprising in 1794 only to be captured. Upon his release, he settled in France in 1798, where he resisted Napoleon's plans for Poland. He was a hero to British liberals, with Coleridge writing a sonnet on him in *Sonnets on Eminent Characters* (1774), Hunt writing a sonnet to him (*Examiner*, November 19, 1815) and displaying his bust in his Hampstead cottage, and Keats celebrating him in "Sleep and Poetry" (below, p. 68, ll. 387–88) as well as here.
2. This is the *Examiner* reading; *Poems* has "and changed," which Woodhouse (*1817*, p. 94) corrected to "and change," noting (opposite) that both "burst" and "change" are verbs.
3. See p. 42, n. 3.

To a loud hymn, that sounds far, far away
To where the great God lives for evermore.[4]

XVII.
[Happy is England! I could be content][1]

HAPPY is England! I could be content
    To see no other verdure[2] than its own;
    To feel no other breezes than are blown
Through its tall woods with high romances blent:
Yet do I sometimes feel a languishment   5
    For skies Italian, and an inward groan
    To sit upon an Alp as on a throne,
And half forget what world or worldling meant.[3]
Happy is England, sweet her artless daughters;
    Enough their simple loveliness for me,   10
        Enough their whitest arms in silence clinging:
Yet do I often warmly burn to see
    Beauties of deeper glance, and hear their singing,
And float with them about the summer waters.

SLEEP AND POETRY.[1]

"As I lay in my bed slepe full unmete
"Was unto me, but why that I ne might
"Rest I ne wist, for there n'as erthly wight
"[As I suppose] had more of hertis ese
"Than I, for I n'ad sicknesse nor disese."
                                CHAUCER.

WHAT is more gentle than a wind in summer?
What is more soothing than the pretty hummer
That stays one moment in an open flower,
And buzzes cheerily from bower to bower?
What is more tranquil than a musk-rose blowing   5

4. One of the very few straightforward references to a Judeo-Christian God in Keats's poetry.
1. This untitled sonnet was perhaps written in 1816. There is a holograph fair copy at Harvard (MS Keats 2.11; *JKPMH*, p. 7).
2. Green vegetation.
3. This desire to escape the world and worldliness for the warm south might remind us of Wordsworth's "The world is too much with us" (1807).
1. This concluding couplet poem, balancing the opening "I stood tip-toe upon a little hill," was written from October to December 1816 during Keats's first acquaintance with Hunt. Clarke (*Recollections*, pp. 133–34) recalls that "It was in the library at Hunt's cottage, where an extemporary bed had been made up for him on the sofa, that he composed the framework and main lines of the poem . . . the last sixty or seventy lines being an inventory of the art garniture of the room." In *Poems*, the epigraph appears on a half title preceding the first page of the text; Woodhouse (*1817*, p. 97), in identifying the passage as from the Chaucerian "The Floure & the Leafe" (ll. 17–21), added part of l. 16, "Upon a certain night." This poem is no longer believed to be by Chaucer, but it was a favorite of the Hunt circle (see Roe, pp. 134–40), prompting another poem by Keats ("Written on a Blank Space at the End of Chaucer's Tale of 'The Floure and the Leaf'"; see p. 72, below) and a responsive sonnet by Reynolds ("Sonnet to Keats, on Reading His Sonnet Written In Chaucer"; February 27, 1817). In his interleaved copy of *Poems*, opposite the final page of "Sleep and Poetry," which he thought "incomparably the best in the volume," Woodhouse wrote out his "To Apollo, written after reading Keats's 'Sleep and Poetry.'" For the poem's debt to visual art, see Jack, pp. 130–41.

In a green island, far from all men's knowing?
More healthful than the leafiness of dales?
More secret than a nest of nightingales?
More serene than Cordelia's[2] countenance?
More full of visions than a high romance?   10
What, but thee Sleep? Soft closer of our eyes!
Low murmurer of tender lullabies!
Light hoverer around our happy pillows!
Wreather of poppy buds, and weeping willows!
Silent entangler of a beauty's tresses!   15
Most happy listener! when the morning blesses
Thee for enlivening all the cheerful eyes
That glance so brightly at the new sun-rise.[3]

But what is higher beyond thought than thee?
Fresher than berries of a mountain tree?   20
More strange, more beautiful, more smooth, more regal,
Than wings of swans, than doves, than dim-seen eagle?
What is it? And to what shall I compare it?
It has a glory, and nought else can share it:
The thought thereof is awful, sweet, and holy,   25
Chacing away all worldliness and folly;
Coming sometimes like fearful claps of thunder,
Or the low rumblings earth's regions under;
And sometimes like a gentle whispering
Of all the secrets of some wond'rous thing   30
That breathes about us in the vacant air;
So that we look around with prying stare,
Perhaps to see shapes of light, aerial lymning,[4]
And catch soft floatings from a faint-heard hymning;
To see the laurel wreath, on high suspended,   35
That is to crown our name when life is ended.
Sometimes it gives a glory to the voice,
And from the heart up-springs, rejoice! rejoice!
Sounds which will reach the Framer of all things,
And die away in ardent mutterings.   40

No one who once the glorious sun has seen,
And all the clouds, and felt his bosom clean
For his great Maker's presence, but must know
What 'tis I mean, and feel his being glow:
Therefore no insult will I give his spirit,   45
By telling what he sees from native merit.

O Poesy! for thee I hold my pen
That am not yet a glorious denizen[5]
Of thy wide heaven—Should I rather kneel
Upon some mountain-top until I feel   50

2. Cordelia is Lear's faithful daughter in Shakespeare's *King Lear*.
3. Allott suggests the description of sleep (ll. 11–18) owes something to Sidney's *Astrophel and Stella*,
Sonnet 39, and Iris's address to Morpheus, the god of sleep, in Ovid's *Metamorphoses* 11:623–26.
Shelley opens his *Queen Mab* (1813) with a discussion of sleep and death.
4. Limning: painting, illuminated writing.
5. An inhabitant but also an alien admitted to rights of citizenship.

A glowing splendour round about me hung,
And echo back the voice of thine own tongue?
O Poesy! for thee I grasp my pen
That am not yet a glorious denizen
Of thy wide heaven; yet, to my ardent prayer,   55
Yield from thy sanctuary some clear air,
Smoothed for intoxication by the breath
Of flowering bays,[6] that I may die a death
Of luxury, and my young spirit follow
The morning sun-beams to the great Apollo[7]   60
Like a fresh sacrifice; or, if I can bear
The o'erwhelming sweets, 'twill bring to me the fair
Visions of all places: a bowery nook
Will be elysium—an eternal book[8]
Whence I may copy many a lovely saying   65
About the leaves, and flowers—about the playing
Of nymphs in woods, and fountains; and the shade
Keeping a silence round a sleeping maid;
And many a verse from so strange influence
That we must ever wonder how, and whence   70
It came. Also imaginings will hover
Round my fire-side, and haply there discover
Vistas of solemn beauty, where I'd wander
In happy silence, like the clear meander[9]
Through its lone vales; and where I found a spot   75
Of awfuller shade, or an enchanted grot,[1]
Or a green hill o'erspread with chequered dress
Of flowers, and fearful from its loveliness,
Write on my tablets all that was permitted,
All that was for our human senses fitted.   80
Then the events of this wide world I'd seize
Like a strong giant, and my spirit teaze
Till at its shoulders it should proudly see
Wings to find out an immortality.

Stop and consider! life is but a day;   85
A fragile dew-drop on its perilous way
From a tree's summit; a poor Indian's sleep
While his boat hastens to the monstrous steep
Of Montmorenci.[2] Why so sad a moan?
Life is the rose's hope while yet unblown;   90
The reading of an ever-changing tale;
The light uplifting of a maiden's veil;
A pigeon tumbling in clear summer air;
A laughing school-boy, without grief or care,
Riding the springy branches of an elm.   95

6. Trees resembling the laurel and a source of garlands or crowns given as prizes to, for example, poets.
7. See p. 6, n. 1.
8. *nook . . . book*: Keats and Hunt both employ this conjoining of nature and culture, of place and
   text; *elysium*: the abode of the virtuous dead in the classical underworld.
9. Most editions capitalize the printed "meander" to make clear the allusion to the river in Asia Minor
   famous in classical antiquity for its wandering course.
1. Grotto, a cave or artificial recess made to resemble a cave.
2. Waterfall in Quebec, known as a site from the French and Indian War.

O for ten years, that I may overwhelm
Myself in poesy;[3] so I may do the deed
That my own soul has to itself decreed.
Then will I pass the countries that I see
In long perspective, and continually   100
Taste their pure fountains. First the realm I'll pass
Of Flora, and old Pan:[4] sleep in the grass,
Feed upon apples red, and strawberries,
And choose each pleasure that my fancy sees;
Catch the white-handed nymphs in shady places,   105
To woo sweet kisses from averted faces,—
Play with their fingers, touch their shoulders white
Into a pretty shrinking with a bite
As hard as lips can make it: till agreed,
A lovely tale of human life we'll read.   110
And one will teach a tame dove how it best
May fan the cool air gently o'er my rest;
Another, bending o'er her nimble tread,
Will set a green robe floating round her head,
And still will dance with ever varied ease,   115
Smiling upon the flowers and the trees:
Another will entice me on, and on
Through almond blossoms and rich cinnamon;
Till in the bosom of a leafy world
We rest in silence, like two gems upcurl'd   120
In the recesses of a pearly shell.

And can I ever bid these joys farewell?
Yes, I must pass them for a nobler life,
Where I may find the agonies, the strife
Of human hearts: for lo! I see afar,   125
O'er sailing the blue cragginess, a car[5]
And steeds with steamy manes—the charioteer
Looks out upon the winds with glorious fear:
And now the numerous tramplings quiver lightly
Along a huge cloud's ridge; and now with sprightly   130
Wheel downward come they into fresher skies,
Tipt round with silver from the sun's bright eyes.
Still downward with capacious whirl they glide;
And now I see them on a green-hill's side
In breezy rest among the nodding stalks.   135
The charioteer with wond'rous gesture talks
To the trees and mountains; and there soon appear
Shapes of delight, of mystery, and fear,
Passing along before a dusky space

3. Lines 96–125 suggest, as Woodhouse (1817, opposite p. 104) notes, that Keats will apply himself
   "to all the species of poetry." Wordsworth's "Tintern Abbey" is often cited as a precursor, and the
   passage is often read in conjunction with Keats's letter to Reynolds of May 3, 1818 (L,1: esp.
   281–83 and below, pp. 245–46). More simply, Keats imagines here his poetic development moving from pastoral (and erotic) romance to tragedy (though identified by Woodhouse as epic).
4. The god of shepherds and huntsmen and more broadly of universal nature; *Flora*: the goddess of
   flowers and gardens. They rule a realm of pastoral and sensual poetry. Allott suggests that ll.
   101–21 may owe something to William Browne's *Britannia's Pastorals* 2, Song 3, and to Nicholas
   Poussin's painting, *L'Empire de Flore*.
5. Chariot.

Made by some mighty oaks: as they would chase 140
Some ever-fleeting music on they sweep.
Lo! how they murmur, laugh, and smile, and weep:
Some with upholden hand and mouth severe;
Some with their faces muffled to the ear
Between their arms; some, clear in youthful bloom, 145
Go glad and smilingly athwart the gloom;
Some looking back, and some with upward gaze;
Yes, thousands in a thousand different ways
Flit onward—now a lovely wreath of girls
Dancing their sleek hair into tangled curls; 150
And now broad wings. Most awfully intent
The driver of those steeds is forward bent,
And seems to listen: O that I might know
All that he writes with such a hurrying glow.

The visions all are fled—the car is fled 155
Into the light of heaven, and in their stead
A sense of real things comes doubly strong,
And, like a muddy stream, would bear along
My soul to nothingness: but I will strive
Against all doubtings, and will keep alive 160
The thought of that same chariot, and the strange
Journey it went.[6]

           Is there so small a range
In the present strength of manhood, that the high
Imagination cannot freely fly
As she was wont of old? prepare her steeds, 165
Paw up against the light, and do strange deeds
Upon the clouds? Has she not shewn us all?
From the clear space of ether,[7] to the small
Breath of new buds unfolding? From the meaning
Of Jove's large eye-brow, to the tender greening 170
Of April meadows? Here her altar shone,
E'en in this isle; and who could paragon[8]
The fervid choir that lifted up a noise
Of harmony, to where it aye will poise
Its mighty self of convoluting sound, 175
Huge as a planet, and like that roll round,
Eternally around a dizzy void?
Ay, in those days the Muses were nigh cloy'd

6. In ll. 125–62, Keats offers an account of the imagination's interaction with nature that will be echoed elsewhere in his poetry (i.e., his verse epistle to Reynolds, below pp. 133–36). The Apollo-like charioteer "talks / To the trees and mountains" (ll. 136–37), engaging in a dialogue with nature that produces an imaginative response in the "Shapes of delight, of mystery, and fear" (l. 138). The poet creates something beyond what nature provides, but the fear is that when the imaginative experience is over a "sense of real things" (l. 157), now seemingly less than the world of vision, will overwhelm the poet.
7. The sky.
8. Surpass; Allott cites Shakespeare's *Othello*, 2.1.61–62: "a maid / That paragons description." In ll. 171–80, Keats celebrates the power of Elizabethan poetry (Woodhouse [*1817*, opposite p. 108] identifies "Shaksp: Milton Beaumont & Fletcher, Spencer &c.") that is then betrayed by the "French school" of neoclassicists (ll. 181–206). This is the same position that Hunt argued in his "Young Poets" review (see above, pp. 11–14).

With honors; nor had any other care
Than to sing out and sooth[9] their wavy hair.   180

Could all this be forgotten? Yes, a schism
Nurtured by foppery and barbarism,
Made great Apollo blush for this his land.
Men were thought wise who could not understand
His glories: with a puling infant's force   185
They sway'd about upon a rocking horse,
And thought it Pegasus.[1] Ah dismal soul'd!
The winds of heaven blew, the ocean roll'd
Its gathering waves—ye felt it not. The blue
Bared its eternal bosom,[2] and the dew   190
Of summer nights collected still to make
The morning precious: beauty was awake!
Why were ye not awake? But ye were dead
To things ye knew not of,—were closely wed
To musty laws lined out with wretched rule   195
And compass vile: so that ye taught a school
Of dolts to smooth, inlay, and clip, and fit,
Till, like the certain wands of Jacob's wit,[3]
Their verses tallied. Easy was the task:
A thousand handicraftsmen wore the mask   200
Of Poesy. Ill-fated, impious race!
That blasphemed the bright Lyrist[4] to his face,
And did not know it,—no, they went about,
Holding a poor, decrepid standard out
Mark'd with most flimsy mottos, and in large   205
The name of one Boileau![5]

                    O ye whose charge
It is to hover round our pleasant hills!
Whose congregated majesty so fills
My boundly[6] reverence, that I cannot trace
Your hallowed names, in this unholy place,   210
So near those common folk; did not their shames
Affright you? Did our old lamenting Thames
Delight you? Did ye never cluster round
Delicious Avon, with a mournful sound,
And weep? Or did ye wholly bid adieu   215
To regions where no more the laurel grew?

---

9. For "soothe," meaning here "smooth," "compose."
1. Pegasus is a winged horse from Greek mythology who opened up Hippocrene, a stream on Mount
   Helicon, sacred to the muses; Pegasus is thus an emblem of poetic inspiration. Keats's attack upon
   the sing-song quality of the heroic couplet echoes Hazlitt's comment from his "On Milton's versification" in the *Examiner* (August 20, 1815, p. 542): "Dr. Johnson and Pope would have converted
   his vaulting Pegasus into a rocking horse."
2. Echo of Wordsworth's "The world is too much with us" (1807): "This Sea that bares her bosom to
   the moon" (l. 5).
3. See Genesis 30. 27–43; Jacob uses wands of poplar, hazel, and chestnut, all peeled to reveal white
   streaks, to control the breeding of cattle, making himself wealthy at Laban's expense.
4. Apollo; see p. 6, n. 1.
5. Nicolas Boileau (1636–1711), French critic and poet; his *Art Poétique* (1674), a four-canto poem,
   set forth neoclassical principles of taste and composition that would be followed by Dryden, Pope,
   and Addison.
6. A coinage probably meaning "boundless" but perhaps "bounden."

Or did ye stay to give a welcoming
To some lone spirits who could proudly sing
Their youth away, and die?[7] 'Twas even so:
But let me think away those times of woe: 220
Now 'tis a fairer season; ye have breathed
Rich benedictions o'er us; ye have wreathed
Fresh garlands: for sweet music has been heard
In many places;—some has been upstirr'd
From out its crystal dwelling in a lake,   225
By a swan's ebon bill;[8] from a thick brake,
Nested and quiet in a valley mild,
Bubbles a pipe;[9] fine sounds are floating wild
About the earth: happy are ye and glad.

These things are doubtless: yet in truth we've had   230
Strange thunders from the potency of song;[1]
Mingled indeed with what is sweet and strong,
From majesty: but in clear truth the themes
Are ugly clubs, the Poets Polyphemes[2]
Disturbing the grand sea. A drainless shower   235
Of light is poesy; 'tis the supreme of power;
'Tis might half slumb'ring on its own right arm.
The very archings of her eye-lids charm
A thousand willing agents to obey,
And still she governs with the mildest sway: 240
But strength alone though of the Muses born
Is like a fallen angel: trees uptorn,
Darkness, and worms, and shrouds, and sepulchres
Delight it; for it feeds upon the burrs,
And thorns of life; forgetting the great end   245
Of poesy, that it should be a friend
To sooth the cares, and lift the thoughts of man.[3]

Yet I rejoice: a myrtle fairer than
E'er grew in Paphos,[4] from the bitter weeds

7. Woodhouse (1817, opposite p. 111) identifies the "lone spirits" as "H. Kirke White—Chatterton—
  & other poets of great promise, neglected by the age, who died young." The earlier references to
  the Thames and Avon call to mind the renowned poets Spenser and Shakespeare.
8. Woodhouse (1817, opposite p. 111) identifies the poet as "Wordsworth, who resides near one of
  the lakes in Cumberland."
9. Woodhouse (1817, opposite p. 111) complains "Leigh Hunt's poetry is here alluded to, in terms
  too favorable."
1. Woodhouse (1817, opposite p. 111) finds an "Allusion to Lord Byron, & his terrific stile of poetry—
  to Christabel by Coleridge &c."
2. Keats suggests here that some modern poets resemble Homer's one-eyed giant Polyphemus. Most
  critics have seen Keats referring specifically to Byron, who, according to Woodhouse (1817, opposite p. 112) is also alluded to in ll. 241–45. Anne Grant, in her rebuke to Barbauld's *Eighteen Hundred and Eleven* entitled *Eighteen Hundred and Thirteen* (1814), also refers to Byron as "Like
  Polyphemus with destructive might, / Revenging thus thy loss of mental sight" (ll. 958–59). Woodhouse also refers to Coleridge, and Hunt's review of Coleridge in the *Examiner* (June 2, 1816)
  makes a similar complaint about "Christabel." Hunt's review of Keats's *Poems* cites these lines as
  a comment "on the morbidity that taints the productions of the Lake Poets" (*Examiner*, July 13,
  1817, p. 444).
3. In ll. 242–47, Keats contrasts the taste for Gothic romance and Byronic melancholy with what
  Hunt would later identify as the poetry of cheerfulness.
4. A city in Cyprus, famous for its temple to Venus. Woodhouse (1817, opposite p. 112) sees ll.
  248–50 referring "to the coming age of poetry under the type of a myrtle. The author appears to
  think (perhaps justly) very favorably of the approaching generation of poets"; he refers the reader
  to the sonnet "Addressed to the Same," above, p. 56.

Lifts its sweet head into the air, and feeds   250
A silent space with ever sprouting green.
All tenderest birds there find a pleasant screen,
Creep through the shade with jaunty fluttering,
Nibble the little cupped flowers and sing.
Then let us clear away the choaking thorns   255
From round its gentle stem; let the young fawns,
Yeaned[5] in after times, when we are flown,
Find a fresh sward beneath it, overgrown
With simple flowers: let there nothing be
More boisterous than a lover's bended knee;   260
Nought more ungentle than the placid look
Of one who leans upon a closed book;
Nought more untranquil than the grassy slopes
Between two hills. All hail delightful hopes!
As she was wont, th' imagination   265
Into most lovely labyrinths will be gone,
And they shall be accounted poet kings
Who simply tell the most heart-easing things.[6]
O may these joys be ripe before I die.

Will not some say that I presumptuously   270
Have spoken? that from hastening disgrace
'Twere better far to hide my foolish face?
That whining boyhood should with reverence bow
Ere the dread thunderbolt could reach? How!
If I do hide myself, it sure shall be   275
In the very fane,[7] the light of Poesy:
If I do fall, at least I will be laid
Beneath the silence of a poplar shade;
And over me the grass shall be smooth shaven;
And there shall be a kind memorial graven.   280
But off Despondence![8] miserable bane!
They should not know thee, who, athirst to gain
A noble end, are thirsty every hour.
What though I am not wealthy in the dower
Of spanning wisdom; though I do not know   285
The shiftings of the mighty winds that blow
Hither and thither all the changing thoughts
Of man: though no great minist'ring reason sorts
Out the dark mysteries of human souls
To clear conceiving: yet there ever rolls   290
A vast idea before me, and I glean
Therefrom my liberty; thence too I've seen
The end and aim of Poesy. 'Tis clear
As any thing most true; as that the year
Is made of the four seasons—manifest   295
As a large cross, some old cathedral's crest,

5. Born, brought forth.
6. An echo of Milton's "L'Allegro" (1631?, 1645), where the goddess Euphrosyne is called by men "heart-easing Mirth" (l. 13).
7. Temple.
8. Book 4 of Wordsworth's *Excursion* (1814), entitled "Despondency Corrected," identified despondency as the illness of the age.

Lifted to the white clouds. Therefore should I
Be but the essence of deformity,
A coward, did my very eye-lids wink
At speaking out what I have dared to think.   300
Ah! rather let me like a madman run
Over some precipice; let the hot sun
Melt my Dedalian wings,[9] and drive me down
Convuls'd and headlong! Stay! an inward frown
Of conscience bids me be more calm awhile.   305
An ocean dim, sprinkled with many an isle,
Spreads awfully before me. How much toil!
How many days! what desperate turmoil!
Ere I can have explored its widenesses.
Ah, what a task! upon my bended knees,   310
I could unsay those—no, impossible!
Impossible!

      For sweet relief I'll dwell
On humbler thoughts, and let this strange assay
Begun in gentleness die so away.
E'en now all tumult from my bosom fades: 315
I turn full hearted to the friendly aids
That smooth the path of honour; brotherhood,
And friendliness the nurse of mutual good.
The hearty grasp that sends a pleasant sonnet
Into the brain ere one can think upon it;   320
The silence when some rhymes are coming out;
And when they're come, the very pleasant rout:[1]
The message certain to be done to-morrow.
'Tis perhaps as well that it should be to borrow
Some precious book from out its snug retreat,   325
To cluster round it when we next shall meet.
Scarce can I scribble on; for lovely airs
Are fluttering round the room like doves in pairs;
Many delights of that glad day recalling,
When first my senses caught their tender falling.   330
And with these airs come forms of elegance
Stooping their shoulders o'er a horse's prance,
Careless, and grand—fingers soft and round
Parting luxuriant curls;—and the swift bound
Of Bacchus from his chariot, when his eye   335
Made Ariadne's cheek look blushingly.[2]
Thus I remember all the pleasant flow
Of words at opening a portfolio.

9. In Greek myth, Daedalus, builder of the Cretan labyrinth, made wings of wax and feathers to
   enable his and his son Icarus's escape from King Minos; when Icarus flew too near the sun, the
   wax melted and he fell. Keats would have known the story from both Lemprière and Ovid, *Meta-*
   morphoses 8.183–235.
1. Here, "fuss, clamour, noise" (*OED*). Keats describes Hunt's sonnet contests (ll. 319–22), and the
   passage as a whole celebrates the sociality of the Hunt household—"pleasure's temple" (l. 355)—
   with its music, poetry, and art.
2. Bacchus, the god of wine who rode a chariot drawn by a lion and a tiger, took Minos's daughter
   Ariadne as his lover after she was abandoned by Theseus. Keats may draw visual details from Titian's *Bacchus and Ariadne* exhibited at the British Institution in 1816. As line 338 suggests, Keats
   came to know reproductions of visual art through Hunt's collection of engravings and busts (see
   Jack, pp. 1–22). Hunt published his "Bacchus and Ariadne" in 1819.

Things such as these are ever harbingers
To trains of peaceful images: the stirs   340
Of a swan's neck unseen among the rushes:
A linnet starting all about the bushes:
A butterfly, with golden wings broad parted,
Nestling a rose, convuls'd as though it smarted
With over pleasure—many, many more,   345
Might I indulge at large in all my store
Of luxuries: yet I must not forget
Sleep, quiet with his poppy coronet:
For what there may be worthy in these rhymes
I partly owe to him: and thus, the chimes   350
Of friendly voices had just given place
To as sweet a silence, when I 'gan retrace
The pleasant day, upon a couch at ease.
It was a poet's house who keeps the keys
Of pleasure's temple. Round about were hung   355
The glorious features of the bards who sung
In other ages—cold and sacred busts
Smiled at each other. Happy he who trusts
To clear Futurity his darling fame!
Then there were fauns and satyrs[3] taking aim   360
At swelling apples with a frisky leap
And reaching fingers, 'mid a luscious heap
Of vine leaves. Then there rose to view a fane
Of liny[4] marble, and thereto a train
Of nymphs approaching fairly o'er the sward: 365
One, loveliest, holding her white hand toward
The dazzling sun-rise: two sisters sweet
Bending their graceful figures till they meet
Over the trippings of a little child:
And some are hearing, eagerly, the wild   370
Thrilling liquidity of dewy piping.
See, in another picture, nymphs are wiping
Cherishingly Diana's timorous limbs;[5]—
A fold of lawny mantle dabbling swims
At the bath's edge, and keeps a gentle motion   375
With the subsiding crystal: as when ocean
Heaves calmly its broad swelling smoothiness o'er
Its rocky marge,[6] and balances once more
The patient weeds; that now unshent[7] by foam
Feel all about their undulating home.   380

Sappho's meek head[8] was there half smiling down
At nothing; just as though the earnest frown
Of over thinking had that moment gone
From off her brow, and left her all alone.

---

3. See p. 20, n. 4, and p. 24, n. 6.
4. "Full of lines, marked with lines" (*OED*).
5. See p. 25, n. 1.
6. See above, p. 38, n. 2.
7. "Uninjured, unharmed, unspoiled" (*OED*).
8. A bust of the Greek woman poet Sappho (b. Lesbos c. 620 B.C.E.).

Great Alfred's too, with anxious, pitying eyes,   385
As if he always listened to the sighs
Of the goaded world; and Kosciusko's[9] worn
By horrid suffrance—mightily forlorn.

Petrarch, outstepping from the shady green,
Starts at the sight of Laura;[1] nor can wean   390
His eyes from her sweet face. Most happy they!
For over them was seen a free display
Of out-spread wings, and from between them shone
The face of Poesy: from off her throne
She overlook'd things that I scarce could tell.   395
The very sense of where I was might well
Keep Sleep aloof: but more than that there came
Thought after thought to nourish up the flame
Within my breast; so that the morning light
Surprised me even from a sleepless night;   400
And up I rose refresh'd, and glad, and gay,
Resolving to begin that very day
These lines; and howsoever they be done,
I leave them as a father does his son.

FINIS

9. See p. 57, n. 1; Alfred: see p. 42, n. 3.
1. For Laura and Petrarch, see p. 53, n. 4.

Between *Poems* (1817)
and *Endymion* (1818)

TO A YOUNG LADY WHO SENT ME
A LAUREL CROWN.[1]

FRESH morning gusts have blown away all fear
From my glad bosom,—now from gloominess
I mount for ever—not an atom less
Than the proud laurel shall content my bier.
No! by the eternal stars! or why sit here   5
    In the Sun's eye, and 'gainst my temples press
    Apollo's very leaves, woven to bless
By thy white fingers and thy spirit clear.
Lo! who dares say, "Do this?"—Who dares call down
    My will from its high[2] purpose? Who say, "Stand,"   10
Or "Go?" This mighty[3] moment I would frown
    On abject Cæsars[4]—not the stoutest band
Of mailed heroes should tear off my crown:—
    Yet would I kneel and kiss thy gentle hand!

On Receiving a Laurel Crown from Leigh Hunt[1]

Minutes are flying swiftly; and as yet
    Nothing unearthly has enticed my brain

---

1. Written in 1816 or 1817, but perhaps (as Allott suggests) in March 1817 as Keats fully commits himself to poetry. The young lady could be one of the Reynolds sisters or perhaps Georgiana Wylie. First published as Sonnet II in 1848, 2: 288; text from 1848 with emendations from W², f. 19r (*MYR: JK* 6: 15).
2. W² originally had "own," corrected to "high."
3. This is Milnes's suggestion for a gap in W²; W¹ adds "very," which might be in Keats's hand.
4. See Horace Smith's "Addressed by the Statue of Jupiter, Lately Arrived from Rome, to his Royal Highness the Prince Regent," (*Examiner*, October 27, 1816, p. 681): "Cæsars, whene'er I frown'd, stood petrified."
1. This poem is usually dated from the spring of 1817 but may have been written in late 1816. At some point, Hunt crowned Keats with laurel, while Keats offered Hunt ivy; when some ladies arrived (see the next poem), Hunt removed his crown but Keats kept his. Woodhouse's account of this story (W², f. 9v) is often used to explain this and the following poem, but Woodhouse's note is linked directly to "God of the golden bow" (pp. 70–71, below). The sonnet's references to time in ll. 1 and 9 suggest that it was written later, perhaps with one of Hunt's sonnets about receiving a crown of ivy from Keats, dated March 1, 1817, and published in *Foliage* (1818). Hunt has an earlier (December 1, 1816) sonnet, also in *Foliage*, that imagines Keats with "a flowering laurel on your brow." Motion relates the occasion to Keats's receiving his first copy of *Poems* on March 1 (pp. 147–49); see also Bate, pp. 138–39n. Keats's sonnet was first published in the *Times*,

Into a delphic[2] labyrinth—I would fain
Catch an immortal thought to pay the debt
I owe to the kind poet who has set   5
     Upon my ambitious head a glorious gain.
Two bending laurel sprigs—'tis nearly pain
To be conscious of such a coronet.
Still time is fleeting, and no dream arises
     Gorgeous as I would have it—only I see   10
A trampling down of what the world most prizes,
     Turbans and crowns, and blank regality;
And then I run into most wild surmises
     Of all the many glories that may be.

To the Ladies Who Saw Me Crowned[1]

What is there in the universal earth
     More lovely than a wreath from the bay tree?
Haply[2] a halo round the moon—a glee
Circling from three sweet pair of lips in mirth;
And haply you will say the dewy birth   5
     Of morning roses—riplings tenderly
     Spread by the halcyon's[3] breast upon the sea—
But these comparisons are nothing worth.
Then is there nothing in the world so fair?
     The silvery tears of April?—Youth of May?   10
Or June that breathes out life for buttlerflies?
     No—none of these can from my favorite bear
Away the palm—yet shall it ever pay
     Due reverence to your most sovereign eyes.

Ode to Apollo[1]

God of the golden bow,
     And of the golden lyre,

May 18, 1914, pp. 9–10; text from the *Times* with emendations from Keats's fair copy in Reynolds's copy of *Poems* (Harvard MS Keats *EC8.K2262.817p (G), p. 78; *JKPMH*, p. 47).
2. From Delphi, the seat of Apollo's oracle.
1. For the poem's composition see the preceding poem. The ladies with their "three sweet pair of lips" are probably three of Reynolds's four sisters, Jane (later the wife of Thomas Hood), Mariane (a favorite of George Keats and jilted by Benjamin Bailey), and Charlotte (whose piano playing has been seen as inspiring "I had a dove and the sweet dove died" and "Hush, hush! tread softy"; see, below, pp. 296–97). First published in the *Times*, May 18, 1914, pp. 9–10; text from the *Times* with emendations from Keats's fair copy in Reynolds's copy of *Poems* (Harvard MS Keats *EC8.K2262.817p(G), p. 78; *JKPMH*, p. 47).
2. Perhaps, maybe.
3. A bird associated with calm.
1. This poem, labeled a fragment by Reynolds and Woodhouse, was written late in 1816 or early in 1817, sometime after the last three poems. Woodhouse (W[2], f. 9v) offers a note opposite his transcript: "As Keats & Leigh Hunt were taking their Wine together after dinner, at the house of the latter, the whim seized them (probably at Hunt's instigation) to crown themselves with laurel after the fashion of the elder bards.—While they were thus attired, two of Hunt's friends happened to call upon him—Just before their entrance H. removed the wreath from his own brows, and sug-

And of the golden hair,
And of the golden fire;
Charioteer   5
Of[2] the patient year;
Where, where slept thine ire
When like a blank idiot I put on thy wreath,
Thy laurel, thy glory,
The light of thy story;   10
Or was I a worm, too low crawling[3] for death?
    O delphic[4] Apollo!

The Thunderer grasp'd and grasp'd,
The Thunderer frown'd and frown'd,
The eagle's feathery mane   15
For wrath became stiffen'd—the sound
Of breeding thunder
Went drowsily under,
Muttering to be unbound—
O why didst thou pity, and for a worm[5]   20
Why touch thy soft lute
Till the thunder was mute?
Why was I not crush'd—such a pitiful germ—
    O delphic Apollo!

The Pleiades[6] were up,   25
Watching the silent air,
The seeds and roots in the earth[7]
Were swelling for summer fare,
The ocean, its neighbour,
Was at its[8] old labor,   30
When—who, who did dare
To tie like a madman[9] thy plant round his brow?
And grin and look proudly,
And blaspheme so loudly,
And live for that honor to stoop to thee now,   35
    O delphic Apollo!

gested to K. that he might as well do the same. K however in his mad enthusiastic way, vowed he would not take off his crown for any human being: and he accordingly wore it, without any explanation, as long as their visit lasted.—He mentioned the circumstance afterwards to some of his friends, along with his sense of the folly (and I believe presumption) of his conduct—And he said he was determined to record it, by an apologetic Ode to Apollo on the occasion—He shortly after wrote this fragment" (*MYR: JK*, 6: 4). First published in the *Western Messenger* 1 (June 1836), p. 763, with this note: "The following beautiful poem is for the first time published from the original manuscript, presented to the Editor by the Poet's brother." Text from *Western Messenger* with emendations from Keats's draft (Harvard MS Keats 2.13; *JKPMH*, p. 51, 53), which Keats's brother George had given to J. F. Clarke; key variants from the Morgan fair copy (MA 211) are given in the notes.
2. The Morgan FC has "Round."
3. The Morgan FC has "low-creeping."
4. See p. 70, n. 2.
5. The Morgan FC has "beg for a worm?"
6. The seven daughters of Atlas transformed into a constellation of stars.
7. The Morgan FC has "in earth."
8. The draft and the Morgan FC have "his."
9. The Morgan FC has "for a moment" for "like a madman."

WRITTEN ON A BLANK SPACE AT THE END OF CHAUCER'S TALE OF "THE FLOURE AND THE LEAFE."[1]

THIS pleasant Tale is like a little Copse:
The honied Lines do freshly interlace
To keep the Reader in so sweet a place,
So that he here and there full-hearted stops;
And oftentimes he feels the dewy drops   5
Come cool and suddenly against his face,
And by the wand'ring Melody may trace
Which way the tender-legged Linnet hops.

O what a power has white Simplicity!
What mighty power has this gentle story!   10
I that do ever feel a thirst[2] for glory,
Could at this moment be content to lie
Meekly upon the grass, as those whose sobbings
Were heard of none beside the mournful Robins.[3]

TO HAYDON
WITH A SONNET WRITTEN ON SEEING THE ELGIN MARBLES[1]

HAYDON! Forgive me[2] that I cannot speak
Definitively on these mighty things;
Forgive me that I have not Eagle's wings—
That what I want I know not where to seek:

1. Written in February 1817 (perhaps before the 27th, the day that Reynolds wrote a sonnet in response) in Clarke's copy of Chaucer, this sonnet was, according to Clarke, "an extempore effusion and without the alteration of a single word" (*Recollections*, p. 139). It was first published over the initials "J.K." in the *Examiner*, March 16, 1817, p. 173: "The following exquisite Sonnet, as well as one or two others that have lately appeared under the same signature, is from the pen of a young poet (KEATS), who was mentioned not long ago in this paper, and who may already lay true claim to that title:—

> The youngest he,
> That sits in shadow of Apollo's tree."

"The Floure and the Leafe," which celebrates the "white Simplicity" (l. 9) of the leaf as an emblem of chastity, though no longer thought to be by Chaucer, was a favorite of the Hunt circle; Keats quoted it as the motto to "Sleep and Poetry" (above, p. 58), and Allott identifies echoes of the poem here in ll. 5–6 and 8. Text from the *Examiner*; the holograph (signed "J. K. Feby. 1815") in Clarke's copy of *The Poetical Works of Geoffrey Chaucer*, 14 vols. (Edinburgh, 1782), 12: 104–105, after "The Floure and the Leafe," is now in the British Library (Add. 33516, vol 6: 150–51).
2. The holograph version in Clarke's Chaucer has "athirst."
3. An allusion to the story of the "Babes in the Woods," where crying children are covered by a blanket of leaves by robins.
1. Written March 1 or 2, 1817. Keats's friend Haydon had been a central figure in the battle to convince the government to buy the marbles from the Parthenon in Athens. Lord Elgin had shipped what came to be known as the "Elgin Marbles" to England in 1803 for his private collection; when he sought to sell them to the government in 1812, a controversy arose over the provenance of the marbles, over the aesthetic worth of what Byron called "Phidian freaks," and over the legitimacy of keeping Greek artifacts in London. Keats "went again and again to see the Elgin Marbles, and would sit for an hour or more at a time beside them rapt in revery" (W. Sharp, *Life of Severn* [1892], p. 32). See Jack, pp. 31–36 165–67, and Stephen Larrabee, *English Bards and Grecian Marbles* (1943). First published over Keats's initials in the *Examiner*, March 9, 1817, p. 155 and the *Champion*, March 9, 1817, p. 78, and reprinted in *Annals of the Fine Arts* 3 (April 1818), pp. 171–72; text from the *Examiner* with some variants noted from the *Champion* and Keats's fair copy (FC) in Reynolds's copy of *Poems* (Harvard MS Keats *EC8.K2262.817p(G), p. 122; *JKPMH*, p. 49).
2. The FC and the *Champion* have "Forgive me, Haydon."

And think that I would not be overmeek   5
    In rolling out upfollow'd thunderings,
        Even to the steep of Heliconian springs,[3]
Were I of ample strength for such a freak—
Think too, that all those numbers should be thine;
    Whose else? In this who touch thy vesture's hem?   10
For when men star'd at what was most divine
    With browless idiotism—o'erwise[4] phlegm—
Thou hadst beheld the Hesperean[5] shine
    Of their star in the East, and gone to worship them.[6]

ON SEEING THE ELGIN MARBLES[1]

My spirit is too weak—Mortality
    Weighs heavily on me like unwilling sleep,
    And each imagined pinnacle and steep
Of godlike hardship, tells me I must die
Like a sick Eagle looking at the sky.[2]   5
    Yet 'tis a gentle luxury to weep
    That I have not the cloudy winds to keep,
Fresh for the opening of the morning's eye.
Such dim-conceived glories of the brain
    Bring round the heart an undescribable feud;   10
So do these wonders a most dizzy pain,
    That mingles Grecian grandeur with the rude
Wasting of old time—with a billowy main[3]—
    A sun—a shadow of a magnitude.

JOHN HAMILTON REYNOLDS

Champion Review of *Poems*[1]

Here is a little volume filled throughout with very graceful and genuine
poetry. The author is a very young man, and one, as we augur from the
present work, that is likely to make a great addition to those who would

---

3. The Hippocrene, a spring sacred to the Muses, is found on Mount Helicon.
4. The FC and the *Champion* have "o'erweening Phlegm." Keats refers to the fierce argument over the Parthenon marbles, with Haydon arguing for their artistic merit against such figures as Richard Payne Knight (1751–1824), antiquarian and author of *Discourse on the Worship of Priapus* (1786).
5. From Hesperus, the planet Venus as the evening star.
6. Allott suggests a comparison between Haydon and the Magi following their star.
1. Written shortly before March 3, 1817 with the previous poem (see p. 72, n. 1). On the poem's historical context, see Grant F. Scott, *The Sculpted Word: Keats, Ekphrasis and the Visual Arts* (1994), pp. 44–72. First published over Keats's initials in the *Examiner*, March 9, 1817, p. 155, and the *Champion*, March 9, 1817, p. 78, and reprinted in *Annals of the Fine Arts* 3 (April 1818), p. 172; text from the *Examiner*. There is a fair copy MS in the copy of *Poems* Keats gave to Reynolds (Harvard MS Keats *EC8.K2262.817p(G), p. 122; *JKPMH*, p. 49).
2. Haydon (*L*, 1: 122) wrote to Keats, "I know not a finer image than the comparison of a Poet unable to express his high feelings to a sick eagle looking at the Sky!" High-flying eagles were thought to be able to look directly into the sun.
3. The high seas.
1. An unsigned review by Keats's friend Reynolds that seeks to establish Keats's unique voice against "society" poets such as Rogers, Byron, and perhaps Wordsworth and the Lake Poets. Keats thanked Reynolds for the review in a letter, March 9, 1817 (*L*, 1: 123–24). Text from the *Champion*, March 9, 1817, 78–81.

overthrow that artificial taste which French criticism has long planted amongst us. At a time when nothing is talked of but the power and passion of Lord Byron, and the playful and elegant fancy of Moore, and the correctness of Rogers, and the sublimity and pathos of Campbell (these terms we should conceive are kept ready composed in the Edinburgh Review-shop)[2] a young man starts suddenly before us, with a genius that is likely to eclipse them all. He comes fresh from nature,—and the originals of his images are to be found in her keeping. Young writers are in general in their early productions imitators of their favourite poet; like young birds that in their first songs, mock the notes of those warblers, they hear the most, and love the best; but this youthful poet appears to have tuned his voice in solitudes,—to have sung from the pure inspiration of nature. In the simple meadows he has proved that he can

"—See shapes of light aerial lymning
And catch soft floating from a faint heard hymning."[3]

We find in his poetry the glorious effect of summer days and leafy spots on rich feelings, which are in themselves a summer. He relies directly and wholly on nature. He marries poesy to genuine simplicity. He makes her artless,—yet abstains carefully from giving her an uncomely homeliness:— that is, he shows he can be familiar with nature, yet perfectly strange to the habits of common life. Mr. Keats is faced, or "we have no judgment in an honest face;"[4] to look at natural objects with his mind, as Shakspeare and Chaucer did,—and not merely with his eye as nearly all modern poets do;— to clothe his poetry with a grand intellectual light,—and to lay his name in the lap of immortality. Our readers will think that we are speaking too highly of this young poet,—but luckily we have the power of making good the ground on which we prophesy so hardily. We shall extract largely from his volume:—it will be seen how familiar he is with all that is green, light, and beautiful in nature;—and with what an originality his mind dwells on all great or graceful objects. His imagination is very powerful,—and one thing we have observed with pleasure, that it never attempts to soar on undue occasions. The imagination, like the eagle on the rock, should keep its eye constantly on the sun,[5]—and should never be started heavenward, unless something magnificent marred its solitude. Again, though Mr Keats' poetry is remarkably abstracted it is never out of reach of the mind; there are one or two established writers of this day who think that mystery is the soul of poetry—that artlessness is a vice—and that nothing can be graceful that is not metaphysical;—and even young writers have sunk into this error, and endeavoured to puzzle the world with a confused sensibility. We must however hasten to the consideration of the little volume before us, and not fill up our columns with observations, which extracts will render unnecessary. * * *[6]

---

2. Reynolds refers to the key reviewing organ of the day, the *Edinburgh Review*. Frequently praised there and elsewhere were the poets Thomas Moore (1779–1852), Samuel Rogers (1763–1855), and Thomas Campbell (1777–1844).
3. Keats, "Sleep and Poetry," ll. 33–34.
4. See Shakespeare, *Othello*, 3.3.50.
5. See the image in Keats's "On Seeing the Elgin Marbles," l. 5, which Reynolds quotes below.
6. Reynolds quotes from or refers to the following pieces from *Poems*: "I stood tip-toe upon a little hill," "Specimen on an Induction to a Poem," "Calidore," "To Some Ladies," "On receiving a curious Shell, and a Copy of Verses, from the same Ladies," "To * * *" ("Hadst thou liv'd in days of old"),

But the last poem in the volume, to which we are now come, is the most powerful and the most perfect. It is entitled "Sleep and Poetry." The poet passed a wakeful night at a brother poet's house,[7] and has in this piece embodied the thoughts which passed over his mind. He gives his opinion of the Elizabethan age,—of the Pope's school,[8]— and of the poetry of the present day. We scarcely know what to select,—we are so confused with beauties. In speaking of poetry, we find the following splendid passage:—

[Quotes "Sleep and Poetry," lines 71–84.]

The following passage relating to the same event, is even greater. It is the very magic of imagination.

[Quotes "Sleep and Poetry," lines 125–37.]

We have not room to extract the passages on Pope and his followers, who,

> "—With a pulling force,
> Sway'd them about upon a rocking horse,
> And thought it Pegasus." [lines 185–87]

Nor can we give those on modern poets. We shall conclude our extracts with the following perfect and beautiful lines on the busts and pictures which hung around the room in which he was resting.

[Quotes "Sleep and Poetry," lines 381–95.]

We conclude with earnestly recommending the work to all our readers. It is not without defects, which may be easily mentioned, and as easily rectified. The author, from his natural freedom of versification at times passes to an absolute faultiness of measure:—This he should avoid. He should also abstain from the use of compound epithets as much as possible. He has a few of the faults which youth must have;—he is apt occasionally to make his descriptions overwrought,—But on the whole we never saw a book which had so little reason to plead youth as its excuse. The best poets of the day might not blush to own it.

We have had two Sonnets presented to us, which were written by Mr Keats, and which are not printed in the present volume. We have great pleasure in giving them to the public,—as well on account of their own power and beauty, as of the grandeur of the subjects; on which we have ourselves so often made observations.

[Reprints the sonnets "To Haydon with a Sonnet Written on Seeing the Elgin Marbles" and "On Seeing the Elgin Marbles."]

ON A PICTURE OF LEANDER.
[On a Leander which Miss Reynolds my kind friend gave me][1]

Come hither all sweet maidens soberly
Down-looking—aye, and with a chasten'd light

"To Hope," and the three verse epistles. Quoting the sonnet "To My Brother George" and Sonnet IX ("Keen, fitful gusts are whisp'ring here and there"), Reynolds notes "A few Sonnets follow these epistles, and, with the exception of Milton's and Wordsworth's, we think them the most powerful ones in the whole range of English poetry."

7. Hunt's.

8. That is, the poets who imitated Alexander Pope (1688–1744).

1. Keats wrote this sonnet in March 1817 when he received from Jane Reynolds one of James Tassie's popular paste reproductions of gems carved with classical images, here Leander swimming across

Hid in the fringes of your eyelids white,
And meekly let your fair hands joined be,
As if so gentle that ye could not see,[2]   5
Untouch'd, a victim of your beauty bright,
Sinking away to his young spirit's night,—
Sinking bewilder'd 'mid the dreary sea:
'Tis young Leander toiling to his death;
Nigh swooning, he doth purse his weary lips   10
For Hero's cheek, and smiles against her smile.
O horrid dream—see how his body dips
Dead-heavy—arms and shoulders gleam awhile—
He's gone—up bubbles all his amorous breath!

ON LEIGH HUNT'S POEM, THE "STORY OF RIMINI."[1]

WHO loves to peer up at the morning sun,
With half-shut eyes and comfortable cheek,
Let him, with this sweet tale full often seek
For meadows where the little rivers run;
Who loves to linger with that brightest one   5
Of heaven—Hesperus[2]—let him lowly speak
These numbers[3] to the night, and starlight meek,
Or moon, if that her hunting be begun.
He who knows these delights, and, too, is prone
To moralise upon a smile or tear,   10
Will find at once a region of his own,
A bower for his spirit, and will steer
To alleys where the fir-tree drops its cone,
Where robins hop, and fallen leaves are sere.[4]

---

the Hellespont in an attempt to meet his love, Hero. (Hunt published his own "Hero and Leander" in 1819.) Woodhouse (W[2], f. 193r) indicates "it was once Keats's intention to write a series of Sonnets & short poems on Some of Tassie's gems." He gave his sister a set of Tassie cameo gems in 1819, and the gems were popular in his circle, with Hunt recommending them in the *Indicator* of November 17, 1819 and Shelley writing to Peacock to send him "£2 worth of Tassie's gems" (Shelley, *Letters* 2: 276–77). The poem, identified as by the "LATE JOHN KEATS," was first published in the *Gem* 1 (1829), p. 108, a journal edited by Thomas Hood, who married Jane Reynolds in 1825. Hood also published in his journal (p. 145) his own "On a Picture of Hero and Leander," which proceeds through a series of puns. Text from the *Gem* with emendations from its probable source, Keats's holograph draft (Harvard MS Keats 2.12; *JKPMH*, p. 55), which supplies the longer title.

2. The draft ends the previous line with a period and offers a difficult-to-decipher text that might read: "So gentle are ye that ye could not see."

1. Written in March 1817, this poem, again reflecting Hunt's importance to Keats, was part of a series of admiring poems on *Rimini*: a sonnet by Reynolds in the *Champion*, December 8, 1816, p. 390, and Shelley's 1816 "Lines to Leigh Hunt." First published as Sonnet VI in 1848, 2: 292; text from 1848 with emendations from Hunt's transcript in his copy of Galignani (Harvard MS Keats *EC 8.K2262.B829pa (B)), where Hunt notes, "Written by Keats in a blank page of the 'presentation-copy' of his first volume of poems."

2. See p. 32, n. 7.

3. Verses.

4. Withered.

Letter to J. H. Reynolds, April 17, 18, 1817[1]

Carisbrooke April 17th

My dear Reynolds,

Ever since I wrote to my Brothers from Southampton I have been in a taking, and at this moment I am about to become settled. For I have unpacked my books, put them into a snug corner—pinned up Haydon—Mary Queen of Scotts, and Milton with his daughters in a row.[2] In the passage I found a head of Shakspeare which I had not before seen—It is most likely the same that George spoke so well of; for I like it extremely—Well—this head I have hung over my Books, just above the three in a row, having first discarded a french Ambassador—Now this alone is a good morning's work—Yesterday I went to Shanklin, which occasioned a great debate in my mind whether I should live there or at Carisbrooke. Shanklin is a most beautiful place— sloping wood and meadow ground reaches round the Chine, which is a cleft between the Cliffs of the depth of nearly 300 feet at least. This cleft is filled with trees & bushes in the narrow part; and as it widens becomes bare, if it were not for primroses on one side, which spread to the very verge of the Sea, and some fishermen's huts on the other, perched midway in the Ballustrades of beautiful green Hedges along their steps down to the sands.—But the sea, Jack, the sea—the little waterfall—then the white cliff—then St Catherine's Hill[3]—"the sheep in the meadows, the cows in the corn."—Then, why are you at Carisbrooke? say you—Because, in the first place, I sho^d be at twice the Expense, and three times the inconvenience—next that from here I can see your continent—from a little hill close by, the whole north Angle of the Isle of Wight, with the water between us. In the 3^d place, I see Carisbrooke Castle from my window, and have found several delightful wood-alleys, and copses, and quick freshes[4]—As for Primroses—the Island ought to be called Primrose Island: that is, if the nation of Cowslips agree thereto, of which there are diverse Clans just beginning to lift up their heads and if an how the Rain holds whereby that is Birds eyes abate—another reason of my fixing is that I am more in reach of the places around me—I intend to walk over the island east—West— North South—I have not seen many specimens of Ruins—I dont think however I shall ever see one to surpass Carisbrooke Castle. The trench is o'ergrown with the smoothest turf, and the walls with ivy— The Keep within side is one Bower of ivy—a Colony of Jackdaws[5] have been there many years—I dare say I have seen many a descendant of some old cawer who peeped through the Bars at Charles the first, when he was there in Confinement.[6] On the road from Cowes to Newport I saw some extensive Barracks[7] which disgusted me extremely with Government for placing such

---

1. Keats wrote this letter shortly after finding lodgings on the road between Newport and Carisbrooke on the Isle of Wight (having traveled from London via Southhampton), where he hoped to make progress on *Endymion*. Text from Woodhouse's letter-book, pp. 43–45.
2. Keats brought various pictures with him, perhaps including a reproduction of George Romney's *Milton and his Daughters* (1792) or early sketches by Haydon of later paintings: Haydon's portrait of *Mary Queen of Scots, when an Infant* would not be painted until 1841, but there may have been an earlier sketch; he painted *Milton at the Organ, or Milton and His Daughters* around 1839, but there is a sketch that is dated 1823, which could have been done even earlier as this was one of the possible subjects Haydon listed for future paintings when he arrived in London in 1804.
3. St. Catherine's Hill near the health resort of Ventnor rises to 781 feet and is topped by the remains of a fourteenth-century beacon. Keats goes on to cite the nursery rhyme of "Little Boy Blue."
4. See Shakespeare's *Tempest* 3.2.65: "Where the quick freshes [fast-flowing springs] are."
5. Common black and gray birds related to the crow; grackles.
6. Charles I was confined in Carisbrooke Castle from November 1647 until September 1648 after being seized by the New Model Army seeking to prevent Charles from making overtures to the Presbyterians.

a Nest of Debauchery in so beautiful a place—I asked a man on the Coach about this—and he said that the people had been spoiled—In the room where I slept at Newport I found this on the Window "O Isle spoilt by the Mil*a*tary"—I must in honesty however confess that I did not feel very sorry at the idea of the Women being a little profligate—The Wind is in a sulky fit, and I feel that it would be no bad thing to be the favorite of some Fairy, who would give one the power of seeing how our Friends got on, at a Distance— I should like, of all Loves, a sketch of you and Tom and George in ink which Haydon will do if you tell him how I want them—From want of regular rest, I have been rather *narvus*—and the passage in Lear—"Do you not hear the Sea?"[8]—has haunted me intensely.

[A draft of "On the Sea" follows.][9]

April 18th

Will you have the goodness to do this? Borrow a Botanical Dictionary— turn to the words Laurel and Prunus show the explanations to your sisters and Mrs Dilk[1] and without more ado let them send me the Cups Basket and Books they trifled and put off and off while I was in Town—ask them what they can say for themselves—ask Mrs Dilk wherefore she does so distress me—Let me know how Jane has her health—the Weather is unfavorable for her—Tell George and Tom to write.—I'll tell you what—On the 23rd was Shakespeare born—now If I should receive a Letter from you and another from my Brothers on that day 'twould be a parlous[2] good thing—Whenever you write say a Word or two on some Passage in Shakespeare that may have come rather new to you; which must be continually happening, notwithstand[g] that we read the same Play forty times—for instance, the following, from the Tempest, never struck me so forcibly as at present,

> "Urchins
> *Shall, for that vast of Night that they may work,*
> All exercise on thee[3]—"

How can I help bringing to your mind the Line—

> *In the dark backward and abysm of time[4]—"*

I find that I cannot exist without poetry—without eternal poetry—half the day will not do—the whole of it—I began with a little, but habit has made me a Leviathan[5]—I had become all in a Tremble from not having written any thing of late—the Sonnet over leaf did me some good. I slept the better last night for it—this Morning, however, I am nearly as bad again—Just now I opened Spencer, and the first Lines I saw were these.—

> "The noble Heart that harbors vertuous thought,
> And is with Child of glorious great intent,

---

7. A facility with housing for 3,000 troops and a military hospital built during the Napoleonic Wars. The government stationed troops across England and particularly near its coasts to prevent a French invasion.
8. Shakespeare, *King Lear*, 4.6.4, Edgar to Gloucester: "Hark, do you hear the sea?"
9. See p. 79, below.
1. Reference to Reynolds's sisters Jane, Mariane, Eliza and Charlotte, and to the wife of Keats's friend, the antiquarian and civil servant Charles Wentworth Dilke (1789–1864).
2. Exceedingly.
3. Shakespeare, *The Tempest* 1.2.329–31.
4. Shakespeare, *The Tempest* 1.2.50.
5. The sea monster mentioned in the Bible.

Can never rest, until it forth have brought
Th' eternal Brood of Glory excellent—"[6]

Let me know particularly about Haydon; ask him to write to me about
Hunt, if it be only ten lines—I hope all is well—I shall forthwith begin my
Endymion, which I hope I shall have got some way into by the time you
come, when we will read our verses in a delightful place I have set my heart
upon near the Castle—Give my Love to your Sisters severally—To George
and Tom—Remember me to Rice[7] M^r & Mrs Dilk and all we know.——

Your sincere Friend
John Keats.

SONNET.
ON THE SEA.[1]

It keeps eternal whisperings around
Desolate shores,—and with its mighty swell,
Gluts twice ten thousand caverns,—till the spell
Of Hecate[2] leaves them their old shadowy sound.
Often 'tis in such gentle temper found,   5
That scarcely will the very smallest shell
Be lightly moved,[3] from where it sometime fell,
When last the winds of heaven were unbound.

Ye, that[4] have your eye-balls vexed and tir'd,
Feast them upon the wideness of the sea;—   10
Or are your hearts disturb'd[5] with uproar rude,
Or fed too much with cloying melody,—
Sit ye near some old cavern's mouth, and brood
Until ye start, as the sea nymphs quired![6]

LINES.[1]

UNFELT, unheard, unseen,
I've left my little queen,
Her languid arms in silver slumber lying:[2]
Ah! through their nestling touch,

6. Spenser, *Faerie Queene*, 1.5.1.
7. James Rice (1792–1832), a friend of Reynolds, and later his law parter, who would spend a month
with Keats on the Isle of Wight in 1819.
1. This sonnet was most likely written on April 17, 1817, when Keats included it in a letter to
Reynolds (above, p. 78). First published in the *Champion*, August 17, 1817, p. 261: "The following Sonnet is from the pen of Mr. Keats. It is quite sufficient, we think, to justify all the praise we
have given him,—and to prove to our correspondent Pierre, his superiority over any poetical writer
in the *Champion*.—J. H. R. would be the first to acknowledge this himself." Text from the *Champion* with variants noted from the transcript of the letter to Reynolds, April 17, 18, 1817, in Woodhouse's letter-book, pp. 43–45.
2. The infernal persona of Diana, goddess of the moon, who here controls the tides through her "spell."
3. Keats's letter to Reynolds has "Be moved for days."
4. Keats's letter to Reynolds has "O ye who"; the *Champion* version lacks the initial "O," needed for
the metre.
5. Keats's letter to Reynolds has "O ye whose ears are dinned."
6. For "choired"; *as*: Keats's letter to Reynolds has "as if."
1. Written in 1817 before Reynolds quoted a part of a line in the *Champion* for August 17, 1817. First
published in 1848, 2: 258; text from 1848 with emendations from Keats's fair copy (FC) at the
Morgan Library (MA 211) and some punctuation from the W³ transcript (f. 91r, *MYR: JK*, 4: 254).
2. The FC seems to read "dying."

Who—who could tell how much   5
There is for madness—cruel or complying?

Those faery lids how sleek,
Those lips how moist—they speak,
In ripest quiet, shadows of sweet sounds;
Into my fancy's ear   10
Melting a burden dear,
How "Love doth know no fullness nor[3] no bounds."

True tender monitors,
I bend unto your laws:
This sweetest day for dalliance was born;   15
So, without more ado,
I'll feel my heaven anew,
For all the blushing of the hasty morn.

[You say you love; but with a voice][1]

You say you love; but with a voice
    Chaster than a nun's, who singeth
The soft Vespers to herself
    While the chime-bell ringeth—
        O love me truly!   5

You say you love; but with a smile
    Cold as sunrise in September,
As you were Saint Cupid's nun,
    And kept his weeks of Ember.[2]
        O love me truly!   10

You say you love; but then your lips
    Coral tinted teach no blisses,
More than coral in the sea—
    They never pout for kisses—
        O love me truly!   15

You say you love; but then your hand
    No soft squeeze for squeeze returneth,
It is like a statue's, dead,—
    While mine for passion burneth—
        O love me truly!   20

3. 1848 misreads as "and." The quotation has not been identified.
1. Perhaps written in the summer of 1817 and perhaps written for Isabella Jones (Woodhouse's note
   on sources for his transcript in W², "and Mrs. Jones," suggests Keats wrote out the poem for her).
   Isabella Jones, whom Keats met at the end of May or the beginning of June in Hastings (when he
   had "warmed with her"; see p. 293, below) and with whom he became acquainted again beginning
   in October 1818, was a beautiful, intelligent woman known to various of Keats's friends and
   attached in some way to an elderly Irishman, Donat O'Callaghan, and later to John Taylor; Woodhouse indicated that she suggested the subject of *The Eve of St. Agnes*. Colvin (pp. 157–158)
   argues the poem echoes the Elizabethan "A Proper Wooing Song." Colvin first published Keats's
   poem in *TLS*, April 16, 1914, p. 181; text from *TLS* with emendations from the transcript by Charlotte Reynolds in the Reynolds-Hood Commonplace Book, f. 39 (Bristol Central Library).
2. "Periods of abstinence and fasting" (*OED*) in the Catholic and Anglican Churches, as in Ember
   days or Ember weeks.

O breathe a word or two of fire!
　Smile, as if those words should burn me,
　Squeeze as lovers should—O kiss
　And in thy heart inurn me—
　　O love me truly!　　　　　　　　　　　25

Letter to Leigh Hunt, May 10, 1817[1]

Margate May 10th—

My dear Hunt,
　The little Gentleman that sometimes lurks in a gossips bowl ought to
have come in very likeness of a *coasted* crab[2] and choaked me outright for
not having answered your Letter ere this—however you must not suppose
that I was in Town to receive it; no, it followed me to the isle of Wight and
I got it just as I was going to pack up for Margate, for reasons which you
anon shall hear. On arriving at this treeless affair I wrote to my Brother
George to request C. C .C.[3] to do the thing you wot of respecting Rimini;
and George tells me he has undertaken it with great Pleasure; so I hope
there has been an understanding between you for many Proofs——C. C.
C. is well acquainted with Bensley.[4] Now why did you not send the key of
your Cupboard which I know was full of Papers? We would have lock'd
them all in a trunk together with those you told me to destroy; which indeed
I did not do for fear of demolishing Receipts. There not being a more
unpleasant thing in the world (saving a thousand and one others) than to
pay a Bill twice. Mind you—Old Wood's a very Varmant—sharded in
Covetousness[5]—And now I am upon a horrid subject—what a horrid one
you were upon last Sunday and well you handled it. The last Examiner was
Battering Ram against Christianity—Blasphemy—Tertullian—Erasmus—
S[r] Philip Sidney. And then the dreadful Petzelians and their expiation by
Blood—and do Christians shudder at the same thing in a Newspaper which
the attribute to their God in its most aggravated form? What is to be the
end of this?[6]—I must mention Hazlitt's Southey—O that he had left out the
grey hairs!—Or that they had been in any other Paper not concluding with

---

1. A rare extant letter to Keats's friend and mentor, Leigh Hunt. Keats had left London to work on
Endymion, arriving at the Isle of Wight on April 15, sleeping at Newport that night, and visiting
Shanklin on the 16th, before moving to Carisbrooke for about a week and then settling at Margate
around April 23 or 24 (see above, pp. 77–79). Text from ALS, British Library (Ashley 4869).
2. Shakespeare, *A Midsummer Night's Dream*, 2.1.47–48: "sometime lurk I in a gossip's bowl, / In very
likeness of a roasted crab." Keats may have written "coasted" because he was living at the shore at
Margate.
3. Charles Cowden Clarke.
4. For Hunt's *Story of Rimini*, see p. 21, n. 2. Keats seems to be discussing proofreading the second
edition (1817) of Hunt's poem printed by Thomas Bensley for Taylor and Hessey.
5. Perhaps a reference to Sir George Wood (1743–1824), a judge presiding over a libel case being covered at the time in Hunt's *Examiner*. Rollins cites Swift's "Wood an Insect," an attack upon William
Wood (1671–1730), who held the patent for making copper coins in Ireland from 1722–25. It might
also be a reference to Hunt's schoolboy friend John Wood, whom he had seen at least as recently as
1811 (see Roe, *Fiery Heart*, p. 125), but as Motion, p. 155, suggests, it is probably the name of a
bailiff; *sharded*: "Of a beetle: Living in dung" (*OED*); a "shard" can also be the hard shell of a beetle.
6. A reference to Hunt's "To the English People, Letter VII," in the May 4, 1817, *Examiner*, which
took up religious intolerance and included references to Tertullian (Quintus Septimus Florens Ter-
tullianus, c. 160–c. 230, Roman theologian and Christian apologist who ultimately formed his own
sect), Desidirius Erasmus (1466?–1536, Dutch humanist and reformer who remained a member
of the Catholic Church during the Reformation), and Sir Philip Sidney (1554–1586, author of
Arcadia, *Astrophel and Stella*, and *The Defense of Poesey*). The *Examiner* also took up the story of
"Petzel, a Priest of Branau" who apparently urged his Austrian followers to use human sacrifice as
a way of purifying others of their sins.

such a Thunderclap—that sentence about making a Page of the feelings of a whole life appears to me like a Whale's back in the Sea of Prose.[7] I ought to have said a word on Shakspeare's Christianity—there are two, which I have not looked over with you, touching the thing: the one for, the other against: That in favor is in Measure for Measure Act. 2. S. 2 Isab. Alas! Alas!

> Why all the Souls that were; were forfeit once
> And he that might the vantage best have took,
> Found out the Remedy—

That against is in Twelfth Night. Act. 3. S 2. Maria—for there is no Christian, that means to be saved by believing rightly, can ever believe such impossible Passages of grossness!'[8] Before I come to the Nymphs[9] I must get through all disagreeables—I went to the Isle of Wight—thought so much about Poetry so long together that I could not get to sleep at night—and moreover, I know not how it was, I could not get wholesome food—By this means in a Week or so I became not over capable in my upper Stories, and set off pell mell for Margate, at least 150 Miles—because forsooth I fancied that I should like my old Lodging here, and could contrive to do without Trees. Another thing I was too much in Solitude, and consequently was obliged to be in continual burning of thought as an only resource. However Tom is with me at present and we are very comfortable. We intend though to get among some Trees. How have you got on among them? How are the Nymphs? I suppose they have led you a fine dance—Where are you now. In Judea, Cappadocia, or the Parts of Lybia about Cyrene. Strangers from "Heaven, Hues and Prototypes.[1] I wager you have given given several new turns to the old saying "Now the Maid was fair and pleasant to look on"[2] as well as mad[e] a little variation in "once upon a time" perhaps too you have rather varied "thus endeth the first Lesson" I hope you have made a Horse shoe business of— "unsuperfluous lift" "faint Bowers" and fibrous roots.[3] I vow that I have been down in the Mouth lately at this Work. These last two day however I have felt more confident—I have asked myself so often why I should be a Poet more than other Men,—seeing how great a thing it is,—how great things are to be gained by it—What a thing to be in the Mouth of Fame[4]—that at last the Idea has grown so monstrously beyond my seeming Power of attainment that the other day I nearly consented with myself to drop into a Phæton[5]—yet 't is a

7. A reference to Hazlitt's review (*Examiner*, May 4, 11, 18, 1817) of Southey's *Letter to William Smith, Esq. M. P.* (1817), part of the dispute over the pirated publication of Southey's youthful and radical *Wat Tyler*. Hazlitt (1788–1830), a critic and essayist in the Hunt Circle, imagines a kind of phrenological examination of the poet laureate's head, where "you see the organ of vanity triumphant" "concealed under withered bay-leaves and a few contemptible, grey hairs." The sentence Keats refers to is "Why should not one make a sentence of a page long, out of the feelings of one's whole life?"
8. In arguments over Christianity on January 20, 1817, Keats, Hunt, Shelley, Haydon, and Horace Smith used such quotations from Shakespeare. See Haydon, *Diary*, 2:80–87.
9. Hunt's "Nymphs" appeared in his *Foliage* (1818). It has been suggested that Hunt wrote "The Nymphs" in a competition with Shelley, who was working on *Laon and Cythna/The Revolt of Islam* and Keats who, as he indicates below, was starting his long poem, *Endymion*.
1. See Acts 2.10: "strangers of Rome, Jews and proselytes."
2. See Genesis 24.16: "And the damsel was very fair to look upon."
3. Phrases from "The Nymphs," 1: 229, 257, 196.
4. An often-used phrase that Keats could have known from, for example, Ben Jonson's Epode IX, l. 79.
5. A phaeton is a light, four-wheeled carriage, so Keats could be saying that he is so exhausted by his attempts that he would take a carriage rather than walk. However, it seems more likely he has misspelled Phaethon, the son of Apollo and Clymene, who, in order to prove his parentage, demanded that his father allow him to drive the chariot of the sun for one day, only to find himself unable to control the flying horses; Zeus struck him with a thunderbolt to prevent the world from being destroyed. Keats would then be invoking Phaethon as an emblem of overreaching, his own concern in taking up *Endymion*.

disgrace to fail even in a huge attempt, and at this moment I drive the thought from me. I began my Poem about a Fortnight since and have done some every day except travelling ones—Perhaps I may have done a good deal for the time but it appears such a Pin's Point to me that I will not coppy any out. When I consider that so many of these Pin points go to form a Bodkin point (God send I end not my Life with a bare Bodkin,[6] in its modern sense) and that it requires a thousand bodkins to make a Spear bright enough to throw any light to posterity—I see that nothing but continual uphill Journeying? Now is there any thing more unpleasant (it may come among the thousand and one) than to be so journeying and miss the Goal at last—But I intend to whistle all these cogitations into the Sea where I hope they will breed Storms violent enough to block up all exit from Russia. Does Shelley go on telling strange Stories of the Death of kings?[7] Tell him there are strange Stories of the death of Poets— some have died before they were conceived "how do you make that out Master Vellum"[8] Does M[rs] S—[9] cut Bread and Butter as neatly as ever? Tell her to procure some fatal Scissars and cut the thread of Life of all to be disappointed Poets. Does M[rs] Hunt tear linen in half as straight as ever? Tell her to tear from the book of Life all blank Leaves. Remember me to them all—to Miss Kent and the little ones all—[1]

Your sincere friend
John Keats alias Junkets[2]—

You shall know where we move—

Letter to B. R. Haydon, May 10, 11, 1817[1]

Margate Saturday Eve

My dear Haydon,

> Let Fame, which all hunt after in their Lives,
> Live register'd upon our brazen tombs,
> And so grace us in the disgrace of death:
> When spite of cormorant devouring time
> The endeavour of this present breath may buy
> That Honor which shall bate his Scythe's keen edge
> And make us heirs of all eternity.[2]

To think that I have no right to couple myself with you in this speech would be death to me so I have e'en written it—and I pray God that our brazen Tombs be nigh neighbors.[3] It cannot be long first the endeavor of this present breath will soon be over—and yet it is as well to breathe freely during

6. Shakespeare, *Hamlet*, 3.1.77–78: "he himself might his quietus make / with a bare bodkin [dagger]." A "bodkin" can be a needle or pin as well as a dagger.
7. Hunt was staying with the Shelleys at Great Marlow. Keats refers to a story of Shelley and Hunt traveling in a stage-coach when Shelley suddenly cried out to Hunt, quoting Shakespeare's *Richard II*, 3.2.151–52, "For God's sake, let us sit upon the ground, / And tell sad stories of the death of kings."
8. See Addison, *The Drummer; Or The Haunted House* (1716), 4.1.
9. Mary Wollstonecraft Godwin Shelley; Keats imagines her in the role of Atropos, one of the Parcae or Fates, who cuts the thread of life when someone is to die.
1. Elizabeth Kent, sister of Hunt's wife and author of *Flora Domestica* (1823) and *Sylvan Sketches* (1825); Hunt's children at this time were Thorton (born 1810), John (1812), and Mary Florimel Leigh (1814).
2. A nickname used in the group from a play on John Keats's name.
1. Text from ALS (Harvard MS Keats 1.7).
2. Shakespeare, *Love's Labor's Lost*, 1.1.1–7.
3. Haydon annotated this: "I wonder if they will be."

our sojourn—it is as well if you have not been teased with that Money affair—that bill-pestilence. However I must think that difficulties nerve the Spirit of a Man—they make our Prime Objects a Refuge as well as a Passion. The Trumpet of Fame is as a tower of Strength the ambitious bloweth it and is safe—I suppose by your telling me not to give way to forebodings George has mentioned to you what I have lately said in my Letters to him— truth is I have been in such a state of Mind as to read over my Lines and hate them. I am "one that gathers Samphire dreadful trade"[4] the Cliff of Poesy Towers above me—yet when, Tom who meets with some of Pope's Homer in Plutarch's Lives[5] reads some of those to me they seem like Mice to mine. I read and write about eight hours a day. There is an old saying well begun is half done"[6]—'t is a bad one. I would use instead—Not begun at all 'till half done" so according to that I have not begun my Poem and consequently (a priori) can say nothing about it. Thank God! I do begin arduously where I leave off, notwithstanding occasional depressions: and I hope for the support of a High Power while I clime this little eminence and especially in my Years of more momentous Labor. I remember your saying that you had notions of a good Genius presiding over you—I have of late had the same thought. for things which I do half at Random are afterwards confirmed by my judgment in a dozen features of Propriety—Is it too daring to Fancy Shakspeare this Presider? When in the Isle of Wight I met with a Shakspeare in the Passage of the House at which I lodged[7]—it comes nearer to my idea of him than any I have seen—I was but there a Week yet the old Woman made me take it with me though I went off in a hurry—Do you not think this is ominous of good? I am glad you say every Man of great Views is at times tormented as I am—

Sunday Aft. This Morning I received a letter from George by which it appears that Money Troubles are to follow us up for some time to come perhaps for always—these vexations are a great hindrance to one—they are not like Envy and detraction stimulants to further exertion as being immediately relative and reflected on at the same time with the prime object—but rather like a nettle leaf or two in your bed. So now I revoke my Promise of finishing my Poem by the Autumn which I should have done had I gone on as I have done—but I cannot write while my spirit is fevered in a contrary direction and I am now sure of having plenty of it this Summer. At this moment I am in no enviable Situation. I feel that I am not in a Mood to write any to day; and it appears that the loss of it is the beginning of all sorts of irregularities. I am extremely glad that a time must come when every thing will leave not a wrack behind.[8] You tell me never to despair—I wish it was as easy for me to observe the saying—truth is I have a horrid Morbidity of Temperament which has shown itself at intervals—it is I have no doubt the greatest Enemy and stumbling block I have to fear—I may even say that it is likely to be the cause of my disappointment. How ever every ill has its share of good—this very bane would at any time enable me to look with an obstinate eye on the Devil Himself—ay to be as proud of being the lowest

---

4. Shakespeare, *King Lear*, 4.6.15. Samphire or "sampire": seaweed.
5. Tom was reading a translation of Plutarch's *Parallel Lives*, matching key Greek and Roman figures, either in an edition "By Several Hands" reissued in 1758 or in Langhorne's version of 1770; see John Livingston Lowes, "LXII: Moneta's Temple," *PMLA* 51 (1936): 1098–1103.
6. A proverbial saying that may echo Horace, *Epistles*, 1.2.40: "Dimidium facti, qui coepit, habet."
7. The engraving of Shakespeare Keats mentions in his letter to Reynolds April 17, 18, 1817, above, p. 77.
8. Shakespeare, *The Tempest* 4.1.156; *wrack*: a wisp of cloud.

of the human race as Alfred[9] could be in being of the highest. I feel confident I should have been a rebel Angel[1] had the opportunity been mine. I am very sure that you do love me as your own Brother—I have seen it in your continual anxiety for me—and I assure you that your wellfare and fame is and will be a chief pleasure to me all my Life. I know no one but you who can be fully sensible of the turmoil and anxiety, the sacrifice of all what is called comfort the readiness to Measure time by what is done and to die in 6 hours could plans be brought to conclusions.—the looking upon the Sun the Moon the Stars, the Earth and its contents as materials to form greater things—that is to say ethereal things—but here I am talking like a Madman greater things that our Creator himself made!! I wrote to Hunt yesterday[2]—scarcely know what I said in it. I could not talk about Poetry in the way I should have liked for I was not in humor with either his or mine. His self delusions are very lamentable they have inticed him into a Situation which I should be less eager after than that of a galley Slave—what you observe thereon is very true must be in time. Perhaps it is a self delusion to say so—but I think I could not be deceived in the Manner that Hunt is—may I die tomorrow if I am to be. There is no greater Sin after the 7 deadly than to flatter oneself into an idea of being a great Poet—or one of those beings who are privileged to wear out their Lives in the pursuit of Honor—how comfortable a feel it is that such a Crime must bring its heavy Penalty? That if one be a Self deluder accounts will be balanced? I am glad you are hard at Work—'t will now soon be done— I long to see Wordsworth's as well as to have mine in:[3] but I would rather not show my face in Town till the end of the Year—if that will be time enough— if not I shall be disappointed if you do not write for me even when you think best—I never quite despair and I read Shakspeare—indeed I shall I think never read any other Book much—Now this might lead me into a long Confab but I desist. I am very near Agreeing with Hazlit that Shakspeare is enough for us—By the by what a tremendous Southean Article his last was— I wish he had left out "grey hairs."[4] It was very gratifying to meet your remarks of the Manuscript[5]—I was reading Anthony and Cleopatra when I got the Paper and there are several Passages applicable to the events you commentate. You say that he arrived by degrees, and not by any single Struggle to the height of his ambition—and that his Life had been as common in particulars as other Mens—Shakspeare makes Enobarb say—Where's Antony Eros— He's walking in the garden—thus: *and spurns the rush that lies* before him, cries fool, Lepidus! In the same scene we find: "let determined things to destiny hold unbewailed their way".[6] Dolabella says of Antony's Messenger

"An argument that he is pluck'd when hither
He sends so poor a pinion of his wing"—Then again,
     Eno—"I see Men's Judgments are
     A parcel of their fortunes; and things outward
     Do draw the inward quality after them,
     To suffer all alike"[7]—The following applies well to Bertram[8]

---

9. See p. 42, n. 3.
1. The rebel angels sided with Lucifer in his battle with God.
2. See above, p. 81–83.
3. Haydon included portraits of Wordsworth and Keats in his painting *Christ's Entry into Jerusalem.*
4. See above, pp. 82 n. 7.
5. Haydon reviewed "Bonaparte. 'Manuscrit venu de St. Helene'" in the *Examiner,* May 4, 1817, pp. 275–76.
6. Shakespeare, *Antony and Cleopatra,* 3.5.14–16; the second quotation is not from the same scene but from 3.6.84–85.

"Yet he that can endure
To follow with allegience a fallen Lord,
Does conquer him that did his Master conquer,
And earns a place i' the story"

But how differently does Buonap bear his fate from Antony!

'T is good too that the Duke of Wellington has a good Word or so in the
Examiner. A Man ought to have the Fame he deserves—and I begin to think
that detracting from him as well as from Wordsworth is the same thing. I
wish he had a little more taste—and did not in that respect "deal in Lieu-
tenantry."[9] You should have heard from me before this—but in the first
place I did not like to do so before I had got a little way in the 1ˢᵗ Book[1] and
in the next as G. told me you were going to write I delayed till I had heard
from you—Give my Respects the next time you write to the North and also
to John Hunt[2]—Remember me to Reynolds and tell him to write, Ay, and
when you sent Westward tell your Sister[3] that I mentioned her in this—So
now in the Name of Shakespeare Raphael[4] and all our Saints I commend
you to the care of heaven!

Your everlasting friend
John Keats—

Letter to J. H. Reynolds, September 21, 1817[1]

My dear Reynolds./   Oxford Sunday Morn
    So you are determined to be my mortal foe—draw a Sword at me, and I
will forgive—Put a Bullet in my Brain, and I will shake it out as a dewdrop
from the Lion's Mane;[2]—put me on a Gridiron, and I will fry with great
complancency—but, oh horror! to come upon me in the shape of a Dun!
Send me Bills! as I say to my Taylor send me Bills and I'll never employ you
more[3]—However, needs must when the devil drives: and for fear of "before
and behind Mʳ Honeycomb"[4] I'll proceed—I have not time to elucidate the
forms and shapes of the grass and trees; for, rot it! I forgot to bring my

7. Shakespeare, *Antony and Cleopatra*, 3.12.3–4, 3.13.30–33, then 42–45. *Eno*: Enobarbus, one of
   Antony's commanders.
8. Napoleon's friend, General Count Henri Gratien Bertrand (1773–1844).
9. Shakespeare, *Antony and Cleopatra*, 3.11.39
1. Of *Endymion*.
2. Leigh Hunt's brother (1775–1848) and co-proprietor of the *Examiner*; *to the North*: to
   Wordsworth.
3. Harriett Cobley Haydon (1789–1869) married James Haviland in 1815 and lived to the West in
   Bridgwater, near Bristol.
4. Raphael Santi (1483–1520), the great Italian Renaissance painter and Haydon's model in the same
   way that Keats is invoking Shakespeare as his.
1. Written while Keats was in Oxford, which he called "the finest City in the world" (*L*, 1: 154), where
   he stayed with his friend Benjamin Bailey who later recalled their time together: Keats "wrote, & I read,
   sometimes at the same table, & sometimes at separate desks or tables, from breakfast to the time of
   our going out for exercise,—generally two or three o'clock. He sat down to his task,—which was about
   50 lines [of *Endymion*] a day, with his paper before, & wrote with as much regularity, & apparently
   with as much ease, as he wrote his letters" (*KC*, 2: 270). Text from Woodhouse's letter-book, pp. 46–48.
2. Shakespeare, *Troilus and Cressida*, 3.3.217–18: "And like a dew-drop from the lion's mane / Be
   shook to air."
3. For "tailor," with Keats owing his tailor money upon his death. *Gridiron*: a metal grate for broiling
   food. *Dun*: a bill collector.
4. An allusion to Oliver Goldsmith's comedy *The Good Natur'd Man* (1768), 3.1.252–54, though
   Keats mistakes the name of the hero, Honeywood, who is being led off by the Bailiff and his assis-
   tant, before and behind.

mathematical case with me; which unfortunately contained my triangular Prism so that the hues of the grass cannot be dissected for you—
    For these last five or six days, we have had regularly a Boat on the Isis,[5] and explored all the streams about, which are more in number than your eye lashes. We sometimes skim into a Bed of rushes, and there become naturalized riverfolks,—there is one particularly nice nest which we have christened "Reynolds's Cove"—in which we have read Wordsworth and talked as may be.[6] I think I see you and Hunt meeting in the Pit.[7]—What a very pleasant fellow he is, if he would give up the sovereignty of a Room pro bono—What Evenings we might pass with him, could we have him from M^rs H—Failings I am always rather rejoiced to find in a Man than sorry for; for they bring us to a Level—He has them,—but then his makes-up are very good. He agrees with the Northe[r]n Poet in this, "He is not one of those who much delight to season their fireside with personal talk"[8]—I must confess however having a little itch that way. and at this present I have a few neighbourly remarks to make—The world, and especially our England, has within the last thirty year's been vexed and teased by a set of Devils, whom I detest so much that I almost hunger after an acherontic[9] promotion to a Torturer, purposely for their accomodation; These Devils are a set of Women, who having taken a snack or Luncheon of Literary scraps, set themselves up for towers of Babel in Languages Sapphos in Poetry—Euclids in Geometry[1]—and everything in nothing. Among such the Name of Montague[2] has been preeminent. The thing has made a very uncomfortable impression on me.—I had longed for some real feminine Modesty in these things, and was therefore gladdened in the extreme on opening the other day one of Bayley's Books—a Book of Poetry written by one beautiful Mrs Philips, a friend of Jeremy Taylor's, and called "the matchless Orinda."[3]—You must have heard of her, and most likely read her Poetry—I wish you have not, that I may have the pleasure of treating you with a few stanzas—I do it at a venture:—You will not regret reading them once more. The following to her friend Mrs M. A. at parting you will Judge of.

-1-

I have examined and do find
    of all that favour me
There's none I grieve to leave behind
    But only, only thee
To part with thee I needs must die
Could parting sep'rate thee and I.

5. Poetical name for the upper part of the Thames river.
6. Perhaps an allusion to the practice of writing poems, in imitation of Wordsworth's "Poems on the Naming of Places," about places named for friends pursued by a circle around the Leigh sisters of Slade Hall, Sidmouth, of which Bailey and Reynolds were a part.
7. The part of the theater we would now call the orchestra.
8. Wordsworth, the "Northern Poet," opens his "Personal Talk" (1807), "I am not One who much or oft delight / To season my fireside with personal talk."
9. Infernal; from Acheron, a river in the classical underworld.
1. Euclid was a Greek mathematician who flourished around 300 B.C.E. and whose *Elements* are the foundation of geometry; Sappho wrote in the sixth century B.C.E. and is considered the greatest of early Greek lyric poets and the first great female poet.
2. Elizabeth (Robinson) Montagu (1720–1800), a member of the Blue Stocking Circle, a gathering around a core of learned, sociable women such as Elizabeth Carter, Hester Chapone, and Hannah More that sometimes included Samuel Johnson, David Garrick, and Sir Joshua Reynolds.
3. Katherine (Fowler) Philips (1631–1664), a poet whose circle adopted coterie names, hers being "Orinda," while Jeremy Taylor (1613–1667; author and chaplain to Charles I) was known as "Palæmon." Keats quotes her "To Mrs. M. A. [Mary Aubrey] at Parting." He may have known the poem in the 1710 edition by Tonson, *Poems by the most deservedly admired Mrs. Katherine Philips, the matchless Orinda*, where this poem (with some differences in punctuation and capitalization) appears on p. 94.

-2-

But neither chance nor Compliment
      Did *element* our Love;
'Twas sacred sympathy was lent
      Us from the Quire above.
That friendship fortune did create,
Still fears a wound from time or fate.

3

Our chang'd and mingled souls are grown
      To such acquaintance now,
That if each would resume her own
      Alas! we know not how.
We have each other so engrost
That each is in the union lost

-4-

And thus we can no absence know
      Nor shall we be confin'd;
Our active souls will daily go
      To learn each others mind.
Nay should we never meet to sense
Our souls would hold intelligence.

5

Inspired with a flame divine
      I scorn to court a stay;
For from that noble soul of thine
      I ne'er can be away.
But I shall weep when thou dost grieve
Nor can I die whilst thou dost live

6

By my own temper I shall guess
      At thy felicity,
And only like my happiness
      Because it pleaseth thee.
Our hearts at any time will tell
If thou, or I be sick or well.

-7-

All honour sure I must pretend,
      All that is good or great;
She that would be Rosania's friend,
      Must be at least compleat,†4

---

4. †A compleat friend—this Line sounded very oddly to me at first [Keats's note].

If I have any Bravery,
'Tis cause I have so much of thee.

8

Thy Leiger[5] Soul in me shall lie,
    And all thy thoughts reveal;
Then back again with mine shall flie
    And thence to me shall steal.
Thus still to one another tend;
Such is the sacred name of friend.

9-

Thus our twin souls in one shall grow,
    And teach the world new Love,
Redeem the age and sex, and show
    A Flame Fate dares not move:
And courting death to be our friend,
Our Lives together too shall end

10

A Dew shall dwell upon our Tomb
    of such a Quality
That fighting Armies thither come
    Shall reconciled be
We'll ask no epitaph but say
Orinda and Rosannia.

In other of her Poems there is a most delicate fancy of the Fletcher[6] Kind—which we will con over together: So Haydon is in Town—I had a letter from him yesterday—We will contrive as the Winter comes on—but that [is] neither here nor there. Have you heard from Rice?[7] Has Martin met with the Cumberland Beggar or been wondering at the old Leech gatherer?[8] Has he a turn for fossils? that is, is he capable of sinking up to his Middle in a Morass?—I have longed to peep in and see him at supper after some tolerable fatigue. How is Hazlitt? We were reading his Table[9] last night—I know he thinks himself not estimated by ten People in the world—I wishe he knew he is—I am getting on famous with my third Book—have written 800 lines thereof, and hope to finish it next week—Bailey likes what I have done very much—Believe me, my Dear Reynolds, one of my chief layings-up is the pleasure I shall have in showing it to you; I may now say, in a few days—I have heard twice from my Brothers, they are going on very well, and send their Remembrances to you. We expected to have had notices from little

---

5. Ledger in its sense of a permanent resident.
6. John Fletcher (1579–1625), playwright who often collaborated with Francis Beaumont.
7. James Rice (1792–1832), a friend Keats met through Reynolds; he was a lawyer and amateur poet.
8. John Martin (1791–1855), publisher, bookseller, and bibliographer. Keats refers to Wordsworth's "Old Cumberland Beggar" (1800) and "Resolution and Independence" (1807).
9. Hazlitt and Hunt wrote a series of essays in the *Examiner* under the title of *The Round Table*, published as a volume in 1817.

Hampton[1] this Morning—we must wait till Tuesday. I am glad of their Days with the Dilks.[2] You are I know very much teased in that precious London, and want all the rest possible; so shall be content with as brief a scrall—a word or two—till there comes a pat hour.—

Send us a few of your Stanzas to read in "Reynolds's cove." Give my Love and respects to your Mother and remember me kindly to all at home.
Yours faithfully

John Keats
I have left the doublings[3] for Bailey who is going to say that he will write to you to Morrow

LEIGH HUNT

To the Grasshopper and the Cricket[1]

Green little vaulter in the sunny grass,
   Catching your heart up at the feel of June,
   Sole voice that's left stirring midst the lazy noon,
When even the bees lag at the summoning brass[2]
And you, warm little housekeeper, who class   5
   With those who think the candles come too soon,
   Loving the fire, and with your tricksome tune
Nick the glad silent moments as they pass;

Oh sweet and tiny cousins, that belong,
   One to the fields, the other to the hearth,   10
Both have your sunshine; both, though small, are strong
   At your clear hearts; and both were sent on earth
To ring in thoughtful ears this natural song—
   In doors and out,—summer and winter,—Mirth.

December 30, 1816

JOSIAH CONDER

Review of *Poems*[1]

There is perhaps no description of publication that comes before us, in which there is for the most part discovered less of what is emphatically denominated *thought*, than in a volume of miscellaneous poems. * * * it

1. Reynolds's sisters Jane and Mariane were staying at Littlehampton, Sussex.
2. For the Dilkes, see p.78, n. 1.
3. The "doubling" created by Bailey's cross-written contribution to the letter is transcribed in Woodhouse's letter-book, p. 49; see *KC*, 1:6–7.
1. First published in the *Examiner*, September 21, 1817, p. 599, and reprinted in *Foliage* (1818), this poem was written in a sonnet competition with Keats (for his poem and the event, see p. 57); Hunt reprinted Keats's poem along with his own. The text is from the *Examiner*.
2. Country folk would attempt to encourage bees to swarm by banging on kitchen utensils.
1. This unsigned review, criticizing Keats's ideas and morality while praising his style, appeared in the *Eclectic Review*, n.s. 8 (September 1817): 267–75; it was written by Josiah Conder (1789–1855), a journalist and preacher who ran the *Eclectic Review*.

would be travelling too far out of the record, to make this notice of a small volume of poems, a pretence for instituting an examination of all the popular poets of the day. Suffice it to refer to the distinct schools into which they and their imitators, as incurable mannerists, are divided, as some evidence that mode of expression has come to form too much the distinguishing characteristic of modern poetry. Upon an impartial estimate of the intellectual quality of some of those poems which rank the highest in the public favour, it will be found to be really of a very humble description. As works of genius, they may deservedly rank high, because there is as much scope for genius in the achievements of art as in the energies of thought; but as productions of mind, in which respect their real value must after all be estimated, they lay the reader under small obligations. Wordsworth is by far the deepest thinker of our modern poets, yet he has been sometimes misled by a false theory, to adopt a puerile style of composition; and it is remarkable, that the palpable failure should be charged on his diction, which is attributable rather to the character of the thoughts themselves; they were not adapted to any form of poetical expression, inasmuch as they are not worth being expressed at all. Scott, of all our leading poets, though the most exquisite artist, occupies the lowest rank in respect to the intellectual quality of his productions. Scarcely an observation or a sentiment escapes him, in the whole compass of his poetry, that even the beauty of expression can render striking or worth being treasured up by the reader for after reference. The only passages recurred to with interest, or cited with effect, are those admirable specimens of scenic painting in which he succeeds beyond almost every poet, in making one see and hear whatever he describes. But when we descend from such writers as confessedly occupy the first rank, to the οι πολλοι[2] of their imitators, respectable as many of them are, and far above mediocrity considered as artists, the characters of sterling thought, of intellect in action, become very faint and rare. It is evident that, in their estimation, to write poetry is an achievement which costs no laborious exercise of faculty; is an innocent recreation rather, to which the consideration of any moral purpose would be altogether foreign.

Now, on turning from the polished versification of the elegant *artists* of the present day, to the rugged numbers of our early poets, the most obvious feature in the refreshing contrast is, the life and the vividness of thought diffused over their poetry. We term this originality, and ascribe the effect either to their pre-eminent genius, or to the early age in which they flourished, which forced upon them the toil of invention. But originality forms by no means a test of intellectual pre-eminence; and we have proof sufficient, that originality does not necessarily depend on priority of time. Provided the person be capable of the requisite effort of abstraction, nothing more is necessary in order to his attaining a certain degree of originality, than that his thoughts should bear the stamp of individuality, which is impressed by self-reflective study. In the earlier stages of the arts, we behold mind acting from itself; through the medium of outward forms, consulting its own purpose as the rule of its working, and referring to nature as its only model. But when the same arts have reached the period of more refined cultivation, they cease to be considered as means through which to convey to other minds the energies of thought and feeling: the productions

2. Greek for "hoi polloi"; the masses, the riffraff.

of art become themselves the ultimate objects of imitation, and the mind is acted upon by them instead of acting through them from itself. Mind cannot be imitated; art can be: and when imitative skill has brought an art the nearest to perfection, it is then that its cultivation is the least allied to mind: its original purpose, as a mode of expression, becomes wholly lost in the artificial object,—the display of skill.

We consider poetry as being in the present day in this very predicament; as being reduced by the increased facilities of imitation, to an elegant art, and as having suffered a forcible divorce from thought. Some of our young poets have been making violent efforts to attain originality, and in order to accomplish this, they have been seeking with some success for new models of imitation in the earlier poets, presenting to us as the result, something of the quaintness, as well as the freedom and boldness of expression characteristic of those writers, in the form and with the effect of novelties. But after all, this specious sort of originality lies wholly in the turn of expression; it is only the last effort of the cleverness of skill to turn eccentric, when the perfection of correctness is no longer new. We know of no path to legitimate originality, but one, and that is, by restoring poetry to its true dignity as a vehicle for noble thoughts and generous feelings, instead of rendering meaning the mere accident of verse. Let the comparative insignificance of art be duly appreciated, and let the purpose and the meaning be considered as giving the expression all its value; and then, so long as men think and feel for themselves, we shall have poets truly and simply original.

We have no hesitation in pronouncing the Author of these Poems, to be capable of writing good poetry, for he has the requisite fancy and skill which constitute the talent. We cannot, however, accept this volume as any thing more than an immature promise of possible excellence. There is, indeed, little in it that is positively good, as to the quality of either the thoughts or the expressions. Unless Mr. Keats has designedly kept back the best part of his mind, we must take the narrow range of ideas and feelings in these Poems, as an indication of not having yet entered in earnest on the business of intellectual acquirement, or attained the full development of his moral faculties. To this account we are disposed to place the deficiencies in point of sentiment sometimes bordering upon childishness, and the nebulous character of the meaning in many passages which occur in the present volume. Mr. Keats dedicates his volume to Mr. Leigh Hunt, in a sonnet which, as possibly originating in the warmth of gratitude, may be pardoned its extravagance; and he has obviously been seduced by the same partiality, to take him as his model in the subsequent poem, to which is affixed a motto from the "Story of Rimini." To Mr. Hunt's poetical genius we have repeatedly borne testimony,[3] but the affectation which vitiates his style must needs be aggravated to a ridiculous excess in the copyist. Mr. Hunt is sometimes a successful imitator of the manner of our elder poets, but this imitation will not do at second hand, for ceasing then to remind us of those originals, it becomes simply unpleasing.

Our first specimen of Mr. Keats's powers, shall be taken from the opening of the poem alluded to.

[Quotes "I stood tip-toe upon a little hill," ll. 1–60.]

---

3. See, for example, Conder's reviews of Hunt's *Feast of the Poets* in the *Eclectic Review*, n.s. 1 (June 1814): 628–29, and of his *Rimini* in the *Eclectic Review*, n.s. 5 (April 1816): 380–85.

There is certainly considerable taste and sprightliness in some parts of this description, and the whole poem has a sort of summer's day glow diffused over it, but it shuts up in mist and obscurity.

After a 'specimen of an induction to a poem,' we have next a fragment, entitled Calidore, which, in the same indistinct and dreamy style, describes the romantic adventure of a Sir Somebody, who is introduced 'paddling o'er a lake,' edged with easy slopes and 'swelling leafiness,' and who comes to a castle gloomy and grand, with halls and corridor, where he finds 'sweet-lipped ladies,' and so forth; and all this is told with an air of mystery that holds out continually to the reader the promise of something interesting just about to be told, when, on turning the leaf, the Will o' the Wisp vanishes, and leaves him in darkness. However ingenious such a trick of skill may be, when the writer is too indolent, or feels incompetent to pursue his story, the production cannot claim to be read a second time; and it may therefore be questioned, without captiousness, whether it was worth printing for the sake of a few good lines which ambitiously aspired to overleap the portfolio.

The 'epistles' are much in the same style, *all about* poetry, and seem to be the first efflorescence of the unpruned fancy, which must pass away before anything like genuine excellence can be produced. The sonnets are perhaps the best things in the volume. We subjoin one addressed 'To my brother George.'

[Quotes the sonnet in full.]

The 'strange assay' entitled Sleep and Poetry, if its forming the closing poem indicates that it is to be taken as the result of the Author's latest efforts, would seem to shew that he is indeed far gone, beyond the reach of the efficacy either of praise or censure, in affectation and absurdity. We must indulge the reader with a specimen

[Quotes "Sleep and Poetry," ll 270–93.]

We must be allowed, however, to express a doubt whether its nature has been as clearly perceived by the Author, or he surely would never have been able to impose even upon himself as poetry the precious nonsense which he has here decked out in rhyme. Mr Keats speaks of

> 'The silence when some rhymes are coming out,
> And when they're come, *the very pleasant rout;*' [ll. 321–22]

and to the dangerous fascination of this employment we must attribute this half-awake rhapsody. Our Author is a very facetious rhymer. We have *Wallace* and *solace, tenderness* and *slenderness, burrs* and *sepulchres, favours* and *behaviours, livers* and *rivers;*—and again,

> 'Where we may soft humanity put on,
> And sit and rhyme, and think on *Chatterton.*'

Mr Keats has satirized certain *pseudo* poets, who,

> 'With a puling infant's force,
> Sway'd about upon a rocking horse,
> And thought it Pegasus.'[4]

---

4. He quotes the epistle to Mathew, ll. 55–56, and "Sleep and Poetry," ll. 185–87.

Satire is a two-edged weapon: the lines brought irresistibly to our imagination the Author of these poems in the very attitude he describes. Seriously, however, we regret that a young man of vivid imagination and fine talents, should have fallen into so bad hands, as to have been flattered into the resolution to publish verses, of which a few years hence he will be glad to escape from the remembrance. The lash of a critic is the thing the least to be dreaded, as the penalty of premature publication. To have committed one's self in the character of a versifier, is often a formidable obstacle to be surmounted in after-life, when other aims require that we should obtain credit for different, and what a vulgar prejudice deems opposite qualifications. No species of authorship is attended by equal inconvenience in this respect. When a man has established his character in any useful sphere of exertion, the fame of the poet may be safely sought as a finish to his reputation. When he has shewn that he can do something else besides writing poetry, then, and not till then, may he safely trust the public with his secret. But the sound of a violin from a barrister's chamber, is not a more fatal augury than the poet's lyre strummed by a youth whose odes are as yet all addressed to Hope and Fortune.

But perhaps the chief danger respects the individual character, a danger which equally attends the alternative of success or failure. Should a young man of fine genius, but of half-furnished mind, succeed in conciliating applause by his first productions, it is a fearful chance that his energies are not dwarfed by the intoxication of vanity, or that he does not give himself up to the indolent day-dream of some splendid achievement never to be realized. Poetical fame, when conceded to early productions, is, if deserved, seldom the fruit of that patient self-cultivation and pains-taking, which in every department of worthy exertion are the only means of excellence; and it is but the natural consequence of this easy acquisition of gratification, that it induces a distaste for severer mental labour. Should, however, this fatal success be denied, the tetchy aspirant after fame is sometimes driven to seek compensation to his mortified vanity, in the plaudits of some worthless coterie, whose friendship consists in mutual flattery, or in community in crime, or, it may be, to vent his rancour in the satire of envy, or in the malignity of *patriotism*.

Exceptions, brilliant exceptions, are to be found in the annals of literature, and these make the critic's task one of peculiar delicacy. The case has occurred, when a phlegmatic Reviewer, in a fit of morning spleen, or of after-dinner dulness, has had it in his power to dash to the ground, by his pen, the innocent hopes of a youth struggling for honourable distinction amid all the disadvantages of poverty, or to break the bruised reed of a tender and melancholy spirit; but such an opportunity of doing mischief must of necessity be happily rare. Instances have also been, in which the performances of maturer life have fully redeemed the splendid pledge afforded by the young Author, in his first crude and unequal efforts, with which he has had to thank the stern critic that he did not rest self-satisfied. Upon the latter kind of exceptions, we would wish to fix Mr. Keats's attention, feeling perfectly confident, as we do, that the patronage of the friend he is content to please, places him wholly out of the danger of adding to the number of those who are lost to the public for want of the smile of praise.

Mr. Keats has, however, a claim to leave upon our readers the full impression of his poetry; and we shall therefore give insertion to another of his sonnets, which we have selected as simple and pleasing.

[Quotes the sonnet "Happy is England! I could be content" in full.]

ANONYMOUS

Review in *Edinburgh Magazine, and Literary Miscellany*, October 1817[1]

Of the author of this small volume we know nothing more than that he is said to be a very young man, and a particular friend of the Messrs Hunt, the editors of the *Examiner*, and of Mr Hazlitt. His youth accounts well enough for some injudicious luxuriancies and other faults in his poems; and his intimacy with two of the wittiest writers of their day, sufficiently vouches both for his intellect and his taste. Going altogether out of the road of high raised passion and romantic enterprise, into which many ordinary versifiers have been drawn after the example of the famous poets of our time, he has attached himself to a model more pure than some of these, we imagine; and, at the same time, as poetical as the best of them. "Sage, serious" *Spencer*, the most melodious and mildly fanciful of our old English poets, is Mr Keats's favourite. He takes his motto from him,—puts his head on his title-page,—and writes one of his most luxurious descriptions of nature in his measure.[2] We find, indeed, *Spencerianisms* scattered through all his other verses, of whatsoever measure or character. But, though these things sufficiently point out where Mr K. has caught his inspiration, they by no means determine the general character of his manner, which partakes a great deal of that *picturesqueness* of fancy and licentious brilliancy of epithet which distinguish the early Italian novelists and amorous poets. For instance, those who know the careless, sketchy, capricious, and yet archly-thoughtful manner of *Pulci* and *Ariosto*,[3] will understand what we mean from the following specimens, better than from any laboured or specific assertion of ours.

[Quotes "I stood tip-toe," ll. 61–106, and "Epistle to my brother George," ll. 110–42.]

This is so easy, and so like the ardent fancies of an aspiring and poetical spirit, that we have a real pleasure in quoting, for the benefit of our readers, another fragment of one of Mr Keats's *epistles*:

[Quotes "Epistle to Charles Cowden Clarke," ll. 1–14.]

All this is just, and brilliant too,—though rather ambitious to be kept up for any length of time in a proper and fitting strain. What follows appears to us the very pink of the smart and flowing conversational style. It is truly such elegant *badinage*[4] as should pass between scholars and gentlemen who can feel as well as judge.

[Quotes ll. 109–32.]

These specimens will be enough to shew that Mr K. has ventured on ground very dangerous for a young poet;—calculated, we think, to fatigue

---

1. This anonymous review offers an early and largely sympathetic description of the experimental style that came to be identified with Hunt's "Cockney School." Text from *Edinburgh Magazine, and Literary Miscellany* (*Scots Magazine*), October 1817, 1: 254–57.
2. For the epigraph and illustration, see headnote to *Poems*, above, p. 17, and for "Imitation of Spenser," see above, pp. 38–39; for Keats's debt to Spenser, see Kucich. Milton referred in his *Areopagitica* (1644) to "our sage and serious Poet Spencer."
3. Ludovico Ariosto (1474–1535), Italian poet whose epic *Orlando Furioso* (1532) was admired by the romantics; Luigi Pulci (1432–1484), Italian poet whose ottava rima *Morgante Maggiore* (1483) influenced, among other works, *Don Juan* by Byron, who translated the first canto of Pulci's poem (1822).
4. Banter.

his ingenuity, and try his resources of fancy, without producing any permanent effect adequate to the expenditure of either. He seems to have
formed his poetical predilections in exactly the same direction as Mr Hunt;
and to write, from personal choice, as well as emulation, at all times, in that
strain which can be most recommended to the favour of the general readers of poetry, only by the critical ingenuity and peculiar refinements of Mr
Hazlitt. That style is vivacious, smart, witty, changeful, sparkling, and
learned—full of bright points and flashy expressions that strike and even
seem to please by a sudden boldness of novelty,—rather abounding in
familiarities of conception and oddnesses of manner which shew ingenuity, even though they be perverse, or common, or contemptuous. The writers themselves seem to be persons of considerable taste, and of comfortable
pretensions, who really appear as much alive to the socialities and sensual
enjoyments of life, as to the contemplative beauties of nature. In addition
to their familiarity, though,—they appear to be too full of conceits and
sparkling points, ever to excite any thing more than a cold approbation at the
long-run—and too fond, even in their favourite descriptions of nature, of a
reference to the factitious resemblances of society, ever to touch the heart.
Their verse is straggling and uneven, without the lengthened flow of blank
verse, or the pointed connection of couplets. They aim laudably enough at
force and freshness, but are not so careful of the inlets of vulgarity, nor so
self-denying to the temptations of indolence, as to make their force a merit.
In their admiration of some of our elder writers, they have forgot the fate of
Withers and Ben Jonson, and May:[5] And, without forgetting that Petrarch
and Cowley[6] are hardly read, though it be decent to profess admiration of
them,—they seem not to bear in mind the appalling doom which awaits the
faults of mannerism or the ambition of a sickly refinement. To justify the conclusions of their poetical philosophy, they are brave enough to sacrifice the
sympathetic enthusiasm of their art, and that common fame which recurs to
the mind with the ready freshness of remembered verse,—to a system of
which the fruits come, at last, to make us exclaim with Lycidas,

"*Numeros* memini, si verba tenerem."[7]

If Mr Keats does not forthwith cast off the uncleannesses of this school,
he will never make his way to the truest strain of poetry in which, taking him
by himself, it appears he might succeed. We are not afraid to say before the
good among our readers, that we think this true strain dwells on features of
manly singleness of heart, or feminine simplicity and constancy of
affection,—mixed up with feelings of rational devotion, and impressions
of independence spread over pictures of domestic happiness and social
kindness,—more than on the fiery and resolute, the proud and repulsive

---

5. Thomas May (1595–1650), poet and historian, who became identified with the parliamentary
   cause during the Civil War (he was secretary for the Parliament in 1646) and whose writings lost
   favor at his death and with changing political times. George Withers (1588–1667), poet and pam-
   phleteer whose early satires led to his imprisonment and whose later religious poetry led him to be
   parodied as "Chronomastrix" in Jonson's masque, "Time Vindicated" (1623). Ben Jonson
   (1572/3–1637), playwright and poet, who was the unofficial poet laureate to James I but whose
   reputation declined after 1700 as Shakespeare's grew.
6. Abraham Cowley (1618–1667), royalist scholar and poet of, for example, "Pindarique Odes."
   Francesco Petrarca (1304–1374), key Italian humanist and poet, who was deeply influential in the
   development of the English sonnet. While Cowley's reputation suffered after the mid-eighteenth
   century, Petrarch was admired by the romantic poets.
7. Virgil, *Eclogue* 9: 45: "I remember the song, if the words would come."

aspects of misnamed humanity. It is something which bears, in fact, the direct impress of natural passion,—which depends for its effect on the shadowings of unsophisticated emotion, and takes no merit from the refinements of a metaphysical wit, or the giddy wanderings of an untamed imagination,—but is content with the glory of stimulating, rather than of oppressing, the sluggishness of ordinary conceptions.

It would be cold and contemptible not to hope well of one who has expressed his love of nature so touchingly as Mr K. has done in the following sonnets:

[Quotes "O Solitude! if I must with thee dwell";
"To one who has been long in city pent."]

Another sonnet, addressed to Mr Haydon the painter, appears to us very felicitous. *The thought*, indeed, of the first eight lines is altogether admirable; and the whole has a veritable air of Milton about it which has not been given, in the same extent, to any other poet except Wordsworth.

[Quotes "Addressed to Haydon."]

We are sorry that we can quote no more of these sweet verses which have in them so deep a tone of moral energy, and such a zest of the pathos of genius. We are loth to part with this poet of promise, and are vexed that critical justice requires us to mention some passages of considerable affectation, and marks of offensive haste, which he has permitted to go forth into his volume. "Leafy luxury," "jaunty streams," "lawny slope," "the moonbeamy air," "a sun-beamy tale;"[8] these, if not namby-pamby, are, at least, the "holiday and lady terms" of those poor affected creatures who write verses "in spite of nature and their stars."[9]—

> "*A little noiseless noise among the leaves,*
> *Born of the very sigh that silence heaves.*"[1]

This is worthy only of the Rosa Matildas whom the strong-handed Gifford put down.[2]

> "To possess but a span of the hour of leisure."
> "No sooner had I stepped into these pleasures."[3]

These are two of the most unpoetical of Mr K.'s lines,—but they are not single. We cannot part, however, on bad terms with the author of such a glorious and Virgilian conception as this:

> "The moon lifting her silver rim
> Above a cloud, and with a gradual swim
> Coming into the blue with all her light."[4]

8. The reviewer cites the "Dedication," l. 13; "I stood tip-toe," l. 22; "Specimen of an Induction to a Poem," l. 66; "To Some Ladies," l. 12; and "On receiving a curious Shell, and a copy of Verses From the same Ladies," l. 22.
9. *Hudibras* (1663), 1.1.641–42 by Samuel Butler (1613–1680); "*holiday and lady terms*": from Shakespeare, 1 *Henry IV* 1.3.45.
1. "I stood tip-toe," ll. 11–12.
2. Reference to the Della Cruscans, a school of late-eighteenth-century poets led by Robert Merry (1755–1798) and that included Hannah Cowley (1743–1809), who engaged as "Anna Matilda" in a poetic correspondence with Merry in *The World*; "Rosa Matilda" was the pseudonym of Charlotte Dacre (1782–1825); William Gifford (1756–1826) satirized the school in *The Baeviad* (1791).
3. "To Some Ladies," l. 27; "To Charles Cowden Clarke," l. 97.
4. "I stood tip-toe," ll. 113–15.

A striking natural vicissitude has hardly been expressed better by Virgil himself,—though the severe simpleness of his age, and the compact structure of its language, do so much for him in every instance:

> "*Ipse Pater*, mediâ nimborum in nocte, *coruscâ*
> *Fulmina molitur dextra.*"[5]

Letter to Benjamin Bailey, October 8, 1817[1]

Hampstead Octr Wednesday

My dear Bailey,

After a tolerable journey I went from Coach to Coach to as far as Hampstead where I found my Brothers—the next Morning finding myself tolerably well I went to Lambs Conduit Street[2] and delivered your Parcel—Jane and Marianne were greatly improved Marianne especially she has no unhealthy plumpness in the face—but she comes me healthy and angular to the Chin—I did not see John I was extremely sorry to hear that poor Rice after having had capital Health During his tour, was very ill. I dare say you have heard from him. From No. 19 I went to Hunt's and Haydon's who live now neighbours.[3] Shelley was there—I know nothing about any thing in this part of the world—every Body seems at Loggerheads. There's Hunt infatuated—theres Haydon's Picture in statu quo.[4] There's Hunt walks up and down his painting room criticising every head most unmercifully— There's Horace Smith[5] tired of Hunt. "The web of our Life is of mingled Yarn."[6] Haydon having removed entirely from Marlborough street Crips[7] must direct his Letter to Lisson Grove North Paddington. Yesterday Morning while I was at Brown's[8] in came Reynolds—he was pretty bobbish[9] we had a pleasant day—but he would walk home at night that cursed cold distance. M[rs] Bentley's children are making a horrid row—whereby I regret I cannot be transported to your Room to write to you. I am quite disgusted with literary Men and will never know another except Wordsworth—no not even Byron—Here is an instance of the friendships of such—Haydon and Hunt have known each other many years—now they live pour ainsi dire[1] jealous Neighbours. Haydon says to me Keats dont show your Lines to Hunt on any account or he will have done half for you—so it appears Hunt

---

5. Virgil, *Georgics* 1: 328–29: "The father himself [Jupiter], throned in the midnight storm-clouds, hurls thunderbolts with his flashing right hand."
1. Written after Keats's return on October 5 to Hampstead where he lived with his brothers at 1 Well Walk in the house of a postman, Benjamin Bentley, and his family. Text from ALS (Harvard MS Keats 1.13); also a transcript in Woodhouse's letter-book, pp. 76–79.
2. No. 19 was the home of the Reynolds family.
3. Haydon had moved in late September to 22 Lisson Grove North where Hunt also resided.
4. Haydon's *Christ's Entry into Jerusalem*, into which Haydon had painted the heads of Keats, Wordsworth, and Hazlitt among others onto figures in the crowd.
5. Horace (Horatio) Smith (1779–1849), banker and poet, a member of the Hunt circle and a particular friend of Shelley's, wrote with his brother James *Rejected Addresses* (1812) and *Horace and London* (1813), published his own interesting volume, *Amarynthus the Nympholept: A Pastoral Drama, in Three Acts, with Other Poems* (1821), and later turned to writing fiction.
6. Shakespeare, *All's Well That Ends Well*, 4.3.69.
7. Charles Cripps (b. 1796?) was a young painter Haydon wished to patronize.
8. Charles Armitage Brown (1787–1842) had been in business with his brother John, who died in 1815, leaving Brown enough money to pursue his literary interests, including a comic opera, *Narensky; or, the Road to Yaroslaf* (1814), and his much later, influential *Shakespeare's Autobiographical Poems* (1838). He became a friend of Keats's in 1817 and later lived, traveled, and collaborated with him. He spent most of the 1820s in Italy and later died in New Zealand.
9. "Well; in good health and spirits" (*OED*).
1. "So to speak" (French).

wishes it to be thought. When he met Reynolds in the Theatre John told him that I was getting on to the completion of 4000 Lines. Ah! says Hunt, had it not been for me they would have been 7000! If he will say this to Reynolds what would he to other People? Haydon received a Letter a little while back on this subject from some Lady—which contains a caution to me through him on this subject—Now is not all this a most paultry thing to think about? You may see the whole of the case by the following extract from a Letter I wrote to George in the spring "As to what you say about my being a Poet, I can return no answer but by saying that the high Idea I have of poetical fame makes me think I see it towering to high above me. At any rate I have no right to talk until Endymion is finished—it will be a test, a trial of my Powers of Imagination and chiefly of my invention which is a rare thing indeed—by which I must make 4000 Lines of one bare circumstance and fill them with Poetry; and when I consider that this is a great task, and that when done it will take me but a dozen paces towards the Temple of Fame—it makes me say—God forbid that I should be without such a task! I have heard Hunt say and may be asked—why endeavour after a long Poem? To which I should answer—Do not the Lovers of Poetry like to have a little Region to wander in where they may pick and choose, and in which the images are so numerous that many are forgotten and found new in a second Reading: which may be food for a Week's stroll in the Summer? Do not they like this better than what they can read through before Mrs Williams comes down stairs? a Morning work at most. Besides a long Poem is a test of Invention which I take to be the Polar Star of Poetry, as Fancy is the Sails, and Imagination the Rudder. Did our great Poets ever write short Pieces? I mean in the shape of Tales—This same invention seems indeed of late Years to have been forgotten as a Poetical excellence. But enough of this, I put on no Laurels till I shall have finished Endymion, and I hope Apollo is not angered at my having made a Mockery at him at Hunt's."[2] You see Bailey how independant my writing has been—Hunts dissuasion was of no avail—I refused to visit Shelley, that I might have my own unfetterd scope—and after all I shall have the Reputation of Hunt's elevé[3]—His corrections and amputations will by the knowing ones be trased in the Poem—This is to be sure the vexation of a day—nor would I say so many Words about it to any but those whom I know to have my wellfare and Reputation at Heart—Haydon promised to give directions for those Casts[4] and you may expect to see them soon—with as many Letters You will soon hear the dinning of Bells—never mind you and Gleg[5] will defy the foul fiend—But do not sacrifice your health to Books do take it kindly and not so voraciously. I am certain if you are your own Physician your stomach will resume its proper strength and then what great Benefits will follow. My Sister wrote a Letter to me which I think must be at ye post office Ax Will[6] to see. My Brothers kindest remembrances to you—we are going to dine at Brown's where I have some hopes of meeting Reynolds. The little Mercury I have taken has corrected the Poison and improved my Health[7]—

---

2. See the various poems on this incident, pp. 69–71.
3. For "élève," student (French).
4. Perhaps copies of the life mask Haydon had made of Keats.
5. George Robert Gleig (1796–1888), after serving in the Peninsular and American Wars, was a student with Bailey at Magdalen Hall, Oxford, later Bailey's brother-in-law, a novelist, and chaplain-general of the forces (1844–1875).
6. Presumably, "Ask Will," a college porter.
7. Gittings (1968), pp. 446–50, argues that the mercury was taken for gonorrhea contracted while Keats was at Oxford.

though I feel from my employment that I shall never be again secure in Robustness—would that you were as well as

> your sincere friend & brother
> John Keats

The Dilkes are expected to day—

Letter to Benjamin Bailey, November 3, 1817[1]

> Monday—Hampstead

My dear Bailey,

Before I received your Letter I had heard of your disappointment[2]—an unlook'd for piece of villainy. I am glad to hear there was an hindrance to your speaking your Mind to the Bishop: for all may go straight yet—as to being ordained—but the disgust consequent cannot pass away in a hurry— it must be shocking to find in a sacred Profession such barefaced oppression and impertinence—The Stations and Grandeurs of the World have taken it into their heads that they cannot commit themselves towards and inferior in rank—but is not the impertinence from one above to one below more wretchedly mean than from the low to the high? There is something so nauseous in self-willed yawning impudence in the shape of conscience—it sinks the Bishop of Lincoln into a smashed frog putrifying: that a rebel against common decency should escape the Pillory! That a mitre should cover a Man guilty of the most coxcombical, tyranical and indolent impertinence! I repeat this word for the offence appears to me most especially *impertinent*—and a very serious return would be the Rod. Yet doth he sit in his Palace. Such is this World—and we live—you have surely [been] in a continual struggle against the suffocation of accidents— we must bear (and my Spleen is mad at the thought thereof) the Proud Mans Contumely[3]—O for a recourse somewhat human independant of the great Consolations of Religion and undepraved Sensations—of the Beautiful—the poetical in all things—O for a Remedy against such wrongs within the pale of the World! Should not those things be pure enjoyment, should they stand the chance of being contaminated by being called in as antagonists to Bishops? Would not earthly thing do? By Heavens my dear Bailey, I know you have a spice of what I mean—you can set me and have set it in all the rubs that may befal me you have I know a sort of Pride which would kick the Devil on the Jaw Bone and make him drunk with the kick— There is nothing so balmy to a soul imbittered as yours must be, as Pride. When we look at the Heavens we cannot be proud—but shall stocks and stones be impertinent and say it does not become us to kick them? At this Moment I take your hand; let us walk up yon Mountain of common sense—now if our Pride be vainglorious such a support woud fail—yet you feel firm footing—now look beneath at that parcel of knaves and fools. Many a Mitre is moving among them. I cannot express how I despise the Man who would wrong or be impertinent to you—The thought that we are mortal makes us groan. I will speak of something else or my Spleen will get higher and higher—and I am not a bearer of the two egded Sword. I hope

---

1. Text from ALS (Harvard MS Keats 1.15); also partial transcript in Woodhouse's letter-book, p. 79.
2. Keats had learned from Rice and Reynolds that Bailey had not received an expected curacy in Lincoln, apparently through the intervention of George Pretyman Tomline (1750–1827), mentioned below, who had recently been made Bishop of Lincoln and delayed his ordination.
3. Scornful abuse; Shakespeare, *Hamlet*, 3.1.73, from Hamlet's "To be, or not to be" speech.

you will recieve an answer from Haydon soon—if not Pride! Pride! Pride! I have received no more subscription[4]—but shall soon have a full health, Liberty and leisure to give a good part of my time to him—I will certainly be in time for him—We have promised him one year—let that have elapsed and then do as we think proper. If I did not know how impossible it is, I should say 'do not at this time of disappointments disturb yourself about others.'

There has been a flaming attack upon Hunt in the Endinburgh Magazine[5]—I never read any thing so virulent—accusing him of the greatest Crimes—depreciating his Wife his Poetry—his Habits—his company, his Conversation—These Philipics are to come out in Numbers—calld 'the Cockney School of Poetry.' There has been but one Number published—that on Hunt to which they have prefixed a Motto from one Cornelius Webb Poetaster—who unfortunately was of our Party occasionally at Hampstead and took it into his head to write the following—something about—"we'll talk on Wordsworth Byron—a theme we never tire on" and so forth till he comes to Hunt and Keats. In the Motto they have put Hunt and Keats in large Letters—I have no doubt that the second Number was intended for me: but have hopes of its non appearance from the following advertisement in last Sunday's Examiner. "To Z. The writer of the Article signed Z in Blackwood's Edinburgh magazine for October 1817 is invited to send his address to the printer of the Examiner, in order that Justice may be executed of the proper person."[6] I dont mind the thing much—but if he should go to such lengths with me as he has done with Hunt I must infalibly call him to an account—if he be a human being and appears in Squares and Theatres where we might possibly meet—I dont relish his abuse.

Yesterday Rice and I were at Reynolds—John was to be articled tomorrow.[7] I suppose by this time it is done. Jane was much better—At one time or other I will do you a Pleasure and the Poets a little Justice—but it ought to be in a Poem of greater moment than Endymion—I will do it some day—I have seen two Letters of a little Story Reynolds is writing—I wish he would keep at it—Here is the song I enclosed to Jane if you can make it out in this cross wise writing.[8]

[Includes a draft of *Endymion* 4.146–81.]

O that I had Orpheus lute[9]—and was able to charm away all your Griefs and Cares—but all my power is a Mite—amid all you troubles I shall ever be—

your sincere and affectionate friend
John Keats

My brothers remembrances to you
Give my respects to Gleig and Whitehead[1]

4. For the subscription for Cripps; see p. 98, n. 7.
5. "On the Cockney School of Poetry. No. 1," *Blackwood's Edinburgh Magazine* 2 (October 1817): 38–41. The attack opens with the lines Keats cites: "Our talk shall be (a theme we never tire on) / Of Chaucer, Spenser, Shakespeare, Milton, Byron, / (Our England's Dante)—Wordsworth—HUNT, and KEATS, / The Muses' son of promise; and of what feats / He may yet do." The lines were signed Cornelius Webb (1789?–1848?), a sometime member of the Hunt circle and an active writer of minor verse (see Cox, pp. 16–18); these lines have not been found outside *Blackwood's*, though Roe (p. 129n.) suggests they were part of a lost "Epistle to a Friend" sent to *Blackwood's* in September 1817 or they may have been included in the announced (but now unknown) volume *Heath Flowers* (1817) by Webb.
6. The *Examiner*, November 2, 1817, p. 693; see also November 16, 1817, p. 729 and December 14, 1817, p. 788 (*SWLH* 2: 142–43).
7. As a lawyer.
8. Writing across the already written text to save paper.
9. See p. 167, n. 5.
1. The Reverend Joseph Charles Frederick Whitehead (1784–1825) was at Magdalen Hall, Oxford. For Gleig, see p. 99, n. 5.

Letter to Benjamin Bailey, November 22, 1817[1]

My dear Bailey,

I will get over the first part of this (*un*said)[2] Letter as soon as possible for it relates to the affair of poor Crips—To a Man of your nature, such a Letter as Haydon's must have been extremely cutting—What occasions the greater part of the World's Quarrels? simply this, two Minds meet and do not understand each other time enough to prevent any shock or surprise at the conduct of either party—As soon as I had known Haydon three days I had got enough of his character not to have been surpised at such a Letter as he has hurt you with. Nor when I knew it was it a principle with me to drop his acquaintance although with you it would have been an imperious feeling. I wish you knew all that I think about Genius and the Heart—and yet I think you are thoroughly acquainted with my innermost breast in that respect or you could not have known me even thus long and still hold me worthy to be your dear friend. In passing however I must say of one thing that has pressed upon me lately and encreased my Humility and capability of submission and that is this truth—Men of Genius are great as certain ethereal Chemicals operating on the Mass of neutral intellect—by[3] they have not any individuality, any determined Character. I would call the top and head of those who have a proper self Men of Power—

But I am running my head into a Subject which I am certain I could not do justice to under five years study and 3 vols octavo—and moreover long to be talking about the Imagination—so my dear Bailey do not think of this unpleasant affair if possible—do not—I defy any harm to come of it—I defy—I'll shall write to Crips this Week and request him to tell me all his goings on from time to time by Letter wherever I may be—it will all go on well—so dont because you have suddenly discover'd a Coldness in Haydon suffer yourself to be teased. Do not my dear fellow. O I wish I was as certain of the end of all your troubles as that of your momentary start about the authenticity of the Imagination. I am certain of nothing but of the holiness of the Heart's affections and the truth of Imagination—What the imagination seizes as Beauty must be truth[4]—whether it existed before or not—for I have the same Idea of all our Passions as of Love; they are all in their sublime, creative of essential Beauty. In a Word, you may know my favorite Speculation by my first Book and the little song I sent in my last[5]— which is a representation from the fancy of the probable mode of operating in these Matters. The Imagination may be compared to Adam's dream—he awoke and found it truth.[6] I am the more zealous in this affair, because I have never yet been able to perceive how any thing can be known for truth by consequitive reasoning—and yet it must be—Can it be that even the greatest Philosopher ever arrived at his goal without putting aside numerous objections—However it may be, O for a Life of Sensations rather than of Thoughts! It is 'a Vision in the form of Youth,' a Shadow of reality to come—and this consideration has further convinced me for it has come

1. Written after Keats left London and the quarrels among his friends to seek some peace at the Fox and Hounds, Burford Bridge, in Surrey, at the foot of Box Hill, this is one of Keats's best-known letters, exploring poetic imagination through "Adam's dream." Text from ALS (Harvard MS Keats 1.16); also a transcript in Woodhouse's letter-book, pp. 80–83.
2. Rollins argues this is a pun on the legal use of "said," with the "said letter" being a letter from Haydon to Bailey and the "unsaid letter," Keats's present one to Bailey. For Cripps, see p. 98, n. 7.
3. For "but."
4. See the end of "Ode on a Grecian Urn," below p. 462.
5. Book I of *Endymion* and the "Ode to Sorrow" from Book 4 included in his November 8 letter.
6. See Milton, *Paradise Lost*, 8. 309–11, 452–90: Adam dreams of Eve and awakes to find her beside him.

as auxiliary to another favorite Speculation of mine, that we shall enjoy ourselves here after by having what we called happiness on Earth repeated in
a finer tone and so repeated—And yet such a fate can only befall those who
delight in sensation rather than hunger as you do after Truth—Adam's
dream will do here and seems to be a conviction that Imagination and its
empyreal reflection is the same as human Life and its spiritual repetition.
But as I was saying—the simple imaginative Mind may have its rewards in
the repetition of its own silent Working coming continually on the spirit
with a fine suddenness—to compare great things with small—have you
never by being surprised with an old Melody—in a delicious place—by a
delicious voice, felt over again your very speculations and surmises at the
time it first operated on your soul—do you not remember forming to yourself the singer's face more beautiful than it was possible and yet with the
elevation of the Moment you did not think so—even then you were
mounted on the Wings of Imagination so high—that the Prototype must be
here after—that delicious face you will see—What a time! I am continually
running away from the subject—sure this cannot be exactly the case with
a complex Mind—one that is imaginative and at the same time careful of
its fruits—who would exist partly on sensation partly on thought—to whom
it is necessary that years should bring the philosophic Mind[7]—such an one
I consider your's and therefore it is necessary to your eternal Happiness
that you not only drink this old Wine of Heaven which I shall call the redi-
gestion of our most ethereal Musings on Earth; but also increase in knowledge and know all things. I am glad to hear you are in a fair Way for
Easter— you will soon get through your unpleasant reading and then!—but
the world is full of troubles and I have not much reason to think myself pes-
terd with many—I think Jane or Marianne has a better opinion of me than
I deserve—for really and truly I do not think my Brothers illness connected
with mine—you know more of the real Cause than they do—nor have I any
chance of being rack'd as you have been[8]—you perhaps at one time thought
there was such a thing as Worldly Happiness to be arrived at, at certain
periods of time marked out—you have of necessity from your disposition
been thus led away—I scarcely remember counting upon any Happiness—
I look not for it if it be not in the present hour—nothing startles me beyond
the Moment. The setting sun will always set me to rights—or if a Sparrow
come before my Window I take part in its existence and pick about the Gravel.
The first thing that strikes me on hearing a Misfortune having befalled
another is this. 'Well it cannot be helped.[9]—he will have the pleasure of trying the resources of his spirit, and I beg now my dear Bailey that hereafter
should you observe any thing cold in me not to put it to the account of heart-
lessness but abstraction—for I assure you I sometimes feel not the influence
of a Passion or Affection during a whole week—and so long this sometimes
continues I begin to suspect myself and the genuiness of my feelings at other
times—thinking them a few barren Tragedy-tears—My Brother Tom is much
improved—he is going to Devonshire—whither I shall follow him—at present I am just arrived at Dorking to change the Scene—change the Air and give

---

7. See Wordsworth, "Ode: Intimations of Immortality" (1807), l. 189–90: "In the faith that looks
   through death, / In the years that bring the philosophic mind."
8. The Reynolds sisters fear Keats has tuberculosis, but he and Bailey know he is currently suffering
   from another malady, perhaps gonorrhea (see p. 99, n. 7); Bailey's troubles may be a failed love
   affair (as Lowell 1:513 argues) or his failure to get a curacy.
9. There is an initial quotation mark, so this may be a reference to George Colman's *Two to One*
   (1784), 3.2: "Well, it cannot be helped.—It is always a maxim in the city, to make the best of a bad
   bargain; and so there's an end of the business."

me a spur to wind up my Poem, of which there are wanting 500 Lines. I should have been here a day sooner but the Reynoldses persuaded me to stop in Town to meet your friend Christie—There were Rice and Martin—we talked about Ghosts—I will have some talk with Taylor and let you know—when please God I come down at Christmas—I will find that Examiner if possible. My best regards to Gleig—My Brothers to you and Mrs Bentley[1]

Your affectionate friend
John Keats—

I want to say much more to you—a few hints will set me going
Direct Burford Bridge near dorking

[Before he went to feed with owls and bats][1]

Before he went to feed[2] with owls and bats,
  Nebuchadnezzar had an ugly dream,
  Worse than an Hus'ifs[3] when she thinks her cream
Made a Naumachia[4] for mice and rats:
So scared, he sent for that "good King of Cats,"[5]   5
  Young Daniel, who soon did pluck[6] the beam
  From out his eye,[7] and said he did not deem
His scepter worth a straw—his Cushions old door mats.[8]
A horrid nightmare, similar somewhat,
  Of late has haunted a most worthy[9] crew   10
    Of Loggerheads and Chapmen[1]—we are told
That any Daniel, though he be a sot,
  Can make their lying lips turn pale of hue
    By belching out—"ye are that head of gold."[2]

---

1. For the Bentleys see p. 98, n. 1. Jonathan Henry Christie (d. 1876) is best known for mortally wounding John Scott in 1821, who had been editor of the *Champion* and was later editor of the *London Magazine*, in a duel over J. G. Lockhart's Cockney School attacks in *Blackwood's*. Christie was tried for murder, defended by Reynolds and Rice, and acquitted. For Rice see p. 79, n. 7; Martin, p. 89, n. 8; Taylor, p. 12, n. 9; Gleig, p. 99, n. 5.
1. This sonnet, labeled a "satire" in the Huntington Library's bound copy of the holograph draft (Huntington MS 1985) and called "Nebuchadnezzar's Dream" by Garrod and Allott, was written in 1817, according to Brown's transcript (Harvard MS Keats 3.6, p. 62; *MYR: JK*, 7: 64). Ward, in "Keats's Sonnet, 'Nebuchadnezzar's Dream'" (*Philological Quarterly* 34 [1955]: 177–88), suggests it was written to celebrate William Hone's legal victory over the government that prosecuted him (and earlier Thomas Wooler) for publishing anti-government satires (see Keats's letter of December 21, 27?, p. 108). In this view, Hone and Wooler and other radical journalists can be seen as Daniels prophesying the collapse of Pittite rule. The biblical text is Daniel 2–4. First published in *Literary Anecdotes of the Nineteenth Century*, ed. W. Robertson Nicoll and Thomas J. Wise, 2 vols. (1896; rpt. New York: AMS Press, 1967), 2: 277–78, where it is labeled "One of Keats's 'Nonsense Sonnets'" and where they argue it is a riposte to the Cockney School attacks. Text from Nicoll and Wise with emendations from the Huntington draft and variants in the notes from Brown's transcript, which also provides some of the punctuation.
2. Brown's transcript has "live."
3. For "housewife's," the reading in Brown's transcript.
4. A staged sea battle such as could be seen at the theater at Sadler's Wells where a tank had been installed for the staging of naval spectaculars.
5. See Shakespeare, *Romeo and Juliet*, 3.1.72, where Mercutio asks for one of Tybalt's nine lives as the "Good King of Cats"; Daniel in the lion's den (l. 6) is an ironic king of cats.
6. Nicoll and Wise read this as "pluck away," from "way" left undeleted in the interlined "straightway"; Brown's transcript has "did straightway pluck."
7. See Luke 6.42.
8. Brown's transcript has "and said—'I do not deem / Your scepter worth a straw, your cushions old door mats.'"
9. Nicoll and Wise have "motley"; the draft deleted "worshipful" for "worthy"; Brown has "valiant."
1. Blockheads and traders, here of political offices.
2. Nebuchadnezzar dreamed of an idol with a golden head and clay feet; Daniel proclaims, "Thou art this head of gold" (Daniel 2.38); *belching*: Brown's transcript has "drawling."

STANZAS.[1]

In drear-nighted December,[2]
Too happy, happy tree,
Thy branches ne'er remember
Their green felicity:
The north cannot undo them,   5
With a sleety whistle through them;
Nor frozen thawings glue them
From budding at the prime.

In drear-nighted December,
Too happy, happy brook,   10
Thy bubblings ne'er remember
Apollo's summer look;
But with a sweet forgetting,
They stay their crystal fretting,
Never, never petting[3]   15
About the frozen time.

Ah! would 'twere so with many
A gentle girl and boy!
But were there ever any
Writhed not at passed joy?   20
The feel of not to feel it,[4]
When there is none to heal it,
Nor numbed sense to steel it,
Was never said in rhyme.

Mr. Kean[1]

"In our unimaginative days,"—Habeas Corpus'd[2] as we are, out of all wonder, uncertainty and fear;—in these fireside, delicate, gilded days,—these days of sickly safety and comfort, we feel very grateful to Mr. Kean for giving us some excitement by his old passion in one of the old plays. He is a relict of romance;—a Posthumous ray of chivalry, and always seems just

---

1. Written in December 1817 at Burford Bridge about the time Keats finished *Endymion*. The poem's form looks back to the song "Farewell ungratefull Traytor," in Dryden's *The Spanish Friar* (1681). First published in the *London Literary Gazette and Journal of Belles Lettres*, September 19, 1829, p. 618; text from the *Literary Gazette* with emendations from Forman's account of the lost holograph draft (the Law MS, a possible source of the printed text) in the Hampstead Keats 4: 61–62.
2. This is the reading of the lost draft; the printed text has "In a" and the same at l. 9.
3. Complaining.
4. This is the reading of the lost draft; the printed text has a revision, "To know the change and feel it." The revision may well be the work of Woodhouse, who complained in a letter to Taylor, November 23, 1818 (*KC*, 1: 64), of Keats's use of the word "feel" for "feeling." An extant fair copy (Bristol MS; see facsimile in Alvin Whitley, *Harvard Library Bulletin* 5 [1951], facing p. 120) has "of" for "at" in the preceding line.
1. Keats's review, written in Reynolds's absence from his duties as a theater critic, was first published in the *Champion* for December 21, 1817. Edmund Kean (1787–1833) was a controversial actor celebrated by Hunt and Hazlitt as revolutionizing acting. Keats saw Kean in a production of Shakespeare's *Richard III* on December 16, when the actor returned to the theater after an illness. See Keats's letter to his brothers of December 21, 27? (below, pp. 107–109), for the context of this review. Text from the *Champion*.
2. Keats adapts Wordsworth, *The Excursion*, 2.26. He also refers to the government's suspension of habeas corpus after a demonstration against the Prince Regent early in the year.

arrived from the camp of Charlemagne.[3] In Richard he is his sword's dear cousin; in Hamlet his footing is germain to the platform. In Macbeth his eye laughs siege to scorn; in Othello he is welcome to Cyprus. In Timon he is of the palace—of Athens—of the woods, and is worthy to sleep in a grave "which once a day with its embossed froth, the turbulent surge doth cover."[4] For all these was he greeted with enthusiasm on his re-appearance in Richard; for all these, his sickness will ever be a public misfortune. His return was full of power. He is not the man to "bate a jot."[5] On Thursday evening, he acted Luke in Riches,[6] as far as the stage will admit, to perfection. In the hypocritical self-possession, in the caution, and afterwards the pride, cruelty and avarice, Luke appears to us a man incapable of imagining to the extreme heinousness of crimes. To him, they are mere magic-lantern horrors. He is at no trouble to deaden his conscience.

Mr. Kean's two characters of this week, comprising as they do, the utmost of quiet and turbulence, invite us to say a few words on his acting in general. We have done this before, but we do it again without remorse. Amid his numerous excellencies, the one which at this moment most weighs upon us, is the elegance, gracefulness and music of elocution. A melodious passage in poetry is full of pleasures both sensual and spiritual. The spiritual is felt when the very letters and points of charactered language show like the hieroglyphics of beauty;—the mysterious signs of an immortal freemasonry! "A thing to dream of, not to tell!"[7] The sensual life of verse springs warm from the lips of Kean, and to one learned in Shakespearean hieroglyphics,[8]—learned in the spiritual portion of those lines to which Kean adds a sensual grandeur: his tongue must seem to have robbed "the hybla bees, and left them honeyless."[9] There is an indescribable gusto[1] in his voice, by which we feel that the utterer is thinking of the past and future, while speaking of the instant. When he says in Othello, "put up your bright swords, for the dew will rust them,"[2] we feel that his throat had commanded where swords were as thick as reeds. From eternal risk, he speaks as though his body were unassailable. Again, his exclamation of "blood, blood, blood!"[3] is direful and slaughterous to the deepest degree, the very words appear stained and gory. His nature hangs over them, making a prophetic repast. His voice is loosed on them, like the wild dog on the savage relics of an eastern conflict; and we can distinctly hear it "gorging, and growling o'er carcase and limb."[4] In Richard, "Be stirring with the lark to-morrow, gentle Norfolk!"[5] comes from him, as through the morning atmosphere, towards which he yearns. We could cite a volume of such immortal scraps, and dote upon them with our remarks; but as an end must come, we will content ourselves with a single syllable. It is in

3. Charles the Great or Charles I (742?–814), emperor of the West (800–814), Carolingian king of the Franks (768–814). Charlemagne's army is depicted in the twelfth-century *Chanson de Roland*.
4. Shakespeare, *The Life of Timon of Athens*, 5.2.102–103.
5. The most likely source is Milton's sonnet "To Cyriack Skinner," l. 7.
6. Kean was known for his performance of this part in *Riches; or the Wife and Brother*, Burges's adaptation of Massinger's *The City Madam*. Keats saw Kean in this part on December 18.
7. Keats adapts Coleridge, "Christabel," 1.247.
8. See Keats's contrast between Shakespeare and Byron: "Lord Byron cuts a figure—but he is not figurative—Shakespeare led a life of Allegory; his works are the comments on it" (spring 1819 journal letter to the George Keatses, p. 315).
9. Shakespeare, *Julius Caesar*, 5.1.34–35.
1. See Hazlitt's essay "On Gusto," included in *The Round Table* (1817), 2: 20–21.
2. Shakespeare, *Othello*, 1.2.60.
3. Shakespeare, *Othello*, 3.3.454.
4. Byron, *Siege of Corinth* (1816), l.456.
5. Shakespeare, *Richard III*, 5.5.10.

those lines of impatience to the night who "like a foul and ugly witch, doth limp so tediously away."[6] Surely this intense power of anatomizing the passion of every syllable—of taking to himself the wings of verse, is the means by which he becomes a storm with such fiery decision; and by which, with a still deeper charm, he "does his spiriting gently."[7] Other actors are continually thinking of their sum-total effect throughout a play. Kean delivers himself up to the instant feeling, without the shadow of a thought about any thing else. He feels his being as deeply as Wordsworth, or any of our intellectual monopolists.[8] From all his comrades he stands alone, reminding us of him, whom Dante has so finely described in his Hell:

> "And sole apart retir'd, the Soldan fierce!"[9]

Although so many times he has lost the Battle of Bosworth Field,[1] we can easily conceive him really expectant of victory, and a different termination of the piece. Yet we are as moths about a candle, in speaking of this great man. "Great, let us call him, for he conquered us!"[2] We will say no more. Kean! Kean! have a carefulness of thy health, an in-nursed respect for thy own genius, a pity for us in these cold and enfeebling times! Cheer us a little in the failure of our days! for romance lives but in books. The goblin is driven from the heath, and the rainbow is robbed of its mystery![3]

Letter to George and Tom Keats, December 21, 27?, 1817[1]

Hampstead Sunday
22 December 1818

My dear Brothers

I must crave your pardon for not having written ere this & &. I saw Kean return to the public in Richard III, & finely he did it, & at the request of Reynolds I went to criticise his Luke in Riches[2]—the critique is in todays champion, which I send you with the Examiner in which you will find very proper lamentation on the obsoletion of christmas Gambols & pastimes: but it was mixed up with so much egotism of that drivelling nature that pleasure is entirely lost.[3] Hone the publisher's trial, you must find very amusing; & as Englishmen very encouraging—his *Not Guilty* is a thing,

---

6. Shakespeare, *Henry V*, 4.0.21–22.
7. Shakespeare, *The Tempest*, 1.2.300.
8. See Keats's comment on Wordsworth in his February 3, 1818, letter to Reynolds (pp. 121–22), where he calls the older poet an "egotist."
9. Cary's translation of Dante's *Inferno*, 4.126.
1. The final defeat of Richard III, August 22, 1485.
2. Keats adapts Edward Young's adaptation of *Othello* as *Revenge* (1721), 1.1.
3. See Keats's comments in *Lamia*, 2.229–38.
1. One of Keats's most famous letters, setting forth his notion of "Negative Capability." It was written after Keats had returned to Hampstead, his brothers had left for Devon, and Reynolds had left for a Christmas holiday, with Keats writing theatrical reviews in his absence. Text from the transcript by Jeffrey (Harvard MS Keats 3.9, f. 5r). Jeffrey dated the letter "22 December 1818," but it must have been written beginning December 21, 1817. Jeffrey also omitted anything from a few words to a few pages which he indicates by "& &."
2. Edmund Kean (1787/90–1833) was an innovative performer and the greatest tragic actor of the day. Kean had been ill but returned on December 15 to play in *Richard III*; Keats's review of Kean's performance of December 18 as Luke Traffic in Sir James Bland Burges' *Riches; or, The Wife and Brother* (an adaptation of Massinger's *City Madam*) appeared in the *Champion*, December 21, 1817 (see pp. 105–107).
3. Hunt published his "Christmas and Other Old National Merry-Makings Considered, with Reference to the Nature of the Age, and to the Desirableness of Their Revival" in the *Examiner*, December 21, 1817, pp. 801–803 and December 28, 1817, pp. 817–19.

which not to have been, would have dulled still more Liberty's Emblazoning. Lord Ellenborough has been paid in his own coin—Wooler & Hone have done us an essential service.[4] I have had two very pleasant evenings with Dilke yesterday & today; & am at this moment just come from him & feel in the humour to go on with this, began in the morning, & from which he came to fetch me. I spent Friday evening with Wells[5] & went the next morning to see *Death on the Pale horse*. It is a wonderful picture, when West's[6] age is considered; But there is nothing to be intense upon; no women one feels mad to kiss; no face swelling into reality. The excellence of every Art is its intensity, capable of making all disagreeables evaporate, from their being in close relationship with Beauty & Truth. Examine King Lear & you will find this examplified throughout; but in this picture we have unpleasantness without any momentous depth of speculation excited, in which to bury its repulsiveness. The picture is larger than Christ rejected. I dined with Haydon the sunday after you left, & had a very pleasant day, I dined too (for I have been out too much lately) with Horace Smith & met his two Brothers with Hill & Kingston & one Du Bois,[7] they only served to convince me, how superior humour is to wit in respect to enjoyment. These men say things which make one start, without making one feel, they are all alike; their manners are alike; they all know fashionables; they have a mannerism in their very eating & drinking, in their mere handling a Decanter—They talked of Kean & his low company. Would I were with that company instead of yours said I to myself! I know such like acquaintance will never do for me & yet I am going to Reynolds, on Wednesday. Brown & Dilke walked with me & back from the Christmas pantomime.[8] I had not a dispute but a disquisition with Dilke, on various

4. Keats echoes Hunt's defense of the "Liberty of the Press," in the *Examiner*, December 7, 1817, pp. 769–71 (*SWLH* 2: 137–41). Thomas Jonathan Wooler (1786?–1853), journalist, politician, and editor of *The Black Dwarf*, had been tried on June 5 for libeling the ministry in a piece entitled "Past, Present, and Future"; he was acquitted (see the *Examiner*, June 8, 1817, pp. 361, 366–68). William Hone (1780–1842), journalist and antiquarian, was tried December 18–20 (see the *Examiner*, December 21, 1817, pp. 805–806) on three counts of blasphemous libel for having printed in his *Reformer's Register* three political parodies that drew on the litany, the Athanasian creed, and the church catechism. He defended himself successfully before Lord Ellenborough (1750–1818), the lord chief justice, who had sentenced the Hunt brothers to prison in 1813. It had been a year in which the government had sought to suppress the radical press: on March 27, 1817, Sidmouth issued a ruling that granted a Justice of the Peace the right to arrest anyone suspected of selling treasonous or seditious material, invited local officials to raid booksellers, and removed the protections of Fox's Libel Act of 1792 which had insured jury trials in cases of seditious libel; there were twenty-six prosecutions for seditious libel and sixteen *ex officio* informations filed in 1817; and Cobbett fled the country fearing imprisonment after the suspension of *habeas corpus*.
5. Charles Jeremiah Wells (1800?–1879), poet and lawyer, had attended Enfield School with Tom Keats. He became friends with Wells (who wrote a sonnet to him, see p. 51), Hazlitt, and especially Hazlitt, but he and Keats broke over Wells's joke on Tom over some faked love letters. Wells was the author of *Stories after Nature* (1822) and *Joseph and his Brethren* (1823), which he claimed he wrote to impress Keats after their falling out.
6. Benjamin West (1738–1820), an American historical painter who rose to be president of the Royal Academy; also Leigh Hunt's uncle. West's *Death on the Pale Horse* (which he had begun as early as 1802 when he exhibited a sketch in Paris) was on exhibit at 125 Pall Mall under royal patronage. Hazlitt commented on the painting in *Edinburgh Magazine* for December 1817 (*Works* 18: 135–40). West's *Christ Rejected*, which Keats mentions later, was painted in 1814.
7. Edward Dubois (1774–1850), wit and literary man, was the editor of the *Monthly Mirror*. For Smith, see p. 9, n. 3; his brothers are his coauthor James Smith (1775–1839) and Leonard Smith (1778–1837). Thomas Hill (1760–1840), drysalter and bookseller, and proprietor of the *Monthly Mirror*, entertained a literary set, including the Smiths and Hunt, at his home in Sydenham, south of London. John Kingston was a comptroller of stamps who was Wordsworth's immediate supervisor in the poet's role as distributor of stamps.
8. Keats saw *Harlequin's Vision; Or, The Feast of the Statue* at Drury Lane probably when it opened on December 26, 1817. Keats wrote a review of the performance along with John Dillon's *Retribution; or, The Chieftain's Daughter* (premiered January 1, 1818, at Covent Garden) in the *Champion*, January 4, 1818 (see Hampsted Edition 5: 247–56), and Hunt called it "decidedly the worst and dullest [opera] we ever saw" in the *Examiner*, January 11, 1818, pp. 25–26. See p. 109, n. 2.

subjects; several things dovetailed in my mind, & at once it struck me, what quality went to form a Man of Achievement especially in Literature & which Shakespeare posessed so enormously—I mean *Negative Capability*, that is when man is capable of being in uncertainties, Mysteries, doubts, without any irritable reaching after fact & reason—Coleridge, for instance, would let go by a fine isolated verisimilitude caught from the Penetralium[9] of mystery, from being incapable of remaining content with half knowledge. This pursued through Volumes would perhaps take us no further than this, that with a great poet the sense of Beauty overcomes every other consideration, or rather obliterates all consideration.

possibility of poet to lose him/herself through other works

Shelley's poem[1] is out & there are words about its being objected too, as much as Queen Mab was. Poor Shelley I think he has his Quota of good qualities, in sooth la!! Write soon to your most sincere friend & affectionate Brother

John

Letter to George and Tom Keats, January 5, 1818[1]

Featherstone Build^{gs}, Monday

My dear Brothers,

I ought to have written before, and you should have had a long Letter last week; but I undertook the Champion for Reynolds who is at Exeter. I wrote two articles, one on the Drury Lane Pantomime, the other on the Covent Garden New Tragedy, which they have not put in.[2] The one they have inserted is so badly punctuated that, you perceive, I am determined never to write more without some care in that particular. Wells tells me that you are licking your Chops, Tom, in expectation of my Book coming out; I am sorry to say I have not begun my corrections yet: tomorrow I set

---

9. The innermost part.
1. Shelley's *Laon and Cythna*, released in December 1817, was revised as *The Revolt of Islam* after his publishers, the Olliers, objected to its treatment of incest and religion. Shelley's visionary and radical *Queen Mab* (1813) had gained notice in 1817 as it had figured in the custody case over Shelley's children with Harriet Shelley.
1. Written to George and Tom, who had left London on December 13, 1817, for a trip to Devon. Text from ALS at the Carl H. Pforzheimer Library Collection of Shelley and His Circle, The New York Public Library, Astor, Lenox and Tilden Foundation (SC 444); the manuscript is reproduced and transcribed in *Shelley and his Circle*, vol. 5, ed. Donald H. Reiman (Cambridge: Harvard University Press, 1973): 428–36. Reiman (p. 438) argues that the body of the letter was completed before Keats went to dine, but it was left at the Featherstone Buildings (where Tom Keats's friend Charles Jeremiah Wells [see p. 108, n. 5] lived); in Reiman's reconstruction, Keats, probably having bought a copy of the *Champion* while out, wrote the postscript upon his return and mailed the letter.
2. Keats took over Reynolds's reviewing duties at the *Champion* while Reynolds was in Exeter for Christmas. As Keats notes in his postscript, both reviews mentioned here appeared in the January 4 issue; they are reprinted in the Hampstead Keats, 5: 247–56. The tragedy was *Retribution; or The Chieftain's Daughter* by John Dillon, which opened at Covent Garden on January 1, 1818, and was a reasonable success for a new tragedy, receiving nine performances; the play was set in Persia and had a talented cast including Charles Young, Eliza O'Neill, Charles Kemble, Daniel Terry, and Charles Macready. Drury Lane's Christmas pantomime opened as was traditional on Boxing Day, December 26, 1817. Keats called it *Don Giovanni* in his review, Nicoll lists it as *The Feast of the Statue; or, Harlequin Libertine*, and it is most often referred to as *Harlequin's Vision; or, The Feast of the Statue*. A successful harlequinade, performed twenty-eight times, it drew on the popularity of the Don Juan story after Mozart's *Don Giovanni* premiered at the King's Theatre on April 12, 1817. While Nicoll lists its author as anonymous, it was apparently created by Lethbridge, Drury Lane's property man, and the pantomimic actor T. P. Cooke, who played Don Pedro (and later the Monster in Peake's adaptation of Shelley's *Frankenstein*), with the dancing and combat choreographed by Ridgway (who also played Don Juan/Harlequin) and the music composed by G. Lanza, presumably Gesualdo Lanza (1779–1859), a well-known singing teacher and author of *The Elements of Singing* (1813). In the next sentence, Keats objects to the way his review of Kean's acting was printed in the *Champion* for December 21, 1817 (see above, pp. 105–08).

out.[3] I called on Sawrey[4] this morning. He did not seem to be at all out at any thing I said and the enquiries I made with regard to your spitting of Blood: and, moreover, desired me to ask you to send him a correct account of all your sensations and symptoms concerning the Palpitation and the spitting and the Cough—if you have any. Your last Letter gave me a great Pleasure for I think the Invalid is in a better spirit there along the Edge[5]—and as for George I must immediately, now I think of it, correct a little misconception of a part of my last Letter. The Miss Reynolds have never said one word against me about you, or by any means endeavoured to lessen you in my estimation. That is not what I referred to: but the manner and thoughts which I knew they internally had towards you— time will show. Wells and Severn dined with me yesterday: we had a very pleasant day. I pitched upon another bottle of claret—Port—we enjoyed ourselves very much were all very witty and full of Rhyme—we played a Concert from 4 o'clock till 10—drank your Healths, the Hunts, and N. B. Severn, Peter Pindar's.[6] I said on that day the only good thing I was ever guilty of—we were talking about Stephens and the 1[s] Gallery.[7] I said I wondered that careful Folks would go there for although it was but a Shilling still you had to pay through the Nose. I saw the Peachey family in a Box at Drury one Night.[8] I have got such a curious—or rather I had such, now I am in my own hand.[9] I have had a great deal of pleasant time with Rice lately, and am getting initiated into a little Cant[1]—they call drinking deep-dying scarlet, and when you breathe in you're wartering they bid you cry hem and play it off. They call good Wine a pretty tipple, and call getting a Child knocking out an apple; stopping at a Tavern they call hanging out. Where do you sup? is where do you hang out? This day I promised to dine with Wordsworth and the Weather is so bad that I am undecided for he lives at Mortimer street. I had an invitation to meet him at Kingstons, but not liking that place I sent my excuse.[2] What I think of doing today is to dine in Mortimer Street (words[th]) and sup here in Feathers[ne] Buildg[s] as M[r] Wells has invited me. On Saturday I called on Wordsworth before he went to Kingstons and was surprised to find him with a stiff Collar. I saw his Spouse and I think his Daughter.[3] I forget whether I had written my last before my Sunday Evening at Haydon's[4]—

3. That is, the corrections to *Endymion*, which he recopied and corrected from January to March 1818.
4. Rollins identifies Sawrey as Solomon Sawrey (1765–1825), a surgeon and specialist on venereal diseases; Reiman (pp. 440–41) argues it was this Sawrey's son who was treating Tom for consumption.
5. An escarpment, presumably overlooking the harbor at Teignmouth.
6. The pen name of the great satirist John Wolcot (1738–1819). Severn: Joseph Severn (1793–1879) painter who accompanied Keats to Italy.
7. The one-shilling gallery offered the cheapest seats in the theater, but Keats puns on "paying through the nose," here the high price of enduring bad odors. Catherine Stephens (1794–1882), a popular soprano who had studied with Lanza, which is perhaps why this Covent Garden singer was at Drury Lane, assuming Lanza wrote the music for the Christmas pantomime. Stephens had sung in the first English-language performances of Mozart's *Don Giovanni*.
8. Keats had gone to school with a Peachey, perhaps James Peachey, an attorney.
9. That is, Keats changed from a bad pen.
1. The jargon or slang of a particular group or class. After quoting Shakespeare, *1 Henry IV*, 2.5.13–15 on drinking deep, Keats gives several examples, some of which appear in the 1811 *Dictionary of the Vulgar Tongue*.
2. Keats dined at Wordsworth's lodgings near Thomas Monkhouse's at 48 Mortimer Street; Monkhouse (1783–1825) was a merchant and a cousin of Wordsworth's wife. For Kingston, see p. 108, n. 7.
3. Apparently, when Keats saw Wordsworth in his stiff collar, he also saw his wife and her sister, Sara Hutchinson, rather than Wordsworth's daughter who was not then in London.
4. Keats offers here his description of Haydon's "Immortal Dinner" on December 28, 1817. See Haydon, *Diary*, 2.173–76, and Penelope Hughes-Hallet, *The Immortal Dinner: A Famous Evening of Genius and Laughter in Literary London, 1817* (London: Viking, 2000).

no, I did not or I should have told you Tom of a y[oung] Man you met at Paris at Scott's of the n[ame of] Richer I—think he is going to Fezan in Africa there to proceed if possible like Mungo Park[5]—he was very polite to me and enquired very particularly after you. Then there was Wordsworth, Lamb, Monkhouse, Landseer, Kingston and your humble Sarvant.[6] Lamb got tipsey and blew up Kingston—proceeding so far as to take the Candle across the Room hold it to his face and show us wh-a-at—sor[t]-fello he-waas. I astonished Kingston at supper with a pertinacity in favour of drinking—keeping my two glasses at work in a knowing way.

I have seen Fanny twice lately—she enquired particularly after you and wants a Co-partnership Letter from you—she has been unwell but is improving—I think she will be quick. Mrs. Abbey was saying that the Keatses were ever indolent, that they would ever be so and that it was born in them. Well whispered fanny to me 'If it is born with us how can we help it. She seems very anxious for a Letter. I asked her what I should get for her, she said a Medal of the Princess.[7] I called on Haslam—we dined very snugly together—he sent me a Hare last Week which I sent to M[rs] Dilk. Brown is not come back.[8] I and Dilk are getting capital Friends—he is going to take the Champion—he has sent his farce to Covent Garden.[9] I met Bob Harris in the Slips at Covent Garden[1]—we had a good deal of curious chat. He came out with his old humble Opinion—the Covent Garden Pantomime is a very nice one but they have a middling Harlequin, a bad Pantaloon, a worse Clown and a shocking Columbine who is one of the Miss Dennets.[2] I suppose you will see my Critique on the new Tragedy in the next Week's Champion. It is a shocking bad one. I have not seen Hunt; he was out when I called. M[rs] Hunt looks as well as ever I saw her after her Confinement.[3] There is an article in the sennight Examiner on Godwin's Mandeville, signed E. K. I think it Miss Kents.[4] I will send it. There are fine Subscriptions going on for Hone.[5] You ask me what degrees there are between Scott's Novels and those of

5. The most famous explorer of Africa in the period. Tom and George Keats had been in Paris in September 1817 and visited John Scott (see p. 104, n. 1), where they met Joseph Ritchie (1788?–1819), a surgeon who joined an expedition to reach central Africa from the North. He would die at Murzuq, the capital of Fezzan (in southwest Libya), on March 22, 1819. Ritchie promised to carry a copy of *Endymion* into the depths of the Sahara; a letter from Richie praising Keats as "the great poetical luminary of the age to come" was published in Lowell, 1.282.

6. Landseer is one (probably the father John but perhaps Thomas) of a family of artists: the father John Landseer (1769–1852) and his three sons, Charles (1799–1879), Sir Edwin Henry (1802–1873), and Thomas (1795–1880), all of whom were pupils of Haydon. For Monkhouse and Kingston, see p. 108, n. 7 and p. 110, n. 2. Ritchie, Landseer, and Kingston all dropped in for tea after dinner. Charles Lamb: (1775–1834) essayist.

7. Princess Charlotte had died on November 6, 1817, which evoked an outpouring of grief expressed in commemorative medals as well as verses; see Stephen Behrendt, *Royal Mourning and Regency Culture: Elegies and Memorials of Princess Charlotte* (New York: St. Martin's Press, 1997).

8. Brown (see p. 98, n. 8) was visiting the Snooks at Bedhampton, Hampshire. For Haslam, see p. 117, n. 1; for Dilke, see p. 78, n. 1.

9. Dilke's farce has not been identified.

1. Keats saw *Harlequin Gulliver; or, The Flying Island* which opened on December 26, 1817. *Slips*: the side portions of the stage from whence scenery was pushed onto the stage. Thomas Harris (d. 1820) was the long time manager of Covent Garden, but Bob Harris has not been identified.

2. Frances Dennett, one of three popular Dennett sisters, played Columbine. John P. "Jack" Bologna played Harlequin (and may have been the author of a *Lilliput Island* at the Sans Pareil in 1811). Mr. Ryalls played Pantaloon and Mr. Norman the clown.

3. She had given birth to Percy Shelley Hunt on December 4, 1817.

4. The piece was not written by Hunt's sister-in-law Elizabeth Kent but by Shelley writing under the pseudonym of the "Elfin Knight"; *sennight*: last week's *Examiner* for December 28, 1817.

5. See above, p. 108, n. 4.

Smollet.[6] They appear to me to be quite distinct in every particular, more especially in their aim. Scott endeavours to throw so interesting and ramantic a colouring into common and low Characters as to give them a touch of the Sublime. Smollet on the contrary pulls down and levels what with other Men would continue Romance. The Grand parts of Scott are within the reach of more Minds than the finest humours in Humphrey Clunker. I forget whether that fine thing of the Sargeant is Fielding's or Smollet's but it gives me more pleasure than the whole Novel of the Antiquary—you must remember what I mean. Some one says to the Sargeant, "that's a non sequiter," "if you come to that" replies the Sargeant "you're another."[7] I see by Wells' Letter, Mr Abbey does not overstock you with Money. You must insist. I have not seen Loveless[8] yet, but expect it on Wednesday. I am afraid it is gone. Severn tells me he has an order for some drawings for the Emperor of Russia. I was at a Dance at Redhall's and passed a pleasant time enough, drank deep and won 10.6 at cutting for Half Guineas.[9] There was a younger Brother of the Squibs made him self very conspicuous after the Ladies had retired from the supper table by giving Mater Omnium.[1] Mr Redhall said he did not understand any thing but plain english, whereat Rice egged the young fool on to say the World plainly out. After which there was an enquiry about the derivation of the Word C—t when while two parsons and Grammarians were sitting together and settling the matter, Wm Squibs[2] interrupting them said a very good thing: 'Gentleman,' says he, 'I have always understood it to be a Root and not a Derivitive.' On proceeding to the Pot in the Cupboard it soon became full, on which the Court door was opened. Frank Floodgate bawls out, Hoollo! Here's an opposition pot. Ay, says Rice, in one you have a Yard for your pot, and in the other a pot for your Yard. Bailey was there and seemed to enjoy the Evening. Rice said he cared less about the hour than anyone and the proof is his dancing. He cares not for time, dancing as if he was deaf. Old Redall, not being used to give parties, had no idea of the Quantity of wine that would be drank and he actually put in readiness on the kitchen Stairs 8 dozen. Everyone enquires after you and everyone desires their remembrances to you. You must get well, Tom, and then I shall feel 'Whole and general as the casing Air.'[3] Give me as many Letters as you like and write to Sawrey soon. I received a short Letter from Bailey about Crips and one from Haydon ditto.[4] Haydon thinks he improves very much. Here a happy twelve days to you and may we pass the next together. Mrs Wells desires remembrances particularly to Tom and her respects to George, and I desire no better than to be ever your most affectionate

Brother John—

I had not opened the Champion before—I find both my articles in it—

6. Keats compares the novels of Walter Scott (1771–1832) with those of Tobias Smollett (1721–1771), noting Smollet's 1771 *Expedition of Humphry Clinker* (here, "Clunker") and Scott's *Antiquary* (1816).
7. See Fielding's *Tom Jones*, 9.6.
8. Reference uncertain; Lovelace is a character in Richardson's *Clarissa*.
9. Presumably a game of cutting for the high card.
1. Every mother (Latin).
2. Rollins identifies Squibb senior as G. Squibb, auctioneer, of Boyle Street, Saville Row. Mr. *Redhall:* identified in Gittings, *Letters*, as G. S. Reddall, sword-cutler, of 236 Picadilly.
3. See Shakespeare, *Macbeth*, 3.4.22: "As Broad and general as the casing air."
4. For Cripps, see p. 98. n. 7.

LINES ON SEEING A LOCK OF MILTON'S HAIR.[1]

Chief of organic numbers![2]
Old scholar of the Spheres![3]
Thy spirit never slumbers,
But rolls about our ears
For ever, and for ever!   5
O, what a mad endeavour
Worketh he,
Who, to thy sacred and ennobled hearse,
Would offer a burnt sacrifice of verse
And melody!   10

How heavenward thou soundest,[4]
Live temple of sweet noise,
And discord unconfoundest,
Giving delight new joys,
And pleasure nobler pinions![5]   15
O, where are thy dominions?
Lend thine ear
To a young Delian[6] oath,—aye, by thy soul,
By all that from thy mortal lips did roll,
And by the kernel of thy earthly love,   20
Beauty, in things on earth and things above,
I swear,—[7]
When every childish fashion
Has vanish'd from my rhyme,
Will I, grey-gone in passion,   25
Leave to an after time
Hymning and harmony
Of thee, and of thy works, and of thy life;
But vain is now the burning and the strife,
Pangs are in vain, until I grow high-rife   30
With old philosophy,
And mad with glimpses of futurity!

For many years my offerings must be hush'd;
When I do speak, I'll think upon this hour,
Because I feel my forehead hot and flush'd,   35

1. Written on January 21, 1818, when Keats visited Hunt, who had a lock of Milton's hair and asked Keats to write a poem on it. Keats copied the poem into his 1808 facsimile of Shakespeare's First Folio and then into a letter to Benjamin Bailey of January 23, 1818 (see p. 115, below), where it is called an "ode." First published in the *Plymouth and Devonport Weekly Journal*, November 15, 1838, with an erratum for the dropping of l. 6 published on November 29, 1838; text from *PDWJ* with emendations from Brown's transcript (Harvard MS Keats 3.6, p. 46; *MYR: JK*, 7: 48–49) and Keats's holograph on the last page of his 1808 facsimile of Shakespeare's First Folio (LMA K/BK/01/011/57).
2. Poetic or musical meter; *organic*: "organ-like" (Allott cites Milton's "Nativity Ode," l. 130: "And let the Base of Heav'n's deep Organ blow").
3. Refers to both the celestial bodies and the music of the spheres (Allott cites Milton, "Arcades," ll. 62–73).
4. The holograph has "soundedest" and then "unconfoundedest" in l. 13.
5. Wings.
6. From the birthplace of Apollo, as god of poetry, on the island of Delos.
7. This line, not in the Shakespeare MS. or originally in the letter to Bailey, appears to have been added by Woodhouse in W², who indicated in a note opposite f. 155 that "a short line to rhyme with 'ear'" was needed; the line was added into Brown's transcript in pencil and then gone over in ink, perhaps indicating that Keats accepted the change.

Even at the simplest vassal of thy power,—
    A lock of thy bright hair!
Sudden it came,
And I was startled, when I caught thy name
    Coupled so unaware;   40
Yet, at the moment, temperate was my blood,—
Methought I had beheld it from the flood.[8]

SONNET.
ON SITTING DOWN TO READ KING LEAR
ONCE AGAIN.[1]

O golden-tongued romance, with serene lute,
    Fair plumed syren, queen of far-away,
    Leave melodising on this wintry day,
Shut up thine olden pages, and be mute.
Adieu! for, once again, the fierce dispute   5
    Betwixt damnation[2] and impassion'd clay
    Must I burn through; once more humbly essay[3]
The bitter-sweet of this Shakespearean fruit.
    Chief Poet! and ye clouds of Albion,[4]
Begetters of our deep eternal theme,   10
    When through the old oak forest I am gone,
Let me not wander in a barren dream,
But, when I am consumed in the fire,
Give me new Phœnix[5] wings to fly at my desire.

Letter to Benjamin Bailey, January 23, 1818[1]

My dear Bailey,   Friday Jany 23rd
    Twelve days have pass'd since your last reached me—what has gone
through the myriads of human Minds since the 12th. We talk of the immense number of Books, the Volumes ranged thousands by thousands—
but perhaps more goes through the human intelligence in 12 days than ever
was written. How has that unfortunate Family lived through the twelve?[2]
One saying of your's I shall never forget—you may not recollect it—it being
perhaps said when you were looking on the surface and seeming of Humanity alone, without a thought of the past or the future—or the deeps of good

8. Presumably the biblical deluge; Keats seems to suggest that when he saw the lock he was first
    startled, then calm, as if he had always known of it; the emotion behind the poem came later.
1. Written January 22, 1818, and copied out in a letter to George and Tom Keats, January 23, 24,
    1818 (see p. 117, below), where he offers it as a "prologue" to Shakespeare's play. For a similar con-
    trast between romance and tragedy, see, for example, "Sleep and Poetry," ll. 96–124 (above, p. 61).
    First published in the *Plymouth and Devonport Weekly Journal*, November 8, 1838; text from *PDWJ*
    with emendations from Keats's fair copy opposite the first page of *King Lear* in his 1808 facsimile
    of Shakespeare's First Folio (LMA K/BK/01/011/57: p. 280).
2. The letter version has "Hell-torment."
3. The FC has "assay"; in either case, "test," "attempt."
4. A poetic name for England.
5. A mythical bird that is reborn from its ashes.
1. Written while Keats was revising *Endymion* for publication as well as reconnecting with his Lon-
    don friends including Haydon and Hunt. Text from ALS (Harvard MS Keats 1.20); there is also a
    transcript in Woodhouse's letter-book, p. 83.
2. Bailey marked this sentence and indicated on the address fold that Keats had helped a poor fam-
    ily: "This letter opens the excellent feelings of an excellent heart."

and evil—you were at the moment estranged from speculation and I think you have arguments ready for the Man who would utter it to you—this is a formidable preface for a simple thing—merely you said; "*Why should Woman suffer?*" Aye. Why should she? "By heavens I'd coin my very Soul and drop my Blood for Drachmas."!³ These things are, and he who feels how incompetent the most skyey Knight errantry is to heal this bruised fairness is like a sensitive leaf on the hot hand of thought. Your tearing, my dear friend, a spiritless and gloomy Letter up to rewrite to me is what I shall never forget—it was to me a real thing. Things have happen'd lately of great Perplexity—You must have heard of them—Reynolds and Haydon retorting and recrimminating—and parting for ever—the same thing has happened between Haydon and Hunt⁴—It is unfortunate—Men should bear with each other—there lives not the Man who may not be cut up, aye hashed to pieces on his weakest side. The best of Men have but a portion of good in them—a kind of spiritual yeast in their frames which creates the ferment of existence—by which a Man is propell'd to act and strive and buffet with Circumstance. The sure way Bailey, is first to know a Man's faults, and then be passive, if after that he insensibly draws you towards him then you have no Power to break the link. Before I felt interested in either Reynolds or Haydon—I was well read in their faults yet knowing them I have been cementing gradually with both—I have an affection for them both for reasons almost opposite—and to both must I of necessity cling—supported always by the hope that when a little time—a few years shall have tried me more fully in their esteem I may be able to bring them together—the time must come because they have both hearts—and they will recollect the best parts of each other when this gust is overblown. I had a Message from you through a Letter to Jane, I think about Cripps—there can be no idea of binding⁵ till a sufficient sum is sure for him—and even then the thing should be maturely consider'd by all his helpers. I shall try my luck upon as many fat-purses as I can meet with—Cripps is improving very fast—I have the greater hopes of him because he is so slow in devellopment—a Man of great executing Powers at 20—with a look and a speech almost stupid is sure to do something. I have just look'd through the second side of your Letter—I feel a great content at it. I was at Hunt's the other day, and he surprised me with a real authenticated Lock of *Milton's Hair*. I know you would like what I wrote thereon—so here it is—*as they say of a Sheep in a Nurse*ry Book

[A draft of "Lines on seeing a Lock of Milton's Hair" called "On seeing a Lock of Milton's Hair—Ode." follows.]⁶

This I did at Hunt's at his request—perhaps I should have done something better alone and at home—I have sent my first book to the Press⁷—and this afternoon shall begin preparing the second—my visit to you will be a great spur to quicken the Proceeding—I have not had your Sermon returned⁸—I

---

3. Shakespeare, *Julius Caesar*, 4.2.127–128; Brutus complains to Cassius about the latter's refusal to send money for Brutus's troops and explains that he will not use devious means to raise funds.
4. Haydon was angry with Reynolds for having failed to attend his "Immortal Dinner" of December 28, 1817, where Keats, Lamb, and Wordsworth had been present. Haydon was also arguing with Hunt over some silverware he claimed Mrs. Hunt had not returned to him.
5. Bailey had written to Jane Reynolds about Cripps being bound or apprenticed to Haydon; see p. 98, n. 7.
6. See p. 113–14.
7. He delivered a revised version of Book I of *Endymion* to Taylor on January 20; Keats did not visit Bailey as he goes on to suggest.
8. Bailey's *A Discourse Inscribed to the Memory of the Princess Charlotte Augusta* (published anonymously by Taylor and Hessey in 1817) was part of the outpouring of writing on the death of the Regent's daughter; see Stephen C. Behrendt, *Royal Mourning and Regency Culture: Elegies and Memorials of Princess Charlotte* (New York: St. Martin's Press, 1997).

long to make it the subject of a Letter to you—What do they say at Oxford?

I trust you and Gleig pass much fine time together. Remember me to him and Whitehead.[9] My Brother Tom is getting stronger but his Spitting of blood continues—I sat down to read King Lear yesterday, and felt the greatness of the thing up to the writing of a Sonnet preparatory thereto[1]—in my next you shall have it There were some miserable reports of Rice's health— I went and lo! Master Jemmy had been to the play the night before and was out at the time—he always comes on his Legs like a Cat—I have seen a good deal of Wordsworth. Hazlitt is lecturing on Poetry at the Surry institution—I shall be there next Tuesday.[2]

Your most affectionate Friend
John Keats—

Letter to George and Tom Keats, January 23, 24, 1818[1]

Friday, 23[d] January 1818
My dear Brothers.

I was thinking what hindered me from writing so long, for I have many things to say to you & know not where to begin. It shall be upon a thing most interesting to you my Poem.[2] Well! I have given the 1st book to Taylor; he seemed more than satisfied with it, & to my surprise proposed publishing it in Quarto if Haydon would make a drawing of some event therein, for a Frontispeice.[3] I called on Haydon, he said he would do anything I liked, but said he would rather paint a finished picture, from it, which he seems eager to do; this in a year or two will be a glorious thing for us; & it will be, for Haydon is struck with the 1st Book. I left Haydon & the next day received a letter from him, proposing to make, as he says, with all his might, a finished chalk sketch of my head, to be engraved in the first style & put at the head of my Poem, saying at the same time he had never done the thing for any human being, & that it must have considerable effect as he will put the name to it. I begin to day to copy my 2nd Book "thus far into the bowels of the Land"[4]—You shall hear whether it will be Quarto or non Quarto, picture or non Picture. Leigh Hunt I showed my 1st Book to, he allows it not much merit as a whole; says it is unnatural & made ten objections to it in the mere skimming over. He says the conversation is unnatural & too high-flown for the Brother & Sister. Says it should be simple, forgetting do ye mind, that they are both overshadowed by a Supernatural Power, & of force could not speak like Franchesca in the Rimini.[5] He must first prove that Caliban's poetry is unnatural,[6]—This with me completely overturns his objections—the fact is he & Shelley are hurt & perhaps justly, at my not having showed them the affair officiously & from several hints I have had they appear much disposed to dissect & anatomize, any trip

9. For Whitehead and Gleig, see p. 101, n. 1 and p. 99, n. 5.
1. See p. 114 for the poem.
2. Hazlitt gave the lectures that became *Lectures on the English Poets* (1818) at the Surrey Institution, Blackfriars Road, from January 13 to March 3, 1818.
1. Text from Jeffrey's transcript (Harvard MS Keats 3.9, f. 3v).
2. *Endymion*, which he was redrafting at the time.
3. Keats broached the idea with Haydon around January 21, but Haydon did not produce the drawing, and Keats later suggested he wait to illustrate *Hyperion*; see also p. 475.
4. Shakespeare, *Richard III*, 5.2.3.
5. Allusion to the heroine of Hunt's *Story of Rimini* (1816).
6. Caliban appears in Shakespeare's *Tempest*.

or slip I may have made.—But whose afraid Ay! Tom! demme if I am.[7] I went last tuesday, an hour too late, to Hazlitt's Lecture on poetry,[8] got there just as they were coming out, when all these pounced upon me. Hazlitt, John Hunt & son, Wells, Bewick, all the Landseers, Bob Harris, Rox of the Burrough.[9] Aye & more; the Landseers enquired after you particularly. I know not whether Wordsworth has left town. But sunday I dined with Hazlitt & Haydon, also that I took Haslam[1] with me. I dined with Brown lately. Dilke having taken the Champion, Theatricals[2] was obliged to be in Town. Fanny has returned to Walthamstow.—Mr Abbey appeared very glum, the last time I went to see her, & said in an indirect way, that I had no business there. Rice has been ill, but has been mending much lately. I think a little change has taken place in my intellect lately—I cannot bear to be uninterested or unemployed, I, who for so long a time, have been addicted to passiveness. Nothing is finer for the purposes of great productions, than a very gradual ripening of the intellectual powers. As an instance of this—observe—I sat down yesterday to read King Lear once again. The thing appeared to demand the prologue of a Sonnet, I wrote it & began to read—(I know you would like to see it) [A draft entitled "On sitting down to King Lear once Again" follows.][3]

So you see I am getting at it, with a sort of determination & strength, though verily I do not feel it at this moment—this is my fourth letter this morning & I feel rather tired & my head rather swimming—so I will leave it open till tomorrow's post.——

I am in the habit of taking my papers to Dilkes & copying there; so I chat & proceed at the same time. I have been there at my work this evening, & the walk over the Heath takes off all sleep, so I will even proceed with you. I left off short in my last, just as I began an account of a private theatrical. Well it was of the lowest order, all greasy & oily, insomuch that if they had lived in olden times, when signs were hung over the doors; the only appropriate one for that oily place would have been—a guttered Candle—they played John Bull, The Review. & it was to conclude with Bombastes Furioso[4]—I saw from a Box the 1st Act of John Bull, then I went to Drury & did not return till it was over; when by Wells' interest we got behind the scenes, there was not a yard wide all the way round for actors, scene shifters & interlopers to move in; for 'Note Bene'[5] the Green Room was under the stage & there was I threatened over & over again to be turned

7. Rollins cites Horace Smith's anti-Methodist satire *Nehemiah Muggs,* which Keats read in manuscript (now in the Essex County Record Office): "Pooh! Nonsense! Damme! Who's afraid."
8. See p. 116, n. 2.
9. Rollins suggests a George Rokes or Richard Rokes who lived in the Borough; Cook, following Gittings, feels it was a copyist mistake for "Cox," a medical bookseller who lived in the Borough near where Keats lived as a medical student. John Hunt, Leigh's brother, was there with his son, Henry Leigh Hunt. William Bewick (1795–1866) was a pupil of Haydon's. John Landseer (1769–1852), painter and engraver, had three sons who he placed with Haydon: Charles (1799–1879), a history painter; Sir Edwin Henry (1802–1873), known for his paintings of animals; and Thomas (1795–1880), an engraver. Keats had earlier met Bob Harris at Covent Garden (see p. 111, n. 1).
1. William Haslam (1795/8?–1851) was a schoolfellow of Keats's who helped Keats and his brothers in various ways, including in aiding Keats to make arrangements and pay for his trip to Italy.
2. That is, Dilke replaced Reynolds as the theatrical reviewer for the *Champion.*
3. See p. 114.
4. Keats attended a private theater, popular at the time, with some, such as the one run by Elizabeth Craven at Brandenburg House, being quite grand; Harry R. Beaudry, *The English Theatre and John Keats* (Salzburg: University of Salzburg, 1973), p. 26, suggests Keats attended either the Dominion of Fancy Theatre, between Southampton-street and Exeter 'Change, Strand, or the Minor Theatre, Catherine-street, Strand. There was a triple bill: George Colman's extremely popular *John Bull; or, The Englishman's Fireside* (1803), his musical farce *The Review; or, The Wags of Windsor* (1801), and William Barnes Rhodes's *Bombastes Furioso* (1810), a burlesque opera. After watching the first act of *John Bull,* Keats left for Drury Lane, one of the patent theatres royal, to see Kean in *Richard III;* he returned for *Bombastes Furioso,* but it was not performed.
5. "Note well" or "take notice" (Latin).

out by the oily scene shifters. There did I hear a little painted Trollop own, very candidly, that she had failed in Mary, with a "damned if she'd play a serious part again, as long as she lived," & at the same time she was habited as the Quaker in the Review. There was a quarrel & a fat good natured looking girl in soldiers Clothes wished she had only been a man for Tom's sake.[6] One fellow began a song but an unlucky finger-point from the Gallery sent him off like a shot, One chap was dressed to kill for the King in Bombastes. & he stood at the edge of the scene in the very sweat of anxiety to show himself, but Alas the thing was not played. The sweetest morsel of the night[7] moreover was, that the musicians began pegging & fagging away at an overture—never did you see faces more in earnest, three times did they play it over, dropping all kinds of correctness & still did not the curtain draw up. Well then they went into a country-dance then into a region they well knew, into their old boonsome Pothouse.[8] & then to see how pompous o'the sudden they turned; how they looked about, & chatted; how they did not care a Damn; was a great treat. I hope I have not tired you by this filling up of the dash in my last,—Constable the Bookseller has offered Reynolds ten gineas a sheet to write for his magazine, it is an Edinburgh one which, Blackwoods started up in opposition to. Hunt said he was nearly sure that the 'Cockney School' was written by Scott, so you are right Tom![9]—There are no more little bits of news I can remember at present

  I remain

    My dear Brothers Your very affectionate Brother

                 John

Messrs Keats
Teignmouth Devonshire.

[When I have fears that I may cease to be][1]

WHEN I have fears that I may cease to be
 Before my pen has glean'd my teeming brain,
Before high piled books, in charactry,[2]
 Hold like rich garners[3] the full-ripen'd grain;
When I behold, upon the night's starr'd face,   5
 Huge cloudy symbols of a high romance,
And think that I may never live to trace
 Their shadows, with the magic hand of chance;
And when I feel, fair creature of an hour,[4]

6. Keats refers to the parts of Mary Thornberry in *John Bull*, the Quaker Grace Gaylove in *The Review*, Phoebe Whitethorne, who appears as a private soldier in *The Review*, and Tom Shuffleton in *John Bull*.
7. Shakespeare, *2 Henry IV*, 2.4.336.
8. A tavern.
9. John Gibson Lockhart was the author, not Sir Walter Scott nor John Scott, the editor of the *Champion* with whom Hunt had clashed in 1816 over Byron's separation from his wife. Archibald Constable (1774–1827) published both the *Scots Magazine*, also called the *Edinburgh Magazine, and Literary Miscellany*, for which Reynolds did write, and the more famous *Edinburgh Review*. William Blackwood (1776–1834) started *Blackwood's Edinburgh Magazine* in 1817 as a conservative response to the *Edinburgh Review*; in October 1817, *Blackwood's* launched the "Cockney School" attacks under the pseudonym of Z.
1. This Shakespearean sonnet was written at the end of January 1818 (see Keats's letter to Reynolds, January 31, 1818, *L*, 1: 222). For Woodhouse's comments on how this poem illustrates Keats's mode of composition, see *KC*, 1: 128–30. First published in 1848, 2: 293 as Sonnet VII; text from 1848 with emendations from Brown's transcript (Harvard MS Keats 3.6, p. 39; *MYR: JK*, 7:41).
2. Handwriting or printing.
3. Granaries.
4. Woodhouse suggests the "fair creature" is the same woman Keats had seen at Vauxhall in 1814; see "Fill for me a brimming bowl," p. 4.

That I shall never look upon thee more,   10
Never have relish in the faery power
    Of unreflecting love;—then on the shore
Of the wide world I stand alone, and think
Till love and fame to nothingness do sink.

Song.[1]

1.

O BLUSH not so! O blush not so!
    Or I shall think you knowing;
And if you smile the blushing while,
    Then maidenheads are going.

2.

There's a blush for won't,[2] and a blush for shan't,   5
    And a blush for having done it;
There's a blush for thought and a blush for nought,[3]
    And a blush for just begun it.

3.

O sigh not so! O sigh not so!
    For it sounds of Eve's sweet pippin;[4]   10
By those loosen'd hips,[5] you have tasted the pips,
    And fought in an amorous nipping.

4.

Will you play once more at nice cut-core,
    For it only will last our youth out;
And we have the prime of the kissing time,   15
    We have not one sweet tooth out.

5.

There's a sigh for yes, and a sigh for no,
    And a sigh for I can't bear it!
O what can be done? Shall we stay or run?
    O cut the sweet apple and share it!   20

1. Written on January 31, 1818, in a letter to Reynolds, this "song" (as Brown labels it in his transcript) has been compared to Elizabethan songs and was objected to by Swinburne as a "short bawdy song which was unfit for publication" (*The Swinburne Letters*, ed. Cecil Y. Lang, 6 vols. [New Haven: Yale University Press, 1959], 2: 113). It was first published in Forman's 1883 edition, 2: 279–80, as "Sharing Eve's Apple" and with this note: "This song, belonging to the year 1818, has not, I believe, been published till now. . . . notwithstanding the brilliant qualities of some of the stanzas, I should have hesitated to be instrumental in adding it to the poet's published works, had it not been handed about in manuscript and more than once copied." Text from 1883 with emendations from Brown's transcript (Harvard MS Keats 3.6, p. 6; *MYR: JK*, 7:8) and some variants from the transcript of the January 31, 1818, letter to Reynolds in Woodhouse's letter-book, pp. 53–55, indicated in the notes.
2. The transcript has "want."
3. The transcript has "naught" with thus a suggestion of "naughty."
4. Apple; "pips" are small seeds.
5. 1883 seems to bowdlerize this to "lips"; "hips" from Brown's transcript.

[Hence Burgundy, Claret, and Port][1]

Hence Burgundy, Claret, and Port,
　　Away with old Hock and Madeira,
Too earthly[2] ye are for my sport;
　　There's a beverage brighter and clearer.
Instead of a pitiful rummer,[3]   5
My wine overbrims a whole summer;
　　My bowl is the sky,
　　And I drink at my eye,
　　Till I feel in the brain
　　A delphian[4] pain—   10
Then follow, my Caius![5] then follow:
　　On the green of the hill
　　We will drink our fill
　　Of golden sunshine,
Till our brains intertwine   15
With the glory and grace of Apollo!

[God of the Meridian][1]

God of the Meridian,[2]
　　And of the East and West,
To thee my soul is flown,
　　And my body is earthward press'd.—
It is an awful mission,   5
A terrible division;
And leaves a gulf austere
To be filled with worldly fear.[3]
Aye, when the soul is fled
To[4] high above our head,   10
Affrighted do we gaze
After its airy maze—
As doth a mother wild
When her young infant child
Is in an eagle's claws—   15
And is not this the cause
Of madness?—God of Song,

1. Written on January 31, 1818, in a letter to Reynolds (*L*, 1: 219–22). First published as part of this letter in 1848, 1: 81–82, though Milnes runs this and the next poem together; text from 1848 with emendations from the transcript in Woodhouse's letter-book, p. 54; in Brown's transcript (Harvard MS Keats 3.6, p. 5; *MYR: JK*, 7: 7), it is labeled a "song."
2. The transcript has "couthly."
3. "A kind of large drinking-glass" (*OED*).
4. From Apollo's oracle at Delphi: poetic.
5. Reynolds used "Caius" as a pseudonym in John Hunt's *Yellow Dwarf*.

1. Written on January 31, 1818, in the same letter as the last piece, this poem is sometimes printed as a continuation of the last, but a break in Keats's letter and metrical differences suggest they are two different pieces. First published as part of the letter to Reynolds in 1848, 1: 82–83; text from 1848 with emendations from the transcript in Woodhouse's letter-book, p. 54.
2. Apollo, god of song in l. 17, and here god of the sun at noonday.
3. See similar accounts of a visionary moment resulting in a diminishment of earthly experience in "Sleep and Poetry," ll. 125–62 (pp. 61–62) and the verse epistle to Reynolds, ll. 67–106 (p. 135–36).
4. Stillinger changes to "Too"; Charlotte Reynolds's transcript (Reynolds-Hood Commonplace Book, Bristol Central Library, f. 25a) has "So."

> Thou bearest me along
> Through sights I scarce can bear:
> O let me, let me share   20
> With the hot lyre and thee
> The staid Philosophy.
> Temper my lonely hours
> And let me see thy bow'rs
> More unalarm'd![5]   25

Letter to J. H. Reynolds, February 3, 1818[1]

Hampstead Tuesday.

My dear Reynolds,

I thank you for your dish of Filberts—Would I could get a basket of them by way of desert every day for the sum of two pence—Would we were a sort of ethereal Pigs, & turn'd loose to feed upon spiritual Mast[2] & Acorns—which would be merely being a squirrel & feed upon filberts. For what is a squirrel but an airy pig, or a filbert but a sort of archangelical acorn. About the nuts being worth cracking, all I can say is that where there are a throng of delightful Images ready drawn simplicity is the only thing. The first is the best on account of the first line, and the "arrow-foil'd of its antler'd food"— and moreover (and this is the only word or two I find fault with, the more because I have had so much reason to shun it as a quicksand) the last has "tender and true"[3]—We must cut this, and not be rattlesnaked into any more of the like. It may be said that we ought to read our Contemporaries, that Wordsworth &c should have their due from us. But for the sake of a few fine imaginative or domestic passages, are we to be bullied into a certain Philosophy engendered in the whims of an Egotist.[4] Every man has his speculations, but every man does not brood and peacock over them till he makes a false coinage and deceives himself—Many a man can travel to the very bourne of Heaven, and yet want confidence to put down his halfseeing. Sancho[5] will invent a Journey heavenward as well as any body. We hate poetry that has a palpable design upon us—and if we do not agree, seems to put its hand in its breeches pocket. Poetry should be great & unobtrusive, a thing which enters into one's soul, and does not startle it or amaze it with itself but with its subject.—How beautiful are the retired flowers! how would they lose

---

5. Cook suggests an echo of Wordsworth's claim that he can "pass . . . unalarmed" heaven and hell to explore the mind of man; see "Prospectus" to *The Recluse*, l. 35, published with *The Excursion* (1814). Woodhouse's W[2] transcript includes a series of x's, after "unalarm'd," perhaps indicating that the poem is a fragment.

1. This letter was written after Keats received (by the two-penny post, as he notes) two sonnets (the "dish of filberts" or hazelnuts) by Reynolds on Robin Hood, "The trees in Sherwood forest are old and good" and "With coat of Lincoln green and mantle too," which were later printed in John Hunt's *Yellow Dwarf*, February 21, 1818, p. 64 and then in Reynolds's *The Garden of Florence* (1821), pp. 124–127. Keats responds at the end of the letter with two poems of his own (though Woodhouse's clerk did not copy them), "Robin Hood" and "Lines on the Mermaid Tavern," published in his 1820 volume (see p. 469–71 below). Text from Woodhouse's letter-book, pp. 28–30.

2. Pig fodder made from the fruit of the oak, beech, and other trees.

3. Keats cites l. 5 of Reynolds's first sonnet, "No arrow found,—foil'd of its antler'd food"; he criticizes l. 8 of the second, which Reynolds emended to "young as the dew."

4. Keats echoes the sentiments of Hazlitt's review of *The Excursion* in the *Examiner*, August 21 and 28, 1814, where he attacks Wordsworth's "intense intellectual egotism" that "swallows up every thing" and refuses to "share the palm with his subject."

5. Sancho Panza, Don Quixote's squire in Cervantes' novel (1605, 1615), imagines a heavenly voyage after being tricked to ride on a wooden horse, Clavileno (Part 2, Chapter 41). The phrase "the very bourne of heaven" is from Keats's stanzaic hymn to Pan in *Endymion* 1:295.

their beauty were they to throng into the highway crying out, "admire me I am a violet! dote upon me I am a primrose!" Modern poets differ from the Elizabethans in this. Each of the moderns like an Elector of Hanover[6] governs his petty state, & knows how many straws are swept daily from the Causeways in all his dominions & has a continual itching that all the Housewives should have their coppers well scoured: the antients were Emperors of vast Provinces, they had only heard of the remote ones and scarcely cared to visit them.—I will cut all this—I will have no more of Wordsworth or Hunt in particular—Why should we be of the tribe of Manasseh, when we can wander with Esau?[7] why should we kick against the Pricks,[8] when we can walk on Roses? Why should we be owls, when we can be Eagles? Why be teased with "nice Eyed wagtails," when we have in sight "the Cherub Contemplation"?[9]—Why with Wordsworths "Matthew with a bough of wilding in his hand" when we can have Jacques "under an oak &c"[1]—The secret of the Bough of Wilding will run through your head faster than I can write it—Old Matthew spoke to him some years ago on some nothing, & because he happens in an Evening Walk to imagine the figure of the old man—he must stamp it down in black & white, and it is henceforth sacred—I don't mean to deny Wordsworth's grandeur & Hunt's merit, but I mean to say we need not be teazed with grandeur & merit—when we can have them uncontaminated & unobtrusive. Let us have the old Poets, & robin Hood.[2] Your letter and its sonnets gave me more pleasure than will the 4th Book of Childe Harold[3] & the whole of any body's life & opinions. In return for your dish of filberts, I have gathered a few Catkins,[4] I hope they'll look pretty.

To J. H. R. In answer to his Robin Hood Sonnets.

"No those days are gone away &c"—

I hope you will like them they are at least written in the Spirit of Outlawry.—Here are the Mermaid lines

"Souls of Poets dead & gone, &c"—[5]

I will call on you at 4 tomorrow, and we will trudge together for it is not the thing to be a stranger in the Land of Harpsicols.[6] I hope also to bring you

---

6. The Electorate of Hanover, the popular name for the Electorate of Brunswick-Lüneburg, was a principality within the Holy Roman Empire, with the duke serving as an elector who with other princes "elected" the emperor; in 1714, the Hanoverian electors became kings of England, creating the Hanoverian dynasty of which George III was a member.
7. The oldest son of Isaac and Rebekah and a hunter. *Manasseh:* a tribe descended from Joseph and referred to as a "half-tribe" in Joshua, i.e., 13.8; later conquered by the Assyrians and exiled.
8. See Acts 9.5, 26.14.
9. Keats opposes a phrase from Hunt's "The Nymphs," 2.169, with one from Milton's "Il Penseroso," l. 54.
1. Keats places a phrase from Wordsworth's "Two April Mornings," l. 59–60, against one from Shakespeare's *As You Like It*, 2.1.31.
2. Legendary medieval outlaw who robbed from the rich to give to the poor, and who became a popular figure in romantic literature after the antiquarian Joseph Ritson (1752–1803) published his edition of Robin Hood ballads in 1795.
3. The fourth canto of Byron's poem was published in April 1818.
4. A plant with a long, spiky arrangement of flowers and leaves (as in willows), looking something like a cat's tail.
5. The clerk copied only the first lines of the poems (see pp. 469–71) and provided a reference to W².
6. For harpsichord; apparently, Keats and Reynolds were to have a musical evening, perhaps at Vincent Novello's.

my 2ᵈ book[7]—In the hope that these Scribblings will be some amusement for you this Evening—I remain copying on the Hill

Yʳ sincere friend and Coscribbler
John Keats.

FRAGMENT.[1]

"Under the flag
Of each his faction, they to battle bring
Their embryo atoms."
MILTON.[2]

Welcome joy, and welcome sorrow,
    Lethe's weed, and Hermes' feather;[3]
Come to-day, and come to-morrow,
    I do love you both together!—
I love to mark sad faces in fair weather,   5
And hear a merry laugh amid the thunder;
    Fair and foul I love together:
Meadows sweet where flames burn[4] under,
And a giggle at a wonder;
Visage sage at pantomime;   10
Funeral and steeple-chime;
Infant playing with a skull;
Morning fair and shipwreck'd[5] hull;
Nightshade with the woodbine kissing;[6]
Serpents in red roses hissing;   15
Cleopatra regal-dress'd
With the aspics at her breast;[7]
Dancing music, music sad,
Both together, sane and mad;
Muses bright, and Muses pale;   20
Sombre Saturn, Momus[8] hale;—
Laugh and sigh; and laugh again;
Oh the sweetness of the pain!

7. Of *Endymion*, which he was revising.
1. Written in 1818, according to Allott probably in October in part because of similarities to Keats's letter to Woodhouse of October 27, 1818 (see below, p. 295). First printed in 1848, 1: 285–86; text from 1848 with emendations from the Withey MS (now at Princeton University Library, Robert H. Taylor Collection, RTC01, Box K) and a variant noted from Brown's transcript (Harvard MS Keats 3.6, p. 52; *MYR: JK*, 7: 54–55).
2. Misquotation of Milton's *Paradise Lost* 2. 898–301: "For hot, cold, moist, and dry, four Champions fierce / Strive here for Maistrie, and to Battel bring / Their embryon Atoms; they around the flag / Of each his faction"; the passage is marked in Keats's copy of Milton at Keats House (LMA K/BK/01/014/127). The poem also seems to recall the paired exploration of joy and sorrow in Milton's "L'Allegro" and "Il Penseroso."
3. Also known as Mercury, Hermes is the messenger of the gods; he has winged feet. Lethe: a river in the classical underworld that brings forgetfulness to those who drink from it.
4. 1848 has "are."
5. Brown's transcript has "storm-wreck'd."
6. The poisonous deadly nightshade or belladonna, and the honeysuckle.
7. For Cleopatra's suicide by applying a poisonous asp to her breast, see Shakespeare, *Antony and Cleopatra*, 5.2.
8. The classical god of merriment who satirizes the other gods. *Saturn*: the leader of the Titans overthrown by the Olympians, as in Keats's *Hyperion*.

Muses bright, and Muses pale,
Bare your faces of the veil;   25
Let me see, and let me write
Of the day, and of the night—
Both together:—let me slake
All my thirst for sweet heart-ache!
Let my bower be of yew,   30
Interwreath'd with myrtles new;
Pines and lime-trees full in bloom,
And my couch a low grass tomb.[9]

SONNET.[1]

LIFE'S[2] sea hath been five times at its slow ebb,
    Long hours have to and fro let creep the sand,
Since I was tangled in thy beauty's web,
    And snared by the ungloving of thy hand.
And yet I never look on midnight sky,   5
    But I behold thine eyes' well-memoried light;
I never gaze[3] upon the rose's dye,
    But to thy cheek my soul doth take its flight.
I never gaze on any budding flower,
    But my fond ear, in fancy at thy lips   10
And hearkening for a love sound, doth devour
    Its sweets in the wrong sense;—thou dost eclipse
Other delights with thy remembering,
And sorrow to my darling joys dost bring.[4]

SONNET.—TO THE NILE.[1]

Son of the old moon-mountains African![2]
Stream[3] of the Pyramid and Crocodile!

9. Perhaps an echo of *Hamlet* 4.5.31–32: "At his head a grass-green turf; / At his heels a stone." The yew tree was often planted in graveyards as a symbol of sadness. The myrtle was sacred to Venus and was an emblem of love; Keats may echo Milton's "Lycidas," l. 2: "myrtles brown." Pine trees and lime trees thrive in different climates.

1. Written on February 4, 1818, this is Keats's second Shakespearean sonnet. Woodhouse links this poem with "Fill for me a brimming bowl" and "When I have fears that I may cease to be" as he finds all three reflecting "the circumstance of obtaining a casual sight of [a lady] at Vauxhall" (W², f. 221v). First published in *Hood's Magazine* 2 (September 1844): 240 "By The Late John Keats"; text from *Hood's* (which Hood notes "was sent me, *copied*, from [Keats's lost] M.S." (*Letters of Thomas Hood*, ed. Peter F. Morgan [Toronto: University of Toronto Press, 1973], p. 652) with emendations to the punctuation from W² where it is entitled "To——" (f. 28r; *MYR: JK*, 6:33) and with some variants noted.

2. W² has "Time's sea hath been five years"; the image of passing time owes something both to Shakespeare's sonnets (see 60.1–2: "Like as the waves make towards the pebbled shore, / So do our minutes hasten to their end") and Wordsworth's "Tintern Abbey" (1798), ll. 1–3: "Five years have past . . . again I hear / These waters."

3. W² has "I cannot look" here and again in l. 7.

4. W² has "Every delight with sweet remembering, / And grief unto my darling joys dost bring."

1. A Petrarchan sonnet written on February 4, 1818, in a fifteen-minute sonnet contest with Shelley and Hunt (see p. 57, n. 1). First published in the *Plymouth and Devonport Weekly Journal*, July 19, 1838; text from *PDWJ* with emendations from Brown's transcript with Keats's corrections (Harvard MS Keats 3.6, p. 54; *MYR: JK*, 7: 56). Hunt's "The Nile" appeared in *Foliage* (1818), p. cxxxiv; Shelley's "To The Nile" appeared in *St. James Magazine* (1876).

2. The Mountains of the Moon stand at the source of the Nile.

3. *PDWJ* chooses the earlier variant "Stream," provided in a note to Brown's transcript, over the transcript's "Chief."

We call thee fruitful, and, that very while,
A desert fills our seeing's inward span;
Nurse of swart[4] nations since the world began,   5
Art thou so fruitful? or dost thou beguile
Such men to honour thee, who, worn with toil,
Rest them[5] a space 'twixt Cairo and Decan?[6]
O may dark fancies err!—they surely do;
'Tis ignorance that makes a barren waste   10
Of all beyond itself.[7] Thou dost bedew
Green rushes like our rivers, and dost taste
The pleasant sun-rise; green isles hast thou too,
And to the sea as happily dost haste.

[Spenser, a jealous honorer of thine][1]

Spenser, a jealous honorer of thine,
A forester[2] deep in thy midmost trees,
Did last eve ask my promise to refine
Some English that might strive thine ear to please.
But, Elfin-poet,[3] 'tis impossible   5
For an inhabitant of wintry earth
To rise, like Phœbus, with a golden quell,[4]
Fire-wing'd, and make a morning in his mirth.
It is impossible to escape[5] from toil
O' the sudden, and receive thy spiriting: 10
The flower must drink the nature of the soil
Before it can put forth its blossoming:
Be with me in the summer days, and I
Will for thine honor and his pleasure try.

4. Black, swarthy.
5. *PDWJ* adopts a penciled "them" (perhaps by Woodhouse) in Brown's transcript over the transcript's "for."
6. Keats suggests the course of an English traveler going to Alexandria, sailing up the Nile to Cairo, crossing the desert to Suez and the Rea Sea, and then sailing on to Deccan in India.
7. Cook cites Shakespeare, *Twelfth Night*, 4.2.40: "This house is as dark as ignorance." See also Shelley, "Mont Blanc" (1817), ll. 142–44: "And what were thou, and earth, and stars, and sea, / If to the human mind's imaginings / Silence and solitude were vacancy?"
1. Written on February 5, 1818, after a visit from Reynolds the day before. First published in 1848, 1: 11; text from 1848 with emendations from Keats's fair copy (Morgan MA 213; there is an earlier draft in Harvard's Dumbarton Oaks Research Library, Washington, D.C.).
2. Reynolds, who had recently sent Keats his Robin Hood sonnets. The Dumbarton Oaks draft originally had a "wanderer" in "midmost Wood," which might have been an allusion to Dante at the beginning of the *Inferno*.
3. Spenser as author of *The Faerie Queene*.
4. 1848 has "quill" but Keats uses "quell" as "a means to quell," here Phoebus Apollo's ability to quell or dispel the night with the fire of the morning sun.
5. 1848 has " 'scape," for the meter; the Dumbarton Oaks draft originally ended this line "leave this world."

ANSWER TO A SONNET ENDING THUS:—[1]

"Dark eyes are dearer far
Than those that mock the hyacinthine bell;"
                    By J. H. Reynolds
                    Feb. 1818

BLUE!—'Tis the life of heaven,—the domain
    Of Cynthia,[2]—the wide palace of the sun,—
The tent of Hesperus and all his train,[3]—
    The bosomer of clouds, gold, grey, and dun.
Blue!—'Tis the life of waters—Ocean,   5
    And all its vassal streams, pools numberless,
May rage, and foam, and fret, but never can
    Subside, if not to dark blue nativeness.
Blue!—Gentle cousin of[4] the forest green,
    Married to green in all the sweetest flowers—   10
Forget-me-not,—the blue-bell,—and, that queen
    Of secrecy, the violet:—what strange powers
Hast thou, as a mere shadow?—But how great,
When in an eye thou art alive with fate!

Letter to J. H. Reynolds, February 19, 1818[1]

My dear Reynolds,

I have an idea that a Man might pass a very pleasant life in this manner—
let him on any certain day read a certain Page of full Poesy or distilled Prose
and let him wander with it, and muse upon it, and reflect from it, and bring
home to it, and prophesy upon it, and dream upon it—until it becomes
stale—but when will it do so? Never. When Man has arrived at a certain
ripeness in intellect any one grand and spiritual passage serves him as a starting post towards all "the two-and thirty Pallaces."[2] How happy is such a voyage of conception! what delicious diligent Indolence! A doze upon a Sofa
does not hinder it, and a napp upon Clover engenders ethereal finger-
pointings—the prattle of a child gives it wings, and the converse of middle
age a strength to beat them—a strain of musick conducts to 'an odd angle of
the Isle'[3] and when the leaves whisper it puts a 'girdle round the earth.[4] Nor
will this sparing touch of noble Books be any irreverance to their Writers—
for perhaps the honors paid by Man to Man are trifles in comparison to the

---

1. Written on February 8, 1818, in response to a sonnet by Reynolds. Reynolds's sonnet, "Sweet poets
   of the gentle antique line," was published in his *Garden of Florence*, pp. 128–29. A note in W[2]
   states that "The preference expressed in the last 2 lines—of Dark eyes to blue—excited poetic
   indignation in [Keats]—who on the opposite page in the collection [of poems by Reynolds, Keats,
   and others], entered his energetic protest against this opinion." First published as Sonnet IX in
   1848, 2: 295; text from 1848 with a correction from the errata and emendations from W[2], f. 23r
   (*MYR: JK*, 6: 23). 1848 misreads "orbs" in Reynolds's second line as "those."
2. See p. 25, n. 1.
3. Hesperus, the evening star, is followed by all the other stars.
4. W[2] has "to."
1. Text from ALS, Robert H. Taylor Collection, Manuscript Division, Department of Rare Books and
   Special Collections, Princeton University Library (RTC01, 10/#24).
2. Keats might be referring to the "two and thirty palaces" of delight in Buddhism, but it is not clear
   how much he would have known about Buddhism.
3. Shakespeare, *The Tempest*, 1.2.224.
4. See Puck's claim in Shakespeare, *A Midsummer Night's Dream*, 2.1.175.

Benefit done by great Works to the 'Spirit and pulse of good'[5] by their mere passive existence. Memory should not be called Knowledge. Many have original Minds who do not think it—they are led away by Custom. Now it appears to me that almost any Man may like the Spider spin from his own inwards his own airy Citadel—the points of leaves and twigs on which the Spider begins her work are few and she fills the Air with a beautiful circuiting: man should be content with as few points to tip with the fine Webb of his Soul and weave a tapestry empyrean[6]—full of Symbols for his spiritual eye, of softness for his spiritual touch, of space for his wandering, of distinctness for his Luxury. But the Minds of Mortals are so different and bent on such diverse Journeys that it may at first appear impossible for any common taste and fellowship to exist between two or three under these suppositions. It is however quite the contrary. Minds would leave each other in contrary directions, traverse each other in Numberless points, and all last greet each other at the Journeys end. A old Man and a child would talk together and the old Man be led on his Path, and the child left thinking—Man should not dispute or assert but whisper results to his neighbour, and thus by every germ of Spirit sucking the Sap from mould ethereal every human might become great, and Humanity instead of being a wide heath of Furse and Briars with here and there a remote Oak or Pine, would become a grand democracy of Forest Trees. It has been an old Comparison for our urging on—the Bee hive—however it seems to me that we should rather be the flower than the Bee—for it is a false notion that more is gained by receiving than giving[7]—no the receiver and the giver are equal in their benefits. The flower I doubt not receives a fair guerdon[8] from the Bee—its leaves blush deeper in the next spring—and who shall say between Man and Woman which is the most delighted? Now it is more noble to sit like Jove than to fly like Mercury[9]—let us not therefore go hurrying about and collecting honey-bee like, buzzing here and there impatiently from a knowledge of what is to be arrived at: but let us open our leaves like a flower and be passive and receptive—budding patiently under the eye of Apollo[1] and taking hints from evey noble insect that favors us with a visit—sap will be given us for Meat and dew for drink. I was led into these thoughts, my dear Reynolds, by the beauty of the morning operating on a sense of Idleness—I have not read any Books—the Morning said I was right—I had no Idea but of the Morning and the Thrush said I was right—seeming to say—

[A draft of "O thou whose face hath felt the Winter's wind" follows.][2]

Now I am sensible all this is a mere sophistication, however it may neighbour to any truths, to excuse my own indolence—so I will not deceive myself that Man should be equal with jove—but think himself very well off as a sort of scullion-Mercury[3] or even a humble Bee. It is not matter whether I am right or wrong either one way or another, if there is sufficient to lift a little time from your Shoulders.   Your affectionate friend

John Keats—

5. Wordsworth, "Old Cumberland Beggar" (1800), l. 77.
6. "Of or pertaining to the sphere of fire or highest heaven" (OED).
7. Rollins cites Acts 20.35.
8. Reward.
9. Messenger of Jove or Jupiter, king of the gods. Jupiter debated with his wife, Juno, over the question of whether men or women took greater pleasure in sex.
1. For Apollo, see p. 6, n. 1. In this passage, Keats may be thinking of Wordsworth's idea of "wise passiveness" in "Expostulation and Reply" (1798), l. 24.
2. See, below, p. 128.
3. A scullion is a kitchen helper.

[O thou whose face hath felt the Winter's wind][1]

O thou whose face hath felt the Winter's wind,
Whose eye hath seen the snow clouds hung in mist,
And the black-elm tops 'mong the freezing stars:
To thee the Spring will be a harvest-time.
O thou whose only book has been the light   5
Of supreme darkness which thou feddest on
Night after night, when Phœbus[2] was away,
To thee the Spring shall be a triple morn.
O fret not after knowledge—I have none,
And yet my song comes native with the warmth.   10
O fret not after knowledge—I have none,
And yet the Evening listens. He who saddens
At thought of idleness cannot be idle,
And he's awake who thinks himself asleep.

Letter to John Taylor, February 27, 1818[1]

Hampstead 27 Feby—

My dear Taylor,

Your alteration strikes me as being a great improvement—the page looks much better. And now I will attend to the Punctuations you speak of—the comma should be at *soberly*, and in the other passage the comma should follow *quiet*,.[2] I am extremely indebted to you for this attention and also for your after admonitions. It is a sorry thing for me that any one should have to overcome Prejudices in reading my Verses—that affects me more than any hypercriticism on any particular Passage. In *Endymion* I have most likely but moved into the Go-cart from the leading strings.[3] In Poetry I have a few Axioms, and you will see how far I am from their Centre. 1st I think Poetry should surprise by a fine excess and not by Singularity—it should strike the Reader as a wording of his own highest thoughts, and appear almost a Remembrance—2nd Its touches of Beauty should never be half way therby making the reader breathless instead of content: the rise, the progress, the setting of imagery should like the Sun come natural natural too him—shine over him and set soberly although in magnificence leaving him in the Luxury of twilight—but it is easier to think what Poetry should be than to write it—and this leads me on to another axiom. That if Poetry comes not as naturally as the Leaves to a tree it had better not come at all. However it may be with me I cannot help looking into new countries with 'O for a Muse of fire to ascend!'[4]—If Endymion serves me as a Pioneer per-

---

1. Written on Feburary 19, 1818, as part of the previous letter. First printed as part of that letter in 1848, 1: 90; text from 1848 with emendations from the holograph letter, Robert H. Taylor Collection, Manuscripts Division, Department of Rare Books and Special Collections, Princeton University Library (RTC01, 10/#24).
2. Phœbus Apollo as the sun.
1. In this letter, written as he revised *Endymion*, Keats sets forth his axioms for poetry. Text from ALS (Morgan Library MA 828); there is also a transcript in Woodhouse's letter-book, pp. 4–5.
2. See *Endymion*, 1.149, 247.
3. That is, he has developed from relying on strings, "with which children used to be guided and supported when learning to walk," to using a "light frame-work, without bottom, moving on castors or rollers, in which a child may learn to walk without danger of falling" (*OED*).
4. Shakespeare, *Henry V*, Prologue. 1–2: "O for a muse of fire, that would ascend / The brightest heaven of invention."

haps I ought to be content. I have great reason to be content, for thank God I can read and perhaps understand Shakspeare to his depths, and I have I am sure many friends, who, if I fail, will attribute any change in my Life and Temper to Humbleness rather than to Pride—to a cowering under the Wings of great Poets rather than to a Bitterness that I am not appreciated. I am anxious to get Endymion printed that I may forget it and proceed. I have coppied the 3rd Book and have begun the 4th. On running my Eye over the Proofs—I saw one Mistake. I will notice it presently and also any others if there be any. There should be no comma in 'the raft branch down sweeping from a tall Ash top.'[5] I have besides made one or two alterations and also altered the 13 Line Page 32 to make sense of it as you will see. I will take care the Printer shall not trip up my Heels—There should be no dash after Dryope in the Line 'Dryope's lone lulling of her Child.[6] Remember me to Percy Street.[7]

Your sincere and obligd friend
John Keats—

P.S. You shall have a short *Preface* in good time—

Letter to Benjamin Bailey, March 13, 1818[1]

My dear Bailey,   Teignmouth Friday
    When a poor devil is drowning, it is said he comes thrice to the surface, ere he makes his final sink if however, even at the third rise, he can manage to catch hold of a piece of weed or rock, he stands a fair chance,—as I hope I do now, of being saved. I have sunk twice in our Correspondence, have risen twice and been too idle, or something worse, to extricate myself—I have sunk the third time and just now risen again at this two of the Clock P.M. and saved myself from utter perdition—by beginning this, all drench'd as I am and fresh from the Water—and I would rather endure the present inconvenience of a Wet Jacket, than you should keep a laced one in store for me. Why did I not stop at Oxford in my Way?—How can you ask such a Question? Why did I not promise to do so? Did I not in a Letter to you make a promise to do so? Then how can you be so unreasonable as to ask me why I did not? This is the thing—(for I have been rubbing up my invention; trying several sleights—I first polish'd a cold, felt it in my fingers tried it on the table, but could not pocket it: I tried Chilblains, Rheumatism, Gout,[2] tight Boots, nothing of that sort would do, so this is, as I was going to say, the thing.—I had a Letter from Tom saying how much better he had got, and thinking he had better stop—I went down to prevent his coming up—Will not this do? Turn it which way you like—it is salvaged all round—I have used it these three last days to keep out the abominable Devonshire Weather—by the by you may say what you will of devonshire: the truth is, it is a splashy, rainy, misty, snowy,

---

5. See *Endymion*, 1.334–35.
6. See *Endymion*, 1.495.
7. Home of De Wint and Hilton (see above, p. 141, n. 7).
1. Written after Keats left London to take care of his brother Tom in Devonshire and at the time he was completing the revisions of *Endymion*. Text from ALS (Harvard MS Keats 1.23); there is also a transcript in Woodhouse's letter-book, pp. 95–99.
2. A disease that causes inflammation of the joints, particularly in the feet. *Chilblains*: inflammations or sores of the hands or feet caused by exposure to the cold.

foggy, haily floody, muddy, slipshod County[3]—the hills are very beautiful, when you get a sight of 'em—the Primroses are out, but then you are in—the Cliffs are of a fine deep Colour; but then the Clouds are continually vieing with them—The Women like your London People in a sort of negative way—because the native men are the poorest creatures in England—because Government never have thought it worth while to send a recruiting party among them. When I think of Wordsworth's Sonnet 'Vanguard of Liberty! ye Men of Kent!' the degenerated race about me are Pulvis Ipecac. Simplex a strong dose[4]—Were I a Corsair I'd make a descent on the South Coast of Devon, if I did not run the chance of having Cowardice imputed to me: as for the Men they'd run away into the methodist meeting houses, and the Women would be glad of it—Had England been a large devonshire we should not have won the Battle of Waterloo—There are knotted oaks—there are lusty rivulets there are Meadows such as are not—there are vallies of feminine Climate—but there are no thews and Sinews[5]—Moor's Almanack[6] is here a curiosity—Arms Neck and shoulders may at least be seen there, and The Ladies read it as some out of the way romance—Such a quelling Power have these thoughts over me, that I fancy the very Air of a deteriorating quality—I fancy the flowers, all precocious, have an Acrasian[7] spell about them—I feel able to beat off the devonshire waves like soap froth—I think it well for the honor of Britain that Julius Cæsar did not first land in this County[8]—A Devonshirer standing on his native hills is not a distinct object—he does not show against the light—a wolf or two would dispossess him. I like, I love England, I like its strong Men—Give me a "long brown plain" for my Morning so I may meet with some of Edmond Iron side's desendants[9]—Give me a barren mould so I may meet with some shadowing of Alfred in the shape of a Gipsey, a Huntsman or as Shepherd.[1] Scenery is fine—but human nature is finer—The Sward is richer for the tread of a real, nervous, english foot—the eagles nest is finer for the Mountaineer has look'd into it—Are these facts or prejudices? Whatever they are, for them I shall never be able to relish entirely any devonshire scenery—Homer is very fine, Achilles is fine, Diomed is fine, Shakspeare is fine, Hamlet is fine, Lear is fine, but dwindled englishmen are not fine—Where too the Women are so passable, and have such english names, such as Ophelia, Cordelia &—that they should have such Paramours or rather Imparamours[2]—As for them I cannot, in thought help wishing as did the cruel Emperour, that they had but one head and I might cut it off to deliver them from any horrible Courtesy they may do their undeserving Countrymen[3]—I wonder I meet with no

3. Keats had left London on March 4 to prevent Tom from ending his convalescence to return to the capital; while traveling through Exeter, Keats was soaked by a violent storm.
4. "Pure powder of Ipecacuanha," a South American plant used as an emetic. Keats quotes the first line of Wordsworth's "To the Men of Kent. October 1803" (1807), a patriotic call to arms following the failure of the Peace of Amiens. He is saying the "degenerated" men of Devon nauseate him.
5. The phrase "thewes and sinews" is used in Scott's *Rob Roy* (1818); "thews" refer to the "bodily powers or forces of a man" and in "modern use after Scott" to "muscular development, associated with *sinews*, and hence materialized as if=muscles or tendons" (*OED*).
6. Francis Moore (1657–1715?) first issued his almanac in 1699.
7. Acrasia is the enchantress who creates the deceptive Bowre of Blisse in Spenser's *Faerie Queene*.
8. Julius Caesar (100?–44 B.C.E.) invaded Britain via Kent in 55 and again in 54 B.C.E.
9. Edmund Ironside (d. 1016) was king of the English (1016) in their war against Canute and the Danes. "*long brown plain*": Keats quotes from Chatterton's *Battle of Hastings*, 2: 544.
1. For Alfred the Great, see p. 42, n. 3. To keep the parallel, "barren mould" would seem to be a quotation, with a not very likely source being Sir Arthur Gorges's translation of Lucan's *Pharsalia* (1614), 3:431.
2. A Keatsian neologism.
3. Keats alludes to a story about the Roman emperor Caligula (12–41 C.E.), which he could have read in the *Spectator* 16 (March 19, 1711), 246 (December 12, 1711), and 435 (July 19, 1712).

born Monsters—O Devonshire, last night I thought the Moon had dwindled in heaven—I have never had your Sermon[4] from Wordsworth but M[rs] Dilke lent it me—You know my ideas about Religion—I do not think myself more in the right than other people and that nothing in this world is proveable. I wish I could enter into all your feelings on the subject merely for one short 10 Minutes and give you a Page or two to your liking. I am sometimes so very sceptical as to think Poetry itself a mere Jack a lanthern to amuse whoever may chance to be struck with its brilliance. As Tradesmen say every thing is worth what it will fetch, so probably every mental pursuit takes its reality and worth from the ardour of the pursuer—being in itself a nothing—Ethereal thing may at least be thus real, divided under three heads—Things real—things semireal—and no things—Things real—such as existences of Sun Moon & Stars and passages of Shakspeare—Things semireal such as Love, the Clouds &c which require a greeting of the Spirit to make them wholly exist—and Nothings which are made Great and dignified by an ardent pursuit— Which by the by stamps the burgundy mark on the bottles of our Minds, insomuch as they are able to "*consecrate whate'er they look upon.*"[5] I have written a Sonnet here of a somewhat collateral nature—so don't imagine it an a propos des bottes.[6]

> Four Seasons fill the Measure of the year;
>   Four Seasons are there in the mind of Man.
> He hath his lusty spring when fancy clear
>   Takes in all beauty with an easy span:
> He hath his Summer, when luxuriously
>   He chews the honied cud of fair spring thoughts,
> Till, in his Soul dissolv'd they come to be
>   Part of himself. He hath his Autumn ports
> And Havens of repose, when his tired wings
>   Are folded up, and he content to look
> On Mists in idleness: to let fair things
>   Pass by unheeded as a threshold brook.
> He hath his Winter too of pale Misfeature,
> Or else he would forget his mortal nature.[7]

Aye this may be carried—but what am I talking of—it is an old maxim of mine and of course must be well known that every point of thought is the centre of an intellectual world—the two uppermost thoughts in a Man's mind are the two poles of his World—he revolves on them and every thing is southward or northward to him through their means—We take but three steps from feathers to iron. Now my dear fellow I must once for all tell you I have not one Idea of the truth of any of my speculations—I shall never be a Reasoner because I care not to be in the right, when retired from bickering and in a proper philosophical temper—So you must not stare if in any future letter I endeavour to prove that Apollo as he had a cat gut string to his Lyre used a cats' paw as a Pecten[8]—and further from said Pecten's reit-

4. See p. 115, n. 8.
5. Keats alludes to Shelley's "Hymn to Intellectual Beauty" (which he could have read in the *Examiner* for January 19, 1817): "Spirit of BEAUTY, that dost consecrate / With thine own hues all thou dost shine upon" (ll. 13–14).
6. About nothing.
7. For the print version of this poem, see p. 132.
8. For plectrum, used to pluck a stringed instrument.

erated and continual teasing came the term Hen peck'd. My Brother Tom desires to be remember'd to you—he has just this moment had a spitting of blood poor fellow—Remember me to Greig and Whitehed[9]—

Your affectionate friend
John Keats—

The Human Seasons.[1]

Four seasons fill the measure of the year;
   There are four seasons in the mind of man:
He has his lusty Spring, when fancy clear
   Takes in all beauty with an easy span:
He has his Summer, when luxuriously   5
   Spring's honied cud of youthful thought he loves
To ruminate, and by such dreaming nigh
   His[2] nearest unto heaven: quiet coves
His soul has in its Autumn, when his wings
   He furleth close; contented so to look   10
On mists in idleness—to let fair things
   Pass by unheeded as a threshold brook.
   He has his Winter too of pale misfeature,
   Or else he would forget[3] his mortal Nature.

[Where be ye going, you Devon maid][1]

1

Where be ye going, you Devon maid,
   And what have ye there i' the basket?
Ye tight little fairy—just fresh from the dairy,
   Will ye give me some cream if I ask it?

2

I love your meads, and I love your flowers,[2]   5
   And I love your junkets[3] mainly,
But 'hind the door, I love kissing more,
   O look not so disdainly![4]

9. For Whitehouse and Gleig, see p. 101, n. 1., p. 99, n. 5.
1. Written between Keats's arrival at Teignmouth on March 6 or 7 and when he included it in his letter to Bailey of March 13 (see p. 131 above). First published in Leigh Hunt's *Literary Pocket-Book for 1819* (1818), p. 225, over the initial "I" (for "Iohannes"?); text from the *Pocket-Book*; I have included the manuscript version in the letter above since it varies substantially from the print text.
2. Stillinger argues that "nigh / His" is an error for "high / Is."
3. Misprinted as "forge" but corrected in the Keats House copy of the *Pocket-Book* (LMA K/BK/01/016/115).
1. Written March 21, 1818, in a letter to Haydon along with "For there's Bishop's Teign," which Keats in the letter calls "doggrel," coining the word "Bitchrell" to describe the present poem (*L*, 1: 250). First published in Tom Taylor, *Life of Benjamin Robert Haydon* (1853), 1: 363–64; text from Taylor with emendations from the letter to Haydon (Harvard MS Keats 1.24).
2. Taylor reads "flowers" as "dales," probably from the next stanza.
3. A "dish consisting of curds sweetened and flavoured, served with a layer of scalded cream on the top. Popularly associated with Devonshire" (*OED*).
4. Taylor reads this as "divinely."

3

I love your hills, and I love your dales,
And I love your flocks a-bleating,   10
But oh, on the heather, to lie together,
With both our hearts a-beating.

4

I'll put your basket all safe in a *nook*,
And your shawl I hang up *on this willow*,[5]
And we will sigh in the daisy's eye,   15
And kiss on a grass green pillow.

[Dear Reynolds, as last night I lay in bed][1]

Dear Reynolds, as last night I lay in bed,
There came before my eyes that wonted thread
Of shapes, and shadows, and remembrances,
That every other minute vex and please:
Things all disjointed come from north and south,—   5
Two witch's eyes above a cherub's mouth,
Voltaire with casque and shield and habergeon,
And Alexander with his night-cap on;
Old Socrates a tying his cravat,
And Hazlitt playing with Miss Edgeworth's cat;   10
And Junius Brutus pretty well so so,
Making the best of 's way towards Soho.[2]

---

5. Taylor read this line as "Your shawl I'll hang on the willow"; Keats underlines the end of the line
   and "nook" in the line before, perhaps to suggest sexual connotations, with "to wear the willow"
   referring to being abandoned by a lover.
1. Written at Teignmouth and sent on March 25, 1818, to Reynolds who was ailing at the time; as
   Keats's prose, promised at the end of the poem, indicates, it was written "In hopes of cheering you
   through a Minute or two" (Woodhouse's letter-book, p. 74). Modern criticism of the poem, which
   mixes playfulness with an exploration of how a Keatsian poetic seeks a ground somewhere between
   the "Purgatory blind" (l. 80) of a wish-fulfilling imagination ungrounded in the material world and
   the "core / Of an eternal fierce destruction" (ll. 96–97) of an inhuman nature untouched by imaginative vision, begins with Stuart Sperry's essay, below, pp. 583–92; see also Scott, *The Sculpted Word*
   (1994), pp. 73–86. First published as part of a letter to Reynolds in 1848, 1: 113–16 without the final
   four lines; text from 1848 (with ll. 73, 90, 94 corrected in Milnes's 1867 *Life*) with emendations
   (since Milnes's copytext is not known) from W², fols. 65–68 (*MYR: JK*, 6: 107–113), where it is
   labeled "To J. H. Reynolds Esqʳ."
2. Keats offers a series of incongruities (perhaps, as Allott suggests, recalling Horace's *Ars Poetica*,
   ll. 1–5): the French philosopher François-Marie Arouet Voltaire (1694–1778), a leading figure of
   the Enlightenment and author of such works as *Lettres Philosophiques* (1733) and *Candide*
   (1759) and before whose portrait in Haydon's *Christ's Entry into Jerusalem* Keats bowed (Haydon,
   Diary, 2: 317), is imagined dressed as a warrior, including a harbegeon, a "sleeveless coat or jacket
   of mail or scale armour" (*OED*); the warrior Alexander the Great (356–323 B.C.E.) is seen in his
   nightclothes; the Greek philosopher Socrates (469–399 B.C.E.) is found dressing for a fashionable dinner; Keats's friend Hazlitt is depicted with the cat of novelist Maria Edgeworth
   (1767/8–1849), author of such works as *Castle Rackrent* (1800) and *Belinda* (1801) and criticized
   by Hazlitt in his *On The English Comic Writers* (1819) in *Works* 6: 123; and finally either Lucius
   Junius Brutus (fl. 520 B.C.E.), the morally upright founder of the Roman Republic, or the actor
   Junius Brutus Booth (1796–1852), whose arrival at Covent Garden in 1817 established him as
   Kean's rival (and whose son would assassinate Lincoln), is depicted as wandering towards Soho
   in London drunk ("so so").

Few are there who escape these visitings,—
P'rhaps one or two whose lives have patient[3] wings,
And thro' whose curtains peeps no hellish nose,   15
No wild-boar tushes,[4] and no Mermaid's toes;
But flowers bursting out with lusty pride,
And young Æolian harps[5] personified;
Some Titian[6] colours touch'd into real life.—
The sacrifice goes on; the pontif knife   20
Gleams[7] in the sun, the milk-white heifer lows,
The pipes go shrilly, the libation flows:[8]
A white sail shows above the green-head cliff,
Moves round the point, and throws her anchor stiff;
The mariners join hymn with those on land.   25

You know the Enchanted Castle,[9]—it doth stand
Upon a rock on the border of a lake
Nested in trees, which all do seem to shake
From some old magic like Urganda's Sword.[1]
O Phœbus![2] that I had thy sacred word   30
To show this Castle in fair dreaming wise
Unto my friend, while sick and ill he lies.

You know it well enough, where it doth seem
A mossy place, a Merlin's[3] Hall, a dream;
You know the clear lake, and the little Isles,   35
The mountains blue, and cold near neighbour rills,
All which elsewhere are but half animate;
Here do they look alive to love and hate,
To smiles and frowns; they seem a lifted mound
Above some giant, pulsing underground.   40

Part of the building was a chosen See,
Built by a banished santon of Chaldee;[4]

---

3. 1848 and W² have "patent" here; for the correction see S. R. Swaminathan, *N&Q*, August 1967: 306–307.
4. Archaic form of tusks.
5. See p. 7, n. 6.
6. Tiziano Vecellio (c. 1490–1576), Venetian painter known for his use of rich, vibrant colors and much admired by Hunt, Hazlitt, and Keats.
7. W² had "gloams," marked "so," to indicate that is what Keats wrote, but then corrected it to "gleams"; Cook argues for "gloams" as a Scots verb meaning "darkens."
8. Jack, pp. 127–31, suggests Keats is remembering Claude Lorrain's "Landscape with the Father of Psyche sacrificing at the Milesian Temple of Apollo," exhibited at the British Institution in 1816. The images also seem to echo the description of Francesca's retreat in Hunt's *Story of Rimini* (1816, 3: 456–85) and look forward to "Ode on a Grecian Urn" (pp. 461–62).
9. W² lacks the break at the beginning of the line, though Woodhouse has marked it in pencil. In his prose at the close of the poem, Keats writes, "You know, I am sure, Claude's Enchanted Castle, and I wish you may be pleased with my remembrance of it" (*L*, 1: 263); Keats would have known this painting from the 1782 engraving by William Woollett and François Vivares (see Jack, pp. 67–68, 127–30 for the interest of Keats and his friends in this painting).
1. Urganda the Unknown, the enchantress from the sixteenth-century romance *Amadis of Gaul*, abridged by Southey in 1803.
2. Apollo, here as the god of poetry.
3. The wizard in the cycle of stories around King Arthur.
4. A "santon" is an Islamic monk or hermit; Keats could have found mention of santons in Beckford's *Vathek* (1786) or Byron's *Childe Harold* 2:56. The allusion to the Chaldeans might recall Wordsworth's *Excursion* (1814) 4: 694 or Byron's *Childe Harold* 3: 91 where there are more serious exercises in comparative religion. *See*: the official seat or dwelling of the "santon." W² gives a canceled line here: "Poor Man he left the Terrace Walks of Ur."

The other part, two thousand years from him,
Was built by Cuthbert de Saint Aldebrim;[5]
Then there's a little wing, far from the Sun,   45
Built by a Lapland Witch[6] turn'd maudlin nun—
And many other juts of aged stone
Founded with many a mason-devil's[7] groan.

    The doors all look as if they oped themselves,
The windows as if latched by fays[8] and elves,   50
And from them comes a silver flash of light
As from the westward of a Summer's night;
Or like a beauteous woman's large blue eyes
Gone mad thro' olden songs and poesies.

    See what is coming from the distance dim!   55
A golden galley all in silken trim!
Three rows of oars are lightening moment-whiles
Into the verd'rous bosoms of those isles;
Towards the shade under the Castle wall
It comes in silence—now 'tis hidden all.   60
The clarion sounds, and from a postern grate[9]
An echo of sweet music doth create
A fear in the poor herdsman who doth bring
His beasts to trouble the enchanted spring:
He tells of the sweet music and the spot   65
To all his friends, and they believe him not.

    O, that our dreamings all of sleep or wake
Would all their colours from the sunset take:
From something of material sublime,[1]
Rather than shadow our own soul's day-time   70
In the dark void of night. For in the world
We jostle,—but my flag is not unfurl'd
On the Admiral-staff,[2]—and to philosophize
I dare not yet!—Oh, never will the prize,
High reason, and the lore[3] of good and ill,   75
Be my award. Things cannot to the will
Be settled, but they tease us out of thought;
Or is it that imagination brought

---

5. While there was a St. Cuthbert (635–687), this appears to be an invented name.
6. See Milton, *Paradise Lost* 2.664–65: "Lur'd with the smell of infant blood, to dance / With *Lapland* witches."
7. "Mason-devil" does not appear in the *OED*; a mason is a skilled worker in stone, so a "mason-devil" is probably an apprentice or aid to a stone-worker on analogy to the use of "printer's devil" to indicate a publisher's errand boy.
8. Fairies.
9. 1848 misreads/corrects this to "postern-gate," which would give us a back door, but the W² reading offers a "rear grate," a "framework of bars or laths, parallel to or crossing each other, fixed in a door, window, or other opening, to permit communication while preventing ingress" (*OED*).
1. Keats echoes Wordsworth, "Tintern Abbey," ll. 95–97, "a sense sublime / Of something far more deeply interfused, / Whose dwelling is the light of setting suns," and the "Intimations Ode," ll. 200–202, "The clouds that gather round the setting sun / Do take a sober colouring from an eye / That hath kept watch o'er man's mortality." There is disagreement over whether this should be read as "sublime material" or as a materialized sublime.
2. J. L. Lowes, "Moneta's Temple," *PMLA* 51 (1936): 1100, cites North's translation of Plutarch's *Lives* (1676), p. 178: "Alcidiades setting up a Flag in the top of his Admiral Galley, to show what he was."
3. 1848 has "love."

Beyond its proper bound, yet still confined,—
Lost in a sort of Purgatory blind,   80
Cannot refer to any standard law
Of either earth or heaven?—It is a flaw
In happiness to see beyond our bourn,—
It forces us in summer skies to mourn,
It spoils the singing of the Nightingale.[4]   85

Dear Reynolds! I have a mysterious tale
And cannot speak it. The first page I read
Upon a Lampit[5] rock of green sea-weed
Among the breakers; 'twas a quiet eve;
The rocks were silent—the wide sea did weave   90
An untumultuous fringe of silver foam
Along the flat brown sand. I was at home
And should have been most happy,—but I saw
Too far into the sea, where every maw
The greater on the less feeds evermore,—   95
But I saw too distinct into the core
Of an eternal fierce destruction,
And so from happiness I far was gone.
Still am I sick of it: and tho' to-day
I've gathered young spring-leaves, and flowers gay   100
Of periwinkle and wild strawberry,
Still do I that most fierce destruction see,—
The Shark at savage prey,—the hawk at pounce,—
The gentle Robin, like a pard or ounce,
Ravening a worm,[6]—Away, ye horrid moods,   105
Moods of one's mind![7] You know I hate them well,
You know I'd sooner be a clapping bell
To some Kamschatkan missionary church,[8]
Than with these horrid moods be left in lurch[9]—
Do you get health—and Tom the same—I'll dance,   110
And from detested moods in new romance[1]
Take refuge.—Of bad lines a centaine[2] dose
Is sure enough—and so "here follows prose."[3]—

---

4. Lines 76–85 look both back to Book 1: 294–95 ("solitary thinkings—such as dodge / Conception to the very bourne of heaven") of *Endymion*, which Keats had just finished, and forward to the "Ode to a Nightingale" and "Ode on a Grecian Urn," ll. 44–45 ("Thou, silent form, dost tease us out of thought / As doth eternity").
5. Scottish spelling of "limpet," a mollusk found on rocks.
6. See Shakespeare, *Pericles*, Scene 5, ll. 66–68: "I marvel how the fishes live in the sea . . . Why, as men do a-land—the great ones eat up the little ones." *pard*: a leopard; *ounce*: an ocelot.
7. Wordsworth entitled a gathering of thirteen pieces in his 1807 *Poems* as "Moods of my own mind."
8. A. D. Atkinson, *N&Q*, August 4 (1951): 343–45, points to Keats's readings in Buffon's *Histoire Naturelle* (English translation, 1792) and Robertson's *History of America* (1777) about the Kamschatka peninsula on the east coast of Russia on the Pacific Ocean and the Bering Sea, where there was a Christian mission.
9. 1848 concludes its text with "i' the lurch."
1. *Isabella*, on which Keats was currently working.
2. One hundred lines.
3. See Shakespeare, *Twelfth Night* 2.5.124: "Soft, here follows prose."

Letter to B. R. Haydon, April 8, 1818[1]

Wednesday—

My dear Haydon,

I am glad you were pleased with my nonsense[2] and if it so happen that the humour takes me when I have set down to prose to you I will not gainsay it. I should be (god forgive me) ready to swear because I cannot make use of your assistance in going through Devon if I was not in my own Mind determined to visit it thoroughly at some more favorable time of the year.[3] But now Tom (who is getting greatly better) is anxious to be in Town therefore I put off my threading the County. I purpose within a Month to put my knapsack at my back and make a pedestrian tour through the North of England, and part of Scotland[4]—to make a sort of Prologue to the Life I intend to pursue— that is to write, to study and to see all Europe at the lowest expence. I will clamber through the Clouds and exist. I will get such an accumulation of stupendous recollolections that as I walk through the suburbs of London I may not see them—I will stand upon Mount Blanc and remember this coming Summer when I intend to straddle ben Lomond[5]—with my Soul!— galligaskins[6] are out of the Question—I am nearer myself to hear your Christ[7] is being tinted into immortality—Believe me Haydon your picture is a part of myself—I have ever been too sensible of the labyrinthian path to eminence in Art (judging from Poetry) ever to think I understood the emphasis of Painting. The innumerable compositions and decompositions which take place between the intellect and its thousand materials before it arrives at that trembling delicate and snail-horn perception of Beauty[8]—I know not your many havens of intenseness—nor ever can know them—but for this I hope not you atchieve is lost upon me: for when a Schoolboy the abstract Idea I had of an heroic painting—was what I cannot describe I saw it somewhat sideways large prominent round and colour'd with magnificence—somewhat like the feel I have of Anthony and Cleopatra. Or of Alcibiades, leaning on his Crimson Couch in his Galley, his broad shoulders imperceptibly heaving with the Sea[9]—What passage in Shakspeare is finer than this

'See how the surly Warwick mans the Wall'[1]

I like your consignment of Corneille[2]—that's the humor of it—They shall be called your Posthumous Works. I don't understand your bit of Italian.[3]

1. Written in response to a letter from Haydon of March 25 (*L*, 1: 257–59). Text from ALS (Harvard MS Keats 1.26).
2. In his letter, Haydon had praised Keats's "bitcherell," "Where be ye going, you Devon Maid," that Keats had included in his letter of March 21.
3. In his letter, Haydon offered to make introductions for Keats in Plymouth and Bridgewater.
4. Tom insisted upon returning to London on May 4 or 5. Keats would voyage north with Brown in June.
5. Ben Lomond, or "Beacon Hill," towers over Loch Lomond and gives fine views of the southern Scottish highlands. *Mont Blanc*, celebrated by Wordsworth, Coleridge, and Shelley, is the highest point in the Alps.
6. Loose breeches.
7. Haydon's painting of *Christ's Entry into Jerusalem*.
8. See Hazlitt, "On Shakespeare and Milton," *Works*, 5: 51, "In Shakespeare there is a continual composition and decomposition [of character]"; for the snail image, see Shakespeare, "Venus and Adonis," ll. 1033–38.
9. For Keats's source in Plutarch, see p. 135, n. 2.
1. Shakespeare, 3 *Henry VI* (*The True Tragedy of Richard Duke of York and the Good King Henry the Sixth*), 5.1.17.
2. In his letter to Keats, Haydon attacked the great French dramatist Pierre Corneille (1606–1684), author of *Le Cid* among other works, as "a heartless tirade maker."
3. In his letter to Keats, Haydon had praised Mrs. John Scott "con occhi neri" ("with black eyes").

I hope she will awake from her dream and flourish fair—my respects to her. The Hedges by this time are beginning to leaf—Cats are becoming more vociferous—young Ladies that wear Watches are always looking at them—Women about forty five think the Season very back ward—Lady's Mares have but half an allowance of food—It rains here again, has been doing so for three days—however as I told you I'll take a trial in June July or August next year. I am afraid Wordsworth went rather huff 'd out of Town—I am sorry for it. He cannot expect his fireside Divan to be infallible he cannot expect but that every Man of worth is as proud as himself. O that he had not fit with a Warrener that is din'd at Kingston's.[4] I shall be in town in about a fortnight and then we will have a day or so now and then before I set out on my northern expedition—we will have no more abominable Rows[5]—for they leave one in a fearful silence having settled the Methodists let us be rational—not upon compulsion—no if it will out let it—but I will not play the Bassoon any more deliberately—Remember me to Hazlitt, and Bewick[6]—Your affectionate friend

John Keats—

Letter to J. H. Reynolds, April 9, 1818[1]

My Dear Reynolds.   Th^y Morn^g
Since you all agree that the thing[2] is bad, it must be so—though I am not aware there is any thing like Hunt in it, (and if there is, it is my natural way, and I have something in common with Hunt) look it over again and examine into the motives, the seeds from which any one sentence sprung—I have not the slightest feel of humility towards the Public—or to any thing in existence,—but the eternal Being, the Principle of Beauty,—and the Memory of great Men—When I am writing for myself for the mere sake of the Moment's enjoyment, perhaps nature has its course with me—but a Preface is written to the Public; a thing I cannot help looking upon as an Enemy, and which I cannot address without feelings of Hostility—If I write a Preface in a supple or subdued style, it will not be in character with me as a public speaker—I wo^d be subdued before my friends, and thank them for subduing me—but among Multitudes of Men—I have no feel of stooping, I hate the idea of humility to them—
I never wrote one single Line of Poetry with the least Shadow of public thought. Forgive me for vexing you and making a Trojan Horse of such a Trifle, both with respect to the matter in Question, and myself—but it eases me to tell you—I could not live without the love of my friends—I would jump down Ætna for any great Public good—but I hate a Mawkish Popularity.[3]—I cannot be subdued before them—My glory would be to daunt and dazzle the

---

4. Keats echoes Shakespeare's *Merry Wives of Windsor*, 1.4.23 ("He hath fought with a warrener [gamekeeper]"), in order to tweak the comptroller of stamps, and Wordsworth's boss, John Kingston (see p. 108, n. 7), whom Keats clearly disliked.
5. Apparently a double reference both to the fights going on in the circle (see above, pp. 115, 116) and to musical evenings in which the circle imitated various instruments such as the bassoon.
6. See p. 117, n. 9.
1. Written from Teignmouth. Text from Woodhouse's letter-book, pp. 58–60.
2. The initial preface to *Endymion* (see pp. 147–48).
3. Keats alludes to the pre-Socratic philosopher Empedocles (c. 495–435 B.C.E.), who according to legend hurled himself into the volcanic crater of Mount Aetna so that no one would know how he died and that he might then be taken for a god.

thousand jabberers about Pictures and Books—I see swarms of Porcupines with their Quills erect "like lime-twigs set to catch my Winged Book"[4] and I would fright 'em away with a torch—You will say my preface is not much of a Torch. It would have been too insulting "to begin from Jove" and I could not set a golden head upon a thing of clay[5]—if there is any fault in the preface it is not affectation: but an undersong of disrespect to the Public.—If I write another preface, it must be done without a thought of those people—I will think about it. If it should not reach you in four—or five days—tell Taylor to publish it without a preface, and let the dedication simply stand "inscribed to the memory of Thomas Chatterton." I had resolved last night to write to you this morning—I wish it had been about something else—something to greet you towards the close of your long illness—I have had one or two intimations of your going to Hampstead for a space; and I regret to see your confounded Rheumatism keeps you in Little Britain where I am sure the air is too confined—Devonshire continues rainy. As the drops beat against the window, they give me the same sensation as a quart of cold water offered to revive a half drowned devil—No feel of the clouds dropping fatness; but as if the roots of the Earth were rotten cold and drench'd—I have not been able to go to Kents' Cave at Babbicun[6]—however on one very beautiful day I had a fine Clamber over the rocks all along as far as that place: I shall be in Town in about Ten days.—We go by way of Bath on purpose to call on Bailey. I hope soon to be writing to you about the things of the north, purposing to wayfare all over those parts.[7] I have settled my accoutrements in my own mind, and will go to gorge wonders: However we'll have some days together before I set out—

I have many reasons for going wonder-ways: to make my winter[8] chair free from spleen—to enlarge my vision—to escape disquisitions on Poetry and Kingston Criticism.[9]—to promote digestion and economise shoe leather—I'll have leather buttons and belt; and if Brown holds his mind, over the Hills we go.—If my Books will help me to it,—thus will I take all Europe in turn, and see the Kingdoms of the Earth and the glory of them—Tom is getting better he hopes you may meet him at the top o' the hill—My Love to your nurses.[1] I am ever

Your affectionate Friend,
John Keats.

4. See Cardinal Beaufort's mad speech in Shakespeare, 2 Henry VI (The First Part of the Contention of the Two Famous Houses of York and Lancaster), 3.3.16, "Like lime twigs set to catch my wingèd soul," with the twigs smeared with birdlime, a sticky substance used to trap birds.
5. Allusion to Robert Herrick's "Evensong" which opens his Hesperides (1648): "Beginne with Jove; then is the worke halfe done; / And runnes most smoothly, when tis well begunne" (ll. 1–2); Keats also draws upon the image of the figure with a golden head and feet of clay in Daniel 2.
6. Kents Cavern, in Babbacombe, Torquay, is a stalactite cavern in which important discoveries were made of bones and flint implements.
7. See p. 137, n. 4, for Keats's plan to travel to Scotland.
8. This word is hard to read in the transcript and might be "writer."
9. For Kingston, see p. 108, n. 7.
1. Reynolds's sisters.

To J. R.[1]

O THAT a week could be an age, and we
    Felt parting and warm meeting every week,
Then one poor year a thousand years would be,
    The flush of welcome ever on the cheek.
So could we live long life in little space,   5
    So time itself would be annihilate,
So a day's journey in oblivious haze
    To serve our joys would lengthen and dilate.
O to arrive each Monday morn from Ind![2]
    To land each Tuesday from the rich Levant,[3]   10
In little time a host of joys to bind,
    And keep our souls in one eternal pant!
This morn, my friend, and yester-evening taught
Me how to harbour such a happy thought.[4]

Letter to John Taylor, April 24, 1818[1]

Teignmouth Friday

My dear Taylor,

I think I Did very wrong to leave you to all the trouble of Endymion—
but I could not help it then—another time I shall be more bent to all sort
of troubles and disagreeables. Young Men for some time have an idea that
such a thing as happiness is to be had and therefore are extremely impatient under any unpleasant restraining—in time however, of such stuff is
the world about them, they know better and instead of striving from
Uneasiness greet it as an habitual sensation, a pannier[2] which is to weigh
upon them through life.

And in proportion to my disgust at the task is my sense of your kindness
& anxiety—the book pleased me much—it is very free from faults; and
although there are one or two words I should wish replaced, I see in many
places an improvement greatly to the purpose—

I think those speeches which are related—those parts where the speaker
repeats a speech—such as Glaucus' repetition of Circe's words,[3] should
have inverted commas to every line. In this there is a little confusion. If we
divide the speeches into *identical* and *related*: and to the former put merely
one inverted comma at the beginning and another at the end; and to the
latter inverted commas before every line, the book will be better understood
at the first glance. Look at pages 126 and 127 you will find in the 3 line the

---

1. A Shakespearean sonnet written perhaps in April 1818 when, many argue, James Rice (J.R.) was
visiting Keats at Teignmouth and presented him with a copy of the Spanish romance *Guzman D'Al-
farache* (1634). First published in 1848, 2: 296, as Sonnet X and mistakenly entitled "To J. H.
Reynolds"; text from 1848 with emendations from Keats's holograph draft (Harvard MS Keats
2.18; *JKPMH*, p. 69).
2. For India.
3. The East, particularly the lands of the eastern Mediterranean commonly referred to as the Middle
East.
4. The draft offers "This morn and yester eve my friend has taught / Such Greediness of Pleasure."
1. Written from Teignmouth after Keats had received an advance copy of *Endymion*; see the headnote to the poem (pp. 143–46) for publication details. Text from ALS (Morgan Library MA 791);
there is also a transcript in Woodhouse's letter-book, pp. 7–8).
2. A basket carried by a beast of burden.
3. Keats refers to characters in his *Endymion*.

beginning of a *related* speech marked thus "Ah! art awake[4]—while at the same time in the next page the continuation of the *identical speech* is mark'd in the same manner "Young Man of Latmos[5]—You will find on the other side all the parts which should have inverted commas to every line— I was purposing to travel over the north this Summer—there is but one thing to prevent me. I know nothing, I have read nothing and I mean to follow Solomon's directions of 'get Wisdom—get understanding'[6]—I find cavalier days are gone by. I find that I can have no enjoyment in the World but continual drinking of Knowledge—I find there is no worthy pursuit but the idea of doing some good for the world—some do it with their society—some with their wit—some with their benevolence—some with a sort of power of conferring pleasure and good humour on all they meet and in a thousand ways all equally dutiful to the command of Great Nature—there is but one way for me—the road lies through application study and thought. I will pursue it and to that end purpose retiring for some years. I have been hovering for some time between an exquisite sense of the luxurious and a love for Philosophy—were I calculated for the former I should be glad—but as I am not I shall turn all my soul to the latter. My Brother Tom is getting better and I hope I shall see both him and Reynolds well before I retire from the World. I shall see you soon and have some talk about what Books I shall take with me—

Your very sincere friend
John Keats

Remember me to Hessey—Woodhouse and Percy Street[7]

---

4. 3: 429.
5. 3: 449. Keats provided an errata sheet on the reverse (not reproduced but see headnote to the poem).
6. Proverbs 4.5.
7. The occupants of 10 Percy Street, Rathbone Place: Peter De Wint (1784–1849), watercolor painter, his wife Harriet and her brother William Hilton (1786–1839), a historical painter. *Hessey*: James Hessey, Taylor's business partner; *Woodhouse*: Richard Woodhouse (1788–1834), lawyer, scholar, and Keats's friend, who played an essential role in collecting and preserving Keats's poetry and letters.

Endymion (1818)

In the spring of 1817, Keats left London for the Isle of Wight to work on a long poem, knowing that Taylor and Hessey were interested in publishing the fruits of his labors and that his brothers were secure together in Hampstead. Keats began *Endymion* after April 18, 1817, when he was at Carisbrooke, Isle of Wight (see letters to Reynolds, p. 79, and Hunt, p. 83); he continued work on the first book as he moved to Margate, Canterbury, Hastings, and then back to Hampstead. He wrote Book II at Hampstead during the summer (see *L,* 1: 149). He drafted Book III while visiting Bailey at Oxford in September (see letter to Reynolds, p. 89; for Keats's work habits at Oxford, see *KC,* 2: 270). He worked on Book IV at Hampstead in October and then completed it at Burford Bridge, Surrey, in November, as indicated by a note at the end of the lost draft manuscript recorded by Woodhouse in his interleaved copy of *Endymion*: "Burford Bridge Novr 28. 1817" (*MYR: JK,* 3: 421). Keats thus adhered to the timetable he set forth at the opening of the poem (1.39–57), where he parallels his quest to write a romance within a year to the quest romance of Endymion. His relative speed in completing such a long poem may have been due in part to competitive pressure. Thomas Medwin (not always a reliable source) claims that "Shelley told me that he and Keats had mutually agreed, in the same given time, (six months each,) to write a long poem, and that the *Endymion* and *Revolt of Islam* were the fruits of this rivalry" (*The Life of Percy Bysshe Shelley,* ed. H. Buxton Forman [London: Oxford University Press, 1913], pp. 178–79). Edmund Blunden ("The Keats-Shelley Poetry Contests," *N&Q,* 199 [December 1954]: 546) has argued that Hunt's "The Nymphs," written at the same time as Keats's and Shelley's poems, was also part of this competition, a sort of extension of Hunt's sonnet contests; Clayton E. Hudnall ("John Hamilton Reynolds, James Rice, and Benjamin Bailey in the Leigh Browne-Lockyer Collection," *KSJ* 19 [1970]: 21) notes that "Keats and Reynolds . . . worked concurrently on their long poems [*Endymion* and "The Romance of Youth"] in 1817." Whether there was a contest or not, key poets in Keats's circle were all at work on long poems, and Keats saw writing the poem as "a test, a trial of my Powers of Imagination and chiefly of my invention which is a rare thing indeed—by which I must make 4000 Lines of one bare circumstance and fill them with Poetry," arguing that "a test of Invention . . . [is] the Polar Star of Poetry, as Fancy is the Sails, and Imagination the Rudder" (see letter to Bailey, p. 99); in the same letter, he argues for writing a long poem as "Lovers of Poetry like to have a little Region to wander in where they may pick and choose, and in which images are so numerous that many are forgotten and found new in a second Reading."

Keats copied and reworked his poem from January to March 1818 (see letters, pp. 109, 115, 116, 128). He began receiving the proofs of Book I in

February, while he was still at work on redrafting the later books. Reynolds indicated to Milnes that he helped with some revisions (*KC*, 2: 178), and Taylor made suggestions as Keats sent him the fair copy; it is not clear that Keats read the proofs of Books III and IV, and he did ask Taylor to send C. C. Clarke the proofs of Book 3 (*KC*, 1: 12)—all of which is to indicate that this book, like all others, is a product of many hands. Keats sent a first version of the preface (included after the printed preface, pp. 147–48) to his publishers on March 21, 1817 (*L*, 1: 253), but upon their advice and Reynolds's he wrote a new one (see letter to Reynolds, p. 138). The book was published by Taylor and Hessey in late April 1818; T. Miller of Noble Street, Cheapside, printed it. The title page carried as its motto (below) a misquotation of Shakespeare, Sonnet 17.12. The dedication to Chatterton originally read "Inscribed, / with every feeling of pride and regret, / and with 'a bowed mind,' [Coleridge, "Ode on the Departing Year" (1797), l. 6] / To the memory of / The most English of Poets except Shakespeare, / Thomas Chatterton." After seeing an advance copy, Keats sent an errata list to Taylor on April 24 (*L*, 1: 270–73); an errata list with five items was included in a second issue. The volume (priced at nine shillings) appears to have been made available on May 19 in an edition of five hundred copies (though St. Clair, *The Reading Nation in the Romantic Period* [2004], p. 611, indicates there may have been as many as 750); copies were still being offered at the original price in 1821.

Keats was first drawn to the story of Endymion when he wrote "I stood tip-toe upon a little hill," which he initially referred to as "Endymion" and which concludes with a version of the myth. He would have known the story in which the shepherd Endymion becomes the object of love for the goddess known as Diana, Cynthia, and Phoebe from Ovid's *Metamorphoses* (1801 Latin ed; 1640 ed. of Sandys's translation) and classical handbooks such as Lemprière's *Classical Dictionary* (6th ed., 1806) and Tooke's *Pantheon* ("New Edition," 1809). Scholars have tracked allusions in *Endymion* to various Elizabethan poets, including Shakespeare, Spenser, Marlowe and Fletcher; Keats owed a larger debt to Michael Drayton's *The Man in the Moone* (1606), which takes up Endymion's voyages with Phoebe. Details of Endymion's exotic journeys in Keats's poem can be traced to contemporary narratives such as Landor's *Gebir* (1798) and Southey's *Thalaba the Destroyer* (1801) and *The Curse of Kehama* (1810). Ian Jack has suggested the pictorial debts of the poem to painters such as Titian, Claude Lorrain, and Poussin (Jack, pp. 143–60).

Keats found inspiration closer at hand as well. It has long been recognized (see, for example, A. C. Bradley's 1909 *Oxford Lectures on Poetry*) that *Endymion* responds to Shelley's *Alastor* (1816), with Keats seeking to move beyond the divide between imaginative ideal and sensuous reality that Shelley's poem explores. Behind Shelley's poem is Wordsworth's *Excursion* (1814), and Keats, too, takes up Wordsworth and particularly his treatment of myth in Book IV of that poem; in a sense, Keats seeks to correct Shelley's correction of Wordsworth. *Endymion* can then be seen as part of a post-Waterloo body of poetry that hopes to contest Wordsworth's version of what is to be learned from the era of the French Revolution. Keats's couplet romance also owes a debt to Hunt's experiments with opening up the heroic couplet in *The Story of Rimini* (1816) and to Hunt's celebration in that romance of the erotic and the poetic (see Vincent Newey, "Keats, history, and the poets," in Roe, *KH*, pp. 165–93). If it is a poem that takes up classical myth as mediated by the Elizabethans, it is also a work firmly involved with contemporary aesthetic, cultural, and political debates. Such engagements are perhaps clearest in the proems that open each of *Endymion*'s four books. In the first passage (1.1–62), Keats not only sets forth the task in writing the poem but also pronounces that "A thing of beauty is a joy forever" with a power to "bind us to earth" "Spite of [the] despondence" that marks the post-revolutionary world of Wordsworth's *Excursion* and the "gloomy days" that Newey has identified with the post-Napoleonic Restoration attacked by Hunt. The proem to Book II (2.1–43) argues that the histories of love "Doth more avail" than the tales of "the death-day of empires," as Keats embraces what we might see as a "Make love, not war" stance. Book III's proem (3.1–71) has always been seen as the most overtly political—Woodhouse records that "K. said, with much simplicity, 'It will easily be seen what I think of the present Ministers by the beginning of the 3d Book'" (*MYR: JK*, 3: 220)—and he pits the poetic inspiration identified with Cynthia as the moon against the "gilded masks" of "regalities." The final proem (4.1–29) invokes the "Muse of my native land" to combat the Wordsworthian "Despondency [that] besets / Our pillows" as we find ourselves confined within "dull, uninspired, snail-paced lives." These passages set forth the poem's central themes that love and poetry represent our best hope to displace oppressive regimes and the despondency that follows upon the collapse of revolutionary ideals.

The poem proper traces the love of Endymion and his goddess. The "one bare circumstance" that inspired the poem is that the goddess of the moon was said to have fallen in love with the shepherd Endymion as he slept upon a mountaintop. In Keats's poem, Endymion is the shepherd king of the land of Latmos, a kind of Arcadian paradise where the people celebrate Pan in a hymn (1.232–306) derided by Wordsworth as "a Very pretty piece of paganism" (*KC*, 2: 143–44). Endymion has fallen out of the innocent harmony of the Latmians after being visited by the goddess who awakens in him a desire that leads to both self-consciousness and a thirst for a "fellowship with essence" (1.779) analyzed through what Keats called his "pleasure-thermometer" (1.777–842); he wrote to Taylor (January 30, 1818) of these lines, "The whole thing must I think have appeared to you, who are a consequitive Man, as a thing almost of mere words—but I assure you that when I wrote it, it was a regular stepping of the Imagination towards a Truth. My having written that Argument will perhaps be of the greatest Service to me of any thing I ever did—It set before me at once the gradations of Happiness even like a kind of Pleasure Thermometer—and is my first step towards the chief Attempt in the Drama—the playing of different Natures with Joy and Sorrow."

The sense that Diana/Cynthia/Phoebe as a triple goddess rules on earth, in the underworld, and in heaven structures Endymion's quest for his goddess, as he moves through an earthly sensuous garden in Book II, under the sea to the hellish confinement of Glaucus in Book III, and into the air and to the Cave of Quietude in Book IV. The poem appears to sample various forms of romance—the pastoral romance of the Latmians, the erotic romance of the Bower of Adonis, the apocalyptic romance of Glaucus—and various relationships between the real and the ideal—the naïve unity of a kind of Blakean innocence, the all-too-bodily sensuous ideal of "lips" as "slippery blisses," an attempt to enact the ideal through the communal action of the Glaucus section—before asserting a discovery of the ideal in the real as the earthly Indian Maid is revealed to be Endymion's goddess. A particularly pointed summary of the poem's vision is found in a comment by Benjamin Bailey, in whose rooms Keats composed much of Book III, and who later wrote to Taylor that in *Endymion* Keats embraced "that abominable principle of *Shelley's*—that *Sensual Love* is the principle of *things*" (*KC*, 1: 35).

Endymion received at least thirteen notices, ranging from Reynolds's praise in the *Champion* to attacks in *Blackwood's* and the *Quarterly Review* (see a selection, pp. 246–50, 272–80, 283–86). Much earlier scholarly discussion of the poem focused on whether the poem was allegorical or not: see for example, Claude Finney, *The Evolution of Keats's Poetry*, 2 vols. (Cambridge: Harvard University Press, 1936), pp. 291–319, Clarence Thorpe, *The Mind of John Keats* (New York: Oxford University Press, 1926), and Newell Ford, "*Endymion*—A Neo-Platonic Allegory?" *ELH* 14 (1947): 64–76. Modern criticism includes chapters by Aske (pp. 53–72), Bush (1966, pp. 38–52), Dickstein (pp. 53–129), Northrop Frye (*A Study of English Romanticism* [New York: Random House, 1968], pp. 125–65), Kucich (pp. 165–83), Newey (in Roe, *KH*, pp. 165–93), Ricks (pp. 69–114), Sperry (pp. 90–116), Stillinger (1971; pp. 14–30), Watkins (35–53), and Wolfson (pp. 227–52); and Karen Swann, "*Endymion's* Beautiful Dreamers," in *The Cambridge Companion to Keats*, ed. Susan J. Wolfson (Cambridge: Cambridge University Press, 2001), pp. 20–36. For a discussion of the "poetics of dissent" in *Endymion*, see Nicholas Roe's essay included here (pp. 573–83).

The text is taken from the edition of 1818, with corrections from Keats's errata list (except for his request that 1.943–59, 3.429–43, and 3.570–600 have "inverted commas" or quotation marks on every line) and the list included in the second issue; some corrections are made from the fair copy. The manuscript of Keats's first draft (the last three books of which were still extant in 1847) is now lost, but Woodhouse recorded variants and cancellations from the draft of Books II–IV (together with variants from the revised fair copy) in his interleaved copy of *Endymion*, described by Stillinger as "in effect a variorum edition begun during the poet's lifetime by a scholarly friend" (*MYR: JK*, 3: ix); it is now in the Berg Collection, New York Public Library (Berg *Endymion* Copy 3; *MYR: JK*, vol. 3). I have cited some of Woodhouse's annotations in the notes. Keats's revised fair copy of the poem along with the title page, dedication, and draft preface sent to Taylor are held at the Morgan Library (MA 208, 209). Passages of the poem were copied into five letters: 1.777–81 in a letter to Taylor of January 30, 1818 (*L*, 1: 218), 4.1–29 in a letter to Bailey of October 28–30, 1817 (*L*, 1: 172–73), 4.146–61 in a letter to Jane Reynolds of October 31, 1817 (*L*, 1: 176–77), and 4.146–81 in a letter to Bailey of November 3, 1817 (*L*, 1: 181–82). For a discussion of the texts and an analysis of needed corrections, see Stillinger, pp. 571–83. Stephen T. Steinhoff produced *Keats's Endymion: A Critical Edition* (Troy, NY: Whitson, 1987).

ENDYMION:

A Poetic Romance.

"THE STRETCHED METRE OF AN ANTIQUE SONG."

INSCRIBED
TO THE MEMORY
OF
THOMAS CHATTERTON

Preface

KNOWING within myself the manner in which this Poem has been produced, it is not without a feeling of regret that I make it public.

What manner I mean, will be quite clear to the reader, who must soon perceive great inexperience, immaturity, and every error denoting a feverish attempt, rather than a deed accomplished. The two first books, and indeed the two last, I feel sensible are not of such completion as to warrant their passing the press; nor should they if I thought a year's castigation would do them any good; it will not: the foundations are too sandy. It is just that this youngster should die away: a sad thought for me, if I had not some hope that while it is dwindling I may be plotting, and fitting myself for verses fit to live.

This may be speaking too presumptuously, and may deserve a punishment: but no feeling man will be forward to inflict it: he will leave me alone, with the conviction that there is not a fiercer hell than the failure in a great object. This is not written with the least atom of purpose to forestall criticisms of course, but from the desire I have to conciliate men who are competent to look, and who do look with a zealous eye, to the honour of English literature.

The imagination of a boy is healthy, and the mature imagination of a man is healthy; but there is a space of life between, in which the soul is in a ferment, the character undecided, the way of life uncertain, the ambition thick-sighted: thence proceeds mawkishness, and all the thousand bitters which those men I speak of must necessarily taste in going over the following pages.

I hope I have not in too late a day touched the beautiful mythology of Greece, and dulled its brightness: for I wish to try once more, before I bid it farewel.

Teigmouth,
April 10, 1818

Original Preface

In a great nation, the work of an individual is of so little importance; his pleadings and excuses are so uninteresting; his 'way of life'[1] such a nothing that a preface seems a sort of impertinent bow to strangers who care nothing about it.

1. Shakespeare, *Macbeth*, 5.3.23.

A preface however should be down in so many words; and such a one
that by an eye glance over the type, the Reader may catch an idea of an
Author's modesty; and non opinion of himself—which I sincerely hope may
be seen in the few lines I have to write, notwithstanding certain proverbs
of many ages' old which men find a great pleasure in receiving for gospel.

About a twelve month since, I published a little book of verses; it was
read by some dozen of my friends who lik'd it; and some dozen who I was
unacquainted with, who did not. Now when a dozen human beings, are at
words with another dozen, it becomes a matter of anxiety to side with one's
friends;—more especially when excited thereto by a great love of Poetry.

I fought under disadvantages. Before I began I had no inward feel of
being able to finish; and as I proceeded my steps were all uncertain. So this
Poem must rather be consider'd as an endeavour than a thing accomplish'd;
a poor prologue to what, if I live, I humbly hope to do. In duty to the Public I should have kept it back for a year or two, knowing it to be faulty: but
I really cannot do so:—by repetition my favorite Passages sound vapid in my
ears, and I would rather redeem myself with a new Poem—should this one
be found of any interest.

I have to apologise to the lovers of simplicity for touching the spell of
loveliness that hung about Endymion: if any of my lines plead for me with
such people I shall be proud.

It has been too much the fashion of late to consider men bigotted and
addicted to every word that may chance to escape their lips: now I here
declare that I have not any particular affection for any particular phrase,
word or letter in the whole affair. I have written to please myself and in
hopes to please others, and for a love of fame; if I neither please myself, nor
others nor get fame, of what consequence is Phraseology?

I would fain escape the bickering that all Works, not exactly in chime,
bring upon their begetters:—but this is not fair to expect, there must be conversation of some sort and to object shows a Man's consequence. In case of
a London drizzle or a Scotch Mist, the following quotation from Marston
may perhaps 'stead me as an umbrella for an hour or so: 'let it be the Curtesy
of my peruser rather to pity my self hindering labours than to malice me.'[2]

One word more—for we cannot help seeing our own affairs in every
point of view—. Should any one call my dedication to Chatterton affected
I answer as followeth:

"Were I dead Sir I should like a Book dedicated to me."

Teignmouth March 19th 1818—

ENDYMION.

BOOK I.

A THING of beauty is a joy for ever:
Its loveliness increases; it will never
Pass into nothingness; but still will keep
A bower quiet for us, and a sleep

---

2. John Marston, "To My Equal Reader," the preface to *The Fawn* (1606).

Full of sweet dreams, and health, and quiet breathing.   5
Therefore, on every morrow, are we wreathing
A flowery band to bind us to the earth,
Spite of despondence,[1] of the inhuman dearth
Of noble natures, of the gloomy days,[2]
Of all the unhealthy and o'er-darkened ways   10
Made for our searching: yes, in spite of all,
Some shape of beauty moves away the pall
From our dark spirits. Such the sun, the moon,
Trees old, and young sprouting a shady boon
For simple sheep; and such are daffodils   15
With the green world they live in; and clear rills[3]
That for themselves a cooling covert[4] make
'Gainst the hot season; the mid forest brake,
Rich with a sprinkling of fair musk-rose blooms:
And such too is the grandeur of the dooms   20
We have imagined for the mighty dead;[5]
All lovely tales that we have heard or read:
An endless fountain of immortal drink,
Pouring unto us from the heaven's brink.

Nor do we merely feel these essences   25
For one short hour; no, even as the trees
That whisper round a temple become soon
Dear as the temple's self, so does the moon,
The passion poesy, glories infinite,
Haunt us till they become a cheering light   30
Unto our souls, and bound to us so fast,
That, whether there be shine, or gloom o'ercast,
They alway must be with us, or we die.

Therefore, 'tis with full happiness that I
Will trace the story of Endymion.   35
The very music of the name has gone
Into my being, and each pleasant scene
Is growing fresh before me as the green
Of our own vallies: so I will begin
Now while I cannot hear the city's din;   40
Now while the early budders are just new,
And run in mazes of the youngest hue
About old forests; while the willow trails
Its delicate amber; and the dairy pails
Bring home increase of milk. And, as the year   45
Grows lush in juicy stalks, I'll smoothly steer

---

1. Allott notes that the opening of the poem may owe something to Wordsworth's "Prospectus to *The Recluse*," ll. 42–47, published with *The Excursion* (1814). The theme of despondency may also echo Book IV of *The Excursion*, "Despondency Corrected."
2. See Vincent Newey's argument that Keats refers here to Hunt's account of the post-Napoleonic Restoration, in "Keats, history, and the poets," in Roe, *KH*, pp. 165–93.
3. Small streams, brooks especially when "formed temporarily in soil or sand after rain or tidal ebb" (*OED*).
4. A shelter, hiding place.
5. In ll. 13–21 Keats seems to repeat the division found in "Sleep and Poetry" between the realm of "Flora and old Pan"—here the "green world"—and that of tragedy, here the "dooms" of the "mighty dead."

My little boat, for many quiet hours,
With streams that deepen freshly into bowers.
Many and many a verse I hope to write,
Before the daisies, vermeil[6] rimm'd and white,   50
Hide in deep herbage; and ere yet the bees
Hum about globes of clover and sweet peas,
I must be near the middle of my story.
O may no wintry season, bare and hoary,
See it half finished: but let Autumn bold,   55
With universal tinge of sober gold,
Be all about me when I make an end.
And now at once, adventuresome, I send
My herald thought into a wilderness:
There let its trumpet blow, and quickly dress   60
My uncertain path with green, that I may speed
Easily onward, thorough flowers and weed.

    Upon the sides of Latmos[7] was outspread
A mighty forest; for the moist earth fed
So plenteously all weed-hidden roots   65
Into o'er-hanging boughs, and precious fruits.
And it had gloomy shades, sequestered deep,
Where no man went; and if from shepherd's keep
A lamb strayed far a-down those inmost glens,
Never again saw he the happy pens   70
Whither his brethren, bleating with content,
Over the hills at every nightfall went.
Among the shepherds, 'twas believed ever,
That not one fleecy lamb which thus did sever
From the white flock, but pass'd unworried   75
By angry wolf, or pard[8] with prying head,
Until it came to some unfooted plains
Where fed the herds of Pan: ay[9] great his gains
Who thus one lamb did lose. Paths there were many,
Winding through palmy fern, and rushes fenny,   80
And ivy banks; all leading pleasantly
To a wide lawn, whence one could only see
Stems thronging all around between the swell
Of turf and slanting branches: who could tell
The freshness of the space of heaven above,   85
Edg'd round with dark tree tops? through which a dove

---

6. A Spenserianism for crimson.
7. Mountain in Caria, Asia Minor, associated with Endymion.
8. Leopard.
9. Here, and elsewhere in the poem, "ay" means ever; Keats uses "aye" for the interjections "yes" or
   "ah." For the pronunciation of such words, see Kucich, "Cockney chivalry: Hunt, Keats and the
   aesthetics of excess," in Leigh Hunt: Life, Poetics, Politics, ed. Nicholas Roe (London: Routledge,
   2003), pp. 118–34. Pan: a goat from the waist down and a man from the waist up who sports horns
   on his head, Pan is the god of shepherds; in Greek, his name means "all" or "everything," and thus
   he was also the god of universal nature. As Allott suggests, Keats may have taken details of the following festival of and hymn to Pan (ll. 89–392) from various Elizabethan sources including Drayton's The Man in the Moone (1606), Jonson's Pan's Anniversarie (1623), Fletcher's Faithfull
   Shepherdess (1610), and Chapman's translation of Homer's "Hymn to Pan" (1616). Jack (p. 149)
   suggests an influence on the visual details from Titian's The Worship of Venus (1518–20) and
   Rubens's Feast of Venus (1639–40).

Would often beat its wings, and often too
A little cloud would move across the blue.

    Full in the middle of this pleasantness
There stood a marble altar, with a tress   90
Of flowers budded newly; and the dew
Had taken fairy phantasies to strew
Daisies upon the sacred sward last eve,
And so the dawned light in pomp receive.
For 'twas the morn: Apollo's upward fire   95
Made every eastern cloud a silvery pyre
Of brightness so unsullied, that therein
A melancholy spirit well might win
Oblivion, and melt out his essence fine
Into the winds: rain-scented eglantine[1]   100
Gave temperate sweets to that well-wooing sun;
The lark was lost in him; cold springs had run
To warm their chilliest bubbles in the grass;
Man's voice was on the mountains; and the mass
Of nature's lives and wonders puls'd tenfold,   105
To feel this sun-rise and its glories old.

    Now while the silent workings of the dawn
Were busiest, into that self-same lawn
All suddenly, with joyful cries, there sped
A troop of little children garlanded;   110
Who gathering round the altar, seemed to pry
Earnestly round as wishing to espy
Some folk of holiday: nor had they waited
For many moments, ere their ears were sated[2]
With a faint breath of music, which ev'n then   115
Fill'd out its voice, and died away again.
Within a little space again it gave
Its airy swellings, with a gentle wave,
To light-hung leaves, in smoothest echoes breaking
Through copse-clad vallies,—ere their death, o'ertaking   120
The surgy murmurs of the lonely sea.

    And now, as deep into the wood as we
Might mark a lynx's eye, there glimmered light
Fair faces and a rush of garments white,
Plainer and plainer shewing, till at last   125
Into the widest alley they all past,
Making directly for the woodland altar.
O kindly muse! let not my weak tongue faulter
In telling of this goodly company,
Of their old piety, and of their glee: 130
But let a portion of ethereal dew
Fall on my head, and presently unmew[3]

1. Sweetbriar.
2. Satisfied, with the suggestion that one is glutted, cloyed by overabundance.
3. Woodhouse *E*, p. 36: "To mew—is to encage, or confine—from Mew (a cage)"; he cites Shakespeare, *Romeo and Juliet* 3.4.11 and Ronsard, *Odes*, I.x.515.

My soul; that I may dare, in wayfaring,
To stammer where old Chaucer used to sing.[4]

Leading the way, young damsels danced along,   135
Bearing the burden of a shepherd song;[5]
Each having a white wicker over brimm'd
With April's tender younglings: next, well trimm'd,
A crowd of shepherds with as sunburnt looks
As may be read of in Arcadian books;[6]   140
Such as sat listening round Apollo's pipe,
When the great deity, for earth too ripe,
Let his divinity o'er-flowing die
In music, through the vales of Thessaly:[7]
Some idly trailed their sheep-hooks on the ground,   145
And some kept up a shrilly mellow sound
With ebon-tipped flutes: close after these,
Now coming from beneath the forest trees,
A venerable priest full soberly,
Begirt with ministring looks: alway his eye   150
Stedfast upon the matted turf he kept,
And after him his sacred vestments swept.
From his right hand there swung a vase, milk-white,
Of mingled wine, out-sparkling generous light;
And in his left he held a basket full   155
Of all sweet herbs that searching eye could cull:
Wild thyme, and valley-lilies whiter still
Than Leda's love,[8] and cresses from the rill.
His aged head, crowned with beechen wreath,
Seem'd like a poll of ivy in the teeth   160
Of winter hoar.[9] Then came another crowd
Of shepherds, lifting in due time aloud
Their share of the ditty. After them appear'd,
Up-followed by a multitude that rear'd
Their voices to the clouds, a fair wrought car,   165
Easily rolling so as scarce to mar
The freedom of three steeds of dapple brown:
Who stood therein did seem of great renown
Among the throng. His youth was fully blown,
Shewing like Ganymede[1] to manhood grown;   170
And, for those simple times, his garments were
A chieftain king's: beneath his breast, half bare,
Was hung a silver bugle, and between
His nervy[2] knees there lay a boar-spear keen.

4. In his fair copy, Keats marked ll. 127–34 for deletion; restored by Taylor with a penciled "stet."
   Keats, "wayfaring" while "telling of this goodly company," recalls the stories of Chaucer's Canterbury pilgrims; Keats went to Canterbury on May 17, 1817 (L, 1: 146–47).
5. "Bearing the burden" means "singing the refrain"; as Allott points out, there is a pun here.
6. Pastoral poems; Arcadia is the pastoral home of Pan.
7. Apollo, having angered Jupiter by killing the Cyclops, spent a period of exile as a shepherd in Thessaly. Keats could have read this tale in Ovid's *Metamorphoses* 2.677–82 or Lemprière. Apollo's
   divinity dying into music looks forward to his dying into life in *Hyperion* (3: 130).
8. Jupiter, who appeared in the form of a white swan.
9. Frost.
1. The boy cupbearer to the gods, who was brought to Olympus by Jupiter, enamored of his beauty
   (Ovid, *Metamorphoses* 10.155–61).
2. "Vigorous, sinewy" (*OED*).

A smile was on his countenance; he seem'd,   175
To common lookers on, like one who dream'd
Of idleness in groves Elysian:[3]
But there were some who feelingly could scan
A lurking trouble in his nether lip,
And see that oftentimes the reins would slip   180
Through his forgotten hands: then would they sigh,
And think of yellow leaves, of owlet's cry,
Of logs piled solemnly.—Ah, well-a-day,
Why should our young Endymion pine away!

   Soon the assembly, in a circle rang'd,   185
Stood silent round the shrine: each look was chang'd
To sudden veneration: women meek
Beckon'd their sons to silence; while each cheek
Of virgin bloom paled gently for slight fear.
Endymion too, without a forest peer,   190
Stood, wan, and pale, and with an awed face,
Among his brothers of the mountain chase.
In midst of all, the venerable priest
Eyed them with joy from greatest to the least,
And, after lifting up his aged hands,   195
Thus spake he: "Men of Latmos! shepherd bands!
Whose care it is to guard a thousand flocks:
Whether descended from beneath the rocks
That overtop your mountains; whether come
From vallies where the pipe is never dumb;   200
Or from your swelling downs, where sweet air stirs
Blue hare-bells lightly, and where prickly furze
Buds lavish gold; or ye, whose precious charge
Nibble their fill at ocean's very marge,[4]
Whose mellow reeds are touch'd with sounds forlorn   205
By the dim echoes of old Triton's horn:[5]
Mothers and wives! who day by day prepare
The scrip, with needments,[6] for the mountain air;
And all ye gentle girls who foster up
Udderless[7] lambs, and in a little cup   210
Will put choice honey for a favoured youth:
Yea, every one attend! for in good truth
Our vows are wanting to our great god Pan.
Are not our lowing heifers sleeker than
Night-swollen mushrooms? Are not our wide plains   215
Speckled with countless fleeces? Have not rains
Green'd over April's lap? No howling sad
Sickens our fearful ewes; and we have had
Great bounty from Endymion our lord.

---

3. In classical mythology, Elysium is the portion of the afterworld reserved for the souls of the virtuous.
4. Edge.
5. Triton is a sea-god, half-man and half-dolphin, whose horn is a seashell; Keats may echo Spenser's
   "Colin Clout's Come Home Againe" (1595), ll. 244–45, or Wordsworth's echo of Spenser in "The
   world is too much with us" (1807), l. 14: "hear old Triton blow his wreathèd horn."
6. Necessities, such as food. Woodhouse, E, p. 44, quotes Spenser's Faerie Queene 1.6.35 (9) to
   refute the Quarterly Review's claim that Keats invented this word; scrip: a small bag or satchel.
7. Motherless.

The earth is glad: the merry lark has pour'd   220
His early song against yon breezy sky,
That spreads so clear o'er our solemnity."

Thus ending, on the shrine he heap'd a spire
Of teeming sweets, enkindling sacred fire;
Anon he stain'd the thick and spongy sod   225
With wine, in honour of the shepherd-god.
Now while the earth was drinking it, and while
Bay leaves were crackling in the fragrant pile,
And gummy frankincense was sparkling bright
'Neath smothering parsley, and a hazy light   230
Spread greyly eastward, thus a chorus sang:[8]

"O THOU, whose mighty palace roof doth hang
From jagged trunks, and overshadoweth
Eternal whispers, glooms, the birth, life, death
Of unseen flowers in heavy peacefulness;   235
Who lov'st to see the hamadryads[9] dress
Their ruffled locks where meeting hazels darken;
And through whole solemn hours dost sit, and hearken
The dreary melody of bedded reeds—
In desolate places, where dank moisture breeds   240
The pipy hemlock[1] to strange overgrowth;
Bethinking thee, how melancholy loth
Thou wast to lose fair Syrinx[2]—do thou now,
By thy love's milky brow!
By all the trembling mazes that she ran,   245
Hear us, great Pan!

"O thou, for whose soul-soothing quiet, turtles[3]
Passion[4] their voices cooingly 'mong myrtles,
What time thou wanderest at eventide
Through sunny meadows, that outskirt the side   250
Of thine enmossed realms: O thou, to whom
Broad leaved fig trees even now foredoom[5]
Their ripen'd fruitage; yellow girted bees
Their golden honeycombs; our village leas[6]
Their fairest blossom'd beans and poppied corn;[7]   255
The chuckling linnet[8] its five young unborn,

---

8. The stanzaic "Hymn to Pan" that follows (ll. 232–306) has been one of the most admired parts of the poem, but when Keats, at Haydon's urging, recited the poem to Wordsworth, "which he did in his usual half chant, (most touching) walking up and down . . . Wordsworth drily said 'a Very pretty piece of Paganism'" (KC, 2: 143–44). In a copy of Galignani's 1829 edition (at Harvard *EC 8 K 2262 B829 pac [A]), Woodhouse dated this hymn April 26, 1817.
9. Nymphs who preside over trees.
1. A poisonous plant that has hollow stems.
2. For Pan and Syrinx, see p. 25, n. 7.
3. Turtle doves, small wild pigeons known for plaintive cooing.
4. Used as a verb; Woodhouse E, p. 48, cites Shakespeare's The Two Gentleman of Verona 4.4.167–68, The Tempest 5.1.22–24, Venus and Adonis 1059, and Spenser's The Faerie Queene 2.9.41(9) to show that Keats was following precedents.
5. Determine beforehand.
6. Pastures.
7. That is, the corn field has poppies mixed in; the OED cites, in addition to Keats, Richard Polwhele's 1797 Old English Gentleman (8): "Poppied cornfields redd'ning to the sky."
8. A finch; chuckling: "clucking."

To sing for thee; low creeping strawberries
Their summer coolness; pent up butterflies
Their freckled wings; yea, the fresh budding year
All its completions—be quickly near,   260
By every wind that nods the mountain pine,
O forester divine!

"Thou, to whom every fawn and satyr[9] flies
For willing service; whether to surprise
The squatted hare while in half sleeping fit;   265
Or upward ragged precipices flit
To save poor lambkins from the eagle's maw;
Or by mysterious enticement draw
Bewildered shepherds to their path again;
Or to tread breathless round the frothy main,   270
And gather up all fancifullest shells
For thee to tumble into Naiads'[1] cells,
And, being hidden, laugh at their out-peeping;
Or to delight thee with fantastic leaping,
The while they pelt each other on the crown   275
With silvery oak apples, and fir cones brown—
By all the echoes that about thee ring,[2]
Hear us, O satyr king!

"O Hearkener to the loud clapping shears,
While ever and anon to his shorn peers   280
A ram goes bleating: Winder of the horn,
When snouted wild-boars routing tender corn
Anger our huntsmen: Breather round our farms,
To keep off mildews, and all weather harms:
Strange ministrant of undescribed sounds,   285
That come a swooning over hollow grounds,
And wither drearily on barren moors:
Dread opener of the mysterious doors
Leading to universal knowledge—see,
Great son of Dryope,[3]   290
The many that are come to pay their vows
With leaves about their brows!

"Be still the unimaginable lodge
For solitary thinkings; such as dodge
Conception to the very bourne[4] of heaven,   295

9. See p. 20, n. 4; *fawn*: an archaic spelling of "faun."
1. Minor goddesses of woods and streams.
2. One of Keats's classical sources, Baldwin's *Pantheon* (p. 105), notes that "All the strange, mysterious and unaccountable sounds which were heard in solitary places, were attributed to Pan."
3. While there are various accounts of Pan's parents, Keats follows the story in which he is the child of Hermes and the nymph Dryope. Pan, meaning "all," is here invoked as the source of "universal knowledge."
4. A boundary; Allott cites Shakespeare, *Hamlet* 3.1.81–82: "The undiscover'd country from whose bourne / No traveler returns." See Keats's letter to Reynolds, February 3 1818 (p. 121), where, writing of Wordsworth, he complains of being "bullied into a certain philosophy engendered in the whims of an Egotist": "Many a man can travel to the very bourne of Heaven, and yet want confidence to put down his halfseeing. Sancho will invent a Journey heavenward as well as any body. We hate poetry that has a palpable design upon us—and if we do not agree, seems to put its hand in its breeches pocket."

Then leave the naked brain: be still the leaven,
That spreading in this dull and clodded earth
Gives it a touch ethereal—a new birth:
Be still a symbol of immensity;
A firmament reflected in a sea;   300
An element filling the space between;
An unknown—but no more: we humbly screen
With uplift hands our foreheads, lowly bending,
And giving out a shout most heaven rending,
Conjure thee to receive our humble Pæan,   305
Upon thy Mount Lycean!"[5]

    Even while they brought the burden to a close,
A shout from the whole multitude arose,
That lingered in the air like dying rolls
Of abrupt thunder, when Ionian[6] shoals   310
Of dolphins bob their noses through the brine.
Meantime, on shady levels, mossy fine,
Young companies nimbly began dancing
To the swift treble pipe, and humming string.
Aye, those fair living forms swam heavenly   315
To tunes forgotten—out of memory:
Fair creatures! whose young children's children bred
Thermopylæ[7] its heroes—not yet dead,
But in old marbles ever beautiful.
High genitors,[8] unconscious did they cull   320
Time's sweet first-fruits—they danc'd to weariness,
And then in quiet circles did they press
The hillock turf, and caught the latter end
Of some strange history, potent to send
A young mind from its bodily tenement.   325
Or they might watch the quoit-pitchers,[9] intent
On either side; pitying the sad death
Of Hyacinthus, when the cruel breath
Of Zephyr slew him,—Zephyr penitent,
Who now, ere Phœbus mounts the firmament,   330
Fondles the flower amid the sobbing rain.[1]
The archers too, upon a wider plain,
Beside the feathery whizzing of the shaft,
And the dull twanging bowstring, and the raft[2]

---

5. Lycaeus, a mountain in Arcadia sacred to Pan whose festivals were called Lycaea. *Pæan:* a hymn of praise or thanksgiving, particularly when addressed to Apollo as Pæan, physician of the gods.
6. Ionia in Asia Minor was colonized by the Greeks; the Aegean and Icarian seas bounded it on the west. Of the next line, Woodhouse W[2] 239v (*MYR: JK,* 6: 427) notes, "The words *raise push* were suggested to the author: but he insisted on retaining *bob.*"
7. Site of famous Spartan stand against Xerxes and the Persians in 480 B.C.E.
8. For "progenitors."
9. Keats refers to a Greek and Roman test of skill in throwing a quoit: "In original and widest sense (now only with reference to the Greek and Roman discus), a flat disc of stone or metal, thrown as an exercise of strength or skill" (*OED*).
1. Woodhouse *E,* p. 56 notes: "Hyacinthus; a youth beloved by Apollo, and by Zephyrus. The latter finding himself slighted in favor of Apollo, resolved to be revenged upon his rival—Accordingly, as Apollo, who was entrusted with the Education of young Hyacinthus, was playing at Quoits with his pupil, Zephyrus [the West Wind] blew the quoit, as soon as it was thrown by Apollo, upon the head of Hyacinthus, who was killed by the blow. Apollo changed the blood of the Youth into a flower bearing the name of Hyacinth."
2. Archaic form of "reft," "torn."

Branch down sweeping from a tall ash top, 335
Call'd up a thousand thoughts to envelope
Those who would watch. Perhaps, the trembling knee
And frantic gape of lonely Niobe,[3]
Poor, lonely Niobe! when her lovely young
Were dead and gone, and her caressing tongue 340
Lay a lost thing upon her paly lip,
And very, very deadliness did nip
Her motherly cheeks. Arous'd from this sad mood
By one, who at a distance loud halloo'd,
Uplifting his strong bow into the air, 345
Many might after brighter visions stare:
After the Argonauts,[4] in blind amaze
Tossing about on Neptune's restless ways,
Until, from the horizon's vaulted side,
There shot a golden splendour far and wide, 350
Spangling those million poutings of the brine
With quivering ore: 'twas even an awful shine
From the exaltation of Apollo's bow;
A heavenly beacon in their dreary woe.
Who thus were ripe for high contemplating, 355
Might turn their steps towards the sober ring
Where sat Endymion and the aged priest
'Mong shepherds gone in eld,[5] whose looks increas'd
The silvery setting of their mortal star.
There they discours'd upon the fragile bar 360
That keeps us from our homes ethereal;
And what our duties there: to nightly call
Vesper,[6] the beauty-crest of summer weather;
To summon all the downiest clouds together
For the sun's purple couch; to emulate 365
In ministring the potent rule of fate
With speed of fire-tailed exhalations;[7]
To tint her pallid cheek with bloom, who cons
Sweet poesy by moonlight: besides these,
A world of other unguess'd offices. 370
Anon they wander'd, by divine converse,
Into Elysium;[8] vieing to rehearse
Each one his own anticipated bliss.
One felt heart-certain that he could not miss
His quick gone love, among fair blossom'd boughs, 375
Where every zephyr-sigh pouts, and endows

3. Niobe, who ridiculed Latona—the mother of Apollo and Diana—for only having two children when she had seven daughters and seven sons, was punished for her presumption when Diana killed all but one of her daughters and Apollo slew all her sons; Niobe was changed into stone.
4. Sailed with Jason in the first ship, the *Argo*, in search of the Golden Fleece. Woodhouse *E*, p. 59 suggests Apollonius Rhodius's *Argonautica* (Greene's translation of 1780) as the source for Apollo's presence, as he is not mentioned in this regard in Keats's usual sources. De Selincourt (pp. 423–24) suggests that Keats learned of this episode from Shelley, who admired Apollonius Rhodius's description of Apollo. Horace Smith wrote a poem, "The Shriek of Prometheus" (1821), that draws on the *Argonautica*.
5. Old age.
6. The evening star; also known as Hesperus.
7. Comets.
8. See p. 60, n. 8.

Her lips with music for the welcoming.
Another wish'd, mid that eternal spring,
To meet his rosy child, with feathery sails,
Sweeping, eye-earnestly, through almond vales: 380
Who, suddenly, should stoop through the smooth wind,
And with the balmiest leaves his temples bind;
And, ever after, through those regions be
His messenger, his little Mercury.
Some were athirst in soul to see again   385
Their fellow huntsmen o'er the wide champaign[9]
In times long past; to sit with them, and talk
Of all the chances in their earthly walk;
Comparing, joyfully, their plenteous stores
Of happiness, to when upon the moors,   390
Benighted, close they huddled from the cold,
And shar'd their famish'd scrips.[1] Thus all out-told
Their fond imaginations,—saving him
Whose eyelids curtain'd up their jewels dim,[2]
Endymion: yet hourly had he striven   395
To hide the cankering venom, that had riven
His fainting recollections. Now indeed
His senses had swoon'd off: he did not heed
The sudden silence, or the whispers low,
Or the old eyes dissolving at his woe,   400
Or anxious calls, or close of trembling palms,
Or maiden's sigh, that grief itself embalms:
But in the self-same fixed trance he kept,
Like one who on the earth had never stept:
Aye, even as dead-still as a marble man,   405
Frozen in that old tale Arabian.[3]

Who whispers him so pantingly and close?
Peona,[4] his sweet sister: of all those,
His friends, the dearest. Hushing signs she made,
And breath'd a sister's sorrow to persuade   410
A yielding up, a cradling on her care.[5]
Her eloquence did breathe away the curse:
She led him, like some midnight spirit nurse
Of happy changes in emphatic dreams,
Along a path between two little streams,—   415
Guarding his forehead, with her round elbow,
From low-grown branches, and his footsteps slow
From stumbling over stumps and hillocks small;
Until they came to where these streamlets fall,

9. A plain; level, open country.
1. See p. 153, n. 6.
2. Allott cites Shakespeare, *The Tempest* 1.2.402 and *Pericles* Scene 12.99–101.
3. Woodhouse *E*, p. 63 cites "The Story of Zobeide in the Arabian Nights' Entertainments"; Allott quotes "The History of the Young King of the Black Isles" from the 1811 edition of *The Arabian Nights*, 1: 117–18.
4. Keats invents the figure of Peona, though Chapman, in his continuation of Marlowe's *Hero and Leander* (1598), indicates Endymion had a sister, and Lemprière lists Pæon or Peon as one of Endymion's sons.
5. An unrhymed line which probably resulted from Keats's revisions of this passage in the fair copy.

With mingled bubblings and a gentle rush,   420
Into a river, clear, brimful, and flush
With crystal mocking of the trees and sky.
A little shallop,[6] floating there hard by,
Pointed its beak over the fringed bank;
And soon it lightly dipt, and rose, and sank,   425
And dipt again, with the young couple's weight,—
Peona guiding, through the water straight,
Towards a bowery island opposite;
Which gaining presently, she steered light
Into a shady, fresh, and ripply cove,   430
Where nested was an arbour, overwove
By many a summer's silent fingering;
To whose cool bosom she was used to bring
Her playmates, with their needle broidery,
And minstrel memories of times gone by.   435

     So she was gently glad to see him laid
Under her favourite bower's quiet shade,
On her own couch, new made of flower leaves,
Dried carefully on the cooler side of sheaves
When last the sun his autumn tresses shook,   440
And the tann'd harvesters rich armfuls took.
Soon was he quieted to slumbrous rest:
But, ere it crept upon him, he had prest
Peona's busy hand against his lips,
And still, a sleeping, held her finger-tips   445
In tender pressure. And as a willow keeps
A patient watch over the stream that creeps
Windingly by it, so the quiet maid
Held her in peace: so that a whispering blade
Of grass, a wailful gnat, a bee bustling   450
Down in the blue-bells, or a wren light rustling
Among sere leaves and twigs, might all be heard.

     O magic sleep! O comfortable[7] bird,
That broodest o'er the troubled sea of the mind
Till it is hush'd and smooth! O unconfin'd   455
Restraint! imprisoned liberty! great key
To golden palaces, strange minstrelsy,
Fountains grotesque, new trees, bespangled caves,
Echoing grottos, full of tumbling waves
And moonlight; aye, to all the mazy world   460
Of silvery enchantment!—who, upfurl'd
Beneath thy drowsy wing a triple hour,
But renovates and lives?—Thus, in the bower,
Endymion was calm'd to life again.
Opening his eyelids with a healthier brain,   465
He said: "I feel this thine endearing love
All through my bosom: thou art as a dove

---

6. A small open boat; Keats could have found the word in Spenser's *The Faerie Queene* 3.7.27 or Shelley's *Alastor* (1816), l. 299.
7. Archaism for "consolatory."

Trembling its closed eyes and sleeked wings
About me; and the pearliest dew not brings
Such morning incense from the fields of May,   470
As do those brighter drops that twinkling stray
From those kind eyes,—the very home and haunt
Of sisterly affection. Can I want
Aught else, aught nearer heaven, than such tears?
Yet dry them up, in bidding hence all fears   475
That, any longer, I will pass my days
Alone and sad. No, I will once more raise
My voice upon the mountain-heights; once more
Make my horn parley from their foreheads hoar:[8]
Again my trooping hounds their tongues shall loll   480
Around the breathed boar: again I'll poll[9]
The fair-grown yew tree, for a chosen bow:
And, when the pleasant sun is getting low,
Again I'll linger in a sloping mead
To hear the speckled thrushes, and see feed   485
Our idle sheep. So be thou cheered, sweet,
And, if thy lute is here, softly intreat
My soul to keep in its resolved course."

    Hereat Peona, in their silver source,
Shut her pure sorrow drops with glad exclaim,   490
And took a lute, from which there pulsing came
A lively prelude, fashioning the way
In which her voice should wander. 'Twas a lay
More subtle cadenced, more forest wild
Than Dryope's[1] lone lulling of her child;   495
And nothing since has floated in the air
So mournful strange. Surely some influence rare
Went, spiritual, through the damsel's hand;
For still, with Delphic[2] emphasis, she spann'd
The quick invisible strings, even though she saw   500
Endymion's spirit melt away and thaw
Before the deep intoxication.
But soon she came, with sudden burst, upon
Her self-possession—swung the lute aside,
And earnestly said: "Brother, 'tis vain to hide   505
That thou dost know of things mysterious,
Immortal, starry; such alone could thus
Weigh down thy nature. Hast thou sinn'd in aught
Offensive to the heavenly powers? Caught
A Paphian[3] dove upon a message sent?   510
Thy deathful bow against some deer-herd bent,
Sacred to Dian? Haply, thou hast seen
Her naked limbs among the alders green;

8. Gray or white with age.
9. To cut off the top of.
1. Woodhouse *E*, p. 71 identifies Dryope as the mother of Pan, but Allott suggests this is the other Dryope, a nymph who was metamorphized into a tree while nursing a child (Ovid, *Metamorphoses* 9.371–79).
2. Delphi was the site of an oracle sacred to Apollo.
3. From the temple in Paphos dedicated to Venus, to whom the dove was sacred.

And that, alas! is death.[4] No, I can trace
Something more high perplexing in thy face!"   515

    Endymion look'd at her, and press'd her hand,
And said, "Art thou so pale, who wast so bland[5]
And merry in our meadows? How is this?
Tell me thine ailment: tell me all amiss!—
Ah! thou hast been unhappy at the change   520
Wrought suddenly in me. What indeed more strange?
Or more complete to overwhelm surmise?
Ambition is no sluggard: 'tis no prize,
That toiling years would put within my grasp,
That I have sigh'd for: with so deadly gasp   525
No man e'er panted for a mortal love.
So all have set my heavier grief above
These things which happen. Rightly have they done:
I, who still saw the horizontal sun
Heave his broad shoulder o'er the edge of the world,   530
Out-facing Lucifer,[6] and then had hurl'd
My spear aloft, as signal for the chace—
I, who, for very sport of heart, would race
With my own steed from Araby; pluck down
A vulture from his towery perching; frown   535
A lion into growling, loth retire—
To lose, at once, all my toil breeding fire,
And sink thus low! but I will ease my breast
Of secret grief, here in this bowery nest.

    "This river does not see the naked sky,   540
Till it begins to progress silverly[7]
Around the western border of the wood,
Whence, from a certain spot, its winding flood
Seems at the distance like a crescent moon:
And in that nook, the very pride of June,   545
Had I been used to pass my weary eves;
The rather for the sun unwilling leaves
So dear a picture of his sovereign power,
And I could witness his most kingly hour,
When he doth lighten[8] up the golden reins,   550
And paces leisurely down amber plains
His snorting four. Now when his chariot last
Its beams against the zodiac-lion[9] cast,
There blossom'd suddenly a magic bed

---

4. Allusion to the myth of Actaeon who was transformed into a stag and hunted down by his own dogs after he saw Diana, the goddess of the moon, naked (Ovid, *Metamorphoses*, 3.173–252).
5. Having a soothing effect.
6. Woodhouse *E*, p. 75 notes, "the morning star, the last that leaves heaven."
7. In his fair copy, Keats put "progress silverly" in quotation marks; the echo is of Shakespeare's *King John* 5.2.46.
8. Stillinger changes this to "tighten," arguing you tighten up the reins when you wish to slow down as in the next line; dressage experts suggest, however, that "lighten" is correct, as tightening the reins would encourage the horse to speed up, while lightening them would allow the horse to relax and slow down.
9. Leo, a constellation; on Keats's knowledge of astronomy, see Roe, pp. 33–45.

Of sacred ditamy, and poppies red:[1] 555
At which I wondered greatly, knowing well
That but one night had wrought this flowery spell;
And, sitting down close by, began to muse
What it might mean. Perhaps, thought I, Morpheus,[2]
In passing here, his owlet pinions shook; 560
Or, it may be, ere matron Night uptook
Her ebon urn, young Mercury, by stealth,
Had dipt his rod in it:[3] such garland wealth
Came not by common growth. Thus on I thought,
Until my head was dizzy and distraught. 565
Moreover, through the dancing poppies stole
A breeze, most softly lulling to my soul;
And shaping visions all about my sight
Of colours, wings, and bursts of spangly light;
The which became more strange, and strange, and dim, 570
And then were gulph'd in a tumultuous swim:
And then I fell asleep. Ah, can I tell
The enchantment that afterwards befel?
Yet it was but a dream: yet such a dream
That never tongue, although it overteem 575
With mellow utterance, like a cavern spring,
Could figure out and to conception bring
All I beheld and felt. Methought I lay
Watching the zenith, where the milky way
Among the stars in virgin splendour pours; 580
And travelling my eye, until the doors
Of heaven appear'd to open for my flight,
I became loth and fearful to alight
From such high soaring by a downward glance:
So kept me stedfast in that airy trance, 585
Spreading imaginary pinions wide.
When, presently, the stars began to glide,
And faint away, before my eager view:
At which I sigh'd that I could not pursue,
And dropt my vision to the horizon's verge; 590
And lo! from opening clouds, I saw emerge
The loveliest moon, that ever silver'd o'er
A shell for Neptune's goblet: she did soar
So passionately bright, my dazzled soul
Commingling with her argent[4] spheres did roll 595
Through clear and cloudy, even when she went
At last into a dark and vapoury tent—
Whereat, methought, the lidless-eyed train
Of planets all were in the blue again.
To commune with those orbs, once more I rais'd 600
My sight right upward: but it was quite dazed
By a bright something, sailing down apace,

1. Lemprière: "Among plants the poppy and the ditamy [the Cretan dittany, "famous for its alleged medicinal virtues," OED] were sacred to" Diana.
2. The god of sleep, often pictured with wings and holding poppies.
3. The caduceus, the magic wand carried by Mercury; Night or Nox, the goddess of the night, was "crowned with poppies and carried on a chariot drawn by owls and bats" (Lemprière).
4. Silvery.

Making me quickly veil my eyes and face:
Again I look'd, and, O ye deities,
Who from Olympus watch our destinies!   605
Whence that completed form of all completeness?
Whence came that high perfection of all sweetness?
Speak, stubborn earth, and tell me where, O where
Hast thou a symbol of her golden hair?
Not oat-sheaves drooping in the western sun;   610
Not—thy soft hand, fair sister! let me shun
Such follying before thee—yet she had,
Indeed, locks bright enough to make me mad;
And they were simply gordian'd[5] up and braided,
Leaving, in naked comeliness, unshaded,   615
Her pearl round ears, white neck, and orbed brow;
The which were blended in, I know not how,
With such a paradise of lips and eyes,
Blush-tinted cheeks, half smiles, and faintest sighs,
That, when I think thereon, my spirit clings   620
And plays about its fancy, till the stings
Of human neighbourhood envenom all.
Unto what awful power shall I call?
To what high fane?[6]—Ah! see her hovering feet,
More bluely vein'd, more soft, more whitely sweet   625
Than those of sea-born Venus, when she rose
From out her cradle shell.[7] The wind out-blows
Her scarf into a fluttering pavilion;
'Tis blue, and over-spangled with a million
Of little eyes, as though thou wert to shed,   630
Over the darkest, lushest blue-bell bed,
Handfuls of daisies."—"Endymion, how strange!
Dream within dream!"—"She took an airy range,
And then, towards me, like a very maid,
Came blushing, waning, willing, and afraid,   635
And press'd me by the hand: Ah! 'twas too much;
Methought I fainted at the charmed touch,
Yet held my recollection, even as one
Who dives three fathoms where the waters run
Gurgling in beds of coral: for anon,   640
I felt upmounted in that region
Where falling stars dart their artillery forth,
And eagles struggle with the buffeting north[8]
That balances the heavy meteor-stone;—
Felt too, I was not fearful, nor alone,   645
But lapp'd and lull'd along the dangerous sky.
Soon, as it seem'd, we left our journeying high,
And straightway into frightful eddies swoop'd;
Such as ay muster where grey time has scoop'd
Huge dens and caverns in a mountain's side: 650

---

5. Knotted, a Keatsian coinage from the famously intricate Gordian Knot.
6. Temple.
7. In most versions of her myth, Venus is "sprung from the froth of the sea, after the mutilated part of the body of Uranus had been thrown there by Saturn" (Lemprière).
8. The north wind, which, here, is strong enough to hold up a meteor.

There hollow sounds arous'd me, and I sigh'd
To faint once more by looking on my bliss—
I was distracted; madly did I kiss
The wooing arms which held me, and did give
My eyes at once to death: but 'twas to live,   655
To take in draughts of life from the gold fount
Of kind and passionate looks; to count, and count[9]
The moments, by some greedy help that seem'd
A second self, that each might be redeem'd
And plunder'd of its load of blessedness.   660
Ah, desperate mortal! I ev'n dar'd to press
Her very cheek against my crowned lip,
And, at that moment, felt my body dip
Into a warmer air: a moment more,
Our feet were soft in flowers. There was store   665
Of newest joys upon that alp. Sometimes
A scent of violets, and blossoming limes,
Loiter'd around us; then of honey cells,
Made delicate from all white-flower bells;
And once, above the edges of our nest,   670
An arch face peep'd,—an Oread[1] as I guess'd.

          "Why did I dream that sleep o'er-power'd me
In midst of all this heaven? Why not see,
Far off, the shadows of his pinions dark,
And stare them from me? But no, like a spark   675
That needs must die, although its little beam
Reflects upon a diamond, my sweet dream
Fell into nothing—into stupid sleep.
And so it was, until a gentle creep,
A careful moving caught my waking ears,   680
And up I started: Ah! my sighs, my tears,
My clenched hands;—for lo! the poppies hung
Dew-dabbled on their stalks, the ouzel[2] sung
A heavy ditty, and the sullen day
Had chidden herald Hesperus[3] away,   685
With leaden looks: the solitary breeze
Bluster'd, and slept, and its wild self did teaze
With wayward melancholy; and I thought,
Mark me, Peona! that sometimes it brought
Faint fare-thee-wells, and sigh-shrilled adieus!—   690
Away I wander'd—all the pleasant hues
Of heaven and earth had faded: deepest shades
Were deepest dungeons; heaths and sunny glades
Were full of pestilent light; our taintless rills
Seem'd sooty, and o'er-spread with upturn'd gills   695
Of dying fish; the vermeil rose had blown
In frightful scarlet, and its thorns out-grown
Like spiked aloe. If an innocent bird

9. Cook suggests a "serious play on 'cunt.'"
1. A mountain nymph; the Oreads accompanied Diana on her hunts.
2. Blackbird.
3. The evening star.

Before my heedless footsteps stirr'd, and stirr'd
In little journeys, I beheld in it   700
A disguis'd demon, missioned to knit
My soul with under darkness; to entice
My stumblings down some monstrous precipice:
Therefore I eager followed, and did curse
The disappointment.[4] Time, that aged nurse,   705
Rock'd me to patience. Now, thank gentle heaven!
These things, with all their comfortings, are given
To my down-sunken hours, and with thee,
Sweet sister, help to stem the ebbing sea
Of weary life."

          Thus ended he, and both   710
Sat silent: for the maid was very loth
To answer; feeling well that breathed words
Would all be lost, unheard, and vain as swords
Against the enchased[5] crocodile, or leaps
Of grasshoppers against the sun. She weeps,   715
And wonders; struggles to devise some blame;
To put on such a look as would say, *Shame
On this poor weakness!* but, for all her strife,
She could as soon have crush'd away the life
From a sick dove. At length, to break the pause,   720
She said with trembling chance: "Is this the cause?
This all? Yet it is strange, and sad, alas!
That one who through this middle earth should pass
Most like a sojourning demi-god, and leave
His name upon the harp-string, should achieve   725
No higher bard than simple maidenhood,
Singing alone, and fearfully,—how the blood
Left his young cheek; and how he used to stray
He knew not where; and how he would say, *nay*,
If any said 'twas love: and yet 'twas love;   730
What could it be but love? How a ring-dove
Let fall a sprig of yew tree in his path;
And how he died: and then, that love doth scathe
The gentle heart, as northern blasts do roses;
And then the ballad of his sad life closes   735
With sighs, and an alas!—Endymion!
Be rather in the trumpet's mouth,—anon
Among the winds at large—that all may hearken!
Although, before the crystal heavens darken,
I watch and dote upon the silver lakes   740
Pictur'd in western cloudiness, that takes
The semblance of gold rocks and bright gold sands,
Islands, and creeks, and amber-fretted strands
With horses prancing o'er them, palaces
And towers of amethyst,—would I so tease   745

---

4. This sense of despair about earthly things following a visionary experience is found throughout
Keats's poetry, e.g. "Sleep and Poetry" (p. 62, ll. 157–59) and his verse epistle to Reynolds (pp.
135–36, ll. 67–106).
5. Hunted.

My pleasant days, because I could not mount
Into those regions? The Morphean fount
Of that fine element that visions, dreams,
And fitful whims of sleep are made of,[6] streams
Into its airy channels with so subtle,   750
So thin a breathing, not the spider's shuttle,
Circled a million times within the space
Of a swallow's nest-door, could delay a trace,
A tinting of its quality: how light
Must dreams themselves be; seeing they're more slight   755
Than the mere nothing that engenders them!
Then wherefore sully the entrusted gem
Of high and noble life with thoughts so sick?
Why pierce high-fronted honour to the quick
For nothing but a dream?" Hereat the youth   760
Look'd up: a conflicting of shame and ruth[7]
Was in his plaited brow: yet, his eyelids
Widened a little, as when Zephyr bids
A little breeze to creep between the fans[8]
Of careless butterflies: amid his pains   765
He seem'd to taste a drop of manna-dew,[9]
Full palatable; and a colour grew
Upon his cheek, while thus he lifeful spake.

    "Peona! ever have I long'd to slake
My thirst for the world's praises: nothing base,   770
No merely slumberous phantasm, could unlace
The stubborn canvas for my voyage prepar'd—
Though now 'tis tatter'd; leaving my bark bar'd
And sullenly drifting: yet my higher hope
Is of too wide, too rainbow-large a scope,   775
To fret at myriads of earthly wrecks.
Wherein lies happiness?[1] In that which becks
Our ready minds to fellowship divine,
A fellowship with essence; till we shine,
Full alchemiz'd, and free of space. Behold   780
The clear religion of heaven! Fold
A rose leaf round thy finger's taperness,
And soothe thy lips: hist, when the airy stress
Of music's kiss impregnates the free winds,
And with a sympathetic touch unbinds   785
Eolian magic[2] from their lucid wombs:

---

6. Allott suggests ll. 747–49 echo Shakespeare, *The Tempest* 4.1.156–57: "We are such stuff / As dreams are made on ["of" in the Folio reading in Keats's copy]." *Morphean:* see p. 59, n. 3.
7. Remorse or, perhaps, dismay.
8. Wings.
9. For "manna," see Exodus 17.21; Allott suggests the compound was suggested by Coleridge's "Kubla Khan" (1816), l. 53, "he on honey-dew hath fed."
1. For Keats's description of this passage (ll. 777–842) as his "Pleasure Thermometer," see headnote above, p. 145. Byron said of this passage (esp. ll. 834–42), "Keats says . . . 'flowers would not blow, leaves bud' etc. if man and woman did not kiss. How sentimental" (Thomas Medwin, *Conversations of Lord Byron* [1824], p. 239). Keats's friend and churchman Benjamin Bailey objected to what he saw as Keats's "inclination to that abominable principle of *Shelley's*—that *Sensual Love* is the principle of *things*" (*KC*, 1: 34–35).
2. The music of the Aeolian wind harp.

Then old songs waken from enclouded tombs;
Old ditties sigh above their father's grave;
Ghosts of melodious prophecyings rave
Round every spot where trod Apollo's foot;   790
Bronze clarions awake, and faintly bruit,[3]
Where long ago a giant battle[4] was;
And, from the turf, a lullaby doth pass
In every place where infant Orpheus[5] slept.
Feel we these things?—that moment have we stept   795
Into a sort of oneness, and our state[6]
Is like a floating spirit's. But there are
Richer entanglements, enthralments far
More self-destroying, leading, by degrees,
To the chief intensity: the crown of these   800
Is made of love and friendship, and sits high
Upon the forehead of humanity.
All its more ponderous and bulky worth
Is friendship, whence there ever issues forth
A steady splendour; but at the tip-top,   805
There hangs by unseen film, an orbed drop
Of light, and that is love: its influence,
Thrown in our eyes, genders a novel sense,
At which we start and fret; till in the end,
Melting into its radiance, we blend,   810
Mingle, and so become a part of it,—
Nor with aught else can our souls interknit
So wingedly: when we combine therewith,
Life's self is nourish'd by its proper pith,
And we are nurtured like a pelican brood.[7]   815
Aye, so delicious is the unsating[8] food,
That men, who might have tower'd in the van
Of all the congregated world, to fan
And winnow from the coming step of time
All chaff of custom,[9] wipe away all slime   820
Left by men-slugs and human serpentry,
Have been content to let occasion die,
Whilst they did sleep in love's elysium.
And, truly, I would rather be struck dumb,
Than speak against this ardent listlessness: 825
For I have ever thought that it might bless
The world with benefits unknowingly;
As does the nightingale, upperched high,
And cloister'd among cool and bunched leaves—

3. Report, noise.
4. Perhaps the war between the Titans and Olympians that Keats would take up in *Hyperion*.
5. A legendary Greek hero and the son of Apollo and Calliope, Orpheus was known for his music, which had the power to move everything in nature; when his wife, Eurydice, died, he journeyed to the underworld where the power of his song so affected Hades that he released her back to life, but Orpheus lost her when he forgot Hades's injunction not to look back for his wife until they reached the light of day.
6. An unrhymed line.
7. Legend had it that the pelican would wound itself to feed its children with its own blood.
8. See p. 151, n.2.
9. For ll. 818–20, Allott cites Shakespeare, *Troilus and Cressida* 1.3.26–27: "Distinction with a loud and powerful fan, / Puffing at all, winnows the light [chaff] away."

She sings but to her love, nor e'er conceives   830
How tiptoe Night holds back her dark-grey hood.
Just so may love, although 'tis understood
The mere commingling of passionate breath,
Produce more than our searching witnesseth:
What I know not: but who, of men, can tell   835
That flowers would bloom, or that green fruit would swell
To melting pulp, that fish would have bright mail,
The earth its dower of river, wood, and vale,
The meadows runnels,[1] runnels pebble-stones,
The seed its harvest, or the lute its tones,   840
Tones ravishment, or ravishment its sweet,
If human souls did never kiss and greet?

      "Now, if this earthly love has power to make
Men's being mortal, immortal; to shake
Ambition from their memories, and brim   845
Their measure of content; what merest whim,
Seems all this poor endeavour after fame,
To one, who keeps within his stedfast aim
A love immortal, an immortal too.
Look not so wilder'd; for these things are true,   850
And never can be born of atomies[2]
That buzz about our slumbers, like brain-flies,
Leaving us fancy-sick. No, no, I'm sure,
My restless spirit never could endure
To brood so long upon one luxury,   855
Unless it did, though fearfully, espy
A hope beyond the shadow of a dream.
My sayings will the less obscured seem,
When I have told thee how my waking sight
Has made me scruple whether that same night   860
Was pass'd in dreaming. Hearken, sweet Peona!
Beyond the matron-temple of Latona,[3]
Which we should see but for these darkening boughs,
Lies a deep hollow, from whose ragged brows
Bushes and trees do lean all round athwart,   865
And meet so nearly, that with wings outraught,
And spreaded tail, a vulture could not glide
Past them, but he must brush on every side.
Some moulder'd steps lead into this cool cell,
Far as the slabbed margin of a well,   870
Whose patient level peeps its crystal eye
Right upward, through the bushes, to the sky.
Oft have I brought thee flowers, on their stalks set
Like vestal primroses, but dark velvet
Edges them round, and they have golden pits:[4]   875
'Twas there I got them, from the gaps and slits

---

1. Small streams.
2. Small beings, mites, but also skeletons.
3. The mother of Apollo and Diana/Cynthia/Phoebe.
4. Woodhouse E, p. 107 notes that Hunt's sister-in-law Elizabeth Kent quoted Keats's ll. 873–75 in
   her *Flora Domestica* (1823) and identified the flower as either the Auricula or the Polyanthus.

In a mossy stone, that sometimes was my seat,
When all above was faint with mid-day heat.
And there in strife no burning thoughts to heed,
I'd bubble up the water through a reed;   880
So reaching back to boy-hood: make me ships
Of moulted feathers, touchwood, alder chips,
With leaves stuck in them; and the Neptune be
Of their petty ocean. Oftener, heavily,
When love-lorn hours had left me less a child,   885
I sat contemplating the figures wild
Of o'er-head clouds melting the mirror through.[5]
Upon a day, while thus I watch'd, by flew
A cloudy Cupid, with his bow and quiver;
So plainly character'd, no breeze would shiver   890
The happy chance: so happy, I was fain
To follow it upon the open plain,
And, therefore, was just going; when, behold!
A wonder, fair as any I have told—
The same bright face I tasted in my sleep,   895
Smiling in the clear well. My heart did leap
Through the cool depth.—It moved as if to flee—
I started up, when lo! refreshfully,
There came upon my face, in plenteous showers,
Dew-drops, and dewy buds, and leaves, and flowers,   900
Wrapping all objects from my smothered sight,
Bathing my spirit in a new delight.
Aye, such a breathless honey-feel of bliss
Alone preserved me from the drear abyss
Of death, for the fair form had gone again.   905
Pleasure is oft a visitant; but pain
Clings cruelly to us, like the gnawing sloth[6]
On the deer's tender haunches: late, and loth,
'Tis scar'd away by slow returning pleasure.
How sickening, how dark the dreadful leisure   910
Of weary days, made deeper exquisite,
By a fore-knowledge of unslumbrous night!
Like sorrow came upon me, heavier still,
Than when I wander'd from the poppy hill:
And a whole age of lingering moments crept   915
Sluggishly by, ere more contentment swept
Away at once the deadly yellow spleen.[7]
Yes, thrice have I this fair enchantment seen;
Once more been tortured with renewed life.
When last the wintry gusts gave over strife   920
With the conquering sun of spring, and left the skies
Warm and serene, but yet with moistened eyes
In pity of the shatter'd infant buds,—
That time thou didst adorn, with amber studs,[8]

5. The crystal pool of ll. 870–72 above.
6. Since sloths are vegetarians, Cook suggests that "Keats puns on the sense of [sloth as the sin of] 'idleness' to make sloth a deadly predator."
7. In the theory of the four humours, the spleen was seen as the seat of melancholy.
8. Allott cites Marlowe's "Passionate Shepherd to his Love," ll. 17–18.

My hunting cap, because I laugh'd and smil'd,   925
Chatted with thee, and many days exil'd
All torment from my breast;—'twas even then,
Straying about, yet, coop'd up in the den
Of helpless discontent,—hurling my lance
From place to place, and following at chance,   930
At last, by hap, through some young trees it struck,
And, plashing among bedded pebbles, stuck
In the middle of a brook,—whose silver ramble
Down twenty little falls, through reeds and bramble,
Tracing along, it brought me to a cave,   935
Whence it ran brightly forth, and white did lave
The nether sides of mossy stones and rock,—
'Mong which it gurgled blythe adieus, to mock
Its own sweet grief at parting.[9] Overhead,
Hung a lush screen[1] of drooping weeds, and spread   940
Thick, as to curtain up some wood-nymph's home.
"Ah! impious mortal, whither do I roam?"
Said I, low voic'd: "Ah, whither! 'Tis the grot
Of Proserpine, when Hell, obscure and hot,
Doth her resign;[2] and where her tender hands   945
She dabbles, on the cool and sluicy sands:
Or 'tis the cell of Echo,[3] where she sits,
And babbles thorough silence, till her wits
Are gone in tender madness, and anon,
Faints into sleep, with many a dying tone   950
Of sadness. O that she would take my vows,
And breathe them sighingly among the boughs,
To sue her gentle ears for whose fair head,
Daily, I pluck sweet flowerets from their bed,
And weave them dyingly—send honey-whispers   955
Round every leaf, that all those gentle lispers
May sigh my love unto her pitying!
O charitable echo! hear, and sing
This ditty to her!—tell her"—so I stay'd
My foolish tongue, and listening, half afraid,   960
Stood stupefied with my own empty folly,
And blushing for the freaks of melancholy.
Salt tears were coming, when I heard my name
Most fondly lipp'd, and then these accents came:
"Endymion! the cave is secreter   965
Than the isle of Delos.[4] Echo hence shall stir
No sighs but sigh-warm kisses, or light noise
Of thy combing hand, the while it travelling cloys
And trembles through my labyrinthine hair."
At that oppress'd I hurried in.—Ah! where   970
Are those swift moments? Whither are they fled?

9. Allott cites Shakespeare, *Romeo and Juliet* 2.1.229: "Parting is such sweet sorrow."
1. The printed text has "scene"; the errata list offers "screne."
2. Proserpine, the daughter of Ceres, was abducted by Hades, who made her his queen in the underworld; Ceres, goddess of the harvest, refused to aid the crops until Proserpine was returned for half
   the year, giving us the seasons.
3. See p. 25, n. 8.
4. Island in the Cyclades reputed to be the birthplace of Apollo and Diana/Cynthia/Phoebe.

I'll smile no more, Peona; nor will wed
Sorrow the way to death; but patiently
Bear up against it: so farewel, sad sigh;
And come instead demurest meditation,   975
To occupy me wholly, and to fashion
My pilgrimage for the world's dusky brink.
No more will I count over, link by link,
My chain of grief: no longer strive to find
A half-forgetfulness in mountain wind   980
Blustering about my ears: aye, thou shalt see,
Dearest of sisters, what my life shall be;
What a calm round of hours shall make my days.
There is a paly flame of hope that plays
Where'er I look: but yet, I'll say 'tis naught—   985
And here I bid it die. Have not I caught,
Already, a more healthy countenance?
By this the sun is setting; we may chance
Meet some of our near-dwellers with my car."[5]

This said, he rose, faint-smiling like a star   990
Through autumn mists, and took Peona's hand:
They stept into the boat, and launch'd from land.

BOOK II.

O SOVEREIGN power of love! O grief! O balm!
All records, saving thine, come cool, and calm,
And shadowy, through the mist of passed years:
For others, good or bad, hatred and tears
Have become indolent; but touching thine,   5
One sigh doth echo, one poor sob doth pine,
One kiss brings honey-dew from buried days.
The woes of Troy, towers smothering o'er their blaze,
Stiff-holden shields, far-piercing spears, keen blades,
Struggling, and blood, and shrieks—all dimly fades   10
Into some backward corner of the brain;
Yet, in our very souls, we feel amain[1]
The close of Troilus and Cressid sweet.[2]
Hence, pageant history! hence, gilded cheat!
Swart[3] planet in the universe of deeds!   15
Wide sea, that one continuous murmur breeds
Along the pebbled shore of memory!
Many old rotten-timber'd boats there be
Upon thy vaporous bosom, magnified
To goodly vessels; many a sail of pride,   20
And golden keel'd, is left unlaunch'd and dry.
But wherefore this? What care, though owl did fly

---

5. That is, others will be nearby with his chariot.
1. "In, or with, full force" (*OED*).
2. The story of the doomed love of Troilus and Cressida, portrayed by Chaucer and Shakespeare, is
   more powerful than the history of the Trojan War; *close*: embrace.
3. Black, dark.

About the great Athenian admiral's mast?[4]
What care, though striding Alexander past
The Indus with his Macedonian numbers?[5]   25
Though old Ulysses tortured from his slumbers
The glutted Cyclops, what care?[6]—Juliet leaning
Amid her window-flowers,—sighing,—weaning
Tenderly her fancy from its maiden snow,
Doth more avail than these: the silver flow   30
Of Hero's tears, the swoon of Imogen,
Fair Pastorella in the bandit's den,[7]
Are things to brood on with more ardency
Than the death-day of empires.[8] Fearfully
Must such conviction come upon his head,   35
Who, thus far, discontent, has dared to tread,
Without one muse's smile, or kind behest,
The path of love and poesy. But rest,
In chaffing[9] restlessness, is yet more drear
Than to be crush'd, in striving to uprear   40
Love's standard on the battlements of song.
So once more days and nights aid me along,
Like legion'd soldiers.

                    Brain-sick shepherd prince,
What promise hast thou faithful guarded since
The day of sacrifice? Or, have new sorrows   45
Come with the constant dawn upon thy morrows?
Alas! 'tis his old grief. For many days,
Has he been wandering in uncertain ways:
Through wilderness, and woods of mossed oaks;
Counting his woe-worn minutes, by the strokes   50
Of the lone woodcutter; and listening still,
Hour after hour, to each lush-leav'd rill.
Now he is sitting by a shady spring,
And elbow-deep with feverous fingering
Stems the upbursting cold: a wild rose tree   55
Pavilions him in bloom, and he doth see
A bud which snares his fancy: lo! but now
He plucks it, dips its stalk in the water: how!
It swells, it buds, it flowers beneath his sight;
And, in the middle, there is softly pight[1]   60
A golden butterfly; upon whose wings
There must be surely character'd strange things,
For with wide eye he wonders, and smiles oft.

---

4. Plutarch's *Life of Themistocles* reports that while Themistocles was trying to urge his officers to engage in battle, an owl landed on the mast, convincing everyone they should fight.
5. Alexander the Great, with his army, here, "numbers," crossed the Indus in 326 B.C.E.
6. See Homer, *The Odyssey*, 9 for the account of Odysseus's blinding of the sleeping cyclops, Polyphemus.
7. Doomed lovers (ll. 27–32), with Juliet appearing in Shakespeare's play, Hero in poems by Marlowe and Hunt (1819), Imogen (or Innogen) in Shakespeare's *Cymbeline* (see esp. 4.2.196f.), and Pastorella in *The Faerie Queene* 6.11.
8. Including the "death-day" of Napoleon's empire in 1815.
9. Then-acceptable spelling of "chafing."
1. Archaic form of "pitched," here meaning "placed."

Lightly this little herald flew aloft,
Follow'd by glad Endymion's clasped hands: 65
Onward it flies. From languor's sullen bands
His limbs are loos'd, and eager, on he hies
Dazzled to trace it in the sunny skies.
It seem'd he flew, the way so easy was;
And like a new-born spirit did he pass   70
Through the green evening quiet in the sun,
O'er many a heath, through many a woodland dun,
Through buried paths, where sleepy twilight dreams
The summer time away. One track unseams
A wooded cleft, and, far away, the blue   75
Of ocean fades upon him; then, anew,
He sinks adown a solitary glen,
Where there was never sound of mortal men,
Saving, perhaps, some snow-light cadences
Melting to silence, when upon the breeze   80
Some holy bark let forth an anthem sweet,
To cheer itself to Delphi.[2] Still his feet
Went swift beneath the merry-winged guide,
Until it reached a splashing fountain's side
That, near a cavern's mouth, for ever pour'd   85
Unto the temperate air: then high it soar'd,
And, downward, suddenly began to dip,
As if, athirst with so much toil, 'twould sip
The crystal spout-head: so it did, with touch
Most delicate, as though afraid to smutch[3]   90
Even with mealy gold[4] the waters clear.
But, at that very touch, to disappear
So fairy-quick, was strange! Bewildered,
Endymion sought around, and shook each bed
Of covert flowers in vain; and then he flung   95
Himself along the grass. What gentle tongue,
What whisperer disturb'd his gloomy rest?
It was a nymph uprisen to the breast
In the fountain's pebbly margin, and she stood
'Mong lilies, like the youngest of the brood.   100
To him her dripping hand she softly kist,
And anxiously began to plait and twist
Her ringlets round her fingers, saying: "Youth!
Too long, alas, hast thou starv'd on the ruth,[5]
The bitterness of love: too long indeed,   105
Seeing thou art so gentle. Could I weed
Thy soul of care, by heavens, I would offer
All the bright riches of my crystal coffer
To Amphitrite;[6] all my clear-eyed fish,
Golden, or rainbow-sided, or purplish,   110

2. Pilgrims crossed the Aegean in a boat or "bark" to reach Apollo's oracle at Delphi.
3. Smudge.
4. Powdery dust on a butterfly's wing (see Shakespeare, *Troilus and Cressida* 3.3.72–73: "Men like
   butterflies / Show not their mealy wings but to the summer").
5. Pity; also sorrow.
6. Neptune's wife.

Vermilion-tail'd, or finn'd with silvery gauze;
Yea, or my veined pebble-floor, that draws
A virgin light to the deep; my grotto-sands
Tawny and gold, ooz'd slowly from far lands
By my diligent springs; my level lilies, shells,   115
My charming rod, my potent river spells;
Yes, every thing, even to the pearly cup
Meander⁷ gave me,—for I bubbled up
To fainting creatures in a desert wild.
But woe is me, I am but as a child   120
To gladden thee; and all I dare to say,
Is, that I pity thee; that on this day
I've been thy guide; that thou must wander far
In other regions, past the scanty bar
To mortal steps, before thou canst be ta'en   125
From every wasting sigh, from every pain,
Into the gentle bosom of thy love.
Why it is thus, one knows in heaven above:
But, a poor Naiad,⁸ I guess not. Farewel!
I have a ditty for my hollow cell."   130

    Hereat, she vanished from Endymion's gaze,
Who brooded o'er the water in amaze:
The dashing fount pour'd on, and where its pool
Lay, half asleep, in grass and rushes cool,
Quick waterflies and gnats were sporting still,   135
And fish were dimpling,⁹ as if good nor ill
Had fallen out that hour. The wanderer,
Holding his forehead, to keep off the burr¹
Of smothering fancies, patiently sat down;
And, while beneath the evening's sleepy frown   140
Glow-worms began to trim their starry lamps,
Thus breath'd he to himself: "Whoso encamps
To take a fancied city of delight,²
O what a wretch is he! and when 'tis his,
After long toil and travelling,³ to miss   145
The kernel of his hopes, how more than vile:
Yet, for him there's refreshment even in toil;
Another city doth he set about,
Free from the smallest pebble-bead⁴ of doubt
That he will seize on trickling honey-combs: 150
Alas, he finds them dry; and then he foams,
And onward to another city speeds.
But this is human life: the war, the deeds,
The disappointment, the anxiety,
Imagination's struggles, far and nigh,   155
All human; bearing in themselves this good,

---

7. See p. 60, n. 9.
8. Water nymph; Reynolds published his *Naiad*, dedicated to Haydon, in 1816.
9. Forming dimples or ripples, here as the fish rise to the surface to eat.
1. A "circle," "a nebulous or nimbus disk of light enfolding" the moon, or a "rough edge" (*OED*).
2. Unrhymed line.
3. Then an acceptable spelling of "travailing" (the reading of the draft), with a possible pun.
4. "Pebble-head" in printed version, corrected on the second issue errata sheet.

That they are still the air, the subtle food,
To make us feel existence, and to shew
How quiet death is. Where soil is men grow,
Whether to weeds or flowers; but for me,   160
There is no depth to strike in: I can see
Nought earthly worth my compassing; so stand
Upon a misty, jutting head of land—
Alone? No, no; and by the Orphean lute,
When mad Eurydice is listening to't;[5]   165
I'd rather stand upon this misty peak,
With not a thing to sigh for, or to seek,
But the soft shadow of my thrice-seen love,
Than be—I care not what. O meekest dove
Of heaven! O Cynthia, ten-times bright and fair!   170
From thy blue throne, now filling all the air,
Glance but one little beam of temper'd light
Into my bosom, that the dreadful might
And tyranny of love be somewhat scar'd!
Yet do not so, sweet queen; one torment spar'd,   175
Would give a pang to jealous misery,
Worse than the torment's self: but rather tie
Large wings upon my shoulders, and point out
My love's far dwelling. Though the playful rout
Of Cupids shun thee, too divine art thou,   180
Too keen in beauty, for thy silver prow
Not to have dipp'd in love's most gentle stream.
O be propitious, nor severely deem
My madness impious; for, by all the stars
That tend thy bidding, I do think the bars   185
That kept my spirit in are burst—that I
Am sailing with thee through the dizzy sky!
How beautiful thou art! The world how deep!
How tremulous-dazzlingly the wheels sweep
Around their axle! Then these gleaming reins,   190
How lithe! When this thy chariot attains
Its airy goal, haply some bower veils
Those twilight eyes? Those eyes!—my spirit fails—
Dear goddess, help! or the wide-gaping air
Will gulph me—help!"—At this with madden'd stare,   195
And lifted hands, and trembling lips he stood;
Like old Deucalion mountain'd o'er the flood,
Or blind Orion[6] hungry for the morn.
And, but from the deep cavern there was borne
A voice, he had been froze to senseless stone;   200
Nor sigh of his, nor plaint, nor passion'd moan
Had more been heard. Thus swell'd it forth: "Descend,[7]

---

5. For Eurydice and Orpheus, see p. 167, n. 5.
6. A Giant who had been blinded by Œnopion and who recovered his sight by staring at the rising
   sun. *Deucalion*: with his wife Pyrrha, Deucalion ("the Noah of the heathen deluge" as Woodhouse
   puts it, *E*, p. 139), was a survivor of a flood ordered by Jupiter to punish mankind; Ovid has him
   waiting for the flood waters to subside (*Metamorphoses* 1.316–19).
7. Endymion is called upon to descend into another world, a common motif in quest romance. Cook
   suggests that ll. 211–14 reflect Keats's reading of Dante's journey to hell in Cary's translation of
   The Divine Comedy.

Young mountaineer! descend where alleys bend
Into the sparry[8] hollows of the world!
Oft hast thou seen bolts of the thunder hurl'd   205
As from thy threshold; day by day hast been
A little lower than the chilly sheen
Of icy pinnacles, and dipp'dst thin arms
Into the deadening ether that still charms
Their marble being: now, as deep profound   210
As those are high, descend! He ne'er is crown'd
With immortality, who fears to follow
Where airy voices lead: so through the hollow,
The silent mysteries of earth, descend!"

He heard but the last words, nor could contend   215
One moment in reflection: for he fled
Into the fearful deep, to hide his head
From the clear moon, the trees, and coming madness.

'Twas far too strange, and wonderful for sadness;
Sharpening, by degrees, his appetite   220
To dive into the deepest. Dark, nor light,
The region;[9] nor bright, nor sombre wholly,
But mingled up; a gleaming melancholy;
A dusky empire and its diadems;
One faint eternal eventide of gems.   225
Aye, millions sparkled on a vein of gold,
Along whose track the prince quick footsteps told,
With all its lines abrupt and angular:
Out-shooting sometimes, like a meteor-star,
Through a vast antre; then the metal woof,[1]   230
Like Vulcan's[2] rainbow, with some monstrous roof
Curves hugely: now, far in the deep abyss,
It seems an angry lightning, and doth hiss
Fancy into belief: anon it leads
Through winding passages, where sameness breeds   235
Vexing conceptions of some sudden change;
Whether to silver grots, or giant range
Of sapphire columns, or fantastic bridge
Athwart a flood of crystal. On a ridge
Now fareth he, that o'er the vast beneath   240
Towers like an ocean-cliff, and whence he seeth
A hundred waterfalls, whose voices come
But as the murmuring surge. Chilly and numb
His bosom grew, when first he, far away,
Descried an orbed diamond, set to fray[3]   245
Old darkness from his throne: 'twas like the sun
Uprisen o'er chaos: and with such a stun

---

8. Rich with crystalline minerals, as in Reynolds's *The Eden of the Imagination* (1814): "Some sparry grot."
9. Allott suggests this underground region (ll. 221–39) owes something to Keats's reading of such works as *The Arabian Nights* and Beckford's *Vathek* (1786).
1. The crosswise threads of woven fabric; *antre*: a cave; see Shakespeare's *Othello*'s "antres vast" (1.3.139).
2. The blacksmith of the gods, able to cast a metallic rainbow.
3. Archaism for "to frighten."

Came the amazement, that, absorb'd in it,
He saw not fiercer wonders—past the wit
Of any spirit to tell, but one of those   250
Who, when this planet's sphering time⁴ doth close,
Will be its high remembrancers: who they?
The mighty ones who have made eternal day
For Greece and England.⁵ While astonishment
With deep-drawn sighs was quieting, he went   255
Into a marble gallery, passing through
A mimic temple, so complete and true
In sacred custom, that he well nigh fear'd
To search it inwards; whence far off appear'd,
Through a long pillar'd vista, a fair shrine,   260
And, just beyond, on light tiptoe divine,
A quiver'd Dian.⁶ Stepping awfully,
The youth approach'd; oft turning his veil'd eye
Down sidelong aisles, and into niches old.
And when, more near against the marble cold   265
He had touch'd his forehead, he began to thread
All courts and passages, where silence dead
Rous'd by his whispering footsteps murmured faint:
And long he travers'd to and fro, to acquaint
Himself with every mystery, and awe;   270
Till, weary, he sat down before the maw
Of a wide outlet, fathomless and dim,
To wild uncertainty and shadows grim.
There, when new wonders ceas'd to float before,
And thoughts of self came on, how crude and sore   275
The journey homeward to habitual self!
A mad-pursuing of the fog-born elf,⁷
Whose flitting lantern, through rude nettle-briar,
Cheats us into a swamp, into a fire,
Into the bosom of a hated thing.   280

    What misery most drowningly doth sing
In lone Endymion's ear, now he has raught⁸
The goal of consciousness? Ah, 'tis the thought,
The deadly feel of solitude: for lo!
He cannot see the heavens, nor the flow   285
Of rivers, nor hill-flowers running wild
In pink and purple chequer, nor, up-pil'd,
The cloudy rack slow journeying in the west,
Like herded elephants; nor felt, nor prest
Cool grass, nor tasted the fresh slumberous air;   290
But far from such companionship to wear
An unknown time, surcharg'd with grief, away,
Was now his lot. And must he patient stay,
Tracing fantastic figures with his spear?

---

4. Time needed to complete an orbit.
5. That is, these countries' poets.
6. Diana/Cynthia/Phoebe as huntress.
7. A will-o-the-wisp or *ignis fatuus*.
8. Reached. This is the fair copy reading; the printed version has "caught."

"No!" exclaimed he, "why should I tarry here?"   295
No! loudly echoed times innumerable.
At which he straightway started, and 'gan tell
His paces back into the temple's chief;[9]
Warming and glowing strong in the belief
Of help from Dian: so that when again   300
He caught her airy form, thus did he plain,[1]
Moving more near the while. "O Haunter chaste
Of river sides, and woods, and heathy waste,
Where with thy silver bow and arrows keen
Art thou now forested? O woodland Queen,   305
What smoothest air thy smoother forehead woos?
Where dost thou listen to the wide halloos
Of thy disparted nymphs? Through what dark tree
Glimmers thy crescent? Wheresoe'er it be,
'Tis in the breath of heaven: thou dost taste   310
Freedom as none can taste it, nor dost waste
Thy loveliness in dismal elements;
But, finding in our green earth sweet contents,
There livest blissfully. Ah, if to thee
It feels Elysian, how rich to me,   315
An exil'd mortal, sounds its pleasant name!
Within my breast there lives a choking flame—
O let me cool it the zephyr-boughs among![2]
A homeward fever parches up my tongue—
O let me slake it at the running springs!   320
Upon my ear a noisy nothing rings—
O let me once more hear the linnet's note!
Before mine eyes thick films and shadows float—
O let me 'noint them with the heaven's light!
Dost thou now lave thy feet and ankles white?   325
O think how sweet to me the freshening sluice!
Dost thou now please thy thirst with berry-juice?
O think how this dry palate would rejoice!
If in soft slumber thou dost hear my voice,
O think how I should love a bed of flowers!—   330
Young goddess! let me see my native bowers!
Deliver me from this rapacious deep!"

        Thus ending loudly, as he would o'erleap
His destiny, alert he stood: but when
Obstinate silence came heavily again,   335
Feeling about for its old couch of space
And airy cradle, lowly bow'd his face
Desponding, o'er the marble floor's cold thrill.
But 'twas not long; for, sweeter than the rill
To its old channel, or a swollen tide   340
To margin sallows,[3] were the leaves he spied,

9. "Head, top, upper end" (OED).
1. Complain.
2. This is Woodhouse's correction for the rhyme (on verso of fair copy) of the printed version's "among the zephyr-boughs."
3. Willows.

And flowers, and wreaths, and ready myrtle crowns
Up heaping through the slab: refreshment drowns
Itself, and strives its own delights to hide—
Nor in one spot alone; the floral pride   345
In a long whispering birth enchanted grew
Before his footsteps; as when heav'd anew
Old ocean rolls a lengthened wave to the shore,
Down whose green back the short-liv'd foam, all hoar,
Bursts gradual, with a wayward indolence.   350

    Increasing still in heart, and pleasant sense,
Upon his fairy journey on he hastes;
So anxious for the end, he scarcely wastes
One moment with his hand among the sweets:
Onward he goes—he stops—his bosom beats   355
As plainly in his ear, as the faint charm
Of which the throbs were born. This still alarm,
This sleepy music, forc'd him walk tiptoe:
For it came more softly than the east could blow
Arion's magic to the Atlantic isles;   360
Or than the west, made jealous by the smiles
Of thron'd Apollo, could breathe back the lyre
To seas Ionian and Tyrian.[4]

    O did he ever live, that lonely man,
Who lov'd—and music slew not? 'Tis the pest   365
Of love, that fairest joys give most unrest;
That things of delicate and tenderest worth
Are swallow'd all, and made a seared dearth,
By one consuming flame: it doth immerse
And suffocate true blessings in a curse.   370
Half-happy, by comparison of bliss,
Is miserable. 'Twas even so with this
Dew-dropping melody, in the Carian's[5] ear;
First heaven, then hell, and then forgotten clear,
Vanish'd in elemental passion.   375

    And down some swart[6] abysm he had gone,
Had not a heavenly guide benignant led
To where thick myrtle branches, 'gainst his head
Brushing, awakened: then the sounds again
Went noiseless as a passing noontide rain   380

---

4. The rhyme at the end of this line ("Dire / Was the lovelorn despair") was lost in revision. Arion: a legendary poet who had accumulated great riches in Italy. Seeking to return to his home on Lesbos, he was seized by the sailors who intended to kill him and seize his wealth; requesting to sing one last song, he so charmed a school of dolphins that he jumped into the sea and rode off on one of their backs. Woodhouse compared this description of Arion's music wafting on the winds to the Atlantic only to be blown back to Greece by a jealous Zephyr favorably to Shakespeare's account of music's power that opens *Twelfth Night*. *seas Ionian and Tyrian*: the Ionian Sea is an arm of the Mediterranean, south of the Adriatic and bounded by southern Italy and Albania; the Mediterranean Sea was sometimes called the Tyrian Sea, given the prevalence of ships from Tyre crossing its waterways.
5. Endymion's.
6. Black, dark; Allott suggests Shakespeare, *The Tempest* 1.2.50: "the dark backward and abysm of time."

Over a bower, where little space he stood;
For as the sunset peeps into a wood
So saw he panting light, and towards it went
Through winding alleys; and lo, wonderment!
Upon soft verdure saw, one here, one there,   385
Cupids a slumbering on their pinions fair.

After a thousand mazes overgone,
At last, with sudden step, he came upon
A chamber,[7] myrtle wall'd, embowered high,
Full of light, incense, tender minstrelsy,   390
And more of beautiful and strange beside:
For on a silken couch of rosy pride,
In midst of all, there lay a sleeping youth
Of fondest beauty; fonder, in fair sooth,
Than sighs could fathom, or contentment reach: 395
And coverlids gold-tinted like the peach,
Or ripe October's faded marigolds,
Fell sleek about him in a thousand folds—
Not hiding up an Apollonian curve
Of neck and shoulder, nor the tenting swerve   400
Of knee from knee,[8] nor ankles pointing light;
But rather, giving them to the filled sight
Officiously. Sideway his face repos'd
On one white arm, and tenderly unclos'd,
By tenderest pressure, a faint damask mouth   405
To slumbery pout; just as the morning south
Disparts[9] a dew-lipp'd rose. Above his head,
Four lily stalks did their white honours wed
To make a coronal; and round him grew
All tendrils green, of every bloom and hue,   410
Together intertwin'd and trammel'd fresh:
The vine of glossy sprout; the ivy mesh,
Shading its Ethiop berries; and woodbine,
Of velvet leaves and bugle-blooms divine;
Convolvulus in streaked vases flush;   415
The creeper, mellowing for an autumn blush;
And virgin's bower, trailing airily;
With others of the sisterhood.[1] Hard by,
Stood serene Cupids watching silently.
One, kneeling to a lyre, touch'd the strings,   420
Muffling to death the pathos with his wings;
And, ever and anon, uprose to look
At the youth's slumber; while another took
A willow-bough, distilling odorous dew,
And shook it on his hair; another flew   425

---

7. Keats's Bower of Adonis draws upon the Garden of Adonis in Spenser's *The Faerie Queene* 3.6,
   Shakespeare's *Venus and Adonis*, and Ovid's *Metamorphoses* 10.
8. Woodhouse *E*, p. 159: "i.e. in the form of the top of a tent—So explained by the author to me."
9. Opens up but also separates (see 2.308 above).
1. Various forms of climbing plant intertwine (ll. 409–18), including ivy with dark berries, the convolvulus, which is an herb of the morning-glory family, and the virgin's bower, a species of clema-
   tis also known as Traveler's Joy and Old Man's Beard.

In through the woven roof, and fluttering-wise
Rain'd violets upon his sleeping eyes.

At these enchantments, and yet many more,
The breathless Latmian wonder'd o'er and o'er;
Until, impatient in embarrassment,   430
He forthright pass'd, and lightly treading went
To that same feather'd lyrist, who straightway,
Smiling, thus whisper'd: "Though from upper day
Thou art a wanderer, and thy presence here
Might seem unholy, be of happy cheer!   435
For 'tis the nicest touch of human honour,
When some ethereal and high-favouring donor
Presents immortal bowers to mortal sense;
As now 'tis done to thee, Endymion. Hence
Was I in no wise startled. So recline   440
Upon these living flowers. Here is wine,
Alive with sparkles—never, I aver,
Since Ariadne was a vintager,[2]
So cool a purple: taste these juicy pears,
Sent me by sad Vertumnus, when his fears   445
Were high about Pomona:[3] here is cream,
Deepening to richness from a snowy gleam;
Sweeter than that nurse Amalthea skimm'd
For the boy Jupiter:[4] and here, undimm'd
By any touch, a bunch of blooming plums   450
Ready to melt between an infant's gums:
And here is manna pick'd from Syrian trees,
In starlight, by the three Hesperides.[5]
Feast on, and meanwhile I will let thee know
Of all these things around us." He did so,   455
Still brooding o'er the cadence of his lyre;
And thus: "I need not any hearing tire
By telling how the sea-born goddess pin'd
For a mortal youth, and how she strove to bind
Him all in all unto her doting self.[6]   460
Who would not be so prison'd? but, fond elf,[7]

2. Ariadne was abandoned by Theseus on Naxos after she helped him escape from the Cretan labyrinth. Bacchus then took her as a lover, as Hunt relates in his "Bacchus and Ariadne" (1819). Woodhouse *E*, p. 163 notes "The happy idea of supposing her to have become a Vintager belongs, I believe, wholly to the Poet."
3. Woodhouse *E*, p. 163: "Vertumnus, the God of orchards (whom the Poet in the exuberance of his fancy supposes to have bribed Love to be propitious) succeeded in his addresses & married Pomona." See Ovid, *Metamorphoses* 14.623–771.
4. Woodhouse *E*, p. 163: "Amalthea, was the Daughter of Melissus, King of Crete. She had the care of the Infant Jupiter, whilst he was concealed, on Mount Ida in Crete, from his father Saturn, & fed him on goat's milk & honey." She was rewarded with one of the goat's horns, known as the horn of plenty.
5. Woodhouse *E*, p. 163: the Hesperides "were so called from their father Hesperus [the evening star]; & were appointed to preserve the golden apples in a garden teeming with all kinds of delicious fruits." See Ovid, *Metamorphoses*, 4.637–38, 11.113–14.
6. Keats's account of the love of "sea-born" Venus for the mortal Adonis (ll. 457–80) draws on Shakespeare's *Venus and Adonis*, Spenser's *The Faerie Queene* 3.1.34–38, 6.46–49, and Ovid's *Metamorphoses* 10.519–52, 708–39. The detail of Venus pleading with Jupiter is not in these sources but in Baldwin's *Pantheon*, chap. xxiii.
7. "Fond" can be both "loving" and "foolish"; with "elf," Keats seems to be thinking of the knights in *The Faerie Queene*, as in Shelley's pseudonym, "Elfin Knight."

He was content to let her amorous plea
Faint through his careless arms; content to see
An unseiz'd heaven dying at his feet;
Content, O fool! to make a cold retreat,   465
When on the pleasant grass such love, lovelorn,
Lay sorrowing; when every tear was born
Of diverse passion; when her lips and eyes
Were clos'd in sullen moisture, and quick sighs
Came vex'd and pettish through her nostrils small.   470
Hush! no exclaim—yet, justly mightst thou call
Curses upon his head.—I was half glad,
But my poor mistress went distract and mad,
When the boar tusk'd him: so away she flew
To Jove's high throne, and by her plainings drew   475
Immortal tear-drops down the thunderer's beard;
Whereon, it was decreed he should be rear'd
Each summer time to life. Lo! this is he,
That same Adonis, safe in the privacy
Of this still region all his winter-sleep.   480
Aye, sleep; for when our love-sick queen did weep
Over his waned corse, the tremulous shower
Heal'd up the wound, and, with a balmy power,
Medicined death to a lengthened drowsiness:
The which she fills with visions, and doth dress   485
In all this quiet luxury; and hath set
Us young immortals, without any let,
To watch his slumber through. 'Tis well nigh pass'd,
Even to a moment's filling up, and fast
She scuds with summer breezes, to pant through   490
The first long kiss, warm firstling, to renew
Embower'd sports in Cytherea's isle.[8]
Look! how those winged listeners all this while
Stand anxious: see! behold!"—This clamant[9] word
Broke through the careful silence; for they heard   495
A rustling noise of leaves, and out there flutter'd
Pigeons and doves: Adonis something mutter'd,
The while one hand, that erst upon his thigh
Lay dormant, mov'd convuls'd and gradually
Up to his forehead. Then there was a hum   500
Of sudden voices, echoing, "Come! come!
Arise! awake! Clear summer has forth walk'd
Unto the clover-sward, and she has talk'd
Full soothingly to every nested finch:
Rise, Cupids! or we'll give the blue-bell pinch   505
To your dimpled arms. Once more sweet life begin!"
At this, from every side they hurried in,
Rubbing their sleepy eyes with lazy wrists,
And doubling over head their little fists
In backward yawns. But all were soon alive: 510
For as delicious wine doth, sparkling, dive
In nectar'd clouds and curls through water fair,

8. The island where "sea-born" Venus first appeared.
9. Noisy, clamorous.

So from the arbour roof down swell'd an air
Odorous and enlivening; making all
To laugh, and play, and sing, and loudly call   515
For their sweet queen: when lo! the wreathed green
Disparted, and far upward could be seen
Blue heaven, and a silver car, air-borne,
Whose silent wheels, fresh wet from clouds of morn,
Spun off a drizzling dew,—which falling chill   520
On soft Adonis' shoulders, made him still
Nestle and turn uneasily about.
Soon were the white doves plain, with necks stretch'd out,
And silken traces lighten'd[1] in descent;
And soon, returning from love's banishment,   525
Queen Venus leaning downward open arm'd:
Her shadow fell upon his breast, and charm'd
A tumult to his heart, and a new life
Into his eyes. Ah, miserable strife,
But for her comforting! unhappy sight,   530
But meeting her blue orbs! Who, who can write
Of these first minutes? The unchariest muse
To embracements warm as theirs makes coy excuse.[2]

       O it has ruffled every spirit there,
Saving love's self, who stands superb to share   535
The general gladness: awfully he stands;
A sovereign quell[3] is in his waving hands;
No sight can bear the lightning of his bow;
His quiver is mysterious, none can know
What themselves think of it; from forth his eyes   540
There darts strange light of varied hues and dyes;
A scowl is sometimes on his brow, but who
Look full upon it feel anon the blue
Of his fair eyes run liquid through their souls.
Endymion feels it, and no more controls   545
The burning prayer within him; so, bent low,
He had begun a plaining of his woe.
But Venus, bending forward, said: "My child,
Favour this gentle youth; his days are wild
With love—he—but alas! too well I see   550
Thou know'st the deepness of his misery.
Ah, smile not so, my son: I tell thee true,
That when through heavy hours I used to rue
The endless sleep of this new-born Adon',
This stranger ay I pitied. For upon   555
A dreary morning once I fled away
Into the breezy clouds, to weep and pray
For this my love: for vexing Mars had teaz'd
Me even to tears:[4] thence, when a little eas'd,

---

1. See p. 161, n. 8.
2. Allott cites Milton's use of "coy excuse" in "Lycidas," ll. 18–20.
3. Archaic word meaning the power to subdue; here, Cupid's bow and arrows have the ability to subdue others to love. Venus fell in love with Adonis when Cupid accidentally hit her with an arrow.
4. Venus's affair with Mars, Cupid's father, was the most notorious of her amours.

Down-looking, vacant, through a hazy wood,   560
I saw this youth as he despairing stood:
Those same dark curls blown vagrant in the wind;
Those same full fringed lids a constant blind
Over his sullen eyes: I saw him throw
Himself on wither'd leaves, even as though   565
Death had come sudden; for no jot he mov'd,
Yet mutter'd wildly. I could hear he lov'd
Some fair immortal, and that his embrace
Had zoned her through the night. There is no trace
Of this in heaven: I have mark'd each cheek,   570
And find it is the vainest thing to seek;
And that of all things 'tis kept secretest.
Endymion! one day thou wilt be blest:
So still obey the guiding hand that fends
Thee safely through these wonders for sweet ends.   575
'Tis a concealment needful in extreme;
And if I guess'd not so, the sunny beam
Thou shouldest mount up to with me. Now adieu!
Here must we leave thee."—At these words up flew
The impatient doves, up rose the floating car,   580
Up went the hum celestial.[5] High afar
The Latmian saw them minish[6] into nought;
And, when all were clear vanish'd, still he caught
A vivid lightning from that dreadful bow.
When all was darkened, with Etnean[7] throe   585
The earth clos'd—gave a solitary moan—
And left him once again in twilight lone.

  He did not rave, he did not stare aghast,
For all those visions were o'ergone, and past,
And he in loneliness: he felt assur'd   590
Of happy times, when all he had endur'd
Would seem a feather to the mighty prize.
So, with unusual gladness, on he hies
Through caves, and palaces of mottled ore,
Gold dome, and crystal wall, and turquois floor,   595
Black polish'd porticos of awful shade,
And, at the last, a diamond balustrade,
Leading afar past wild magnificence,
Spiral through ruggedest loopholes, and thence
Stretching across a void, then guiding o'er   600
Enormous chasms, where, all foam and roar,
Streams subterranean tease their granite beds;
Then heighten'd just above the silvery heads
Of a thousand fountains,[8] so that he could dash

5. Clarke recalls Keats reading "the description of the 'Bower of Adonis'; and the conscious pleasure
   with which he looked up when he came to the passage that tells the ascent of the car of Venus"
   (KC, 2: 151).
6. Diminish. Keats has a number of cases where he uses aphaeresis for metrical reasons.
7. Mount Ætna, a volcano in Sicily, was sometimes thought of as housing the forge of Vulcan, Venus's
   husband.
8. For ll. 601–604, Allott cites Coleridge's "Kubla Khan" (1816), ll. 17–19, and Shelley's Alastor
   (1816), ll. 377–81.

The waters with his spear; but at the splash,   605
Done heedlessly, those spouting columns rose
Sudden a poplar's height, and 'gan to enclose
His diamond path with fretwork, streaming round
Alive, and dazzling cool, and with a sound,
Haply, like dolphin tumults, when sweet shells   610
Welcome the float of Thetis.[9] Long he dwells
On this delight; for, every minute's space,
The streams with changed magic interlace:
Sometimes like delicatest lattices,
Cover'd with crystal vines; then weeping trees,   615
Moving about as in a gentle wind,
Which, in a wink, to watery gauze refin'd,
Pour'd into shapes of curtain'd canopies,
Spangled, and rich with liquid broideries
Of flowers, peacocks, swans, and naiads[1] fair.   620
Swifter than lightning went these wonders rare;
And then the water, into stubborn streams
Collecting, mimick'd the wrought oaken beams,
Pillars, and frieze, and high fantastic roof,
Of those dusk places in times far aloof   625
Cathedrals call'd. He bade a loth farewel
To these founts Protean,[2] passing gulph, and dell,
And torrent, and ten thousand jutting shapes,
Half seen through deepest gloom, and griesly gapes,[3]
Blackening on every side, and overhead   630
A vaulted dome like Heaven's, far bespread
With starlight gems: aye, all so huge and strange,
The solitary felt a hurried change
Working within him into something dreary,—
Vex'd like a morning eagle, lost, and weary,   635
And purblind amid foggy, midnight wolds.[4]
But he revives at once: for who beholds
New sudden things, nor casts his mental slough?[5]
Forth from a rugged arch, in the dusk below,
Came mother Cybele![6] alone—alone—   640
In sombre chariot; dark foldings thrown
About her majesty, and front death-pale,
With turrets crown'd. Four maned lions hale
The sluggish wheels; solemn their toothed maws,
Their surly eyes brow-hidden, heavy paws   645
Uplifted drowsily, and nervy tails

9. Conch shells are blown for the arrival of Thetis, a sea goddess married to Peleus and the mother of Achilles.
1. See p. 41, n. 6.
2. Constantly changing; from Proteus, a shape-shifting sea god who plays a part in the story of Peleus and Thetis (Ovid's *Metamorphoses* 11.235–65).
3. Grisly or horrifying openings in the rocks; chasms.
4. Upland plains.
5. A state of extreme depression, as in the "Slough of Despond" in John Bunyan's *Pilgrim's Progress*.
6. Wife of Saturn and often conceived as mother earth and mother of the Olympian gods, Cybele is depicted on a chariot drawn by lions (in some accounts these are the transformed Hippomenes and Atalanta as in Ovid's *Metamorphoses* 10.560–707). She had a famous amour with Atys. Atys, Thetis, and other figures mentioned here appear in poems of Catullus most likely known to Keats. Bailey admired the sublimity of this passage (*KC*, 2: 284).

Cowering their tawny brushes. Silent sails
This shadowy queen athwart, and faints away
In another gloomy arch.

               Wherefore delay,
Young traveller, in such a mournful place?   650
Art thou wayworn, or canst not further trace
The diamond path? And does it indeed end
Abrupt in middle air? Yet earthward bend
Thy forehead, and to Jupiter cloud-borne
Call ardently! He was indeed wayworn;   655
Abrupt, in middle air, his way was lost;
To cloud-borne Jove he bowed, and there crost
Towards him a large eagle, 'twixt whose wings,
Without one impious word, himself he flings,
Committed to the darkness and the gloom: 660
Down, down, uncertain to what pleasant doom,
Swift as a fathoming plummet down he fell
Through unknown things; till exhaled asphodel,[7]
And rose, with spicy fannings interbreath'd,
Came swelling forth where little caves were wreath'd   665
So thick with leaves and mosses, that they seem'd
Large honey-combs of green, and freshly teem'd
With airs delicious. In the greenest nook
The eagle landed him, and farewel took.

       It was a jasmine bower, all bestrown   670
With golden moss. His every sense had grown
Ethereal for pleasure; 'bove his head
Flew a delight half-graspable; his tread
Was Hesperean;[8] to his capable ears
Silence was music from the holy spheres;   675
A dewy luxury[9] was in his eyes;
The little flowers felt his pleasant sighs
And stirr'd them faintly. Verdant cave and cell
He wander'd through, oft wondering at such swell
Of sudden exaltation: but, "Alas!"   680
Said he, "will all this gush of feeling pass
Away in solitude? And must they wane,
Like melodies upon a sandy plain,
Without an echo? Then shall I be left
So sad, so melancholy, so bereft!   685
Yet still I feel immortal! O my love,
My breath of life, where art thou? High above,
Dancing before the morning gates of heaven?[1]
Or keeping watch among those starry seven,

---

7. A type of lily.
8. Westward from Hesperus, the evening or westward star, but Cook, following Bush, suggests "Hes-
   peridean" for "as in the garden of the Hesperides," home of the golden apples.
9. For such expressions, see Ricks, *Keats and Embarrassment*.
1. Not knowing that his love is Diana, Endymion speculates she may be one of the Horae, the three
   daughters of Themis and Jupiter, identified with the seasons of spring, summer, and winter and
   imagined as opening the gates of heaven and Olympus when Apollo rides forth at dawn.

Old Atlas' children?[2] Art a maid of the waters,   690
One of shell-winding Triton's bright-hair'd daughters?
Or art, impossible! a nymph of Dian's,[3]
Weaving a coronal of tender scions[4]
For very idleness? Where'er thou art,
Methinks it now is at my will to start   695
Into thine arms; to scare Aurora's[5] train,
And snatch thee from the morning; o'er the main
To scud like a wild bird, and take thee off
From thy sea-foamy cradle; or to doff
Thy shepherd vest, and woo thee mid fresh leaves.[6]   700
No, no, too eagerly my soul deceives
Its powerless self: I know this cannot be.
O let me then by some sweet dreaming flee
To her entrancements: hither sleep awhile!
Hither most gentle sleep! and soothing foil   705
For some few hours the coming solitude."

    Thus spake he, and that moment felt endued
With power to dream deliciously; so wound
Through a dim passage, searching till he found
The smoothest mossy bed and deepest, where   710
He threw himself, and just into the air
Stretching his indolent arms, he took, O bliss!
A naked waist:[7] "Fair Cupid, whence is this?"
A well-known voice sigh'd, "Sweetest, here am I!"
At which soft ravishment, with doating cry   715
They trembled to each other.—Helicon![8]
O fountain'd hill! Old Homer's Helicon!
That thou wouldst spout a little streamlet o'er
These sorry pages; then the verse would soar
And sing above this gentle pair, like lark   720
Over his nested young: but all is dark
Around thine aged top, and thy clear fount
Exhales in mists to heaven. Aye, the count
Of mighty Poets is made up; the scroll
Is folded by the Muses; the bright roll   725
Is in Apollo's hand: our dazed eyes
Have seen a new tinge in the western skies:
The world has done its duty. Yet, oh yet,
Although the sun of poesy is set,

---

2. The Pleiades, the seven daughters of Atlas and Pleione who were turned into a constellation upon their death.
3. He asks whether his love is a sea-nymph serving the powerful ocean god Triton, usually pictured blowing a shell, or a nymph attending the huntress goddess, Diana.
4. Branches.
5. The dawn, whose chariot precedes that of Apollo, the sun.
6. If his love is a Horae, he will search for her at dawn, if a sea-nymph, he will "scud" or skim across the ocean looking for her, and if she is a nymph, he will "doff" or remove the "shepherd vest" she would wear in service to Diana.
7. Finney, *The Evolution of Keats's Poetry* (1936), p. 296, finds Endymion's erotic encounter with Diana/Cynthia/Phoebe to be a crude, Cockney imitation of the Poet's erotic dream in Shelley's *Alastor*.
8. A mountain in Boeotia sacred to the muses and the site of the fountain Hippocrene. Keats longs for the inspiration of ancient poetry (ll. 716–32).

These lovers did embrace, and we must weep   730
That there is no old power left to steep
A quill immortal in their joyous tears.
Long time in silence did their anxious fears
Question that thus it was; long time they lay
Fondling and kissing every doubt away;   735
Long time ere soft caressing sobs began
To mellow into words, and then there ran
Two bubbling springs of talk from their sweet lips.
"O known Unknown! from whom my being sips
Such darling essence, wherefore may I not   740
Be ever in these arms? in this sweet spot
Pillow my chin for ever? ever press
These toying hands and kiss their smooth excess?
Why not for ever and for ever feel
That breath about my eyes? Ah, thou wilt steal   745
Away from me again, indeed, indeed—
Thou wilt be gone away, and wilt not heed
My lonely madness. Speak, my delicious⁹ fair!
Is—is it to be so? No! Who will dare
To pluck thee from me? And, of thine own will,   750
Full well I feel thou wouldst not leave me. Still
Let me entwine thee surer, surer—now
How can we part? Elysium!¹ who art thou?
Who, that thou canst not be for ever here,
Or lift me with thee to some starry sphere?   755
Enchantress! tell me by this soft embrace,
By the most soft completion of thy face,
Those lips, O slippery blisses,² twinkling eyes,
And by these tenderest, milky sovereignties—
These tenderest, and by the nectar-wine,   760
The passion"—"O lov'd Ida³ the divine!
Endymion! dearest! Ah, unhappy me!
His soul will 'scape us—O felicity!
How he does love me! His poor temples beat
To the very tune of love—how sweet, sweet, sweet.   765
Revive, dear youth, or I shall faint and die;
Revive, or these soft hours will hurry by
In tranced dulness; speak, and let that spell
Affright this lethargy! I cannot quell
Its heavy pressure, and will press at least   770
My lips to thine, that they may richly feast
Until we taste the life of love again.
What! dost thou move? dost kiss? O bliss! O pain!
I love thee, youth, more than I can conceive;
And so long absence from thee doth bereave   775
My soul of any rest: yet must I hence:

9. From Keats's errata list; the printed version has "my kindest."
1. See p. 60, n. 8.
2. Lips are "slippery blisses" because of the moisture involved in kissing; see Ricks, *Keats and Embar-rassment.*
3. The mountain near Troy where Paris awarded the golden apple to Venus, so perhaps here a reference to Venus herself. The fair copy has "dov'd" for "lov'd"; the dove was sacred to Venus.

Yet, can I not to starry eminence
Uplift thee; nor for very shame can own
Myself to thee. Ah, dearest, do not groan
Or thou wilt force me from this secrecy,   780
And I must blush in heaven. O that I
Had done't already; that the dreadful smiles
At my lost brightness, my impassion'd wiles,
Had waned from Olympus' solemn height,
And from all serious Gods; that our delight   785
Was quite forgotten, save of us alone!
And wherefore so ashamed? 'Tis but to atone
For endless pleasure, by some coward blushes:
Yet must I be a coward!—Horror[4] rushes
Too palpable before me—the sad look   790
Of Jove—Minerva's[5] start—no bosom shook
With awe of purity—no Cupid pinion
In reverence veiled[6]—my crystalline dominion
Half lost, and all old hymns made nullity!
But what is this to love? O I could fly   795
With thee into the ken of heavenly powers,
So thou wouldst thus, for many sequent hours,
Press me so sweetly. Now I swear at once
That I am wise, that Pallas is a dunce—
Perhaps her love like mine is but unknown—   800
O I do think that I have been alone
In chastity: yes, Pallas has been sighing,
While every eve saw me my hair uptying
With fingers cool as aspen leaves. Sweet love,
I was as vague as solitary dove,   805
Nor knew that nests were built. Now a soft kiss—
Aye, by that kiss, I vow an endless bliss,
An immortality of passion's thine:
Ere long I will exalt thee to the shine
Of heaven ambrosial; and we will shade   810
Ourselves whole summers by a river glade;
And I will tell thee stories of the sky,
And breathe thee whispers of its minstrelsy.
My happy love will overwing all bounds!
O let me melt into thee; let the sounds   815
Of our close voices marry at their birth;
Let us entwine hoveringly—O dearth
Of human words! roughness of mortal speech!
Lispings empyrean will I sometime teach
Thine honied tongue—lute-breathings, which I gasp   820
To have thee understand, now while I clasp
Thee thus, and weep for fondness—I am pain'd,
Endymion: woe! woe! is grief contain'd
In the very deeps of pleasure, my sole life?"—
Hereat, with many sobs, her gentle strife   825

---

4. The errata list replaces the printed version's "honour."
5. Also known as Pallas (l. 799), Minerva is the goddess of wisdom, known for her chastity.
6. Then-acceptable spelling of "vailed," here meaning "lowered."

Melted into a languor. He return'd
Entranced vows and tears.

                    Ye who have yearn'd
With too much passion, will here stay and pity,
For the mere sake of truth; as 'tis a ditty
Not of these days, but long ago 'twas told   830
By a cavern wind unto a forest old;
And then the forest told it in a dream
To a sleeping lake, whose cool and level gleam
A poet caught as he was journeying
To Phœbus' shrine; and in it he did fling   835
His weary limbs, bathing an hour's space,
And after, straight in that inspired place
He sang the story up into the air,
Giving it universal freedom.[7] There
Has it been ever sounding for those ears   840
Whose tips are glowing hot. The legend cheers
Yon centinel stars; and he who listens to it
Must surely be self-doomed or he will rue it:
For quenchless burnings come upon the heart,
Made fiercer by a fear lest any part   845
Should be engulphed in the eddying wind.
As much as here is penn'd doth always find
A resting place, thus much comes clear and plain;
Anon the strange voice is upon the wane—
And 'tis but echo'd from departing sound,   850
That the fair visitant at last unwound
Her gentle limbs, and left the youth asleep.—
Thus the tradition of the gusty deep.

          Now turn we to our former chroniclers.[8]—
Endymion awoke, that grief of hers   855
Sweet paining on his ear: he sickly guess'd
How lone he was once more, and sadly press'd
His empty arms together, hung his head,
And most forlorn upon that widow'd bed
Sat silently. Love's madness he had known: 860
Often with more than tortured lion's groan
Moanings had burst from him; but now that rage
Had pass'd away: no longer did he wage
A rough-voic'd war against the dooming stars.
No, he had felt too much for such harsh jars: 865
The lyre of his soul Eolian[9] tun'd
Forgot all violence, and but commun'd
With melancholy thought: O he had swoon'd
Drunken from pleasure's nipple; and his love
Henceforth was dove-like.—Loth was he to move   870

7. This account (ll. 830–839) of the origin of myth looks back to "I stood tip-toe" (pp. 21–27) and to
   Book 4 of Wordsworth's *Excursion* (1814).
8. Earlier writers who took up the story of Endymion; Allott suggests that Drayton's *The Man in the
   Moone*, ll. 114–16 in particular is being echoed in ll. 855–60.
9. For the Aeolian harp, see p. 7, n. 6.

From the imprinted couch, and when he did,
'Twas with slow, languid paces, and face hid
In muffling hands. So temper'd, out he stray'd
Half seeing visions that might have dismay'd
Alecto's serpents;[1] ravishments more keen   875
Than Hermes' pipe, when anxious he did lean
Over eclipsing eyes:[2] and at the last
It was a sounding grotto, vaulted, vast,
O'er studded with a thousand, thousand pearls,
And crimson mouthed shells with stubborn curls,   880
Of every shape and size, even to the bulk
In which whales arbour[3] close, to brood and sulk
Against an endless storm. Moreover too,
Fish-semblances, of green and azure hue,
Ready to snort their streams. In this cool wonder   885
Endymion sat down, and 'gan to ponder
On all his life: his youth, up to the day
When 'mid acclaim, and feasts, and garlands gay,
He stept upon his shepherd throne: the look
Of his white palace in wild forest nook,   890
And all the revels he had lorded there:
Each tender maiden whom he once thought fair,
With every friend and fellow-woodlander—
Pass'd like a dream before him. Then the spur
Of the old bards to mighty deeds: his plans   895
To nurse the golden age 'mong shepherd clans:
That wondrous night: the great Pan-festival:
His sister's sorrow; and his wanderings all,
Until into the earth's deep maw he rush'd:
Then all its buried magic, till it flush'd   900
High with excessive love. "And now," thought he,
"How long must I remain in jeopardy
Of blank amazements that amaze no more?
Now I have tasted her sweet soul to the core
All other depths are shallow: essences,   905
Once spiritual, are like muddy lees,
Meant but to fertilize my earthly root,
And make my branches lift a golden fruit
Into the bloom of heaven: other light,
Though it be quick and sharp enough to blight   910
The Olympian eagle's vision, is dark,
Dark as the parentage of chaos. Hark!
My silent thoughts are echoing from these shells;
Or they are but the ghosts, the dying swells
Of noises far away?—list!"—Hereupon   915
He kept an anxious ear. The humming tone
Came louder, and behold, there as he lay,

1. Alecto, one of the Furies, is depicted with snakes covering her head.
2. Hermes (Mercury) charmed the hundred-eyed Argus to sleep with his pipe; see "A Dream, After Reading Dante's Episode of Paulo and Francesca" ("As Hermes once took to his feathers light"), p. 336.
3. Stillinger, following Woodhouse, changes this to "harbour." While the *OED* has no definition for "arbour" as a verb, it does offer "arboured": "Placed in or as in an arbour, arched over as by an arbour; embowered." This would be in keeping with Keats's language of bowers and a "green world."

On either side outgush'd, with misty spray,
A copious spring; and both together dash'd
Swift, mad, fantastic round the rocks, and lash'd   920
Among the conchs and shells of the lofty grot,
Leaving a trickling dew. At last they shot
Down from the ceiling's height, pouring a noise
As of some breathless racers whose hopes poize
Upon the last few steps, and with spent force   925
Along the ground they took a winding course.
Endymion follow'd—for it seem'd that one
Ever pursued, the other strove to shun—
Follow'd their languid mazes, till well nigh
He had left thinking of the mystery,—   930
And was now rapt in tender hoverings
Over the vanish'd bliss. Ah! what is it sings
His dream away? What melodies are these?
They sound as through the whispering of trees,
Not native in such barren vaults. Give ear!   935

      "O Arethusa,[4] peerless nymph! why fear
Such tenderness as mine? Great Dian, why,
Why didst thou hear her prayer? O that I
Were rippling round her dainty fairness now,
Circling about her waist, and striving how   940
To entice her to a dive! then stealing in
Between her luscious lips and eyelids thin.
O that her shining hair was in the sun,
And I distilling from it thence to run
In amorous rillets[5] down her shrinking form!   945
To linger on her lily shoulders, warm
Between her kissing breasts, and every charm
Touch raptur'd!—See how painfully I flow:
Fair maid, be pitiful to my great woe.
Stay, stay thy weary course, and let me lead,   950
A happy wooer, to the flowery mead
Where all that beauty snar'd me."—"Cruel god,
Desist! or my offended mistress' nod
Will stagnate all thy fountains:—tease me not
With syren words—Ah, have I really got   955
Such power to madden thee? And is it true—
Away, away, or I shall dearly rue
My very thoughts: in mercy then away,
Kindest Alpheus, for should I obey
My own dear will, 'twould be a deadly bane.   960
O, Oread-Queen![6] would that thou hadst a pain
Like this of mine, then would I fearless turn

---

4. Keats (ll. 936–1009) retells the Ovidian story (*Metamorphoses* 5.572–641) of the love of the river
   Alpheus for Arethusa, a nymph who follows Diana. Alpheus became enamored when Arethusa
   bathed in his waters and pursued her until she was transformed into a fountain by Diana. The legend recounts that the river Alpheus, rising in Arcadia, passes under ground to rise in Sicily near
   the fountain in order to join with its stream. Their story was also taken up by P. B. Shelley in lines
   written for M. Shelley's *Midas* and by Horace Smith in his "Sicilian Arethusa."
5. Rivulets.
6. Diana, queen over the nymphs known as Oreads.

And be a criminal. Alas, I burn,
I shudder—gentle river, get thee hence.
Alpheus! thou enchanter! every sense 965
Of mine was once made perfect in these woods.
Fresh breezes, bowery lawns, and innocent floods,
Ripe fruits, and lonely couch, contentment gave;
But ever since I heedlessly did lave
In thy deceitful stream, a panting glow 970
Grew strong within me: wherefore serve me so,
And call it love? Alas, 'twas cruelty.
Not once more did I close my happy eye
Amid the thrush's song. Away! Avaunt!
O 'twas a cruel thing."—"Now thou dost taunt 975
So softly, Arethusa, that I think
If thou wast playing on my shady brink,
Thou wouldst bathe once again. Innocent maid!
Stifle thine heart no more;—nor be afraid
Of angry powers: there are deities 980
Will shade us with their wings. Those fitful sighs
'Tis almost death to hear: O let me pour
A dewy balm upon them!—fear no more,
Sweet Arethusa! Dian's self must feel
Sometimes these very pangs. Dear maiden, steal 985
Blushing into my soul, and let us fly
These dreary caverns for the open sky.
I will delight thee all my winding course,
From the green sea up to my hidden source
About Arcadian forests; and will shew 990
The channels where my coolest waters flow
Through mossy rocks; where, 'mid exuberant green,
I roam in pleasant darkness, more unseen
Than Saturn in his exile;[7] where I brim
Round flowery islands, and take thence a skim 995
Of mealy[8] sweets, which myriads of bees
Buzz from their honied wings: and thou shouldst please
Thyself to choose the richest, where we might
Be incense-pillow'd every summer night.
Doff all sad fears, thou white deliciousness, 1000
And let us be thus comforted; unless
Thou couldst rejoice to see my hopeless stream
Hurry distracted from Sol's temperate beam,
And pour to death along some hungry sands."—
"What can I do, Alpheus? Dian stands 1005
Severe before me: persecuting fate!
Unhappy Arethusa! thou wast late
A huntress free in"—At this, sudden fell
Those two sad streams adown a fearful dell.
The Latmian listen'd, but he heard no more, 1010
Save echo, faint repeating o'er and o'er
The name of Arethusa. On the verge

7. Saturn after his defeat by the Olympians; see *Hyperion* pp. 475–95.
8. Powdery, with the "mealy sweets" being pollen.

Of that dark gulph he wept, and said: "I urge
Thee gentle Goddess of my pilgrimage,
By our eternal hopes, to soothe, to assuage,   1015
If thou art powerful, these lovers' pains;
And make them happy in some happy plains."

   He turn'd—there was a whelming sound—he stept,
There was a cooler light; and so he kept
Towards it by a sandy path, and lo!   1020
More suddenly than doth a moment go,
The visions of the earth were gone and fled—
He saw the giant sea above his head.[9]

BOOK III.

THERE are who lord it o'er their fellow-men
With most prevailing tinsel:[1] who unpen
Their baaing vanities,[2] to browse away
The comfortable green and juicy hay
From human pastures; or, O torturing fact!   5
Who, through an idiot blink, will see unpack'd
Fire-branded foxes to sear up and singe
Our gold and ripe-ear'd hopes.[3] With not one tinge
Of sanctuary splendour, not a sight
Able to face an owl's, they still are dight   10
By the blear-eyed nations in empurpled vests,
And crowns, and turbans.[4] With unladen breasts,
Save of blown self-applause, they proudly mount
To their spirit's perch, their being's high account,
Their tiptop nothings, their dull skies, their thrones—   15
Amid the fierce intoxicating tones
Of trumpets, shoutings, and belabour'd drums,
And sudden cannon.[5] Ah! how all this hums,
In wakeful ears, like uproar past and gone—
Like thunder clouds that spake to Babylon,   20

9. Gittings (p. 146) cites Cary's translation of Dante's *Inferno*, where Canto 26 closes, "And over us the booming billow clos'd"; Gittings finds that Keats's line "has the sudden sharp isolated echo of the great single lines with which Dante finishes each canto."
1. Keats (ll. 1–21) attacks the current government and its European allies which, in the wake of the defeat of Napoleon, had pursued a reactionary course, working to stamp out liberation movements abroad and to fight reform at home through a policy of suppressing political dissent and of supporting the building of new churches in impoverished areas. As Woodhouse notes (*E*, p. 220), "K said, with much simplicity, 'It will be easily seen what I think of the present Ministers, by the beginning of the 3ᵈ Book.'" As Allott points out, Keats echoes here the ideas of his friend Hunt, whose *Examiner* was a major voice in opposition to the Liverpool government.
2. Bailey, in objecting to the political message of these lines, also criticizes the phrase "baaing vanities" as an example of "Cockney" poetics (*KC*, 2: 269). Keats imagines the ministers as foxes in sheep's clothing, who will destroy the human community through lies and spectacle and, if that does not work, through violence.
3. See Judges 15.4–5, where Sampson unleashes foxes with firebrands tied to their tails to destroy the crops of the Philistines.
4. Hunt had recently attacked the French clergy for adopting Cardinal's hats of "Roman purple . . . the garb of the Antonines,—and of the Neros!" (*Examiner*, August 31, 1817, pp. 550–51). See Keats's "On Receiving a Laurel Crown from Leigh Hunt" (above, ll. 11–12), where he imagines a "trampling down of . . . Turbans and crowns and blank regality." *dight:* adorned.
5. Allott suggests these lines refer to the celebrations of the victory over Napoleon, particularly the "national jubilee" on August 1, 1814.

And set those old Chaldeans to their tasks.[6]—
Are then regalities all gilded masks?[7]
No, there are throned seats unscalable
But by a patient wing, a constant spell,
Or by ethereal things that, unconfin'd,   25
Can make a ladder of the eternal wind,
And poise about in cloudy thunder-tents
To watch the abysm-birth of elements.
Aye, 'bove the withering of old-lipp'd Fate
A thousand Powers keep religious state,   30
In water, fiery realm, and airy bourne;
And, silent as a consecrated urn,
Hold sphery sessions for a season due.
Yet few of these far majesties, ah, few!
Have bared their operations to this globe—   35
Few, who with gorgeous pageantry enrobe
Our piece of heaven—whose benevolence
Shakes hand with our own Ceres;[8] every sense
Filling with spiritual sweets to plenitude,
As bees gorge full their cells. And, by the feud   40
'Twixt Nothing and Creation,[9] I here swear,
Eterne Apollo! that thy Sister fair
Is of all these the gentlier-mightiest.
When thy gold breath is misting in the west,
She unobserved steals unto her throne,   45
And there she sits most meek and most alone;
As if she had not pomp subservient;
As if thine eye, high Poet! was not bent
Towards her with the Muses in thine heart;
As if the ministring stars kept not apart,   50
Waiting for silver-footed messages.
O Moon! the oldest shades 'mong oldest trees
Feel palpitations when thou lookest in:
O Moon! old boughs lisp forth a holier din
The while they feel thine airy fellowship.   55
Thou dost bless every where, with silver lip
Kissing dead things to life. The sleeping kine,[1]
Couched in thy brightness, dream of fields divine:
Innumerable mountains rise, and rise,
Ambitious for the hallowing of thine eyes;   60
And yet thy benediction passeth not
One obscure hiding-place, one little spot
Where pleasure may be sent: the nested wren
Has thy fair face within its tranquil ken,
And from beneath a sheltering ivy leaf   65
Takes glimpses of thee; thou art a relief
To the poor patient oyster, where it sleeps

6. The Chaldeans worshipped a thunder god, Rammon, also an oracle.
7. For power and theatricality, see Hazlitt's review of Shakespeare's *Coriolanus* in the *Examiner*,
   December 15, 1816, *Works*, 5: 347–50.
8. The goddess of the harvest and mother of Proserpine.
9. See Ovid's *Metamorphoses* 1.7–21 for the account of the creation behind this passage.
1. Cows.

Within its pearly house.—The mighty deeps,
The monstrous sea is thine—the myriad sea!
O Moon! far-spooming[2] Ocean bows to thee,   70
And Tellus[3] feels his forehead's cumbrous load.

    Cynthia! where art thou now? What far abode
Of green or silvery bower doth enshrine
Such utmost beauty? Alas, thou dost pine
For one as sorrowful: thy cheek is pale   75
For one whose cheek is pale: thou dost bewail
His tears, who weeps for thee. Where dost thou sigh?
Ah! surely that light peeps from Vesper's[4] eye,
Or what a thing is love! 'Tis She, but lo!
How chang'd, how full of ache, how gone in woe!   80
She dies at the thinnest cloud; her loveliness
Is wan on Neptune's blue: yet there's a stress
Of love-spangles, just off yon cape of trees,
Dancing upon the waves, as if to please
The curly foam with amorous influence.   85
O, not so idle: for down-glancing thence
She fathoms eddies, and runs wild about
O'erwhelming flung water-courses; scaring out
The thorny sharks from hiding-holes, and fright'ning
Their savage eyes with unaccustomed lightning.   90
Where will the splendor be content to reach?
O love! how potent hast thou been to teach
Strange journeyings! Wherever beauty dwells,
In gulf or aerie, mountains or deep dells,
In light, in gloom, in star or blazing sun,   95
Thou pointest out the way, and straight 'tis won.
Amid his toil thou gav'st Leander breath;
Thou leddest Orpheus through the gleams of death;
Thou madest Pluto bear thin element;[5]
And now, O winged Chieftain![6] thou hast sent   100
A moon-beam to the deep, deep water-world,
To find Endymion.

        On gold sand impearl'd
With lily shells, and pebbles milky white,
Poor Cynthia greeted him, and sooth'd her light
Against his pallid face: he felt the charm   105
To breathlessness, and suddenly a warm
Of his heart's blood: 'twas very sweet; he stay'd
His wandering steps, and half-entranced laid
His head upon a tuft of straggling weeds,
To taste the gentle moon, and freshening beads,   110
Lashed from the crystal roof by fishes' tails.
And so he kept, until the rosy veils

---

2. Foaming; Shelley also refers to the sea as a "Monster" in *Prometheus Unbound* (1820) 3.2.50.
3. The Earth who gives birth to the Titans.
4. The planet Venus as the evening star.
5. Pluto rose up into the "thin" air of earth in pursuit of Proserpine; Leander swam the Hellespont
   to reach his love, Hero; Orpheus descended into the underworld to win back his wife, Eurydice.
6. Cupid.

Mantling the east, by Aurora's[7] peering hand
Were lifted from the water's breast, and fann'd
Into sweet air; and sober'd morning came   115
Meekly through billows:—when like taper-flame
Left sudden by a dallying breath of air,
He rose in silence, and once more 'gan fare
Along his fated way.

           Far had he roam'd,
With nothing save the hollow vast, that foam'd   120
Above, around, and at his feet; save things
More dead than Morpheus'[8] imaginings:
Old rusted anchors, helmets, breast-plates large
Of gone sea-warriors; brazen beaks and targe;[9]
Rudders that for a hundred years had lost   125
The sway of human hand; gold vase emboss'd
With long-forgotten story, and wherein
No reveller had ever dipp'd a chin
But those of Saturn's vintage;[1] mouldering scrolls,
Writ in the tongue of heaven, by those souls   130
Who first were on the earth; and sculptures rude
In ponderous stone, developing the mood
Of ancient Nox;[2]—then skeletons of man,
Of beast, behemoth, and leviathan,[3]
And elephant, and eagle, and huge jaw   135
Of nameless monster. A cold leaden awe
These secrets struck into him; and unless
Dian had chaced away that heaviness,
He might have died: but now, with cheered feel,
He onward kept; wooing these thoughts to steal   140
About the labyrinth in his soul of love.

    "What is there in thee, Moon! that thou shouldst move
My heart so potently? When yet a child
I oft have dried my tears when thou hast smil'd.
Thou seem'dst my sister: hand in hand we went   145
From eve to morn across the firmament.
No apples would I gather from the tree,
Till thou hadst cool'd their cheeks deliciously:
No tumbling water ever spake romance,
But when my eyes with thine thereon could dance: 150
No woods were green enough, no bower divine,
Until thou liftedst up thine eyelids fine:
In sowing time ne'er would I dibble[4] take,
Or drop a seed, till thou wast wide awake;
And, in the summer tide of blossoming,   155

7. See p. 41, n. 6.
8. The son of Somnus, god of sleep. Allott argues that this passage (ll. 119–36) echoes Shakespeare's
    Richard III 1.4.22–28 and is echoed in Shelley's *Prometheus Unbound* 4.283–95.
9. A shield; *brazen beaks*: bronze-pointed beams used on ancient warships to pierce enemy vessels.
1. Wine from the Golden Age ruled over by Saturn.
2. Night, the daughter of Chaos as in Milton's *Paradise Lost* 2.970: "*Chaos and ancient Night.*"
3. Monsters from the Bible (see Job 40.15, Isaiah 27.1); Endymion's despair at viewing the wreckage
    of ages past is similar to the response of Byron's hero in *Cain* (1821).
4. A small tool used to make holes for planting seeds.

No one but thee hath heard me blithely sing
And mesh my dewy flowers all the night.
No melody was like a passing spright
If it went not to solemnize thy reign.
Yes, in my boyhood, every joy and pain   160
By thee were fashion'd to the self-same end;
And as I grew in years, still didst thou blend
With all my ardours: thou wast the deep glen;
Thou wast the mountain-top—the sage's pen—
The poet's harp—the voice of friends—the sun;   165
Thou wast the river—thou wast glory won;
Thou wast my clarion's blast—thou wast my steed—
My goblet full of wine—my topmost deed:—
Thou wast the charm of women, lovely Moon!
O what a wild and harmonized tune   170
My spirit struck from all the beautiful!
On some bright essence could I lean, and lull
Myself to immortality: I prest
Nature's soft pillow in a wakeful rest.
But, gentle Orb! there came a nearer bliss—   175
My strange love came—Felicity's abyss!
She came, and thou didst fade, and fade away—
Yet not entirely; no, thy starry sway
Has been an under-passion to this hour.
Now I begin to feel thine orby power   180
Is coming fresh upon me: O be kind,
Keep back thine influence, and do not blind
My sovereign vision.—Dearest love, forgive
That I can think away from thee and live!—
Pardon me, airy planet, that I prize   185
One thought beyond thine argent luxuries!
How far beyond!" At this a surpris'd start
Frosted the springing verdure of his heart;
For as he lifted up his eyes to swear
How his own goddess was past all things fair,   190
He saw far in the concave green of the sea
An old man sitting calm and peacefully.
Upon a weeded rock this old man sat,[5]
And his white hair was awful, and a mat
Of weeds were cold beneath his cold thin feet;   195
And, ample as the largest winding-sheet,
A cloak of blue wrapp'd up his aged bones,
O'erwrought with symbols by the deepest groans
Of ambitious magic: every ocean-form
Was woven in with black distinctness; storm,   200
And calm, and whispering, and hideous roar,
Quicksand and whirlpool, and deserted shore[6]

---

5. Allott suggests that the description of Glaucus and his cloak (ll. 197–217) echoes Drayton's *Man in the Moone* (ll. 145–220). The story of Glaucus and Scylla, recounted in ll. 318–68, is based on Ovid's *Metamorphoses* 13.898–968, 14.1–74. Glaucus, at moments, resembles the Leech Gatherer from Wordsworth's "Resolution and Independence" (1807).
6. This line, taken from the draft recorded in Woodhouse's interleaved copy of *Endymion* and needed to complete the couplet, is missing in the printed version.

Were emblem'd in the woof;[7] with every shape
That skims, or dives, or sleeps, 'twixt cape and cape.
The gulphing whale was like a dot in the spell,   205
Yet look upon it, and 'twould size and swell
To its huge self; and the minutest fish
Would pass the very hardest gazer's wish,
And shew his little eye's anatomy.
Then there was pictur'd the regality   210
Of Neptune; and the sea nymphs round his state,
In beauteous vassalage, look up and wait.
Beside this old man lay a pearly wand,
And in his lap a book, the which he conn'd
So stedfastly, that the new denizen   215
Had time to keep him in amazed ken,
To mark these shadowings, and stand in awe.

    The old man rais'd his hoary head and saw
The wilder'd stranger—seeming not to see,
His features were so lifeless. Suddenly   220
He woke as from a trance; his snow-white brows
Went arching up, and like two magic ploughs
Furrow'd deep wrinkles in his forehead large,
Which kept as fixedly as rocky marge,
Till round his wither'd lips had gone a smile.   225
Then up he rose, like one whose tedious toil
Had watch'd for years in forlorn hermitage,
Who had not from mid-life to utmost age
Eas'd in one accent his o'er-burden'd soul,
Even to the trees. He rose: he grasp'd his stole,   230
With convuls'd clenches waving it abroad,
And in a voice of solemn joy, that aw'd
Echo into oblivion, he said:—

    "Thou art the man![8] Now shall I lay my head
In peace upon my watery pillow: now   235
Sleep will come smoothly to my weary brow.
O Jove! I shall be young again, be young!
O shell-borne Neptune, I am pierc'd and stung
With new-born life! What shall I do? Where go,
When I have cast this serpent-skin of woe?—   240
I'll swim to the syrens,[9] and one moment listen
Their melodies, and see their long hair glisten;
Anon upon that giant's arm I'll be,
That writhes about the roots of Sicily:[1]
To northern seas I'll in a twinkling sail,   245
And mount upon the snortings of a whale
To some black cloud; thence down I'll madly sweep

---

7. The crosswise threads of woven fabric.
8. An echo of Nathan's statement to David in 2 Samuel 7.7.
9. "Sea nymphs who charmed so much with their melodious voice, that all forgot their employments to listen with more attention and at last died for want of food" (Lemprière).
1. Either Typhon or Briareus, both giants who rebelled against the Olympian gods and were consequently imprisoned beneath Mount Aetna in Sicily, where their struggles and hot breath cause the volcano's eruptions.

On forked lightning, to the deepest deep,
Where through some sucking pool I will be hurl'd
With rapture to the other side of the world!   250
O, I am full of gladness! Sisters three,[2]
I bow full hearted to your old decree!
Yes, every god be thank'd, and power benign,
For I no more shall wither, droop, and pine.
Thou art the man!" Endymion started back   255
Dismay'd; and, like a wretch from whom the rack
Tortures hot breath, and speech of agony,
Mutter'd: "What lonely death am I to die
In this cold region? Will he let me freeze,
And float my brittle limbs o'er polar seas?   260
Or will he touch me with his searing hand,
And leave a black memorial on the sand?
Or tear me piece-meal with a bony saw,
And keep me as a chosen food to draw
His magian[3] fish through hated fire and flame?   265
O misery of hell! resistless, tame,
Am I to be burnt up? No, I will shout,
Until the gods through heaven's blue look out!—
O Tartarus![4] but some few days agone
Her soft arms were entwining me, and on   270
Her voice I hung like fruit among green leaves:
Her lips were all my own, and—ah, ripe sheaves
Of happiness! ye on the stubble droop,
But never may be garner'd. I must stoop
My head, and kiss death's foot. Love! love, farewel!   275
Is there no hope from thee? This horrid spell
Would melt at thy sweet breath.—By Dian's hind
Feeding from her white fingers, on the wind
I see thy streaming hair! and now, by Pan,
I care not for this old mysterious man!"   280

    He spake, and walking to that aged form,
Look'd high defiance. Lo! his heart 'gan warm
With pity, for the grey-hair'd creature wept.
Had he then wrong'd a heart where sorrow kept?
Had he, though blindly contumelious, brought   285
Rheum to kind eyes, a sting to human[5] thought,
Convulsion to a mouth of many years?
He had in truth; and he was ripe for tears.
The penitent shower fell, as down he knelt
Before that care-worn sage, who trembling felt   290
About his large dark locks, and faultering spake:

    "Arise, good youth, for sacred Phœbus' sake!
I know thine inmost bosom, and I feel
A very brother's yearning for thee steal

2. The three Fates.
3. Magical.
4. The portion of the classical underworld where the impious and guilty were punished.
5. The fair copy has "humane."

Into mine own: for why? thou openest 295
The prison gates that have so long opprest
My weary watching. Though thou know'st it not,
Thou art commission'd to this fated spot
For great enfranchisement. O weep no more;
I am a friend to love, to loves of yore: 300
Aye, hadst thou never lov'd an unknown power,
I had been grieving at this joyous hour.
But even now most miserable old,
I saw thee, and my blood no longer cold
Gave mighty pulses: in this tottering case 305
Grew a new heart, which at this moment plays
As dancingly as thine. Be not afraid,
For thou shalt hear this secret all display'd,
Now as we speed towards our joyous task."

    So saying, this young soul in age's mask 310
Went forward with the Carian side by side:
Resuming quickly thus; while ocean's tide
Hung swollen at their backs, and jewel'd sands
Took silently their foot-prints.

                "My soul stands
Now past the midway from mortality, 315
And so I can prepare without a sigh
To tell thee briefly all my joy and pain.
I was a fisher once, upon this main,
And my boat danc'd in every creek and bay;
Rough billows were my home by night and day,— 320
The sea-gulls not more constant; for I had
No housing from the storm and tempests mad,
But hollow rocks,—and they were palaces
Of silent happiness, of slumberous ease:
Long years of misery have told me so. 325
Aye, thus it was one thousand years ago.
One thousand years!—Is it then possible
To look so plainly through them? to dispel
A thousand years with backward glance sublime?
To breathe away as 'twere all scummy slime 330
From off a crystal pool, to see its deep,
And one's own image from the bottom peep?
Yes: now I am no longer wretched thrall,
My long captivity and moanings all
Are but a slime, a thin-pervading scum, 335
The which I breathe away, and thronging come
Like things of yesterday my youthful pleasures.

    "I touch'd no lute, I sang not, trod no measures:
I was a lonely youth on desert shores.
My sports were lonely, 'mid continuous roars, 340
And craggy isles, and sea-mew's[6] plaintive cry

6. Seagull's.

Plaining discrepant between sea and sky.
Dolphins were still my playmates; shapes unseen
Would let me feel their scales of gold and green,
Nor be my desolation; and, full oft,   345
When a dread waterspout[7] had rear'd aloft
Its hungry hugeness, seeming ready ripe
To burst with hoarsest thunderings, and wipe
My life away like a vast sponge of fate,
Some friendly monster, pitying my sad state,   350
Has dived to its foundations, gulph'd it down,
And left me tossing safely. But the crown
Of all my life was utmost[8] quietude:
More did I love to lie in cavern rude,
Keeping in wait whole days for Neptune's voice,   355
And if it came at last, hark, and rejoice!
There blush'd no summer eve but I would steer
My skiff along green shelving coasts, to hear
The shepherd's pipe come clear from aery[9] steep,
Mingled with ceaseless bleatings of his sheep: 360
And never was a day of summer shine,
But I beheld its birth upon the brine:
For I would watch all night to see unfold
Heaven's gates, and Æthon[1] snort his morning gold
Wide o'er the swelling streams: and constantly   365
At brim of day-tide, on some grassy lea,
My nets would be spread out, and I at rest.
The poor folk of the sea-country I blest
With daily boon of fish most delicate:
They knew not whence this bounty, and elate   370
Would strew sweet flowers on a sterile beach.

        "Why was I not contented? Wherefore reach
At things which, but for thee, O Latmian!
Had been my dreary death? Fool! I began
To feel distemper'd longings: to desire   375
The utmost privilege that ocean's sire
Could grant in benediction: to be free
Of all his kingdom. Long in misery
I wasted, ere in one extremest fit
I plung'd for life or death. To interknit   380
One's senses with so dense a breathing stuff
Might seem a work of pain; so not enough
Can I admire how crystal-smooth it felt,
And buoyant round my limbs. At first I dwelt
Whole days and days in sheer astonishment;   385
Forgetful utterly of self-intent;
Moving but with the mighty ebb and flow.

---

7. "A gyrating column of mist, spray, and water, produced by the action of a whirlwind on a portion of the sea and the clouds immediately above it" (*OED*).
8. On his errata sheet, Keats changed this to "tiptop" and then changed his mind again.
9. "Aerial; hence etherial, spiritual, incorporeal, unsubstantial, visionary" (*OED*). Stillinger believes this is a compositor's error for "airy," which is also Woodhouse's reading.
1. One of Apollo's horses.

Then, like a new fledg'd bird that first doth shew
His spreaded feathers to the morrow chill,
I tried in fear the pinions of my will.   390
'Twas freedom! and at once I visited
The ceaseless wonders of this ocean-bed.
No need to tell thee of them, for I see
That thou hast been a witness—it must be—
For these I know thou canst not feel a drouth,   395
By the melancholy corners of that mouth.
So I will in my story straightway pass
To more immediate matter. Woe, alas!
That love should be my bane! Ah, Scylla fair!
Why did poor Glaucus ever—ever dare   400
To sue thee to his heart? Kind stranger-youth!
I lov'd her to the very white of truth,
And she would not conceive it. Timid thing!
She fled me swift as sea-bird on the wing,
Round every isle, and point, and promontory,   405
From where large Hercules wound up his story[2]
Far as Egyptian Nile. My passion grew
The more, the more I saw her dainty hue
Gleam delicately through the azure clear:
Until 'twas too fierce agony to bear;   410
And in that agony, across my grief
It flash'd, that Circe[3] might find some relief—
Cruel enchantress! So above the water
I rear'd my head, and look'd for Phœbus' daughter.
Æææa's isle was wondering at the moon:—   415
It seem'd to whirl around me, and a swoon
Left me dead-drifting to that fatal power.

    "When I awoke, 'twas in a twilight bower;
Just when the light of morn, with hum of bees,
Stole through its verdurous matting of fresh trees.   420
How sweet, and sweeter! for I heard a lyre,
And over it a sighing voice expire.
It ceased—I caught light footsteps; and anon
The fairest face that morn e'er look'd upon
Push'd through a screen of roses. Starry Jove!   425
With tears, and smiles, and honey-words she wove
A net whose thraldom was more bliss than all
The range of flower'd Elysium. Thus did fall
The dew of her rich speech: "Ah! Art awake?
O let me hear thee speak, for Cupid's sake!   430
I am so oppress'd with joy! Why, I have shed

---

2. Probably Mount Oeta, between Thessaly and Macedonia, where Hercules burnt himself on a pyre;
   but Woodhouse *E*, p. 259 offers "The Pillars of Hercules. The separation of Calpe & Abyla was that
   hero's last labour."
3. A powerful witch, the daughter of Phoebus (l. 414), the sun, and Perseis (one of the Oceanides),
   who lived on the island of Aeaea (l. 415), off the Italian coast. She was famous for transforming
   men, such as Odysseus's shipmates, into beasts after they ate at her table. In Ovid's account of
   Glaucus's story, which Keats changes, Glaucus, loving Scylla, resists Circe's advances, so she turns
   him into a monster; Scylla was also transformed into a monster in Ovid, while in Keats's version
   she falls into a trance.

An urn of tears, as though thou wert cold dead;
And now I find thee living, I will pour
From these devoted eyes their silver store,
Until exhausted of the latest drop,   435
So it will pleasure thee, and force thee stop
Here, that I too may live: but if beyond
Such cool and sorrowful offerings, thou art fond
Of soothing warmth, of dalliance supreme;
If thou art ripe to taste a long love dream;   440
If smiles, if dimples, tongues for ardour mute,
Hang in thy vision like a tempting fruit,
O let me pluck it for thee." Thus she link'd
Her charming syllables, till indistinct
Their music came to my o'er-sweeten'd soul;   445
And then she hover'd over me, and stole
So near, that if no nearer it had been
This furrow'd visage thou hadst never seen.

     "Young man of Latmos! thus particular
Am I, that thou may'st plainly see how far   450
This fierce temptation went: and thou may'st not
Exclaim, How then, was Scylla quite forgot?

     "Who could resist? Who in this universe?
She did so breathe ambrosia; so immerse
My fine existence in a golden clime.   455
She took me like a child of suckling time,
And cradled me in roses. Thus condemn'd,
The current of my former life was stemm'd,
And to this arbitrary queen of sense
I bow'd a tranced vassal: nor would thence   460
Have mov'd, even though Amphion's[4] harp had woo'd
Me back to Scylla o'er the billows rude.
For as Apollo each eve doth devise
A new appareling for western skies;
So every eve, nay every spendthrift hour   465
Shed balmy consciousness within that bower.
And I was free of haunts umbrageous;[5]
Could wander in the mazy forest-house
Of squirrels, foxes shy, and antler'd deer,
And birds from coverts innermost and drear   470
Warbling for very joy mellifluous sorrow—
To me new born delights!

                   "Now let me borrow,
For moments few, a temperament as stern
As Pluto's sceptre, that my words not burn
These uttering lips, while I in calm speech tell   475
How specious heaven was changed to real hell.

---

4. Amphion was the son of Jupiter, often considered as the inventor of music, whose lyre was so powerful that he used it to move stones to build the walls of Thebes.
5. Shady.

"One morn she left me sleeping: half awake
I sought for her smooth arms and lips, to slake[6]
My greedy thirst with nectarous camel-draughts;[7]
But she was gone. Whereat the barbed shafts   480
Of disappointment stuck in me so sore,
That out I ran and search'd the forest o'er.
Wandering about in pine and cedar gloom
Damp awe assail'd me; for there 'gan to boom
A sound of moan, an agony of sound,   485
Sepulchral from the distance all around.
Then came a conquering earth-thunder, and rumbled
That fierce complain to silence: while I stumbled
Down a precipitous path, as if impell'd.
I came to a dark valley.—Groanings swell'd   490
Poisonous about my ears, and louder grew,
The nearer I approach'd a flame's gaunt blue,
That glar'd before me through a thorny brake.
This fire, like the eye of gordian[8] snake,
Bewitch'd me towards; and I soon was near   495
A sight too fearful for the feel of fear:
In thicket hid I curs'd the haggard scene—
The banquet of my arms, my arbour queen,
Seated upon an uptorn forest root;
And all around her shapes, wizard and brute,   500
Laughing, and wailing, groveling, serpenting,
Shewing tooth, tusk, and venom-bag, and sting!
O such deformities! Old Charon's[9] self,
Should he give up awhile his penny pelf,
And take a dream 'mong rushes Stygian,   505
It could not be so phantasied. Fierce, wan,
And tyrannizing was the lady's look,
As over them a gnarled staff she shook.
Oft-times upon the sudden she laugh'd out,
And from a basket emptied to the rout   510
Clusters of grapes, the which they raven'd quick
And roar'd for more; with many a hungry lick
About their shaggy jaws. Avenging, slow,
Anon she took a branch of mistletoe,[1]
And emptied on't a black dull-gurgling phial: 515
Groan'd one and all, as if some piercing trial
Was sharpening for their pitiable bones.
She lifted up the charm: appealing groans
From their poor breasts went sueing to her ear
In vain; remorseless as an infant's bier   520
She whisk'd against their eyes the sooty oil.
Whereat was heard a noise of painful toil,

6. To satisfy.
7. A Keatsian coinage, presumably suggesting large amounts of liquid such as would satisfy a thirsty
camel.
8. Intricately tied; see p. 163, n. 5.
9. The ferryman of the dead, who is paid an obolus (here anglicized to "penny pelf") to take the shades
across the rivers Styx and Acheron.
1. While we think of mistletoe as a Christmas decoration, it was traditionally thought to have medicinal and magical powers; it can also be poisonous.

Increasing gradual to a tempest rage,
Shrieks, yells, and groans of torture-pilgrimage;
Until their grieved bodies 'gan to bloat   525
And puff from the tail's end to stifled throat:
Then was appalling silence: then a sight
More wildering than all that hoarse affright;
For the whole herd, as by a whirlwind writhen,
Went through the dismal air like one huge Python   530
Antagonizing Boreas,²—and so vanish'd.
Yet there was not a breath of wind: she banish'd
These phantoms with a nod. Lo! from the dark
Came waggish fauns, and nymphs, and satyrs stark,
With dancing and loud revelry,—and went   535
Swifter than centaurs after rapine bent.—
Sighing an elephant appear'd and bow'd
Before the fierce witch, speaking thus aloud
In human accent: "Potent goddess! chief
Of pains resistless! make my being brief,   540
Or let me from this heavy prison fly:
Or give me to the air, or let me die!
I sue not for my happy crown again;
I sue not for my phalanx on the plain;
I sue not for my lone, my widow'd wife;   545
I sue not for my ruddy drops of life,
My children fair, my lovely girls and boys!
I will forget them; I will pass these joys;
Ask nought so heavenward, so too—too high:
Only I pray, as fairest boon, to die,   550
Or be deliver'd from this cumbrous flesh,
From this gross, detestable, filthy mesh,
And merely given to the cold bleak air.
Have mercy, Goddess! Circe, feel my prayer!"

        "That curst magician's name fell icy numb   555
Upon my wild conjecturing: truth had come
Naked and sabre-like against my heart.
I saw a fury whetting a death-dart;
And my slain spirit, overwrought with fright,
Fainted away in that dark lair of night.   560
Think, my deliverer, how desolate
My waking must have been! disgust, and hate,
And terrors manifold divided me
A spoil amongst them. I prepar'd to flee
Into the dungeon core of that wild wood: 565
I fled three days—when lo! before me stood
Glaring the angry witch. O Dis,³ even now,
A clammy dew is beading on my brow,
At mere remembering her pale laugh, and curse.
"Ha! ha! Sir Dainty! there must be a nurse   570

---

2. The North Wind; *Python:* a huge serpent that arose from the slime after Deucalion's flood and that
was eventually slain by Apollo.
3. Pluto, god of the underworld.

Made of rose leaves and thistledown, express,
To cradle thee, my sweet, and lull thee: yes,
I am too flinty-hard for thy nice touch:
My tenderest squeeze is but a giant's clutch.
So, fairy-thing, it shall have lullabies   575
Unheard of yet; and it shall still its cries
Upon some breast more lily-feminine.
Oh, no—it shall not pine, and pine, and pine
More than one pretty, trifling thousand years;
And then 'twere pity, but fate's gentle shears   580
Cut short its immortality. Sea-flirt!
Young dove of the waters! truly I'll not hurt
One hair of thine: see how I weep and sigh,
That our heart-broken parting is so nigh.
And must we part? Ah, yes, it must be so.   585
Yet ere thou leavest me in utter woe,
Let me sob over thee my last adieus,
And speak a blessing: Mark me! Thou hast thews[4]
Immortal, for thou art of heavenly race:
But such a love is mine, that here I chase   590
Eternally away from thee all bloom
Of youth, and destine thee towards a tomb.
Hence shalt thou quickly to the watery vast;
And there, ere many days be overpast,
Disabled age shall seize thee; and even then   595
Thou shalt not go the way of aged men;
But live and wither, cripple and still breathe
Ten hundred years: which gone, I then bequeath
Thy fragile bones to unknown burial.
Adieu, sweet love, adieu!"—As shot stars fall,   600
She fled ere I could groan for mercy. Stung
And poisoned was my spirit: despair sung
A war-song of defiance 'gainst all hell.
A hand was at my shoulder to compel
My sullen steps; another 'fore my eyes   605
Moved on with pointed finger. In this guise
Enforced, at the last by ocean's foam
I found me; by my fresh, my native home.
Its tempering coolness, to my life akin,
Came salutary as I waded in;   610
And, with a blind voluptuous rage, I gave
Battle to the swollen billow-ridge, and drave
Large froth before me, while there yet remain'd
Hale strength, nor from my bones all marrow drain'd.

       "Young lover, I must weep—such hellish spite   615
With dry cheek who can tell? While thus my might
Proving upon this element, dismay'd,
Upon a dead thing's face my hand I laid;
I look'd—'twas Scylla! Cursed, cursed Circe!
O vulture-witch, hast never heard of mercy?   620

4. Might, vigor.

Could not thy harshest vengeance be content,
But thou must nip this tender innocent
Because I lov'd her?—Cold, O cold indeed
Were her fair limbs, and like a common weed
The sea-swell took her hair. Dead as she was   625
I clung about her waist, nor ceas'd to pass
Fleet as an arrow through unfathom'd brine,
Until there shone a fabric⁵ crystalline,
Ribb'd and inlaid with coral, pebble, and pearl.
Headlong I darted; at one eager swirl   630
Gain'd its bright portal, enter'd, and behold!
'Twas vast, and desolate, and icy-cold;
And all around—But wherefore this to thee
Who in few minutes more thyself shalt see?—
I left poor Scylla in a niche and fled.   635
My fever'd parchings up, my scathing dread
Met palsy half way: soon these limbs became
Gaunt, wither'd, sapless, feeble, cramp'd, and lame.

　　　"Now let me pass a cruel, cruel space,
Without one hope, without one faintest trace   640
Of mitigation, or redeeming bubble
Of colour'd phantasy; for I fear 'twould trouble
Thy brain to loss of reason: and next tell
How a restoring chance came down to quell
One half of the witch in me.

　　　　　　　　"On a day,   645
Sitting upon a rock above the spray,
I saw grow up from the horizon's brink
A gallant vessel: soon she seem'd to sink
Away from me again, as though her course
Had been resum'd in spite of hindering force—   650
So vanish'd: and not long, before arose
Dark clouds, and muttering of winds morose.
Old Eolus⁶ would stifle his mad spleen,
But could not: therefore all the billows green
Toss'd up the silver spume against the clouds.   655
The tempest came: I saw that vessel's shrouds
In perilous bustle; while upon the deck
Stood trembling creatures. I beheld the wreck;
The final gulphing; the poor struggling souls:
I heard their cries amid loud thunder-rolls.   660
O they had all been sav'd but crazed eld⁷
Annull'd my vigorous cravings: and thus quell'd
And curb'd, think on't, O Latmian! did I sit
Writhing with pity, and a cursing fit
Against that hell-born Circe. The crew had gone,   665
By one and one, to pale oblivion;
And I was gazing on the surges prone,

5. Building.
6. The god of the winds, who keeps them trapped in a cave on his island.
7. Old age.

With many a scalding tear and many a groan,
When at my feet emerg'd an old man's hand,
Grasping this scroll, and this same slender wand.   670
I knelt with pain—reached out my hand—had grasp'd
These treasures—touch'd the knuckles—they unclasp'd—
I caught a finger: but the downward weight
O'erpowered me—it sank. Then 'gan abate
The storm, and through chill aguish gloom outburst   675
The confortable sun. I was athirst
To search the book, and in the warming air
Parted its dripping leaves with eager care.
Strange matters did it treat of, and drew on
My soul page after page, till well-nigh won   680
Into forgetfulness; when, stupefied,
I read these words, and read again, and tried
My eyes against the heavens, and read again.
O what a load of misery and pain
Each Atlas-line bore off![8]—a shine of hope   685
Came gold around me, cheering me to cope
Strenuous with hellish tyranny. Attend!
For thou hast brought their promise to an end.

    "In the wide sea there lives a forlorn wretch,
Doom'd with enfeebled carcase to outstretch   690
His loath'd existence through ten centuries,
And then to die alone. Who can devise
A total opposition? No one. So
One million times ocean must ebb and flow,
And he oppressed. Yet he shall not die,   695
These things accomplish'd:—If he utterly
Scans all the depths of magic, and expounds
The meanings of all motions, shapes, and sounds;
If he explores all forms and substances
Straight homeward to their symbol-essences;   700
He shall not die. Moreover, and in chief,
He must pursue this task of joy and grief
Most piously;—all lovers tempest-tost,
And in the savage overwhelming lost,
He shall deposit side by side, until   705
Time's creeping shall the dreary space fulfil:
Which done, and all these labours ripened,
A youth, by heavenly power lov'd and led,
Shall stand before him; whom he shall direct
How to consummate all. The youth elect   710
Must do the thing, or both will be destroy'd."—

    "Then," cried the young Endymion, overjoy'd,
"We are twin brothers in this destiny!
Say, I intreat thee, what achievement high
Is, in this restless world, for me reserv'd.   715

---

8. Each line carries a weight as heavy as the burden of Atlas, the Titan who holds up the world.

What! if from thee my wandering feet had swerv'd,
Had we both perish'd ?"—"Look!" the sage replied,
"Dost thou not mark a gleaming through the tide,
Of divers brilliances? 'tis the edifice
I told thee of, where lovely Scylla lies;   720
And where I have enshrined piously
All lovers, whom fell storms have doom'd to die
Throughout my bondage." Thus discoursing, on
They vent till unobscur'd the porches shone;
Which hurryingly they gain'd, and enter'd straight.   725
Sure never since king Neptune held his state
Was seen such wonder underneath the stars.
Turn to some level plain where haughty Mars
Has legion'd all his battle; and behold
How every soldier, with firm foot, doth hold   730
His even breast: see, many steeled squares,
And rigid ranks of iron—whence who dares
One step? Imagine further, line by line,
These warrior thousands on the field supine:—
So in that crystal place, in silent rows,   735
Poor lovers lay at rest from joys and woes.—
The stranger from the mountains, breathless, trac'd
Such thousands of shut eyes in order plac'd;
Such ranges of white feet, and patient lips
All ruddy,—for here death no blossom nips.   740
He mark'd their brows and foreheads; saw their hair
Put sleekly on one side with nicest care;
And each one's gentle wrists, with reverence,
Put cross-wise to its heart.

                              "Let us commence,"
Whisper'd the guide, stuttering with joy, "even now."   745
He spake, and, trembling like an aspen-bough,
Began to tear his scroll in pieces small,
Uttering the while some mumblings funeral.
He tore it into pieces small as snow
That drifts unfeather'd when bleak northerns blow;   750
And having done it, took his dark blue cloak
And bound it round Endymion: then struck
His wand against the empty air times nine.—
"What more there is to do, young man, is thine:
But first a little patience; first undo   755
This tangled thread, and wind it to a clue.[9]
Ah, gentle! 'tis as weak as spider's skein;
And shouldst thou break it—What, is it done so clean?
A power overshadows thee! Oh, brave!
The spite of hell is tumbling to its grave.   760
Here is a shell; 'tis pearly blank to me,
Nor mark'd with any sign or charactery—
Canst thou read aught? O read for pity's sake!

---

9. Nail. Frye, *A Study of English Romanticism* (1968), p. 144, finds allusions to the story of Theseus
and Ariadne here and elsewhere in this book.

Olympus! we are safe! Now, Carian, break
This wand against yon lyre on the pedestal."   765

   'Twas done: and straight with sudden swell and fall
Sweet music breath'd her soul away, and sigh'd
A lullaby to silence.—"Youth! now strew
These minced leaves on me, and passing through
Those files of dead, scatter the same around,   770
And thou wilt see the issue."—'Mid the sound
Of flutes and viols, ravishing his heart,
Endymion from Glaucus stood apart,
And scatter'd in his face some fragments light.
How lightning-swift the change! a youthful wight[1]   775
Smiling beneath a coral diadem,
Out-sparkling sudden like an upturn'd gem,
Appear'd, and, stepping to a beauteous corse,
Kneel'd down beside it, and with tenderest force
Press'd its cold hand, and wept,—and Scylla sigh'd!   780
Endymion, with quick hand, the charm applied—
The nymph arose: he left them to their joy,
And onward went upon his high employ,
Showering those powerful fragments on the dead.
And, as he pass'd, each lifted up its head,   785
As doth a flower at Apollo's touch.
Death felt it to his inwards: 'twas too much:
Death fell a weeping in his charnel-house.
The Latmian persever'd along, and thus
All were re-animated. There arose   790
A noise of harmony, pulses and throes
Of gladness in the air—while many, who
Had died in mutual arms devout and true,
Sprang to each other madly; and the rest
Felt a high certainty of being blest.   795
They gaz'd upon Endymion. Enchantment
Grew drunken, and would have its head and bent.
Delicious symphonies, like airy flowers,
Budded, and swell'd, and, full-blown, shed full showers
Of light, soft, unseen leaves of sounds divine.   800
The two deliverers tasted a pure wine
Of happiness, from fairy-press ooz'd out.
Speechless they eyed each other, and about
The fair assembly wander'd to and fro,
Distracted with the richest overflow   805
Of joy that ever pour'd from heaven.

                        —"Away!"
Shouted the new born god; "Follow, and pay
Our piety to Neptunus supreme!"—
Then Scylla, blushing sweetly from her dream,
They led on first, bent to her meek surprise,   810
Through portal columns of a giant size,

---

1. Creature, being.

Into the vaulted, boundless emerald.
Joyous all follow'd, as the leader call'd,
Down marble steps; pouring as easily
As hour-glass sand,—and fast, as you might see   815
Swallows obeying the south summer's call,
Or swans upon a gentle waterfall.

    Thus went that beautiful multitude, nor far,
Ere from among some rocks of glittering spar,
Just within ken, they saw descending thick   820
Another multitude. Whereat more quick
Moved either host. On a wide sand they met,
And of those numbers every eye was wet;
For each their old love found. A murmuring rose,
Like what was never heard in all the throes   825
Of wind and waters: 'tis past human wit
To tell; 'tis dizziness to think of it.

    This mighty consummation made, the host
Mov'd on for many a league; and gain'd, and lost
Huge sea-marks; vanward swelling in array,   830
And from the rear diminishing away,—
Till a faint dawn surpris'd them. Glaucus cried,
"Behold! behold, the palace of his pride!
God Neptune's palaces!" With noise increas'd,
They shoulder'd on towards that brightening cast.   835
At every onward step proud domes arose
In prospect,—diamond gleams, and golden glows
Of amber 'gainst their faces levelling.
Joyous, and many as the leaves in spring,
Still onward; still the splendour gradual swell'd.   840
Rich opal domes were seen, on high upheld
By jasper pillars, letting through their shafts
A blush of coral. Copious wonder-draughts
Each gazer drank; and deeper drank more near:
For what poor mortals fragment up, as mere   845
As marble was there lavish, to the vast
Of one fair palace, that far far surpass'd,
Even for common bulk, those olden three,
Memphis, and Babylon, and Nineveh.[2]

    As large, as bright, as colour'd as the bow   850
Of Iris,[3] when unfading it doth shew
Beyond a silvery shower, was the arch
Through which this Paphian army[4] took its march,
Into the outer courts of Neptune's state:
Whence could be seen, direct, a golden gate,   855
To which the leaders sped; but not half raught

---

2. Neptune's palace surpasses even the greatest palaces of the ancient world, such as those found in the Egyptian city of Memphis, Babylon with its hanging gardens, and Nineveh, capital of Assyria. Shelley mentions the three cities together in *Alastor* (1816), ll. 110–12.
3. An Oceanide, the goddess of the rainbow.
4. An army of lovers, from Paphos, Venus's birthplace.

Ere it burst open swift as fairy thought,
And made those dazzled thousands veil their eyes
Like callow eagles at the first sunrise.
Soon with an eagle nativeness their gaze   860
Ripe from hue-golden swoons took all the blaze,
And then, behold! large Neptune on his throne
Of emerald deep: yet not exalt alone;
At his right hand stood winged Love, and on
His left sat smiling Beauty's paragon.[5]   865

    Far as the mariner on highest mast
Can see all round upon the calmed vast,
So wide was Neptune's hall: and as the blue
Doth vault the waters, so the waters drew
Their doming curtains, high, magnificent,   870
Aw'd from the throne aloof;—and when storm-rent
Disclos'd the thunder-gloomings in Jove's air;
But sooth'd as now, flash'd sudden everywhere,
Noiseless, sub-marine cloudlets, glittering
Death to a human eye: for there did spring   875
From natural west, and east, and south, and north,
A light as of four sunsets, blazing forth
A gold-green zenith 'bove the Sea-God's head.
Of lucid depth the floor, and far outspread
As breezeless lake, on which the slim canoe   880
Of feather'd Indian darts about, as through
The delicatest air: air verily,
But for the portraiture of clouds and sky:
This palace floor breath-air,—but for the amaze
Of deep-seen wonders motionless,—and blaze   885
Of the dome pomp, reflected in extremes,
Globing a golden sphere.[6]

          They stood in dreams
Till Triton blew his horn. The palace rang;
The Nereids danc'd; the Syrens[7] faintly sang;
And the great Sea-King bow'd his drippng head.   890
Then Love took wing, and from his pinions shed
On all the multitude a nectarous dew.
The ooze-born Goddess[8] beckoned and drew
Fair Scylla and her guides to conference;
And when they reach'd the throned eminence   895
She kist the sea-nymph's cheek,—who sat her down
A toying with the doves. Then,—"Mighty crown
And sceptre of this kingdom!" Venus said,
"Thy vows were on a time to Nais[9] paid:

---

5. Venus, with her son Cupid, the "winged Love" of the previous line.
6. The palace floor would seem like air if it were not for the images of the palace reflected in it.
7. See p. 199, n. 9. *Triton*: see p. 153, n. 5. The fifty Nereides were sea nymphs, the daughters of Nereus and Doris.
8. Venus.
9. As Lemprière indicates, in some versions of the myth, Glaucus is the child of Neptune and the sea-nymph Nais.

Behold!"—Two copious tear-drops instant fell   900
From the God's large eyes; he smil'd delectable,
And over Glaucus held his blessing hands.—
"Endymion! Ah! still wandering in the bands
Of love? Now this is cruel. Since the hour
I met thee in earth's bosom, all my power   905
Have I put forth to serve thee. What, not yet
Escap'd from dull mortality's harsh net?
A little patience, youth! 'twill not be long,
Or I am skilless quite: an idle tongue,
A humid eye, and steps luxurious,   910
Where these are new and strange, are ominous.
Aye, I have seen these signs in one of heaven,
When others were all blind; and were I given
To utter secrets, haply I might say
Some pleasant words:—but Love will have his day.   915
So wait awhile expectant. Pr'ythee soon,
Even in the passing of thine honey-moon,
Visit my Cytherea:[1] thou wilt find
Cupid well-natured, my Adonis kind;
And pray persuade with thee—Ah, I have done,   920
All blisses be upon thee, my sweet son!"—
Thus the fair goddess: while Endymion
Knelt to receive those accents halcyon.

        Meantime a glorious revelry began
Before the Water-Monarch. Nectar ran   925
In courteous fountains to all cups outreach'd;
And plunder'd vines, teeming exhaustless, pleach'd[2]
New growth about each shell and pendent lyre;
The which, in disentangling for their fire,
Pull'd down fresh foliage and coverture   930
For dainty toying. Cupid, empire-sure,
Flutter'd and laugh'd, and oft-times through the throng
Made a delighted way. Then dance, and song,
And garlanding grew wild; and pleasure reign'd.
In harmless tendril they each other chain'd,   935
And strove who should be smother'd deepest in
Fresh crush of leaves.

                O 'tis a very sin
For one so weak to venture his poor verse
In such a place as this. O do not curse,
High Muses! let him hurry to the ending.   940

        All suddenly were silent. A soft blending
Of dulcet instruments came charmingly;
And then a hymn.

1. For Cythera, an island sacred to Venus.
2. Interwove.

"King of the stormy sea!
Brother of Jove, and co-inheritor
Of elements! Eternally before   945
Thee the waves awful bow. Fast, stubborn rock,
At thy fear'd trident shrinking, doth unlock
Its deep foundations, hissing into foam.
All mountain-rivers lost in the wide home
Of thy capacious bosom ever flow.   950
Thou frownest, and old Eolus³ thy foe
Skulks to his cavern, 'mid the gruff complaint
Of all his rebel tempests. Dark clouds faint
When, from thy diadem, a silver gleam
Slants over blue dominion. Thy bright team   955
Gulphs in the morning light, and scuds along
To bring thee nearer to that golden song
Apollo singeth, while his chariot
Waits at the doors of heaven. Thou art not
For scenes like this: an empire stern hast thou;   960
And it hath furrow'd that large front: yet now,
As newly come of heaven, dost thou sit
To blend and interknit
Subdued majesty with this glad time.
O shell-borne King sublime!   965
We lay our hearts before thee evermore—
We sing, and we adore!

    "Breathe softly, flutes;
Be tender of your strings, ye soothing lutes;
Nor be the trumpet heard! O vain, O vain;   970
Not flowers budding in an April rain,
Nor breath of sleeping dove, nor river's flow,—
No, nor the Eolian twang of Love's own bow,
Can mingle music fit for the soft ear
Of goddess Cytherea!⁴   975
Yet deign, white Queen of Beauty, thy fair eyes
On our souls' sacrifice.

    "Bright-winged Child!⁵
Who has another care when thou hast smil'd?
Unfortunates on earth, we see at last   980
All death-shadows, and glooms that overcast
Our spirits, fann'd away by thy light pinions.
O sweetest essence! sweetest of all minions!
God of warm pulses, and dishevell'd hair,
And panting bosoms bare!   985
Dear unseen light in darkness! eclipser
Of light in light! delicious poisoner!
Thy venom'd goblet will we quaff until

---

3. Aeolus is Neptune's foe as the god of storms and winds that trouble the seas.
4. Venus.
5. Cupid.

We fill—we fill!
And by thy Mother's lips——"   990

                  Was heard no more
For clamour, when the golden palace door
Opened again, and from without, in shone
A new magnificence. On oozy throne
Smooth-moving came Oceanus[6] the old,
To take a latest glimpse at his sheep-fold,   995
Before he went into his quiet cave
To muse for ever—Then a lucid wave,
Scoop'd from its trembling sisters of mid-sea,
Afloat, and pillowing up the majesty
Of Doris, and the Egean seer, her spouse—[7]   1000
Next, on a dolphin, clad in laurel boughs,
Theban Amphion leaning on his lute:
His fingers went across it—All were mute
To gaze on Amphitrite, queen of pearls,
And Thetis[8] pearly too.—

               The palace whirls   1005
Around giddy Endymion; seeing he
Was there far strayed from mortality.
He could not bear it—shut his eyes in vain;
Imagination gave a dizzier pain.
"O I shall die! sweet Venus, be my stay!   1010
Where is my lovely mistress? Well-away!
I die—I hear her voice—I feel my wing—"
At Neptune's feet he sank. A sudden ring
Of Nereids were about him, in kind strife
To usher back his spirit into life: 1015
But still he slept. At last they interwove
Their cradling arms, and purpos'd to convey
Towards a crystal bower far away.

   Lo! while slow carried through the pitying crowd,
To his inward senses these words spake aloud;   1020
Written in star-light on the dark above:
Dearest Endymion! my entire love!
How have I dwelt in fear of fate: 'tis done—
Immortal bliss for me too hast thou won.
Arise then! for the hen-dove shall not hatch   1025
Her ready eggs, before I'll kissing snatch
Thee into endless heaven. Awake! awake!

   The youth at once arose: a placid lake
Came quiet to his eyes; and forest green,

---

6. A Titan, Oceanus was "a powerful deity of the sea, son of Cœlus and Terra. . . . Oceanus presided over every part of the sea, and even the rivers were subjected to his power" (Lemprière). He appears in Keats's *Hyperion*.
7. Doris is married to Nereus, who is identified with the Aegean Sea and has the gift of prophecy.
8. See p. 185, n. 9; *Amphion*: see p. 204, n. 4; *Amphitrite*: see p. 173, n. 6.

Cooler than all the wonders he had seen,   1030
Lull'd with its simple song his fluttering breast.
How happy once again in grassy nest!

BOOK IV.

MUSE of my native land! loftiest Muse![1]
O first-born on the mountains! by the hues
Of heaven on the spiritual air begot:
Long didst thou sit alone in northern grot,
While yet our England was a wolfish den;   5
Before our forests heard the talk of men;
Before the first of Druids[2] was a child;—
Long didst thou sit amid our regions wild
Rapt in a deep prophetic solitude.
There came an eastern voice of solemn mood:—   10
Yet wast thou patient. Then sang forth the Nine,
Apollo's garland:—yet didst thou divine
Such home-bred glory, that they cry'd in vain,
"Come hither, Sister of the Island!" Plain
Spake fair Ausonia; and once more she spake   15
A higher summons:—still didst thou betake
Thee to thy native hopes. O thou hast won
A full accomplishment! The thing is done,
Which undone, these our latter days had risen
On barren souls. Great Muse, thou know'st what prison,   20
Of flesh and bone, curbs, and confines, and frets
Our spirit's wings: despondency[3] besets
Our pillows; and the fresh to-morrow morn
Seems to give forth its light in very scorn
Of our dull, uninspired, snail-paced lives.   25
Long have I said, how happy he who shrives[4]
To thee! But then I thought on poets gone,[5]
And could not pray:—nor can I now—so on
I move to the end in lowliness of heart.——

"Ah, woe is me! that I should fondly part   30
From my dear native land! Ah, foolish maid!
Glad was the hour, when, with thee, myriads bade
Adieu to Ganges and their pleasant fields!
To one so friendless the clear freshet[6] yields
A bitter coolness; the ripe grape is sour: 35

1. Keats's invocation of an indigenous muse may have been influenced by his recent reading of Milton's *Paradise Lost*. Keats traces the "westerning" of the imagination (perhaps with a debt to Gray's *Progress of Poesy* [1754]) from the "eastern voice" (l. 10; "hebrew voice" in his letter of Bailey of October 28, 1817) of the Bible to the Greek poets (ll. 11–13, where the nine classical muses are mentioned) and the poets of Ausonia or Italy (ll. 14–15; Woodhouse *E*, p. 327, suggests that Keats alludes to both the Roman poets and Dante) and then on to England.
2. Ancient poet-priests of England, often alluded to in romantic poetry.
3. A central theme of Wordsworth's *Excursion* (1814).
4. Here, "confesses," though "shrives" usually means "grants absolution."
5. Cook suggests Chatterton and Burns, which might make this an echo of Wordsworth's "Resolution and Independence" (1807), ll. 43–49.
6. "A small stream of fresh water" (*OED*).

Yet I would have, great gods! but one short hour
Of native air—let me but die at home."

Endymion to heaven's airy dome
Was offering up a hecatomb[7] of vows,
When these words reach'd him. Whereupon he bows   40
His head through thorny-green entanglement
Of underwood, and to the sound is bent,
Anxious as hind towards her hidden fawn.

"Is no one near to help me? No fair dawn
Of life from charitable voice? No sweet saying   45
To set my dull and sadden'd spirit playing?
No hand to toy with mine? No lips so sweet
That I may worship them? No eyelids meet
To twinkle on my bosom? No one dies
Before me, till from these enslaving eyes   50
Redemption sparkles!—I am sad and lost."

Thou, Carian[8] lord, hadst better have been tost
Into a whirlpool. Vanish into air,
Warm mountaineer! for canst thou only bear
A woman's sigh alone and in distress?   55
See not her charms! Is Phœbe[9] passionless?
Phœbe is fairer far—O gaze no more:—
Yet if thou wilt behold all beauty's store,
Behold her panting in the forest grass!
Do not those curls of glossy jet surpass   60
For tenderness the arms so idly lain
Amongst them? Feelest not a kindred pain,
To see such lovely eyes in swimming search
After some warm delight, that seems to perch
Dovelike in the dim cell lying beyond   65
Their upper lids?[1]—Hist!

                    "O for Hermes' wand,[2]
To touch this flower into human shape!
That woodland Hyacinthus[3] could escape
From his green prison, and here kneeling down
Call me his queen, his second life's fair crown!   70
Ah me, how I could love!—My soul doth melt
For the unhappy youth—Love! I have felt
So faint a kindness, such a meek surrender
To what my own full thoughts had made too tender,
That but for tears my life had fled away!—   75
Ye deaf and senseless minutes of the day,
And thou, old forest, hold ye this for true,

---

7. A great number; from the Greco-Roman practice of making a public sacrifice of one hundred oxen.
8. From Endymion's country, Caria.
9. Another name for Diana as the moon, "on account of the brightness of that luminary" (Lemprière).
1. Allott suggests ll. 57–66 echo Shelley's *Alastor* (1816), ll. 178–82, 489–92.
2. See p. 21, n. 5.
3. See p. 156, n. 1.

There is no lightning, no authentic dew
But in the eye of love: there's not a sound,
Melodious howsoever, can confound 80
The heavens and earth in one to such a death
As doth the voice of love: there's not a breath
Will mingle kindly with the meadow air,
Till it has panted round, and stolen a share
Of passion from the heart!"—

                  Upon a bough 85
He leant, wretched. He surely cannot now
Thirst for another love: O impious,
That he can even dream upon it thus!—
Thought he, "Why am I not as are the dead,
Since to a woe like this I have been led 90
Through the dark earth, and through the wondrous sea?
Goddess! I love thee not the less: from thee
By Juno's smile I turn not—no, no, no—
While the great waters are at ebb and flow.—
I have a triple soul! O fond pretence— 95
For both, for both my love is so immense,
I feel my heart is cut for them in twain."[4]

    And so he groan'd, as one by beauty slain.
The lady's heart beat quick, and he could see
Her gentle bosom heave tumultuously. 100
He sprang from his green covert: there she lay,
Sweet as a muskrose upon new-made hay;
With all her limbs on tremble, and her eyes
Shut softly up alive. To speak he tries.
"Fair damsel, pity me! forgive that I 105
Thus violate thy bower's sanctity!
O pardon me, for I am full of grief—
Grief born of thee, young angel! fairest thief!
Who stolen hast away the wings wherewith
I was to top the heavens. Dear maid, sith[5] 110
Thou art my executioner, and I feel
Loving and hatred, misery and weal,
Will in a few short hours be nothing to me,
And all my story that much passion slew me;
Do smile upon the evening of my days: 115
And, for my tortur'd brain begins to craze,
Be thou my nurse; and let me understand
How dying I shall kiss that lily hand.—
Dost weep for me? Then should I be content.
Scowl on, ye fates! until the firmament 120
Outblackens Erebus,[6] and the full-cavern'd earth

---

4. *1818* has "in twain for them"; the fair copy provides the adopted emendation, probably by Woodhouse, to supply the rhyme. Endymion is divided in his love for his mysterious goddess and for this
Indian maid; he has a "triple soul" because he also is devoted to the moon. He, of course, does not
yet know that all three are the same woman.
5. From "sithence," "since."
6. A "deity of hell, son of Chaos and Darkness. He married Night. . . . The poets often used the word
Erebus to signify hell itself" (Lemprière).

Crumbles into itself. By the cloud girth
Of Jove, those tears have given me a thirst
To meet oblivion."—As her heart would burst
The maiden sobb'd awhile, and then replied:　　　125
"Why must such desolation betide
As that thou speakest of? Are not these green nooks
Empty of all misfortune? Do the brooks
Utter a gorgon voice? Does yonder thrush,
Schooling its half-fledg'd little ones to brush　　　130
About the dewy forest, whisper tales?—
Speak not of grief, young stranger, or cold snails
Will slime the rose to night. Though if thou wilt,
Methinks 'twould be a guilt—a very guilt—
Not to companion thee, and sigh away　　　135
The light—the dusk—the dark—till break of day!"
"Dear lady," said Endymion, " 'tis past:
I love thee! and my days can never last.
That I may pass in patience still speak:
Let me have music dying, and I seek　　　140
No more delight—I bid adieu to all.
Didst thou not after other climates call,
And murmur about Indian streams?"—Then she,
Sitting beneath the midmost forest tree,
For pity sang this roundelay————　　　145

　　　"O Sorrow,[7]
　　　Why dost borrow
The natural hue of health, from vermeil lips?—
　　　To give maiden blushes
　　　To the white rose bushes?　　　150
Or is't thy dewy hand the daisy tips?

　　　"O Sorrow,
　　　Why dost borrow
The lustrous passion from a falcon-eye?—
　　　To give the glow-worm light?　　　155
　　　Or, on a moonless night,
To tinge, on syren shores, the salt sea-spry?[8]

　　　"O Sorrow,
　　　Why dost borrow
The mellow ditties from a mourning tongue?—　　　160
　　　To give at evening pale
　　　Unto the nightingale,
That thou mayst listen the cold dews among?

　　　"O Sorrow,
　　　Why dost borrow　　　165

7. Keats copied out this "Ode to Sorrow" (ll. 146–81) in letters to Jane Reynolds (October 31, 1817;
　　L, 1: 176–77) and Bailey (November 3, 1817; L, 1: 181–82), and comments on it in a letter to Bai-
　　ley of November 22, 1817 (L, 1: 184–86 and above, p. 102). For a similar treatment of the min-
　　gling of joy and sorrow, see "Ode to Melancholy," pp. 473–74.
8. Sea-spray.

Heart's lightness from the merriment of May?—
A lover would not tread
A cowslip on the head,[9]
Though he should dance from eve till peep of day—
Nor any drooping flower   170
Held sacred for thy bower,
Wherever he may sport himself and play.

"To Sorrow,
I bade good-morrow,
And thought to leave her far away behind;   175
But cheerly, cheerly,
She loves me dearly;
She is so constant to me, and so kind:
I would deceive her
And so leave her,   180
But ah! she is so constant and so kind.

"Beneath my palm trees, by the river side,
I sat a weeping: in the whole world wide
There was no one to ask me why I wept,—
And so I kept   185
Brimming the water-lily cups with tears
    Cold as my fears.

"Beneath my palm trees, by the river side,
I sat a weeping: what enamour'd bride,
Cheated by shadowy wooer from the clouds,   190
    But hides and shrouds
Beneath dark palm trees by a river side?

"And as I sat, over the light blue hills
There came a noise of revellers: the rills
Into the wide stream came of purple hue—   195
'Twas Bacchus and his crew![1]

---

9. Keats, ll. 167–68, echoes Milton's *Comus* (1637), ll. 897–99: "Thus I set my printless feet / O'er the Cowslips velvet head, / That bends not as I tread"; for Keats's thoughts on *Comus*, see pp. 245–46. Milton's "Lycidas," l. 150, is echoed at l. 186, and Milton's "Nativity Ode" is an important source for the narrative of Bacchus's triumph (ll. 193–272).

1. Keats in depicting Bacchus's triumph (ll. 193–272) draws upon a number of sources (see Finney, *The Evolution of Keats's Poetry*, pp. 272–91, and Jack, pp. 159–60), including Titian's *Bacchus and Ariadne* (see W. Sharp, *Life of Severn* [1892], p. 32), Sandys's translation of Ovid's *Metamorphoses*, and Milton's "Nativity Ode," which supplies both a suggestion for the irregular stanzaic form and the image of one religion overcoming earlier ones, with Bacchus here playing the role of Milton's Jesus. The Indian Maid's "rescue" by Bacchus recalls in particular the story of Bacchus saving Ariadne after she was abandoned by Theseus, a story taken up in Catullus 64 and later by Hunt in his "Bacchus and Ariadne." Lemprière (quoted by Woodhouse in *E*, p. 339) suggests many of the details: "But of all the achievements of Bacchus, his expedition into the East is most celebrated. He marched at the head of an army composed of men as well as of women, all inspired with divine fury, and armed with thyrsi [the thyrsus is the "ivy-dart" of l. 210], cymbals, and other musical instruments. The leader was drawn in a chariot by a lion and a tiger, and was accompanied by Pan, Silenus, and all the Satyrs. His conquests were easy, and without bloodshed; the people cheerfully submitted, and gratefully elevated to the rank of a god the hero who taught them the use of the vine, the cultivation of the earth, and the manner of making honey. . . . He is generally represented crowned with vine and ivy leaves, with a thyrsus in his hand. His figure is that of an effeminate young man, to denote the joys which commonly prevail at feasts. . . . The panther is sacred to him, because he went on his expedition covered with the skin of that beast." Bacchus was also known as Bromius, the noisy one (see ll. 194–98), and Lyaeus, the deliverer from care (see l. 203).

The earnest trumpet spake, and silver thrills
From kissing cymbals made a merry din—
    'Twas Bacchus and his kin!
Like to a moving vintage down they came,   200
Crown'd with green leaves, and faces all on flame;
All madly dancing through the pleasant valley,
    To scare thee, Melancholy!
O then, O then, thou wast a simple name!
And I forgot thee, as the berried holly   205
By shepherds is forgotten, when, in June,
Tall chestnuts keep away the sun and moon:—
    I rush'd into the folly!

"Within his car, aloft, young Bacchus stood,
Trifling his ivy-dart, in dancing mood,   210
    With sidelong laughing;
And little rills of crimson wine imbrued
His plump white arms, and shoulders, enough white
    For Venus' pearly bite:
And near him rode Silenus[2] on his ass,   215
Pelted with flowers as he did pass
    Tipsily quaffing.

"Whence came ye, merry Damsels! whence came ye!
So many, and so many, and such glee?
Why have ye left your bowers desolate,   220
    Your lutes, and gentler fate?—
'We follow Bacchus! Bacchus on the wing,
    A conquering!
Bacchus, young Bacchus! good or ill betide,
We dance before him thorough kingdoms wide:—   225
Come hither, lady fair, and joined be
    To our wild minstrelsy!'

"Whence came ye, jolly Satyrs![3] whence came ye!
So many, and so many, and such glee?
Why have ye left your forest haunts, why left   230
    Your nuts in oak-tree cleft?—
'For wine, for wine we left our kernel tree;
For wine we left our heath, and yellow brooms,
    And cold mushrooms;
For wine we follow Bacchus through the earth;   235
Great God of breathless cups and chirping mirth!—
Come hither, lady fair, and joined be
    To our mad minstrelsy!'

---

2. "[A] demi-god, who became the nurse, the preceptor, and the attendant of the god Bacchus. . . .
   Silenus is generally represented as a fat and jolly old man, riding on an ass, crowned with flowers, and always intoxicated" (Lemprière).
3. "[D]emi-gods of the country, whose origin is unknown. They are represented like men, but with
   the feet and legs of goats, short horns on the head, and the whole body covered with hair. They
   chiefly attended upon Bacchus, and rendered themselves known in his orgies by their riot and lasciviousness" (Lemprière).

"Over wide streams and mountains great we went,
And, save when Bacchus kept his ivy tent, 240
Onward the tiger and the leopard pants,
 With Asian elephants:
Onward these myriads—with song and dance,
With zebras striped, and sleek Arabians' prance,
Web-footed alligators, crocodiles, 245
Bearing upon their scaly backs, in files,
Plump infant laughers mimicking the coil
Of seamen, and stout galley-rowers' toil:[4]
With toying oars and silken sails they glide,
 Nor care for wind and tide. 250

"Mounted on panthers' furs and lions' manes,
From rear to van[5] they scour about the plains;
A three days' journey in a moment done:
And always, at the rising of the sun,
About the wilds they hunt with spear and horn, 255
 On spleenful unicorn.

"I saw Osirian Egypt[6] kneel adown
 Before the vine-wreath crown!
I saw parch'd Abyssinia[7] rouse and sing
 To the silver cymbals' ring! 260
I saw the whelming vintage hotly pierce
 Old Tartary[8] the fierce!
The kings of Inde their jewel-sceptres vail,[9]
And from their treasures scatter pearled hail;
Great Brahma[1] from his mystic heaven groans, 265
 And all his priesthood moans;
Before young Bacchus' eye-wink turning pale.—
Into these regions came I following him,
Sick hearted, weary—so I took a whim
To stray away into these forests drear 270
 Alone, without a peer:
And I have told thee all thou mayest hear.

 "Young stranger!
 I've been a ranger
In search of pleasure throughout every clime: 275
 Alas, 'tis not for me!
 Bewitch'd I sure must be,
To lose in grieving all my maiden prime.

---

4. Bush (1959) suggests an echo in ll. 245–49 of Shakespeare's *Antony and Cleopatra* 2.2.199–214
 and of W. S. Landor's *Gebir* (1798), IV.157–58: "Crown'd were tame crocodiles, and boys white-
 robed / Guided their creaking crests across the stream."
5. The vanguard; the foremost detachment of a military force.
6. Lemprière notes that Bacchus was often identified with Osiris, a key Egyptian god.
7. A large African kingdom near the source of the Nile; modern Ethiopia.
8. The kingdom of the Tatars, the area of Central Asia conquered by the Mongols, Tatars, and Turks
 under Genghis Khan.
9. Lower.
1. The creator god in Hindu mythology, the ground of all being; Keats could have read of Brahma in
 the work of Sir William Jones.

"Come then, Sorrow!
Sorrow!
Sweetest Sorrow!   280
Like an own babe I nurse thee on my breast:
    I thought to leave thee
    And deceive thee,
But now of all the world I love thee best.

    "There is not one,   285
    No, no, not one
But thee to comfort a poor lonely maid;
    Thou art her mother,
    And her brother,
Her playmate, and her wooer in the shade."   290

    O what a sigh she gave in finishing,
And look, quite dead to every worldly thing!
Endymion could not speak, but gazed on her;
And listened to the wind that now did stir
About the crisped oaks full drearily,   295
Yet with as sweet a softness as might be
Remember'd from its velvet summer song.
At last he said: "Poor lady, how thus long
Have I been able to endure that voice?
Fair Melody! kind Syren! I've no choice;   300
I must be thy sad servant evermore:
I cannot choose but kneel here and adore.
Alas, I must not think—by Phœbe, no!
Let me not think, soft Angel! shall it be so?
Say, beautifullest, shall I never think?   305
O thou could'st foster me beyond the brink
Of recollection! make my watchful care
Close up its bloodshot eyes, nor see despair!
Do gently murder half my soul, and I
Shall feel the other half so utterly!—   310
I'm giddy at that cheek so fair and smooth;
O let it blush so ever! let it soothe
My madness! let it mantle rosy-warm
With the tinge of love, panting in safe alarm.—
This cannot be thy hand, and yet it is;   315
And this is sure thine other softling—this
Thine own fair bosom, and I am so near!
Wilt fall asleep? O let me sip that tear!
And whisper one sweet word that I may know
This is this world—sweet dewy blossom!"—*Woe!*   320
Woe! Woe to that Endymion! Where is he?—
Even these words went echoing dismally
Through the wide forest—a most fearful tone,
Like one repenting in his latest moan;
And while it died away a shade pass'd by,   325
As of a thunder cloud. When arrows fly
Through the thick branches, poor ring-doves sleek forth
Their timid necks and tremble; so these both
Leant to each other trembling, and sat so

Waiting for some destruction—when lo,   330
Foot-feather'd Mercury appear'd sublime
Beyond the tall tree tops; and in less time
Than shoots the slanted hail-storm, down he dropt
Towards the ground; but rested not, nor stopt
One moment from his home: only the sward   335
He with his wand light touch'd, and heavenward
Swifter than sight was gone—even before
The teeming earth a sudden witness bore
Of his swift magic. Diving swans appear
Above the crystal circlings white and clear;   340
And catch the cheated eye in wild[2] surprise,
How they can dive in sight and unseen rise—
So from the turf outsprang two steeds jet-black,
Each with large dark blue wings upon his back.
The youth of Caria plac'd the lovely dame   345
On one, and felt himself in spleen to tame
The other's fierceness. Through the air they flew,
High as the eagles. Like two drops of dew
Exhal'd to Phœbus' lips, away they are gone,
Far from the earth away—unseen, alone,   350
Among cool clouds and winds, but that the free,
The buoyant life of song can floating be
Above their heads, and follow them untir'd.—
Muse of my native land, am I inspir'd?
This is the giddy air, and I must spread   355
Wide pinions to keep here; nor do I dread
Or height, or depth, or width, or any chance
Precipitous: I have beneath my glance
Those towering horses and their mournful freight.
Could I thus sail, and see, and thus await   360
Fearless for power of thought, without thine aid?—

        There is a sleepy dusk, an odorous shade
From some approaching wonder, and behold
Those winged steeds, with snorting nostrils bold
Snuff at its faint extreme, and seem to tire,   365
Dying to embers from their native fire!

        There curl'd a purple mist around them; soon,
It seem'd as when around the pale new moon
Sad Zephyr[3] droops the clouds like weeping willow:
'Twas Sleep[4] slow journeying with head on pillow.   370
For the first time, since he came nigh dead born
From the old womb of night, his cave forlorn
Had he left more forlorn; for the first time,
He felt aloof the day and morning's prime—
Because into his depth Cimmerian[5]   375

---

2. The fair copy has "wide," so the print text may reflect a printer's error.
3. See p. 8, n. 2.
4. Somnus, or Sleep, the "son of Erebus and Nox, was one of the infernal deities. . . . His palace . . .
   is a dark cave, where the sun never penetrated" (Lemprière).
5. Misty, gloomy; from Cimmerius, an ancient Asian town imagined to be perpetually surrounded by
   clouds.

There came a dream, shewing how a young man,
Ere a lean bat could plump its wintery skin,
Would at high Jove's empyreal footstool win
An immortality, and how espouse
Jove's daughter,[6] and be reckon'd of his house.　　　　380
Now was he slumbering towards heaven's gate,
That he might at the threshold one hour wait
To hear the marriage melodies, and then
Sink downward to his dusky cave again.
His litter of smooth semilucent mist,　　　　　　　385
Diversely ting'd with rose and amethyst,
Puzzled those eyes that for the centre sought;
And scarcely for one moment could be caught
His sluggish form reposing motionless.
Those two on winged steeds, with all the stress　　390
Of vision search'd for him, as one would look
Athwart the sallows[7] of a river nook
To catch a glance at silver throated eels,—
Or from old Skiddaw's[8] top, when fog conceals
His rugged forehead in a mantle pale,　　　　　395
With an eye-guess towards some pleasant vale
Descry a favourite hamlet faint and far.

　　These raven horses, though they foster'd are
Of earth's splenetic fire, dully drop
Their full-veined ears, nostrils blood wide, and stop;　400
Upon the spiritless mist have they outspread
Their ample feathers, are in slumber dead,—
And on those pinions, level in mid air,
Endymion sleepeth and the lady fair.
Slowly they sail, slowly as icy isle　　　　　405
Upon a calm sea drifting: and meanwhile
The mournful wanderer dreams. Behold! he walks
On heaven's pavement; brotherly he talks
To divine powers: from his hand full fain
Juno's proud birds[9] are pecking pearly grain:　　410
He tries the nerve of Phœbus' golden bow,
And asketh where the golden apples grow:
Upon his arm he braces Pallas' shield,[1]
And strives in vain to unsettle and wield
A Jovian thunderbolt: arch Hebe[2] brings　　　415
A full-brimm'd goblet, dances lightly, sings
And tantalizes long; at last he drinks,
And lost in pleasure at her feet he sinks,
Touching with dazzled lips her starlight hand.
He blows a bugle,—an ethereal band　　　　420

6. Diana/Cynthia/Phoebe is the daughter of Jupiter (Jove) and Latona.
7. Willows.
8. A mountain in the Lake District, which Keats did not visit until the summer of 1818; he would
　have known of it from Wordsworth's poetry.
9. Peacocks, sacred to Juno.
1. Pallas Athena, the goddess of wisdom and war, is usually represented wearing armor.
2. Daughter of Jupiter and Juno and cupbearer of the gods until dismissed in favor of Ganymede.

Are visible above: the Seasons four,—
Green-kyrtled Spring, flush Summer, golden store
In Autumn's sickle, Winter frosty hoar,
Join dance with shadowy Hours; while still the blast,
In swells unmitigated, still doth last   425
To sway their floating morris.[3] "Whose is this?
Whose bugle?" he inquires: they smile—"O Dis![4]
Why is this mortal here? Dost thou not know
Its mistress' lips? Not thou?—'Tis Dian's: lo!
She rises crescented!" He looks, 'tis she,   430
His very goddess: good-bye earth, and sea,
And air, and pains, and care, and suffering;
Good-bye to all but love! Then doth he spring
Towards her, and awakes—and, strange, o'erhead,
Of those same fragrant exhalations bred,   435
Beheld awake his very dream: the gods
Stood smiling; merry Hebe laughs and nods;
And Phœbe bends towards him crescented.
O state perplexing! On the pinion bed,
Too well awake, he feels the panting side   440
Of his delicious lady. He who died
For soaring too audacious in the sun,[5]
When that same treacherous wax began to run,
Felt not more tongue-tied than Endymion.
His heart leapt up as to its rightful throne,   445
To that fair shadow'd passion puls'd its way—
Ah, what perplexity! Ah, well a day!
So fond, so beauteous was his bed-fellow,
He could not help but kiss her: then he grew
Awhile forgetful of all beauty save   450
Young Phœbe's, golden hair'd; and so 'gan crave
Forgiveness: yet he turn'd once more to look
At the sweet sleeper,—all his soul was shook,—
She press'd his hand in slumber; so once more
He could not help but kiss her and adore.   455
At this the shadow wept, melting away.
The Latmian started up: "Bright goddess, stay!
Search my most hidden breast! By truth's own tongue,
I have no dædale[6] heart: why is it wrung
To desperation? Is there nought for me,   460
Upon the bourne of bliss, but misery?"

      These words awoke the stranger of dark tresses:
Her dawning love-look rapt Endymion blesses
With 'haviour soft. Sleep yawned from underneath.
"Thou swan of Ganges, let us no more breathe   465
This murky phantasm! thou contented seem'st
Pillow'd in lovely idleness, nor dream'st

3. An English folk dance performed by men wearing costumes and bells.
4. See p. 206, n. 3.
5. Icarus; see p. 66, n. 9.
6. Labyrinthine; from Daedalus, constructor of the Minotaur's maze.

What horrors may discomfort thee and me.
Ah, shouldst thou die from my heart-treachery!—
Yet did she merely weep—her gentle soul   470
Hath no revenge in it: as it is whole
In tenderness, would I were whole in love!
Can I prize thee, fair maid, all price above,
Even when I feel as true as innocence?
I do, I do.—What is this soul then? Whence   475
Came it? It does not seem my own, and I
Have no self-passion or identity.
Some fearful end must be: where, where is it?
By Nemesis,[7] I see my spirit flit
Alone about the dark—Forgive me, sweet: 480
Shall we away?" He rous'd the steeds: they beat
Their wings chivalrous into the clear air,
Leaving old Sleep within his vapoury lair.

The good-night blush of eve was waning slow,
And Vesper, risen star, began to throe   485
In the dusk heavens silverly, when they
Thus sprang direct towards the Galaxy.
Nor did speed hinder converse soft and strange—
Eternal oaths and vows they interchange,
In such wise, in such temper, so aloof   490
Up in the winds, beneath a starry roof,
So witless of their doom, that verily
'Tis well nigh past man's search their hearts to see;
Whether they wept, or laugh'd, or griev'd, or toy'd—
Most like with joy gone mad, with sorrow cloy'd.   495

Full facing their swift flight, from ebon streak,
The moon put forth a little diamond peak,
No bigger than an unobserved star,
Or tiny point of fairy scymetar;
Bright signal that she only stoop'd to tie   500
Her silver sandals, ere deliciously
She bow'd into the heavens her timid head.
Slowly she rose, as though she would have fled,
While to his lady meek the Carian turn'd,
To mark if her dark eyes had yet discern'd   505
This beauty in its birth—Despair! despair!
He saw her body fading gaunt and spare
In the cold moonshine. Straight he seiz'd her wrist;
It melted from his grasp: her hand he kiss'd,
And, horror! kiss'd his own—he was alone.   510
Her steed a little higher soar'd, and then
Dropt hawkwise to the earth.

There lies a den,
Beyond the seeming confines of the space
Made for the soul to wander in and trace

---

7. "One of the infernal deities, daughter of Nox. She was the goddess of vengeance" (Lemprière).

Its own existence, of remotest glooms.   515
Dark regions are around it, where the tombs
Of buried griefs the spirit sees, but scarce
One hour doth linger weeping, for the pierce
Of new-born woe it feels more inly smart:
And in these regions many a venom'd dart   520
At random flies; they are the proper home
Of every ill: the man is yet to come
Who hath not journeyed in this native hell.
But few have ever felt how calm and well
Sleep may be had in that deep den of all.   525
There anguish does not sting; nor pleasure pall:
Woe-hurricanes beat ever at the gate,
Yet all is still within and desolate.
Beset with plainful gusts, within ye hear
No sound so loud as when on curtain'd bier   530
The death-watch[8] tick is stifled. Enter none
Who strive therefore: on the sudden it is won.
Just when the sufferer begins to burn,
Then it is free to him; and from an urn,
Still fed by melting ice, he takes a draught—   535
Young Semele[9] such richness never quaft
In her maternal longing! Happy gloom!
Dark Paradise! where pale becomes the bloom
Of health by due; where silence dreariest
Is most articulate; where hopes infest;   540
Where those eyes are the brightest far that keep
Their lids shut longest in a dreamless sleep.
O happy spirit-home! O wondrous soul!
Pregnant with such a den to save the whole
In thine own depth. Hail, gentle Carian!   545
For, never since thy griefs and woes began,
Hast thou felt so content: a grievous feud
Hath led thee to this Cave of Quietude.
Aye, his lull'd soul was there, although upborne
With dangerous speed: and so he did not mourn   550
Because he knew not whither he was going.
So happy was he, not the aerial blowing
Of trumpets at clear parley from the east
Could rouse from that fine relish, that high feast.
They stung the feather'd horse: with fierce alarm   555
He flapp'd towards the sound. Alas, no charm
Could lift Endymion's head, or he had view'd
A skyey mask,[1] a pinion'd multitude,—
And silvery was its passing: voices sweet
Warbling the while as if to lull and greet   560

8. Name of "various insects which make a noise like the ticking of a watch, supposed by the ignorant
   and superstitious to portend death" (*OED*).
9. The mother of Bacchus by Jupiter; she was consumed by fire when, urged on by Juno, she convinced Jupiter to come to her in all his glory, which as a mortal she could not bear.
1. A "masque," a form of spectacular and allegorical dramatic entertainment particularly popular in
   the sixteenth- and seventeenth-century English court, used by Shakespeare in *The Tempest*
   (4.1.60–138), Milton in *Comus*, and in Keats's time by Hunt in *The Descent of Liberty* (1815) and
   later by Shelley in *The Mask of Anarchy* (1819; 1832).

The wanderer in his path. Thus warbled they,
While past the vision went in bright array.

"Who, who from Dian's feast would be away?
For all the golden bowers of the day
Are empty left? Who, who away would be   565
From Cynthia's wedding and festivity?
Not Hesperus:[2] lo! upon his silver wings
He leans away for highest heaven and sings,
Snapping his lucid fingers merrily!—
Ah, Zephyrus! art here, and Flora[3] too!   570
Ye tender bibbers of the rain and dew,
Young playmates of the rose and daffodil,
Be careful, ere ye enter in, to fill
     Your baskets high
With fennel green, and balm, and golden pines,   575
Savory, latter-mint, and columbines,
Cool parsley, basil sweet, and sunny thyme;
Yea, every flower and leaf of every clime,
All gather'd in the dewy morning: hie
     Away! fly, fly!—   580
Crystalline brother of the belt of heaven,
Aquarius![4] to whom king Jove has given
Two liquid pulse streams 'stead of feather'd wings,
Two fan-like fountains,—thine illuminings
     For Dian play: 585
Dissolve the frozen purity of air;
Let thy white shoulders silvery and bare
Shew cold through watery pinions; make more bright
The Star-Queen's crescent on her marriage night:
     Haste, haste away!—   590
Castor has tamed the planet Lion, see!
And of the Bear has Pollux mastery:[5]
A third is in the race! who is the third,
Speeding away swift as the eagle bird?
     The ramping Centaur![6]   595
The Lion's mane's on end: the Bear how fierce!
The Centaur's arrow ready seems to pierce
Some enemy: far forth his bow is bent
Into the blue of heaven. He'll be shent,
     Pale unrelentor,   600
When he shall hear the wedding lutes a playing.—
Andromeda![7] sweet woman! why delaying

2. See p. 32, n. 7.
3. See p. 61, n. 4; *Zephyrus*: see p. 8, n. 2.
4. Keats draws on the figures and constellations of the Zodiac. *Aquarius*, the "Water Carrier," was
   sometimes identified with Ganymede, cupbearer to the gods after Hebe.
5. Castor and Pollux, the Gemini or twins, were the sons of Leda by Jupiter; Keats imagines them tam-
   ing the Zodiac figure of Leo the lion and the constellation Ursa Major, the Great Bear.
6. The constellation Sagittarius is imagined as a centaur, half man and half horse, shooting an arrow.
7. Woodhouse *E*, p. 383 notes, "Andromeda was the daughter of Cepheus, King of Œthiopia, by
   Cassiope.—In obedience to the oracle, & to stay the resentment of Neptune, who had sent a Sea
   Monster to depopulate her father's kingdom, she was exposed to the Monster; when Perseus, the
   son of Danae by Jupiter [l. 606], as he was returning thro' the air from the conquest of the Gorgons, saw her, & was captivated with her beauty: he attacked & slew the Monster, & received her
   hand as his reward. They were both changed into constellations after death."

So timidly among the stars: come hither!
Join this bright throng, and nimbly follow whither
   They all are going.   605
Danae's Son, before Jove newly bow'd,
Has wept for thee, calling to Jove aloud.
Thee, gentle lady, did he disenthral:
Ye shall for ever live and love, for all
   Thy tears are flowing.—   610
By Daphne's fright, behold Apollo!—"[8]

                          More
Endymion heard not: down his steed him bore,
Prone to the green head of a misty hill.

   His first touch of the earth went nigh to kill.
"Alas!" said he, "were I but always borne   615
Through dangerous winds, had but my footsteps worn
A path in hell, for ever would I bless
Horrors which nourish an uneasiness
For my own sullen conquering: to him
Who lives beyond earth's boundary, grief is dim,   620
Sorrow is but a shadow: now I see
The grass; I feel the solid ground—Ah, me!
It is thy voice—divinest! Where?—who? who
Left thee so quiet on this bed of dew?
Behold upon this happy earth we are;   625
Let us ay love each other; let us fare
On forest-fruits, and never, never go
Among the abodes of mortals here below,
Or be by phantoms duped. O destiny!
Into a labyrinth now my soul would fly,   630
But with thy beauty will I deaden it.
Where didst thou melt to? By thee will I sit
For ever: let our fate stop here—a kid
I on this spot will offer: Pan[9] will bid
Us live in peace, in love and peace among   635
His forest wilderness. I have clung
To nothing, lov'd a nothing, nothing seen
Or felt but a great dream! O I have been
Presumptuous against love, against the sky,
Against all elements, against the tie   640
Of mortals each to each, against the blooms
Of flowers, rush of rivers, and the tombs
Of heroes gone! Against his proper glory
Has my own soul conspired: so my story
Will I to children utter, and repent.   645
There never liv'd a mortal man, who bent
His appetite beyond his natural sphere,
But starv'd and died. My sweetest Indian, here,
Here will I kneel, for thou redeemed hast

8. Daphne, daughter of the river Peneus, begged her father to transform her into a laurel tree to escape the pursuit of Apollo.
9. See p. 20, n. 4.

My life from too thin breathing: gone and past   650
Are cloudy phantasms. Caverns lone, farewel!
And air of visions, and the monstrous swell
Of visionary seas! No, never more
Shall airy voices cheat me to the shore
Of tangled wonder, breathless and aghast.   655
Adieu, my daintiest Dream! although so vast
My love is still for thee. The hour may come
When we shall meet in pure elysium.
On earth I may not love thee; and therefore
Doves will I offer up, and sweetest store   660
All through the teeming year: so thou wilt shine
On me, and on this damsel fair of mine,
And bless our simple lives. My Indian bliss!
My river-lily bud! one human kiss!
One sigh of real breath—one gentle squeeze,   665
Warm as a dove's nest among summer trees,
And warm with dew at ooze from living blood!
Whither didst melt? Ah, what of that!—all good
We'll talk about—no more of dreaming.—Now,
Where shall our dwelling be? Under the brow   670
Of some steep mossy hill, where ivy dun
Would hide us up, although spring leaves were none;
And where dark yew trees, as we rustle through,
Will drop their scarlet berry cups of dew?
O thou wouldst joy to live in such a place;   675
Dusk for our loves, yet light enough to grace
Those gentle limbs on mossy bed reclin'd:
For by one step the blue sky shouldst thou find,
And by another, in deep dell below,
See, through the trees, a little river go   680
All in its mid-day gold and glimmering.
Honey from out the gnarled hive I'll bring,
And apples, wan with sweetness, gather thee,—
Cresses that grow where no man may them see,
And sorrel untorn by the dew-claw'd[1] stag: 685
Pipes will I fashion of the syrinx flag,[2]
That thou mayst always know whither I roam,
When it shall please thee in our quiet home
To listen and think of love. Still let me speak;
Still let me dive into the joy I seek,—   690
For yet the past doth prison me. The rill,
Thou haply mayst delight in, will I fill
With fairy fishes from the mountain tarn,
And thou shalt feed them from the squirrel's barn.
Its bottom will I strew with amber shells,   695
And pebbles blue from deep enchanted wells.
Its sides I'll plant with dew-sweet eglantine,

---

1. Allott glosses this as "Dappled with dew"; Woodhouse E, p. 391 offers, "the small short claw in the
   back part of the animals leg, above the foot," and the OED provides, "The false hoof of deer and
   other ungulates, consisting of two rudimentary toes."
2. A plant growing in a moist place; for the story of Syrinx being transformed into a river reed, see
   p. 25, n. 7.

And honeysuckles full of clear bee-wine.
I will entice this crystal rill to trace
Love's silver name upon the meadow's face.   700
I'll kneel to Vesta,[3] for a flame of fire;
And to god Phœbus, for a golden lyre;
To Empress Dian, for a hunting spear;
To Vesper, for a taper silver-clear,
That I may see thy beauty through the night;   705
To Flora, and a nightingale shall light
Tame on thy finger; to the River-gods,
And they shall bring thee taper fishing-rods
Of gold, and lines of Naiads' long bright tress.
Heaven shield thee for thine utter loveliness!   710
Thy mossy footstool shall the altar be
'Fore which I'll bend, bending, dear love, to thee:
Those lips shall be my Delphos,[4] and shall speak
Laws to my footsteps, colour to my cheek,
Trembling or stedfastness to this same voice,   715
And of three sweetest pleasurings the choice:
And that affectionate light, those diamond things,
Those eyes, those passions, those supreme pearl springs,
Shall be my grief, or twinkle me to pleasure.
Say, is not bliss within our perfect seisure?   720
O that I could not doubt!"

               The mountaineer
Thus strove by fancies vain and crude to clear
His briar'd path to some tranquillity.
It gave bright gladness to his lady's eye,
And yet the tears she wept were tears of sorrow;   725
Answering thus, just as the golden morrow
Beam'd upward from the vallies of the east:
"O that the flutter of this heart had ceas'd,
Or the sweet name of love had pass'd away.
Young feather'd tyrant![5] by a swift decay   730
Wilt thou devote this body to the earth:
And I do think that at my very birth
I lisp'd thy blooming titles inwardly;
For at the first, first dawn and thought of thee,
With uplift hands I blest the stars of heaven.   735
Art thou not cruel? Ever have I striven
To think thee kind, but ah, it will not do!
When yet a child, I heard that kisses drew
Favour from thee, and so I kisses gave[6]
To the void air, bidding them find out love: 740
But when I came to feel how far above
All fancy, pride, and fickle maidenhood,
All earthly pleasure, all imagin'd good,

---

3. The Roman goddess of hearth and home.
4. "My oracle," from Apollo's oracle at Delphi.
5. Cupid.
6. This unrhymed line is the corrected version from Keats's errata slip; the print version has "so I gave
   and gave."

Was the warm tremble of a devout kiss,—
Even then, that moment, at the thought of this,   745
Fainting I fell into a bed of flowers,
And languish'd there three days. Ye milder powers,
Am I not cruelly wrong'd? Believe, believe
Me, dear Endymion, were I to weave
With my own fancies garlands of sweet life,   750
Thou shouldst be one of all. Ah, bitter strife!
I may not be thy love: I am forbidden—
Indeed I am—thwarted, affrighted, chidden,
By things I trembled at, and gorgon wrath.
Twice hast thou ask'd whither I went: henceforth   755
Ask me no more! I may not utter it,
Nor may I be thy love. We might commit
Ourselves at once to vengeance; we might die;
We might embrace and die: voluptuous thought!
Enlarge not to my hunger, or I'm caught   760
In trammels of perverse deliciousness.
No, no, that shall not be: thee will I bless,
And bid a long adieu."

                    The Carian
No word return'd: both lovelorn, silent, wan,
Into the vallies green together went.   765
Far wandering, they were perforce content
To sit beneath a fair lone beechen tree;
Nor at each other gaz'd, but heavily
Por'd on its hazle cirque of shedded leaves.

        Endymion! unhappy! it nigh grieves   770
Me to behold thee thus in last extreme:
Ensky'd ere this, but truly that I deem
Truth the best music in a first-born song.
Thy lute-voic'd brother will I sing ere long,[7]
And thou shalt aid—hast thou not aided me?   775
Yes, moonlight Emperor! felicity
Has been thy meed for many thousand years;
Yet often have I, on the brink of tears,
Mourn'd as if yet thou wert a forester;—
Forgetting the old tale.

                    He did not stir   780
His eyes from the dead leaves, or one small pulse
Of joy he might have felt. The spirit culls
Unfaded amaranth,[8] when wild it strays
Through the old garden-ground of boyish days.
A little onward ran the very stream   785
By which he took his first soft poppy dream;
And on the very bark 'gainst which he leant

7. Woodhouse *E*, p. 399 reads this line as looking forward to Keats's writing of *Hyperion* and its
   account of Apollo.
8. A mythological flower that never dies.

A crescent he had carv'd, and round it spent
His skill in little stars. The teeming tree
Had swollen and green'd the pious charactery,   790
But not ta'en out. Why, there was not a slope
Up which he had not fear'd[9] the antelope;
And not a tree, beneath whose rooty shade
He had not with his tamed leopards play'd:
Nor could an arrow light, or javelin,   795
Fly in the air where his had never been—
And yet he knew it not.

          O treachery!
Why does his lady smile, pleasing her eye
With all his sorrowing? He sees her not.
But who so stares on him? His sister sure!   800
Peona of the woods!—Can she endure—
Impossible—how dearly they embrace!
His lady smiles; delight is in her face;
It is no treachery.

          "Dear brother mine!
Endymion, weep not so! Why shouldst thou pine   805
When all great Latmos so exalt will be?
Thank the great gods, and look not bitterly;
And speak not one pale word, and sigh no more.
Sure I will not believe thou hast such store
Of grief, to last thee to my kiss again.   810
Thou surely canst not bear a mind in pain,
Come hand in hand with one so beautiful.
Be happy both of you! for I will pull
The flowers of autumn for your coronals.
Pan's holy priest for young Endymion calls;   815
And when he is restor'd, thou, fairest dame,
Shalt be our queen. Now, is it not a shame
To see ye thus,—not very, very sad?
Perhaps ye are too happy to be glad:
O feel as if it were a common day;   820
Free-voic'd as one who never was away.
No tongue shall ask, whence come ye? but ye shall
Be gods of your own rest imperial.
Not even I, for one whole month, will pry
Into the hours that have pass'd us by,   825
Since in my arbour I did sing to thee.
O Hermes! on this very night will be
A hymning up to Cynthia, queen of light;
For the soothsayers old saw yesternight
Good visions in the air,—whence will befal,   830
As say these sages, health perpetual
To shepherds and their flocks; and furthermore,
In Dian's face they read the gentle lore:

9. Frightened.

Therefore for her these vesper-carols are.
Our friends will all be there from nigh and far.   835
Many upon thy death have ditties made;
And many, even now, their foreheads shade
With cypress, on a day of sacrifice.
New singing for our maids shalt thou devise,
And pluck the sorrow from our huntsmen's brows.   840
Tell me, my lady-queen, how to espouse
This wayward brother to his rightful joys!
His eyes are on thee bent, as thou didst poise
His fate most goddess-like. Help me, I pray,
To lure—Endymion, dear brother, say   845
What ails thee?" He could bear no more, and so
Bent his soul fiercely like a spiritual bow,
And twang'd it inwardly, and calmly said:
"I would have thee my only friend, sweet maid!
My only visitor! not ignorant though,   850
That those deceptions which for pleasure go
'Mong men, are pleasures real as real may be:
But there are higher ones I may not see,
If impiously an earthly realm I take.
Since I saw thee, I have been wide awake   855
Night after night, and day by day, until
Of the empyrean I have drunk my fill.
Let it content thee, Sister, seeing me
More happy than betides mortality.
A hermit young, I'll live in mossy cave,   860
Where thou alone shalt come to me, and lave
Thy spirit in the wonders I shall tell.
Through me the shepherd realm shall prosper well;
For to thy tongue will I all health confide.
And, for my sake, let this young maid abide   865
With thee as a dear sister. Thou alone,
Peona, mayst return to me. I own
This may sound strangely: but when, dearest girl,
Thou seest it for my happiness, no pearl
Will trespass down those cheeks. Companion fair!   870
Wilt be content to dwell with her, to share
This sister's love with me?" Like one resign'd
And bent by circumstance, and thereby blind
In self-commitment, thus that meek unknown:
"Aye, but a buzzing by my ears has flown,   875
Of jubilee to Dian:—truth I heard?
Well then, I see there is no little bird,
Tender soever, but is Jove's own care.[1]
Long have I sought for rest, and, unaware,
Behold I find it! so exalted too!   880
So after my own heart! I knew, I knew
There was a place untenanted in it:
In that same void white Chastity shall sit,

---

1. A pagan adaptation of Matthew 10.29–30: "Are not two sparrows sold for a farthing? And one of them shall not fall to the ground without your Father."

And monitor me nightly to lone slumber.
With sanest lips I vow me to the number   885
Of Dian's sisterhood; and, kind lady,
With thy good help, this very night shall see
My future days to her fane² consecrate."

    As feels a dreamer what doth most create
His own particular fright, so these three felt: 890
Or like one who, in after ages, knelt
To Lucifer or Baal,³ when he'd pine
After a little sleep: or when in mine
Far under-ground, a sleeper meets his friends
Who know him not. Each diligently bends   895
Towards common thoughts and things for very fear;
Striving their ghastly malady to cheer,
By thinking it a thing of yes and no,
That housewives talk of. But the spirit-blow
Was struck, and all were dreamers. At the last   900
Endymion said: "Are not our fates all cast?
Why stand we here? Adieu, ye tender pair!
Adieu!" Whereat those maidens, with wild stare,
Walk'd dizzily away. Pained and hot
His eyes went after them, until they got   905
Near to a cypress grove, whose deadly maw,
In one swift moment, would what then he saw
Engulph for ever. "Stay!" he cried, "ah, stay!
Turn, damsels! hist! one word I have to say.
Sweet Indian, I would see thee once again.   910
It is a thing I dote on: so I'd fain,
Peona, ye should hand in hand repair
Into those holy groves, that silent are
Behind great Dian's temple. I'll be yon,
At vesper's earliest twinkle—they are gone—   915
But once, once, once again—" At this he press'd
His hands against his face, and then did rest
His head upon a mossy hillock green,
And so remain'd as he a corpse had been
All the long day; save when he scantly lifted   920
His eyes abroad, to see how shadows shifted
With the slow move of time,—sluggish and weary
Until the poplar tops, in journey dreary,
Had reach'd the river's brim. Then up he rose,
And, slowly as that very river flows,   925
Walk'd towards the temple grove with this lament:
"Why such a golden eve? The breeze is sent
Careful and soft, that not a leaf may fall
Before the serene father of them all
Bows down his summer head below the west.   930
Now am I of breath, speech, and speed possest,
But at the setting I must bid adieu

2. See p. 65, n. 7.
3. Name given to a number of Canaanite and Phoenician deities.

To her for the last time. Night will strew
On the damp grass myriads of lingering leaves,
And with them shall I die; nor much it grieves   935
To die, when summer dies on the cold sward.
Why, I have been a butterfly, a lord
Of flowers, garlands, love-knots, silly posies,
Groves, meadows, melodies, and arbour roses;
My kingdom's at its death, and just it is   940
That I should die with it: so in all this
We miscal grief, bale, sorrow, heartbreak, woe,
What is there to plain of? By Titan's foe[4]
I am but rightly serv'd." So saying, he
Tripp'd lightly on, in sort of deathful glee;   945
Laughing at the clear stream and setting sun,
As though they jests had been: nor had he done
His laugh at nature's holy countenance,
Until that grove appear'd, as if perchance,
And then his tongue with sober seemlihed[5]   950
Gave utterance as he entered: "Ha! I said,
King of the butterflies; but by this gloom,
And by old Rhadamanthus'[6] tongue of doom,
This dusk religion, pomp of solitude,
And the Promethean clay by thief endued,[7]   955
By old Saturnus'[8] forelock, by his head
Shook with eternal palsy, I did wed
Myself to things of light from infancy;
And thus to be cast out, thus lorn to die,
Is sure enough to make a mortal man   960
Grow impious." So he inwardly began
On things for which no wording can be found;
Deeper and deeper sinking, until drown'd
Beyond the reach of music: for the choir
Of Cynthia he heard not, though rough briar   965
Nor muffling thicket interpos'd to dull
The vesper hymn, far swollen, soft and full,
Through the dark pillars of those sylvan aisles.
He saw not the two maidens, nor their smiles,
Wan as primroses gather'd at midnight   970
By chilly finger'd spring. "Unhappy wight!
Endymion!" said Peona, "we are here!
What wouldst thou ere we all are laid on bier?"
Then he embrac'd her, and his lady's hand
Press'd, saying: "Sister, I would have command,   975
If it were heaven's will, on our sad fate."
At which that dark-eyed stranger stood elate
And said, in a new voice, but sweet as love,
To Endymion's amaze: "By Cupid's dove,

---

4. Jupiter.
5. Archaic word for "seemliness," probably borrowed from Spenser.
6. Mythological judge of the dead in the underworld.
7. Prometheus stole fire from the gods for man; in one version of the myth, he uses fire to animate clay to create the first man and woman.
8. Saturn; see p. 123, n. 8.

And so thou shalt! and by the lily truth   980
Of my own breast thou shalt, beloved youth!"
And as she spake, into her face there came
Light, as reflected from a silver flame:
Her long black hair swell'd ampler, in display
Full golden; in her eyes a brighter day   985
Dawn'd blue and full of love. Aye, he beheld
Phœbe, his passion! joyous she upheld
Her lucid bow, continuing thus: "Drear, drear
Has our delaying been; but foolish fear
Withheld me first; and then decrees of fate;   990
And then 'twas fit that from this mortal state
Thou shouldst, my love, by some unlook'd for change
Be spiritualiz'd. Peona, we shall range
These forests, and to thee they safe shall be
As was thy cradle; hither shalt thou flee   995
To meet us many a time." Next Cynthia bright
Peona kiss'd, and bless'd with fair good night:
Her brother kiss'd her too, and knelt adown
Before his goddess, in a blissful swoon.
She gave her fair hands to him, and behold,   1000
Before three swiftest kisses he had told,
They vanish'd far away!—Peona went
Home through the gloomy wood in wonderment.

THE END.

Between *Endymion* (1818) and *Lamia, Isabella, The Eve of St. Agnes, and Other Poems* (1820)

[Mother of Hermes! and still youthful Maia!][1]

Mother of Hermes! and still youthful Maia![2]
    May I sing to thee
As thou wast hymned on the shores of Baiæ?[3]
    Or may I woo thee
In earlier Sicilian?[4] or thy smiles   5
Seek, as they once were sought, in Grecian isles,
By bards who died content in pleasant sward,[5]
Leaving great verse unto a little clan?
O, give me their old vigour, and unheard,
Save of the quiet Primrose, and the span   10
    Of heaven, and few ears,
Rounded[6] by thee, my song should die away
    Content as theirs,
Rich in the simple worship of a day.[7]

TO HOMER.[1]

STANDING aloof in giant ignorance,
  Of thee I hear and of the Cyclades,[2]

---

1. Written on May 1, 1818, at Teignmouth and sent in a letter to Reynolds on May 3 (see below, p. 243) where Keats calls the poem an unfinished ode. First published as part of that letter in 1848, 1: 135; the text is from 1848 with emendations from the transcript in Woodhouse's letter-book, p. 65. The line breaks creating rhymes for lines 11–14, transcribed differently in the letter, follow emendations made by Woodhouse and used in 1848; Bate (pp. 335–37) suggests the fourteen-line poem thus revealed is a transition between Keats's work on the sonnet and the famous odes of the following May.
2. "[A] daughter of Asia and Pleione, mother of Mercury [Hermes, the messenger of the gods] by Jupiter" (Lemprière).
3. The bay of Naples, associated with the Italian poet, Tasso, who was born in Naples.
4. Theocritus, the father of pastoral verse, was from Sicily.
5. "A growth of grass" (*OED*).
6. "Whispered" or "whispered to."
7. See Wordsworth's "Prospectus to *The Recluse*" published with *The Excursion*, where beauty and an earthly paradise are found to be "A simple produce of the common day" (l. 55).
1. Written in 1818, in April or May, at Teignmouth, according to Allott (see Keats's comments on learning Greek in his letter to Reynolds, April 27, 1818, *L*, 1: 274), as Keats takes up the subject of his earlier sonnet on Chapman's Homer (see pp. 54–55). First printed as Sonnet VIII in 1848, 2: 294; text from 1848 with emendations from Brown's transcript with revisions by Keats (Harvard MS Keats 3.6, p. 40; *MYR: JK*, 7: 42).
2. Greek island chain.

As one who sits ashore and longs perchance
To visit dolphin-coral in deep seas.
So wast thou blind;—but then the veil was rent,   5
    For Jove uncurtain'd Heaven to let thee live,
And Neptune made for thee a spumy³ tent,
    And Pan made sing for thee his forest-hive;⁴
Aye, on the shores of darkness there is light,
    And precipices show untrodden green,   10
There is a budding morrow in midnight,
    There is a triple sight in blindness keen;
Such seeing hadst thou, as it once befel,
To Dian, Queen of Earth, and Heaven, and Hell.⁵

Letter to J. H. Reynolds, May 3, 1818¹

Teignmouth May 3ᵈ
My dear Reynolds.
    What I complain of is that I have been in so an uneasy a state of Mind as
not to be fit to write to an invalid. I cannot write to any length under a dis-
guised feeling. I should have loaded you with an addition of gloom, which I
am sure you do not want. I am now thank God in a humour to give you a good
groats worth²—for Tom, after a Night without a Wink of sleep, and overbur-
dened with fever, has got up after a refreshing day sleep and is better than he
has been for a long time; and you I trust have been again round the Common³
without any effect but refreshment.—As to the Matter I hope I can say with
Sir Andrew "I have matter enough in my head"⁴ in your favor. And now, in the
second place, for I reckon that I have finished my Imprimis, I am glad you
blow up the weather—all through your letter there is a leaning towards a
climate-curse, and you know what a delicate satisfaction there is in having a
vexation anathematized: one would think there has been growing up for these
last four thousand years, a grandchild Scion of the old forbidden tree, and that
some modern Eve had just violated it; and that there was come with double
charge, "Notus and Afer black with thunderous clouds from Sierra-leona"⁵—
I shall breathe worsted stockings sooner than I thought for.⁶ Tom wants to be
in Town—we will have some such days upon the heath like that of last summer and why not with the same book: or what say you to a black Letter
Chaucer printed in 1596: aye I've got one huzza! I shall have it bounden goth-
ique a nice sombre binding—it will go a little way to unmodernize. And also
I see no reason, because I have been away this last month, why I should not

---

3. 1848 reads this as "spermy."
4. Lines 6–8 invoke Jove/Jupiter's realm in the heavens, Neptune's kingdom in the sea, and the wood-
    land god Pan's earthly sphere. Homer has "triple sight" (l. 12) in being able to write of all three.
5. Allusion to Diana/Cynthia's threefold powers in the heavens, on earth, and in hell; see p. 25, n. 1.
1. Posted from Teignmouth at the end of Keats's stay there, this is one of Keats's most famous letters;
    he creates the image of human life as "a large mansion of Many Apartments" and discusses "a grand
    march of intellect." Text from Woodhouse's letter-book, pp. 64–70.
2. A small amount, from the old coin, the groat, worth four pence.
3. Kennington Common, where Reynolds was staying.
4. While Keats seems to recall Sir Andrew Aguecheek from Shakespeare's *Twelfth Night*, it is Abraham
    Slender in *The Merry Wives of Windsor*, 1.1.105, who says, "I have matter in my head against you."
5. Milton, *Paradise Lost*, 10.702–703; Keats and Reynolds have been complaining about the unusu-
    ally stormy weather of the past months.
6. That is, Keats and his brother are returning to the Bentley household with all its children.

have a peep at your Spencerian[7]—notwithstanding you speak of your office, in my thought a little too early, for I do not see why a Mind like yours is not capable of harbouring and digesting the whole Mystery of Law as easily as Parson Hugh does Pepins—which did not hinder him from his poetic Canary[8]— Were I to study physic or rather Medicine again,—I feel it would not make the least difference in my Poetry; when the Mind is in its infancy a Bias is in reality a Bias, but when we have acquired more strength, a Bias becomes no Bias. Every department of knowledge we see excellent and calculated towards a great whole. I am so convinced of this, that I am glad at not having given away my medical Books, which I shall again look over to keep alive the little I know thitherwards; and moreover intend through you and Rice to become a sort of Pip-civilian.[9] An extensive knowledge is needful to thinking people—it takes away the heat and fever; and helps, by widening speculation, to ease the Burden of the Mystery:[1] a thing I begin to understand a little, and which weighed upon you in the most gloomy and true sentence in your Letter. The difference of high Sensations with and without knowledge appears to me this—in the latter case we are falling continually ten thousand fathoms deep and being blown up again without wings and with all the horror of a bare shoulderd Creature—in the former case, our shoulders are fledge, and we go thro' the same air and space without fear.[2] This is running one's rigs on[3] the score of abstracted benefit—when we come to human Life and the affections it is impossible to know how a parallel of breast and head can be drawn—(you will forgive me for thus privately treading out my depth and take it for treading as schoolboys tread the water)—it is impossible to know how far knowledge will console us for the death of a friend and the ill "that flesh is heir to."[4]—With respect to the affections and Poetry you must know by a sympathy my thoughts that way; and I dare say these few lines will be but a ratification: I wrote them on May-day—and Intend to finish the ode all in good time.—

["Mother of Hermes! And still youthful Maia!" follows.][5]

You may be anxious to know for fact to what sentence in your Letter I allude. You say "I fear is little chance of any thing else in this life." You seem by that to have been going through with a more painful and acute zest the same labyrinth that I have—I have come to the same conclusion thus far. My Branchings out therefrom have been numerous: one of them is the consideration of Wordsworth's genius and as a help, in the manner of gold being the meridian Line of worldly wealth,—how he differs from Milton.—And here I have nothing but surmises, from an uncertainty whether Milton's apparently less anxiety for Humanity proceeds from his seeing further or no than Wordsworth: And whether Wordsworth has in truth epic passion, and martyrs himself to the human heart, the main region of his song[6]—In regard

7. Reynolds's "Garden of Florence," in Spenserian stanzas, published in *The Garden of Florence* (1821).
8. A wine. *Parson Hugh does Pepins*: Sir Hugh Evans in Shakespeare's *Merry Wives of Windsor*, 1.2.10, says, "I will make an end of my dinner; there's pippins [apples] and cheese to come." Keats worried that Reynolds's training in the law would lead him from poetry.
9. As Rice and Reynolds learn the law, Keats will get some "pips" or seeds of understanding.
1. Wordsworth, "Tintern Abbey" (1798), l. 38.
2. See Milton, *Paradise Lost*, 3.627; *bare shoulderd Creature*: see Shakespeare, *King Lear*, 3.4.99–100, "bare, forked animal."
3. To make sport or game of something.
4. Shakespeare, *Hamlet*, 3.1.64–65: "The heartache and the thousand natural shocks / That flesh is heir to."
5. See p. 241, above.
6. Wordsworth's "Prospectus to *The Recluse*," published with *The Excursion* (1814), ll. 40–41: "the Mind of Man— / My haunt, and the main region of my song."

to his genius alone—we find what he says true as far as we have experienced and we can judge no further but by larger experience—for axioms in philosophy are not axioms until they are proved upon our pulses: We read fine—— things but never feel them to the full until we have gone the same steps as the Author.—I know this is not plain; you will know exactly my meaning when I say, that now I shall relish Hamlet more than I ever have done—Or, better— You are sensible no man can set down Venery[7] as a bestial or joyless thing until he is sick of it and therefore all philosophizing on it would be mere wording. Until we are sick, we understand not;—in fine, as Byron says, "Knowledge is Sorrow";[8] and I go on to say that "Sorrow is Wisdom"—and further for aught we can know for certainty! "Wisdom is folly."—So you see how I have run away from Wordsworth, and Milton; and shall still run away from what was in my head, to observe, that some kind of letters are good squares, others handsome ovals, and others some orbicular, others spheroid—and why should there not be another species with two rough edges like a Rat-trap? I hope you will find all my long letters of that species, and all will be well; for by merely touching the spring delicately and etherially, the rough edged will fly immediately into a proper compactness, and thus you may make a good wholesome loaf, with your own leven in it, of my fragments—If you cannot find this said Rat-trap sufficiently tractable—alas for me, it being an impossibility in grain for my ink to stain otherwise: If I scribble long letters I must play my vagaries. I must be too heavy, or too light, for whole pages—I must be quaint and free of Tropes and figures—I must play my draughts as I please, and for my advantage and your erudition, crown a white with a black, or a black with a white, and move into black or white, far and near as I please[9]—I must go from Hazlitt to Patmore, and make Wordsworth and Coleman play at leap-frog—or keep one of them down a whole half holiday at fly the garter—"From Gray to Gay, from Little to Shakespeare"[1]—Also as a long cause requires two or more sittings of the Court, so a long letter will require two or more sittings of the Breech wherefore I shall resume after dinner.—

Have you not seen a Gull, an orc, a sea Mew,[2] or any thing to bring this Line to a proper length, and also fill up this clear part; that like the Gull I may *dip*—I hope, not out of sight—and also, like a Gull, I hope to be lucky in a good sized fish—This crossing a letter is not without its association— for chequer work leads us naturally to a Milkmaid, a Milkmaid to Hogarth, Hogarth to Shakespeare, Shakespear to Hazlitt—Hazlitt to Shakespeare and thus by merely pulling an apron string we set a pretty peal of Chimes at work—Let them chime on while, with your patience,—I will return to Wordsworth—whether or no he has an extended vision or a circumscribed grandeur—whether he is an eagle in his nest, or on the wing—And to be

7. The pursuit of sexual pleasure.
8. Byron, *Manfred* (1817), 1.1.10: "Sorrow is knowledge."
9. Woodhouse's note later on this page indicates that the letter was cross-written ("dipping" into the previous writing at the point he writes "dip" below), so Keats seems to be playing off the interplay of ink and white space in his original.
1. Keats plays off Pope's *Essay on Man* 4.380, "From grave to gay, from lively to severe," moving from the poet Thomas Gray (1716–1771) to John Gay (1685–1732), author of *The Beggar's Opera*, from Thomas Moore (1779–1852) in his pseudonymous guise as "Thomas Little" to Shakespeare. Peter George Patmore (1786–1855), journalist and friend of Hazlitt, who dedicated *Liber Amoris* to him. George Colman the Younger (1762–1836), a leading playwright of the period and a manager of the Haymarket. *fly the garter*: like leap frog, "A game in which the players leap from one side of a 'garter' or line of stones over the back of one of their number" (*OED*).
2. See Milton, *Paradise Lost*, 11.835, "The haunt of Seals and Orcs [ferocious sea creatures], and Sea-mews' clang."

more explicit and to show you how tall I stand by the giant, I will put down a simile of human life as far as I now perceive it; that is, to the point to which I say we both have arrived at—'Well—I compare human life to a large Mansion of Many Apartments,[3] two of which I can only describe, the doors of the rest being as yet shut upon me—The first we step into we call the infant or thoughtless Chamber, in which we remain as long as we do not think—We remain there a long while, and notwithstanding the doors of the second Chamber remain wide open, showing a bright appearance, we care not to hasten to it; but are at length imperceptibly impelled by the awakening of the thinking principle—within us—we no sooner get into the second Chamber, which I shall call the Chamber of Maiden-Thought, than we become intoxicated with the light and the atmosphere, we see nothing but pleasant wonders, and think of delaying there for ever in delight: However among the effects this breathing is father of is that tremendous one of sharpening one's vision into the heart and nature of Man—of convincing ones nerves that the World is full of Misery and Heartbreak, Pain, Sickness and oppression— whereby This Chamber of Maiden Thought becomes gradually darken'd and at the same time on all sides of it many doors are set open—but all dark—all leading to dark passages—We see not the ballance of good and evil. We are in a Mist—*We* are now in that state—We feel the "burden of the Mystery." To this point was Wordsworth come, as far as I can conceive when he wrote 'Tintern Abbey' and it seems to me that his Genius is explorative of those dark Passages. Now if we live, and go on thinking, we too shall explore them. He is a Genius and superior to us, in so far as he can, more than we, make discoveries, and shed a light in them—Here I must think Wordsworth is deeper than Milton—though I think it has depended more upon the general and gregarious advance of intellect, than individual greatness of Mind—From the Paradise Lost and the other Works of Milton, I hope it is not too presuming, even between ourselves to say, his Philosophy, human and divine, may be tolerably understood by one not much advanced in years, In his time englishmen were just emancipated from a great superstition—and Men had got hold of certain points and resting places in reasoning which were too newly born to be doubted, and too much opposed by the Mass of Europe not to be thought etherial and authentically divine—who could gainsay his ideas on virtue, vice, and Chastity in Comus,[4] just at the time of the dismissal of Cod-pieces and a hundred other disgraces? who would not rest satisfied with his hintings at good and evil in the Paradise Lost, when just free from the inquisition and burrning in Smithfield?[5] The Reformation produced such immediate and great benefits, that Protestantism was considered under the immediate eye of heaven, and its own remaining Dogmas and superstitions, then, as it were, regenerated, constituted those resting places and seeming sure points of Reasoning—from that I have mentioned, Milton, whatever he may have thought in the sequel, appears to have been content with these by his writings—He did not think into the human heart, as Wordsworth has done— Yet Milton as a Philosopher, had sure as great powers as Wordsworth—What is then to be inferr'd? O many things—It proves there is really a grand march of intellect—, It proves that a mighty providence subdues the mightiest

---

3. See John 14.2: "In my Father's house are many mansions."
4. Milton's masque (1634, 1637) celebrating chastity.
5. West Smithfield, north of St. Paul's in London, was a place of execution where 200 Protestants were burnt at the stake in the 1550s under Queen Mary.

Minds to the service of the time being, whether it be in human Knowledge
or Religion—I have often pitied a Tutor who has to hear "Nom^e: Musa"[6]—
so often dinn'd into his ears—I hope you may not have the same pain in this
scribbling—I may have read these things before, but I never had even a
thus dim perception of them; and moreover I like to say my lesson to one
will endure my tediousness for my own sake—After all there is certainly
something real in the World—Moore's present to Hazlitt is real—I like that
Moore, and am glad I saw him at the Theatre just before I left Town. Tom
has spit a leetle blood this afternoon, and that is rather a damper—but I
know—the truth is there is something real in the World. Your third Chamber of Life shall be a lucky and a gentle one—stored with the wine of love—
and the Bread of Friendship—When you see George if he should not have
recēd a letter from me tell him he will find one at home most likely—tell
Bailey I hope soon to see him—Remember me to all The leaves have been
out here, for MONY a day—I have written to George for the first stanzas of
my Isabel—I shall have them soon and will copy the whole out for you.

Your affectionate friend
John Keats.

JOHN HAMILTON REYNOLDS?

Review of *Endymion*[1]

Although this poem has very lately appeared, the short delay between its
publication and our notice, was intentional. We are sincerely anxious for
its ultimate success: we were willing that the age should do honour to itself
by its reception of it; and cared little for having been the first to notice it.
We were fearful, that if we ventured to decide on it, and could induce *the
few* to take its consideration into their own hands, our great critical authorities would choose, as usual, to maintain an obstinate silence, or to speak
slightingly, perhaps contemptuously, to keep up the etiquette; for they have
a spice of Cicero, and "never follow any thing that other men begin."[2] Neither have we now altered our opinion, but having seen more than one
public notice of the work, do not choose longer to delay it. That the consequences will be pretty nearly as we predict we have little doubt. If the
reviews play the sure game and say nothing, to nothing can we object; but
if they really notice it, let us have something like a fair and liberal
criticism—something that can be subjected to examination itself. Let them
refer to principles: let them shew us the philosophic construction of poetry,
and point out its errors by instance and application. To this we shall not
object: but this we must think they owe to Mr. Keats himself; and all those
who have written and spoken highly of his talent. If however, they follow
their old course, and having tacked the introduction of the first book, to the
fag end of the last, swear the whole is an unintelligible jumble, we will at
least exert ourselves to stop their chuckling and self congratulation.

---

6. "Nominative: Musa": the words a student would speak in beginning the declension of the Latin
noun "*musa*."
1. Published in the *Champion*, June 7, 1818, pp. 362–64, this review was perhaps written by John
Hamilton Reynolds, who was attached to that journal. Richard Woodhouse has also been suggested
as a possible author.
2. So says Brutus of Cicero in Shakespeare's *Julius Caesar*, 2.1.150–51.

We cannot, however, disguise from ourselves that the conduct that may be pursued by these reviews will have its influence, and a great influence, on public opinion: but, excepting as to the effect that opinion may have on the poet himself; we care not two straws for it. Public opinion is not a comprehensive or comprehending thing; it is neither a wit nor a wise man: a poet nor a philosopher: it is the veriest "king of shadows:"[3] it is nothing but the hollow echoing of some momentary oracle: and if we estimate the work of the reviews themselves, we have it, for they are the things now in authority: they are your only substantials: they give currency to our poets: and what chance has an original genius that differs from all our poets, when nearly all our poets write for one or other of them. These men have it in their own hands, to mete out praise and censure, for half the population. We only hope they do not flatter themselves on the general assent: if they really mistake their popularity for immortality, they trick out an ideot in motley, and having stuck a Bartholomew trumpet[4] in his hand, persuade themselves it is fame. But we do fear even public opinion from our knowledge of human nature. No man ever lived but he had a consciousness of his own power, and if he chose to make a fair estimate was perhaps a better judge than any other of his own ability. If then with this consciousness he find nothing in unison with his own feeling, no fair and liberal estimate made of his worth, no concessions made, no deference paid to him by the opinion that for the time passes current, he is driven by necessity upon his self-love for satisfaction, his indignation lashes his pride, he is unsupported by others w[h]ere he has an undoubted assurance of being right, and he maintains those errors that have been justly objected against him, because they have been urged too far, and refuses to concede any thing because too much has been demanded. This, however, is a speculation, and we trust, it will remain so.

It is ever hazardous to predict the fate of a great original work; and of Endymion, all we dare venture in this way is an opinion, that an inferior poem is likely to excite a more general interest. The secret of the success of our modern poets, is their universal presence in their poems—they give to every thing the colouring of their own feeling; and what a man has felt intensely—the impressions of actual existence—he is likely to describe powerfully: what he has felt we can easily sympathize with.[5] But Mr. Keats goes out of himself into a world of abstractions:—his passions, feelings, are all as much imaginative as his situations. Neither is it the mere outward signs of passions that are given: there seems ever present some being that was equally conscious of its internal and most secret imaginings. There is another objection to its ever becoming popular, that it is, as the Venus and Adonis of Shakespeare, a *representation* and not a *description* of passion. Both these poems would, we think, be more generally admired had the poets been only veiled instead of concealed from us. Mr. Keats conceives the scene before him, and represents it as it appears. This is the excellence of dramatic poetry; but to feel its truth and power in any other, we must abandon our ordinary feeling and common consciousness, and identify

---

3. Puck uses this phrase for Oberon, king of the fairies, in Shakespeare's A *Midsummer Night's Dream*, 3.2.348.
4. Presumably a trumpet from Bartholomew Fair in West Smithfield; *motley*: the multicolored costume of a jester or harlequin.
5. These comments parallel those by Hazlitt in his review of Wordsworth's *Excursion* in the *Examiner*, August 21 and 28, 1814; reprinted in *The Round Table* (1817).

ourselves with the scene. Few people can do this. In representation, which is the ultimate purpose of dramatic poetry, we should feel some thing of sympathy though we could merely observe the scene, or the gesticulation, and no sound could reach us; but to make an ordinary *reader* sensible of the excellence of a poem, he must be told what the poet felt; and he is affected by him and not by the scene. Our modern poets are the shewmen of their own pictures, and point out its beauties.

Mr. Keats' very excellence, we fear, will tell against him. Each scene bears so actually the immediate impress of truth and nature, that it may be said to be local and peculiar, and to require some extrinsic feeling for its full enjoyment:—perhaps we are not clear in what we say. Every man then, according to his particular habit of mind, not only gives a correspondent colouring to all that surrounds him, but seeks to surround himself with corresponding objects, in which he has more than other people's enjoyment. In everything then that art or nature may present to man, though gratifying to all, each man's gratification and sympathy will be regulated by the disposition and bent of his mind. Look at Milton's Sonnets. With what a deep and bitter feeling would a persecuted religious enthusiast select and dwell "On the late Massacre in Piemont." Has a social man no particular enjoyment in those to Laurence and Skynner? or a patriot in those to Fairfax, Cromwell, and Vane?[6] What is common to humanity we are all readily sensible of; and all men proportioned to their intelligence, will receive pleasure on reading that on his birth day:—it wants nothing exclusive either in persons or age:— but would not a young and fearful lover find a thousand beauties in his address to the nightingale that must for ever escape the majority?[7] In further illustration, we would adduce the first meeting of Endymion and Cynthia in the poem before us; which, though wonderfully told, we do not think most likely to be generally liked. It is so true to imagination, that passion absorbs every thing. Now, as we have observed, to transfer the mind to the situation of another, to feel as he feels, requires an enthusiasm, and an abstraction, beyond the power or the habit of most people. It is in this way eloquence differs from poetry, and the same speech on delivery affects people, on an after reading would appear tame and unimpassioned. We have certain sympathies with the person addressing us, and what he feels, we feel in an inferior degree; but he is afterwards to describe to us his passion; to make us feel by *telling us what he felt*: and this is to be done by calculating on the effect on *others'* feelings, and not by abandoning ourselves to our own. If Mr. Keats can do this, he has not done it. When he writes of passion, it seems to have possessed him. This, however, is what Shakespeare did, and if Endymion bears any general resemblance to any other poem in the language, it is to Venus and Adonis on this very account. In the necessarily abrupt breaking off of this scene of intense passion, however, we think he has exceeded even his ordinary power. It is scarcely possible to conceive any thing more poetically imaginative; and though it may be brought in rather abruptly, we cannot refuse ourselves the pleasure of immediately extracting it.

6. References to a number of Milton's sonnets (*Poems*, 1673): his great sonnet (later Sonnet 18) on the massacre of some 1700 Vaudois in April 1655, lighter pieces to "Lawrence of virtuous father" (later Sonnet 20) and to Cyriack Skinner (later Sonnets 21 and 22), and poems to Lord General Fairfax (later Sonnet 15), written while the general besieged Colchester in the summer of 1648, "To the Lord General Cromwell" (later Sonnet 16), and to Sir Henry Vane the younger (later Sonnet 17). See Hazlitt's essay on Milton's sonnets in *Works* 8: 174–81.
7. Milton's "Sonnet to a Nightingale" (later Sonnet 1).

[Quotes *Endymion*, Book 2.827–54.]

The objection we have here stated is equally applicable to the proper and full appreciation of many other beautiful scenes in this poem; but having acknowledged this, we shall extract the hymn to Pan, that our readers may be satisfied there are others to which universal assent must be given as among the finest specimens of classic poetry in our language.

[Quotes *Endymion*, Book 1.232–62, 279–306.]

We shall trespass a little beyond the hymn itself; and must then postpone our further observations.

[Quotes *Endymion*, Book 1.307–19.]

This last line is as fine as that in Shakespeare's Sonnets,

And beauty making beautiful old rhyme:[8]

and there are not a dozen finer in Shakespeare's poems.

ANONYMOUS

British Critic Review of *Endymion*[1]

This is the most delicious poem, of its kind, which has fallen within our notice, and if Mr. Leigh Hunt had never written, we believe we might have pronounced it to be *sui generis* without fear of contradiction. That gentleman, however, has talked so much about "daisies and daffodils, clover and sweet peas, blossomings and lushiness,"[2] that we fear Mr. Keats must be content to share but half the laurel, provided always, and we can most conscientiously assert it, that the disciple be recognized as not one whit inferior to his mighty master. All the world knows that the moon fell in love with Endymion * * * but it remained for a muse of modern days to acquaint us with the whole progress of this demi-celestial amour. "A thing of beauty (as Mr. Keats says, or sings, we know not which, in the first line of his poem,) is a joy for ever!" And, "as the year grows lush in juicy stalks," "many and many a verse he hopes to write." * * * Mr. Keats is not contented with a half initiation into the school he has chosen. And he can strike from unmeaning absurdity into the gross slang of voluptuousness with as much skill as the worthy prototype whom he has selected. We will assure him, however, that not all the flimsy veil of words in which he would involve immoral images, can atone for their impurity; and we will not disgust our readers by retailing to them the artifices of vicious refinement, by which, under the semblance of "slippery blisses, twinkling eyes, soft completion of faces, and smooth excess of hands,"[3] he would palm upon the unsuspicious and the innocent imaginations better adapted to the stews.[4] * * *

The third book begins in character, with a jacobinical apostrophe to "crowns, turbans, and tiptop nothings;"[5] we wonder how mitres escaped from their usual place. * * *

---

8. Shakespeare, Sonnet 106, l. 3.
1. This anonymous review, excerpted from the *British Critic* n.s. 9 (June 1818): 649–54, is the first of the assaults launched on *Endymion*. It was indexed as "*Endymion*, a monstrously droll poem, analysis of." The reviewer's mocking summary of the poem's action has been cut.
2. For example, see Hunt's description of "flowers on all their beds" in *The Descent of Liberty* (1815), scene three, ll. 87–112.
3. *Endymion* 2.743, 756–58.
4. Brothels.
5. *Endymion* 3.12, 15.

We do most solemnly assure our readers that this poem, containing 4074 lines, is printed on very nice hot-pressed paper, and sold for nine shillings, by a very respectable London bookseller. Moreover, that the author has put his name in the title page, and told us, that though he is something between man and boy, he means by and by to be "plotting and fitting himself for verses fit to live."[6] We think it necessary to add that it is all written in rhyme, and, for the most part, (when there are syllables enough) in the heroic couplet.

Letter to Benjamin Bailey, June 10, 1818[1]

My dear Bailey,   London—

I have been very much gratified and very much hurt by your Letters in the Oxford Paper: because independant of that unlawful and mortal feeling of pleasure at praise, there is a glory in enthusiam; and because the world is malignant enough to chuckle at the most honorable Simplicity. Yes on my Soul my dear Bailey you are too simple for the World—and that Idea makes me sick of it—How is it that by extreme opposites we have as it were got discontented nerves—you have all your Life (I think so) believed every Body—I have suspected every Body—and although you have been so deceived you make a simple appeal—the world has something else to do, and I am glad of it—were it in my choice I would reject a petrarchal coronation—on account of my dying day, and because women have Cancers. I should not by rights speak in this tone to you—for it is an incendiary spirit that would do so. Yet I am not old enough or magnanimous enough to annihilate self—and it would perhaps be paying you an ill compliment. I was in hopes some little time back to be able to relieve your dullness by my spirits—to point out things in the world worth your enjoyment—and now I am never alone without rejoicing that there is such a thing as death—without placing my ultimate in the glory of dying for a great human purpose. Perhaps if my affairs were in a different state I should not have written the above—you shall judge—I have two Brothers one is driven by the 'burden of Society' to America the other, with an exquisite love of Life, is in a lingering state. My Love for my Brothers from the early loss of our parents and even for earlier Misfortunes has grown into a affection 'passing the Love of Women.'[2]—I have been ill temper'd with them, I have vex'd them—but the thought of them has always stifled the impression that any woman might otherwise have made upon me—I have a Sister too and may not follow them, either to America or to the Grave—Life must be undergone, and I certainly derive a consolation from the thought of writing one or two more Poems before it ceases. I heard some hints of your retireing to Scotland—I should like to know your feeling on it—it seems rather remote—perhaps Gleg[3] will have a duty near you. I am not certain whether I shall be able to go my Journey on account of my Brother Tom and a little indisposition of my own—If I do not you shall

6. See the preface to *Endymion* (p. 147).
1. Written to Bailey in Oxford after Keats read Bailey's two letters (signed "N.Y.") to the editor of the *Oxford University & City Herald, and Midland Country Chronicle*, May 30, June 6, 1818, serving as a kind of advertisement for *Endymion*, which Bailey calls "the most original production I ever read." Keats was preparing for his trip to Scotland and dreading his brother George's and new sister-in-law Georgiana's departure for the United States on June 25. Text from ALS (Harvard MS Keats 1.30).
2. 2 Samuel 1.26: "I am distressed for thee, my brother Jonathan . . . thy love to me was wonderful, passing the love of women."
3. For Gleg, see p. 99, n. 5.

see me soon—if not on my return—or I'll quarter myself upon you in Scotland next Winter. I had known my sister in Law some time before she was my Sister and was very fond of her. I like her better and better—she is the most disinterrested woman I ever knew—that is to say she goes beyond degree in it. To see an entirely disinterrested Girl quite happy is the most pleasant and extraordinary thing in the world—it depends upon a thousand Circumstances—on my word 'tis extraordinary. Women must want Imagination and they may thank God for it—and so may we that a delicate being can feel happy without any sense of crime. It puzzles me and I have no sort of Logic to comfort me—I shall think it over. I am not at home and your letter being there I cannot look it over to answer any particular—only I must say I felt that passage of Dante—if I take any book with me it shall be those minute volumes of Carey[4] for they will go into the aptest corner. Reynolds is getting I may say robust—his illness has been of service to him—like eny one just recovered he is high-spirited. I hear also good accounts of Rice. With respects to domestic Literature—the Endinburgh Magasine in another blow up against Hunt calls me 'the amiable Mister Keats' and I have more than a Laurel from the Quarterly Reviewers for they have smothered me in 'Foliage.'[5] I want to read you my 'Pot of Basil' if you go to scotland I should much like to read it there to you among the Snows of next Winter. My Brothers' remembrances to you.

Your affectionate friend
John Keats—

Letter to Tom Keats, June 25–27, 1818[1]

Here beginneth my journal, this Thursday, the 25th day of June, Anno Domini 1818. This morning we arose at 4, and set off in a Scotch mist; put up once under a tree, and in fine, have walked wet and dry to this place, called in the vulgar tongue Endmoor, 17 miles; we have not been incommoded by our knapsacks; they serve capitally, and we shall go on very well.

June 26—I merely put pro forma, for there is no such thing as time and space, which by the way came forcibly upon me on seeing for the first hour the Lake and Mountains of Winander[2]—I cannot describe them—they surpass my expectation—beautiful water—shores and islands green to the marge—mountains all round up to the clouds. We set out from Endmoor this morning, breakfasted at Kendal with a soldier who had been in all the wars for the last seventeen years—then we have walked to Bowne's[3] to

---

4. H. F. Carey's translation of the *Divine Comedy* reprinted in 1814 by Taylor and Hessey in three very transportable 32mo. volumes.
5. Keats refers here to the ongoing battle over the "Cockney School." In a "Letter from Z. to Leigh Hunt," *Blackwood's* 3 (May 1818): 197, Lockhart called Keats the "amiable but infatuated bardling, Mister John Keats" and mocked him for being part of Hunt's exchange of ivy crowns. Hunt was also attacked in the *Quarterly Review* 14 (January 1816): 473–81 and 18 (January 1818): 324–35, which takes up Hunt's *Foliage*, mentioned here; *Endymion* was the subject of a review by John Wilson Croker, 19 (April 1818): 204–208, which was actually published in September (see pp. 277–80).
1. Written as Keats and Brown began their northern tour after they had traveled by coach from London on June 22 to Liverpool (to see off Keats's brother George) and then to Lancaster on the 24th. Brown published his "Walks in the North, During the Summer of 1818," in the *Plymouth and Devonport Weekly Journal*, October 1, 8, 15, 22, 1840 (L, 1: 421–42). See also Carol Kyros Walker, *Walking North with Keats* (New Haven: Yale University Press, 1992). The original letter is lost; text from the Louisville, Kentucky, *Western Messenger* 1 (June 1836): 772–77.
2. Now known by its alternate name of Windermere (also Winandermere below).
3. Bowness-on-Windermere, on the east side of the lake.

dinner—said Bowne's situated on the Lake where we have just dined, and I am writing at this present. I took an oar to one of the islands to take up some trout for dinner, which they keep in porous boxes. I enquired of the waiter for Wordsworth—he said he knew him, and that he had been here a few days ago, canvassing for the Lowthers. What think you of that—Wordsworth versus Brougham!! Sad—sad—sad—and yet the family has been his friend always. What can we say? We are now about seven miles from Rydale, and expect to see him to-morrow. You shall hear all about our visit.[4]

There are many disfigurements to this Lake—not in the way of land or water. No; the two views we have had of it are of the most noble tenderness—they can never fade away—they make one forget the divisions of life; age, youth, poverty and riches; and refine one's sensual vision into a sort of north star which can never cease to be open lidded and stedfast over the wonders of the great Power. The disfigurement I mean is the miasma of London. I do suppose it contaminated with bucks and soldiers, and women of fashion—and hat-band ignorance. The border inhabitants are quite out of keeping with the romance about them, from a continual intercourse with London rank and fashion. But why should I grumble? They let me have a prime glass of soda water—O they are as good as their neighbors. But Lord Wordsworth, instead of being in retirement, has himself and his house full in the thick of fashionable visitors quite convenient to be pointed at all the summer long. When we had gone about half this morning, we began to get among the hills and to see the mountains grow up before us—the other half brought us to Wynandermere, 14 miles to dinner. The weather is capital for the views, but is now rather misty, and we are in doubt whether to walk to Ambleside to tea—it is five miles along the borders of the Lake. Loughrigg will swell up before us all the way—I have an amazing partiality for mountains in the clouds. There is nothing in Devon like this, and Brown says there is nothing in Wales to be compared to it. I must tell you, that in going through Cheshire and Lancashire, I saw the Welsh mountains at a distance. We have passed the two castles, Lancaster and Kendal. 27th—We walked here to Ambleside yesterday along the border of Winandermere all beautiful with wooded shores and Islands—our road was a winding lane, wooded on each side, and green overhead, full of Foxgloves—every now and then a glimpse of the Lake, and all the while Kirkstone and other large hills nestled together in a sort of grey black mist. Ambleside is at the northern extremity of the Lake. We arose this morning at six, because we call it a day of rest, having to call on Wordsworth who lives only two miles hence— before breakfast we went to see the Ambleside water fall. The morning beautiful—the walk easy among the hills. We, I may say, fortunately, missed the direct path, and after wandering a little, found it out by the noise—for, mark you, it is buried in trees, in the bottom of the valley—the stream itself is interesting throughout with "mazy error over pendant shades."[5] Milton

---

4. In the 1818 general election, the Whig Henry Brougham (1778–1868), known for opposing the slave trade and for supporting parliamentary reform (and the Hunt brothers' lawyer), challenged the Tory William Lowther (1787–1872), the son of Lord Londsdale to whom Wordsworth had dedicated *The Excursion*. Lowther held onto the seat (perhaps through electoral shenanigans) long controlled by his family. Hunt's *Examiner* backed Brougham. Wordsworth strongly supported his patron's family. Rydal Mount, Westmorland, was the Wordsworth family home from 1817 on. Keats did not see Wordsworth, who was at Lowther Hall, but left a note stuck above a portrait of Dorothy Wordsworth.
5. Milton, *Paradise Lost*, 4.239.

meant a smooth river—this is buffetting all the way on a rocky bed ever various—but the waterfall itself, which I came suddenly upon, gave me a pleasant twinge. First we stood a little below the head about halfway down the first fall, buried deep in trees, and saw it streaming down two more descents to the depth of near fifty feet—then we went on a jut of rock nearly level with the second fall-head, where the first fall was above us, and the third below our feet still—at the same time we saw that the water was divided by a sort of cataract island on whose other side burst out a glorious stream—then the thunder and the freshness. At the same time the different falls have as different characters; the first darting down the slate-rock like an arrow; the second spreading out like a fan—the third dashed into a mist—and the one on the other side of the rock a sort of mixture of all these. We afterwards moved away a space, and saw nearly the whole more mild, streaming silverly through the trees. What astonishes me more than any thing is the tone, the coloring, the slate, the stone, the moss, the rock-weed; or, if I may so say, the intellect, the countenance of such places. The space, the magnitude of mountains and waterfalls are well imagined before one sees them; but this countenance or intellectual tone must surpass every imagination and defy any remembrance. I shall learn poetry here and shall henceforth write more than ever, for the abstract endeavor of being able to add a mite to that mass of beauty which is harvested from these grand materials, by the finest spirits, and put into etherial existence for the relish of one's fellows. I cannot think with Hazlitt that these scenes make man appear little.[6] I never forgot my stature so completely—I live in the eye; and my imagination, surpassed, is at rest—We shall see another waterfall near Rydal to which we shall proceed after having put these letters in the post office. I long to be at Carlisle, as I expect there a letter from George and one from you. Let any of my friends see my letters—they may not be interested in descriptions—descriptions are bad at all times—I did not intend to give you any; but how can I help it? I am anxious you should taste a little of our pleasure; it may not be an unpleasant thing, as you have not the fatigue. I am well in health. Direct henceforth to Port Patrick till the 12th July. Content that probably three or four pair of eyes whose owners I am rather partial to will run over these lines I remain; and moreover that I am your affectionate brother John.

[Give me your patience, sister, while I frame][1]

Give me your patience, sister, while I frame
Exact in capitals your golden name:
Or sue the fair Apollo and he will
Rouse from his heavy slumber and instill
Great love in me for thee and Poesy.   5

---

6. See Hazlitt's comment in his review of Wordsworth's *Excursion*, *Works*, 19: 23–24: "The immensity of their mountains makes the human form seem little and insignificant."

1. This acrostic ("the first and most likely the last I ever shall do") on the name of Keats's sister-in-law was written at the "Foot of Helvellyn" on June 27, 1818, and sent in a letter of June 27, 28, 1818 to George and Georgiana Augusta Keats (*L*, 1: 303–304); as this letter was returned, Keats recopied the poem with revisions into the journal letter of September 1819 to the George Keatses (*L*, 2: 195). First published in the New York *World* June 25, 1877: 2; text from the *World* with emendations from the later holograph letter (Morgan Library MA 212).

Imagine not that greatest mastery
And kingdom over all the realms of verse
Nears more to heaven in aught than when we nurse
And surety give to love and Brotherhood.

Anthropophagi in Othello's mood;[2]   10
Ulysses stormed, and his enchanted belt[3]
Glow with the Muse, but they are never felt
Unbosom'd so and so eternal made,
Such tender incense in their laurel shade,
To all the regent sisters of the Nine,[4]   15
As this poor offering to you sister mine.

Kind sister! aye, this third name says you are;
Enchanted has it been the Lord knows where.
And may it taste to you like good old wine,
Take you to real happiness and give   20
Sons, daughters and a home like honied hive.

ON VISITING THE TOMB OF BURNS.[1]

The town, the churchyard, and the setting sun,
The clouds, the trees, the rounded hills all seem,
Though beautiful, cold—strange—as in a dream,
I dreamed long ago, now new begun.[2]
The short-lived, paly summer is but won   5
From winter's ague, for one hour's gleam;
Though[3] sapphire-warm, their stars do never beam:
All is cold Beauty; pain is never done:[4]
For who has mind to relish, Minos-wise,[5]
The real of Beauty, free from that dead hue   10
Sickly[6] imagination and sick pride[7]

---

2. See Shakespeare, *Othello*, 1.3.142–43: "And of the cannibals, that each other eat, / The Anthropophagi [eaters of men]."
3. Perhaps the magic "veil" Ulysses/Odysseus receives from the goddess Leucothea in the *Odyssey*, Book 5, which saves him from drowning; he is often tossed by storms at sea.
4. The nine muses.
1. Written on July 1, 1818, when Keats visited Burns's tomb at Dunfries. Robert Burns (1759–1796) was born into poverty before becoming perhaps Scotland's most beloved poet; his 1786 *Poems, chiefly in the Scottish Dialect* was an immediate success, with his rapid rise, his struggles to remain true to his own voice while being fêted by society, and his early death making him one model of the young poet who ends tragically. The poem was included in a (lost) letter to Tom Keats of June 29–July 2, 1818 (*L*, 1: 308–309) where Keats notes, "Burns' tomb is in the Churchyard corner, not very much to my taste, though on a scale, large enough to show they wanted to honour him. . . . This Sonnet I have written in a strange mood, half asleep. I know not how it is, the Clouds, the sky, the Houses, all seem anti Grecian & anti Charlemagnish." First published as part of the letter to Tom in 1848, 1: 156–57; text from 1848 with emendations from Jeffrey's transcript (Harvard MS Keats 3.9, f.7r).
2. This is the punctuation of this line from 1848; Jeffrey's transcript has no end punctuation. Allott and Stillinger change the transcript's comma into a period after "ago" and drop 1848's period at the end of the line.
3. Jeffrey's transcript reads "Through," which Allott defends as correct.
4. Jeffrey's transcript has a period here; Allott and Stillinger have no punctuation at the end of the line.
5. With the wisdom of Minos, one of the classical judges of the dead.
6. While 1848 and most editors offer "Sickly," the Jeffrey transcript reads "Fickly," which, as J. C. Maxwell (*KSJ* 4 [1955]: 77) points out, is an appropriate word meaning "deceitful."
7. Allott suggests an echo of Shakespeare, *Hamlet*, 3.1.86–87: "the native hue of resolution / Is sicklied o'er with the pale cast of thought."

Cast[8] wan upon it! Burns! with honour due
I have oft honoured thee. Great shadow, hide
Thy face; I sin against thy native skies.

MEG MERRILIES.

A Ballad, written for the amusement of his young sister[1]

Old Meg she was a gipsey,
    And lived upon the moors;
Her bed it was the brown heath turf,
    And her house was out of doors!
Her apples were swart blackberries,   5
    Her currants, pods o' broom;
Her wine was dew o' the wild white rose,
    Her book a churchyard tomb!

Her brothers were the craggy hills,
    Her sisters larchen trees—   10
Alone with her great family,
    She liv'd as she did please.
No breakfast had she many a morn,
    No dinner many a noon,
And, 'stead of supper, she would stare   15
    Full hard against the moon!

But every morn of woodbine fresh
    She made her garlanding,
And every night the dark glen yew
    She wove, and she would sing;   20
And with her fingers, old and brown,
    She plaited mats o' rushes,
And gave them to the cottagers
    She met among the bushes.

Old Meg was brave as Margaret Queen,   25
    And tall as Amazon:[2]
An old red blanket cloak she wore;
    A chip-hat[3] had she on;
God rest her aged bones somewhere—
    She died full long agone!   30

8. There is a blank in the Jeffrey transcript; this is 1848's conjecture.
1. Written on July 3, 1818, in a letter to Fanny Keats as Keats and Brown walked to Kirkcudbright via Auchencairn. Meg Merrilies is a character in Scott's *Guy Mannering* (1815), which Keats had not read but about which Brown chatted; they were walking through the landscape of the novel, and Keats at one point said to Brown, "There . . . in that very spot, without a shadow of a doubt, has old Meg Merrilies often boiled her kettle!" (*KC*, 2: 61). First published in the *Plymouth and Devonport Weekly Journal*, November 22, 1838; text from *PDWJ* with emendations from the draft version in the letter to Fanny (Morgan Library MA 975).
2. A type of female warrior from Greek myth who supposedly lived in Scythia. *Margaret Queen*: possibly Margaret, Queen of Scots (1240–1275), Margaret, Queen of Edward 1 (1282?–1318), Margaret of Anjou, Queen Consort to Henry VI (1430–1482), or Margaret Tudor (1489–1541), the daughter of Henry VII who married James IV of Scotland in 1503.
3. A hat made of thin strips of wood.

Letter to Tom Keats, July 3, 5, 7, 9, 1818[1]

My dear Tom,   Auchencairn July 3rd
    I have not been able to keep up my journal completely on account of
other letters to George and one which I am writing to Fanny from which I
have turned to loose no time whilst Brown is coppying a song about Meg
Merrilies[2] which I have just written for her—We are now in Meg Merrilies
county and have this morning passed through some parts exactly suited to
her—Kirkudbright County is very beautiful, very wild with craggy hills
somewhat in the westmoreland fashion—we have come down from Dum-
fries to the sea coast part of it. The song I mention you would have from
Dilke: but perhaps you would like it here—
          [A copy of "Old Meg she was a gipsy" follows.][3]
Now I will return to Fanny—it rains. I may have time to go on here
presently. July 5—You see I have missed a day from fanny's Letter. Yesterday was passed in Kircudbright—the Country is very rich—very fine—and
with a little of Devon—I am now writing at Newton Stuart six Miles into
Wigton[4]—Our Landlady of yesterday said very few Southrens passed these
ways—The children jabber away as in a foreign Language—The barefooted
Girls look very much in keeping—I mean with the Scenery about them—
Brown praises their cleanliness and appearance of comfort—the neatness
of their cottages &c. It may be—they are very squat among trees and fern
and heaths and broom, on levels slopes and heights—They are very pleasant because they are very primitive—but I wish they were as snug as those
up the Devonshire vallies—We are lodged and entertained in great
varieties—we dined yesterday on dirty bacon dirtier eggs and dirtiest Potatoes with a slice of Salmon—we breakfast this morning in a nice carpeted
Room with Sofa hair bottomed chairs and green-baized mehogany—A spring
by the road side is always welcome—we drink water for dinner diluted with
a Gill of wiskey. July 7th Yesterday Morning we set out from Glenluce going
some distance round to see some Ruins[5]—they were scarcely worth the
while—we went on towards Stranrawier in a burning sun and had gone
about six Miles when the Mail overtook us—we got up—were at Portpatrick in a jiffy, and I am writing now in little Ireland.[6] The dialect on the
neighbouring shores of Scotland and Ireland is much the same—yet I can
perceive a great difference in the nations from the Chambermaid at this
nate Inn kept by Mr Kelly—She is fair, kind and ready to laugh, because she
is out of the horrible dominion of the Scotch kirk[7]—A Scotch Girl stands
in terrible awe of the Elders—poor little Susannas[8]—They will scarcely
laugh—they are greatly to be pitied and the kirk is greatly to be damn'd.
These kirkmen have done scotland good (Query?) they have made Men,
Women, Old Men Young Men old Women, young women boys, girls and
infants all careful—so that they are formed into regular Phalanges of savers
and gainers—such a thrifty army cannot fail to enrich their Country and

  1. Begun at the same time as a letter to his sister, Fanny, on a stop between Dalbeattie and Kirkcud-
      bright. Text from ALS (Harvard MS Keats 1.33); there is also a Jeffrey transcript (Harvard MS
      Keats 3.9, f. 7v.).
  2. Character in Scott's *Guy Mannering* (1815).
  3. See p. 255.
  4. For Wigtown, Cumberland; he appears to have walked six miles into Wigtownshire.
  5. Of Glenluce Abbey (1192).
  6. Keats and Brown took the postal packet boat from Portpatrick to Donaghadee, Ireland.
  7. Church of Scotland.
  8. In the Book of Daniel, the elders leer at the bathing Susanna.

give it a greater apperance of comfort than that of their poor irish neighbours. These kirkmen have done Scotland harm—they have banished puns
and laughing and kissing (except in cases where the very danger and crime
must make it very fine and gustful. I shall make a full stop at kissing for
after that there should be a better parent-thesis: and go on to remind you
of the fate of Burns. Poor unfortunate fellow—his disposition was
southern—how sad it is when a luxurious imagination is obliged in self
defence to deaden its delicacy in vulgarity, and riot in thing attainable that
it may not have leisure to go mad after things which are not. No Man in
such matters will be content with the experience of others. It is true that
out of suffrance there is no greatness, no dignity; that in the most
abstracted Pleasure there is no lasting happiness: yet who would not like
to discover over again that Cleopatra was a Gipsey, Helen a Rogue and
Ruth a deep one? I have not sufficient reasoning faculty to settle the doctrine of thrift—as it is consistent with the dignity of human Society—with
the happiness of Cottagers—All I can do is by plump contrasts—Were the
fingers made to squeeze a guinea or a white hand? Were the Lips made to
hold a pen or a kiss? And yet in Cities Man is shut out from his fellows if
he is poor, the Cottager must be dirty and very wretched if she be not
thrifty—The present state of society demands this and this convinces me
that the world is very young and in a verry ignorant state—We live in a bar-
barous age. I would sooner be a wild deer than a Girl under the dominion
of the kirk, and I would sooner be a wild hog than be the occasion of a Poor
Creatures pennance before those execrable elders. It is not so far to the
Giant's Cause way[9] as we supposed—we thought it 70 and hear it is only
48 Miles—so we shall leave one of our knapsacks here at Donoghadee, take
our immediate wants and be back in a week—when we shall proceed to the
County of Ayr. In the Packet Yesterday we heard some Ballads from two old
Men—one was a romance which seemed very poor—then there was the
Battle of the Boyne[1]—then Robin Huid as they call him—'Before the king
you shall go, go, go, before the king you shall go.'[2] There were no Letters
for me at Port Patrick so I am behind hand with you I dare say in news from
George. Direct to Glasgow till the 17th of this month.
9th We stopped very little in Ireland and that you may not have leisere to
marvel at our speedy return to Portpatrick I will tell you that is it as dear
living in Ireland as at the Hummums[3]—thrice the expence of Scotland—it
would have cost us £15 before our return—Moreover we found those 48
Miles to be irish ones which reached to 70 english—So having walked to
Belfast one day and back to Donoghadee the next we left Ireland with a fair
breeze—We slept last night at Port patrick where I was gratified by a letter
from you. On our walk in Ireland we had too much opportunity to see the
worse than nakedness, the rags, the dirt and misery of the poor common
Irish—A Scotch cottage, though in that some times the Smoke has no exit
but at the door, is a pallace to an irish one—We could observe that
impetiosity in Man and boy and Woman—We had the pleasure of finding
our way through a Peat-Bog—three miles long at least—dreary, black, dank,
flat and spongy: here and there were poor dirty creatures and a few strong

9. Due to costs in Ireland, they did not go to the Giant's Causeway, a promontory made up of basalt
   columns and a major tourist site.
1. The Battle of the Boyne (July 1, 1690) saw the defeat of King James II by William III, ending the
   Jacobite effort in Ireland. For ballads on the battle, see Rollins, *The Pepys Ballads* 5 (Harvard University Press, 1931): 186, 191, 195.
2. From the tenth stanza of "Robin Hood and the Bishop of Hereford."
3. An expensive London hotel in Covent Garden.

men cutting or carting peat. We heard on passing into Belfast through a most wretched suburb that most disgusting of all noises worse than the Bag pipe, the laugh of a Monkey, the chatter of women *solus* the scream of Macaw—I mean the sound of the Shuttle[4]—What a tremendous difficulty is the improvement of the condition of such people. I cannot conceive how a mind 'with child'[5] of Philanthrophy could grasp at possibility—with me it is absolute despair. At a miserable house of entertainment half way between Donaghadee and Bellfast were two Men Sitting at Whiskey one a Laborer and the other I took to be a drunken Weaver—The Laborer took me for a Frenchman and the other hinted at Bounty Money saying he was ready to take it—On calling for the Letters at Port patrick the man snapp'd out 'what Regiment'? On our return from Bellfast we met a Sadan[6]—the Duchess of Dunghill—It is no laughing matter tho—Imagine the worst dog kennel you ever saw placed upon two poles from a mouldy fencing—In such a wretched thing sat a squalid old Woman squat like an ape half starved from a scarcity of Buiscuit in its passage from Madagascar to the cape,—with a pipe in her mouth and looking out with a round-eyed skinny lidded, inanity—with a sort of horizontal idiotic movement of her head—squab[7] and lean she sat and puff 'd out the smoke while two ragged tattered Girls carried her along. What a thing would be a history of her Life and sensations. I shall endeavour when I know more and have thought a little more, to give you my ideas of the difference between the scotch and irish—The two Irishmen I mentioned were speaking of their treatment in England when the Weaver said—'Ah you were a civil Man but I was a drinker.' Remember me to all—I intend writing to Haslam[8]—but dont tell him for fear I should delay—We left a notice at Portpatrick that our Letters should be thence forwarded to Glasgow—Our quick return from Ireland will occasion our passing Glasgow sooner than we thought—so till further notice you must direct to Inverness

Your most affectionate Brother John—
Remember me to the Bentleys[9]

SONNET TO AILSA ROCK[1]

Hearken, thou craggy ocean pyramid!
Give answer from[2] thy voice, the sea fowls' screams!
When were thy shoulders mantled in huge streams?
When, from the sun, was thy broad forehead hid?

4. Keats's reference to the unnatural sounds coming from one of Belfast's large cotton factories gestures toward the terrible working conditions for weavers.
5. Spenser, *Faerie Queene*, 1.5.1–2: "The noble hart, that harbours vertuous thought, / And is with child of glorious great intent."
6. Sedan chair.
7. Short and stout; Jeffrey reads as "squat."
8. See p. 117, n. 1.
9. See p. 98, n. 1.
1. Written at an inn at Girvan, July 10, 1818, about Ailsa Craig, seventeen miles out to sea in the Firth of Clyde, near the Ayrshire Coast, 1109 feet in height. Keats wrote "The effect of Ailsa with the peculiar perspective of the Sea in connection with the ground we stood on, and the misty rain then falling gave me a complete Idea of a deluge—Ailsa struck me very suddenly—really I was a little alarmed"; he indicates, "This is the only Sonnet of any worth I have of late written" (letter to Tom Keats, July 10–14, 1818 (*L*, 1: 329, 330). First published in Hunt's *Literary Pocket-Book for 1819* (1818), p. 225; text from *Literary Pocket-Book* with a variant from the letter to Tom (British Museum, Add. 45510).
2. The letter to Tom has "by."

How long is't since the mighty power bid   5
    Thee heave to airy sleep from fathom dreams?
  Sleep in the lap of thunder or sunbeams,
Or when grey clouds are thy cold coverlid.

Thou answer'st not, for thou are dead asleep;
    Thy life is but two dead eternities—   10
  The last in air, the former in the deep;
    First with the whales, last with the eagle-skies—
  Drown'd wast thou till an earthquake made thee steep,
    Another cannot wake thy giant size.

SONNET.[1]

This mortal body of a thousand days
    Now fills, O Burns, a space in thine own room,
  Where thou didst dream alone on budded bays,
    Happy and thoughtless of thy day of doom!
My pulse is warm with thine old Barley-bree,[2]   5
    My head is light with pledging a great soul,
My eyes are wandering, and I cannot see,
    Fancy is dead and drunken at its goal;
Yet can I stamp my foot upon thy floor,
    Yet can I ope thy window-sash to find   10
The meadow thou hast tramped o'er and o'er,—
    Yet can I think of thee till thought is blind,—
Yet can I gulp a bumper to thy name,—
O smile among the shades, for this is fame!

The Gadfly[1]

1

ALL gentle folks who owe a grudge
    To any living thing
Open your ears and stay your trudge
    Whilst I in dudgeon sing.

2

The gadfly he hath stung me sore—   5
    O may he ne'er sting you!

1. Written on July 11, 1818, when Keats visited the cottage where Burns was born at Ayr; see his
   journal letter to Reynolds for July 13: "We went to the Cottage and took some Whiskey—I wrote
   a sonnet for the mere sake of writing some lines under the roof" (*L*, 1: 324). He refused to copy the
   poem for Reynolds or his brother Tom, but Brown made a transcript (now lost), noting that
   the cottage's "conversion into a whiskey-shop, together with its drunken landlord, went far
   towards the annihilation of his poetic power" (*KC*, 2: 62). First published in 1848, 1: 159; text
   from 1848 (there are no extant MSS.).
2. Ale.
1. Written at Cairndow, Argyllshire, on July 17, 1818, in a letter to Tom Keats of July 17–21, 1818,
   after Keats had been bathing in Loch Fyne and been attacked by "cursed Gad flies" (*L*, 1: 334).
   First published in Forman (1883) 2: 303–306; text from Forman with emendations from the holograph letter (LMA: K/MS/02/003/6571).

But we have many a horrid bore
He may sting black and blue.

3

Has any here an old grey Mare
With three legs all her store,   10
O put it to her Buttocks bare
And straight she'll run on four.

4

Has any here a Lawyer suit
Of 1743,[2]
Take Lawyer's nose and put it to't   15
And you the end will see.

5

Is there a Man in Parliament
Dumb-founder'd in his speech,[3]
O let his neighbour make a rent
And put one in his breech.   20

6

O Lowther[4] how much better thou
Hadst figur'd t'other day
When to the folks thou mad'st a bow
And hadst no more to say

7

If lucky gadfly had but ta'en   25
His seat upon thine a—e
And put thee to a little pain
To save thee from a worse.

8

Better than Southey[5] it had been,
Better than Mr. D—,   30
Better than Wordsworth too, I ween,
Better than Mr. V—.[6]

---

2. A long-running legal case, started supposedly in 1743.
3. Perhaps Viscount Castlereagh (Robert Stewart) (1769–1822), Foreign Secretary under Liverpool and long-time Pittite leader until he committed suicide; known as a blunt, irregular speaker and often attacked by Hunt, Byron, and Shelley.
4. William Lowther (1787–1872), second earl of Lonsdale, and an anti-Reform Member of Parliament for Westmorland elected in 1813, 1818, 1820, and 1826; Wordsworth had campaigned for him against Brougham, much to Keats's disgust (see p. 252).
5. Robert Southey (1774–1843), Lake Poet and Poet Laureate, who had earned the enmity of the left by deserting his early political positions for conservative ones.
6. Forman, *The Letters of John Keats* (1935), pp. 186–87n, suggests that Keats refers to Robert Dundas, Viscount Melville (1771–1851), whom Wordsworth mentions in *Two Addresses to the Freeholders of Westmoreland* (1818), and Nicholas Vansittart (1766–1851), Chancellor of the Exchequer from 1812–1822 and another favorite target of writers such as Hunt.

9

Forgive me pray good people all
    For deviating so—
In spirit sure I had a call—   35
    And now I on will go.

10

Has any here a daughter fair
    Too fond of reading novels,
Too apt to fall in love with care
    And charming Mister Lovels,[7]   40

11

O put a gadfly to that thing
    She keeps so white and pert—
I mean the finger for the ring,
    And it will breed a wert.[8]

12

Has any here a pious spouse   45
    Who seven times a day
Scolds as King David pray'd, to chouse[9]
    And have her holy way—

13

O let a gadfly's little sting
    Persuade her sacred tongue   50
That noises are a common thing,
    But that her bell has rung.

14

And as this is the summum bo-
    Num[1] of all conquering,
I leave "withouten wordes mo"[2]   55
    The gadfly's little sting.

[Of late two dainties were before me placed][1]

Of late two dainties were before me placed,
    Sweet, holy, pure, sacred and innocent,

---

7. The hero of Scott's *The Antiquary* (1816).
8. Wart.
9. To cheat. For David praying, see Psalms 119.164: "Seven times a day do I praise thee."
1. Greatest good.
2. A Chaucerian turn.
1. Written on July 17 or 18, 1818, after going to a "Barn alone where I saw the Stranger accompanied by a bag-pipe" (*L*, 1: 336); Keats probably drafted the sonnet in his letter of July 17, 18, 20, 21, 1818, to Tom Keats. *The Stranger*, adapted from *Menschenhass und Reue* by Kotzebue (1761–1819), was one the best-known plays of the period, having first appeared in London in

From the ninth sphere[2] to me benignly sent,
That Gods might know my own particular taste.
First the soft bagpipe mourned with zealous haste,   5
The Stranger next, with head on bosom bent,
Sighed; rueful again the piteous bagpipe went,
Again the Stranger sighings fresh did waste.
O Bagpipe, thou didst steal my heart away;
O Stranger, thou my nerves from Pipe didst charm;   10
O Bagpipe, thou did'st reassert thy sway;
Again thou, Stranger, gav'st me fresh alarm;
Alas! I could not choose. Ah! my poor heart,
Mum-chance[3] art thou with both obliged to part.

LINES WRITTEN IN THE SCOTCH HIGHLANDS.[1]

There is a charm[2] in footing slow across a silent plain,
Where patriot battle has been fought, where[3] glory had the gain;
There is a pleasure on the heath, where Druids[4] old have been,
Where mantles grey have rustled by and swept the nettles green;
There is a joy in every spot, made known in days[5] of old,   5
New to the feet, although each tale a hundred times be told;
There is a deeper joy than all, more solemn in the heart,
More parching to the tongue than all, of more divine a smart,
When weary steps[6] forget themselves upon a pleasant turf,
Upon hot sand, or flinty road, or sea-shore iron scurf,[7]   10
Toward the castle or the cot, where long ago was born
One who was great through mortal days, and died of fame
    unshorn.[8]

1798. In the letter, Keats writes of "the horrors of a solo on the Bag-pipe" and how it was used to accompany the production. First published in the *Athenaeum*, June 7, 1873, p. 725; text from *Athenaeum* with emendations from the version in the letter to Tom (LMA K/MS/02/003/6571).
2. The nine spheres of Ptolemaic astronomy.
3. Archaic word for "tongue-tied."
1. Written around July 18–22, 1818, when Keats copied it into a letter to Bailey (see p. 266, n. 3 below) to express his strong reaction to visiting Burns's cottage and the surrounding countryside. Feeling that his sonnet written in the cottage, "This mortal body of a thousand days" (p. 259), was "wretched," Keats "a few days afterwards . . . wrote some lines cousin-german to the Circumstance." The poem's rhyming fourteeners or heptameters recall Keats's reading of Renaissance authors such as Chapman. Published in part at the end of an article by Brown on "Mountain Scenery" in the *New Monthly Magazine*, March 4, 1822, p. 252 (where the poem is given in alternating tetrameters and trimeters), the complete text in heptameters first appeared in the *Examiner*, July 14, 1822, p. 445, where the earlier printing is criticized as "mutilated," and the poem is found, "exclusive of its rare poetic merits," to be "valuable as an index to the mind of the lamented Author, while under the excitation of the powerful scenery of the Highlands"; text from the *Examiner* with emendations from Keats's holograph draft (Harvard MS Keats 2.19; *JKPMH*, pp. 89–91), where it is given the title at the end of "Lines written in the highlands after a visit to Burns's Country," and with some variants from the letter version (Harvard MS Keats 1.34) indicated in the notes.
2. The letter version alters to "joy," presumably to parallel ll. 5 and 7.
3. The draft has "when."
4. See p. 41, n. 8.
5. The draft has "by times."
6. The letter version has "feet."
7. Salt deposit.
8. Literally uncut, but here undiminished.

Light heather-bells[9] may tremble then—but they are far away;
Wood-lark may sing from sandy fern,—the sun may hear his lay;[1]
Runnels[2] may kiss the grass on shelves and shallows clear,—   15
But their low voices are not heard, though come on travels drear;
Blood-red the sun may set behind black mountain peaks;
Blue tides may sluice and drench their time in caves and weedy
   creeks;
Eagles may seem to sleep wing-wide upon the air;
Ring-doves[3] may fly convulsed across to some high cedar'd lair;   20
But the forgotten eye is still fast lidded[4] to the ground,
As Palmer's,[5] that, with weariness, mid-desert shrine hath found.

At such a time the soul's a child, in childhood is the brain;
Forgotten is the worldly heart—alone, it beats in vain.—
Aye, if a madman could have leave to pass a healthful day,   25
To tell his forehead's swoon and faint when first began decay,
He might make tremble many a one[6] whose spirit had gone forth
To find a Bard's[7] low cradle place about the silent North.—

Scanty the hour and few the steps beyond the bourn[8] of care,
Beyond the sweet and bitter world,—beyond it unaware!   30
Scanty the hour, and few the steps, because a longer stay
Would bar return, and make a man forget his mortal way.
O horrible! to lose the sight of well remembered face,
Of brother's eyes, of sister's brow,—constant to every place;
Filling the air, as on we move, with portraiture intense,   35
More warm than those heroic tints that pain[9] a painter's sense,
When shapes of old come striding by, and visages of old,
Locks shining black, hair scanty grey, and passions manifold.

No, no, that horror cannot be,—for at the cable's length
Man feels the gentle anchor pull and gladdens in its strength.   40
One hour, half-ideot, he stands by mossy waterfall,
But in the very next he reads his soul's memorial:—
He reads it on the mountain's height, where chance he may sit
   down
Upon rough marble diadem,—that hill's eternal crown.
Yet be his anchor e'er so fast, room is there for a prayer   45
That man may never lose his mind on mountains black[1] and bare;
That he may stray, league after league, some great birth-place
   to find,
And keep his vision clear from speck, his inward sight unblind.

9. The blossoms of the heather; a word Keats could have found in Burns, "To W. Simpson" (1785),
   l. 56 or Scott, *Marmion* (1808), 1.18.
1. Song.
2. Small streams, brooklets.
3. Wood pigeons; perhaps they are "convulsed" or "agitated" because of the eagles drifting above.
4. The letter version has "fast wedded."
5. Pilgrim's.
6. The letter version has "man."
7. Burns [*Examiner* note].
8. Boundary, limit.
9. The letter version has "fill."
1. The letter version has "bleak."

Letter to Benjamin Bailey, July 18, 22, 1818[1]

My Dear Bailey,   Inverary July 18th
    The only day I have had a chance of seeing you when you were last in
London I took every advantage of—some devil led you out of the way—Now
I have written to Reynolds to tell me where you will be in Cumberland—
so that I cannot miss you—and when I see you the first thing I shall do will
be to read that about Milton and Ceres and Proserpine[2]—for though I am
not going after you to John o' Grotts[3] it will be but poetical to say so. And
here Bailey I will say a few words written in a sane and sober Mind, a very
scarce thing with me, for they may hereafter save you a great deal of trouble
about me, which you do not deserve, and for which I ought to be bastina-
doed.[4] I carry all matters to an extreme—so that when I have any little vexation it grows in five Minutes into a theme for Sophocles—then and in that
temper if I write to any friend I have so little self-possession that I give him
matter for grieving at the very time perhaps when I am laughing at a Pun.
Your last Letter made me blush for the pain I had given you—I know my
own disposition so well that I am certain of writing many times hereafter
in the same strain to you—now you know how far to believe in them—you
must allow for imagination—I know I shall not be able to help it. I am sorry
you are grieved at my not continuing my visits to little Britain[5]—yet I think
I have as far as a Man can do who has Books to read and subjects to think
upon—for that reason I have been no where else except to Wentworth place
so nigh at hand—moreover I have been too often in a state of health that
made me think it prudent not to hazard the night Air. Yet further I will confess to you that I cannot enjoy Society small or numerous. I am certain that
our fair friends are glad I should come for the mere sake of my coming; but
I am certain I bring with me a Vexation they are better without—If I can
possibly at any time feel my temper coming upon me I refrain even from a
promised visit. I am certain I have not a right feeling towards Women—at
this moment I am striving to be just to them but I cannot—Is it because
they fall so far beneath my Boyish imagination? When I was a Schoolboy I
thought a fair Woman a pure Goddess, my mind was a soft nest in which
some one of them slept though she knew it not—I have no right to expect
more than their reality. I thought them etherial above Men—I find them
perhaps equal—great by comparison is very small—Insult may be inflicted
in more ways than by Word or action—one who is tender of being insulted
does not like to think an insult against another. I do not like to think insults
in a Lady's Company—I commit a Crime with her which absence would
have not known—Is it not extraordinary? When among Men I have no evil
thoughts, no malice, no spleen—I feel free to speak or to be silent—I can
listen and from every one I can learn—my hands are in my pockets I am
free from all suspicion and comfortable. When I am among Women I have

1. Written to Bailey at his father's house in Peterborough but forwarded on to Carlisle in Cumber-
    land where Bailey had been given a curacy; as the letter makes clear, Keats intended to stop to see
    Bailey on his way back to London but, because of his health, he did not do so. Text from ALS (Har-
    vard MS Keats 1.34); there is also a transcript in Woodhouse's letter-book, pp. 90–95.
2. Milton, in *Paradise Lost*, 4.268–72, tells the story of the abduction of Proserpine, the daughter of
    Ceres, by Hades (Dis), the god of the underworld, leaving Ceres "To seek her through the world."
3. The northern extremity of Scotland and a phrase for land's end.
4. To be beaten upon the soles of the feet with a stick.
5. Reynolds's family, including his sisters, lived on this street in London; Wentworth Place, mentioned
    below, was the home of Brown and Dilke in Hampstead, near where Keats and his brother lived
    and Keats's future home.

evil thoughts, malice, spleen—I cannot speak or be silent—I am full of Suspicions & therefore listen to no thing—I am in a hurry to be gone—You must be charitable and put all this perversity to my being disappointed since Boyhood—Yet with such feelings I am happier alone among Crowds of men, by myself or with a friend or two—With all this trust me Bailey I have not the least idea that Men of different feelings and inclinations are more short sighted than myself—I never rejoiced more than at my Brother's Marriage and shall do so at that of any of my friends—. I must absolutely get over this—but how? The only way is to find the root of evil, and so cure it "with backward mutters of dissevering Power."[6]—That is a difficult thing; for an obstinate Prejudice can seldom be produced but from a gordian[7] complication of feelings, which must take time to unravel and care to keep unravelled—I could say a good deal about this but I will leave it in hopes of better and more worthy dispositions—and also content that I am wronging no one, for after all I do think better of Womankind than to suppose they care whether Mister John Keats five feet hight likes them or not. You appeard to wish to avoid any words on this subject—don't think it a bore my dear fellow—it shall be my Amen—I should not have consented to myself these four Months[8] tramping in the highlands but that I thought it would give me more experience, rub off more Prejudice, use me to more hardship, identify finer scenes, load me with grander Mountains, and strengthen more my reach in Poetry, than would stopping at home among Books even though I should reach Homer. By this time I am comparitively a mountaineer—I have been among wilds and Mountains too much to break out much about their Grandeur. I have fed upon Oat cake—not long enough to be very much attached to it—The first Mountains I saw, though not so large as some I have since seen, weighed very solemnly upon me. The effect is wearing away—yet I like them mainly—We have come this evening with a Guide, for without was impossible, into the middle of the Isle of Mull, pursuing our cheap journey to Iona and perhaps Staffa—We would not follow the common and fashionable mode from the great imposition of expense.[9] We have come over heath and rock and river and bog to what in England would be called a horrid place—yet it belongs to a Shepherd pretty well off perhaps—The family speak not a word but gælic and we have not yet seen their faces for the smoke which after visiting every cranny, (not excepting my eyes very much incommoded for writing), finds its way out at the door. I am more comfortable than I could have imagined in such a place, and so is Brown—The People are all very kind. We lost our way a little yesterday and enquiring at a Cottage, a young Woman without a word threw on her cloak and walked a Mile in a missling[1] rain and splashy way to put us right again. I could not have had a greater pleasure in these parts than your mention of my Sister—She is very much prisoned from me—I am affraid it will be some time before I can take her to many places I wish—I trust we shall see you ere long in Cumberland—at least I hope I shall before my visit to America more than once I intend to pass a whole year with

6. Milton, *Comus* (1634, 1637), l. 817.
7. See p. 163, n. 5.
8. The planned length of the trip; he would in fact return to London in August.
9. The fashionable route would have been by boat from Oban to Aros where one would hire a guide and ponies. Keats and Brown found a guide to take them directly from Oban to Mull at a cheaper rate than they had thought possible. They traveled on to Iona, the first Christian settlement in what would become Great Britain and a burial place for the Kings of Scotland, and then Staffa and Fingal's Cave, which he would describe in "Not Alladin magian" (see pp. 266–68; also his letter to Tom Keats July 23, 26, *L*, 1: 346–51).
1. For mizzling, "falling in fine particles; drizzling" (*OED*).

George if I live to the completion of the three next—My sister's well-fare and the hopes of such a stay in America will make me observe your advice—I shall be prudent and more careful of my health than I have been—I hope you will be about paying your first visit to Town after settling when we come into Cumberland—Cumberland however will be no distance to me after my present journey—I shall spin to you a minute—I begin to get rather a contempt for distances. I hope you will have a nice convenient room for a Library. Now you are so well in health do keep it up by never missing your dinner, by not reading hard and by taking proper exercise. You'll have a horse I suppose so you must make a point of sweating him. You say I must study Dante—well the only Books I have with me are those three little Volumes.[2] I read that fine passage you mention a few days ago. Your Letter followed me from Hampstead to Port Patrick and thence to Glasgow—you must think me by this time a very pretty fellow—One of the pleasantest bouts we have had was our walk to Burns's Cottage, over the Doon and past Kirk Alloway—I had determined to write a Sonnet in the Cottage. I did but lauk it was so wretched I destroyed it—howev[r] in a few days afterwards I wrote some lines cousin-german to the Circumstance which I will transcribe or rather cross scribe in the front of this[3]— Reynolds's illness has made him a new Man—he will be stronger than ever—before I left London he was really getting a fat face—Brown keeps on writing volumes of adventures to Dilke—when we get in of an evening and I have perhaps taken my rest on a couple of Chairs he affronts my indolence and Luxury by pulling out of his knapsack 1st his paper—2nd his pens and last his ink—Now I would not care if he would change about a little— I say now, why not Bailey take out his pens first sometimes—But I might as well tell a hen to hold up her head before she drinks instead of afterwards—Your affectionate friend

John Keats—

[Not Aladdin magian][1]

Not Aladdin magian
Ever such a work began.
Not the Wizard of the Dee[2]

2. See p. 251, n. 4.
3. Keats cross-wrote "There is a charm in footing slow across a silent plain"; see above, pp. 262–63.
1. Written between July 24, 1818, when Keats visited Fingal's Cave on the island of Staffa, and July 26 when he copied the poem into a letter to Tom Keats written on the island of Mull (*L*, 1: 346–51; he recopied the poem, with changes and without ll. 43–55, into his journal letter to the George Keatses of September 1819, *L*, 2: 199–200). He introduces the poem to Tom with a description, "I am puzzled how to give you an Idea of Staffa. . . . One may compare the surface of the Island to a roof—this roof is supported by grand pillars of basalt standing together as thick as honey combs. The finest thing is Fingal's Cave—it is entirely a hollowing out of Basalt Pillars. Suppose now the Giants who rebelled against Jove had taken a whole Mass of black Columns and bound them together like bunches of matches—and then with immense Axes had made a cavern in the body of these columns—of course the roof and floor must be composed of the broken ends of the Columns—such is fingal's Cave except that the Sea has done the work of excavations and is continually dashing there. . . . For Solemnity and grandeur it far surpasses the finest Cathedrall. . . . As we approached in the boat there was such a fine swell of the sea that the pillars appeared rising immediately out of the crystal—But it is impossible to describe it" (*L*, 1: 348–49). Finn or Fingal had been celebrated by Macpherson in the Ossian poems as a defender of the oppressed. First published as part of the transcribed letter in the *Western Messenger* 1 (July 1836): 822–23; text from *Western Messenger* with emendations from the letter to Tom (Harvard MS Keats 1.35).
2. Merlin, who is associated with the area of Wales around the River Dee.

Ever such a dream could see.
Not St. John in Patmos Isle,   5
In the passion of his toil,
When he saw the churches seven,
Golden aisled, built up in heaven,[3]
Gazed at such a rugged wonder.
As I stood its roofing under   10
Lo! I saw one sleeping there
On the marble cold and bare;
While the ocean[4] washed his feet
And his garments white did beat
Drenched about the sombre rocks.   15
On his neck his well grown locks
Lifted dry upon[5] the main
Were upon the curl again.
"What is this, and what art thou?"
Whisper'd I and touched his brow.   20
"What art thou, and what is this?"
Whisper'd I and strove to kiss
The spirit's hand to wake his eyes.
Up he started in a trice.
"I am Lycidas,"[6] said he,   25
"Fam'd in funeral minstrelsy.
This was architected thus
By the great Oceanus.[7]
Here the[8] mighty waters play
Hollow organs all the day.   30
Here by turns his dolphins all,
Finny palmers[9] great and small,
Come to pay devotion due—
Each a month of mass most rue.[1]
Many a mortal of these days   35
Dares to pass our sacred ways,
Dares to touch audaciously
This cathedral of the sea.
I have been the pontiff priest
Where the waters never rest,   40
Where a fledgy sea-bird choir
Soars forever—holy fire
I have hid from mortal man.
Proteus[2] is my sacristan.
But the stupid eye of mortal   45
Hath pass'd beyond the rocky portal,
So for ever will I leave

3. John wrote the book of Revelation on the Island of Patmos; see Revelation 1.9–12.
4. The letter has "surges."
5. The letter has "above."
6. Milton's "Lycidas" (1638) is a pastoral elegy written about the drowned Edward King, a fellow student at Cambridge; Milton describes him "under the whelming tide," visiting "the bottom of the monstrous world" (ll. 157–58).
7. The Titan who ruled the seas; see *Hyperion*, below.
8. The letter has "his."
9. Fish that swim to this site as "palmers" or pilgrims.
1. The letter has "Each a mouth of pearls must strew."
2. A sea god able to change his shape; *sacristan*: a church sexton.

Such a taint and soon unweave
All the magic of the place—
'Tis now free to stupid face,   50
To cutters and to fashion boats,
To cravats and to petticoats.
The great sea shall wear[3] it down,
For its fame shall not be blown
At every farthing quadrille dance."[4]   55
So saying with a spirit's glance
He dived—[5]

SONNET, WRITTEN ON THE SUMMIT
OF BEN NEVIS.[1]

Read me a lesson, Muse, and speak it loud
    Upon the top of Nevis, blind in mist!
I look into the chasms, and a shroud
    Vaporous doth hide them,—just so much, I wist,[2]
Mankind do know of Hell: I look o'erhead,   5
    And there is sullen mist,—even so much
Mankind can tell of Heaven: mist is spread
    Before the earth beneath me,—even such,
Even so vague is man's sight of himself.
    Here are the craggy stones beneath my feet,—   10
Thus much I know, that, a poor witless elf,[3]
    I tread on them,—that all my eye doth meet
Is mist and crag, not only on this height,
But in the world of thought and mental might!

STANZAS ON SOME SKULLS IN BEAULEY
ABBEY, INVERNESS.[1]

_____I shed no tears;
Deep thought, or awful vision, I had none;

3. The letter has "war."
4. In his letter to Tom, Keats noted that Staffa had become a tourist spot, with people arriving in "cutters," or small passenger boats, and going to "farthing quadrilles," or cheap square dances.
5. Keats breaks off the poem here, writing to Tom, "I am sorry I am so indolent as to write such stuff
   as this" (*L*, 1: 351). Brown identifies it as a fragment: "Keats wrote some lines on this cave, a fragment of a poem, which I never could induce him to finish" (*KC*, 2: 63).
1. Written August 2, 1818, after Keats and Brown scaled Ben Nevis, the highest mountain in the
   British isles; according to Brown, they were "enveloped in a cloud" and Keats "sat on the stones,
   a few feet from the edge of that fearful precipice, fifteen hundred feet perpendicular from the valley below, and wrote this sonnet" (*KC*, 2: 63). First published in the *Plymouth and Devonport
   Weekly Journal*, September 6, 1838; text from *PDWJ* with emendations from Keats's draft in his
   letter to Tom Keats, August 3, 6, 1818 (Harvard MS Keats 1.36).
2. Know.
3. A Spenserianism for "man" or "person."
1. A collaborative piece by Keats and Brown, this poem was perhaps written in Inverness or Cromarty
   as they waited for a boat to take the ill Keats back to London; Stillinger points out that it could
   have been written weeks or even months later as it was not included in any of the Scottish tour letters. Colvin, working from a lost Woodhouse transcript, identified as Keats's contributions lines 1,
   the first four words of 2, 7–12, 43–48, and 55–60. Beauly Priory is about ten miles from Inverness; it was a Valliscaulian monastery (a French order that followed the Carthusian rule but wore
   the Cistercian habit; they practiced silence and privation). The abbey was destroyed by Cromwell, who

By thousand petty fancies I was crossed;[2]
And mock'd the dead bones that lay scatter'd by.[3]

1

In silent barren synod met
Within these roofless walls, where yet
The sever'd[4] arch and carved fret
    Cling to the ruin,
The brethren's skulls mourn, dewy wet,   5
    Their Creed's undoing.[5]

2

The mitred ones of Nice and Trent[6]
Were not so tongue-tied,—no, they went
Hot to their Councils, scarce content
    With orthodoxy;   10
But ye, poor tongueless things, were meant
    To speak by proxy.

3

Your chronicles no more exist,
For[7] Knox, the revolutionist,[8]
Destroy'd the work of every fist   15
    That scrawl'd black letter;[9]
Well! I'm a craniologist,[1]
    And may do better.

4

This skull-cap wore the cowl from sloth,
Or discontent, perhaps from both;   20
And yet one day, against his oath,
    He tried escaping;
For men, though idle, may be loth
    To live on gaping.

---

used its stone for his fort at Inverness. The poem owes something to the gravediggers scene in *Hamlet* 5.1 and uses a stanzaic form from Burns. First published in the *New Monthly Magazine*, 4 (January, 1822), pp. 47–48 from a text supplied by Brown; text from the *New Monthly Magazine* with emendations, epigraph, and stanza numbers from Brown's transcript in W³, f. 75 (*MYR: JK*, 4: 309–12).

2. Brown inserts "Wordsworth" here; he quotes Wordsworth's sonnet, " 'Beloved Vale,' I said, 'when I shall con' " (1807): "from mine eyes escaped no tears; / Deep thought, or dread remembrance, had I none. / By doubts and thousand petty fancies crost" (ll. 7–9).
3. Brown inserts "Shakspeare"; he quotes *Richard III*, 1.4.33.
4. Brown's transcript has "shafted."
5. Keats refers to the Protestant Reformation as the undoing of the Catholic Church.
6. The First Council of Nicea (325) brought together three hundred bishops, the "mitred ones," to settle the Arian Controversy and resulted in the Nicean creed on the Trinity. The Council of Trent (1545–1563) set forth Counter-Reformation doctrines and a new discipline for the clergy.
7. Brown's transcript has "Since."
8. John Knox (c. 1513–1572), the Scottish protestant reformer who helped create the Presbyterian church; with the Pope's authority abolished in Scotland and the Catholic mass forbidden, monasteries were often pillaged, though Beauly itself was not destroyed under the Civil War.
9. Strictly the type used by early printers and sometimes called "Gothic"; here he seems to refer to the work of the monks in copying and illuminating manuscripts as in stanza 8.
1. A phrenologist who can interpret personality based on the bumps of the skull.

5

A toper[2] this! he plied his glass　　　　　　25
More strictly than he said the mass,
And lov'd to see a tempting lass
　　　　　Come to confession,
Letting her absolution pass
　　　　　O'er fresh transgression.　　　　30

6

This crawl'd through life in feebleness,
Boasting he never knew excess,
Cursing those crimes he scarce could guess,
　　　　　Or feel but faintly,
With prayers that Heaven would cease to bless　　35
　　　　　Men so unsaintly.

7

Here's a true churchman!—he'd affect
Much charity, and ne'er neglect
To pray for mercy on th' elect,
　　　　　But thought no evil　　　　40
In sending heathen, Turk, and Sect
　　　　　All to the Devil!

8

Poor skull, thy fingers set ablaze,
With silver Saint in golden rays,
The holy Missal; thou didst craze　　　　　45
　　　　　'Mid bead and spangle,
While others pass'd their idle days
　　　　　In coil[3] and wrangle.

9

Long time this sconce a helmet wore,—
But sickness smites the conscience sore;　　　50
He broke his sword, and hither bore
　　　　　His gear and plunder,
Took to the cowl,—then rav'd and swore
　　　　　At his damn'd blunder!

10

This lily-colour'd skull, with all　　　　　55
The teeth complete, so white and small,
Belong'd to one whose early pall
　　　　　A lover shaded;
He died ere superstition's gall
　　　　　His heart invaded.　　　　60

2. Drunkard.
3. Noisy disturbance, turmoil.

11

Ha! here is "undivulged crime!"[4]
Despair forbad his soul to climb
Beyond this world, this mortal time
    Of fever'd sadness,
Until their monkish pantomime   65
    Dazzled his madness!

12

A younger brother this!—a man
Aspiring as a Tartar Khan,[5]
But, curb'd and baffled, he began
    The trade of frightening;   70
It smack'd of power!—and here he ran
    To deal Heaven's lightning.

13

This idiot-skull belong'd to one,
A buried miser's only son,
Who penitent, ere he'd begun   75
    To taste of pleasure,
And hoping Heaven's dread wrath to shun,
    Gave Hell his treasure.

14

Here is the forehead of an ape,
A robber's mark,—and near the nape   80
That bone, fie on't! bears just the shape
    Of carnal passion;
Ah! he was one for theft and rape,
    In monkish fashion!

15

This was the porter!—he could sing,   85
Or dance, or play, do any thing,
And what the friars bade him bring
    They ne'er were balk'd of,
Matters not worth remembering,
    And seldom talk'd of.   90

16

Enough! why need I farther[6] pore?
This corner holds at least a score,
And yonder twice as many more
    Of reverend brothers;
'Tis the same story o'er and o'er,—   95
    They're like the others!

4. Shakespeare, *King Lear*, 3.2.50.
5. The supreme ruler of the Tatar tribes as a successor of Genghis Khan.
6. Brown's transcript has "further."

"Z."

Review of *Endymion*[1]

COCKNEY SCHOOL OF POETRY
No. IV

_____ OF KEATS,
THE MUSES' SON OF PROMISE, AND WHAT FEATS
HE YET MAY DO, &c.
CORNELIUS WEBB.

Of all the manias of this mad age, the most incurable, as well as the most common, seems to be no other than the *Metromanie*. The just celebrity of Robert Burns and Miss Baillie[2] has had the melancholy effect of turning the heads of we know not how many farm-servants and unmarried ladies; our very footmen compose tragedies, and there is scarcely a superannuated governess in the island that does not leave a roll of lyrics behind her in her band-box. To witness the disease of any human understanding, however feeble, is distressing; but the spectacle of an able mind reduced to a state of insanity is of course ten times more afflicting. It is with such sorrow as this that we have contemplated the case of Mr John Keats. This young man appears to have received from nature talents of an excellent, perhaps even of a superior order—talents which, devoted to the purposes of any useful profession, must have rendered him a respectable, if not an eminent citizen. His friends, we understand, destined him to the career of medicine, and he was bound apprentice some years ago to a worthy apothecary in town. But all has been undone by a sudden attack of the malady to which we have alluded. Whether Mr John had been sent home with a diuretic or composing draught to some patient far gone in the poetical mania, we have not heard. This much is certain, that he has caught the infection, and that thoroughly. For some time we were in hopes, that he might get off with a violent fit or two; but of late the symptoms are terrible. The phrenzy of the "Poems" was bad enough in its way; but it did not alarm us half so seriously as the calm, settled, imperturbable drivelling idiocy of "Endymion." We hope, however, that in so young a person, and with a constitution originally so good, even now the disease is not utterly incurable. Time, firm treatment, and rational restraint, do much for many apparently hopeless invalids; and if Mr Keats should happen, at some interval of reason, to cast his eye upon our pages, he may perhaps be convinced of the existence of his malady, which, in such cases, is often all that is necessary to put the patient in a fair way of being cured.

The readers of the Examiner newspaper were informed, some time ago, by a solemn paragraph, in Mr Hunt's best style, of the appearance of two new stars of glorious magnitude and splendour in the poetical horizon of

---

1. "Z." was a pseudonym of John Gibson Lockhart (1794–1854), a lawyer and friend of Sir Walter Scott, whose daughter he married in 1820. This was the fourth in a series of attacks upon the "Cockney School," the group of poets and intellectuals around Leigh Hunt (See Cox, pp. 16–37 and Roe, pp. 11–12, 119–20). For the quotation from Webb, see p. 101, n. 5. Text from *Blackwood's Edinburgh Magazine* 3 (August 1818): 519–24.

2. Joanna Baillie (1762–1851), Scottish dramatist and poet, who was considered by many the greatest playwright of the period. Robert Burns: see p. 42, n. 4.

the land of Cockaigne.[3] One of these turned out, by and by, to be no other than Mr John Keats. This precocious adulation confirmed the wavering apprentice in his desire to quit the gallipots,[4] and at the same time excited in his too susceptible mind a fatal admiration for the character and talents of the most worthless and affected of all the versifiers of our time. One of his first productions was the following sonnet, "*written on the day when Mr Leigh Hunt left prison.*"[5] It will be recollected, that the cause of Hunt's confinement was a series of libels against his sovereign, and that its fruit was the odious and incestuous *Story of Rimini.*

[Quotes "Written on the day that Mr. Leigh Hunt left Prison"
in its entirety.]

The absurdity of the thought in this sonnet is, however, if possible, surpassed in another, "*addressed to Haydon*" the painter,[6] that clever, but most affected artist, who as little resembles Raphael in genius as he does in person, notwithstanding the foppery of having his hair curled over his shoulders in the old Italian fashion. In this exquisite piece it will be observed, that Mr Keats classes together WORDSWORTH, HUNT, and HAYDON, as the three greatest spirits of the age, and that he alludes to himself, and some others of the rising brood of Cockneys, as likely to attain hereafter an equally honourable elevation. Wordsworth and Hunt! what a juxta-position! The purest, the loftiest, and, we do not fear to say it, the most classical of living English poets, joined together in the same compliment with the meanest, the filthiest, and the most vulgar of Cockney poetasters. No wonder that he who could be guilty of this should class Haydon with Raphael, and himself with Spencer.

[Quotes "Great spirits now on earth are sojourning" in its entirety.]

The nations are to listen and be dumb! and why, good Johnny Keats? because Leigh Hunt is editor of the Examiner, and Haydon has painted the judgment of Solomon, and you and Cornelius Webb, and a few more city sparks, are pleased to look upon yourselves as so many future Shakspeares and Miltons! The world has really some reason to look to its foundations! Here is a *tempestas in matulâ*[7] with a vengeance. At the period when these sonnets were published, Mr Keats had no hesitation in saying, that he looked on himself as '*not yet* a glorious denizen of the wide heaven of poetry,'[8] but he had many fine soothing visions of coming greatness, and many rare plans of study to prepare him for it. The following we think is very pretty raving.

[Quotes "Sleep and Poetry," ll. 89–121.]

Having cooled a little from this "fine passion,"[9] our youthful poet passes very naturally into a long strain of foaming abuse against a certain class of English Poets, whom, with Pope at their head, it is much the fashion with the ignorant unsettled pretenders of the present time to undervalue.[1] Begging these gentlemens' pardon, although Pope was not a poet of the same high order with some who are now living, yet, to deny his genius, is just

---

3. "Name of an imaginary country, the abode of luxury and idleness"; "humorously applied to London, as the country of Cockneys; Cockneydom" (OED).
4. Small earthen pots used by apothecaries for medicines.
5. See p. 50.
6. See pp. 55–56.
7. "Tempest in a pot."
8. Misquotes "Sleep and Poetry," ll. 48–49, p. 59.
9. Boswell speaks of "love as a thing that could not be controlled by reason, as a fine passion" in the December 16, 1762, entry in *Boswell's London Journal 1762–1763,* ed. Frederick A. Pottle (New York: McGraw-Hill, 1950), p. 88.
1. See "Sleep and Poetry," ll. 181–206.

about as absurd as to dispute that of Wordsworth, or to believe in that of Hunt. Above all things, it is most pitiably ridiculous to hear men, of whom their country will always have reason to be proud, reviled by uneducated and flimsy striplings, who are not capable of understanding either their merits, or those of any other *men of power*—fanciful dreaming tea-drinkers, who, without logic enough to analyse a single idea, or imagination enough to form one original image, or learning enough to distinguish between the written language of Englishmen and the spoken jargon of Cockneys, presume to talk with contempt of some of the most exquisite spirits the world ever produced, merely because they did not happen to exert their faculties in laborious affected descriptions of flowers seen in window-pots, or cascades heard at Vauxhall;[2] in short, because they chose to be wits, philosophers, patriots, and poets, rather than to found the Cockney school of versification, morality, and politics, a century before its time. After blaspheming himself into a fury against Boileau, &c. Mr Keats comforts himself and his readers with a view of the present more promising aspect of affairs; above all, with the ripened glories of the poet of Rimini.[3] Addressing the manes of the departed chiefs of English poetry, he informs them, in the following clear and touching manner, of the existence of 'him of the Rose,' &c.

[Quotes "Sleep and Poetry," ll.226–29.]

From this he diverges into a view of "things in general." We smile when we think to ourselves how little most of our readers will understand of what follows.

[Quotes "Sleep and Poetry," ll. 248–76.]

From some verses addressed to various amiable individuals of the other sex, it appears, notwithstanding all this gossamer-work, that Johnny's affections are not entirely confined to objects purely etherial. Take, by way of specimen, the following prurient and vulgar lines, evidently meant for some young lady east of Temple-bar.

[Quotes "TO * * *" ("Hadst thou liv'd in days of old"), ll. 23–40.]

Who will dispute that our poet, to use his own phrase (and rhyme),

> Can mingle music fit for the soft *ear*
> Of Lady *Cytherea*.[4]

So much for the opening bud; now for the expanded flower. It is time to pass from the juvenile "Poems," to the mature and elaborate "Endymion, a Poetic Romance." The old story of the moon falling in love with a shepherd, so prettily told by a Roman Classic, and so exquisitely enlarged and adorned by one of the most elegant of German poets, has been seized upon by Mr John Keats, to be done with as might seem good unto the sickly fancy of one who never read a single line either of Ovid or of Wieland.[5] If the quantity, not the quality, of the verses dedicated to the story is to be taken into account, there can be no doubt that Mr John Keats may now claim Endymion entirely to himself. To say the truth, we do not suppose either

---

2. A London pleasure garden which had a famous artificial cascade.
3. Hunt.
4. *Endymion*, 3.974–75.
5. Christoph Martin Wieland (1733–1813), German novelist, dramatist, and poet and here the author of the epic poem *Oberon* (1780). Publius Ovidus Naso (43 B.C.E.–18 C.E.), Roman poet, author of the *Amores, Heroides, Ars Amatoria*, and here the *Metamorphoses*.

the Latin or the German poet would be very anxious to dispute about the property of the hero of the "Poetic Romance." Mr Keats has thoroughly appropriated the character, if not the name. His Endymion is not a Greek shepherd, loved by a Grecian goddess; he is merely a young Cockney rhymester, dreaming a phantastic dream at the full of the moon. Costume, were it worth while to notice such a trifle, is violated in every page of this goodly octavo. From his prototype Hunt, John Keats has acquired a sort of vague idea, that the Greeks were a most tasteful people, and that no mythology can be so finely adapted for the purposes of poetry as theirs. It is amusing to see what a hand the two Cockneys make of this mythology; the one confesses that he never read the Greek Tragedians, and the other knows Homer only from Chapman,[6] and both of them write about Apollo, Pan, Nymphs, Muses, and Mysteries, as might be expected from persons of their education. We shall not, however, enlarge at present upon this subject, as we mean to dedicate an entire paper to the classical attainments and attempts of the Cockney poets. As for Mr Keats' "Endymion," it has just as much to do with Greece as it has with "old Tartary the fierce;"[7] no man, whose mind has ever been imbued with the smallest knowledge or feeling of classical poetry or classical history, could have stooped to profane and vulgarise every association in the manner which has been adopted by this "son of promise." Before giving any extracts, we must inform our readers, that this romance is meant to be written in English heroic rhyme. To those who have read any of Hunt's poems, this hint might indeed be needless. Mr Keats has adopted the loose, nerveless versification, and Cockney rhymes of the poet of Rimini; but in fairness to that gentle man, we must add, that the defects of the system are tenfold more conspicuous in his disciple's work than in his own. Mr Hunt is a small poet, but he is a clever man. Mr Keats is a still smaller poet, and he is only a boy of pretty abilities, which he has done every thing in his power to spoil.

The poem sets out with the following exposition of the reasons which induced Mr Keats to compose it.

[Quotes *Endymion*, 1.1–35.]

After introducing his hero to us in a procession, and preparing us, by a few mystical lines, for believing that his destiny has in it some strange peculiarity, Mr Keats represents the beloved of the Moon as being conveyed by his sister Peona into an island in a river. This young lady has been alarmed by the appearance of the brother, and questioned him thus:

[Quotes *Endymion*, 1.505–515.]

Endymion replies in a long speech, wherein he describes his first meeting with the Moon. We cannot make room for the whole of it, but shall take a few passages here and there.

[Quotes *Endymion*, 1.554–67, 598–616, 633–45.]

Not content with the authentic love of the Moon, Keats makes his hero captivate another supernatural lady, of whom no notice occurs in any of his predecessors.

---

6. References to Hunt's preface to *Foliage* (1818) and Keats's "On first looking into Chapman's Homer," pp. 54–55. Keats's critics often wrote condescendingly of his education.

7. *Endymion*, 4.262.

[Quotes *Endymion*, 2.100–132.]

But we find that we really have no patience for going over four books filled with such amorous scenes as these, with subterraneous journeys equally amusing, and submarine processions equally beautiful; but we must not omit the most interesting scene of the whole piece.

[Quotes *Endymion*, 2.709–743.]

After all this, however, the "modesty," as Mr Keats expresses it,[8] of the Lady Diana prevented her from owning in Olympus her passion for Endymion. Venus, as the most knowing in such matters, is the first to discover the change that has taken place in the temperament of the goddess. 'An idle tale,' says the laughter-loving dame,

> "A humid eye, and steps luxurious,
> When these are new and strange, are ominous."[9]

The inamorata, to vary the intrigue, carries on a romantic intercourse with Endymion, under the disguise of an Indian damsel. At last, however, her scruples, for some reason or other, are all overcome, and the Queen of Heaven owns her attachment.

> "She gave her fair hands to him, and behold,
> Before three swiftest kisses he had told,
> They vanish far away !—Peona went
> Home through the gloomy wood in wonderment."[1]

And so, like many other romances, terminates the "Poetic Romance" of Johnny Keats, in a patched-up wedding.

We had almost forgot to mention, that Keats belongs to the Cockney School of Politics, as well as the Cockney School of Poetry.

It is fit that he who holds *Rimini* to be the first poem, should believe the Examiner to be the first politician of the day. We admire consistency, even in folly. Hear how their bantling has already learned to lisp sedition.

[Quotes *Endymion*, 3.1–22.]

And now, good-morrow to "the Muses' son of Promise;" as for "the feats he yet may do," as we do not pretend to say, like himself, "Muse of my native land am I inspired" we shall adhere to the safe old rule of *pauca verba*.[2] We venture to make one small prophecy, that his book seller will not a second time venture £50 upon any thing he can write. It is a better and a wiser thing to be a starved apothecary than a starved poet; so back to the shop Mr John, back to "plasters, pills, and ointment boxes," &c. But, for Heaven's sake, young Sangrado, be a little more sparing of extenuatives and soporifics in your practice than you have been in your poetry.[3]

---

8. While Keats does not use the word "modesty," Z. appears to be referring to Diana's speech at *Endymion*, 2.779f.
9. *Endymion*, 3.909–911, though Keats writes "idle tongue."
1. *Endymion*, 4.1000–1003.
2. "Few words"; Z. quotes *Endymion*, 4.1.
3. Reference to Sangrado in Le Sage's novel *Gil Blas* (1735), who prescribes the same remedy for all ailments.

JOHN WILSON CROKER

Review of *Endymion* in *Quarterly Review*[1]

Reviewers have been sometimes accused of not reading the works which they affected to criticise. On the present occasion we shall anticipate the author's complaint, and honestly confess that we have not read his work. Not that we have been wanting in our duty—far from it—indeed, we have made efforts almost as superhuman as the story itself appears to be, to get through it; but with the fullest stretch of our perseverance, we are forced to confess that we have not been able to struggle beyond the first of the four books of which this Poetic Romance consists. We should extremely lament this want of energy, or whatever it may be, on our parts, were it not for one consolation—namely, that we are no better acquainted with the meaning of the book through which we have so painfully toiled, than we are with that of the three which we have not looked into.

It is not that Mr. Keats, (if that be his real name, for we almost doubt that any man in his senses would put his real name to such a rhapsody,) it is not, we say, that the author has not powers of language, rays of fancy, and gleams of genius—he has all these; but he is unhappily a disciple of the new school of what has been somewhere called Cockney poetry; which may be defined to consist of the most incongruous ideas in the most uncouth language.

Of this school, Mr. Leigh Hunt, as we observed in a former Number,[2] aspires to be the hierophant. Our readers will recollect the pleasant recipes for harmonious and sublime poetry which he gave us in his preface to *Rimini*, and the still more facetious instances of his harmony and sublimity in the verses themselves; and they will recollect above all the contempt of Pope, Johnson, and such like poetasters and pseudo-critics, which so forcibly contrasted itself with Mr Leigh Hunt's self-complacent approbation of

> —'all the things itself had wrote,
> Of special merit though of little note.'[3]

This author is a copyist of Mr. Hunt, but he is more unintelligible, almost as rugged, twice as diffuse, and ten times more tiresome and absurd than his prototype, who, though he impudently presumed to seat himself in the chair of criticism, and to measure his own poetry by his own standard, yet generally had a meaning. But Mr. Keats had advanced no dogmas which he was bound to support by examples; his nonsense therefore is quite gratuitous; he writes it for its own sake, and, being bitten by Mr. Leigh Hunt's insane criticism, more than rivals the insanity of his poetry.

1. This unsigned review was thought at the time to have been written by the editor of the *Quarterly*, William Gifford, but it was penned by one of the review's cofounders, John Wilson Croker (1780–1857), secretary of the Admiralty and a would-be poet. The *Quarterly* was founded in 1809 by John Murray (Byron's publisher) as a Tory riposte to the Whig *Edinburgh Review*; a staunchly conservative journal, it supported the Lake School and excoriated the Cockneys. Text from *Quarterly Review* 19 (dated April 1818, published September 1818): 204–208.
2. See Croker's review of Hunt's *Foliage* in the *Quarterly Review* 18 (January 1818): 324–35.
3. Charles Churchill (1732–1764), *The Rosciad* (1761), ll. 156–57.

Mr. Keats's preface hints that his poem was produced under peculiar circumstances.

'Knowing within myself (he says) the manner in which this Poem has been produced, it is not without a feeling of regret that I make it public.—What manner I mean, will be quite clear to the reader, who must soon perceive great inexperience, immaturity, and every error denoting a feverish attempt, rather than a deed accomplished.—' *Preface*, p. vii.

We humbly beg his pardon, but this does not appear to us to be quite so clear—we really do not know what he means—but the next passage is more intelligible.

'The two first books, and indeed the two last, I feel sensible are not of such completion as to warrant their passing the press.'—*Preface*, p. vii.

Thus 'the two first books' are, even in his own judgment, unfit to appear, and 'the two last' are, it seems, in the same condition—and as two and two make four, and as that is the whole number of books, we have a clear and, we believe, a very just estimate of the entire work.

Mr. Keats, however, deprecates criticism on this 'immature and feverish work' in terms which are themselves sufficiently feverish; and we confess that we should have abstained from inflicting upon him any of the tortures of the 'fierce hell'[4] of criticism, which terrify his imagination, if he had not begged to be spared in order that he might write more; if we had not observed in him a certain degree of talent which deserves to be put in the right way, or which, at least, ought to be warned of the wrong; and if, finally, he had not told us that he is of an age and temper which imperiously require mental discipline.

Of the story we have been able to make out but little; it seems to be mythological, and probably relates to the loves of Diana and Endymion; but of this, as the scope of the work has altogether escaped us, we cannot speak with any degree of certainty; and must therefore content ourselves with giving some instances of its diction and versification:—and here again we are perplexed and puzzled.—At first it appeared to us, that Mr. Keats had been amusing himself and wearying his readers with an immeasurable game at *bouts-rimés*;[5] but, if we recollect rightly, it is an indispensable condition at this play, that the rhymes when filled up shall have a meaning; and our author, as we have already hinted, has no meaning. He seems to us to write a line at random, and then he follows not the thought excited by this line, but that suggested by the *rhyme* with which it concludes. There is hardly a complete couplet inclosing a complete idea in the whole book. He wanders from one subject to another, from the association, not of ideas but of sounds, and the work is composed of hemistichs[6] which, it is quite evident, have forced themselves upon the author by the mere force of the catchwords on which they turn.

4. While this phrase appears in Shelley's *Queen Mab* (1813) 5.256, it is probably taken from Charles Fitz-Geffry's *Sir Frances Drake, his Honorable Lifes Commendation, and his Tragicall Deathes Lamentation*, l. 398, where detractors of Drake are described.
5. Literally "rhymed-ends"; a game defined by Addison as involving "lists of words that rhyme to one another, drawn up by another hand, and given to a poet, who was to make a poem to the rhymes in the same order that they were placed upon the list" (*OED*).
6. Half lines.

We shall select, not as the most striking instance, but as the least liable to suspicion, a passage from the opening of the poem.

[Quotes *Endymion*, 1.13–21.]

Here it is clear that the word, and not the idea, *moon* produces the simple sheep and their shady *boon*, and that 'the *dooms* of the mighty dead' would never have intruded themselves but for the '*fair musk-rose blooms*.' Again.

[Quotes *Endymion*, 1.95–106.]

Here Apollo's *fire* produces a *pyre*, a silvery pyre of clouds, *wherein* a spirit might *win* oblivion and melt his essence *fine*, and scented *eglantine* gives sweets to the *sun*, and cold springs had *run* into the grass, and then the pulse of the *mass* pulsed *tenfold* to feel the glories *old* of the new-born day, &c. One example more.

[Quotes *Endymion*, 1.293–98.]

Lodge, dodge—*heaven, leaven*—*earth, birth*; such, in six words, is the sum and substance of six lines.

We come now to the author's taste in versification. He cannot indeed write a sentence, but perhaps he may be able to spin a line. Let us see. The following are specimens of his prosodial notions of our English heroic metre.

> Dear as the temple's self; so does the moon,
> The passion poesy, glories infinite.—p.4.
> So plenteously all weed-hidden roots.—p. 6.
> Of some strange history, potent to send.—p. I8.
> Before the deep intoxication.—p. 27.
> Her scarf into a fluttering pavilion.—p. 33.
> The stubborn canvass for my voyage prepared—.—p. 39.
> "Endymion! the cave is secreter
> Than the isle of Delos. Echo hence shall stir
> No sighs but sigh-warm kisses, or light noise
> Of thy combing hand, the while it travelling cloys
> And trembles through my labyrinthine hair."—p. 48.[7]

By this time our readers must be pretty well satisfied as to the meaning of his sentences and the structure of his lines: we now present them with some of the new words with which, in imitation of Mr. Leigh Hunt, he adorns our language.

We are told that 'turtles *passion* their voices,' (p. 15); that 'an arbour was *nested*,' (p. 23); and a lady's locks '*gordian'd* up,' (p. 32); and to supply the place of the nouns thus verbalized Mr Keats, with great fecundity, spawns new ones; such as 'men-slugs and human *serpentry*,' (p. 41); the '*honey-feel* of bliss,' (p. 45); 'wives prepare *needments*,' (p. 13)—and so forth.[8]

Then he has formed new verbs by the process of cutting off their natural tails, the adverbs, and affixing them to their foreheads; thus, 'the wine out-sparkled,' (p. 10); the 'multitude up-followed,' (p. 11); and 'night up-took,' (p. 29). 'The wind up-blows,' (p. 32); and the 'hours are down-sunken,' (p. 36.)[9]

But if he sinks some adverbs in the verbs he compensates the language with adverbs and adjectives which he separates from the parent stock.

---

7. He quotes *Endymion*, 1.28–29, 65, 324, 502, 628, 772, 965–69.
8. He refers to *Endymion*, 1.247–48, 431, 613–14, 821, 903, 207–208.
9. He refers to *Endymion*, 1.154, 164, 561, 627, 708.

Thus, a lady 'whispers *pantingly* and close,' makes '*hushing* signs,' and steers her skiff into a '*ripply* cove,' (p. 23); a shower falls '*refreshfully*,' (p. 45); and a vulture has a '*spreaded* tail,' (p. 44).[1]

But enough of Mr. Leigh Hunt and his simple neophyte.—If any one should be bold enough to purchase this 'Poetic Romance,' and so much more patient, than ourselves, as to get beyond the first book, and so much more fortunate as to find a meaning, we entreat him to make us acquainted with his success; we shall then return to the task which we now abandon in despair, and endeavour to make all due amends to Mr. Keats and to our readers.

[Nature withheld Cassandra in the skies][1]

Nature withheld Cassandra in the skies,
For more[2] adornment, a full thousand years;
She took their cream of Beauty's fairest dies,[3]
And shaped and tinted her above all peers:
Meanwhile Love kept[4] her dearly with his wings,   5
And underneath their shadow filled[5] her eyes
With[6] such a richness, that the cloudy Kings
Of high Olympus uttered slavish sighs.
When from the heavens I saw her first descend,[7]
My heart took fire, and only burning pains,[8]   10

1. He refers to *Endymion*, 1.407, 409, 430, 898–99, 867.
1. Keats's translation of Ronsard (except the final two lines added by Milnes) was written during September 1818, as Keats nursed Tom and thought about Jane Cox (in a letter to Reynolds on the 22nd, he wrote of her, "the shape of a woman has haunted me these two days"). Woodhouse loaned him a copy of Ronsard (the seventh edition of his collected works of 1587, where Keats would have found this poem on 1: 2). Pierre de Ronsard (1524–1585) was a French poet and leader of the Pléiade. Keats had written the translation by September 21 when he included line 12 in his letter to Dilke (see p. 282, below); in his letter to Reynolds of September 22, (*L*, 1: 370–71), he copied out the twelve lines he had completed, noting, "Here is a free translation of a Sonnet of Ronsard. . . . I have the loan of his works—they have great Beauties. . . . I had not the original by me when I wrote it, and did not recollect the purport of the last lines." Milnes included the original sonnet at the end of his printing in 1848, noting it is "The second sonnet in the 'Amours de Cassandre:' she was a damosel of Blois—":

> Nature ornant Cassandre, qui deuoit
> De sa douceur forcer les plus rebelles,
> La composa de cent beautez nouuelles
> Que dés mille ans en espargne elle auoit.—
> De tous les biens qu'Amour au Ciel couuoit
> Comme vu tresor cherement sous ces ailles,
> Elle enrichit les Graces immortelles
> De son bel oeil qui les Dieux esmouuoit.—
> Du Ciel à peine elle estoit descenduë
> Quand ie la vey, quand mon asme esperduë
> En deuint folle, et d'un si poignant trait,
> Amour coulet ses beautez en mes veines,
> Qu'autres plaisirs ie ne sens que mes peines,
> Ny autre bien qu'adorer son portrait.

First published as part of the letter to Reynolds in 1848, 1: 241, with the final two lines added by Milnes; text from 1848 (which agrees with the extant transcripts in all but l. 3) with variations indicated in the notes from Keats's holograph fair copy (FC) written on a blank page (236) of his 1806 *Poetical Works of William Shakespeare* (LMA: K/BK/01/010/56).
2. The FC has "meet."
3. Dyes. This is 1848's unique version; FC has "cream of beauty, fairest dies."
4. FC has "Love meanwhile held."
5. FC has "charm'd."
6. FC has "to."
7. FC has "When I beheld her on the Earth descend."
8. FC has "My heart began to burn—and only pains."

They were my pleasures—they my Life's sad[9] end;
Love poured her beauty into my warm veins,
[So that her image in my soul upgrew,
The only thing adorable and true.—*Ed.*][1]

Letter to C. W. Dilke, September 20, 21, 1818[1]

My dear Dilke,

According to the Wentworth place Bulletin you have left Brighton much improved: therefore now a few lines will be more of a pleasure than a bore. I have a few things to say to you and would fain begin upon them in this fourth line: but I have a Mind too well regulated to proceed upon any thing without due preliminary remarks—you may perhaps have observed that in the simple process of eating radishes I never begin at the root but constantly dip the little green head in the salt—that in the Game of Whist if I have an ace I constantly play it first—So how can I with any face begin without a dissertation on letter writing—Yet when I consider that a sheet of paper contains room only for three pages, and a half how can I do justice to such a pregnant subject?[2] however as you have seen the history of the world stamped as it were by a diminishing glass in the form of a chronological Map, so will I 'with retractile claws'[3] draw this in to the form of a table—whereby it will occupy merely the remainder of this first page—

Folio——[4]	Parsons, Lawyers, Statesmen, Physians out of place—Ut—Eustace—Thornton out of practice or on their travels—[5]
Fools cap—	1 superfine! rich or noble poets—ut Byron. 2 common ut egomet—
Quarto—	Projectors, Patentees, Presidents, Potatoe growers—
Bath	Boarding schools, and suburbans in general
Gilt edge	Dandies in general, male female and literary—
Octavo or tears	All who make use of a lascivious seal—
Duodec—	May be found for the most part on Milliners and Dressmakers Parlour tables—
Strip	At the Playhouse doors, or any where—
Slip	Being but a variation—
Snip	So called from its size being disguised by a twist

9. FC has "sad life's."
1. Milnes supplied the last two lines of the translation missing from Keats's version.
1. When Keats returned to London and Hampstead on August 18, 1818, he stopped first at Wentworth Place, where Brown and the Dilkes lived; he learned that Dilke had gone to Brighton for his health (so that he only saw "Mrs. D.," below) and that his brother Tom was so bad that the Dilkes had written a letter to Keats, which he had not received, urging him to return. Text from ALS (LMA K/MS/02/009/6559).
2. The sheet is folded in half, giving four sides; the letter is written on the right recto and both verso sides, with the address on half of the left recto, leaving about one half a page.
3. Cary's translation of Dante's *Inferno*, 17: 101.
4. Keats plays with various terms used to describe paper. Folio is the largest size of paper used in books, with the sheet only folded once; a quarto uses sheets folded twice, giving four pages; an octavo folds the sheet three times, giving eight sheets; a duodecimo book (12mo.) has pages one twelfth the size of a sheet; and foolscap, named for a watermark using a fool's cap device, is a long folio page of varying lengths (usually quarto or octavo). Many of Keats's letters are on paper embossed with the word "Bath," which was a kind of letter or note paper, 8 x 14 inches.
5. Thomas Thornton (d. 1814), author of *The Present State of Turkey* (1807). John Chetwode *Eustace* (1762–1815), antiquarian and author of *A Classical Tour through Italy* (1817; 4th rev. ed of 1813).

I suppose you will have heard that Hazlitt has on foot a prosecution against Blackwood[6]—I dined with him a few days since at Hessey's—there was not a word said about it, though I understand he is excessively vexed—Reynolds by what I hear is almost over happy[7] and Rice is in town. I have not seen him nor shall I for some time as my throat has become worse after getting well, and I am determined to stop at home till I am quite well—I was going to Town tomorrow with M[rs] D. but I thought it best, to ask her excuse this morning—I wish I could say Tom was any better. His identity presses upon me so all day that I am obliged to go out—and although I intended to have given some time to study alone I am obliged to write, and plunge into abstract images to ease myself of his countenance his voice and feebleness—so that I live now in a continual fever—it must be poisonous to life although I feel well. Imagine 'the hateful siege of contraries'[8]—if I think of fame of poetry it seems a crime to me, and yet I must do so or suffer—I am sorry to give you pain—I am almost resolv'd to burn this—but I really have not self possession and magninimity enough to manage the thing otherwise—after all it may be a nervousness proceeding from the Mercury—[9]

Bailey I hear is gaining his Spirits and he will yet be what I once thought impossible a cheerful Man—I think he is not quite so much spoken of in Little Brittain.[1] I forgot to ask M[rs] Dilke if she had any thing she wanted to say immediately to you—This morning look'd so unpromising that I did not think she would have gone—but I find she has on sending for some volumes of Gibbon—I was in a little funk yesterday, for I sent an unseal'd note of sham abuse, until I recollected from what I had heard Charles[2] say, that the servant could neither read nor write—not even to her Mother as Charles observed. I have just had a Letter from Reynolds—he is going on gloriously. The following is a translation of a Line of Ronsard—

'Love poured her Beauty into my warm veins'—.[3]

You have passed your Romance and I never gave into it or else I think this line a feast for one of your Lovers—How goes it with Brown?

Your sincere friend
John Keats—

Modern Love.[1]

And what is love?—It is a doll dress'd up
For idleness to cosset, nurse, and dandle;
A thing of soft misnomers, so divine
That silly youth doth think to make itself

6. *Blackwood's Edinburgh Magazine* 3 (August 1818) contained both the Cockney School piece attacking Keats (519–24; and above, pp. 272–76) and an assault on Hazlitt, "Hazlitt Cross-Questioned" (550–52), where he is called a "quack." Hazlitt brought a suit against the magazine, which was dropped by the following February with Blackwood paying expenses and some damages.
7. Presumably as a result of his engagement to Miss Drewe.
8. Milton, *Paradise Lost*, 9.121–22.
9. If Keats were taking mercury, it might suggest that he and his doctor thought his sore throat was a syphilitic ulcer, marking a return of the disease he had perhaps caught in Oxford.
1. Home to the Reynolds family, where Bailey had courted one of Reynolds's sisters.
2. Dilke's son.
3. See "Nature withheld Cassandra in the Skies" (pp. 280–81).
1. Written in 1818. First published with this title in 1848, 1: 283; text from 1848 with emendations from W[2], f. 75r (*MYR: JK*, 6:127).

Divine by loving,[2] and so goes on   5
Yawning and doting a whole summer long,
Till Miss's comb is made a pearl tiara,
And common Wellingtons turn Romeo boots;[3]
Then[4] Cleopatra lives at Number Seven,
And Anthony resides in Brunswick Square.   10
Fools! if some passions high have warm'd the world,
If Queens and Soldiers have play'd deep[5] for hearts,
It is no reason why such agonies
Should be more common than the growth of weeds.
Fools! make me whole again that weighty pearl   15
The Queen of Egypt melted,[6] and I'll say
That ye may love in spite of beaver hats.[7]

"J. S."

Letter [Responding to the *Quarterly Review*'s Attack on Keats][1]

Although I am aware that literary squabbles are of too uninteresting and *interminable* a nature for your Journal, yet there are occasions when acts of malice and gross injustice towards an author may be properly brought before the public through such a medium.—Allow me, then, without further preface, to refer you to an article in the last Number of *The Quarterly Review*, professing to be a Critique on "The Poems of John Keats."[2] Of John Keats I know nothing; from his Preface I collect that he is very young—no doubt a heinous sin; and I have been informed that he has incurred the additional guilt of an acquaintance with Mr Leigh Hunt. That this latter Gentleman and the Editor of *The Quarterly Review* have long been at war, must be known to every one in the least acquainted with the literary gossip of the day. Mr L. Hunt, it appears, has thought highly of the poetical talents of Mr Keats; hence Mr K. is doomed to feel the merciless tomahawk of the Reviewers, termed Quarterly, I presume from the *modus operandi*. From a perusal of the criticism, I was led to the work itself. I would, Sir, that your limits would permit a few extracts from this poem. I dare appeal to the taste and judgment of your readers, that beauties of the highest order may be found in almost every page—that there are also many, very many passages indicating haste and carelessness, I will not deny; I will go further, and assert that a real friend of the author would have dissuaded him from an immediate publication.

2. Woodhouse (W²) suggests adding "too" for the metre.
3. Popular mud boots named for the Duke of Wellington (also known as "Wellies") are here transformed into boots fit for Romeo.
4. W² has "Till."
5. W² has "high."
6. Cleopatra was said to have dissolved a pearl in vinegar so as to drink it in a toast to Antony.
7. Hats made of beaver fur were popular. Cook suggests an allusion to Richard Abbey's desire that Keats become a hat-maker (see *L*, 2: 77).
1. This letter was presumably written by John Scott (1783–1821), editor of the *Champion* (and later the *London Magazine*) and sometime friend, sometime competitor of Hunt. He would be killed in a duel after he attacked *Blackwood's* in the *London Magazine*. A letter supporting Scott's defense of Keats signed "R. B." appeared in the *Morning Chronicle* five days later. Text from letter to the editor of the *Morning Chronicle*, October 3, 1818.
2. *Quarterly Review* 19 (dated April 1818, published September 1818): 204–208, above, pp. 277–80.

Had the genius of Lord Byron sunk under the discouraging sneers of an *Edinburgh Review* the nineteenth century would scarcely yet have been termed the Augustan æra of Poetry. Let Mr Keats too persevere—he has talents of no common stamp; this is the hastily written tribute of a stranger, who ventures to predict that Mr K. is capable of producing a poem that shall challenge the admiration of every reader of true taste and feeling; nay if he will give up his acquaintance with Mr Leigh Hunt, and apostatise in his friendships, his principles and his politics (if he have any), he may even command the approbation of the *Quarterly Review*.

I have not heard to whom public opinion has assigned this exquisite morceau[3] of critical acumen. If the Translator of Juvenal be its author, I would refer him to the manly and pathetic narrative prefixed to that translation, to the touching history of genius oppressed by and struggling with innumerable difficulties, yet finally triumphing under *patronage and encouragement*. If the Biographer of Kirke White have done Mr Keats this cruel wrong, let him remember his own just and feeling expostulation with the Monthly Reviewer, who "*sat down to blast the hopes of a boy,* who had confessed to him all his hopes and all his difficulties." If the "Admiralty Scribe" (for he too is a Reviewer) be the critic, let him compare the "Battle of Talavera" with "Endymion."[4]

JOHN HAMILTON REYNOLDS

Review of *Endymion*[1]

We have met with a singular instance, in the last number of the *Quarterly Review*, of that unfeeling arrogance, and cold ignorance, which so strangely marked the minds and hearts of Government sycophants and Government writers. The Poem of a young man of genius, which evinces more natural power than any other work of this day, is abused and cried down, in terms which would disgrace any other pens than those used in the defence of an *Oliver* or a *Castles*.[2] We have read the Poetic Romance of *Endymion* (the book in question) with no little delight; and could hardly believe that it was written by so young a man as the preface infers. Mr. Keats, the author of it, is a genius of the highest order; and no one but a Lottery Commissioner and Government Pensioner (both of which Mr. William Gifford, the Editor of the *Quarterly Review*, is) could, with a false and remorseless pen, have striven to frustrate hopes and aims, so youthful and so high as this young Poet nurses. * * *

The cause of the unmerciful condemnation which has been passed on Mr. Keats, is pretty apparent to all who have watched the intrigues of

3. Morsel.
4. J. S. speculates on the identity of the conservative reviewer. William Gifford, editor of the *Quarterly*, translated Juvenal. Robert Southey offered a biography of Henry Kirke White (1807). The actual author was Croker, secretary of the Admiralty and author of the epic, *Battle of Talavera*.
1. Keats's friend John Hamilton Reynolds published this defense of *Endymion* and attack upon the *Quarterly Review* (see its review, pp. 277–80) in *Alfred, West of England Journal and General Advertiser*, October 6, 1818.) It was reprinted in the *Examiner*, October 11, 1818.
2. Government spies. William Oliver (the assumed name of W. J. Richards) helped trap several participants in the Pentridge Rising (June 1817); they were later hanged. John Castle, who had been involved in provoking the Spa Fields Riot of late 1816, was exposed as a government agent.

literature, and the wily and unsparing contrivances of political parties. This young and powerful writer was noticed, some little time back, in the *Examiner*; and pointed out, by its Editor, as one who was likely to revive the early vigour of English poetry.[3] Such a prediction was a fine, but dangerous compliment, to Mr. Keats: it exposed him instantly to the malice of the *Quarterly Review.* Certain it is, that hundreds of fashionable and flippant readers, will henceforth set down this young Poet as a pitiable and nonsensical writer, merely on the assertions of some single heartless critic, who has just energy enough to despise what is good, because it would militate against his pleasantry, if he were to praise it.

The genius of Mr. Keats is peculiarly classical; and, with the exception of a few faults, which are the natural followers of youth, his imaginations and his language have a spirit and an intensity which we should in vain look for in half the popular poets of the day. Lord Byron is a splendid and noble egotist.—He visits classical shores; roams over romantic lands, and wanders through magnificent forests; courses the dark and restless waves of the sea, and rocks his spirit on the midnight lakes; but no spot is conveyed to our minds, that is not peopled by the gloomy and ghastly feelings of one proud and solitary man. It is as if he and the world were the only two things which the air clothed.—His lines are majestic vanities;—his poetry always is marked with a haughty selfishness;—he writes loftily, because he is the spirit of an ancient family;—he is liked by most of his readers, because he is a Lord. If a common man were to dare to be as moody, as contemptuous, and as misanthropical, the world would laugh at him. There must be a coronet marked on all his little pieces of poetical insolence, or the world would not countenance them. Mr. Keats has none of this egotism—this daring selfishness, which is a stain on the robe of poesy—His feelings are full, earnest, and original, as those of the olden writers were and are; they are made for all time, not for the drawing-room and the moment. Mr. Keats always speaks of, and describes nature, with an awe and a humility, but with a deep and almost breathless affection.—He knows that Nature is better and older than he is, and he does not put himself on an equality with her. You do not see him, when you see her. The moon, and the mountainous foliage of the woods, and the azure sky, and the ruined and magic temple; the rock, the desert, and the sea; the leaf of the forest, and the embossed foam of the most living ocean, are the spirits of his poetry; but he does not bring them in his own hand, or obtrude his person before you, when you are looking at them. Poetry is a thing of generalities—a wanderer amid persons and things—not a pauser over one thing, or with one person. The mind of Mr. Keats, like the minds of our older poets, goes round the universe in its speculations and its dreams. It does not set itself a task. The manners of the world, the fictions and the wonders of other worlds, are its subjects; not the pleasures of hope, or the pleasures of memory. The true poet confines his imagination to no one thing—his soul is an invisible ode to the passions.—He does not make a home for his mind in one land—its productions are an universal story, not an eastern tale. The fancies of Moore are exquisitely beautiful, as fancies, but they are always of one colour;—his feelings are pathetic, but they are "still harping on my daughter."[4] The true pathetic is to be found in the

---

3. See Hunt's "Young Poets" review, pp. 11–14.
4. Polonius says this of Hamlet in Shakespeare, *Hamlet*, 2.2.187–88. For Thomas *Moore*, see p. 244, n. 1.

reflections on things, not in the moods and miseries of one person. There is not one poet of the present day, that enjoys any popularity that will live; each writes for his booksellers and the ladies of fashion, and not for the voice of centuries. Time is a lover of old books, and he suffers few new ones to become old. Posterity is a difficult mark to hit, and few minds can send the arrow full home. Wordsworth might have safely cleared the rapids in the stream of time, but he lost himself by looking at his own image in the waters. Coleridge stands bewildered in the cross-road of fame;—his genius will commit suicide, and be buried in it. Southey is Poet Laureate, "so there is no heed to be taken of him."[5] Campbell has relied on two stools, *The Pleasures of Hope*, and *Gertrude of Wyoming*, but he will come to the ground, after the fashion of the old proverb.[6] The journey of fame is an endless one; and does Mr. Rogers[7] think that pumps and silk stockings (which his genius wears) will last him the whole way? Poetry is the coyest creature that ever was wooed by man: she has something of the coquette in her; for she flirts with many, and seldom loves one.

Mr. Keats has certainly not perfected anything yet; but he has the power, we think, within him, and it is in consequence of such an opinion that we have written these few hasty observations. If he should ever see this, he will not regret to find that all the country is not made up of Quarterly Reviewers. All that we wish is, that our Readers could read the Poem, as we have done, before they assent to its condemnation—they will find passages of singular feeling, force, and pathos. We have the highest hopes of this young Poet. We are obscure men, it is true. * * * We live far from the world of letters,—out of the pale of fashionable criticism,—aloof from the atmosphere of a Court; but we are surrounded by a beautiful country, and love Poetry, which we read out of doors, as well as in. We think we see glimpses of a high mind in this young man, and surely the feeling is better that urges us to nourish its strength, than that which prompts the Quarterly Reviewer to crush it in its youth, and for ever. If however, the mind of Mr Keats be of the quality we think it to be of; it will not be cast down by this wanton and empty attack. Malice is a thing of the scorpion kind—It drives the sting into its own heart. The very passages which the *Quarterly Review* quotes as ridiculous, have in them the beauty that sent us to the Poem itself. * * *[8]

Letter to J. A. Hessey, October 8, 1818[1]

My dear Hessey.

You are very good in sending me the letter from the Chronicle—and I am very bad in not acknowledging such a kindness sooner.—Pray forgive me— It has so chanced that I have had that paper every day—I have seen today's.

---

5. Shakespeare, *Julius Caesar*, 1.2.268–69.
6. The proverb is "Between two stools you come to the ground." Thomas Campbell (1777–1844), known primarily for *Pleasures of Hope* (1799) and *Gertrude of Wyoming* (1809).
7. Samuel Rogers (1763–1855), a banker, poet, and friend of Byron's.
8. Reynolds closes by praising Keats's ability to put "a spirit of life and novelty into Heathen Mythology" and the "*sinewy* quality of his thoughts."
1. Written as Keats absorbed negative and positive reactions to *Endymion*. *Blackwood's Edinburgh Magazine* 3 (August 1818): 519–24 had attacked the poem in its Cockney School series, and the *Quarterly Review* 19 (September 1818): 204–208 followed with a savage review by John Wilson Croker (see pp. 272–76 and 277–80). Keats was defended in the *Morning Chronicle* by J. S. (probably John Scott) on October 3 (see, pp. 283–84), who noted that the attacks occurred largely because of Keats's alliance with Hunt, and then by R. B. on October 8. Text from Woodhouse's letter-book, pp. 13–14.

I cannot but feel indebted to those Gentlemen who have taken my part—As for the rest, I begin to get a little acquainted with my own strength and weakness.—Praise or blame has but a momentary effect on the man whose love of beauty in the abstract makes him a severe critic on his own Works. My own domestic criticism has given me pain without comparison beyond what Blackwood or the Quarterly could possibly inflict, and also when I feel I am right, no external praise can give me such a glow as my own solitary reperception & ratification of what is fine. J. S. is perfectly right in regard to the slipshod Endymion.[2] That it is so is no fault of mine.—No!—though it may sound a little paradoxical. It is as good as I had power to make it—by myself—Had I been nervous about its being a perfect piece, & with that view asked advice, & trembled over every page, it would not have been written; for it is not in my nature to fumble—I will write independantly.—I have written independently without Judgment—I may write independently & with judgment hereafter.—The Genius of Poetry must work out its own salvation in a man: It cannot be matured by law & precept, but by sensation & watchfulness in itself—That which is creative must create itself—In Endymion, I leaped headlong into the Sea, and thereby have become better acquainted with the Soundings, the quicksands, & the rocks, than if I had stayed upon the green shore, and piped a silly pipe, and took tea & comfortable advice.—I was never afraid of failure; for I would sooner fail than not be among the greatest—But I am nigh getting into a rant. So, with remembrances to Taylor & Woodhouse &c I am

Yrs very sincerely
John Keats.

From Letter to George and Georgiana Keats, October 14, 16, 21, 24, 31, 1818[1]

My dear George; There was a part in your Letter which gave me a great deal of pain, that where you lament not receiving Letters from England. I intended to have written immediately on my return from Scotland (which was two Months earlier than I had intended on account of my own as well as Tom's health) but then I was told by M^rs W—[2] that you had said you would not wish any one to write till we had heard from you. This I thought odd and now I see that it could not have been so; yet at the time I suffered my unreflecting head to be satisfied and went on in that sort of abstract careless and restless Life with which you are well acquainted. This sentence should it give you any uneasiness do not let it last for before I finish it will be explained away to your satisfaction.

I am grieved to say that I am not sorry you had not Letters at Philadelphia; you could have had no good news of Tom and I have been withheld on his account from beginning these many days; I could not bring myself to say the truth, that he is no better, but much worse—However it must be told, and you must my dear Brother and Sister take example frome me and

---

2. J. S., while praising "beauties of the highest order" on "almost every page," acknowledges "that there are also many, very many passages indicating haste and carelessness."
1. Text excerpted from ALS (Harvard MS Keats 1.39); there is also a transcript by Jeffrey (Harvard MS Keats 3.9, p. 13r.).
2. Mrs. Wylie, the mother of Georgiana Keats.

bear up against any Calamity for my sake as I do for your's. Our's are ties which independent of their own Sentiment are sent us by providence to prevent the deleterious effects of one great, solitary grief. I have Fanny and I have you—three people whose Happiness to me is sacred—and it does annul that selfish sorrow which I should otherwise fall into, living as I do with poor Tom who looks upon me as his only comfort—the tears will come into your Eyes—let them—and embrace each other—thank heaven for what happiness you have and after thinking a moment or two that you suffer in common with all Mankind hold it not a sin to regain your cheerfulness. I will relieve you of one uneasiness of overleaf: I returned I said on account of my health—I am now well from a bad sore throat which came of bog trotting in the Island of Mull—of which you shall hear by the coppies I shall make from my Scotch Letters[3]—Your content in each other is a delight to me which I cannot express—the Moon is now shining full and brilliant—she is the same to me in Matter, what you are to me in Spirit— If you were here my dear Sister I could not pronounce the words which I can write to you from a distance: I have a tenderness for you, and an admiration which I feel to be as great and more chaste than I can have for any woman in the world. You will mention Fanny—her character is not formed; her identity does not press upon me as yours does. I hope from the bottom of my heart that I may one day feel as much for her as I do for you. I know not how it is, but I have never made any acquaintance of my own—nearly all through your medium my dear Brother—through you I know not only a Sister but a glorious human being—And now I am talking of those to whom you have made me known I cannot forbear mentioning Haslam as a most kind and obliging and constant friend. His behaviour to Tom during my absence and since my return has endeared him to me for ever—besides his anxiety about you. Tomorrow I shall call on your Mother[4] and exchange information with her—On Tom's account I have not been able to pass so much time with her as I would otherwise have done—I have seen her but twice—once I dined with her and Charles—She was well, in good Spirits and I kept her laughing at my bad jokes. We went to tea at Mrs Millar's and in going were particularly struck with the light and shade through the Gate way at the Horse Guards.[5] I intend to write you such Volumes that it will be impossible for me to keep any order or method in what I write: that will come first which is uppermost in my Mind, not that which is uppermost in my heart—besides I should wish to give you a picture of our Lives here whenever by a touch I can do it; even as you must see by the last sentence our walk past Whitehall all in good health and spirits—this I am certain of, because I felt so much pleasure from the simple idea of your playing a game at Cricket—At Mrs Millars I saw Henry quite well—there was Miss Keasle—and the goodnatured Miss Waldegrave—Mrs Millar began a long story and you know it is her Daughter's way to help her on as though her tongue were ill of the gout—Mrs M. certainly tells a Story as though she had been taught her Alphabet in Crutched Friars.[6] Dilke has been very unwell;

3. See pp. 251–71.
4. Mrs. Wylie.
5. Located in the middle of a block of government buildings on Whitehall, named for Whitehall Palace, the only remnant of which is Inigo Jones's Banqueting House. Henry Wylie, Georgiana's brother, lived with his aunt, Mrs. Millar, and her daughter, Mary, on Henrietta Street, where apparently Mrs. Millar rented rooms to Miss Keasle and Miss Waldegrave.
6. There is a convent/monastery of Crouched or Crutched Friars in London.

I found him very ailing on my return—he was under Medical care for some time, and then went to the Sea Side whence he has returned well—Poor little Mrs D. has had another gall-stone attack; she was well ere I returned—she is now at Brighton[7]—Dilke was greatly pleased to hear from you and will write a Letter for me to enclose—He seems greatly desirous of hearing from you of the Settlement itself.[8] I came by ship from Inverness[9] and was nine days at Sea without being sick—a little Qualm now and then put me in mind of you—however as soon as you touch the shore all the horrors of sickness are soon forgotten; as was the case with a Lady on board who could not hold her head up all the way. We had not been in the Thames an hour before her tongue began to some tune; paying off as it was fit she should all old scores. I was the only Englishman on board. There was a downright Scotchman who hearing that there had been a bad crop of Potatoes in England had brought some triumphant Specimens from Scotland—these he exhibited with national pride to all the Lightermen, and Watermen from the Nore to the Bridge.[1] I fed upon beef all the way; not being able to eat the thick Porridge which the Ladies managed to manage with large awkward horn spoons into the bargain. Severn has had a narrow escape of his Life from a Typhous fever: he is now gaining strength. Reynolds has returned from a six weeks enjoyment in Devonshire, he is well and persuades me to publish my pot of Basil as an answer to the attacks made on me in Blackwood's Magazine and the Quarterly Review.[2] There have been two Letters in my defence in the Chronicle and one in the Examiner, copied from the Alfred Exeter paper, and written by Reynolds—I do not know who wrote those in the Chronicle.[3] This is a mere matter of the moment—I think I shall be among the English Poets after my death. Even as a Matter of present interest the attempt to crush me in the Quarterly has only brought me more into notice and it is a common expression among book men "I wonder the Quarterly should cut its own throat.'

It does me not the least harm in Society to make me appear little and rediculous: I know when a Man is superior to me and give him all due respect—he will be the last to laugh at me and as for the rest I feel that I make an impression upon them which insures me personal respect while I am in sight whatever they may say when my back is turned. Poor Haydon's eyes will not suffer him to proceed with his picture—he has been in the Country. I have seen him but once since my return—I hurry matters together here because I do not know when the Mail sails—I shall enquire tomorrow and then shall know whether to be particular or general in my letter—you shall have at least two sheets a day till it does sail whether it be three days or a fortnight—and then I will begin a fresh one for the next Month. The Miss Reynoldses are very kind to me—but they have lately

<hr />

7. From whence Dilke had returned before September 20.
8. George planned to join Albion, a settlement founded on 16,000 acres of land in Illinois by Morris Birkbeck (1764–1825); George had read of the settlement in Birkbeck's *Letters from Illinois* (1818).
9. Actually, from Cromarty, twenty miles northeast of Inverness.
1. London Bridge; *Lightermen*: men who worked on a lighter, a flat-bottomed boat that ferried cargo from ships to shore; *the Nore*: a sandbank off Sheerness, which gave its name to a naval command; the site of the Great Mutiny of 1797.
2. For these attacks, see pp. 272–80; for *Severn*, see p. 110, n. 6.
3. For the letters in the *Morning Chronicle*, see p. 286, n. 1; Reynolds published a defense in *The Alfred, West of England Journal*, October 6, 1818, which was reprinted in the *Examiner*, October 12, 1818, pp. 648–49 (see pp. 284–86).

displeased me much and in this way—Now I am coming the Richardson.[4] On my return, the first day I called they were in a sort of taking or bustle about a Cousin of theirs who having fallen out with her Grandpapa in a serious manner, was invited by Mrs R. to take Asylum in her house.[5] She is an east indian and ought to be her Grandfather's Heir. At the time I called Mrs R. was in conference with her up stairs and the young Ladies were warm in her praises down stairs calling her genteel, interresting and a thousand other pretty things to which I gave no heed, not being partial to 9 days wonders. Now all is completely changed—they hate her; and from what I hear she is not without faults—of a real kind: but she has others which are more apt to make women of inferior charms hate her. She is not a Cleopatra; but she is at least a Charmian.[6] She has a rich eastern look; she has fine eyes and fine manners. When she comes into a room she makes an impression the same as the Beauty of a Leopardess. She is too fine and too concious of her Self to repulse any Man who may address her—from habit she thinks that nothing *particular*.[7] I always find myself more at ease with such a woman; the picture before me always gives me a life and animation which I cannot possibly feel with any thing inferiour—I am at such times too much occupied in admiring to be awkward or on a tremble. I forget myself entirely because I live in her. You will by this time think I am in love with her; so before I go any further I will tell you I am not—she kept me awake one Night as a tune of Mozart's might do. I speak of the thing as a passtime and an amuzement than which I can feel none deeper than a conversation with an imperial woman the very 'yes' and 'no' of whose Lips is to me a Banquet.[8] I dont cry to take the moon home with me in my Pocket nor do I fret to leave her behind me. I like her and her like because one has no *sensations*—what we both are is taken for granted—You will suppose I have by this had much talk with her—no such thing—there are the Miss Reynoldses on the look out—They think I dont admire her because I did not stare at her—

They call her a flirt to me—What a want of knowledge? she walks across a room in such a manner that a Man is drawn towards her with a magnetic Power. This they call flirting! they do not know things. They do not know what a Woman is. I believe tho' she has faults—the same as Charmian and Cleopatra might have had—Yet she is a fine thing speaking in a worldly way: for there are two distinct tempers of mind in which we judge of things—the worldly, theatrical and pantomimical; and the unearthly, spiritual and etherial—in the former Buonaparte, Lord Byron and this Charmian hold the first place in our Minds; in the latter John Howard, Bishop Hooker rocking his child's cradle and you my dear Sister are the conquering feelings.[9] As a

---

4. That is, he is becoming like Samuel Richardson (1689–1761), author of the key epistolary novels *Pamela* (1740–41), *Clarissa* (1747–49), and *Sir Charles Grandison* (1753–54).
5. Jane Cox, Mrs. Reynolds's niece. Her father had been employed by the East India Company; upon his death, she became her grandfather's heir, but the older man and the young heiress had quarreled, leading to Mrs. Reynolds's offering Ms. Cox a temporary home. Keats had heard of her on September 1 and was introduced to her on September 19.
6. Cleopatra's attendant, who dies at her side in Shakespeare's *Antony and Cleopatra*.
7. Flirtatious.
8. See Shakespeare, *Much Ado about Nothing*, 2.3.18–19: "His words are a very fantastical [poetic] banquet."
9. Richard Hooker (1554?–1600) was a theologian whose *Laws of Ecclesiastical Politie* (1593, 1597) defended the Church of England; Keats would have known of his life through Izaak Walton's biography. Keats links Jane Cox with Napoleon and Byron as "worldly" and "imperial" presences. *John Howard* (1726?–1790) was a famous philanthropist and prison reformer.

man in the world I love the rich talk of a Charmian; as an eternal being I love the thought of you. I should like her to ruin me, and I should like you to save me. Do not think my dear Brother from this that my Passions are head long or likely to be ever of any pain to you—no

> "I am free from Men of Pleasure's cares
> By dint of feelings far more deep than theirs"[1]

This is Lord Byron, and is one of the finest things he has said. I have no town talk for you, as I have not been much among people—as for Politics they are in my opinion only sleepy because they will soon be too wide awake. Perhaps not—for the long and continued Peace of England itself has given us notions of personal safety which are likely to prevent the reestablishment of our national Honesty—There is of a truth nothing manly or sterling in any part of the Government. There are many Madmen in the Country, I have no doubt, who would like to be beheaded on tower Hill merely for the sake of eclat, there are many Men like Hunt who from a principle of taste would like to see things go on better, there are many like Sir F. Burdett who like to sit at the head of political dinners[2]—but there are none prepared to suffer in obscurity for their Country—the motives of our worst Men are interest and of our best Vanity—We have no Milton, no Algernon Sidney[3]—Governers in these days loose the title of Man in exchange for that of Diplomat and Minister. We breathe in a sort of Officinal Atmosphere. All the departments of Government have strayed far from Spimpicity which is the greatest of Strength—there is as much difference in this respect between the present Government and Oliver Cromwell's, as there is between the 12 Tables of Rome and the volumes of Civil Law which were digested by Justinian.[4] A Man now entitlerd Chancellor has the same honour paid to him whether he be a Hog or a Lord Bacon.[5] No sensation is created by Greatness but by the number of orders a Man has at his Button holes. Notwithstand the part which the Liberals take in the Cause of Napoleon I cannot but think he has done more harm to the life of Liberty than any one else could have done: not that the divine right Gentlemen[6] have done or intend to do any good—no they have taken a Lesson of him and will do all the further harm he would have done without any of the good. The worst thing he has done is, that he has taught them how to organize their monstrous armies—The Emperor Alexander it is said intends to divide his Empire as did Diocletian— creating two Czars besides himself, and continuing the supreme Monarch

---

1. While Keats identifies these lines as by Byron, they are in fact from Hunt's *Story of Rimini* 3.121–22: "And had been kept from men of pleasure's cares / By dint of feelings still more warm than theirs."

2. Sir Francis Burdett (1770–1844) was an independent aristocratic reformer identified with the movement for Radical Reform of Parliament; Burdett often chaired dinners to rally Reformers, such as the annual "Dinner in Commemoration of the Acquital of Messrs. Tooke and Hardy" (*Examiner*, November 17, 1811, pp. 731–32; *SWLH*, 1: 195–98). Keats probably refers to Leigh Hunt here, given the reference to "taste," but Cook believes he means Henry ("Orator") Hunt.

3. See p. 4, n. 2.

4. Keats contrasts what he sees as the "simplicity" of the government of Oliver Cromwell (1599–1658), who became Lord Protector of England after the Civil War, with the present government; he draws on an opposition between the "simplicity" of Rome's "Twelve Tables," its earliest (probably around 450 B.C.E.) legal code written down to protect the people from patrician oppression, and the complexity of the Emperor Justinian's *Corpus Juris Civilis* (529–35 C.E.) which sought to codify 1,000 years of Roman law.

5. Francis Bacon (1561–1626), English philosopher, essayist, and statesman.

6. Those who support the legitimacy of monarchy as ordained by God.

of the whole[7]—Should he do this and they for a series of Years keep peaceable among themselves Russia may spread her conquest even to China—I think a very likely thing that China itself may fall. Turkey certainly will—Meanwhile european north Russia will hold its horns against the rest of Europe, intrieguing constantly with France. Dilke, whom you know to be a Godwin perfectibily Man,[8] pleases himself with the idea that America will be the country to take up the human intellect where england leaves off—I differ there with him greatly—A country like the united states whose greatest Men are Franklins and Washingtons will never do that—They are great Men doubtless but how are they to be compared to those our countrey men Milton and the two Sidneys[9]—The one is a philosophical Quaker full of mean and thrifty maxims the other sold the very Charger who had taken him through all his Battles—Those American's are great but they are not sublime Man—the humanity of the United States can never reach the sublime—Birkbeck's mind is too much in the American Style—you must endeavour to infuse a little Spirit of another sort into the Settlement, always with great caution, for thereby you may do your descendents more good than you may imagine. If I had a prayer to make for any great good, next to Tom's recovery, it should be that one of your Children should be the first American Poet. I have a great mind to make a prophecy and they say prophecies work out their own fulfillment. * * *[1]

Since I wrote thus far I have met with that same Lady again, whom I saw at Hastings and whom I met when we were going to the English Opera.[2] It was in a street which goes from Bedford Row to Lamb's Conduit Street. I passed her and turned back—she seemed glad of it; glad to see me and not offended at my passing her before. We walked on towards Islington where we called on a friend of her's who keeps a Boarding School. She has always been an enigma to me—she has been in a Room with you and with Reynolds and wishes we should be acquainted without any of our common acquaintance knowing it. As we went along, some times through shabby, sometimes through decent Streets I had my guessing at work, not knowing what it would be and prepared to meet any surprise—First it ended at this House at Islington: on parting from which I pressed to attend her home. She consented and then again my thoughts were at work what it might lead to, tho' now they had received a sort of genteel hint from the Boarding

---

7. Alexander I (1777–1825), czar of Russia and architect of the Holy Alliance formed after the defeat of Napoleon. Rollins cites a report in the *Gentleman's Magazine* for September 1818 that Alexander intended to divide Russia into three parts, with his brothers ruling them as kings under his ultimate authority. In 293 C.E., the Roman emperor Diocletian divided the empire into Eastern and Western halves under a "tetrarchy."

8. Dilke was a follower of the political philosopher and novelist William Godwin (1756–1836), the founder of philosophical anarchism and proponent of man's perpetual improvement; Godwin was linked to the circle of which Keats was a part through the Shelleys (Mary Shelley was his daughter) and Hunt. Dilke could have found an image of the Western hemisphere replacing the cultural power of Europe in Barbauld's *Eighteen Hundred and Eleven* (1812).

9. For Algernon Sidney, see p. 4, n. 2; for Sir Philip Sidney, see p. 81, n. 6.

1. Keats includes " 'Tis 'the witching time of night' " (Stillinger, pp. 288–90), in which he imagines a "Little Child / O' the western wild / A Poet"; he then goes on to discuss various comings and goings among his circle.

2. Keats is writing on October 24, 1818 and describes a meeting with Isabella Jones (see p. 80, n. 1). He had met her in Hastings and again on the way to the English Opera House (also known as the Lyceum Theatre) in the Strand. He met her this time on Theobald's Road, Bloomsbury, walking towards Lamb's Conduit Street, Holborn, where Reynolds's family lived. Keats walked with her from Holborn to Islington, and then turned south to her rooms in 34 Gloucester Street, after stopping to see a friend, perhaps Mary Green of Miss Green's Boarding-School near where Isabella Jones lived.

School. Our Walk ended in 34 Gloucester Street Queen Square—not exactly so for we went up stairs into her sitting room—a very tasty sort of place with Books, Pictures a bronze statue of Buonaparte, Music, æolian Harp; a Parrot, a Linnet[3]—A Case of choice Liquers &c &c &. she behaved in the kindest manner—made me take home a Grouse for Tom's dinner—Asked for my address for the purpose of sending more game. As I had warmed with her before and kissed her—I thought it would be living backwards not to do so again—she had a better taste: she perceived how much a thing of course it was and shrunk from it—not in a prudish way but in as I say a good taste. She contrived to disappoint me in a way which made me feel more pleasure than a simple kiss could do—she said I should please her much more if I would only press her hand and go away. Whether she was in a different disposition when I saw her before—or whether I have in fancy wrong'd her I cannot tell. I expect to pass some pleasant hours with her now and then: in which I feel I shall be of service to her in matters of knowledge and taste: if I can I will. I have no libidinous thought about her—she and your George are the only women à peu près de mon age[4] whom I would be content to know for their mind and friendship alone. I shall in a short time write you as far as I know how I intend to pass my Life—I cannot think of those things now Tom is so unwell and weak. Notwithstand your Happiness and your recommendation I hope I shall never marry. Though the most beautiful Creature were waiting for me at the end of a Journey or a Walk; though the carpet were of Silk, the Curtains of the morning Clouds; the chairs and Sofa stuffed with Cygnet's down; the food Manna, the Wine beyond Claret, the Window opening on Winander mere,[5] I should not feel—or rather my Happiness would not be so fine, as my Solitude is sublime. Then instead of what I have described, there is a Sublimity to welcome me home. The roaring of the wind is my wife and the Stars through the window pane are my Children. The mighty abstract Idea I have of Beauty in all things stifles the more divided and minute domestic happiness—an amiable wife and sweet Children I contemplate as a part of that Beauty, but I must have a thousand of those beautiful particles to fill up my heart. I feel more and more every day, as my imagination strengthens, that I do not live in this world alone but in a thousand worlds—No sooner am I alone than shapes of epic greatness are stationed around me, and serve my Spirit the office which is equivalent to a king's body guard—then 'Tragedy, with scepter'd pall, comes sweeping by.'[6] According to my state of mind I am with Achilles shouting in the Trenches or with Theocritus in the Vales of Sicily.[7] Or I throw my whole being into Troilus and repeating those lines, 'I wander, like a lost soul upon the stygian Banks staying for waftage,'[8] I melt into the air with a voluptuousness so delicate that I am content to be alone. These things combined with the opinion I have of the generallity of women—who appear to me as children to whom I would rather give a Sugar Plum than my time, form a barrier

---

3. A songbird; *aeolian Harp*: see p. 7, n. 6.
4. That is, about my own age.
5. Windermere. A cygnet is a young swan.
6. See Milton, "Il Penseroso," ll. 97–98.
7. That is, he is either in an epic mood with Achilles from the *Iliad* 18.228 or in a pastoral mood with the founder of pastoral poetry, Theocritus (see p. 241, n. 4).
8. See Shakespeare, *Troilus and Cressida*, 3.2.7–9; "staying for waftage": waiting to be ferried.

against Matrimony which I rejoice in. I have written this that you might see I have my share of the highest pleasures and that though I may choose to pass my days alone I shall be no Solitary. You see therre is nothing spleenical in all this. The only thing that can ever affect me personally for more than one short passing day, is any doubt about my powers for poetry—I seldom have any, and I look with hope to the nighing time when I shall have none. I am as happy as a Man can be—that is in myself I should be happy if Tom was well, and I knew you were passing pleasant days. Then I should be most enviable—with the yearning Passion I have for the beautiful, connected and made one with the ambition of my intellect. Think of my Pleasure in Solitude, in comparison of my commerce with the world—there I am a child—there they do not know me not even my most intimate acquaintance—I give into their feelings as though I were refraining from irritating a little child—Some think me middling, others silly, others foolish—every one thinks he sees my weak side against my will; when in truth it is with my will—I am content to be thought all this because I have in my own breast so great a resource. This is one great reason why they like me so; because they can all show to advantage in a room, and eclipese from a certain tact one who is reckoned to be a good Poet. I hope I am not here playing tricks 'to make the angels weep':[9] I think not: for I have not the least contempt for my species; and though it may sound paradoxical: my greatest elevations of soul leaves me every time more humbled. Enough of this—though in your Love for me you will not think it enough.* * *[1]

Your anxious and affectionate Brother
John—

This day is my Birth day—
All our friends have been anxious in their enquiries and all send their rembrances

Letter to Richard Woodhouse, October 27, 1818[1]

My dear Woodhouse,
Your Letter gave me a great satisfaction; more on account of its friendliness, than any relish of that matter in it which is accounted so acceptable in the 'genus irritabile.'[2] The best answer I can give you is in a clerklike manner to make some observations on two principle points, which seem to point like indices into the midst of the whole pro and con, about genius, and views and atchievements and ambition and cœtera. 1st As to the poet-

---

9. See Shakespeare, *Measure for Measure*, 2.2.120–25: "Man . . . Plays such fantastic tricks before high heaven / As makes the angels weep."
1. Keats goes on to explain how he will send his letters and takes his leave of his brother and sister-in-law. He notes, "Mind you I mark this Letter A," as the first of a series of journal letters.
1. Keats's famous rejection of the "wordsworthian or egotistical sublime" and identification of himself as the "camelion Poet" was written in response to Woodhouse's letter of October 21, 1818 (*L*, 1: 378–82) in which he complained about the *Quarterly Review*'s attack on *Endymion* (see pp. 277–80, above), praised Keats and his poem, and defended modern poetry against Keats's claim that "there was now nothing original to be written in poetry." Text from ALS (Harvard MS Keats 1.38); there is also a transcript in Woodhouse's letter-book, pp. 15–17.
2. Horace, *Epistles*, 2.2: 102, on the "irritable race" of poets.

ical Character itself, (I mean that sort of which, if I am any thing, I am a Member; that sort distinguished from the wordsworthian or egotistical sublime; which is a thing per se and stands alone[3]) it is not itself—it has no self—it is every thing and nothing—It has no character—it enjoys light and shade; it lives in gusto, be it foul or fair, high or low, rich or poor, mean or eleveated. It has as much delight in conceiving an Iago as an Imogen.[4] What shocks the virtuous philosoper, delights the camelion Poet. It does no harm from its relish of the dark side of things any more than from its taste for the bright one; because they both end in speculation. A Poet is the most unpoetical of any thing in existence; because he has no Identity—he is continually in for—and filling some other Body—The Sun, the Moon, the Sea and Men and Women who are creatures of impulse are poetical and have about them an unchangeable attribute—the poet has none; no identity—he is certainly the most unpoetical of all God's Creatures. If then he has no self, and if I am a Poet, where is the Wonder that I should say I would write no more? Might I not at that very instant been cogitating on the Characters of Saturn and Ops?[5] It is a wretched thing to confess; but is a very fact that not one word I ever utter can be taken for granted as an opinion growing out of my identical nature—how can it, when I have no nature? When I am in a room with People if I ever am free from speculating on creations of my own brain, then not myself goes home to myself: but the identity of every one in the room begins so to press upon me that, I am in a very little time annihilated—not only among Men; it would be the same in a Nursery of children: I know not whether I make myself wholly understood: I hope enough so to let you see that no dependence is to be placed on what I said that day.

In the second place I will speak of my views, and of the life I purpose to myself—I am ambitious of doing the world some good: if I should be spared that may be the work of maturer years—in the interval I will assay to reach to as high a summit in Poetry as the nerve bestowed upon me will suffer. The faint conceptions I have of Poems to come brings the blood frequently into my forehead—All I hope is that I may not lose all interest in human affairs—that the solitary indifference I feel for applause even from the finest Spirits, will not blunt any acuteness of vision I may have. I do not think it will—I feel assured I should write from the mere yearning and fondness I have for the Beautiful even if my night's labours should be burnt every morning and no eye ever shine upon them. But even now I am perhaps not speaking from myself; but from some character in whose soul I now live. I am sure however that this next sentence is from myself. I feel your anxiety, good opinion and friendliness in the highest degree, and am

Your's most sincerely
John Keats

---

3. Shakespeare, *Troilus and Cressida*, 1.2.15–16: "They say he is a very man *per se* [unique man] / And stands alone."
4. That is, the villain of *Othello* and the virtuous heroine of *Cymbeline*. Keats seems to recall some ideas from Hazlitt's lecture on "Shakespeare and Milton" (*Works* 5: 44–68), which he heard in the spring.
5. Characters in *Hyperion*, on which Keats was working.

FRAGMENT.[1]

Where's the Poet? Show him! show him!
Muses nine, that I may know him!
'Tis the man who with a man
Is an equal, be he King,
    Or poorest of the beggar-clan,   5
Or any other wondrous thing
    A man may be 'twixt ape and Plato;
'Tis the man who with a bird,
    Wren or eagle, finds his way to
All its instincts;—he hath heard   10
    The Lion's roaring, and can tell
What his horny throat expresseth;
    And to him the Tiger's yell
Comes articulate and presseth
    On his ear like mother-tongue.   15

* * * * * * * * * * * * * *

SONG.[1]

I HAD a dove, and the sweet dove died,
    And I have thought it died of grieving;
O, what could it grieve[2] for? Its feet were tied[3]
    With a silken thread of my own hand's weaving;
Sweet little red feet! why would you die?[4]   5
    Why would you leave me, sweet bird,[5] why?
You lived alone on the forest tree,
Why, pretty thing! would[6] you not live with me?
    I kiss'd you oft and gave you white peas;
Why not live sweetly as in the green trees?   10

SONG[1]

1

Hush, hush, tread softly! hush, hush, my dear,
All the house is asleep, but we know very well

1. Written in 1818, in October according to Allott because of similarities to ideas in Keats's "came-lion poet" letter of October 27, 1818, to Woodhouse (above, p. 295). First printed in 1848, 1:282–83; text from 1848 with emendations from Brown's transcript (Harvard MS Keats 3.6, p. 35; *MYR: JK*, 7: 37).
1. Written in late 1818 or very early 1819 and copied into a journal letter to George and Georgiana Keats for January 2, 1819, where Keats indicates it was written "to some Music as it was playing" (see p. 306), with the musician perhaps being Fanny Keats and perhaps Charlotte Reynolds. First printed in 1848, 2: 260; text from 1848 with emendations from W², f. 187r (*MYR: JK*, 6: 347), derived from the same lost transcript by Brown as 1848, and with some variants from the letter listed in the notes.
2. The letter has "mourn."
3. The letter has "It was tied."
4. The letter has "why did you die?"; 1848 misreads "would" as "should."
5. The letter has "dove."
6. The letter has "could."
1. Written in 1818, perhaps for a tune played by Charlotte Reynolds, who told Forman, "Keats was passionately fond of music, and would sit for hours while she played piano to him. It was to a Span-ish air which she used to play that the song 'Hush, hush! tread softly!' was composed" (Forman,

That the jealous, the jealous old baldpate may[2] hear,
  Though you've padded his nightcap, O sweet Isabel.
Though your feet are more light than a fairy's feet,   5
  Who[3] dances on bubbles where brooklets meet,
Hush, hush, tread softly, hush, hush, my dear,
For less than a nothing the jealous can hear.

2

No leaf doth tremble, no ripple is there
  On the river—all's still, and the night's sleepy eye   10
Closes up, and forgets all its Lethean[4] care,
  Charmed to death by the drone of the humming may-fly.
And the moon, whether prudish or complaisant,
  Hath fled to her bower, well knowing I want
No light in the darkness, no torch in the gloom,   15
But my Isabel's eyes, and her lips pulp'd with bloom.

3

Lift the latch, ah gently! ah tenderly, sweet,
  We are dead if that latchet gives one little chink:
Well done! now those lips and a flowery seat.
  The old man may sleep,[5] and the planets may wink,   20
    The shut rose shall[6] dream of our loves and awake
    Full blown, and such warmth for the morning take;
The stock-dove shall hatch her soft brace and shall coo,
While I kiss to the melody, aching all through.

From Letter to George and Georgiana Keats, December 16–18, 22, 29?, 31, 1818, January 2–4, 1819[1]

[2] My dear Brother and Sister,
    You will have been prepared, before this reaches you for the worst news you could have, nay if Haslam's letter arrives in proper time, I have a consolation in thinking the first shock will be past before you receive this. The last days of poor Tom were of the most distressing nature; but his last moments were not so painful, and his very last was without a pang. I will not enter into any parsonic comments on death—yet the common observations

---

1883, 1: xxix–xxx). First published in *Hood's Magazine* 3 (April 1845: 339) "By The Late John Keats"; text from *Hood's* with emendations from Fanny Brawne's transcript in the copy of Hunt's *Literary Pocketbook for 1819* (1818) given to her by Keats, who in turn received it from Hunt (LMA, K/BK/01/016/115), and Keats's holograph draft (Harvard, MS Keats 2.20; *JKPMH*, p. 93). Stillinger notes that "Textually this is the strangest poem in the Keats canon" (1974, p. 211); no two versions are identical, so some variants have been used.
2. The reading of the draft and Brawne's transcript; *Hood's* has "can."
3. The reading of the draft and Brawne's transcript; *Hood's* has "That."
4. Lethe is a river in Hades whose waters bring forgetfulness to those about to be reborn.
5. The reading in the draft; *Hood's* and Brawne's transcript have "dream."
6. The reading in the draft; *Hood's* and Brawne's transcript have "may."
1. Written following Tom's death and Keats's acquaintance with Fanny Brawne. Text excerpted from ALS at Harvard (MS Keats 1.45); there is also an excerpted transcript by Jeffrey (Harvard MS Keats 3.9, f.16r).
2. Keats had labeled his October 1818 letter to the George Keatses (see above, p. 294, n. 1) as "A" to mark the first in the series of letters he planned to write to them.

of the commonest people on death are as true as their proverbs. I have scarce a doubt of immortality of some nature or other—neither had Tom. My friends have been exceedingly kind to me every one of them—Brown detained me at his House. I suppose no one could have had their time made smoother than mine has been. During poor Tom's illness I was not able to write and since his death the task of beginning has been a hindrance to me. Within this last Week I have been every where—and I will tell you as nearly as possible how all go on. With Dilke and Brown I am quite thick—with Brown indeed I am going to domesticate—that is we shall keep house together.[3] I Shall have the front parlour and he the back one—by which I shall avoid the noise of Bentley's Children—and be the better able to go on with my Studies—which ave[4] been greatly interrupted lately, so that I have not the Shadow of an idea of a book in my head, and my pen seems to have grown too goutty for verse. How are you going on now? The going on of the world make me dizzy—there you are with Birkbeck[5]—here I am with Brown—sometimes I fancy an immense separation, and sometimes, as at present, a direct communication of spirit with you. That will be one of the grandeurs of immortality—there will be no space and consequently the only commerce between spirits will be by their intelligence of each other—when they will completely understand each other—while we in this world merely comprehend each other in different degrees—the higher the degree of good so higher is our Love and friendship. I have been so little used to writing lately that I am affraid you will not smoke my meaning so I will give an example—Suppose Brown or Haslam or any one whom I understand in the nether degree to what I do you, were in America, they would be so much the farther from me in proportion as their identity was less impressed upon me. Now the reason why I do not feel at the present moment so far from you is that I remember your Ways and Manners and actions; I know your manner of thinking, your manner of feeling: I know what shape your joy or your sorrow would take, I know the manner of your walking, standing, sauntering, sitting down, laughing, punning, and every action so truly that you seem near to me. You will remember me in the same manner—and the more when I tell you that I shall read a passage of Shakspeare every Sunday at ten o Clock—you read one at the same time and we shall be as near each other as blind bodies can be in the same room. * * *[6] Haydon was here yesterday—he amused us much by speaking of young Hopner who went with Captn Ross on a voyage of discovery to the Poles[7]—The Ship was sometimes entirely surrounded with vast mountains and crags of ice and in a few Minutes not a particle was to be seen all round the Horizon. Once they met with with so vast a Mass that they gave themselves over for lost; their last recourse was in meeting it with the Bowspit,[8] which they did, and split it asunder and glided through it as it parted for a great distance—one

---

3. Keats lived with Brown for the next seventeen months in his side of the "double house" on Wentworth Place where Dilke had the other half.
4. Rollins labels this a "Cockneyism."
5. See p. 289. n. 8.
6. Keats writes of various visits with family and friends.
7. John Ross (1777–1856) commanded the *Isabella* while Lieutenant Henry Parkyns Hoppner (1795–1833) served on the *Alexander*, commanded by Lieutenant W. E. Parry, as the boats rediscovered Baffin Bay in trying to find the Northwest Passage; see Captain Sir John Ross's *A Voyage of Discovery* (1819). *Haydon*: see p. 55, n. 1.
8. For "bowsprit," "a large spar or boom running out from the stem of a vessel, to which (and the jib-boom and flying jib-boom, which extend beyond it) the foremast stays are fastened" (*OED*).

Mile and more. Their eyes were so fatigued with the eternal dazzle and whiteness that they lay down on their backs upon deck to relieve their sight on the blue Sky. Hopner describes his dreadful weriness at the continual day—the sun ever moving in a circle round above their heads—so pressing upon him that he could not rid himself of the sensation even in the dark Hold of the Ship—The Esquimaux are described as the most wretched of Beings—they float from the Summer to their winter residences and back again like white Bears on the ice floats—They seem never to have washed, and so when their features move, the red skin shows beneath the cracking peal of dirt. They had no notion of any inhabitants in the World but themselves. The sailors who had not seen a Star for some time, when they came again southwards, on the hailing of the first revision, of one all ran upon deck with feelings of the most joyful nature. Haydon's eyes will not suffer him to proceed with his Picture—his Physician[9] tells him he must remain two months more, inactive. Hunt keeps on in his old way—I am completely tired of it all—He has lately publish'd a Pocket-Book call'd the litrerary Pocket-Book—full of the most sickening stuff you can imagine.[1] Reynolds is well—he has become an edinburgh Reviewer[2]—I have not heard from Bailey. Rice I have seen very little of lately—and I am very sorry for it. The Miss R's are all as usual—Archer above all people called on me one day[3]— he wanted some information, by my means, from Hunt and Haydon, concerning some Man they knew. I got him what he wanted, but know none of the whys and wherefores. Poor Kirkman left wentworth place one evening about half past eight and was stopped, beaten and robbed of his Watch in Pond Street.[4] I saw him a few days since, he had not recovered from his bruize. I called on Hazlitt the day I went to Romney Street[5]—I gave John Hunt extracts from your Letters—he has taken no notice.[6] I have seen Lamb lately—Brown and I were taken by Hunt to Novello's[7]—there we were devastated and excruciated with bad and repeated puns—Brown dont want to go again. We went the other evening to see Brutus a new Trageday by Howard Payne, an American—Kean was excellent—the play was very bad—It is the first time I have been since I went with you to the Lyceum[8]—

M[rs] Brawne who took Brown's house for the Summer, still resides in Hampstead—she is a very nice woman—and her daughter senior is I think beautiful and elegant, graceful, silly, fashionable and strange we have a little tiff now and then—and she behaves a little better, or I must have sheered off[9]—I find by a sidelong report from your Mother that I am to be

9. Dr. George Darling (1779/80–1862).
1. Hunt's quite popular volume, part calendar, almanac, and anthology, included Keats's "The Human Seasons" ("Four seasons fill the measure of the year") and "To Ailsa Rock").
2. It is unclear whether Reynolds actually wrote for the *Edinburgh Review* (see *KC*, 2:235).
3. Archibald Archer, a painter who seems to have flourished between 1810 and 1845. The "Miss R's" are Reynolds's sisters.
4. Blunden identifies George Buchanan Kirkman as a native of Portsmouth and the son of G. F. Mathew's aunt, Rebecca Mathew, and Edward Kirkman; see Blunden, *English* 1 (1936): 51.
5. December 14, 1818, when Keats visited Mrs. Wylie at her Romney Street home.
6. Apparently Keats hoped that John Hunt, Leigh's brother, would publish extracts from their letters from the United States.
7. Vincent Novello (1781–1861), conductor, composer, and founder of a music publishing house; he was at the center of the Hunt's circle's interest in music. Charles *Lamb*: see p. 111, n. 6.
8. The Lyceum or English Opera House was a theater operated by Samuel Arnold in the Strand; Keats had met Isabella Jones for the second time there. John Howard Payne's *Brutus; or, The Fall of Tarquin* opened at Drury Lane, with Kean (see p. 105, n. 1) in the lead, on December 3, 1818, after a period in which the theaters had been closed following the queen's death. The play was a considerable success.
9. Keats's first mention of Fanny Brawne.

invited to Miss Millar's birthday dance—Shall I dance with Miss Walde-grave?[1] Eh! I shall be obliged to shirk a good many there—I shall be the only Dandy there—and indeed I merely comply with the invitation that the party may no be entirely destitute of a specimen of that Race. I shall appear in a complete dress of purple Hat and all—with a list of the beauties I have con-quered embroidered round my Calves.

Thursday This morning[2] is so very fine. I should have walked over to Walthamstow if I had thought of it yesterday[3]—What are you doing this morning? Have you a clear hard frost as we have? How do you come on with the gun? Have you shot a Buffalo? Have you met with any Pheasants? My Thoughts are very frequently in a foreign Country—I live more out of England than in it—The Mountains of Tartary are a favourite lounge, if I happen to miss the Alle-gany ridge, or have no whim for Savoy.[4] There must be great pleasure in pur-suing game—pointing your gun—no, it wont do—now no—rabbit it—now bang—smoke and feathers—where is it? Shall you be able to get a good pointer or so? Have you seen M[r] Trimmer—He is an acquaintance of Peachey's.[5] Now I am not addressing miself to G. minor, and yet I am—for you are one—Have you some warm furs? By your next Letters I shall expect to hear exactly how you go on—smother nothing—let us have all—fair and foul all plain—Will the little bairn have made his entrance before you have this? Kiss it for me, and when it can first know a cheese from a Caterpillar show it my picture twice a Week—You will be glad to hear that Gifford's attack[6] upon me has done me service—it has got my Book among several Sets. * * *[7] Hunt has asked me to meet Tom Moore[8] some day—so you shall hear of him. The night we went to Novello's there was a complete set to of Mozart and punning—I was so completely tired of it that if I were to follow my own inclinations I should never meet any one of that set again, not even Hunt—who is certainly a pleasant fellow in the main when you are with him—but in reallity he is vain, egotistical and disgusting in matters of taste and in morals—He understands many a beautiful thing; but then, instead of giving other minds credit for the same degree of perception as he him-self possesses—he begins an explanation in such a curious manner that our taste and self-love is offended continually. Hunt does one harm by making fine things petty and beautiful things hateful—Through him I am indiffer-ent to Mozart, I care not for white Busts—and many a glorious thing when associated with him becomes a nothing—This distorts one's mind—makes one's thoughts bizarre—perplexes one in the standard of Beauty— * * *—I have been several times thinking whether or not I should send you the examiners as Birkbeck no doubt has all the good periodical Publications—I will save them at all events.— * * * I am passing a Quiet day—which I have not done a long while—and if I do continue so—I feel I must again begin with my poetry—for if I am not in action mind or Body I am in pain—and

1. For Miss Waldegrave and Miss Millar, see p. 288, n. 5.
2. December 17, 1818.
3. Presumably to see Fanny Keats but perhaps Abbey who also lived there.
4. The Haute Savoie are in the French Alps, Tartary refers to central Asia, and the Allegany Moun-tains run from New York to West Virginia.
5. A schoolmate of Keats and his brother.
6. It was actually by Croker; see above, pp. 277–80.
7. Keats copies a letter from Woodhouse and a letter he forwarded from Jane Porter. Porter, sister of Anna Maria and author of such novels as The Scottish Chiefs (1810), had read and admired Endymion and wished to meet Keats.
8. See p. 244, n. 1.

from that I suffer greatly by going into parties where from the rules of society and a natural pride I am obliged to smother my Spirit and look like an Idiot—because I feel my impulses given way to would too much amaze them—I live under an everlasting restraint—Never relieved except when I am composing—so I will write away. Friday.[9] I think you knew before you left England that my next subject would be 'the fall of Hyperion" I went on a little with it last night—but it will take some time to get into the vein again. I will not give you any extracts because I wish the whole to make an impression—I have however a few Poems which you will like and I will copy out on the next sheet—* * *—I think I am in too huge a Mind for study— I must do it—I must wait at home, and let those who wish come to see me. I cannot always be (how do you spell it?) trapsing—Here I must tell you that I have not been able to keep the journal or write the Tale I promised—now I shall be able to do so. I will write to Haslam this morning to know when the Packet sails and till it does I will write something evey day—after that my journal shall go on like clockwork—and you must not complain of its dullness—for what I wish is to write a quantity to you—knowing well that dullness itself will from me be interesting to you—You may conceive how this not having been done has weighed upon me—I shall be able to judge from your next what sort of information will be of most service or amusement to you. Perhaps as you were fond of giving me sketches of character you may like a little pic nic of scandal even across the Atlantic—* * *—Shall I give you Miss Brawn? She is about my height—with a fine style of countenance of the lengthen'd sort—she wants sentiment in every feature—she manages to make her hair look well—her nostrills are fine—though a little painful—he mouth is bad and good—he Profil is better than her full-face which indeed is not full but pale and thin without showing any bone—Her shape is very graceful and so are her movements—her Arms are good her hands badish—her feet tolerable—she is not seventeen[1]—but she is ignorant—monstrous in her behaviour flying out in all directions, calling people such names—that I was forced lately to make use of the term *Minx*—this is I think not from any innate vice but from a penchant she has for acting stylishly. I am however tired of such style and shall decline any more of it—She had a friend to visit her lately—you have known plenty such—Her face is raw as if she was standing out in a frost—her lips raw and seem always ready for a Pullet—she plays the Music without one sensation but the feel of the ivory at her fingers—she is a downright Miss without one set off[2]—we hated her and smoked her and baited her, and I think drove her away—Miss B—thinks her a Paragon of fashion, and says she is the only woman she would change persons with—What a Stupe—She is superior as a Rose to a Dandelion—When we went to bed Brown observed as he put out the Taper what an ugly old woman that Miss Robinson[3] would make— at which I must have groan'd aloud for I'm sure ten minutes. I have not seen the thing Kingston[4] again—George will describe him to you—I shall insinuate some of these Creatures into a Comedy some day—and perhaps have Hunt among them—Scene, a little Parlour—Enter Hunt—Gattie—

---

9. December 18, 1818.
1. She was actually eighteen.
2. Something that would counterbalance something else.
3. Fanny's friend, Caroline Robinson, would marry the wealthy landowner James Ellis.
4. See p. 108, n. 7.

Hazlitt—Mrs Novello—Ollier—Gattie)[5] Ha! Hunt! got into you new house?
Ha! Mrs Novello seen Altam and his Wife?[6] Mrs N. Yes (with a grin) *its* M^{r}
Hunts is'nt it? Gattie. Hunts' no ha! Mr Olier I congratulate you upon the
highest compliment I ever heard paid to the Book. Mr Haslit, I hope you are
well (Hazlitt—yes Sir, no Sir—Mr Hunt (at the Music) La Biondina[7] &c
Hazlitt did you ever hear this—La Biondina &c—Hazlitt—O no Sir—I
never—Olier—Do Hunt give it us over again—divino—Gattie/divino—
Hunt when does your Pocket Book come out—/Hunt/What is this absorbs
me quite? O we are spinning on a little, we shall floridize[8] soon I hope—
Such a thing very much wanting—people think of nothing but money-
getting—now for me I am rather inclined to the liberal side of things—but
I am reckoned lax in my christian principles—& & & &c—[9]

It is some days since I wrote the last page—and what have I been about
since I have no Idea—I dined at Haslam's on sunday—with Haydon yesterday and saw Fanny in the morning—she was well—Just now I took out
my poem to go on with it—but the thought of my writing so little to you
came upon me and I could not get on—so I have began at random—and I
have not a word to say—and yet my thoughts are so full of you that I can
do nothing else. I shall be confined at Hampstead a few days on account of
a sore throat—* * *—I think there will soon be perceptible a change in the
fashionable slang literature of the day—it seems to me that Reviews have
had their day—that the public have been surfeited—there will soon be
some new folly to keep the Parlours in talk—What it is I care not—We have
seen three literary kings in our Time—Scott—Byron—and then the scotch
novels.[1] All now appears to be dead—or I may mistake—literary Bodies may
still keep up the Bustle which I do not hear—Haydon show'd me a letter
he had received from Tripoli—Ritchey was well and in good Spirits, among
Camels, Turbans, Palm Trees and sands—You may remember I promised
to send him an Endymion which I did not—howeever he has one—you
have one—One is in the Wilds of america—the other is on a Camel's back
in the plains of Egypt.[2] I am looking into a Book of Dubois's[3]—he has written directions to the Players—one of them is very good. "In singing never
mind the music—observe what time you please. It would be a pretty degradation indeed if you were obliged to confine your genius to the dull regularity of a fiddler—horse hair and cat's guts—no, let him keep *your* time
and play *your* tune—*dodge him*"—I will now copy out the Letter and Sonnet

---

5. John Byng Gattie (1788–1828), connected by marriage to the Olliers and an amateur singer, was
a member of Hunt's circle who worked for the Treasury; there is a sonnet to him, Novello, and
Henry Robertson in Hunt's *Foliage* (1818). For Hazlitt, see p. 82, n. 7; the Novellos, p. 299, n. 7;
and Ollier, p. 9, n. 3.
6. Charles Ollier's *Altham and his Wife: a Domestic Tale* (1818).
7. "La biondina in gondoleta," a popular Italian ballad.
8. A coinage, "to floridize" would presumably mean "to make florid," that is, "ornate, showy." "What
is this absorbs me quite": from Pope's "The Dying Christian to His Soul" (1730), l. 9.
9. Haydon, among others, criticized Hunt for his religious views. Hunt (and Keats) considered themselves "liberals," a position set forth in the *Liberal*, the journal jointly created by Hunt, Shelley, and
Byron. Hunt often wrote against "money-getting" (i.e., the *Examiner*, January 19, 1817, pp. 33–34;
SWLH, 2: 91–93).
1. The Waverley novels, which Keats did not yet know were written by Scott, though he could have
read in the *Examiner*, May 17, 1818, p. 313, that Scott's anonymous authorship was now an open
secret.
2. Haydon had heard from Joseph Ritchie (1788?–1819), a surgeon and admirer of Keats whom Keats
had met at Haydon's "Immortal Dinner"; Ritchie died while on a government mission exploring
North Africa.
3. See p. 108, n. 7. Keats read the 1808 edition of *My Pocket Book* which contained the "directions"
to which he refers.

I have spoken of—The outside cover was thus directed 'Messʳˢ Taylor and Hessey (Booksellers) No 93 Fleet Street London' and it contained this 'Messʳˢ Taylor and Hessey are requested to forward the enclosed letter by some *safe* mode of conveyance to the Author of Endymion, who is not known at Teignmouth: or if they have not his address, they will return the letter by post, directed as below, within *a fortnight* "Mʳ P. Fenbank P.O. Teignmouth" 9ᵗʰ Novʳ 1818—⁴ In this sheet was enclosed the following— with a superscription 'Mʳ John Keats Teignmouth'—Then came the Sonnet to John Keats—which I would not copy for any in the world but you—who know that I scout "mild light and loveliness" or any such nonsense in myself

> Star of high promise!—not to this dark age
> Do thy mild light and loveliness belong;—
> For it is blind intolerant and wrong;
> Dead to empyreal soarings, and the rage
> Of scoffing spirits bitter war doth wage
> With all that hold integrity of song.
> Yet thy clear beam shall shine through ages strong
> To ripest times a light—and heritage.
> And there breathe now who dote upon thy fame,
> Whom thy wild numbers wrap beyond their being,
> Who love the freedom of thy Lays—their aim
> Above the scope of a dull tribe unseeing—
> And there is one whose hand will never scant
> From his poor store of fruits all thou can'st want.

November, 1818   turn over

I tun'd over and found a £25-note—Now this appears to me all very proper—if I had refused it—I should have behaved in a very bragadochio dunderheaded manner—and yet the present galls me a little. and I do not know whether I shall not return it if I ever meet with the donor—after whom to no purpose I have written—I have your Miniature on the Table George the great—its very like—though not quite about the upper lip—I wish we had a better of you little George⁵—I must not forget to tell you that a few days since I went with Dilke a shooting on the heath and shot a Tomtit—There were as many guns as Birds—I intended to have been at Chichester this Wednesday—but on account of this sore throat I wrote him (Brown) my excuse Yesterday— Thursday⁶ . . . . I will insert any little pieces I may write—though I will not give any extracts from my large poem which is scarce began—I what⁷ to hear very much whether Poetry and literature in general has gained or lost interest with you—and what sort of writing is of the highest gust with you now. With what sensation do you read Fielding?—and do not Hogarth's pictures seem an old thing to you?⁸ Yet you are very little more removed from

---

4. Apparently "Fenbank" is a pseudonym. The sonnet was once thought to be by Woodhouse, but, as Rollins points out, he later requested a copy of it (see *KC*, 1: 66, 85, 146). Gittings (1954, p. 39) suggests Marian Jeffrey of Teignmouth, who was rumored to be in love with Keats.
5. Georgiana; *George the great*: George Keats (the miniature was by Severn).
6. December 30, 1818.
7. For want.
8. William Hogarth (1697–1764), painter and engraver, known for such works as *The Harlot's Progress* (1732), *The Rake's Progress* (1733–35), and *Mariage à la Mode* (1743–45). Henry Fielding (1707–1754), dramatist, novelist, and jurist, and the author of *Shamela* (1741), *Joseph Andrews* (1742), and *Tom Jones* (1749).

general association than I am—recollect that no Man can live but in one society at a time—his enjoyment in the different states of human society must depend upon the Powers of his Mind—that is you can imagine a roman triumph, or an olympic game as well as I can. We with our bodily eyes see but the fashion and Manners of one country for one age—and then we die. Now to me manners and customs long since passed whether among the Babylonians or the Bactrians[9] are as real, or eveven more real than those among which I now live—My thoughts have turned lately this way—The more we know the more inadequacy we discover in the world to satisfy us—this is an old observation; but I have made up my Mind never to take any thing for granted—but even to examine the truth of the commonest proverbs—This however is true—M[rs] Tighe and Beattie once delighted me[1]—now I see through them and can find nothing in them—or weakness—and yet how many they still delight! Perhaps a superior being may look upon Shakspeare in the same light—is it possible? No—This same inadequacy is discovered (forgive me little George you know I don't mean to put you in the mess) in Women with few exceptions—the Dress Maker, the blue Stocking and the most charming sentimentalist differ but in a Slight degree, and are equally smokeable[2]—But I'll go no further—I may be speaking sacrilegiously—and on my word I have thought so little that I have not one opinion upon any thing except in matters of taste—I never can feel certain of any truth but from a clear perception of its Beauty—and I find myself very young minded even in that perceptive power—which I hope will encrease—A year ago I could not understand in the slightest degree Raphael's cartoons[3]—now I begin to read them a little—and how did I learn to do so? By seeing something done in quite an opposite spirit—I mean a picture of Guido's in which all the Saints, instead of that heroic simplicity and unaffected grandeur which they inherit from Raphael, had each of them both in countenance and gesture all the canting, solemn melo dramatic mawkishness of Mackenzie's father Nicholas[4]—When I was last at Haydon's I looked over a Book of Prints taken from the fresco of the Church of Milan the name of which I forget[5]—in it are comprised Specimens of the first and second age of art in Italy—I do not think I ever had a greater treat out of Shakspeare—Full of Romance and the most tender feeling—magnificence of draperies beyond any I ever saw not excepting Raphael's—But Grotesque to a curious pitch—yet still making

9. Bactria is the name of an ancient Greek kingdom in central Asia, in what is now Afghanistan; it had earlier been an eastern province of the Persian empire.
1. James Beattie (1735–1803), Scottish poet and moral philosopher, was best known for his Spenserian poem, *The Minstrel* (1771, 1774). For Mary Tighe, see p. 33, n. 6.
2. "To smoke" something is to see through and to make fun of something. The Bluestockings were a circle of learned and sociable women who gathered in the later eighteenth century that included Mrs. Montague, Mrs. Carter, and Hannah Moore; more generally, a term for women intellectuals or writers.
3. For Raphael, see p. 56, n. 4. The cartoons were designs for tapestries done by Raphael for Leo X in 1515–16; the cartoons had become part of the Royal collection and in the early nineteenth century were on loan to the British Institution in London where painters such as Haydon (who had engineered the loan over the protest of Royal Academicians) brought their students to study and to copy them.
4. *The Story of Father Nicholas* by Henry Mackenzie (1745–1831) appeared in the Edinburgh *Lounger*, 82–84 (August 26, September 2, 9, 1786) and was reprinted in his *Works* (London, 1816), pp. 154–69. Guido Reni (1575–1642), Italian Baroque painter.
5. Sidney Colvin, *John Keats* (1917), p. 325, established that the book was not of Milanese frescos but was instead Haydon's copy of Carlo Lasinio's *Pitture a fresco del Campo Santo di Pisa* (Florence, 1812), a book which Goethe admired and which inspired the Pre-Raphaelites.

up a fine whole—even finer to me than more accomplish'd works—as there was left so much room for Imagination. I have not heard one of this last course of Hazlitt's lecture's—They were upon 'Wit and Humour,' the english comic writers.'[6] Saturday Jan[y] 2nd Yesterday M[r] M[rs] D and myself dined at M[rs] Brawne's—nothing particular passed. I never intend here after to spend any time with Ladies unless they are handsome—you lose time to no purpose— For that reason I shall beg leave to decline going again to Redall's or Butlers or any Squad where a fine feature cannot be mustered among them all—and where all the evening's amusement consists in saying 'your good health,' *your* good health, and YOUR good health—and (o I beg you pardon) your's Miss——. and such things not even dull enough to keep one awake—with respect to amiable speaking I can read—let my eyes be fed or I'll never go out to dinner any where—Perhaps you may have heard of the dinner given to Tho[s] Moore in Dublin, because I have the account here by me in the Philadelphia democratic paper—The most pleasant thing that accured was the speech M[r] Tom made on his Farthers health being drank[7]—I am affraid a great part of my Letters are filled up with promises and what I will do rather than any great deal written—but here I say once for all—that circumstances prevented me from keeping my promise in my last, but now I affirm that as there will be nothing to hinder me I will keep a journal for you. That I have not yet done so you would forgive if you knew how many hours I have been repenting of my neglect—For I have no thought pervading me so constantly and frequently as that of you—my Poeem cannot frequently drive it away—you will retard it much more that You could by taking up my time if you were in England—I never forget you except after seeing now and then some beautiful woman—but that is a fever—the thought of you both is a passion with me but for the most part a calm one—I asked Dilke for a few lines for you—he has promised them—I shall send what I have written to Haslam on Monday Morning. what I can get into another sheet tomorrow I will—there are one or two little poems you might like—I have given up snuff very nearly quite—Dilke has promised to sit with me this evening, I wish he would come this minute for I want a pinch of snuff very much just now—I have none though in my own snuff box—My sore throat is much better to day—I think I might venture on a crust—Here are the Poems— they will explain themselves—as all poeems do without any comment

[A draft of "Fancy" follows.][8]

I did not think this had been so long a Poem—I have another not so long— but as it will more conveniently be coppied on the other side I will just put down here some observations on Caleb Williams by Hazlitt—I mean to say S[t] Leon for although he has mentioned all the Novels of Godwin very finely I do not quote them, but this only on account of its being a specimen of his usual abrupt manner, and fiery laconiscism[9]—* * *—now I will copy the other Poem—it is on the double immortality of Poets—

---

6. Hazlitt's lectures ran from November 3, 1818, to January 5, 1819, and were published in 1819.
7. There was a dinner for Moore on June 7, 1818; the *Democratic Press* of Philadelphia for October 24, 1818, reprinted a piece from the *Dublin Evening Post* about the dinner in which Moore's speech celebrating his father is quoted.
8. See pp. 465–68.
9. Keats goes on to quote with approval Hazlitt's comments on Godwin's *St. Leon* (1799) and *Caleb Williams* (1794) which Keats read in a manuscript of Hazlitt's lecture "On the English Novelists" and which also appeared in the *Examiner*, December 28, 1818, pp. 825–26 (see *Works*, 6: 131, 130); for *Godwin*, see p. 292, n. 8.

[A draft of "Ode" ("Bards of Passion and of Mirth") follows.][1]
These are specimens of a sort of rondeau which I think I shall become partial to—because you have one idea amplified with greater ease and more
delight and freedom than in the sonnet—It is my intention to wait a few
years before I publish any minor poems—and then I hope to have a volume
of some worth—and which those people will realish who cannot bear the
burthen of a long poem—In my journal I intend to copy the poems I write
the days they are written—there is just room I see in this page to copy a
little thing I wrote off to some Music as it was playing—
    [A draft of "I had a dove and the sweet dove died" is written to the side.][2]
    Sunday.[3]
I have been dining with Dilke to day—* * *—Kirkman came down to see
me this morning—his family has been very badly off lately—He told me of
a villainous trick of his Uncle William in Newgate Street who became sole
Creditor to his father under pretence of serving him, and put an execution
on his own Sister's goods—He went in to the family at Portsmouth; con-
versed with them, went out and sent in the Sherif 's officer—He tells me
too of abominable behaviour of Archer to Caroline Mathew—Archer has
lived nearly at the Mathews these two years; he has been amusing Caroline all this time—and now he has written a Letter to M[rs] M— declining
on pretence of inability to support a wife as he would wish, all thoughts of
marriage. What is the worst is, Caroline is 27 years old—It is an abominable matter[4]—He has called upon me twice lately—I was out both
times—What can it be for—There is a letter to day in the Examiner to the
Electors of westminster on M[r] Hobhouse's account—In it there is a good
Character of Cobbet—I have not the paper by me or I would copy it[5]—I do
not think I have mentioned the Discovery of an african kingdom—the
account is much the same as the first accounts of Mexico—all
magnificence—there is a Book being written about it—I will read it and
give you the cream in my next.[6] The ramance we have heard upon it runs
thus: they have window frames of gold—100,000 infantry—human
sacrifices—The Gentleman who is the adventurer has his wife with him—
she I am told is a beautiful little sylphid[7] woman—her husband was to have
been sacrificed to their Gods and was led through a Chamber filled with
different instruments of torture with priveledge to choose what death he
would die, without their having a thought of his aversion to such a death
they considering it a supreme distinction—However he was let off and
became a favorite with the King, who at last openly patronised him; though
at first on account of the Jealousy of his Ministers he was wont to hold conversations with his Majesty in the dark middle of the night—All this sounds

1. See pp. 468–69.
2. See p. 296.
3. January 3, 1819.
4. As noted above (p. 299, n. 4), Kirkman was a relative of George Felton Mathew, cousin to Caro-
    line Mathew; Keats wrote two poems to Caroline and Ann Mathew (see pp. 32–34).
5. "To the Electors of Westminster" by "A Reformer," published in the *Examiner*, January 3, 1819,
    pp. 2–6; the letter discusses William Cobbett (1762–1835), perhaps the most famous radical po-
    litical writer of the day, and Byron's friend John Cam Hobhouse (1786–1869). Hobhouse was con-
    testing the Westminster seat in Parliament with other radicals, Sir William Burdett (1770–1844)
    and Henry "Orator" Hunt (1773–1835), though the seat was won by George Lamb (1784–1834),
    politician and translator of Catullus.
6. See Thomas Edward Bowdich (1791–1824), *Mission from Cape Coast Castle to Ashantee, with a
    Statistical Account of that Kingdom* (1819).
7. Slender, graceful.

a little Blue-beardish[8]—but I hope it is true—* * * I do not think I have any thing to say in the Business way—You will let me know what you would wish done with your property in England—What things you would wish sent out—but I am quite in the dark about what you are doing—if I do not hear soon I shall put on my Wings and be after you—I will in my next, and after I have seen your next letter—tell you my own particular idea of America. Your next letter will be the key by which I shall open your hearts and see what spaces want filling, with any particular information—Whether the affairs of Europe are more or less interesting to you—whether you would like to hear of the Theatre's—of the bear Garden—of the Boxers—the Painters— The Lecturers—the Dress—The Progress of Dandyism—The Progress of Courtship—or the fate of Mary Millar— being a full true and très particular account of Miss M's ten Suitors—How the first tried the effect of swearing; the second of stammering; the third of whispering;—the fourth of sonnets—the fifth of spanish leather boots, the sixth of flattering her body— the seventh of flattering her mind—the eighth of flattering himself—the ninth stuck to the Mother—the tenth kissed the Chambermaid and told her to tell her Mistress—But he was soon discharged his reading lead him into an error—he could not sport the Sir Lucius to any advantage[9]—And now for this time I bid you good by—I have been thing of these sheets so long that I appear in closing them to take my leave of you—but that is not it—I shall immediately as I send this off begin my journal—when some days I shall write no more than 10 lines and others 10 times as much. M[rs] Dilke is knocking at the wall for Tea is ready—I will tell you what sort of a tea it is and then bid you—Good bye—This is Monday morning[1]—no thing particular happened yesterday evening, except that just when the tray came up M[rs] Dilke and I had a battle with celery stalks—she sends her love to you—I shall close this and send it immediately to Haslam—remaining ever

My dearest brother and sister

Your most affectionate Brother

John—

THE EVE OF SAINT MARK.[1]

UPON a Sabbath day it fell;
Twice holy was the Sabbath-bell,
That call'd the folk to evening prayer.
The city streets were clean and fair

---

8. See George Colman the Younger, *Blue-Beard; or, Female Curiosity* (1798).
9. Sir Lucius O'Trigger in Sheridan's *The Rivals* (1775).
1. January 4, 1819.
1. Written between February 13 and 17, 1818, after Keats returned to Hampstead following a visit to Chichester and Bedhampton in Sussex. Keats never finished what he called a "little thing," which he copied in part (ll. 1–114) into his September 1820 journal letter to the George Keatses, noting, "Some time since I began a Poem call'd 'The Eve of S[t] Mark' quite in the spirit of Town quietude. I think it will give you the sensation of walking about an old country Town in a coolish evening" (see p. 367). Keats took some of the descriptive details of the town from his visit to Chichester and the images in Bertha's book from the windows in Stansted Chapel near Bedhampton; Gittings has suggested that some further details come from the rooms of Isabella Jones, who, he believes, also suggested the topic. While the fragment offers descriptive set pieces, it presumably would have gone on to take up the Yorkshire legend of St. Mark's Eve (April 24): if one watches the church porch on that evening for three years in a row, one will see ghosts of all those who will die that year (see John Brand, *Observations on Popular Antiquities* [1813], 1: 166). Keats took up this legend in some draft lines (now at the Morgan Library) clearly related to this poem

From wholesome drench of April rains,[2]   5
And on the western window panes
The chilly sunset faintly told
Of unmatured green vallies cold,
Of the green thorny bloomless hedge,
Of rivers new with springtide sedge,[3]   10
Of primroses by shelter'd rills,
And daisies on the aguish hills.
Twice holy was the Sabbath-bell:
The silent streets were crowded well
With staid and pious companies,   15
Warm from their fireside orat'ries;
And moving, with demurest air,
To even-song, and vesper prayer.
Each arched porch and entry low
Was fill'd with patient folk and slow,   20
With whispers hush and shuffling feet,
While play'd the organ loud and sweet.

The bells had ceased, the prayers begun,
And Bertha had not yet half done
A curious volume, patch'd and torn,   25
That all day long, from earliest morn,
Had taken captive her two eyes
Among its golden broideries;[4]
Perplex'd her with a thousand things,—
The stars of heaven, and angels' wings,   30
Martyrs in a fiery blaze,
Azure saints mid silver rays,
Aaron's[5] breastplate, and the seven
Candlesticks John saw in heaven,
The winged Lion of Saint Mark,   35
And the Covenantal Ark,
With its many mysteries,
Cherubim and golden mice.[6]

Bertha was a maiden fair,
Dwelling in the old Minster Square;   40

---

but never integrated into it; they are given as an addendum at the end of the present text. Keats's
pastiche of Middle English and his octasyllabic couplets recall Chatterton (from whose *Aella, a
Tragic Interlude* [1777] Keats may have taken the name of his heroine, Bertha), Chaucer, and
Gower; Coleridge's "Christabel" has also been suggested as a model. First printed in 1848, 2:
279–83, where it is labeled as "unfinished"; text from 1848 with emendations from the British
Library holograph draft (Egerton 2780, fs. 33–36; *MYR: JK*, 5: 123–29). For Keats's portrait of a
woman reader in the poem, see Margaret Homans's essay included here, pp. 563–72.
2. Allott cites the opening of Chaucer's *Canterbury Tales*, "Whan that Aprille with his shoures sote."
3. "A name for various coarse grassy, rush-like or flag-like plants growing in wet places" (*OED*).
4. She is reading an illuminated volume with interwoven designs.
5. 1848 has "Moses'."
6. This mixture of Jewish and Christian symbols was suggested by the stained glass windows of Lewis
   Way's Stansted Chapel; Christian iconography often drew upon earlier Jewish symbols, and as Way
   was interested in converting the Jews, the imagery was appropriate for the chapel. Aaron's breastplate was a square of embroidery set with precious stones recording the names of the tribes of Israel
   (see Exodus 28.15–30; Leviticus 8.8). In Revelation 1.13–20, John sees the seven-branched can-
   delabra (or menorah) representing the seven churches of Asia. Revelation 4.5–9 identifies the lion
   as the emblem of St. Mark. For the Ark of the Covenant, see Hebrews 9.4–5. In 1 Samuel 6.4, five
   golden mice are sent as an offering by the Philistines when they return the Ark to the Israelites.

From her fireside she could see,
Sidelong, its rich antiquity,
Far as the Bishop's garden-wall;
Where sycamores and elm trees tall,
Full leaved, the forest had outstript,[7]   45
By no sharp north wind ever nipt,
So shelter'd by the mighty pile.
Bertha arose and read awhile,
With forehead 'gainst the window pane.
Again she tried, and then again,   50
Until the dusk eve left her dark
Upon the legend of St. Mark.
From pleated lawn-frill, fine and thin,
She lifted up her soft warm chin,
With aching neck and swimming eyes,   55
And dazed with saintly imag'ries.

All was gloom, and silent all,
Save now and then the still footfall
Of one returning townwards[8] late,
Past the echoing minster gate.   60
The clamorous daws, that all the day
Above tree tops and towers play,
Pair by pair had gone to rest,
Each in its ancient belfry nest,
Where asleep they fall betimes   65
To music and the drowsy chimes.

All was silent, all was gloom,
Abroad and in the homely room:
Down she sat, poor cheated soul!
And struck a lamp from the dismal coal,   70
Leaned forward, with bright drooping hair
And slant book, full against the glare.
Her shadow, in uneasy guise,
Hover'd about, a giant size,
On ceiling beam and old oak chair,   75
The parrot's cage, and panel square;
And the warm angled winter screen,
On which were many monsters seen,
Call'd doves of Siam, Lima mice,
And legless birds of Paradise,   80
Macaw, and tender av'davat,
And silken furr'd Angora cat.[9]
Untired she read; her shadow still
Glower'd about, as it would fill
The room with wildest forms and shades,   85

7. The draft deletes this line, which is needed for the rhyme scheme.
8. 1848 reads the draft with its uncrossed "t" as "homewards."
9. The images on the screen suggest to Allott a Chinese Coromandel lacquer screen (seven-teenth–nineteenth centuries), but Gittings (1954) argues it is Isabella Jones's screen with images from Madagascar. He finds *Lima mice* to be the phonetic spelling of lemur mice, nocturnal mammals from Madagascar. The *birds of Paradise*, from New Guinea, are "legless" because they were thought to be always in flight. The avadavat or amadavat is an Indian song bird.

As though some ghostly queen of spades
Had come to mock behind her back,
And dance, and ruffle her[1] garments black.
Untired she read the legend page
Of holy Mark from youth to age;   90
On land, on sea, in pagan chains,
Rejoicing for his many pains.[2]
Sometimes the learned eremite,[3]
With golden star, or dagger bright,
Referr'd to pious poesies   95
Written in smallest crow-quill[4] size
Beneath the text; and thus the rhyme
Was parcel'd out from time to time:[5]
—"Als writith he of swevenis,[6]
Men han beforne they wake in bliss,   100
Whanne thate hir friendes thinke hem bound
In crimpid shroude farre under grounde;
And how a litling child mote be
A saint er its nativitie,
Gif thate the modre (God her blesse)   105
Kepen in solitarinesse,
And kissen devoute the holy croce.
Of Goddis love, and Sathan's force
He writith; and thinges many mo:
Of swiche thinges I may not shew;   110
Bot I must tellen verilie
Somdel of Saintè Cicilie;
And chieflie whate he auctorethe
Of Saintè Markis life and dethe."

At length her constant eyelids come   115
Upon the fervent martyrdom;
Then lastly to his holy shrine,
Exalt amid the tapers' shine
At Venice,—

Addendum:[7]
Gif ye wol stonden hardie wight—
Amiddes of the blacke night—
Righte in the churche porch, pardie
Ye wol behold a companie
Appouchen thee full dolourouse   5
For sooth to sain from everich house

---

1. The reading in 1848; the draft seems to adopt "their," then "her," then "their."
2. The legends that grew up around St. Mark, including his martyrdom and burial in Alexandria, are first recounted by St. Jerome (c. 342–420).
3. Hermit.
4. A quill from a crow's feather, used in fine writing.
5. In copying the poem to George, Keats breaks off here, noting, "What follows is an imitation of the Authors in Chaucer's time—'tis more ancient than Chaucer himself and perhaps between him and Gower."
6. Dreams.
7. These lines are on the reverse side of a different draft of lines 99–114 (Morgan Library MA 213; facsimile in Forman [1906], after p. 342); first published in E. de Selincourt (ed.), *The Poems of John Keats* (5th ed., 1926), p. 584, and Garrod includes them between the current lines 98 and 99. Text from the Morgan Library draft.

> Be it in City or village
> Wol come the Phantom and image
> Of ilka gent and ilka carle
> Whom coldè Deathè hath in parle   10
> And wol some day that very year
> Touchen with foulè venime spear
> And sadly do them all to die—
> Hem all shalt thou see verilie—
> And everichon shall by thee pass   15
> All who must die that year Alas—

From Letter to George and Georgiana Keats, February 14, 19, March 3?, 12, 13, 17, 19, April 15, 16, 21, 30, May 3, 1819[1]

Letter C[2]—   sunday Morn Feby 14—

My dear Brother & Sister—How is it we have not heard from you from the Settlement[3] yet? The Letters must surely have miscarried. * * * The Literary world I know nothing about—There is a Poem from Rogers dead born— and another satire is expected from Byron call'd Don Giovanni[4]—* * * There are two new tragedies—one by the Apostate Man, and one by Miss Jane Porter.[5]* * * I have not seen Mr Lewis[6] lately for I have shrunk from going up the hill—Mr Lewis went a few morning ago to town with Mrs Brawne they talked about me—and I heard that M^r L Said a thing I am not at all contented with—Says he 'O, he is quite the little Poet' now this is abominable—you might as well say Buonaparte is quite the little Soldier— You see what it is to be under six foot and not a lord—There is a long fuzz to day in the examiner about a young Man who delighted a young woman with a Valentine—I think it must be Ollier's.[7] Brown and I are thinking of passing the summer at Brussels, if we do we shall go about the first of May—We i e Brown and I sit opposite one another all day authorizing (N.B. an s instead of a z would give a different meaning) He is at present writing a Story of an old Woman who lived in a forest and to whom the Devil or one his Aid de feus[8] came one night very late and in disguise—The old Dame sets before him pudding after pudding—mess after mess—which he devours and moreover casts his eyes up at a side of Bacon hanging over his

---

1. Text from ALS (Harvard MS Keats 1.53); there is also a much abbreviated transcript by Jeffrey (Harvard MS 3.9, f.20r).
2. Keats used letters to designate the series of journal letters to the George Keatses (see p. 294, n. 1).
3. See p. 289, n. 8.
4. Byron's *Don Juan*, cantos 1–2, appeared in July 1819. Samuel Rogers (1763–1855), a banker as well as a poet (his *Pleasures of Memory* appeared in 1792 and *Jacqueline* in 1814), had published *Human Life*.
5. Jane Porter (1776–1850), author of *The Scottish Chiefs* (1810), saw her *Switzerland* (ascribed by Nicoll to her sister Anna Maria Porter) fail at Drury Lane on February 15, 1819, perhaps due to Kean's lackluster performance. *Apostate Man*: Richard Lalor Sheil (1791–1851), author of the successful *Apostate* (Covent Garden, May 3, 1817), saw the production of his *Evadne; or, The Statue* at Covent Garden on February 10, 1819.
6. Perhaps a Mr. Israel Lewis who lived at Well Walk or another "Mr. Lewis" who lived in the Vale of Health, both in Keats's neighborhood.
7. See the *Examiner*, February 14, 1819, pp. 108–109; the piece is signed by three asterisks, but is probably by Lamb.
8. Presumably by analogy with "aide-de-camp," these would be assistants from Hell's fires.

head and at the same time asks whither her Cat is a Rabbit—On going he leaves her three pips[9] of eve's apple—and some how—she, having liv'd a virgin all her life, begins to repent of it and wishes herself beautiful enough to make all the world and even the other world fall in love with her—So it happens—she sets out from her smoky Cottage in magnificent apparel; the first city She enters every one falls in love with her—from the Prince to the Blacksmith. A young gentleman on his way to the church to be married leaves his unfortunate Bride and follows this nonsuch—A whole regiment of soldiers are smitten at once and follow her—A whole convent of Monks in corpus christi[1] procession join the Soldiers—The Mayor and Corporation[2] follow the same road—Old and young, deaf and dumb—all but the blind are smitten and form an immense concourse of people who— what Brown will do with them I know not—The devil himself falls in love with her flies away with her to a desert place—in consequence of which she lays an infinite number of Eggs—The Eggs being hatched from time to time fill the world with many nuisances such as John Knox—George Fox— Johanna Southcote—Gifford[3]—There have been within a fortnight eight failures of the highest consequence in London—Brown went a few evenings since to Davenport's and on his coming in he talk'd about bad news in the City with such a face, I began to think of a national Bankruptcy[4]—I did not feel much surprised—and was rather disappointed. Carlisle, a Bookseller on the *Hone* principle has been issuing Pamphlets from his shop in fleet Street Called the Deist—he was conveyed to Newgate last Thursday—he intends making his own defence.[5] I was surprised to hear from Taylor the amount of Murray the Booksellers last sale—what think you of £25,000? He sold 4000 coppies of Lord Byron.[6] I am sitting opposite the Shakspeare I brought from the Isle of wight—and I never look at it but the silk tassels on it give me as much pleasure as the face of the Poet itself—except that I do not know how you are going on—In my next Packet as this is one by the way, I shall send you the Pot of Basil, St Agnes eve, and if I should have finished it a little thing call'd the 'eve of St Mark' you see what fine mother Radcliff[7] names I have—it is not my fault—I did not

9. Apple seeds, from "pippin" or apple: see "O Blush not so! O blush not so! (p. 119), l. 10.
1. The Feast of the Blessed Sacrament or Body of Christ, observed on the Thursday after Trinity Sunday.
2. The civic authorities of the city such as the aldermen, city council members, etc.
3. See p. 97, n. 2 and p. 277, n. 1. *John Knox* (c. 1513–1572), key religious reformer in Scotland. *George Fox* (1624–1691), founder of the Society of Friends or Quakers. *Joanna Southcott* (1750–1814), a farmer's daughter who became the prophetic leader of a millenarian movement; in 1813, at the age of 63, she proclaimed that she was pregnant by her divine husband and would give birth to Shiloh who would rule earth in preparation for Christ's return, but the child never appeared and she died on December 27, 1814.
4. England was still struggling with a post-Waterloo recession. The *Examiner* often listed bankruptcies, as on January 31, 1819, p. 75 and February 7, 1819, p. 88. Mr. Davenport, who may have been called Benjamin, Burrage, or Burridge, was a merchant who lived in Hampstead. Keats and Fanny Brawne attended parties at his house.
5. Richard Carlile (1790–1843) was an important radical journalist and publisher, in large part responsible for the revival of interest in Thomas Paine's political and religious writings as well as for disseminating the works of other republicans and deists. He was arrested on February 11, 1819, and found guilty on October 15, 1819, for blasphemous and seditious libel following his issuing of Paine's *Age of Reason* and Palmer's *Principles of Deism*; for Hunt's defense of Carlile, see the *Examiner*, May 23, 1819, pp. 321–22, SWLH, 2: 196–98 and subsequent pieces listed there. Keats refers to another radical publisher and journalist, William Hone (see p. 108, n. 4).
6. Byron's fourth canto of *Childe Harold's Pilgrimage* was issued in 1818 in a very large run of 10,000 copies; the *Monthly Magazine* 45 (February 1818): 68 indicated that 4,000 copies had been ordered even before the poem was printed.
7. Ann Radcliffe (1764–1823), key Gothic novelist of the 1790s whose works include *The Mysteries of Udolpho* (1794) and *The Italian* (1797). For the various poems Keats mentions, see pp. 429–56, 307–11.

search for them—I have not gone on with Hyperion—for to tell the truth I have not been in great cue for writing lately—I must wait for the spring to rouse me up a little—The only time I went out from Bedhampton was to see a Chapel consecrated[8]—Brown I and John Snook the boy, went in a chaise behind a leaden horse Brown drove, but the horse did not mind him. This Chapel is built by a M.r Way a great Jew converter, who in that line has spent one hundred thousand Pounds. He maintains a great number of poor Jews—Of course his communion plate was stolen—he spoke to the Clerk about it—The Clerk said he was very sorry adding—'I dare shay your honour its among ush.' The Chapel is built in M.r Way's park—The Consecration was—not amusing—there were numbers of carriages, and his house crammed with Clergy—they sanctified the Chapel—and it being a wet day consecrated the burial ground through the vestry window. I begin to hate Parsons—they did not make me love them that day—when I saw them in their proper colours—A Parson is a Lamb in a drawing room and a lion in a Vestry[9]—The notions of Society will not permit a Parson to give way to his temper in any shape—so he festers in himself—his features get a peculiar diabolical self sufficient iron stupid expession—He is continually acting—His mind is against every Man and every Mans mind is against him—He is an Hippocrite to the Believer and a Coward to the unbeliever— He must be either a Knave or an Ideot—And there is no Man so much to be pitied as an ideot parson. The soldier who is cheated into an esprit du corps—by a red coat, a Band and Colours for the purpose of nothing—is not half so pitiable as the Parson who is led by the nose by the Bench of Bishops—and is smothered in absurdities—a poor necessary subaltern of the Church—

Friday Feb.y 18[1]—The day before yesterday I went to Romney Street— your Mother was not at home—but I have just written her that I shall see her on wednesday. I call'd on M.r Lewis this morning—he is very well—and tells me not to be uneasy about Letters the chances being so arbitary—He is going on as usual among his favorite democrat papers—We had a chat as usual about Cobbett: and the westminster electors.[2] Dilke has lately been verry much harrassed about the manner of educating his Son—he at length decided for a public school—and then he did not know what school—he at last has decided for Westminster; and as Charley is to be a day boy, Dilke will remove to Westminster. We lead verry quiet lives here— Dilke is at present in greek histories and antiquities—and talks of nothing but the electors of Westminster and the retreat of the ten-thousand[3]—I never drink now above three glasses of wine—and never any spirits and water. Though by the bye the other day—Woodhouse took me to his coffee house—and ordered a Bottle of Claret—now I like Claret whenever I can have Claret I must drink it—'t is the only palate affair that I am at all sensual

---

8. Lewis Way's Stansted Chapel was consecrated on January 25, 1819; details of the chapel may have influenced "The Eve of St. Mark," see pp. 307–11. Way (1772–1840) used his inheritance to support the London Society for the Promotion of Christianity among the Jews; he lodged a number of Jews at his house in the hopes of making them missionaries and hoped to turn Stansted Park into a college for the conversion of the Jews. See Gittings (1954), pp. 75–82.
9. From the proverb about a man being a lamb in the house but a lion in the field of battle.
1. Friday was the 19th.
2. Cobbett (see p. 306, n. 5) was running for the Westminster seat in Parliament against Byron's friend John Cam Hobhouse (1786–1869) and George Lamb (1784–1834), who won.
3. Xenophon's *Anabasis*, which Keats knew in Edward Spelman's translation, *The Expedition of Cyrus* (1742, 1811, 1813), tells of the defeat of Cyrus and his 20,000-man army in the spring of 401 B.C.E.

in—Would it not be a good Speck[4] to send you some vine roots—could it be done? I'll enquire—If you could make some wine like Claret to drink on summer evenings in an arbour! For really 't is so fine—it fills the mouth one's mouth with a gushing freshness—then goes down cool and feverless—then you do not feel it quarelling with your liver—no it is rather a Peace maker and lies as quiet as it did in the grape—then it is as fragrant as the Queen Bee; and the more ethereal Part of it mounts into the brain, not assaulting the cerebral apartments like a bully in a bad house looking for his trul[5] and hurrying from door to door bouncing against the waist-coat; but rather walks like Aladin about his own enchanted palace so gently that you do not feel his step—Other wines of a heavy and spirituous nature transform a Man to a Silenus; this makes him a Hermes—and gives a Woman the soul and immortality of Ariadne for whom Bacchus always kept a good cellar of claret—and even of that he could never persuade her to take above two cups[6]—I said this same Claret is the only palate-passion I have I forgot game, I must plead guilty to the breast of a Partridge, the back of a hare, the back bone of a grouse, the wing and side of a Pheasant and a Woodcock *passim* Talking of game (I wish I could make it) the Lady whom I met at Hastings and of whom I said something in my last I think,[7] has lately made me many presents of game, and enabled me to make as many—She made me take home a Pheasant the other day which I gave to Mrs Dilke; on which, tomorrow, Rice, Reynolds and the Wentworthians will dine next door—The next I intend for your Mother. These moderate sheets of paper are much more pleasant to write upon than those large thin sheets which I hope you by this time have received—though that cant be now I think of it—I have not said in any Letter yet a word about my affairs—in a word I am in no despair about them—my poem[8] has not at all succeeded—in the course of a year or so I think I shall try the public again—in a selfish point of view I should suffer my pride and my contempt of public opinion to hold me silent—but for your's and fanny's sake I will pluck up a spirit, and try again— I have no doubt of success in a course of years if I persevere—but it must be patience—for the Reviews have enervated and made indolent mens minds—few think for themselves—These Reviews too are getting more and more powerful and especially the Quarterly—They are like a superstition which the more it prostrates the Crowd and the longer it continues the more powerful it becomes just in proportion to their increasing weakness. I was in hopes that when people saw, as they must do now, all the trickery and iniquity of these Plagues they would scout them, but no they are like the spectators at the Westminster cock-pit—they like the battle and do not care who wins or who looses—Brown is going on this morning with the story of his old woman and the Devil—He makes but slow progreess—the fact is it is a Libel on the Devil and as that person is Brown's Muse, look ye, if he libels his own Muse how can he expect to write—Either Brown or his muse must turn tale. . . . this[9] may teach them that the man who rediicules romance is the most romantic of Men—that he who abuses women and

---

4. Speculation.
5. Wench, trollop, prostitute.
6. For Bacchus and Ariadne, see p. 66, n. 2; for Hermes, p. 21, n. 5; for Silenus, p. 222, n. 2.
7. Isabella Jones (see p. 80, n. 1).
8. *Endymion.*
9. Keats has been recounting Bailey's complicated romantic relationships.

slights them—loves them the most—that he who talks of roasting a Man alive would not do it when it came to the push—and above all that they are very shallow people who take every thing literal. A Man's life of any worth is a continual allegory—and very few eyes can see the Mystery of his life—a life like the scriptures, figurative—which such people can no more make out than they can the hebrew Bible. Lord Byron cuts a figure—but he is not figurative—Shakspeare led a life of Allegory; his works are the comments on it—

On Monday we had to dinner Severn & Cawthorn the Bookseller & print virtuoso;[1] in the evening Severn went home to paint & we other three went to the play to see Sheild's new tragedy ycleped Evadné[2]—In the morning Severn & I took a turn round the Museum, There is a Sphinx there of a giant size, & most voluptuous Egyptian expression, I had not seen it before—The play was bad even in comparison with 1818 the Augustan age of the Drama, "Comme on sait" as Voltaire[3] says.—the whole was made up of a virtuous young woman, an indignant brother, a suspecting lover, a libertine prince, a gratuitous villain, a street in Naples, a Cypress grove, lillies & roses, virtue & vice, a bloody sword, a spangled jacket, One Lady Olivia, One Miss ONeil alias Evadné, alias Bellamira, alias—Alias—Yea & I say unto you a greater than Elias—there was Abbot,[4] & talking of Abbot his name puts me in mind of a Spelling book lesson, descriptive of the whole Dramatis personae—Abbot—Abbess—Actor—Actress—The play is a fine amusement as a friend of mine once said to me—"Do what you will" says he "A poor gentleman who wants a guinea, cannot spend his two shillings better than at the playhouse—The pantomime was excellent, I had seen it before & enjoyed it again[5] * * * Don't think I am writing a petition to the Governors of St Lukes;[6] no, that would be in another style. May it please your worships; forasmuch as the undersigned has committed, transferred, given up, made over, consigned, and aberrated himself to the art & mystery of poetry; for as much as he hath cut, rebuffed, affronted, huffed, & shirked, and taken stint, at all other employments, arts, mysteries, & occupations honest, middling & dishonest; for as much as he hath at sundry times, & in diverse places, told truth unto the men of this generation, & eke to the women, moreover; for as much as he hath kept a pair of boots that did not fit, & doth not admire Sheild's play, Leigh Hunt, Tom Moore, Bob Southey & Mr Rogers; & does admire Wm Hazlitt: more over for as more, as he liketh half of Wordsworth, & none of Crabbe;[7] more over-est for for

1. Jeffrey's transcript provides this and the next paragraph which were on a leaf left out of Keats's letter; Jeffrey has Sunday. Severn: see p. 110, n. 6; James Cawthorn (d. 1833) was a publisher of, for example, Byron's English Bards and Scotch Reviewers.
2. Sheil's Evadne, mentioned above.
3. See p. 133, n. 2; the Augustan age, named for the Emperor Caesar Augustus, is a high point in culture; "Comme on sait": "as one knows" (French).
4. Keats mentions various performers: Mrs. John Fawcett (née Gaudry or Gawdry), married to the famous actor and playwright, apparently played the part of Lady Olivia. Eliza O'Neill (1791–1872), hailed as the greatest actress of the moment and considered by Shelley as perfect for the part of Beatrice Cenci, played Evadne and also the title role in Sheil's Bellamira; or, The Fall of Tunis (Covent Garden, 22 April 1818); William Abbot (1790–1843) played the King of Naples.
5. The Christmas pantomime, Harlequin Munchausen; or, The Fountain of Love opened at Covent Garden on December 26, 1818, and was quite successful, receiving at least seventy performances; Keats saw it with Evadne on March 1, 1819.
6. An asylum.
7. George Crabbe (1754–1832) was known for The Village (1783), The Borough (1810), and Tales in Verse (1812); he published Tales of the Hall (1819). His heroic couplet verse attempting to offer a realistic portrait of rural life was seen as a poetic practice in opposition to the experiments of the poets who came to define romanticism.

as most; as he hath written this page of penmanship—he prayeth your Worships to give him a lodging—witnessed by R^d Abbey & Co. cum familiaribus & Consanguiniis (signed) Count de Cockaigne—[8]   The nothing of the day is a machine called the Velocepede[9]—It is a wheel-carriage to ride cock horse upon, sitting astride & pushing it along with the toes, a rudder wheel in hand, they will go seven miles an hour, A handsome gelding will come to eight guineas, however they will soon be cheaper, unless the army takes to them.   I look back upon the last month, & find nothing to write about, indeed I do not recollect one thing particular in it—It's all alike, we keep on breathing. The only amusement is a little scandal of however fine a shape, a laugh at a pun—& then after all we wonder how we could enjoy the scandal, or laugh at the pun,

     I have been at different times turning it in my head whether I should go to Edinburgh & study for a physician; I am afraid I should not take kindly to it, I am sure I could not take fees—& yet I should like to do so; it is not worse than writing poems, & hanging them up to be flyblown on the Reviewshambles[1]—Every body is in his own mess—   Here is a parson at Hampstead[2] quarreling with all the world, he is in the wrong by this same token; when the black Cloth was put up in the Church for the Queen's mourning, he asked the workmen to hang it the wrong side outwards, that it might be better when taken down, it being his perquisite—Parsons will always keep up their Character, but as it is said there are some animals, the Ancients knew, which we do not; let us hope our posterity will miss the black badger with tri-cornered hat; Who knows but some Revisor of Buffon or Pliny,[3] may put an account of the parson in the Appendix; No one will then believe it any more than we beleive in the Phoenix. I think we may class the lawyer in the same natural history of Monsters; a green bag will hold as much as a lawn sleeve[4]—   The only difference is that the one is fustian, & the other flimsy; I am not unwilling to read Church history at present & have Milnes in my eye his is reckoned a very good one— * * *

March 12 Friday—I went to town yesterday chiefly for the purpose of seeing some young Men who were to take some Letters for us to you—through the medium of Peachey. I was surprised and disappointed at hearing they had changed their minds and did not purpose going so far as Birkbeck's—

8. The Cockney School attacks often referred to Hunt as the "King of Cockaigne," so Keats here engages those assaults. The Latin phrase roughly means "with those of the household and those linked by blood."
9. The "swift-walker," a kind of bicycle propelled by the rider running along, was modified to allow for steering by Baron von Drais in 1817; see the *Examiner*, April 11, 1819, pp. 239–40.
1. Rollins suggests an echo of Shakespeare, *Othello*, 4.2.68–69: "as summer flies are in the shambles [slaughterhouse], / That quicken even with blowing."
2. Samuel White (1765–1841), vicar (December 1807–January 1841). Queen Charlotte's death, mentioned below, occurred on November 17,1818.
3. Gaius Plinius Secundus, Pliny the Elder (23–79 C.E.), Roman naturalist and author of the *Historia naturalis*, an encyclopedia of natural science. *Buffon*: Georges-Louis Leclerc, Comte de Buffon (1707–1788), French naturalist, keeper of the Jardin des Plantes, and author of the monumental *Histoire naturelle*, 44 vol. (1749–1804). In a passage sent with his September journal letter to the George Keatses along with the sheet omitted from this letter, Keats notes that the "very singular" "idea about Buffon, above, has been taken up by Hunt in the *Examiner*, in some papers which he calls 'A Preter-Natural History'" (see the *Examiner*, August 1, 8, 15, 1819, pp. 491–92, 506–508, 521–22 for "Praeter-Natural History" by "Harry Brown," a Huntian pseudonym).
4. A sleeve made of fine linen, particularly the sleeve of a bishop and thus an indication of his office; *green bag*: a lawyer's bag for carrying his briefs, including secret evidence held in several famous prosecutions in the period; here made of "fustian," a coarse cloth made of cotton and flax and often dyed olive. The church history Keats goes on to mention is in fact *History of the Church of Christ*, 5 vols. (York, 1794–1809) by Joseph Milner (1745–1797) and his brother Isaac (1750–1820).

I was much disappointed; for I had counted upon seeing some persons who were to see you—and upon your seeing some who had seen me—I have not only lost this opportunity—but the sail of the Post-Packet to new york or Philadelphia—by which last, your Brothers have sent some Letters—The weather in town yesterday was so stifling that I could not remain there though I wanted much to see Kean in Hotspur[5]—I have by me at present Hazlitt's Letter to Gifford[6]—perhaps you would like an extract or two from the high seasoned parts—It begins thus. "Sir, You have an ugly trick of saying what is not true of any one you do not like; and it will be the object of this Letter to cure you of it. You say what you please of others; it is time you were told what you are. In doing this give me leave to borrow the familiarity of your style:—for the fidelity of the picture I shall be answerable. You are a little person, but a considerable cat's paw; and so far worthy of notice. Your clandestine connection with persons high in office constantly influences your opinions, and alone gives importence to them. You are the government critic, a character nicely differing from that of a government spy—the invisible link, that connects literature with the Police." Again— "Your employers Mr Gifford, do not pay their hirelings for nothing—for condescending to notice weak and wicked sophistry; for pointing out to contempt what excites no admiration; for cautiously selecting a few specimens of bad taste and bad grammar where nothing else is to be found. They want your invincible pertness, your mercenary malice, your impenetrable dullness, your barefaced impudence, your pragmatical self sufficiency, your hypocritical zeal, your pious frauds to stand in the gap of their Prejudices and pretensions, to fly blow and taint public opinion, to defeat independent efforts, to apply not the touch of the scorpion but the touch of the Torpedo to youthful hopes, to crawl and leave the slimy track of sophistry and lies over every work that does not 'dedicate its sweet leaves'[7] to some Luminary of the tresury bench, or is not fostered in the hot bed of corruption—This is your office; "this is what is look'd for at your hands and this you do not baulk"—to sacrifice what little honesty and prostitute what little intellect you possess to any dirty job you are commission'd to execute. "They keep you as an ape does an apple in the corner of his jaw, first mouth'd to be at last swallow'd"[8]—You are by appointment literary toad eater to greatness and taster to the court—You have a natural aversion to whatever differs from your own pretensions, and an acquired one for what gives offence to your superiors. Your vanity panders to your interest, and your malice truckles only to your love of Power. If your instinctive or premeditated abuse of your enviable trust were found wanting in a single instance; if you were to make a single slip in getting up your select committee of enquiry and greenbag report of the state of Letters, your occupation would be gone. You would never after obtain a squeeze of the hand from a great man, or a smile

5. Kean (see p. 105, n. 1) appeared at Drury Lane in Shakespeare's *1 Henry IV* as Hotspur on March 9 and 11, 1819.

6. Hazlitt's *A Letter to William Gifford, Esq. from William Hazlitt Esq.*, published in 1819 and excerpted in the *Examiner*, March 7, 14, 1819, pp. 156, 171–73, took on the editor of the *Quarterly Review* which had attacked Hazlitt along with other members of the "Cockney School"; Hunt's later satire on Gifford, *Ultra-Crepidarius* (1823), cites Hazlitt's *Letter*. See *Works*, 9: 13–59; Keats extracts pp. 13, 33–34.

7. Shakespeare, *Romeo and Juliet*, 1.1.145–46: "Ere he can spread his sweet leaves to the air / Or dedicate his beauty to the sun."

8. See Shakespeare, *Hamlet*, 4.2.16–17: Hamlet says of officers or courtiers such as Rosencrantz, "He keeps them, like an ape an apple in the corner of his jaw, first mouthed to be last swallowed."

from a Punk of Quality. The great and powerful (whom you call wise and good) do not like to have the privacy of their self love startled by the obtrusive and unmanageable claims of Literature and Philosophy, except through the intervention of people like you, whom; if they have common penetration, they soon find out to be without any superiority of intellect; or if they do not whom they can despise for their meanness of soul. You "have the office opposite to saint Peter." You "keep a corner in the public mind, for foul prejudice and corrupt power to knot and gender in";[9] you volunteer your services to people of quality to ease scruples of mind and qualmes of conscience; you lay the flattering unction of venal prose and laurell'd verse to their souls[1]—You persuade them that there is neither purity of morals, not depth of understanding, except in themselves and their hangers on; and would prevent unhallow'd names of Liberty and humanity from ever being whispered in years polite! You, sir, do you not all this? I cry you mercy then: I took you for the Editor of the Quarterly Review!"[2] This is the sort of feu de joie[3] he keeps up—there is another extract or two—one especially which I will copy tomorrow—for the candles are burnt down and I am using the wax taper—which has a long snuff on it—the fire is at its last click—I am sitting with my back to it with one foot rather askew upon the rug and the other with the heel a little elevated from the carpet—I am writing this on the Maid's tragedy which I have read since tea with Great pleasure— Besides this volume of Beaumont & Fletcher—there are on the table two volumes of chaucer and a new work of Tom Moores call'd 'Tom Cribb's memorial to Congress'[4]—nothing in it—These are trifles—but I require nothing so much of you as that you will give me a like description of yourselves, however it may be when you are writing to me—Could I see the same thing done of any great Man long since dead it would be a great delight: as to know in what position Shakspeare sat when he began "To be or not to be"[5]—such thing become interesting from distance of time or place. I hope you are both now in that sweet sleep which no two beings deserve more than you do—I must fancy you so—and please myself in the fancy of speaking a prayer and a blessing over you and your lives—God bless you—I whisper good night in your ears and you will dream of me. *Saturday 13 March** * *I know not why Poetry and I have been so distant lately I must make some advances soon or she will cut me entirely. Hazlitt has this fine Passage in his Letter Gifford, in his Review of Hazlitt's characters of Shakspeare's plays,[6] attacks the Coriolanus critique—He says that Hazlitt has slandered Shakspeare in saying that he had a leaning to

9. See Shakespeare, *Othello*, 4.2.94–96: "You, mistress, / That have the office opposite to Saint Peter / And keeps the gate of hell"; 3.3.276: "keep a corner in the thing I love"; 4.2.63–64: "Or keep it as a cistern for foul toads / To knot and gender in."
1. See Shakespeare, *Hamlet*, 3.4.136: "Lay not a flattering unction to your soul."
2. See Shakespeare, *Othello*, 4.2.92–93: "I cry you mercy then / I took you for that cunning whore of Venice."
3. Bonfire.
4. Keats owned *The Dramatic Works of Jonson, and Beaumont and Fletcher*, ed. Peter Whalley, 4 vol. (1811), and a 14-volume (bound as 7) edition of Chaucer (Edinburgh, 1782). Tom Moore's "Tom Crib's Memorial to Congress" was extracted anonymously in the *Examiner*, April 11, 18, 1819, pp. 237–38, 253–54.
5. See Shakespeare, *Hamlet*, 3.1.58. "Sweet sleep" in the next sentence echoes *Othello*, 3.3.336. Perhaps Hazlitt's quotations from these two plays brought these passages into Keats's mind.
6. That is, in Gifford's review of Hazlitt's *Characters of Shakespeare's Plays* (1817) in the *Quarterly Review* 18 (January 1818): 458–66. For the passage from which Keats quotes, see Hazlitt, *Works* 9: 36–38. Hazlitt's review of *Coriolanus*, famous for its assertion that poetry is "right royal," first appeared in the *Examiner* for December 15, 1816.

the arbitary side of the question. Hazlitt thus defends himself "My words are "Coriolanus is a storehouse of political commonplaces. The Arguments for and against aristocracy and democracy, on the Preveleges of the few and the claims of the many, on Liberty and slavery, power and the abuse of it, peace and war, are here very ably handled, with the spirit of a poet and the acuteness of a Philosopher. Shakspeare himself seems to have had a leaning to the arbitrary side of the question, perhaps from some feeling of contempt for his own origin, and to have spared no occasion of baiting the rabble. *What he says of them is very true; what he says of their betters is also very true, though he dwells less upon it.*" I then proceed to account for this by shewing how it is that "the cause of the people is but little calculated for a subject for Poetry; or that the language of Poetry naturally falls in with the language of power." I affirm, Sir, that Poetry, that the imagination, generally speaking, delights in power, in strong excitement, as well as in truth, in good, in right, whereas pure reason and the moral sense approve only of the true and good. I proceed to show that this general love or tendency to immediate excitement or theatrical effect, no matter how produced, gives a Bias to the imagination often consistent[7] with the greatest good, that in Poetry it triumphs over Principle, and bribes the passions to make a sacrifice of common humanity. You say that it does not, that there is no such original Sin in Poetry, that it makes no such sacrifice or unworthy compromise between poetical effect and the still small voice of reason—And how do you prove that there is no such principle giving a bias to the imagination, and a false colouring to poetry? Why by asking in reply to the instances where this principle operates, and where no other can with much modesty and simplicity—"But are these the only topics that afford delight in Poetry &c" No; but these objects do afford delight in poetry, and they afford it in proportion to their strong and often tragical effect, and not in proportion to their strong and often tragical effect,[8] and not in proportion to the good produced, or their desireableness in a moral point of view? "Do we read with more pleasure of the ravages of a beast of prey than of the Shepherds pipe upon the Mountain?" No but we do read with pleasure of the ravages of a beast of prey, and we do so on the principle I have stated, namely from the sense of power abstracted from the sense of good; and it is the same principle that makes us read with admiration and reconciles us in fact to the triumphant progress of the conquerers and mighty Hunters of mankind, who come to stop the shepherd's Pipe upon the Mountains and sweep away his listening flock. Do you mean to deny that there is any thing imposing to the imagination in power, in grandeur, in outward shew, in the accumulation of individual wealth and luxury, at the expense of equal justice and the common weal? Do you deny that there is any thing in the "Pride, Pomp and Circumstance of glorious war, that makes ambition virtue'?[9] in the eyes of admiring multitudes? Is this a new theory of the Pleasures of the imagination which says that the pleasures of the imagination do not take rise soly in calculations of the understanding? Is it a paradox of my creating that "one murder makes a villain millions a

7. "Inconsistent" in Hazlitt.
8. Keats copies this clause out again, though now making it negative.
9. See Shakespeare, *Othello*, 3.3.354–55: "Farewell the plumèd troops and big wars / That makes ambition virtue!"

Hero!"[1] or is it not true that here, as in other cases, the enormity of the evil overpowers and makes a convert of the imagination by its very magnitude? You contradict my reasoning, because you know nothing of the question, and you think that no one has a right to understand what you do not. My offence against purity in the passage alluded to, "which contains the concentrated venom of my malignity," is, that I have admitted that there are tyrants and slaves abroad in the world; and you would hush the matter up, and pretend that there is no such thing in order that there may be nothing else. Farther I have explained the cause, the subtle sophistry of the human mind, that tolerates and pampers the evil in order to guard against its approaches; you would conceal the cause in order to prevent the cure, and to leave the proud flesh about the heart to harden and ossify into one impenetrable mass of selfishness and hypocrisy, that we may not "sympathise in the distresses of suffering virtue" in any case in which they come in competition with the fictitious[2] wants and "imputed weaknesses of the great." You ask "are we gratified by the cruelties of Domitian or Nero?" No, not we—they were too petty and cowardly to strike the imagination at a distance; but the Roman senate tolerated them, addressed their perpetrators, exalted them into gods, the fathers of the people; they had pimps and scribblers of all sorts in their pay, their Senecas, &c till a turbulent rabble thinking that there were no injuries to Society greater than the endurance of unlimited and wanton oppression, put an end to the farce and abated the nuisance as well as they could. Had you and I lived in those times we should have been what we are now, I "a sour mal content," and you "a sweet courtier." The manner in which this is managed: the force and innate power with which it yeasts and works up itself—the feeling for the costume of society; is in a style of genius—He hath a demon as he himself says of Lord Byron[3] * * * *March 17th*—Wednesday—On sunday I went to Davenports'[4] where I dined—and had a nap. I cannot bare a day anhilated in that manner—there is a great difference between an easy and an uneasy indolence—An indolent day—fill'd with speculations even of an unpleasant colour—is bearable and even pleasant alone—when one's thoughts cannot find out any thing better in the world; and experience has told us that locomotion is no change: but to have nothing to do, and to be surrounded with unpleasant human identities; who press upon one just enough to prevent one getting into a lazy position; and not enough to interest or rouse one; is a capital punishment of a capital crime: for is not giving up, through goodnature, one's time to people who have no light and shade a capital crime? Yet what can I do?—they have been very kind and attentive to me. I do not know what I did on monday—nothing—nothing—nothing—I wish this was any thing extraordinary—Yesterday I went to town: I called on Mr Abbey; he began again (he has don it frequently lately) about that hat-making concern—saying he wish you had hearkened to it: he wants to make me a Hat-maker—I really believe 't is all interested: for from the manner he

---

1. Beilby Porteus (1731–1809), Bishop of London, published "The Bishop of London's Opinion on War" in the *Cambridge Intelligencer* (September 14, 1793) which quotes from his 1759 Cambridge prize-winning poem, *Death*,"One murder makes a villain; / Millions, a hero." Porteus was an abolitionist but also preached against Tom Paine and the French Revolution.
2. "Factitious" in Hazlitt.
3. See Hazlitt, *Lectures on the English Poets* (1818), *Works* 5: 153.
4. For Davenport, see p. 312, n. 4.

spoke withal and the card he gave me I think he is concerned in Hat-making himself. He speaks well of Fanny's health. . . . I called at Taylor's and found that he and Hilton[5] had set out to dine with me: so I followed them immediately back—I walk'd with them townwards again as far as Cambden Town and smoak'd home a Segar[6]—This morning I have been reading the '*False one*'[7] I have been up to M[rs] Bentley's—shameful to say I was in bed at ten—I mean this morning—The Blackwood's review has committed themselves in a scandalous heresy—they have been putting up Hogg the ettrick shepherd against Burns[8]—The senseless villains. I have not seen Reynolds, Rice or any of our set lately—. Reynolds is completely limed in the law: he is not only reconcil'd to it but hobbyhorses upon it—Blackwood wanted very much to see him—the scotch cannot manage by themselves at all—they want imagination—and that is why they are so fond of Hogg, who has a little of it—

Friday 19th—Yesterday I got a black eye—the first time I took a Cricket bat—Brown who is always one's friend in a disaster applied a leech to the eyelid, and there is no inflammation this morning though the ball hit me directly on the sight—'t was a white ball—I am glad it was not a clout[9]— This is the second black eye I have had since leaving school—during all my school days I never had one at all—we must eat a peck before we die. This morning I am in a sort of temper indolent and supremely careless: I long after a stanza or two of Thompson's Castle of indolence.[1] My passions are all alseep from my having slumbered till nearly eleven and weakened the animal fibre all over me to a delightful sensation about three degrees on this side of faintness—if I had teeth of pearl and the breath of lillies[2] I should call it langour—but as I am+[3] I must call it Laziness—In this state of effeminacy the fibres of the brain are relaxed in common with the rest of the body, and to such a happy degree that pleasure has no show of enticement and pain no unbearable frown. Neither Poetry, nor Ambition, nor Love have any alertness of countenance as they pass by me: they seem rather like three figures on a greek vase—a Man and two women—whom no one but myself could distinguish in their disguisement. This is the only happiness; and is a rare instance of advantage in the body overpowering the Mind. I have this moment received a note from Haslam in which he expects the death of his Father who has been for some time in a state of insensibility— his mother bears up he says very well—I shall go to town tommorrow to see him. This is the world—thus we cannot expect to give way many hours to pleasure—Circumstances are like Clouds continually gathering and

---

5. Hilton, the historical painter (see p. 141, n. 7) and Taylor, Keats's publisher (see p. 12, n. 9).
6. Cigar.
7. A play (performed c. 1620; printed 1647) attributed to Beaumont and Fletcher but probably by Fletcher in collaboration with Massinger.
8. James Hogg (1770–1835), known from his birthplace and early career as the "Ettrick Shepherd," became known for poetic works such as *The Queen's Wake* (1813) and prose works such as *The Private Memoirs and Confessions of a Justified Sinner* (1824); he was on the editorial board of *Blackwood's Edinburgh Review*, which published "Some Observations on the Poetry of the Agricultural and That of the Pastoral Districts of Scotland, Illustrated by a Comparative View of the Genius of Burns and the Ettrick Shepherd" (4 [February 1819]: 521–29).
9. Perhaps for cleat or a long, powerful hit.
1. A poem (1748) in Spenserian stanzas by James Thomson (1700–1748). This passage has often been seen to parallel ideas and phrases in Keats's "Ode to Indolence" (pp. 334–36, below).
2. Compliments typical of a blazon or poem of praise.
3. + especially as I have a black eye [Keats's note].

bursting—While we are laughing the seed of some trouble is put into the wide arable land of events—while we are laughing it sprouts it grows and suddenly bears a poison fruit which we must pluck—Even so we have leisure to reason on the misfortunes of our friends; our own touch us too nearly for words. Very few men have ever arrived at a complete disinterestedness of Mind: very few have been influenced by a pure desire of the benefit of others—in the greater part of the Benefactors & to Humanity some meretricious motive has sullied their greatness—some melodramatic scenery has facinated them—From the manner in which I feel Haslam's misfortune I perceive how far I am from any humble standard of disinterestedness—Yet this feeling ought to be carried to its highest pitch, as there is no fear of its ever injuring society—which it would do I fear pushed to an extremity—For in wild nature the Hawk would loose his Breakfast of Robins and the Robin his of Worms The Lion must starve as well as the swallow[4]—The greater part of Men make their way with the same instinctiveness, the same unwandering eye from their purposes, the same animal eagerness as the Hawk—The Hawk wants a Mate, so does the Man—look at them both they set about it and procure one in the same manner—They want both a nest and they both set about one in the same manner—they get their food in the same manner—The noble animal Man for his amusement smokes his pipe—the Hawk balances about the Clouds—that is the only difference of their leisures. This it is that makes the Amusement of Life—to a speculative Mind. I go among the Fields and catch a glimpse of a stoat or a fieldmouse peeping out of the withered grass—the creature hath a purpose and its eyes are bright with it—I go amongst the buildings of a city and I see a Man hurrying along—to what? The Creature has a purpose and his eyes are bright with it. But then as Wordsworth says, "We have all one human heart"[5]—there is an ellectric fire in human nature tending to purify—so that among these human creatures there is continually some birth of new heroism—The pity is that we must wonder at it: as we should at finding a pearl in rubbish—I have no doubt that thousands of people never heard of have had hearts completely disinterested: I can remember but two—Socrates and Jesus—their Histories evince it[6]—What I heard a little time ago, Taylor observe with respect to Socrates, may be said of Jesus—That he was so great a man that though he transmitted no writing of his own to posterity, we have his Mind and his sayings and his greatness handed to us by others. It is to be lamented that the history of the latter was written and revised by Men interested in the pious frauds of Religion. Yet through all this I see his splendour. Even here though I myself am pursueing the same instinctive course as the veriest human animal you can think of—I am however young writing at random— straining at particles of light in the midst of a great darkness—without knowing the bearing of any one assertion of any one opinion. Yet may I not in this be free from sin? May there not be superior beings amused with any graceful, though instinctive attitude my mind may fall into, as I am entertained with the alertness of a Stoat or the anxiety of a Deer? Though a quar-

---

4. For a similar juxtaposition of disinterestedness and nature "red in tooth and claw," see Keats's verse epistle to Reynolds (pp. 133–36).
5. See Wordsworth, "The Old Cumberland Beggar" (1800), l. 153.
6. Keats could have read of the parallel between Jesus and the Greek philosopher in Book 2 of Rousseau's *Émile* (1762).

rel in the streets is a thing to be hated, the energies displayed in it are fine; the commonest Man shows a grace in his quarrel—By a superior being our reasoning may take the same tone—though erroneous they may be fine— This is the very thing in which consists poetry; and if so it is not so fine a thing as philosophy—For the same reason that an eagle is not so fine a thing as a truth—Give me this credit—Do you not think I strive—to know myself? Give me this credit—and you will not think that on my own account I repeat Milton's lines

> "How charming is divine Philosophy
> Not harsh and crabbed as dull fools suppose
> But musical as is Apollo's lute"[7]—

No—no for myself—feeling grateful as I do to have got into a state of mind to relish them properly—Nothing ever becomes real till it is experienced—Even a Proverb is no proverb to you till your Life has Illustrated it—I am ever affraid that your anxiety for me will lead you to fear for the violence of my temperament continually smothered down: for that reason I did not intend to have sent you the following sonnet—but look over the two last pages and ask yourselves whether I have not that in me which will well bear the buffets of the world. It will be the best comment on my sonnet; it will show you that it was written with no Agony but that of ignorance; with no thirst of any thing but knowledge when pushed to the point though the first steps to it were through my human passions— they went away, and I wrote with my Mind—and perhaps I must confess a little bit of my heart—

[A copy of "Why did I laugh tonight? No voice will tell" follows.][8] I went to bed, and enjoyed an uninterrupted sleep—Sane I went to bed and sane I arose. ‖ This is the 15th of April—you see what a time it is since I wrote—all that time I have been day by day expecting Letters from you—I write quite in the dark—In the hopes of a Letter daily I have deferred that I might write in the light—I was in town yesterday and at Taylors heard that young Birkbeck had been in Town and was to set forward in six or seven days—so I shall dedicate that time to making up this parcel ready for him— I wish I could hear from you to make me "whole and general as the casing air."[9] A few days after the 19th of april I received a note from Haslam containng the news of his father's death—The Family has all been well— Haslam has his father's situation. The Framptons[1] have behaved well to him—The day before yesterday I went to a rout at Sawrey's[2]—it was made pleasant by Reynolds being there, and our getting into conversation with one of the most beautiful Girls I ever saw—She gave a remarkable prettiness to all those commonplaces which most women who talk must utter—I liked M[rs] Sawrey very well. The Sunday before last your Brothers were to come by a long invitation—so long that for the time I forgot it when I promised M[rs] Brawne to dine with her on the same day—On recollecting my engagement with your Brothers I immediately excused myself with M[rs] Brawn but she

7. Milton, *Comus* (1634, 1637), ll. 475–77.
8. See p. 333.
9. See Shakespeare, *Macbeth*, 3.4.22: "As broad and general as the casing [surrounding] air."
1. Haslam's father's employers.
2. Solomon Sawrey (1765–1825), surgeon specializing in ophthalmic surgery and author of two books on venereal diseases.

would not hear of it and insisted on my bringing my friends with me. so we all dined at Mrs Brawne's. I have been to Mrs Bentley's this morning and put all the Letters two and from you and poor Tom and me—I have found some of the correspondence between him and that degraded Wells and Amena[3]— It is a wretched business. I do not know the rights of it—but what I do know would I am sure affect you so much that I am in two Minds whether I will tell you any thing about it—And yet I do not see why—for any thing tho' it be unpleasant, that calls to mind those we still love, has a compensation in itself for the pain it occasions—so very likely tomorrow I may set about copying thee whole of what I have about it: with no sort of a Richardson[4] self satisfaction—I hate it to a sickness—and I am affraid more from indolence of mind than any thing else. I wonder how people exist with all their worries. * * * A few days ago Hunt dined here and Brown invited Davenport to meet him. Davenport from a sense of weakness thought it incumbent on him to show off—and pursuant to that never ceased talking and boaring all day, till I was completely fagged out—Brown grew melancholy—but Hunt perceiving what a complimentary tendency all this had bore it remarkably well—Brown grumbled about it for two or three days—I went with Hunt to Sir John Leicester's gallery,[5] there I saw Northcote—Hilton—Bewick[6] and many more of great and Little note. Haydons picture is of very little progress this last year—He talk about finishing it next year—Wordsworth is going to publish a Poem called Peter Bell—what a perverse fellow it is! Why wilt he talk about Peter Bells—I was told not to tell—but to you it will not be tellings—Reynolds hearing that said Peter Bell was coming out, took into his head to write a skit upon it call'd Peter Bell. He did it as soon as thought on it is to be published this morning, and comes out before the real Peter Bell, with this admirable motto from the "Bold stroke for a Wife". " 'I am the real Simon Pure' "[7] It would be just as well to trounce Lord Byron in the same manner. I am still at a stand in versifying—I cannot do it yet with any pleasure—I mean however to look round at my resources and means—and see what I can do without poetry—To that end I shall live in Westminster—I have no doubt of making by some means a little to help on or I shall be left in the Lurch—with the burden of a little Pride—However I look in time—The Dilkes like their lodging in Westminster tolerably well. I cannot help thinking what a shame it is that poor Dilke should give up his

3. Keats broke with Charles Wells over a hoax on Tom in which Wells sent Tom love letters supposedly by "Amena Bellefila"; Tom was taken in, and Keats believed that his health suffered when he learned he had been tricked.
4. Samuel Richardson (1689–1761), author of such epistolary novels as *Clarissa* (1747–1749).
5. The private collection of British art of Sir John Fleming Leicester (1762–1827) was open to the public on most Mondays from March 15 to May 17.
6. For Bewick and Hilton, see p. 117, n. 9 and p. 141, n. 7; Bewick also recalled being at the gallery with Hunt, Haydon, the Landseers, and Keats, and their being introduced to Sir John and Lady Leicester (see Thomas Landseer's *Life and Letters of William Bewick* [1871], 2: 169–70). James *Northcote* (1746–1831), history and portrait painter, was a friend of Hazlitt's who later published his *Conversations* (1830).
7. Refers to the Quaker preacher Simon Pure from *Bold Stroke for a Wife* (1718) by Susanna Centlivre (1669?–1723). Wordsworth's *Peter Bell. A Tale in Verse*, written in 1798 but published in 1819, was met with derision by the circle around Hunt. Reynolds published his parodic *Peter Bell* on April 16, 1819, before Wordsworth's poem was released at the end of the month; Keats published a review in the *Examiner*, April 25, 1819, p. 270, which he copies out below, p. 328. Hunt reviewed Wordsworth's poem in the *Examiner*, May 2, 1819, pp. 282–83 (*SWLH*, 2: 186–90) and then contrasted it to Shelley's *Rosalind and Helen* in the *Examiner*, May 9, 1819, pp. 302–303 (*SWLH*, 2: 191–95). Shelley would write his *Peter Bell the Third* by October, though it was not published until 1839.

comfortable house & garden for his Son, whom he will certainly ruin with too much care—The boy has nothing in his ears all day but himself and the importance of his education—Dilke has continually in his mouth "My Boy." This is what spoils princes: it may have the same effect with Commoners. Mrs Dilke has been very well lately—But what a shameful thing it is that for that obstinate Boy Dilke should stifle himself in Town Lodgings and wear out his Life by his continual apprehension of his Boys fate in Westministerschool, with the rest of the Boys and the Masters—Evey one has some wear and tear—One would think Dilke ought to be quiet and happy—but no—this one Boy—makes his face pale, his society silent and his vigilance jealous—He would I have no doubt quarrel with any one who snubb'd his Boy—With all this he has no notion how to manage him. O what a farce is our greatest cares! Yet one must be in the pother for the sake of Clothes food and Lodging. There has been a squabble between Kean and one Mr Bucke[8]—There are faults on both sides—on Bucks the faults are positive to the Question: Keans fault is a want of genteel knowledge and high Policy—The formor writes knavishly foolish and the other silly bombast. It was about a Tragedy written by said Mr Bucke; which it appears Mr Kean kick'd at—it was so bad—. After a little struggle of Mr Bucke's against Kean—drury Lane had the Policy to bring it on and Kean the impolicy not to appear in it—It was damn'd—The people in the Pit had a favouite call on the night of "Buck Buck rise up" and "Buck Buck how many horns do I hold up.[9] Kotzebue the German Dramatist and traitor to his country was murdered lately by a young student whose name I forget—he stabbed himself immediately after crying out Germany! Germany![1] I was unfortunate to miss Richards the only time I have been for many months to see him. Shall I treat you with a little extempore.

[A copy of "When they were come unto the Faery's Court" follows.]
Brown is gone to bed—and I am tired of rhyming—there is a north wind blowing playing young gooseberry with the trees—I dont care so it heps even with a side wind a Letter to me—for I cannot put faith in any reports I hear of the Settlement some are good some bad—Last Sunday I took a Walk towards highgate and in the lane that winds by the side of Lord Mansfield's park I met Mr Green our Demonstrator at Guy's in conversation with Coleridge[2]—I joined them, after enquiring by a look whether it would be agreeable. I walked with him at his alderman-after dinner pace for near two miles I suppose. In those two Miles he broached a thousand things—let me

8. Charles Bucke (1781–1846) had his play *The Italians; or, The Fatal Accusation* accepted for performance at Drury Lane in 1817, but it did not reach the stage until April 3 and 12, 1819, by which time Kean had raised objections to the play and Bucke had tried to have its performance stopped. Bucke complained of his treatment by Kean and the theater in the preface to the printed version of his play, which, because of the controversy, went through seven editions in 1819. Keats could have read of the matter in the *Examiner*, April 4, 11, and 18, 1819, pp. 222–23, 238, 251–52.
9. A children's game.
1. The German playwright August von Kotzebue (1761–1819), author of *The Stranger* and *Lover's Vows*, was murdered by Karl Ludwig Sand who considered the author a tool of the Russian czar. Keats could have read of the assassination in the *Examiner*, April 4 and 11, 1819, pp. 219, 225, and 233.
2. Coleridge recalled the meeting in his *Table Talk* for August 14, 1832. Joseph Henry Green (1791–1863) was a surgeon, natural philosopher, and later coeditor of Coleridge's literary remains. Keats met them near Kenwood, the seat of the lord chief justice, William Murray, first Earl of Mansfield (1705–1793). "Playing *old* gooseberry" means wreaking havoc.

see if I can give you a list—Nightingales, Poetry—on Poetical sensation—
Metaphysics—Different genera and species of Dreams—Nightmare—a
dream accompanied by a sense of touch—single and double touch—A
dream related—First and second consciousness—the difference explained
between will and Volition—so many metaphysicians from a want of smok-
ing the second consiousness—Monsters—the Kraken[3]—Mermaids—
southey believes in them—southeys belief too much diluted—A Ghost
story—Good morning—I heard his voice as he came towards me—I heard
it as he moved away—I had heard it all the interval—if it may be called so.
He was civil enough to ask me to call on him at Highgate Good Night! It
looks so much like rain I shall not go to town to day;[4] but put it off till
tomorrow—Brown this morning is writing some spenserian stanzas against
M[rs] Miss Brawne and me; so I shall amuse myself with him a little: in the
manner of Spenser—

[A copy of "He is to weet a melancholy Carle" follows.]

This character would ensure him a situation in the establishment of patient
Griselda[5]—The servant has come for the little Browns this morning—they
have been a toothache to me which I shall enjoy the riddance of—Their
little voices are like wasps stings—'Some times am I all wound with
Browns'.[6] We had a claret feast some little while ago There were Dilke,
Reynolds, Skinner, Mancur, John Brown, Martin,[7] Brown and I—We all got
a little tipsy—but pleasantly so—I enjoy Claret to a degree—I have been
looking over the correspondence of the pretended Amena and Wells this
evening[8]—I now see the whole cruel deception—I think Wells must have
had an accomplice in it—Amena's letters are in a Man's language, and in a
Man's hand imitating a woman's—The instigations to this diabolical
scheme were vanity, and the love of intrigue. It was no thoughtless hoax—
but a cruel deception on a sanguine Temperament, with every show of
friendship. I do not think death too bad for the villain. The world would
look upon it in a different light should I expose it—they would call it a
frolic—so I must wary—but I consider it my duty to be prudently revengeful. I will hang over his head like a sword by a hair. I will be opium to his
vanity—if I cannot injure his interests—He is a rat and he shall have ratsbane to his vanity—I will harm him all I possibly can—I have no doubt I
shall be able to do so—Let us leave him to his misery alone except when
we can throw in a little more—The fifth canto of Dante pleases me more
and more—it is that one in which he meets with Paulo and Francesca—I
had passed many days in rather a low state of mind and in the midst of them
I dreamt of being in that region of Hell. The dream was one of the most
delightful enjoyments I ever had in my life—I floated about the whirling
atmosphere as it is described with a beautiful figure to whose lips mine
were joined at it seem'd for an age—and in the midst of all this cold and
darkness I was warm—even flowery tree tops sprung up and we rested on

---

3. A mythical sea monster.
4. Keats is now writing on April 16.
5. A figure from folklore who is a character in tales by Boccaccio and Chaucer; Maria Edgeworth published *The Modern Griselda* in 1804.
6. See Shakespeare, *The Tempest*, 2.2.12–13, where Caliban says "sometime am I / All wound with
   adders."
7. See p. 89, n. 8. Skinner is Charles Brown's lawyer. Mancur is perhaps John Mancur, a wholesale
   hosier. John Brown is Charles Brown's brother.
8. See above, p. 324, n. 3.

them sometimes with the lightness of a cloud till the wind blew us away again—I tried a Sonnet upon it—there are fourteen lines but nothing of what I felt in it—o that I could dream it every night—

[A copy of "A dream, after reading Dante's Episode of Paolo and Francesca" follows.][9]

I want very very much a little of your wit my dear sister—a Letter or two of yours just to bandy back a pun or two across the Atlantic and send a quibble over the Floridas—Now you have by this time crumpled up your large Bonnet, what do you wear—a cap! do you put your hair in papers of a night? do you pay the Miss Birkbeck's a morning visit—have you any tea? or to you milk and water with them—What place of Worship do you go to—the Quakers the Moravians, the Unitarians or the Methodists—Are there any flowers in bloom you like—any beautiful heaths—Any Streets full of Corset Makers. What sort of shoes have you to fit those pretty feet of yours? Do you desire Comp^ts to one another? Do you ride on Horseback? What do you have for breakfast, dinner and supper? without mentioning lunch and bever and wet[1] and snack—and a bit to stay one's stomach—Do you get any spirits—now you might easily distill some whiskey—and going into the woods set up a whiskey shop for the Monkeys—Do you and the miss Birkbecks get groggy on any thing—a little so so ish so as to be obliged to be seen home with a Lantern—You may perhaps have a game at puss in the corner—Ladies are warranted to play at this game though they have not whiskers. Have you a fiddle in the Settlement—or at any rate a jew's harp—which will play in spite of ones teeth—When you have nothing else to do for a whole day I tell you how you may employ it—First get up and when you are dress'd, as it would be pretty early, with a high wind in the woods give George a cold Pig[2] with my Complements. Then you may saunter into the nearest coffee-house and after taking a dram and a look at the chronicle—go and frighten the wild boars upon the strength—you may as well bring one home for breakfast serving up the hoofs garnished with bristles and a grunt or two to accompany the singing of the kettle—then if George is not up give him a colder Pig always with my Compliments—When you are both set down to breakfast I advise you to eat your full share—but leave off immediately on feeling yourself inclined to any thing on the other side of the puffy—avoid that for it does not become young women—After you have eaten your breakfast—keep your eye upon dinner—it is the safest way—You should keep a Hawk's eye over your dinner and keep hovering over it till due time then pounce taking care not to break any plates—While you are hovering with your dinner in prospect you may do a thousand things—put a hedgehog into George's hat—pour a little water into his rifle—soak his boots in a pail of water—cut his jacket round into shreds like a roman kilt or the back of my grandmothers stays—sow *off* his buttons.

Yesterday[3] I could not write a line I was so fatigued for the day before, I went to town in the morning called on your Mother, and returned in time for a few friends we had to dinner. There were Taylor Woodhouse,

9. See p. 336, below.
1. A glass of liquor; *bever*: a small repast between meals.
2. Waking someone up by pulling off the covers and dousing him or her with cold water.
3. Keats is writing on April 21.

Reynolds—we began cards at about 9 o'Clock, and the night coming on and continuing dark and rainy they could not think of returning to town—so we played at Cards till very daylight—and yesterday I was not worth a sixpence—Your mother was very well but anxious for a Letter. We had half an hours talk and no more for I was obliged to be home. M^rs and Miss Millar were well—and so was Miss Waldegrave[4]—I have asked your Brothers here for next Sunday—When Reynolds was here on Monday—he asked me to give Hunt a hint to take notice of his Peter Bell in the Examiner—the best thing I can do is to write a little notice of it myself which I will do here and copy it out if it should suit my Purpose[5]—*Peter-Bell* There have been lately advertized two Books both Peter Bell by name; what stuff the one was made of might be seen by the motto, 'I am the real Simon Pure'. This false florimel[6] has hurried from the press and obtruded herself into public notice while for ought we know the real one may be still wandering about the woods and mountains. Let us hope she may soon appear and make good her right to the magic girdle—The Pamphleteering Archimage we can perceive has rather a splenetic love than a downright hatred to real florimels— if indeed they had been so christened—or had even a pretention to play at bob cherry with Barbara Lewthwaite: but he has a fixed aversion to those three rhyming Graces Alice Fell, Susan Gale and Betty Foy;[7] and now at length especially to Peter Bell—fit Apollo. It may be seen from one or two passages in this little skit, that the writer of it has felt the finer parts of Mr Wordsworth and perhaps expatiated with his more remote and sublimer muse; This as far as it relates to Peter Bell is unlucky. The more he may love the sad embroidery of the Excursion; the more he will hate the coarse Samplers of Betty Foy and Alice Fell; and as they come from the same hand, the better will be able to imitate that which can be imitated, to wit Peter Bell— as far as can be imagined from the obstinate Name—We repeat, it is very unlucky—this real Simon Pure is in parts the very Man—There is a pernicious likeness in the scenery a 'pestilent humour' in the rhymes and an inveterate cadence in some of the Stanzas that must be lamented—If we are one part amused at this we are three parts sorry that an appreciator of Wordsworth should show so much temper at this really provoking name of Peter Bell—! This will do well enough—I have coppied it and enclosed it to Hunt—You will call it a little politic—seeing I keep clear of all parties. I say something for and against both parties—and suit it to the tune of the examiner—I mean to say I do not unsuit it—and I believe I think what I say nay I am sure I do—I and my conscience are in luck to day—which is an excellent thing—The other night I went to the Play with Rice, Reynolds and Martin—we saw a new dull and half damnd opera call'd 'the heart of Mid Lothian' that was on Saturday[8]—I stopt at Taylors on sunday with Woodhouse—and passed a quiet sort of pleasant day. I have been very much pleased with the Panorama of the ships at the north Pole—with the icebergs, the Mountains, the Bears the Walrus—the seals the Penguins—

---

4. See p. 288, n. 5.
5. Keats copies, not always precisely, from his review in the *Examiner*, April 25, 1819, p. 270.
6. See Spenser, *The Faerie Queene*, 3.8, for the deceitful copy of Florimel.
7. Betty Foy and Susan Gale appear in "The Idiot Boy"; Barbara Lethwaite is the child heroine of Wordsworth's "The Pet Lamb"; Alice Fell has a poem named for her.
8. Keats saw at Covent Garden Daniel Terry's adaptation of Scott's novel into a musical drama, with the score by Sir Henry Rowley Bishop (1786–1855).

and a large whale floating back above water—it is impossible to describe the place[9]—Wednesday Evening—
[A copy of "La Belle Dame Sans Merci" follows.][1]
Why four kisses—you will say—why four because I wish to restrain the headlong impetuosity of my Muse—she would have fain said 'score' without hurting the rhyme—but we must temper the Imagination as the Critics say with Judgment. I was obliged to choose an even number that both eyes might have fair play: and to speak truly I think two a piece quite sufficient—Suppose I had said seven; there would have been three and a half a piece—a very awkward affair—and well got out of on my side—
[A copy of "Song of Four Fairies" follows.][2]
I have been reading lately two very different books Robertson's America and Voltaire's Siecle De Louis xiv [3] It is like walking arm and arm between Pizarro[4] and the great-little Monarch. In How lementable a case do we see the great body of the people in both instances: in the first, where Men might seem to inherit quiet of Mind from unsophisticated senses; from uncontamination of civilisation; and especially from their being as it were estranged from the mutual helps of Society and its mutual injuries—and thereby more immediately under the Protection of Providence—even there they had mortal pains to bear as bad; or even worse than Baliffs, Debts and Poverties of civilised Life—The whole appears to resolve into this—that Man is originally 'a poor forked creature'[5] subject to the same mischances as the beasts of the forest, destined to hardships and disquietude of some kind or other. If he improves by degrees his bodily accomodations and comforts—at each stage, at each accent there are waiting for him a fresh set of annoyances—he is mortal and there is still a heaven with its Stars above his head. The most interesting question that can come before us is, How far by the persevering endeavours of a seldom appearing Socrates Mankind may be made happy—I can imagine such happiness carried to an extreme—but what must it end in?—Death—and who could in such a case bear with death—the whole troubles of life which are now frittered away in a series of years, would then be accumulated for the last days of a being who instead of hailing its approach, would leave this world as Eve left Paradise—But in truth I do not at all believe in this sort of perfectibility— the nature of the world will not admit of it—the inhabitants of the world will correspond to itself—Let the fish philosophise the ice away from the Rivers in winter time and they shall be at continual play in the tepid delight of summer. Look at the Poles and at the sands of Africa, Whirlpools and volcanoes—Let men exterminate them and I will say that they may arrive at earthly Happiness—The point at which Man may arrive is as far as the paralel state in inanimate nature and no further. For instance suppose a rose to have sensation, it blooms on a beautiful morning, it enjoys itself— but there comes a cold wind, a hot sun—it cannot escape it, it cannot

---

9. Keats went around April 17 to see Henry Aston Barker's panorama "representing the north coast of Spitzbergen" that had opened on April 12 in Leicester Square.
1. See pp. 338–43.
2. See p. 343–45.
3. William Robertson (1721–1793), *The History of America* (1777); Keats owned a copy of Voltaire's five-volume *Le Siècle de Louis XIV*.
4. Francisco Pizarro (c. 1476–1541), Spanish conquistador and conqueror of Peru.
5. See Shakespeare, *King Lear*, 3.4.99–100, where Lear describes man as a "poor, bare, forked animal."

destroy its annoyances—they are as native to the world as itself: no more can man be happy in spite, the worldy elements will prey upon his nature— The common cognomen of this world among the misguided and superstitious is 'a vale of tears' from which we are to be redeemed by a certain arbitrary interposition of God and taken to Heaven—What a little circumscribed straightened notion! Call the world if you Please "The vale of Soulmaking." Then you will find out the use of the world (I am speaking now in the highest terms for human nature admitting it to be immortal which I will here take for granted for the purpose of showing a thought which has struck me concerning it) I say "Soul making." Soul as distinguished from an Intelligence. There may be intelligences or sparks of the divinity in millions—but they are not Souls till they acquire identities, till each one is personally itself. Intelligences are atoms of perception—they know and they see and they are pure, in short they are God—how then are Souls to be made? How then are these sparks which are God to have identity given them—so as ever to possess a bliss peculiar to each ones individual existence? How, but by the medium of a world like this? This point I sincerely wish to consider because I think it a grander system of salvation than the chrystain religion—or rather it is a system of Spirit-creation—This is effected by three grand materials acting the one upon the other for a series of years—These three Materials are the *Intelligence*—the *human heart* (as distinguished from intelligence or Mind) and the *World* or *Elemental space* suited for the proper action of *Mind* and *Heart* on each other for the purpose of forming the *Soul* or *Intelligence destined to possess the sense of Identity*. I can scarcely express what I but dimly perceive—and yet I think I perceive it—that you may judge the more clearly I will put it in the most homely form possible—I will call the *world* a School instituted for the purpose of teaching little children to read—I will call the *human heart* the *horn Book* used in that School—and I will call *the Child able to read, the Soul* made from that *school* and its *hornbook*. Do you not see how necessary a World of Pains and troubles is to school an Intelligence and make it a soul? A Place where the heart must feel and suffer in a thousand diverse ways! Not merely is the Heart a Hornbook, It is the Minds Bible, it is the Minds experience, it is the teat from which the Mind or intelligence sucks its identity. As various as the Lives of Men are—so various become their souls, and thus does God make individual beings, Souls, Identical Souls of the sparks of his own essence. This appears to me a faint sketch of a system of Salvation which does not affront our reason and humanity—I am convinced that many difficulties which christians labour under would vanish before it—There is one which even now Strikes me—the Salvation of Children—In them the Spark or intelligence returns to God without any identity—it having had no time to learn of, and be altered by, the heart— or seat of the human Passions—It is pretty generally suspected that the christian scheme has been coppied from the ancient persian and greek Philosophers. Why may they not have made this simple thing even more simple for common apprehension by introducing Mediators and Personages in the same manner as in the hethen mythology abstractions are personified— Seriously I think it probable that this System of Soul-making—may have been the Parent of all the more palpable and personal Schemes of Redemption, among the Zoroastrians the Christians and the Hindoos. For as one part of the human species must have their carved Jupiter; so another part must have the palpable and named Mediator and saviour, their Christ their Oromanes and their Vishnu[6]—If what I have said should not be plain enough, as I fear it may not be, I will put you in the place where I began in this series of thoughts—I mean, I began by seeing how man was formed by circumstances—and what are circumstances?—but touchstones of his heart—? and what are touch stones?—but proovings of his hearrt?—and what are proovings of his heart but fortifiers or alterers of his nature? and what is his altered nature but his soul?—and what was his soul before it came into the world and had These provings and alterations and perfectionings?—An intelligence—without Identity—and how is this Identity to be made? Through the medium of the Heart? And how is the heart to become this Medium but in a world of Circumstances?— There now I think what with Poetry and Theology you may thank your Stars that my pen is not very long winded—Yesterday I received two Letters from your Mother and Henry which I shall send by young Birkbeck with this—

Friday—April 30—Brown has been rummaging up some of my old sins— that is to say sonnets I do not think you remember them, so I will copy them out as well as two or three lately written—I have just written one on Fame—which Brown is transcribing and he has his book and mine I must employ myself perhaps in a sonnet on the same subject—

[Copies of the two sonnets on fame and "To Sleep" follow.][7]

The following Poem—the last I have written is the first and the only one with which I have taken even moderate pains—I have for the most part dash'd of my lines in a hurry. This I have done leisurely—I think it reads the more richly for it and will I hope encourage me to write other thing in even a more peacable and healthy spirit. You must recollect that Psyche was not embodied as a goddess before the time of Apulieus the Platonist who lived afteir the Agustan age, and consequently the Goddess was never worshipped or sacrificed to with any of the ancient fervour—and perhaps never thought of in the old religion—I am more orthodox than to let a hethen Goddess be so neglected—

[A copy of "Ode to Psyche" follows.][8]
Here endethe yᵉ Ode to Psyche

————

Incipit altera Sonneta.

————

I have been endeavouring to discover a better sonnet stanza than we have. The legitimate does not suit the language over-well from the pouncing rhymes—the other kind appears too elegiac—and the couplet at the end of it has seldom a pleasing effect—I do not pretend to have succeeded—It will explain itself—

6. Keats had read "The History of the Merchant Abudah: Or, The Talisman of Oromanes" in the popular *Tales of the Genii; Or, The Delightful Lessons of Horam, the Son of Asmar* (1764) by James Ridley. Zoroastrianism had also been taken up by Byron in *Manfred* (1817) and Peacock in his unfinished *Ahrimanes*. Keats could have learned of Hinduism from the work of Sir William Jones among other places.
7. See pp. 346–47.
8. For the poem and Keats's source, Apuleius, see pp. 463–65.

[A copy of "If by dull rhymes our English must be chain'd" follows.]⁹
Here endeth the other Sonnet—
This is the 3ᵈ of May & every thing is in delightful forwardness; the violets
are not withered, before the peeping of the first rose—Yesterday I walked
to Walhamstow through the fields, through Highgate, Horsey—and
Tottenham—I call'd in my way on the Hamptons—they were well; but she
has grown so much bodily as to be thin and I not think very strong. Mʳˢ
Abbey was ill, and Miss Abby looks not much better—Fanny is very sensible in my mind—she does not grow very pretty. We took a walk in the Garden and about the Village. She complains about Mrs. Abbey's behaviour—I
long to send her some Letters from you. I only want some Letters from you
to make the spring in proper time.
Wednesday May 4—I went to Town this morning and calling at Taylors
they tell me that I must let young Birbeck have the Packet immediately—
so I shall seal it tonight and be in Town early tomorrow morning—I hope
I shall see him—for the sake of his seeing you afterwards. I have been
waiting for Taylor to perform his promise of inviting young B. to meet me
at his House—I suppose he has had no opportunity. I have heard to day
that the Packets from Illinois had been robbed and that accounts for
my not having received any Letters. This I have been very uneasy about;
and have constantly kept your mother from any despondence about it.
Rice and Reynolds came with me from Town and drank Tea—they
both desire particularly their Remembrances. You must let me know
every thing, how parcels come and go—what Papers Birbeck has and
what newspapers you want and other things. God bless you, my dear
Brother & Sister.

Your ever Affectionate Brother
John Keats—

Letter to B. R. Haydon, March 8, 1819¹

Wentworth Place.

My dear Haydon,
    You must be wondering where I am and what I about! I am mostly at
Hampstead, and about nothing; being in a sort of qui bono² temper, not
exactly on the road to an epic poem. Nor must you think I have forgotten
you. No, I have about every three days been to Abbey's and to the
Lawyers. Do let me know how you have been getting on, and in what spirits you are.
    You got out gloriously in yesterday's Examiner.³ What a set of little people
we live amongst. I went the other day into an ironmonger's shop, without any

9. See p. 347.
1. Text from Forman's 1901 edition, 5: 14–15, with a transcript of the next to last paragraph, begin-
    ning with the second sentence, appearing in Sotheby's sale catalogue, *Catalogue of Valuable Auto-
    graph Letters and Historical Documents*, March 11–12, 1898 (London: Sotheby, Wilkinson, and
    Hodge, 1898), p. 17, #179.
2. "Cui bono": "to whose advantage" (see Cicero, *Pro Milone*, 12); the principle that responsibility
    for an event lies with the person who has something to gain.
3. In January and February 1819, Haydon and his pupils exhibited chalk copies of Raphael's cartoons
    and the Elgin Marbles, first privately at 29 St. James's Street and then at 87 Pall Mall. They were
    attacked in the *New Monthly Magazine* 9 (May 1819): 321–24, and Haydon responded to these
    attacks in "Attacks on Mr. Haydon," the *Examiner*, March 7, 1819, pp. 157–58.

change in my sensations—men and tin kettles are much the same in these days. They do not study like children at five and thirty, but they talk like men at twenty. Conversation is not a search after knowledge, but an endeavour at effect. In this respect two most opposite men, Wordsworth and Hunt, are the same. A friend of mine observed the other day that if Lord Bacon[4] were to make any remark in a party of the present day, the conversation would stop on the sudden. I am convinced of this, and from this I have come to the resolution never to write for the sake of writing, or making a poem, but from running over with any little knowledge and experience which many years of reflection may perhaps give me—otherwise I will be dumb. What Imagination I have I shall enjoy, and greatly, for I have experienced the satisfaction of having great conceptions without the toil of sonnetteering. I will not spoil my love of gloom by writing an ode to darkness; and with respect to my livelihood I will not write for it, for I will not mix with that most vulgar of all crowds the literary. Such things I ratify by looking upon myself, and trying myself at lifting mental weights, as it were. I am three and twenty with little knowledge and middling intellect. It is true that in the height of enthusiasm I have been cheated into some fine passages, but that is nothing.

I have not been to see you because all my going out has been to town, and that has been a great deal. Write soon.

Yours constantly,
John Keats

[Why did I laugh to-night? No voice will tell][1]

WHY did I laugh tonight? No voice will tell:
　No God, no Demon of severe response,
Deigns to reply from Heaven or from Hell.
　Then to my human heart I turn at once—
Heart! thou and I are here sad and alone;　　　　　　　5
　Say, wherefore[2] did I laugh? O mortal pain!
O Darkness! Darkness! ever must I moan,
　To question Heaven and Hell and Heart in vain!
Why did I laugh? I know this being's lease,
　My fancy to its utmost blisses spreads:　　　　　　10
Yet could I on this very midnight cease,
　And the world's gaudy ensigns see in shreds.
Verse, Fame, and Beauty are intense indeed,
But Death intenser—Death is Life's high meed.

---

4. Francis Bacon (1561–1626), Baron Verulam and Viscount St. Albans, English philosopher, essayist, and statesman.
1. Written in March 1819 before being included in a journal letter to George and Georgiana Keats on the 19th, where Keats says, "I did not intend to have sent you the following sonnet—but . . . ask yourselves whether I have not that in me which will bear the buffets of the world. It will be the best comment on my poem; it will show you that it was written with no Agony but that of ignorance; with no thirst of any thing but knowledge . . . the first steps to it were through my human passions—they went away, and I wrote with my Mind—and perhaps I must confess a little bit of my heart" (see p. 323, above). First printed as Sonnet XV in 1848, 2: 301; text from 1848 with emendations from the letter holograph (Harvard MS Keats 1.53).
2. 1848 has a corrupted reading, "I say, why."

ODE ON INDOLENCE.[1]

"They toil not, neither do they spin."[2]

I

ONE morn before me were three figures seen,
    With bowed necks, and joined hands, side-faced;
And one behind the other stepp'd serene,
    In placid sandals, and in white robes graced:
    They pass'd, like figures on a marble urn,   5
When shifted round to see the other side;[3]
They came again; as when the urn once more
    Is shifted round, the first seen shades return;
    And they were strange to me, as may betide
With vases, to one deep in Phidian[4] lore.   10

II

How is it, Shadows, that I knew ye not?
    How came ye muffled in so hush a masque?[5]
Was it a silent deep-disguised plot
    To steal away, and leave without a task
    My idle days? Ripe was the drowsy hour;   15
The blissful cloud of summer-indolence
Benumb'd my eyes; my pulse grew less and less;
    Pain had no sting, and pleasure's wreath no flower:[6]
    O, why did ye not melt, and leave my sense
Unhaunted quite of all but—nothingness?[7]   20

1. Written in the spring of 1819, this ode, the only one of the Spring odes not included by Keats in his 1820 volume, has often been seen as being written after the others, with Allott, for example, arguing that the adoption of the stanza form of "Ode on a Grecian Urn" and "Ode on Melancholy" and the reference in l. 46 to May suggest it was written at the end of that month. It was certainly written by June 9, 1819, when Keats wrote to Sarah Jeffrey, "You will judge of my 1819 temper when I tell you that the thing I have most enjoyed this year has been writing an ode to Indolence" (L, 2: 116). However, it seems plausible that Keats wrote the ode as early as mid-March, for he wrote to the George Keatses on March 19, "This morning I am in a sort of temper indolent and supremely careless: I long after a stanza or two of Thompson's Castle of Indolence. . . . Neither Poetry, nor Ambition, nor Love have any alertness of countenance as they pass by me: they seem rather like figures on a greek vase—A man and two women—whom no one but myself could distinguish in their disguisement" (see above, p. 321; he spoke of "indolence" on March 17 as well, see p. 320). Similarities between phrases in this ode and the wording of other odes may suggest either that Keats "languidly echoes" (Bate, p. 528) earlier poems or that he developed these images in later odes. First published in 1848, 2: 276–78; text from 1848 with emendations from Brown's transcript (Harvard MS Keats 3.6, p. 19–22; MYR: JK, 7:21–24). Brown initially had the stanzas in the wrong order, suggesting he copied the ode from several sheets, and thus Gittings (1968, 311n.) argues that Brown confused the composition of "Indolence" with that of the Nightingale ode when he wrote of an ode being recovered from "some scraps of paper" (KC, 2: 65).
2. Matthew 6.28: "Consider the lilies of the field, how they grow; they toil not, neither do they spin."
3. These lines bring to mind the "Ode on a Grecian Urn"; the language may also recall Hunt's description of Francesca's Grecian temple in Story of Rimini (1816) 3: 464–85 with its nymphs "sidelong-eyed" and their "forgotten urns."
4. Phidias (c. 490–c. 448 B.C.E.), famed Athenian sculptor whose works included the sculptures of the Parthenon known as the Elgin Marbles (see p. 72, n. 1).
5. A "form of courtly dramatic entertainment, often richly symbolic, in which music and dancing played a substantial part, costumes and stage machinery tended to be elaborate, and the audience might be invited to contribute to the action or the dancing" (OED). Also written as "mask."
6. Keats wrote of indolence to the George Keatses on March 19, "In this state of effeminacy the fibres of the brain are relaxed in common with the rest of the body, and to such a happy degree that pleasure has no show of enticement and pain no unbearable frown" (see p. 321).
7. See "Ode to a Nightingale," ll. 19–21: "That I might drink, and leave the world unseen, / And with thee fade away into the forest dim: / Fade far away, dissolve, and quite forget."

III

A third time pass'd they by, and, passing, turn'd
  Each one the face a moment whiles to me;
Then faded, and to follow them I burn'd
  And ached for wings,[8] because I knew the three:
    The first was a fair Maid, and Love her name;   25
  The second was Ambition, pale of cheek,
And ever watchful with fatigued eye;
    The last, whom I love more, the more of blame
  Is heap'd upon her, maiden most unmeek,—
I knew to be my demon Poesy.   30

IV

They faded, and, forsooth! I wanted wings:
  O folly! What is Love? and where is it?
And for that poor Ambition! it springs
  From a man's little heart's short fever-fit;[9]
    For Poesy!—no,—she has not a joy,—   35
  At least for me,—so sweet as drowsy noons,
And evenings steep'd in honied indolence;
    O, for an age so shelter'd from annoy,
  That I may never know how change the moons,
Or hear the voice of busy common-sense!   40

V

A third time[1] came they by;—alas! wherefore?
  My sleep had been embroider'd with dim dreams;
My soul had been a lawn besprinkled o'er
  With flowers, and stirring shades, and baffled beams:
    The morn was clouded, but no shower fell,   45
  Tho' in her lids hung the sweet tears of May;
The open casement[2] press'd a new-leaved vine,
  Let in the budding warmth and throstle's lay;[3]
    O Shadows! 'twas a time to bid farewell!
Upon your skirts had fallen no tears of mine.   50

VI

So, ye three Ghosts, adieu! Ye cannot raise
  My head cool-bedded in the flowery grass;[4]
For I would not be dieted with praise,
  A pet-lamb in a sentimental farce![5]

---

8. See "wings of Poesy" in "Ode to a Nightingale" (l. 33).
9. See "the weariness, the fever, and the fret" in "Ode to a Nightingale" (l. 23); Allott suggests the ambitious Macbeth's words on Duncan's death, *Macbeth* 3.2.24: "After life's fitful fever he sleeps well."
1. Milnes emended this to "And once more."
2. See the use of "casement" in both "Ode to Psyche," open "to let the warm Love in" (ll. 66–67), and "Ode to a Nightingale" (l. 69), "opening on the foam / Of perilous seas."
3. The thrush's song.
4. See the "cool-rooted flowers" and the "bedded grass" of the "Ode to Psyche" (ll. 13, 15).
5. In his letter to Mary-Ann Jeffrey of June 9, 1819, Keats wrote, "I hope I am a little more of a Philosopher than I was, consequently a little less of a versifying Pet-Lamb" (see p. 349).

Fade softly from my eyes, and be once more   55
In masque-like figures on the dreamy urn;
Farewell! I yet have visions for the night,
And for the day faint visions there is store;
Vanish, ye Phantoms, from my idle spright,
Into the clouds, and never more return!   60

A DREAM,
AFTER READING DANTE'S EPISODE
OF PAULO AND FRANCESCA[1]

As Hermes once took to his feathers light,
When lulled Argus, baffled, swoon'd and slept,[2]
So on a Delphic reed my idle spright
So play'd, so charm'd, so conquer'd, so bereft
The dragon world of all its hundred eyes;   5
And, seeing it asleep, so fled away—
Not unto Ida[3] with its snow-cold skies,
Nor unto Tempe where Jove griev'd a day;
But to that second circle of sad hell,
Where 'mid the gust, the world-wind, and the flaw[4]   10
Of rain and hailstones, lovers need not tell
Their sorrows.[5] Pale were the sweet lips I saw,
Pale were the lips I kiss'd, and fair the form
I floated with about that melancholy storm.

1. Written in April 1819 sometime before Keats included the poem in a letter to the George Keatses on April 16 (see pp. 327), where he offers the following comments: "The fifth canto of Dante pleases me more and more—it is that one in which he meets with Paulo and Francesca—I had passed many days in rather a low state of mind and in the midst of them I dreamt of being in that region of Hell. The dream was one of the most delightful enjoyments I ever had in my life—I floated about the whirling atmosphere as it is described with a beautiful figure to whose lips mine were joined at it seem'd for an age—and in the midst of all this cold and darkness I was warm—even flowery tree tops sprung up and we rested on them sometimes with the lightness of a cloud till the wind blew us away again—I tried a Sonnet upon it—there are fourteen lines but nothing of what I felt in it—o that I could dream it every night." Hunt's Story of Rimini had taken up the story of Paolo and Francesca, and Byron translated the fifth canto of The Inferno which includes their story. First published over the pseudonym "Caviare" in the Indicator, June 28, 1820, p. 304; text from the Indicator with some variants noted from Keats's draft on the end paper of volume one of his copy of Cary's translation of Dante which he gave to Fanny Brawne, now at Yale (Beinecke In K226 Zz814D; facsimile in Rare Books, original Drawings, Autograph Letters and Manuscripts Collected by the Late A. Edward Newton, Parke-Bernet Sale Catalogue [New York 1941], Part Two, p. 157).
2. Hermes or Mercury, the messenger of the gods with winged feet, rescued Io, a nymph after whom Jupiter lusted, from her hundred-eyed guardian, Argus, set to watch her by Jupiter's jealous wife, Juno; Mercury lulled Argus to sleep by playing music on his pipe, a "Delphic reed" (l. 3). as it was made by Pan from reeds and Apollo's main temple was at Delphos (see Ovid, Metamorphoses, 1.688–720).
3. The draft has "Not to pure Ida." Ida is a mountain near Troy, the site of Paris's decision to award Venus the prize as the most beautiful of the gods. Tempe (l. 8) was Io's home in Thessaly, famed for its beauty; Keats may have confused it with the equally edenic Arcadia, where Ovid has Jupiter and Io meet.
4. A blast of wind, appropriate to the second circle of hell where the lovers are blown about; the rain and hail of the next line come from the third circle. The draft has "whirlwind" in this line (and "in" for "mid"), and most editors have adopted that reading. Jerome McGann, however, in The Beauty of Inflections, pp. 37–39, argues persuasively for keeping the Indicator text.
5. Though Dante's Francesca does tell her tale.

[Bright star! would I were steadfast as thou art!]

The first version of perhaps Keats's most famous sonnet has been assigned to a range of different dates, from October 1818, in Gittings's argument that the poem takes up at least in part Keats's feelings for Isabella Jones, to late 1819, when Keats's letters express his strong feelings for Fanny Brawne. Lines 7–8 have been linked to a heavy snowfall on October 22, 1819, to place the poem in the later part of that month. In order to argue for various datings, the sonnet's language has been found to echo or predict that of Keats's letter (among others) to Tom Keats of June 25–27, 1818 (pp. 251–53), Shakespeare's *Troilus and Cressida*, *Hyperion*, "Ode to a Nightingale," and "Ode on a Grecian Urn." Allott finds Keats echoing Wordsworth's *Excursion* 4: 697–99, where "Chaldean shepherds" "Looked on the polar star, as on a guide / And guardian of their course, that never closed / His steadfast eye," in ll. 1–6; and Byron's *Childe Harold* 2.27.1–3, "godly eremite / Such as on lonely Athos may be seen, / Watching at eve upon the giant height, / Which looks o'er waves," in l. 5. For most readers, the poem is now firmly associated with Keats's relationship with Fanny Brawne.

There are two quite different versions of the poem. The first version appeared in the *Plymouth and Devonport Weekly Journal* for September 27, 1838, and is derived from a transcript, dated 1819, by Brown (Harvard MS Keats 3.6, p. 60; *MYR: JK*, 7: 62); this is the first text below, from *PDWJ* with emendations from Brown's transcript. The other version of the poem appeared in facsimile in the *Union Magazine* 1 (February 1846): 156, and then as "Keats's Last Sonnet" in 1848, 2: 306. This second version was, according to Severn, written out onto a blank page in Keats's 1806 *Poetical Works of William Shakespeare*, opposite "A Lover's Complaint," while Keats was on board the *Maria Crowther* on the way to Italy in late September or early October 1820; it is also represented by Fanny Brawne's transcript on the endpaper of volume one of her copy of Cary's 1814 translation of Dante (now at Yale Beinecke Rare Book and Manuscript Library, IN K226 Zz814D). The second version below is from Keats's holograph in his Shakespeare (LMA K/BK/01/010/56, p. 220).

SONNET.

Bright star! would I were steadfast as thou art!
  Not in lone splendour hung amid the night;
Not watching, with eternal lids apart,
  Like nature's devout sleepless eremite,[1]
The morning-waters at their priestlike task   5
  Of pure ablution[2] round earth's human shores;
Or, gazing on the new soft fallen mask
  Of snow upon the mountains and the moors:—
No;—yet still steadfast, still unchangeable,
  Cheek-pillow'd on my love's white ripening breast,   10
To touch, for ever, its warm sink and swell,
  Awake, for ever, in a sweet unrest,

---

1. Hermit.
2. Act of washing clean, usually as part of a ceremony or rite.

To hear, to feel her tender taken breath,
Half passionless, and so swoon on to death.

Holograph Version

Bright Star, would I were stedfast as thou art—
    Not in lone splendor hung aloft the night,
And watching, with eternal lids apart,
    Like nature's patient, sleepless Eremite,
The moving waters at their priestlike task   5
    Of pure ablution round earth's human shores,
Or gazing on the new soft-fallen masque
    Of snow upon the mountains and the moors—
No—yet still stedfast, still unchangeable
    Pillow'd upon my fair love's ripening breast,   10
To feel for ever its soft swell and fall,
    Awake for ever in a sweet unrest,
Still, still to hear her tender-taken breath,
And so live ever—or else swoon to death—

La Belle Dame Sans Merci

"La Belle Dame Sans Merci," one of Keats best-known poems, was apparently written in a single sitting in a journal letter to George and Georgiana Keats on either April 21, 1819 (the date assigned by Rollins), or April 28 (the dating depends upon which Saturday production of Daniel Terry's *Heart of Midlothian* Keats saw; he saw it "on Saturday," and the play was performed on both the 17th and the 24th, with the poem being composed on a following Wednesday evening). The poem has been read autobiographically, as taking up "Love [for Fanny Brawne], Death by Consumption . . . and Poetry" (as Robert Graves put it in *The White Goddess* [1948], p. 378), and as a distillation of a romance tradition running from Alain Chartier, whose "La Belle Dame Sans Merci" (1424) provided the title, through Dante, Spenser and the various enchantresses in *The Faerie Queene*, William Browne's *Britannia's Pastorals*, and Robert Burton's *Anatomy of Melancholy* to the poetry of Wordsworth, Coleridge, and Hunt; it also draws on the ballad tradition, as represented, for example, in Scott's *Minstrelsy of the Scottish Border* (1802) and the reworking of that tradition in *Lyrical Ballads* (1798). As Allott notes, it was a particular favorite among the Pre-Raphaelites, with Rossetti, for example, praising its "real medievalism" and William Morris identifying it as the "germ" from which the group's poetry had developed.

The poem was first published in Hunt's *Indicator* 1 (May 10, 1820): 248 in a piece by Hunt entitled "La Belle Dame Sans Mercy" (*SWLH* 2: 257–60, whose editors point out that the issue also contained an English translation of Rousseau's monodrama on art and desire, *Pygmalion*); it appeared over the signature, "Caviare," which echoes *Hamlet* 2.2.418, where Hamlet notes of a play that was not popular, " 'Twas caviare to the general." Hunt's comments accompanying Keats's poem are worth excerpting at length:

> Among the pieces printed at the end of Chaucer's works [the 1782 edition of *The Poetical Works of Geoffrey Chaucer* would have been

known to Keats], and attributed to him, is a translation, under this title, of a poem of the celebrated Alan Chartier, Secretary to Charles the Sixth and Seventh. It was the title which suggested to a friend the verses at the end of the present number. We wish Alain could have seen them. He would have found a Troubadour air for them, and sung them to La Belle Dame Agnes Sorel, who was however not Sans Mercy. The union of the imaginative and the real is very striking throughout, particularly in the dream. The wild gentleness of the rest of the thoughts and of the music are all alike old; and they are also alike young; for love and imagination are always young, let them bring with them what time and accompaniments they may. If we take real flesh and blood with us, we may throw ourselves, on the facile wings of our sympathy, into what age we please. It is only by trying to feel, as well as to fancy, through the medium of a costume, that writers become mere fleshless masks and cloaks,—things like the trophies of the ancients, when they hung up the empty armour of an enemy. A hopeless lover would still feel these verses, in spite of the introduction of something unearthly. Indeed any lover, truly touched, or any body capable of being so, will feel them; because love itself resembles a visitation; and the kindest looks, which bring with them an inevitable portion of happiness because they seem happy themselves, haunt us with a spell-like power, which makes us shudder to guess at the sufferings of those who can be fascinated by unkind ones.

People however need not be much alarmed at the thought of such suffering now-a-days; not at least in some countries. Since the time when ladies, and cavaliers, and poets, and the lovers of nature, felt that humanity was a high and not a mean thing, love in general has become either a grossness or a formality. The modern systems of morals would ostensibly divide women into two classes, those who have no charity, and those who have no restraint; while men, poorly conversant with the latter, and rendered indifferent to the former, acquire bad ideas of both. Instead of the worship of Love, we have the worship of Mammon; and all the difference we can see between the sufferings attending on either is, that the sufferings from the worship of Love exalt and humanize us, and those from the worship of Mammon debase and brutalize. Between the delights there is no comparison.—Still our uneasiness keeps our knowledge going on.

The *Indicator* version differs significantly from the letter draft that, according to Stillinger's recreation of the poem's composition, led to a now lost holograph copied both by Woodhouse in W^2 and by Brown, who supplied the text for 1848. The Brown/1848 version—based on Keats's earlier handling of the poem—has been preferred by most commentators, with Bate (following Colvin's earlier attack on the *Indicator* text), for example, arguing that "The revisions [in the *Indicator*] were made when Keats was far too ill to have any confidence at all in his own judgment (early May, 1820). . . . One can only suppose that Hunt—possibly Woodhouse—thought, with myopic good-will, that the magic, dreamlike quality of the poem would be considered 'sentimental' and wished him to take a less ambiguous stand" (p. 479n.). Jerome McGann, however, in "Keats and the Historical Method in Literary Criticism," in *The Beauty of Inflections* (Oxford: Clarendon Press, 1988), pp. 25–65, argues for taking into account the calculated, self-conscious irony of the *Indicator* version, and Marjorie Levinson grounds her discussion of the poem in the existence of the two versions, with the *Indicator* standing as a parodic reconstitution of the earlier version (*Keats's Life of Allegory: The Origins of a Style* [Oxford: Basil Blackwell, 1988], pp. 45–95). For other readings of the poem, see John Barnard, "Keats's Belle Dame and the Sexual Politics of Leigh Hunt's *Indicator*," *Romanticism* 1 (1995): 34–49; Karen Swann, "Harassing the Muse," in *Romanticism and Feminism*, ed. Anne K. Mellor (Bloomington: University of Indiana Press, 1988), pp. 81–92; and Theresa M. Kelley, "Poetics and the Politics of Reception: Keats's 'La Belle Dame sans Merci'," *ELH* 54 (Summer 1987): 333–62.

Both texts are provided below, the version from the *Indicator* as printed, and the 1848 version with emendations from Brown's transcript (Harvard, MS Keats 3.6, pp. 9–11; *MYR: JK*, 7: 11–13); notes that apply to both versions appear only in the first text.

Indicator version:

LA BELLE DAME SANS MERCY.

Ah, what can ail thee, wretched wight,[1]
    Alone and palely loitering;
The sedge[2] is wither'd from the lake,
    And no birds sing.[3]

Ah, what can ail thee, wretched wight,   5
    So haggard and so woe-begone?
The squirrel's granary is full,
    And the harvest's done.

I see a lily on thy brow,
    With anguish moist and fever dew;   10
And on thy cheek a fading rose
    Fast withereth too.

I met a Lady in the meads
    Full beautiful, a fairy's child;
Her hair was long, her foot was light,   15
    And her eyes were wild.[4]

I set her on my pacing steed,
    And nothing else saw all day long;
For sideways would she lean, and sing
    A fairy's song.   20

I made a garland for her head,
    And bracelets too, and fragrant zone:
She look'd at me as she did love,
    And made sweet moan.

---

1. A person, usually with a contemptuous or derogatory tone; as McGann (see headnote) argues, "wight" evoked a double tradition, that of heroic romance and that of an ironic reworking of romance.
2. See p. 308, n. 3.
3. See William Browne, *Britannia's Pastorals* (1613), 2.1.244–45: "Within the shady woods / Let no birds sing!"
4. See Wordsworth, "Her eyes are wild" (1798).

She found me roots of relish sweet,   25
    And honey wild, and manna dew;[5]
And sure in language strange she said,
    I love thee true.

She took me to her elfin grot,
    And there she gaz'd and sighed deep,   30
And there I shut her wild sad eyes—
    So kiss'd to sleep.

And there we slumber'd on the moss,
    And there I dream'd, ah woe betide,
The latest dream I ever dream'd   35
    On the cold hill side.

I saw pale kings, and princes too,
    Pale warriors, death-pale were they all;
Who cried, "La belle Dame sans mercy[6]
    Hath thee in a thrall!"   40

I saw their starv'd lips in the gloom
    With horrid warning gaped wide,
And I awoke, and found me here
    On the cold hill side.

And this is why I sojourn here   45
    Alone and palely loitering,
Though the sedge is withere'd from the lake,
    And no birds sing.

                                    CAVIARE.

1848/Brown Version:

LA BELLE DAME SANS MERCI. A BALLAD.

I.

O WHAT can ail thee, knight-at-arms,
    Alone and palely loitering?
The sedge has wither'd from the lake,
    And no birds sing.

II.

O what can ail thee, knight-at-arms,   5
    So haggard and so woe-begone?
The squirrel's granary is full,
    And the harvest's done.

---

5. See Coleridge, "Kubla Khan," l. 53: "For he on honey-dew hath fed."
6. That is, the beautiful woman without pity.

III.

I see a lily on thy brow
  With anguish moist and fever dew, 10
And on thy cheeks a fading rose
  Fast withereth too.

IV.

I met a lady in the meads,
  Full beautiful, a fairy's child,
Her hair was long, her foot was light, 15
  And her eyes were wild.

V.

I made a garland for her head,
  And bracelets too, and fragrant zone;
She look'd at me as she did love,
  And made sweet moan. 20

VI.

I set her on my pacing steed,
  And nothing else saw all day long,
For sidelong would she bend, and sing
  A fairy's song.

VII.

She found me roots of relish sweet, 25
  And honey wild, and manna dew,
And sure in language strange she said—
  "I love thee true."

VIII.

She took me to her elfin grot,
  And there she wept, and sigh'd full sore, 30
And there I shut her wild wild eyes
  With kisses four.[7]

IX.

And there she lulled me asleep,
  And there I dream'd—Ah! woe betide!
The latest dream I ever dream'd 35
  On the cold hill's side.

---

7. In his journal letter to the George Keatses, Keats wrote, "Why four kisses—you will say—why four because I wish to restrain the headlong impetuosity of my Muse—she would fain said 'score' without hurting the rhyme—but we must temper the Imagination as the Critics say with Judgment. I was obliged to choose an even number that both eyes might have fair play: and to speak truly I think two a piece quite sufficient—Suppose I had said seven; there would have been three and a half a piece—a very awkward affair—and well got out of on my side" (see p. 329).

X.

I saw pale kings, and princes too,
   Pale warriors, death pale were they all;
They cried—"La Belle Dame sans Merci
   Hath thee in thrall!"   40

XI.

I saw their starved lips in the gloam[8]
   With horrid warning gaped wide,
And I awoke and found me here
   On the cold hill's side.

XII.

And this is why I sojourn here,   45
   Alone and palely loitering,
Though the sedge is wither'd from the lake,
   And no birds sing.

SONG OF FOUR FAIRIES,[1]

FIRE, AIR, EARTH, AND WATER,
SALAMANDER, ZEPHYR, DUSKETHA, AND BREAMA.

Sal.	HAPPY, happy glowing fire!
Zep.	Fragrant air! Delicious light!
Dus.	Let me to my glooms retire!
Bre.	I to green-weed rivers bright!
Sal.	Happy, happy glowing fire, 5

     Dazzling bowers of soft retire,
     Ever let my nourish'd wing,
     Like a bat's, still wandering,
     Faintly[2] fan your fiery spaces,
     Spirit sole in deadly places.   10
     In unhaunted roar and blaze,
     Open eyes that never daze:
     Let me see the myriad shapes
     Of men, and beasts, and fish, and apes,
     Portray'd in many a fiery den,   15

---

8. Twilight.
1. A poem in the octasyllabic couplets used in "The Eve of St. Mark," this piece was written on April 21 or 28, 1819 (see the question of the date for "La Belle Dame Sans Merci," above, p. 338). The Fairies represent the four classical elements of fire (the Salamander was a mythical being able to live in fire), air (Zephyr is the west wind), earth (Dusketha, presumably from the idea that the earth is not a light-producing body, thus dusky), and water (Breama from bream, a freshwater fish); they also reflect the idea of the bodily humours and have features of the elves of folklore and perhaps recall the first four elemental spirits who appear to Byron's Manfred. First published in 1848, 2: 271–75; text from 1848 with emendations from Brown's transcript (Harvard MS Keats 3.6, pp. 11–14; *MYR: JK*, 7: 13–16) and with some variants in the notes from Keats's fair copy (FC) (Harvard MS Keats 2.23) which Woodhouse (W², f. 164r) says was "Keats's copy for the press," suggesting that Keats at some point intended to include this poem in his 1820 volume.
2. FC changes this to "Nimbly."

And wrought by spumy bitumen[3]
On the deep intenser roof,
Arched every way aloof;
Let me breathe upon their skies,
And anger their live tapestries;   20
Free from cold and every care
Of chilly rain, and shivering air.

Zep.   Spirit of Fire—away! away!
Or your very roundelay[4]
Will sear my plumage newly budded   25
From its quilled sheath, all studded
With the self-same dews that fell
On the May-grown Asphodel.[5]
Spirit of Fire—away! away!

Bre.   Spirit of Fire—away! away!   30
Zephyr, blue-eyed fairy, turn,
And see my cool sedge-buried urn,[6]
Where it rests its mossy brim
'Mid water-mint and cresses dim;
And the flowers, in sweet troubles,   35
Lift their eyes above the bubbles,
Like our Queen when she would please
To sleep and Oberon will tease.[7]
Love me, blue-eyed Fairy, true,
Soothly I am sick for you.   40

Zep.   Gentle Breama! by the first
Violet young nature nurst,
I will bathe myself with thee,
So you sometimes follow me
To my home, far, far in west,   45
Beyond the nimble-wheeled quest
Of the golden-browed[8] sun.
Come with me, o'er tops of trees,
To my fragrant palaces,
Where they ever floating are   50
Beneath the cherish of a star
Call'd Vesper,[9] who with silver veil
Ever hides his brilliance pale,
Ever gently drows'd doth keep
Twilight for the Fays to sleep.   55
Fear not that your watry hair
Will thirst in drouthy ringlets there;
Clouds of stored summer rains

---

3. 1848, following Brown's transcript, has a full stop at the end of line 16 and commas at the end of lines 17 and 18. For ll. 15–16, Allott offers Thomson's *The Seasons* (1730), "Summer," ll. 1108–09: "The fiery spume / Of fat bitumen."
4. A song or poem with a refrain.
5. The immortal flower of the Elysian Fields in classical myth.
6. Perhaps an echo of Hunt's *Story of Rimini* (1816), 3: 482–83: "forgotten urns, lying about / In the green herbage"; *sedge*: see p. 308, n. 3.
7. For Oberon and his queen, Titania, see p. 34, n. 7.
8. FC has "golden-presenc'd"; since this line does not form a rhyming couplet, Woodhouse (W²) offered "When his arched course is run."
9. The evening star.

Thou shalt taste, before the stains
Of the mountain soil they take,   60
And too unlucent for thee make.
I love thee, crystal Fairy true;
Sooth I am as sick for you!

Sal.   Out, ye aguish Fairies, out!

Chilly lovers, what a rout   65
Keep ye with your frozen breath,
Colder than the mortal death.
Adder-eyed Dusketha, speak,
Shall we leave these and go seek
In the earth's wide entrails old   70
Couches warm as theirs are cold?
O for a fiery gloom and thee,
Dusketha, so enchantingly
Freckle-wing'd and lizard-sided!

Dus.   By thee, Sprite, will I be guided!   75

I care not for cold or heat;
Frost and flame, or sparks, or sleet
To my essence are the same;
But I honour more the flame.
Sprite of Fire! I follow thee   80
Wheresoever it may be,
To the torrid spouts and fountains
Underneath earth-quaked mountains;
Or, at thy supreme desire,
Touch the very pulse of fire   85
With my bare unlidded eyes.

Sal.   Sweet Dusketha! paradise!

Off, ye icy Spirits, fly!
Frosty creatures of the sky!

Dus.   Breathe upon them, fiery sprite!   90
Zep.}

Away! away to our delight!

Bre.}
Sal.   Go, feed on icicles, while we

Bedded in tongue-flames[1] will be.

Dus.   Lead me to these fevrous glooms,

Sprite of Fire!

Bre.   Me to the blooms,   95

Blue-eyed Zephyr, of those flowers
Far in the west where the May-cloud lowers,
And the beams of still Vesper, when winds are
        all whist,[2]
Are shed thro' the rain and the milder mist,
And twilight your floating bowers.   100

1. FC has "tongued flames."
2. 1848 has "wist"; the word means "silent."

SONNET.—TO SLEEP.[1]

O soft embalmer of the still midnight,
  Shutting, with careful fingers and benign,
Our gloom-pleas'd eyes, embower'd from the light,
  Enshaded in forgetfulness divine:[2]
O soothest Sleep! if so it please thee, close,   5
  In midst of this thine hymn, my willing eyes,
Or wait the amen, ere thy poppy throws
  Around my head[3] its lulling charities.[4]
Then save me, or the passed day will rise[5]
  Upon my pillow, breeding many woes;   10
Save me from curious conscience, that still lords[6]
  Its strength for darkness, burrowing like a mole;
Turn the key deftly in the oiled wards,
  And seal the hushed casket of my soul.

On Fame[1]

Fame, like a wayward girl, will still be coy
  To those who woo her with too slavish knees,
But makes surrender to some thoughtless boy,
  And dotes the more upon a heart at ease;
She is a Gipsey, will not speak to those   5
  Who have not learnt to be content without her;
A Jilt, whose ear was never whisper'd close,
  Who thinks they scandal her who talk about her;
A very Gipsey is she, Nilus born,[2]
  Sister-in-law to jealous Potiphar.[3]   10
Ye love-sick Bards, repay her scorn for scorn,
  Ye lovelorn Artists,[4] madmen that ye are,

---

1. Written in April 1819, shortly before Keats copied it into a letter to the George Keatses on April 30 (see above, p. 331). First published in the *Plymouth and Devonport Weekly Journal*, October 11, 1838; text from *PDWJ* with emendations from Brown's transcript (Harvard MS Keats 3.6, p. 48; *MYR: JK*, 7: 50) and Keats's original draft (on the flyleaf of Volume 2 of the 1807 *Paradise Lost* Keats gave to Mrs. Dilke, LMA K/BK/01/014/127) and some variants from a fair copy cased in the Berg Collection of English and American Literature, The New York Public Library, Astor, Lenox and Tilden Foundations: John Keats Collection of Papers, 1816–1948 Bulk (1816–1924).
2. The draft has "As wearisome as darkness is divine."
3. This is a unique variant in *PDWJ*; other texts have "bed."
4. The draft has "Its sweet-dark dews o'er every pulse and limb."
5. This is a unique variant in *PDWJ*, possibly for rhyme; other texts have "shine."
6. Woodhouse changed this to "hoards," which Keats accepted for the Berg album copy.
1. Written in April 1819, probably toward the end of the month, as Keats indicates it was "just written" when he copies it with the next sonnet, also on fame, into his journal letter to the George Keatses on April 30, 1819 (see p. 331). Allott suggests the influence of Dryden's *Conquest of Granada* (1672), Epilogue to Part 1: 5–22, where "Fame, like a little Mistress of the town, / Is gained with ease; but then she's lost as soon." First published as "UNPUBLISHED SONNET ON FAME, BY JOHN KEATS," in an article by the American playwright John Howard Payne, who had met George Keats and seen his collection of manuscripts, in the *Ladies Companion* 7 (August 1838), p. 186; text from the *Ladies Companion* with title and emendations from the letter holograph (Harvard MS Keats 1.53) and also from Brown's transcript, copied from the same lost source as Keats's version sent in the letter (Harvard MS Keats 3.6, p. 49; *MYR: JK*, 7:51).
2. Gypsies were thought to originate in Egypt, thus born from the land of the Nile.
3. See Genesis 39, where Potiphar, an Egyptian captain of the guard who has bought Joseph as a slave, becomes jealous of Joseph after his wife becomes attracted to him.
4. Brown's transcript has "Artists lovelorn."

Make your best bow to her and bid adieu,
Then, if she likes it, she will follow you.

ON FAME.[1]

"You cannot eat your cake and have it too."—Proverb.

How fever'd is the man, who cannot look
   Upon his mortal days with temperate blood,
Who vexes all the leaves of his life's book,
   And robs his fair name of its maidenhood;
It is as if the rose should pluck herself,   5
   Or the ripe plum finger its misty bloom,
As if a Naiad,[2] like a meddling elf,
   Should darken her pure grot with muddy gloom:[3]
But the rose leaves herself upon the briar,
   For winds to kiss and grateful bees to feed,   10
And the ripe plum still wears its dim attire,
   The undisturbed lake has crystal space;
Why then should man, teasing the world for grace,
   Spoil his salvation for a fierce miscreed?

[If by dull rhymes our English must be chain'd][1]

If by dull rhymes our English must be chain'd,
And, like Andromeda,[2] the sonnet sweet
Fetter'd, in spite of pained loveliness;
Let us find out, if we must be constrain'd,
Sandals more interwoven and complete   5
To fit the naked foot of Poesy;
Let us inspect the lyre, and weigh the stress
Of every chord, and see what may be gain'd
By ear industrious, and attention meet;
Misers of sound and syllable, no less   10
Than Midas[3] of his coinage, let us be
Jealous of dead leaves in the bay wreath crown;
So, if we may not let the Muse be free,
She will be bound with garlands of her own.

1. Written on April 30, 1819, in a journal letter to the George Keatses (p. 331). First published as Sonnet XIV in 1848, 2: 300; text from 1848 with emendations from Brown's transcript (Harvard MS Keats 3.6, p. 51; *MYR: JK*, 7: 53), which reflects Keats's corrections to his letter holograph (Harvard MS Keats 1.53).
2. A water nymph.
3. The letter version had "As if a clear Lake meddling with itself / Should Cloud its pureness with a muddy gloom"; Woodhouse (W² f. 152v) notes that in altering these lines Keats "forgot that he left an allusion in the 12th line to those erased."
1. Written toward the end of April or the beginning of May 1819 and copied out in the spring 1819 letter to the George Keatses (*L*, 2: 108–109). It is labeled "Sonnet" or "On the Sonnet" in various transcripts. Woodhouse notes "Irregular" next to the headings in W¹ and W². First published in the *Plymouth, Devonport, and Stonehouse News*, October 15, 1836; text from *PDSN* with emendations from Brown's transcript (MS Keats 3.6, p. 55; *MYR: JK*, 7: 57).
2. Having claimed she was more beautiful than Juno, Andromeda was chained to a rock and left for a sea monster sent by Neptune; she was rescued by Perseus.
3. Miserly king of Phrygia who was granted by Bacchus the ability to turn anything he touched into gold; the subject of a play by Mary Shelley.

Letter to Mary-Ann Jeffery, June 9, 1819[1]

Wentworth Place.

My Dear young Lady,—I am exceedingly obliged by your two letters—Why I did not answer your first immediately was that I have had a little aversion to the South of Devon from the continual remembrance my Brother Tom. On that account I do not return to my old Lodgins in Hampstead though the people of the house have become friends of mine[2]—This however I could think nothing of, it can do no more than keep one's thoughts employed for a day or two. I like your description of Bradley[3] very much and I dare say shall be there in the course of the summer; it would be immediately but that a friend with ill health and to whom I am greatly attached[4] call'd on me yesterday and proposed my spending a Month with him at the back of the Isle of Wight. This is just the thing at present—the morrow will take care of itself—I do not like the name of Bishop's Teigntown[5]—I hope the road from Teignmouth to Bradley does not lie that way—Your advice about the Indiaman[6] is a very wise advice, because it just suits me, though you are a little in the wrong concerning its destroying the energies of Mind: on the contrary it would be the finest thing in the world to strengthen them—To be thrown among people who care not for you, with whom you have no sympathies forces the Mind upon its own resourses, and leaves it free to make its speculations of the differences of human character and to class them with the calmness of a Botanist. An Indiaman is a little world. One of the great reasons that the english have produced the finest writers in the world; is, that the English world has ill-treated them during their lives and foster'd them after their deaths. They have in general been trampled aside into the bye paths of life and seen the festerings of Society. They have not been treated like the Raphaels of Italy.[7] And where is the Englishman and Poet who has given a magnificent Entertainment at the christening of one of his Hero's Horses as Boyardo did?[8] He had a Castle in the Appenine. He was a noble Poet of Romance; not a miserable and mighty Poet of the human Heart. The middle age of Shakspeare was all clouded over; his days were not more happy than Hamlet's who is perhaps more like Shakspeare himself in his common every day Life than any other of his Characters—Ben Johnson was a common Soldier and in the Low countries, in the face of two armies, fought a single combat with a french Trooper and slew him[9]—For all this I will not go on board an Indiaman, nor for examples sake run my head into dark alleys: I dare say my discipline is to come, and plenty of it too. I have been very idle

---

1. The Keats brothers had lodged in Teignmouth, Devon, with a Mrs. Jeffery, and Tom and George had struck up a flirtation with the two daughters, Mary-Ann and Sarah (also known as Fanny); some have felt Mary-Ann fell in love with Keats. Text from transcript in A. F. Sieveking, "Some Unedited Letters of John Keats," *Fortnightly Review* 60 (1893): 734–35. Rollins identifies the recipient as Sarah Jeffrey, corrected by Gittings (1970), p. 402.
2. The Bentleys (see p. 98, n. 1).
3. Perhaps the fifteenth-century Bradley Manor near Newton Abbot.
4. For Rice, see p. 79, n. 7.
5. Bishopsteignton, to the west of Teignmouth and four miles south of Newton Abbot.
6. At the time, Keats was considering taking a job as a surgeon on a ship bound for India.
7. In general, Italy's great painters; for Raphael, see p. 56, n. 4.
8. Matteo Maria Boiardo (1441?–1494), an Italian writer of chivalric romance whose major work was the unfinished *Orlando Innamorato*. Keats probably learned of him from Hunt, who would later write of Boiardo in *Stories of the Italian Poets* (1846).
9. Rollins cites the version of this story in William Gifford's edition of Jonson's *Works* (1816), 1: xii–xiv.

lately, very averse to writing; both from the overpowering idea of our dead poets and from abatement of my love of fame. I hope I am a little more of a Philosopher than I was, consequently a little less of a versifying Pet-lamb.[1] I have put no more in Print or you should have had it. You will judge of my 1819 temper when I tell you that the thing I have most enjoyed this year has been writing an ode to Indolence. Why did you not make your long-haired sister put her great brown hard fist to paper and cross your Letter?[2] Tell her when you write again that I expect chequer-work—My friend Mr Brown is sitting opposite me employed in writing a Life of David. He reads me passages as he writes them stuffing my infidel mouth as though I were a young rook—Infidel Rooks do not provender with Elisha's Ravens.[3] If he goes on as he has begun your new Church had better not proceed, for parsons will be superseeded—and of course the Clerks must follow. Give my love to your Mother with the assurance that I can never forget her anxiety for my Brother Tom. Believe also that I shall ever remember our leave-taking with *you*.

Ever sincerely yours'
John Keats.

Letter to Fanny Brawne, July 1, 1819[1]

Shanklin,
Isle of Wight, Thursday.

My dearest Lady,
    I am glad I had not an opportunity of sending off a Letter which I wrote for you on Tuesday night—'twas too much like one out of Rousseau's Heloise.[2] I am more reasonable this morning. The morning is the only proper time for me to write to a beautiful Girl whom I love so much: for at night, when the lonely day has closed, and the lonely, silent, unmusical Chamber is waiting to receive me as into a Sepulchre, then believe me my passion gets entirely the sway, then I would not have you see those Rhapsodies which I once thought it impossible I should ever give way to, and which I have often laughed at in another, for fear you should [think me] either too unhappy or perhaps a little mad. I am now at a very pleasant Cottage window, looking onto a beautiful hilly country, with a glimpse of the sea; the morning is very fine. I do not know how elastic my spirit might be, what pleasure I might have in living here and breathing and wandering as free as a stag about this beautiful Coast if the remembrance of you did not weigh so upon me. I have never known any unalloy'd Happiness for many days together: the death or sickness of some one has always spoilt my hours—and now when none such troubles oppress me, it is you must confess very hard that another sort of pain should haunt me. Ask yourself my love whether you are not very cruel to have so entrammelled me, so

---

1. See "Ode to Indolence," l. 54, referred to below.
2. That is, cross-write it to produce "chequer-work."
3. 1 Kings 17.6. For Brown's "Life of David," see *The Letters of Charles Armitage Brown*, ed. Jack Stillinger (Cambridge: Harvard University Press, 1966), p. 7.
1. The first of Keats's love letters to Fanny Brawne, this was written from Shanklin, Isle of Wight, where Keats had traveled to join Rice and to work on *Lamia, Hyperion*, and his collaboration with Brown, *Otho the Great*. Text from HBF (1883) 4: 125–27.
2. Jean-Jacques Rousseau's (1712–1778) novel, *Julie, ou la Nouvelle Héloïse* (1761), which tells of the love between the tutor St. Preux and his student Julie.

destroyed my freedom. Will you confess this in the Letter you must write immediately and do all you can to console me in it—make it rich as a draught of poppies to intoxicate me—write the softest words and kiss them that I may at least touch my lips where yours have been. For myself I know not how to express my devotion to so fair a form: I want a brighter word than bright, a fairer word than fair. I almost wish we were butterflies and liv'd but three summer days—three such days with you I could fill with more delight than fifty common years could ever contain. But however selfish I may feel, I am sure I could never act selfishly: as I told you a day or two before I left Hampstead, I will never return to London if my Fate does not turn up Pam or at least a Court-card.[3] Though I could centre my Happiness in you, I cannot expect to engross your heart so entirely—indeed if I thought you felt as much for me as I do for you at this moment I do not think I could restrain myself from seeing you again tomorrow for the delight of one embrace. But no—I must live upon hope and Chance. In case of the worst that can happen, I shall still love you—but what hatred shall I have for another! Some lines I read the other day are continually ringing a peal in my ears:

> To see those eyes I prize above mine own
> Dart favors on another—
> And those sweet lips (yielding immortal nectar)
> Be gently press'd by any but myself—
> Think, think Francesca, what a cursed thing
> It were beyond expression![4]

J.

Do write immediately. There is no Post from this Place, so you must address Post Office, Newport, Isle of Wight. I know before night I shall curse myself for having sent you so cold a Letter; yet it is better to do it as much as in my senses as possible. Be as kind as the distance will permit to your

J. Keats.

Present my Compliments to your mother, my love to Margaret and best remembrances to your Brother—if you please so.[5]

Letter to Fanny Brawne, July 8, 1819[1]

July 8th

My sweet Girl,

Your Letter gave me more delight, than any thing in the world but yourself could do; indeed I am almost astonished that any absent one should have that luxurious power over my senses which I feel. Even when I am not thinking of you I receive your influence and a tenderer nature steeling upon me. All my thoughts, my unhappiest days and nights have I find not at all

---

3. Forman cites Pope's *Rape of the Lock*, 3: 61–64; *Pam*: the knave of hearts, the highest trump card in five-card Loo; a *Court-card*: any face card.
4. As Forman notes, Keats misquotes Philip Massinger's *Duke of Milan* 1.3.203–208, probably from Gifford's 1805 edition of Massinger's *Plays*.
5. Frances Rickets (Mrs. Samuel) Brawne (d. 1829); Margaret Brawne (1809–1887); and Samuel Brawne (1804–1828).
1. Written like the last letter from the Isle of Wight, where Keats stayed with the ailing Rice. Text from ALS in the Ferdinand Julius Dreer Collection, Coll. 175, English Poets, The Historical Society of Pennsylvania.

cured me of my love of Beauty, but made it so intense that I am miserable that you are not with me: or rather breathe in that dull sort of patience that cannot be called Life. I never knew before, what such a love as you have made me feel, was; I did not believe in it; my Fancy was affraid of it, lest it should burn me up. But if you will fully love me, though there may be some fire, 't will not be more than we can bear when moistened and bedewed with Pleasures. You mention 'horrid people' and ask me whether it depend upon them, whether I see you again. Do understand me, my love, in this— I have so much of you in my heart that I must turn Mentor when I see a chance of harm beffaling you. I would never see any thing but Pleasure in your eyes, love on your lips, and Happiness in your steps. I would wish to see you among those amusements suitable to your inclinations and spirits; so that our loves might be a delight in the midst of Pleasures agreeable enough, rather than a resource from vexations and cares. But I doubt much, in case of the worst, whether I shall be philosopher enough to fol- low my own Lessons: if I saw my resolution give you a pain I could not. Why may I not speak of your Beauty, since without that I could never have lov'd you. I cannot conceive any beginning of such love as I have for you but Beauty. There may be a sort of love for which, without the least sneer at it, I have the highest respect and can admire it in others: but it has not the richness, the bloom, the full form, the enchantment of love after my own heart. So let me speak of your Beauty, though to my own endangering; if you could be so cruel to me as to try elsewhere its Power. You say you are affraid I shall think you do not love me—in saying this you make me ache the more to be near you. I am at the diligent use of my faculties here, I do not pass a day without sprawling some blank verse or tagging some rhymes; and here I must confess, that, (since I am on that subject,) I love you the more in that I believe you have liked me for my own sake and for nothing else. I have met with women whom I really think would like to be married to a Poem and to be given away by a Novel. I have seen your Comet,[2] and only wish it was a sign that poor Rice would get well whose illness makes him rather a melancholy companion: and the more so as so to conquer his feelings and hide them from me, with a forc'd Pun. I kiss'd your writing over in the hope you had indulg'd me by leaving a trace of honey—What was your dream? Tell it me and I will tell you the interpretation thereof.

Ever yours my love!

John Keats—

Do not accuse me of delay—we have not here an opportunity of sending letters every day. Write speedily.

Letter to Fanny Brawne, July 15 ?, 1819[1]

Shanklin

Thursday Evening

My love,

I have been in so irritable a state of health these two or three last days, that I did not think I should be able to write this week. Not that I was so

2. A comet appeared on July 3 (see *Gentleman's Magazine* 89 [July 1819]: 64) and was apparently seen by both Fanny and Keats.
1. Text from HBF (1883) 4: 130–33.

ill, but so much so as only to be capable of an unhealthy teasing letter. To night I am greatly recovered only to feel the languor I have felt after you touched with ardency. You say you perhaps might have made me better: you would then have made me worse: now you could quite effect a cure: What fee my sweet Physician would I not give you to do so. Do not call it folly, when I tell you I took your letter last night to bed with me. In the morning I found your name on the sealing wax obliterated. I was startled at the bad omen till I recollected that it must have happened in my dreams, and they you know fall out by contraries. You must have found out by this time I am a little given to bode ill like the raven; it is my misfortune not my fault; it has proceeded from the general tenor of the circumstances of my life, and rendered every event suspicious. However I will no more trouble either you or myself with sad Prophecies; though so far I am pleased at it as it has given me opportunity to love your disinterestedness towards me. I can be a raven no more; you and pleasure take possession of me at the same moment. I am afraid you have been unwell. If through me illness have touched you (but it must be with a very gentle hand) I must be selfish enough to feel a little glad at it. Will you forgive me this? I have been read-ing lately an oriental tale of a very beautiful color—It is of a city of melan-choly men, all made so by this circumstance. Through a series of adventures each one of them by turns reach some gardens of Paradise where they meet with a most enchanting Lady; and just as they are going to embrace her, she bids them shut their eyes—they shut them—and on opening their eyes again find themselves descending to the earth in a magic basket. The remembrance of this Lady and their delights lost beyond all recovery render them melancholy ever after.[2] How I applied this to you, my dear; how I palpitated at it; how the certainty that you were in the same world with myself, and though as beautiful, not so talismanic as that Lady; how I could not bear you should be so you must believe because I swear it by yourself. I cannot say when I shall get a volume ready. I have three or four stories half done, but as I cannot write for the mere sake of the press, I am obliged to let them progress or lie still as my fancy chooses. By Christ-mas perhaps they may appear, but I am not yet sure they ever will. 'Twill be no matter, for Poems are as common as newspapers and I do not see why it is a greater crime in me than in another to let the verses of an half-fledged brain tumble into the reading-rooms and drawing room windows. Rice has been better lately than usual: he is not suffering from any neglect of his par-ents who have for some years been able to appreciate him better than they did in his first youth, and are now devoted to his comfort. Tomorrow I shall, if my health continues to improve during the night, take a look farther about the country, and spy at the parties about here who come hunting after the picturesque like beagles. It is astonishing how they raven down scenery like children do sweetmeats. The wondrous Chine[3] here is a very great Lion: I wish I had as many guineas as there have been spy-glasses in it. I have been, I cannot tell why, in capital spirits this last hour. What rea-son? When I have to take my candle and retire to a lonely room, without the thought as I fall asleep, of seeing you tomorrow morning? or the next

---

2. Keats refers to "The History of the Basket," which he would have found in Henry Weber's *Tales of the East* (Edinburgh, 1812), 2: 666–82.
3. The Shanklin Chine is a narrow, wooded fissure in the sandstone opening onto the sea.

day, or the next—it takes on the appearance of impossibility and eternity—
I will say a month—I will say I will see you in a month at most, though no
one but yourself should see me; if it be but for an hour. I should not like to
be so near you as London without being continually with you: after having
once more kissed you Sweet I would rather be here alone at my task than
in the bustle and hateful literary chitchat. Meantime you must write to
me—as I will every week—for your letters keep me alive. My sweet Girl I
cannot speak my love for you. Good night! and

Ever yours
John Keats.

Letter to Fanny Brawne, July 25, 1819[1]

Sunday Night

My sweet Girl,
    I hope you did not blame me much for not obeying your request of a Let-
ter on Saturday: we have had four in our small room playing cards night and
morning leaving me no undisturb'd opportunity to write. Now Rice and
Martin[2] are gone, I am at liberty. Brown[3] to my sorrow confirms the
account you give of your ill health. You cannot conceive how I ache to be
with you: how I would die for one hour—for what is in the world? I say you
cannot conceive; it is impossible you should look with such eyes upon me
as I have upon you: it cannot be. Forgive me if I wander a little this evening
for I have been all day employ'd in a very abstract Poem[4] and I am in deep
love with you—two things which must excuse me. I have, believe me, not
been an age in letting you take possession of me; the very first week I knew
you I wrote myself your vassal; but burnt the Letter as the very next time I
saw you I thought you manifested some dislike to me. If you should ever
feel for Man at the first sight what I did for you, I am lost. Yet I should not
quarrel with you, but hate myself if such a thing were to happen—only I
should burst if the thing were not as fine as a Man as you are as a Woman.
Perhaps I am too vehement, then fancy me on my knees, especially when
I mention a part of your Letter which hurt me; you say speaking of Mr. Severn "but you must be satisfied in knowing that I admired you much more
than your friend." My dear love, I cannot believe there ever was or ever
could be any thing to admire in me especially as far as sight goes—I cannot be admired, I am not a thing to be admired. You are, I love you; all I can
bring you is a swooning admiration of your Beauty. I hold that place among
Men which snubnos'd brunettes with meeting eyebrows do among
women—they are trash to me—unless I should find one among them with
a fire in her heart like the one that burns in mine. You absorb me in spite
of myself—you alone: for I look not forward with any pleasure to what is
call'd being settled in the world; I tremble at domestic cares—yet for you I
would meet them though if it would leave you the happier I would rather die
than do so. I have two luxuries to brood over in my walks, your Loveliness

---

1. Text from ALS (Harvard MS Keats 1.57).
2. Rice's and Reynolds's friend, John Martin (1791–1855), a partner in the publishing firm of Rod-
   well and Martin.
3. Brown had come to Shanklin to work with Keats on *Otho the Great*.
4. Probably *Hyperion*.

and the hour of my death. O that I could have possession of them both in the same minute. I hate the world: it batters too much the wings of my self will, and would I could take a sweet poison from your lips to send me out of it. From no others would I take it. I am indeed astonish'd to find myself so careless of all charms but yours—remembring as I do the time when even a bit of ribband was a matter of interest with me. What softer words can I find for you after this—what it is I will not read. Nor will I say more here, but in a Postscript answer any thing else you may have mentioned in your Letter in so many words—for I am distracted with a thousand thoughts. I will imagine you Venus to night and pray, pray, pray to your star like a Hethen.

Your's ever, fair Star,
John Keats.

My seal is mark'd like a family table cloth with my mother's initial F for Fanny: put between my Father's initials. You will soon hear from me again. My respectful Compts to your Mother. Tell Margaret I'll send her a reef of best rocks and tell Sam I will give him my light bay hunter if he will tie the Bishop hand and foot and pack him in a hamper and send him down for me to bathe him for his health with a Necklace of good snubby stones about his Neck.[5]

Letter to Benjamin Bailey, August 14, 1819[1]

* * *

We removed to Winchester for the convenience of a Library and find it an exceeding pleasant Town, enriched with a beautiful Cathedrall and surrounded by a fresh-looking country. We are in tolerably good and cheap Lodgings. Within these two Months I have written 1500 Lines, most of which besides many more of prior composition you will probably see by next Winter. I have written two Tales, one from Boccacio call'd the Pot of Basil; and another call'd St Agnes' Eve on a popular superstition; and a third call'd Lamia—(half finished—I have also been writing parts of my Hyperion and completed 4 Acts of a Tragedy. It was the opinion of most of my friends that I should never be able to write a scene—I will endeavour to wipe away the prejudice—I sincerely hope you will be pleased when my Labours since we last saw each other shall reach you. One of my Ambitions is to make as great a revolution in modern dramatic writing as Kean has done in acting[2]—another to upset the drawling of the blue stocking literary world—if in the course of a few years I do these two things I ought to

---

5. For the members of Fanny's family, see p. 350, n. 5. Various explanations for this private joke have been offered with "the Bishop" being identified as either a mutual acquaintance, a Wentworth Place dog, or a rat.
1. Text from ALS (Harvard MS Keats 1.58); there is also transcript in Woodhouse's letter-book, p. 99, where it is labeled a fragment.
2. For Edmund Kean, see p. 105, n. 1. Keats and Brown hoped that Kean would star in *Otho the Great*, but they learned he was going on tour in the United States. Keats wrote to Fanny Keats (August 28, 1819), "What can we do now? There is not another actor of Tragedy in all London or Europe—The Covent Garden Company is execrable—[Charles Mayne] Young is the best among them and is a ranting, coxcombical tasteless Actor—A Disgust A Nausea—and yet the very best after Kean" (*L*, 2: 149).

die content—and my friends should drink a dozen of Claret on my Tomb—
I am convinced more and more every day that (excepting the human friend
Philosopher) a fine writer is the most genuine Being in the World. Shakspeare and the paradise Lost every day become greater wonders to me.[3] I
look upon fine Phrases like a Lover. I was glad to see, by a Passage in one
of Brown's Letters some time ago from the north that you were in such
good Spirits—Since that you have been married and in congratulating you
I wish you every continuance of them—Present my Respects to M[rs] Bailey.
This sounds oddly to me, and I dare say I do it awkwardly enough: but I suppose by this time it is nothing new to you—Brown's remembrances to you—
As far as I know we shall remain at Winchester for a goodish while—

Ever your sincere friend
John Keats.

RICHARD WOODHOUSE

From Letter to John Taylor, September 19, 20, 1819[1]

* * * [Keats] wanted I believe to publish the Eve of S[t] Agnes & Lamia
immediately: but Hessey[2] told him it could not answer to do so now. I wondered why he said nothing of Isabella: & assured him it would please more
than the Eve of S[t] Agnes. He said he could not bear the former now. It
appeared to him mawkish. This certainly cannot be so. The feeling is very
likely to come across an author on review of a former work of his own, particularly where the objects of his present meditations are of a more sobered
& unpassionate Character. The feeling of mawkishness seems to me to be
that which comes upon us where any thing of great tenderness & excessive
simplicity is met with when we are not in a sufficiently tender & simple
frame of mind to bear it: when we experience a sort of revulsion, or
resiliency (if there be such a word) from the sentiment or expression. Now
I believe there is nothing in any of the most passionate parts of Isabella to
excite this feeling. It may, as may Lear, leave the reader far behind: but
there is none of that sugar & butter sentiment, that cloys & disgusts.—He
had the Eve of S[t] A. copied fair: He has made trifling alterations, inserted
an additional stanza early in the poem to make the *legend* more intelligible,
and correspondent with what afterwards takes place, particularly with
respect to the supper & the playing on the lute.—He retains the name of
Porphyro[3]—has altered the last 3 lines to leave on the reader a sense of pettish disgust, by bringing old Angela in (only) dead stiff & ugly.—He says he
likes that the poem should leave off with this Change of Sentiment—it was
what he aimed at, & was glad to find from my objections to it that he had
succeeded.—I apprehend he had a fancy for trying his hand at an attempt
to play with his reader, & fling him off at last—I sho[d] have thought, he

---

3. See the similar comment to Reynolds in Keats's letter of August 24, 1819, "I am convinced more
   and more day by day that fine writing is next to fine doing the top thing in the world; the Paradise
   Lost becomes a greater wonder" (*L*, 2: 146).
1. Woodhouse reports Keats's famous comments on *Isabella, The Eve of* St. *Agnes*, and *Lamia*. Text
   from ALS (Morgan Library, MA 215[14]).
2. James August Hessey (1785–1870), along with Taylor, Keats's publisher.
3. Keats had originally used the name "Lionel."

affected the "Don Juan"[4] style of mingling up sentiment & sneering: but that he had before asked Hessey if he co^d procure him a sight of that work, as he had not met with it, and if the E. of St A. had not in all probability been altered before his Lordship had thus flown in the face of the public. There was another alteration, which I abused for "a full hour by the *Temple* clock."[5] You know if a thing has a decent side, I generally look no further. As the Poem was orig^y written, *we* innocent ones (ladies & myself) might very well have supposed that Porphyro, when acquainted with Madeline's love for him, & when "he arose, Etherial flush^d &c &c (turn to it) set himself at once to persuade her to go off with him, & succeeded & went over the "Dartmoor black" (now changed for some other place) to be married, in right honest chaste & sober wise.[6] But, as it is now altered, as soon as M. has confessed her love, P. winds by degrees his arms around her, presses breast to breast, and acts all the acts of a bonâ fide husband, while she fancies she is only playing the part of a Wife in a dream. This alteration is of about 3 stanzas; and tho' there are no improper expressions but all is left to inference and tho' profanely speaking, the Interest on the reader's imagination is greatly heightened, yet I do apprehend it will render the poem unfit for ladies, & indeed scarcely to be mentioned to them among the "things that are."[7]—He says he does not want ladies to read his poetry: that he writes for men—& that if in the former poem there was an opening for doubt what took place, it was his fault for not writing clearly & comprehensibly—that he sh^d despise a man who would be such an eunuch in sentiment as to leave a maid, with that Character about her, in such a situation: & sh^d despise himself to write about it &c &c &c—and all this sort of Keats-like rhodomontade.—But you will see the work I dare say.[8]— He then read to me Lamia, which he has half fair copied: the rest is rough. I was much pleased with it. I can use no other terms for you know how badly he reads his own poetry: & you know how slow I am in Catching, even the sense of poetry read by the best reader for the 1st time. And his poetry really must be studied to be properly appreciated. The story is to this effect—Hermes is hunting for a Nymph, when from a wood he hears his name & a song relating to his loss—Mercury finds out that it comes from a serpent, who promises to shew him his Nymph if he will turn the serpent into a Woman; This he agrees to: upon which the serpent breathes on his eyes when he sees his Nymph who had been beside them listening invisibly—The serpent had seen a young Man of Corinth with whom she had fallen desperately in Love. She is metamorphosed into a beautiful

4. Byron's great satiric poem, the first two cantos of which appeared in 1819; of course, Keats could have found a similar style in the earlier *Beppo*, published in 1818 around the time Keats began *Isabella*.
5. Rollins offers Shakespeare, *1 Henry IV*, 5.4.141–42: "fought a long hour by Shrewsbury clock." See also Tobias Smollett, *Humphry Clinker* (Dublin, 1771), "he plays a full hour by the clock" (2: 88).
6. Woodhouse refers to Keats's attempts to revise stanzas 35–36. He changed "Dartmoor black" to "southern moors" (l. 351).
7. Rollins cites Proclus Lycius, *On Plato's Timaeus*, "I am the things that are." See also *Things as They Are, or Caleb Williams* (1794) by Godwin, whom Woodhouse mentions at the opening of the letter (*L*, 2: 161).
8. Taylor would write back to Woodhouse (September 25, 1819) about the proposed changes: "This Folly of Keats is the most stupid piece of Folly I can conceive. . . . I don't know how the Meaning of the new Stanzas is wrapped up, but I will not be necessary (I can answer also for H. I think) towards publishing any thing which can only be read by men, since even on their Minds a bad Effect must follow the Encouragement of those Thoughts which cannot be rased without Impropriety" (*L*, 2: 182). Keats would acquiesce when his publishers forced the restoration of the original wording. *Rhodomontade*: "an extravagantly boastful or arrogant saying or speech" (*OED*).

Woman, the Change is quite Ovidian, but better,—She then finds the Youth, & they live together in a palace in the Middle of Corinth (described, or rather pictured out in very good costume) the entrance of which no one can see (like the Cavern Prince Ahmed found in the Arabian Nights, when searching for his lost arrow).[9] Here they live & love, "the world forgetting; of the world forgot."[1] He wishes to marry her & introduce her to his friends as his wife, But this would be a forfeiture of her immortality & she refuses but at length (for—says K—"Women love to be forced to do a thing, by a fine fellow—*such as this*—I forget his name—*was*") she consents. The Palace door becomes visible—to the "astonishment of the Natives"—the friends are invited to the wedding feast—& K. wipes the Cits[2] & the low lived ones: of some of whom he says "who make their mouth a napkin to their thumb" in the midst of this Imperial splendour.[3]—The lover had seen his tutor Appollonius that morning, while in a car with his Lamia; he had a scowl on his brow, which makes the hearts of the lovers sink: & she asks him, who that frowning old fellow was, as soon as A. passed.—He appears at the feast: damps the joy of the two by his presence—sits over against the woman: He is a Magician—He looks earnestly at the woman: so intently & to such effect, that she reads in his eyes that she is discovered: & vanishes away, shrieking.—The lover is told she was a "Lamia" & goes mad for the loss of her, & dies—You may suppose all these Events have given K. scope for some beautiful poetry: which even in this Cursory hearing of it, came every now & then upon me, & made me "start, as tho' a Sea Nymph quired."[4] The metre is Drydenian heroic—with many triplets, & many alexandrines.[5] But this K. observed, & I agreed, was required, or rather quite in character with the language & sentiment in those particular parts.—K. has a fine feeling when & where he may use poetical licences with effect* * *

[Pensive they sit, and roll their languid eyes][1]

> Pensive they sit, and roll their languid eyes,
> Nibble their toasts, and cool their tea with sighs,
> Or else forget the purpose of the night,
> Forget their tea—forget their appetite.
> See, with cross'd arms they sit—ah hapless crew,   5

9. "The Story of Prince Ahmed, and the Fairy Pari Banou," from *The Arabian Nights*.
1. Pope, "Eloisa to Abelard" (1717), l. 208.
2. Plural of "cit," which is "short for *citizen*; usually applied, more or less contemptuously, to a townsman" (*OED*).
3. Woodhouse refers to a passage following 2.162 that Keats dropped from the print version of *Lamia*.
4. Allusion to the final line of Keats's "On the Sea" (p. 79).
5. Woodhouse points out that Keats imitates Dryden's use of the heroic couplet (a pair of rhymed iambic pentameter lines). An alexandrine, borrowed from French heroic verse and named for twelfth- and thirteenth-century French poems on Alexander the Great that used the meter, is an iambic line of six feet; a triplet is composed of three rhyming lines.
1. Written on September 17, 1819, in the September journal letter to the George Keatses (see p. 364), after noting, "Nothing strikes me so forcibly with a sense of the rediculous as love—A Man in love I do think cuts the sorryest figure in the world—Even when I know a poor fool to be really in pain about it, I could burst out laughing in his face. . . . Somewhere in the Spectator is related an account of a Man inviting a party of stutterers and squinters to his table. 'twould please me more to scrape together a party of Lovers, not to dinner—no to tea. There would be no fighting as among Knights of old"; after the poem, he writes, "You see I cannot get on without writing as boys do at school a few nonsense verses—I begin them and before I have written six the whim has pass'd." First published in the New York *World*, June 25, 1877, p. 2, with extracts from the letter; text from the *World* with emendations from Keats's holograph letter (Morgan Library MA 212).

The fire is going out, and no one rings
For coals, and therefore no coals Betty brings.
A fly is in the milk pot—must he die
Circled by a humane society?[2]
No, no, there Mr. Werter[3] takes his spoon,   10
Inverts[4] it, dips the handle, and lo, soon
The little struggler,[5] sav'd from perils dark,
Across the teaboard draws a long wet mark.
Romeo![6] Arise! take snuffers by the handle;
There's a large cauliflower in each candle,   15
A winding-sheet[7]—Ah me! I must away
To No. 7, just beyond the Circus gay.[8]
"Alas, my friend! your coat sits very well:
Where may your taylor[9] live?" "I may not tell—
O pardon me—I'm absent now and then.   20
Where *might* my taylor live?—I say again
I cannot tell. Let me no more be teas'd—
He lives in Wapping,[1] *might* live where he pleas'd."

Letter to J. H. Reynolds, September 21, 1819[1]

Winchester. Tuesday

My dear Reynolds,
    I was very glad to hear from Woodhouse that you would meet in the
Country. I hope you will pass some pleasant time together. Which I wish to
make pleasanter by a brace of letters, very highly to be estimated, as really
I have had very bad luck with this sort of game this season. I "kepen in solitarinesse,"[2] for Brown has gone a visiting.[3] I am surprised myself at the
pleasure I live alone in. I can give you no news of the place here, or any
other idea of it but what I have to this effect written to George. Yesterday I
say to him was a grand day for Winchester. They elected a Mayor—It was
indeed high time the place should receive some sort of excitement. There
was nothing going on: all asleep: not an old maid's sedan returning from a
card party: and if any old woman got tipsy at Christenings they did not
expose it in the streets. The first night tho' of our arrival here, there was a
slight uproar took place at about 10 o' the Clock. We heard distinctly a
noise patting down the high Street as of a walking cane of the good old

2. The Royal Humane Society was founded in 1774 to aid those in danger of drowning; the *World*
lacks "Circled."
3. Allusion to Goethe's famous novel, *The Sorrows of Young Werter,* translated by either Richard
Graves or Daniel Malthus and published by J. Dodsley in 1783 (4th ed.). Rollins cites Werter's
sense that "Every moment I am myself a destroyer. The most innocent walk deprives of life thousands of poor insects" (1: 144–45).
4. The *World* has "Inserts."
5. The *World* has "straggler."
6. Omitted in the *World.*
7. A "mass of solidified drippings of grease clinging to the side of a candle, resembling a sheet folded
in creases, and regarded as an omen of death or calamity" (*OED*); *cauliflower* (l. 15) can then
describe the untrimmed wick producing the drippings and needing to be snuffed out.
8. Probably Piccadilly Circus in London.
9. For tailor, with perhaps a nod to Keats's publisher, John Taylor.
1. The garment district in East London near the docks on the Thames.
1. Text from Woodhouse's letter-book, pp. 33–37.
2. "The Eve of St. Mark," l. 106 (see p. 310).
3. Brown was in Chichester from c. September 7 to October 1.

Dowager breed; and a little minute after we heard a less voice observe "What a noise the ferril made—it must be loose"—Brown wanted to call the Constables, but I observed 'twas only a little breeze,[4] and would soon pass over.—The side streets here are excessively maiden-lady like: the door steps always fresh from the flannel. The knockers have a staid serious, nay almost awful quietness about them.—I never saw so quiet a collection of Lions' & Rams' heads—The doors most part black, with a little brass handle just above the keyhole, so that in Winchester a man may very quietly shut himself out of his own house. How beautiful the season is now—How fine the air. A temperate sharpness about it. Really, without joking, chaste weather—Dian[5] skies—I never lik'd stubble fields so much as now—Aye better than the chilly green of the spring. Somehow a stubble plain looks warm—in the same way that some pictures look warm—this struck me so much in my sunday's walk that I composed upon it.[6] I hope you are better employed than in gaping after weather. I have been at different times so happy as not to know what weather it was—No I will not copy a parcel of verses. I always somehow associate Chatterton with autumn. He is the purest writer in the English Language. He has no French idiom, or particles like Chaucer—'tis genuine English Idiom in English words. I have given up Hyperion[7]—there were too many Miltonic inversions in it—Miltonic verse cannot be written but in an artful or rather artist's humour. I wish to give myself up to other sensations. English ought to be kept up. It may be interesting to you to pick out some lines from Hyperion and put a mark ▶ to the false beauty proceeding from art, and one ‖ to the true voice of feeling. Upon my soul 'twas imagination I cannot make the distinction—Every now & then there is a Miltonic intonation—But I cannot make the division properly. The fact is I must take a walk; for I am writing so long a letter to George; and have been employed at it all the morning. You will ask, have I heard from George. I am sorry to say not the best news—I hope for better— This is the reason among others that if I write to you it must be in such a scraplike way. I have no meridian to date Interests from, or measure circumstances—To night I am all in a mist; I scarcely know what's what— But you knowing my unsteady & vagarish disposition, will guess that all this turmoil will be settled by tomorrow morning. It strikes me to night that I have led a very odd sort of life for the two or three last years—Here & there—No anchor—I am glad of it.—If you can get a peep at Babbicomb before you leave the country,[8] do.—I think it the finest place I have seen, or—is to be seen in the South. There is a Cottage there I took warm water at, that made up for the tea. I have lately skirk'd some friends of ours, and I advise you to do the same, I mean the blue-devils—I am never at home to them. You need not fear them while you remain in Devonshire. There will be some of the family waiting for you at the Coach office—but go by another Coach.—I shall beg leave to have a third opinion in the first discussion you have with Woodhouse—just half way—between both. You

---

4. Slang for a disturbance, a row; *ferril*: for "ferrule," the metal cap at the end of a cane.
5. For Diana, goddess of chastity, see p. 25, n. 1.
6. Woodhouse notes on the transcript that Keats alludes to the "Ode to Autumn," which he sent Woodhouse in a letter of the same date.
7. That is, his revision of it as *The Fall of Hyperion*, see pp. 497–510.
8. Reynolds was at the Woodhouse home in Bath. Babbacome is a suburb of Torquay, above Babbacombe Bay and known for its views.

know I will not give up my argument—In my walk to day I stoop'd under a rail way that lay across my path, and ask'd myself "Why I did not get over." Because, answered I, "no one wanted to force you under."—I would give a guinea to be a reasonable man—good sound sense—a says what he thinks, and does what he says man—and did not take snuff—They say men near death however mad they may have been, come to their senses—I hope I shall here in this letter—there is a decent space to be very sensible in— many a good proverb has been in less—Nay I have heard of the statutes at large being chang'd into the Statutes at Small and printed for a watch paper.[9] Your sisters by this time must have got the Devonshire ees—short ees—you know 'em—they are the prettiest ees in the Language. O how I admire the middle siz'd delicate Devonshire girls of about 15. There was one at an Inn door holding a quartern of brandy—the very thought of her kept me warm a whole stage—and a 16 miler too—"You'll pardon me for being jocular."[1]

Ever your affectionate friend
John Keats—

Letter to C. W. Dilke, September 22, 1819[1]

My dear Dilke,　　　　　　　　　　　Winchester Wednesday Eve—
　　Whatever I take too for the time I cannot leave off in a hurry; letter writing is the go now; I have consumed a Quire at least. You must give me credit, now, for a free Letter when it is in reality an interested one, on two points, the one requestive, the other verging to the pros and cons—As I expect they will lead me to seeing and conferring with you in a short time, I shall not enter at all upon a letter I have lately received from george of not the most comfortable intelligence:[2] but proceed to these two points, which if you can theme out in sexions and subsexions, for my edification, you will oblige me. The first I shall begin upon, the other will follow like a tail to a Comet. I have written to Brown on the subject, and can but go over the same Ground with you in a very short time, it not being more in length than the ordinary paces between the Wickets. It concerns a resolution I have taken to endeavour to acquire something by temporary writing in periodical works.[3] You must agree with me how unwise it is to keep feeding upon hopes, which depending so much on the state of temper and imagination, appear gloomy or bright, near or afar off just as it happens—Now an act has three parts—to act, to do, and to perform—I mean I should *do* something for my immediate welfare—Even if I am swept away like a Spider from a

9. Keats plays with the idea that "Statutes at Large," that is, official versions of law printed for citation, have been reduced to be used as a watch paper, "a disc of paper, silk, or other material, inscribed or painted with an ornamental design, a picture, rhyme, or other device, inserted as a lining or pad in the outer case of an old-fashioned watch" (*OED*).
1. A remark of Mr. Vellum in Addison's comedy, *The Drummer; or, The Haunted House* (1716), 1.2.
1. Keats wrote on similar subjects the same day to Woodhouse and Brown, as indicated in the notes. This letter was not sent. Text from ALS (LMA/KH: K/MS/02/010/6562).
2. On September 10, Keats had received a letter from his brother George indicating he was out of money; Keats immediately left for London to meet with Abbey.
3. Keats wrote to Brown, "I will write, on the liberal side of the question, for whoever will pay me" and "If I can get an article in the 'Edinburg' I will" (*L*, 2: 176, 177); to Woodhouse, he wrote that he planned to "get employment in some of our elegant Periodical Works" (*L*, 2: 174).

drawing room I am determined to spin—home spun any thing for sale. Yea I will trafic. Any thing but Mortgage my Brain to Blackwood.[4] I am determined not to lie like a dead lump. If Reynolds had not taken to the law, would he not be earning something? Why cannot I. You may say I want tact—that is easily acquired. You may be up to the slang of a cock pit in three battles. It is fortunate I have not before this been tempted to venture on the common.[5] I should a year or two ago have spoken my mind on every subject with the utmost simplicity. I hope I have learnt a little better and am confident I shall be able to cheat as well as any literary Jew of the Market and shine up an article on any thing without much knowledge of the subject, aye like an orange. I would willingly have recourse to other means. I cannot; I am fit for nothing but literature. Wait for the issue of this Tragedy? No—there cannot be greater uncertainties east west, north, and south than concerning dramatic composition. How many months must I wait! Had I not better begin to look about me now? If better events supersede this necessity what harm will be done? I have no trust whatever on Poetry. I dont wonder at it—the marvel is to me how people read so much of it. I think you will see the reasonableness of my plan. To forward it I purpose living in cheap Lodging in Town, that I may be in the reach of books and information, of which there is here a plentiful lack.[6] If I can [find] any place tolerably comfitable I will settle myself and fag till I can afford to buy Pleasure—which if [I] never can afford I must go Without. Talking of Pleasure, this moment I was writing with one hand, and with the other holding to my Mouth a Nectarine—good god how fine. It went down soft, pulpy, slushy, oozy—all its delicious embonpoint melted down my throat like a large beatified Strawberry. I shall certainly breed. Now I come to my request. Should you like me for a neighbour again? Come, plump it out, I wont blush. I should also be in the neighbourhood of M[rs] Wylie, which I should be glad of, though that of course does not influence me. Therefore will you look about Marsham, or rodney street for a couple of rooms for me.[7] Rooms like the gallants legs in massingers time "as good as the times allow, Sir."[8] I have written to day to Reynolds, and to Woodhouse. Do you know him? He is a Friend of Taylors at whom Brown has taken one of his funny odd dislikes. I'm sure he's wrong, because Woodhouse likes my Poetry—conclusive. I ask your opinion and yet I must say to you as to him, Brown that if you have any thing to say against it I shall be as obstinate & heady as a Radical. By the Examiner coming in your hand writing you must be in Town. They have put [me] into spirits: Notwithstand my aristocratic temper I cannot help being verry much pleas'd with the present public proceedings.[9] I hope sincerely I shall be able to put a Mite of help to the

4. *Blackwood's Edinburgh Magazine* was the reactionary journal that launched the Cockney School attacks.
5. To prostitute oneself.
6. Keats wrote to Woodhouse, "I shall live in Westminster—from which a walk to the British Museum will be noisy and muddy—but otherwise pleasant enough—I shall enquire of Hazlitt how the figures of the market stand" (*L*, 2: 174).
7. Rollins notes that Keats miswrites "Romney" Street, which intersected Marsham Street; Dilke had moved from Hampstead to Westminster.
8. Philip Massinger (1583–1640), *A Very Woman*, 3.1.104, "Strong as the time allows sir" (in Gifford's edition of *Plays* [1813], 4: 284).
9. Following the Peterloo Massacre of August 16, there were outcries against the attack and intensified calls for Reform, covered of course in Hunt's *Examiner*; Keats had been in London on September 13 when Henry Hunt, who had led the meeting at St. Peter's Fields, Manchester, entered London to be greeted by a crowd of three hundred thousand.

Liberal side of the Question before I die. If you should have left Town again (for your Holidays cannot be up yet) let me know—when this is forwarded to you. A most extraordinary mischance has befallen two Letters I wrote Brown—one from London whither I was obliged to go on business for George; the other from this place since my return. I cant make it out. I am excessively sorry for it. I shall hear from Brown and from you almost together for I have sent him a Letter to day: you must positively agree with me or by the delicate toe nails of the virgin I will not open your Letters. If they are as David says 'suspicious looking letters"[1] I wont open them. If S[t] John had been half as cunning he might have seen the revelations comfortably in his own room, without giving Angels the trouble of breaking open Seals.[2] Remember me to M[rs] D.—and the Westmonisteranian[3] and believe me

Ever your sincere friend
John Keats—

From Letter to George and Georgiana Keats, September 17, 18, 20, 21, 24, 25, 27, 1819[1]

My dear George,   Winchester Sept[r] Friday—
I was closely employed in reading and composition, in this place, whither I had come from Shanklin, for the convenience of a library, when I received your last, dated July 24th. You will have seen by the short Letter I wrote from Shanklin, how matters stand beetween us and M[rs] Jennings.[2] They had not at all mov'd and I knew no way of overcoming the inveterate obstinacy of our affairs. On receiving your last I immediately took a place in the same night's coach for London—M[r] Abbey behaved extremely well to me, appointed Monday evening at 7 to meet me and observed that he should drink tea at that hour. I gave him the inclosed note and showed him the last leaf of yours to me. He really appeared anxious about it; promised he would forward your money as quickly as possible—I think I mention'd that Walton was dead—He will apply to M[r] Gliddon the partner; endeavour to get rid of M[rs] Jennings's claim and be expeditious. He has received an answer from my Letter to Fry[3]—that is something. We are certainly in a very low estate: I say we, for I am in such a situation that were it not for the assistance of Brown & Taylor, I must be as badly off as a Man can be. I could not raise any sum by the promise of any Poem—no, not by the mortgage of my intellect. We must wait a little while. I really have hopes of success. I have finish'd a Tragedy which if it succeeds will enable me to sell what I

---

1. See Sheridan, *The Rivals* (1775), 4.1.74–75, "malicious-looking letter."
2. See Revelation, 5–6.
3. Dilke's son went to Westminster School.
1. Written after Keats returned to Winchester on September 15, 1819, following a trip into London on September 10 after receiving word from George that he needed money. Text from ALS, Morgan Library (MA 212); there is also a much abbreviated Jeffrey transcript (Harvard MS Keats 3.9, 29r).
2. Mrs. Margaret Midgley Jennings, widow of Keats's uncle, Captain Jennings; she had filed a bill in Chancery against the Keats siblings' inheritance.
3. Fry may have been a trustee for the Keats inheritance; Rollins suggest Thomas Fry, a stock broker, or Thomas Fry, commercial and general broker. The lawyers mentioned formed the law firm of Walton and Gliddon, 28 Basinghall Street.

may have in manuscript to a good avantage. I have pass'd my time in reading, writing and fretting—the last I intend to give up and stick to the other two. They are the only chances of benefit to us. Your wants will be a fresh spur to me. I assure you you shall more than share what I can get, whilst I am still young—the time may come when age will make me more selfish. I have not been well treated by the world—and yet I have capitally well—I do not know a Person to whom so many purse strings would fly open as to me—if I could possibly take advantage of them—which I cannot do for none of the owners of these purses are rich—Your present situation I will not suffer myself to dwell upon—when misfortunes are so real we are glad enough to escape them, and the thought of them. I cannot help thinking Mr Audubon a dishonest man[4]—Why did he make you believe that he was a Man of Property? How is it his circumstances have altered so suddenly? In truth I do not believe you fit to deal with the world; or at least the american worrld—But good God—who can avoid these chances—You have done your best—Take matters as coolly as you can and confidently expecting help from England, act as if no help was nigh. Mine I am sure is a tolerable tragedy—it would have been a bank to me, if just as I had finish'd it I had not heard of Kean's resolution to go to America.[5] That was the worst news I could have had. There is no actor can do the principal character besides Kean. At Covent Garden there is a great chance of its being damn'd. Were it to succeed even there it would lift me out of the mire. I mean the mire of a bad reputation which is continually rising against me. My name with the literary fashionables is vulgar—I am a weaver boy to them—a Tragedy would lift me out of this mess. And mess it is as far as it regards our Pockets—But be not cast down any more than I am. I feel I can bear real ills better than imaginary ones. Whenever I find myself growing vapourish, I rouse myself, wash and put on a clean shirt brush my hair and clothes, tie my shoestrings neatly and in fact adonize[6] as I were going out—then all clean and comfortable I sit down to write. This I find the greatest relief—Besides I am becoming accustom'd to the privations of the pleasures of sense. In the midst of the world I live like a Hermit. I have forgot how to lay plans for enjoyment of any Pleasure. I feel I can bear any thing, any misery, even imprisonment—so long as I have neither wife nor child. Perpaps you will say yours are your only comfort—they must be. * * * I had been so long in retirement that London appeared a very odd place I could not make out I had so many acquaintance, and it was a whole day before I could feel among Men—I had another strange sensation there was not one house I felt any pleasure to call at. * * * I saw Haslam he is very much occupied with love and business being one of Mr Saunders executors and Lover to a young woman He show'd me her Picture by Severn—I think she is, though not very cunning, too cunning for him. Nothing strikes me so forcibly with a sense of the rediculous as love—A Man in love I do think cuts the sorryest figure in the world—Even when I know a poor fool to be really in pain about it, I could burst out laughing in his face—His pathetic visage becomes irrisistable. Not that I take Haslam as a pattern for

4. John James Audubon (1785–1851), the famous naturalist, had convinced George to invest in a riverboat working the Ohio and Mississippi rivers, but when the boat sank, George lost all his money.
5. For Kean, see p. 105, n. 1; he toured North America successfully in 1820–21.
6. From Adonis, the beautiful youth loved by Venus.

Lovers—he is a very worthy man and a good friend. His love is very amusing. Somewhere in the Spectator is related an account of a Man inviting a party of stutterers and squinters to his table.[7] 't would please me more to scrape together a party of Lovers, not to dinner—no to tea. There would be no fighting as among Knights of old—
[A copy of "Pensive they sit, and roll their languid eyes" follows.][8]
You see I cannot get on without writing as boys do at school a few nonsense verses—I begin them and before I have written six the whim has pass'd—if there is any thing deserving so respectable a name in them. I shall put in a bit of information any where just as it strikes me. Mr Abbey is to write to me as soon as he can bring matters to bear, and then I am to go to Town to tell him the means of forwarding to you through Capper and Hazlewood[9]—I wonder I did not put this before—I shall go on tomorrow—it is so fine now I must take a bit of a walk—

Saturday—
With my inconstant disposition it is no wonder that this morning, amid all our bad times and misfortunes, I should feel so alert and well spirited. At this moment you are perhaps in a very different state of Mind. It is because my hopes are very paramount to my despair. I have been reading over a part of a short poem I have composed lately call'd 'Lamia'—and I am certain there is that sort of fire in it which must take hold of people in some way—give them either pleasant or unpleasant sensation. What they want is a sensation of some sort. I wish I could pitch the key of your spirits as high as mine is—but your organ loft is beyond the reach of my voice— * * * This Winchester is a place tolerably well suited to me; there is a fine Cathedral, a College, a Roman-Catholic Chapel, a Methodist do, an independent do,[1]—and there is not one loom or any thing like manufacturing beyond bread & butter in the whole City. There are a number of rich Catholics in the place. It is a respectable, ancient aristocratical place—and moreover it contains a nunnery—Our set are by no means so hail fellow, well met, on literary subjects as we were wont to be. Reynolds has turn'd to the law. Bye the bye, he brought out a little piece at the Lyceum call'd *one, two, three, four, by advertisement*.[2] It met with complete success. The meaning of this odd title is explained when I tell you the principal actor is a mimic who takes off four of our best performers in the course of the farce—Our stage is loaded with mimics. I did not see the Piece being out of Town the whole time it was in progress. . . . I have been reading lately Burton's Anatomy of Melancholy; and I think you will be very much amused with a page I here coppy for you.[3] * * * When I left Mr Abbey on monday evening I walk'd up Cheapside but returned to put some letters in the Post and met him again

7. See the *Spectator*, May 6, 1712, for the story of a wit who hosts dinners for "stammerers" and "oglers."
8. See pp. 357–58.
9. Stockbrokers who apparently handled mail for the Birkbeck settlement.
1. "Something done in a set or formal manner; a performance; *esp.* an entertainment, show; a party; hence (orig. *jocular*), a military engagement, raid, or other 'show'"; but also "A cheat, fraud, swindle, imposture" (OED); *independent*: a Dissenting chapel, particularly a Congregational one.
2. Reynolds saw the production of his farce *One, Two, Three, Four, Five: By Advertisement* at the Lyceum or English Opera House on the Strand on July 17, 1819.
3. Keats quotes from Burton's *Anatomy of Melancholy* (1621–51; Keats owned an 1813 ed.), 3.2.4.1. He drew on Burton's *Anatomy* for the story of Lamia (see p. 429); for Burton's general influence on Keats, see Gittings, *The Living Year* (1954), pp. 215–23.

in Bucklersbury: we walk'd together through the Poultry as far as the hatter's shop he has some concern in—He spoke of it in such a way to me, I thought he wanted me to make an offer to assist him in it. I do believe if I could be a hatter I might be one. He seems anxious about me. He began blowing up Lord Byron while I was sitting with him, however Says he the fellow says true things now & then; at which he took up a Magasine and read me some extracts from Don Juan, (Lord Byron's last flash poem) and particularly one against literary ambition.[4] I do think I must be well spoken of among sets, for Hodgkinson is more than polite, and the coffee-german endeavour'd to be very close to me the other night at covent garden where I went at half-price before I tumbled into bed[5]—Every one however distant an acquaintance behaves in the most conciliating manner to me—You will see I speak of this as a matter of interest. On the next Sheet I will give you a little politics. In every age there has been in England for some two or three centuries subjects of great popular interest on the carpet: so that however great the uproar one can scarcely prophesy any material change in the government; for as loud disturbances have agitated this country many times. All civiled countries become gradually more enlighten'd and there should be a continual change for the better. Look at this Country at present and remember it when it was even thought impious to doubt the justice of a trial by Combat—From that time there has been a gradual change—Three great changes have been in progress—First for the better, next for the worse, and a third time for the better once more. The first was the gradual annihilation of the tyranny of the nobles, when kings found it their interest to conciliate the common people, elevate them and be just to them. Just when baronial Power ceased and before standing armies were so dangerous, Taxes were few. Kings were lifted by the people over the heads of their nobles, and those people held a rod over kings. The change for the worse in Europe was again this. The obligation of kings to the Multitude began to be forgotten—Custom had made noblemen the humble servants of kings—Then kings turned to the Nobles as the adorners of their power, the slaves of it, and from the people as creatures continually endeavouring to check them. Then in every kingdom therre was a long struggle of kings to destroy all popular privileges. The english were the only people in europe who made a grand kick at this. They were slaves to Henry 8th but were freemen under william 3rd at the time the french were abject slaves under Lewis 14th.[6] The example of England, and the liberal writers of france and england sowed the seed of opposition to this Tyranny—and it was swelling in the ground till it burst out in the french revolution—That has had an unlucky termination. It put a stop to the rapid progress of free sentiments in England; and gave our Court hopes of turning back to the despotism of

4. See Byron, *Don Juan*, Canto 1, stanza 218: "What is the end of fame? 'tis but to fill / A certain portion of uncertain paper"; Byron's poem was excerpted in various journals. *flash*: the use of cant or slang language.
5. Keats most likely saw the second show on the bill at Covent Garden on September 14, which was Colman the Younger's *Blue-Beard; or, Female Curiosity*. Cadman *Hodgkinson*: Abbey's junior partner, with whom George Keats had quarreled; *coffee-german* would seem to mean a relative in the coffee business.
6. Louis XIV (1638–1715), king of France (1643–1715), is often seen as the strongest example of absolute monarchy. Henry VIII (1491–1547), king of England (1509–47), broke with the Catholic Church and strengthened the king's power. William III (1650–1702), king of England, Scotland, and Ireland (1689–1702), gained power through the "Glorious Revolution" that brought about a constitutional monarchy.

the 16 century. They have made a handle of this event in every way to undermine our freedom. They spread a horrid superstition against all inovation and improvement—The present struggle in England of the people is to destroy this superstition. What has rous'd them to do it is their distresses—Perpaps on this account the present distresses of this nation are a fortunate thing—tho' so horrid in their experience. You will see I mean that the french Revolution put a temporry stop to this third change, the change for the better—Now it is in progress again and I think it an effectual one. This is no contest beetween whig and tory—but between right and wrong. There is scarcely a grain of party spirit now in England—Right and Wrong considered by each man abstractedly is the fashion. I know very little of these things. I am convinced however that apparently small causes make great alterations. There are little signs wherby we many know how matters are going on—This makes the business about Carlisle the Bookseller[7] of great moment in my mind. He has been selling deistical pamphlets, republished Tom Payne and many other works held in superstitious horror. He even has been selling for some time immense numbers of a work call 'The Deist' which comes out in weekly numbers—For this Conduct he I think has had above a dozen inditements issued against him; for which he has found Bail to the amount of many thousand Pounds—After all they are affraid to prosecute: they are affraid of his defence: it would be published in all the papers all over the Empire: they shudder at this: the Trials would light a flame they could not extinguish. Do you not think this of great import? You will hear by the papers of the proceedings at Manchester and Hunt's triumphal entry into London[8]—It would take me a whole day and a quire of paper to give you any thing like detail—I will merely mention that it is calculated that 30.000 people were in the streets waiting for him—The whole distance from the Angel Islington to the Crown and anchor[9] was lined with Multitudes. As I pass'd Colnaghi's window I saw a profil Portraict of Sands the destroyer of Kotzebue.[1] His very look must interest every one in his favour—I suppose they have represented him in his college dress— He seems to me like a young Abelard[2]—A fine Mouth, cheek bones (and this is no joke) full of sentiment; a fine unvulgar nose and plump temples. On looking over some Letters I found the one I wrote intended for you from the foot of Helvellyn to Liverpool—but you had sail'd and therefore It was returned to me.[3] * * *
You speak of Lord Byron and me—There is this great difference between us. He describes what he sees—I describe what I imagine—Mine is the

7. For Richard Carlile, see p. 312, n. 5.
8. Henry "Orator" Hunt (1773–1835) had presided on the platform at a reform meeting in St. Peter's Fields, Manchester, on August 16, 1819, that was broken up violently by the yeomanry at what came to be known as the "Peterloo Massacre." He was arrested, but, upon being released on bond, he traveled to London on September 13, where he was met by a crowd (including Keats) of as many as 300,000.
9. A famous tavern on the Strand known as a site for political meetings; *Angel*: an inn near the toll gate on the Great North Road, and now gives its name to a section of London called Angel Islington.
1. For Sand and Kotzebue, see p. 325, n. 1. Paul and Dominic Colnaghi were print dealers at 23 Cockspur Street.
2. Peter Abelard (1079–1142), brilliant lecturer at Notre Dame de Paris and author of *Sic et Non*; he fell in love with his student Héloïse, which led to their forced separation and a famous correspondence, the subject of Pope's "Eloisa to Abelard" (1717).
3. Here Keats copies his acrostic poem to Georgiana (see pp. 253–54) and much of his July 23, 26, 1818 letter to Tom.

hardest task. You see the immense difference—The Edinburgh review are affraid to touch upon my Poem[4]—They do not know what to make of it—they do not like to condemn it and they will not praise it for fear—They are as shy of it as I should be of wearing a Quaker's hat—The fact is they have no real taste—they dare not compromise their Judgements on so puzzling a Question—If on my next Publication they should praise me and so lug in Endymion—I will address in a manner they will not at all relish—The Cowardliness of the Edinburgh is worse than the abuse of the Quarterly. Monday[5]—This day is a grand day for winchester—they elect the Mayor. It was indeed high time the place should have some sort of excitement. There was nothing going on—all asleep—Not an old Maids Sedan returning from a card party—and if any old women have got tipsy at christenings they have not exposed themselves in the Street—The first night tho' of our arrival here there was a slight uproar took place at about ten of the clock—We heard distinctly a noise patting down the high Street as of a walking Cane of the good old dowager breed; and a little minute after we heard a less voice observe 'what a noise the ferril made.—it must be loose." Brown wanted to call the Constables, but I observed 't was only a little breeze and would soon pass over. The side-streets here are excessively maiden lady like—The door steps always fresh from the flannel. The knockers have a very staid serious, nay almost awful quietness about them—I never saw so quiet a collection of Lions, and rams heads—The doors most part black with a little brass handle just above the key hole—so that you may easily shut yourself out of your own house—he! he! There is none of your Lady Bellaston[6] rapping and ringing here—no thundering-Jupiter footmen no opera-trebble-tattoos—but a modest lifting up of the knocker by a set of little wee old fingers that peep through the grey mittens, and a dying fall thereof—The great beauty of Poetry is, that it makes every thing every place interesting—The palatine venice and the abbotine Winchester are equally interesting—Some time since I began a Poem call'd "the Eve of St Mark" quite in the spirit of Town quietude. I think it will give you the sensation of walking about an old county Town in a coolish evening. I know not yet whether I shall ever finish it—I will give it far as I have gone. *Ut tibi placent!*[7]
   [A copy of "The Eve of St. Mark" follows.][8]
What follows is an imitation of the Authors in Chaucer's time—'t is more ancient than Chaucer himself and perhaps between him and Gower
   [A copy of lines 99–114 of "The Eve of St. Mark" follows.]
I hope you will like this for all its Carelessness—I must take an opportunity here to observe that though I am *to* you I am all the while writing *at* your Wife—This explanation will account for my speaking sometimes *hoity-toityishly*. Whereas if you were alone I should sport a little more sober sadness. I am like a squinting gentleman who saying soft things to one Lady ogles another—or what is as bad in arguing with a person on his left hand appeals with his eyes to one on the right. His Vision is elastic he bends it

4. *Endymion.*
5. September 20. Keats copied this description into his September 21 letter to Reynolds (see pp. 358–59 for notes for this passage).
6. A character in Fielding's *Tom Jones.*
7. "May they be pleasing to you."
8. See pp. 307–11.

to a certain object but having a patent spring it flies off. Writing has this disadvantage of speaking. One cannot write a wink, or a nod, or a grin, or a purse of the Lips, or a *smile*—*O law!* One can-not put ones finger to one's nose, or yerk ye in the ribs,[9] or lay hold of your button in writing—but in all the most lively and titterly parts of my Letter you must not fail to imagine me as the epic poets say—now here, now there, now with one foot pointed at the ceiling, now with another—now with my pen on my ear, now with my elbow in my mouth—O my friends you loose the action—and attitude is every thing as Fusili[1] said when he took up his leg like a Musket to shoot a Swallow just darting behind his shoulder. And yet does not the word mum! go for ones finger beside the nose—I hope it does. I have to make use of the word Mum! before I tell you that Severn has got a little Baby—all his own let us hope—He told Brown he had given up painting and had turn'd modeller. I hope sincerely tis not a party concern; that no M[r]—or **** is the real *Pinxit* and Severn the poor *Sculpsit* to this work of art—You know he has long studied in the Life-Academy.[2] Haydon—yes your wife will say, 'here is a sum total account of Haydon again I wonder your Brother don't put a monthly bulleteen in the Philadelphia Papers about him—I wont hear—no—skip down to the bottom—aye and there are some more of his verses, skip (lullaby-by) them too." "No, lets go regularly through." "I wont hear a word about Haydon—bless the child, how rioty she is!—there go on there." Now pray go on here for I have a few words to say about Haydon— Before this Chancery threat had cut of every legitimate supply of Cash from me I had a little at my disposal: Haydon being very much in want I lent him 30£ of it. Now in this se-saw game of Life I got nearest to the ground and this chancery business rivetted me there so that I was sitting in that uneasy position where the seat slants so abominably. I applied to him for payment— he could not—that was no wonder. but goodman Delver,[3] where was the wonder then, why marry, in this, he did not seem to care much about it— and let me go without my money with almost nonchalance when he aught to have sold his drawings to supply me. I shall perhaps still be acquainted with him, but for friendship that is at an end. Brown has been my friend in this he got him to sign a Bond payable at three Months—Haslam has assisted me with the return of part of the money you lent him. * * *

Tuesday[4]—You see I keep adding a sheet daily till I send the packet off— which I shall not do for a few days as I am inclined to write a good deal: for there can be nothing so remembrancing and enchaining as a good long letter be it composed of what it may—From the time you left me, our friends say I have altered completely—am not the same person—perhaps in this letter I am for in a letter one takes up one's existence from the time we last met—I dare say you have altered also—evey man does—Our bodies every seven years are completely fresh-materiald—seven years ago it was not this

---

9. See Shakespeare, *Othello*, 1.2.5: "I had thought to've yerked [stabbed] him here, under the ribs"; "titterly," which appears later in the sentence, is a Keatsian coinage, presumably from "titter."
1. Henry Fuseli (1741–1825), a Swiss artist who came to England and became a friend of Blake's; he was known to Hunt as part of the circle around Rowland Hunter, who took over Joseph Johnson's radical salon of the 1790s. A "fusil" is a light musket.
2. In a "life class," one paints nude models. It is not clear why Keats raises questions about the paternity of this child, as Severn (see p. 110, n. 6) had been married since 1809. He draws on the Latin terms used on engravings to designate the original artist ("pictor") and the engraver who copied him ("sculptor").
3. See Shakespeare, *Hamlet*, 5.1.13, "Nay, but hear you, Goodman Delver [Master Digger]."
4. September 21.

hand that clench'd itself against Hammond[5]—We are like the relict garments of a Saint: the same and not the same: for the careful Monks patch
it and patch it: till there's not a thread of the original garment left, and still
they show it for S[t] Anthony's shirt. This is the reason why men who had
been bosom friends, on being separated for any number of years, afterwards
meet coldly, neither of them knowing why—The fact is they are both
altered—Men who live together have a silent moulding and influencing
power over each other—They interassimulate. 'T is an uneasy thought that
in seven years the same hands cannot greet each other again. All this may
be obviated by a willful and dramatic exercise of our Minds towards each
other. Some think I have lost that poetic ardour and fire 't is said I once
had—the fact is perhaps I have: but instead of that I hope I shall substitute
a more thoughtful and quiet power. I am more frequently, now, contented
to read and think—but now & then, haunted with ambitious thoughts. Quieter in my pulse, improved in my digestion; exerting myself against vexing
speculations—scarcely content to write the best verses for the fever they
leave behind. I want to compose without this fever. I hope I one day shall.
You would scarcely imagine I could live alone so comfortably "Kepen in
solitarinesse."[6] I told Anne, the servent here, the other day, to say I was not
at home if any one should call. I am not certain how I should endure loneliness and bad weather together. Now the time is beautiful. I take a walk
every day for an hour before dinner and this is generally my walk—I go out
at the back gate across one street, into the Cathedral yard, which is always
interesting; then I pass under the trees along a paved path, pass the beautiful front of the Cathedral, turn to the left under a stone door way—then
I am on the other side of the building—which leaving behind me I pass on
through two college-like squares seemingly built for the dwelling place of
Deans and Prebendaries[7]—garnished with grass and shaded with trees.
Then I pass through one of the old city gates and then you are in one
College-Street through which I pass and at the end thereof crossing some
meadows and at last a country alley of gardens I arrive, that is, my worship
arrives at the foundation of Saint Cross, which is a very interesting old
place, both for its gothic tower and alms-square and for the appropriation
of its rich rents to a relation of the Bishop of Winchester[8]—Then I pass
across St Cross meadows till you come to the most beautifully clear river—
now this is only one mile of my walk I will spare you the other two till after
supper when they would do you more good—You must avoid going the first
mile just after dinner. I could almost advise you to put by all this nonsense
until you are lifted out of your difficulties—but when you come to this part
feel with confidence what I now feel that though there can be no stop put
to troubles we are inheritors of there can be and must be and end to immediate difficulties. Rest in the confidence that I will not omit any exertion to
benefit you by some means or other. If I cannot remit you hundreds, I will
tens and if not that ones. Let the next year be managed by you as well as
possible—the next month I mean for I trust you will soon receive Abbey's
remittance. What he can send you will not be a sufficient capital to ensure

5. Thomas Hammond, a surgeon with whom Keats had been apprenticed seven years earlier.
6. "The Eve of St. Mark," l. 106.
7. Canons supported by a prebend, a portion of the revenue of a cathedral or collegiate church.
8. The son of Brownlow North (1741–1820), bishop of Winchester, was Francis North, the sixth Earl
   of Guilford, who was master of St. Cross Hospital. Keats then comes to the river Itchen.

you any command in America. What he has of mine I nearly have anticipated by debts. So I would advise you not to sink it, but to live upon it in
hopes of my being able to encrease it—To this end I will devote whatever I
may gain for a few years to come—at which period I must begin to think of
a security of my own comforts when quiet will become more pleasant to me
than the World—Still I would have you doubt my success—'T is at present
the cast of a die with me. You say 'these things will be a great torment to
me.' I shall not suffer them to be so. I shall only exert myself the more—
while the seriousness of their nature will prevent me from missing up imaginary griefs. I have not had the blue devils[9] once since I received your
last—I am advised not to publish till it is seen whether the Tragedy will or
not succeed—Should it, a few months may see me in the way of acquiring
property; should it not it will be a drawback and I shall have to perform a
longer literary Pilgrimage—You will perceive that it is quite out of my interest to come to America—What could I do there? How could I employ
myself? Out of the reach of Libraries. You do not mention the name of the
gentleman who assists you.[1] 'T is an extraordinary thing. How could you do
without that assistance? I will not trust myself with brooding over this. The
following is an extract from a Letter of Reynolds to me "I am glad to hear
you are getting on so well with your writings. I hope you are not neglecting
the revision of your Poems for the press: from which I expect more than you
do"—the first thought that struck me on reading your last, was to mortgage
a Poem to Murray:[2] but on more consideration I made up my mind not to
do so: my reputation is very low: he would perhaps not have negociated my
bill of intellect or given me a very small sum. I should have bound myself
down for some time. 'T is best to meet present misfortunes; not for a
momentary good to sacrifice great benefits which one's own untramell'd
and free industry may bring one in the end. In all this do never think of me
as in any way unhappy: I shall not be so. I have a great pleasure in thinking of my responsibility to you and shall do myself the greatest luxury if I
can succeed in any way so as to be of assistance to you. We shall look back
upon these times—even before our eyes are at all dim—I am convinced of
it. But be careful of those Americans—I could almost advise you to come
whenever you have the sum of 500£ to England—Those Americans will I
am affraid still fleece you—If ever you should think of such a thing you
must bear in mind the very different state of society here—The immense
difficulties of the times—The great sum required per annum to maintain
yourself in any decency. In fact the whole is with Providence. I know not
how to advise you but by advising you to advise with yourself. In your next
tell me at large your thoughts, about america; what chance there is of succeeding there: for it appears to me you have as yet been somehow deceived.
I cannot help thinking M[r] Audubon has deceived you. I shall not like the
sight of him—I shall endeavour to avoid seeing him—You see how puzzled
I am—I have no meridian to fix you to—being the Slave of what is to happen. I think I may bid you finally remain in good hopes: and not teise yourself with my changes and variations of Mind—If I say nothing decisive in
any one particular part of my Letter, you may glean the truth from the

9. Depression.
1. Rollins identifies him as Audubon's brother-in-law, William Bakewell.
2. John Murray, Byron's publisher.

whole pretty correctly—You may wonder why I had not put your affairs with Abbey in train on receiving your Letter before last, to which there will reach you a short answer dated from shanklin. I did write and speak to Abbey but to no purpose. You last, with the enclosed note has appealed home to him— He will not see the necessity of a thing till he is hit in the mouth. 'T will be effectual—I am sorry to mix up foolish and serious things together—but in writing so much I am obliged to do so—and I hope sincerely the tenor of your mind will maintain itself better. In the course of a few months I shall be as good an Italian Scholar as I am a french one—I am reading Ariosto[3] at present: not manageing more than six or eight stanzas at a time. When I have done this language so as to be able to read it tolerably well—I shall set myself to get complete in latin and there my learning must stop. I do not think of venturing upon Greek. I would not go even so far if I were not persuaded of the power the knowlege of any language gives one. The fact is I like to be acquainted with foreign languages. It is besides a nice way of filling up intervals &c. Also the reading of Dante is well worth the while. And in latin there is a fund of curious literature of the middle ages—The Works of many great Men Aretine and Sanazarius and Machievel[4]—I shall never become attach'd to a foreign idiom so as to put it into my writings. The Paradise lost though so fine in itself is a curruption of our Language— it should be kept as it is unique—a curiosity, a beautiful and grand Curiosity. The most remarkable Production of the world—A northern dialect accommodating itself to greek and latin inversions and intonations. The purest english I think—or what ought to be the purest—is Chatterton's— The Language had existed long enough to be entirely uncorrupted of Chaucer's gallicisms and still the old words are used—Chatterton's language is entirely northern—I prefer the native music of it to Milton's cut by feet I have but lately stood on my guard against Milton. Life to him would be death to me. Miltonic verse cannot be written but in the vein of art—I wish to devote myself to another sensation—

I have been obliged to intermiten your Letter for two days (this being Friday morn) from having had to attend to other correspondence. Brown who was at Bedhampton, went thence to Chichester, and I still directing my letters Bedhampton—there arose a misunderstand about them—I began to suspect my Letters had been stopped from curiosity. However yesterday Brown had four Letters from me all in a Lump—and the matter is clear'd up—Brown complained very much in his Letter to me of yesterday of the great alteration the Disposition of Dilke has undergone—He thinks of nothing but 'Political Justice'[5] and his Boy—Now the first political duty a Man ought to have a Mind to is the happiness of his friends. I wrote Brown a comment on the subject, wherein I explained what I thought of Dilke's Character. Which resolved itself into this conclusion. That Dilke was a Man who cannot feel he has a personal identity unless he has made up his Mind about every thing. The only means of strengthening one's intellect is to make up one's mind about nothing—to let the mind be a thoroughfare

3. See p. 95, n. 3.
4. Niccolò Machiavelli (1469–1527), Italian statesman and author, known primarily as the author of *The Prince* (1532). Pietro Aretino (1492–1556), Italian satirist. Jacopo Sannazaro (1456?–1530), Italian humanist and author of *Arcadia* and *Piscatoriae*, eclogues with fisherman instead of shepherds.
5. Key work (1793) of philosophical anarchism by William Godwin (1756–1836); Keats had earlier referred to Dilke's devotion to Godwin (see p. 292).

for all thoughts. Not a select party. The genus is not scarce in population. All the stubborn arguers you meet with are of the same brood—They never begin upon a subject they have not preresolved on. They want to hammer their nail into you and if you turn the point, still they think you wrong. Dilke will never come at a truth as long as he lives; because he is always trying at it. He is a Godwin-methodist. I must not forget to mention that your mother show'd me the lock of hair—'t is of a very dark colour for so young a creature. When it is two feet in length I shall not stand a barley corn higher. That's not fair—one ought to go on growing as well as others— At the end of this sheet I shall stop for the present—and sent it off. you may expect another Letter immediately after it. As I never know the day of the month but by chance I put here that this is *the 24th September.* I would wish you here to stop your ears, for I have a word or two to say to your Wife— My dear sister, In the first place I must quarrel with you for sending me such a shabby sheet of paper—though that is in some degree made up for by the beautiful impression of the seal. You should like to know what I was doing—The first of May—let me see—I cannot recollect. I have all the Examiners ready to send—They will be a great treat to you when they reach you—I shall pack them up when my Business with Abbey has come to a good conclusion and the remittance is on the road to you—I have dealt round your best wishes to our friends, like a pack of cards but being always given to cheat, myself, I have turned up ace. You see I am making game of you. I see you are not all all happy in that America. England however would not be over happy for us if you were here. Perpaps 'twould be better to be teased herre than there. * * * My Dear George—This Monday morning the 27th I have received your last dated July 12th You say you have not heard from England these three months—Then my Letter from Shanklin written I think at the end of July cannot have reach'd you. You shall not have cause to think I neglect you. I have kept this back a little time in expectation of hearing from Mr Abbey—You will say I might have remained in Town to be Abbey's messenger in these affairs. That I offer'd him—but he in his answer convinced me he was anxious to bring the Business to an issue—He observed that by being himself the agent in the whole, people might be more expeditious. You say you have not heard for three months and yet you letters have the tone of knowing how our affairs are situated by which I conjecture I acquainted you with them in a Letter previous to the Shanklin one. That I may not have done. To be certain I will here state that it is in consequence of Mrs Jennings threatning a Chancery suit that you have been kept from the receipt of monies and myself deprived of any help from Abbey—I am glad you say you keep up your Spirits—I hope you make a true statement on that score—Still keep them up—for we are all young—I can only repeat here that you shall hear from me again immediately— Notwithstanding their bad intelligence I have experienced some pleasure in receiving so correctly two Letters from you, as it gives me if I may so say a distant Idea of Proximity. This last improves upon my little niece—Kiss her for me. Do not fret yourself about the delay of money on account of any immediate opportunity being lost: for in a new country whoever has money must have opportunity of employing it in many ways. The report runs now more in favor of Kean stopping in England. If he should I have confident hopes of our Tragedy—If he smokes the hotblooded character of

Ludolph[6]—and he is the only actor that can do it—He will add to his own fame, and improve my fortune—I will give you a half dozen lines of it before I part as a specimen—

> "Not as a Swordsman would I pardon crave,
> But as a Son: the bronz'd Centurion
> Long-toil'd in foreign wars, *and whose high deeds*
> *Are shaded in a forest of tall spears,*
> *Known only to his troop*, hath greater plea
> Of favour with my Sire than I can have—"

Believe me my dear brother and Sister—

Your affectionate and anxious Brother

[John Keats]

Letter to Fanny Brawne, October 13, 1819[1]

25 College Street.

My dearest Girl,

This moment I have set myself to copy some verses out fair. I cannot proceed with any degree of content. I must write you a line or two and see if that will assist in dismissing you from my Mind for ever so short a time. Upon my Soul I can think of nothing else. The time is passed when I had power to advise and warn you against the unpromising morning of my Life. My love has made me selfish. I cannot exist without you. I am forgetful of every thing but seeing you again—my Life seems to stop there—I see no further. You have absorb'd me. I have a sensation at the present moment as though I was dissolving—I should be exquisitely miserable without the hope of soon seeing you, I should be affraid to separate myself far from you. My sweet Fanny, will your heart never change? My love, will it? I have no limit now to my love. You note came in just here. I cannot be happier away from you. 'T is richer than an Argosy of Pearles. Do not threat me even in jest. I have been astonished that Men could die Martyrs for religion—I have shudder'd at it—I shudder no more—I could be martyr'd for my Religion—Love is my religion—I could die for that—I could die for you. My Creed is Love and you are its only tenet. You have ravish'd me away by a Power I cannot resist; and yet I could resist till I saw you; and even since I have seen you I have endeavoured often "to reason against the reasons of my Love."[2] I can do that no more—the pain would be too great. My Love is selfish. I cannot breathe without you.

Yours for ever

John Keats

---

6. The lead part in *Otho the Great*. He goes on to quote 1.3.24–29.
1. Written from the rooms Keats took when he returned to London around October 8, 1819, at 25 College Street in Westminster; he had visited Fanny on October 10 and "was in a complete fascination. . . . You dazzled me" (*L*, 2: 222). He would quit his rooms and return to Hampstead by the end of the month. Text from ALS (Haverford College Special Collections, MS 115; facsimile in A. E. Hancock, *John Keats* [New York, 1908], facing p. 188).
2. John Ford (1586–after 1639), *'Tis Pity She's a Whore*, 1.3.78.

Letter to John Taylor, November 17, 1819[1]

Wentworth Place
Wednesday,

My dear Taylor,

I have come to a determination not to publish any thing I have now ready written; but for all that to publish a Poem before long and that I hope to make a fine one.[2] As the marvellous is the most enticing and the surest guarantee of harmonious numbers I have been endeavouring to persuade myself to untether Fancy and let her manage for herself—I and myself cannot agree about this at all. Wonders are no wonders to me. I am more at home amongst Men and women. I would rather read Chaucer than Ariosto.[3] The little dramatic skill I may as yet have however badly it might show in a Drama would I think be sufficient for a Poem. I wish to diffuse the colouring of St Agnes eve throughout a Poem in which Character and Sentiment would be the figures to such drapery. Two or three such Poems, if God should spare me, written in the course of the next six years, would be a famous gradus ad Parnassum altissimum.[4] I mean they would nerve me up to the writing of a few fine Plays—my greatest ambition—when I do feel ambitious. I am sorry to say that is very seldom. The subject we have once or twice talked of appears a promising one, The Earl of Leicester's historry. I am this morning reading Holingshed's Elisabeth,[5] You had some Books awhile ago, you promised to lend me, illustrative of my Subject. If you can lay hold of them or any others which may be serviceable to me I know you will encourage my low-spirited Muse by sending them—or rather by letting me know when our Errand cart Man shall call with my little Box. I will endeavour to set my self selfishly at work on this Poem that is to be—

Your sincere friend
John Keats—

SONNET.[1]

The day is gone, and all its sweets are gone!
   Sweet voice, sweet lips, soft hand, and softer breast,
Warm breath, light whisper, tender semi-tone,
   Bright eyes, accomplish'd shape, and lang'rous waist!

---

1. Written after Keats had returned to Wentworth Place to live with Brown and near Fanny Brawne. Keats was depressed and frustrated, waiting for news about a possible production of *Otho the Great* and making little progress with *King Stephen*; he had dined with Taylor and the painter William Hilton on November 15 to discuss his next volume of poems. Text from ALS (Morgan Library 210[2]); there is also a transcript in Woodhouse's letter-book, p. 37–38 and 104–105.
2. Perhaps "The Jealousies" (see pp. 378–402).
3. For Ariosto, see p. 95, n. 3.
4. "A step towards the highest Parnassus," home of the Muses.
5. Raphael Holinshed's *Chronicles of England, Scotland, and Ireland* (1577). Keats and Taylor had apparently discussed a possible play about Robert Dudley, Earl of Leicester (1532?–1588), a favorite of Elizabeth I involved in court intrigues of the period.
1. Written in 1819, presumably toward the end of the year after Keats had returned to Hampstead and was again seeing Fanny Brawne, whom he first visited upon his return on October 10. First published in the *Plymouth and Devonport Weekly Journal*, October 4, 1838; text from *PDWJ* with emendations from Brown's transcript (Harvard MS Keats 3.6, p. 57; *MYR: JK*, 7: 59).

Faded the flower and all its budded charms,　　　　　　　5
　　Faded the sight of beauty from my eyes,
Faded the shape[2] of beauty from my arms,
　　Faded the voice, warmth, whiteness, paradise,
Vanish'd unseasonably at shut of eve,
　　When the dusk holiday—or holinight—　　　　　　　10
Of fragrant curtained love begins to weave
　　The woof[3] of darkness, thick, for hid delight;
But, as I've read Love's Missal[4] through to-day,
He'll let me sleep, seeing I fast and pray.

TO————.[1]

What can I do to drive away
Remembrance from my eyes? for they have seen,
Aye, an hour ago, my brilliant Queen!
Touch has a memory. O say, love, say,
What can I do to kill it and be free　　　　　　　　5
In my old liberty?
When every fair one that I saw was fair,
Enough to catch me in but half a snare,
Not keep me there:
When, howe'er poor or particolour'd things,　　　　　10
My muse had wings,[2]
And ever ready was to take her course
Whither I bent her force,
Unintellectual, yet divine to me;—
Divine, I say!—What sea-bird o'er the sea　　　　　15
Is a philosopher the while he goes
Winging along where the great water throes?

How shall I do
To get anew
Those moulted feathers, and so mount once more　　　20
Above, above
The reach of fluttering Love,
And make him cower lowly while I soar?
Shall I gulp wine?[3] No, that is vulgarism,
A heresy and schism,　　　　　　　　　　　　　　25
Foisted into the canon law of love;—
No,—wine is only sweet to happy men;
More dismal cares
Seize on me unawares,—
Where shall I learn to get my peace again?　　　　　30

2. *PDWJ* misreads as "shade."
3. *PDWJ* misreads as "roof."
4. A book containing the service for the Mass for the entire year.
1. Probably written in 1819, with Milnes speculating that it was written around October 1, 1819, Forman (1883) dating it on October 12, and Allott placing it between October 15 and 31, linking it to the feelings Keats expresses in, for example, his October 13 letter (see p. 373). First published in 1848, 2: 34–35; text from 1848, the poem's sole source.
2. See Keats's "wings of poesy" in "Ode to a Nightingale," l. 33.
3. See "Ode to a Nightingale," l. 11, "Oh, for a draught of vintage."

To banish thoughts of that most hateful land,[4]
Dungeoner of my friends, that wicked strand
Where they were wreck'd and live a wrecked[5] life;
That monstrous region, whose dull rivers pour,
Ever[6] from their sordid urns unto the shore,   35
Unown'd of any weedy-haired gods;
Whose winds, all zephyrless, hold scourging rods,
Iced in the great lakes, to afflict mankind;
Whose rank-grown forests, frosted, black, and blind,
Would fright a Dryad; whose harsh herbaged meads   40
Make lean and lank the starv'd ox while he feeds;
There bad[7] flowers have no scent, birds no sweet song,
And great unerring Nature once seems wrong.

O, for some sunny spell
To dissipate the shadows of this hell!   45
Say they are gone,—with the new dawning light
Steps forth my lady bright!
O, let me once more rest
My soul upon that dazzling breast!
Let once again these aching arms be placed,   50
The tender gaolers of thy waist!
And let me feel that warm breath here and there
To spread a rapture in my very hair,—
O, the sweetness of the pain!
Give me those lips again!   55
Enough! Enough! it is enough for me
To dream of thee!

TO FANNY.[1]

PHYSICIAN Nature! let my spirit blood![2]
O ease my heart of verse and let me rest;
Throw me upon thy Tripod,[3] till the flood
Of stifling numbers ebbs from my full breast.
A theme! a theme! great nature! give a theme;   5
Let me begin my dream.
I come—I see thee, as thou standest there,
Beckon me out[4] into the wintry air.

Ah! dearest love, sweet home of all my fears,
And hopes, and joys, and panting miseries,—   10

4. The United States, where George and Georgiana Keats had encountered difficulties. Keats imagines the American landscape defeating the kind of mythological imagination he often drew upon,
   as Grecian urns become "sordid" (l. 35), "weedy-haired" (l. 36) sea gods disown the land, the winds
   lack spirits such as Zephyr, and the forest nymphs or Dryads are frightened away.
5. Forman (1939) suggests emending this to "wretched."
6. Forman (1939) suggests emending this to "Even."
7. Forman (1939), arguing that Keats started "bud" and then changed it to "flowers," drops "bad."
1. Written in late 1819 or early 1820, with Allott and Cook assigning it to February 1820 when Keats's
   illness separated him from Fanny Brawne and he was beset with jealousy. First published in 1848,
   2: 284–86; text from 1848 with emendations from Milnes's transcript (Harvard MS Keats 3.10[6]).
2. Blood-letting was a common practice as it was believed to relieve bodily pressure; Keats was bled
   after his February 1820 hemorrhage, for example.
3. The three-legged vessel at Apollo's shrine at Delphi on which the priestess sat to prophesy.
4. 1848 has "not."

To-night, if I may guess, thy beauty wears
    A smile of such delight,
    As brilliant and as bright,
As when with ravished, aching, vassal eyes,
    Lost in a soft amaze,   15
      I gaze, I gaze!

Who now, with greedy looks, eats up my feast?
What stare outfaces now my silver moon!
Ah! keep that hand unravished at the least;
    Let, let, the amorous burn—   20
    But, pr'ythee, do not turn
The current of your heart from me so soon.
    O! save, in charity,
    The quickest pulse for me.

Save it for me, sweet love! though music breathe   25
Voluptuous visions into the warm air,
Though swimming through the dance's dangerous wreath;
    Be like an April day,
    Smiling and cold and gay,
A temperate lily, temperate as fair;   30
    Then, Heaven! there will be
    A warmer June for me.

Why, this—you'll say, my Fanny! is not true;
Put your soft hand upon your snowy side,
Where the heart beats: confess—'tis nothing new—   35
    Must not a woman be
    A feather on the sea,
Sway'd to and fro by every wind and tide?
    Of as uncertain speed
    As blow-ball⁵ from the mead?   40

I know it—and to know it is despair
To one who loves you as I love, sweet Fanny,
Whose heart goes flutt'ring for you every where,
    Nor, when away you roam,
    Dare keep its wretched home: 45
Love, love alone, has pains severe and many;
    Then, loveliest! keep me free,
    From torturing jealousy.

Ah! if you prize my subdued soul above
The poor, the fading, brief, pride of an hour: 50
Let none profane my Holy See of love,
    Or with a rude hand break
    The sacramental cake:⁶
Let none else touch the just new-budded flower;

---

5. The seed head of a dandelion.
6. Keats invokes religious language with "sacramental cake" evoking the wafer used in communion and "Holy See" (l. 51) referring to the Vatican.

If not—may my eyes close,   55
Love! on their last[7] repose!

[This living hand, now warm and capable][1]

THIS living hand, now warm and capable
Of earnest grasping, would, if it were cold
And in the icy silence of the tomb,
So haunt thy days and chill thy dreaming nights
That thou wouldst[2] wish thine own heart dry of blood   5
So in my veins red life might stream again,
And thou be conscience-calm'd—see here it is—
I hold it towards you. —> *a bit aggressive*
—> *from dying speaker —> reader*

Will —> death —> to achieve some sort of connection

THE CAP AND BELLS;
OR, THE JEALOUSIES.
A FAËRY TALE. UNFINISHED.
[The Jealousies: A Faery Tale, by Lucy Vaughan Lloyd of China Walk, Lambeth][1]

This unfinished satire, Keats's last attempt at a long poem, was written in late 1819, while Keats was living with Brown, who reports, "By chance our conversation turned on the idea of a comic faery poem in the Spenser stanza. . . . It was to be published under the feigned authorship of Lucy Vaughan Lloyd, and to bear the title of *The Cap and Bells*, or, which he preferred, *The Jealousies*. This occupied his mornings pleasantly. He wrote it with the greatest facility; in one instance I remember having copied (for I copied as he wrote) as many as twelve stanzas before dinner" (*KC*, 2: 71–72). Brown at times suggests the poem was written without plan (it "was written chiefly for amusement; it appeared to be a relaxation; and it was begun without framing laws in his mind for the supernatural"; *KC*, 2: 99); at other times, he indicates that there was an overall structure and that he was a collaborator in it ("I knew all, and was to assist him in the machinery of one part"; *KC*, 2: 79). There is also an indication that Reynolds was to provide notes for the poem (see letter to Reynolds, February 28, 1820, *L*, 2: 268), so this may have been imagined as a collective effort. In any event, Keats, increasingly ill and with his brother George in London seeking financial aid, had stopped work on the poem by the beginning of the new year (*L*, 2: 268) but was still expressing hope

---

7. 1846 has "lost."
1. Probably written in late 1819, as it is found in the draft MS of "The Jealousies," on which Keats was working at the time. Forman's title, "Lines Supposed to Have Been Addressed to Fanny Brawne," links the poem to Keats's jealousy of Fanny Brawne; others have seen it as associated with Keats's work in the drama. First published in Forman's 1898 one-volume edition, p. 417; text from 1898 with emendations from the holograph (Harvard MS Keats 2.92.2, on last verso; *JKPMH*, p. 259).
2. The holograph MS has "would."
1. The title in W[2].

that he could return to it in June 1820 (see letter to Brown, ca. June 21, 1820, *L*, 2: 299).

While Francis Jeffrey would praise the poem to Milnes for its "beautiful passages," its "strange outbreaks of redundant fancy, and felicitous expression" (*KC*, 2: 249), the poem has not won many modern admirers. There has been disagreement about the subject of the satire. Some have found it joining in the political attacks upon the Prince Regent, soon to be George IV: Elfinan, "famed ev'rywhere / For love of mortal women" (ll. 4–5), can be read as the Regent known for his various amours and his unhappy marriage to Princess Caroline, with Crafticant (the crafty deployer of cant) being a summary figure for such ministers as Castlereagh and Sidmouth, perpetual targets of attacks from the left, and the Regent's opponent Biancopany ("White-Bread") being an Italianized Samuel Whitbread (1764–1815), a strong defender of the Regent's wife. Others, following Gittings (pp. 368–73), have found the poem offering a satirical portrait of the literary scene: in this account, we get portraits of both the Lake Poets—with Crafticant having features of Wordsworth, Coleridge, and particularly Southey—and the opposing writers on the left, particularly Hunt as Hum (a poet who creates Huntian "nows"; l. 560) and Byron as the amorous Elfinan pursuing women other than his wife Bellanaine/Annabella Milbanke (see Keats's parody of Byron's "Fare thee well" to Lady Byron at ll. 609–12), with Eban perhaps being Hazlitt. When we note Keats's comment that if he published this poem, with its fictitious lady author, there "will be some delicate picking for squeamish stomachs" who have found his other poems displeasing women (*L*, 2: 327–28), we might see the poem as a satire on the "blue-stocking" set that Keats disparaged. With its echoes of other Keats poems, particularly *The Eve of St. Agnes* and "The Eve of St. Mark," it can be read as an act of self-parody; it certainly takes a different approach to the union of mortal and immortal often found in his poetry, as in, for example, "I stood tiptoe upon a little hill," *Endymion*, "Ode to Psyche," and *Lamia*. Contemporary issues and fads—from hackney coaches to slavery, empire and Tipoo Sultan (see Phyllis G. Mann, "Keats's Indian Allegory," *KSJ* 6 [1957]: 4–9; and Chandler, *England in 1819* [1998], pp. 233–34)—are also taken up. For a fine account of the poem's satiric valences, see Steven E. Jones, *Satire and Romanticism* (New York: St. Martin's Press, 2000), pp. 125–32.

Written in Spenserian stanzas and drawing on Spenser and Shakespeare's *Midsummer Night's Dream* for its fairies, the poem has been seen to imitate Byron's style in *Beppo* (April 1819) and the first two cantos of *Don Juan* (July 1819). It partakes of the interest in oriental subjects that can be found in Southey's *Thalaba the Destroyer* (1801) and *Curse of Kehama* (1810), Byron's oriental tales, and Tom Moore's *Lalla Rookh* (1817). It may owe something to Hunt's orientalist satire on the Regent and European politics, "Account of the Remarkable Rise and Downfall of the Late Great Khan of Tartary," the *Examiner*, January 14, 1816, pp. 17–20 (*SWLH*, 2: 40–49). It was drafted at a moment of widespread satiric writing that, on one hand, followed upon the "Peterloo Massacre" in August 1819 and, on another, attended the publication of Wordsworth's *Peter Bell* in April 1819, including Reynolds's "prenatal" satire and Shelley's *Peter Bell the Third*, sent to Hunt on November 2,

1819. With its fairy cast, its star-crossed lovers, and its magicians, the piece also seems to owe something to the Christmas pantomime or harlequinade.

Lines 217–56 on hackney coaches were first published in Hunt's *Indicator*, August 23, 1820, p. 368; lines 390–96 and 415–23 were first published as epigraphs for chapters 12 and 48 in E. J. Trewlawny's *Adventures of a Younger Son* (1831). The complete text (except for ll. 793–94) was first published in 1848, 2: 215–51 with a note, "This poem was written subject to future amendments and omissions: it was begun without a plan, and without any prescribed laws for the supernatural machinery.— CHARLES BROWN." The present text is taken from 1848 with emendations drawn from Keats's draft of ll. 1–729 (1–72, 145–398, 460–729 at the Morgan Library, MA 214; 73–108 at the Huntington Library, MS HM 7149; 109–144, 397–459 at Harvard, MS Keats 2.29.1, 2.29.2, *JKPMH* 247–57) and from W² f.196r–210v (*MYR: JK*, 6: 365–94).

I.

In midmost Ind, beside Hydaspes cool,[2]
There stood, or hover'd, tremulous in the air,
A faery city, 'neath the potent rule
Of Emperor Elfinan;[3] famed ev'rywhere
For love of mortal women, maidens fair,   5
Whose lips were solid, whose soft hands were made
Of a fit mould and beauty, ripe and rare,
To pamper his slight wooing, warm yet staid:
He lov'd girls smooth as shades, but hated a mere shade.

II.

This was a crime forbidden by the law;[4]   10
And all the priesthood of his city wept,
For ruin and dismay they well foresaw,
If impious prince no bound or limit kept,
And faery Zendervester[5] overstept;
They wept, he sinn'd, and still he would sin on,   15
They dreamt of sin, and he sinn'd while they slept;
In vain the pulpit thunder'd at the throne,
Caricature was vain, and vain the tart lampoon.[6]

---

2. Keats sets his fairy story in India, on the river Hydaspes (modern Jhelum, the Punjabi river flowing through India and Pakistan); in classical mythology, the god of the river helped India's resistance against Dionysus, and it was also the site where Alexander the Great fought his last great battle in 326 B.C.E. against Porus, a powerful Indian king. Keats could have adopted the name from Horace, *Odes*, Book 1, Carmen 22, ll. 7–8, or Milton, *Paradise Lost*, 3.436: "Ganges, or Hydaspes, Indian streams."
3. See Spenser's "rolles of Elfin Emperours" in *The Faerie Queene*, 2.10, especially 72: "*Elfin*; him all India obayd, / And all that now *America* men call: / Next him was noble *Elfinan*."
4. Political readings have focused on the Regent's tortured marriage to Princess Caroline, whom he would attempt to divorce upon becoming King in 1820; his "forbidden" love, however, was his secret marriage in 1785 to the widow Mrs. Fitzherbert, a Catholic.
5. Zend-Avesta is the sacred book of Zoroastrianism, the ancient Persian religion.
6. There was a long history of satires on the Prince Regent (if we read him as Elfinan), including Lamb's "Triumph of the Whale" (*Examiner*, March 15, 1812, p. 173), Hone's *Political House that Jack Built* (1819), and many pieces by Peter Pindar (John Wolcott).

III.

Which seeing, his high court of parliament
Laid a remonstrance at his Highness' feet,   20
Praying his royal senses to content
Themselves with what in faery land was sweet,
Befitting best that shade with shade should meet:
Whereat, to calm their fears, he promised soon
From mortal tempters all to make retreat,—   25
Aye, even on the first of the new moon,
An immaterial wife to espouse as heaven's boon.

IV.

Meantime he sent a fluttering embassy
To Pigmio, of Imaus[7] sovereign,
To half beg, and half demand, respectfully,   30
The hand of his fair daughter Bellanaine;
An audience had, and speeching done, they gain
Their point, and bring the weeping bride away;
Whom, with but one attendant, safely lain
Upon their wings, they bore in bright array,   35
While little harps were touch'd by many a lyric fay.

V.

As in old pictures tender cherubim
A child's soul thro' the sapphired canvas bear,
So, thro' a real heaven, on they swim
With the sweet Princess on her plumaged lair,   40
Speed giving to the winds her lustrous hair;
And so she journey'd, sleeping or awake,
Save when, for healthful exercise and air,
She chose to "promener à l'aile,"[8] or take
A pigeon's somerset,[9] for sport or change's sake.   45

VI.

"Dear Princess, do not whisper me so loud,"
Quoth Corallina, nurse and confidant,
"Do not you see there, lurking in a cloud,
Close at your back, that sly old Crafticant?
He hears a whisper plainer than a rant: 50
Dry up your tears, and do not look so blue;
He's Elfinan's great state-spy militant,
He's running, lying, flying foot-man too,—
Dear mistress, let him have no handle against you!

7. A name the ancients used for any large mountain chain in Asia, particularly bordering India; the Hindu Kush. Lemprière gives, "a large mountain of Scythia, which is part of mount Taurus. It divides Scythia." Dibdin's Christmas pantomime, *Harlequin and Humpo* (1812/13) that usually followed Coleridge's *Remorse* on stage, tells the story of a match between a princess and Prince Humpino, son of Humpo, king of the dwarves.
8. To go for a walk in the air; to exercise her wings.
9. Somersault.

VII.

"Show him a mouse's tail, and he will guess,   55
With metaphysic swiftness, at the mouse;
Show him a garden, and with speed no less,
He'll surmise sagely of a dwelling-house,
And plot, in the same minute, how to chouse
The owner out of it; show him a—" "Peace!   60
Peace! nor contrive thy mistress' ire to rouse;"
Return'd the Princess, "my tongue shall not cease
Till from this hated match I get a free release.

VIII.

"Ah, beauteous mortal!" "Hush!" quoth Coralline,
"Really you must not talk of him, indeed."   65
"You hush!" replied the mistress, with a shine
Of anger in her eyes, enough to breed
In stouter hearts than nurse's fear and dread:
'Twas not the glance itself made nursey flinch,
But of its threat she took the utmost heed;   70
Not liking in her heart an hour-long pinch,
Or a sharp needle run into her back an inch.

IX.

So she was silenced, and fair Bellanaine,
Writhing her little body with ennui,
Continued to lament and to complain,   75
That Fate, cross-purposing, should let her be
Ravish'd away far from her dear countree;
That all her feelings should be set at nought,
In trumping up this match so hastily,
With lowland blood; and lowland blood she thought   80
Poison, as every staunch true-born Imaian ought.

X.

Sorely she grieved, and wetted three or four
White Provence rose-leaves with her faery tears,
But not for this cause;—alas! she had more
Bad reasons for her sorrow, as appears   85
In the famed memoirs of a thousand years,
Written by Crafticant, and published
By Parpaglion and Co., (those sly compeers
Who raked up ev'ry fact against the dead,)
In Scarab Street, Panthea, at the Jubal's Head.[1]   90

---

1. Parpaglion may derive from "parpagliòne," Italian for butterfly, particularly a large nocturnal one. The scarab beetle was considered by the Egyptians to be sacred to the god Ra. Panthea is a "Christall" city of the fairies in Spenser's *Faerie Queene* 2.10.73. For Jubal, See Genesis 4.21: "And his brother's name was Jubal: he was the father of all such as handle the harp and organ."

XI.

Where, after a long hypercritic howl
Against the vicious manners of the age,
He goes on to expose, with heart and soul,
What vice in this or that year was the rage,
Backbiting all the world in ev'ry page;   95
With special strictures on the horrid crime,
(Section'd and subsection'd with learning sage,)
Of faeries stooping on their wings sublime
To kiss a mortal's lips, when such were in their prime.

XII.

Turn to the copious index, you will find   100
Somewhere in the column, headed letter B.,
The name of Bellanaine, if you're not blind;
Then pray refer to the text, and you will see
An article made up of calumny
Against this highland princess, rating her   105
For giving way, so over fashionably,
To this new-fangled vice, which seems a burr
Stuck in his moral throat, no coughing e'er could stir.

XIII.

There he says plainly that she loved a man!
That she around him flutter'd, flirted, toy'd,   110
Before her marriage with great Elfinan;
That after marriage too, she never joy'd
In husband's company, but still employ'd
Her wits to 'scape away to Angle-land;[2]
Where liv'd the youth, who worried and annoy'd   115
Her tender heart, and its warm ardors fann'd
To such a dreadful blaze, her side would scorch her hand.

XIV.

But let us leave this idle tittle-tattle
To waiting-maids, and bed-room coteries,
Nor till fit time against her fame wage battle.   120
Poor Elfinan is very ill at ease,
Let us resume his subject if you please:
For it may comfort and console him much,
To rhyme and syllable his miseries;
Poor Elfinan! whose cruel fate was such,   125
He sat and cursed a bride he knew he could not touch.

XV.

Soon as (according to his promises)
The bridal embassy had taken wing,

2. England.

And vanish'd, bird-like, o'er the suburb trees,
The Emperor, empierced with the sharp sting   130
Of love, retired, vex'd and murmuring
Like any drone shut from the fair bee-queen,
Into his cabinet, and there did fling
His limbs upon a sofa, full of spleen,
And damn'd his House of Commons, in complete chagrin.   135

XVI.

"I'll trounce some of the members," cried the Prince,
I'll put a mark against some rebel names,
I'll make the opposition-benches wince,
I'll show them very soon, to all their shames,
What 'tis to smother up a prince's flames;   140
That ministers should join in it, I own,
Surprises me!—they too at these high games!
Am I an Emperor? Do I wear a crown?
Imperial Elfinan, go hang thyself or drown!

XVII.

"I'll trounce 'em!—there's the square-cut chancellor,[3]   145
His son shall never touch that bishopric;
And for the nephew of old Palfior,
I'll show him that his speeches made me sick,
And give the colonelcy to Phalaric;[4]
The tiptoe marquis, moral and gallant,   150
Shall lodge in shabby taverns upon tick;[5]
And for the Speaker's second cousin's aunt,
She sha'n't be maid of honour,—by heaven that she sha'n't!

XVIII.

"I'll shirk the Duke of A.; I'll cut his brother;
I'll give no garter[6] to his eldest son;   155
I won't speak to his sister or his mother!
The Viscount B. shall live at cut-and-run;
But how in the world can I contrive to stun
That fellow's voice, which plagues me worse than any,
That stubborn fool, that impudent state-dun,   160
Who sets down ev'ry sovereign as a zany,—
That vulgar commoner, Esquire Biancopany?[7]

XIX.

"Monstrous affair! Pshaw! pah! what ugly minx
Will they fetch from Imaus for my bride?

3. Perhaps Nicholas Vansittart (1766–1851), Chancellor of the Exchequer, unpopular for his poli-
cies on taxation and a supporter of Christian missionary societies.
4. A "javelin or dart wrapped in tow and pitch, set on fire, and thrown by the catapult or by hand, in
order to set fire to a fortified place, a ship, etc." (OED). *Palfior*=friend+bloom (Italian)? Benjamin
Bloomfield (1768–1846), gentleman-in-waiting, chief equerry and clerk-marshal to the Regent?
5. On credit.
6. The Order of the Garter.
7. See headnote above.

Alas! my wearied heart within me sinks,   165
To think that I must be so near allied
To a cold dullard fay,—ah, woe betide!
Ah, fairest of all human loveliness!
Sweet Bertha! what crime can it be to glide
About the fragrant plaitings of thy dress,   170
Or kiss thine eyes, or count thy locks, tress after tress?"

XX.

So said, one minute's while his eyes remain'd
Half lidded, piteous, languid, innocent;
But, in a wink, their splendour they regain'd,
Sparkling revenge with amorous fury blent.   175
Love thwarted in bad temper oft has vent:
He rose, he stampt his foot, he rang the bell,
And order'd some death-warrants to be sent
For signature:—somewhere the tempest fell,
As many a poor fellow[8] does not live to tell.   180

XXI.

"At the same time, Eban,"—(this was his page,
A fay of colour, slave from top to toe,
Sent as a present, while yet under age,
From the Viceroy of Zanguebar,[9]—wise, slow,
His speech, his only words were "yes" and "no,"   185
But swift of look, and foot, and wing was he,)—
"At the same time, Eban, this instant go
To Hum[1] the soothsayer, whose name I see
Among the fresh arrivals in our empery.

XXII.

"Bring Hum to me! But stay—here take my ring,   190
The pledge of favour, that he not suspect
Any foul play, or awkward murdering,[2]
Though I have bowstrung[3] many of his sect;
Throw in a hint, that if he should neglect
One hour, the next shall see him in my grasp,   195
And the next after that shall see him neck'd,[4]
Or swallow'd by my hunger-starved asp,—
And mention ('tis as well) the torture of the wasp."[5]

---

8. The draft and W[2] have "felon."
9. Zanguebar (Zanzibar), meaning "black coast," was used to designate the East African coastline and
   islands from the Sudan to Mozambique. Eban's name (which started as Amorio and then Amorico
   in the draft) comes from "ebony."
1. For humbug. Hum may have been suggested by Hunt's essay, referred to in the headnote, where
   an orientalized England worships "JUSDY-VINUM [Divine Right], or that is to say in English the
   DIVINE HUM" (*SWLH*, 2: 45).
2. The draft has "handling."
3. Garroted or strangled with a bowstring.
4. Beheaded.
5. Similar imagery can be found in Shelley's *Oedipus Tyrannus; or Swellfoot the Tyrant* (1820) and
   William Hone's *The Political Showman—At Home! Exhibiting His Cabinet of Curiosities and
   Creatures—All Alive!* (1821).

XXIII.

These orders given, the Prince, in half a pet,
Let o'er the silk his propping elbow slide,   200
Caught up his little legs, and, in a fret,
Fell on the sofa on his royal side.
The slave retreated backwards, humble-eyed,
And with a slave-like silence closed the door,
And to old Hum thro' street and alley hied;   205
He "knew the city," as we say, of yore,
And for short cuts and turns, was nobody knew more.

XXIV.

It was the time when wholesale houses[6] close
Their shutters with a moody sense of wealth,
But retail dealers, diligent, let loose   210
The gas (objected to on score of health),
Convey'd in little solder'd pipes by stealth,
And make it flare in many a brilliant form,
That all the power of darkness it repell'th,
Which to the oil-trade doth great scaith and harm,   215
And supersedeth quite the use of the glow–worm.[7]

XXV.

Eban, untempted by the pastry-cooks,
(Of pastry he got store within the palace,)
With hasty steps, wrapp'd cloak, and solemn looks,
Incognito upon his errand sallies,   220
His smelling-bottle ready for the allies;[8]
He pass'd the hurdy-gurdies[9] with disdain,
Vowing he'd have them sent on board the gallies;
Just as he made his vow, it 'gan to rain,
Therefore he call'd a coach, and bade it drive amain.   225

XXVI.

"I'll pull the string,"[1] said he, and further said,
"Polluted jarvey![2] Ah, thou filthy hack!
Whose springs of life are all dried up and dead,
Whose linsey-woolsey[3] lining hangs all slack,
Whose rug is straw, whose wholeness is a crack;   230
And evermore thy steps go clatter-clitter;
Whose glass once up can never be got back,

---

6. This is the draft reading; 1848's "dealers" seems a misreading, probably from l. 210.
7. The first public gas street lights were in Pall Mall in 1807; on December 31, 1813, the Westminster Bridge was lighted by gas.
8. Alleys.
9. Kinds of barrel organ. He wants to send these street musicians as criminals to row in the galleys.
1. The check-string pulled to tell the driver the stop.
2. Perhaps derived from Jarvis, a driver of a hackney coach, also a "hack," though the latter can also refer to the horses.
3. A cheap cloth made of wool and flax.

Who prov'st, with jolting arguments and bitter,
That 'tis of modern use[4] to travel in a litter.[5]

XXVII.

"Thou inconvenience! thou hungry crop[6]   235
For all corn! thou snail-creeper to and fro,
Who while thou goest ever seem'st to stop,
And fiddle-faddle standest while you go;
I' the morning, freighted with a weight of woe,
Unto some lazar-house[7] thou journeyest,   240
And in the evening tak'st a double row
Of dowdies, for some dance or party drest,
Besides the goods meanwhile thou movest east and west.

XXVIII.

"By thy ungallant bearing and sad mien,
An inch appears the utmost thou couldst budge: 245
Yet at the slightest nod, or hint, or sign,
Round to the curb-stone patient dost thou trudge,
School'd in a beckon, learned in a nudge,
A dull-eyed Argus[8] watching for a fare;
Quiet and plodding, thou dost bear no grudge   250
To whisking tilburies, or phaetons rare,
Curricles, or mail-coaches, swift beyond compare."[9]

XXIX.

Philosophising thus, he pull'd the check,
And bade the coachman wheel to such a street,
Who, turning much his body, more his neck,   255
Louted[1] full low, and hoarsely did him greet:
"Certes, Monsieur were best take to his feet,
Seeing his servant can no further drive
For press of coaches, that to-night here meet,
Many as bees about a straw-capp'd hive,   260
When first for April honey into faint flowers they dive."

XXX.[2]

Eban then paid his fare, and tiptoe went
To Hum's hotel; and, as he on did pass

---

4. The *Indicator* lines have "of vile no-use."
5. The draft has an uncancelled version of ll. 231–34: "thy steps are clattering / Whose glass once up can never be got back, / Whose number stuck above my head a thing / (The number of the beast) gives trembling to my wing."
6. The craw and thus the maw or stomach.
7. A place for diseased persons, particularly lepers; Lazar is derived from Lazarus.
8. The hundred-eyed watchman placed to guard Io.
9. Various light, open coaches, with the tilbury and curricle both having two wheels and the phaeton four. Mail coaches had come into use in 1787.
1. Bent, bowed.
2. A cancelled version of stanza XXX in the draft reads in part, "Signor Hum / A Converzazione holds tonight / Whene'er he beats his literary drum / The learned muster round all light and tight / Drest in best black to talk by candle light."

With head inclined, each dusky lineament
Show'd in the pearl-paved street, as in a glass;   265
His purple vest, that ever peeping was
Rich from the fluttering crimson of his cloak,
His silvery trowsers, and his silken sash
Tied in a burnish'd knot, their semblance took
Upon the mirror'd walls, wherever he might look.   270

XXXI.

He smiled at self, and, smiling, show'd his teeth,
And seeing his white teeth, he smiled the more;
Lifted his eye-brows, spurn'd the path beneath,
Show'd teeth again, and smiled as heretofore,
Until he knock'd at the magician's door;   275
Where, till the porter answer'd, might be seen,
In the clear panel, more he could adore,—
His turban wreath'd of gold, and white, and green,
Mustachios, ear-ring, nose-ring, and his sabre keen.

XXXII.

"Does not your master give a rout to-night?"   280
Quoth the dark page; "Oh, no!" return'd the Swiss,
"Next door but one to us, upon the right,
The *Magazin des Modes* now open is
Against the Emperor's wedding;—and, sir, this
My master finds a monstrous horrid bore;   285
As he retired, an hour ago I wis,[3]
With his best beard and brimstone, to explore
And cast a quiet figure[4] in his second floor.

XXXIII.

"Gad! he's obliged to stick to business!
For chalk, I hear, stands at a pretty price;   290
And as for aqua vitæ[5]—there's a mess!
The *dentes sapientiæ*[6] of mice
Our barber tells me too are on the rise,—
Tinder's a lighter article,—nitre[7] pure
Goes off like lightning,—grains of paradise[8]   295
At an enormous figure!—stars not sure!—
Zodiac will not move without a slight douceur![9]

3. Know (pseudo-archaic).
4. Cast a horoscope or draw a magical sign.
5. A "term of the alchemists applied to ardent spirits or unrectified alcohol" (*OED*).
6. Wisdom teeth.
7. A "supposed volatile substance or chemical principle related to or present in saltpetre, said to exist in the air or in plants and to give rise to various physico-chemical or vital phenomena" (*OED*).
8. Also known as Guinea grains, the seeds of an aromatic West African plant used as a spice and a medicine.
9. A sweetener. The draft and W² have "sly" for "slight."

XXXIV.

"Venus won't stir a peg without a fee,
And master is too partial, *entre nous*,
To—" "Hush—hush!" cried Eban, "sure that is he   300
Coming down stairs,—by St. Bartholomew![1]
As backwards as he can,—is't something new?
Or is't his custom, in the name of fun?"
"He always comes down backward, with one shoe"—
Return'd the porter—"off, and one shoe on,   305
Like, saving shoe for sock or stocking, my man John!"[2]

XXXV.

It was indeed the great Magician,
Feeling, with careful toe, for every stair,
And retrograding careful as he can,
Backwards and downwards from his own two pair:[3]   310
"Salpietro!"[4] exclaim'd Hum, "is the dog there?
He's always in my way upon the mat!"
"He's in the kitchen, or the Lord knows where,"—
Replied the Swiss,—"the nasty, whelping[5] brat!"
"Don't beat him!" return'd Hum, and on the floor came pat.   315

XXXVI.

Then facing right about, he saw the Page,
And said: "Don't tell me what you want, Eban;
The Emperor is now in a huge rage,—
'Tis nine to one he'll give you the rattan![6]
Let us away!" Away together ran   320
The plain-dress'd sage and spangled blackamoor,
Nor rested till they stood to cool, and fan,
And breathe themselves at th' Emperor's chamber door,
When Eban thought he heard a soft imperial snore.

XXXVII.

"I thought you guess'd, foretold, or prophesied,   325
That 's Majesty was in a raving fit."
"He dreams," said Hum, "or I have ever lied,
That he is tearing you, sir, bit by bit."
"He's not asleep, and you have little wit,"
Replied the Page, "that little buzzing noise,   330

---

1. One of the twelve apostles; Hunt mentions the St. Bartholomew's Day Massacre of French Protestants of August 24, 1572, in his orientalist satire on the Regent (*SWLH*, 2: 48). St. Bartholomew Fair had been a carnivalesque site appropriate to the poem.
2. Keats apparently knew a version of the nursery rhyme, "Diddle, diddle, dumpling, my son John," with "sock" or "stocking" replacing "shoe" in the line "One shoe off, and one shoe on." Lamb apparently recited the rhyme at Haydon's "Immortal Dinner"; see Penelope Hughes-Hallett, *The Immortal Dinner: A Famous Evening of Genius and Laughter in Literary London, 1817* (Chicago: New Amsterdam Books, 2002), pp. 278–80.
3. "Situated above two 'pairs' or flights of stairs, i.e. on the second floor" (*OED*).
4. Saltpeter is used to make gunpowder.
5. Forman (1883) emends to "yelping," as the dog is male.
6. A switch made from a palm tree used in giving someone a beating.

Whate'er your palmistry may make of it,
Comes from a play-thing of the Emperor's choice,
From a Man-Tiger-Organ, prettiest of his toys."[7]

XXXVIII.

Eban then usher'd in the learned Seer:
Elfinan's back was turn'd, but, ne'ertheless,　335
Both, prostrate on the carpet, ear by ear,
Crept silently, and waited in distress,
Knowing the Emperor's moody bitterness;
Eban especially, who on the floor 'gan
Tremble and quake to death,—he feared less　340
A dose of senna-tea, or nightmare Gorgon,[8]
Than the Emperor when he play'd on his Man-Tiger-Organ.

XXXIX.

They kiss'd nine times the carpet's velvet face
Of glossy silk, soft, smooth, and meadow-green,
Where the close eye in deep rich fur might trace　345
A silver tissue, scantly to be seen,
As daisies lurk'd in June-grass, buds in green;[9]
Sudden the music ceased, sudden the hand
Of majesty, by dint of passion keen,
Doubled into a common fist, went grand,　350
And knock'd down three cut glasses, and his best ink-stand.

XL.

Then turning round, he saw those trembling two:
"Eban," said he, "as slaves should taste the fruits
Of diligence, I shall remember you
To-morrow, or the next day, as time suits,　355
In a finger conversation with my mutes,[1]—
Begone!—for you, Chaldean![2] here remain;
Fear not, quake not, and as good wine recruits
A conjurer's spirits, what cup will you drain?
Sherry in silver, hock[3] in gold, or glass'd champagne?"　360

XLI.

"Commander of the faithful!"[4] answer'd Hum,
"In preference to these, I'll merely taste
A thimble-full of old Jamaica rum."

7. Allusion to Tipoo Sultan's mechanical "toy" (now in the Victoria and Albert Museum), which depicts a tiger devouring an English officer and which has a bellows organ that emits both shrieks and music. Keats could have seen it in the public reading-room of the East India Company. Jones (see headnote) suggests a sexual play on "man-tiger-organ."
8. A mythical female, such as Medusa, with snakes for hair and a look capable of turning the beholder to stone; *senna-tea*: made with an infusion of the Cassia shrub and used as an emetic.
9. The draft and W² have "treen," or trees.
1. Sign language had been introduced at the London Asylum in 1792.
2. Astrologer. See p. 337.
3. The German wine called Hochheimer, and by extension German white wines.
4. A title taken by the caliphs, first by Omar I c. 640.

"A simple boon!" said Elfinan, "thou may'st
Have Nantz,[5] with which my morning-coffee's laced."[6]   365
"I'll have a glass of Nantz, then,"—said the Seer,—
"Made racy—(sure my boldness is misplaced!)—
With the third part—(yet that is drinking dear!)—
Of the least drop of *crème de citron*[7] crystal clear."

XLII.

"I pledge you, Hum! and pledge my dearest love,   370
My Bertha!" "Bertha! Bertha!" cried the sage,
"I know a many Berthas!" "Mine's above
All Berthas!" sighed the Emperor. "I engage,"
Said Hum, "in duty, and in vassalage,
To mention all the Berthas in the earth;—   375
There's Bertha Watson,—and Miss Bertha Page,—
This famed for languid eyes, and that for mirth,—
There's Bertha Blount of York,—and Bertha Knox of Perth."

XLIII.

"You seem to know"—"I do know," answer'd Hum,
"Your Majesty's in love with some fine girl   380
Named Bertha; but her surname will not come,
Without a little conjuring." "'Tis Pearl,
'Tis Bertha Pearl! What makes my brains so whirl?
And she is softer, fairer than her name!"
"Where does she live?" ask'd Hum. "Her fair locks curl   385
So brightly, they put all our fays to shame!—
Live!—O! at Canterbury, with her old grand-dame."

XLIV.

"Good! good!" cried Hum, "I've known her from a child!
She is a changeling of my management;
She was born at midnight in an Indian wild;   390
Her mother's screams with the striped tiger's blent,
While the torch-bearing slaves a halloo sent
Into the jungles; and her palanquin,[8]
Rested amid the desert's dreariment,
Shook with her agony, till fair were seen   395
The little Bertha's eyes ope on the stars serene."

XLV.

"I can't say," said the monarch, "that may be
Just as it happen'd, true or else a bam![9]
Drink up your brandy, and sit down by me,

5. A brandy from the Nantes region of France.
6. "Mr. Nisby is of opinion that laced coffee is bad for the head." Spectator. [Note from Keats's text, perhaps by Reynolds (see headnote).] From *Spectator* 317 (March 4, 1712).
7. A syrupy liqueur with a lemon flavor.
8. "A covered conveyance, usually for one person, consisting of a large box carried on two horizontal poles by four or six (rarely two) bearers, used esp. in South, South-East, and East Asia" (*OED*).
9. Hoax.

Feel, feel my pulse, how much in love I am;   400
And if your science is not all a sham,
Tell me some means to get the lady here."
"Upon my honor!" said the son of Cham,[1]
"She is my dainty changeling, near and dear,
Although her story sounds at first a little queer."   405

XLVI.

"Convey her to me, Hum, or by my crown,
My sceptre, and my cross-surmounted globe,
I'll knock you—" "Does your Majesty mean—*down*?
No, no, you never could my feelings probe
To such a depth!" The Emperor took his robe,   410
And wept upon its purple palatine,[2]
While Hum continued, shamming half a sob,—
"In Canterbury doth your lady shine?
But let me cool your brandy with a little wine."

XLVII.

Whereat a narrow Flemish glass he took,   415
That since belong'd to Admiral De Witt,[3]
Admired it with a connoisseuring look,
And with the ripest claret crowned it,
And, ere the lively bead could burst and flit,
He turned it quickly, nimbly upside down,   420
His mouth being held conveniently fit
To catch the treasure: "Best in all the town!"
He said, smack'd his moist lips, and gave a pleasant frown.

XLVIII.

"Ah! good my Prince, weep not!" And then again
He fill'd a bumper. "Great sire, do not weep!   425
Your pulse is shocking, but I'll ease your pain."
"Fetch me that ottoman, and prithee keep
Your voice low," said the Emperor, "and steep
Some lady's fingers nice in Candy wine;[4]
And prithee, Hum, behind the screen do peep   430
For the rose-water vase, magician mine!
And sponge my forehead,—so my love doth make me pine."

1. "Cham is said to have been the inventor of magic. Lucy learnt this from Bayle's Dictionary, and had copied a long Latin note from that work." [Note in Keats's text, perhaps by Reynolds (see headnote).] Cham is the youngest son of Noah. See Pierre Bayle's *Dictionnaire Historique* (1695–97; rev. 1702), where there is a long article on Cham, including citations from Latin sources.
2. Royal.
3. Johan de Witt (1625–1672), a leader of the Dutch states-rights party against the federalism of the House of Orange, was named Grand Pensionary of Holland in 1653, essentially running the country and its relations and wars with England over the next nineteen years. After a French invasion of the United Provinces in 1672, William III won the support of the people; when de Witt's brother was imprisoned and John de Witt went to visit him, a crowd seized both men and dismembered them.
4. Also known as Kandy wine, a sweet wine from Ceylon (Sri Lanka) and named for the capital of a Sinhalese kingdom; England had taken the island from the Dutch in 1796 and had established total control of it with the capture of Kandy in 1815. *lady's fingers*: lady fingers, a kind of oblong cake or biscuit.

XLIX.

"Ah, cursed Bellanaine!" "Don't think of her,"
Rejoin'd the Mago, "but on Bertha muse;
For, by my choicest best barometer,
You shall not throttled be in marriage noose;   435
I've said it, sire; you only have to choose
Bertha or Bellanaine." So saying, he drew
From the left pocket of his threadbare hose,
A sampler hoarded slyly, good as new,   440
Holding it by his thumb and finger full in view.

L.

"Sire, this is Bertha Pearl's neat handy-work,
Her *name*, see here, *Midsummer*, *ninety-one*."
Elfinan snatch'd it with a sudden jerk,
And wept as if he never would have done,   445
Honouring with royal tears the poor homespun;
Whereon were broider'd tigers with black eyes,
And long-tail'd pheasants, and a rising sun,
Plenty of posies, great stags, butterflies
Bigger than stags,—a moon,—with other mysteries.   450

LI.

The monarch handled o'er and o'er again
These day-school hieroglyphics with a sigh;
Somewhat in sadness, but pleas'd in the main,
Till this oracular couplet met his eye
Astounded,—*Cupid, I—do thee defy!*   455
It was too much. He shrunk back in his chair,
Grew pale as death, and fainted—very nigh!
"Pho! nonsense!" exclaim'd Hum, "now don't despair:
She does not mean it really. Cheer up, hearty—there!

LII.

"And listen to my words. You say you won't,   460
On any terms, marry Miss Bellanaine;
It goes against your conscience—good! Well, don't.
You say, you love a mortal. I would fain
Persuade your honour's Highness to refrain
From peccadilloes. But, sire, as I say,   465
What good would that do? And, to be more plain,
You would do me a mischief some odd day,
Cut off my ears and hands, or head too, by my fay![5]

LIII.

"Besides, manners forbid that I should pass any
Vile strictures on the conduct of a prince   470

---

5. Archaic form of "faith," but also a word for "fairy."

Who should indulge his genius, if he has any,
Not, like a subject, foolish matters mince.
Now I think on't, perhaps I could convince
Your Majesty there is no crime at all
In loving pretty little Bertha, since   475
She's very delicate,—not over tall,—
A fairy's hand, and in the waist, why—very small."

LIV.

"Ring the repeater,[6] gentle Hum!" " 'Tis five,"
Said gentle Hum; "the nights draw in apace;
The little birds I hear are all alive;   480
I see the dawning touch'd upon your face;
Shall I put out the candles, please your Grace?"
"Do put them out, and, without more ado,
Tell me how I may that sweet girl embrace,—
How you can bring her to me." "That's for you,   485
Great Emperor! to adventure, like a lover true."

LV.

"I fetch her!"—"Yes, an't like your Majesty;
And as she would be frighten'd wide awake
To travel such a distance through the sky,
Use of some soft manœuvre you must make,   490
For your convenience, and her dear nerves' sake;
Nice way would be to bring her in a swoon,
Anon, I'll tell what course were best to take;
You must away this morning." "Hum! so soon?"
"Sire, you must be in Kent by twelve o'clock at noon."   495

LVI.

At this great Cæsar started on his feet,
Lifted his wings, and stood attentive-wise.
"Those wings to Canterbury you must beat,
If you hold Bertha as a worthy prize.
Look in the Almanack—*Moore*[7] never lies—   500
April the twenty-fourth,—this coming day,
Now breathing its new bloom upon the skies,
Will end in St. Mark's eve;—you must away,
For on that eve alone can you the maid convey."

LVII.

Then the magician solemnly 'gan frown,   505
So that his frost-white eyebrows, beetling low,
Shaded his deep green eyes, and wrinkles brown
Plaited upon his furnace-scorched brow:

---

6. A repeating watch that strikes the time by means of a mechanism operated by a push-piece or bolt. This appears to be a Grande sonnerie or "grand strike" repeater that struck every quarter hour and would repeat the time if the push-piece was pressed.
7. *Old Moore's Almanac*, begun by Francis Moore (1657–1715?), astrologer and physician, in 1699.

Forth from his hood that hung his neck below,
He lifted a bright casket of pure gold,   510
Touch'd a spring-lock, and there in wool, or snow
Charm'd into ever freezing, lay an old
And legend-leaved book, mysterious to behold.

LVIII.

"Take this same book,—it will not bite you, sire;
There, put it underneath your royal arm;   515
Though it's a pretty weight, it will not tire,
But rather on your journey keep you warm:
This is the magic, this the potent charm,
That shall drive Bertha to a fainting fit!
When the time comes, don't feel the least alarm,   520
But lift her from the ground, and swiftly flit
Back to your palace, where I wait for guerdon fit."[8]

LIX.

"What shall I do with that same book?" "Why merely
Lay it on Bertha's table, close beside
Her work-box, and 'twill help your purpose dearly;   525
I say no more." "Or good or ill betide,
Through the wide air to Kent this morn I glide!"
Exclaim'd the Emperor, "When I return,
Ask what you will,—I'll give you my new bride!
And take some more wine, Hum;—O, Heavens! I burn   530
To be upon the wing! Now, now, that minx I spurn!"

LX.

"Leave her to me," rejoin'd the magian:
But how shall I account, illustrious fay!
For thine imperial absence? Pho! I can
Say you are very sick, and bar the way   535
To your so loving courtiers for one day;
If either of their two Archbishops' graces
Should talk of extreme unction, I shall say
You do not like cold pig with Latin phrases,[9]
Which never should be used but in alarming cases."   540

LXI.

"Open the window, Hum; I'm ready now!"
"Zooks!" exclaim'd Hum, as up the sash he drew,
"Behold, your Majesty, upon the brow
Of yonder hill, what crowds of people!" "Whew!"[1]
The monster's always after something new,"   545

---

8. The second half of the line, from the draft, is missing in 1848; *guerdon*: a "reward," a "recompense."
9. The sacrament of Last Rites is reduced to giving a "cold pig"; that is, awakening a sluggard by pulling off the sheets and dousing with cold water, here accompanied by the Latin phrases of the Last Sacrament.
1. This is the reading of the draft and W[2]; 1848 has the unrhymed "Where?"

Return'd his Highness, "they are piping hot
To see my pigsney[2] Bellanaine. Hum! do
Tighten my belt a little,—so, so,—not
Too tight,—the book!—my wand!—so, nothing is forgot."

LXII.

"Wounds![3] how they shout!" said Hum, "and there,—see, see,   550
Th'Ambassador's return'd from Pigmio!
The morning's very fine,—uncommonly!
See, past the skirts of yon white cloud they go,
Tinging it with soft crimsons! Now below
The sable-pointed heads of firs and pines   555
They dip, move on, and with them moves a glow
Along the forest side! Now amber lines
Reach the hill top, and now throughout the valley shines."

LXIII.

"Why, Hum, you're getting quite poetical!
Those *nows*[4] you managed in a special style."   560
"If ever you have leisure, sire, you shall
See scraps of mine will make it worth your while,
Tit-bits for Phœbus!—yes, you well may smile.
Hark! hark! the bells!" "A little further yet,[5]
Good Hum, and let me view this mighty coil."[6]   565
Then the great Emperor full graceful set
His elbow for a prop, and snuff'd his mignionette.[7]

LXIV.

The morn was full of holiday; loud bells
With rival clamours rang from every spire;
Cunningly-station'd music dies and swells   570
In echoing places; when the winds respire,
Light flags stream out like gauzy tongues of fire;
A metropolitan murmur, lifeful, warm,
Came from the northern suburbs; rich attire
Freckled with red and gold the moving swarm;   575
While here and there clear trumpets blew a keen alarm.

LXV.

And now the fairy escort was seen clear,
Like the old pageant of Aurora's[8] train,
Above a pearl-built minster,[9] hovering near;
First wily Crafticant, the chamberlain,   580

2. A "darling, pet; commonly used as an endearing form of address" (*OED*).
3. For "Swounds," an oath from "God's wounds."
4. Perhaps an allusion to the style of Leigh Hunt. See Hunt's "A Now, Descriptive of Hot Day" (pp. 510–13), written with Keats.
5. The draft and W[2] have "get."
6. Disturbance, turmoil.
7. For "mignonette," a perfume made from a West African flower.
8. See p. 41, n. 6.
9. Church.

Balanced upon his grey-grown pinions[1] twain,
His slender wand officially reveal'd;
Then black gnomes scattering sixpences like rain;
Then pages three and three; and next, slave-held,
The Imaian 'scutcheon bright,—one mouse in argent field.[2]   585

LXVI.

Gentlemen pensioners next; and after them,
A troop of winged Janizaries[3] flew;
Then slaves, as presents bearing many a gem;
Then twelve physicians fluttering two and two;
And next a chaplain in a cassock new;   590
Then lords in waiting; then (what head not reels
For pleasure?)—the fair Princess in full view,
Borne upon wings,—and very pleased she feels
To have such splendour dance attendance at her heels.

LXVII.

For there was more magnificence behind: 595
She waved her handkerchief. "Ah, very grand!"
Cried Elfinan, and closed the window-blind;
"And, Hum, we must not shilly-shally stand,—
Adieu! adieu! I'm off for Angle-land!
I say, old Hocus,[4] have you such a thing   600
About you,—feel your pockets, I command,—
I want, this instant, an invisible ring,—
Thank you, old mummy!—now securely I take wing."

LXVIII.

Then Elfinan swift vaulted from the floor,
And lighted graceful on the window-sill;   605
Under one arm the magic book he bore,
The other he could wave about at will;
Pale was his face, he still look'd very ill:
He bow'd at Bellanaine, and said—"Poor Bell!
Farewell! farewell! and if for ever! still   610
For ever fare thee well!"—and then he fell
A laughing!—snapp'd his fingers!—shame it is to tell![5]

LXIX.

"By 'r Lady! he is gone!" cries Hum, "and I,—
(I own it,)—have made too free with his wine;
Old Crafticant will smoke[6] me, by-the-bye!   615

---

1. Wings.
2. An escutcheon is the field upon which a coat of arms is displayed, here a mouse on silvery white (argent) background.
3. Turkish infantry comprising the Sultan's guard.
4. For "hocus-pocus," a conjurer or juggler.
5. An echo of Byron's controversial poem to his wife, "Fare Thee Well" (1816), which Keats could have read in Hunt's *Examiner*, April 21, 1816, p. 250.
6. Smoke out, but also suspect and make fun of.

This room is full of jewels as a mine,—
Dear valuable creatures, how ye shine!
Sometime to-day I must contrive a minute,
If Mercury[7] propitiously incline,
To examine his scrutoire, and see what's in it,   620
For of superfluous diamonds I as well may thin it.

LXX.

"The Emperor's horrid bad; yes, that's my cue!"
Some histories say that this was Hum's last speech;
That, being fuddled, he went reeling through
The corridor, and scarce upright could reach   625
The stair-head; that being glutted as a leach,
And used, as we ourselves have just now said,
To manage stairs reversely, like a peach
Too ripe, he fell, being puzzled in his head
With liquor and the staircase: verdict—*found stone dead*.   630

LXXI.

This as a falsehood Crafticanto treats;
And as his style is of strange elegance,
Gentle and tender, full of soft conceits,
(Much like our Boswell's),[8] we will take a glance
At his sweet prose, and, if we can, make dance   635
His woven periods into careless rhyme;
O, little faery Pegasus![9] rear—prance—
Trot round the quarto—ordinary time!
March, little Pegasus, with pawing hoof sublime!

LXXII.

Well, let us see,—*tenth book and chapter nine*,—   640
Thus Crafticant pursues his diary:—
" 'Twas twelve o'clock at night, the weather fine,
Latitude thirty-six; our scouts descry
A flight of starlings making rapidly
Tow'rds Thibet. Mem.:—birds fly in the night;   645
From twelve to half-past—wings not fit to fly
For a thick fog—the Princess sulky quite—
Call'd for an extra shawl, and gave her nurse a bite.

LXXIII.

"Five minutes before one—brought down a moth
With my new double-barrel—stew'd the thighs,   650

7. Here as god of thieves.
8. James Boswell (1740–1795), lawyer and author of *The Life of Samuel Johnson* (1791); the draft
   has "Cowley's."
9. The winged horse of classical myth. Keats may allude to Wordsworth's rejection of a visionary "flying horse" in l. 1 of *Peter Bell* (1819); *Peter Bell* was subject to repeated attacks by Keats's circle,
   and Wordsworth's turn to a "little Boat" over Pegasus in particular would be ridiculed by Byron in
   Canto 3.98–100 of *Don Juan*.

And made a very tolerable broth—
Princess turn'd dainty, to our great surprise,
Alter'd her mind, and thought it very nice:
Seeing her pleasant, tried her with a pun—
She frown'd; a monstrous owl across us flies   655
About this time,—a sad old figure of fun;
Bad omen—this new match can't be a happy one.

LXXIV.

"From two to half-past, dusky way we made,
Above the plains of Gobi,—desert, bleak;
Beheld afar off, in the hooded shade   660
Of darkness, a great mountain (strange to speak),
Spitting, from forth its sulphur-baken peak,
A fan-shaped burst of blood-red, arrowy fire,
Turban'd with smoke, which still away did reek,
Solid and black from that eternal pyre,   665
Upon the laden winds that scantly could respire.

LXXV.

"Just upon three o'clock, a falling star
Created an alarm among our troop,
Kill'd a man-cook, a page, and broke a jar,
A tureen, and three dishes, at one swoop,   670
Then passing by the Princess, singed her hoop:
Could not conceive what Coralline was at—
She clapp'd her hands three times, and cried out 'Whoop!'—
Some strange Imaian custom. A large bat
Came sudden 'fore my face, and brush'd against my hat.   675

LXXVI.

"Five minutes thirteen seconds after three,
Far in the west a mighty fire broke out—
Conjectured, on the instant, it might be
The city of Balk[1]—'twas Balk beyond all doubt:
A griffin, wheeling here and there about,   680
Kept reconnoitring us—doubled our guard—
Lighted our torches, and kept up a shout,
Till he sheer'd off—the Princess very scared—
And many on their marrow-bones[2] for death prepared.

LXXVII.

"At half-past three arose the cheerful moon—   685
Bivouac'd for four minutes on a cloud—
Where from the earth we heard a lively tune

1. Balkh was a major ancient Persian city in what is now Afghanistan; reputed to be the birthplace or
burial site of Zoroaster, it was conquered on various occasions, two being by Alexander the Great
and the forces of Islam.
2. On their knees.

Of tambourines and pipes, serene and loud,
While on a flowery lawn a brilliant crowd
Cinque-parted[3] danced, some half asleep reposed   690
Beneath the green-fan'd cedars, some did shroud
In silken tents, and 'mid light fragrance dozed,
Or on the open turf their soothed eyelids closed.

LXXVIII.

"Dropp'd my gold watch, and kill'd a kettle-drum—
It went for apoplexy—foolish folks!—   695
Left it to pay the piper—a good sum—
(I've got a conscience, maugre people's jokes:)
To scrape a little favour, 'gan to coax
Her Highness' pug-dog—got a sharp rebuff—
She wish'd a game at whist—made three revokes[4]—   700
Turn'd from myself, her partner, in a huff;
His Majesty will know her temper time enough.

LXXIX.

"She cried for chess—I play'd a game with her—
Castled her king with such a vixen look,
It bodes ill to his Majesty—(refer   705
To the second chapter of my fortieth book,
And see what hoity-toity airs she took:)
At half-past four the morn essay'd to beam—
Saluted, as we pass'd, an early rook—
The Princess fell asleep, and, in her dream,   710
Talk'd of one Master Hubert, deep in her esteem.

LXXX.

"About this time,—making delightful way,—
Shed a quill-feather from my larboard wing—
Wish'd, trusted, hoped 'twas no sign of decay—
Thank heaven, I'm hearty yet!—'twas no such thing:—   715
At five the golden light began to spring,
With fiery shudder through the bloomed east;
At six we heard Panthea's churches ring—
The city all her unhived swarms had cast,
To watch our grand approach, and hail us as we pass'd.   720

LXXXI.

"As flowers turn their faces to the sun,
So on our flight with hungry eyes they gaze,
And, as we shaped our course, this, that way run,
With mad-cap pleasure, or hand-clasp'd amaze:
Sweet in the air a mild-toned music plays,   725
And progresses through its own labyrinth;

---

3. In groups of five; the cinquepace had been an early modern dance.
4. Failures to follow suit in the card game whist.

Buds gather'd from the green spring's middle-days,
They scatter'd,—daisy, primrose, hyacinth,—
Or round white columns wreath'd from capital to plinth.

LXXXII.

"Onward we floated o'er the panting streets,   730
That seem'd throughout with upheld faces paved;
Look where we will, our bird's-eye vision meets
Legions of holiday; bright standards waved,
And fluttering ensigns emulously craved
Our minute's glance; a busy thunderous roar,   735
From square to square, among the buildings raved,
As when the sea, at flow, gluts up once more
The craggy hollowness of a wild-reefed shore.

LXXXIII.

"And 'Bellanaine for ever!' shouted they!
While that fair Princess, from her winged chair,   740
Bow'd low with high demeanour, and, to pay
Their new-blown loyalty with guerdon fair,
Still emptied, at meet distance, here and there,
A plenty horn of jewels. And here I
(Who wish to give the devil her due) declare   745
Against that ugly piece of calumny,
Which calls them Highland pebble-stones not worth a fly.

LXXXIV.

"Still 'Bellanaine!' they shouted, while we glide
'Slant to a light Ionic portico,
The city's delicacy, and the pride   750
Of our Imperial Basilic;[5] a row
Of lords and ladies, on each hand, make show
Submissive of knee-bent obeisance,
All down the steps; and, as we enter'd, lo!
The strangest sight—the most unlook'd-for chance—   755
All things turn'd topsy-turvy in a devil's dance.

LXXXV.

" 'Stead of his anxious Majesty and court
At the open doors, with wide saluting eyes,
Congées and scrape-graces[6] of every sort,
And all the smooth routine of gallantries,   760
Was seen, to our immoderate surprise,
A motley crowd thick gather'd in the hall,
Lords, scullions, deputy-scullions, with wild cries

---

5. Basilica, a royal palace with a large oblong hall, double colonnades (here with Ionic columns) and
   semicircular apse at the end.
6. While editors usually change this to "scape-graces," Stillinger suggests that Keats intended the pun
   "scapegraces who bow and scrape"; Congées: bows.

Stunning the vestibule from wall to wall,
Where the Chief Justice on his knees and hands doth crawl.   765

LXXXVI.

"Counts of the palace, and the state purveyor
Of moth's down, to make soft the royal beds,
The Common Council and my fool Lord Mayor
Marching a-row, each other slipshod treads;
Powder'd bag-wigs and ruffy-tuffy[7] heads   770
Of cinder wenches meet and soil each other;
Toe crush'd with heel ill-natured fighting breeds,
Frill-rumpling elbows brew up many a bother,
And fists in the short ribs keep up the yell and pother.

LXXXVII.

"A Poet, mounted on the Court-Clown's back,   775
Rode to the Princess swift with spurring heels,
And close into her face, with rhyming clack,
Began a Prothalamion;[8]—she reels,
She falls, she faints!—while laughter peals
Over her woman's weakness. 'Where,' cried I,   780
'Where is his Majesty?' No person feels
Inclined to answer; wherefore instantly
I plunged into the crowd to find him or to die.

LXXXVIII.

"Jostling my way I gain'd the stairs, and ran
To the first landing, where, incredible!   785
I met, far gone in liquor, that old man,
That vile impostor Hum,——"
          So far so well,—
For we have proved the Mago never fell
Down stairs on Crafticanto's evidence;
And therefore duly shall proceed to tell,   790
Plain in our own original mood and tense,
The sequel of this day, though labor 'tis immense![9]

LXXXIX

Now Hum, new fledg'd with high Authority,
Came forth to quell the Hubbub in the Hall.

✻ ✻

---

7. Disheveled; *bag-wigs*: popular in the eighteenth century, a wig of black hair enclosed in an ornamental bag.
8. A pre-nuptial poem.
9. 1848 breaks off here with the note, "*No more was written*"; last two lines from W².

[In after time, a sage of mickle lore][1]

In after time a sage of mickle lore,[2]
Yclep'd Typographus, the Giant took
And did refit his limbs as heretofore,
And made him read in many a learned book,
And into many a lively legend look;   5
Thereby in goodly themes so training him,
That all his brutishness he quite forsook,
When, meeting Artegall and Talus grim,
The one he struck stone-blind, the other's eyes wox dim.

Letter to Fanny Brawne, February? 1820[1]

My dearest Girl,
    According to all appearances I am to be separated from you as much as possible. How I shall be able to bear it, or whether it will not be worse than your presence now and then, I cannot tell. I must be patient, and in the mean time you must think of it as little as possible. Let me not longer detain you from going to Town—there may be no end to this emprisoning of you. Perhaps you had better not come before tomorrow evening: send me however without fail a good night.
    You know our situation—what hope is there if I should be recovered ever so soon—my very health will not suffer me to make any great exertion. I am recommended not even to read poetry much less write it. I wish I had even a little hope. I cannot say forget me—but I would mention that there are impossibilities in the world. No more of this—I am not strong enough to be weaned—take no notice of it in your good night. Happen what may I shall ever be my dearest Love

Your affectionate
J—K—

Letter to Fanny Brawne, February 27?, 1820[1]

My dearest Fanny,
    I had a better night last night than I have had since my attack, and this morning I am the same as when you saw me. I have been turning over two

---

1. Written in 1820 in a lost copy of Spenser that Keats gave to Fanny Brawne, this is perhaps Keats's last poem, for Brown wrote (in *PDWJ*) that it was "the last stanza, of any kind, that he wrote before his lamented death." Brown also notes that Keats "died with his pen wielded in the cause of Reform," for the poem responds to *The Faerie Queene* 5.2.30–54, where the Giant is seen as undermining justice as he "all things would reduce unto equality"; he is destroyed by Artegall, the knight of justice, and his squire, Talus. Keats imagines the Giant liberated by Typographus, standing for print culture and the dissemination of knowledge. For a similar sense that the "spirit" of "knowledge" will prove stronger than "kings, or armies, or all the most predominant shapes of prejudice and force," see Hunt's "Political Examiner," in the *Examiner*, January 3, 1819, 1–2, *SWLH*, 2: 173–77. First published in the *Plymouth and Devonport Weekly Journal*, July 4, 1839; text from *PDWJ* with emendations from Brown's transcript in his copy of Spenser's *Poetical Works* (1788) at the end of *Faerie Queene* 5.2, vol. 3: 38 (LMA K/BK/01/039b/151).
2. Much learning.
1. Text from ALS (Harvard MS Keats 1.72).
1. Perhaps written on February 27, 1820, when Keats received a copy of *Dramatic Scenes and Other Poems* (1819), which he mentions below, by "Barry Cornwall," the pseudonym of Bryan Waller

volumes of Letters written between Rousseau and two Ladies in the perplexed strain of mingled finesse and sentiment in which the Ladies and gentlemen of those days were so clever, and which is still prevalent among Ladies of this Country who live in a state of reasoning romance.[2] The Likeness however only extends to the mannerism not to the dexterity. What would Rousseau have said at seeing our little correspondence![3] What would his Ladies have said! I don't care much—I would sooner have Shakespeare's opinion about the matter. The common gossiping of washerwomen must be less disgusting than the continual and eternal fence and attack of Rousseau and these sublime Petticoats. One calls herself Clara and her friend Julia two of Rousseau's Heroines—they all the same time christen poor Jean Jacques St Preux—who is the pure cavalier of his famous novel.[4] Thank God I am born in England with our own great Men before my eyes. Thank god that you are fair and can love me without being Letter-written and sentimentaliz'd into it. Mr Barry Cornwall has sent me another Book,[5] his first, with a polite note. I must do what I can to make him sensible of the esteem I have for his kindness. If this north east would take a turn it would be so much the better for me. Good bye, my love, my dear love, my beauty—

love me for ever—

J—K—

Letter to J. H. Reynolds, February 28, 1820[1]

My dear Reynolds,

I have been improving since you saw me: my nights are better which I think is a very encouraging thing. You mention your cold in rather too slighting a manner—if you travel outside have some flannel against the wind—which I hope will not keep on at this rate when you are in the Packet boat. Should it rain do not stop upon deck though the Passengers should vomit themselves inside out. Keep under Hatches from all sort of wet.

I am pretty well provided with Books at present, when you return I may give you a commission or two—Mr B. C. has sent me not only his Sicilian Story but yesterday his Dramatic Scenes.[2] This is very polite and I shall do

Proctor (1787–1874), a member of Hunt's circle. Text from ALS in Robert H. Taylor Collection, Manuscripts Division, Department of Rare Books and Special Collections, Princeton University Library (RTCOI, Box 10, Last Folder).

2. Keats refers to *Correspondence originale et inédit de J. J. Rousseau avec Mme. Latour de Franqueville et M. du Peyrou*, 2 vols. (Paris, 1803). Rousseau: see p. 349, n. 2.

3. See also his joking suggestion that he might have Byron's publisher Murray compile an edition of their letters (*L*, 2.282).

4. That is, Rousseau's *Julie, ou La Nouvelle Héloïse* (1761).

5. This suggests that Proctor had already sent Keats his *Sicilian Story: with Diego de Montilla, and other poems* (1820) with the opening poem taking up the same story from Boccaccio as Keats's *Isabella*.

1. Written as Reynolds prepared to leave for Brussels and France and as Keats dealt with the certainty that he had tuberculosis. ALS at the University of Texas, Humanities Research Center, Miriam Luther Stark Collection.

2. "Barry Cornwall," the pen name of Bryan Waller Proctor (1787–1874), was a member of the Hunt circle whom Keats came to know during the spring of 1820. Proctor had sent his *Dramatic Scenes* (1819) to Keats via Hunt, but Hunt had forgotten to deliver it; when Proctor, sending his *A Sicilian Story* (1820) directly to Keats, learned of this, he sent the earlier volume as well. There are various parallels between the work of Proctor and Keats, including the fact that the *Sicilian Story* treats the same tale from Boccaccio as *Isabella*. Proctor's *Literary Recollections*, ed. R. W. Armour (1936), provides accounts of members of Hunt's circle, including Keats.

what I can to make him sensible I think so. I confess they tease me. They are composed of Amiability, the Seasons, the Leaves, the Moon &c. upon which he rings (according to Hunt's expression) triple bob majors.[3] However that is nothing—I think he likes poetry for its own sake, not his. I hope I shall soon be well enough to proceed with my fairies and set you about the notes on Sundays and Stray-days.[4] If I had been well enough I should have liked to cross the water with you. Brown wishes you a pleasant voyage—Have fish for dinner at the sea ports, and don't forget a bottle of Claret. You will not meet with so much to hate at Brussels as at Paris. Remember me to all my friends. If I were well enough I would paraphrase an Ode of Horace's for you, on your embarking in the seventy years ago style—the Packet will bear a comparison with a roman galley at any rate.[5]

Ever yours affectionately,
J. Keats

Letter to Fanny Brawne, March? 1820[1]

Sweetest Fanny,

You fear, sometimes, I do not love you so much as you wish? My dear Girl I love you ever and ever and without reserve. The more I have known you the more have I lov'd. In every way—even my jealousies have been agonies of Love, in the hottest fit I ever had I would have died for you. I have vex'd you too much. But for Love! Can I help it? You are always new. The last of your kisses was ever the sweetest; the last smile the brightest; the last movement the gracefullest. When you pass'd my window home yesterday, I was fill'd with as much admiration as if I had then seen you for the first time. You uttered a half complaint once that I only lov'd your Beauty. Have I nothing else then to love in you but that? Do not I see a heart naturally furnish'd with wings imprison itself with me? No ill prospect has been able to turn your thoughts a moment from me. This perhaps should be as much a subject of sorrow as joy—but I will not talk of that. Even if you did not love me I could not help an entire devotion to you: how much more deeply then must I feel for you knowing you love me. My Mind has been the most discontented and restless one that ever was put into a body too small for it. I never felt my Mind repose upon anything with complete and undistracted enjoyment—upon no person but you. When you are in the room my thoughts never fly out of window: you always concentrate my whole senses. The anxiety shown about our Loves in your last note is an immense pleasure to me: however you must not suffer such speculations to molest you any more: nor will I any more believe you can have the least pique against me. Brown is gone out—but here is Mrs. Wylie[2]— when she is gone I shall be awake for you.—Remembrances to your Mother.

Your affectionate
J. Keats.

---

3. For "treble bob major": "*treble bob* is a method in which the bells, and more especially the 'Treble', have a dodging course" (*OED*); a bob major is rung on eight bells.
4. Keats refers to his "The Cap and Bells" (see p. 378–402) for which he apparently intended to have Reynolds write the notes (in his spare time, on Sundays and holidays).
5. See Horace's *Odes* 1.3 where the poet addresses Virgil setting out for Greece.
1. From HBF (1883), 4: 164–65.
2. George Keats's mother-in-law. HBF suggests that here Keats is acknowledging that he and Fanny must have a chaperone.

Letter to Fanny Brawne, May? 1820[1]

Tuesday Morn—

My dearest Girl,

I wrote a Letter for you yesterday expecting to have seen your mother. I shall be selfish enough to send it though I know it may give you a little pain, because I wish you to see how unhappy I am for love of you, and endeavour as much as I can to entice you to give up your whole heart to me whose whole existence hangs upon you. You could not step or move an eyelid but it would shoot to my heart—I am greedy of you. Do not think of any thing but me. Do not live as if I was not existing—Do not forget me—But have I any right to say you forget me? Perhaps you think of me all day. Have I any right to wish you to be unhappy for me? You would forgive me for wishing it, if you knew the extreme passion I have that you should love me—and for you to love me as I do you, you must think of no one but me, much less write that sentence. Yesterday and this morning I have been haunted with a sweet vision. I have seen you the whole time in your shepherdess dress. How my senses have ached at it![2] How my heart has been devoted to it! How my eyes have been full of Tears at it! Indeed I think a real Love is enough to occupy the widest heart. Your going to town alone, when I heard of it was a shock to me—yet I expected it—*promise me you will not for some time, till I get better.* Promise me this and fill the paper full of the most endearing names. If you cannot do so with good will, do my Love tell me—say what you think—confess if your heart is too much fasten'd on the world. Perhaps then I may see you at a greater distance, I may not be able to appropriate you so closely to myself. Were you to loose a favorite bird from the cage, how would your eyes ache after it as long as it was in sight; when out of sight you would recover a little. Perhaps if you would, if so it is, confess to me how many things are necessary to you besides me, I might be happier, by being less tantaliz'd. Well may you exclaim, how selfish, how cruel, not to let me enjoy my youth! to wish me to be unhappy! You must be so if you love me—upon my Soul I can be contented with nothing else. If you could really what is call'd enjoy yourself at a Party—if you can smile in peoples faces, and wish them to admire you *now*, you never have nor ever will love me. I see *life* in nothing but the certainty of your Love—convince me of it my sweetest. If I am not somehow convinc'd I shall die of agony. If we love we must not live as other men and women do. I cannot brook the wolfsbane[3] of fashion and foppery and tattle. You must be mine to die upon the rack if I want you. I do not pretend to say I have more feeling than my fellows—but I wish you seriously to look over my letters kind and unkind and consider whether the Person who wrote them can be able to endure much longer the agonies and uncertainties which you are so peculiarly made to create—My recovery of bodily health will be of no benefit to me if you are not all mine when I am well. For god's sake save me—or tell me my passion is of too awful a nature for you. Again God bless you

J.K.

---

1. Text from ALS (LMA K/MS/02/013/6565). Rollins speculates the letter was written on May 30.
2. See Shakespeare, *Othello*, 4.2.71, where Othello says to Desdemona, "the senses ache at thee."
3. Aconite, used as a sedative.

No—my sweet Fanny—I am wrong. I do not want you to be unhappy—and yet I do, I must while there is so sweet a Beauty—my loveliest my darling! Good bye! I kiss you—O the torments!

Letter to Fanny Brawne, June? 1820[1]

My dearest Fanny,

My head is puzzled this morning, and I scarce know what I shall say though I am full of a hundred things. 'T is certain I would rather be writing to you this morning, notwithstanding the alloy of grief in such an occupation, than enjoy any other pleasure, with health to boot, unconnected with you. Upon my soul I have loved you to the extreme. I wish you could know the Tenderness with which I continually brood over your different aspects of countenance, action and dress. I see you come down in the morning: I see you meet me at the Window—I see every thing over again eternally that I ever have seen. If I get on the pleasant clue I live in a sort of happy misery, if on the unpleasant 'tis miserable misery. You complain of my illtreating you in word thought and deed—I am sorry,—at times I feel bitterly sorry that I ever made you unhappy—my excuse is that those words have been wrung from me by the sharpness of my feelings. At all events and in any case I have been wrong; could I believe that I did it without any cause, I should be the most sincere of Penitents. I could give way to my repentant feelings now, I could recant all my suspicions, I could mingle with you heart and Soul though absent, were it not for some parts of your Letters. Do you suppose it possible I could ever leave you? You know what I think of myself and what of you. You know that I should feel how much it was my loss and how little yours—My friends laugh at you![2] I know some of them—when I know them all I shall never think of them again as friends or even acquaintance. My friends have behaved well to me in every instance but one, and there they have become tattlers, and inquisitors into my conduct: spying upon a secret I would rather die than share it with any body's confidence. For this I cannot wish them well, I care not to see any of them again. If I am the Theme, I will not be the Friend of idle Gossips. Good gods what a shame it is our Loves should be so put into the microscope of a Coterie. Their laughs should not affect you (I may perhaps give you reasons some day for these laughs, for I suspect a few people to hate me well enough, *for reasons I know of,* who have pretended a great friendship for me) when in competition with one, who if he never should see you again would make you the saint of his memory—These Laughers, who do not like you, who envy you for your Beauty, who would have God-bless'd-me from you for ever: who were plying me with disencouragements with respect to you eternally. People are revengeful—do not mind them—do nothing but love me—if I knew that for certain life and health will in such event be a heaven, and death itself will be less painful. I long to believe in immortality I shall never be able to bid you an entire farewell. If I am destined to be happy with you here—how short is the longest Life—I wish to believe in immortality—I wish to live with you for ever. Do not let my name

---

1. Text from ALS (Harvard MS Keats 1.79).
2. Fanny Brawne believed that the Reynoldses at least opposed her.

ever pass between you and those laughers, if I have no other merit than the great Love for you, that were sufficient to keep me sacred and unmentioned in such society. If I have been cruel and injust I swear my love has ever been greater than my cruelty which last but a minute whereas my Love come what will shall last for ever. If concessions to me has hurt your Pride, god knows I have had little pride in my heart when thinking of you. Your name never passes my Lips—do not let mine pass yours. Those People do not like me. After reading my Letter you even then wish to see me. I am strong enough to walk over—but I dare not. I shall feel so much pain in parting with you again. My dearest love, I am afraid to see you, I am strong but not strong enough to see you. Will my arm be ever round you again. And if so shall I be obliged to leave you again. My sweet Love! I am happy whilst I believe your first Letter. Let me be but certain that you are mine heart and soul, and I could die more happily than I could otherwise live. If you think me cruel—if you think I have slighted you—do muse it over again and see into my heart. My Love to you is "true as truth's simplicity and simpler than the infancy of truth"[3] as I think I once said before. How could I slight you? How threaten to leave you? not in the spirit of a Threat to you—no—but in the spirit of Wretchedness in myself. My fairest, my delicious, my angel Fanny! do not believe me such a vulgar fellow. I will be as patient in illness and as believing in Love as I am able—

Yours for ever my dearest
John Keats—

Letter to Fanny Brawne, June? 1820[1]

My dearest Girl,

I endeavour to make myself as patient as possible. Hunt amuses me very kindly—besides I have your ring on my finger and your flowers on the table. I shall not expect to see you yet because it would be so much pain to part with you again. When the Books you want come you shall have them. I am very well this afternoon. My dearest

[signature cut out]

---

3. Shakespeare, *Troilus and Cressida*, 3.2.156–57.
1. This brief letter was written between June 23, when Keats moved in with Leigh Hunt due to his health, and August 12, when he left over a dispute about one of Hunt's children opening a letter from Fanny. As he wrote to Fanny Keats on July 22, "Mr Hunt does every thing in his power to make the time pass as agreeably with me as possible" (*L*, 2: 309). Text from AL (Harvard MS Keats 1.81).

Lamia, Isabella, The Eve of St. Agnes, and Other Poems (1820)

Keats's final volume, appearing over his name as the "Author of Endymion," was released in 12mo. on July 1 or 2, 1820 (the preface is dated June 26), in a run of perhaps one thousand copies and priced at seven and one half shillings; it was printed by Thomas Davison for Keats's publishers, Taylor and Hessey, with the following "Advertisement":

> IF any apology be thought necessary for the appearance of the unfin-ished poem of HYPERION, the publishers beg to state that they alone are responsible, as it was printed at their particular request, and con-trary to the wish of the author. The poem was intended to have been of equal length with ENDYMION, but the reception given to that work discouraged the author from proceeding.

> *Fleet-Street, June* 26, 1820.

At the top of this statement in a copy he gave to his acquaintance Burridge Davenport, a banker in Hampstead, Keats wrote, "I had no part in this; I was ill at the time," and next to the final comment, he indicated, "This is a lie" (Harvard, Houghton Keats*EC8.K2262.820*l* [G]; facsimile in Motion, p. 522).

The volume appeared when Keats was ill and contemplating a trip to Italy for his health. He wrote to Brown on June 21 that "This shall be my last trial; not succeeding, I shall try what I can do in the Apothecary line" (*L*, 2: 298). He suffered a serious hemorrhage on June 22 and, following doctor's orders, moved in with his long-time friend Leigh Hunt on June 23. During this period, Hunt published Keats's Dante sonnet (see above, p. 336) and some lines from *The Jealousies* (see above, p. 380) in the *Indica-tor*, wrote with Keats a "Now" (see pp. 510–13, below), and dedicated his translation of *Amyntas* to Keats. Keats would leave Hunt's house on August 12 when he became upset that Hunt's son Thorton had opened a letter from Fanny Brawne; though he said he intended to return to the Bentleys' house in Well Walk, he in fact stayed with the Brawnes until he departed for Italy.

While the volume appeared in the summer of 1820, the poems in it had been first composed in 1818 and in 1819: *Isabella* was written in Febru-ary–April 1818, Keats began *Hyperion* in late 1818 and set it aside in April 1819, he drafted *The Eve of St. Agnes* January–February 1819, and *Lamia* had been begun in July 1819 and finished in September and then revised in March 1820; of the shorter poems "Lines of the Mermaid Tavern" and "Robin Hood" had been written in February 1818, "Fancy" and "Ode" ("Bards of pas-sion and of mirth") at the end of 1818, four of the great odes in April–May of 1819, and "To Autumn" on September 19, 1819. Keats worked on revising the poems in the spring of 1820 as he readied them for publication; he presented a fair copy of the volume to Taylor at the end of April, and the poems were typeset at the end of May and in the first two weeks of June.

The volume is most famous for its odes, but Keats named the volume for its three opening romances; he identified himself on the title page as the author of the poetic romance of *Endymion*, and he closed the volume with the narrative of *Hyperion*. The volume can thus be usefully read in the context of the popularity of romances by Byron and Scott that also brought forth efforts by Hunt (*Story of Rimini*), Moore (*Lalla Rookh*), and Wordsworth (*Peter Bell*). Keats's handling of romance in the volume has received considerable critical attention, particularly in response to Jack Stillinger's argument (included here, pp. 604–14) that Keats created a kind of antiromance capable of confronting the sorrows of life beyond the wish-fulfilling enchantments offered by conventional romances.

Keats's friend Charles Lamb, reviewing the volume (*New Times* [July 19, 1820]; below pp. 515–16), expressed an opinion that would be shared by many throughout the nineteenth century, that *Isabella* was the "finest thing in the volume." However, for most of the twentieth century, *Isabella* has been ranked far below the other two narratives, with the *The Eve of St. Agnes* frequently praised as the most perfect of Keats's poems and with *Lamia* lauded as the most interesting and most "mature" of the three tales. This modern accounting reiterates Keats's own concerns about these poems. While friends such as John Hamilton Reynolds were impressed with *Isabella*—Reynolds praised its "simplicity and quiet pathos" and thought it would "annul" the negative criticism Keats had received in conservative journals (letter to Keats, October 14, 1818, *L*, 1: 376)—Keats became anxious that the poem would be misunderstood by his readers. His friend and literary advisor Richard Woodhouse reported in a letter to Keats's publisher John Taylor (September 19, 20, 1819; above, pp. 355–57) that, while Keats wished to publish *The Eve* and *Lamia* immediately, he now found *Isabella; or, The Pot of Basil* "mawkish." Woodhouse disagreed, praising *Isabella* and fretting more about what he saw as the indelicacy of *The Eve*, but Keats continued to worry:

> I will give you a few reasons why I shall persist in not publishing The Pot of Basil—I[t] is too smokeable. . . . There is too much inexperience of live, and simplicity of knowledge in it—which might do very well after one's death—but not while one is alive. There are very few would look to the reality. I intend to use more finesse with the Public. It is possible to write fine things which cannot be laugh'd at in any way. Isabella is what I should call were I a reviewer 'A weak-sided Poem' with an amusing sober-sadness about it. Not that I do not think Reynolds and you are quite right about it—it is enough for me. But this will not do to be public—If I may so say, in my dramatic capacity I enter fully into the feeling: but in Propria Persona I should be apt to quiz it myself—There is no objection of this kind to Lamia—A good deal to St Agnes Eve—only not so glaring—(letter to Woodhouse, September 22, 1819, *L*, 2: 174)

Of course, Keats did not persist in not publishing *Isabella*, which suggests that finally his friends and advisors convinced him of the poem's worth, but his concerns have tended nevertheless to shape the evaluation of these three poems by modern scholars. The romances as a whole can be better understood as experiments within a range of contemporary efforts on the romance. Keats can then be seen offering three different kinds of narrative of desire and imagination: one that draws on classical myth, one that turns to an Italian source in Boccaccio, and one that evokes English medieval romance and the medievalism of Spenser.

Keats seems less concerned about the "other poems," that is, the famous odes. Stuart Curran's account of romantic experimentation on the ode in *Poetic Form and British Romanticism* (New York: Oxford University Press, 1986), pp. 56–84, provides a good context for understanding Keats's work in that form, which should be seen to include "Bards of passion and of mirth," which is labeled in the volume simply as "Ode" and "Fancy," which Brown entitled "Ode to Fancy." Keats also refers to these two poems in a letter to his brother of January 2, 1819 (above, p. 306) as "specimens of a sort of rondeau which I think I shall become partial to—because you have one idea amplified with greater ease and more delight and freedom than in the sonnet." The great odes have also been seen as arising from Keats's experimentation with the sonnet, so we might understand one goal of the volume as the discovery of a larger lyric form. We should remember the wide range of uses poets of the day found for the ode. While we think primarily of the philosophical or sublime ode, poems such as Byron's "Ode to Napoleon Bonaparte," Wordsworth's Thanksgiving ode of 1816, and the various odes Southey wrote during his tenure as poet laureate remind us that the ode could serve political purposes. Odes could be amorous, as in Moore's *Odes of Anacreon*, and even satiric, as in the widely admired odes of "Peter Pindar" (John Wolcott).

While criticism tends to focus on particular poems or groups of poems in the 1820 volume, Neil Fraistat's essay, included here (pp. 592–604), explores the organization of the volume and argues for a reading of the volume as a whole. On the narrative poems, see John Spencer Hill, ed., *Keats: Narrative Poems* (London: Macmillan, 1983); Tilottama Rajan, *Dark Interpreter: The Discourse of Romanticism* (Ithaca: Cornell University Press, 1980); Bennett, Cox, and Wolfson. For a comprehensive account of romance in the period, see Stuart Curran, *Poetic Form and British Romanticism*, pp. 128–57. On the odes, see Paul Fry, *The Poets Calling in the English Ode* (New Haven: Yale University Press, 1980); Robert Gittings, ed., *The Odes of Keats and Their Earliest Known Manuscripts* (Ohio: Kent State University Press, 1970); James O'Rourke, *Keats's Odes and Contemporary Criticism* (Gainesville: University of Florida Press, 1998); Jack Wright Rhodes, *Keats's Major Odes: An Annotated Bibliography of the Criticism* (Westport, CT: Greenwood Press, 1984); and Helen Vendler, *The Odes of John Keats* (Cambridge: Harvard University Press, 1983). On *Hyperion,* see, for example, Stuart Ende, *Keats and the Sublime* (New Haven: Yale University Press, 1976), pp. 98–115; Walter Evert, *Aesthetic and Myth in the Poetry of Keats* (Princeton: Princeton University Press, 1965), pp. 225–43; Geoffrey Hartman, "Spectral Symbolism and the Authorial Self: An Approach to *Hyperion*", *Essays in Criticism* 24 (1974), pp. 1–19; John Jones, *John Keats's Dream of Truth* (London: Chatto and Windus, 1969), pp. 74–104; Levinson (pp. 191–226); Sperry (pp. 155–97); Watkins (pp. 85–103); and Wolfson (pp. 253–69).

The volume received twelve reviews in the first two months after its publication, with only four of them being hostile (see pp. 515–16, 518–23, 525–29). Woodhouse praised *Hyperion,* Hunt admired both that poem and the nightingale ode, and Lamb, as noted, found *Isabella* the "finest thing in the volume." The *Edinburgh Review* finally gave Keats's poetry its due, and the *London Magazine* praised Keats while admonishing his attackers in *Blackwood's* and the *Quarterly Review*. The volume sold somewhere around 500 copies but was still being offered at the original price in 1828.

The texts of the poems are taken from the 1820 volume. Additional information about composition, extant holograph manuscripts, and some additional criticism will be given with individual poems.

[handwritten: Keats wrote this when he knew - igoing to die]

LAMIA.   *[handwritten: Historical Allegory]*

Lamia was the last of the romances in the 1820 volume to be written. Keats had left London on June 17, 1819, and traveled to Shanklin on the Isle of Wight, where Rice had arranged for their lodgings. After working on the first act of *Otho the Great*, he took up *Lamia*, finishing the first part by July 11. Keats left Shanklin for Winchester on August 12, and there he completed the poem by September 5. In between writing the two parts of the poem, he worked on *Otho* and his recasting of the *Hyperion* project. Keats made a fair copy of *Lamia* sometime between September and March, making final revisions in March 1820 for publication. Differences between the draft and the final copy indicate a move away from a satiric tone that still is present in the Byronic turn of the opening of Part II.

In the fair copy, Keats notes that "The groundwork of the story will be found in Burton's *Anatomy of Melancholy*," and he appended the appropriate passage to the end of the poem (below, p. 429). Other sources include classical handbooks, such as Potter's *Antiquities of Greece* (1697) and Ovid's *Metamorphoses*, and *The Arabian Nights*. The figure of Lamia, an enchantress with whom readers sympathize, can be compared to Geraldine in Coleridge's *Christabel* (1816) and the enchantress in Thomas Love Peacock's *Rhododaphne* (1818). Brown indicated that Keats modeled the poem on Dryden's versification (*KC*, 2: 67), and Woodhouse wrote Taylor on September 19, 20, 1819, saying, "The metre is Drydenian heroic—with many triplets, & many alexandrines. But this K. observ'd, & I agreed, was required, or rather quite in character with the language & sentiment in those particular parts.—K. has a fine feeling when & where he may use poetical licenses with effect" (p. 357). For Keats's sense that this poem avoided the pitfalls of his other romances, see the headnote to the volume (p. 410). With its opening portrayal of Hermes' love of a nymph that appears perfect because it exists outside the vicissitudes of human desire, its account of an erotic enthrallment between Lamia and Lycius that turns to possessiveness and destruction, and its Byronic view that love—whether in a palace or a hut— is flawed, the poem offers a sober account of love's frailties.

On *Lamia*, see, in addition to the pieces mentioned in the headnote to the volume, Garrett Stewart, "*Lamia* and the Language of Metamorphosis," *Studies in Romanticism* 15 (1976): 3–41, and Watkins, pp. 135–55.

The text is from the 1820 volume. Only portions of Keats's draft remain; the surviving pieces seem to have been in the possession of Severn (and perhaps Brown), who gave them to various people. Fragments are now located at the University of Texas (1.185a), the Keats-Shelley Memorial House, Rome (1.185b–90; 2.67b–74), the Berg Collection at the New York Public

Library (1.324–29; 2. 293–94), the Rosenbach Museum and Library (1.386b–397; EL3 f.K25 MS2), Harvard (2.26–49; 2.85–92, with ten discarded lines and two moved to 2.104–105; 2.122–47; 2.191–98), and the Robert H. Taylor Collection, Manuscripts Division, Department of Rare Books and Special Collections, Princeton University Library (2.50–61; 2.62–67a); see Stillinger, p. 665. Keats included a different draft of ` 2.122–62 (with some cancelled lines) in a letter to Taylor of September 5, 1819 (Harvard MS Keats 1.63). The fair copy, with revisions, is held at Harvard (MS Keats 2.26), which also holds the page proofs with corrections and annotations by Keats, Woodhouse, and Taylor (*EC8.K2262.8201a).

1820 = end of Romantic period

PART I.

UPON a time, before the faery broods
Drove Nymph and Satyr from the prosperous woods,
Before King Oberon's bright diadem,
Sceptre, and mantle, clasp'd with dewy gem,
Frighted away the Dryads and the Fauns[1]   5
From rushes green, and brakes, and cowslip'd lawns,[2]
The ever-smitten Hermes[3] empty left
His golden throne, bent warm on amorous theft:
From high Olympus had he stolen light,
On this side of Jove's clouds, to escape the sight   10
Of his great summoner, and made retreat
Into a forest on the shores of Crete.[4]
For somewhere in that sacred island dwelt
A nymph, to whom all hoofed Satyrs knelt;
At whose white feet the languid Tritons[5] poured   15
Pearls, while on land they wither'd and adored.
Fast by the springs where she to bathe was wont,
And in those meads where sometime she might haunt,
Were strewn rich gifts, unknown to any Muse,
Though Fancy's casket were unlock'd to choose.   20
Ah, what a world of love was at her feet!
So Hermes thought, and a celestial heat
Burnt from his winged heels to either ear,
That from a whiteness, as the lily clear,
Blush'd into roses 'mid his golden hair,   25
Fallen in jealous curls about his shoulders bare.

1. Keats links the nymphs, satyrs, dryads, and fauns of classical mythology with the fairies—here represented by Oberon, who appears in Shakespeare's *Midsummer Night's Dream*—of English folklore, perhaps following the example of Spenser's *Faerie Queene* 2.10.70–76, Burton's *Anatomy of Melancholy* 1. 2. 1. 2, Sandys's translation of Ovid's *Metamorphoses*, or Dryden's *The Wife of Bath Her Tale*, ll. 1–4; whatever his source, Keats constructs a movement from Greek and Roman myth to English folk culture that historicizes the legendary material.
2. Cowslips, a common British primrose, bloom here amidst the grass; *rushes*: marsh plants; *brakes*: tall ferns.
3. Also known as Mercury, the patron god of travelers, shepherds, orators, merchants, and thieves and the messenger of the gods and particularly of Jove, "his great summoner" (l. 11), Hermes wears a winged hat, has winged heels, and carries a wand, the caduceus. He was known for his many loves. This amour with the nymph uses details from Ovid's *Metamorphoses* 2.708ff.
4. An island in the eastern Mediterranean where, according to Lemprière, Jupiter was secretly educated in a cave on Mount Ida.
5. Sea gods, part men and part fish, named for the son of Neptune and Amphitrite.

From vale to vale, from wood to wood, he flew,
Breathing upon the flowers his passion new,
And wound with many a river to its head,
To find where this sweet nymph prepar'd her secret bed: 30
In vain; the sweet nymph might nowhere be found,
And so he rested, on the lonely ground,
Pensive, and full of painful jealousies
Of the Wood-Gods, and even the very trees.
There as he stood, he heard a mournful voice,   35
Such as once heard, in gentle heart, destroys
All pain but pity:[6] thus the lone voice spake:
"When from this wreathed tomb shall I awake!
"When move in a sweet body fit for life,
"And love, and pleasure, and the ruddy strife   40
"Of hearts and lips! Ah, miserable me!"
The God, dove-footed, glided silently
Round bush and tree, soft-brushing, in his speed,
The taller grasses and full-flowering weed,
Until he found a palpitating snake,   45
Bright, and cirque-couchant[7] in a dusky brake.

She was a gordian[8] shape of dazzling hue,
Vermilion-spotted, golden, green, and blue;
Striped like a zebra, freckled like a pard,[9]
Eyed like a peacock, and all crimson barr'd;   50
And full of silver moons, that, as she breathed,
Dissolv'd, or brighter shone, or interwreathed
Their lustres with the gloomier tapestries—
So rainbow-sided, touch'd with miseries,
She seem'd, at once, some penanced lady elf,[1]   55
Some demon's mistress, or the demon's self.
Upon her crest she wore a wannish fire
Sprinkled with stars, like Ariadne's tiar:[2]
Her head was serpent, but ah, bitter-sweet!
She had a woman's mouth with all its pearls complete: 60
And for her eyes: what could such eyes do there
But weep, and weep, that they were born so fair?
As Proserpine still weeps for her Sicilian air.[3]
Her throat was serpent, but the words she spake
Came, as through bubbling honey, for Love's sake,   65
And thus; while Hermes on his pinions lay,
Like a stoop'd falcon ere he takes his prey.

"Fair Hermes, crown'd with feathers, fluttering light,
"I had a splendid dream of thee last night:

6. See Chaucer's *Knight's Tale*, l. 903: "For pitee renneth soone in gentil herte."
7. Keats's coinage, meaning lying in coils.
8. Intricately interwoven; from the famous Gordian Knot that could not be untangled.
9. Leopard.
1. A fairy transformed into a snake for penance or punishment.
2. Ariadne is given a crown of stars by Bacchus (see p. 66, n. 2), as depicted in Titian's *Bacchus and Ariadne* and Leigh Hunt's 1819 poem of the same title, ll. 344–53.
3. Proserpine was abducted by Hades from Sicily to live in the underworld.

"I saw thee sitting, on a throne of gold,   70
"Among the Gods, upon Olympus old,
"The only sad one; for thou didst not hear
"The soft, lute-finger'd Muses chaunting clear,
"Nor even Apollo when he sang alone,
"Deaf to his throbbing throat's long, long melodious moan.   75
"I dreamt I saw thee, robed in purple flakes,
"Break amorous through the clouds, as morning breaks,
"And, swiftly as a bright Phœbean dart,[4]
"Strike for the Cretan isle; and here thou art!
"Too gentle Hermes, hast thou found the maid?"   80
Whereat the star of Lethe[5] not delay'd
His rosy eloquence, and thus inquired:
"Thou smooth-lipp'd serpent, surely high inspired!
"Thou beauteous wreath, with melancholy eyes,
"Possess whatever bliss thou canst devise,   85
"Telling me only where my nymph is fled,—
"Where she doth breathe!" "Bright planet, thou hast said,"
Return'd the snake, "but seal with oaths, fair God!"
"I swear," said Hermes, "by my serpent rod,[6]
"And by thine eyes, and by thy starry crown!"   90
Light flew his earnest words, among the blossoms blown.
Then thus again the brilliance feminine:
"Too frail of heart! for this lost nymph of thine,
"Free as the air, invisibly, she strays
"About these thornless wilds; her pleasant days   95
"She tastes unseen; unseen her nimble feet
"Leave traces in the grass and flowers sweet;
"From weary tendrils, and bow'd branches green,
"She plucks the fruit unseen, she bathes unseen:
"And by my power is her beauty veil'd   100
"To keep it unaffronted, unassail'd
"By the love-glances of unlovely eyes,
"Of Satyrs, Fauns, and blear'd Silenus'[7] sighs.
"Pale grew her immortality, for woe
"Of all these lovers, and she grieved so   105
"I took compassion on her, bade her steep
"Her hair in weïrd syrops, that would keep
"Her loveliness invisible, yet free
"To wander as she loves, in liberty.
"Thou shalt behold her, Hermes, thou alone,   110
"If thou wilt, as thou swearest, grant my boon!"
Then, once again, the charmed God began
An oath, and through the serpent's ears it ran
Warm, tremulous, devout, psalterian.[8]

---

4. A ray of sunshine, from Phoebus Apollo's role as god of the sun.
5. The river of forgetfulness leading into Hades; the reference here is to Hermes's role as the psychopomp who conducts the souls of the dead into the underworld.
6. His wand or caduceus, which has wings at its tip and two serpents entwined on the rod.
7. The fat, perpetually intoxicated follower of Bacchus, who is also accompanied by riotous satyrs and fauns.
8. From psaltery, an antique stringed instrument, though Keats also seems to have "psalm" in mind.

Ravish'd, she lifted her Circean[9] head,   115
Blush'd a live damask, and swift-lisping said,
"I was a woman, let me have once more
"A woman's shape, and charming as before.
"I love a youth of Corinth—O the bliss!
"Give me my woman's form, and place me where he is.   120
"Stoop, Hermes, let me breathe upon thy brow,
"And thou shalt see thy sweet nymph even now."
The God on half-shut feathers sank serene,
She breath'd upon his eyes, and swift was seen
Of both the guarded nymph near-smiling on the green. 125
It was no dream; or say a dream it was,
Real are the dreams of Gods, and smoothly pass
Their pleasures in a long immortal dream.
One warm, flush'd moment, hovering, it might seem
Dash'd by the wood-nymph's beauty, so he burn'd;   130
Then, lighting on the printless verdure, turn'd
To the swoon'd serpent, and with languid arm,
Delicate, put to proof the lythe Caducean[1] charm.
So done, upon the nymph his eyes he bent
Full of adoring tears and blandishment,   135
And towards her stept: she, like a moon in wane,
Faded before him, cower'd, nor could restrain
Her fearful sobs, self-folding like a flower
That faints into itself at evening hour:
But the God fostering her chilled hand,   140
She felt the warmth, her eyelids open'd bland,
And, like new flowers at morning song of bees,
Bloom'd, and gave up her honey to the lees.
Into the green-recessed woods they flew;
Nor grew they pale, as mortal lovers do.   145

    Left to herself, the serpent now began
To change;[2] her elfin blood in madness ran,
Her mouth foam'd, and the grass, therewith besprent,[3]
Wither'd at dew so sweet and virulent;
Her eyes in torture fix'd, and anguish drear,   150
Hot, glaz'd, and wide, with lid-lashes all sear,
Flash'd phosphor and sharp sparks, without one cooling tear.
The colours all inflam'd throughout her train,
She writh'd about, convuls'd with scarlet pain:
A deep volcanian yellow took the place   155
Of all her milder-mooned body's grace;
And, as the lava ravishes the mead,[4]
Spoilt all her silver mail, and golden brede;[5]
Made gloom of all her frecklings, streaks and bars,

---

9. Either dangerously beautiful like the powerful witch Circe or transformed into an animal as were Circe's victims.
1. See p. 415, n. 6 above.
2. Of her change, Woodhouse wrote to Taylor, "She is metamorphosed into a beautiful Woman, the Change is quite Ovidian, but better" (pp. 356–57).
3. Sprinkled over (archaic); Allott suggests an echo of Milton's *Comus*, ll. 541–42.
4. Meadow.
5. Something interwoven, plaited; embroidery.

Eclips'd her crescents, and lick'd up her stars: 160
So that, in moments few, she was undrest
Of all her sapphires, greens, and amethyst,
And rubious-argent:[6] of all these bereft,
Nothing but pain and ugliness were left.
Still shone her crown; that vanish'd, also she   165
Melted and disappear'd as suddenly;
And in the air, her new voice luting soft,
Cried, "Lycius! gentle Lycius!"—Borne aloft
With the bright mists about the mountains hoar
These words dissolv'd: Crete's forests heard no more.   170

　　Whither fled Lamia, now a lady bright,
A full-born beauty new and exquisite?
She fled into that valley they pass o'er
Who go to Corinth from Cenchreas'[7] shore;
And rested at the foot of those wild hills,   175
The rugged founts of the Peræan[8] rills,
And of that other ridge whose barren back
Stretches, with all its mist and cloudy rack,
South-westward to Cleone.[9] There she stood
About a young bird's flutter from a wood,   180
Fair, on a sloping green of mossy tread,
By a clear pool, wherein she passioned
To see herself escap'd from so sore ills,
While her robes flaunted with the daffodils.

　　Ah, happy Lycius!—for she was a maid[1]   185
More beautiful than ever twisted braid,
Or sigh'd, or blush'd, or on spring-flowered lea
Spread a green kirtle[2] to the minstrelsy:
A virgin purest lipp'd, yet in the lore
Of love deep learned to the red heart's core: 190
Not one hour old, yet of sciential brain
To unperplex bliss from its neighbour pain;
Define their pettish limits, and estrange
Their points of contact, and swift counterchange;
Intrigue with the specious chaos, and dispart   195
Its most ambiguous atoms with sure art;
As though in Cupid's college she had spent
Sweet days a lovely graduate, still unshent,[3]
And kept his rosy terms in idle languishment.

---

6. Reddish silver (Keats's coinage).
7. The port of Corinth on the Saronic Gulf.
8. This word has escaped identification. Lemprière for Peræa gives a "part of Caria," which is a mountainous region in southwest Asia Minor. Keats might be suggesting that the hills near Corinth are
the beginnings of a mountain chain that appears on the other side of the Aegean sea.
9. A village on the road from Corinth to Argos.
1. The fair copy has a longer version: "Ah! never heard of, delight never known, / Save of one happy
mortal! Only one; / Lycius the happy: for she was a Maid."
2. Long gown.
3. Unspoilt. Gittings (1954) finds a parallel between ll. 197–98 and Dryden's *The First Book of Ovid's
Art of Love*, ll. 1–2: "in *Cupid's* school whoe'er would take Degree, / Must learn his Rudiments by
reading me"; Gittings (1968) also notes that "Graduate was the slang term for 'an unmarried
woman who has taken her degree in carnal love'" (p. 491).

Why this fair creature chose so fairily   200
By the wayside to linger, we shall see;
But first 'tis fit to tell how she could muse
And dream, when in the serpent prison-house,[4]
Of all she list, strange or magnificent:
How, ever, where she will'd, her spirit went;   205
Whether to faint Elysium,[5] or where
Down through tress-lifting waves the Nereids[6] fair
Wind into Thetis'[7] bower by many a pearly stair;
Or where God Bacchus drains his cups divine,
Stretch'd out, at ease, beneath a glutinous[8] pine;   210
Or where in Pluto's gardens palatine
Mulciber's columns gleam in far piazzian line.[9]
And sometimes into cities she would send
Her dream, with feast and rioting to blend;
And once, while among mortals dreaming thus,   215
She saw the young Corinthian Lycius
Charioting foremost in the envious race,
Like a young Jove with calm uneager face,
And fell into a swooning love of him.
Now on the moth-time of that evening dim   220
He would return that way, as well she knew,
To Corinth from the shore; for freshly blew
The eastern soft wind, and his galley now
Grated the quaystones with her brazen prow
In port Cenchreas, from Egina isle[1]   225
Fresh anchor'd; whither he had been awhile
To sacrifice to Jove, whose temple there
Waits with high marble doors for blood and incense rare.
Jove heard his vows,[2] and better'd his desire;
For by some freakful chance he made retire   230
From his companions, and set forth to walk,
Perhaps grown wearied of their Corinth talk:
Over the solitary hills he fared,
Thoughtless at first, but ere eve's star appeared
His phantasy was lost, where reason fades,   235
In the calm'd twilight of Platonic shades.[3]
Lamia beheld him coming, near, more near—
Close to her passing, in indifference drear,
His silent sandals swept the mossy green;
So neighbour'd to him, and yet so unseen   240

4. Keats noted in the margins of his copy of *Paradise Lost* 9.179–91: "Whose head is not dizzy at the
   probable speculations of satan in this serpent prison"; see Beth Lau, *Keats's "Paradise Lost"*
   (Gainesville: University of Florida Press, 1998), p. 153.
5. Classical paradise for the virtuous dead.
6. Sea nymphs, the daughters of Nereus.
7. The Nereid who was the mother of Achilles.
8. Gummy, here from pine resin.
9. As Allott notes, Keats (ll. 211–12) recalls Mulciber or Vulcan's construction of Pandemonium in
   Paradise Lost (1.713–15). *palatine*: suggests palatial; the coinage *piazzian line*, from a piazza or
   square surrounded by buildings, probably means a colonnade.
1. Located in the Saronic Gulf, opposite Athens; the first Greek coins were struck there.
2. Allott suggests Lycius prays for a mate to Jupiter as one of the gods who oversees marriage.
3. Perhaps an allusion to Platonic philosophizing but also perhaps to thoughts of "Platonic" (that is,
   non-erotic) love, in contrast to his friend's "Corinth talk" (l. 232); Corinth was known for its lasciviousness, its Temple of Venus, as Burton notes, functioning as a whore house.

She stood: he pass'd, shut up in mysteries,
His mind wrapp'd like his mantle, while her eyes
Follow'd his steps, and her neck regal white
Turn'd—syllabling thus, "Ah, Lycius bright,
"And will you leave me on the hills alone?   245
"Lycius, look back! and be some pity shown."
He did; not with cold wonder fearingly,
But Orpheus-like at an Eurydice;[4]
For so delicious were the words she sung,
It seem'd he had lov'd them a whole summer long: 250
And soon his eyes had drunk her beauty up,[5]
Leaving no drop in the bewildering cup,
And still the cup was full,—while he, afraid
Lest she should vanish ere his lip had paid
Due adoration, thus began to adore;   255
Her soft look growing coy, she saw his chain so sure:
"Leave thee alone! Look back! Ah, Goddess, see
"Whether my eyes can ever turn from thee!
"For pity do not this sad heart belie—
"Even as thou vanishest so I shall die.   260
"Stay! though a Naiad of the rivers,[6] stay!
"To thy far wishes will thy streams obey:
"Stay! though the greenest woods be thy domain,
"Alone they can drink up the morning rain:
"Though a descended Pleiad,[7] will not one   265
"Of thine harmonious sisters keep in tune
"Thy spheres, and as thy silver proxy shine?
"So sweetly to these ravish'd ears of mine
"Came thy sweet greeting, that if thou shouldst fade
"Thy memory will waste me to a shade:—   270
"For pity do not melt!"—"If I should stay,"
Said Lamia, "here, upon this floor of clay,
"And pain my steps upon these flowers too rough,
"What canst thou say or do of charm enough
"To dull the nice remembrance of my home?   275
"Thou canst not ask me with thee here to roam
"Over these hills and vales, where no joy is,—
"Empty of immortality and bliss!
"Thou art a scholar, Lycius, and must know
"That finer spirits cannot breathe below   280
"In human climes, and live: Alas! poor youth,
"What taste of purer air hast thou to soothe
"My essence? What serener palaces,
"Where I may all my many senses please,
"And by mysterious sleights[8] a hundred thirsts appease? 285

4. Orpheus, son of Calliope and Apollo, played music so moving that he convinced Hades to allow
   him to attempt to rescue his wife Eurydice from the underworld, but he failed when, against orders,
   he looked back to be sure that she followed him.
5. Allott notes that Keats marked his copy of Burton's *Anatomy of Melancholy* 3. 2. 4.1, "she will . . .
   drink to him with her eyes, nay drink him up, devour him," and then cited Jonson's "To Celia,"
   "Drinke to me, onely, with thine eyes."
6. See Reynolds's *Naiad* (1816), where a river nymph lures a knight to his death in the water.
7. One of the seven daughters of Atlas, who, after their deaths, made up the constellation Pleiades,
   and who appear here to participate in the harmonious music of the spheres.
8. Artifices but also deceitful strategems.

"It cannot be—Adieu!" So said, she rose
Tiptoe with white arms spread. He, sick to lose
The amorous promise of her lone complain,
Swoon'd, murmuring of love, and pale with pain.
The cruel lady, without any show   290
Of sorrow for her tender favourite's woe,
But rather, if her eyes could brighter be,
With brighter eyes and slow amenity,
Put her new lips to his, and gave afresh
The life she had so tangled in her mesh: 295
And as he from one trance was wakening
Into another, she began to sing,
Happy in beauty, life, and love, and every thing,
A song of love, too sweet for earthly lyres,
While, like held breath, the stars drew in their panting fires.   300
And then she whisper'd in such trembling tone,
As those who, safe together met alone
For the first time through many anguish'd days,
Use other speech than looks; bidding him raise
His drooping head, and clear his soul of doubt,   305
For that she was a woman, and without
Any more subtle fluid in her veins
Than throbbing blood, and that the self-same pains
Inhabited her frail-strung heart as his.
And next she wonder'd how his eyes could miss   310
Her face so long in Corinth, where, she said,
She dwelt but half retir'd, and there had led
Days happy as the gold coin could invent
Without the aid of love; yet in content
Till she saw him, as once she pass'd him by,   315
Where 'gainst a column he leant thoughtfully
At Venus' temple porch, 'mid baskets heap'd
Of amorous herbs and flowers, newly reap'd
Late on that eve, as 'twas the night before
The Adonian feast;⁹ whereof she saw no more,   320
But wept alone those days, for why should she adore?
Lycius from death awoke into amaze,
To see her still, and singing so sweet lays;
Then from amaze into delight he fell
To hear her whisper woman's lore so well;   325
And every word she spake entic'd him on
To unperplex'd delight and pleasure known.
Let the mad poets say whate'er they please
Of the sweets of Fairies, Peris,¹ Goddesses,
There is not such a treat among them all,   330
Haunters of cavern, lake, and waterfall,
As a real woman, lineal indeed
From Pyrrha's pebbles² or old Adam's seed.

---

9. The feast that honors Adonis, Venus's lover; see Marlowe's *Hero and Leander*, 1: 91–134, and Dryden's *The First Book of Ovid's Art of Love*, ll. 80–81.
1. Persian genii.
2. In classical myth, following a flood by which Jupiter destroyed the world, Deucalion and Pyrrha recreated humankind by throwing stones which were transformed into people. The pairing of the Biblical Adam and the mythic Pyrrha echoes the kind of comparative mythology popular in the period.

Thus gentle Lamia judg'd, and judg'd aright,
That Lycius could not love in half a fright,   335
So threw the goddess off, and won his heart
More pleasantly by playing woman's part,
With no more awe than what her beauty gave,
That, while it smote, still guaranteed to save.
Lycius to all made eloquent reply,   340
Marrying to every word a twinborn sigh;
And last, pointing to Corinth, ask'd her sweet,
If 'twas too far that night for her soft feet.
The way was short, for Lamia's eagerness
Made, by a spell, the triple league decrease   345
To a few paces; not at all surmised
By blinded Lycius, so in her comprized.
They pass'd the city gates, he knew not how,
So noiseless, and he never thought to know.

As men talk in a dream, so Corinth all,   350
Throughout her palaces imperial,
And all her populous streets and temples lewd,[3]
Mutter'd, like tempest in the distance brew'd,
To the wide-spreaded night above her towers.
Men, women, rich and poor, in the cool hours,   355
Shuffled their sandals o'er the pavement white,
Companion'd or alone; while many a light
Flared, here and there, from wealthy festivals,
And threw their moving shadows on the walls,
Or found them cluster'd in the corniced shade   360
Of some arch'd temple door, or dusky colonnade.

Muffling his face, of greeting friends in fear,
Her fingers he press'd hard, as one came near
With curl'd gray beard, sharp eyes, and smooth bald crown,
Slow-stepp'd, and robed in philosophic gown: 365
Lycius shrank closer, as they met and past,
Into his mantle, adding wings to haste,
While hurried Lamia trembled: "Ah," said he,
"Why do you shudder, love, so ruefully?
"Why does your tender palm dissolve in dew?"—   370
"I'm wearied," said fair Lamia: "tell me who
"Is that old man? I cannot bring to mind
"His features:—Lycius! wherefore did you blind
"Yourself from his quick eyes?" Lycius replied,
" 'Tis Apollonius[4] sage, my trusty guide   375

3. Can mean "lay, not in holy orders" and "unlearned" (*OED*) and thus refer to the temples' pagan status, but can also mean "lascivious," for, as noted above, Corinth's Temple of Venus was considered little better than a brothel.
4. Apollonius of Tyana in Asia Minor, a first-century C.E. philosopher. He is mentioned in Burton and has an entry in Lemprière, and Keats may also have read Edward Bewick's 1809 translation of Philostratus's *Life of Apollonius of Tyana*. Lemprière describes Apollonius as "a Pythagorean philosopher, well skilled in magic. . . . By renouncing the common indulgencies of age . . . he aspired to the name of a reformer of mankind. . . . Hierocles had the presumption to compare the impostures of Apollonius, with the miracles of Christ." Gibbon had made similar comparisons, which were challenged by Bewick in his translation. Peacock's *Rhododaphne* (1818) also has a seer who warns the hero against enchantment.

"And good instructor; but to-night he seems
"The ghost of folly haunting my sweet dreams."

While yet he spake they had arrived before
A pillar'd porch, with lofty portal door,
Where hung a silver lamp, whose phosphor glow   380
Reflected in the slabbed steps below,
Mild as a star in water; for so new,
And so unsullied was the marble hue,
So through the crystal polish, liquid fine,
Ran the dark veins, that none but feet divine   385
Could e'er have touch'd there. Sounds Æolian[5]
Breath'd from the hinges, as the ample span
Of the wide doors disclos'd a place unknown
Some time to any, but those two alone,
And a few Persian mutes, who that same year   390
Were seen about the markets: none knew where
They could inhabit; the most curious
Were foil'd, who watch'd to trace them to their house:[6]
And but the flitter-winged verse must tell,
For truth's sake, what woe afterwards befel,   395
'Twould humour many a heart to leave them thus,
Shut from the busy world of more incredulous.

PART II.

LOVE in a hut, with water and a crust,
Is—Love, forgive us!—cinders, ashes, dust;
Love in a palace is perhaps at last
More grievous torment than a hermit's fast:—
That is a doubtful tale from faery land,   5
Hard for the non-elect to understand.[1]
Had Lycius liv'd to hand his story down,
He might have given the moral a fresh frown,
Or clench'd it quite: but too short was their bliss
To breed distrust and hate, that make the soft voice hiss. 10
Besides, there, nightly, with terrific glare,
Love, jealous grown of so complete a pair,
Hover'd and buzz'd his wings, with fearful roar,
Above the lintel of their chamber door,
And down the passage cast a glow upon the floor.   15

For all this came a ruin: side by side
They were enthroned, in the even tide,
Upon a couch, near to a curtaining
Whose airy texture, from a golden string,
Floated into the room, and let appear   20

5. For the Aeolian harp, see p. 7, n. 6.
6. Woodhouse, in a letter to Taylor (*L*, 2: 164), compares Lamia's house to the "Cavern Prince Ahmed found in the Arabian Nights" (in "The Story of Prince Ahmed and the Fairy Pari Banou," which Allott finds echoed elsewhere in the poem).
1. Commentators often find these opening lines echoing the tactics and sentiments of Byron's satiric *Don Juan.*

Unveil'd the summer heaven, blue and clear,
Betwixt two marble shafts:—there they reposed,
Where use had made it sweet, with eyelids closed,
Saving a tythe² which love still open kept,
That they might see each other while they almost slept;   25
When from the slope side of a suburb hill,
Deafening the swallow's twitter, came a thrill
Of trumpets—Lycius started—the sounds fled,
But left a thought, a buzzing in his head.
For the first time, since first he harbour'd in   30
That purple-lined palace of sweet sin,
His spirit pass'd beyond its golden bourn
Into the noisy world almost forsworn.
The lady, ever watchful, penetrant,
Saw this with pain, so arguing a want   35
Of something more, more than her empery³
Of joys; and she began to moan and sigh
Because he mused beyond her, knowing well
That but a moment's thought is passion's passing bell.
"Why do you sigh, fair creature?" whisper'd he: 40
"Why do you think?" return'd she tenderly:
"You have deserted me;—where am I now?
"Not in your heart while care weighs on your brow:
"No, no, you have dismiss'd me; and I go
"From your breast houseless: ay, it must be so."   45
He answer'd, bending to her open eyes,
Where he was mirror'd small in paradise,
"My silver planet, both of eve and morn!
"Why will you plead yourself so sad forlorn,
"While I am striving how to fill my heart   50
"With deeper crimson, and a double smart?
"How to entangle, trammel⁴ up and snare
"Your soul in mine, and labyrinth you there
"Like the hid scent in an unbudded rose?
"Ay, a sweet kiss—you see your mighty woes.   55
"My thoughts! shall I unveil them? Listen then!
"What mortal hath a prize, that other men
"May be confounded and abash'd withal,
"But lets it sometimes pace abroad majestical,
"And triumph, as in thee I should rejoice   60
"Amid the hoarse alarm of Corinth's voice.
"Let my foes choke, and my friends shout afar,
"While through the thronged streets your bridal car
"Wheels round its dazzling spokes."—The lady's cheek
Trembled; she nothing said, but, pale and meek,   65
Arose and knelt before him, wept a rain
Of sorrows at his words; at last with pain
Beseeching him, the while his hand she wrung,
To change his purpose. He thereat was stung,

2. Tithe, 10 percent of one's income, especially when given in support of the church. See "Ode to
  Psyche" (p. 464, ll. 17–20) for a similar image.
3. Empire.
4. Enmesh, confine.

Their relationship turns into masochism

Perverse, with stronger fancy to reclaim   70
Her wild and timid nature to his aim:
Besides, for all his love, in self despite,
Against his better self, he took delight
Luxurious in her sorrows, soft and new.
His passion, cruel grown, took on a hue   75
Fierce and sanguineous as 'twas possible
In one whose brow had no dark veins to swell.
Fine was the mitigated fury, like
Apollo's presence when in act to strike
The serpent—Ha, the serpent! certes,⁵ she   80
Was none. She burnt, she lov'd the tyranny,
And, all subdued, consented to the hour
When to the bridal he should lead his paramour.
Whispering in midnight silence, said the youth,
"Sure some sweet name thou hast, though, by my truth,   85
"I have not ask'd it, ever thinking thee
"Not mortal, but of heavenly progeny,
"As still I do. Hast any mortal name,
"Fit appellation for this dazzling frame?
"Or friends or kinsfolk on the citied earth,   90
"To share our marriage feast and nuptial mirth?"
"I have no friends," said Lamia, "no, not one;
"My presence in wide Corinth hardly known:
"My parents' bones are in their dusty urns
"Sepulchred, where no kindled incense burns,   95
"Seeing all their luckless race are dead, save me,
"And I neglect the holy rite for thee.
"Even as you list invite your many guests;
"But if, as now it seems, your vision rests
"With any pleasure on me, do not bid   100
"Old Apollonius—from him keep me hid."
Lycius, perplex'd at words so blind and blank,
Made close inquiry; from whose touch she shrank,
Feigning a sleep; and he to the dull shade
Of deep sleep in a moment was betray'd.   105

     It was the custom then to bring away
The bride from home at blushing shut of day,
Veil'd, in a chariot, heralded along
By strewn flowers, torches, and a marriage song,
With other pageants: but this fair unknown   110
Had not a friend. So being left alone,
(Lycius was gone to summon all his kin)
And knowing surely she could never win
His foolish heart from its mad pompousness,
She set herself, high-thoughted, how to dress   115
The misery in fit magnificence.
She did so, but 'tis doubtful how and whence
Came, and who were her subtle servitors.
About the halls, and to and from the doors,

---

5. Certainly; *serpent*: the Python, the monster that arose after the flood in classical myth, slain by
Apollo.

There was a noise of wings, till in short space   120
The glowing banquet-room shone with wide-arched grace.
A haunting music, sole perhaps and lone
Supportress of the faery-roof, made moan
Throughout, as fearful the whole charm might fade.
Fresh carved cedar, mimicking a glade   125
Of palm and plantain, met from either side,
High in the midst, in honour of the bride:
Two palms and then two plantains, and so on,
From either side their stems branch'd one to one
All down the aisled place; and beneath all   130
There ran a stream of lamps straight on from wall to wall.
So canopied, lay an untasted feast
Teeming with odours.[6] Lamia, regal drest,
Silently paced about, and as she went,
In pale contented sort of discontent,   135
Mission'd her viewless servants to enrich
The fretted splendour of each nook and niche.
Between the tree-stems, marbled plain at first,
Came jasper pannels; then, anon, there burst
Forth creeping imagery of slighter trees,   140
And with the larger wove in small intricacies.
Approving all, she faded at self-will,
And shut the chamber up, close, hush'd and still,
Complete and ready for the revels rude,
When dreadful guests would come to spoil her solitude.   145

   The day appear'd, and all the gossip rout.
O senseless Lycius! Madman! wherefore flout
The silent-blessing fate, warm cloister'd hours,
And show to common eyes these secret bowers?
The herd approach'd; each guest, with busy brain,   150
Arriving at the portal, gaz'd amain,
And enter'd marveling: for they knew the street,
Remember'd it from childhood all complete
Without a gap, yet ne'er before had seen
That royal porch, that high-built fair demesne;[7]   155
So in they hurried all, maz'd, curious and keen:
Save one, who look'd thereon with eye severe,
And with calm-planted steps walk'd in austere;
'Twas Apollonius: something too he laugh'd,
As though some knotty problem, that had daft   160
His patient thought, had now begun to thaw,
And solve and melt:—'twas just as he foresaw.

   He met within the murmurous vestibule
His young disciple. "'Tis no common rule,
"Lycius," said he, "for uninvited guest   165

---

6. The magic palace with its magnificent banquet room recalls similar scenes in Peacock's *Rhododaphne* (1818) and Southey's *Thalaba the Destroyer* (1801), Book 6, as well as Potter's *Antiquities of Greece* (1697), 2.376–77, and perhaps also recalls elaborate entertainments hosted by the Prince Regent, such as that described by Hunt in the *Reflector* 2 (March–December 1811): 1–13 (*SWLH*, 1: 183–94).
7. Estate, domain.

"To force himself upon you, and infest
"With an unbidden presence the bright throng
"Of younger friends; yet must I do this wrong,
"And you forgive me." Lycius blush'd, and led
The old man through the inner doors broad-spread;   170
With reconciling words and courteous mien
Turning into sweet milk the sophist's[8] spleen.

Of wealthy lustre was the banquet-room,
Fill'd with pervading brilliance and perfume:
Before each lucid pannel fuming stood   175
A censer fed with myrrh and spiced wood,
Each by a sacred tripod held aloft,
Whose slender feet wide-swerv'd upon the soft
Wool-woofed carpets: fifty wreaths of smoke
From fifty censers their light voyage took   180
To the high roof, still mimick'd as they rose
Along the mirror'd walls by twin-clouds odorous.
Twelve sphered tables, by silk seats insphered,
High as the level of a man's breast rear'd
On libbard's[9] paws, upheld the heavy gold   185
Of cups and goblets, and the store thrice told
Of Ceres' horn,[1] and, in huge vessels, wine
Come from the gloomy tun[2] with merry shine.
Thus loaded with a feast the tables stood,
Each shrining in the midst the image of a God.   190

When in an antichamber every guest
Had felt the cold full sponge to pleasure press'd,
By minist'ring slaves, upon his hands and feet,
And fragrant oils with ceremony meet
Pour'd on his hair, they all mov'd to the feast   195
In white robes, and themselves in order placed
Around the silken couches, wondering
Whence all this mighty cost and blaze of wealth could spring.

Soft went the music the soft air along,
While fluent Greek a vowel'd undersong   200
Kept up among the guests, discoursing low
At first, for scarcely was the wine at flow;
But when the happy vintage touch'd their brains,
Louder they talk, and louder come the strains
Of powerful instruments:—the gorgeous dyes,   205
The space, the splendour of the draperies,
The roof of awful richness, nectarous cheer,
Beautiful slaves, and Lamia's self, appear,
Now, when the wine has done its rosy deed,
And every soul from human trammels freed,   210

8. Most generally a wise man but more particularly someone who taught the tools of success—
whether rhetoric, memory training, or virtue—for a fee; sophist has come to mean someone who
makes specious or false arguments.
9. Leopard's.
1. Horn of Plenty or cornucopia.
2. Large cask or barrel.

No more so strange; for merry wine, sweet wine,
Will make Elysian shades[3] not too fair, too divine.

    Soon was God Bacchus at meridian height;
Flush'd were their cheeks, and bright eyes double bright:
Garlands of every green, and every scent   215
From vales deflower'd, or forest-trees branch-rent,
In baskets of bright osier'd gold[4] were brought
High as the handles heap'd, to suit the thought
Of every guest; that each, as he did please,
Might fancy-fit his brows, silk-pillow'd at his ease.   220

    What wreath for Lamia? What for Lycius?
What for the sage, old Apollonius?
Upon her aching forehead be there hung
The leaves of willow and of adder's tongue;
And for the youth, quick, let us strip for him   225
The thyrsus, that his watching eyes may swim
Into forgetfulness; and, for the sage,
Let spear-grass and the spiteful thistle[5] wage
War on his temples. Do not all charms fly
At the mere touch of cold philosophy?   230
There was an awful rainbow once in heaven:
We know her woof, her texture; she is given
In the dull catalogue of common things.
Philosophy will clip an Angel's wings,
Conquer all mysteries by rule and line,   235
Empty the haunted air, and gnomed mine—
Unweave a rainbow, as it erewhile made
The tender-person'd Lamia melt into a shade.[6]

    By her glad Lycius sitting, in chief place,
Scarce saw in all the room another face,   240
Till, checking his love trance, a cup he took
Full brimm'd, and opposite sent forth a look
'Cross the broad table, to beseech a glance
From his old teacher's wrinkled countenance,
And pledge him. The bald-head philosopher   245
Had fix'd his eye, without a twinkle or stir
Full on the alarmed beauty of the bride,
Brow-beating her fair form, and troubling her sweet pride.
Lycius then press'd her hand, with devout touch,
As pale it lay upon the rosy couch: 250

3. The dead, who may not look "too fair" without the aid of wine.
4. The baskets are made of gold woven in imitation of willow branches.
5. A prickly plant that can be as abundant as a weed; *willow*: associated with deserted lovers; *adder's-tongue*: either a fern or a dog-tooth violet, both of which have the shape of a serpent's tongue; *thyrsus*: the god of wine Bacchus's wand, woven with vine and ivy; *spear-grass*: a troublesome weed.
6. See Hazlitt's 1818 lecture, "On Poetry in General": "the progress of knowledge and refinement has a tendency to circumscribe the limits of the imagination, and to clip the wings of poetry" (*Works*, 5: 9); Haydon, in his *Diary* (2:72), reports that at the "Immortal Dinner" of December 28, 1817, Keats had agreed with Lamb that Newton "destroyed all the Poetry of the rainbow by reducing it to a prism." See also the close of Keats's December 21, 1817, review of Kean (p. 107), where he writes that "romance lives but in books. The goblin is driven from the heath, and the rainbow is robbed of its mystery!"

'Twas icy, and the cold ran through his veins;
Then sudden it grew hot, and all the pains
Of an unnatural heat shot to his heart.
"Lamia, what means this? Wherefore dost thou start?
"Know'st thou that man?" Poor Lamia answer'd not.   255
He gaz'd into her eyes, and not a jot
Own'd they the lovelorn piteous appeal:
More, more he gaz'd: his human senses reel:
Some hungry spell that loveliness absorbs;
There was no recognition in those orbs.   260
"Lamia!" he cried—and no soft-toned reply.
The many heard, and the loud revelry
Grew hush; the stately music no more breathes;
The myrtle sicken'd in a thousand wreaths.
By faint degrees, voice, lute, and pleasure ceased;   265
A deadly silence step by step increased,
Until it seem'd a horrid presence there,
And not a man but felt the terror in his hair.
"Lamia!" he shriek'd; and nothing but the shriek
With its sad echo did the silence break.   270
"Begone, foul dream!" he cried, gazing again
In the bride's face, where now no azure vein
Wander'd on fair-spaced temples; no soft bloom
Misted the cheek; no passion to illume
The deep-recessed vision:—all was blight;   275
Lamia, no longer fair, there sat a deadly white.
"Shut, shut those juggling eyes, thou ruthless man!
"Turn them aside, wretch! or the righteous ban
"Of all the Gods, whose dreadful images
"Here represent their shadowy presences,   280
"May pierce them on the sudden with the thorn
"Of painful blindness; leaving thee forlorn,
"In trembling dotage to the feeblest fright
"Of conscience, for their long offended might,
"For all thine impious proud-heart sophistries,   285
"Unlawful magic, and enticing lies.
"Corinthians! look upon that gray-beard wretch!
"Mark how, possess'd, his lashless eyelids stretch
"Around his demon eyes! Corinthians, see!
"My sweet bride withers at their potency."   290
"Fool!" said the sophist, in an under-tone
Gruff with contempt; which a death-nighing moan
From Lycius answer'd, as heart-struck and lost,
He sank supine beside the aching ghost.
"Fool! Fool!" repeated he, while his eyes still   295
Relented not, nor mov'd; "from every ill
"Of life have I preserv'd thee to this day,
"And shall I see thee made a serpent's prey?"
Then Lamia breath'd death breath; the sophist's eye,
Like a sharp spear, went through her utterly,   300
Keen, cruel, perceant,[7] stinging: she, as well

7. Piercing.

As her weak hand could any meaning tell,
Motion'd him to be silent; vainly so,
He look'd and look'd again a level—No!
"A Serpent!" echoed he; no sooner said,   305
Than with a frightful scream she vanished:
And Lycius' arms were empty of delight,
As were his limbs of life, from that same night.
On the high couch he lay!—his friends came round—
Supported him—no pulse, or breath they found,   310
And, in its marriage robe, the heavy body wound.*

*"Philostratus, in his fourth book *de Vita Apollonii*, hath a memorable instance in this kind, which I may not omit, of one Menippus Lycius, a young man twenty-five years of age, that going betwixt Cenchreas and Corinth, met such a phantasm in the habit of a fair gentlewoman, which taking him by the hand, carried him home to her house, in the suburbs of Corinth, and told him she was a Phœnician by birth, and if he would tarry with her, he should hear her sing and play, and drink such wine as never any drank, and no man should molest him; but she, being fair and lovely, would live and die with him, that was fair and lovely to behold. The young man, a philosopher, otherwise staid and discreet, able to moderate his passions, though not this of love, tarried with her a while to his great content, and at last married her, to whose wedding, amongst other guests, came Apollonius; who, by some probable conjectures, found her out to be a serpent, a lamia; and that all her furniture was, like Tantalus' gold, described by Homer, no substance but mere illusions. When she saw herself descried, she wept, and desired Apollonius to be silent, but he would not be moved, and thereupon she, plate, house, and all that was in it, vanished in an instant: many thousands took notice of this fact, for it was done in the midst of Greece."

Burton's 'Anatomy of Melancholy.' *Part 3. Sect. 2.*
Memb. 1. Subs. 1.

ISABELLA;
OR,
THE POT OF BASIL.
A STORY FROM BOCCACCIO.

Keats began *Isabella* in late February or early March 1818 and, after finishing *Endymion*, completed it by April 27. Keats took up the project as he and his friend John Hamilton Reynolds contemplated co-writing a volume of tales versified from Boccaccio's *Decameron*, with the idea probably suggested by Hazlitt's lecture of February 3, 1818 (attended by Keats) "On Dryden and Pope" (published in the 1818 *Lectures on the English Poets*); noting that Dryden's tales were popular, Hazlitt adds, "I should think that a translation of some of the other serious tales in Boccaccio and Chaucer, as that of Isabella, the Falcon, of Constance, the Prioress's Tale, and others, if executed with taste and spirit, could not fail to succeed" (*Works* 5: 82). Keats's poem takes up the fifth story of the fourth day in Boccaccio's

Decameron; Keats's fellow in Hunt's Cockney School, Barry Cornwall (Proctor), adapted the same tale in his *Sicilian Story*, also published in 1820. Reynolds completed two tales, "The Garden of Florence" and "The Ladye of Provence," both published in his 1821 *The Garden of Florence; and Other Poems*. These efforts are part of the larger effort within the Hunt circle to engage Italian literature, begun by Hunt's key *Story of Rimini* (1816). For the larger contemporary interest in Boccaccio, see Herbert G. Wright, *Boccaccio in England from Chaucer to Tennyson* (London: University of London, The Athlone Press, 1958), and F. S. Stych, *Boccaccio in English: A Bibliography of Editions, Adaptations, and Criticism* (Westport, CT: Greenwood Press, 1995).

Keats's poem is a free adaptation of his source, which he knew through a 1684 edition of the first English translation (1620). In seeking to explore the privatization of love in a world dominated by the money-getting private enterprise of Isabella's brothers, Keats makes a number of changes, for example, moving the tale from Messina to Florence and reducing the number of Isabella's brothers from three to two (see Allott's notes for the ways in which Keats differs from his original). Keats adopts *ottava rima* for his poem, a meter popular with Italian writers, including Tasso whose *Gerusalemme Liberata* (1600) Keats knew in a translation by Fairfax. Hookham Frere's *The Monks and the Giants* (1818) had suggested the possibilities of the verse form for English writers, and Byron had adopted *ottava rima* for his *Beppo*, published on February 28, 1818, as Keats began *Isabella*.

In addition to the criticism cited in the headnote for the 1820 volume, see Kelvin Everest, "Isabella in the Market-Place: Keats and Feminism," in Roe (ed.), *Keats and History*, pp. 107–26; Kurt Heinzelmann, "Self-Interest and the Politics of Composition in Keats's *Isabella*," *ELH* 55 (1988): 159–93; and Stillinger, "Keats and His Helpers: The Multiple Authorship of *Isabella*," *Multiple Authorship and the Myth of Solitary Genius* (New York: Oxford University Press, 1991), pp. 25–49.

The text is from 1820. Keats's draft was once in the possession of Severn, who distributed fragments to various people; for a listing of the known fragments, held at Texas Christian University, the Historical Society of Pennsylvania, Cornell University, the University of Texas, the Carl H. Pforzheimer Library, the National Library of Scotland, the Martin Bodmer Foundation, and Harvard, see Stillinger, pp. 602–04. Keats's fair copy is found in George Keats's notebook, now at the British Museum (Egerton 2780, 1–28; *MYR: JK*, 5: 59–113). Woodhouse's W[1] transcript with Keats's corrections (Harvard MS Keats 3.1, ff. 86r–107) appears to have been used as the printer's copy.

I.

FAIR Isabel, poor simple[1] Isabel!
Lorenzo, a young palmer[2] in Love's eye!
They could not in the self-same mansion dwell
Without some stir of heart, some malady;
They could not sit at meals but feel how well   5

---

1. Innocent, unspoiled, but also intellectually dim.
2. A pilgrim, as in Shakespeare, *Romeo and Juliet*, 1.5.96–97, "For saints have hands that pilgrims' hands do touch, / And palm to palm is holy palmers' kiss"; also someone who cheats by palming cards.

It soothed each to be the other by;
They could not, sure, beneath the same roof sleep
But to each other dream, and nightly weep.

II.

With every morn their love grew tenderer,
    With every eve deeper and tenderer still;   10
He might not in house, field, or garden stir,
    But her full shape would all his seeing fill;
And his continual voice was pleasanter
    To her, than noise of trees or hidden rill;
Her lute-string gave an echo of his name,   15
She spoilt her half-done broidery with the same.

III.

He knew whose gentle hand was at the latch,
    Before the door had given her to his eyes;
And from her chamber-window he would catch
    Her beauty farther than the falcon spies;   20
And constant as her vespers would he watch,
    Because her face was turn'd to the same skies;
And with sick longing all the night outwear,
To hear her morning-step upon the stair.

IV.

A whole long month of May in this sad plight   25
    Made their cheeks paler by the break of June:
"To-morrow will I bow to my delight,
    "To-morrow will I ask my lady's boon."—
"O may I never see another night,
    "Lorenzo, if thy lips breathe not love's tune."—   30
So spake they to their pillows; but, alas,
Honeyless days and days did he let pass;

V.

Until sweet Isabella's untouch'd cheek
    Fell sick within the rose's just domain,
Fell thin as a young mother's, who doth seek   35
    By every lull to cool her infant's pain:
"How ill she is," said he, "I may not speak,
    "And yet I will, and tell my love all plain:
"If looks speak love-laws, I will drink her tears,
"And at the least 'twill startle off her cares."   40

VI.

So said he one fair morning, and all day
    His heart beat awfully against his side;
And to his heart he inwardly did pray
    For power to speak; but still the ruddy tide
Stifled his voice, and puls'd resolve away—   45

Fever'd his high conceit of such a bride,
Yet brought him to the meekness of a child:
Alas! when passion is both meek and wild!

VII.

So once more he had wak'd and anguished
    A dreary night of love and misery,   50
If Isabel's quick eye had not been wed
    To every symbol on his forehead high;
She saw it waxing very pale and dead,
    And straight all flush'd; so, lisped tenderly,
"Lorenzo!"—here she ceas'd her timid quest,   55
But in her tone and look he read the rest.[3]

VIII.

"O Isabella, I can half perceive[4]
    "That I may speak my grief into thine ear;
"If thou didst ever any thing believe,
    "Believe how I love thee, believe how near   60
"My soul is to its doom: I would not grieve
    "Thy hand by unwelcome pressing, would not fear
"Thine eyes by gazing; but I cannot live
    "Another night, and not my passion shrive.[5]

IX.

"Love! thou art leading me from wintry cold,   65
    "Lady! thou leadest me to summer clime,
"And I must taste the blossoms that unfold
    "In its ripe warmth this gracious morning time."
So said, his erewhile timid lips grew bold,
    And poesied with hers in dewy rhyme: 70
Great bliss was with them, and great happiness
Grew, like a lusty flower in June's caress.

X.

Parting they seem'd to tread upon the air,
    Twin roses by the zephyr[6] blown apart

3. In the fair copy, these lines are handled differently and there is a deleted stanza:

> "Lorenzo I would clip my ringlet hair
>   To make thee laugh again & debonair—
>
> "Then should I be," said he, "full deified
>   And yet I would not have it clip it not—
> For Lady I do love it, where 'tis tied
>   About the Neck I dote on—and that spot
> That anxious dimple it doth take a pride
>   To play about—Aye Lady I have got
> Its shadow in my heart and every sweet
> Its Mistress owns there summed all complete—"

4. See Wordsworth, "Tintern Abbey." ll. 105–107: "the mighty world / Of eye, and ear,—both what they half-create, / And what perceive."
5. Confess.
6. West wind.

Only to meet again more close, and share   75
    The inward fragrance of each other's heart.
She, to her chamber gone, a ditty fair
    Sang, of delicious love and honey'd dart;
He with light steps went up a western hill.
And bade the sun farewell; and joy'd his fill.   80

XI.

All close they met again, before the dusk
    Had taken from the stars its pleasant veil,
All close they met, all eves, before the dusk
    Had taken from the stars its pleasant veil,
Close in a bower of hyacinth and musk,   85
    Unknown of any, free from whispering tale.
Ah! better had it been for ever so,
Than idle ears should pleasure in their woe.

XII.

Were they unhappy then?—It cannot be—
    Too many tears for lovers have been shed,   90
Too many sighs give we to them in fee,
    Too much of pity after they are dead,
Too many doleful stories do we see,
    Whose matter in bright gold were best be read;
Except in such a page where Theseus' spouse   95
Over the pathless waves towards him bows.[7]

XIII.

But, for the general award of love,
    The little sweet doth kill much bitterness;
Though Dido silent is in under-grove,[8]
    And Isabella's was a great distress,   100
Though young Lorenzo in warm Indian clove
    Was not embalm'd, this truth is not the less—
Even bees, the little almsmen[9] of spring-bowers,
Know there is richest juice in poison-flowers.

XIV.

With her two brothers this fair lady dwelt,   105
    Enriched from ancestral merchandize,
And for them many a weary hand did swelt
    In torched mines and noisy factories,

---

7. Ariadne saved Theseus from the Minotaur (her half brother) by helping him find his way through the labyrinth on Crete; she fled with him, but he abandoned her on the island of Naxos, where she was rescued by Bacchus. Keats would have known the story from Ovid's *Metamorphoses* 8.172–82, though the image of Ariadne watching Theseus depart over the sea may come from Catullus's "Epithalamion of Peleus and Thetis," ll. 50–266; see also Hunt's "Bacchus and Ariadne" (1819).
8. Virgil's *Aeneid*, written in part in response to Catullus's "Epithalamion of Peleus and Thetis," which offers an account of Theseus abandoning Ariadne, tells of Aeneas's desertion of Dido to found Rome, after which she kills herself (see esp. *Aeneid* 6.450–51, where Aeneas sees Dido in the underworld "wandering in a great forest").
9. The bees receive "alms" or "gifts" of honey from the flowers.

And many once proud-quiver'd loins[1] did melt
   In blood from stinging whip;—with hollow eyes   110
Many all day in dazzling river stood,
   To take the rich-ored driftings of the flood.

XV.

For them the Ceylon diver held his breath,
   And went all naked to the hungry shark;
For them his ears gush'd blood; for them in death   115
   The seal on the cold ice with piteous bark
Lay full of darts; for them alone did seethe
   A thousand men in troubles wide and dark:
Half-ignorant, they turn'd an easy wheel,
That set sharp racks at work, to pinch and peel.   120

XVI.

Why were they proud? Because their marble founts
   Gush'd with more pride than do a wretch's tears?—
Why were they proud? Because fair orange-mounts
   Were of more soft ascent than lazar stairs?[2]—
Why were they proud? Because red-lin'd accounts   125
   Were richer than the songs of Grecian years?—
Why were they proud? again we ask aloud,
Why in the name of Glory were they proud?

XVII.

Yet were these Florentines[3] as self-retired
   In hungry pride and gainful cowardice,   130
As two close Hebrews in that land inspired,[4]
   Paled in and vineyarded from beggar-spies;
The hawks of ship-mast forests—the untired
   And pannier'd mules for ducats and old lies—
Quick cat's-paws on the generous stray-away,—   135
Great wits in Spanish, Tuscan, and Malay.[5]

1. These men once proudly carried quivers of arrows at their hip, perhaps suggesting they were warriors sold into slavery.
2. Could be stairs in a lazar-house for the sick and poor or steps upon which lepers beg; *orange-mounts*: perhaps hills in an orange grove.
3. In Boccaccio, the brothers come from Messina, but Keats may adopt this locale because the *Decameron* is set in the neighborhood of Florence.
4. Palestine; the "ducats" of l. 134 suggest that Shakespeare's Shylock lies behind the anti-Semitic comment; *close*: see stanza XI above, as both the lovers and the broters live "closed" lives.
5. A difficult passage: the brothers hide behind their walls and estates to escape from both the needy and spies; they are mercenary, swooping like hawks on merchandise among the forest of masts at a port; they are like mules carrying baskets of money and gossip; like cats, they seize upon their victims quickly, here the generous and the lost; as merchants they know a bit of various languages used by sailors. The fair copy follows these lines with a dropped stanza:

> Two young Orlandos far away they seem'd,
>   But on a near inspect their vapid Miens—
> Very alike,—at once themselves redeem'd
>   From all suspicion of Romantic spleens—
> No fault of theirs, for their good Mother dream'd
>   In the longing time of Units in their teens
> Of proudly-bas'd addition and of net—
> And both their backs were mark'd with tare and tret.

XVIII.

How was it these same ledger-men could spy
    Fair Isabella in her downy nest?
How could they find out in Lorenzo's eye
    A straying from his toil? Hot Egypt's pest   140
Into their vision covetous and sly!⁶
    How could these money-bags see east and west?—
Yet so they did—and every dealer fair
Must see behind, as doth the hunted hare.

XIX.

O eloquent and famed Boccaccio!   145
    Of thee we now should ask forgiving boon,
And of thy spicy myrtles as they blow,
    And of thy roses amorous of the moon,
And of thy lilies, that do paler grow
    Now they can no more hear thy ghittern's⁷ tune,   150
For venturing syllables that ill beseem
The quiet glooms of such a piteous theme.

XX.

Grant thou a pardon here, and then the tale
    Shall move on soberly, as it is meet;
There is no other crime, no mad assail   155
    To make old prose in modern rhyme more sweet:
But it is done—succeed the verse or fail—
    To honour thee, and thy gone spirit greet;
To stead thee as a verse in English tongue,
An echo of thee in the north-wind sung.⁸   160

XXI.

These brethren having found by many signs
    What love Lorenzo for their sister had,
And how she lov'd him too, each unconfines
    His bitter thoughts to other, well nigh mad
That he, the servant of their trade designs,   165
    Should in their sister's love be blithe and glad,
When 'twas their plan to coax her by degrees
To some high noble and his olive-trees.

XXII.

And many a jealous conference had they,
    And many times they bit their lips alone,   170

---

6. Keats may allude to the plague of flies brought on the Egyptians (Exodus 8.21), the plague of darkness (Exodus 10.21–23), or infections bringing blindness prevalent along the Nile.
7. A kind of guitar.
8. See Reynolds's statement about his adaptation of Boccaccio in "The Ladye of Provence," which he offers as a "Provence tale . . . tamed into Northern verse" (*The Garden of Florence; and Other Poems* [1821], p. 156).

Before they fix'd upon a surest way
　　To make the youngster for his crime atone;
And at the last, these men of cruel clay
　　Cut Mercy with a sharp knife to the bone;
For they resolved in some forest dim　　　　　　175
To kill Lorenzo, and there bury him.

XXIII.

So on a pleasant morning, as he leant
　　Into the sun-rise, o'er the balustrade
Of the garden-terrace, towards him they bent
　　Their footing through the dews; and to him said,　　180
"You seem there in the quiet of content,
　　"Lorenzo, and we are most loth to invade
"Calm speculation; but if you are wise,
"Bestride your steed while cold is in the skies.

XXIV.

"To-day we purpose, ay, this hour we mount　　　185
　　"To spur three leagues towards the Apennine;[9]
"Come down, we pray thee, ere the hot sun count
　　"His dewy rosary on the eglantine."[1]
Lorenzo, courteously as he was wont,
　　Bow'd a fair greeting to these serpents' whine;　　190
And went in haste, to get in readiness,
With belt, and spur, and bracing huntsman's dress.

XXV.

And as he to the court-yard pass'd along,
　　Each third step did he pause, and listen'd oft
If he could hear his lady's matin-song,　　　　　195
　　Or the light whisper of her footstep soft;
And as he thus over his passion hung,
　　He heard a laugh full musical aloft;
When, looking up, he saw her features bright
Smile through an in-door lattice, all delight.　　200

XXVI.

"Love, Isabel!" said he, "I was in pain
　　"Lest I should miss to bid thee a good morrow:
"Ah! what if I should lose thee, when so fain
　　"I am to stifle all the heavy sorrow
"Of a poor three hours' absence? but we'll gain　　205
　　"Out of the amorous dark what day doth borrow.
"Goodbye! I'll soon be back."—"Goodbye!" said she:—
And as he went she chanted merrily.

---

9. The mountains traversing the center of Italy.
1. Before the sun causes the beads of dew to evaporate off the sweetbriar.

XXVII.

So the two brothers and their murder'd man[2]
 Rode past fair Florence, to where Arno's stream   210
Gurgles through straiten'd banks, and still doth fan
 Itself with dancing bulrush, and the bream
Keeps head against the freshets.[3] Sick and wan
 The brothers' faces in the ford did seem,
Lorenzo's flush with love.—They pass'd the water   215
Into a forest quiet for the slaughter.

XXVIII.

There was Lorenzo slain and buried in,
 There in that forest did his great love cease;
Ah! when a soul doth thus its freedom win,
 It aches in loneliness—is ill at peace   220
As the break-covert blood-hounds of such sin:[4]
 They dipp'd their swords in the water, and did tease
Their horses homeward, with convulsed spur,
Each richer by his being a murderer.

XXIX.

They told their sister how, with sudden speed,   225
 Lorenzo had ta'en ship for foreign lands,
Because of some great urgency and need
 In their affairs, requiring trusty hands.
Poor Girl! put on thy stifling widow's weed,
 And 'scape at once from Hope's accursed bands;   230
To-day thou wilt not see him, nor to-morrow,
And the next day will be a day of sorrow.

XXX.

She weeps alone for pleasures not to be;
 Sorely she wept until the night came on,
And then, instead of love, O misery!   235
 She brooded o'er the luxury alone:
His image in the dusk she seem'd to see,
 And to the silence made a gentle moan,
Spreading her perfect arms upon the air,
And on her couch low murmuring "Where? O where?"   240

XXXI.

But Selfishness, Love's cousin, held not long
 Its fiery vigil in her single breast;

---

2. A phrase admired by Lamb in the *New Times*, July 19, 1820 ("The anticipation of the assassination is wonderfully conceived in one epithet"), and Hunt in "What is Poetry" (1844).
3. Small, fresh-water streams; *Arno's stream*: a river in Tuscany, Italy, which runs through Florence; *bream*: the common name of a fresh water fish, yellowish in color and with a high-arched back.
4. The ghost of a murdered man is as uneasy as bloodhounds seeking to find where the murderer has hidden.

She fretted for the golden hour, and hung
  Upon the time with feverish unrest—
Not long for soon into her heart a throng   245
  Of higher occupants, a richer zest,
Came tragic; passion not to be subdued,
And sorrow for her love in travels rude.

XXXII.

In the mid days of autumn, on their eves
  The breath of Winter comes from far away,   250
And the sick west continually bereaves
  Of some gold tinge, and plays a roundelay
Of death among the bushes and the leaves,
  To make all bare before he dares to stray
From his north cavern. So sweet Isabel   255
By gradual decay from beauty fell,

XXXIII.

Because Lorenzo came not. Oftentimes
  She ask'd her brothers, with an eye all pale,
Striving to be itself, what dungeon climes
  Could keep him off so long? They spake a tale   260
Time after time, to quiet her. Their crimes
  Came on them, like a smoke from Hinnom's vale;[5]
And every night in dreams they groan'd aloud,
To see their sister in her snowy shroud.

XXXIV.

And she had died in drowsy ignorance,   265
  But for a thing more deadly dark than all;
It came like a fierce potion, drunk by chance,
  Which saves a sick man from the feather'd pall
For some few gasping moments; like a lance,
  Waking an Indian from his cloudy hall   270
With cruel pierce, and bringing him again
Sense of the gnawing fire at heart and brain.[6]

XXXV.

It was a vision.—In the drowsy gloom,
  The dull of midnight, at her couch's foot
Lorenzo stood, and wept: the forest tomb   275
  Had marr'd his glossy hair which once could shoot
Lustre into the sun, and put cold doom
  Upon his lips, and taken the soft lute

---

5. A valley into which the Israelites threw refuse and the bodies of criminals; see 2 Chronicles 28.3:
   "he burnt incense in the valley of the son of Hinnom, and burnt his children in the fire, after the
   abominations of the heathen."
6. Allott suggests that Keats alludes to William Robertson's account of tests of physical endurance
   practiced by American Indians in his *History of America* (1777), 2: 156–57, 163.

From his lorn voice, and past his loamed ears
Had made a miry channel for his tears. 280

XXXVI.

Strange sound it was, when the pale shadow spake;
 For there was striving, in its piteous tongue,
To speak as when on earth it was awake,
 And Isabella on its music hung:
Languor there was in it, and tremulous shake, 285
 As in a palsied Druid's[7] harp unstrung;
And through it moan'd a ghostly under-song,
Like hoarse night-gusts sepulchral briars among.

XXXVII.

Its eyes, though wild, were still all dewy bright
 With love, and kept all phantom fear aloof 290
From the poor girl by magic of their light,
 The while it did unthread the horrid woof
Of the late darken'd time,—the murderous spite
 Of pride and avarice,—the dark pine roof
In the forest,—and the sodden turfed dell, 295
Where, without any word, from stabs he fell.

XXXVIII.

Saying moreover, "Isabel, my sweet!
 "Red whortle-berries droop above my head,
"And a large flint-stone weighs upon my feet;
 "Around me beeches and high chestnuts shed 300
"Their leaves and prickly nuts; a sheep-fold bleat
 "Comes from beyond the river to my bed:
"Go, shed one tear upon my heather-bloom,
"And it shall comfort me within the tomb.

XXXIX.

"I am a shadow now, alas! alas! 305
 "Upon the skirts of human-nature dwelling
"Alone: I chant alone the holy mass,
 "While little sounds of life are round me knelling,
"And glossy bees at noon do fieldward pass,
 "And many a chapel bell the hour is telling, 310
"Paining me through: those sounds grow strange to me,
"And thou art distant in Humanity.

XL.

"I know what was, I feel full well what is,
 "And I should rage, if spirits could go mad;

7. See p. 41, n. 8.

"Though I forget the taste of earthly bliss,   315
     "That paleness warms my grave, as though I had
"A Seraph chosen from the bright abyss
     "To be my spouse: thy paleness makes me glad;
"Thy beauty grows upon me, and I feel
"A greater love through all my essence steal."[8]   320

XLI.

The Spirit mourn'd "Adieu!"—dissolv'd, and left
     The atom darkness in a slow turmoil;
As when of healthful midnight sleep bereft,
     Thinking on rugged hours and fruitless toil,
We put our eyes into a pillowy cleft,   325
     And see the spangly gloom froth up and boil:
It made sad Isabella's eyelids ache,
And in the dawn she started up awake;

XLII.

"Ha! ha!" said she, "I knew not this hard life,
     "I thought the worst was simple misery;   330
"I thought some Fate with pleasure or with strife
     "Portion'd us—happy days, or else to die;
"But there is crime—a brother's bloody knife!
     "Sweet Spirit, thou hast school'd my infancy:
"I'll visit thee for this, and kiss thine eyes,   335
"And greet thee morn and even in the skies."

XLIII.

When the full morning came, she had devised
     How she might secret to the forest hie;[9]
How she might find the clay, so dearly prized,
     And sing to it one latest lullaby;   340
How her short absence might be unsurmised,
     While she the inmost of the dream would try.
Resolv'd, she took with her an aged nurse,
And went into that dismal forest-hearse.[1]

XLIV.

See, as they creep along the river side,   345
     How she doth whisper to that aged Dame,
And, after looking round the champaign wide,
     Shows her a knife.—"What feverous hectic flame
"Burns in thee, child?—What good can thee betide,
     "That thou should'st smile again?"—The evening came,   350
And they had found Lorenzo's earthy bed;
The flint was there, the berries at his head.

---

8. Keats quoted ll. 319–20 in his letter to Fanny Brawne of February? 1820 (*L*, 2: 256): "In my present state of Health I feel too much separated from you and could almost speak to you in the words of Lorenzo's Ghost to Isabella."
9. Hasten, speed.
1. The forest as the bearer of Lorenzo's corpse.

XLV.

Who hath not loiter'd in a green church-yard,
    And let his spirit, like a demon-mole,
Work through the clayey soil and gravel hard,   355
    To see scull, coffin'd bones, and funeral stole;
Pitying each form that hungry Death hath marr'd,
    And filling it once more with human soul?
Ah! this is holiday to what was felt
When Isabella by Lorenzo knelt.   360

XLVI.

She gaz'd into the fresh-thrown mould, as though
    One glance did fully all its secrets tell;
Clearly she saw, as other eyes would know
    Pale limbs at bottom of a crystal well;
Upon the murderous spot she seem'd to grow,   365
    Like to a native lily of the dell:
Then with her knife, all sudden, she began
To dig more fervently than misers can.

XLVII.

Soon she turn'd up a soiled glove, whereon
    Her silk had play'd in purple phantasies,[2]   370
She kiss'd it with a lip more chill than stone,
    And put it in her bosom, where it dries
And freezes utterly unto the bone
    Those dainties made to still an infant's cries:
Then 'gan she work again; nor stay'd her care,   375
But to throw back at times her veiling hair.

XLVIII.

That old nurse stood beside her wondering,
    Until her heart felt pity to the core
At sight of such a dismal labouring,
    And so she kneeled, with her locks all hoar,   380
And put her lean hands to the horrid thing:
    Three hours they labour'd at this travail sore;
At last they felt the kernel of the grave,
And Isabella did not stamp and rave.[3]

XLIX.

Ah! wherefore all this wormy circumstance?   385
    Why linger at the yawning tomb so long?
O for the gentleness of old Romance,
    The simple plaining of a minstrel's song!

2. Isabella had embroidered the glove with purple silk thread.
3. Lamb in his review in *New Times*, July 19, 1820, particularly admired stanzas XLVI–XLVIII: "there
   is nothing more awfully simple in diction, more nakedly grand and moving in sentiment, in Dante,
   in Chaucer, or in Spenser."

Fair reader, at the old tale take a glance,
   For here, in truth, it doth not well belong   390
To speak:—O turn thee to the very tale,
And taste the music of that vision pale.

L.

With duller steel than the Perséan[4] sword
   They cut away no formless monster's head,
But one, whose gentleness did well accord   395
   With death, as life. The ancient harps have said,
Love never dies, but lives, immortal Lord:
   If Love impersonate was ever dead,
Pale Isabella kiss'd it, and low moan'd.
'Twas love; cold,—dead indeed, but not dethroned.   400

LI.

In anxious secrecy they took it home,
   And then the prize was all for Isabel:
She calm'd its wild hair with a golden comb,
   And all around each eye's sepulchral cell
Pointed each fringed lash; the smeared loam   405
   With tears, as chilly as a dripping well,
She drench'd away:—and still she comb'd, and kept
Sighing all day—and still she kiss'd, and wept.

LII.

Then in a silken scarf,—sweet with the dews
   Of precious flowers pluck'd in Araby,   410
And divine liquids come with odorous ooze
   Through the cold serpent-pipe refreshfully,—
She wrapp'd it up; and for its tomb did choose
   A garden-pot, wherein she laid it by,
And cover'd it with mould, and o'er it set   415
Sweet Basil, which her tears kept ever wet.

LIII.

And she forgot the stars, the moon, and sun,
   And she forgot the blue above the trees,
And she forgot the dells where waters run,
   And she forgot the chilly autumn breeze;   420
She had no knowledge when the day was done,
   And the new morn she saw not: but in peace
Hung over her sweet Basil evermore,
And moisten'd it with tears unto the core.[5]

LIV.

And so she ever fed it with thin tears,   425
   Whence thick, and green, and beautiful it grew,

---

4. The sword given by Mercury to the mythical hero Perseus, who used it to behead the Gorgon.
5. Isabella and her basil perhaps recall Wordsworth's Martha Ray in "The Thorn" (1798), esp. ll. 69–74.

So that it smelt more balmy than its peers
  Of Basil-tufts in Florence; for it drew
Nurture besides, and life, from human fears,
  From the fast mouldering head there shut from view: 430
So that the jewel, safely casketed,
  Came forth, and in perfumed leafits spread.

LV.

O Melancholy, linger here awhile!
  O Music, Music, breathe despondingly!
O Echo, Echo, from some sombre isle,   435
  Unknown, Lethean,[6] sigh to us—O sigh!
Spirits in grief, lift up your heads, and smile;
  Lift up your heads, sweet Spirits, heavily,
And make a pale light in your cypress glooms,
Tinting with silver wan your marble tombs.   440

LVI.

Moan hither, all ye syllables of woe,
  From the deep throat of sad Melpomene![7]
Through bronzed lyre in tragic order go,
  And touch the strings into a mystery;
Sound mournfully upon the winds and low;   445
  For simple Isabel is soon to be
Among the dead: She withers, like a palm
Cut by an Indian for its juicy balm.

LVII.

O leave the palm to wither by itself;
  Let not quick Winter chill its dying hour!—   450
It may not be—those Baälites of pelf,[8]
  Her brethren, noted the continual shower
From her dead eyes; and many a curious elf,
  Among her kindred, wonder'd that such dower
Of youth and beauty should be thrown aside   455
By one mark'd out to be a Noble's bride.

LVIII.

And, furthermore, her brethren wonder'd much
  Why she sat drooping by the Basil green,
And why it flourish'd, as by magic touch;
  Greatly they wonder'd what the thing might mean: 460
They could not surely give belief, that such
  A very nothing would have power to wean
Her from her own fair youth, and pleasures gay,
And even remembrance of her love's delay.

---

6. Lethe is a river in Hades whose waters bring forgetfulness to souls about to be reborn.
7. The muse of tragedy.
8. Worshippers of the false god (Baal is an idol worshipped by the Israelites) of money (pelf).

LIX.

Therefore they watch'd a time when they might sift   465
   This hidden whim; and long they watch'd in vain;
For seldom did she go to chapel-shrift,
   And seldom felt she any hunger-pain;
And when she left, she hurried back, as swift
   As bird on wing to breast its eggs again;   470
And, patient as a hen-bird, sat her there
   Beside her Basil, weeping through her hair.

LX.

Yet they contriv'd to steal the Basil-pot,
   And to examine it in secret place:
The thing was vile with green and livid spot,   475
   And yet they knew it was Lorenzo's face:
The guerdon[9] of their murder they had got,
   And so left Florence in a moment's space,
Never to turn again.—Away they went,
   With blood upon their heads, to banishment.   480

LXI.

O Melancholy, turn thine eyes away!
   O Music, Music, breathe despondingly!
O Echo, Echo, on some other day,
   From isles Lethean, sigh to us—O sigh!
Spirits of grief, sing not your "Well-a-way!"   485
   For Isabel, sweet Isabel, will die;
Will die a death too lone and incomplete,
Now they have ta'en away her Basil sweet.

LXII.

Piteous she look'd on dead and senseless things,
   Asking for her lost Basil amorously;   490
And with melodious chuckle in the strings
   Of her lorn voice, she oftentimes would cry
After the Pilgrim in his wanderings,
   To ask him where her Basil was; and why
'Twas hid from her: "For cruel 'tis," said she,   495
"To steal my Basil-pot away from me."

LXIII.

And so she pined, and so she died forlorn,
   Imploring for her Basil to the last.
No heart was there in Florence but did mourn
   In pity of her love, so overcast.
And a sad ditty of this story born   500
   From mouth to mouth through all the country pass'd:

9. Reward, recompense.

Still is the burthen sung—"O cruelty,
"To steal my Basil-pot away from me!"

THE
EVE OF ST. AGNES.

Keats left London on January 19, 1819, traveling to Chichester to visit the Dilkes and then to Bedhampton on January 23. He began work on a new poem, which he called "St. Agnes Eve," the subject of which had been suggested by Isabella Jones (see p. 80, n. 1). He drafted *The Eve of St. Agnes* in the last two weeks of January and perhaps the first few days of February. He would return to revise it when he was in Winchester in September 1819.

As Keats indicated to Bailey (*L*, 2: 139), the poem is based "on a popular superstition," in which women will dream of their future husbands if they fast on St. Agnes's Eve; Keats would have most likely known of this tradition, but he could have read of it in the 1813 edition of John Brand's 1777 *Observations on Popular Antiquities* (pp. 32–34). The situation of the lovers, Madeline and Porphyro (originally called Lionel), beset as they are by warring families, owes something to Shakespeare's *Romeo and Juliet*. The Gothic setting can be traced to the novels of Ann Radcliffe and poems by Scott (*The Lay of the Last Minstrel*) and Coleridge (*Christabel*). See Jerrold Hogle's "The Gothic-Romantic Relationship: Underground Histories in The *Eve of St. Agnes*," *European Romantic Review* 14 (June 2003): 205–23. Keats adopts a Spenserian stanza for the poem, which he had not used since his earliest extant poem (on Keats and Spenser, see Kucich).

Criticism of the poem begins with Woodhouse's comment that in its original form it was "unfit for ladies" (see above, p. 356). Stillinger's seminal essay, cited in the headnote to the volume and included here, suggested that Porphyro is a kind of rapist, hoodwinking the gullible Madeline. See also readings by Sperry, Wolfson, Levinson, and Timothy Morton, *The Poetics of Spice: Romantic Consumerism and the Exotic* (Cambridge: Cambridge University Press, 2000), pp. 148–70. For a complete account of the poem, see Stillinger, *Reading "The Eve of St. Agnes": The Multiples of Complex Literary Transaction* (New York: Oxford University Press, 1999).

The text is from 1820. Keats's draft of lines 64–378 is held at Harvard (MS Keats 2.21). There are transcripts in both W[1] and W[2]. The fair copy, which was probably the printer's copy, has been lost but can be reconstructed at least in part from George Keats's transcript at the British Library (Egerton 2780, 31–32, 37–51v; *MYR: JK*, 5: 119–21, 131–60).

I.

sᴛ. Agnes' Eve—Ah, bitter chill it was!
The owl, for all his feathers, was a-cold;
The hare limp'd trembling through the frozen grass,
And silent was the flock in woolly fold:
Numb were the Beadsman's fingers, while he told   5

His rosary, and while his frosted breath,
Like pious incense from a censer old,
Seem'd taking flight for heaven, without a death,
Past the sweet Virgin's picture, while his prayer he saith.[1]

II.

His prayer he saith, this patient, holy man;   10
Then takes his lamp, and riseth from his knees,
And back returneth, meagre, barefoot, wan,
Along the chapel aisle by slow degrees:
The sculptur'd dead, on each side, seem to freeze,
Emprison'd in black, purgatorial rails:[2]   15
Knights, ladies, praying in dumb orat'ries,
He passeth by; and his weak spirit fails
To think how they may ache in icy hoods and mails.

III.

Northward he turneth through a little door,
And scarce three steps, ere Music's golden tongue   20
Flatter'd to tears this aged man and poor;
But no—already had his deathbell rung;
The joys of all his life were said and sung:
His was harsh penance on St. Agnes' Eve:
Another way he went, and soon among   25
Rough ashes sat he for his soul's reprieve,
And all night kept awake, for sinners' sake to grieve.[3]

IV.

That ancient Beadsman heard the prelude soft;
And so it chanc'd, for many a door was wide,
From hurry to and fro. Soon, up aloft,   30
The silver, snarling trumpets 'gan to chide:
The level chambers, ready with their pride,
Were glowing to receive a thousand guests:
The carved angels, ever eager-eyed,
Star'd, where upon their heads the cornice rests,   35
With hair blown back, and wings put cross-wise on their breasts.

---

1. A beadsman is paid to pray for others; sometimes a pensioner who prays for his benefactors' souls. Allott suggests an echo of Spenser's description of "old January" in *The Faerie Queene*, 7.7.42: "Yet did he quake and quiuer like to quell, / And blowe his nayles to warm them . . . For, they were numbed." Gittings (p. 280) suggests the beadsman is based on the hermit depicted in Orcagna's fresco, *The Triumph of Death*, which Keats would have seen in an engraving at Haydon's studio.
2. Woodhouse in W² opposite f. 110 notes, "The stone figures of the Temple Church probably suggested these lines," but Keats could also have seen sculptured tombs at Chichester Cathedral.
3. There is a cancelled stanza in Woodhouse's transcripts:

> But there are ears may not hear sweet melodies,
> And there are eyes to brighten festivals,
> And there are feet for nimble minstrelsies,
> And many a lip that for the red wine calls.—
> Follow, then follow to the illumined halls,
> Follow me youth—and leave the Eremite—
> Give him a tear—then trophied banneral,
> And many a brilliant tasseling light,
> Shall droop from arched ways this Baronial night.

V.

At length burst in the argent[4] revelry,
With plume, tiara, and all rich array,
Numerous as shadows haunting fairly
The brain, new stuff 'd, in youth, with triumphs gay   40
Of old romance. These let us wish away,
And turn, sole-thoughted, to one Lady there,
Whose heart had brooded, all that wintry day,
On love, and wing'd St. Agnes' saintly care,
As she had heard old dames full many times declare.   45

VI.

They told her how, upon St. Agnes' Eve,
Young virgins might have visions of delight,
And soft adorings from their loves receive
Upon the honey'd middle of the night,
If ceremonies due they did aright;   50
As, supperless to bed they must retire,
And couch supine their beauties, lily white;
Nor look behind, nor sideways, but require
Of Heaven with upward eyes for all that they desire.[5]

VII.

Full of this whim was thoughtful Madeline:
The music, yearning like a God in pain,   55
She scarcely heard: her maiden eyes divine,
Fix'd on the floor, saw many a sweeping train
Pass by—she heeded not at all: in vain
Came many a tiptoe, amorous cavalier,
And back retir'd, not cool'd by high disdain;   60
But she saw not: her heart was otherwhere:
She sigh'd for Agnes' dreams, the sweetest of the year.

conjoining of opposites — mixture of divine + earthly

VIII.

She danc'd along with vague, regardless eyes,
Anxious her lips, her breathing quick and short:
The hallow'd hour was near at hand: she sighs   65
Amid the timbrels, and the throng'd resort
Of whisperers in anger, or in sport;
'Mid looks of love, defiance, hate, and scorn,

---

4. Heraldic term for silver.
5. There is a dropped stanza in Woodhouse's transcripts:

> 'Twas said her future lord would there appear
> Offering, as sacrifice—all in the dream—
> Delicious food, even to her lips brought near,
> Viands, and wine, and fruit, and sugar'd cream,
> To touch her palate with the fine extreme
> Of relish: then soft music heard, and then
> More pleasures follow'd in a dizzy stream
> Palpable almost: then to wake again
> Warm in the virgin morn, no weeping Magdalen.

Hoodwink'd with faery fancy; all amort,[6]   70
Save to St. Agnes and her lambs unshorn,
And all the bliss to be before to-morrow morn.

IX.

So, purposing each moment to retire,
She linger'd still. Meantime, across the moors,
Had come young Porphyro, with heart on fire   75
For Madeline. Beside the portal doors,
Buttress'd from moonlight, stands he, and implores
All saints to give him sight of Madeline,
But for one moment in the tedious hours,
That he might gaze and worship all unseen;   80
Perchance speak, kneel, touch, kiss—in sooth such things have been.

X.

He ventures in: let no buzz'd whisper tell:
All eyes be muffled, or a hundred swords
Will storm his heart, Love's fev'rous citadel:
For him, those chambers held barbarian hordes,   85
Hyena foemen, and hot-blooded lords,
Whose very dogs would execrations howl
Against his lineage: not one breast affords
Him any mercy, in that mansion foul,
Save one old beldame,[7] weak in body and in soul.   90

XI.

Ah, happy chance! the aged creature came,
Shuffling along with ivory-headed wand,
To where he stood, hid from the torch's flame,
Behind a broad hall-pillar, far beyond
The sound of merriment and chorus bland: 95
He startled her; but soon she knew his face,
And grasp'd his fingers in her palsied hand,
Saying, "Mercy, Porphyro! hie[8] thee from this place;
"They are all here to-night, the whole blood-thirsty race!

XII.

"Get hence! get hence! there's dwarfish Hildebrand;   100
"He had a fever late, and in the fit
"He cursed thee and thine, both house and land:
"Then there's that old Lord Maurice, not a whit
"More tame for his gray hairs—Alas me! flit!
"Flit like a ghost away."—"Ah, Gossip[9] dear,   105

6. Dead.
7. A grandmother, and thus any old woman; sometimes a hag, sometimes a nurse. Allott suggests
   Angela is derived from both the nurse in Shakespeare's *Romeo and Juliet* and various aged female
   servants in the novels of Ann Radcliffe.
8. Go quickly.
9. From "god-sib" or "god-relation," so a godmother; also a female friend, and a talkative woman.

"We're safe enough; here in this arm-chair sit,
"And tell me how"—"Good Saints! not here, not here;
"Follow me, child, or else these stones will be thy bier."

XIII.

He follow'd through a lowly arched way,
Brushing the cobwebs with his lofty plume,   110
And as she mutter'd "Well-a—well-a-day!"
He found him in a little moonlight room,
Pale, lattic'd, chill, and silent as a tomb.
"Now tell me where is Madeline," said he,
"O tell me, Angela, by the holy loom   115
"Which none but secret sisterhood may see,
"When they St. Agnes' wool are weaving piously."

XIV.

"St. Agnes! Ah! it is St. Agnes' Eve—
"Yet men will murder upon holy days:
"Thou must hold water in a witch's sieve,   120
"And be liege-lord of all the Elves and Fays,
"To venture so: it fills me with amaze
"To see thee, Porphyro!—St. Agnes' Eve!
"God's help! my lady fair the conjuror plays
"This very night: good angels her deceive!   125
"But let me laugh awhile, I've mickle[1] time to grieve."

XV.

Feebly she laugheth in the languid moon,
While Porphyro upon her face doth look,
Like puzzled urchin on an aged crone
Who keepeth clos'd a wond'rous riddle-book,   130
As spectacled she sits in chimney nook.
But soon his eyes grew brilliant, when she told
His lady's purpose; and he scarce could brook
Tears, at the thought of those enchantments cold,
And Madeline asleep in lap of legends old.   135

XVI.

Sudden a thought came like a full-blown rose,
Flushing his brow, and in his pained heart
Made purple riot: then doth he propose
A stratagem, that makes the beldame start:
"A cruel man and impious thou art: 140
"Sweet lady, let her pray, and sleep, and dream
"Alone with her good angels, far apart
"From wicked men like thee. Go, go!—I deem
"Thou canst not surely be the same that thou didst seem."

1. Much.

XVII.

"I will not harm her, by all saints I swear,"   145
Quoth Porphyro: "O may I ne'er find grace
"When my weak voice shall whisper its last prayer,
"If one of her soft ringlets I displace,
"Or look with ruffian passion in her face:
"Good Angela, believe me by these tears;   150
"Or I will, even in a moment's space,
"Awake, with horrid shout, my foemen's ears,
"And beard them, though they be more fang'd than wolves and bears."

XVIII.

"Ah! why wilt thou affright a feeble soul?
"A poor, weak, palsy-stricken, churchyard thing,   155
"Whose passing-bell may ere the midnight toll;
"Whose prayers for thee, each morn and evening,
"Were never miss'd."—Thus plaining, doth she bring
A gentler speech from burning Porphyro;
So woful, and of such deep sorrowing,   160
That Angela gives promise she will do
Whatever he shall wish, betide her weal or woe.[2]

XIX.

Which was, to lead him, in close secrecy,
Even to Madeline's chamber, and there hide
Him in a closet, of such privacy   165
That he might see her beauty unespied,
And win perhaps that night a peerless bride,
While legion'd fairies pac'd the coverlet,
And pale enchantment held her sleepy-eyed.
Never on such a night have lovers met,   170
Since Merlin paid his Demon all the monstrous debt.[3]

XX.

"It shall be as thou wishest," said the Dame:
"All cates[4] and dainties shall be stored there
"Quickly on this feast-night: by the tambour frame[5]
"Her own lute thou wilt see: no time to spare,   175
"For I am slow and feeble, and scarce dare
"On such a catering trust my dizzy head.
"Wait here, my child: with patience; kneel in prayer
"The while: Ah! thou must needs the lady wed,
"Or may I never leave my grave among the dead."   180

2. Whether good or evil befalls her.
3. Hunt in *Imagination and Fancy* (*SWLH*, 4: 117n) admitted that he did not understand this reference. Allott suggests an allusion to Spenser's *Faerie Queene*, 3.3.7–11, where Merlin is imprisoned
in a cave by his false love, the Lady of the Lake; the Lady of the Lake is, in some versions of the
Arthurian stories, Vivien, who enchants Merlin and imprisons him in a cave or tree. As a fairy and
enchantress, the Lady of the Lake/Vivien is a "demon." Keats owned a "Hist. of Arthur" according
to Brown, which Rollins identifies as an 1816 edition of Malory's *Morte d'Arthur* called *The History of the Renowned Prince Arthur, King of Britain*" (*KC*, 1: 259n.).
4. Foodstuffs, delicacies; etymologically connected with "catering" in l. 177.
5. A circular frame used for embroidery.

XXI.

So saying, she hobbled off with busy fear.
The lover's endless minutes slowly pass'd;
The dame return'd, and whisper'd in his ear
To follow her; with aged eyes aghast
From fright of dim espial. Safe at last,   185
Through many a dusky gallery, they gain
The maiden's chamber, silken, hush'd, and chaste;
Where Porphyro took covert, pleas'd amain.[6]
His poor guide hurried back with agues in her brain.

XXII.

Her falt'ring hand upon the balustrade,   190
Old Angela was feeling for the stair,
When Madeline, St. Agnes' charmed maid,
Rose, like a mission'd spirit, unaware:
With silver taper's light, and pious care,
She turn'd, and down the aged gossip led   195
To a safe level matting. Now prepare,
Young Porphyro, for gazing on that bed;
She comes, she comes again, like ring-dove fray'd[7] and fled.

XXIII.

Out went the taper as she hurried in;
Its little smoke, in pallid moonshine, died: 200
She clos'd the door, she panted, all akin
To spirits of the air, and visions wide:
No uttered syllable, or, woe betide!
But to her heart, her heart was voluble,
Paining with eloquence her balmy side;   205
As though a tongueless nightingale[8] should swell
Her throat in vain, and die, heart-stifled, in her dell.

XXIV.

A casement high and triple-arch'd there was,
All garlanded with carven imag'ries
Of fruits, and flowers, and bunches of knot-grass,   210
And diamonded with panes of quaint device,
Innumerable of stains and splendid dyes,
As are the tiger-moth's deep-damask'd wings;
And in the midst, 'mong thousand heraldries,
And twilight saints, and dim emblazonings,   215
A shielded scutcheon blush'd with blood of queens and kings.[9]

6. Exceedingly but also violently, with force; *took covert*: hid himself.
7. Frightened, afraid.
8. On the myth of Procne and Philomel, see p. 32, n. 6.
9. This stanza has been seen to reflect both the architecture of the neo-Gothic chapel at Stansted and
   Scott's *Lay of the Last Minstrel* (1805), 2.11. *Casement*: window frame; *knot-grass*: "a common weed
   in waste ground, with numerous intricately-branched creeping stems, and small pale pink flowers"
   (*OED*); *tiger-moth*: "a large scarlet and brown moth spotted and streaked with white" (*OED*); *deep-
   damask*'d: damask is "rich silk fabric woven with elaborate designs and figures, often of a variety

XXV.

Full on this casement shone the wintry moon,
And threw warm gules on Madeline's fair breast,
As down she knelt for heaven's grace and boon;
Rose-bloom fell on her hands, together prest,   220
And on her silver cross soft amethyst,
And on her hair a glory, like a saint:
She seem'd a splendid angel, newly drest,
Save wings, for heaven:—Porphyro grew faint:
She knelt, so pure a thing, so free from mortal taint.   225

XXVI.

Anon his heart revives: her vespers done,
Of all its wreathed pearls her hair she frees;
Unclasps her warmed jewels one by one;
Loosens her fragrant boddice; by degrees
Her rich attire creeps rustling to her knees: 230
Half-hidden, like a mermaid in sea-weed,
Pensive awhile she dreams awake, and sees,
In fancy, fair St. Agnes in her bed,
But dares not look behind, or all the charm is fled.

[handwritten margin notes: elevation + objectification of woman; right onto this stanza, Keats writes about her undressing]

XXVII.

Soon, trembling in her soft and chilly nest,   235
In sort of wakeful swoon, perplex'd she lay,
Until the poppied warmth of sleep oppress'd
Her soothed limbs, and soul fatigued away;
Flown, like a thought, until the morrow-day;
Blissfully haven'd both from joy and pain;   240
Clasp'd like a missal where swart Paynims pray;[1]
Blinded alike from sunshine and from rain,
As though a rose should shut, and be a bud again.

XXVIII.

Stol'n to this paradise, and so entranced,
Porphyro gazed upon her empty dress,   245
And listen'd to her breathing, if it chanced
To wake into a slumberous tenderness;
Which when he heard, that minute did he bless,
And breath'd himself: then from the closet crept,

---

of colours" originally produced at Damascus (OED); *emblazonings*: heraldic devices; *scutcheon*: shield on which a coat of arms is depicted, with the vertical lines in gules (l. 218, the heraldic term for red) indicating they are of royal blood.

1. Of this line, Hunt wrote (*Imagination and Fancy; SWLH*, 4: 119n.), "Clasp'd like a missal in a land of *Pagans*: that is to say, where Christian prayer-books must not be seen, and are, therefore, doubly cherished for the danger." The line could also refer to a prayer book shut with clasps in a pagan or Moslem country. Lowell, 2: 173–74, suggests that Keats was referring to *Missale mixtum secundum regulam beati Isidori dictum Mozarabes . . . In regali civitate Toleti, 1500*, a prayer book used by the Goths under Moorish rule, which was discussed by the antiquarian Thomas Frognall Dibdin in his *Bibliotheca Spenceriana* (1814) and could have been known to Keats through Dilke.

Noiseless as fear in a wide wilderness,   250
And over the hush'd carpet, silent, stept,
And 'tween the curtains peep'd, where, lo!—how fast she slept.

XXIX.

Then by the bed-side, where the faded moon
Made a dim, silver twilight, soft he set
A table, and, half anguish'd, threw thereon   255
A cloth of woven crimson, gold, and jet:—
O for some drowsy Morphean amulet![2]
The boisterous, midnight, festive clarion,
The kettle-drum, and far-heard clarionet,[3]
Affray his ears, though but in dying tone:—   260
The hall door shuts again, and all the noise is gone.

XXX.

And still she slept an azure-lidded sleep,
In blanched linen, smooth, and lavender'd,
While he from forth the closet brought a heap
Of candied apple, quince, and plum, and gourd;   265
With jellies soother[4] than the creamy curd,
And lucent syrops, tinct with cinnamon;
Manna and dates, in argosy[5] transferr'd
From Fez; and spiced dainties, every one,
From silken Samarcand to cedar'd Lebanon.[6]   270

XXXI.

These delicates he heap'd with glowing hand
On golden dishes and in baskets bright
Of wreathed silver: sumptuous they stand
In the retired quiet of the night,
Filling the chilly room with perfume light.—   275
"And now, my love, my seraph fair, awake!
"Thou art my heaven, and I thine eremite:[7]
"Open thine eyes, for meek St. Agnes' sake,
"Or I shall drowse beside thee, so my soul doth ache."

XXXII.

Thus whispering, his warm, unnerved arm   280
Sank in her pillow. Shaded was her dream

2. A charm administered by Morpheus, god of sleep.
3. Diminutive form of "clarion," a trumpet. Clarke (*Recollections*, p. 143) noted that when Keats read him the poem, he said that this passage "came into my head when I remembered how I used to listen in bed to your music at school."
4. Keats's coinage from "smoother" and "more soothing." Hunt (*Autobiography*, 1850) remembers Keats reading this passage "with great relish and particularly, conscious of what he had set forth."
5. A merchant ship, from the *Argus*, the first ship.
6. For Lebanon as "cedar'd," see Psalms 104.16. *Fez*: also known as Fès, a city in north central Morocco, noted for its Islamic art and handicrafts. *Samarcand*: an ancient Persian city in Uzbekistan famous in the Middle Ages for its palaces and gardens and its silk industry.
7. A hermit devoted to prayer; *seraph*: an angel.

By the dusk curtains:—'twas a midnight charm
Impossible to melt as iced stream:
The lustrous salvers[8] in the moonlight gleam;
Broad golden fringe upon the carpet lies: 285
It seem'd he never, never could redeem
From such a stedfast spell his lady's eyes;
So mus'd awhile, entoil'd in woofed phantasies.

XXXIII.

Awakening up, he took her hollow lute,—
Tumultuous,—and, in chords that tenderest be,   290
He play'd an ancient ditty, long since mute,
In Provence call'd, "La belle dame sans mercy":[9]
Close to her ear touching the melody;—
Wherewith disturb'd, she utter'd a soft moan:
He ceased—she panted quick—and suddenly   295
Her blue affrayed eyes wide open shone:
Upon his knees he sank, pale as smooth-sculptured stone.

XXXIV.

Her eyes were open, but she still beheld,
Now wide awake, the vision of her sleep:
There was a painful change, that nigh expell'd   300
The blisses of her dream so pure and deep
At which fair Madeline began to weep,
And moan forth witless words with many a sigh;
While still her gaze on Porphyro would keep;
Who knelt, with joined hands and piteous eye,   305
Fearing to move or speak, she look'd so dreamingly.

XXXV.

"Ah, Porphyro!" said she, "but even now
"Thy voice was at sweet tremble in mine ear,
"Made tuneable with every sweetest vow;
"And those sad eyes were spiritual and clear: 310
"How chang'd thou art! how pallid, chill, and drear!
"Give me that voice again, my Porphyro,
"Those looks immortal, those complainings dear!
"Oh leave me not in this eternal woe,
"For if thou diest, my Love, I know not where to go."[1]   315

[handwritten marginalia: ½ awake / ½ asleep; not fully conscious; Rape]

---

8. Trays or dishes.
9. The title of a poem by Alain Chartier (1424) and of a later poem by Keats (see pp. 338–43).
1. For lines 314–22, the draft has:

> See, while she speaks his arms encroaching slow,
> Have zoned her, heart to hear,—loud, loud the dark winds blow!
>
> For on the midnight came a tempest fell;
> More sooth, for that his quick rejoinder flows
> Into her burning ear: and still the spell
> Unbroken guards her in serene repose.
> With her wild dream he mingled, as a rose
> Marrieth its odour to a violet.
> Still, still, she dreams, louder the frost wind blows.

XXXVI.

Beyond a mortal man impassion'd far
At these voluptuous accents, he arose,
Ethereal, flush'd, and like a throbbing star
Seen mid the sapphire heaven's deep repose;
Into her dream he melted, as the rose   320
Blendeth its odour with the violet,—
Solution sweet: meantime the frost-wind blows
Like Love's alarum[2] pattering the sharp sleet
Against the window-panes; St. Agnes' moon hath set.

XXXVII.

'Tis dark: quick pattereth the flaw-blown sleet:[3]   325
"This is no dream, my bride, my Madeline!"
'Tis dark: the iced gusts still rave and beat:
"No dream, alas! alas! and woe is mine!
"Porphyro will leave me here to fade and pine.—
"Cruel! what traitor could thee hither bring?   330
"I curse not, for my heart is lost in thine,
"Though thou forsakest a deceived thing;—
"A dove forlorn and lost with sick unpruned wing."

[handwritten: what a creeper → Rape]

XXXVIII.

"My Madeline! sweet dreamer! lovely bride!
"Say, may I be for aye thy vassal blest?   335
"Thy beauty's shield, heart-shap'd and vermeil[4] dyed?
"Ah, silver shrine, here will I take my rest
"After so many hours of toil and quest,
"A famish'd pilgrim,—saved by miracle.
"Though I have found, I will not rob thy nest   340
"Saving of thy sweet self; if thou think'st well
"To trust, fair Madeline, to no rude infidel.

[handwritten: marriage = her only choice after him raping her]

XXXIX.

"Hark! 'tis an elfin-storm from faery land,
"Of haggard[5] seeming, but a boon indeed:
"Arise—arise! the morning is at hand;—   345
"The bloated wassaillers will never heed:—
"Let us away, my love, with happy speed;
"There are no ears to hear, or eyes to see,—
"Drown'd all in Rhenish[6] and the sleepy mead:
"Awake! arise! my love, and fearless be,   350
"For o'er the southern moors I have a home for thee."

[handwritten: "One must experience trauma in order to experience beauty" → So is woman's rape justified in this way by Keats?]

---

2. A call to arms, a military alarm often sounded on a drum.
3. See Cary's translation of Dante, *Inferno*, 6.9: "Large hail, discolour'd water, sleety flaw"; a flaw is a gust of wind.
4. Vermilion, a bright scarlet color.
5. Wild.
6. Rhine wine.

XL.

She hurried at his words, beset with fears,
For there were sleeping dragons all around,
At glaring watch, perhaps, with ready spears—
Down the wide stairs a darkling way they found.— 355
In all the house was heard no human sound.
A chain-droop'd lamp was flickering by each door;
The arras,[7] rich with horseman, hawk, and hound,
Flutter'd in the besieging wind's uproar;
And the long carpets rose along the gusty floor. 360

XLI.

They glide, like phantoms, into the wide hall;
Like phantoms, to the iron porch, they glide;
Where lay the Porter, in uneasy sprawl,
With a huge empty flaggon[8] by his side:
The wakeful bloodhound rose, and shook his hide, 365
But his sagacious eye an inmate owns:
By one, and one, the bolts full easy slide:—
The chains lie silent on the footworn stones;—
The key turns, and the door upon its hinges groans.

XLII.

And they are gone: ay, ages long ago 370
These lovers fled away into the storm.
That night the Baron dreamt of many a woe,
And all his warrior-guests, with shade and form
Of witch, and demon, and large coffin-worm,
Were long be-nightmar'd. Angela the old 375
Died palsy-twitch'd, with meagre face deform;
The Beadsman, after thousand aves told,
For aye unsought for slept among his ashes cold.[9]

ODE TO A NIGHTINGALE.

Often thought of as the second of the spring odes, "Ode to a Nightingale" was written in May 1819. Brown gives a now disputed story (he may be remembering the writing of "Ode on Indolence") of the poem's composition (*KC*, 2: 65): he notes that Keats, feeling "a continual and tranquil joy" in the song of a nightingale in their yard, returned one morning from sitting on "the grass-plot under a plum-tree" with "some scraps of paper in his

---

7. A hanging tapestry, perhaps used as a screen along the walls of a room allowing people to walk hidden behind it. For lines 357–60 Allott suggests Byron's *Siege of Corinth* (1816), ll. 620–27, which read in part, "Like the figures on arras, that gloomily glare, / Stirred by the breath of the wintry air . . . Fearfully flitting to and fro, / As the gusts on the tapestry come and go."
8. A large wine bottle.
9. For ll. 375–78, Woodhouse records:

     Angela went off
  Twitch'd by the palsy:—and with face deform
  The Beadsman stiffen'd—'twixt a sigh and laugh,
  Ta'en sudden from his beads by one weak little cough.

hand, and these he was quietly thrusting behind the books. On inquiry, I found these scraps, four or five in number, contained his poetic feeling on the song of the nightingale." Brown's statement that it was "difficult to arrange the stanzas" has suggested to some the difficulties in tracking the movements between the poem's sections, which might be thought of as moving from a sense of opposition between the poet's self-conscious numbness and the happiness of the nightingale through alternating synecdochal, idealizing turns (as when a glass of wine becomes a "draught of vintage" filled from "the true, the blushful Hippocrene") and metonymic, "realistic" ones (as when life is reduced to the "weariness, the fever, and the fret"), to an equilibrium of the ideal in the real of stanza 5, that must still admit the fact of death (first idealized as "easeful Death" but finally confronted as the fact that one dies to "become a sod"), with poetry perhaps offering a way of tackling even death, though the poem closes on the question of whether this is "a vision, or a waking dream."

As Bate points out (pp. 497–98), Keats here and in the other spring odes other than "Psyche," uses a stanza that combines a Shakespearean quatrain (*a b a b*) with a Petrarchan sestet (*c d e c d e*). The odes can thus be seen as arising from Keats's experimentations with the sonnet and his search for a larger lyric form.

Keats could have looked back to a long tradition of poems about nightingales including those by Anne Finch, Mary Hays, Joseph Warton, George Dyer, three by Charlotte Smith in her *Elegiac Sonnets* (1784), two odes by Mary Robinson, "Eastern Ode" by Anna Seward (in *Poetical Works* of 1810), and two by Coleridge, the 1796 "To the Nightingale" and the 1798 "The Nightingale: A Conversation Poem." Keats reports that when he met Coleridge on Hampstead Heath on April 11, 1819 (see pp. 325–26), they talked of "nightingales" among a "thousand things" including poetry and metaphysics. The influence of Wordsworth and Hazlitt has been identified in the final two stanzas in particular. For criticism on the poem, see the headnote to the volume.

The ode was first published as "Ode to the Nightingale" in *The Annals of the Fine Arts* 4 (1819): 354–56 and then in 1820. There is a holograph draft (with a cancelled beginning, "Small, winged Dryad") at the Fitzwilliam Museum, Cambridge (a facsimile can be found in Gittings, *The Odes of John Keats and Their Earliest Known Manuscripts* [Kent, Ohio: Kent State University Press, 1970], pp. 36–43). The printer's copy appears to have been a lost fair copy by Keats or Brown. The text is from 1820.

1.

My heart aches, and a drowsy numbness pains
  My sense, as though of hemlock I had drunk,
Or emptied some dull opiate to the drains
  One minute past, and Lethe-wards had sunk:[1]

[handwritten margin note: struggle bet. actual experience + imagination → hard to keep images together because of negation through out]

---

1. For Lethe, see p. 4, n. 3. Keats may echo Horace, *Epodes*, 14.1–4 where the poet downs a cup that brings "Lethean slumber"; and Marlowe's translation of Ovid's *Amores* as *Elegies*, 3.6.14: "like as if cold *hemlock* I had drunk." *hemlock*: a strong sedative that can be poisonous (as when it was used to execute Socrates). Keats could have read in John Potter's *Archaeologia Graeca: Or the Antiquities of Greece* (1697; new ed. 1795), "The Hierophantae at Athens, after their admission, enfeebled themselves by a draught of the juice of hemlock" (1: 204); the Hierophantes was the head of the Eleusinian mystery cult and the most revered priest in Attica.

'Tis not through envy of thy happy lot,   5
  But being too happy in thine happiness,—
    That thou, light-winged Dryad[2] of the trees,
          In some melodious plot
  Of beechen green, and shadows numberless,
    Singest of summer in full-throated ease.   10

2.

O, for a draught of vintage! that hath been
  Cool'd a long age in the deep-delved earth,
Tasting of Flora and the country green,
  Dance, and Provençal song, and sunburnt mirth!
O for a beaker full of the warm South,   15
  Full of the true, the blushful Hippocrene,[3]
    With beaded bubbles winking at the brim,
          And purple-stained mouth;
  That I might drink, and leave the world unseen,
    And with thee fade away into the forest dim: 20

3.

Fade far away, dissolve, and quite forget
  What thou among the leaves hast never known,
The weariness, the fever, and the fret
  Here, where men sit and hear each other groan;
Where palsy shakes a few, sad, last gray hairs,   25
  Where youth grows pale, and spectre-thin, and dies;[4]
    Where but to think is to be full of sorrow[5]
          And leaden-eyed despairs,
  Where Beauty cannot keep her lustrous eyes,
    Or new Love pine at them beyond to-morrow.   30

4.

Away! away! for I will fly to thee,
  Not charioted by Bacchus and his pards,[6]
But on the viewless[7] wings of Poesy,
  Though the dull brain perplexes and retards:
Already with thee! tender is the night,   35
  And haply the Queen-Moon is on her throne,

2. See p. 376, n. 4.
3. Keats offers a series of figures for a glass of wine, from a "draught of vintage," which tastes of,
   among other things, Flora (the Roman goddess of flowers mentioned in "Sleep and Poetry," l. 102,
   as embodying the world of romance) and Provence (in the south of France and famous for the love
   songs of the Troubadours), to a beaker filled with all the warmth and vitality of Mediterranean
   culture as well as of the waters of the Hippocrene (a fountain sacred to the muses on Mount
   Helicon).
4. Allott hears Wordsworth's "Tintern Abbey," ll. 52–53, "the fretful stir / Unprofitable, and the fever
   of the world" behind l. 23, and Wordsworth's Excursion 4.760, "While man grows old, and dwin-
   dles, and decays" behind l. 26.
5. See Byron, Manfred, 1.1.10, "Sorrow is knowledge," quoted in Keats's letter to Reynolds, May 3,
   1818 (above, p. 244).
6. Bacchus is sometimes portrayed in a chariot drawn by leopards as in Titian's Bacchus and Ariadne.
7. Invisible.

Cluster'd around by all her starry Fays;[8]
But here there is no light,
Save what from heaven is with the breezes blown
Through verdurous glooms and winding mossy ways.   40

5.

I cannot see what flowers are at my feet,
Nor what soft incense hangs upon the boughs,
But, in embalmed darkness, guess each sweet
Wherewith the seasonable month endows
The grass, the thicket, and the fruit-tree wild;   45
White hawthorn, and the pastoral eglantine;[9]
Fast fading violets cover'd up in leaves;
And mid-May's eldest child,
The coming musk-rose, full of dewy wine,
The murmurous haunt of flies on summer eves.[1]   50

6.

Darkling[2] I listen; and, for many a time
I have been half in love with easeful Death,
Call'd him soft names in many a mused rhyme,
To take into the air my quiet breath;
Now more than ever seems it rich to die,   55
To cease upon the midnight with no pain,
While thou art pouring forth thy soul abroad
In such an ecstasy!
Still wouldst thou sing, and I have ears in vain—
To thy high requiem become a sod.   60

7.

Thou wast not born for death, immortal Bird!
No hungry generations tread thee down;
The voice I hear this passing night was heard
In ancient days by emperor and clown:
Perhaps the self-same song that found a path   65
Through the sad heart of Ruth, when, sick for home,
She stood in tears amid the alien corn;[3]
The same that oft-times hath
Charm'd magic casements, opening on the foam
Of perilous seas, in faery lands forlorn.[4]   70

[handwritten margin note: mvmts all the way to Romanticism]

---

8. Fairies.
9. See p. 151, n. 1.
1. For ll. 46–50, see Shakespeare, *A Midsummer Night's Dream*, 2.1.249–52: "I know a bank where
   the wild thyme blows, / Where oxlips and the nodding violet grows, / Quite overcanopied with luscious woodbine, / With sweet musk-roses, and with eglantine"; and Milton, "Lycidas," ll. 145–46:
   "The glowing Violet. / The Musk-rose, and the well attir'd Woodbine."
2. In the dark.
3. See Ruth 2.1–3; Ruth flees her native Moab, beset by famine, to work as a gleaner of corn (grain)
   for her kinsman Boaz. See also Wordsworth's "Solitary Reaper" (1807), where the Highland Lass
   is "Reaping and singing" and the nightingale's "chaunt" is mentioned; Wordsworth's poem also
   seems to be echoed in the last stanza.
4. Lost but also wretched.

8.

Forlorn! the very word is like a bell
    To toll me back from thee to my sole self!
Adieu! the fancy cannot cheat so well
    As she is fam'd to do, deceiving elf.
Adieu! adieu! thy plaintive anthem fades   75
    Past the near meadows, over the still stream,
        Up the hill-side; and now 'tis buried deep
            In the next valley-glades:
Was it a vision, or a waking dream?[5]
Fled is that music:—Do I wake or sleep?   80

ODE ON A GRECIAN URN.

Keats wrote this ode in 1819, and critics usually assign it to May of that year and consider it as having been written after "Ode to a Nightingale." Various prototypes for the urn in the poem have been sought: the Townley Vase, which Keats could have seen at the British Museum; the Sosibos Vase (from the Musée Napoléon), which Keats drew in outline, probably from Henry Moses's *A Collection of Antique Vases, Altars, etc* . . . (Taylor, 1814); the Holland House Urn, which depicts a sacrifice; the Borghese Vase, in the Louvre but often reproduced; and the Portland Vase, also at the British Museum and reproduced by Wedgwood. (For images, see Jack, pp. 214–24.) Many critics have found it more plausible that Keats was inspired by the Elgin Marbles, particularly a section of the south frieze showing a heifer being led to sacrifice. The poem's engagement with the ekphrastic tradition is taken up by Grant F. Scott in *The Sculpted Word* (1994) and Theresa Kelley, "Keats, ekphrasis, and history," in Roe (ed.), *Keats and History*, pp. 212–37. McGann, in *Beauty of Inflections*, pp. 42–45, suggests how an interpretation of the poem depends at least upon the fiction that the poem describes an actual urn.

Moses's volume may have been a particularly rich source for Keats. In it, Moses notes:

> Few remains of antiquity have excited more interest than vases. The variety and the elegance of their forms, the singularity of the designs, the beauty of the compositions with which they are adorned, and the important instruction which the subjects of these pictures convey, have conspired to render them peculiarly attractive. By attentively studying the stories they record, the scholar has been enabled to throw much light upon the mythology, the history, the manners and customs of the ancients; the artist has derived high improvement from copying their beautiful designs . . . (p. 1)

He goes on to note that "Of the sepulchral vases, the most celebrated is that known by the name of the *Portland vase*," and he notes that one interpretation of that vase is that it represents the marriage of Peleus and Thetis, also taken up in Catullus's epithalamium (64). Moses's volume also offers

---

5. See Hazlitt's 1818 lecture "On Chaucer and Spenser," where "Spenser was the poet of our waking dreams" (*Works* 5: 44); see also Wordsworth's "Intimations Ode," ll. 56–57: "Whither is fled the visonary gleam? / Where is it now, the glory and the dream?"

in plate 48 a vase from Piranesi that has on it various images similar to those in Keats's poem: a pipe player, a sacrifice, two heifers (one of which is about to be slaughtered), and people entering from both sides. The final plate 50 is of the Portland vase. This rich visual and literary context might help to understand Keats's ode, as is suggested in Cox's essay on the poem included here (pp. 614–25).

There is a voluminous critical literature on the poem. A major line of criticism has seen the ode engaged not with any particular vase but with an ideal of art, a view set forth most strikingly in Cleanth Brooks's seminal piece of "new criticism," "Keats's Sylvan Historian: History without Footnotes," *The Well-Wrought Urn* (New York: Harcourt Brace, 1947), pp. 139–52.

The poem was first published in *The Annals of the Fine Arts* 4 (January 1820), pp. 638–39, where it is called "On a Grecian Urn." The *Annals* version differs in a number of ways, most famously in the closing lines, which do not have internal quotation marks and thus read "Beauty is Truth,—Truth Beauty.—That is all / Ye know on earth, and all ye need to know." See Stillinger, "Who Says What to Whom at the End of *Ode on a Grecian Urn*," (1971), pp. 167–73. There is no extant holograph of the poem, though Brown's transcript (Harvard MS Keats 3.6, p. 25–27; *MYR: JK*, 7: 27–29) was taken from a Keats manuscript; we also have a transcript by George Keats in the British Museum (Egerton 2780, ff. 55–56; *MYR: JK*, 5: 167–69). Text from 1820.

1.

THOU still unravish'd bride of quietness,
    Thou foster-child of silence and slow time,
  Sylvan historian, who canst thus express
    A flowery tale[1] more sweetly than our rhyme:
What leaf-fring'd legend haunts about thy shape   5
      Of deities or mortals, or of both,
        In Tempe or the dales of Arcady?[2]
      What men or gods are these? What maidens loth?
    What mad pursuit? What struggle to escape?
      What pipes and timbrels?[3] What wild ecstasy?   10

2.

Heard melodies are sweet, but those unheard
    Are sweeter; therefore, ye soft pipes, play on;
Not to the sensual ear, but, more endear'd,
    Pipe to the spirit ditties of no tone:
Fair youth, beneath the trees, thou canst not leave   15
    Thy song, nor ever can those trees be bare;

---

1. Could refer to a pastoral narrative, or an ornate, overly poetic story, or, when linked with "leaf-fring'd legend" in the next line, a tale embellished with a floral design, as is often the case with Greek vases where the images of the mythological subject are decorated with vegetation. *Sylvan historian*: literally a historian of the woods, presumably a teller of stories about the pastoral world, which is usually thought of as lacking a history.
2. Tempe, a valley in Thessaly, and Arcadia in the Peloponnesus are both sites of a classical pastoral, edenic realm.
3. Percussion instruments such as tambourines. Pipes and timbrels often accompany the "wild ecstasy" of Bacchic revels.

Bold Lover, never, never canst thou kiss,
Though winning near the goal—yet, do not grieve;
She cannot fade, though thou hast not thy bliss,
For ever wilt thou love, and she be fair!   20

Ah, happy, happy boughs! that cannot shed
Your leaves, nor ever bid the Spring adieu;
And, happy melodist, unwearied,[4]
For ever piping songs for ever new;
More happy love! more happy, happy love!   25
For ever warm and still to be enjoy'd,
For ever panting, and for ever young;
All breathing human passion far above,[5]
That leaves a heart high-sorrowful and cloy'd,
A burning forehead, and a parching tongue.   30

4.

Who are these coming to the sacrifice?
To what green altar, O mysterious priest,
Lead'st thou that heifer lowing at the skies,
And all her silken flanks with garlands drest?
What little town by river or sea shore,   35
Or mountain-built with peaceful citadel,
Is emptied of this folk, this pious morn?
And, little town, thy streets for evermore
Will silent be; and not a soul to tell
Why thou art desolate, can e'er return.[6]   40

5.

O Attic shape! Fair attitude! with brede[7]
Of marble men and maidens overwrought,
With forest branches and the trodden weed;
Thou, silent form, dost tease us out of thought
As doth eternity: Cold Pastoral!   45
When old age shall this generation waste,
Thou shalt remain, in midst of other woe
Than ours, a friend to man, to whom thou say'st,
"Beauty is truth, truth beauty,"—that is all
Ye know on earth, and all ye need to know.[8]   50

4. Allott suggests an echo of Collins's "The Passions: An Ode for Music" (1747), l. 88: "To some
   unwearied Minstrel dancing."
5. See Hazlitt's comment on Greek statues in "On Gusto" (1816): "By their beauty they are raised
   above the frailties of pain or passion" (Works 4: 79).
6. Among the possible sources of the images here are Claude's Landscape with the Father of Psyche
   sacrificing at the Temple of Apollo and the Parthenon frieze, which Keats would have seen as part
   of the Elgin Marbles and which depicts a procession including a heifer "lowing at the skies." See
   also Hunt's Story of Rimini (1816) 3. 464–85, where he describes a temple that "o'er the door was
   carved a sacrifice."
7. Something interwoven, embroidered, literally applied to the figures "overwrought" or "written over"
   the circumference of the vase, but Keats also puns on the sexual possibilities of overexcited men
   and women breeding. Fair attitude: see the essay by Cox (pp. 621–25, below).
8. For the famous dispute over the punctuation of these final lines, see the headnote.

ODE TO PSYCHE.

Usually considered the first of the great spring odes, "Ode to Psyche" was written toward the end of April 1819, before its inclusion in Keats's journal letter to the George Keatses on April 30, where he refers to it as "the last [poem] I have written" (see above, p. 331). He also identified the poem as "the first and the only one with which I have taken even moderate pains," and much discussion has gone into the pains he took here to create a new stanza form out of his experimentations with the sonnet. As with the other odes, it needs to be understood in relation to the history of the ode proper, as here Keats uses the irregular stanza identified with the Pindaric ode to address a classical deity, as he draws on Milton's ode "On the Morning of Christ's Nativity" and as he learns from his contemporaries' experiments with the ode, perhaps particularly Wordsworth's innovative use of the tradition of the Horatian ode in "Tintern Abbey."

Keats's source for the story of Cupid and Psyche is an episode in Apuleius' *Golden Ass*, which he knew in William Adlington's translation (1566); he would also have known the story from Mary Tighe's *Psyche, or the Legend of Love* (1805). Keats refers only indirectly to the main line of the story: while ordered by his mother, Venus, to unite Psyche with a serpent, Cupid falls in love with Psyche, though she is a mortal, and visits her at night, as she is not to see him; persuaded by her sisters that she is being visited by a monster, she conceals an oil lantern in her bedchamber and looks upon Cupid as he sleeps, but, dripping hot oil, she awakes him, and he leaves in anger; she undergoes many trials at the hands of Venus, until Jupiter rescues her, makes her immortal, and unites her with Cupid. It is, as Lemprière notes, a late myth. Keats wrote to his brother and sister-in-law (above, p. 331), "You must recollect that Psyche was not embodied as a goddess before the time of Apulieus the Platonist . . . and consequently the Goddess was never worshipped or sacrificed to with any of the ancient fervour—and perhaps never thought of in the old religion—I am more orthodox than to let a hethen Goddess be so neglected." Keats invokes the culture of classical myth, the time of "antique vows" (l. 36), but, as Milton argued in his Nativity ode, he recognizes the passing of those "happy pieties" (l. 41) with the coming of Christianity. Addressing Psyche, whose name signifies "soul," as Lemprière notes, Keats wonders whether a modern, Wordsworthian poetry of the "Mind of Man," the "haunt, and the main region" of Wordsworth's song ("Prospectus" to *The Recluse*, ll. 40–41) has not now moved beyond Milton's Christian culture; and in the poem's close, Keats explores how we might gesture beyond what he called the "wordsworthian or egotistical sublime" (see above, p. 295). See James Choudler's essay included here, pp. 625–34.

The ode was first published in 1820. There are two holographs: Keats's draft at the Morgan Library (MA 210 [1]) and his copy in the letter to the George Keatses (Harvard MS Keats 1.53). The text is from 1820.

> O GODDESS! hear these tuneless numbers,[1] wrung
>   By sweet enforcement and remembrance dear,
> And pardon that thy secrets should be sung
>   Even into thine own soft-conched ear:

1. Verses.

Surely I dreamt to-day, or did I see   5
    The winged Psyche with awaken'd eyes?[2]
I wander'd in a forest thoughtlessly,
    And, on the sudden, fainting with surprise,
Saw two fair creatures, couched side by side
    In deepest grass, beneath the whisp'ring roof   10
Of leaves and trembled blossoms, where there ran
    A brooklet, scarce espied:
'Mid hush'd, cool-rooted flowers, fragrant-eyed,
    Blue, silver-white, and budded Tyrian,[3]
They lay calm-breathing on the bedded grass;   15
    Their arms embraced, and their pinions[4] too;
Their lips touch'd not, but had not bade adieu,
As if disjoined by soft-handed slumber,
And ready still past kisses to outnumber
    At tender eye-dawn of aurorean love:[5]   20
        The winged boy[6] I knew;
But who wast thou, O happy, happy dove?
        His Psyche true!

O latest born and loveliest vision far
    Of all Olympus' faded hierarchy!   25
Fairer than Phœbe's sapphire-region'd star,
    Or Vesper,[7] amorous glow-worm of the sky;
Fairer than these, though temple thou hast none,
    Nor altar heap'd with flowers;
Nor virgin-choir to make delicious moan   30
    Upon the midnight hours;
No voice, no lute, no pipe, no incense sweet
    From chain-swung censer teeming;
No shrine, no grove, no oracle, no heat
    Of pale-mouth'd prophet dreaming.[8]   35

O brightest! though too late for antique vows,
    Too, too late for the fond believing lyre,[9]

2. Allott cites Spenser's *Amoretti* 77: "Was it a dreame, or did I see it playne"; see also "Ode to a Nightingale," l. 79.
3. A purple dye once made in the Phoenician city of Tyre.
4. Wings. Lemprière notes, "Psyche is generally represented with the wings of a butterfly, to intimate the lightness of the soul."
5. Keats plays with the name of Aurora, goddess of the dawn, and with the image of the opening of the eyelids to reveal the pupils as a kind of dawn.
6. Cupid, known because part of the traditional classical pantheon of gods, while Psyche is "latest born" (l. 24) of the gods.
7. Venus, the goddess of love, as the evening star; Phœbe: also known as Diana, the goddess of chastity and the moon.
8. Describing a time after "Olympus' faded hierachy" (l. 25), Keats echoes Milton's ode "On the Morning of Christ's Nativity" with its account of the disappearance of pagan religions upon Christ's arrival on earth, esp. ll. 173–80:

> The Oracles are dumm,
> No voice or hideous humm
>   Runs through the arched roof in words deceiving.
> *Apollo* from his shrine
> Can no more divine,
>   With hollow shriek the steep of *Delphos* leaving.
> No nightly trance, or breathed spell,
> Inspires the pale-ey'd Priest from the prophetic cell.

9. Keats puns on both "fond"—caring, devoted but also foolish—and "lyre"/liar.

When holy were the haunted forest boughs,
    Holy the air, the water, and the fire;[1]
Yet even in these days so far retir'd   40
    From happy pieties, thy lucent fans,[2]
    Fluttering among the faint Olympians,
I see, and sing, by my own eyes inspired.
So let me be thy choir, and make a moan
       Upon the midnight hours;   45
Thy voice, thy lute, thy pipe, thy incense sweet
    From swinged censer teeming;
Thy shrine, thy grove, thy oracle, thy heat
    Of pale-mouth'd prophet dreaming.

Yes, I will be thy priest, and build a fane[3]   50
    In some untrodden region of my mind,
Where branched thoughts, new grown with pleasant pain,
    Instead of pines shall murmur in the wind:
Far, far around shall those dark-cluster'd trees
    Fledge the wild-ridged mountains steep by steep;   55
And there by zephyrs, streams, and birds, and bees,
    The moss-lain Dryads[4] shall be lull'd to sleep;
And in the midst of this wide quietness
A rosy sanctuary will I dress
With the wreath'd trellis of a working brain,   60
    With buds, and bells, and stars without a name,
With all the gardener Fancy e'er could feign,[5]
    Who breeding flowers, will never breed the same:
And there shall be for thee all soft delight
    That shadowy thought can win,   65
A bright torch, and a casement ope at night,
    To let the warm Love in![6]

FANCY.[1]

EVER let the Fancy roam,
Pleasure never is at home:

---

1. Keats evokes the four classical elements of earth, air, water, and fire; Allott cites Milton's "On the Morning of Christ's Nativity," ll. 184–91, and also Wordsworth's account of pagan mythology in Book 4 of *The Excursion*, esp. ll. 735–44.
2. Gleaming or translucent wings; *happy pieties* suggest the "natural piety" of Wordsworth's "My Heart Leaps Up," in lines also used as an epigraph for the "Intimations Ode" (1807).
3. Temple.
4. Tree nymphs; *zephyrs*: the west winds.
5. To fashion or invent, but also to fashion deceptively. Fancy as a gardener is a commonplace in early modern accounts of the imagination.
6. In the myth, Cupid/Love visits Psyche only in the dark. Keats's imagery recalls that of Hunt's "Hero and Leander" (1819), where Hero shows Leander the way to land with a torch and where his death becomes certain "when the casement, at the dawn of light, / Began to shew a square of ghastly white" (ll. 284–85).
1. Written at end of 1818 and copied out in a journal letter to the George Keatses on January 2, 1819 (see p. 305), along with the next poem, identifying the two pieces as "specimens of a sort of rondeau which I think I shall become partial to—because you have one idea amplified with greater ease and more delight and freedom than in the sonnet." Brown in his transcript labels the poem "Ode to Fancy." The trochaic four-stress couplets, used here and in the next three poems, owe something to Milton's "L'Allegro" and "Il Penseroso." There was a long tradition of poems on the fancy, including pieces by Thomas Carey, Mark Akenside, Joseph Warton, Bernard Barton,

At a touch sweet Pleasure melteth,
Like to bubbles when rain pelteth;
Then let winged Fancy wander   5
Through the thought still spread beyond her:
Open wide the mind's cage-door,
She'll dart forth, and cloudward soar.
O sweet Fancy! let her loose;
Summer's joys are spoilt by use,   10
And the enjoying of the Spring
Fades as does its blossoming;
Autumn's red-lipp'd fruitage too,
Blushing through the mist and dew,
Cloys with tasting: What do then?   15
Sit thee by the ingle, when
The sear faggot[2] blazes bright,
Spirit of a winter's night;
When the soundless earth is muffled,
And the caked snow is shuffled   20
From the ploughboy's heavy shoon;[3]
When the Night doth meet the Noon
In a dark conspiracy
To banish Even from her sky.
Sit thee there, and send abroad,   25
With a mind self-overaw'd,
Fancy, high-commission'd:—send her!
She has vassals to attend her:
She will bring, in spite of frost,
Beauties that the earth hath lost;   30
She will bring thee, all together,
All delights of summer weather;
All the buds and bells of May,
From dewy sward or thorny spray;[4]
All the heaped Autumn's wealth,   35
With a still, mysterious stealth:
She will mix these pleasures up
Like three fit wines in a cup,
And thou shalt quaff it:—thou shalt hear
Distant harvest-carols clear;   40
Rustle of the reaped corn;
Sweet birds antheming the morn:
And, in the same moment—hark!
'Tis the early April lark,
Or the rooks, with busy caw,   45
Foraging for sticks and straw.
Thou shalt, at one glance, behold
The daisy and the marigold;

Hemans, Hunt, Charlotte Smith, Anna Seward, and Mary Robinson. On the poem, see Jeffrey
Robinson, *Unfettering Poetry: The Fancy in British Romanticism* (New York: Palgrave Macmillan,
2006) and Neil Fraistat's essay included here (pp. 592–604). First published in 1820 with a holograph copy in the letter cited above; text from 1820.
2. A bundle of dry sticks; *ingle*: a fire burning on the hearth.
3. Shoes.
4. Brushwood; *sward*: turf.

White-plum'd lilies, and the first
Hedge-grown primrose that hath burst;   50
Shaded hyacinth, alway
Sapphire queen of the mid-May;
And every leaf, and every flower
Pearled with the self-same shower.
Thou shalt see the field-mouse peep   55
Meagre from its celled sleep;
And the snake all winter-thin
Cast on sunny bank its skin;
Freckled nest-eggs thou shalt see
Hatching in the hawthorn-tree,   60
When the hen-bird's wing doth rest
Quiet on her mossy nest;
Then the hurry and alarm
When the bee-hive casts its swarm;
Acorns ripe down-pattering,   65
While the autumn breezes sing.[5]

   Oh, sweet Fancy! let her loose;
Every thing is spoilt by use:[6]
Where's the cheek that doth not fade,
Too much gaz'd at? Where's the maid   70
Whose lip mature is ever new?
Where's the eye, however blue,
Doth not weary? Where's the face
One would meet in every place?
Where's the voice, however soft,   75
One would hear so very oft?
At a touch sweet Pleasure melteth
Like to bubbles when rain pelteth.
Let, then, winged Fancy find
Thee a mistress to thy mind: 80
Dulcet-eyed as Ceres' daughter,[7]
Ere the God of Torment taught her
How to frown and how to chide;
With a waist and with a side
White as Hebe's, when her zone[8]   85
Slipt its golden clasp, and down
Fell her kirtle[9] to her feet,
While she held the goblet sweet,
And Jove grew languid.[1]—Break the mesh

---

5. The letter version has an additional couplet: "For the same sleek throated mouse / To store up in its winter house."
6. The letter version has an additional couplet: "Every pleasure, every joy— / Not a Mistress but doth cloy."
7. For Proserpine, the daughter of Ceres and Jupiter, who was abducted by Pluto, the "God of Torment" (l.82), see p. 170, n. 2.
8. Girdle; *Hebe's*: the goddess of youth and cupbearer to the gods, until, in this version of the myth, she was accidentally exposed, and Jupiter replaced her with Ganymede.
9. Gown.
1. The letter version inserts the following lines here:

               —Mistress fair,
      Thou shalt have that tressed hair
      Adonis tangled all for spite;
      And the mouth he would not kiss,

Of the Fancy's silken leash;   90
Quickly break her prison-string
And such joys as these she'll bring.—
Let the winged Fancy roam,
Pleasure never is at home.

ODE.[1]

BARDS of Passion and of Mirth,
Ye have left your souls on earth!
Have ye souls in heaven too,
Double-lived in regions new?
Yes, and those of heaven commune   5
With the spheres of sun and moon;
With the noise of fountains wond'rous,
And the parle[2] of voices thund'rous;
With the whisper of heaven's trees
And one another, in soft ease   10
Seated on Elysian lawns
Brows'd by none but Dian's fawns;[3]
Underneath large blue-bells tented,
Where the daisies are rose-scented,
And the rose herself has got   15
Perfume which on earth is not;
Where the nightingale doth sing
Not a senseless, tranced thing,
But divine melodious truth;
Philosophic numbers smooth;[4]   20
Tales and golden histories
Of heaven and its mysteries.

Thus ye live on high, and then
On the earth ye live again;

And the treasure he would miss;
And the hand he would not press,
And the warmth he would distress,
    O the Ravishment—the Bliss!
Fancy has her there she is—
Never fulsome, ever new,
There she steps! and tell me who
Has a Mistress so divine?
Be the palate ne'er so fine
She cannot sicken.

1. Written at end of 1818 and copied out in Keats's journal letter to the George Keatses on January 2, 1819 (see p. 306), with the preceding poem (see p. 465, n. 1), where Keats describes it as treating "the double immortality of Poets." In addition to the journal letter copy, there is a holograph copy written opposite the first page of Fletcher's *The Fair Maid of the Inn. A Tragi-Comedy* in volume 4 of the 1811 *Dramatic Works of Ben Jonson, and Beaumont and Fletcher* in the Keats House Collection (LMA KB.03 JON 1811 Vol. 4/2758). Perhaps that tragicomedy had some influence on this poem about passion and mirth. The prologue to the play discusses the fate of plays (and thus playwrights), noting "A worthy story, howsoever writ . . . Meets oftentimes the sweet commendation / Of 'hang't! 'tis scurvy!' . . . Let ignorance and laughter dwell together / They are beneath the muses' pity: hither / Come nobler judgments, and to those the strain / Of our invention is not bent in vain." On the poem, see Neil Fraistat's essay, included here (pp. 592–604). First published 1820; text from 1820.
2. Speech, discussion.
3. The goddess of the hunt; *Elysian*: Elysium is the home of the virtuous in the classical underworld.
4. Allott cites Milton's *Comus*, ll. 476–78: "How charming is divine Philosophy! / Not harsh, and crabbed as dull fools suppose, / But musical as is *Apollo's* lute." *Numbers*: verses.

And the souls ye left behind you   25
Teach us, here, the way to find you,
Where your other souls are joying,
Never slumber'd, never cloying.
Here, your earth-born souls still speak
To mortals, of their little week;   30
Of their sorrows and delights;
Of their passions and their spites;
Of their glory and their shame;
What doth strengthen and what maim.
Thus ye teach us, every day,   35
Wisdom, though fled far away.

    Bards of Passion and of Mirth,
Ye have left your souls on earth!
Ye have souls in heaven too,
Double-lived in regions new!   40

LINES
ON
THE MERMAID TAVERN.[1]

SOULS of Poets dead and gone,
What Elysium[2] have ye known,
Happy field or mossy cavern,
Choicer than the Mermaid Tavern?
Have ye tippled drink more fine   5
Than mine host's Canary wine?[3]
Or are fruits of Paradise
Sweeter than those dainty pies
Of venison? O generous food!
Drest as though bold Robin Hood   10
Would, with his maid Marian,
Sup and bowse[4] from horn and can.

    I have heard that on a day
Mine host's sign-board flew away,
Nobody knew whither, till   15
An astrologer's old quill
To a sheepskin gave the story,
Said he saw you in your glory,
Underneath a new old-sign[5]

---

1. Written at beginning of February 1818 and copied in a letter to Reynolds on February 3 (p. 122) as part of Keats's response to Reynolds's poems on Robin Hood (see the next poem). The Mermaid Tavern, Cheapside, was reputed to be a gathering place for Elizabethan dramatists such as Beaumont and Fletcher; see Beaumont's "Letter to Ben Jonson." There are two holograph copies, an early fair copy at Harvard (MS Keats 2.16) and a revised version (labeled "Ode. 1818") in George Keats's notebook at the British Library (Egerton 2780, ff. 29, 30; *MYR: JK,* 5: 115, 117). First published in 1820; text from 1820.
2. See p. 60, n. 8.
3. A sweet white wine from the Canary Islands.
4. Sip and booze.
5. Stillinger eliminates the hyphen, following the Harvard MS; Gillham suggests that the "sign of the Mermaid, one of the constellations in the Zodiac, is as old as the heavens themselves, though now it has been renewed in being replaced by the sign-board from the tavern."

Sipping beverage divine,   20
And pledging with contented smack
The Mermaid in the Zodiac.

Souls of Poets dead and gone,
What Elysium have ye known,
Happy field or mossy cavern,   25
Choicer than the Mermaid Tavern?

ROBIN HOOD.[1]

TO A FRIEND.

No! those days are gone away,
And their hours are old and gray,
And their minutes buried all
Under the down-trodden pall
Of the leaves of many years: 5
Many times have winter's shears,
Frozen North, and chilling East,
Sounded tempests to the feast
Of the forest's whispering fleeces,
Since men knew nor rent nor leases.   10

No, the bugle sounds no more,
And the twanging bow no more;
Silent is the ivory[2] shrill
Past the heath and up the hill;
There is no mid-forest laugh,   15
Where lone Echo gives the half
To some wight,[3] amaz'd to hear
Jesting, deep in forest drear.

On the fairest time of June
You may go, with sun or moon,   20
Or the seven stars to light you,
Or the polar ray to right you;
But you never may behold

---

1. Written at beginning of February 1818 and copied into a letter to Reynolds of February 3 (see p. 122) as "To J. H. R. In answer to his Robin Hood Sonnets," which Reynolds had sent to Keats. Reynolds's poems, "The trees in Sherwood forest are old and good" and "With coat of Lincoln green and mantle too," were later printed in John Hunt's *Yellow Dwarf*, February 21, 1818, p. 64 and then in Reynolds's *The Garden of Florence* (1821), pp. 124–27. Robin Hood, known for his defiance of Norman rule, became an often-invoked figure by liberals of the period. This interest was spurred in part by Joseph Ritson's *Robin Hood: A Collection of All the Ancient Poems, Songs and Ballads* (1795). Hunt wrote a series of "Songs of Robin Hood," published in the *Indicator*, November 15, 22, 1820, pp. 41–47, 52–54; John Taylor wrote three poems on Sherwood Forest; and Thomas Love Peacock wrote a romance, *Maid Marian* (1822). See John Barnard, "Keats's 'Robin Hood,' John Hamilton Reynolds, and the 'Old Poets,'" *Proceedings of the British Academy* 75 (1989), pp. 181–200; Thomas Mitchell, "Keats's 'Outlawry' in 'Robin Hood,'" *SEL* 34 (1994): 753–69; and Neil Fraistat's essay included here (pp. 592–604). There are no extant holographs. First published 1820; text from 1820.
2. Presumably a hunting horn.
3. Archaic word for a living being.

Little John, or Robin bold;
Never one, of all the clan,   25
Thrumming on an empty can
Some old hunting ditty, while
He doth his green way beguile
To fair hostess Merriment,
Down beside the pasture Trent;[4]   30
For he left the merry tale
Messenger for spicy ale.

  Gone, the merry morris din;[5]
Gone, the song of Gamelyn;[6]
Gone, the tough-belted outlaw   35
Idling in the "grenè shawe";[7]
All are gone away and past!
And if Robin should be cast
Sudden from his turfed grave,
And if Marian should have   40
Once again her forest days,
She would weep, and he would craze:
He would swear, for all his oaks,
Fall'n beneath the dockyard strokes,
Have rotted on the briny seas;   45
She would weep that her wild bees
Sang not to her—strange! that honey
Can't be got without hard money!

  So it is: yet let us sing,
Honour to the old bow-string!   50
Honour to the bugle-horn!
Honour to the woods unshorn!
Honour to the Lincoln green![8]
Honour to the archer keen!
Honour to tight[9] little John,   55
And the horse he rode upon!
Honour to bold Robin Hood,
Sleeping in the underwood!
Honour to maid Marian,
And to all the Sherwood-clan!   60
Though their days have hurried by
Let us two a burden try.

---

4. A river near Sherwood Forest; *pasture Trent*: either "the pastoral Trent" or "pasture along the Trent."
5. The music that accompanies a morris dance, a "lively traditional English dance performed in formation by a group of dancers in a distinctive costume (usually wearing bells and ribbons and carrying handkerchiefs or sticks, to emphasize the rhythm and movement), often accompanied by a character who generally represents a symbolic or legendary figure (as the Fool, Hobby Horse, Maid Marian, etc.)" (*OED*).
6. The "Tale of Gamelyn" (c. 1350) is a metrical romance about a band of forest outlaws.
7. Quoted from Chaucer's "Friar's Tale," l. 86, "Wher rydestow, under this grene-wode shawe"; it means "green wood."
8. A middle-grade cloth, manufactured in Lincoln and dyed green; it was known as the uniform of Robin Hood's band.
9. Capable, skillful, stout.

TO AUTUMN.

Keats wrote "To Autumn" on September 19, 1819, in Winchester (after a short trip to and from London). He describes the occasion in his letter to Reynolds of September 21 (p. 359); he copied the poem into a letter to Woodhouse of September 21, 22 (*L*, 2: 170–71). The ode is often read as the most perfect of Keats's poems. Vendler, *The Odes of John Keats*, p. 234, suggests that the poem draws upon Shakespeare's sonnets "That time of year thou mayst in me behold" (73) and "How like a winter hath my absence been" (97), Spenser's Mutability Cantos, Wordsworth's "Intimations Ode," and Coleridge's "Frost at Midnight." Jack, pp. 232–43, suggests various visual representations that might have influenced Keats's imagery, particularly in the second stanza. Keats himself, in the letter to Reynolds, links the poem to Chatterton. He also owes something to Hunt's description of September in his "Calendar of Nature" from the September 5, 1819, *Examiner*, and the poem is written in the shadow of the events known as the Peterloo Massacre of August 16.

Beyond the pieces listed in the headnote to the volume, there is an interesting line of critical debate around the poem that includes Geoffrey Hartman, "Poem and Ideology: A Study of Keats's 'To Autumn,'" *The Fate of Reading* (Chicago: University of Chicago Press, 1975), pp. 57–73; Paul Frye, "History, Existence and 'To Autumn,'" *Studies in Romanticism* 25 (1986): 211–19; McGann, *Beauties of Inflection*, pp. 57–62; and Roe, pp. 230–67. For a recent reading of the poem in relation to issues of colonialism, medicine, and disease, see the essay by Alan Bewell here (pp. 634–42).

The text is from 1820. There are two holographs, a draft (Harvard MS Keats 2.27; *JKPMH*, pp. 223–25) and the version in the letter to Woodhouse (Harvard MS Keats 1.64).

1.

SEASON of mists and mellow fruitfulness,
    Close bosom-friend of the maturing sun;
Conspiring with him how to load and bless
    With fruit the vines that round the thatch-eves run;
To bend with apples the moss'd cottage-trees,   5
    And fill all fruit with ripeness to the core;
        To swell the gourd, and plump the hazel shells
With a sweet kernel; to set budding more,
    And still more, later flowers for the bees,
    Until they think warm days will never cease,   10
        For Summer has o'er-brimm'd their clammy[1] cells.

2.

Who hath not seen thee oft amid thy store?
    Sometimes whoever seeks abroad may find
Thee sitting careless on a granary floor,
    Thy hair soft-lifted by the winnowing wind;   15

---

1. "Soft, moist, and sticky" (*OED*).

Or on a half-reap'd furrow sound asleep,
    Drows'd with the fume of poppies, while thy hook[2]
    Spares the next swath and all its twined flowers:
And sometimes like a gleaner[3] thou dost keep
    Steady thy laden head across a brook;   20
    Or by a cyder-press, with patient look,
    Thou watchest the last oozings hours by hours.

3.

Where are the songs of Spring? Ay, where are they?
    Think not of them, thou hast thy music too,—
    While barred clouds bloom the soft-dying day,   25
    And touch the stubble-plains with rosy hue;
Then in a wailful choir the small gnats mourn
    Among the river sallows,[4] borne aloft
    Or sinking as the light wind lives or dies;
And full-grown lambs loud bleat from hilly bourn;[5]   30
    Hedge-crickets sing; and now with treble soft
    The red-breast whistles from a garden-croft;
    And gathering swallows twitter in the skies.

ODE ON MELANCHOLY.

Keats wrote this ode in 1819, and critics have tended to think of it as written in May after "Ode on a Grecian Urn." Keats could have drawn on a long
tradition of poems on melancholy, including Elizabeth Carter's "Ode to
Melancholy" (1739), Thomas Warton's *Pleasures of Melancholy* (1747),
James Beattie's *The Triumph of Melancholy* (1760), and Byron's friend Robert Charles Dallas's "The Cavern of Melancholy: An Ode" (1813). The
dropped stanza, below, suggests a satiric stance toward this tradition. For
criticism on the poem, see the headnote to the volume.
    The text is from 1820. There is a holograph draft of the poem (stanzas 1
and 2 are in the Robert H. Taylor Collection, Manuscripts Division, Department of Rare Books and Special Collections, Princeton University Library
[RTCOL 10/#19] and stanza 3 is cased in the Berg Collection of English
and American Literature, The New York Public Library, Astor, Lenox and
Tilden Foundations: John Keats Collection of Papers, 1816–1948 Bulk
[1816–1924]). Brown's transcript (Harvard MS Keats 3.6, p. 7) has the following deleted stanza (first published in 1848 1: 287):

Tho' you should build a bark of dead men's bones,
    And rear a phantom gibbet for a mast,
Stitch creeds [shrouds interlined above] together for a sail, with groans
    To fill it out, bloodstained and aghast;
Altho' your rudder be a Dragon's tail,

---

2. An agricultural tool with a curved blade and an inner cutting edge.
3. Someone who picks up grain or ears of corn or other produce left by reapers.
4. Low-growing willows.
5. Hills define the horizon.

Long sever'd, yet still hard with agony,
    Your cordage large uprootings from the skull
Of bald Medusa; certes you would fail
    To find the Melancholy, whether she
        Dreameth in any isle of Lethe dull.

1.

No, no, go not to Lethe, neither twist
    Wolf 's-bane, tight-rooted, for its poisonous wine;
Nor suffer thy pale forehead to be kiss'd
    By nightshade, ruby grape of Proserpine;[1]
Make not your rosary of yew-berries,   5
    Nor let the beetle, nor the death-moth be
        Your mournful Psyche,[2] nor the downy owl
A partner in your sorrow's mysteries;
    For shade to shade will come too drowsily,
        And drown the wakeful anguish of the soul.   10

2.

But when the melancholy fit shall fall
    Sudden from heaven like a weeping cloud,
That fosters the droop-headed flowers all,
    And hides the green hill in an April shroud;
Then glut thy sorrow on a morning rose,   15
    Or on the rainbow of the salt sand-wave,
        Or on the wealth of globed peonies;
Or if thy mistress some rich anger shows,
    Emprison her soft hand, and let her rave,
        And feed deep, deep upon her peerless eyes.   20

3.

She dwells with Beauty—Beauty that must die;
    And Joy, whose hand is ever at his lips
Bidding adieu; and aching Pleasure nigh,
    Turning to poison while the bee-mouth sips:
Ay, in the very temple of Delight   25
    Veil'd Melancholy has her sovran shrine,
        Though seen of none save him whose strenuous tongue
Can burst Joy's grape against his palate fine;
    His soul shall taste the sadness of her might,
        And be among her cloudy trophies hung.[3]   30

---

1. For Proserpine's abduction to the underworld, see p. 170, n. 2. *Lethe*: see p. 4, n. 3; *Wolf 's-bane*: also known as aconite, a yellow-flowered plant found in Europe's mountainous regions; its root is poisonous as are the nightshade's purple berries and the yew-berries of the next line, with yew trees often being planted in graveyards.
2. See "Ode to Psyche" (p. 463–65). Psyche, the soul, is often represented by a butterfly, so the death's-head moth, with markings representing a human skull, would invert the traditional image.
3. Emblems of victory were hung in Greek and Roman temples, as Keats could have read in John Potter's *Archaeologia Graeca: Or the Antiquities of Greece* (1697; new ed. 1795). See also Shakespeare, Sonnet 31, ll. 9–10: "Thou art the grave where buried love doth live, / Hung with the trophies of my lovers gone."

HYPERION.
A FRAGMENT.

Keats began work on *Hyperion* by October 27, 1818, when he mentions the poem in a letter to Woodhouse (see p. 295); he had given up work on this version by April 20, 1819, when Woodhouse copied it. Reynolds (*KC*, 2: 234) later indicated that Keats intended to publish the poem with pieces by Hunt, presumably his "Hero and Leander" and "Bacchus and Ariadne," but many commentators have seen the poem striving to move away from a Huntian manner. In a letter to Haydon of January 23, 1818, where Keats suggests that the painter do a frontispiece of his work in progress, he notes that where "in Endymion I think you may have many bits of the deep and sentimental cast—the nature of *Hyperion* will lead me to treat it in a more naked and grecian Manner" (*L*, 1: 207). The return to a more "Cockney" style in the unfinished third book has been seen as one reason why Keats may have abandoned the poem, though one might also read the third book as a turn from a Miltonic to a modern style. Woodhouse noted in his interleaved copy of *Endymion*, opposite 4.774 (780 in original; *MYR: JK*, 3: 399), that "the Fragment here alluded to . . . contains 2 books & ½. . . . He said he was dissatisfied with what he had done of it; and should not complete it." Keats would write often in the spring of 1819 of his inability to make progress on the poem. He would try to rework the poem as *The Fall of Hyperion* in August and September of 1819 (see p. 354). When he finally gave up the project, he wrote to Reynolds that "there were too many Miltonic inversions in it—Miltonic verse cannot be written but in an artful or rather artist's humour. I wish to give myself up to other sensations" (p. 359).

The poem takes up the fall of the pre-Olympian Titans. Keats begins his story late in the mythic account. The Titans, the offspring of Heaven (Coelus) and Earth (Tellus), led by Saturn, often seen as the ruler of a golden age, have been overturned by the next generation, the Olympian gods, with Jupiter as their king. We learn that Jupiter has displaced his father Saturn, and Neptune has overturned Oceanus, but Hyperion, Saturn's brother and the sun god, still rules, as his successor, Apollo, wanders the world in Book 3, where a meeting with Titan Mnemosyne "makes a God of me" (3.113). Keats contrasted his new hero to Endymion in the letter to Haydon, cited above, "the Hero of the written tale being mortal is led on, like Buonaparte, by circumstance; whereas the Apollo in Hyperion being a fore-seeing God will shape his actions like one." We meet the fallen Saturn in Book 1, where he is tended by Hyperion's wife, Thea, who leads him to meet others of the fallen Titans; they gather in Book 2 (in an imitation of the congress of fallen angels in Milton's *Paradise Lost*), where different perspectives on the struggle between the generations are offered by Oceanus, Clymene, and Enceladus, the mightiest of the Titans who was eventually imprisoned under Mount Ætna by Jupiter. We learn of Hyperion's troubled but continuing reign at the end of Book 1, and he appears before his fellow Titans at the end of Book 2 before Book 3 turns to Apollo and then breaks off. In a note to his annotated *Endymion* (*MYR: JK*, 3: 426), Woodhouse writes, "The poem, if completed would have treated of the dethronement of Hyperion, the former God of the Sun, by Apollo—and incidentally of those of Oceanus by Neptune, of Saturn by Jupiter &c and of the war of the Giants for Saturn's reestablishment—with other events, of which we have but very dark hints in the Mythological poets of Greece & Rome. In fact, the incidents would have been pure creations of the Poet's brain."

Keats would have gleaned such "dark hints" from his usual mythological sources such as Lemprière as well as from Hesiod's *Theogony* (he could have seen Cooke's 1728 translation in Chalmer's 1810 *English Poets*) and Hyginus's *Fabulae* in the 1742 *Auctores Mythographi Latini* which he acquired in 1819. The style of the poem is influenced by his study of Milton (see Lau, *Keats's* Paradise Lost) and by Cary's translation of Dante.

The poem has been praised since it first appeared, with Hunt, Shelley, and Byron all singling it out in their comments on Keats's poetry. The poem is addressed in most modern treatments of Keats as well as in Geoffrey Hartman's "Spectral Symbolism and the Authorial Self: An Approach to *Hyperion*," *The Fate of Reading* (Chicago: University of Chicago Press, 1974), pp. 124–46, and essays by Terence Hoagwood, Michael O'Neill, and Vincent Newey in Roe (ed.), *Keats and History*, pp. 127–93. For a reading of the poem in the context of Keats's development as a poet in relation to his audience, see Andrew Bennet's essay included in this Norton Critical Edition (pp. 643–52).

Hyperion was published as a fragment in 1820, perhaps over Keats's objections. There is a Keats holograph, mostly at the British Museum (Add. MS. 37000, *MYR: JK*, 5: 3–55), with ll. 116–27 at the Morgan Library (MA 925). Woodhouse's transcript, mentioned above (W², f. 79r–109r; *MYR: JK*, 6: 135–95), was made from this holograph, as indicated in Woodhouse's note: "Copied 20 Ap¹ 1819 from J. K.'s Manuscript written in 1818/19" and then, "The Copy from which I took the above was the original & only copy—The alterations are noted in the margin—With the exception of these, it was composed & written down as once it now stands." Woodhouse's second copy, W¹, was printer's copy for the 1820 volume. The text is from 1820.

BOOK I.

DEEP in the shady sadness of a vale
Far sunken from the healthy breath of morn,
Far from the fiery noon, and eve's one star,
Sat gray-hair'd Saturn, quiet as a stone,
Still as the silence round about his lair;   5
Forest on forest hung about his head
Like cloud on cloud.¹ No stir of air was there,
Not so much life as on a summer's day

---

1. Bailey uses ll. 1–7 to demonstrate Keats's "principle of melody in Verse . . . particularly in the management of open & close vowels. . . . Keats's theory was, that the vowels should be so managed as not to clash one with another so as to mar the melody,—& yet that they should be interchanged, like differing notes of music to prevent monotony" (*KC*, 2: 277). *Vale*: valley, see Keats's marginal note on the word in *Paradise Lost* 1.321, "To slumber here, as in the Vales of Heaven" (see Lau, *Keats's Paradise Lost*, p. 77): "There is a cool pleasure in the very sound of vale. The English word is of the happiest chance. Milton has put vales in heaven and hell with the . . . affection and yearning of a great Poet." Many editors adopt "above" from Keats's draft for "about" in l. 6.

Robs not one light seed from the feather'd grass,
But where the dead leaf fell, there did it rest.   10
A stream went voiceless by, still deadened more
By reason of his fallen divinity
Spreading a shade: the Naiad[2] 'mid her reeds
Press'd her cold finger closer to her lips.

   Along the margin-sand large foot-marks went,   15
No further than to where his feet had stray'd,
And slept there since. Upon the sodden ground
His old right hand lay nerveless, listless, dead,
Unsceptred; and his realmless eyes were closed;
While his bow'd head seem'd list'ning to the Earth,   20
His ancient mother, for some comfort yet.

   It seem'd no force could wake him from his place;
But there came one, who with a kindred hand
Touch'd his wide shoulders, after bending low
With reverence, though to one who knew it not.   25
She was a Goddess of the infant world;
By her in stature the tall Amazon
Had stood a pigmy's height: she would have ta'en
Achilles by the hair and bent his neck;
Or with a finger stay'd Ixion's wheel.   30
Her face was large as that of Memphian sphinx,
Pedestal'd haply in a palace court,
When sages look'd to Egypt for their lore.[3]
But oh! how unlike marble was that face:
How beautiful, if sorrow had not made   35
Sorrow more beautiful than Beauty's self.
There was a listening fear in her regard,
As if calamity had but begun;
As if the vanward clouds of evil days
Had spent their malice, and the sullen rear   40
Was with its stored thunder labouring up.
One hand she press'd upon that aching spot
Where beats the human heart, as if just there,
Though an immortal, she felt cruel pain:
The other upon Saturn's bended neck   45
She laid, and to the level of his ear
Leaning with parted lips, some words she spake
In solemn tenour and deep organ tone:
Some mourning words, which in our feeble tongue
Would come in these like accents; O how frail   50

2. See p. 41, n. 6.
3. Following Napoleon's 1798 expedition into Egypt, there was great interest in Egyptian artifacts;
   Keats saw some recently acquired pieces, including a sphinx "of a giant size, and most voluptuous
   Egyptian expression" at the British Museum in early 1819 (see p. 315). *Amazon*: see p. 255, n. 2.
   Achilles: the greatest of Greek warriors who died in the Trojan war; in other versions of his story,
   he either kills or is killed by Penthesilea, the queen of the Amazons who fought on the Trojan side
   in the war. *Ixion's*: a mortal invited by Jupiter to the table of the gods, Ixion sought to seduce Juno,
   for which he was banished to Hades and tied to a perpetually revolving wheel. *Memphian*: Memphis, ancient Egypt's second great city, was home to the colossal statue of the Sphinx, half woman,
   half lion.

To that large utterance of the early Gods!
"Saturn, look up!—though wherefore, poor old King?
"I have no comfort for thee, no not one:
"I cannot say, 'O wherefore sleepest thou?'
"For heaven is parted from thee, and the earth   55
"Knows thee not, thus afflicted, for a God;
"And ocean too, with all its solemn noise,
"Has from thy sceptre pass'd; and all the air
"Is emptied of thine hoary majesty.
"Thy thunder, conscious of the new command,   60
"Rumbles reluctant o'er our fallen house;
"And thy sharp lightning in unpractised hands
"Scorches and burns our once serene domain.[4]
"O aching time! O moments big as years!
"All as ye pass swell out the monstrous truth,   65
"And press it so upon our weary griefs
"That unbelief has not a space to breathe.
"Saturn, sleep on:—O thoughtless, why did I
"Thus violate thy slumbrous solitude?
"Why should I ope thy melancholy eyes?   70
"Saturn, sleep on! while at thy feet I weep."

　　As when, upon a tranced summer-night,
Those green-rob'd senators of mighty woods,
Tall oaks, branch-charmed by the earnest stars,
Dream, and so dream all night without a stir,   75
Save from one gradual solitary gust
Which comes upon the silence, and dies off,
As if the ebbing air had but one wave;
So came these words and went; the while in tears
She touch'd her fair large forehead to the ground,   80
Just where her falling hair might be outspread
A soft and silken mat for Saturn's feet.
One moon, with alteration slow, had shed
Her silver seasons four upon the night,
And still these two were postured motionless,   85
Like natural sculpture in cathedral cavern;
The frozen God still couchant[5] on the earth,
And the sad Goddess weeping at his feet:
Until at length old Saturn lifted up
His faded eyes, and saw his kingdom gone,   90
And all the gloom and sorrow of the place,
And that fair kneeling Goddess; and then spake,
As with a palsied tongue, and while his beard
Shook horrid with such aspen-malady:[6]
"O tender spouse of gold Hyperion,   95
"Thea, I feel thee ere I see thy face;

---

4. Jupiter, "unpractised" since newly in power, now commands thunder and lightning. Keats in his
    marginal note to Milton's use of "reluctant" in *Paradise Lost*, 6.58 (Lau, *Keats's Paradise Lost*,
    p. 132) praises the "powerful effect" of weaving together the "original and modern meaning" of the
    word, which can mean "struggling," "offering resistance" as well as "unwilling."
5. A heraldic term for lying down; see Keats's praise of Milton's "*stationing* or *statuary*" in his note to
    Paradise Lost 7.422–23 (Lau, *Keats's Paradise Lost*, pp. 142–43).
6. Aspen leaves shake with the slightest breeze.

"Look up, and let me see our doom in it;
"Look up, and tell me if this feeble shape
"Is Saturn's; tell me, if thou hear'st the voice
"Of Saturn; tell me, if this wrinkling brow,   100
"Naked and bare of its great diadem,
"Peers like the front of Saturn. Who had power
"To make me desolate? whence came the strength?
"How was it nurtur'd to such bursting forth,
"While Fate seem'd strangled in my nervous[7] grasp?   105
"But it is so; and I am smother'd up,
"And buried from all godlike exercise
"Of influence benign on planets pale,
"Of admonitions to the winds and seas,
"Of peaceful sway above man's harvesting,   110
"And all those acts which Deity supreme
"Doth ease its heart of love in.—I am gone
"Away from my own bosom: I have left
"My strong identity, my real self,
"Somewhere between the throne, and where I sit   115
"Here on this spot of earth. Search, Thea, search!
"Open thine eyes eterne, and sphere them round
"Upon all space: space starr'd, and lorn of light;
"Space region'd with life-air; and barren void;
"Spaces of fire, and all the yawn of hell.—   120
"Search, Thea, search! and tell me, if thou seest
"A certain shape or shadow, making way
"With wings or chariot fierce to repossess
"A heaven he lost erewhile: it must—it must
"Be of ripe progress—Saturn must be King.   125
"Yes, there must be a golden victory;
"There must be Gods thrown down, and trumpets blown
"Of triumph calm, and hymns of festival
"Upon the gold clouds metropolitan,
"Voices of soft proclaim, and silver stir   130
"Of strings in hollow shells; and there shall be
"Beautiful things made new, for the surprise
"Of the sky-children; I will give command:
"Thea! Thea! Thea! where is Saturn?"

This passion lifted him upon his feet,   135
And made his hands to struggle in the air,
His Druid[8] locks to shake and ooze with sweat,
His eyes to fever out, his voice to cease.
He stood, and heard not Thea's sobbing deep;
A little time, and then again he snatch'd   140
Utterance thus.—"But cannot I create?
"Cannot I form? Cannot I fashion forth
"Another world, another universe,
"To overbear and crumble this to nought?
"Where is another chaos? Where?"—That word   145
Found way unto Olympus, and made quake

7. Carries the sense of "muscular," "vigorous."
8. See p. 41, n. 8.

The rebel three.[9]—Thea was startled up,
And in her bearing was a sort of hope,
As thus she quick-voic'd spake, yet full of awe.

"This cheers our fallen house: come to our friends,   150
"O Saturn! come away, and give them heart;
"I know the covert, for thence came I hither."
Thus brief; then with beseeching eyes she went
With backward footing through the shade a space:
He follow'd, and she turn'd to lead the way   155
Through aged boughs, that yielded like the mist
Which eagles cleave upmounting from their nest.

Meanwhile in other realms big tears were shed,
More sorrow like to this, and such like woe,
Too huge for mortal tongue or pen of scribe: 160
The Titans fierce, self-hid, or prison-bound,
Groan'd for the old allegiance once more,
And listen'd in sharp pain for Saturn's voice.
But one of the whole mammoth-brood still kept
His sov'reignty, and rule, and majesty;—   165
Blazing Hyperion on his orbed fire
Still sat, still snuff'd the incense, teeming up
From man to the sun's God; yet unsecure:
For as among us mortals omens drear
Fright and perplex, so also shuddered he—   170
Not at dog's howl, or gloom-bird's hated screech,[1]
Or the familiar visiting of one
Upon the first toll of his passing-bell,
Or prophesyings of the midnight lamp;
But horrors, portion'd to a giant nerve,   175
Oft made Hyperion ache. His palace bright
Bastion'd with pyramids of glowing gold,
And touch'd with shade of bronzed obelisks,
Glar'd a blood-red through all its thousand courts,
Arches, and domes, and fiery galleries;   180
And all its curtains of Aurorian clouds
Flush'd angerly:[2] while sometimes eagle's wings,
Unseen before by Gods or wondering men,
Darken'd the place; and neighing steeds were heard,
Not heard before by Gods or wondering men.   185
Also, when he would taste the spicy wreaths
Of incense, breath'd aloft from sacred hills,
Instead of sweets, his ample palate took
Savour of poisonous brass and metal sick:
And so, when harbour'd in the sleepy west,   190

9. Saturn's sons: Jupiter, ruler of the heavens, Neptune, god of the sea, and Pluto, lord of the underworld.
1. The hooting of the owl, often thought to presage death. In the following lines, friends and relatives
("familiar" can stand for "familial") visit someone for whom the "passing-bell" has been rung to call
for prayers as the person is dying.
2. Hyperion's palace, which includes orientalist, perhaps particularly Egyptian (see p. 477, n. 3),
motifs owes something to Mulciber's palace in Milton's *Paradise Lost* 1.702–30 as well as to eastern palaces in Southey's *Thalaba the Destroyer* (1801) and Beckford's *Vathek* (1786). *Aurorian*:
from Aurora, goddess of the dawn, thus here "rose-colored" like the dawn.

After the full completion of fair day,—
For rest divine upon exalted couch
And slumber in the arms of melody,
He pac'd away the pleasant hours of ease
With stride colossal, on from hall to hall;   195
While far within each aisle and deep recess,
His winged minions in close clusters stood,
Amaz'd and full of fear; like anxious men
Who on wide plains gather in panting troops,
When earthquakes jar their battlements and towers.   200
Even now, while Saturn, rous'd from icy trance,
Went step for step with Thea through the woods,
Hyperion, leaving twilight in the rear,
Came slope upon the threshold of the west;
Then, as was wont, his palace-door flew ope   205
In smoothest silence, save what solemn tubes,
Blown by the serious Zephyrs, gave of sweet
And wandering sounds, slow-breathed melodies;[3]
And like a rose in vermeil tint and shape,
In fragrance soft, and coolness to the eye,   210
That inlet to severe magnificence
Stood full blown, for the God to enter in.

　　He enter'd, but he enter'd full of wrath;
His flaming robes stream'd out beyond his heels,
And gave a roar, as if of earthly fire,   215
That scar'd away the meek ethereal Hours[4]
And made their dove-wings tremble. On he flared,
From stately nave to nave, from vault to vault,
Through bowers of fragrant and enwreathed light,
And diamond-paved lustrous long arcades,   220
Until he reach'd the great main cupola;
There standing fierce beneath, he stampt his foot,
And from the basements deep to the high towers
Jarr'd his own golden region; and before
The quavering thunder thereupon had ceas'd,   225
His voice leapt out, despite of godlike curb,
To this result: "O dreams of day and night!
"O monstrous forms! O effigies of pain!
"O spectres busy in a cold, cold gloom!
"O lank-eared Phantoms of black-weeded pools!   230
"Why do I know ye? why have I seen ye? why
"Is my eternal essence thus distraught
"To see and to behold these horrors new?
"Saturn is fallen, am I too to fall?
"Am I to leave this haven of my rest,   235
"This cradle of my glory, this soft clime,
"This calm luxuriance of blissful light,
"These crystalline pavilions, and pure fanes,[5]

---

3. The Zephyrs, or west winds, create music when they blow across the tubes. Allott suggests a rec-
　　ollection of the sounds uttered by the statue of Memnon when struck by the sun.
4. The Horae, goddesses of the seasons and attendants on the sun.
5. Temples.

"Of all my lucent empire? It is left
"Deserted, void, nor any haunt of mine.   240
"The blaze, the splendor, and the symmetry,
"I cannot see—but darkness, death and darkness.
"Even here, into my centre of repose,
"The shady visions come to domineer,
"Insult, and blind, and stifle up my pomp.—   245
"Fall!—No, by Tellus and her briny robes![6]
"Over the fiery frontier of my realms
"I will advance a terrible right arm
"Shall scare that infant thunderer, rebel Jove,
"And bid old Saturn take his throne again."—   250
He spake, and ceas'd, the while a heavier threat
Held struggle with his throat but came not forth;
For as in theatres of crowded men
Hubbub increases more they call out "Hush!"[7]
So at Hyperion's words the Phantoms pale   255
Bestirr'd themselves, thrice horrible and cold;
And from the mirror'd level where he stood
A mist arose, as from a scummy marsh.
At this, through all his bulk an agony
Crept gradual, from the feet unto the crown,   260
Like a lithe serpent vast and muscular
Making slow way, with head and neck convuls'd
From over-strained might. Releas'd, he fled
To the eastern gates, and full six dewy hours
Before the dawn in season due should blush,   265
He breath'd fierce breath against the sleepy portals,
Clear'd them of heavy vapours, burst them wide
Suddenly on the ocean's chilly streams.
The planet orb of fire, whereon he rode
Each day from east to west the heavens through,   270
Spun round in sable curtaining of clouds;
Not therefore veiled quite, blindfold, and hid,
But ever and anon the glancing spheres,
Circles, and arcs, and broad-belting colure,[8]
Glow'd through, and wrought upon the muffling dark   275
Sweet-shaped lightnings from the nadir deep
Up to the zenith,—hieroglyphics old,
Which sages and keen-eyed astrologers
Then living on the earth, with labouring thought
Won from the gaze of many centuries: 280
Now lost, save what we find on remnants huge
Of stone, or marble swart; their import gone,
Their wisdom long since fled.—Two wings this orb
Possess'd for glory, two fair argent[9] wings,
Ever exalted at the God's approach: 285

6. Tellus is the earth, mother of Hyperion and the other Titans, here clothed in the seas.
7. Allott suggests an echo of the satiric *Rejected Addresses* (1812) by Keats's friend Horace Smith and his brother James, "The Theatre," ll. 50–51: "He who, in quest of quiet, 'Silence!' hoots, / Is apt to make the hubbub he imputes."
8. An astronomical term: "Each of two great circles which intersect each other at right angles at the poles, and divide the equinoctial and the ecliptic into four equal parts" (*OED*).
9. Silvery.

And now, from forth the gloom their plumes immense
Rose, one by one, till all outspreaded were;
While still the dazzling globe maintain'd eclipse,
Awaiting for Hyperion's command.
Fain would he have commanded, fain took throne   290
And bid the day begin, if but for change.
He might not:—No, though a primeval God:
The sacred seasons might not be disturb'd.
Therefore the operations of the dawn
Stay'd in their birth, even as here 'tis told.   295
Those silver wings expanded sisterly,
Eager to sail their orb; the porches wide
Open'd upon the dusk demesnes[1] of night;
And the bright Titan, phrenzied with new woes,
Unus'd to bend, by hard compulsion bent   300
His spirit to the sorrow of the time;
And all along a dismal rack of clouds,
Upon the boundaries of day and night,
He stretch'd himself in grief and radiance faint.
There as he lay, the Heaven with its stars   305
Look'd down on him with pity, and the voice
Of Cœlus,[2] from the universal space,
Thus whisper'd low and solemn in his ear.
"O brightest of my children dear, earth-born
"And sky-engendered, Son of Mysteries   310
"All unrevealed even to the powers
"Which met at thy creating; at whose joys
"And palpitations sweet, and pleasures soft,
"I, Cœlus, wonder, how they came and whence;
"And at the fruits thereof what shapes they be,   315
"Distinct, and visible; symbols divine,
"Manifestations of that beauteous life
"Diffus'd unseen throughout eternal space:[3]
"Of these new-form'd art thou, oh brightest child!
"Of these, thy brethren and the Goddesses!   320
"There is sad feud among ye, and rebellion
"Of son against his sire. I saw him fall,
"I saw my first-born tumbled from his throne!
"To me his arms were spread, to me his voice
"Found way from forth the thunders round his head!   325
"Pale wox[4] I, and in vapours hid my face.
"Art thou, too, near such doom? vague fear there is:
"For I have seen my sons most unlike Gods.
"Divine ye were created, and divine
"In sad demeanour, solemn, undisturb'd,   330
"Unruffled, like high Gods, ye liv'd and ruled:

1. Domains.
2. The ancient god of the heavens, the father of Hyperion and the other Titans; with Tellus, the "powers" in l. 311. Keats does not draw upon the myth of Saturn's murder and dismemberment of Cœlus.
3. Allott points to Wordsworth's evocation of a Christian "Principle" that "subsists / In all things" (from *The Excursion*, 9.1–9) but also to pagan conceptions of a universal principle revealed, for example, in the worship of Ceres.
4. Archaic past tense of "wax," "grew."

"Now I behold in you fear, hope, and wrath;
"Actions of rage and passion; even as
"I see them, on the mortal world beneath,
"In men who die.—This is the grief, O Son!   335
"Sad sign of ruin, sudden dismay, and fall!
"Yet do thou strive; as thou art capable,
"As thou canst move about, an evident God;
"And canst oppose to each malignant hour
"Ethereal presence:—I am but a voice;   340
"My life is but the life of winds and tides,
"No more than winds and tides can I avail:—
"But thou canst.—Be thou therefore in the van
"Of circumstance; yea, seize the arrow's barb
"Before the tense string murmur.—To the earth!   345
"For there thou wilt find Saturn, and his woes.
"Meantime I will keep watch on thy bright sun,
"And of thy seasons be a careful nurse."—
Ere half this region-whisper[5] had come down,
Hyperion arose, and on the stars   350
Lifted his curved lids, and kept them wide
Until it ceas'd; and still he kept them wide:
And still they were the same bright, patient stars.
Then with a slow incline of his broad breast,
Like to a diver in the pearly seas,   355
Forward he stoop'd over the airy shore,
And plung'd all noiseless into the deep night.

BOOK II.

Just at the self-same beat of Time's wide wings
Hyperion slid into the rustled air,
And Saturn gain'd with Thea that sad place
Where Cybele[1] and the bruised Titans mourn'd.
It was a den where no insulting light   5
Could glimmer on their tears; where their own groans
They felt, but heard not, for the solid roar
Of thunderous waterfalls and torrents hoarse,
Pouring a constant bulk, uncertain where.
Crag jutting forth to crag, and rocks that seem'd   10
Ever as if just rising from a sleep,
Forehead to forehead held their monstrous horns;
And thus in thousand hugest phantasies
Made a fit roofing to this nest of woe.
Instead of thrones, hard flint they sat upon,   15
Couches of rugged stone, and slaty ridge
Stubborn'd with iron. All were not assembled:
Some chain'd in torture, and some wandering.
Cœus, and Gyges, and Briareüs,

---

5. Cœlus is the region of the heavens (unlike Hyperion, who rules over the sun), so his whisper comes from the sky; see the treatment of the voice of Earth in Shelley's *Prometheus Unbound* (1820).
1. Saturn's sister and wife, also called Ops and Rhea; she is sometimes confused with her mother, Tellus, the mother of the Titans.

Typhon, and Dolor, and Porphyrion,[2]   20
With many more, the brawniest in assault,
Were pent in regions of laborious breath;
Dungeon'd in opaque element, to keep
Their clenched teeth still clench'd, and all their limbs
Lock'd up like veins of metal, crampt and screw'd;   25
Without a motion, save of their big hearts
Heaving in pain, and horribly convuls'd
With sanguine feverous boiling gurge of pulse.
Mnemosyne was straying in the world;
Far from her moon had Phœbe[3] wandered;   30
And many else were free to roam abroad,
But for the main, here found they covert drear.
Scarce images of life, one here, one there,
Lay vast and edgeways; like a dismal cirque
Of Druid stones, upon a forlorn moor,[4]   35
When the chill rain begins at shut of eve,
In dull November, and their chancel vault,[5]
The Heaven itself, is blinded throughout night.
Each one kept shroud, nor to his neighbour gave
Or word, or look, or action of despair.   40
Creüs was one;[6] his ponderous iron mace
Lay by him, and a shatter'd rib of rock
Told of his rage, ere he thus sank and pined.
Iäpetus[7] another; in his grasp,
A serpent's plashy neck; its barbed tongue   45
Squeez'd from the gorge, and all its uncurl'd length
Dead; and because the creature could not spit
Its poison in the eyes of conquering Jove.
Next Cottus:[8] prone he lay, chin uppermost,
As though in pain; for still upon the flint   50
He ground severe his skull, with open mouth

---

2. The gathering of the Titans is based on Milton's convocation of the fallen angels in Hell, *Paradise Lost*, I.376–521. Keats would have found lists and accounts of the Titans in various sources, including Lemprière, Hesiod's *Theogony*, Baldwin's *Pantheon*, and Hyginus's *Fabulae*; Woodhouse in W² cites Sandys's *Ovid's Metamorphosis Englished* (1640) opposite these lines and at the end of the poem quotes Ronsard's account of the war of the Titans from his ode "A Michel de l'Hospital" (1597). *Cœus*: a Titan married to Phœbe, mentioned below. *Gyges and Briareüs*: active in the resistance to the Olympians, both are represented with fifty heads and one hundred hands; Gyges is punished in the underworld by Zeus, while in some accounts Briareüs is buried under Mount Ætna. *Typhon*: sometimes considered a Titan, sometimes a giant, and in some accounts is imprisoned under Mount Ætna. *Dolor*: identified in Hyginus as born from Heaven and Earth, "from Air and Earth, Grief," but he is not listed as a Titan. *Porphyrion*: sometimes a Titan, sometimes a giant; he threatens Jupiter to such a degree that Jupiter has Juno seduce him in order to lure him into a trap.
3. Married to Cœus, above, Phœbe is the mother of Diana, who is often called by her name. *Mnemosyne*: Titan and the mother of the nine Muses by Jupiter; she is seeking Apollo. Her name means "memory."
4. Keats seems to be thinking of something similar to Stonehenge. *Druid*: see p. 41, n. 8. See Keats's visit to a Druid temple, mentioned in his letter to Tom Keats, June 29, 1818 (*L*, 1: 306). Keats would have read of Druids in Edward Davies's *Celtic Researches* (1804), where the Titans and the Celts are linked.
5. The stones form a vault such as would be found in the chancellery of a Gothic cathedral.
6. Keats adds to his list of Titans some figures who are often identified as children of Cœlus and Tellus but not necessarily as Titans. *Creüs*: also known as Crius, he married Eurybia, daughter of Tellus, who bore three sons: Astreus, the husband of Aurora; Pallas, the husband of Stylx; and Perses, the father of Asteria by Hecate. The sufferings of the Titans owe something to Keats's reading of Cary's Dante.
7. Also known as Japetus, Iäpetus was looked upon by the Greeks as the father of mankind; he married Asia or perhaps Clymene and was father to Atlas and Prometheus.
8. One of the giants who stormed Olympus.

And eyes at horrid working. Nearest him
Asia, born of most enormous Caf,
Who cost her mother Tellus keener pangs,
Though feminine, than any of her sons:[9]   55
More thought than woe was in her dusky face,
For she was prophesying of her glory;
And in her wide imagination stood
Palm-shaded temples, and high rival fanes,
By Oxus or in Ganges' sacred isles.   60
Even as Hope upon her anchor leans,
So leant she, not so fair, upon a tusk
Shed from the broadest of her elephants.
Above her, on a crag's uneasy shelve,
Upon his elbow rais'd, all prostrate else,   65
Shadow'd Enceladus;[1] once tame and mild
As grazing ox unworried in the meads;
Now tiger-passion'd, lion-thoughted, wroth,
He meditated, plotted, and even now
Was hurling mountains in that second war,   70
Not long delay'd, that scar'd the younger Gods
To hide themselves in forms of beast and bird.
Not far hence Atlas; and beside him prone
Phorcus, the sire of Gorgons. Neighbour'd close
Oceanus, and Tethys, in whose lap   75
Sobb'd Clymene among her tangled hair.
In midst of all lay Themis, at the feet
Of Ops[2] the queen all clouded round from sight;
No shape distinguishable, more than when
Thick night confounds the pine-tops with the clouds: 80
And many else whose names may not be told.
For when the Muse's wings are air-ward spread,
Who shall delay her flight? And she must chaunt
Of Saturn, and his guide, who now had climb'd
With damp and slippery footing from a depth   85
More horrid still. Above a sombre cliff
Their heads appear'd, and up their stature grew
Till on the level height their steps found ease:

---

9. Asia is here depicted as the daughter of Tellus and the mountain Caf, which was supposed to surround the world and was sometimes associated with the Caucasus; she is imagining herself as the
goddess of a future Asian cult which will stretch from the Oxus (the Greek name for the river Amu
Darya on the border of Uzbekistan) to the islands of the river Ganges (the holy river of Northern
India). See Shelley's depiction of Asia in *Prometheus Unbound* (1820).
1. Considered the mightiest of the Titans; during the assault upon Mount Olympus, when the Giants
caused such fear in the Olympians that they transformed themselves into birds and beasts (l. 72),
Enceladus was struck down by Jupiter's lightning and buried under Mount Ætna, like Typhon with
whom he is sometimes identified. He imagines the future war between the Olympians and the
Giants in which island-size rocks were thrown at the Olympian gods and the Giants heaped up the
mountains Pelion and Ossa to reach Olympus; in Milton's *Paradise Lost*, mountains are also
weapons in the war in Heaven.
2. Also known as Cybele; see p. 185, n. 6. *Atlas*: identified with the mountain range in north Africa,
the son of Iäpetus and Clymene or Asia and the father of the Atlantides; in one version of the myth,
he joined the assault upon Olympus only to be punished by Jupiter by having to bear the heavens
on his shoulders. Lemprière identifies *Phorcus* as a "sea deity, son of Pontus [sometimes identified
with Oceanus] and Terra, who married his sister Ceto, by whom he had the Gorgons, [and] the
dragon that kept the apples of the Hesperides." *Oceanus and Tethys*: ancient deities of the sea; their
offspring were the Oceanides and the presiding gods of all rivers. *Clymene*: one of their daughters,
a sea nymph and the wife of Iäpetus. *Themis*: though a Titan, she had a number of children by
Jupiter, including the Parcæ or fates and the Horæ.

Then Thea spread abroad her trembling arms
Upon the precincts of this nest of pain,   90
And sidelong fix'd her eye on Saturn's face:
There saw she direst strife; the supreme God
At war with all the frailty of grief,
Of rage, of fear, anxiety, revenge,
Remorse, spleen, hope, but most of all despair.   95
Against these plagues he strove in vain; for Fate
Had pour'd a mortal oil upon his head,
A disanointing poison: so that Thea,
Affrighted, kept her still, and let him pass
First onwards in, among the fallen tribe.   100

      As with us mortal men, the laden heart
Is persecuted more, and fever'd more,
When it is nighing to the mournful house
Where other hearts are sick of the same bruise;
So Saturn, as he walk'd into the midst,   105
Felt faint, and would have sunk among the rest,
But that he met Enceladus's eye,
Whose mightiness, and awe of him, at once
Came like an inspiration; and he shouted,
"Titans, behold your God!" at which some groan'd;   110
Some started on their feet; some also shouted;
Some wept, some wail'd, all bow'd with reverence;
And Ops, uplifting her black folded veil,
Show'd her pale cheeks, and all her forehead wan,
Her eye-brows thin and jet, and hollow eyes.   115
There is a roaring in the bleak-grown pines
When Winter lifts his voice; there is a noise
Among immortals when a God gives sign,
With hushing finger, how he means to load
His tongue with the full weight of utterless thought,   120
With thunder, and with music, and with pomp:
Such noise is like the roar of bleak-grown pines;
Which, when it ceases in this mountain'd world,
No other sound succeeds; but ceasing here,
Among these fallen, Saturn's voice therefrom   125
Grew up like organ, that begins anew
Its strain, when other harmonies, stopt short,
Leave the dinn'd air vibrating silverly.
Thus grew it up—"Not in my own sad breast,
"Which is its own great judge and searcher out,   130
"Can I find reason why ye should be thus:
"Not in the legends of the first of days,
"Studied from that old spirit-leaved book
"Which starry Uranus with finger bright
"Sav'd from the shores of darkness, when the waves   135
"Low-ebb'd still hid it up in shallow gloom;—
"And the which book ye know I ever kept
"For my firm-based footstool:—Ah, infirm!
"Not there, nor in sign, symbol, or portent
"Of element, earth, water, air, and fire,—   140

"At war, at peace, or inter-quarreling
"One against one, or two, or three, or all
"Each several one against the other three,
"As fire with air loud warring when rain-floods
"Drown both, and press them both against earth's face,   145
"Where, finding sulphur, a quadruple wrath
"Unhinges the poor world;—not in that strife.
"Wherefrom I take strange lore, and read it deep,
"Can I find reason why ye should be thus:
"No, no-where can unriddle, though I search,   150
"And pore on Nature's universal scroll
"Even to swooning, why ye, Divinities,
"The first-born of all shap'd and palpable Gods,
"Should cower beneath what, in comparison,
"Is untremendous might. Yet ye are here,   155
"O'erwhelm'd, and spurn'd, and batter'd, ye are here!
"O Titans, shall I say 'Arise!'—Ye groan:
"Shall I say 'Crouch!'—Ye groan. What can I then?
"O Heaven wide! O unseen parent dear!
"What can I? Tell me, all ye brethren Gods,   160
"How we can war, how engine our great wrath!
"O speak your counsel now, for Saturn's ear
"Is all a-hunger'd. Thou, Oceanus,
"Ponderest high and deep; and in thy face
"I see, astonied, that severe content   165
"Which comes of thought and musing: give us help?"

So ended Saturn; and the God of the Sea,
Sophist and sage, from no Athenian grove,
But cogitation in his watery shades,
Arose, with locks not oozy, and began,   170
In murmurs, which his first-endeavouring tongue
Caught infant-like from the far-foamed sands.
"O ye, whom wrath consumes! who, passion-stung,
"Writhe at defeat, and nurse your agonies!
"Shut up your senses, stifle up your ears,   175
"My voice is not a bellows unto ire.
"Yet listen, ye who will, whilst I bring proof
"How ye, perforce, must be content to stoop:
"And in the proof much comfort will I give,
"If ye will take that comfort in its truth.   180
"We fall by course of Nature's law, not force
"Of thunder, or of Jove, Great Saturn, thou
"Hast sifted well the atom-universe;
"But for this reason, that thou art the King,
"And only blind from sheer supremacy,   185
"One avenue was shaded from thine eyes,
"Through which I wandered to eternal truth.
"And first, as thou wast not the first of powers,
"So art thou not the last; it cannot be:
"Thou art not the beginning nor the end.   190
"From chaos and parental darkness came

"Light, the first fruits of that intestine broil,
"That sullen ferment, which for wondrous ends
"Was ripening in itself. The ripe hour came,
"And with it light, and light, engendering   195
"Upon its own producer, forthwith touch'd
"The whole enormous matter into life.
"Upon that very hour, our parentage,
"The Heavens and the Earth, were manifest:
"Then thou first-born, and we the giant-race,   200
"Found ourselves ruling new and beauteous realms.
"Now comes the pain of truth, to whom 'tis pain;
"O folly! for to bear all naked truths,
"And to envisage circumstance, all calm,
"That is the top of sovereignty. Mark well!   205
"As Heaven and Earth are fairer, fairer far
"Than Chaos and blank Darkness, though once chiefs;
"And as we show beyond that Heaven and Earth
"In form and shape compact and beautiful,
"In will, in action free, companionship,   210
"And thousand other signs of purer life;
"So on our heels a fresh perfection treads,
"A power more strong in beauty, born of us
"And fated to excel us, as we pass
"In glory that old Darkness: nor are we   215
"Thereby more conquer'd, than by us the rule
"Of shapeless Chaos. Say, doth the dull soil
"Quarrel with the proud forests it hath fed,
"And feedeth still, more comely than itself?
"Can it deny the chiefdom of green groves?   220
"Or shall the tree be envious of the dove
"Because it cooeth, and hath snowy wings
"To wander wherewithal and find its joys?
"We are such forest-trees, and our fair boughs
"Have bred forth, not pale solitary doves,   225
"But eagles golden-feather'd, who do tower
"Above us in their beauty, and must reign
"In right thereof; for 'tis the eternal law
"That first in beauty should be first in might:
"Yea, by that law, another race may drive   230
"Our conquerors to mourn as we do now.
"Have ye beheld the young God of the Seas,
"My dispossessor? Have ye seen his face?
"Have ye beheld his chariot, foam'd along
"By noble winged creatures he hath made?   235
"I saw him on the calmed waters scud,
"With such a glow of beauty in his eyes,
"That it enforc'd me to bid sad farewell
"To all my empire: farewell sad I took,
"And hither came, to see how dolorous fate   240
"Had wrought upon ye; and how I might best
"Give consolation in this woe extreme.
"Receive the truth, and let it be your balm."

Whether through poz'd conviction, or disdain,
They guarded silence, when Oceanus   245
Left murmuring, what deepest thought can tell?
But so it was, none answer'd for a space,
Save one whom none regarded, Clymene;
And yet she answer'd not, only complain'd,
With hectic lips, and eyes up-looking mild,   250
Thus wording timidly among the fierce:
"O Father, I am here the simplest voice,
"And all my knowledge is that joy is gone,
"And this thing woe crept in among our hearts,
"There to remain for ever, as I fear: 255
"I would not bode of evil, if I thought
"So weak a creature could turn off the help
"Which by just right should come of mighty Gods;
"Yet let me tell my sorrow, let me tell
"Of what I heard, and how it made me weep,   260
"And know that we had parted from all hope.
"I stood upon a shore, a pleasant shore,
"Where a sweet clime was breathed from a land
"Of fragrance, quietness, and trees, and flowers.
"Full of calm joy it was, as I of grief;   265
"Too full of joy and soft delicious warmth;
"So that I felt a movement in my heart
"To chide, and to reproach that solitude
"With songs of misery, music of our woes;
"And sat me down, and took a mouthed shell   270
"And murmur'd into it, and made melody—
"O melody no more! for while I sang,
"And with poor skill let pass into the breeze
"The dull shell's echo, from a bowery strand
"Just opposite, an island of the sea,   275
"There came enchantment with the shifting wind,
"That did both drown and keep alive my ears.
"I threw my shell away upon the sand,
"And a wave fill'd it, as my sense was fill'd
"With that new blissful golden melody.   280
"A living death was in each gush of sounds,
"Each family of rapturous hurried notes,
"That fell, one after one, yet all at once,
"Like pearl beads dropping sudden from their string:
"And then another, then another strain,   285
"Each like a dove leaving its olive perch,
"With music wing'd instead of silent plumes,
"To hover round my head, and make me sick
"Of joy and grief at once. Grief overcame,
"And I was stopping up my frantic ears,   290
"When, past all hindrance of my trembling hands,
"A voice came sweeter, sweeter than all tune,
"And still it cried, 'Apollo! young Apollo!
"'The morning-bright Apollo! young Apollo!'
"I fled, it follow'd me, and cried 'Apollo!'   295
"O Father, and O Brethren, had ye felt

"Those pains of mine; O Saturn, hadst thou felt,
"Ye would not call this too indulged tongue
"Presumptuous, in thus venturing to be heard."

   So far her voice flow'd on, like timorous brook   300
That, lingering along a pebbled coast,
Doth fear to meet the sea: but sea it met,
And shudder'd; for the overwhelming voice
Of huge Enceladus swallow'd it in wrath:
The ponderous syllables, like sullen waves   305
In the half-glutted hollows of reef-rocks,
Came booming thus, while still upon his arm
He lean'd; not rising, from supreme contempt.
"Or shall we listen to the over-wise,
"Or to the over-foolish giant, Gods?   310
"Not thunderbolt on thunderbolt, till all
"That rebel Jove's whole armoury were spent,
"Not world on world upon these shoulders piled,
"Could agonize me more than baby-words
"In midst of this dethronement horrible.   315
"Speak! roar! shout! yell! ye sleepy Titans all.
"Do ye forget the blows, the buffets vile?
"Are ye not smitten by a youngling arm?
"Dost thou forget, sham Monarch of the Waves,
"Thy scalding in the seas? What, have I rous'd   320
"Your spleens with so few simple words as these?
"O joy! for now I see ye are not lost:
"O joy! for now I see a thousand eyes
"Wide glaring for revenge!"—As this he said,
He lifted up his stature vast, and stood,   325
Still without intermission speaking thus:
"Now ye are flames, I'll tell you how to burn,
"And purge the ether of our enemies;
"How to feed fierce the crooked stings of fire,
"And singe away the swollen clouds of Jove,   330
"Stifling that puny essence in its tent.
"O let him feel the evil he hath done;
"For though I scorn Oceanus's lore,
"Much pain have I for more than loss of realms:
"The days of peace and slumberous calm are fled;   335
"Those days, all innocent of scathing war,
"When all the fair Existences of heaven
"Came open-eyed to guess what we would speak:—
"That was before our brows were taught to frown,
"Before our lips knew else but solemn sounds;   340
"That was before we knew the winged thing,
"Victory, might be lost, or might be won.
"And be ye mindful that Hyperion,
"Our brightest brother, still is undisgraced—
"Hyperion, lo! his radiance is here!"   345

   All eyes were on Enceladus's face,
And they beheld, while still Hyperion's name

Flew from his lips up to the vaulted rocks,
A pallid gleam across his features stern:
Not savage, for he saw full many a God   350
Wroth as himself. He look'd upon them all,
And in each face he saw a gleam of light,
But splendider in Saturn's, whose hoar locks
Shone like the bubbling foam about a keel
When the prow sweeps into a midnight cove.   355
In pale and silver silence they remain'd,
Till suddenly a splendour, like the morn,
Pervaded all the beetling gloomy steeps,
All the sad spaces of oblivion,
And every gulf, and every chasm old,   360
And every height, and every sullen depth,
Voiceless, or hoarse with loud tormented streams:
And all the everlasting cataracts,
And all the headlong torrents far and near,
Mantled before in darkness and huge shade,   365
Now saw the light and made it terrible.
It was Hyperion:—a granite peak
His bright feet touch'd, and there he stay'd to view
The misery his brilliance had betray'd
To the most hateful seeing of itself.   370
Golden his hair of short Numidian[3] curl,
Regal his shape majestic, a vast shade
In midst of his own brightness, like the bulk
Of Memnon's image at the set of sun
To one who travels from the dusking East: 375
Sighs, too, as mournful as that Memnon's harp
He utter'd, while his hands contemplative
He press'd together, and in silence stood.
Despondence seiz'd again the fallen Gods
At sight of the dejected King of Day,   380
And many hid their faces from the light:
But fierce Enceladus sent forth his eyes
Among the brotherhood; and, at their glare,
Uprose Iäpetus, and Creüs too,
And Phorcus, sea-born, and together strode   385
To where he towered on his eminence.
There those four shouted forth old Saturn's name;
Hyperion from the peak loud answered, "Saturn!"
Saturn sat near the Mother of the Gods,
In whose face was no joy, though all the Gods   390
Gave from their hollow throats the name of "Saturn!"

BOOK III.

Thus in alternate uproar and sad peace,
Amazed were those Titans utterly.

---

3. Numidia was an ancient kingdom in North Africa, in the area of Algeria; Memnon, below: the
   Egyptian statue of Memnon, the son of Aurora who was slain by Achilles, was said to produce music
   when struck by the rising or setting sun.

O leave them, Muse! O leave them to their woes;
For thou art weak to sing such tumults dire:
A solitary sorrow best befits   5
Thy lips, and antheming a lonely grief.
Leave them, O Muse! for thou anon wilt find
Many a fallen old Divinity
Wandering in vain about bewildered shores.
Meantime touch piously the Delphic harp,   10
And not a wind of heaven but will breathe
In aid soft warble from the Dorian⁴ flute;
For lo! 'tis for the Father of all verse.
Flush every thing that hath a vermeil hue,
Let the rose glow intense and warm the air,   15
And let the clouds of even and of morn
Float in voluptuous fleeces o'er the hills;
Let the red wine within the goblet boil,
Cold as a bubbling well; let faint-lipp'd shells,
On sands, or in great deeps, vermilion turn   20
Through all their labyrinths; and let the maid
Blush keenly, as with some warm kiss surpris'd.
Chief isle of the embowered Cyclades,
Rejoice, O Delos,⁵ with thine olives green,
And poplars, and lawn-shading palms, and beech,   25
In which the Zephyr breathes the loudest song,
And hazels thick, dark-stemm'd beneath the shade:
Apollo is once more the golden theme!
Where was he, when the Giant of the Sun
Stood bright, amid the sorrow of his peers?   30
Together had he left his mother fair
And his twin-sister sleeping in their bower,
And in the morning twilight wandered forth
Beside the osiers of a rivulet,
Full ankle-deep in lilies of the vale.   35
The nightingale had ceas'd, and a few stars
Were lingering in the heavens, while the thrush
Began calm-throated. Throughout all the isle
There was no covert, no retired cave
Unhaunted by the murmurous noise of waves,   40
Though scarcely heard in many a green recess.
He listen'd, and he wept, and his bright tears
Went trickling down the golden bow he held.
Thus with half-shut suffused eyes he stood,
While from beneath some cumbrous boughs hard by   45
With solemn step an awful Goddess came,
And there was purport in her looks for him,
Which he with eager guess began to read
Perplex'd, the while melodiously he said:
"How cam'st thou over the unfooted sea?   50
"Or hath that antique mien and robed form
"Mov'd in these vales invisible till now?
"Sure I have heard those vestments sweeping o'er

4. "[O]ne of the ancient Grecian modes [of music], characterized by simplicity and solemnity" (*OED*).
5. The island birthplace of Apollo.

"The fallen leaves, when I have sat alone
"In cool mid-forest. Surely I have traced   55
"The rustle of those ample skirts about
"These grassy solitudes, and seen the flowers
"Lift up their heads, as still the whisper pass'd.
"Goddess! I have beheld those eyes before,
"And their eternal calm, and all that face,   60
"Or I have dream'd."—"Yes," said the supreme shape,
"Thou hast dream'd of me; and awaking up
"Didst find a lyre all golden by thy side,
"Whose strings touch'd by thy fingers, all the vast
"Unwearied ear of the whole universe   65
"Listen'd in pain and pleasure at the birth
"Of such new tuneful wonder. Is't not strange
"That thou shouldst weep, so gifted? Tell me, youth,
"What sorrow thou canst feel; for I am sad
"When thou dost shed a tear: explain thy griefs   70
"To one who in this lonely isle hath been
"The watcher of thy sleep and hours of life,
"From the young day when first thy infant hand
"Pluck'd witless the weak flowers, till thine arm
"Could bend that bow heroic to all times.   75
"Show thy heart's secret to an ancient Power
"Who hath forsaken old and sacred thrones
"For prophecies of thee, and for the sake
"Of loveliness new born."—Apollo then,
With sudden scrutiny and gloomless eyes,   80
Thus answer'd, while his white melodious throat
Throbb'd with the syllables.—"Mnemosyne!
"Thy name is on my tongue, I know not how;
"Why should I tell thee what thou so well seest?
"Why should I strive to show what from thy lips   85
"Would come no mystery? For me, dark, dark,
"And painful vile oblivion seals my eyes:
"I strive to search wherefore I am so sad,
"Until a melancholy numbs my limbs;
"And then upon the grass I sit, and moan,   90
"Like one who once had wings.—O why should I
"Feel curs'd and thwarted, when the liegeless air
"Yields to my step aspirant? why should I
"Spurn the green turf as hateful to my feet?
"Goddess benign, point forth some unknown thing: 95
"Are there not other regions than this isle?
"What are the stars? There is the sun, the sun!
"And the most patient brilliance of the moon!
"And stars by thousands! Point me out the way
"To any one particular beauteous star,   100
"And I will flit into it with my lyre,
"And make its silvery splendour pant with bliss.
"I have heard the cloudy thunder: Where is power?
"Whose hand, whose essence, what divinity
"Makes this alarum in the elements,   105
"While I here idle listen on the shores

"In fearless yet in aching ignorance?
"O tell me, lonely Goddess, by thy harp,
"That waileth every morn and eventide,
"Tell me why thus I rave, about these groves!   110
"Mute thou remainest—Mute! yet I can read
"A wondrous lesson in thy silent face:
"Knowledge enormous makes a God of me.
"Names, deeds, gray legends, dire events, rebellions
"Majesties, sovran voices, agonies,   115
"Creations and destroyings, all at once
"Pour into the wide hollows of my brain,
"And deify me, as if some blithe wine
"Or bright elixir peerless I had drunk,
"And so become immortal."—Thus the God,   120
While his enkindled eyes, with level glance
Beneath his white soft temples, stedfast kept
Trembling with light upon Mnemosyne.
Soon wild commotions shook him, and made flush
All the immortal fairness of his limbs;   125
Most like the struggle at the gate of death;
Or liker still to one who should take leave
Of pale immortal death, and with a pang
As hot as death's is chill, with fierce convulse
Die into life: so young Apollo anguish'd: 130
His very hair, his golden tresses famed,
Kept undulation round his eager neck.
During the pain Mnemosyne upheld
Her arms as one who prophesied.—At length
Apollo shriek'd;—and lo! from all his limbs   135
Celestial⁶   *   *   *   *   *   *
 *   *   *   *   *   *   *   *

THE END.

---

6. Woodhouse and Taylor tried to complete the line, offering "from all his limbs / Celestial glory
dawn'd. He was a god!"

Last Writings

THE FALL OF HYPERION—A DREAM

Keats left London on June 17, 1819, and traveled to Shanklin on the Isle of Wight, where Rice had arranged for their lodgings; on August 12 he moved on to Winchester. During this period, while he wrote *Lamia* and made progress with his drama, *Otho the Great*, he also adapted his earlier poem, *Hyperion*, starting work toward the end of July and finishing this version by September 21, when he wrote to Reynolds that he was abandoning the project (see p. 359); he may have made some revisions in November–December 1819.

As indicated in the headnote to *Hyperion* (p. 475), Keats abandoned the project because he felt it was too "Miltonic." If *Hyperion* is clearly modeled on *Paradise Lost*, *The Fall* tries to recast that poem in a visionary mode influenced by Dante's work, which Keats was rereading, particularly the *Purgatorio*, in Cary's version (Keats was also working on his Italian at this point and may have read Dante in the original). Allott suggests Keats drew upon Coleridge's "Allegoric Vision"—reprinted in his 1817 *A Lay Sermon*—and Addison's 1710 *Vision of Mirzah*, while Cook points to medieval dream poems. As in *The Divine Comedy*, the poem is cast as a quest by the poet-narrator, who finds himself in a kind of fallen paradise before undergoing a test that earns him the right to engage the goddess Moneta in a dialogue. After a debate over the nature of poets, she presents him with a vision which is essentially the story of *Hyperion*. Similar debates about the status of poetry can be found throughout Keats's works, for example, in *Endymion* or the early "Sleep and Poetry."

Keats's friends preferred the earlier version of the poem and prevailed on him to include it in his 1820 volume. The redrafted fragment was first published as *ANOTHER VERSION OF KEATS'S "HYPERION"* and entitled *The Fall of Hyperion, a Vision* in *Miscellanies of the Philobiblon* Society 3 (1856–57), pp. 5–24; it was also issued as a separate pamphlet (a copy is held by Keats House; LMA K/BK/01/035/73). Milnes made some corrections when he republished the poem in his one-volume *Life* in 1867. A group of omitted lines (1: 187–210) were first published in de Selincourt's *Hyperion: A Facsimile* (Oxford: Clarendon Press, 1905). These lines had been marked by Woodhouse as possibly deleted by Keats, so Milnes dropped them, and some critics have also argued against their inclusion, with Bate, for example, finding them "departing from the course of the poem—to some extent conflicting with it" (p. 599). I have included the lines as germane to the fragment's discussion of contemporary poetry and Keats's place in it. The only portion of the poem that we have in Keats's hand (1.1–11a, 61–86; 2.1–4, 6) was copied in a letter to Woodhouse of

September 21, 22, 1819 (*L*, 2: 169–75). The text is from Milnes's 1857 texts (with his corrections) and the omitted lines from de Selincourt; title and emendations from their ultimate source in Woodhouse's transcript in W² 165–81 (*MYR: JK*, 6: 305–37). Milnes notes parallels between the two versions and sometimes adopts the earlier version (and both Milnes and Allott provide useful notes comparing the two poems, while Stillinger lists the corresponding lines, p. 672); in these cases I have followed W². On the Hyperion poems, see Andrew Bennett's essay included here (pp. 643–52).

Canto I

FANATICS have their dreams, wherewith they weave
A paradise for a sect; the savage, too,
From forth the loftiest fashion of his sleep
Guesses at Heaven: pity these have not
Trac'd upon vellum or wild Indian leaf[1]   5
The shadows of melodious utterance.
But bare of laurel they live, dream, and die;
For Poesy alone can tell her dreams,
With the fine spell of words alone can save
Imagination from the sable charm[2]   10
And dumb enchantment. Who alive can say,
"Thou art no Poet; may'st not tell thy dreams?"
Since every man whose soul is not a clod
Hath visions, and would speak, if he had lov'd
And been well nurtured in his mother tongue.   15
Whether the dream now purposed to rehearse
Be Poet's or Fanatic's will be known
When this warm scribe, my hand, is in the grave.

Methought I stood where trees of every clime,
Palm, myrtle, oak, and sycamore, and beech,   20
With plantane[3] and spice-blossoms, made a screen,
In neighbourhood of fountains, by the noise
Soft-showering in mine ears, and by the touch
Of scent, not far from roses. Turning[4] round,
I saw an arbour with a drooping roof   25
Of trellis vines, and bells, and larger blooms,
Like floral-censers swinging light in air;
Before its wreathed doorway, on a mound
Of moss, was spread a feast of summer fruits,
Which, nearer seen, seem'd refuse of a meal   30
By angel tasted, or our Mother Eve;[5]

1. "[T]he aromatic leaf of a species of *Cinnamomum*" (*OED*), but Keats may be referring to hand-made papers from India where the impressions of leaves are visible on the paper's surface. *vellum*: a "fine kind of parchment prepared from the skins of calves (lambs or kids) and used especially for writing, painting, or binding; also, any superior quality of parchment or an imitation of this" (*OED*).
2. Woodhouse notes opposite a word that looks like "cham": "probably charm"; Milnes offers "chain."
3. For "plaintain," a tree that bears a variety of banana.
4. Milnes reads this as "Twining."
5. For Eve preparing a meal, see Milton, *Paradise Lost*, 5.303–307, 326–28; Keats marked both passages in his copy of the poem. On the poem's general debt to Milton, particularly dense in this passage, see the headnote.

For empty shells were scatter'd on the grass,
And grapestalks but half-bare, and remnants more,
Sweet smelling, whose pure kinds I could not know.
Still was more plenty than the fabled horn[6]   35
Thrice emptied could pour forth, at banqueting,
For Proserpine return'd to her own fields,
Where the white heifers low.[7] And appetite,
More yearning than on earth I ever felt
Growing within, I ate deliciously;   40
And, after not long, thirsted, for thereby
Stood a cool vessel of transparent juice,
Sipp'd by the wander'd bee, the which I took,
And, pledging all the mortals of the world,
And all the dead whose names are in our lips,   45
Drank. That full draught is parent of my theme.
No Asian poppy, nor elixir fine
Of the soon-fading, jealous Caliphat;[8]
No poison gender'd in close monkish cell
To thin the scarlet conclave[9] of old men,   50
Could so have rapt unwilling life away.
Among the fragrant husks and berries crush'd,
Upon the grass I struggled hard against
The domineering potion; but in vain.
The cloudy swoon came on, and down I sunk,   55
Like a Silenus on an antique vase.[1]
How long I slumber'd 'tis a chance to guess.
When sense of life return'd, I started up
As if with wings; but the fair trees were gone,
The mossy mound and arbour were no more;   60
I look'd around upon the carved[2] sides
Of an old sanctuary with roof august,[3]
Builded so high, it seem'd that filmed clouds
Might spread beneath, as o'er the stars of heaven;
So old the place was, I remembered none   65
The like upon the earth: what I had seen
Of grey cathedrals, buttress'd walls, rent towers,
The superannuations[4] of sunk realms,
Or nature's rocks toil'd hard in waves and winds,

6. The cornucopia, identified with Ceres, Roman goddess of grain; see *Lamia*, 2.187: "Ceres' horn."
7. For Proserpine, daughter of Ceres, see p. 170, n. 2; see also "Ode on a Grecian Urn," l. 33: "heifer lowing at the skies." Allott finds an echo of Dante's description of Proserpine in *Purgatorio*, 28.49–51; for Keats's general debt to Dante, see the headnote.
8. Probably for caliph, a title given to the chief civil and religious leader in an Islamic country; a caliphate is his kingdom. Allott cites "The History of Ganem" in *The Arabian Nights*, which Keats would have known from Weber's *Tales of the East* (1812), 1: 280.
9. The gathering of cardinals to elect a pope; various commentators have found the monkish poison used in a plot during the papal succession to be an element borrowed from the Gothic, just as the Caliph comes from Oriental tales.
1. Jack cites the Borghese vase, p. 227 and pl. xxxvii. *Silenus:* see p. 222, n. 2.
2. Milnes reads as "curved."
3. Woodhouse notes that this is "The Temple of Saturn."
4. Here, antiquated structures; *rent towers*: those towers that have been pulled down. Keats also appears to recollect medieval buildings with flying buttresses that he could have seen in Winchester in July 1819 when he was working on the poem. Allott suggests that in line 69 he is thinking of the rocks of Iona and Staffa, which he saw during his trip in the summer of 1818 (see pp. 265 and 266, n. 1).

Seem'd but the faulture[5] of decrepit things   70
To that eternal domed monument.
Upon the marble at my feet there lay
Store of strange vessels, and large draperies,
Which needs had been of dyed asbestos[6] wove,
Or in that place the moth could not corrupt,[7]   75
So white the linen; so, in some, distinct
Ran imageries from a sombre loom.
All in a mingled heap confus'd there lay
Robes, golden tongs, censer, and chafing-dish,
Girdles, and chains, and holy jewelries.   80

    Turning from these with awe, once more I rais'd
My eyes to fathom the space every way;
The embossed roof, the silent massy range
Of columns north and south,[8] ending in mist
Of nothing, then to eastward, where black gates   85
Were shut against the sunrise evermore.
Then to the west I look'd, and saw far off
An image, huge of feature as a cloud,
At level of whose feet an altar slept,[9]
To be approach'd on either side by steps,   90
And marble balustrade, and patient travail
To count with toil the innumerable degrees.
Towards the altar sober-pac'd I went,
Repressing haste, as too unholy there;
And, coming nearer, saw beside the shrine   95
One minist'ring; and there arose a flame.
When in mid-May[1] the sickening east wind
Shifts sudden to the south, the small warm rain
Melts out the frozen incense from all flowers,
And fills the air with so much pleasant health   100
That even the dying man forgets his shroud;
Even so that lofty sacrificial fire,
Sending forth Maian incense,[2] spread around
Forgetfulness of every thing but bliss,
And clouded all the altar with soft smoke,   105
From whose white fragrant curtains thus I heard
Language pronounc'd: "If thou canst not ascend
These steps, die on that marble where thou art.
Thy flesh, near cousin to the common dust,
Will parch for lack of nutriment; thy bones   110
Will wither in few years, and vanish so

---

5. Keats coined this term to bring together the idea of failings or weakness with the image of a geological fault.
6. Asbestos: "A mineral of fibrous texture, capable of being woven into an incombustible fabric" (*OED*).
7. See Matthew 6.19–20 for the image of heavenly things beyond the corruption of the moth.
8. Allott cites Milton's "Il Penseroso," ll. 157–58: "the high embowed Roof, / With antick Pillars massy proof"; *embossed*: carved or molded in relief.
9. Potter's *Antiquities of Greece* (1697) noted that Greek temples were built toward the east so that one would see the rising sun upon opening the doors and that one paid devotion to the west; images, here that of Saturn, were placed in the middle of the temple.
1. Milnes originally had "As in midday." W^2 offers what appears to be "mid-way." A. E. Housman suggested "mid-May" (*TLS*, May 8, 1924, p. 286), which connects with "Maian incense" in l. 103.
2. The scent of spring flowers; *Maian*: from the goddess Maia; see Keats's "Ode to May" (p. 241).

That not the quickest eye could find a grain
Of what thou now art on that pavement cold.
The sands of thy short life are spent this hour,
And no hand in the universe can turn   115
Thy hour glass, if these gummed leaves be burnt
Ere thou canst mount up these immortal steps."
I heard, I look'd: two senses both at once
So fine, so subtle, felt the tyranny
Of that fierce threat, and the hard task proposed.   120
Prodigious seem'd the toil; the leaves were yet
Burning,—when suddenly a palsied chill
Struck from the paved level up my limbs,
And was ascending quick to put cold grasp
Upon those streams that pulse beside the throat.   125
I shriek'd; and the sharp anguish of my shriek
Stung my own ears—I strove hard to escape
The numbness; strove to gain the lowest step.
Slow, heavy, deadly was my pace: the cold
Grew stifling, suffocating, at the heart;   130
And when I clasp'd my hands I felt them not.
One minute before death, my iced foot touch'd
The lowest stair; and, as it touch'd, life seem'd
To pour in at the toes: I mounted up,
As once fair angels on a ladder flew   135
From the green turf to heaven.[3]—"Holy Power,"
Cried I, approaching near the horned shrine,[4]
"What am I that should so be sav'd from death?
What am I that another death come not
To choke my utterance, sacrilegious, here?"   140
Then said the veiled shadow—"Thou hast felt
What 'tis to die and live again before
Thy fated hour. That thou hadst power to do so
Is thy own safety; thou hast dated on[5]
Thy doom."—"High prophetess," said I, "purge off,   145
Benign, if so it please thee, my mind's film."[6]
"None can usurp this height," return'd that shade,
"But those to whom the miseries of the world
Are misery, and will not let them rest.[7]
All else who find a haven in the world,   150
Where they may thoughtless sleep away their days,
If by a chance into this fane they come,
Rot on the pavement where thou rotted'st half."—
"Are there not thousands in the world," said I,
Encourag'd by the sooth[8] voice of the shade,   155

---

3. Reference to Jacob's Ladder with ascending and descending angels in Genesis 28.12.
4. Keats could have read in John Potter's *Antiquities of Greece* (1697) that "[t]he most ancient alters were adorned with horns" (1: 229).
5. Postponed.
6. He asks Moneta to please clarify things. Allott cites this as one of the Miltonic inversions that bothered Keats.
7. A. C. Bradley ("The Letters of John Keats," *Oxford Lecture on Poetry* [1909], p. 242) found this passage echoing Shelley's preface to *Alastor* (1816), where he distinguishes between the self-concentration of the poet and the selfishness of the "unforeseeing multitudes" (*Shelley's Poetry and Prose*, p. 73).
8. Soothing but also truthful.

"Who love their fellows even to the death;
Who feel the giant agony of the world;[9]
And more, like slaves to poor humanity,
Labour for mortal good? I sure should see
Other men here: but I am here alone."   160
"They whom thou spak'st of are no vision'ries,"
Rejoin'd that voice—"They are no dreamers weak;
They seek no wonder but the human face;
No music but a happy-noted voice.
They come not here, they have no thought to come—   165
And thou art here, for thou art less than they.
What benefit canst thou do,[1] or all thy tribe,
To the great world? Thou art a dreaming thing;
A fever of thyself—think of the earth;
What bliss even in hope is there for thee?   170
What haven? every creature hath its home;
Every sole man hath days of joy and pain,
Whether his labours be sublime or low—
The pain alone, the joy alone; distinct:
Only the dreamer venoms all his days,   175
Bearing more woe than all his sins deserve.
Therefore, that happiness be somewhat shar'd,
Such things as thou art are admitted oft
Into like gardens thou didst pass erewhile,
And suffer'd in these temples; for that cause   180
Thou standest safe beneath this statue's knees."
"That I am favoured for unworthiness,
By such propitious parley medicin'd
In sickness not ignoble, I rejoice,
Aye, and could weep for love of such award."   185
So answer'd I, continuing, "If it please,
Majestic shadow, tell me: sure not all[2]
Those melodies sung into the world's ear
Are useless: sure a poet is a sage;
A humanist, physician to all men.[3]   190
That I am none I feel, as vultures feel
They are no birds when eagles are abroad.
What am I then? Thou spakest of my tribe:
What tribe?"—The tall shade veil'd in drooping white
Then spake, so much more earnest, that the breath   195
Mov'd the thin linen folds that drooping hung
About a golden censer from the hand
Pendent.—"Art thou not of the dreamer tribe?
The poet and the dreamer are distinct,
Diverse, sheer opposite, antipodes.   200
The one pours out a balm upon the world,

---

9. Allott cites "Sleep and Poetry," ll. 122–25 (p. 61).
1. Woodhouse suggests omitting this word, presumably for the meter. The original MS. apparently
   had "do" both here and at the opening of the next line, which was corrected to "To" by Woodhouse.
2. Milnes omits lines 187–210 which were first published by de Selincourt (see headnote). Woodhouse had marked these lines with a pencil note, "Keats seems to have intended to erase this &
   the 21 follow⁸ verses," but he has merely surmised this based on the repetition of 187 and 194–98
   at 211 and 216–20.
3. See "Sleep and Poetry," ll. 246–47 (p. 64).

The other vexes it." Then shouted I[4]
Spite of myself, and with a Pythia's spleen,
"Apollo! faded, far flown Apollo!
Where is thy misty pestilence[5] to creep   205
Into the dwellings, thro' the door crannies,
Of all mock lyrists, large self worshipers,
And careless Hectorers in proud bad verse.[6]
Tho' I breathe death with them it will be life
To see them sprawl before me into graves.   210
Majestic shadow, tell me where I am:
Whose altar this; for whom this incense curls;
What image this, whose face I cannot see,
For the broad marble knees; and who thou art,
Of accent feminine, so courteous."   215
Then the tall shade, in drooping linens veil'd,
Spoke out, so much more earnest, that her breath
Stirr'd the thin folds of gauze that drooping hung
About a golden censer from her hand
Pendent; and by her voice I knew she shed   220
Long treasured tears. "This temple, sad and lone,
Is all spar'd from the thunder of a war
Foughten long since by giant hierarchy
Against rebellion:[7] this old image here,
Whose carved features wrinkled as he fell,   225
Is Saturn's; I, Moneta,[8] left supreme,
Sole priestess of his desolation."[9]
I had no words to answer; for my tongue,
Useless, could find about its roofed home
No syllable of a fit majesty   230
To make rejoinder to Moneta's mourn.
There was a silence, while the altar's blaze
Was fainting for sweet food:[1] I look'd thereon,
And on the paved floor, where nigh were pil'd
Faggots of cinnamon, and many heaps   235
Of other crisped spice-wood—then again
I look'd upon the altar, and its horns
Whiten'd with ashes, and its lang'rous flame,
And then upon the offerings again;

---

4. W[2] originally finished this line "Apollo mine" and lacked the next two lines. Woodhouse crossed out this half line and added the present 202b–204, suggesting adding "O" before "far flown" for the meter. He glosses Pythia as "the Priestess of Apollo at Delphi"; she delivers Apollo's oracles while in an ecstatic frenzy.
5. Apollo is here the bringer of plagues, as in the *Iliad*, 1.9–12 or Sophocles' *Oedipus*.
6. Commentators have found various contemporary poets alluded to here. There is some agreement that the "hectorer" in "proud bad verse" is Byron (see "Sleep and Poetry," ll. 233–35, p. 64). Hunt and Tom Moore have been offered as the "mock lyrist." Given Keats's comments on the "wordsworthian or egotistical sublime" (see p. 295), the "self-worshipper" may be Wordsworth.
7. The war between the Titans and the Olympian gods.
8. The name that Keats now gives to Mnemosyne from *Hyperion*; the two were linked as Titans in Hyginus's *Fabulae*. Moneta was sometimes linked to Minerva; according to Lemprière, Moneta is a "first name of Juno among the Romans," "from assuring the Romans, when in war against Pyrrhus they complained of want of pecuniary resources, that money could never fail to those who cultivated justice." See K. K. Ruthven, "Keats's *Dea Moneta*," *SiR* 15 (1976): 445–59.
9. Milnes offers "Sole goddess of this desolation."
1. The fire on the altar is dying because it has not been "fed" with fuel. Keats follows Potter's *Antiquities of Greece* in restricting sacrifices in this ancient temple to wood and herbs rather than, say, animals.

And so by turns—till sad Moneta cried,   240
"The sacrifice is done, but not the less
Will I be kind to thee for thy good will.
My power, which to me is still a curse,
Shall be to thee a wonder; for the scenes
Still swooning vivid through my globed brain   245
With an electral changing misery
Thou shalt with those dull mortal eyes behold,
Free from all pain, if wonder pain thee not."
As near as an immortal's sphered words
Could to a mother's soften, were these last: 250
But yet I had a terror of her robes,
And chiefly of the veils, that from her brow
Hung pale, and curtain'd her in mysteries
That made my heart too small to hold its blood.
This saw that Goddess, and with sacred hand   255
Parted the veils. Then saw I a wan face,
Not pin'd by human sorrows, but bright blanch'd
By an immortal sickness which kills not;
It works a constant change, which happy death
Can put no end to; deathwards progressing   260
To no death was that visage; it had pass'd
The lily and the snow; and beyond these
I must not think now, though I saw that face—
But for her eyes I should have fled away.
They held me back, with a benignant light,   265
Soft mitigated by divinest lids
Half closed, and visionless entire they seem'd
Of all external things—they saw me not,
But in blank splendour beam'd like the mild moon,
Who comforts those she sees not, who knows not   270
What eyes are upward cast. As I had found
A grain of gold upon a mountain's side,
And twing'd with avarice strain'd out my eyes
To search its sullen entrails rich with ore,
So, at the view of sad Moneta's brow,   275
I ached to see what things the hollow brain[2]
Behind enwombed:[3] what high tragedy
In the dark secret chambers of her skull
Was acting, that could give so dread a stress
To her cold lips, and fill with such a light   280
Her planetary eyes; and touch her voice
With such a sorrow. "Shade of Memory!"[4]
Cried I, with act adorant[5] at her feet,
"By all the gloom hung round thy fallen house,
By this last temple, by the golden age,   285
By great Apollo, thy dear foster child,[6]

2. Milnes offers "asked . . . brow."
3. Milnes offers "environed."
4. Mnemosyne means "memory" and in some accounts Moneta is the child of Jupiter and Memory.
5. Keats's coinage, for adoring.
6. Moneta is imagined as the last (the "Omega," l. 298) of the Titans, outliving the Golden Age of
   Saturn's reign; she is also seen as foster mother to Apollo, as in *Hyperion*, for as mother of the
   Muses she deserts the Titans to help deify the future god of poetry.

And by thyself, forlorn divinity,
The pale Omega of a wither'd race,
Let me behold, according as thou said'st,
What in thy brain so ferments to and fro."—   290
No sooner had this conjuration pass'd
My devout lips, than side by side we stood
(Like a stunt bramble by a solemn pine)
Deep in the shady sadness of a vale,[7]
Far sunken from the healthy breath of morn,   295
Far from the fiery noon, and eve's one star.
Onward I look'd beneath the gloomy boughs,
And saw, what first I thought an image huge,
Like to the image pedestal'd so high
In Saturn's temple. Then Moneta's voice   300
Came brief upon mine ear,—"So Saturn sat
When he had lost his realms."—Whereon there grew
A power within me of enormous ken,
To see as a god sees,[8] and take the depth
Of things as nimbly as the outward eye   305
Can size and shape pervade. The lofty theme
At those few words hung vast before my mind,
With half unravell'd web. I set[9] myself
Upon an eagle's watch, that I might see,
And seeing ne'er forget. No stir of life   310
Was in this shrouded vale,—not so much air
As in the zoning of a summer's day
Robs not one light seed from the feather'd grass,
But where the dead leaf fell there did it rest:
A stream went voiceless[1] by, still deaden'd more   315
By reason of the fallen divinity
Spreading more shade: the Naiad[2] mid her reeds
Press'd her cold finger cider to her lips.
Along the margin sand large footmarks went
No farther than to where old Saturn's feet   320
Had rested, and there slept, how long a sleep!
Degraded, cold, upon the sodden ground
His old right hand lay nerveless, listless, dead,
Unsceptred; and his realmless eyes were close'd;
While his bow'd head seem'd listening to the Earth,   325
His ancient mother, for some comfort yet.

It seem'd no force could wake him from his place;
But there came one who, with a kindred hand
Touch'd his wide shoulders, after bending low
With reverence, though to one who knew it not.   330
Then came the griev'd voice of Mnemosyne,
And griev'd I hearken'd. "That divinity
Whom thou saw'st step from yon forlornest wood,

7. Keats returns to his account in *Hyperion* here.
8. See *Hyperion*, 3.113, where it is Apollo who is transformed.
9. Milnes offers "sat."
1. Milnes offers "noiseless."
2. See p. 41, n. 6.

And with slow pace approach our fallen king,
Is Thea,[3] softest-natur'd of our brood."   335
I mark'd the goddess, in fair sanctuary
Surpassing wan Moneta by the head,
And in her sorrow nearer woman's tears.
There was a listening fear in her regard,
As if calamity had but begun;   340
As if the vanward[4] clouds of evil days
Had spent their malice, and the sullen rear
Was with its stored thunder labouring up.
One hand she press'd upon that aching spot
Where heats the human heart; as if just there,   345
Though an immortal, she felt cruel pain;
The other upon Saturn's bended neck
She laid, and to the level of his hollow ear[5]
Leaning, with parted lips, some words she spake
In solemn tenour and deep organ tune;[6]   350
Some mourning words, which in our feeble tongue
Would come in this-like accenting; how frail
To that large utterance of the early gods!—
"Saturn! look up—and for what, poor lost king?
I have no comfort for thee; no, not one;   355
I cannot cry,[7] *Wherefore thus sleepest thou?*
For heaven is parted from thee, and the earth
Knows thee not, so afflicted, for a god;
And ocean, too, with all its solemn noise,
Has from thy sceptre pass'd, and all the air   360
Is emptied of thine hoary majesty.
Thy thunder, captious at the new command,
Rumbles reluctant o'er our fallen house;
And thy sharp lightning in unpracticed hands
Scorches[8] and burns our once serene domain.   365
With such remorseless speed still come new woes
That unbelief has not a space to breathe.
Saturn, sleep on:—Me thoughtless, why should I
Thus violate thy slumbrous solitude?
Why should I ope thy melancholy eyes?   370
Saturn, sleep on, while at thy feet I weep."

    As when, upon a tranced summer night,
Forests, branch-charmed by the earnest stars,
Dream, and so dream all night, without a noise,
Save from one gradual solitary gust,   375
Swelling upon the silence, dying off,
As if the ebbing air had but one wave,
So came these words, and went; the while in tears
She press'd her fair large forehead to the earth,

---

3. Hyperion's wife.
4. Milnes offers "venom'd."
5. Following *Hyperion*, Milnes drops "hollow," as this line is hypermetrical.
6. Milnes offers "organ-tone," which follows Woodhouse's query to this line in W[2] and *Hyperion*,
   1.48.
7. Milnes offers "say" from *Hyperion*, 1.54.
8. Milnes offers "Scourges."

Just where her fallen hair might spread in curls,   380
A soft and silken mat[9] for Saturn's feet.
Long, long those two were postured motionless,
Like sculpture builded up upon the grave
Of their own power. A long awful time
I look'd upon them; still they were the same;   385
The frozen God still bending to the earth,
And the sad Goddess weeping at his feet;
Moneta silent. Without stay or prop
But my own weak mortality, I bore
The load of this eternal quietude,   390
The unchanging gloom, and the three fixed shapes
Ponderous upon my senses a whole moon.
For by my burning brain I measured sure
Her silver seasons shedded on the night,
And every day by day methought I grew   395
More gaunt and ghostly. Oftentimes I pray'd
Intense, that death would take me from the vale
And all its burthens. Gasping with despair
Of change, hour after hour I curs'd myself:
Until old Saturn raised his faded eyes,   400
And look'd around and saw his kingdom gone,
And all the gloom and sorrow of the place,
And that fair kneeling Goddess at his feet.
As the moist scent of flowers, and grass, and leaves,
Fills forest dells with a pervading air   405
Known to the woodland nostril, so the words
Of Saturn fill'd the mossy glooms around,
Even to the hollows of time-eaten oaks,
And to the windings in the foxes' hole,
With sad, low tones, while thus he spake, and sent   410
Strange musings to the solitary Pan.[1]
"Moan, brethren, moan; for we are swallow'd up
And buried from all godlike exercise
Of influence benign on planets pale,
And peaceful sway above man's harvesting,   415
And all those acts which Deity supreme
Doth ease its heart of love in. Moan and wail.
Moan, brethren, moan; for lo! the rebel spheres
Spin round; the stars their antient courses keep,
Clouds still with shadowy moisture haunt the earth,   420
Still suck their fill of light from sun and moon,
Still buds the tree, and still the sea-shores murmur.
There is no death in all the universe,
No smell of death—there shall be death—Moan, moan,
Moan, Cybele,[2] moan, for thy pernicious babes   425
Have chang'd a God into a shaking[3] palsy.
Moan, brethren, moan; for I have no strength left,

9. Milnes offers "net."
1. See p. 20, n. 4. It is not clear why Pan, usually surrounded by celebrants, is "solitary"; the sense
   may be that this nature god is bereft after the end of Saturn's Golden Age. *musings*: Milnes offers
   "moanings."
2. The mother of the Olympian gods who have turned upon the older generation.
3. Milnes offers "an aching."

Weak as the reed—weak—feeble as my voice—
O, O, the pain, the pain of feebleness.
Moan, moan; for still I thaw—or give me help: 430
Throw down those imps and give me victory.
Let me hear other groans, and trumpets blown
Of triumph calm, and hymns of festival
From the gold peaks of heaven's high piled clouds;
Voices of soft proclaim, and silver stir   435
Of strings in hollow shells; and let there be
Beautiful things made new, for the surprize
Of the sky-children."—So he feebly ceas'd,
With such a poor and sickly sounding pause,
Methought I heard some old man of the earth   440
Bewailing earthly loss; nor could my eyes
And ears act with that pleasant unison of sense
Which marries sweet sound with the grace of form,
And dolorous accent from a tragic harp
With large-limb'd visions. More I scrutinized: 445
Still fix'd he sat beneath the sable trees,
Whose arms spread straggling in wild serpent forms,
With leaves all hush'd; his awful presence there
(Now all was silent) gave a deadly lie
To what I erewhile heard: only his lips   450
Trembled amid the white curls of his beard.
They told the truth, though, round the snowy locks
Hung nobly, as upon the face of heaven
A mid-day fleece of clouds. Thea arose
And stretch'd her white arm through the hollow dark,   455
Pointing some whither: whereat he too rose,
Like a vast giant seen by men at sea
To grow pale from the waves at dull midnight.
They melted from my sight into the woods;
Ere I could turn, Moneta cried—"These twain   460
Are speeding to the families of grief,
Where roof 'd in by black rocks they waste in pain
And darkness, for no hope."—And she spake on,
As ye may read who can unwearied pass
Onward from the antichamber[4] of this dream,   465
Where even at the open doors awhile
I must delay, and glean my memory
Of her high phrase: perhaps no further dare.

END OF CANTO I.

Canto II.

"Mortal, that thou may'st understand aright,
I humanize my sayings to thine ear,

---

4. For "antechamber"; see Keats's letter to Reynolds of May 3, 1818, where he discusses the "chambers" of life (p. 245).

Making companions of earthly things;
Or thou might'st better listen to the wind,
Whose language is to thee a barren noise,   5
Though it blows legend-laden through the trees.
In melancholy realms big tears are shed,
More sorrow like to this, and such like woe,
Too huge for mortal tongue, or pen of scribe.
The Titans fierce, self-hid, or prison-bound,   10
Groan for the old allegiance once more,
Listening in their doom for Saturn's voice.
But one of our whole eagle-broods still keeps
His sovereignty, and rule, and majesty;
Blazing Hyperion on his orbed fire   15
Still sits, still snuffs the incense teeming up
From man to the Sun's God: yet unsecure,
For as upon the earth dire prodigies
Fright and perplex, so also shudders he:
Nor at dog's howl, or gloom-bird's even[1] screech,   20
Or the familiar visitings of one
Upon the first toll of his passing bell:[2]
But horrors, portion'd to a giant nerve
Make great Hyperion ache. His palace bright,
Bastion'd with pyramids of glowing[3] gold,   25
And touch'd with shade of bronzed obelisks,
Glares a blood red through all the thousand courts,
Arches, and domes, and fiery galleries:
And all its curtains of Aurorian clouds
Flush[4] angerly: when he would taste the wreaths   30
Of incense breath'd aloft from sacred hills,
Instead of sweets, his ample palate takes
Savour of poisonous brass and metals sick.
Wherefore when harbour'd in the sleepy west,
After the full completion of fair day,   35
For rest divine upon exalted couch
And slumber in the arms of melody,
He paces through the pleasant hours of ease,
With strides colossal, on from hall to hall;
While, far within each aisle and deep recess,   40
His winged minions in close clusters stand
Amaz'd, and full of fear; like anxious men
Who on a wide plain gather in sad troops,
When earthquakes jar their battlements and towers.
Even now, while Saturn, rous'd from icy trance,   45
Goes, step for step, with Thea from yon woods,
Hyperion, leaving twilight in the rear,
Is sloping to the threshold of the west.—
Thither we tend."—Now in clear light I stood,
Reliev'd from the dusk vale. Mnemosyne   50

---

1. Milnes offers "hated" from *Hyperion*, l. 171.
2. Milnes inserts "Or prophesyings of the midnight lamp" from *Hyperion*, 1.174.
3. Milnes offers "shining."
4. Milnes offers "Flash," and "rich" for "sick" in l. 33.

Was sitting on a square edg'd polish'd stone,
That in its lucid depth reflected pure
Her priestess-garments. My quick eyes ran on
From stately nave to nave, from vault to vault,
Through bowers of fragrant and enwreathed light,   55
And diamond paved[5] lustrous long arcades.
Anon rush'd by the bright Hyperion;
His flaming robes stream'd out beyond his heels,
And gave a roar, as if of earthy fire,
That scar'd away the meek ethereal hours   60
And made their dove-wings tremble: on he flared

****

LEIGH HUNT [WITH KEATS]

A Now, Descriptive of a Hot Day[1]

Now the rose- (and lazy-) fingered Aurora,[2] issuing from her saffron house, calls up the moist vapours to surround her, and goes veiled with them as long as she can; till Phoebus,[3] coming forth in his power, looks every thing out of the sky, and holds sharp uninterrupted empire from his throne of beams. Now the mower begins to make his sweeping cuts more slowly, and resorts oftener to the beer. Now the carter[4] sleeps a-top of his load of hay, or plods with double slouch of shoulder; looking out with his eyes winking under his shading hat, and with a hitch upward of one side of his mouth. Now the little girl at her grandmother's cottage-door watches the coaches that go by, with her hand held up over her sunny forehead. Now labourers look well resting in their white shirts at the doors of rural alehouses. Now an elm is fine there, with a seat under it; and horses drink out of the trough, stretching their yearning necks with loosened collars; and the traveller calls for his glass of ale, having been without one for more than ten minutes; and his horse stands wincing at the flies, giving sharp shivers of his skin, and moving to and fro his ineffectual docked[5] tail; and now Miss Betty Wilson, the host's daughter, comes streaming forth in a flowered gown and ear-rings, carrying with four of her beautiful fingers the foaming glass, for which, after the traveller has drank it, she receives with an indifferent eye, looking another way, the lawful two-pence: that is to say, unless the traveller, nodding his ruddy face, pays some gallant compliment to her before he drinks, such

---

5. Milnes offers "diamond-paned."
1. This piece, created collaboratively by Keats and Hunt (who indicated that Keats contributed one or two passages to the essay) while Keats was staying at Hunt's house in Kentish Town, was first published in the *Indicator*, June 28, 1820, pp. 300–304. Keats had used the adverb "Now" in "The Cap and Bells," in what is perhaps a parody of Hunt, the preceding winter (see p. 396). The editors of *SWLH* suggest that there are echoes of that poem as well as of "To Autumn" in the essay. Hunt published Keats's sonnet on Paulo and Francesca at the close of the essay (see p. 336).
2. Roman goddess of the dawn.
3. Apollo, the sun.
4. The driver of a cart.
5. Cropped.

as "I'd rather kiss you, my dear, than the tumbler,"—or "I'll wait for you, my love, if you'll marry me;" upon which, if the man is good-looking and the lady in good-humour, she smiles and bites her lips, and says "Ah—men can talk fast enough;" upon which the old stage-coachman, who is buckling something near her, before he sets, says in a hoarse voice, "So can women too for that matter," and John Boots grins through his ragged red locks, and doats on the repartee all the day after. Now grasshoppers "fry," as Dryden says.[6] Now cattle stand in water, and ducks are envied. Now boots and shoes, and trees by the road side, are thick with dust; and dogs, rolling in it, after issuing out of the water, into which they have been thrown to fetch sticks, come scattering horror among the legs of the spectators. Now a fellow who finds he has three miles further to go in a pair of tight shoes, is in a pretty situation. Now rooms with the sun upon them become intolerable; and the apothecary's apprentice, with a bitterness beyond aloes,[7] thinks of the pond he used to bathe in at school. Now men with powdered heads (especially if thick) envy those that are unpowdered, and stop to wipe them up hill, with countenances that seem to expostulate with destiny. Now boys assemble round the village pump with a ladle to it, and delight to make a forbidden splash and get wet through the shoes. Now also they make suckers[8] of leather, and bathe all day long in rivers and ponds, and follow the fish into their cool corners, and say millions of "MY eyes!" at "tittle-bats."[9] Now the bee, as he hums along, seems to be talking heavily of the heat. Now doors and brick-walls are burning to the hand; and a walled lane, with dust and broken bottles in it, near a brick-field, is a thing not to be though of. Now a green lane, on the contrary, thick-set with hedge-row elms, and having the noise of a brook "rumbling in pebble-stone,"[1] is one of the pleasantest things in the world. Now youths and damsels walk through hay-fields, by chance; and the latter say, "Ha' done then, William;" and the overseer in the next field calls out to "let thic thear hay thear bide;" and the girls persist, merely to plague "such a frumpish old fellow."

Now, in town, gossips talk more than ever to one another, in rooms, in doorways, and out of window, always beginning the conversation with saying that the heat is overpowering. Now blinds are let down, and doors thrown open, and flannel waistcoats left off, and cold meat preferred to hot, and wonder expressed why tea continues so refreshing, and people delight to sliver lettuces into bowls, and apprentices water door-ways with tin-canisters that lay several atoms of dust. Now the water-cart, jumbling along the idle of the street, and jolting the showers out of it's box of water, really does something. Now boys delight to have a water-pipe let out, and see it bubbling away in a tall and frothy volume. Now fruiterers' shops and dairies look pleasant, and ices are the only things to those who can get

---

6. Hunt appears to refer to Dryden's translation of Horace's Ode 29, "To Maecenas": "The Sun is in the Lion mounted high . . . The Ground below is parch'd, the Heavens above us fry. / The Shepherd drives his fainting Flock / Beneath the Covert of a Rock, / And seeks refreshing Rivulets nigh" (ll. 29–36).
7. The drug made from the juice of the aloe plant is bitter with a strong odor.
8. Pipes or tubes.
9. Child's name for stickleback, a small fish.
1. SWLH cites Robert Baron's prose work, Erotopaignion, or the Cyprian Academy (1647): "silver streames . . . gently tumbled over their beds of pebble stone" (Book I, p. 38).

them. Now ladies loiter in baths; and people make presents of flowers; and wine is put into ice; and the after-dinner lounger recreates his head with applications of perfumed water out of long-necked bottles. Now the lounger who cannot resist riding his ne horse feels his boots burn him. Now buck-skins are not the lawn of Cos.[2] Now jockies, walking in great coats to lose flesh, curse inwardly. Now five fat people in a stage coach, hate the sixth fat one who is coming in, and think he has no right to be so large. Now clerks in offices do nothing, but drink soda-water and spruce-beer, and read the newspaper. Now the old clothes-man drops his solitary cry more deeply into the areas on the hot and forsaken side of the street; and bakers look vicious; and cooks are aggravated and the steam of a tavern kitchen catches hold of one like the breath of Tartarus.[3] Now delicate skins are beset with gnats; and boys make their sleeping companion start up, with playing a burning-glass[4] on his hand; and black-smiths are super-carbonated; and cobblers in their stalls almost feel a wish to be transplanted; and butter is too easy to spread; and the dragoons wonder whether the Romans liked their helmets; and old ladies, with their lappets[5] unpinned, walk along in a state of dilapidation; and the servant-maids are afraid they look vulgarly hot; and the author who has a plate of strawberries brought him, finds that he has come to the end of his writing.

We cannot conclude this article however without returning thanks, both on our own account and on that of our numerous predecessors who have left so large a debt of gratitude unpaid, to this very useful and ready— "Now." We are sure that there is not a didactic poet, ancient or modern, who if he possessed a decent share of candour would not be happy to own his acknowledgments to that masterly conjunction, which possesses the very essence of wit, for it has the talent of bringing the most remote things together. And it's generosity is in due proportion to it's talent, for it always is most profuse of it's aid, where it is most wanted.

We must enjoy a pleasant passage with the reader on the subject of this "eternal Now" in Beaumont and Fletcher's play of the Woman Hater.[6]— Upon turning to it, we perceive that our illustrious particle does not make quite so great a figure as we imagined; but the whole passage is in so analogous a taste, and affords such an agreeable specimen of the wit and humour with which fine poets could rally the common-places of their art, that we cannot help proceeding with it. Lazarello, a foolish table-hunter, has requested an introduction to the Duke of Milan, who has had a fine lamprey presented him. Before the introduction takes place, he finds that the Duke has given the fish away; so that his wish to be known to him goes with it; and part of the drollery of the passage arises from his uneasiness at being detained by the consequences of his own request, and his fear lest he should be too late for the lamprey elsewhere.

COUNT. (Aside to the Duke.) Let me entreat your Grace to stay a little,
To know a gentleman, to whom yourself

2. *Cos vestis*, referred to by Horace, is a thin kind of silk or gauze made on the Greek island of Cos (near the Turkish coast and famous for being the home of Hippocrates, the founder of medicine).
3. In Greek mythology, the place of punishment in Hades.
4. Magnifying glass.
5. Overlapping pieces of garment.
6. Francis Beaumont and John Fletcher, *The Woman Hater* (1607), 2.1.

Is much beholding. He hath made the sport
For your whole court these eight years, on my knowledge.
   DUKE. His name?
   COUNT. Lazarello.
   DUKE. I heard of him this morning:—which is he?
   COUNT. (Aside to Laz.) Lazarello, pluck up they spirits. Thy fortune is
now raising. The Duke calls for thee, and thou shalt be acquainted with
him.
   LAZ. He's going away, and I must of necessity stay here upon business.
   COUNT. 'Tis all one: thou shalt know him first.
   LAZ. Stay a little. If he should offer to take me with him, and by that
means I should lose that I seek for! But if he should, I will not go with
him.
   COUNT. Lazarello, the Duke stays. Wilt thou lose this opportunity?
   LAZ. How must I speak to him?
   COUNT. 'Twas well thought of. You must talk to him as you do to an
ordinary man, honest plain sense; but you must wind about him. For
example if he should ask you what o'clock it is, you must not say, "If it
please your Grace, 'tis nine";—but thus;—"Thrice three o'clock, so please
my Sovereign":—or thus;—

> "Look how many Muses there doth dwell
> Upon the sweet banks of the learned well,
> And just so many strokes the clock hath struck";—

And so forth. And you must now and then enter into a description.
   LAZ. I hope I shall do it.
   COUNT. Come.—May it please your Grace to take note of a gentleman,
well seen, deeply read, and thoroughly grounded, in the hidden knowledge
of all sallets[7] and pot-herbs whatsoever?
   DUKE. I shall desire to know him more inwardly.
   LAZ. I kiss the ox-hide of your Grace's foot.
   COUNT. (Aside to Laz.) Very well.—Will your Grace question him a
little?
   DUKE. How old are you?
   LAZ. Full eight-and-twenty several almanacks
Have been compiled, all for several years,
Since first I drew this breath. Four prenticeships
Have I most truly served in this world:
And eight-and-twenty times hath Phoebus' car
Run out his yearly course, since—
   DUKE. I understand you, Sir.
   LUCIO. How like an ignorant poet he talks!
   DUKE. You are eight-and-twenty years old? What time of the day do you
hold it to be?
   LAZ. About the time that mortals whet their knives
On thresholds, on their shoe-soles, and on stairs.
Now bread is grating, and the testy cook
Hath much to do now: now the tables all—
   DUKE. 'Tis almost dinner-time?
   LAZ. You Grace doth apprehend me very rightly.

---

7. Late medieval war helmets.

Letter to Fanny Brawne, July 5?, 1820[1]

Wednesday Morng.

My dearest Girl,

I have been a walk this morning with a book in my hand, but as usual I have been occupied with nothing but you: I wish I could say in an agreeable manner. I am tormented day and night. They talk of my going to Italy.[2] 'Tis certain I shall never recover if I am to be so long separate from you: yet with all this devotion to you I cannot persuade myself into any confidence of you. Past experience connected with the fact of my long separation from you gives me agonies which are scarcely to be talked of. When your mother comes I shall be very sudden and expert in asking her whether you have been to Mrs. Dilke's, for she might say no to make me easy. I am literally worn to death, which seems my only recourse. I cannot forget what has pass'd. What? nothing with a man of the world, but to me deathful. I will get rid of this as much as possible. When you were in the habit of flirting with Brown you would have left off, could your own heart have felt one half of one pang mine did. Brown is a good sort of Man—he did not know he was doing me to death by inches. I feel the effect of every one of those hours in my side now; and for that cause, though he has done me many services, though I know his love and friendship for me, though at this moment I should be without pence were it not for his assistance, I will never see or speak to him until we are both old men, if we are to be. I *will* resent my heart having been made a football. You will call this madness. I have heard you say that it was not unpleasant to wait a few years—you have amusements—your mind is away—you have not brooded over one idea as I have, and how should you? You are to me an object intensely desirable— the air I breathe in a room empty of you is unhealthy. I am not the same to you—no—you can wait—you have a thousand activities—you can be happy without me. Any party, any thing to fill up the day has been enough. How have you pass'd this month? Who have you smil'd with? All this may seem savage in me. You do not feel as I do—you do not know what it is to love— one day you may—your time is not come. Ask yourself how many unhappy hours Keats has caused you in Loneliness. For myself I have been a Martyr the whole time, and for this reason I speak; the confession is forc'd from me by the torture. I appeal to you by the blood of that Christ you believe in: Do not write to me if you have done anything this month which it would have pained me to have seen. You may have altered—if you have not—if you still behave in dancing rooms and other societies as I have seen you—I do not want to live—if you have done so I wish this coming night may be my last. I cannot live without you, and not only you but *chaste you*; *virtuous you.* The Sun rises and sets, the day passes, and you follow the bent of your inclination to a certain extent—you have no conception of the quantity of miserable feeling that passes through me in a day.—Be serious! Love is not a plaything—and again do not write unless you can do it with a crystal conscience. I would sooner die for want of you than——

Yours for ever
J. Keats.

---

1. Text from HBF (1883), 4: 181–83.
2. Keats had suffered a major hemorrhage on June 22 and his doctors, William Lambe and George Darling, recommended he go to Italy for his health.

CHARLES LAMB

Review of *Lamia, Isabella, The Eve of St. Agnes and Other Poems.*[1]

[The review opens with quotations from *Eve of St. Agnes*, stanzas 24, 25.1–8, 26–27.]
Such is the description which Mr. Keats has given us, with a delicacy worthy of Christabel,[2] of a high-born damsel, in one of the apartments of a baronial castle, laying herself down devoutly to dream, on the charmed Eve of St Agnes; and like the radiance, which comes from those old windows upon the limbs and garments of the damsel, is the almost Chaucer-like painting, with which this poet illumes every subject he touches. We have scarcely any thing like it in modern description. It brings us back to ancient days, and

> *Beauty making-beautiful old rhymes.*[3]

The finest thing in the volume is the paraphrase of Boccaccio's story of the Pot of Basil. Two Florentines, merchants, discovering that their sister Isabella has placed her affections upon Lorenzo, a young factor[4] in their employ, when they had hopes of procuring for her a noble match, decoy Lorenzo, under pretence of a ride, into a wood, where they suddenly stab and bury him. The anticipation of the assassination is wonderfully conceived in one epithet, in the narration of the ride—

> So the two brothers, and their *murder'd* man,
>   Rode past fair Florence, to where Arno's stream
> Gurgles—[5]

Returning to their sister, they delude her with a story of their having sent Lorenzo abroad to look after their merchandises; but the spirit of her lover appears to Isabella in a dream, and discovers how and where he was stabbed, and the spot where they have buried him. To ascertain the truth of the vision, she sets out to the place, accompanied by her old nurse, ignorant as yet of her wild purpose. Her arrival at it, and digging for the body, is described in the following stanzas, than which there is nothing more awfully simple in diction, more nakedly grand and moving in sentiment, in Dante, in Chaucer, or in Spenser:—
[Quotes *Isabella*, stanzas 46–48.]
To pursue the story in prose.—They find the body, and with their joint strengths sever from it the head, which Isabella takes home, and wrapping it in a silken scarf, entombs it in a garden-pot, covers it with mould, and over it she plants sweet basil, which, watered with her tears, thrives so that no other basil tufts in all Florence throve like her basil. How her brothers, suspecting something mysterious in this herb, which she watched day and

1. This unsigned review by Charles Lamb (see p. 111, n. 6) was published in the Tory daily the *New Times* for July 19, 1820 (reprinted in the *Examiner* for July 30); three days later, the paper published extracts from the odes and *Hyperion*, not discussed here.
2. Coleridge's poem of that name was published in 1816.
3. Shakespeare, Sonnet 106.3.
4. Agent.
5. Lines 209–11.

night, at length discover the head, and secretly convey the basil from her; and how from the day that she loses her basil she pines away, and at last dies, we must refer our readers to the poem, or to the divine germ of it in Boccaccio. It is a great while ago since we read the original; and in this affecting revival of it we do but

> *weep again a long-forgotten woe.*[6]

More exuberantly rich in imagery and painting is the story of the Lamia. It is of as gorgeous stuff as ever romance was composed of. Her first appearance in serpentine form—

> —a beauteous wreath with melancholy eyes[7]—

her dialogue with Hermes, the *Star of Lethe*, as he is called by one of those prodigal phrases which Mr Keats abounds in, which are each a poem in a word, and which in this instance lays open to us at once, like a picture, all the dim regions and their inhabitants, and the sudden coming of a celestial among them; the charming of her into woman's shape again by the God; her marriage with the beautiful Lycius; her magic palace, which those who knew the street, and remembered it complete from childhood, never remembered to have seen before; the few Persian mutes, her attendants,

> —who that same year
> Were seen about the markets: none knew where
> They could inhabit;[8]—

the high-wrought splendours of the nuptial bower, with the fading of the whole pageantry, Lamia, and all, away, before the glance of Apollonius,— are all that fairy land can do for us. They are for younger impressibilities. To *us* an ounce of feeling is worth a pound of fancy; and therefore we recur again, with a warmer gratitude, to the story of Isabella and the pot of basil, and those never-cloying stanzas which we have cited, and which we think should disarm criticism, if it be not in its nature cruel; if it would not deny to honey its sweetness, nor to roses redness, nor light to the stars in Heaven; if it would not bay the moon out of the skies, rather than acknowledge she is fair.

PERCY BYSSHE SHELLEY

Letter to Keats, July 27, 1820[1]

Pisa—July 27, 1820

My dear Keats
    I hear with great pain the dangerous accident that you have undergone, & Mr Gisborne who gives me the account of it, adds that you continue to

---

6. Shakespeare, Sonnet 30.7.
7. *Lamia*, 1.84; the reviewer refers in the next sentence to l.81.
8. *Lamia*, 1.390–92.
1. Written from Italy after Shelley heard from his friends the Gisbornes, who were in London, of Keats's serious hemorrhage of June 22 (see *Maria Gisborne & Edward E. Williams, Shelley's Friends: Their Journals and Letters*, ed. F. L. Jones [Norman, OK, 1951], pp. 35–37) and sent to Keats via Leigh Hunt with whom Keats had been staying. Text from ALS (Harvard Keats MS 4.17.1).

wear a consumptive appearance. This consumption is a disease particularly fond of people who write such good verses as you have done, and with the assistance of an English winter it can often indulge its selection;—I do not think that young & amiable poets are at all bound to gratify its taste; they have entered into no bond with the Muses to that effect . . . But seriously (for I am joking on what I am very anxious about) I think you would do well to pass the winter after so tremendous an accident in Italy, & (if you thinks it as necessary as I do) so long as you could find Pisa or its neighbourhood agreeable to you, Mrs Shelley unites with myself in urging the request, that you would take up your residence with us.—You might come by sea to Leghorn, (France is not worth seeing, & the sea air is particularly good for weak lungs) which is within a few miles of us. You ought at all events to see Italy, & your health which I suggest as a motive, might be an excuse to you.—I spare declamation about the statues & the paintings & the ruins—& what is a greater piece of forbearance—about the mountains the Streams & the fields, the colours of the sky, & the sky itself—

I have lately read your Endymion again & ever with a new sense of the treasures of poetry it contains, though treasures poured forth with indistinct profusion. This, people in general will not endure, & that is the cause of the comparatively few copies which have been sold.—I feel persuaded that you are capable of the greatest things, so you but will.

I always tell Ollier to send you Copies of my books.[2]—"Prometheus Unbound" I imagine you will receive nearly at the same time with this letter. The Cenci I hope you have already received—it was studiously composed in a different style "below the *good* how far! but far above the *great*."[3] In poetry *I* have sought to avoid system & mannerism; I wish those who excel me in genius, would pursue the same plan—

Whether you remain in England, or journey to Italy,—believe that you carry with you my anxious wishes for your health happiness & success, wherever you are or whatever you undertake—& that I am

Yours sincerely P. B. Shelley

Letter to Fanny Brawne, August? 1820[1]

I do not write this till the last, that no eye may catch it.[2]

My dearest Girl,

I wish you could invent some means to make me at all happy without you. Every hour I am more and more concentrated in you; every thing else tastes like chaff in my Mouth. I feel it almost impossible to go to Italy— the fact is I cannot leave you, and shall never taste one minute's content until it pleases chance to let me live with you for good. But I will not go on at this rate. A person in health as you are can have no conception of

2. See Shelley's letter of August 20, 1819, to his publisher, Charles Ollier in *The Letters of of Percy Bysshe Shelley*, ed. Frederick L. Jones, 2 vols. (Oxford: Clarendon Press, 1964), 2: 119–21.
3. See the last line of Thomas Gray's *Progress of Poesy* (1754).
1. This is perhaps Keats's last letter to Fanny Brawne. Text from ALS (cased in the Berg Collection of English and American Literature, The New York Public Library, Astor, Lenox and Tilden Foundations: John Keats Collection of Papers, 1816–1948 Bulk [1816–1924]).
2. This suggests the letter was written at Hunt's house, where Keats was concerned the large family would intrude on his private matters.

the horrors that nerves and a temper like mine go through. What Island do your friends propose retiring to? I should be happy to go with you there alone, but in company I should object to it; the backbitings and jealousies of new colonists who have nothing else to amuse them selves, is unbearable. Mᵣ Dilke came to see me yesterday, and gave me a very great deal more pain than pleasure. I shall never be able any more to endure to society of any of those who used to meet at Elm Cottage and Wentworth Place.³ The last two years taste like brass upon my Palate. If I cannot live with you I will live alone. I do not think my health will improve much while I am separated from you. For all this I am averse to seeing you—I cannot bear flashes of light and return into my glooms again. I am not so unhappy now as I should be if I had seen you yesterday. To be happy with you seems such an impossibility! it requires a luckier Star than mine! it will never be. I enclose a passage from one of your Letters which I want you to alter a little—I want (if you will have it so) the matter express'd less coldly to me. If my health would bear it, I could write a Poem which I have in my head, which would be a consolation for people in such a situation as mine. I would show some one in Love as I am, with a person living in such Liberty as you do. Shakspeare always sums up matters in the most sovereign manner. Hamlet's heart was full of such Misery as mine is when he said to Ophelia "Go to a Nunnery, go, go!"⁴ Indeed I should like to give up the matter at once—I should like to die. I am sickened at the brute world which you are smiling with. I hate men and women more. I see nothing but thorns for the future—wherever I may be next winter in Italy or nowhere Brown will be living near you with his indecencies⁵—I see no prospect of any rest. Suppose me in Rome—well, I should there see you as in a magic glass going to and from town at all hours,—I wish you could infuse a little confidence in human nature into my heart. I cannot muster any—the world is too brutal for me—I am glad there is such a thing as the grave—I am sure I shall never have any rest till I get there. At any rate I will indulge myself by never seeing any more Dilke or Brown or any of their Friends. I wish I was either in your arms full of faith or that a Thunder bolt would strike me.

God bless you—J.K—

LEIGH HUNT

Review of *Lamia, Isabella, The Eve of St. Agnes and Other Poems.*¹

In laying before our readers an account of another new publication, it is fortunate that the nature of the work again falls in with the character of our miscellany; part of the object of which is to relate the stories of old times. We shall therefore abridge into prose the stories which Mr Keats has told in poetry, only making up for it, as we go, by cutting some of the richest pas-

---

3. For Dilke, see p. 78, n.1. The Brawnes lived at both Elm Cottage and Wentworth Place, where Keats also once lived.
4. *Hamlet*, 3.1.122.
5. A reference to Brown's affair with Abigail O'Donaghue.
1. Published in the *Indicator* for August 2, 1820, pp. 337–44, and August 9, 1820, pp. 345–52. Hunt's long summaries of the plots of the three opening narratives have been cut.

sages out of his verse, and fitting them in to our plainer narrative. They are such as would leaven a much greater lump. Their drops are rich and vital, the essence of a heap of fertile thoughts.

The first story, entitled Lamia, was suggested to our author by a passage in Burton's Anatomy of Melancholy, which he has extracted at the end of it. * * *

Mr. Keats has departed as much from common-place in the character and moral of this story, as he has in the poetry of it. He would see fair play to the serpent, and makes the power of the philosopher an ill-natured and disturbing thing. Lamia though liable to be turned into painful shapes had a soul of humanity; and the poet does not see why she should not have her pleasures accordingly, merely because a philosopher saw that she was not a mathematical truth. This is fine and good. It is vindicating the greater philosophy of poetry. At the same time, we wish that for the purpose of his story he had not appeared to give in to the common-place of supposing that Apollonius's sophistry must always prevail, and that modern experiment has done a deadly thing to poetry by discovering the nature of the rainbow, the air, &c.: that is to say, that the knowledge of natural history and physics, by shewing us the nature of things, does away the imaginations that once adorned them.[2] This is a condescension to a learned vulgarism, which so excellent a poet as Mr. Keats ought not to have made. The world will always have fine poetry, as long as it has events, passions, affections, and a philosophy that sees deeper than this philosophy. There will be a poetry of the heart, as long as there are tears and smiles: there will be a poetry of the imagination, as long as the first causes of things remain a mystery. A man who is no poet, may think he is none, as soon as he finds out the physical cause of the rainbow; but he need not alarm himself:—he was none before. The true poet will go deeper. He will ask himself what is the cause of that physical cause; whether truths to the senses are after all to be taken as truths to the imagination; and whether there is not room and mystery enough in the universe for the creation of infinite things, when the poor matter-of-fact philosopher has come to the end of his own vision. It is remarkable that an age of poetry has grown up with the progress of experiment; and that the very poets, who seem to countenance these notions, accompany them by some of their finest effusions. Even if there were nothing new to be created,—if philosophy, with its line and rule, could even score the ground, and say to poetry "Thou shalt go no further," she would look back to the old world, and still find it inexhaustible. The crops from its fertility are endless. But these alarms are altogether idle. The essence of poetical enjoyment does not consist in belief, but in a voluntary power to imagine.

The next story, that of the Pot of Basil, is from Boccaccio. * * *

Our author can pass to the most striking imaginations from the most delicate and airy fancy. He says of the lovers in their happiness,

[Quotes *Isabella*, ll. 73–76.]

These pictures of their intercourse terribly aggravate the gloom of what follows. Lorenzo, when lured away to be killed, is taken unknowingly out of his joys, like a lamb out of the pasture. The following masterly anticipation of his end, conveyed in a single word, has been justly admired:[3]—

---

2. See *Lamia*, 2.229–38.
3. By Lamb; see his review, pp. 515–16; he quotes *Isabella*, ll. 209–11, 215–16.

> So the two brothers and their *murder'd* man
>   Rode past fair Florence, to where Arno's stream
> Gurgles through straitened banks.
>   They passed the water
> Into a forest quiet for the slaughter.

When Mr. Keats errs in his poetry, it is from the ill management of a good thing,—exuberance of ideas. Once or twice, he does so in a taste positively bad, like Marino or Cowley,[4] as in a line in his Ode to Psyche

> At tender eye-dawn of aurorean love;

but it is once or twice only, in his present volume. Nor has he erred much in it in a nobler way. What we allude to is one or two passages in which he over-informs the occasion or the speaker; as where the brothers, for instance, whom he describes as a couple of mere "money-bags," are gifted with the power of uttering the following exquisite metaphor:—

> "To-day we purpose, ay, this hour we mount
>   To spur three leagues towards the Apennine:
> Come down, we pray thee, ere the hot sun count
>   His dewy rosary on the eglantine."[5]

*   *   *

The Eve of St. Agnes, which is rather a picture than a story, may be analysed in a few words. It is an account of a young beauty, who going to bed on the eve in question to dream of her lover, while her rich kinsmen, the opposers of his love, are keeping holiday in the rest of the house, finds herself waked by him in the night, and in the hurry of the moment agrees to elope with him. The portrait of the heroine, preparing to go to bed, is remarkable for its union of extreme richness and good taste; not that those two properties of description are naturally distinct; but that they are too often separated by very good poets and that the passage affords a striking specimen of the sudden and strong maturity of the author's genius. When he wrote Endymion he could not have resisted doing too much. To the description before us, it would be a great injury either to add or diminish. It falls at once gorgeously and delicately upon us, like the colours of the painted glass. Nor is Madeline hurt by all her encrusting jewelry and rustling silks. Her gentle, unsophisticated heart is in the midst, and turns them into so many ministrants to her loveliness.
    [Quotes *Eve of St Agnes*, stanzas 24–27.]
Is not this perfectly beautiful?
    As a specimen of the Poems, which are all lyrical, we must indulge ourselves in quoting entire the Ode to a Nightingale. There is that mixture in it of real melancholy and imaginative relief which poetry alone presents us in her "charmed cup,"[6] and which some over-rational critics have undertaken to find wrong because it is not true. It does not follow that what is

---

4. Abraham Cowley (1618–1667), author and scholar, was known in particular for his "Pindarique Odes," which introduced the irregular ode into English literature. Giambattista Marino (1569–1625), Neapolitan poet, whose style of "marinismo" was considered extremely mannered and full of conceits. Hunt goes on to quote Keats's "Ode to Psyche," l. 20.
5. *Isabella*, ll. 142, 185–88.
6. This phrase appears in a number of places, but probably should be traced back to Milton's *Comus* (1637), scene 1, l. 51.

not true to them, is not true to others. If the relief is real, the mixture is good and sufficing. A poet finds refreshment in his imaginary wine, as other men do in their real; nor have we the least doubt, that Milton found his grief for the loss of his friend King, more solaced by the allegorical recollections of Lycidas, (which were exercises of his mind, and recollections of a friend who would have admired them) than if he could have anticipated Dr. Johnson's objections, and mourned in nothing but broadcloth and matter of fact.[7] He yearned after the poetical as well as social part of his friend's nature; and had as much right to fancy it straying in the wilds and oceans of romance, where it had strayed, as in the avenues of Christ's College where his body had walked. In the same spirit the imagination of Mr. Keats betakes itself like the wind, "where it listeth,"[8] and is as truly there, as if his feet could follow it. The poem will be the more striking to the reader, when he understands what we take a friend's liberty in telling him, that the author's powerful mind has for some time past been inhabiting a sickened and shaken body, and that in the mean while it has had to contend with feelings that make a fine nature ache for its species, even when it would disdain to do so for itself;—we mean, critical malignity,—that unhappy envy, which would wreak its own tortures upon others, especially upon those that really feel for it already.

[Quotes "Ode to a Nightingale."]

The Hyperion is a fragment,—a gigantic one, like a ruin in the desart, or the bones of the mastodon. It is truly of a piece with its subject, which is the downfall of the elder gods. It opens with Saturn, dethroned, sitting in a deep and solitary valley, benumbed in spite of his huge powers with the amazement of the change.

*   *   *

The fragment ends with the deification of Apollo. It strikes us that there is something too effeminate and human in the way in which Apollo receives the exaltation which his wisdom is giving him. He weeps and wonders somewhat too fondly; but his powers gather nobly on him as he proceeds. * * *

If any living poet could finish this fragment, we believe it is the author himself. But perhaps he feels that he ought not. A story which involves passion, almost of necessity involves speech; and though we may well enough describe beings greater than ourselves by comparison, unfortunately we cannot make them speak by comparison.* * * The moment the Gods speak, we forget that they did not speak like ourselves. The fact is, they feel like ourselves; and the poet would have to make them feel otherwise, even if he could make them speak otherwise, which he cannot, unless he venture upon an obscurity which would destroy our sympathy: and what is sympathy with a God, but turning him into a man? We allow, that superiority and inferiority are, after all, human terms, and imply something not so truly fine and noble as the levelling of a great sympathy and love; but poems of the present nature, like Paradise Lost, assume a different principle; and fortunately perhaps, it is one which it is impossible to reconcile with the other.

We have now to conclude the surprise of the reader, who has seen what solid stuff these poems are made of; with informing him of what the book

---

7. Samuel Johnson criticized Milton's "Lycidas" in *Lives of the English Poets* (1779–81).
8. John 3.8.

has not mentioned,—that they were almost all written four years ago, when the author was but twenty. Ay, indeed! cries a critic, rubbing his hands delighted (if indeed even criticism can do so, any longer); "then that accounts for the lines you speak of; written in the taste of Marino."—It does so; but, sage Sir, after settling the merits of those one or two lines you speak of what accounts, pray, for a small matter which you leave unnoticed, namely, all the rest?—The truth is, we rather mention this circumstance as a matter of ordinary curiosity, than any thing else; for great faculties have great privileges, and leap over time as well as other obstacles. Time itself; and its continents, are things yet to be discovered. There is no knowing even how much duration one man may crowd into a few years, while others drag out their slender lines. There are circular roads full of hurry and scenery, and straight roads full of listlessness and barrenness; and travellers may arrive by both, at the same hour. The Miltons, who begin intellectually old, and still intellectual, end physically old, are indeed Methusalems;[9] and may such be our author, their son.

Mr. Keats's versification sometimes reminds us of Milton in his blank verse, and sometimes of Chapman[1] both in his blank verse and rhyme; but his faculties, essentially speaking, though partaking of the unearthly aspirations and abstract yearnings of both these poets, are altogether his own. They are ambitious, but less directly so. They are more social, and in the finer sense of the word, sensual, than either. They are more coloured by the modern philosophy of sympathy and natural justice. Endymion, with all its extraordinary powers, partook of the faults of youth, though the best ones; but the reader of Hyperion and these other stories would never guess that they were written at twenty. The author's versification is now perfected, the exuberances of his imagination restrained, and a calm power, the surest and loftiest of all power, takes place of the impatient workings of the younger god within him. The character of his genius is that of energy and voluptuousness, each able at will to take leave of the other, and possessing, in their union, a high feeling of humanity not common to the best authors who can less combine them. Mr. Keats undoubtedly takes his seat with the oldest and best of our living poets.

We have carried our criticism to much greater length than we intended; but in truth, whatever the critics might think, it is a refreshment to us to get upon other people's thoughts, even though the rogues be our contemporaries. Oh! how little do those minds get out of themselves, and what fertile and heaven-breathing prospects do they lose, who think that a man must be confined to the mill-path of his own homestead, merely that he may avoid seeing the abundance of his neighbours! Above all, how little do they know of us eternal, weekly, and semi-weekly writers! We do not mean to say that it is not very pleasant to run upon a smooth road, seeing what we like, and talking what we like; but we do say, that it is pleasanter than all, when we are tired, to hear what we like, and to be lulled with congenial thoughts and higher music, till we are fresh to start again upon our journey. What we would not give to have a better Examiner and a better Indicator than our own twice every week, uttering our own thoughts in

9. Methuselah is the longest-lived person in the Bible, credited with 969 years.
1. See p. 54, n. 1.

a finer manner, and altering the world faster and better than we can alter it! How we should like to read our present number, five times bettered; and to have nothing to do, for years and years, but to pace the green lanes, forget the tax-gatherer, and vent ourselves now and then in a verse.

Letter to Leigh Hunt, August 13?, 1820[1]
(An Amyntas)[2]

Wentworth Place

My dear Hunt,

You will be glad to hear I am going to delay a little time at M[rs] Brawnes. I hope to see you whenever you can get time for I feel really attach'd to you for your many sympathies with me, and patience at my lunes.[3] Will you send by the Bearess Lucy Vaughn Lloyd:[4] My best rem[cs] to M[rs] Hunt—

Your affectionate friend
John Keats

LEIGH HUNT

Letter to Keats, August 13, 1820[1]

Mortimer Terrace.

Giovanni mio,

I shall see you this afternoon, & most probably every day. You judge rightly when you think I shall be glad at your putting up awhile where you are, instead of that solitary place.[2] There are humanities in the house; & if wisdom loves to live with children round her knees (the tax-gatherer apart), *sick* wisdom, I think, should love to live with arms about its waist. I need not say how you gratify me by the impulse which led you to write a particular sentence in your letter, for you must have seen by this time how much I am attached to yourself.

I am indicating at as dull a rate as a battered finger-post in wet weather.[3] Not that I am ill: for I am very well altogether.

Your affectionate friend,
Leigh Hunt.

1. Written after Keats left Hunt's house (where he had been convalescing since June) when he became angry that one of Hunt's children had opened a letter from Fanny Brawne. Keats had earlier written to his sister Fanny not only about that incident (August 13, 1820, *L,* 2: 313) but also about the fact that "M[r] Hunt does every thing in his power to make the time pass as agreeably with me as possible" (July 22, 1820, *L,* 2: 309). Text from ALS (manuscript box in the Berg Collection of English and American Literature, The New York Public Library, Astor, Lenox and Tilden Foundations: John Keats Collection of Papers, 1816–1948 Bulk [1816–1924]).
2. Hunt had just published a translation of Tasso's *Amyntas, A Tale of the Woods,* dedicated to Keats.
3. Lunatic outbursts.
4. Rollins speculates that Fanny Brawne was sent to get the manuscript of *The Cap and Bells* (see *L,* 2.317, n.1)

1. An answer to the last letter. Text from Hunt's holograph (LMA K/MS/02/088/6587) with an addition from *Papers of a Critic. Selected from the Writings of the Late Charles Wentworth Dilke,* 2 vols. (1875), 1:9–10.
2. That is, Hunt is glad Keats is at the Brawnes' rather than the Bentleys'.
3. That is, he is laboring at writing for his journal the *Indicator,* which had recently reviewed Keats's new volume (see p. 518–23); *finger-post:* a "post set up at the parting of roads, with one or more arms, often terminating in the shape of a finger, to indicate the directions of the several roads" (*OED*).

Letter to Percy Bysshe Shelley, August 16, 1820[1]

Hampstead August 16th

My dear Shelley,

I am very much gratified that you, in a foreign country, and with a mind almost over occupied, should write to me in the strain of the Letter beside me. If I do not take advantage of your invitation it will be prevented by a circumstance I have very much at heart to prophesy—There is no doubt that an english winter would put an end to me, and do so in a lingering hateful manner, therefore I must either voyage or journey to Italy as a soldier marches up to a battery. My nerves at present are the worst part of me, yet they feel soothed when I think that come what extreme may, I shall not be destined to remain in one spot long enough to take a hatred of any four particular bed-posts. I am glad you take any pleasure in my poor Poem;— which I would willingly take the trouble to unwrite, if possible, did I care so much as I have done about Reputation. I received a copy of the Cenci, as from yourself from Hunt. There is only one part of it I am judge of; the Poetry, and dramatic effect, which by many spirits now a days is considered the mammon. A modern work it is said must have a purpose, which may be the God—*an artist* must serve Mammon[2]—he must have "self concentration" selfishness perhaps. You I am sure will forgive me for sincerely remarking that you might curb your magnanimity and be more of an artist, and 'load every rift' of your subject with ore.[3] The thought of such discipline must fall like cold chains upon you, who perhaps never sat with your wings furl'd for six Months together. And is not this extraordinary talk for the writer of Endymion? whose mind was like a pack of scattered cards—I am pick'd up and sorted to a pip.[4] My Imagination is a Monastry and I am its Monk—you must explain my metap[cs5] to yourself. I am in expectation of Prometheus every day. Could I have my own wish for its interest effected you would have it still in manuscript—or be but now putting an end to the second act. I remember you advising me not to publish my first-blights, on Hampstead heath[6]—I am returning advice upon your hands. Most of the Poems in the volume I send you have been written above two years, and would never have been publish'd but from a hope of gain; so you see I am inclined enough to take your advice now. I must express once more my deep sense of your kindness, adding my sincere thanks and respects for M[rs] Shelley. In the hope of soon seeing you I remain

most sincerely
John Keats—

---

1. A response to Shelley's letter, pp. 516–17. As Hunt wrote Shelley, Keats "is sensible of your kindness, and has sent you a letter and a fine piece of poetry [the 1820 volume] by the Gisbornes. He is advised to go to Rome, but will call on you in the Spring" (*Correspondence* [1862], 1:158). The Gisbornes sailed for Europe on September 3 and returned to Leghorn and Shelley around October 10. For an analysis of this exchange of letters, see Cox, *Poetry and Politics*, pp. 187–218. Text from ALS at Oxford, Bodleian Library, [Abinger] S. N.
2. See Matthew 6.24 and Luke 16.13. Mammon represents material wealth.
3. See Spenser, *The Faerie Queene*, 2.7.28, l. 5, where Mammon "with rich metall loaded euery rift."
4. Arranged in order, with all the cards matched up.
5. Difficult to read: perhaps an abbreviation of "metaphysics," but perhaps of "metaphor."
6. While Shelley may have advised against the publication of *Poems*, Keats's publisher recalled Shelley speaking to him "about the printing of a little volume of Keats's first poems" (see John Dix, *Pen and Ink Sketches of Poets, Preachers, and Politicians* [1846], p. 144 and SC, 5: 408).

JOSIAH CONDER

Review of *Lamia, Isabella, The Eve of St. Agnes and Other Poems*[1]

It is just three years since we were called upon to review Mr. Keats's first production. We then gave it as our opinion, that he was not incapable of writing good poetry, that he possessed both the requisite fancy and skill; but we regretted that a young man of his vivid imagination and promising talents should have been flattered into the resolution to publish verses of which he would probably be glad a few years after to escape from the remembrance. It is our practice, when a young writer appears for the first time as a candidate for public favour, to look to the indications of ability which are to be detected in his performance, rather than to its intrinsic merits. There is a wasteful efflorescence that must be thrown off before the intellect attains its maturity. The mind is then at a critical period: there is equal danger of its lavishing all its strength in the abortive promise of excellence, and of its being blighted by unjust discouragement. Such appeared to us to be then the situation of Mr. Keats; and in the spirit of candour and of kindness, we made those remarks on his volume which were designed at once to guide and to excite his future exertions, but for which he manfully disdained to be the wiser. His next production had the good fortune to fall into the hands of critics who rarely deal in either half-praise or half-censure, and whose severity of censure can at least confer notoriety upon the offender. According to his own account, the Author of Endymion must, while smarting under their unsparing lash, have claimed pity almost equally on account of his mortified feelings and his infidel creed; for, in the preface to that 'feverish attempt,' he avows his conviction that there is not a fiercer hell than the failure in a great object.[2] How complete was his failure in that matchless tissue of sparkling and delicious nonsense, his Publishers frankly confess in an Advertisement prefixed to the present volume, wherein they take upon themselves the responsibility of printing an unfinished poem in the same strain, from proceeding with which the Author was discouraged by the reception given to that poem. And yet, under the sanction, we presume, of the same advisers, Mr. Keats has ventured to proclaim himself in his title-page as the unfortunate 'Author of *Endymion*.' Are we to gather from this, that he is vain and foolish enough to wish that production not to be forgotten?

The present volume, however, we have been assured, contains something much better. Startled as we were at the appearance of the ghost of Endymion in the title, we endeavoured, on renewing our acquaintance with its Author, to banish from our recollection the unpropitious circumstances under which we had last met, and, as it is now too late to expect that he will exhibit any material change as the result of further intellectual growth, to take a fresh and final estimate of his talents and pretensions as they may be judged of from the volume before us. The evidence on which our opinion is formed, shall now be laid before our readers. One naturally turns first

1. This unsigned review by Josiah Conder, who also reviewed *Poems* (see pp. 90–94), appeared in the *Eclectic Review* n.s. 14 (September 1820): 158–71.
2. See "Preface" to *Endymion* (p. 147).

to the shorter pieces, in order to taste the flavour of the poetry. The following ode to Autumn is no unfavourable specimen.

[Quotes "To Autumn."]

Fancy has again and again been hymned in lays Pindaric or Anacreontic,[3] but not often in more pleasing and spirited numbers than the following.

[Quotes "Fancy," ll.1–66.]

The lines addressed to a friend,[4] on Robin Hood, are in the same light and sportive style.

[Quotes "Robin Hood."]

Of the longer pieces, Lamia is decidedly the best. * * *

This sort of semi-allegorical legend is of the same family of fictions as the Vampire. The plain matter of fact which it envelops, would seem to be, the case of a young man of good talents and respectable connexions, that falls in love with a rich courtezan who has the address to persuade him to marry her. The spell of her charms and her ill-gotten wealth naturally enough dissolve together, and her victim at last discovers her to be—a *lamia*. The story thus interpreted is not without a moral; though Keats does not make use of it. * * *

* * *

Isabella, or the Pot of Basil, is founded on a tale in the Decameron. A poetical rival of Mr Keats, whose volumes are now on our table, has taken the same subject in his 'Sicilian Story;' and in a future Number, we shall, perhaps, afford our readers the opportunity of comparing the different versions.[5] The Eve of St Agnes, is the story of a young damsel of high degree, who loves the son of her father's foe. Having heard that upon St Agnes' eve, young virgins might, if they would go to bed supperless, and perform certain other rites, enjoy a vision of their lovers, she determines to try the spell; and Young Porphyro, who learns her purpose from her Duenna, resolves to fulfil the legend *in propriâ personâ.*[6] Every thing succeeds to admiration; Madeline is quite delighted when she finds the supposed vision is a palpable reality; and while all in the castle are asleep, they elope together; the old nurse dies in the night; and thus endeth the tale. A few stanzas must suffice for further extracts:—

[Quotes *The Eve of St Agnes*, stanzas 25, 27–28, 33–35, 40–42.]

We have laid before our readers these copious extracts from Mr. Keats's present volume, without any comment, in order that he might have the full benefit of pleading his own cause: there they are, and they can be made to speak neither more nor less in his favour than they have already testified.

Mr. Keats, it will be sufficiently evident, is a young man—whatever be his age, we must consider him as still but a young man,—possessed of an elegant fancy, a warm and lively imagination, and something above the average talents of persons who take to writing poetry. Poetry is his mistress,—we were going to say, his *Lamia*, for we suspect that she has proved a syren, that her

3. Odes written in the style of Pindar (as in Abraham Cowley's "Pindarique Odes") or amusing, erotic poems in the style of Anacreon (as in Thomas Moore's verses by "Thomas Little").
4. John Hamilton Reynolds.
5. "Barry Cornwall" (Proctor), another member of Hunt's circle, published his *Sicilian Story* in 1820 which included an adaptation of the same story from Boccaccio that Keats took up in *Isabella*; Cornwall's volume along with his *Dramatic Scenes* and *Marcian Colonna* was reviewed in the *Eclectic Review* n.s. 14 (1820): 323–33.
6. In his own person.

wine is drugged, and that her treasures will be found to be like the gold of Tantalus.[7] Mr. Keats has given his whole soul to 'plotting and fitting himself for verses fit to live';[8] and the consequence is, that he has produced verses which, if we mistake not, will not live very long, though they will live as long as they deserve. The exclusive cultivation of the imagination is always attended by a dwindling or contraction of the other powers of the mind. This effect has often been remarked upon: it is the penalty which second-rate genius pays for the distinction purchased by the exhaustion of its whole strength in that one direction, or upon that one object, that has seized upon the fancy; and it is the true source of affectation and eccentricity. In no other way can we account for the imbecility of judgement, the want of sober calculation, the intense enthusiasm about mean or trivial objects, and the real emptiness of mind, which are sometimes found connected with distinguishing talents. Poetry, after all, if pursued as an end, is but child's play; and no wonder that those who seem not to have any higher object than to be poets, should sometimes be very childish. What better name can we bestow on the nonsense that Mr. Keats, and Mr. Leigh Hunt, and Mr. Percy Bysshe Shelley, and some other poets about town, have been talking of 'the beautiful mythology of Greece?'[9] To some persons, although we would by no means place Mr. Keats among the number, that mythology comes recommended chiefly by its grossness—its alliance to the sensitive pleasures which belong to the animal. With our Author, this fondness for it proceeds, we very believe, from nothing worse than a school boy taste for the stories of the Pantheon and Ovid's Metamorphoses, and the fascination of the word *classical*. Had he passed through the higher forms of a liberal education, he would have *shed* all these puerilities; his mind would have received the rich alluvial deposit of such studies, but this would only have formed the soil for its native fancies; and he would have known that the last use which a full-grown scholar thinks of making of his classical acquirements, is to make a parade of them either in prose or verse. There is nothing gives a greater richness to poetry, we admit, than classical allusions, if they are not of a common-place kind; but they will generally be found to please in proportion to their slightness and remoteness: it is as illustrations, sometimes highly picturesque illustrations of the subject, not as distinct objects of thought,—it is as metaphor, never in the broad and palpable shape of simile, that they please. It was reserved for the Author of Endymion to beat out the gold of ancient fable into leaf thin enough to cover four long cantos of incoherent verse. And now, in the present volume, we have Hyperion, books one, two, and three! We do not mean to deny that there is a respectable degree of inventive skill and liveliness of fancy displayed in this last poem, but they are most miserably misapplied; nor should we have imagined that any person would have thrown away his time in attempting such a theme, unless it were some lad with his fancy half full of Homer and half full of Milton, who might, as a school exercise, try to frame something out of the compound ideas of the Titan and the Demon, of Olympus and Pandemonium. But Mr. Keats, seemingly, can think or write of scarcely any thing else than the 'happy pieties'[1] of Paganism. A Grecian Urn

---

7. That is, an illusion; mentioned in the passage from Burton's *Anatomy of Melancholy* included with *Lamia* (see p. 429).
8. See "Preface" to *Endymion* (p. 147).
9. See "Preface" to *Endymion* (p. 147).
1. "Ode to Psyche," l. 41.

throws him into an ecstasy: its 'silent form,' he says, 'doth tease us out of thought as doth Eternity,'[2]—a very happy description of the bewildering effect which such subjects have at least had upon his own mind; and his fancy having thus got the better of his reason, we are the less surprised at the oracle which the Urn is made to utter:

> ' "Beauty is truth, truth beauty,"—that is all
> Ye know on earth, and all ye need to know.'

That is, all that Mr. Keats knows or cares to know.—But till he knows much more than this, he will never write verses fit to live.

We wish to say little of the affectation which still frequently disfigures Mr. Keats's phraseology, because there is very much less of it in the present volume than in his former poems. We are glad to notice this indication of *growth*. An imperfect acquaintance with the genuine resources of the language, or an impatience of its poverty and weakness as a vehicle for his teeming fancies, is still occasionally discernible in the violence he lays upon words and syllables forced to become such: *e. g.* 'rubious-argent?' 'milder-moon'd'; 'frail-strung heart'; a 'tithe' of eye-sight,—

> '————With eye-lids closed,
> Saving a tythe which love still open kept.'[3]

(N. B. An American Keats would have said, '*a balance*') 'trembled blossoms'; 'honey'd middle of the night';[4] and other splendid novelties.

We would, however, be the last persons to lay great stress on such *minutiæ* in estimating the merits of a writer; but we feel it our duty to warn off all persons who are for breaking down the fences which language interposes between sense and nonsense.

The true cause of Mr. Keats's failure is, not the want of talent, but the misdirection of it; and this circumstance presents the only chance there is that some day or other he will produce something better: whether he ever does or not, is a matter of extreme insignificance to the public, for we have surely poets enough; but it would seem to be not so to himself. At present, there is a sickliness about his productions, which shews there is a mischief at the core. He has with singular ingenuousness and correctness described his own case in the preface to Endymion: 'The imagination of a boy,' he says, 'is healthy, and the *mature* imagination of a man is healthy; but there is a space of life between, in which the soul is in a ferment, the character undecided, the way of life uncertain, the ambition thick-sighted: thence proceeds mawkishness'. The diagnosis of the complaint is well laid down; his is a diseased state of feeling, arising from the want of a sufficient and worthy object of hope and enterprise, and of the regulating principle of religion. Can a more unequivocal proof of this be given, than that there does not occur, if our recollection serves us, throughout his present volume, a single reference to any one object of *real* interest, a single burst of virtuous affection or enlightened sentiment, a single reference, even of the most general kind, to the Supreme Being, or the slenderest indication that the Author is allied by any one tie to his family, his country, or his kind?

---

2. "Ode on a Grecian Urn," ll. 44–45; he goes on to quote the last two lines.
3. He cites phrases from *Lamia*, 1.163, 156, 309; 2.23–24
4. "Ode to Psyche," l. 11; *Eve of St. Agnes*, l. 49.

Mr. Keats, we doubt not, *has* attachments and virtuous feelings, and we would fain hope, notwithstanding the silly expressions which would justify a presumption to the contrary, that he is a Christian: if he is not, it will matter very little to him in a few years what else he may or may not be. We will, however, take it for granted that he is an amiable and well principled young man; and then we have but one piece of advice to offer him on parting, namely, to let it appear in his future productions.

LEIGH HUNT

Farewell to Keats[1]

Ah, dear friend, as valued a one as thou art a poet,—John Keats,—we cannot, after all, find it in our hearts to be glad, now thou art gone away with the swallows to seek a kindlier clime. The rains began to fall heavily, the moment thou wast to go;—we do not say, poet-like, for thy departure. One tear in an honest eye is more precious to thy sight, than all the metaphorical weepings in the universe; and thou didst leave many starting to think how many months it would be till they saw thee again. And yet thou didst love metaphorical tears too, in their way; and couldst always liken every thing in nature to something great or small; and the rains that beat against thy cabin-window will set, we fear, they over-working wits upon many comparisons that ought to be much more painful to others than thyself;—Heaven mend their envious and ignorant numskulls. But thou has "a mighty soul in a little body;"[2] and the kind cares of the former for all about thee shall no longer subject the latter to the chance of impressions which it scorns; and the soft skies of Italy shall breathe balm upon thee; and thou shalt return with thy friend the nightingale, and make all thy other friends as happy with thy voice as they are sorrowful to miss it. The little cage thou didst sometimes share with us, looks as deficient without thee, as thy present one may do without us; but—farewell for awhile: thy heart is in our fields: and thou will soon be back to rejoin it.

Letter to Charles Brown, September 30, 1820[1]

Saturday Septr 28[2]
Maria Crowther
off Yarmouth isle
of wight—

My dear Brown,
    The time has not yet come for a pleasant Letter from me. I have delayed writing to you from time to time because I felt how impossible it was to enliven you with one heartening hope of my recovery; this morning in bed the matter struck me in a different manner; I thought I would write

---

1. Published in the *Indicator* for September 20, 1820, pp. 399–400 on Keats's departure for Italy.
2. See Joseph Addison's translation of Virgil, *Georgics*, 4.97
1. Text From ALS (Harvard MS Keats 1.87).
2. Saturday was the 30th.

"while I was in some liking"[3] or I might become too ill to write at all and then if the desire to have written should become strong it would be a great affliction to me. I have many more Letters to write and I bless my stars that I have begun, for time seems to press,—this may be my best opportunity. We are in a calm and I am easy enough this morning. If my spirits seem too low you may in some degree impute it to our having been at sea a fortnight without making any way. I was very disappointed at not meeting you at Bedhampton, and am very provoked at the thought of you being at Chichester to day.[4] I should have delighted in setting off for London for the sensation merely—for what should I do there? I could not leave my lungs or stomach or other worse things behind me. I wish to write on subjects that will not agitate me much—there is one I must mention and have done with it. Even if my body would recover of itself, this would prevent it. The very thing which I want to live most for will be a great occasion of my death. I cannot help it. Who can help it? Were I in health it would make me ill, and how can I bear it in my state? I dare say you will be able to guess on what subject I am harping—you know what was my greatest pain during the first part of my illness at your house. I wish for death every day and night to deliver me from these pains, and then I wish death away, for death would destroy even those pains which are better than nothing. Land and Sea, weakness and decline are great seperators, but death is the great divorcer for ever. When the pang of this thought has passed through my mind, I may say the bitterness of death is passed. I often wish for you that you might flatter me with the best. I think without my mentioning it for my sake you would be a friend to Miss Brawne when I am dead. You think she has many faults—but, for my sake, think she has not one——if there is any thing you can do for her by word or deed I know you will do it. I am in a state at present in which woman merely as woman can have no more power over me than stocks and stones, and yet the difference of my sensations with respect to Miss Brawne and my Sister is amazing. The one seems to absorb the other to a degree incredible. I seldom think of my Brother and Sister in america. The thought of leaving Miss Brawne is beyond every thing horrible—the sense of darkness coming over me—I eternally see her figure eternally vanishing. Some of the phrases she was in the habit of using during my last nursing at Wentworth place ring in my ears—Is there another Life? Shall I awake and find all this a dream? There must be we cannot be created for this sort of suffering. The receiving of this letter is to be one of yours—I will say nothing about our friendship or rather yours to me more than that as you deserve to escape you will never be so unhappy as I am. I should think of—you in my last moments. I shall endeavour to write to Miss Brawne if possible to day. A sudden stop to my life in the middle of one of these Letters would be no bad thing for it keeps one in a sort of fever awhile. Though fatigued with a Letter longer than any I have written for a long while it would be better to go on for ever than awake to a sense of contrary winds. We expect to put into Portland roads to night.[5] The Capt[n] the Crew and the Passengers are all illtemper'd and weary. I

---

3. Shakespeare, *1 Henry IV*, 3.3.4–5.
4. With the *Maria Crowther* detained at Portsmouth, Keats went to Bedhampton to stay with Dilke's brother-in-law, John Snook, but Brown was at Chichester visiting Dilke's parents.
5. The ship entered the open sea on October 1, a fortnight after its departure from Tower Dock, London.

shall write to dilke. I feel as if I was closing my last letter to you—My dear Brown

Your affectionate friend
John Keats

Letter to Mrs. Brawne, October 24, 1820[1]

Oct[r] 24 Naples Harbour—
care Giovanni

My dear M[rs] Brawne,

A few words will tell you what sort of a Passage we had, and what situation we are in, and few they must be on account of the Quarantine, our Letters being liable to be opened for the purpose of fumigation at the Health Office. We have to remain in the vessel ten days[2] and are, at present shut in a tier of ships. The sea air has been beneficial to me about to as great an extent as squally weather and bad accommodations and provisions has done harm. So I am about as I was. Give my Love to Fanny and tell her, if I were well there is enough in this Port of Naples to fill a quire of Paper—but it looks like a dream—every man who can row his boat and walk and talk seems a different being from myself. I do not feel in the world. It has been unfortunate for me that one of the Passengers is a young Lady in a Consumption[3]—her imprudence has vexed me very much—the knowledge of her complaint—the flushings in her face, all her bad symptoms have preyed upon me—they would have done so had I been in good health. Severn now is a very good fellow but his nerves are too strong to be hurt by other peoples illnesses—I remember poor Rice wore me in the same way in the isle of Wight. I shall feel a load off me when the Lady vanishes out of my sight. It is impossible to describe exactly in what state of health I am—at this moment I am suffering from indigestion very much, which makes such stuff of this Letter. I would always wish you to think me a little worse than I really am; not being of a sanguine disposition I am likely to succeed. If I do not recover your regret will be softened, if I do your pleasure will be doubled. I dare not fix my Mind upon Fanny, I have not dared to think of her. The only comfort I have had that way has been in thinking for hours together of having the knife she gave me put in a silver-case—the hair in a Locket—and the Pocket Book in a gold net. Show her this. I dare say no more. Yet you must not believe I am so ill as this Letter may look for if ever there was a person born without the faculty of hoping I am he. Severn is writing to Haslam, and I have just asked him to request Haslam to send you his account of my health. O what an account I could give you of the Bay of Naples if I could once more feel myself a Citizen of this world—I feel a Spirit in my Brain would lay it forth pleasantly—O what a misery it is to have an intellect in splints! My Love again to Fanny—tell Tootts[4] I wish I could pitch her a basket of grapes—and tell Sam the fellows catch here with a line a little fish much like an anchovy, pull them up fast.

---

1. Written while the *Maria Crowther* was in quarantine due to an outbreak of typhus in London. Text from ALS (LMA K/MS/02/014/6569). For Keats's companion Severn, see p. 110, n. 6.
2. They were in quarantine October 21–31; Rollins believes the letter was written on the 22nd.
3. Miss Cotterell, who would die in Naples before 1825.
4. Rollins identifies her as Mrs. Brawne's daughter, Margaret.

Remember me to M^rs and Mr Dilke—mention to Brown that I wrote him
a letter at Portsmouth which I did not send and am in doubt if he ever will
see it.

my dear Mrs Brawne
Yours sincerely and affectionate
John Keats—
Good bye Fanny! god bless you

Letter to Charles Brown, November 1, 2, 1820[1]

Naples. Wednesday first in November.
My dear Brown,
Yesterday we were let out of Quarantine, during which my health suffered more from bad air and a stifled cabin than it had done the whole voyage. The fresh air revived me a little, and I hope I am well enough this
morning to write to you a short calm letter;—if that can be called one, in
which I am afraid to speak of what I would the fainest dwell upon. As I have
gone thus far into it, I must go on a little;—perhaps it may relieve the load
of WRETCHEDNESS which presses upon me. The persuasion that I shall
see her no more will kill me. I cannot q—*(Note)[2] My dear Brown, I should
have had her when I was in health, and I should have remained well. I can
bear to die—I cannot bear to leave her. Oh, God! God! God! Every thing I
have in my trunks that reminds me of her goes through me like a spear. The
silk lining she put in my travelling cap scalds my head. My imagination is
horribly vivid about her—I see her—I hear her. There is nothing in the
world of sufficient interest to divert me from her a moment. This was the
case when I was in England; I cannot recollect, without shuddering, the
time that I was prisoner at Hunt's, and used to keep my eyes fixed on Hampstead all day. Then there was a good hope of seeing her again—Now!—O
that I could be buried near where she lives! I am afraid to write to her—to
receive a letter from her—to see her hand writing would break my heart—
even to hear of her any how, to see her name written would be more than
I can bear. My dear Brown, what am I to do? Where can I look for consolation or ease? If I had any chance of recovery, this passion would kill me.
Indeed through the whole of my illness, both at your house and at Kentish
Town, this fever has never ceased wearing me out. When you write to me,
which you will do immediately, write to Rome (poste restante[3])—if she is
well and happy, put a mark thus +,—if—Remember me to all. I will endeavour to bear my miseries patiently. A person in my state of health should not
have such miseries to bear. Write a short note to my sister, saying you have
heard from me. Severn is very well. If I were in better health I should urge
your coming to Rome. I fear there is no one can give me any comfort. Is
there any news of George? O, that something fortunate had ever happened
to me or my brothers!—then I might hope,—but despair is forced upon me
as a habit. My dear Brown, for my sake, be her advocate for ever. I cannot
say a word about Naples; I do not feel at all concerned in the thousand novelties around me. I am afraid to write to her. I should like her to know that

---

1. Text from Brown's *Life of John Keats* (*KC*, 2: 83–84).
2. "* (Note) He could not go on with this sentence, nor even write the word 'quit',—as I suppose. The
   word WRETCHEDNESS above he himself wrote in large characters" [Brown's note].
3. A department in a post office where the letters of travelers are kept until called for.

I do not forget her. Oh, Brown, I have coals of fire in my breast. It surprised me that the human heart is capable of containing and bearing so much misery. Was I born for this end? God bless her, and her mother, and my sister, and George, and his wife, and you, and all!

Your ever affectionate friend,
John Keats.

Thursday. I was a day too early for the courier. He sets out now. I have been more calm to-day, though in a half dread of not continuing so. I said nothing of my health; I know nothing of it; you will hear Severn's account from xxxxxx.[4] I must leave off. You bring my thoughts too near to——

God bless you!

Letter to Charles Brown, November 30, 1820[1]

Rome. 30 November 1820.

My dear Brown,

'Tis the most difficult thing in the world to me to write a letter. My stomach continues so bad, that I feel it worse on opening any book,—yet I am much better than I was in Quarantine. Then I am afraid to encounter the proing and conning of any thing interesting to me in England. I have an habitual feeling of my real life having past, and that I am leading a posthumous existence. God knows how it would have been—but it appears to me—however, I will not speak of that subject. I must have been at Bedhampton nearly at the time you were writing to me from Chichester[2]—how unfortunate—and to pass on the river too! There was my star predominant![3] I cannot answer any thing in your letter, which followed me from Naples to Rome, because I am afraid to look it over again. I am so weak (in mind) that I cannot bear the sight of any hand writing of a friend I love so much as I do you. Yet I ride the little horse,[4]—and, at my worst, even in Quarantine, summoned up more puns, in a sort of desperation, in one week than in any year of my life. There is one thought enough to kill me—I have been well, healthy, alert &c, walking with her—and now—the knowledge of contrast, feeling for light and shade, all that information (primitive sense) necessary for a poem are great enemies to the recovery of the stomach. There, you rogue, I put you to the torture,—but you must bring your philosophy to bear—as I do mine, really—or how should I be able to live? Dr Clarke is very attentive to me; he says, there is very little the matter with my lungs, but my stomach, he says, is very bad. I am well disappointed in hearing good news from George,—for it runs in my head we shall all die young. I have not written to xxxxx yet, which he must think very neglectful; being anxious to send him a good account of my health, I have delayed it from week to week. If I recover, I will do all in my power to correct the mistakes made

---

4. Haslam.

1. After clearing quarantine, Keats and Severn (see p. 110, n. 6) left Naples for Rome on November 7 or 8, reaching Terracina on November 12 and then Rome on November 15. They stayed in rooms (now the Keats-Shelley House) on the Spanish Steps, arranged by Dr.Clark. Text from Brown's *Life of John Keats* (*KC*, 2: 85–86). Brown has dropped various proper names (Rollins suggests Haslam, Dilke, Woodhouse, Reynolds) and probably substitutes "her" for Fanny Brawne's name.

2. See p. 530, n. 4.

3. Rollins cites Shakespeare, *The Winter's Tale*, 1.2.202–203: "It is a bawdy planet, that will strike / Where 'tis predominant."

4. Dr. Clark recommended that Keats hire a horse (for the high price of £6 a month); he often rode with a fellow consumptive, Lieutenant Isaac Elton.

during sickness; and if I should not, all my faults will be forgiven. I shall write to xxx to-morrow, or next day. I will write to xxxxx in the middle of next week. Severn is very well, though he leads so dull a life with me. Remember me to all friends, and tell xxxx I should not have left London without taking leave of him, but from being so low in body and mind. Write to George as soon as you receive this, and tell him how I am, as far as you can guess;—and also a note to my sister—who walks about my imagination like a ghost—she is so like Tom. I can scarcely bid you good bye even in a letter. I always made an awkward bow.

God bless you!

John Keats.

CRITICISM

PAUL DE MAN

[The Negative Path]†

* * *

The pattern of Keats's work is prospective rather than retrospective; it consists of hopeful preparations, anticipations of future power rather than meditative reflections on past moments of insight or harmony. His poems frequently climax in questions—"Was there a poet born?", "Do I wake or sleep?"—or in statements such as: "and beyond these / I must not think now . . .", "but now no more, / My wand'ring spirit must no further soar"— that suggest he has reached a threshold, penetrated to the borderline of a new region which he is not yet ready to explore but toward which all his future efforts will be directed. *I Stood Tiptoe* announces *Endymion*, *Endymion* announces *Hyperion*, *Hyperion* prefigures *The Fall of Hyperion*, etc.; Keats is steadily moving forward, trying to pull himself up to the level and the demands of his own prospective vision. None of the larger works— and we know that the larger works mattered most to him—can in any sense be called finished. The circle never seems to close, as if he were haunted by a dream that always remains in the future.

The dream is dramatically articulated from the very start, in a naïve but clear mythological outline that even the awkward diction of the early poems cannot altogether hide from sight. It reveals Keats's original conception of the poet's role and constitutes the thematic center around which the history of his development is organized.* * *

* * * [P]oetry is always the means by which an excess is tempered, a flight checked, a separation healed. * * *

The early Keats discovers the narrative equivalence of this restoring, balancing power of poetry in the Greek myths, which he interprets at the time as tales in which the distance between mortals and immortals is overcome by an act of erotic union. As a story of love between a goddess and a mortal shepherd, Endymion attracts him even more than Psyche or Narcissus, and he announces it as his main theme before embarking on the narrative poem *Endymion* itself. But the symbolic function of the poet as a narrator of myths immediately widens in significance: since he can "give meek Cynthia her Endymion," he not only restores the natural balance of things, but his exemplary act extends to the whole of mankind. The union between the goddess and the shepherd prefigures directly the communal celebration of mankind liberated from its suffering. By telling "one wonder of [Cynthia's] bridal night," the poet causes the "languid sick" to awake and

> Young men, and maidens at each other gaz'd
> With hands held back, and motionless, amaz'd
> To see the brightness in each other's eyes;
> And so they stood, fill'd with a sweet surprise,
> Until their tongues were loos'd in poesy.
> Therefore no lover did of anguish die:

† From "Introduction," by Paul de Man, *The Selected Poetry of Keats* (New York: Signet Classics; The New American Library, Inc., 1966), pp. ix–xxxvi. Reprinted by permission of Penguin Group (USA).

> But the soft numbers, in that moment spoken,
> Made silken ties, that never may be broken.
>   (*I Stood Tiptoe*, ll. 231–38)

Here we have Keats's original dream in all its naïve clarity: it is a dream about poetry as a redeeming force, oriented toward others in a concern that is moral but altogether spontaneous, rooted in the fresh sensibility of love and sympathy and not in abstract imperatives. The touching tale of a lovelorn goddess replaces the Ten Commandments, a humanized version of Hellenic myth replaces biblical sternness, in an optimistic belief that the universe naturally tends toward the mood of temperate balance and that poetry can always recapture the freshness of ever-rising springs.

The optimism of this myth is tempered, however, by the negative implications it contains: if poetry is to redeem, it must be that there is a need for redemption, that humanity is indeed "languid sick" and "with temples bursting." The redemption is the happier future of a painful present. One of the lines of development that Keats's poetry will follow reaches a deeper understanding of this pain which, in the earlier texts, is merely a feverish restlessness, a discordance of the sensations that creates a tension between warring extremes of hot and cold. Some of his dissatisfaction with the present is transposed in Keats's image of his own situation as a beginning poet on the contemporary literary scene: the greatness of the major predecessors—Spenser, Shakespeare and Milton—measures his own inadequacy and dwarfs the present:

> Is there so small a range
> In the present strength of manhood, that the high
> Imagination cannot freely fly
> As she was wont of old?
>   (*Sleep and Poetry*, ll. 162–65)

Totally oriented toward the future, Keats cannot draw strength from this past grandeur; his use of earlier models will always be more a sympathetic imitation than a dialogue between past and present, as between Milton and Wordsworth in *The Prelude*. Hence that Keats's use of earlier poets is more technical than thematic: however Spenserian or Miltonic the diction of *The Eve of St. Agnes* and *Hyperion* may be, Spenser and Milton are not present as such in the poems; Keats has to derive all his power from energy he finds in himself or in his immediate vicinity. But he experiences his own times as literarily deficient: a curious passage from *Sleep and Poetry*, where the entire movement of the poem, as well as the allegiance to Leigh Hunt, would demand the unmixed praise of contemporary poetry, turns into a criticism of Byron and Wordsworth for failing to deliver the message of hope that Keats would like to hear. As a criticism of *The Excursion* the observation would be valid enough, but it is presented instead as a source of personal discouragement. A certain form of despondency and stagnation seems to threaten Keats from the start and forces him to take shelter in falsely idyllic settings like the one at the end of *Sleep and Poetry*, where the problem that concerns him can be temporarily forgotten but not resolved.

Retreats of this kind recur throughout the work, but they gain in poetic significance as the predicament from which he retreats grows in universality. This progression can be traced in the changed use of Ovidian myth from *Endymion* on, as compared to the earliest poems. Originally, the myths serve to gain access to the idyllic aspects of nature: they are "delightful stories" about "the fair paradise of Nature's light." The sad tales alternate with joyful ones merely for the sake of variety. This, of course, is by no means the dominant mood in Ovid himself, who often reports acts of refined cruelty with harsh detachment. From *Endymion* on, the movement of mythical metamorphosis, practically absent from the early poems, achieves a striking prominence that will maintain itself to the end; the very narrative pattern of *Endymion*, of *Lamia* and, in a more hidden way, of *Hyperion* and the Odes, is based on a series of transformations from one order of being into another. The various metamorphic combinations between the inanimate, the animal, human and divine world keep appearing, and the moment of transformation always constitutes the dramatic climax toward which the story is oriented. Far from being merely picturesque, the metamorphoses acquire an obsessive intensity in which one recognizes a more mature version of the original, happy dream of redemption.

The erotic contact between the gods and man in Ovid is anything but the idyllic encounter between Cynthia and Endymion in *I Stood Tiptoe*; it results instead in the brutal degradation of the human being to a lower order of life, his imprisonment in the rigid forms of the inanimate world: Niobe's "very tongue frozen to her mouth's roof" (*Metamorphoses* VI, l. 306), Daphne's "swift feet grown fast in sluggish roots" (I, l. 551), Myrrha, the mother of Adonis, watching her skin change to hard bark (X, l. 494). This state of frozen immobility, of paralysis under the life-destroying impact of eternal powers, becomes the obsessive image of a human predicament that poetry is to redeem. A long gallery of human beings thus caught in poses of frozen desire appear throughout the work: the lovers in Book III of *Endymion* imprisoned in a sea cave "vast, and desolate, and icy-cold" (III, l. 632), the figures on the Grecian Urn, the knight-at-arms of "La Belle Dame Sans Merci" caught "On the cold hillside," the knights and ladies at the beginning of *The Eve of St. Agnes* "sculptur'd dead, on each side, [who] seem to freeze, / Emprison'd in black, purgatorial rails," Saturn at the beginning of *Hyperion* "quiet as a stone, / Still as the silence round about his lair." There hardly exists a single of Keats's important poems in which a version of this recurrent theme fails to appear, though the outward form may vary. It is most frequently associated with the sensation of cold, as if the cooling breeze of *I Stood Tiptoe* heralding the benevolent arrival of the gods had suddenly turned icy and destructive. The myth is a paradoxical version of the mutability theme: the passage of time, the loss of power, death, are the means by which the gods announce their presence; time is the only eternal force and it strips man of his ability to move freely in the direction of his own desire; generations are wasted by old age, "youth grows pale, and spectre-thin, and dies" and "Every thing is spoilt by use" ("Fancy," l. 68). Under the impact of this threat, mankind is made powerless in the stagnation that Keats felt at times in himself and saw around him. Mutability causes paralysis.

His dream then becomes a kind of reversal of the Ovidian metamorphosis, in which man was frozen into a natural form: the poet is the one who can reverse the metamorphosis and reanimate the dead forms into life. Again, Book III of *Endymion* gives a clear mythological outline of this process: by a mere touch of his wand, warmth is restored to the frozen lovers and the reanimated figures rejoice in an exact repetition of the redemption scene from *I Stood Tiptoe* (*Endymion*, III, ll. 780ff.). This dream, by which dead nature is restored to life and refinds, as it were, the human form that was originally its own, is Keats's fondest reverie. A large measure of his poetical power stems from this. It allows him to give nature such an immediate and convincing presence that we watch it take on effortlessly human form: the ode "To Autumn" is the supreme achievement of this Ovidian metamorphosis in reverse. His ability to make his conceits and metaphors spring out of a genuine identity of nature with man, rather than out of an intellectual awareness of an analogy between both, is also rooted in this dream. It is so strong that it forces itself upon the narrative of his longer poems, even when the original story does not allow for it. In *Hyperion*, one can never conceive of Apollo as the warring opponent of the Titans. Instead, the story inevitably turns toward a repetition of the Glaucus episode in *Endymion*: Apollo tends to become the young man whose task it is to free and rejuvenate Saturn, the victim of old age. We are dealing with still another version of Keats's humanitarian dream. He will reach maturity at the end of a rather complicated itinerary, when the last trace of naïveté is removed from this vision.

The power by means of which the poet can redeem the suffering of mankind is called love, but love, in Keats, is a many-sided force. On the simplest level, love is merely the warmth of sensation: Endymion's ardor is such that it seems to melt the curse of time away at sheer contact. Till the later "Ode to Psyche" when love has been internalized to such an extent that it bears only the remotest relationship to anything physical, the epithet "warm," associated with Eros, preserves the link with sensation in a world that is otherwise entirely mental.

> A bright torch, and a casement ope at night,
> To let the warm Love in!
> ("Ode to Psyche," ll. 66–67)

The importance of sensuality to Keats has been abundantly stressed; when some biographers, with the laudable intention of rescuing Keats from the Victorian reproach of coarseness, have tried to minimize the importance of erotic elements in his poetry, they present an oddly distorted picture. Yet, even his most straightforward eroticism easily turns into something more than sensation. First of all, sensuous love for him is more readily imagined than experienced; therefore it naturally becomes one of the leading symbols for the workings of the imagination. One of his most elaborate conceits on the activity of the mind, the final stanza of the "Ode to Psyche," spontaneously associates Eros with fancy; the same is true of the poem "Fancy," in which Eros is present as an activity of the mind. Moreover, since Keats is the least narcissistic of romantic poets, love is easily transferred by him to others and becomes a communal bond: one remembers how the union of Cynthia and Endymion spontaneously turns into a public feast, the kind of Rousseauistic brotherhood that recurs in romantic poetry as a symbol of reconciliation. In *Endymion* also, one passes without tension from love to a communal spirit of friendship with social and political overtones; something of the spirit of the French Revolution still echoes in these passages. In the optimistic world of *Endymion*, love and history act together as positive forces and historical redemption goes hand in hand with sensuous fulfillment.

Another aspect of the love experience, however, leads to more complex involvements. Aside from sensation, love also implies sympathy, a forgetting of the self for the sake of others, especially when the other is in a state of suffering. In the earlier poems, when the poet's sympathy goes out to Narcissus, to Psyche or to Pan, or even when Endymion is moved to tears over the sad fate of the wood-nymph Arethusa, these movements of the heart could still be considered a conventional form of sensibility. But in the recurrent image of frozen immobility, the suffering is not just an arbitrary trick of fate or a caprice of the gods: it becomes the generalized statement of the human predicament, man stifled by the awareness of his mortality. Sympathetic understanding of these threatened figures, the attempt "To think how they may ache in icy hoods and mails" (*St. Agnes*, l. 18), tears us away from the safety of everyday experience and forces us to enter a realm that is in fact the realm of death. The ordinary life of consciousness is then suspended and its continuity disrupted. Hence that the experience can only be expressed in metaphors such as "trance" or "sleep," suspended states of consciousness in which the self is momentarily absent. The "romantic" setting of certain dream episodes in *Endymion* or in "La Belle Dame Sans Merci" should not mislead us into misunderstanding the connection between love and death that prevails here: love is not a temptation to take us out of the finite world of human experiences, still less an impulse toward a platonic heaven. Keats's love impulse is a very human sense of sympathy and pity, chivalrous perhaps, but devoid of transcendental as well as escapist dimensions. Endymion cannot resist the "sorrow" of the Indian maiden, Glaucus is taken in by the feigned tears of Circe, the knight of "La Belle Dame . . ." is definitely lulled to sleep only after his lady has "wept, and sighed full sore," and Lamia, also, woos her lover Lucius by appealing to his pity as well as to his senses. Keats's imagination is fired by a mixture of sensation and sympathy in which the dual nature of love is reunited. The sympathy, however, is even more important than the sensation: love can exist without the latter but not without the former, and some of Keats's heroes are motivated by sympathy alone. This adds an important dimension to our understanding of the relationship between love, poetry and death in his work: because poetry is essentially an act of sympathy, of human redemption, it must move through the death-like trances that abound in Keats. One misunderstands these moments altogether if one interprets them as a flight from human suffering; to the contrary, they are the unmistakable sign of a sympathetic identification with the human predicament. There are moments of straightforward escape in Keats: we mentioned the end of *Sleep and Poetry* as one instance; several of the more trivial poems fulfill the same function. But the "tranced summer night" of *Hyperion*, the Cave of Quietude in Book IV of *Endymion*, the "drowsy numbness" of the Nightingale Ode, the "cloudy swoon" of *The Fall of Hyperion*, do not stand in opposition to human sympathy; as the subsequent dramatic action of these poems indicates, they represent a necessary first step toward the full unfolding of humanitarian love as it grows into a deeper understanding of the burden of mortality.

*   *   *

* * * Keats's gift for sympathy has a negative aspect, and the significance of his complete evolution can only be understood if one takes this into account.

Already in *Endymion*, when Keats is speaking of love and friendship as central formative experiences, he refers to these experiences as "self-destroying":

> But there are
> Richer entanglements, enthrallments far
> More self-destroying, leading, by degrees,
> To the chief intensity: the crown of these
> Is made of love and friendship . . .
>
> (*Endymion*, I, ll. 797–801)

"Self-destroying" is obviously used in a positive sense here, to designate the moral quality of disinterestedness—yet "destroying" is a curiously strong term. The phrase is revealing, for a recurrent pattern in the poetry indicates a strong aversion to a direct confrontation with his own self; few poets have described the act of self-reflection in harsher terms. For Endymion, the most miserable condition of man is that in which he is left to consider his own self in solitude, even when this avowedly takes him close to teaching the "goal of consciousness" (2.283). * * *

* * * The experience of being "tolled back to one's sole self" is always profoundly negative. He almost succeeds in eliminating himself from his poetry altogether. There is, of course, much that is superficially autobiographical in *Endymion* and even in *Hyperion*, but one never gains an intimate sense of Keats's own selfhood remotely comparable to that conveyed by other romantic poets. The "I" of the Nightingale Ode, for instance, is always seen in the movement that takes it away from its own center. The emotions that accompany the discovery of the authentic self, feelings of guilt and dread as well as sudden moments of transparent clarity, are lacking in Keats. Poetic "sleep" or "trance" is a darkening, growing opacity of the consciousness. Suffering plays a very prominent role in his work, but it is always the suffering of others, sympathetically but objectively perceived and so easily generalized into historical and universal pain that it rarely appears in its subjective immediacy: a passage such as the opening scene of *Hyperion* gains its poetic effectiveness from the controlled detachment of an observer who is not directly threatened. The only threat that Keats seems to experience subjectively is that of self-confrontation.

Keats's sympathetic love thus appears less simple than it may seem at first sight: his intense and altogether genuine concern for others serves, in a sense, to shelter him from the self-knowledge he dreads. He is a man distracted from the awareness of his own mortality by the constant spectacle of the death of others. * * * Although it would be entirely false to say of Keats that he escaped out of human suffering into the idealized, trance-like condition of poetry, one can say, with proper caution, that he moves away from the burden of self-knowledge into a world created by the combined powers of the sympathetic imagination, poetry and history, a world that is ethically impeccable, but from which the self is excluded.

* * *

Interpreters of Keats have difficulty agreeing on the significance of his latest work: after the almost miraculous outburst of creative activity in May, 1819, when he wrote practically all the great odes in quick succession, there still followed a period of nearly six months until the final onset of his illness. *The Fall of Hyperion*, *Lamia* and several other shorter poems were written at that time. There is some logic in considering the entire period from June till the end of the year as one single unit—the "late" Keats—that includes the poems to Fanny Brawne, dating from the fall of 1819, and frequently considered as poetically unimportant and slightly embarrassing documents written when he was no longer in full control of his faculties. In truth, it is from *The Fall of Hyperion* on that a sharp change begins to take place. * * * The particular difficulty and obscurity of *The Fall of Hyperion* and *Lamia* stems from the fact that they are works of transition toward a new phase that is fully revealed only in the last poems Keats wrote.

The striking fact about Keats's last poems is that they contain an attack on much that had been held sacred in the earlier work. * * * We must understand that, far from detracting from his stature, the negativity of Keats's last poems shows that he was about to add another dimension to a poetic development that, up till then, had not been altogether genuine.

We can take as an example the poem dated October, 1819, and entitled "To —," sometimes referred to as "Ode" or "Second Ode to Fanny Brawne." The term "Ode" in the title is fitting, for the dramatic organization of the poem is very similar to that of the famous great odes; it is, in fact, the exact negative counterpart of the "Ode to a Nightingale." The paradox that was partly concealed by the richness of the language in the earlier odes is now fully revealed: the poems in fact set out to destroy the entities they claim to praise; or, to put it less bluntly, the ambiguity of feeling toward these entities is such that the poems fall apart. In the October poem, the absurdity of the dramatic situation is apparent from the first lines, in which Keats begs Fanny to assist him, by her presence, in curing a suffering of which this very presence is the sole cause:

> What can I do to drive away
> Remembrance from my eyes? for they have seen,
> Aye, an hour ago, my brilliant Queen!
> Touch has a memory. O say, love, say,
> What can I do to kill it and be free
> In my old liberty?
>
> ("To —," ll. 1–6)

The prospective character of Keats's poetry, which we stressed from the start, stands out here in its full meaning. The superiority of the future over the past expresses, in fact, a rejection of the experience of actuality. Memory, being founded on actual sensations, is for Keats the enemy of poetic language, which thrives instead on dreams of pure potentiality. In the last stanzas, the poem turns from past to future, with all the ardor of the sensuous desire that tormented Keats at the time, and with an immediacy that produces the kind of language that already proved so cumbersome in the erotic passages of *Endymion*:

> O, let me once more rest
> My soul upon that dazzling breast!
> Let once again these aching arms be placed,
> The tender gaolers of thy waist! . . .
> Give me those lips again!
>
> (*Idem.*, ll. 48–51, 55)

The interest of the passage is that the desire it names has already been canceled out by the statement made at the onset of the poem. The passion that produces these lines is precisely what has been rejected at the start as the main obstacle to the "liberty" of poetic creation. Before Fanny's presence had put the poet within "the reach of fluttering love," his poetic faculties could grow unimpaired:

> My muse had wings,
> And ever ready was to take her course
> Whither I bent her force, . . .
> (*Idem.*, ll. 11–13)

This belongs to a past that preceded his involvement; the movement toward the future is checked by the awareness of a contradiction that opposes love to poetry as memory is opposed to dream. Contradicting the prayer for her return, the poem concludes by stating a preference for imaginary passion over actual presence:

> Enough! Enough! it is enough for me
> To dream of thee!
>
> (ll. 56–57)

It is certainly true that the poem destroys itself in a hopeless conflict between temptation and rejection, between praise and blame, that no language can hope to resolve. What is so revealing, however, is that the contradiction so crudely manifest here is potentially present in the earlier odes as well.

The difference in situation between this late poem and the odes "On a Grecian Urn" and "To a Nightingale" is obvious enough: the urn and the nightingale are general, impersonal entities, endowed with significance by an act of the poet's imagination; Fanny Brawne, on the other hand, is a highly distinct and specific person whose presence awakens in him an acute sense of threatened selfhood. The temptation she incarnates clashes directly with his desire to forget his own self. In the earlier odes, this conflict is avoided by keeping carefully apart what the urn and the nightingale signify for Keats himself, and what they signify for Keats in relation to humanity in general. The poetic effectiveness of the odes depends entirely on the positive temptation that emanates from the symbolic entities: the world to which they give access is a world of happiness and beauty, and it is by the suggestive evocation of this world that beauty enters the poems. * * *

* * *

As a humanist, he can lay claim to a good conscience and write poems that have reassured generations of readers, willing to be authoritatively told about the limits of their knowledge ("that is all / Ye know on earth, and all ye need to know"); but as a poet, he can indulge in the wealth of a soaring imagination whose power of metamorphosis knows no limits. The poet of the Grecian Urn would hardly be able to evoke the happy world on the urn if he were himself the creature "lowing at the skies" about to be sacrificed.

We can see, from the poem "To —" what happens when this distance between the private self and its moral stance vanishes: the late poem is the "Ode to a Nightingale" with the metamorphic power of the imagination destroyed by a sense of real selfhood. This destruction now openly coincides with the appearance of love on the scene, in an overt admission that, up to this point, the moral seriousness of the poems had not, in fact, been founded on love at all:

> How shall I do
> To get anew

> Those moulted feathers, and so mount once more
> Above, above
> The reach of fluttering Love,
> And make him cower lowly while I soar?
>   ("To —," ll. 18–23)

The violence of the feeling is reminiscent of the hostile language in which Endymion refers to solitary self-knowledge. In the experience of love, the self comes to know itself without mask, and when this happens the care-free movement of the poetic imagination falters. Before, as we know from the Nightingale Ode, the intoxication of the imagination, like that of wine, was able to fuse the familiar Keatsian tension between heat and cold into one single sensation:

> O, for a draught of vintage! that hath been
>   Cool'd a long age in the deep-delved earth,
> Tasting of Flora and the country green,
>   Dance, and Provençal song, and sunburnt mirth!
>   ("Ode to a Nightingale," ll. 11–14)

But now, in a world ruled by the law of love, such easy syntheses are no longer within our power:

> Shall I gulp wine? No, that is vulgarism,
>   A heresy and schism,
> Foisted into the canon law of love;—
> No—wine is only sweet to happy men; . . .
>   ("To —," ll. 24–27)

Consequently, the metamorphosis of the landscape, achieved in Stanza 5 of the Nightingale Ode under the impact of the trancelike song, fails, and we are confronted instead with the bleakness of a totally de-mythologized world:

> That monstrous region, whose dull rivers pour,
> Ever from their sordid urns unto the shore,
> Unowned of any weedy-haired gods;
> Whose winds, all zephyrless, hold scourging rods,
> Iced in the great lakes, to afflict mankind;
> Whose rank-grown forests, frosted, black, and blind,
> Would fright a Dryad; whose harsh herbaged meads
> Make lean and lank the starv'd ox while he feeds;
> There bad flowers have no scent, birds no sweet song,
> And great unerring nature once seems wrong.
>   (*Idem.*, ll. 34–43)

The landscape, at last, is that of Keats's real self, which he had kept so carefully hidden up till now under poetic myth and moral generosity. It is still an imagined landscape, but rooted this time in an experience that is both intimate and painful: his brother's financial disaster near the very "Great Lakes" here evoked was caused by such a landscape and it is certain that Keats equated his own miseries with the calamitous misadventures of his brother in America. This does not make this landscape less "symbolic" than the world of the nightingale or the Grecian Urn, but it dramatizes the distinction between a symbol rooted in the self and one rooted in an abstract dream.

    The power which forces a man to see himself as he really is, is also called "philosophy" in the later Keats; the term receives the same ambiguous value-emphasis as does the word "love." In the same poem "To —," the previous poetry, written when he was free of the burden of love, is called "unintellectual" and the confining power of self-awareness is stressed again in the rhetorical question:

> What sea-bird o'er the sea
> Is a philosopher the while he goes
> Winging along where the great water throes?
> (*Idem.*, ll. 15–17)

We have come a long way since the early days of *Endymion* when Keats thought of philosophy as a means to help him carry out his generous dream of human redemption. Apollonius, the philosopher in *Lamia*, has all the outward attributes of villainy, yet there can be no doubt that truth is on his side: Lucius is about to mistake the seductiveness of a serpent for real love and it is, after all, his own weakness that is to blame for his inability to survive the revelation of the truth. In this poem, Truth and Beauty are indeed at odds, but one may well conjecture that, as Keats's sense of truth grew, he would have been able to discover a beauty that would have surpassed that of Lamia. Fanny Brawne may well have looked to him more like Moneta than like La Belle Dame sans Merci.

With the development that stood behind him, this final step could only take the violently negative form of his last poems. It is morally consistent that he would have rebelled against a generosity that offered more protection than it cost him. After having acted, in all his dreams of human redemption, as the one who rescues others from their mortal plight, his last poem reverses the parts. Taking off from an innocuous line in *The Fall of Hyperion* ("When this warm scribe my hand is in the grave") he now offers his hand no longer in a gesture of assistance to others, but as the victim who defies another to take away from him the weight of his own death:

> This living hand, now warm and capable
> Of earnest grasping, would, if it were cold
> And in the icy silence of the tomb,
> So haunt thy days and chill thy dreaming nights
> That thou wouldst wish thine own heart dry of blood
> So in my veins red life might stream again,
> And thou be conscience-calm'd—see here it is—
> I hold it towards you.
> ("This Living Hand," ll. 1–8)

Romantic literature, at its highest moments, encompasses the greatest degree of generality in an experience that never loses contact with the individual self in which it originates. * * * Nowadays, we are less than ever capable of philosophical generality rooted in genuine self-insight, while our sense of selfhood hardly ever rises above self-justification. Hence that our criticism of romanticism so often misses the mark: for the great romantics, consciousness of self was the first and necessary step toward moral judgment. Keats's last poems reveal that he reached the same insight; the fact that he arrived at it by a negative road may make him all the more significant for us.

*   *   *

MARJORIE LEVINSON

Keats's Life of Allegory: The Origins of a Style†

* * *

* * * Keats, like Shakespeare, is a name for the figure of the capable poet. The best Keats criticism (Lionel Trilling, John Bayley, Christopher Ricks), and the smartest (the Harvard Keatsians), mark out the canonical extremes and define a range of problems.[1] * * * These greatly disparate critiques * * * are both founded on a single premise, one which opposes *tout court* the governing thesis of the contemporary criticism of Keats's poetry. We all agree to know the man and his writing by their eminent authenticity: Bayley's "Gemeine," Ricks's "unmisgiving" imagination, Eliot's epistolary *idiot savant*, Vendler's true craftsman. In order to produce this knowledge, we put what the contemporary reviews called Keats's "vulgarity" under the sign of psychic, social, and textual unself-consciousness: roughly, the sign of sensuous sincerity. Further, by the providential tale of intellectual, moral, and artisanal development we find coded in Keats's letters, we put the vulgarity which cannot be so sublimed in the early verse and show its gradual sea-change into the rich, inclusive seriousness that distinguishes the great poetry. Thus do we rescue Keats's deep meanings from his alluring surfaces, his poetic identity from his poetical identifications. By and large, we read the poetry as a sweet solution to a bitter life: a resolution of the actual contradictions. The writing is not, we say, an escape from the real but a constructive operation performed upon it so as to bring out its Truth, which is also a new and deeply human Beauty. We describe, in short, a transformation of experience by knowledge and by the aesthetic practice which that knowledge promotes. The word that best describes this critical plot is romance: a march from alienation to identity. The governing figure of this narrative is the Coleridgean or Romantic symbol and its rhetorical device the oxymoron: irreducibly syncretic ideas. The hero of our critical history is a profoundly associated sensibility and his gift to us is the exemplary humanism of his life and art.

Trilling, Bayley and Ricks have discriminated a stylistic "badness" that occurs throughout Keats's poetry: a certain remove whereby Keats signifies his *interest* in his representations and, we might add, in his own expressiveness. In so doing, these critics approximate the response of Keats's contemporaries, analyzed below. However, by emphasizing the psychic investment rather than the social remove which prompts it (and, by focusing on mimetic and rhetorical rather than subjective disorders), Bayley and Ricks bring Keats's discursive alienations into the dominant romance. Following these powerful writers, we read Keats's lapses from the good taste of innocent, object-related representation and transparent subjectivity as a determined consent to his own voluptuous inwardness *and* to the self-conscious recoil. By this willed abandon, Keats transcends both enthrallments, thereby releasing the reader into a more generous (in today's

† From *Keats's Life of Allegory: The Origins of a Style*, (Oxford and New York: Basil Blackwell, 1988), pp. 1–17. Reprinted by permission of the author and Basil Blackwell. The author's notes have been edited.
1. See Bate, Bayley, Bush, Perkins, Ricks, Trilling, Vendler, and Wasserman in the selected bibliography at the back of this Norton Critical Edition.

parlance, "intersubjective") relational mode. In other words, those critics who acknowledge the stylistic vulgarity of Keats's writing put it in the redeemable field of creaturely instinct and defense, and not in the really unsettling category of externality, materiality, and ambitious reflexiveness. When Keats nods, we say, it is because he *dares* to nod ("swoon," "sink," or "cease"), not because he tries too hard.

The early reviews tell a different story. The most casual survey of this commentary (1817–35) reveals a response so violent and sustained, so promiscuous in its blending of social, sexual, and stylistic critique, and so sharply opposed to mainstream modern commentary as to imply a determinate insight on the part of Keats's contemporaries and a determined oversight on the part of his belated admirers. While we're all familiar with *Blackwood's* Cockney School attack (Lockhart's rebuke of Keats's literary presumption ["so back to the shop Mr. John, back to 'plasters, pills, and ointment boxes, . . . ' "]), we have not attended very closely to the sexual invective, and not at all to the relation between those two discourses. Time and again, the poetry is labelled "profligate," "puerile," "unclean," "disgusting," "recklessly luxuriant and wasteful," "unhealthy," "abstracted," and "insane."[2] More specifically, it is graphed as a stylistically self-indulgent verse: prolix, repetitive, metrically and lexically licentious, overwrought. The diatribes culminate in the epithet "nonsense."

We have always related the savaging of the early poetry to the anomaly of Keats's social position and to the literary blunders which follow from that fact: generally, problems of diction, rhetoric, and subject matter, all of them reducible to the avoidable (and, finally, avoided) misfortune of Keats's coterie. Because we situate these blunders at a certain level and within a very contained biographical field, and because we isolate them from the beauties of the so-called great poetry, we have not understood the deeper insult of Keats's writing, that which explains the intensity and displacements of the early response and the equal but opposite distortions of the twentieth-century view.

From the distance of today, one can detect in those vituperative catalogues a governing discursive and even cognitive model. Keats's poetry was characterized as a species of masturbatory exhibitionism, an offensiveness further associated with the self-fashioning gestures of the petty bourgeoisie. The erotic opprobrium pinpoints the self-consciousness of the verse: its autotelic reflection on its own fine phrases, phrases stylistically objectified as acquired, and therefore *mis*acquired property. The sexual language of the reviews was, of course, an expedient way to isolate Keats, but it is also a telling index to the social and existential project outlined by Keats's style. In his overwrought inscriptions of canonical models, the early readers sensed the violence of Keats's raids upon that empowering system, a violence driven by the strongest desire for an authorial manner and means, and for the social legitimacy felt to go with it. In the alienated reflexiveness of Keats's poetry, the critics read the signature of a certain

---

2. All excerpts from contemporary notices are drawn from Donald Reiman, *The Romantics Reviewed: Contemporary Reviews of British Romantic Writers* (New York: Garland Publishing, 1972), and from G. M. Matthews, ed., *Keats, The Critical Heritage* (London: Routledge and Kegan Paul, 1971). A sampling is included in this Norton Critical Edition. Censored Byron material checked against Leslie Marchand, *Byron's Letters and Journals*, vol. 7, 1820 (Cambridge, Mass.: Belknap Press, 1977), p. 217 (from letter to John Murray, 4 November 1820).

kind of life, itself the sign of a new social phenomenon. Byron's famous epithet for the style of the Cockney writers, "shabby genteel," puts the matter plainly.

> The grand distinction of the under forms of the new school of poets is their *vulgarity*. By this I do not mean that they are *coarse*, but "shabby-genteel," as it is termed. A man may be *coarse* and yet not *vulgar*, and the reverse . . . It is in their *finery* that the new under school are *most* vulgar, and they may be known by this at once; as what we called at Harrow "a Sunday blood" might be easily distinguished from a gentleman . . . In the present case, I speak of writing, not of persons. (Extract from letter to John Murray, 25 March 1821)

If we were not already convinced of Byron's ear for social nuance, we would only have to recall Keats's confession, "I look upon fine Phrases like a Lover."

Like our own criticism, the early reviews read in Keats's poetry "a life of Allegory," but the meaning they develop by that allegory lies in the realm of social production, not aesthetics, metaphysics, or humanistic psychology. To those early readers, "Keats" was the allegory of a man belonging to a certain class and aspiring, as that entire class was felt to do, to another: a man with particular but typical ambitions and with particular but typical ways of realizing them. A world of difference separates this hermeneutic from the "poignantly allegorical life," an adventure in soul-making, which has become today's John Keats.[3] By respecting the social-sexual compounding evidenced by those reviews, we recover the sense of danger underlying our formalist and rhetorical readings of Keats's middling states: his adolescence, his literariness, his stylistic suspensions, his pronounced reflexiveness. We focus Keats's position—sandwiched between the Truth of the working class and the Beauty of the leisure class—not as a healthy both/and but as the monstrous neither/nor constructed in the reviews. We see that the problem of Keats's early poetry is not its regressive escapism (its instincts, so to speak), but its stylistic project: a social-ego enterprise. The deep contemporary insult of Keats's poetry, and its deep appeal (and long opacity) for the modern reader, is its idealized enactment of the conflicts and solutions which defined the middle class at a certain point in its development and which still to some extent obtain. We remember that Keats's style can delineate that station so powerfully because of his marginal, longing relation to the legitimate bourgeoisie (and its literary exemplars) of his day. In emulating the condition of the accomplished middle class (the phrase is itself an oxymoron), Keats isolated the constitutive contradictions of that class. The final fetish in Keats's poetry is precisely that stationing tension.

By the stylistic contradictions of his verse, Keats produces a writing which is aggressively *literary* and therefore not just "not Literature" but, in effect, *anti*-Literature: a parody. We will see that Keats's most successful poems are those most elaborately estranged from their own materials and procedures and thus from both a writerly and readerly subjectivity. * * * The triumph of the great poetry is not its capacious, virile, humane authenticity

---

3. The much-quoted phrase "poignantly allegorical life" is Bate's allusion to Keats's own observation that Shakespeare led "a life of Allegory" (See p. 315 above; page numbers for letters refer to this Norton Critical Edition.)

but its subversion of those authoritarian values, effects which it could not in any case, and for the strongest social reasons, realize. This is the triumph of the double-negative. The awfulness of the early work, by contrast, is explained as an expression of the *single*, or suffered negative: a nondynamic reflection of Keats's multiple estrangements and of the longing they inspired. The accomplished poetry may be considered the negative knowledge of Keats's actual life: the production of his freedom by the figured negation of his given being, natural and social. To say this is not to consecrate Keats a precocious post-modernist, only to take seriously the social facts and meanings embedded in his representations and in the contemporary reception. It is to see in "the continuous manner in which the whole is elaborated" a parodic reproduction of the social restrictions that marked Keats as *wanting*: unequipped, ineffectual, and deeply fraudulent.[4]

Keats did not accomplish by this greatly overdetermined stratagem the goodness he craved: that plenitude of being he worshipped in the great canonical models and which he images in Autumn's breeding passiveness. What he did produce by what Shelley called "the bad sort of style" was a truly *negative* capability. I call this power "virtual" to bring out its parodic relation to authorized forms of power, "virtuoso" to suggest its professional, technically preoccupied character, and "virtuous" by reference to its imposed and contrived limitations. * * * To generate this verbal sequence is also, of course, to put as the ruling stylistic and social question the question of Keats's virility: to begin, that is, where the early commentary leaves off. We will take Keats's own phrase, the "wreathed trellis of a working brain," as a figure for Keats's negative power: his inside-out, thoroughly textualized and autotelic accomplishment. In the celebrated poise of Keats's poetry, we read the effect of the impossible project set him by his interests and circumstances: to become by (mis)acquiring; to become by his writing at once authorized (properly derivative) and authorial (original); to turn his suffered objectivity into a sign of his self-estranged psyche, and to wield that sign as a shield and an ornament.

* * *

To observe that Keats's circumstances put him at a severe remove from the canon is to remark not only his educational deficits but his lack of those skills prerequisite to a transparent mode of appropriation: guiltless on the one side, imperceptible on the other. He knew some French and Latin, little Italian, no Greek. His Homer was Chapman, his Dante was Cary, his Provençal ballads translations in an edition of Chaucer, his Boccaccio Englished. Keats's art education was largely by engravings and, occasionally, reproductions. His absorption of the accessible English writers was greatly constrained by his ignorance of the originals upon which they drew and by his nonsystematic self-education. To say all this is to observe Keats's literally corrupt relation to the languages of poetry: his means of production.

* * *

Before we can begin re-reading Keats, we must really imagine what we know. We must see very clearly, as John Bayley saw, that Keats was a man

---

4. Fredric Jameson, *Sartre: The Origins of a Style* (New York: Columbia University Press, 1961; 1984), p. vii.

whose almost complete lack of control over the social code kept him from living his life. He could not write his poetry in the manner he required, marry the woman he loved, claim his inheritance, hold his family together, or assist his friends. He could not, in short, seize any of the appurtenances of manhood. Keats was as helplessly and ignominiously a "boy" poet as Chatterton, and Byron's "Mankin" was a viciously knowing insult.

The range of paradoxes which Byron and his contemporaries observed in Keats's poetry is ultimately referrable to the fact that it was not given to Keats, a poet in Shelley's "general sense," to be a poet in the most pedestrian, professional, "restricted" sense. Keats had to make for himself a life (the training at Guy's; then, getting by on his allowance; finally, when the money ran out, the projected career of ship's surgeon), while writing a poetry that was, structurally, a denial of that life. At no time did Keats make any money from his writing. (One wonders *how*, exactly, Keats applied the title of "poet" to himself. How did he introduce himself in ordinary social interactions?) The oddly abstract materialism of the poetry—its overinvestment in its signs—takes on a new look when we remember both Keats's remove from his representational manner and means, and also his want of those real things that help people live their lives. Is it any wonder that the poetry produced by this man should be so autotelic, autoerotic, so fetishistic and so stuck? Should it surprise us to find that his dearest fantasy—a picture of somebody reading, a window on the one side, a goldfish bowl on the other—takes the form of a multiply framed, *trompe-l'oeil* still life? "Find the subject," we might call it; or, what is the same thing, "Find the frame."

Keats's poetry was at once a tactical activity, or an escape route from an actual life, and a final construction: the concrete imaginary to that apparitional actual. What was, initially, a substitute *for* a grim life became for Keats a substitute life: a real life of substitute things—simulacra—which, though they do not nourish, neither do they waste. At the very end of his career, Keats began, I believe, to position this parodic solution as part of the problem. *Lamia* is Keats's attempt to frame the problematic of his life and writing and thus to set it aside.

It is crucial to see, as Bayley saw, that the deep desire in Keats's poetry is not for aesthetic things or languages *per se* (that is, Byron's "finery"), but for the social code inscribed in them, a code which was, to Keats, a human transformational grammar. Indeed, all Keats's meditations on art and identity (typically, plasticity), should be related to his abiding desire, to live. The real perversion of Keats's poetry is not its display of its cultural fetishes but its preoccupation with the system felt to organize those talismanic properties. Keats could have had all the urns, Psyches, nightingales, Spenserianisms, Miltonisms, Claudes, and Poussins he wanted; he was not, however, permitted possession of the social grammar inscribed in that aesthetic array, and this was just what Keats was after.

We illuminate Keats's legitimacy problem by way of the originality anxiety that seems to have beset most of the Romantic and what used to be called pre-Romantic poets. The past only lies like a weight on the brain of those who inherit it. Or rather, the past imposes a special *kind* of burden on those individual talents who feel themselves disinherited by the Tradition, and, thus, excluded from the dialectic of old and new, identity and difference. Wordsworth's celebrated defense of his poetical innovations—"every author, as far as he is great and at the same time *original*, has had the task of *creating* the taste by which he is to be enjoyed"—must be understood as the statement of a man so assured of his entitlement that he can trust his originality to be received as intelligible and valuable. (That Wordsworth's confidence was not always confirmed is not the issue here.) Keats, by contrast, could not begin to invent an original voice without first and *throughout* establishing his legitimacy: roughly, his derivativeness.

* * *

* * * By the self-signifying *imperfection* of his canonical reproductions (a parodic return upon his own derivativeness), Keats drew upon the licensing primacy of the code even as his *representation* of that total form changed the nature of its authority. The pronounced badness of Keats's writing figures the mythic goodness of the canon and, by figuring, at once exalts and delimits it. Thus did Keats plot for himself a scene of writing. By the double unnaturalness of his style, Keats projects the authority of an *anti*-nature, stable by virtue of its continuous self-revolutionizing and secured by its contradictions.* * * [L]et me offer as a critical instance a reading of "Chapman's Homer."[5] * * *

Even if we were ignorant of Keats's social disadvantages, this fulsome claim to literary ease would give us pause. The very act of assertion, as well as its histrionically commanding and archly literary style, undermine the premise of natural authority and erudition. The contemporary reader might have observed as well some internal contradictions; not only *is* Homer the Golden Age, but not to "have" Greek and not to have encountered Homer by the age of twenty-three is to make one's claim to any portion of the literary empire suspect. (Keats's acquaintance with Pope's translation is suppressed by the sonnet.) Keats effectively assumes the role of the literary adventurer (with the commercial nuance of that word) as opposed to the mythic explorer: Odysseus, Cortes, Balboa. More concretely, he advertises his corrupt access to the literary system and to those social institutions which inscribe that system systematically in the hearts and minds of young men. To read Homer in translation and after having read Spenser, Coleridge, Cary, and whoever else is included in Keats's travelogue, is to read Homer badly (in a heterodox and alienated way), and to subvert the system which installs Homer in a particular and originary place. Moreover, to "look into" Chapman's Homer is to confess—in this case, *profess*—one's fetishistic relation to the great Original. Keats does not *read* even the translation. To "look into" a book is to absorb it idiosyncratically at best, which is to say, with casual or conscious opportunism. Similarly, the substitution of "breathe" for the expected "read" in line 7 marks the rejection of a sanctioned mode of literary acquisition. To "breathe" a text is to take it in, take from it, and let it out, somewhat the worse for wear. It is, more critically, to miscategorize the object and in such a way as to proclaim one's intimacy with it. Both the claim and the title of Keats's sonnet are, in a word, vulgar.

One is reminded of Valéry's appraisal of museum pleasure: "For anyone who is close to works of art, they are no more objects of delight than his own breathing".[6] Keats, we observe, rejoices in his respiration and goes so

---

5. For the poem, see pp. 54–55.
6. Quoted in Theodor Adorno, *Prisms*, trans. Weber and Weber (Cambridge, Mass.: MIT Press, 1967; 1983). The essay from which that quotation derives, "Valery Proust Museum," deeply informs my discussion.

far as to fetishize the very air he admits. I single out the phrase "pure serene" not only because it is structurally foregrounded but because it reproduces in miniature the method—the working contradiction—of the sonnet. What Keats "breathes" is, of course, anything but pure and Homeric (since he reads in translation and perversely with respect to canon protocol), and the phrase formally exposes that fact. We cannot help but see that "pure serene," a primary reification, further calls attention to itself as a fine phrase, that Keats clearly looks upon as a lover. Not only is the phrase a Miltonic construction, but more recent usage would have characterized it as a sort of translator-ese. One thinks of Pope's "vast profound" and indeed, of Cary's own "pure serene," a description of Dante's ether (1814). Coleridge uses the phrase in his "Hymn before Sunrise in the Vale of Chamouni," 1802. Keats's reproduction of the phrase designates both his access to the literary system and his mode of access—that of translator to Original. In effect, he intentionalizes the alienation he suffers by his social deficits. By signifying the restriction, he converts it into restraint: "might half-slumb'ring on its own right arm." Let me note here that the translation of an adjective into a noun, while etymologically justifiable, transforms Homer's pure and therefore insensible atmosphere—his aura—into a palpable particular: a detached literary style and a self-reflexive one at that. What figures in Homer as a natural and epochal expressiveness is in Keats, and first, a represented object. Only by performing that office does the Homeric value assume for Keats an expressive function.

The thing to remark is the way Keats produces the virtues of his alienated access to the canon. The consummate image of the poem—that which accounts for its overall effect of "energetic . . . calmness"—is, obviously, that of Cortes/Balboa "star[ing] at the Pacific" while "all his men / Looked [Look'd] at each other with a wild surmise — / Silent, upon a peak in Darien." Cortes, we notice, is a "stout" and staring fellow: a solid citizen. "Stout" means, of course, "stout-hearted," but in the context, where Cortes's direct stare at the object of his desire is juxtaposed against the "surmise" of his men (and the alliteration reinforces these visual connections), one feels the energy of the men and the stuck or frozen state of their leader. By their surmise—a liminal, semi-detached state—the men are "wild," a word which in the Romantic idiom means "free." We clearly see that the relation of the men to that (etymologically) literal "pure serene," the Pacific, is indirect and perverse. Who in that situation would avert his gaze?

Claude Finney has reminded us that according to Keats's sources, Balboa's men were forbidden the prospect until their leader had had his full gaze.[7] We can see that the social discrepancy vividly sketched by Keats's original gets translated in the sonnet into an existential and self-imposed difference, and one that inverts the given power ratio by rendering the men, not the master, free and vital. One does not, I think, go too far in associating Keats with those capably disenfranchised men.

It is the stillness and strangeness of the men—their peculiar *durée*— which stations Keats's sonnet, all the gregarious exploration metaphors notwithstanding. Homer enters the poem as the Pacific enters the sensibilities of Cortes's men: through Chapman's/Cortes's more direct possession of/by the object of desire. Odysseus's extrovert energy animates Keats's

7. Finney, *The Evolution of Keats' Poetry*, 2 vols. (New York: Russell & Russell, 1963), 1: 126.

sonnet but, again, perversely. In the Keatsian space, that energy turns self-reflexive, reminding us perhaps of Tennyson's "Ulysses." The poem looks at itself as the men look at each other. The virtue of both looks is their impropriety; what they refuse by that gesture is the Gorgon stare, the direct embrace of and by the authorizing Original. Keats's poem "speak[s] out loud and bold" by not speaking "out" at all. We finish the sonnet, which seems to be predicated on such a simple *donnée*, and we wonder where we have travelled. What happened to Homer, and to Keats for that matter? Why does Keats interpose between himself and his ostensible subject Chapman, Cary, Coleridge, Gilbert, Robertson, Herschel, Balboa, Cortes, and Cortes's men? Why does Keats leave us with this off-center cameo, an image of turbulent stasis among the extras of the cast when what we expect is a "yonder lie the Azores" flourish by the principal? What *is* this poem? By the conventions it sets, it should strike us as a graceful display of literary inspiration and gratitude. But it seems other, and otherwise. How do we explain the real power of its slant rhyme?

Let me recall Hunt's comment on the sonnet: "prematurely masculine." By emphasizing the adverb for a change, we begin to see that Keats's unnatural (illicit) assumption of power, signified by the "poetical" octet, does not *qualify* the "masculinity" of the sestet, it constitutes it. The direct and natural compression of the sestet is the stylistic effect of the displayed disentitlement that is the functional representation of the opening eight lines. The pivot which constructs this before-and-after dynamic (the coordinates for a range of ratios: imitation-genuine, protest-power, struggle-ease) is, of course, the experience of reading Chapman. The experience takes place, significantly, in the breach between the two movements of the sonnet. Rather than imitate Chapman, Keats reproduces Chapman's necessarily parodic (that is, Elizabethan) inscription of Homer. The queerness of Chapman's "mighty line, loud-and-bold" version is rewritten in Keats's own parodic Elizabethan*ism*, and, through the queerness of the Cortes/Balboa image. It is the self-reflexive, fetishistic inscription of the canon—the display of bad access and misappropriation—that emancipates Keats's words. Keats's sonnet breaks free of Homer and Chapman by mis-giving both. By the English he puts on Homer's serenity (he reifies it) and on Chapman's "masculine" extrovert energy, Keats produces the perpetual imminence which is the hero of his sonnet. In the Keatsian idiom, we could call that imminence or suspension a "stationing," with an ear for the full social resonance of Keats's aesthetic word.[8]

The instance of this poem would suggest that Keats's relation to the Tradition is better conceived as dialogic (Bakhtin) than dialectic (Bloom). The poetry does not clear a space for itself by a phallic agon; it opens itself to the Tradition, defining itself as a theater wherein such contests may be eternally and inconclusively staged. The authority of this poetry consists in its detachment from the styles or voices it entertains. By this detachment, these styles become *signatures*: not audible voices but visible, material *signs* of canonical voices. These signs—like all such marks, inauthentic and incomplete—are not, ultimately, mastered by the master-of-ceremonies. And because they remain external to authorial consciousness, theirs is the

---

8. In his notes on Milton, Keats comments on "what may be called his stationing or statuary. He is not content with simple description, he must station . . .," quoted in Jack, *Keats and the Mirror of Art*, p. 142.

empowering virtue of the supplement. In these magic supplements, "Things semi-real," lies the terrific charm of Keats's poetry.

The contained badness of "Chapman's Homer" constitutes its goodness, which is to say, its rhetorical force. The paradox hinges, naturally, on the word "contained." When Keats is great, it is because he *signifies* his alienation from his *materia poetica*, a fact that modern criticism and textual studies have suppressed.[9] This alienation—inevitable, given Keats's education, class, and opportunities—was highly expedient. By it, Keats could possess the "stuff of creativity" without becoming possessed by it. By "stuff," I do not mean Bloom's primary, inspirational matter but the means and techne for exercises in literary production. Keats's poetry, inspired by translations, engravings, reproductions, schoolroom mythologies, and Tassie's gems, delivers itself through these double and triple reproductions as the "true, the blushful Hippocrene." That phrase describes, ironically, *precisely* a substitute truth. Again, Byron understood these things; "You know my opinion of *that second-hand* school of poetry."

* * *

GRANT F. SCOTT

Keats in His Letters[†]

For most modern readers it is hard to see Keats's poems for the sheen of their language. They appear too much like bright monuments in winter sun. No one, I suspect, could mistake a line like "And still she slept an azure-lidded sleep"—from *The Eve of St. Agnes*—for anything but poetry. Indeed, Keats has come to represent the poet of "silken Phrases, and silver sentences," exploiting language, rhyme, and allusion in ways that terrify students but thrill the ranks of professional scholars.

On first looking into Keats's letters, however, readers who bring with them some memory of the formal difficulty of his poems will be pleasantly surprised. Rather than the stately elegance of "Ode on a Grecian Urn" or the finely wrought agonies of "Ode to a Nightingale," the letters yield the spontaneous and frank observations of a young man: his insecurities, doubts, fears, enthusiasms, prejudices, ambitions, opinions, and ideas. If his greatest poems are characterized by their stillness and poise, his letters are masterpieces of motion. They read like mountain rivers: ragged, rough, full of raw energy, dangerous. They are alive with improvisational wit and verbal gusto, revealing an agile mind happily willing to dwell in contradiction or, as he says, "remain content with half knowledge" (21, 27 [?] December 1817; p. 109). Keats never commits his speculations to the casket of a theory. A remarkable fact of the letters is that his most famous ideas—Negative Capability, the Chameleon Poet, the Vale of Soul-making,

9. See Jerome McGann, "Keats and the Historical Method in Literary Criticism", *MLN*, 94 (1979), pp. 988–1032.
† "Introduction," *Selected Letters of John Keats,* rev. ed. Grant F. Scott (Cambridge: Harvard University Press, 2002), pp. xxi–xxxiii. Reprinted by permission of the author and Harvard University Press. Page numbers for letters refer to this Norton Critical Edition; *L* refers to Rollins's edition. Scott modernizes spelling and punctuation.

the Mansion of Many Apartments—appear only once. They are neither repeated to other correspondents nor formalized in published essays, but remain provisional, bound within the specific human context of a letter. Perhaps what is most surprising and delightful about Keats's letters, especially next to the polished, anthology-ready gems of his poetry, is their unpredictability. In *The Use of Poetry and the Use of Criticism*, T. S. Eliot remarked that the letters "are what letters ought to be; the fine things come in unexpectedly, neither introduced nor shown out, but between trifle and trifle" (100). And he is right. What is so striking about the famous "Negative Capability" letter is not so much the term itself, though it has generated hundreds of pages of commentary, as the casual way in which it emerges out of the quotidian detail of Keats's life. He goes to see a play, mentions a publisher's trial for libel, talks about dining out with friends, and then—like a thunderclap—"I had not a dispute but a disquisition with Dilke on various subjects; several things dovetailed in my mind, and at once it struck me what quality went to form a Man of Achievement especially in Literature and which Shakespeare possessed so enormously—I mean *Negative Capability*, that is when man is capable of being in uncertainties, Mysteries, doubts, without any irritable reaching after fact and reason." Yet the sentence that immediately precedes this one is marvelously ordinary, providing not a clue of what is about to follow: "Brown and Dilke walked with me and back from the Christmas pantomime" (21, 27 [?] December 1817; pp. 108–109).

The proximity of the mundane and the profound leads to another salient feature of Keats's letters: their seamless integration of everyday life with the life of the mind. Today we have grown accustomed to think of intelligence as necessitating a special time and place. Thinking is segregated from other activities and has become the unique preserve of institutions such as the university, the foundation, and the "think tank," where it is carried out by a camera-friendly team of "experts" and "knowledge workers." In our time we have come to witness the complete professionalization of the intellect as well as the allotment of designated time to "mental work." The weekends are now reserved for the strenuous fun that constitutes authentic living. Such a belief makes Keats's letters all the more astonishing for their insistence that there need be no distinction between living and thinking; that thinking *is* living and in fact works best when it takes its measure directly from life. "Axioms in philosophy," he writes to his friend John Hamilton Reynolds, "are not axioms until they are proved upon our pulses" (3 May 1818; p. 244). This is one of the signs of Keats's health: that he can find no essential difference between the body and the mind, that such a split would be unnatural, and that the mind's activities are in every way as sensuous and exhilarating as the body's. In the same letter, Keats illustrates the danger of separating body and mind in a metaphor that suggests a scene out of Dante: "The difference of high Sensations with and without knowledge appears to me this: in the latter case we are falling continually ten thousand fathoms deep and being blown up again without wings and with all the horror of a bare-shouldered Creature. In the former case, our shoulders are fledged, and we go thro' the same air and space without fear" (p. 243). Only in tandem do "high Sensations" and "knowledge" equip the human creature with wings capable of navigating the abyss.

If the letters show no embarrassment in mingling serious ideas with bits of idle gossip, light-hearted banter, comments on women and the weather, they also seem perfectly at ease with the inclusion of poetry—Keats's own and that of others. For those who have encountered Keats's poems only in weighty anthologies, it is refreshing to come upon them in this warmer human environment. In this context they seem to breathe again, to take on new life and interest. Here the poems are not isolated aesthetic events or solemn attempts at initiation into the "Temple of Fame" so much as natural extensions of his ordinary existence. Some of Keats's most supple and original sonnets—for example, "On the Sea," "On Sitting Down to Read *King Lear* Once Again," "O thou whose face hath felt the winter's wind," "Four seasons fill the measure of the year"—grow organically out of specific contexts, reflecting both the patterns of his thought at the moment of writing and the interests of individual correspondents. His own commentary on works such as *The Eve of St. Agnes* and "La Belle Dame Sans Merci" is also highly suggestive and serves to humanize poems that have become dauntingly canonical. The happy marriage of poetry and prose in the letters tells us that for Keats, poetry was not a job or a career but a necessity, like breathing. "I find that I cannot exist without poetry, without eternal poetry," he admits to Reynolds, "half the day will not do, the whole of it." Poetry becomes a physical appetite, almost an addiction: "I began with a little, but habit has made me a Leviathan." If he cannot get his fix, either by reading or writing it, he becomes "all in a Tremble" (17, 18 April 1817; p. 78).

This attitude will no doubt surprise the modern reader who has been taught to see poetry like Keats's as a luxury, to be classed with opera or haute cuisine. Keats's poetry—serious poetry—is not a part of most people's workaday lives. It is a sign of his complexity that Keats too could share this belief in poetry as an elite club; indeed, he once signed one of his poems "Caviare" and was fond of playing the connoisseur, even the collector, of the beautiful. He notes, for instance, that "though a quarrel in the streets is a thing to be hated, the energies displayed in it are fine" (14 February–4 May 1819; p. 322–23), and on his walking tour with Charles Brown he relates to his brother Tom their first sight of a Scottish country dancing school: "There was as fine a row of boys and girls as you ever saw, some beautiful faces, and one exquisite mouth" (29 June, 1, 2 July 1818).

But more often Keats saw a vital connection between poetry and the "real world," the world of suffering and misfortune that beset those closest to him. "I am ambitious of doing the world some good," he confesses to his friend Richard Woodhouse, and he meant *through his poetry*. He begins his adult life in training to be an apothecary, what we would consider today a family doctor; he ends it determined to be a poet-physician, healing with the balm of his words. Poetry is what Keats prescribes but not exclusively for spiritual health (as we might do today, insisting that it is "good for the soul"); rather, he sees it as genuinely medicinal and therapeutic. In a memorable passage Keats concludes the early poem "I stood tiptoe" with a vision of ethereal breezes reviving "the languid sick" as they lie feverish in their hospital beds. "Springing up," these invalids awake "clear eyed" to greet their friends, their tongues "loos'd in poesy." This powerfully vivid image tells us that for Keats, poetry was both a cure for disease—those breezes bear the burden of Apollo's song—and a vital sign of a person's health.

In his letters this association of poetry with health is made explicit on a number of occasions. The poems are conceived not only as diversions or amusements for his friends, but also as a means of speeding the time and soothing their cares. The poetic epistle to J. H. Reynolds of 25 March 1818, for example, is sent "in hopes of cheering [him] through a Minute or two" and "pleas[ing] his friend, who is confined to his bed, "sick and ill." In an-other letter he calls his poems "Scribblings" and hopes that they "will be some amusement for you this Evening" (3 February 1818; p. 123), and in yet an-other feels content if his words have been "sufficient to lift a little time from your Shoulders" (19 February 1818, p. 127). He is continually jotting down nonsense rhymes for his brother Tom, who is battling tuberculosis, and his young sister, Fanny, who is "imprisoned" by their legal guardian, Richard Abbey. And it is clear that he sees these poems as a way of consol-ing his family, combating and ameliorating their respective hardships.

The epistolary context of his poems as well as their function as antidote suggests another important dimension of Keats's letters: their sociability. The stereotype of the isolated romantic poet—confined to some lonely hut in the wilds, generating poems in a visionary frenzy with "flashing eyes" and "floating hair"—could hardly be less appropriate for Keats. He is genial and gregarious, inseparable from the tight network of his friends. He goes to plays, public lectures, dinner parties, dances, exhibitions, picture galleries, concerts, "claret feasts," even boxing matches and bear-baitings. He is always dining with the Brawnes or the Dilkes, going to "routs" at the Reynoldses', visiting Haydon's studio or the British Museum with Severn, attending Hazlitt's lectures, or reciting his poetry for Bailey or Wordsworth. He cuts short his first sojourn at the Isle of Wight (where he had repaired to write *Endymion*) because he "was too much in Solitude, and conse-quently was obliged to be in continual burning of thought as an only resource" (10 May 1817; p. 82), and a year later confides to Reynolds, "I could not live without the love of my friends" (April 19, 1818; p. 138).

Although literary critics have recently stressed the political aspect of Keats's life and thought, it is important to remember that Keats himself felt that "the first political duty a Man ought to have a Mind to is the happiness of his friends" (17–27 September 1819; p.371). That his friends felt the same way about him is poignantly illustrated in a letter of December 1820 William Haslam sent to Joseph Severn, who was ministering to his dying companion in Italy: "Keats must get himself again, Severn, if but for us. I for one cannot afford to lose him. If I know what it is to love, I truly love John Keats." This sort of devotion speaks well both of Haslam and of Keats's other close friends, who eventually win their own collective fame as the "Keats Circle."

Keats occasionally yearned for solitude, it is true. He announces to George and Georgiana that he will never marry, and in a beautifully evoca-tive image says that "the roaring of the wind is my wife and the Stars through the window pane are my Children" (14–31 October 1818; p. 293). But it is only in his last year that he begins to sequester himself, and this is more the result of financial distress and the burden of his illness than any permanent streak of misanthropy in his character. In health, Keats's sensibility was pro-foundly social. Even when he decides to embark on a well-deserved walking tour with Charles Brown in the summer of 1818, he feels some guilt at abandoning his friends; as he says to Mrs. Wylie, "It was a great regret to me that I should leave all my friends just at the moment when I might have helped to soften away the time for them" (6 August 1818; *L*, 1:358).

It is more than a measure of compensation, however, that the tour itself takes on the character of a larger humanitarian mission. Keats vows to his brother Tom that he shall "learn poetry here and shall henceforth write more than ever, for the abstract endeavour of being able to add a mite to that mass of beauty which is harvested from these grand materials by the finest spirits and put into ethereal existence for the relish of one's fellows" (25–27 June 1818; p. 253). For Keats the "abstract endeavour" of art is always tempered by "the relish of one's fellows"; the pursuit of beauty always fulfills a social obligation that benefits humanity. It is not for nothing that Keats calls both Milton and the Grecian Urn the "friend[s] of man." Nor is it accidental that his famous prediction—"I think I shall be among the English Poets after my death"—pivots on the word *among*, as if immortality were a congenial gathering of geniuses rather than a row of marble busts.

Keats's conception of fame is similarly inflected by this social imperative. He was always saddened by the quarrels of his friends and frequently tried to reconcile them, but nothing depressed him more than the bickering of artists. He writes to Benjamin Bailey that he is "quite disgusted with literary Men" because they envy one another's work and as a result are constantly "at Loggerheads" (8 October 1817; p. 98). Keats sees fame not as the culmination of a competitive struggle, or as the image of a glorious trophy held aloft in individual triumph, but rather as an aesthetic heaven where great spirits may converse with one another. "So now in the Name of Shakespeare, Raphael, and all our Saints," he concludes a letter to Haydon, "I commend you to the care of heaven!" (10, 11 May 1817; p. 86). No matter how much "Minds [will] leave each other in contrary directions, traverse each other in Numberless points," he muses in another letter, they will nevertheless "greet each other at the Journey's end" (19 February 1818; p. 127). Such camaraderie advocates the "*gregarious* advance of intellect" (3 May 1818, my emphasis; p. 245) while exposing—for Keats at least—the bankruptcy of the "egotistical sublime."

Even as he is dying of consumption, it testifies to the fundamentally social character of his mind that the genial Keats returns. The last sentence of his will, provided to his publisher John Taylor before he sailed for Italy, reads, "My Chest of Books divide among my friends" (14 August 1820). And he signs off his final letter to Charles Brown by admitting that he "always made an awkward bow" (30 November 1820; p. 534), as if even in the end he was trying to close the gap between letter and life, write a gesture that would place him for one last moment in the physical presence of his friend. It is precisely the *awkwardness* of this final bow—especially coming from the Poet of Beauty—that lends it so much quiet grace.

It would be a mistake to conclude from these examples that because Keats was so generous and warm-hearted, he was also consistently amiable or overly compliant. In fact, he was possessed of a fiery temper and could get magnificently pissed off. Commentators have politely ignored this side of the man, perhaps because it does not square with the noble Keats of "exquisite manners" and "profound tolerance" that Lionel Trilling has portrayed, or perhaps because it is difficult to reconcile the person who claimed that he would "jump down Aetna for any great Public good" (9 April 1818; p. 138) with the one who remarks bitterly that he likes "man" but hates "Men." But the Keats who confesses to "the violence of my temperament" (14 February–4 May 1819; p 323) is a very real presence in the letters, and we ignore him at the risk of painting an idealized or sanitized portrait.

In truth, Keats had a great capacity for anger, particularly when it came to acts of injustice against others. When he learns that his friend Benjamin

Bailey's curacy has been delayed because of snobbery, for example, he can hardly contain his rage: "There is something so nauseous in self-willed yawning impudence in the shape of conscience, it sinks the Bishop of Lincoln into a smashed frog putrifying. That a rebel against common decency should escape the Pillory! That a mitre should cover a Man guilty of the most coxcombical, tyrannical and indolent impertinence!" (3 November 1817; p. 100). This "Keats-like rhodomontade" (19, 20 September 1819; p. 356), as one of his friends called it, goes on for another page. He demonstrates similar loathing for the figure of the parson, who "is an Hippocrite to the Believer and a Coward to the unbeliever" and "must be either a Knave or an Ideot" (14 February–4 May 1819; p. 313), and he vehemently damns the Scottish Church elders for banishing "puns and laughing and kissing" in order to create "regular Phalanges of savers and gainers" (7 July 1818; pp. 256–57). In other letters he vents his spleen on the public, Devonshire men, the caretaker of Burns's cottage ("I hate the rascal . . . he is a mahogany-faced old Jackass who knew Burns"), and bluestocking women writers, whom he decries as "a set of Devils whom I detest so much that I almost hunger after an acherontic promotion to a Torturer purposefully for their accommodation" (21 September 1817; p. 87).

Keats saves the brunt of his wrath, however, for Charles Wells, the perpetrator of a romantic hoax against his brother Tom. Though the man who impersonated Amena Bellafila in a series of trumped-up love letters no doubt meant the whole affair as a practical joke, Keats was furious at the deception and called it a "diabolical scheme." What most enraged him was that it was carried out "with every show of friendship," exploiting Tom's open and generous nature. It is this manipulation of the sacred bond of friendship that elicits an ire appearing nowhere else in Keats's letters: "I do not think death too bad for the villain," he writes to his brother and sister-in-law. "I consider it my duty to be prudently revengeful. I will hang over his head like a sword by a hair. I will be opium to his vanity, if I cannot injure his interests. He is a rat and he shall have ratsbane to his vanity. I will harm him all I possibly can. I have no doubt I shall be able to do so. Let us leave him to misery alone except when we can throw in a little more" (14 February–4 May 1819; p. 326). This is Keats's "incendiary spirit" with a vengeance; it is the ready pugilist who as a five-year-old boy reputedly defended his mother's sickroom with a sword, "clench'd" his fist against his master Thomas Hammond, and knocked down an usher who had boxed his brother's ears at school.

If we acknowledge this more explosive side of his character, we need also come to terms with those troubling moments in Keats's letters that commentators have conspicuously overlooked. Because they have laid so much stress on the intellectual strain of his mind, influential critics such as A. C. Bradley, T. S. Eliot, and Lionel Trilling have ignored the darker Keats, the man who could be rash, cruel, unreasonable, jealous, intolerant, misogynistic, and even anti-Semitic. These qualities simply do not square with the man of "moral energy" and "firmness of character" who has been promoted in the last half century. In fact, a remarkable feature of Trilling's highly successful paperback edition of the selected letters is its complete omission of any passage that might contradict his portrait of Keats as the "Poet-Hero." Entire paragraphs simply disappear from the letters without editorial comment.

Such is the case as well with the sequence of notes and love letters that Keats sent to his fiancée, Fanny Brawne, which were not published until 1878 and then created a storm of controversy. Although they now form part of any legitimate edition of the letters, this sequence has been almost completely ignored by scholars. Even as perceptive a reader as W. H. Auden confesses that he is "sorry that they were not published anonymously." After quoting a few of the more distasteful passages, he then attempts to cordon them off like a crime scene: "Any discussion of Keats's letters, therefore, should confine itself to those written before February 3, 1820." These are the texts that embarrass academic critics not only because they cut too close to the bone but also because they thwart the attempt to enshrine Keats as secular humanist and gentleman, a man of "generosity" and "exquisite manners." As we have seen, Keats was certainly possessed of these qualities, but he could also be imperious and antisocial, self-pitying and suspicious. "I enclose a passage from one of your Letters which I want you to alter a little," he writes to Fanny Brawne. "I want (if you will have it so) the matter express'd less coldly to me" (August [?] 1820; p. 518). In these brief notes and letters, Keats is prone to self-dramatization and hyperbole. He can be as melodramatic as a gothic novel—"Good bye! I kiss you—O the torments!" (May [?] 1820; p. 407)—or as jealous as Othello: "How have you pass'd this month? Who have you smil'd with?" (5 July [?] 1820; p. 514). Even as Fanny complains of his "illtreating [her] in word, thought and deed" (June [?] 1820; p. 407), Keats bristles with accusations: "You do not feel as I do. You do not know what it is to love. One day you may, your time is not come . . . Do not write to me if you have done anything this month which it would have pained me to have seen. You may have altered. If you have not, if you still behave in dancing rooms and other societies as I have seen you, I do not want to live" (5 July [?] 1820; p. 514).

It has been argued that Keats's illness distorted his normally sanguine temperament and that it is unfair to judge his character on this basis. But Keats's treatment of Fanny Brawne was no anomaly. The same man who could admire the "grand march of intellect" (3 May 1818; p. 245) and endorse the progressive improvement of civilization could also denigrate and abuse women with disturbing candor. Women "appear to me as children," he writes to George and Georgiana in October 1818, "to whom I would rather give a Sugar Plum than my time," and two months later: "I never intend here after to spend any time with Ladies unless they are handsome, you lose time to no purpose" (2 January 1819; p. 305). To Bailey he confesses that when he is among women he has "evil thoughts, malice, spleen" (18 July 1818; p. 265), and to George that "the Dress Maker, the blue Stocking and the most charming sentimentalist differ but in a Slight degree, and are equally smokeable" (31 December 1818; p. 304). He reserves his most venomous attack, however, for a letter of September 1819 to America. A scant page before an extended meditation on the humane progress of English history, where Keats argues that all civilized "countries become gradually more enlighten'd," he quotes a long passage from Burton's *Anatomy of Melancholy* describing a lover's mistress. It is one of the most extraordinary pieces of misogyny in romantic literature, a detailed catalog of female ailments that Keats patiently copies from Burton's book and then exuberantly endorses for his brother George: "There's a dose for you—fine!!" Perhaps even more remarkable is that the letter is addressed to both his brother *and* his sister-in-law Georgiana, whose response to this gruesome list we can scarcely imagine.

To arrive at a more honest estimation of Keats's character, then, it is important that we acknowledge these moments even (or especially) if they trouble our sense of his spiritual health or appear to compromise "the energy of his heroism." Such acknowledgment, I hasten to add, does not mean that we ought to drag Keats before a firing squad, or scold him for not being sensitive enough to issues of gender and ethnicity. This would demonstrate our own historical amnesia. But it does mean that we should recognize the fullness and complexity of Keats the man, resisting the spell of his considerable charms. To register the dark side of his character also helps us to recognize his capacity for role-playing and the ease with which he assumed a variety of social and psychological identities. In his letters he is finely attuned to his different audiences. By turns he is reflective and philosophical with Bailey and Reynolds, ambitious with Haydon, gossipy and colloquial with George and Georgiana, and paternal with his sister, Fanny. He plays the beleaguered poet with Taylor, the knowing rake with Dilke and Rice, the martyred lover with Fanny Brawne, and the solicitous older brother with Tom. To the Jeffery sisters he shows off, lacing his letters with puns, and to his close friend Charles Brown he reveals his deepest anxieties about writing, about money, and about death.

In sum, the Keats we experience in the letters bears striking similarities to the hypothetical "chameleon Poet" whom he refers to in a letter to Richard Woodhouse: "As to the poetical Character itself," he writes, "it is not itself, it has no self. It is everything and nothing. It has no character. It enjoys light and shade; it lives in gusto, be it foul or fair, high or low, rich or poor, mean or elevated. It has as much delight in conceiving an Iago as an Imogen" (27 October 1818; p. 295). Such protean versatility allows Keats to explore a remarkable range of human character and emotion *without judgment*; that is, it allows him to entertain the very real existence of evil in the world (Iago's hatred, cynicism, and bigotry) alongside the existence of good (Imogen's loyalty and virtue) in isolation from any moral prerogative. It is this kind of disinterestedness—a word Keats liked and borrowed from William Hazlitt—that makes him vulnerable to moral critics, who see Keats sliding into the abyss of absolute aestheticism, art for art's sake. But such openness, really a kind of celebration of the question of the world, also makes him distinctly modern, especially in his efforts to forge an identity out of "uncertainties, Mysteries, doubts."

One of the great ironies of Negative Capability and of Keats's formulation and embodiment of the characterless character is that he leaves behind such a powerful trace of self after his death. Even as he enters what he calls his "posthumous existence" in Italy and stops reading and writing letters, Keats's voice is channeled through the words of his friends. Joseph Severn becomes both the chronicler of his last months and his scribe, writing a series of detailed letters back to England relating the progress of Keats's disease and recording portions of his conversation. These letters are then carefully copied and circulated among Keats's friends and family. Almost immediately after his death, Keats's publisher John Taylor begins collecting material for a biography, as does Charles Brown. So lasting is the impression that Keats leaves on Reynolds that he requests his tombstone bear the words "The Friend of Keats," the same phrase that is eventually included on Brown's stone as well. Although she eventually marries, Fanny Brawne wears mourning for three years after Keats's death and takes his engagement ring to her grave. Fanny Keats carefully collects and preserves all of her brother's letters, and Joseph Severn sustains the poet's memory the length of his long life, writing no fewer than five separate memoirs of his experiences along with countless letters of reminiscence; his many portraits and sketches of Keats now constitute Severn's most enduring legacy.

True to his own theories about the fragility of identity, Keats insists that no name appear on his tombstone but only the words "Here lies one whose name was writ in water." It is one of the saddest epitaphs ever written, expressing Keats's bitter disappointment and his sense of the futility of his career. In this respect, it is consistent with his other request to Severn, "that no mention be made of [me] in any manner publicly—in reviews, magazines or newspapers—that no engraving be taken from any picture of [me]" (Severn to Taylor, 24 December 1820). In both of these requests Keats attempts to erase himself from the world, to ensure that not a trace of his character remain. A similar kind of evanescence appears at the end of a letter he wrote to J. H. Reynolds in March 1818, though it is predicated on air rather than water. Keats apologizes for the brevity of his letter, for not crossing it with "a little innocent bit of metaphysic," but then invites Reynolds to cross the letter himself in his own mind: "If you think for five minutes after having read this, you will find it a long letter and see written in the Air above you, Your most affectionate friend, John Keats." Here is a more accurate forecast of his eventual reception: the body of Keats's life and work inscribed in air, floating above us like a genial spirit, awaiting our imaginative participation to give him presence.

MARGARET HOMANS

Keats Reading Women, Women Reading Keats[†]

* * *

* * * When Keats defines his own poetic ideal against the bullying egotism of "Wordsworth &c," he defines what is not his mode as clearly masculine: "We hate poetry that has a palpable design upon us—and if we do not agree, seems to put its hands in its breeches pocket."[1] Yet while this passage suggests that Keats defines his poetry as a woman, he always makes it clear that it is not he himself who is the woman, but rather that he is the male suitor courting poetry personified as a woman, as in his description of himself "adoniz[ing]" (p. 363)—that is, washing and dressing nicely—before sitting down to write, or in his remark, "I know not why Poetry and I have been so distant lately I must make some advances soon or she will cut me entirely" (p. 318).[2] From the start, Keats defines his project by

---

† From "Keats Reading Women, Women Reading Keats," *Studies in Romanticism* 29 (Fall 1990): 341–70. Reprinted by permission of the author and *Studies in Romanticism*. The author's notes have been edited.

1. p. 121. Page numbers for letters refer to this Norton critical edition; *L* refers to Rollins's edition.

2. On poetry as a woman, see Mario L. D'Avanzo, *Keats's Metaphors for the Poetic Imagination* (Durham, N.C.: Duke University Press, 1967), pp. 25–31. See also Wolfson, "Feminizing Keats," *Critical Essays on John Keats*, ed. Hermione de Almeida (Boston: Hall, 1990), pp. 317–56.

attaching it to a preeminently masculine one: he writes, "The Imagination may be compared to Adam's dream—he awoke and found it truth" (p. 102).

Adam dreams of Eve while God shapes her out of Adam's rib; as Christine Froula has pointed out, our original myth of creativity amounts to the appropriation of female creation, represented as maternity, by two male figures.[3] Keats equates his imaginative project, then, not only with male sexual potency but also with the masculine appropriation of the feminine. That Keats asserts this equation so often suggests how defensively unconfident he is of its truth in his case. Whenever he does describe himself as a woman, his train of thought always counters the identification by juxtaposing to it an assertion of masculinity. For example, when he describes his mood of what he calls "effeminacy" (p. 321), the mood eventually represented in the "Ode on Indolence," he also mentions that his lassitude is due to a black eye, won, apparently, in a fistfight with a butcher. * * * In an earlier passage about poetic identity, an apparent identification of his project with the woman's position turns out to be an appropriation of it for the masculine:

> It has been an old Comparison for our urging on—the Bee hive— however it seems to me that we should rather be the flower than the Bee—for it is a false notion that more is gained by receiving than giving—no the receiver and the giver are equal in their benefits. The flower I doubt not receives a fair guerdon from the Bee—its leaves blush deeper in the next spring—and who shall say between Man and Woman which is the most delighted? Now it is more noble to sit like Jove tha[n] to fly like Mercury—let us not therefore go hurrying about and collecting honey-bee like, buzzing here and there impatiently from a knowledge of what is to be arrived at: but let us open our leaves like a flower and be passive and receptive—(p. 127)

Keats here aligns the passivity of the flower with what he understands to be women's sexual passivity, and if it's better to be like the flower, as he claims, then by the logic of analogy it's better also to be like the woman. This preference accords with Keats's dislike for the "irritable reaching after fact & reason" that he opposes to "*Negative Capability*" (1: 109). * * * But the same logic also aligns with flowers and women the figure of Jove, who sits still in contrast to the bee-like, masculine busyness of Mercury. No one could be less passive or flower-like than Jove, but what the figure accomplishes is to define the passive female position as one that's also powerfully masculine and therefore acceptable to a poet who identifies his project with Adam's. By making Jove's pleasure like a woman's, Keats also realigns Tiresias' claim that the woman is more "delighted" than the man. Here, Jove gets to have not only power, but also an extra measure of pleasure, because his pleasure is female; and so does Keats, writing as Jove-as-a-woman (even though at the end of the letter, modesty requires him to re-position himself as "scullion-Mercury or even a humble Bee").

* * *

Keats's reflections on women readers follow a similar pattern. Keats suffered, both emotionally and financially, from the failure of his three

---

3. See Christine Froula, "When Eve Reads Milton: Undoing the Canonical Economy," *Critical Inquiry* 10 (1983): 321–47.

books of poetry to attract a wide audience during his lifetime. While he and his friends blamed this situation on the poor or nonexistent reviews of his *Poems* of 1817 and of *Endymion*—he speaks of publishing poems as "hanging them up to be flyblown on the Reviewshambles" (p. 316)— his third volume was well reviewed (that is, liked by an elite of educated male readers) but still did not sell. Keats explains the situation in the following way:

> One of the causes, I understand from different quarters, of the unpopularity of this new book, and the others also, is the offence the ladies take at me. On thinking that matter over, I am certain that I have said nothing in a spirit to displease any woman I would care to please: but still there is a tendency to class women in my books with roses and sweetmeats,—they never see themselves dominant. (*L*, 2: 327)

Although he viewed the public in general as an "Enemy" (see *L*, 2: 266–67 and 1: 415), Keats understood a major part of his problem with the public as a failure to attract a female audience. He also understands that power can be given and withheld through figuration, and that a woman who has been made a sweetmeat cannot also be dominant. Although in this way he reminds himself of his imaginative authority, implicitly the passage is about his fear of women's real dominance, for he attributes to women readers, rightly or wrongly, the power to make him succeed or fail in the marketplace. Because of changing patterns of work and leisure, women (whose schooling led them to prefer novels or narrative verse) had been replacing the elite group of classically educated men as the chief consumers of literature. Moreover, class difference often magnifies Keats's sense of the power of women readers: it is chiefly (though not always) "ladies," women from the classes above the one into which he was born, to whom a book must appeal in order to succeed. Far from doing anything to attract a female audience, however, Keats reveals an active disdain for women readers and for the steps he views as necessary to attract them. He identifies "wom[e]n I would care to please" as those who do not mind being turned into sweetmeats and do not seek to dominate. By objectifying and subordinating figures of women in his poems, he strikes back at what he perceives to be real women's dominance.

Quite possibly, the state of affairs depicted in this passage is not so much an after-the-fact analysis as the result of Keats's intentions. For in a recorded conversation to whose full context we will want to return, "[Keats] said he does not want ladies to read his poetry: that he writes for men" (p. 356). His remarks about literary ladies and women bear out this hostility to the prospect of a female readership. In one letter he half-jokingly remarks that one of his "Ambitions" is to "upset the drawling of the blue stocking literary world" (p. 354). Bluestockings he defines elsewhere as "Devils," as "a set of Women, who having taken a snack or Luncheon of Literary scraps, set themselves up for towers of Babel in Languages Sapphos in Poetry" (p. 87), and again he describes as "sublime Petticoats" two literary ladies who published their correspondence with Rousseau (p. 404). In another letter, discussing the shallowness of the many readers who delight in the popular poets Mary Tighe and James Beattie, he remarks (now condemning equally women of all classes) that "This same inadequacy is discovered . . . in Women with few exceptions—the Dress Maker, the blue Stocking and the most charming sentimentalist differ but in a Slight degree, and are equally smokeable—" (p. 304). * * *

* * * To lift himself out of his own class by writing as he does highbrow poetry—poetry that required a Latin education, poetry in the line of Homer and Milton—is also for Keats to rise above all women considered as a class, and he resents being "obliged" to look up to women who write mere romances, just because they are wealthy and upperclass.

Here and elsewhere, one of Keats's habitual defenses against the power of women readers of whatever class is to transform them from reading subjects into objects of (visual) description. He deflates the considerable literary authority of Jane Porter by writing that he would meet her only so as to write about her. Keats makes a similar gesture following his cross-class indictment of the shallow women readers of Mary Tighe and James Beattie.* * * The next day's entry begins with a dinner party about which he comments, "I never intend here after to spend any time with Ladies unless they are handsome—you lose time to no purpose" (p. 305). Over the course of this letter Keats has neutralized the nagging topic of women as opinionated subjects, by assuring himself that women need only be looked at.

As this sequence suggests, much as he equates poetic ability with sexual potency, Keats equates the need to attract a female readership with the need to attract women sexually, and he scorns that compulsion as much as he disdains to seek women readers. These attitudes appear to be the compensatory, defensive forms taken by Keats's feeling of both literary and sexual inadequacy. After a long meditation on how his early idealization of women gave way to his present perplexing distaste for women's company, he writes, "I do think better of Womankind than to suppose they care whether Mister John Keats five feet hight likes them or not" (p. 265).* * * [Keats] maps his anxiety about women readers onto his anxiety about love. This connection finds compressed form in a later statement about audience: "I feel every confidence that if I choose I may be a popular writer; that I will never be; but for all that I will get a livelihood—I equally dislike the favour of the public with the love of a woman—they are both a cloying treacle to the wings of independence" (L, 2: 144).* * *

Mingling thoughts of female readers with thoughts of "the love of a woman," Keats makes Fanny Brawne into the prototype of the woman reader, and he acts out in his relation to her much of his anxiety about women readers at large. Keats directed Fanny Brawne's reading: he taught her to dislike Byron, and his letters to her mention the loan of various books including a Spenser with the most beautiful passages marked (L, 2: 302). He also took great pleasure in educating the literary taste of his young sister Fanny. As Fanny Brawne's letters to Fanny Keats after Keats's death make clear, she enjoyed reading and talking about books, "unless it is to such a very great judge that I am affraid they will think all my delightful criticism nonsense."[4] Such a judge she almost certainly felt Keats himself was—later sending the Spenser to Fanny Keats, she refers to him as "one who I have heard called the best judge of poetry living" (Brawne 84)—and he also quite ferociously directs Fanny Brawne as a reader of *himself*. From the Isle of

---

4. Fanny Brawne, *Letters of Fanny Brawne to Fanny Keats, 1820–1824*, ed. Fred Edgcumbe (New York: Oxford University Press, 1937), p. 49; cited hereafter in the text as "Brawne" followed by pages.

Wight in the summer of 1819 he writes to her, "Why may I not speak of your Beauty, since without that I could never have lov'd you. I cannot conceive any beginning of such love as I have for you but Beauty. * * * So let me speak of you [for your] Beauty, though to my own endangering; if you could be so cruel to me as to try elsewhere its Power" (p. 351). Though Keats often omits the final "r" from "your," his slip here reinforces the conflation he makes here and elsewhere between Fanny and Beauty. Earlier in the same letter, in a remark typical of what had provoked Fanny's objection in the first place, he writes: "All my thoughts, my unhappiest days and nights have I find not at all cured me of my love of Beauty, but made it so intense that I am miserable that you are not with me" (pp. 350–51). Keats, by continuing to speak of her Beauty, shows that she is not to prevail as a reader of him, and invoking the chimera of her supposed erotic power justifies his further disempowering her. She has attempted a critique of his writing—indeed of the central tenet of his creed in his worship of Beauty—and he responds by declaring her reading invalid. And then he effaces her critique further by burning it.[5]

In addition to directing Fanny's reading and her reading of him, he also directs her writing, appropriating her voice in his strongest defense against what he feels is her power over him as object of desire who is also a woman reader. In his first extant letter to her he asks her a question, then denies her freedom as a reader by supplying her answer: "Ask yourself my love whether you are not very cruel to have so entrammelled me, so destroyed my freedom. Will you confess this in the Letter you must write immediately and do all you can to console me in it—make it rich as a draught of poppies to intoxicate me . . ." (pp. 349–50). While it is easy to imagine Fanny wanting to answer "no," the rhetoricization of his question leaves her no room. Many times in their later correspondence he expresses his love through telling her what to say: "Write me ever so few lines and tell you [me] you will never for ever be less kind to me than yesterday" (L, 2: 222); "Send me every evening a written Good night" (L, 2: 262), which it appears she did. In a letter in which he reiterates the exclamations about her beauty that she had attempted to critique, he corrects her writing in another way too: "For some reason or other your last night's note was not so treasureable as former ones. I would fain that you call me *Love* still" (L, 2: 263).

* * *

* * * Keats's assumptions of [Fanny's] voice * * * could be described as gestures of empathetic identification with an other of the kind he names negative capability, through which he also identifies with the sparrow and with Achilles. But they could better be described as acts of self-aggrandizing appropriation. Keats opposes living "in a thousand worlds" to life with any particular woman. * * *

Keats's letters favoring what is usually summarized as negative capability date before the end of 1818. In November 1817 he writes, "Men of Genius . . . have not any individuality, any determined Character" (p. 102). The letter defining negative capability is dated December 1817 (p. 109).

---

5. * * * [See] Sonia Hofkosh, "The Writer's Ravishment: Women and the Romantic Author—The Example of Byron," in Anne K. Mellor, ed., *Romanticism and Feminism* (Bloomington: Indiana University Press, 1988), pp. 93–114.

* * * In October 1818 he describes to George and Georgiana his feeling of living in a thousand worlds, and, writing to Woodhouse, he distinguishes "the Wordsworthian or egotistical sublime" from his own "poetical Character": "it is not itself—it has no self—it is every thing and nothing—It has no character"; and twice he repeats that the poet is "unpoetical" and has "no identity" (pp. 294–95). By abrupt contrast, in April 1819 the term "identity" has become a wholly favorable one, in his account of "the world" as "the vale of Soul-making": "There may be intelligences or sparks of the divinity in millions—but they are not Souls till they acquire identities, till each one is personally itself " (p. 330); and he details the process by which "the sense of Identity" is formed. As time passes, the letters reveal an increasing tendency to seek solitude in life and self-sufficiency in poetry. Living alone in Winchester in August 1819, Keats writes to Reynolds, "My own being which I know to be becomes of more consequence to me than the crowds of Shadows in the Shape of Man and women that inhabit a kingdom. The Soul is a world of itself and has enough to do in its own home" (L, 2: 146). Or again the next summer he writes to Shelley that an artist "must have 'self-concentration,' selfishness perhaps. . . . My imagination is a Monastry and I am its Monk" (p. 524).

One way to explain this change is to note that all along his language for defining negative capability is predominantly negative, so that celebrating a positive sense of identity may be the logical outcome of the ambivalence these negations have expressed all along.[6] Keats's withdrawal into himself has been attributed to depression over his growing illness, although this is not likely the case when he writes the letter about soul-making. In the late fall of 1818, between that letter and the last of the letters celebrating "no identity," Tom died and Keats met and fell in love with Fanny Brawne, and it may be that falling in love—perhaps made possible, for a man who said "the thought of [my Brothers] has always stifled the impression that any woman might otherwise have made upon me" (p. 250), by the death of one brother after the emigration of the other—contributes materially to the radical change in his view of identity and self.[7] The letter of October 1818, about love and marriage, is the first to sound openly self-contradictory about the unboundedness of negative capability. If living in a thousand worlds erects a "barrier" between himself and any women he might love, then his devotion to negative capability has undone itself, by requiring a limit to the outgoing of the self. Because he sometimes formulates negative capability as a defense against and appropriation of women and femininity, the turn toward a self-contained identity may extend or fulfill—not diverge from—that ongoing defensiveness, with the difference that, early on, one woman would seem to limit his entering into others, while later, one woman threatens to carry his negative capability too far. For as several critics have pointed out, in Keats's letters to Fanny from the summer of 1819 and later, he writes of feeling that the "thought of you would uncrystallize and dissolve me"

6. See Paul de Man's essay included here, pp. 537–46.
7. De Man charts what he sees as Keats's not wholly voluntary turn, in the latest poems, to a more rigid sense of selfhood and attributes this turn in part to the influence of Fanny Brawne (p. 544). Susan Wolfson argues that Keats "realized that his love for Fanny had made him exceptionally conscious of himself, or 'selfish' "; "Keats is now aware that this easy self-annihilation [of negative capability], though a creative asset, is an existential liability": "Composition and 'Unrest': The Dynamics of Form in Keats's Last Lyrics," *Keats-Shelley Journal* 34 (1985): 57 and 66.

(*L*, 2: 142); "you absorb me in spite of myself" (p. 353.[8] This sense of dissolution Keats explicitly links to the thought of death: "I have two luxuries to brood over in my walks, your Loveliness and the hour of my death. . . . would I could take a sweet poison from your lips to send me out of [the world]" (pp. 353–54). It is thus as a defense against Fanny's supposed power of life and death that he appropriates her voice as a reader and turns her into a silent Venus. The constitution of his specifically masculine authority and subjectivity is in his view a necessary (if scarcely adequate) antidote to her threat to his identity—a sense of identity he scarcely thought he wanted, until he felt she would take it from him. His final defense against his thought of her power comes when he has her last letters to him buried with him, unopened and unread.

* * *

Keats rehearses * * * his insistence upon his own masculine authority * * * as a lover and as a writer. It is an authority defined through the control of women's sexuality and of their voices, and through the appropriation of these to his interests (figured as the interests of male authority more generally), as we see in his subordination of literary mothers to literary fathers. In *The Eve of St. Agnes,* a poem that borrows more of its language from "mother Radcliff" than just its title,[9] Porphyro seduces Madeleine with the aid of the "ancient ditty . . . La belle dame sans mercy." In some further remarks about *The Eve of St. Agnes,* recorded in September 1819 by Richard Woodhouse, Keats shows himself to be carrying this insistence on male authority even further than we have so far seen. Just prior to the remark I want to discuss, Keats insists that an alteration he made to the poem was not an imitation of Byron, thus bringing competition with Byron into the subtext of what follows. Next, Keats's desired revision would make the poem more sexually explicit (a revision Keats was ultimately persuaded to discard). Originally, "innocent" readers—"ladies and myself"—could have assumed that right after Madeleine confesses her love, the pair go off and, Woodhouse continues:

> marr[y] in right honest chaste & sober wise. But, as it is now altered, as soon as M. has confessed her love, P. winds by degrees his arm round her, presses breast to breast, and acts all the acts of a bonâ fide husband. . . . tho' there are no improper expressions but all is left to inference, and tho' . . . the Interest on the reader's imagination is greatly heightened, yet I do apprehend it will render the poem unfit for ladies, & indeed scarcely to be mentioned to them among the "things that are."—He says he does not want ladies to read his poetry: that he writes for men—& that if in the former poem there was an opening for doubt what took place, it was his fault for not writing clearly & comprehensibly—. . . . (p. 356)

* * * That the poem is so repellently seductive turns out to be by design: Keats hopes to exclude women readers. But would they necessarily have been repelled by such sexual boldness?

8. Wolfson, "Composition and 'Unrest,'" 59 and 65 and Hofkosh, 107, both discuss the passage about dissolving in the context of Keats's resistance to it.
9. See Martha Hale Shackford, "'The Eve of St. Agnes' and *The Mysteries of Udolpho,*" *PMLA* 36 (1921): 104–18.

I have been implying here that Keats hopes that women will not be interested in his poem. But far from speculating accurately about what women readers might feel, Keats and Woodhouse fail to speculate on this subject at all. They focus instead on men as readers and as censors of the reading specifically of "ladies." Woodhouse candidly reveals that what would render the poem unfit for ladies makes it more appealing to him, that is, makes it sexually arousing: "the Interest on the reader's imagination is greatly heightened." * * * Indeed (this seems to be Keats's weird promotional scheme) men will be obliged to read the poem, in order to protect their ladies from it. Keats has not so much made his poem uninteresting to women readers, as made it necessary as well as pleasurable for male readers to control its distribution.

* * *

Keats's most striking image of the woman reader occurs in another of the poems with "mother Radcliff" names, "The Eve of St. Mark." A young woman named Bertha, who lives "in the old Minster Square" of a cathedral town and who is, if not high-born, at least as leisured as the "ladies" of Keats's putative readership, reads, presumably on the eve of St. Mark, from

> A curious volume, patch'd and torn,
> That all day long, from earliest morn,
> Had taken captive her two eyes (25–27).

So intense is her concentration that the fading of the daylight does not break it: she reads "With forehead 'gainst the window pane" (49) and then by the light of the fire, which casts her "giant" shadow on the walls behind her.

> her shadow still
> Glower'd about as it would fill
> The room with wildest forms and shades,
> As though some ghostly queens of spades
> Had come to mock behind her back,
> And dance, and ruffle her garments black. (83–88)

The poem breaks off with a "quotation" not from the book itself, but from its marginalia of "pious poesies," including a verse to the effect that a mother who "Kepen in solitarinesse, / And kissen devoute the holy croce" can make her child "A saint er its nativitie." Bertha, reading about sainthood and female chastity (the description of "her constant eyelids" links her to the pious mother) is among the most chaste of Keats's heroines, and many commentators have noted the poem's restraint and somberness. Yet the giant forms of Bertha's shadows, the ghostly queens of spades who dance and ruffle behind her, belie that restraint. Conflating the deathly ace of spades with the amorous queen of hearts, these images of monstrous, powerful femaleness represent as the fear of death a terrifying sexuality. And because they result from Bertha's fixed position by the flickering fire, they represent what is released in her by her unnatural, obsessive reading. We noted earlier Keats's hope that, by redescribing women's power over him as having originated in their reading of him, he would be in the position of imaginatively controlling that power. This process is dramatized here. A demonic power is elicited from the otherwise chaste and sober

Bertha, but because it is brought out by her reading, she remains under the authority of the text, which can harness this force to its doctrinaire purposes (when her eyes stray to the margin, they stray only into further pieties).

The poem breaks off, but Keats continues it in a grotesquely comic form, his last attempt—an ambivalent one, again—to capture a female audience. As various readers have noted, Bertha, her cathedral town setting, and her book reappear in *The Jealousies* (Keats's preferred title for the poem better known as *The Cap and Bells*).[1] A commoner, but "solid," Bertha Pearl is illicitly loved by Elfinan, the Emperor of the fairies. Elfinan has been read as a figure for the Prince Regent or for Byron or both, since each was, like Elfinan, royalty or nobility involved in publicly scandalous sexual intrigues. While Elfinan is supposed to be awaiting the arrival of his official fiancée, the fairy Bellanaine, he secretly flies off to visit Bertha Pearl. He carries with him a book, "an old / And legend-leaved book, mysterious to behold" (512–13), that is endowed with "the potent charm, / That shall drive Bertha to a fainting fit" (518–19). Elfinan sets out on this mock quest on St. Mark's eve for, the sorcerer Hum tells him, "on that eve alone can you the maid convey" (504).

According to the satirical lens turned on it by *The Jealousies*, Bertha's reading in "The Eve of St. Mark" is sexual: it seduces her, and it seduces her on behalf of a royal and unearthly suitor. The original Bertha's ancient and holy tome turns out to be a fairy Emperor's aid to seduction. The suggestion of a monstrous female power in those shadowy "queens of spades" that mock the original Bertha is made grotesquely explicit as the sexuality that Hum's book will activate in Bertha Pearl, a sexuality that exists for Elfinan. An amorphous, terrifying power released for no clear purpose in the original becomes a submissive sexuality in the revision. Like the sexual interest daughters and sisters might take in a poem like *The Eve of St. Agnes*, female sexuality is released here only to reinforce the authority of the masculine purveyors of books. Bertha Pearl has embroidered on her sampler the words, "*Cupid, I—do thee defy!*" (455), but that Hum has captured it for Elfinan suggests the inefficacy of her protest. The woman's own words will not outweigh the seductive and controlling power of what a man gives her to read. As in his attempted revisions to *The Eve of St. Agnes*, Keats turned his need to cater to female taste aggressively against his idea of the highbrow woman reader. In the letter blaming "the offence the ladies take at me" on his tendency "to class women . . . with roses and sweetmeats" he continues: "If I ever come to publish [*The Jealousies*], there will be some delicate picking for squeamish stomachs" (*L*, 2: 327–28). Keats will avenge his unpopularity on the supposed sources of it: recalcitrant lady readers, women who object to objectification.

We have yet to note one of the most significant features of *The Jealousies*, which is that it is written by a woman, or rather by Keats writing as a woman: Lucy Vaughan Lloyd, of China Walk, Lambeth, a woman whose dainty name and address identify her as a member of the tribe of "sublime Petticoats" who so irritate Keats by their sentimentalism and their failure to buy his poems. That the pseudonym mattered to Keats's conception of

---

1. See, for example, Martin Halpern, "Keats and 'The Spirit that Laughest,'" *Keats-Shelley Journal* 15 (1966): 82.

the poem is shown by his references to the poem. To Charles Brown he writes, "I shall soon begin upon *Lucy Vaughan Lloyd*" (*L*, 2: 299). And in the passage from which I just quoted, Keats actually writes, "If I ever come to publish 'Lucy Vaughan Lloyd,' there will be. . . ." Having spoken in Fanny's * * * voice, having written poems with "fine mother Radcliff names," Keats again appropriates a female voice in order to change a woman reader into a sexual object, in order to reassert his own authority as a masculine subject. Purporting to offer a woman's reading of a woman reading, the poem makes a woman complicitous in the subordination of the woman reader to masculine sexual and literary authority. Keats preempts a woman's voice, and shapes a woman reader, to show what he could perhaps never get Fanny herself to say, that women are Beauty and belong, as the objects of men's gaze, under male proprietorship. And that reading the poetry of Keats can bring about this transformation.

If it seems disappointing to end with the suggestion that this little-liked poem somehow culminates any tendency of Keats's, we might return briefly to *The Fall of Hyperion.* * * * [W]e might think of the vicissitudes of Moneta's power in the context of Bertha Pearl's failure to resist seduction by the book. Moneta is too grand for seduction, yet she is induced (by the speaker-poet's willingness to suffer) to open her womb-brain to him, and her doing so enhances his authority as a poet (even though that authority is defined through his very mortal weakness). Through the poem's carefully orchestrated and undecidable epistemological reversals, Moneta's initial dominance as a reader is subdued, and the very grandeur of Moneta and of this process dignifies the male authority that neutralizes the woman reader in a way that *The Jealousies* could not.

As Keats's motive for treating women and especially lady readers as he does, I have stressed his resentment of their real and imagined power over him and his compensatory wish to assert his own masculine authority. But that assertion of masculinity accomplishes a further aim for him. By invoking an exclusively male readership, by writing only for men, he makes of his poetry a masculine preserve, and in so doing he elects himself a member of the male club that poets in the classical tradition, and especially the high romantics, have always claimed literature to be, but which it is not. If we recall Lockhart's insulting review, we can see why this move might have been crucial for Keats. By asserting his membership in highbrow literature as an exclusively male club, Keats would dissociate himself from the category—female, lower class, and desexualized—in which Lockhart places him: "there is scarcely a superannuated governess in the island that does not leave a roll of lyrics behind in her band-box." Twentieth-century male literary critics of high romanticism such as Harold Bloom have succeeded in fulfilling Keats's wish, by stressing his place in the line of Milton and Wordsworth and by effacing his sources in the writings of women such as Mary Tighe and Ann Radcliffe. It is not only his sense of powerlessness with respect to supposedly powerful women that motivates Keats in his quest for a male readership; it is also his fear of sharing in the cultural powerlessness of women themselves.

* * *

NICHOLAS ROE

Lisping Sedition: *Poems, Endymion,* and the Poetics of Dissent[†]

A Cockney Bantling

Richard Woodhouse wrote in his copy of *Endymion*, "K. said, with much simplicity, 'It will easily be seen what I think of the present Ministers by the beginning of the 3d Book' " [3.1–18].[1] * * * Keats wrote the third book of *Endymion* in September 1817 at Magdalen Hall, Oxford, where he was staying with Benjamin Bailey, and he completed it by 28 September (*L*, 1:168).[2] Many years afterwards Bailey, now Archdeacon at Colombo, Ceylon, wrote a series of letters to Richard Monckton Milnes in which he made much of his short acquaintance with Keats: "I knew his *inner* man so thoroughly that I may be able to throw light upon his genius and character" (15 October 1848, 2:263–64).[3] When he recalled the composition of *Endymion* III, however, Bailey grew thoroughly stern and censorious, claiming that Keats had written "the first few introductory lines which he read to me, before he became my guest":

> I did not then, & I cannot now very much approve that introduction. The "baaing vanities" [l. 3] have something of the character of what was called "the cockney school". Nor do I like many of the forced rhymes, & the apparent effort, by breaking up the lines, to get as far as possible in the opposite direction of the Pope school. (7 May 1849; *KC*, 2.269)

* * * Bailey may indeed have consistently disliked the passage, although in September 1817 he could not have associated "baaing vanities" with "Cockney School" poetics since Z's first essay, inventing and then denouncing the sect, had not appeared in *Blackwood's Magazine*.

It is more probable that Bailey would have been reluctant to approve the introduction to Book III because of its anti-clerical sentiments:

> With not one tinge
> Of sanctuary splendour, not a sight
> Able to face an owl's, they still are dight
> By the blear-eyed nations in empurpled vests . . . (8–11)

These lines are too awkward and convoluted to be effective as anti-clerical polemic, although for Bailey they came to represent one of the "errors of Keats's character" (*KC*, 2. 260). "On *religion*, for instance, he had . . . the most lax notions," Bailey informed Milnes (*KC*, 2.291). * * * When *Endymion* was published in April 1818, the anti-clerical sentiment which so preoccupied Bailey passed almost without notice in reviews. *The*

---

† From *John Keats and the Culture of Dissent*, by Nicholas Roe (Oxford: Oxford University Press, 1997), pp. 202–229. Reprinted by permission of the author and Oxford University Press. The author's notes have been edited.
1. See *The Poems of John Keats*, ed. Miriam Allott (London, 1970), 206 n. Hereafter in this essay referred to as *AP*.
2. *The Letters of John Keats, 1814–1821*, ed. Hyder E. Rollins (2 vols., London, 1848). Hereafter referred to as *L*. Page numbers alone refer to this Norton Critical Edition.
3. *The Keats Circle: Letters and Papers 1816–1878 and More Letters and Poems 1814–1879*, ed. Hyder E. Rollins (2nd ed., 2 vols., Cambridge, MA, 1965). Hereafter referred to as *KC*.

British Critic observed: "The third book begins in character, with a jacobinical apostrophe to 'crowns, turbans, and tiptop nothings'; we wonder how mitres escaped from their usual place."[4] In *Blackwood's*, Z prefaced his quotation from the opening of Book III with these remarks:

> We had almost forgot to mention, that Keats belongs to the Cockney School of Politics, as well as the Cockney School of Poetry. It is fit that he who holds Rimini to be the first poem, should believe the Examiner to be the first politician of the day. We admire consistency, even in folly. Hear how their bantling has already learned to lisp sedition.[5]

The terms of Z's criticism in this passage have received less attention than they deserve. Keats is a "bantling"—a bastard child—taught by the "Cockney School" to versify in a "lisp," associated at this period with childish or "effeminate" sensibility. The beginning of *Endymion* III is indeed characterized by a sort of unstable, childish exuberance. But the verse is clogged with awkward parentheses: "or, O torturing fact! / Who"; forced "Cockney" rhymes "fact! / unpack'd," "past and gone— / Babylon"; archaic words such as "dight"; and elliptical phrases like "There are who lord it," "most prevailing tinsel," "a sight / to face an owl's," "unladen breasts, / Save of blown self-applause." As political invective, the lines are almost wholly obscure. * * * But to Z the poem's marred and imperfect verse, its "lisping" voice, was a further expression of the political agenda which he associated with Hunt and the Cockney School. Was this simply one more gibe to ridicule the "young Cockney rhymester"?—or should we take Z's observation seriously as an insight that reveals the ideological grounds on which Keats's poems were identified with "the Cockney school of versification, morality, and politics"?

* * * *Poems, by John Keats* deliberately announced the author's relationship to Leigh Hunt. * * * [T]he complex design of this volume deserves further consideration here. Keats had divided his book into five parts: following the dedicatory sonnet to Hunt were three sections—"Poems," "Epistles," "Sonnets"—and the book concluded with *Sleep and Poetry*. The contents comprised occasional verses, "To Some Ladies," "On Receiving a Curious Shell," "On Leaving Some Friends"; two imitations of Spenser, the "Specimen of an Induction" and "Calidore"; and familiar and fraternal verse epistles to friends and his brother George. * * * [M]any of these poems were explicit in announcing Keats's politics, most obviously so in the sonnets to Hunt and Kosciusko, and in the epistles to Mathew and George Keats. The ode "To Hope," probably written shortly after Hunt's release from gaol on 2 February 1815, declared:

> Let me not see the patriot's high bequest,
>   Great Liberty! how great in plain attire!
> With the base purple of a court oppress'd,
>   Bowing her head, and ready to expire. (37–40)

"To Hope" is written in a conventional eighteenth-century libertarian idiom and * * * it reinforces the political interests directly voiced by Keats's first

---

4. *British Critic* (June 1818); see above, p. 249.
5. "Cockney School IV", p. 524; see above, p. 276.

book. In some of these early poems Keats interweaves comparably explicit liberal sentiments with passages of luxurious description in which a decorative Spenserian bower is identified as a place of imaginative retirement and recreation:

> a bowery nook
> Will be elysium—an eternal book
> Whence I may copy many a lovely saying
> About the leaves, and flowers—about the playing
> Of nymphs in woods, and fountains; and the shade
> Keeping a silence round a sleeping maid;
> And many a verse from so strange influence
> That we must ever wonder how, and whence
> It came. (*Sleep and Poetry*, 63–71)

This arbour of fancied sequestration may be read as "an eternal book" which expresses Keats's wish to lose the responsibilities of life to erotic enchantment and the "strange influence" of poetry. But * * * the luxurious bower also defined a space of imagined "elysium" comparable to Hunt's "Places of nestling green for Poets made," and intelligible as an expression of the liberal ideals announced more directly elsewhere in the book. When critics noticed Keats's "natural freedom of versification," or observed that "in his enmity to the French school, and to the Augustan age of England, he seems to have a principle, that plan and arrangement are prejudicial to natural poetry," they were responding to the stylistic signature of the "natural freedom" that also defined his opposition to "the present Ministers."[6] * * * A comparably patriotic inflection of retreat appears in *Sleep and Poetry*, where withdrawal into "the bosom of a leafy world" (119) gives rise to thoughts of the fully humanized poetry which Keats hoped to write in the future:

> And can I ever bid these joys farewell?
> Yes, I must pass them for a nobler life,
> Where I may find the agonies, the strife
> Of human hearts . . . (122–5)

Here, and elsewhere in Keats's early poems, the bower serves as a temporary refuge in the poet's quest towards a humane, historicized imagination—indeed, Jack Stillinger has seen the whole of the 1817 collection as a narrative addressing issues related to Keats's career as a poet.[7] A similar progression appears in "Ode to a Nightingale," where "verdurous glooms and winding mossy ways" (40) lead into the "embalmed darkness" of reverie figured as a woodland bower in which the poet may "guess each sweet" (43) * * * —much as he had delighted to catalogue "luxuries" in his earlier poems. But in "Ode to a Nightingale" this child-like poring over "sweets" of the imagination (which Yeats thought was characteristic of Keats) gives way to an awareness of mortality [i.e., "fading violets," 47; "murmurous haunt of flies," 50], the passage of time, and the tread of "hungry generations" of humankind. This movement from "sweets" or "luxuries"

---

6. See the following reviews of *Poems, by John Keats*: J. H. Reynolds in *Champion* (9 Mar. 1817), above, pp. 73–75, and George Felton Mathew in the *European Magazine* (May 1817), rpt. *KCH* 52.
7. See "The Order of Poems in Keats's First Volume," in *The Hoodwinking of Madeline and Other Essays on Keats's Poems* (Urbana, IL, 1971), pp. 1–13.

to a chastened awareness of history is a recurrent pattern in Keatsian romance, and in his early verse it is accompanied by a more evident preoccupation with the political life of England.

A Time when Pan is not Sought

* * *

The title-page of *Poems, by John Keats* was carefully arranged to announce the relationship between liberal politics and the poet's imaginative life. * * * On opening the book, Keats's first readers saw an epigraph from Spenser's complaint *Muiopotmos; or, The Fate of the Butterfly:*

> "What more felicity can fall to creature,
> Than to enjoy delight with liberty"

Just beneath this verse is a laurelled head of William Shakespeare. * * * In bringing together Spenser and Shakespeare, Keats paid tribute to his poetic heroes (two months after *Poems* appeared he "dared" to acknowledge Shakespeare as his "good Genius" [p. 84]) and also made a public declaration of his political allegiances. By coupling "delight" and "liberty" with Shakespeare, Keats neatly focused a theme in Hunt's leaders for the *Examiner* where Shakespeare was invoked as presiding over "our liberties" in a liberal pantheon that included King Alfred, Chaucer, Milton, Sydney, and Marvell.[8] Keats may well have expected his readers to know that in Spenser's poem libertarian "felicity" is immediately succeeded by "mishap," and an elegiac meditation on the vulnerability of joy:

> But what on earth can long abide in state?
> Or who can him assure of happie day;
> Sith morning faire may bringe fowle evening late,
> And least mishap the most blisse alter may? (217–20)[9]

Earthly mutability also characterized the first poem in Keats's volume, the dedicatory sonnet to Leigh Hunt. The sonnet echoes in its first line the "May-morning" festival of Wordsworth's "Immortality" ode, recalling Wordsworth's loss of visionary power ("there hath passed away a glory from the earth") as a comment on the historical moment of Keats's compliment to Hunt:

To Leigh Hunt, Esq.

Glory and loveliness have passed away;
   For if we wander out in early morn,
   No wreathed incense do we see upborne
Into the east, to meet the smiling day:
No crowd of nymphs soft voic'd and young, and gay,
   In woven baskets bringing ears of corn,
   Roses, and pinks, and violets, to adorn
The shrine of Flora in her early May.
But there are left delights as high as these,
   And I shall ever bless my destiny,

---

8. See for example the *Examiner* (2 Mar. 1817), pp. 129, 138, (9 Mar. 1817), p. 145 and (10 May 1818), p. 289.
9. *Spenser: Poetical Works,* ed. J.C. Smith and E. de Selincourt (Oxford, 1912).

> That in a time, when under pleasant trees
> Pan is no longer sought, I feel a free,
> A leafy luxury, seeing I could please
> With these poor offerings, a man like thee.

The impact that this impressive dedicatory poem would have made on Keats's readers and reviewers should not be underestimated. By placing it on the first page of his first collection Keats deliberately identified himself with an outspoken figure of public opposition to the government, but, more than this, he did so in the unsettled period following the Spa Fields riot—"a crisis of . . . general and unexampled pressure and calamity".[1] On 2 March 1817, the day before *Poems* was published in London, the front page of the *Examiner* carried an article "On the Proposed Suspension of the Habeas Corpus Act," denouncing the Foreign Secretary Lord Castlereagh—"a man, who is proved guilty in the House of Commons of violating the Constitution and setting at nought the representative rights of the people, coming forward and asking for a suspension of our most sacred privilege"—and warning that "The Suspension Bill, if it pass, will be an unconstitutional assumption of power by the House of Commons illegally constituted."[2] By appearing the day following Hunt's attack in the *Examiner*, Keats's lyrical compliment to Castlereagh's opponent would have seemed markedly controversial—and not only because of the political stakes it so clearly announced. In the economy of Keats's sonnet national crisis is associated with dislocation from the classical world, with loss of pastoral innocence and "a time, when under pleasant trees / Pan is no longer sought." * * * Against Castlereagh's suppression of "the representative rights of the people," * * * Keats brings his "poor offerings" in *Poems* as a witness to the renewal of what Hunt called "our green and glorious country".[3]

The Suburban School

*   *   *

After the politically motivated attacks on Keats in the *Quarterly* and *Blackwood's*, Keats's friends rallied to his defence. One of their tactics was to insist upon the separation of poetry and history, the aesthetic and the political. John Hamilton Reynolds for example, asserted Keats's rural "independence":

> We have the highest hopes of this young poet. We are obscure men, it is true . . . We live far from the world of letters,—out of the pale of fashionable criticism,—aloof from the atmosphere of a Court; but we are surrounded by a beautiful country, and love Poetry, which we read out of doors, as well as in. We think we see glimpses of a high mind in this young man[4] . . .

The poet's "high mind," by implication, was disengaged from the traffic of letters, criticism, and politics. Yet each of Reynolds's claims for Keats's

---

1. From the first resolution taken at the "Meeting for a Reform" reported in the *Examiner* (26 Jan. 1817), p. 58.
2. *Examiner* (2 Mar. 1817), p. 129–30.
3. *Examiner* (2 Mar. 1817), p. 139.
4. *Alfred, West of England Journal and General Advertiser* (6 Oct. 1818); above, p. 286.

"obscurity" was socially definitive: "fashionable criticism," for instance, denoted criticism which was currently "stylish," but also a manner "current in upper-class society" or "in vogue among persons of the upper class" (*OED*)—that is, the coterie of "fashionables" who contributed to "the atmosphere of a Court". Reynolds's purpose was to defend Keats by insulating him in "beautiful country," although the poet's distance from "fashionable criticism" and "the atmosphere of a court" might readily be interpreted as reprobate—a characteristic of the literary revolution announced in *Sleep and Poetry* and championed by Hunt in his "Young Poets" essay and in the preface to *Foliage*.[5] Certainly, Z took this view and contrived to frustrate Keats and the other Cockneys by banishing them to a cultural limbo on the fringe of metropolitan civilization, yet not quite removed to the country. In retrospect the strategy of enforcing Keats's isolation from "the world," adopted by friends and hostile critics alike, can be seen to have initiated the long-standing critical consensus which agreed that historical analysis was "irrelevant" to the understanding of Keats's poetry.[6]

The London "mob" had always been seen as a vulgar, turbulent mass, and it was probably this historical association with social upheaval that Z wished to invoke with the "Cockney" label. But his criticism displaced the Cockney territory from the inner city to the northerly village of Hampstead, and confined it there by coining the disagreeable adjective "suburban." * * * One might argue * * * that it was Z's essays on the Cockney School * * * that served to fix the modern, pejorative senses of "suburban" as part of his caricatures of Hunt, Hazlitt, Keats, Reynolds, and Webb.

In his first essay, Z writes about Hunt's poetry of nature and place:

> He is the ideal of a Cockney Poet. He raves perpetually about "green fields," "jaunty streams," and "o'er-arching leafiness," exactly as a Cheapside shop-keeper does about the beauties of his box on the Camberwell road. Mr Hunt is altogether unacquainted with the face of nature in her magnificent scenes; he has never seen any mountain higher than Highgate-hill, nor reclined by any stream more pastoral than the Serpentine River. But he is determined to be a poet eminently rural, and he rings the changes—till one is sick of him, on the beauties of the different "high views" which he has taken of God and nature, in the course of some Sunday dinner parties, at which he has assisted in the neighbourhood of London.[7]

Cockney nature poetry, for Z, was a Cheapside sublime expressed in catchphrases and jingles. * * *

* * *

* * * We need also to recognize that Z's criticism succeeded in making suburban life and literature synonymous with cultural vulgarity, for later generations followed him in regarding the "*Suburban School*" of English writing (so Byron termed it) as beyond the pale of serious critical attention.[8]

---

5. See Elizabeth Jones, "The Suburban School: Snobbery and Fear in the Attacks on Keats," *Times Literary Supplement* (27 October 1995), 14.
6. See Jerome McGann, "Keats and the Historical Method in Literary Criticism," in *The Beauty of Inflections: Literary Investigations on Historical Method and Theory* (Oxford, 1985), p. 26.
7. "Cockney School I", p. 39.
8. Byron to John Murray, 4 Aug. 1821, *Byron's Letters and Journals*, ed. Leslie A. Marchand (12 vols., London, 1973–82), viii. 166.

As part of this systematic cultural depreciation, the "Cockney School" essays worked further to prejudice understanding of Keats's politics from an early date, establishing a powerful idea of Keats as an immature poet and thinker.

John Hamilton Reynolds had recommended Keats's poetry by drawing attention to his youth, and other critics made similar points, so that William Rossetti, writing in 1887, could claim that Keats had been "doomed" to "youthfulness".[9] Hunt had introduced Keats in the *Examiner*, 1 December 1816, under the heading "Young Poets": "The last of these young aspirants . . . is, we believe, the youngest of them all, and just of age. His name is JOHN KEATS."[1] Reviews of *Poems* and *Endymion* refer to Keats as "a very young man"; "our young poet"; "the young writer"; "a young poet giving himself up to his own impressions"; "an immature promise of possible excellence"; "sentiments sometimes bordering upon childishness"; "a very young man"; "our young friend"; "the young aspirant"; "a young man of genius."[2] For Wordsworth, too, "young Keats" was "a youth of [great] promise".[3] Nevertheless, in April 1818, when *Endymion* was published, Keats was 22 ½ years old: hardly young any longer, and certainly not "bordering on childhood." Wordsworth had been not quite 23 when he published *An Evening Walk* and *Descriptive Sketches* in 1793; Byron was just 24 when *Childe Harold* was published in 1812, and the reviews certainly did not dwell at length upon his young manhood. So while many of Keats's first reviewers welcomed his poetry, their preoccupation with youth pointed to qualities that other less sympathetic critics found suspect: the callow sentiments of a poet "just of age," the unformed imagination of a man still bordering on childishness, the "lisped" verses of a "bantling."

Keats himself tried to deflect hostile criticism of *Endymion* by alerting readers to his own "great inexperience [and] immaturity". "The imagination of a boy is healthy," Keats wrote in his preface to the poem, "and the mature imagination of a man is healthy; but there is a space of life between, in which the soul is in a ferment, the character undecided, the way of life uncertain, the ambition thick-sighted: thence proceeds mawkishness." "Mawkishness" (denoting sickly sentimentality) is derived from "mawk," a maggot, and in this context may also be related to the auxiliary sense of "maggot," meaning "a whimsical fancy." * * * Z recognized the symptoms of this "maggotty" disease in the "drivelling idiocy" of *Endymion*, responding to the poem's style also to the preface where Keats associated mawkishness with a "space of life between" at which the imagination is "sickly" (and fantastical) in that it lacks character and steadiness of purpose. *Endymion*, according to the preface, is a "feverish attempt," a "youngster" which "should die away." In December 1817 Keats identified a comparable uncertainty of self as one characteristic of imaginative genius, a quality he defined as "negative capability" (p. 109). Reviews of *Poems* and *Endymion*

9. See Rossetti, *Life of John Keats* (London, 1887), p. 209.
1. *Examiner* (1 Dec. 1816), p. 761; see above, p. 13.
2. *Champion* (9 Mar. 1817), *KCH* 45; *European Magazine* (May 1817), *KCH* 52; *Examiner* (1 June 1817), *KCH* 55; *Eclectic Review* (Sept. 1817), *KCH* 67; *Edinburgh Magazine, and Literary Miscellany* (Oct. 1817), *KCH* 71; *Examiner* (27 Sept. 1818), 609; *Chester Guardian*, rpt. in *Examiner* (1 Nov. 1818), p. 696; *Alfred, West of England Journal and General Advertiser* (6 Oct. 1817), *KCH* 117; see above, pp. 73, 92, 95, and 284.
3. See *The Letters of William and Dorothy Wordsworth*, ed. E. de Selincourt, 2nd edn., *The Middle Years Part II, 1812–1820*, rev. M. Moorman and A.G. Hill (Oxford, 1970), pp. 360, 578.

described the poetry as "remarkably abstracted," "indiscriminate," "the shadowings of unsophisticated emotions," and "indistinct and confused"[4]—and some of the reviewers found these effects attractive. For example, the *Edinburgh Magazine*[5] drew attention Keats's "licentious brilliancy of epithet": * * *

> That style is vivacious, smart, witty, changeful, sparkling, and learned—full of bright points and flashy expressions that strike and even seem to please by a sudden boldness of novelty,—rather abounding in familiarities of conception and oddnesses of manner which shew ingenuity, even though they be perverse, or common, or contemptuous.

At a first glance, "vivacious," "smart," "witty," "sparkling," "learned" would seem to be a full approbation for the brisk and lively manner of Keats's poetry. But the critic's unease is registered through a second strand of vocabulary in the review: the poetry is "licentious," "changeful," "flashy," mingling a "boldness of novelty" with familiarities and commonplaces. Evidently, this novel (and "maggotty") style was perceived as a challenge to received literary values, and specifically to the neoclassical ideal of stylistic and intellectual "decorum." But, as Olivia Smith has demonstrated, such criticism had an agenda that extended far beyond linguistic and literary matters. Its core vocabulary had a social register which derived from the preface to Johnson's *Dictionary of the English Language* (1755), in which "such terms as 'elegant,' 'refined,' 'pure,' 'proper,' and 'vulgar' . . . conveyed the assumptions that correct usage belonged to the upper classes and that a developed sensibility and an understanding of moral virtue accompanied it."[6] In direct contrast to this authorized language was what Johnson termed the "fugitive cant" of current usages among "the laborious and mercantile part of the people": "illiterate writers will at one time or other, by publick infatuation, rise into renown, who, not knowing the original import of words, will use them with colloquial licentiousness, confound distinction, and forget propriety."[7] The *Edinburgh's* reviewer makes Keats's poetry conform exactly to Johnson's paradigm of the "illiterate." It is "licentious," which glossed by Johnson as "unrestrained by law or morality"; and when carried over into literary criticism, the word retained its unsettling legal and moral associations. Those senses of "licentious" are echoed by "changeful," defined by Johnson as "Full of change; inconstant; uncertain; mutable; subject to variation; lie," and also by "flashy," that is, "Empty; not solid; showy without substance." The "boldness of novelty" in Keats's poems, which one might expect to be a praiseworthy quality, was in fact a persistent fault: rather than expressing a courageous break with literary precedent, for the *Edinburgh's* critic (as for Johnson) Keats's "boldness of novelty" signalled a lack of caution; an aspiration to liberty without responsibility (after the pattern of revolutionary France) through which proper "distinctions" were overturned and "confounded."

---

4. See J. H. Reynolds in *Champion* (9 Mar. 1817), rpt. *KCH* 46; Hunt in *Examiner* (6 July 1817), p. 429, rpt. *KCH* 73; Baldwin's *London Magazine* (Apr. 1820), *KCH* 137.
5. See *KCH* 72; see above, p. 96.
6. Olivia Smith, *The Politics of Language 1791–1819* (Oxford, 1984), p. 9.
7. From the "Preface" to Samuel Johnson, *A Dictionary of the English Language* (London, 1755), unpaginated.

All of these critical terms show how Keats's vocabulary, poetic idiom, and style were intensely freighted with moral, social, and political meanings. His "mawkishness" was not just the impotence of an adolescent poet; it represented a more radical settlement, the poetics of dissent which defined Keats's opposition to establishment ideology. Like Hunt's and Hazlitt's writings, Keats's innovative poetry is "full of conceits and sparkling points" which were understood as the voice of a reformist political agenda: their writing is "alive to the socialities . . . of life," and is "too fond, even in their favourite descriptions of nature, of a reference to the factitious resemblances of society." John Wilson Croker, reviewing *Endymion* in the *Quarterly*, elucidated the politics of Keats's style by characterizing his poetry as an anarchy of neologisms and run-on couplets, to be understood only in so far as Keats was "a copyist of Hunt, but . . . more unintelligible."[8] Byron, like Croker, felt threatened by Keats's mawkish novelty. But for him Keats's imagination was less involved with "soul . . . character . . . [and] way of life" and rather more absorbed by the sexual awakening of an adolescent "Mankin": his imaginative impotence was integral to his "*Vulgarity* . . . a sad abortive attempt at all things, 'signifying nothing.' "[9] The Tory journals demonstrated a comparable preoccupation with Keats's "mankin" sexuality, but more distinctly in the context of childish and "effeminate" sensibility and seditious politics. And, as with the review from the *Edinburgh Magazine* discussed above, this politically oriented criticism reflected eighteenth-century preoccupations with language.

* * *

* * * [W]hen Keats pondered negative capability in his letter of late December 1817, he concluded: "This pursued through Volumes would perhaps take us no further than this, that with a great poet the sense of Beauty overcomes every other consideration, or rather obliterates all consideration" (p. 109). Here, Keats's idea of beauty authenticated creative genius— especially Shakespeare's—but its power to "overcome" and "obliterate" presented a combative aesthetic appropriate to age of revolutionary struggle. Writing sixty years previously, Edmund Burke had said that beauty invokes ideas of "weakness and imperfection," arguing further that "[w]omen are very sensible of this; for which reason, they learn to lisp, to totter in their walk, to counterfeit weakness, and even sickness."[1] For Keats "feminine" sickliness and imperfection were overcome and assimilated by the imagination as a paradoxical source of human strength which, unlike the French Revolution, might offer a lasting renewal for the world: "a joy for ever." And the diction of Keats's poetry, glossed by reviewers as an "effeminate" and childish lisp, articulated the challenge of beauty to the authorized "masculine" discourses of the political and cultural establishment.

* * * [C]ritics of Keats identified him as the latest offspring of "sickly Fancy": Leigh Hunt's foster-child, or "bantling" illegitimate son, taught to "lisp" sedition not "midst lakes and mountains wild" but in the studio of a

8. See *KCH* 111; see above p. 277.
9. Byron's "Addenda" to his *Letter to John Murray Esqre.* See *Lord Byron: The Complete Miscellaneous Prose,* ed. Andrew Nicholson (Oxford, 1991), p. 160, and Byron to John Murray, 12 Mar. 1821, *BLJ* viii. 92.
1. See Burke, *A Philosophical Enquiry into the Origin of our Ideas of the Sublime and the Beautiful,* ed. Adam Phillips (Oxford 1990), p. 100.

suburban villa at Hampstead—"a poet's house" (*Sleep and Poetry*, 354). By insisting on Keats's "youth" and "effeminacy," these critics sought to disperse the Jacobin potential in his poems. The extent to which later generations have been unwilling to treat Keats's political interests seriously is one measure of the reviewers' success in enforcing earlier, Burkean standards according to which Keats's distinctive poetic voice could be identified with stereotypes of passivity and weakness, and thus accommodated to the prevailing masculine structures of social and cultural authority.

As we have already seen, for Z childishness was a definitive characteristic of the "Cockney School" of "politics, versification and morality," and of Keats in particular as "a young Cockney rhymester." In Z's essays the following profile of Cockney culture is firmly outlined: "exquisitely bad taste," "vulgar modes of thinking," "low birth and low habits," "ignorant," "underbred," "suburban," "paltry," "morally depraved," "indecent and immoral," "licentious," "obscene and traitorous". The occasion for this sexual slander was Hunt's poem *The Story of Rimini*, that "lewd tale of incest, adultery, and murder,"[2] and Byron used much the same language in his abusive remarks about Keats. Yet in Z's essay on Keats, the social-sexual hostility aimed at Hunt gives place to the different, more radical sense of "Cockneyism" associated with childishness. In the fourth Cockney School essay the political charge of "Cockneyism" had less to do with Keats's social circumstances and origins than with Z's recognition of the disruptive possibilities of Keatsian "childishness." But what precisely did Z intend by disparaging Keats as a young Cockney rhymester?

In Samuel Johnson's *Dictionary of the English Language* (1755) the leading sense of "Cockney" is "A native of London" (which fits Keats surely enough). But Johnson also lists a second sense of Cockney, which has obvious gendered and social inflections: "Any effeminate, low citizen." So there we have it: Cockney Keats: effeminate, common, and a Londoner. This tells us a lot about how the "Cockney" tag might be employed in sexual-social conflict, but perhaps not very much, yet, about how the word was intended to apply to Keats's poetry. In the *Oxford English Dictionary*, the four primary senses of "Cockney" are glossed as follows:

> Cockney: egg; lit. "cocks' egg."
> 1. An egg . . . hen's egg . . . one of the small or misshapen eggs occasionally laid by fowls. . . . 2. "A child that sucketh long," "a nestlecock," "a mother's darling" . . . "a child tenderly brought up"; hence, squeamish or effeminate fellow, "a milksop" . . . 3. A derisive appellation for a townsman, as the type of effeminacy in contrast to the hardier inhabitants of the country. 4. One born in the city of London.

For Z Keats was a Cockney not merely because he was supposedly a "young man," and an admirer of Leigh Hunt and Hazlitt. The charge was more specific: Cockney Keats was an unweaned boy-child, unwilling to "bid farewell" to the exuberant joys of early, sensual experience at his mother's breast. His "simplicity" was a token of his opposition to the "artful" duplicity of government (compare William Hone's 1820 *Political House that Jack Built*, dedicated to "The Nursery of Children Six Feet High, His Readers," in which the nursery rhyme was adapted in a satirical exposure of state

---

2. "Cockney School III", p. 453.

oppression after the Peterloo Massacre of August 1819). Keats's vulnerable "tenderness" enervated the discourse of masculine authority, which Z now associated with the one-time republican William Wordsworth, [now] a figure of austere "patriarchal simplicity."[3] * * * Keats, meanwhile, had become potentially more dangerous than his natural father Leigh Hunt, as the "new brood" of treacherous sensibility that had formerly been associated with Rousseau and the French Revolution.

As the political unrest of the post-Waterloo years grew more distant, or moved through different channels, the unsettling aspects of Keats and Hunt (which had seemed so alarming in an age of revolutions) gradually vanished. During the nineteenth century both writers were accommodated by sustaining the stereotypes of childish and effeminate passivity established by Z and others after 1817. In this manner, Hunt and Keats were publicly depoliticized, and disengaged from the ideological context which had so powerfully informed their creativity and their thinking about literature. * * *

* * *[T]he revolutionary potential of [Keats's] "style of babyish effeminacy" has been forgotten: Keats entered the canon as the Romantic poet widely believed to have had no interest in politics and the events of contemporary history. * * *

STUART SPERRY

The Epistle to John Hamilton Reynolds[†]

The period immediately following the revision of *Endymion* for the press was one of dislocation poetically. Keats was relieved to have the major task completed and out of the way, leaving him once more free for new endeavors. At the same time, beyond a sense of general dissatisfaction with the work, he was left with the pressing intellectual and aesthetic questions it had raised which he knew he would have to face in order to make progress. The best evidence of this unsettled state of things is his verse epistle to John Hamilton Reynolds. The verses make up the greater part of a letter he sent his friend on March 25, 1818, about a month before *Endymion* went to press, and recount the effects of a powerful and strangely moving depression he had been suffering. In the past there has been considerable reluctance to view the poem as much more than the reflection of a passing mood.[1] For one thing it is an occasional piece that begins as a playful attempt to provide some humorous distraction for Reynolds, who was ill at the time, starting off with a jocularity Keats is only briefly able to maintain. The poem as a whole seems strangely disjointed and even, at times, incoherent, especially when compared with the poet's more polished work.

---

3. See *Blackwood's Magazine* (Oct. 1817), p. 40.
† From *Keats the Poet* (Princeton: Princeton University Press, 1973), pp. 117–31. Reprinted by permission of Princeton University Press. The author's notes have been edited.
1. *The Letters of John Keats, 1814–1821*, ed. Hyder E. Rollins, 2 vols. (Cambridge, MA, 1958). Hereafter cited in the text as *L*; page numbers alone refer to this Norton Critical Edition. Criticism of the poem has been, relatively speaking, small. I have found especially useful Albert Gerard's "Romance and Reality: Continuity and Growth in Keats's View of Art," *Keats-Shelley Journal*, 11 (1962): 17–29; Walter Evert's *Aesthetic and Myth in the Poetry of Keats* (Princeton, 1964), pp. 194–211; and Mary Visick's "Tease us out of thought': Keats's *Epistle to Reynolds* and the Odes," *Keats-Shelley Journal*, 15 (1966): 87–98. My discussion is in varying ways indebted to all these as well as to Bate.

Indeed it is somewhat unfair, as Bate reminds us, that these hasty and impromptu verses Keats never intended to meet the public eye have been printed alongside his other poetic work "and then approached with formal expectations that are wildly irrelevant."[2] Yet it is precisely the kind of disturbance they succeed in revealing that tells us a great deal about Keats and that, in the study of his development, makes the poem of greater interest than the new romance in which he sought refuge—the longer, more finished, but languid *Isabella*. The *Epistle to Reynolds* goes far toward explaining the sense of mist and darkness, the feeling of the "burden of the Mystery," that was beginning to oppress him while forcing him, at the same time, to extend his vision into the "dark Passages" that were opening on all sides.

In many respects the lines to Reynolds mark a return to the manner of the earlier verse epistles and the longer pieces of the 1817 volume. The poem begins with the very situation that had in the past proved so fruitful for composition: a sleepless evening passed amid a flow of images and associations. One recalls, for example, the origin of "Sleep and Poetry" in a sleepless night spent "upon a couch at ease" (353) in Hunt's study. Once again there is the device Keats had used so often in the past of working into the poem by elaborating a chain of images and associations that he hoped might lead on to a major theme. Again we find the poet ready to spin "that wonted thread / Of shapes, and shadows, and remembrances" (2–3) into the woof of poetry. Yet the opening of the lines to Reynolds reads almost like a caricature of Keats's earlier technique, for the images that now come forward are all perversely incongruous or anachronistic:

> Things all disjointed come from north and south,—
> Two witch's eyes above a cherub's mouth,
> Voltaire with casque and shield and habergeon,
> And Alexander with his nightcap on;
> Old Socrates a tying his cravat,
> And Hazlitt playing with Miss Edgeworth's cat.   (5–10)

The passage seems at first only a bit of admirable fooling intended for Reynolds's diversion until Keats's tone darkens and we realize that what he is describing is a more serious and unaccountable disruption of the usual associative processes of composition. There are few, he proceeds to lament, whose reveries and dreams are not sometimes spoiled by "hellish" apparitions. It is not merely that the images themselves are ludicrously inconsistent with each other; but they neither suggest nor lead on to anything more. They are, in fact, totally inconsistent with that ideal process that, by way of contrast, he proceeds to describe in terms of

> flowers bursting out with lusty pride,
> And young Æolian harps personified;
> Some Titian colours touch'd into real life   (17–19)

that flowering of art into the fullness of reality that is the end of all aesthetic creation. It is this criterion of "aliveness," of higher verisimilitude, that Keats has most in view and that suddenly prompts him, by way of providing an example, to "touch into life" the scene of pagan sacrifice so remarkably

2. *John Keats*, p. 307.

prefigurative of stanza four of the "Ode on a Grecian Urn," a scene full of flashing light, color, movement, and music caught in a moment of ceremony and communal worship:

> The sacrifice goes on; the pontif knife
> Gleams in the sun, the milk-white heifer lows,
> The pipes go shrilly, the libation flows:
> A white sail shows above the green-head cliff,
> Moves round the point, and throws her anchor stiff;
> The mariners join hymn with those on land.   (20–25)

As various commentators have pointed out, there is no painting known by Titian that contains a scene similar to the one Keats describes; and it is commonly assumed that, through some slip of memory, he confused with the Venetian the work of another painter, perhaps the *Sacrifice to Apollo* of Claude Lorrain, whose *Enchanted Castle* Keats is shortly to recall at length.[3] Most probably Keats's description draws upon a general recollection of a number of different prints and canvases. Yet the mention of Hazlitt a few lines earlier strongly suggests there is a deeper logic at work in his allusion to Titian within this particular context and that he had in view, at the same time, central differences between the two painters. In his essay "On Gusto" in *The Round Table*, a collection with which Keats was familiar, Hazlitt had praised Titian for the very ability the poet is attempting to depict. Hazlitt had written of Titian's power to "interpret one sense by another" so as to bring to "the look and texture of flesh" the sense of "feeling in itself,"[4] the power, in short, to bring a scene or a face "swelling into reality" (to use Keats's phrase) by endowing the elements of nature with an intensity of human passion and feeling. A few months earlier, in the Negative Capability letter written near the very end of 1817, Keats had, as we have seen, defined this ability with specific reference to the work of a painter quite different from either Titian or Claude—Benjamin West. Familiar as it may be, the passage must be quoted in full:

> I spent Friday evening with Wells & went the next morning to see *Death on the Pale horse*. It is a wonderful picture, when West's age is considered; But there is nothing to be intense upon; no women one feels mad to kiss; no face swelling into reality. The excellence of every Art is its intensity, capable of making all disagreeables evaporate, from their being in close relationship with Beauty & Truth. Examine King Lear & you will find this examplified throughout; but in this picture we have unpleasantness without any momentous depth of speculation excited, in which to bury its repulsiveness.   (p. 108; Keats's italics)

As Bate has shown, Keats's conception of "intensity" owes a great deal to Hazlitt's "gusto,"[5] although one must add that the two are far from identical. Indeed the *Epistle to Reynolds* represents Keats's working through in a

---

3. See Sir Sidney Colvin, *John Keats* (London, 1920), p. 264, whom most commentators have followed. The *Sacrifice to Apollo*, however, does not depict the mariners who join the hymn; and most recently James Dickie (*Bulletin of the John Rylands Library*, 52 [1969]: 96–114) and Alan Osler (*TLS*, April 16, 1971) have suggested that Keats was remembering as well other specific paintings by Titian or Claude. In *Keats and the Mirror of Art* (Oxford, 1967), Ian Jack takes the sense the poet describes as a composite and thinks "it is certainly most unlikely that Keats is here describing any particular painting" (p. 221).
4. Hazlitt, *Works*, 4: 77. References are hereafter included within the text.
5. *John Keats*, p. 244.

far deeper way some of the notions that had first been suggested to him by the older critic and his own consideration of West's painting. Keats's method in the lines to Reynolds is progression by way of contrasts and oppositions. He turns from Titian and the idealized scene of ritual he has just touched into life to a particular painting that has come to mind, the work of a quite different master—Claude Lorrain. The imaginative scene he has created, in its relation to the two painters, has slowly crystallized the major preoccupation of his poem: the degree of idealization—both in a good and bad sense—that art can achieve in its transcendence of actuality. The theme, of course, is one intimately connected with his growing interest in the sublime, both as a general and long-established ideal of art and in its relation to his own more particular sense of the process of aesthetic sublimation by which the materials of art are purged of "disagreeables," fused in imagination, and "put into etherial existence for the relish of one's fellows" (p. 253). It is natural, then, that he should turn to one of the great neoclassic exemplars of the sublime, not of those aspects associated with scenes of terror and destruction (the conditions he is to touch on at the end) but rather with peace, security, happiness, and a sense of repose.[6] The painting, *The Enchanted Castle*, is one that best epitomizes "the grand quiescence of Claude." Yet Keats's attitude toward the aspect of sublimity, however attractive, that Claude represents is, as we shall see, hardly one of unqualified admiration. Here again our best guide for tracing the chain of association that leads Keats from Titian to Claude and *The Enchanted Castle* is Hazlitt who, in his essay "On Gusto," turns from praising the earlier painter to a more detailed analysis of the peculiar charm of the later:

> Claude's landscapes, perfect as they are, want gusto. This is not easy to explain. They are perfect abstractions of the visible images of things. . . . He saw the atmosphere, but he did not feel it. He painted the trunk of a tree or a rock in the foreground as smooth—with as complete an abstraction of the gross, tangible impression, as any other part of the picture. His trees are perfectly beautiful, but quite immovable; they have a look of enchantment. In short, his landscapes are unequalled imitations of nature, *released from its subjection to the elements*, as if all objects were become a delightful fairy vision, and the eye had *rarefied and refined away the other senses*.(4:79; my italics)

Turning to Keats's long description for Reynolds of the exact impression he holds of Claude's painting, one can see that it is this very quality of enchantment, of abstraction from gross reality, that he singles out as most characteristic. Whereas, however, Hazlitt sees the effect Claude achieves by his mastery as serene and charming, Keats represents the mood as partly frozen, unnatural, even perverse. Claude's trees, which Hazlitt describes as "perfectly beautiful, but quite immovable" with "a look of enchantment," for Keats seem held under a harsh, restraining spell so that they "shake / From some old magic like Urganda's Sword" (28–29). Hazlitt had written that Claude's landscapes "are perfect abstractions of the visible images of things. . . . He saw the atmosphere, but he did not feel it." Keats's impression

---

6. See the contrast drawn between Salvator and Claude in "The Sublime in Painting," ch. 9 of Samuel Monk's *The Sublime* (New York, 1935).

of *The Enchanted Castle*, on the other hand, while once again following the general tenor of Hazlitt's remarks, is more ambivalent and complex:

> You know it well enough, where it doth seem
> A mossy place, a Merlin's Hall, a dream;
> You know the clear lake, and the little Isles,
> The mountains blue, and cold near neighbour rills,
> All which elsewhere are but half animate;
> Here do they look alive to love and hate,
> To smiles and frowns; they seem a lifted mound
> Above some giant, pulsing underground.   (33–40)

At first glance the painting seems perfectly dreamlike in its self-containment and abstraction. Yet this unifying mood is not everywhere maintained. Parts of the landscape seem unnaturally, even morbidly, alive with feeling. The image of some giant pulsing underground in particular creates a sense of titanic forces of upheaval ready at any moment to break into open eruption to destroy the surface placidity. The mood of sublimity the painting creates, in other words, only imperfectly transcends a vast underlying disorder it can only partly repress or conceal.

Other aspects peculiar to Keats's view of *The Enchanted Castle* can be best defined by briefly returning to Hazlitt's remarks. For example, Hazlitt marvels at Claude's ability to transform the elements of nature into "a delightful fairy vision." So Keats develops the idea of enchantment, but with a quite different emphasis:

> The doors all look as if they oped themselves,
> The windows as if latched by fays and elves,
> And from them comes a silver flash of light
> As from the westward of a Summer's night;
> Or like a beauteous woman's large blue eyes
> Gone mad thro' olden songs and poesies.   (49–54)

The note of elvish mischief seems incongruous with the larger theme of calm and sublimity, while the flashing eyes of the woman, like the Abyssinian maid's vision of "flashing eyes" and "floating hair" in Coleridge's "Kubla Khan" (a poem that, in its preoccupation with the balance art struggles to achieve between energy and control, resembles Keats's) introduces a hint of danger and madness. Even the "sweet music" that issues from the castle to greet the "golden galley all in silken trim" (56) as it serenely approaches its port for some reason brings fear to the herdsman who hears it. Hints of dark magic in its more bizarre aspects also color Keats's description of the castle itself. He had noted, of course, that the castle in Claude's painting is very much a conglomerate affair, combining, as Colvin points out,[7] ancient Roman features with medieval battlements and later Palladian elements in the manner of many old structures that have been built onto through the centuries. Though somewhat fanciful, the fusion of styles is not inharmonious in Claude's painting but creates an effect that is calm, mysterious, and imposing. Keats's imaginary account of its architects and history, however, reduces the structure to the level of the macabre and fantastic:

---

7. *John Keats* (London, 1920), p. 264.

> Part of the building was a chosen See,
> Built by a banished Santon of Chaldee;
> The other part, two thousand years from him,
> Was built by Cuthbert de Saint Aldebrim;
> Then there's a little wing, far from the Sun,
> Built by a Lapland Witch turn'd maudlin nun—
> And many other juts of aged stone
> Founded with many a mason-devil's groan.   (41–48)

The same sense of anachronism that characterized the train of disjointed images passing before Keats's eyes at the very outset of the poem in all their ludicrous incongruity now extends itself to his awareness of Claude's painting. There is the same failure of the associative process, now visualized as an aspect of the painting itself, to achieve a harmonious and unified effect.

Critics have at this point generally accepted the failure as Keats's own, an instance of the moodiness and morbidity of which he openly complains to Reynolds at the end. The disordered state of imagination he has described to his friend at the outset has now obtruded itself upon his appreciation of the painting and perversely distorted the values of Claude's landscape.[8] Yet the implications of the poem go a good deal beyond this. Keats obviously recognizes that the creations of art necessarily depend for their success upon a large degree of sympathy and responsiveness. As the poem goes on to make clear, however, the ability to respond can be impaired not merely by a captious state of mind but by a condition of awareness that, in its fullness or complexity, exceeds the powers of any particular work of art to harmonize or satisfy. More specifically, in its effort to expel all "disagreeables," to "swell into reality" and idealize a particular aspect of beauty or truth, the work of art can fatally remove itself from that wealth of human knowledge and experience that provides the substratum of all aesthetic apprehension. As in his remarks some months earlier on West's *Death on the Pale Horse*, what preoccupies Keats in his reflections on *The Enchanted Castle* is a failure in the attempt to achieve the sublime.[9] Yet the problem he now returns to is one he had barely touched on earlier, a problem related to his whole conception of "intensity." The failure as he had analyzed it in West's painting was a lack of anything "to be intense upon," a dearth of material for the imagination to "swell into reality." The problem that confronts him now, however, is a deeper one, for it has to do with the very nature of "intensity" itself: its continual tendency to refine away too much that is fundamental to our general awareness of life, its drift into one-sidedness and subjectivity. Such, at least, is the larger aspect of the problem that, turning away from his immediate consideration of Claude's painting, Keats seeks to sum up for Reynolds in what is the most abstract and in many ways difficult section of his poem:

> O, that our dreamings all of sleep or wake
> Would all their colours from the sunset take:
> From something of material sublime,

---

8. See, e.g., Evert, *Aesthetic and Myth*, pp. 200–201.
9. Bate points out (*John Keats*, p. 243) that West's painting has been praised as a successful effort at the sublime.

> Rather than shadow our own soul's day-time
> In the dark void of night. For in the world
> We jostle. . . .   (67–72)

A key phrase (a consciously ironic one) for elucidating Keats's meaning is "material sublime," expressing as it does the desire of the imagination to possess at once the best of both worlds, the ethereal and the concrete. Here again perhaps our best gloss on the passage as a whole is provided by some general remarks of Hazlitt's on the nature of painting, written, though they were, after the poet's death:

> A fine gallery of pictures is a sort of illustration of Berkeley's Theory of Matter and Spirit. It is like a palace of thought—another universe, built of air, of shadows, of colours. Every thing seems "palpable to feeling as to sight." Substances turn to shadows by the painter's arch-chemic touch; shadows harden into substances. "The eye is made the fool of the other senses, or else worth all the rest." The material is in some sense embodied in the immaterial, or, at least, we see all things in a sort of intellectual mirror. The world of art is an enchanting deception.   (10:19)

Once again the dissimilarity-in-similarity between Keats's lines and Hazlitt's remarks is revealing. What for Hazlitt is an ideal translation of the material into the spiritual is the very aspect of the creative process most troubling to Keats. We long in our reveries, whether those of mere dreaming or those that engross us in our contemplation of the world of art, for the colors of the sunset—some substantial element of the real world that lies outside. Yet instead of such colors we must remain content with fleeting, doubtful moments of inner illumination that fade away into shadows and uncertainty. Hazlitt recognizes and accepts an element of illusion as a part of aesthetic creation: "The world of art is an enchanting deception" tinted into reality by the painter's "arch-chemic touch." Yet it is clear that Keats is unwilling to accept the easy logic of such an equation and that what Hazlitt delights in as enchantment can assume for him the horror of a subjective *enfer*.

For a moment he draws back from some of the metaphysical questions he customarily sought to avoid confronting head-on, then plunges a little further into the problem:

> . . . but my flag is not unfurl'd
> On the Admiral-staff,—and to philosophise
> I dare not yet!—Oh, never will the prize,
> High reason, and the lore of good and ill,
> Be my award. Things cannot to the will
> Be settled, but they tease us out of thought;
> Or is it that imagination brought
> Beyond its proper bound, yet still confined—
> Lost in a sort of Purgatory blind,
> Cannot refer to any standard law
> Of either earth or heaven?—It is a flaw
> In happiness to see beyond our bourn,—
> It forces us in summer skies to mourn,
> It spoils the singing of the Nightingale.   (72–85)

In his remarks a few months earlier prompted by his consideration of West's *Death on the Pale Horse* he had gone on to postulate as an ideal for the artist the state of Negative Capability, that is "when man is capable of being in uncertainties, Mysteries, doubts, without any irritable reaching after fact & reason." More particularly, he had imagined that the great work of art would, like *Lear*, achieve what West's painting had failed to accomplish, that it would bury all "unpleasantness," all "repulsiveness," all disagreeable and insistent questioning, by engrossing the imagination in a "momentous depth of speculation" (pp. 108–109). However it is precisely the failure of this stratagem that now forms the burden of his complaint to Reynolds. Resisting the lure of speculation, the will remains unappeasable in its desire for certainty. Moreover Keats has come to realize that the state of speculation itself can be as vexing in its irresolution as it can be momentous in its implications. The phrase "tease us out of thought," which he was to use again within a subtly different context in the "Ode on a Grecian Urn," here suggests the tantalizing ability of the speculative life to raise, only to defer answering, our final questions. Seen in a different light, that very immunity of the imagination to ordinary kinds of interrogation that had in the past seemed of positive value might suggest corresponding limitations and defects. The "Penetralium of mystery," rich with suggestiveness and undiscovered meaning, could become the poet's "Purgatory blind." The latter phrase, apt like so many of his personal coinages, sums up the dilemma he seeks to convey. Though liberated, the poetic imagination can relate itself to no single "standard law" of either earth or heaven, the material world or the sublime. Lacking the ability to reconcile the two domains, it must experience them as a "hateful siege of contraries"[1] that together spoil whatever consolations either taken singly might afford. Thus we can mourn at the beauty of summer skies or at the singing of the nightingale. The poet is trapped in limbo, somewhere between the uncertain heaven figured by the visionary imagination and the real hell of actual existence when stripped of all romantic possibilities.

It is, of course, to the hell life becomes when viewed in an uncompromisingly realistic and antiromantic light that Keats turns in the final section of the poem. The Darwinian vision of life as an unrelenting struggle for survival waged throughout nature is terrifying and quite unlike anything in his earlier verse. The scene as it unfolds, however, does not stand in isolation but relates itself organically to earlier sections of the poem. The setting in the early evening by the seaside briefly recalls in its pastoral tranquility the mood of Claude's painting. Once again, however, Keats's eye probes beneath the surface to discern signs of sacrifice, oppression, and underlying disorder—not the bloodless and beautifully ceremonial picture of sacrifice that had earlier come alive in his imagination but one of nature "red in tooth and claw." The sublimity and refinement of the painter's ideal world are sensed in contrast to the naked brutality of primeval nature, and the two contexts for conceiving reality develop between them uneasy reverberations in a way now familiar to us as the prevailing method of the poem.

With its abrupt shifts and changes of perspective the *Epistle to Reynolds* reveals an undeniable instability and lack of central focus. The poem may compress only the transitory fantasies of a single evening, but the dislocation

---

1. See Keats's use of this phrase from *Paradise Lost*, 9.121f., in a letter some months later (*L*, 1:369).

it exposes is too fundamental to be written off, as some critics would have it, as a passing case of bad nerves. Although at the very end Keats berates those "horrid moods, / Moods of one's mind" (105–106), the work is much more than a mere poem of mood. The strange distortion of Claude's scene of elysian quiet and the brief, terrifying glimpse of nature reduced to universal rapacity are both, in different ways, troubling and even perverse, but it is not sufficient to dismiss them as unaccountable aberrations from Keats's usual poetic mode, instances of that "horrid Morbidity of Temperament" (p. 84) of which he from time to time complained. There is a logic to the poem's apparent disorder, and if such scenes can justly be described as "morbid," they are so in such a way as to counterbalance and explain each other. If at the end Keats appears more naturalist than poet and sees "Too *far* into the sea" (94), it is in part because he has earlier sensed the treacherous tendency of art to encourage us "to see beyond our bourn" (83) in the opposite extreme. There is a principle of compensation at work by which the imagination struggles to rectify itself and discover a proper balance. The charge of morbidity is unjust if only because the poem itself provides the grounds for understanding how depression and unevenness of vision are to some degree unavoidable to those who struggle to reconcile a full and sympathetic participation in the world of art with a knowledge of the actuality that lies outside. As in Wordsworth's mature reappraisal of the relationship art holds to reality in his "Elegiac Stanzas" on Sir George Beaumont's painting of Peele Castle, a poem that in theme and method must have been in the back of Keats's mind,[2] the true subject is not the vagaries of an errant imagination but the way in which our whole approach to art is radically altered by a change in our perspective on the reality it mirrors. If Keats emphasizes the element of subjectivity in our awareness, he does so with an understanding of the various ways in which, during the centuries spanning Titian, Claude, and his contemporary West, a spontaneous sublimity of style has become increasingly difficult to achieve. His lament is not purely personal but in part historical and cultural.[3]

The deeper questions that lie behind the *Epistle to Reynolds* are philosophic and more particularly aesthetic and reveal how much, during the months following the completion of *Endymion*, Keats had come to question some of his earlier poetic assumptions, especially those concerning the nature of the poetic process. The point now most at issue is his deepening sense of the nature of "intensity" and the role it plays in the creation of art. The central question, to put it simply, is what and how does art "intensify"? Does the imagination, in fact, concentrate and sublime a material and substantial beauty? Or does it rather, in purging away "disagreeables"—all that is discordant or repulsive—distill a vision that, for any complex intelligence, must remain hopelessly tenuous and unreal? Is art a heightening and enrichment, or is it rather an abstraction and evasion, of reality? The chain of associations leading Keats, partly in company with Hazlitt, from Titian, Claude, and the sublime in painting to the terrors of brute nature reveals the degree to which such questions had become of vital concern. It reveals, too, a state of irresolution it would not be too much to call a period

2. So Claude Finney has argued in *The Evolution of Keats's Poetry* (Cambridge, MA, 1936), 1: 391.
3. There is no need to elaborate here a point developed throughout Bate's biography and again by Harold Bloom in "Keats and the Embarrassments of Poetic Tradition," in *From Sensibility to Romanticism: Essays Presented to Frederick A. Pottle*, ed. F. W. Hilles and Harold Bloom (New York, 1965).

of crisis.[4] Although it cannot claim to rank among his major productions, the *Epistle to Reynolds* illuminates more clearly than any other single work the major problems with which Keats wrestled in passing from *Endymion* to his first attempt at *Hyperion*.

NEIL FRAISTAT

"Lamia" Progressing: Keats's 1820 Volume[†]

It is my intention to wait a few years before I publish any minor poems— and then I hope to have a volume of some worth—and which those people will realish [*sic*] who cannot bear the burthen of a long poem.
—Keats to George and Georgiana Keats

That which is creative must create itself.
—Keats to J. A. Hessey

I

After the failure of *Endymion*, Keats—as he later put it—decided "to use more finesse with the Public"[1] In 1820 he would substitute for the often tedious form of the long poem a group of shorter poems that, read together, would be epic in scope but not burden the reader. This time he would indeed use more finesse—and produce "a volume of some worth." * * * [W]ith the possible exception of "Hyperion," Keats oversaw the printing of the collection. * * * More important, finally, than whether Keats assembled the *Lamia* volume alone or jointly with his editors is that it does show sophisticated organization. In general, its thirteen poems are grouped by genre: the three opening romances are followed by clusters of three odes, four rondeaus, and two odes—with the fragment "Hyperion" concluding the whole. Within these groups, poems are positioned without reference to their chronological order of composition. For instance, although it was almost certainly written before the "Ode to a Nightingale" and the "Ode to a Grecian Urn," the "Ode to Psyche" is placed after both; conversely, "Lamia" is the first of the romances, though the last composed. Such positionings, along with the placement of the five odes into two separate groups rather than a single generic block, suggest that the order of the poems is itself important.

In fact, as the reader moves sequentially from the opening "Lamia" to the concluding "Hyperion," [s]he discovers a complex system of verbal echoes, transitional links, and thematic progressions through which each poem revises the meaning of its predecessor. * * * Whereas it is, perhaps, impossible to prove that Keats consciously organized the *Lamia* volume as a progressive and self-revising structure, it can be shown that such a reading

---

4. See Evert's discussion, noted above, and p. 212.
† From *The Poem and the Book* (Chapel Hill: University of North Carolina Press, 1985), pp. 93–140. Reprinted by permission of the author and the University of North Carolina Press. The author's notes have been edited. Page numbers for letters refer to this Norton Critical Edition; *L* refers to Rollins's edition.
1. Quoted above, p. 410; see *L*, 2:174.

is consonant with Keats's own view of the poetic process and the actual movement of the poems themselves.

* * *

Keats's letters show that Milton was very much in his thoughts during the summer of 1819. But so, as always, was Shakespeare. In August he writes to Bailey, "Shakespeare and the paradise Lost every day become greater wonders to me—I look upon fine Phrases like a Lover" (p. 355). It has long been recognized that the council scenes of *Paradise Lost* and *Troilus and Cressida* coalesced in Keats's mind as he wrote the second book of "Hyperion." However, the extent to which Shakespeare's play influenced Keats's vision, particularly in the *Lamia* poems, has for just as long been overlooked.[2] * * * Keats found in this reading a play that, perhaps above all else, concerns enchantment. "Let thy song be love," Helen tells Pandarus in *Troilus and Cressida*, adding, "This love will undo us all. / O Cupid, Cupid, Cupid!" (3.1.102–3).[3] Keats's 1820 volume begins with three long poems about pairs of lovers, each, in a different way, "undone" by love. Just as *Troilus and Cressida* broadens from its microcosmic examination of its lovers' relationships to a depiction of the world gone awry, so, in the examination of the relationships between its lovers, does the *Lamia* volume begin to depict a world with which human beings and their unrealizable desires are forever at odds.

* * *

Troilus and Cressida illustrates the need for an ironic perspective that can prevent the mind from succumbing to enchantment. However, this perspective, as evidenced by Thersites, is not sufficient: it frees the mind from enchantment without rededicating it to anything else. Ironic detachment needs to be transcended by an embrace of the world's sad realities, even, as Hector sees, if it is at the expense of one's own martyrdom. But can the mind sustain this painful embrace? Keats's *Lamia* volume traces these same concerns and, finally, asks a similar question. Dramatized in the movement from poem to poem is Keats's own effort to discover the powers and limitations of both poetry and the imagination and to create a poetic adequate for exploring the "agonies, the strife / Of human hearts."

II

In the concluding speech of *Troilus and Cressida*, Pandarus cynically sums up a world in which every person seems solely concerned with gathering as much "honey" as possible:

> Full merrily the humble-bee doth sing,
> Till he hath lost his honey and his sting;
> And being once subdued in armed tail,
> Sweet honey and sweet notes together fail. (5.10.41–44)

---

2. Bruce Haley is a notable exception to this general neglect; see "The Infinite Will: Shakespeare's *Troilus* and the 'Ode to a Nightingale,'" *KSJ* 21 (1972): 18–23.
3. All quotations from Shakespeare are taken from Harbage, *William Shakespeare: The Complete Works* (hereafter cited in the text by act, scene, and line).

A life devoted to the gathering of honey contains the seeds of its own undoing: "sweet honey and sweet notes" inevitably fail. Harold Bloom remarks
that all "romance, literary and human, is founded upon enchantment."[4]
And the result of that enchantment is often death. In "Isabella," Keats,
using imagery similar to that of *Troilus*, provides the credo for the three
romances beginning the *Lamia* volume:

> But, for the general award of love,
>   The little sweet doth kill much bitterness;
> Though Dido silent is in under-grove,
>   And Isabella's was a great distress,
> Though young Lorenzo in warm Indian clove
>   Was not embalm'd, this truth is not the less—
> Even bees, the little almsmen of spring-bowers,
>   Know there is richest juice in poison-flowers. (ll. 97–104)

All of Keats's mortal lovers discover the cost of drinking from "poison-
flowers"; "Lamia" begins the lesson in enchantment.

"Lamia," itself, commences with a search for honey: Hermes is in desperate pursuit of a "sweet nymph," who will eventually yield to the burning
god "her honey to the lees" (1:31, 143). The "ever-smitten" (1:7) Hermes
is perpetually enchanted, always desiring and always fulfilling desire, never
and ever satiated. An avatar of the erotic turned in upon itself, Hermes
becomes the god of enchantment. And Crete, "the idyllic mythological
home of Venus,"[5] is a fit setting for him.

Crete is a world of pure erotic power. In Keats's vision, love and the
imagination are closely akin. Each springs from the erotic energy necessary to embrace an object outside of the self. Certainly Keats saw in the
self-annihilating, or "identity-destroying," power of the imagination an
analog to love. However, both love and the imagination can fall victims to
enchantment. Then love becomes mere autoeroticism, imagination mere
fancy, both solipsistic. The danger is clear. Both powers can act to cut
individuals off from the world, unless, of course, they are gods, whose
worlds are the sum of their desires. A mortal mind can attempt to absorb
a single object seen as a completion of itself only to find instead a phantom of its own projection. Lycius, and even, Lamia succumb to this fatal
enchantment.

* * *

Ironies are everywhere apparent in "Lamia." The three main characters
all labor under their own misconceptions and limitations. Lamia is the
imagination undoing itself, a victim of its own power to conjure up images
of desire so powerful that they become self-consuming. To satisfy her desire
Lamia takes form from Hermes, limiting herself in the process to a power
of mere enchantment. Her ability to "unperplex bliss from its neighbour
pain" (1:192) belies the very process through which she is incarnated.
While it offers a world in which the "most ambiguous atoms" of "specious
chaos" (1:195) are rearranged into coherent form, it also falsifies very real
complexities.

---

4. Bloom, *The Ringers in the Tower*, (Chicago, 1971), p. 23.
5. Donald Reiman, "Keats and the Humanistic Paradox: Mythological History in *Lamia*," *SEL* 11
   (1971): 23.

Lamia becomes the author of a fiction, creating a romance world that she cohabits with Lycius. She is thus both victimizer and victim, so entrammeled in her own fiction that, when it is exposed as such by Apollonius, she can no longer exist. Lycius, too, is both victimizer and victim, enchanter and enchanted. Unable to forsake his "secret bowers" (2:149) or the world of Corinth, he stakes both his own life and Lamia's on a misguided attempt to wed the two worlds. And Apollonius, Lycius' self-professed protector, enjoys the mental satisfaction of his reductive truth at the cost of his pupil's life. Intent on preventing Lycius from being made "a serpent's prey" (2:298), he makes Lycius his own prey. All three have justifiable motives for their actions: Lamia loves Lycius and apparently intends him no harm, Lycius refuses to forsake a public for a completely private world, and Apollonius desires to save his former pupil from enchantment. All three become murderers. The world refuses to correspond to their simplistically wishful images of it. In the baffling world "Lamia" presents, the dreams of gods are real, those of human beings self-destroying.

Keats, however, locks the poem into an even more baffling dialectic. Pitted against each other are the "rainbow-sided" (1:54) Lamia and the rainbow-destroying Apollonius (2:231–38). It seems as though one can only choose between enchantment and "cold philosophy" (2:230). One either becomes involved in the world and succumbs to it, or one becomes a detached ironist like Thersites or Apollonius, whose harsh laughter is as much at his own expense as at that of others. The imaginative and rational powers battle each other to a deadly standoff in "Lamia." By refusing to take sides, by presenting a dilemma with no possible solutions, Keats himself becomes an ironist. Judging from his letters, it was a role in which he reveled: "I have been reading over a part of a short poem I have composed lately call'd 'Lamia'—and I am certain there is that sort of fire in it which must take hold of people in some way—give them either pleasant or unpleasant sensation. What they want is a sensation of some sort" (p. 364). "Lamia" is a poem intended to produce a "sensation of some sort." As such, it refuses to provide the terms by which it can be evaluated: nowhere can a center of meaning be located in the poem. Perhaps Stuart Sperry is right to say that in "a number of respects Lamia is a work written by a poet against his better self."[6] The witty and detached style of "Lamia" allows Keats to remain aloof from the questions he raises, and in a sense, to abdicate poetic responsibility to meaning, while at the same time deliberately enticing the reader to take a position. Ultimately, the poem's final meaning is its refusal to mean. In its enticement and then frustration of its reader, "Lamia" itself becomes a demon of enchantment, a demon that the rest of the volume attempts to exorcise. This process begins in "Isabella," a work in many ways antithetical to "Lamia."

* * * Whereas the narrator of "Lamia" is ironic and detached from his narrative, the narrator of "Isabella" is sympathetic and involved. That the narrator of "Lamia" has devised a strategy, albeit self-defeating, for facing loss results in his cynicism. That the narrator of "Isabella" can devise no such strategy results in his pathos.

While wishing fervently for the "gentleness of old Romance" (1. 387), the narrator of "Isabella" is fascinated by a far more complex reality that

6. Sperry, *Keats the Poet*, p. 292.

presents him with the mysteries of the "yawning tomb" (1. 386). His many repetitions and digressions signal his own inability to confront successfully the "wormy circumstance" of his tale (1. 385). For the misery he depicts, he knows no remedy. In contrast, the narrator of "Lamia" can be glib about what he perceives to be the inevitable destruction of love in the world:

> Love in a hut, with water and a crust,
> Is—Love, forgive us!—cinders, ashes, dust;
> Love in a palace is perhaps at last
> More grievous torment than a hermit's fast. (2:1–4)

This same perception is a source of great pain to the narrator of "Isabella." His narrative is to begin with the hopefulness of spring and end in the bleakness of approaching winter, detailing the fatal effects of enchantment.

* * *

If Hermes appears as the god of enchantment in "Lamia," he appears by proxy in "Isabella," precipitating a similar tragedy. For Lemprière notes that Hermes is also the god of merchants and commerce. As represented by Isabella's brothers, the public world of commercial interest puts an end to her love. This is a world productive of "ledger-men" (1. 137), whose only interest is self-interest. To such men it is a "crime" (1. 172) punishable by death that "the servant of their trade designs, / Should in their sister's love be blithe and glad" (ll. 165–66) when they intend her instead to marry a rich nobleman. Ambushed in the forest, Lorenzo becomes their helpless victim: "There in that forest did his great love cease" (1. 218). But Isabella proves to be an even greater victim.

* * *

In a letter to Woodhouse, Keats dissociated himself from the narrator's pathos in "Isabella," declaring, "in my dramatic capacity I enter fully into the feeling: but in Propria Persona I should be apt to quiz it myself" (L, 2:174). The pathos of the narrator of "Isabella" is no more satisfactory than the cynicism of the narrator of "Lamia." The two extremes needed to be synthesized in a voice, which could be sympathetic yet wary, from a narrator whose ability to depict a moment of fulfillment is predicated upon his knowledge of the fleetingness of that moment. In his "dramatic capacity," Keats produces such a narrator in "The Eve of St. Agnes."

Like the two preceding poems, "The Eve of St. Agnes" is about enchantment, but unlike the two previous narrators this narrator does not re-create a narrative whose burden he is unable to bear successfully. Rather, he is engaged in a fiction of his own devising that allows him a self-aware playfulness: he can for a time "wish away" (1. 41) a world hostile to his romance because he knows that his poem must inevitably return to that world. Ultimately, "The Eve of St. Agnes" is a romance whose concern is the limitations of romance. The innocent world of young love it depicts survives only through frequent strategic manipulations. * * *

* * *

* * * Madeline and Porphyro cannot, and do not, stay to confront their world. The possibilities for fulfilled desire that they represent are instead apotheosized out of the world presented by the poem into a nebulous world beyond the storm. The lovers' triumph in "The Eve of St. Agnes" is thus ultimately also their defeat. Like the previous lovers of the volume, they find no way to connect their private desires with public reality. Love in the world is formidably beset by darkness and mental death, and Madeline and Porphyro's escape is reminiscent of Albert's in the "Foster-Mother's Tale" of *Lyrical Ballads*. For available to them is a possibility from which the other characters in the volume, as well as the narrator himself, are quite cut off. As the lovers recede in time and immediacy from the narrator—"gone . . . ages long ago"—he is left contemplating a world devoid of enchantment, where the "be-nightmar'd" (1. 375) Baron and his warrior guests hold sway, and where the Beadsman and Angela succumb to deaths that complete the logic of their life-denying lives. The consequence of enchantment is invariably disenchantment. That the narrator can willingly return to the world he has temporarily wished away allows him the joy of participating fully in his fiction. That he must return to this world, his fiction being subject to the limits of all fiction, leaves him trapped between a paradisal vision of fulfilled desire and a hellish reality.

"This love will undo us all." The three romances beginning Keats's 1820 volume show that, at best, romance and the enchantment necessary for romance, both literary and human, offer a temporary respite from reality, a type of wish fulfilling imaginative play. At worst they undo the mind. While it is certain that the mind must desire in order to survive, it is just as certain that, all too often, the desiring mind engages a world produced by its own wishful distortions, the perverted projection of an imagination self-seduced into mere fancy, a love self-projected into mere lust. From such fictions result madness and death.

The world presented by the volume seems knowable only by transposing the physics of Newton's Third Law of Thermodynamics into psychic terms: for every motion of the mind the world responds with an equal and opposite motion. The more the mind desires, the more it will be frustrated; the more it seeks pleasure, the more it will be given pain; the more it retreats into its own fictions, the more it will be destroyed by reality. The self-revising form of the volume assumes in the opening group of romances three different stances to confront this frightening dialectic, ranging from the ironic detachment of "Lamia" to the helpless sympathy of "Isabella" to the self-conscious play of "The Eve of St. Agnes." All are inadequate, though the narrator of "The Eve of St. Agnes," with his understanding of the limitations of his own fiction, seems most successful. His poem begins to illustrate what the volume next begins to consider—that the poet himself must become the meeting ground of the conflicting worlds opposed by the desiring mind and resistant reality; his breast, their battleground.

III

"My heart aches," begins the poet of the "Ode to a Nightingale," the first of three odes grouped together in the 1820 collection. "Ode to a Nightingale" marks the first generic change in the dramatic movement of the volume. Like most dramas, the *Lamia* volume has its soliloquies: the larger scope of narrative poetry gives way to the more focused concerns of the ode; a multiplicity of voices gives way to a single voice—that of the "sole self " of the poet ("Ode to a Nightingale," 1. 72). To confront the disconcerting dialectic emerging from the narratives is the ode, a form founded upon dialectic. "I must take my stand upon some vantage ground and begin to fight" (*L*, 2:113), Keats wrote in the spring of 1819, approximately at the same time he was composing these odes. This statement applies clearly to his poetry as well as to his life. For in the "Ode to a Nightingale," "Ode on a Grecian Urn," and "Ode to Psyche," Keats begins in earnest to take such a stand. The narrator who evades the import of the questions he raises in "Lamia" is at a far remove from the poet of the odes, who takes his place upon a vantage ground where every thought is felt upon his pulse. In the odes Keats is to isolate and examine in closer detail the questions raised in the narratives about the nature of desire, enchantment, and the imagination—all centering around the question of the poet's proper relationship to poetry and to his world.

*   *   *

"My heart aches." Since the "Ode to a Nightingale" follows three romances, much is compressed into its opening three words. All of the aching hearts in the preceding poems are thereby recalled; in fact, the poem itself seems for a moment to be concerned with love and erotic tensions. Through this juxtaposition the volume keeps alive the erotic tensions of the romances while focusing specifically on the problems of the poetic imagination—once again emphasizing that love and the imagination are both erotic powers, the means by which the mind embraces openly its world. Moreover, "Ode to a Nightingale" is the first poem of the volume to center its attention upon the poet himself, the voice behind the narratives. The poem's dialectical progression works out the terms by which an invocation to a muse becomes the means of discovering the muse's own insufficiency. Made explicit in the "high requiem" of the nightingale's song is what has been implicit in the volume all along—that a poetic based upon enchantment, and the escape afforded by enchantment, is, ultimately, a poetic of death. Also made explicit in the poem is the poet's own battle with enchantment, his fight to resist the powers of his own fiction.

Whereas the "Ode to a Nightingale" is the first poem in the *Lamia* volume to be concerned primarily with the poet, the "Ode on a Grecian Urn," the succeeding poem, is the first to concern primarily art itself. Because both activities are dependent on the imagination, the mind can be waylaid by the act of interpretation as easily as by the act of creation. Like the narrators of the first two poems in the volume, the poet of the "Ode on a Grecian Urn" imaginatively reconstitutes a work of art, creating in the process his own work. In the silence of the urn is an enchantment as potent as that of the nightingale's song.

*   *   *

* * * The "Ode on a Grecian Urn" marks both an end and a new beginning to the quest dramatized in the *Lamia* volume for an art that is both beautiful and true. For it discovers that the type of art the urn represents is of only limited value to humanity; while this art temporarily comforts by providing visions of a world without loss, it ultimately reminds one of one's exclusion from such a world. The urn is thus both a "friend to man" and a "Cold Pastoral" (ll. 48, 45). "I must take my stand upon some vantage point and begin to fight." What is needed is a type of art resistant to enchantment,

an art in which the mind halts its retreat from the world and confronts suffering and loss. * * *

*   *   *

The "Ode to Psyche" celebrates the imagination's ability to appoint its own deities and become the arbiter of all human values. As the last of the initial group of odes in the volume, it culminates their search for an authentic stance toward the world, an authentic poetic. However, the "Ode to Psyche" only marks a beginning, and a hesitant beginning at that. If the imagination is to mediate the mind's encounter with a world of process and loss, it has also proven itself vulnerable to enchantment. Psyche's "rosy sanctuary" will be dressed "With all the gardener Fancy e'er could feign" (1. 62); and as the word "feign" indicates, fancy is not only capable of creating but also of falsifying, or enchanting. At the exact center of a volume estimating the cost of enchantment, seventh among its thirteen poems, is a poem concerned with the power of enchantment—"Fancy."

IV

"Fancy" is the first of four poems in the volume to which Keats referred as "specimens of a sort of rondeau which I think I shall become partial to—because you have one idea amplified with greater ease and more delight and freedom than in the sonnet" (p. 306). Usually given scant critical attention, these "rondeaus" take on a greater significance by their position in the *Lamia* volume. There, they form a climax, a turning point begun at the "Ode to Psyche." The mind, contracted to the realm of the "sole self" in the odes, begins to reengage its world along the lines projected by "Psyche," but not before examining the limit of that contraction in "Fancy." "Oh, sweet Fancy! let her loose; / Every thing is spoilt by use," writes Keats in "Fancy" (ll. 67–68). Discontent with a world where "Pleasure never is at home" (1. 2), the mind succumbs to its power to improve upon reality. "Hoodwink'd with faery fancy," Madeline dreams of a Porphyro capable of satisfying all of her desires. Similarly, for one who cannot find a face he "would meet in every place" (1. 74), "winged Fancy" is able to produce "a mistress to thy mind" (ll. 79, 80). Breaking fancy's "prison-string" (1. 91) would, however, allow the mind to collapse into a solipsistic, self-consuming enchantment. "Fancy," writes Stuart Ende, "emerges as a self-sufficient power of mind, the autonomous and self-sufficient quality that enables mind to exist apart from outward circumstance . . . and even to defy it."[7]

*   *   *

* * * In the *Lamia* volume, perhaps the most important transition is the movement from "Fancy" to "Bards of Passion." Fancy is in this way contrasted with imagination, solipsism with empathy and understanding, and the enchanted dreamer and the poet are finally made distinct.

Although fancy promises delights that will never cloy, they are also insubstantial and illusory. In contrast, the "never cloying" pleasures of which "Bards of Passion" speaks (1. 28) result from the poetic imagination's

---

7. Ende, *Keats and the Sublime*, p. 8.

attempt to console and teach humanity. In return for the knowledge they
have left behind on earth in their poetry, poets gain a heaven

> Where the nightingale doth sing
> Not a senseless, tranced thing,
> But divine melodious truth;
> Philosophic numbers smooth;
> Tales and golden histories
> Of heaven and its mysteries (ll. 17–22)

No longer an agent of enchantment, the nightingale has be come, like Urania, a "Voice divine," a true muse singing to the poets of "heaven and its
mysteries." The eternal delight they enjoy is thus constant enlightenment,
a never-ending knowledge progressing toward an understanding of an infinite universe. More important for Keats, these "Double-lived" (1. 4) poets
have gained heaven because of their concern for humanity:

> Here, your earth-born souls still speak
> To mortals, of their little week;
> Of their sorrows and delights;
> Of their passions and their spites;
> Of their glory and their shame;
> What doth strengthen and what maim. (ll. 29–34)

Speaking to humanity of human joys and sorrows—of "What doth strengthen
and what maim"—such poetry and such poets deserve to be celebrated, for
they provide the only true link between earth and heaven: "the souls ye left
behind you / Teach us, here, the way to find you" (ll. 25–26). To turn from
"Fancy" to "Bards" is thus to accept poetic responsibility and begin the project outlined in the "Ode to Psyche" by expanding out of the contracted
world of the sole self. In a letter to Bailey, Keats writes that "Fancy is the
Sails [of Poetry], and Imagination the Rudder" (p. 99). "Bards" marks the
volume's subjection of fancy to the imagination's control. The two rondeaus
that follow show a new kind of playfulness—fancy subjected to the free play
of the imagination—reversing the reduction of imagination begun in
"Lamia."

Though playful, "Lines on the Mermaid Tavern" and "Robin Hood" result
from a serious search for a type of poetry adequate to teach the contemporary world. The two poems first appear in a letter to Reynolds in which Keats
writes:

> It may be said that we ought to read our Contemporaries, that
> Wordsworth &c should have their due from us. But for the sake of a
> few fine imaginative or domestic passages, are we to be bullied into a
> certain Philosophy engendered in the whims of an Egotist. . . . I don't
> mean to deny Wordsworth's grandeur & Hunt's merit, but I mean to
> say we need not be teazed with grandeur & merit—when we can have
> them uncontaminated & unobtrusive. Let us have the old Poets, &
> robin Hood. (pp. 121, 122)

Written, as Keats goes on to say, in "the Spirit of Outlawry" (p. 122),
"Lines on the Mermaid Tavern" and "Robin Hood" spurn contemporary
poetry for the larger, more heroic vision of the past: "Why should we be
owls, when we can be Eagles?" But if Keats celebrates the poetic grandeur
of the Elizabethans, those "Emperors of vast Provinces," and the moral

heroism of Robin Hood, he also recognizes that "All are gone away and past!" ("Robin Hood," 1. 37). Though he can locate himself within a tradition of vision, Keats must still define the shape that tradition is to take in the contemporary world. One of the most daring juxtapositions of the volume comes at the end of "Robin Hood," where the celebration of a past heroism heralds the beginning of a new heroism. Immediately following the last two lines of "Robin Hood"—"Though their days have hurried by / Let us two a burden try"—is "To Autumn." "Robin Hood" is addressed "To a Friend," John Hamilton Reynolds, and the "burden" in which Reynolds is invited to join is thus the creation of a new kind of poetry with all of the imaginative vitality of the old, the kind of poetry represented by "To Autumn."

The four rondeaus as a group, then, move from fancy to imagination. They concern the creation of a poetry true to both poetic tradition and the complexities of the contemporary world. In their commitment to a poetry that is public, educative, and morally courageous, they make the necessary transition from Keats's vow to become Psyche's prophet to his prophecy— "To Autumn," the "Ode on Melancholy," and "Hyperion."

V

"To Autumn" is about a moment of imaginative grace. The third poem from the end of the volume, it balances by antithesis "The Eve of St. Agnes," the third poem of the volume. For, like "The Eve of St. Agnes," the moment of fulfillment "To Autumn" depicts is possible only because the poem allows for the fleetingness of that moment. Not only is the autumn it hymns the transitional season between the fertility of summer and the bareness of winter, but, as numerous critics have remarked, the poem itself moves from early to late autumn, from morning to evening, from life to death, from fulfillment to loss. Thus, unlike "The Eve of St. Agnes," "To Autumn" is a poem that confronts, rather than retreats from, a world of process and loss: its vision is the product of a mind on its way "through." As such, it defines itself against all of the other poems in the volume about enchantment, particularly "Fancy."

* * *

"To Autumn" * * * resolutely resists * * * enchantment, insisting instead on what Keats has elsewhere called "the real of beauty."[8] The poem's triumph is that it can accommodate the songs of autumn without the assurances contained within the songs of spring: "Where are the songs of spring? Ay, where are they? / Think not of them, thou hast thy music too" (ll. 23–24). Composed of the "wailful choir" of mourning gnats (1. 27), the loud bleating of "full-grown lambs" (1. 30), the singing of hedge-crickets, the whistling of robins, and the twittering of "gathering swallows" (1. 33), the music of autumn is the rich, bittersweet melody of a world in flux. That "To Autumn" is able to sustain the burden of its own music is much. And if the gathering swallows at the end of the poem herald the coming of the wintry bleakness attendant upon autumn's ripe fulfillment, the "Ode on Melancholy" insists that the mind not retreat before such a prospect.

8. "On Visiting The Tomb of Burns," l. 10.

"No, no, go not to Lethe," admonishes the "Ode on Melancholy" in its opening line. As their placement in the volume indicates, "To Autumn" and the "Ode on Melancholy" are companion poems. Each deliberately refuses to follow the "star of Lethe" into enchantment. Psyche, not Hermes, is the divinity presiding over these poems. Whereas "To Autumn" shows the vision surpassing enchantment that disenchantment can purchase, the "Ode on Melancholy" begins to estimate the cost of that purchase. For the mind that willfully refuses oblivion gains instead anguish, the "wakeful anguish" (1. 10) of a soul that knows that Joy's hand "is ever at his lips / Bidding adieu" (ll. 22–23). "One begins with 'Joy,' the abstract concept," says Stuart Sperry, "and works toward the informing gesture, the 'adieu' (the theatrical, slightly affected word that occurs in each of the odes of the spring)."[9] As we have seen, this "adieu" is present in the romances as well as in the odes. Implied in every greeting of the mind with the object of its desire is parting: "I eternally see her figure eternally vanishing," Keats wrote of Fanny Brawne. Recalling a prominent metaphor in the volume, the "Ode to Melancholy" recognizes that "aching Pleasure nigh" turns "to poison while the bee-mouth sips" (ll. 23–24). "What is the price of Experience?" Blake asks in *The Four Zoas*, answering: "it is bought with the price of all that a man hath." That the mind is willing to pay this price for those pains that are better than the nothing of oblivion testifies to its courage. That it can continue to bear the pains of disenchantment without breaking, however, is far from certain. For he who bursts "Joy's grape against his palate fine; / . . . shall taste the sadness" of Melancholy's might, "And be among her cloudy trophies hung" (ll. 28–30). "To Autumn" and the "Ode on Melancholy" force the volume's most compelling question: Can the mind sustain the burdens of disenchantment and loss?

VI

With both disenchantment and loss, "Hyperion," the final poem of the volume, begins. For unlike Hermes and his fellow gods in "Lamia," Saturn and the Titans discover that their dreams are not real, nor do their pleasures "smoothly pass / . . . in a long immortal dream" ("Lamia," 1:127–28). The implications of that "shadowy thought" of which the "Ode to Psyche" speaks begin to be made clear in the figures of a despairing Saturn, who sits deep within the "shady sadness of a vale" (1:1), contemplating his loss of power, and a Hyperion who finds himself confronting within his own palace of light "darkness, death and darkness. / Even here . . . / The shady visions come to domineer" (1:242–44).

The Titans thus gain the knowledge of a world "Where but to think is to be full of sorrow / And leaden-eyed despairs." Such knowledge humanizes them. * * *

*   *   *

* * * The Titans find themselves the gods of an "infant world" progressed into maturity, where their power to create "beautiful things" is no longer sufficient. Needed now is the ability "to bear all naked truths," the ability

9. Sperry, *Keats the Poet*, p. 284.

to confront successfully process, loss, and an inexplicable universe. Needed now is the imaginative vitality of Apollo and the younger gods. Recognizing this, Mnemosyne leaves her fellow Titans, traveling to Delos to educate the young Apollo into "naked truth."

Just as the island of Crete is the initial setting of the volume, the island of Delos is the last. And if Crete is the scene of imaginative contraction, Delos is the scene of imaginative expansion. There, Apollo already plays a music filled with "joy and grief " (2:289), containing, as Clymene tells the Titans, "A living death" in "each gush of sounds" (2:281). This music of warring contraries overpowers Clymene, ranging far beyond the limited scope of the most limited Titan. Though Apollo's music is yet in its infancy, its power springs from his "aching ignorance" (3:107), his own painful confrontation with "shadowy thought": "For me, dark, dark, / And painful vile oblivion seals my eyes" (3:86–87). Here, the "Ode to a Nightingale" is recalled. For unlike the poet who seeks escape from flux in the oblivion of the nightingale's "embalmed darkness," Apollo yearns to know about the continual passing of "hungry generations." The process by which the poet sinks "Lethe-wards," "as though of hemlock I had drunk," is reversed as Apollo is deified by the knowledge he gains from Mnemosyne, "as if some blithe wine / Or bright elixir peerless I had drunk" (3:118–19).

* * * Apollo refuses to avert his eyes from a suffering humanity. * * * However, if "Knowledge enormous" (3:113) deifies Apollo, "it is impossible to know," as Keats writes to Reynolds, "how far knowledge will console us for . . , the ill 'that flesh is heir to' " (p. 243). Apollo's transformation into a god is accompanied by all of the fierce pain of Lamia's opposing transformation into a woman: "Soon wild commotions shook him, and made flush / All the immortal fairness of his limbs; / Most like the struggle at the gate of death" (3:124–26).

The knowledge of the past that will center Apollo mentally in the painful realm of the present exacts the anguish spoken of in the "Ode to Melancholy": "so Young Apollo anguish'd" (3:130). At stake in Apollo's confrontation with a universe knowable only through loss is whether the mind can sustain such an encounter. Geoffrey Hartman suggests that " 'Hyperion' [breaks off] when 'bearing' becomes 'overbearing,' when maturing, instead of strengthening the prophetic or foreseeing character, leads to an overload destructive of it."[1] This may well be so; for the "Hyperion" appearing in the Lamia collection does not close the description of Apollo's struggle with the triumphant conclusion still preserved in manuscript: "he was the God!" Instead the poem breaks off abruptly in mid-sentence, with Apollo's anguished shriek followed by the inconclusive conclusion of two rows of asterisks. Ominously, "Hyperion," like "Lamia," ends in a horrifying shriek. The most important question posed by the volume is thus left unanswered. Keats wrote to Bailey that "nothing in this world is proveable" (p. 131). The skeptical position he takes in this letter is provided for the *Lamia* volume by the open-ended form of its final poem. "Hyperion" throws open for questioning any possibilities proposed by the volume for bearing "naked truth."

---

1. Hartman, *Fate of Reading*, (Chicago, 1975), p. 326n.

"That which is creative must create itself." "Hyperion" concludes the self-revising consideration of poetry that takes place in Keats's 1820 volume. The "hierarchy it ["Hyperion"] describes is largely a poetic or aesthetic one," says Sperry, who also asserts, quite correctly, that Keats in "Hyperion" surveys and rejects "the chief poetic attitudes of his day, from stoicism (one of the less appealing aspects of *The Excursion*) to the stormy desolation of a poem like *Childe Harold*."[2] It is true that in the Titans' inability to accommodate loss Keats was criticizing the failure of contemporary poetry to make this same accommodation. Yet in "Hyperion" he was similarly criticizing many of the previous poems of the *Lamia* volume. If, for instance, Oceanus's stoic resignation could be found in the Wordsworth of *The Excursion*, and Enceladus's fiery gloom could be found in the Byron of *Childe Harold*, Clymene's helpless pathos could be found in the Keats of "Isabella." "Hyperion," and hence the volume itself, rejects all poetry that is unable to confront honestly and courageously the complexities of a world resistant to human desire.

The subject of the first sentence of the *Lamia* volume is Hermes, the last Apollo; between these two brother deities lie the major tensions of the collection. The movement from the god of enchantment to the god of poetry is a progression from evasion to confrontation, from fancy to imagination, from solipsism to community, from romance to epic. "Faith in the power of poetry to express the profoundest kind of truth is the necessary condition of all Romantic attempts at epic," writes Karl Kroeber.[3] Such faith motivates not only "Hyperion," but the entire *Lamia* volume. In its progressive movement from poem to poem, the 1820 collection becomes an aggregate greater than the sum of its poems—a drama of poetic discovery truly epic in scope.

* * *

JACK STILLINGER

The Hoodwinking of Madeline: Skepticism in *The Eve of St. Agnes*[†]

I

* * *

According to the popular superstition connected with St. Agnes' Eve, a young maiden who fasts and neither speaks nor looks about before she goes to bed may get sight of her future husband in a dream. Madeline follows

2. Sperry, *Keats the Poet*, pp. 182, 187.
3. Kroeber, *Romantic Narrative Art*, (Madism, 1960), p. 87.
† From *"The Hoodwinking of Madeline" and Other Essays on Keats's Poems* (Urbana: University of Illinois Press, 1971), pp. 67–93. Reprinted by permission of the author. The author's notes have been edited. The argument of this piece has been further developed (and another 58 interpretations of the poem outlined) in Stillinger, *Reading "The Eve of St. Agnes": The Multiples of Complex Literary Transaction* (New York: Oxford University Press, 1999).

this prescription, dreams of her lover, then seems to awaken out of her dream to find him present in her chamber, an actual, physical fact. Her dream in a sense comes true. The events are thought to relate to a passage in the well-known letter to Benjamin Bailey, 22 November 1817, in which Keats expressed his faith in "the truth of Imagination": "What the imagination seizes as Beauty must be truth—whether it existed before or not. . . . The Imagination may be compared to Adam's dream—he awoke and found it truth." For the metaphysical critics, just as Adam dreamed of the creation of Eve, then awoke to find his dream a truth—Eve before him a beautiful reality—so Madeline dreams of Porphyro and awakens to find him present and palpably real.

But the imagination is not merely prophetic: it is "a Shadow of reality to come" hereafter; and in the same letter Keats is led on to "another favorite Speculation"—"that we shall enjoy ourselves here after by having what we called happiness on Earth repeated in a finer tone and so repeated. . . . Adam's dream will do here and seems to be a conviction that Imagination and its empyreal reflection is the same as human Life and its spiritual repetition" (pp. 102–103).[1] The idea is that a trust in the visionary imagination will allow us to "burst our mortal bars," to "dodge / Conception to the very bourne of heaven,"[2] to transcend our earthly confines, guess at heaven, and arrive at some view of the reality to come. If the visionary imagination is valid, the earthly pleasures portrayed in our visions will make up our immortal existence—will be spiritually "repeated in a finer tone and so repeated." In this sense, Madeline's dream of Porphyro is a case history in the visionary imagination. * * *

* * *

In brief summary, the main points of the metaphysical critics' interpretation are that Madeline's awakening to find Porphyro in her bedroom is a document in the validity of the visionary imagination; that Porphyro in the course of the poem makes a spiritual pilgrimage, ascending higher by stages until he arrives at transcendent reality in Madeline's bed; and that there the lovers reenact earthly pleasures that will be stored up for further, still more elevated repetition in a finer tone. * * * [O]ne may suggest reasons for hesitating to accept them.

For one thing, when the imaginative vision of beauty turns out to be a truth—when Madeline awakens to find Porphyro in her bed—she is not nearly so pleased as Adam was when he awoke and discovered Eve. In fact, truth here is seemingly undesirable: Madeline is frightened out of her wits, and she laments, "No dream, alas! alas! and woe is mine! / Porphyro will leave me here to fade and pine" (328–329). For another, it is a reversal of Keats's own sequence to find in the poem the spiritual repetition of earthly pleasures. In Madeline's dream the imaginative enactment of pleasure comes first; it is an earthly repetition of spiritual pleasure that follows, and perhaps in a grosser, rather than a finer, tone. * * *

Much of the critics' interpretation rests on the religious language of the poem. Madeline is "St. Agnes' charmed maid," "a mission'd spirit" (192–193),

1. *The Letters of John Keats*, Hyder E. Rollins, ed. Cambridge: Harvard University Press, 1958. 2 vols. Hereafter cited as *L*. Page numbers above refer to this Norton Critical Edition.
2. *I stood tip-toe*, l. 190; *Endymion*, l.294–295.

"all akin / To spirits of the air" (201–202), "a saint," "a splendid angel, newly drest, / Save wings, for heaven," "so pure a thing, so free from mortal taint" (222–225). To Porphyro, her "eremite," she is "heaven" (277), and from closet to bedchamber he progresses from purgatory to paradise. Finally, Porphyro is "A famish'd pilgrim,—saved by miracle" (339). But the significance of such language is questionable. * * * In other poems Keats, * * * in the manner of hundreds of poets before him, uses religious terms in hyperbolic love language: for example, Isabella's lover Lorenzo is called "a young palmer in Love's eye," he is said to "shrive" his passion, and (in a stanza ultimately rejected from the poem) he declares that he would be "full deified" by the gift of a love token.[3]

What is perhaps most telling against the critics, in connection with the religious language of *The Eve of St. Agnes*, is that when Porphyro calls himself "A famish'd pilgrim,—saved by miracle," his words must be taken ironically, unless Keats has forgotten, or hopes the reader has forgotten, all the action leading to the consummation. The miracle on which Porphyro congratulates himself is in fact a *stratagem* that he has planned and carried out to perfection. Early in the poem, when he first encounters Angela, she is amazed to see him, and says that he "must hold water in a witch's sieve, / And be liege-lord of all the Elves and Fays, / To venture" into a castle of enemies (120–122). Although Porphyro later assures Madeline that he is "no rude infidel" (342), the images in Angela's speech tend to link him with witches and fairies rather than with the Christian pilgrim. By taking a closer look at the poem, we may see that Keats had misgivings about Porphyro's fitness to perform a spiritual pilgrimage and arrive at heaven.

II

Porphyro's first request of Angela, "Now tell me where is Madeline" (114), is followed by an oath upon the holy loom used to weave St. Agnes' wool, and it is implied that he is well aware what night it is. "St. Agnes' Eve," says Angela, "God's help! my lady fair the conjuror plays / This very night: good angels her deceive!" (123–125). While she laughs at Madeline's folly, Porphyro gazes on her, until "Sudden a thought came like a full-blown rose. . . . then doth he propose / A stratagem" (136–139). The full force of "stratagem" comes to be felt in the poem—a ruse, an artifice, a trick for deceiving. For Angela, the deception of Madeline by good angels is funny; but Porphyro's is another kind of deception, and no laughing matter. She is startled, and calls him "cruel," "impious," "wicked" (140, 143); the harshness of the last line of her speech emphasizes her reaction: "Thou canst not surely be the same that thou didst seem" (144).

Porphyro swears "by all saints" not to harm Madeline: "O may I ne'er find grace / When my weak voice shall whisper its last prayer, / If one of her soft ringlets I displace" (146–48). He next enforces his promise with a suicidal threat: Angela must believe him, or he "will . . . Awake, with horrid shout" his foemen, "And beard them" (151–153). Because Angela is "A poor, weak, palsy-stricken, churchyard thing" (155), she presently accedes, promising to do whatever Porphyro wishes—

---

3. Lines 2, 64, and the rejected stanza following l. 56 (*The Poetical Works of John Keats,* ed. H. W. Garrod, 2nd ed., Oxford, 1958, p. 217); for the rejected stanza, see above, p. 432.

Which was, to lead him, in close secrecy,
Even to Madeline's chamber, and there hide
Him in a closet, of such privacy
That he might see her beauty unespied,
And win perhaps that night a peerless bride,
While legion'd fairies pac'd the coverlet,
And pale enchantment held her sleepy-eyed. (163–169)

At this point our disbelief must be suspended if we are to read the poem as an affirmation of romantic love. We must leave our world behind, where stratagems like Porphyro's are frowned on, sometimes punished in the criminal courts, and enter an imaginary world where "in sooth such things have been" (81). But the narrator's summary comment on the stratagem is that "Never on such a night have lovers met, / Since Merlin paid his Demon all the monstrous debt" (170–171). The allusion is puzzling. Commentators feel that the "monstrous debt" is Merlin's debt to his demon-father for his own life, and that he paid it by committing evil deeds, or perhaps specifically by effecting his own imprisonment and death through the misworking of a spell.[4] However it is explained, it strengthens rather than dispels our suspicion, like Angela's, that Porphyro is up to no good; and, with the earlier images of "legion'd fairies" and "pale enchantment," it brings further associations of fairy lore and sorcery to bear on his actions. Then Angela asserts a kind of orthodox middle-class morality: "Ah! thou must needs the lady wed" (179).

She now leads Porphyro to Madeline's chamber, "silken, hush'd, and chaste," where he takes "covert" (187–188). * * * The ideas of viewing love's own domain, or what he may attain, are documents in the peeping-Tomism that occupies the next few stanzas. As Angela is feeling her way toward the stair, she is met by Madeline, who turns back to help her down to "a safe level matting" (196). If the action is significant, its meaning lies in the juxtaposition of Madeline's unselfish act of "pious care" (194) with the leering overtones just before of Porphyro's having hidden himself in her closet, "pleas'd amain" (188) by the success of his stratagem, and with the tone of the narrator's words immediately following: "Now prepare, / Young Porphyro, for gazing on that bed; / She comes, she comes again, like ring-dove fray'd and fled" (196–198).

The mention of "ring-dove" is interesting. Porphyro has taken "covert"—the position of the hunter (or perhaps merely the bird-watcher). There follows a series of bird images that perhaps may be thought of in terms of the hunter's game. * * * [T]he single comparison of Madeline's heart to a "tongueless nightingale" seems significant. * * * For Keats's image embraces the entire story of the rape of Philomel, and with it he introduces a further note of evil that prevents us from losing ourselves in the special morality of fairy romance. Madeline has the status of one of St. Agnes' "lambs unshorn" (71); she is a maiden innocent and pure, but also is about to lose that status through what is in some ways a cruel deception. The comparison with Philomel is not inappropriate.

* * *

4. See, among others, H. Buxton Forman, ed., *The Poetical Works and Other Writings of John Keats* (London, 1889), II, 84 n.; Roy P. Basler, *Explicator*, III (1944), item I.

Madeline undresses, then falls fast asleep. Porphyro creeps to the bed, "Noiseless as fear in a wide wilderness" (250), and "'tween the curtains peep'd, where, lo!—how fast she slept" (252). At the bedside he sets a table, when, in the midst of his preparations, a hall door opens in the castle, and the revelers' music shatters the silence of the room. Porphyro calls for a "drowsy Morphean amulet" (257)—and then "The hall door shuts . . . and all the noise is gone" (261). Madeline continues sleeping, while he brings from the closet the feast of candied apple, quince, plum, and all the rest.

Aside from the unheroic implications of "Noiseless as fear in a wide wilderness" and of the word "peep'd," there are three things worth noting in the stanzas just summarized. One is the relationship the poem has here with *Cymbeline*, II.ii.11–50, in which the villainous Iachimo emerges from the trunk, where he has hidden himself, to gaze on the sleeping Imogen. Readers since Swinburne have noted resemblances.[5] Imogen is "a heavenly angel," and like Madeline a "fresh lily," "whiter than the sheets," as she lies in bed, sleeping, in effect, an "azure-lidded sleep" (262)—and so on. But no critic has been willing to include among the resemblances that Porphyro's counterpart in the scene is a villain. In the speech from which these details have been drawn, Iachimo compares himself with Tarquin, who raped Lucrece, and he notes that Imogen "hath been reading late / The tale of Tereus; here the leaf's turn'd down / Where Philomel gave up."

The second point concerns Porphyro's call for a "drowsy Morphean amulet"—a sleep-inducing charm to prevent Madeline's awakening when the music bursts forth into the room. Earlier he has wished to win Madeline while "pale enchantment held her sleepy-eyed" (169). Here he would assist "pale enchantment" with a "Morphean amulet." * * *

The third point has to do with the feast that Porphyro sets out. In his copy of *The Anatomy of Melancholy*, opposite a passage in which Burton commends fasting as an excellent means of preparation for devotion, "by which chast thoughts are ingendred . . . concupiscence is restrained, vicious . . . lusts and humours are expelled," Keats recorded his approval in the marginal comment "good."[6] It is for some reason of this sort that Madeline fasts, going "supperless to bed" (51). Porphyro's feast seems intended to produce the opposite results, and there is more than a suggestion of pagan sensuality in the strange affair of eastern luxuries that he heaps as if by magic—"with glowing hand" (271)—on the table by the bed.

Next Porphyro tries to awaken Madeline, or so it seems: "And now, my love, my seraph fair, awake! / Thou art my heaven, and I thine eremite" (276–277). * * * It is curious that in the proposition that follows, "Open thine eyes . . . Or I shall drowse beside thee" (278–279), Porphyro does not wait for an answer: "Thus whispering, his warm, unnerved arm / Sank in her pillow" (280–281). "Awakening up" (289), he takes Madeline's lute and plays an ancient ditty, which causes her to utter a soft moan. It would seem that she does at this point wake up: "suddenly / Her blue affrayed eyes wide open shone. . . . Her eyes were open, but she still beheld, / Now wide awake, the vision of her sleep" (295–299). Not unreasonably, we might think, she weeps, sighs, and "moan[s] forth witless words" (303).

5. See Thomas B. Stroup, "Cymbeline, II.ii, and The Eve of St. Agnes," *English Studies*, XVII (1935): 144–145; Claude Lee Finney, *The Evolution of Keats's Poetry* (Cambridge, Mass., 1936), II, 557–558; *Times Literary Supplement*, 6 April, 4 May, 1 June 1946, pp. 163, 211, 259.
6. Hampstead Keats, V, 318.

We shall see in a moment, however, that she has not after all awakened from her trance. The "painful change" she witnesses—the substitution of the genuine Porphyro for the immortal looks and voice of her vision—"*nigh expell'd / The blisses of her dream*" (300–301), came near expelling them, but did not in fact do so. Apparently she is to be thought of as still in her trance, but capable of speaking to the Porphyro before her, when she says, "Ah, Porphyro! . . . but even now / Thy voice was at sweet tremble in mine ear" (307–308). To her request for "that voice again . . . Those looks immortal" (312–313), Porphyro offers neither, but rather impassioned action of god-like intensity. At the end of stanza XXXVI, the image of "St. Agnes' moon" combines the notions of St. Agnes, the patron saint of maidenhood, and Cynthia, the goddess of chastity, and the symbolic combination has "set," gone out of the picture to be replaced by a storm: "meantime the frost-wind blows / Like Love's alarum pattering the sharp sleet / Against the window-panes; St. Agnes' moon hath set" (322–324).

Keats's final manuscript version of the consummation, rejected by his publishers on moral grounds, as making the poem unfit to be read by young ladies, is more graphic. For a rather lame conclusion to Madeline's speech (314–315), he substituted the lines, "See, while she speaks his arms encroaching slow, / Have zoned her, heart to heart,—loud, loud the dark winds blow!" Then he rewrote stanza XXXVI:

> For on the midnight came a tempest fell;
> More sooth, for that his quick rejoinder flows
> Into her burning ear: and still the spell
> Unbroken guards her in serene repose.
> With her wild dream he mingled, as a rose
> Marrieth its odour to a violet.
> Still, still she dreams, louder the frost wind blows,
> Like Love's alarum pattering the sharp sleet
> Against the window panes :—St Agnes' Moon hath set.[7]

The revised version makes clearer that Madeline is still dreaming: "still the spell / Unbroken guards her in serene repose." And it makes clearer the connection between the sexual consummation, the setting of St. Agnes' moon, and the rising of the storm. * * * Madeline by this time has no choice; the revision heightens the contrast between her innocent unconsciousness and the storm raging outside: "Still, still she dreams, louder the frost wind blows."

As printed, the poem continues: " 'Tis dark: quick pattereth the flaw-blown sleet." Then Porphyro: "This is no dream, my bride, my Madeline!" Another line describes the storm: " 'Tis dark: the iced gusts still rave and beat" (325–327). And now Madeline finally does wake up, if she ever does. Her speech shows a mixed attitude toward what has happened, but above all it is the lament of the seduced maiden: "No dream, alas! alas! and woe is mine! / Porphyro will leave me here to fade and pine.— / Cruel! what traitor could thee hither bring?" (328–330). She will curse not, for her heart is lost in his, or, perhaps more accurately, still lost in her romantic idealization of him. But she is aware that her condition is woeful: Porphyro is cruel; Angela is a traitor; and Madeline is a "deceived thing;— / A dove

---

7. I quote the revised stanza from the second Woodhouse transcript (*W*² in Garrod's *Poetical Works*); see above, pp. 454–55.

forlorn and lost" (332–33). In subsequent stanzas Porphyro soothes her
fears, again calls her his bride, and seems to make all wrongs right. He tells
her that the storm outside is really only "an elfin-storm from faery land"
(343) and that she should "Awake! arise! . . . and fearless be, / For o'er the
southern moors I have a home for thee" (350–351). They hurry out of the
chamber, down the wide stairs, through the castle door—"And they are
gone . . . fled away into the storm" (370–371).

III

After giving so much space to Porphyro, in admittedly exaggerated fashion
portraying him as peeping Tom and villainous seducer, I must now confess
that I do not think his stratagem is the main concern of the poem. I have
presented him as villain in order to suggest, in the first place, that he is not,
after all, making a spiritual pilgrimage, unless the poem is to be read as a
satire on spiritual pilgrimages; in the second place, that the lovers, far from
being a single element in the poem, are as much protagonist and antago-
nist as Belinda and the Baron, or Clarissa and Lovelace; and in the third
place, that no matter how much Keats entered into the feelings of his characters, he could not lose touch with the claims and responsibilities of the
world he lived in.
    Certainly he partially identified himself with Porphyro. When Wood-
house found his revisions objectionable, Keats replied that he should
"despise a man who would be such an eunuch in sentiment as to leave a
maid, with that Character about her, in such a situation: & sh^d despise himself to write about it" (p. 356). One may cite the narrator's obvious relish in
Porphyro's situation as Madeline is about to undress—"Now prepare, /
Young Porphyro, for gazing on that bed" (196–197)—and Keats's later
objection to the poem that "in my dramatic capacity I enter fully into the
feeling: but in Propria Persona I should be apt to quiz it myself" (L, 2:174).
But sexual passion worried him: to Bailey he confessed in July 1818,
"When I am among Women I have evil thoughts" (pp. 264–65), and he wrote
in his copy of The Anatomy of Melancholy, "there is nothing disgraces me in
my own eyes so much as being one of a race of eyes nose and mouth beings
in a planet call'd the earth who . . . have always mingled goatish winnyish
lustful love with the abstract adoration of the deity."[8] Though it has touches
of humor, The Eve of St. Agnes is a serious poem; regardless of the extent to
which Keats identified with his hero, he introduced enough overtones of evil
to make Porphyro's actions wrong within the structure of the poem.
    From now on, however, it may be best to think of Porphyro as repre-
senting, like the storm that comes up simultaneously with his conquest, the
ordinary cruelties of life in the world. Like Melville, Keats saw

> Too far into the sea; where every maw
> The greater on the less feeds evermore. . . .
> Still do I that most fierce destruction see,
> The shark at savage prey—the hawk at pounce,
> The gentle Robin, like a pard or ounce,
> Ravening a worm.   (see p. 136, ll. 94–95, 102–105)

8. Hampstead Keats, V, 309.

Let Porphyro represent one of the sharks under the surface. And to borrow another figure from Melville, let the main concern of the poem be the young Platonist dreaming at the masthead: one false step, his identity comes back in horror, and with a half-throttled shriek he drops through transparent air into the sea, no more to rise for ever. There are reasons why we ought not entirely to sympathize with Madeline. She is a victim of deception, to be sure, but of deception not so much by Porphyro as by herself and the superstition she trusts in. Madeline the self-hoodwinked dreamer is, I think, the main concern of the poem, and I shall spend some time documenting this notion and relating it to Keats's other important poems—all of which, in a sense, are about dreaming. If we recall Keats's agnosticism, his sonnet *Written in Disgust of Vulgar Superstition* (Christianity), and his abuse in a spring 1819 journal letter of "the pious frauds of Religion" (p. 322), we may be prepared to see a hoodwinked dreamer in the poem even before we meet Madeline. He is the old Beadsman, so engrossed in an ascetic ritual that he is sealed off from the joys of life. After saying his prayers, he turns first through a door leading to the noisy revelry upstairs. "But no. . . . The joys of all his life were said and sung: / His was harsh penance on St. Agnes' Eve" (22–24). And so he goes another way, to sit among rough ashes, while the focus of the narrative proceeds through the door he first opened, and on into the assembly of revelers, where we are introduced to Madeline and the ritual she is intent on following. * * * Then the poem * * * continues describing Madeline, who scarcely hears the music, and, with eyes fixed on the floor, pays no attention to anyone around her.

Several things deserve notice. By brooding "all that wintry day, / On love, and wing'd St. Agnes' saintly care" (43–44), and by setting herself apart from the revelers, Madeline presents an obvious parallel with the Beadsman. Both are concerned with prayer and an ascetic ritual; both are isolated from the crowd and from actuality. A second point is that the superstition is clearly an old wives' tale: Madeline follows the prescription that "she had heard old dames full many times declare" (45). It is called by the narrator a "whim": "Full of this whim was thoughtful Madeline" (55). * * * Perfunctorily dancing along, she is said to be "Hoodwink'd with faery fancy; all amort, / Save to St. Agnes and her lambs unshorn" (70–71).

The superstition is next mentioned when Angela tells that Madeline "the conjuror plays / This very night: good angels her deceive!" (124–125). Porphyro thinks of the ritual in terms of "enchantments cold" and "legends old" (134–135). Proceeding to her chamber, Madeline is called "St. Agnes' charmed maid," "a mission'd spirit, unaware" (192–193). * * * [S]he is engrossed in a fanciful dream-world. "Pensive awhile she dreams awake, and sees, / In fancy, fair St. Agnes in her bed, / But dares not look behind, or all the charm is fled" (232–234). This last line carries a double meaning: in following her ritual, Madeline must look neither "behind, nor sideways" (53); but the real point is that if she did look behind, she would discover Porphyro, and then "the charm" would be "fled" for a more immediate reason.

Asleep in bed, Madeline is said to be "Blissfully haven'd both from joy and pain . . . Blinded alike from sunshine and from rain, / As though a rose should shut, and be a bud again" (240–243). Her dream is "a midnight charm / Impossible to melt as iced stream," "a stedfast spell" (282–283, 287). It is while she is in this state of stuporous insensibility—while "still the spell / Unbroken guards her in serene repose," "Still, still she dreams, louder the frost wind blows"—that Porphyro makes love to her. On awakening to learn, "No dream, alas! alas! and woe is mine," she calls herself "a deceived thing," echoing Angela's words earlier, "good angels her deceive!" Her condition is pitiful, yet at the same time reprehensible. Her conjuring (perhaps like Merlin's) has backfired upon her, and as hoodwinked dreamer she now gets her reward in coming to face reality a little too late. The rose cannot shut, and be a bud again.

IV

* * * *The Eve of St. Agnes* * * * stands significantly at the beginning of Keats's single great creative year, 1819, and it introduces a preoccupation of all the major poems of this year: that an individual ought not to lose touch with the realities of this world.

In the poems of 1819, Keats's most explicit, unequivocal pronouncement on the conditions of human life comes in the *Ode on Melancholy*. Life in the world, we are told five or six times in the statements and images of the third stanza, is an affair in which pleasure and pain are inseparably mixed. There is no pleasure without pain, and, conversely, if pain is sealed off, so also is pleasure. One accepts life on these terms, or else suffers a kind of moral and spiritual emptiness amounting to death. The former is the better choice: he lives most fully "whose strenuous tongue / Can burst Joy's grape against his palate fine." The images of the first stanza—forgetfulness, narcotics, poisons, death—represent various ways of avoiding pain in life. But they are rejected (the whole stanza is a series of negatives) because they also exclude pleasure and reduce life to nothing ("For shade to shade will come too drowsily, / And drown the wakeful anguish of the soul"). The equivalent of these anodynes elsewhere in Keats's poems is dreaming, trusting in the visionary imagination; and, to cut short further explanation, the dreamer in the works of 1819 is always one who would escape pain, but hopes, wrongly, to achieve pleasure.

Take Madeline as the first instance. In bed, under the delusion that she can achieve bliss in her dream, * * * she is "Blissfully haven'd both from joy and pain" (240)—for all practical purposes in the narcotic state rejected by the *Ode on Melancholy*, experiencing nothing. Keats reiterates the idea two lines later, "Blinded alike from sunshine and from rain," and the folly of her delusion is represented by the reversal of natural process, "As though a rose should shut, and be a bud again" (242–243). As generally in Keats's poems, dreaming is attended by fairy-tale imagery: under the spell of "faery fancy," Madeline plays the conjuror, and Porphyro is linked in several ways with fairy lore, witchcraft, and sorcery, as well as pagan sensuality. It is possible that Madeline never completely awakens from her fanciful dream; for she believes Porphyro when he tells her that the storm is "an elfin-storm from faery land" (343), and she imagines "sleeping dragons all around" (353) when they hurry out of the castle.

* * *

The wretched knight-at-arms in *La Belle Dame Sans Merci* is similarly a hoodwinked dreamer. La Belle Dame is "a faery's child"; she sings "A faery's song," speaks "in language strange," and takes him to an "elfin grot." When he awakens from his vision he finds himself "On the cold hill's side." But he is still the dupe of his dream, still hoodwinked, because he continues, in a barren landscape, "Alone and palely loitering," hoping for a second meeting with La Belle Dame. And he denies himself participation in the actual world, which, in contrast to his bleak surroundings, is represented as a more fruitful scene, where "The squirrel's granary is full, / And the harvest's done."

In *Lamia*, the hoodwinked dreamer is of course Lycius, who falls in love with the serpent-woman Lamia, in whose veins runs "elfin blood," who lingers by the wayside "fairily," with whom he lives in "sweet sin" in a magical palace with a "faery-roof" (I.147, 200; II.31, 123). "She seem'd, at once, some penanced lady elf, / Some demon's mistress, or the demon's self" (I.55–56). What she promises to do for Lycius is what, according to the *Ode on Melancholy*, cannot be done for mortal men: "To unperplex bliss from its neighbour pain; / Define their pettish limits, and estrange / Their points of contact, and swift counterchange." The inseparability of pleasure and pain is for her a "specious chaos"; she will separate them "with sure art" (I.192–196)—or so the blinded Lycius thinks. But "Spells are but made to break," wrote Keats, in a passage subsequently omitted from the text.[9] "A thrill / Of trumpets" reminds Lycius of the claims of the "noisy world almost forsworn" (II.27–33), and he holds a wedding feast, at which "cold philosophy," in the form of his old tutor Apollonius, attends to put "all charms" to flight. The "foul dream" Lamia vanishes under the tutor's piercing eye, and Lycius, too engrossed in his dream to survive, falls dead.

*   *   *

Keats's mature view of dreamers illuminates perhaps most importantly the two best odes, *On a Grecian Urn* and *To a Nightingale*. In each poem the speaker begins as dreamer, hoodwinked with the idea that he can unperplex bliss from its neighbor pain, that he can find an anodyne to the ills of the flesh by joining the timeless life pictured on an urn, or by fading away into the forest with a bird. In each case the result is an awareness that spells are but made to break: the speaker recognizes the falseness of the dream, the shortcomings of the ideal he has created, and he returns to the mortal world. Life on the urn is at first attractive: unheard melodies are sweeter; the lovers will remain young and fair; the trees will never lose their leaves. Yet it is a static situation. Love must be enjoyed, not stopped forever at a point when enjoyment is just out of reach. The final judgment is that the urn is a "Cold Pastoral," a "friend to man" that, as a work of art, teases him out of thought but offers no possible substitute for life in the actual world.

In the *Ode to a Nightingale*, the speaker would fade away with the bird, and forget "The weariness, the fever, and the fret" of the mortal world, "Where Beauty cannot keep her lustrous eyes, / Or new Love pine at them beyond to-morrow." But when he imaginatively joins the bird in the forest, he immediately longs for the world he has just rejected: "Here there is no light. . . . I cannot see what flowers are at my feet." "In embalmed darkness" he is forced to "guess each sweet" of the transient natural world. As he continues musing, the bird takes on for him the fairy-tale associations

9. *Poetical Works*, ed. Garrod, p. 205.

that we saw earlier connected with Madeline's dream, La Belle Dame, and Lamia: its immortal voice has charmed "magic casements . . . in faery lands forlorn." The realization that the faery lands are forlorn of human life tolls the dreamer back to his sole self, and he wakes up. The nightingale, symbol of dreams and the visionary imagination, has turned out to be a "deceiving elf." The fancy "cannot cheat so well."

* * *

The dreamer in Keats is ultimately one who turns his back, not merely on the pains of life, but on life altogether; and in the poems of 1819, beginning with *The Eve of St. Agnes,* his dreaming is condemned. If the major concern in these poems is the conflict between actuality and the ideal, the result is not rejection of the actual, but rather a facing-up to it that amounts, in the total view, to affirmation. It is a notable part of Keats's wisdom that he never lost touch with reality, that he reproved his hoodwinked dreamers who would shut out the world, that he recognized life as a complexity of pleasure and pain, and laid down a rule for action: achievement of the ripest, fullest experience that one is capable of. These qualities make him a saner if in some ways less romantic poet than his contemporaries, and they should qualify him as the Romantic poet most likely to survive in the modern world.

JEFFREY N. COX

Cockney Classicism: History with Footnotes[†]

I

In 1783, Sir William Hamilton, the renowned connoisseur, returned home from his diplomatic post in Naples with what was then known as the Barbarini Vase. Hamilton—who considered the vase his prize possession and as great a work of art as the then revered Apollo Belvedere—found himself forced to sell it to the Duchess of Portland. Its attraction deepened by the controversy over its mysterious frieze, what came to be known as the Portland Vase had then all the powerful allure—what Walter Benjamin calls an object's "aura"—of a unique and great work of art.[1]

However, its mode of cultural existence was soon to change radically. The Duchess of Portland died within a year of purchasing the vase, and thus it was put up for auction along with the rest of her museum of curiosities. Her son, the third Duke of Portland, secretly purchased the vase, and it was he who made two decisions that shaped the vase's future history. In 1810, he decided to place the vase on permanent loan with the British Museum, where it immediately became a favorite attraction, where a regular visitor to the museum such as John Keats could have seen it. This unique art object,

---

† Text and notes revised from *Poetry and Politics in the Cockney School: Keats, Shelley, Hunt and their Circle* (Cambridge: Cambridge University Press, 1998), pp. 146–86. Reprinted by permission of Cambridge University Press.

1. Walter Benjamin, "The Work of Art in the Age of Mechanical Reproduction," in *Illuminations,* ed. Hannah Arendt, trans. Harry Zohn (New York: Schocken, 1968), pp. 217–51.

prized by an aristocratic connoisseur such as Hamilton, was thus given over to the more democratic gaze of the national museum.

More important, the Duke of Portland agreed upon purchasing the vase to loan it to Josiah Wedgwood for twelve months so that the master potter could copy it; while the first edition of the Wedgwood Portland probably ran to no more than forty-five copies, later editions multiplied the replicated images of the Portland. The unique art object suddenly existed in a host of reproductions.

Of course, the Portland Vase later suffered another change in its mode of existence, for on the seventh of February 1845, a young man entered the room in the British Museum where the vase was exhibited and, using a Persian "curiosity in sculpture," smashed it into more than two hundred fragments. When restorers came to reconstruct the vase, they had to rely on reproductions such as Wedgwood's for models. This unique work of art now exists only as it has been mediated through its duplicates.

II

Keats's "Ode on a Grecian Urn" was once thought to represent a particular, unique art object, perhaps the Townley Vase, part of the collection that came to the British Museum in 1805 and which Keats surely saw, perhaps the Sosibos Vase, which Keats apparently traced from an engraving of the piece in the *Musée Napoléon*, perhaps some other Attic urn. As Jerome McGann has pointed out, we are now somewhat embarrassed by the attempt to limit this supposedly universal poem to a specific prototype, but he also reminds us that the poem demands that we consider it as a representation of a concrete object: "Part of the poem's fiction . . . is that the urn it describes is an actual urn comparable to the Townley, Borghese, or Sosibos vases. . . . The poem's fiction—that its *ideal* subject is an *actual* urn—asks its readers to try to visualize, in a concrete way, the urn of the poet's imaginings."[2] McGann thus finds the ode engaging the project of romantic classicism with its sense of Greek art as being simultaneously perfectly ideal and perfectly embodied.[3]

Romantic classicism was not, however, merely an aesthetic doctrine; it was also a practical project, perhaps best represented by Wedgwood's factory, Etruria, which had a classicizing—and romantic—name but which made useful household products. In early nineteenth London, one could view an extraordinary range of reproduced art objects—not just Wedgwood porcelains but statues done in wax, ancient buildings modeled in cork, paintings done in colored wools on linen and hung in Miss Linwood's famous gallery of over sixty needlepoint reproductions of the masters. While Keats knew some art objects first hand, he was more likely to know them through reproductions, such as the copies of statues and paintings in Leigh Hunt's cottage that Keats celebrated in "Sleep and Poetry." The first thing we must realize about Keats's ode is that it confronts the vicissitudes of a thing of beauty in the age of porcelain—and wax, cork, and needlepoint—reproduction.

---

2. Jerome McGann, *The Beauty of Inflections* (Oxford:Oxford University Press, 1985), p. 44.
3. McGann follows Ian Jack's account of the *Annals* in Jack's *Keats and the Mirror of Art* (Oxford: Clarendon Press, 1967), pp. 46–57.

Keats, of course, experienced these vicissitudes first hand each time he ventured into print. In manuscript a Keats poem could be treasured by the supportive circle of friends around Hunt, but once the poem was committed to reproduction in a published book, Keats lost control of its reception and its interpretation as it entered the commercialized, public space of print. As the poems that Keats first showed to the Hunt circle in manuscript came to be printed in his *Poems* of 1817 and *Endymion* of 1818, Keats exchanged his status as a coterie favorite for that of a target of the Cockney School attacks. His unique works of art were through a series of reproductions—the last being the reviewers' mocking quotations—reduced to parody.

Keats responded to this condition of authorship and this mode of cultural existence of the artistic object in the "Ode on a Grecian Urn" by attempting to recreate in fiction the "aura"—the power and attraction—lost to an object such as the Portland Vase. Benjamin tells us in "The Work of Art in the Age of Mechanical Reproduction" that reproduction destroys the physical history of the unique art object, its provenance or ownership history, and its original context or its cultural history. We can perhaps get a sense of what Benjamin's argument means for art in Keats's day if we look at an engraving of the "Portland Museum," the Duchess of Portland's collection of curios and antiquities including the Portland Vase. The vase occupies the central place in the composition, and a mirror is placed behind it in an attempt to re-present the vase as fully as possible; but the engraving cannot offer us the Portland Vase, and not only because three dimensions are collapsed into two; the contrast between the cobalt-blue glass of the vase and the milky-white glass of the relief is lost, the shape is altered, and the figures are not reproduced with accuracy. Moreover, what Benjamin sees as the vase's history as it is inscribed in the physical object is lost: not only are we unaware from the engraving that the figures' "surfaces [were] partially decayed by time," as Wedgwood noted, but also we cannot see that the vase's bottom had broken and been replaced with a glass disk not belonging to the original.[4] The history of its ownership is also obscured: the very renaming of the vase as the Portland Vase reinvents the vase in the present, denying its status as a long-coveted object, formerly owned by and named for the Barbarini. Moreover, the engraving removes the vase from any context that might help us to understand it in a historical sense; the vase is instead placed amongst a mélange of odd, mainly natural objects, and a piece of coral is placed in it. The "aura" of the vase is destroyed as it loses its physical reality, its provenance, and its location in history. It comes as no surprise that this engraving was reproduced as the frontispiece to Mr. Skinner and Co.'s sale catalogue for the auction of the Duchess of Portland's collection.

Keats's ode seeks to reverse this process. Addressing himself to the features that Benjamin finds lost in reproduction, Keats provides his urn with both a physical inviolability—it is "still unravish'd," unlike the Portland Vase with its lost bottom—and a life history, from its "birth" at the hands of its unknown creator through its status as the "foster-child of silence and slow time" to its future status as "a friend to man," "When old age shall this

---

4. Josiah Wedgwood, letter to Sir William Hamilton, 24 June 1786, Wedgwood Museum MS E 18976, excerpted in *The Selected Letters of Josiah Wedgwood*, ed. Ann Finer and George Savage (London: Cory, Adams & Mackay, 1965).

generation waste" (ll. 1–2, 46–48). If the reproduction is the object without history, Keats makes his vase into a "Sylvan historian" offering a legend. Keats would seem in his fiction to heal the damage done to real urns such as the Portland Vase. The great success of Keats's poem is that it convinces us that there is an urn behind it, that it is powerfully re-presenting a unique work of art with its aura intact.

It would be wrong, however, to see Keats's "Ode on a Grecian Urn" as an exercise in cultural nostalgia, an attempt to recreate a lost aesthetic wholeness in his divided age. Keats is always aware of his distance from any idealized past; he knows he is what Schiller called a "sentimental poet," writing—as Keats put it in "Ode to Psyche"—"Too, too late for the fond believing lyre." Keats wants to rescue his urn and his art from the ravages of reproduction, but he does so not through invoking a unified, naive, pure, timeless art object but rather by writing an ironic, sentimental, eroticized, and historicized poem about such an object. Put another way, he creates the fiction of the unique object of romantic classicism—the perfectly embodied, realized ideal—through a poem that is paradoxical, elusive, and distanced. He grants the imagined urn its aura by recognizing that his poem cannot achieve such a state, a fact he recognizes in calling the urn a "Sylvan historian, who canst thus express / A flowery tale more sweetly than our rhyme" (ll. 3–4). "Ode on a Grecian Urn" is a work of what I want to call Cockney classicism that seeks to return passion and power—the aura of the classic— to art beyond the diminution of its allure through endless imitation. But that beyond is a sign of the poem's own belatedness, of its own acts of imitation— and thus reproduction—of another poem and of a woman's performances.

III

The Portland Vase has itself never been a particularly popular candidate for the model behind Keats's "Ode on a Grecian Urn": as a work of the Augustan era done by Alexandrian craftsmen, it is no longer found to be good enough or Greek enough to inspire Keats—we prefer to imagine him responding to the Elgin marbles. However, Keats surely knew the then greatly admired Portland Vase, which his friend Haydon quoted in one of his paintings, which Darwin praised in his *Botanic Garden*, and which was the subject of a heated debate concerning the meaning of its frieze. Most experts then argued that the vase was a "Sepulchral Urn" originally containing the ashes of Alexander Severus and his mother and that the frieze was an allegory of death. No less an authority than Winckelmann, however, as early as 1776 linked the frieze to the legend of Peleus and Thetis, as did Henry Moses in his 1814 *A Collection of Antique Vases*, and W. Watkiss Lloyd (1849) connected the vase directly to a poetic precursor, Catullus 64, the "Ephithalamium of Peleus and Thetis." Recently, Randall L. Skalsky has convincingly established the ties between the Portland Vase and Catullus's poem, finding the vase offering the same kind of witty, learned manipulation of myth that marks Catullus's verse.[5] The vase, which I have

---

5. Randall L. Skalsky, "Visual Trope and the Portland Vase Frieze: A New Reading and Exegesis," *Arion* 19 (Winter 1992): 42–71. W. Watkiss Lloyd in *Classical Museum* 6 (1849): 253–78. J. J. Winckelmann, *Geschichte der Kunst des Altertums* (Vienna, 1776), part 2, pp. 861f. On interpretations of the Portland Vase prior to 1950, see D. E. L. Haynes, *The Portland Vase* (London: Trustees of the British Museum, 1964), pp. 27–31.

been treating as an original, now appears as a cross-media reproduction, an attempt to recreate a poem in the shape of an urn. Keats's ode—which, of course, seeks to recreate an urn in the shape of a poem—tries to recreate the "aura" of an imaginative Portland Vase by taking upon itself the belatedness of imitation, by making itself a reproduction of the vase's great poetic prototype, thus freeing the urn to stand perhaps for itself. Whether Keats knew of the attempts to link the Portland Vase to the story of Peleus and Thetis set forth in Catullus 64, he surely knew Catullus's poem, as Catullus was a key, if little recognized influence on the poetry of the period and particularly on the circle of which Keats was a part.[6]

The Hunt circle's encounter with Catullus was a profound act of self-recognition. Catullus's poetry summons up a coterie of urban experimental poets—the neoteric or new poets—that must have appealed to the Cockneys with their social, communal sense of poetry. Neoteric poetry—with its self-conscious, playfully belated style, with its inversion of traditional myths, with its combination of learned allusions and slangy diction, with its evocation of the natural and the sensual by an urban coterie—almost provides the program for Cockney poetry. It comes as no surprise that Hunt's first major poetic volume, *The Feast of the Poets*, has as its motto a quotation from the neoterics' model, Callimachus, and that among its eight shorter poems are three translations from Catullus.

Catullus 64 is our one great example of the Latin epyllion, or "little epic," one of the innovative forms the neoterics cultivated to engage epic and heroic subject matter without adopting either epic form or a heroic ideology. Catullus's eccentric narrative opens with the voyage of Jason and the Argonauts, only to have the mission left behind as Peleus and Thetis meet and decide to marry. As the wedding guests gather, we discover that one of the wedding presents is a tapestry depicting another hero, Theseus, though we see him at one of his least heroic moments as he abandons Ariadne, who is later swept up by Bacchus. The poem closes with a song by the Parcae, who detail the supposed glories of this marriage that will bring forth the "greatest" hero, Achilles, who is described as a killing machine who will choke the river Scamander with corpses, whose "valour oft, his ever dauntless breast / Shall mothers' grief o'er children's biers attest," and whose death will be mourned by the sacrifice of Polyxena (2: 43, 45).

The poem systematically undercuts the heroic. The Trojan War is imagined as a killing field commanded by Agamemnon. Achilles' heroism raises itself upon slaughter, upon the tears of mothers and the sacrifice of the maiden Polyxena on his tomb. Theseus returns as a hero to rule Thebes, hut he can do so only by abandoning Ariadne. Lawrence Lipking, in *Abandoned Women and Poetic Tradition*, argues that "epics require abandoned women."[7] Catullus's epyllion rejects the epic, heroic tradition as a result. For set against the abandoned Ariadne and the sacrificed Polyxena is Ariadne after she discovers "wild ecstasy" with Bacchus. The only moment of joy in the poem comes as "Bacchus young," followed by dancing Satyrs and Sileni who play "timbrels," "cymbals," and "fifes," appears "With love for thee high

6. See Karl Pomeroy Harrington, *Catullus and His Influence* (New York: Cooper Square, 1963), pp. 196–206. George Lamb's contemporary translation of *Poems of Caius Valerius Catullus*, 2 vols. (London: Murray, 1821), is cited in the text.
7. Lipking, *Abandoned Women and Poetic Tradition* (Chicago: University of Chicago Press, 1988), p. 30.

raging in his heart, / Thee seeking, Ariadne" (2: 37). The poem indicts the heroic choice made by Theseus and Achilles of an epic career over a life of sexual and personal fulfillment, an indictment strong enough to call forth Virgil's reply in the Dido episode of his epic where, echoing in order to "correct" Catullus, he sought to demonstrate that it is the right choice to abandon one's love for the demands of country, home, and *pietas*. "Pius Aeneas" properly escapes Dido's bower of bliss to found Rome.

There are many echoes of this Catullan anti-heroic stand in the poetry of the second generation of romantics, in Shelley's *Prometheus Unbound*, in Keats's *Endymion* with its rejection of the epic subject matter of "the death-day of empires" and its embrace of tales of love, and most directly in Hunt's "Bacchus and Ariadne" (1818), which takes up the scene on Catullus's tapestry. Hunt completes the tale of Bacchus and Ariadne to offer a Catullan counter-response to Virgil's Dido and Aeneas episode, for Hunt attacks Theseus—and by extension, Aeneas—for abandoning their lovers, noting that they will "quote Heaven's orders," saying that "A dream, advised him sternly not to stay / But go and cut up nations limb by limb." The god Bacchus values the "lady and the bower," where they create an erotic paradise, but the traditional hero prefers to "cut up nations limb by limb" (ll. 46–55). Theseus departs in pursuit of epic glory, but Hunt's poem remains with Ariadne to glory in her sexual union with Bacchus.

Keats's engagement with Cockney poetry is usually seen as a juvenile attachment to such poetry by Hunt which Keats abandons as he grows as a poet, but the late "Ode on a Grecian Urn"—as can be seen in its proliferating puns—uses the same "archly-thoughtful manner," the same "licentious brilliancy of epithet" that the *Edinburgh Magazine* (2d ser., 1 [October 1817]: 256; above, p. 95) found in Keats's poetry in 1817. Individual scholars often note a single pun in the poem—Ian Jack reminds us that the phrase "leaf-fringed legend" can refer to either a story or an embellished written statement; William Empson objected to the opening line of the last stanza as "very bad . . . the half pun [of "Attic" with "attitude"] suggesting a false Greek derivation and jammed up against an arty bit of Old English seems . . . affected and ugly"; and Paul Hamilton takes up the phrase "With brede / Of marble men and maidens overwrought" to point out that "overwrought" can be read as "the elevation of the 'brede' above the surface of the urn, the emotions of the 'mad pursuit' of 'men and maidens,' the transference of figures from one work of art 'over' to another, and the overarching umbrage, itself legendary, fringing the urn's narrative."[8] Pursuing Hamilton's point further, we might find the full statement taking up not only the way in which the figures are fashioned on the urn but also the breeding going on between overwrought or worked-up women and men stiffened into "marble."

There are many more puns—for example, "Thou still unravish'd bride of quietness," where "still" could refer to a motionless, quiet quality of the urn or function as a modifier of "unravish'd," indicating that the bride has yet to be ravished; "flowery tale," where we could have a tale embellished with floral designs, an ornate, overly poetic story, or simply a pastoral narrative;

8. Jack, *Keats and the Mirror of Art*, p. 283 n. 13. William Empson, *The Structure of Complex Words* (New York: New Directions, 1951), pp. 368–74. Paul Hamilton, "Keats and Critique," in Marjorie Levinson, Marilyn Butler, Jerome McGann, and Paul Hamilton, *Rethinking Historicism: Critical Readings in Romantic History* (Oxford: Basil Blackwell, 1989), p. 112.

or the "desolate" city which is both abandoned and in despair. If we fail to notice the density of the punning in the ode, we lose a sense of the poem's playfulness, of the experimental, even quirky, nature of Keats's language to which Marjorie Levinson has pointed,[9] of the Catullan and Cockney delight in toying with what others consider serious in the name of a linguistic and also finally an erotic delight.

This witty, extreme, even odd, wordplay, so distinctive of Cockney verse, links Keats back to *doctus* Catullus, and particularly the "Epithalamium of Peleus and Thetis"; for I want to argue that the "legend" which "haunts about" the shape of Keats's urn is the same one depicted on the Portland Vase, that of Catullus's odd wedding poem. For example, we are told that the urn's legend is "Of deities or mortals, or of both"; whereas this might simply express an inability to read the urn, it might recall Catullus 64, with its account of the only marriage between a mortal and a goddess. The action imagined here—"the maidens loth," who "struggle to escape" from the men in "mad pursuit"—could be a reference to Thetis' initial rejection of Peleus and his need to pursue and win her against her will, a facet of their story introduced only elliptically in Catullus ("Nor Thetis *then* a mortal bridegroom spurn'd"; emphasis added) but made clear in such Keatsian source books as Lemprière's *Bibliotheca Classica*. The final line of the stanza ("What pipes and timbrels? What wild ecstasy?") can certainly be linked to the coming of Bacchus to Ariadne as he is accompanied by devotees with pipes, cymbals, and timbrels, a point made in both Catullus 64 and Hunt's "Bacchus and Ariadne."

However, the strongest evidence for a link between the ode and the epyllion comes in stanza four, the most admired part of the poem and one for which we have struggled to discover a model or prototype. Keats's description of the abandoned town is tantalizingly close to Catullus's account of the desertion of Thessaly as everyone journeys to attend the wedding of Peleus and Thetis:

> Thessalia's crowds with gifts the palace seek,
> . . . .
> The earth's untill'd, the bullock's callous throat,
> Free from the yoke, regains its softer coat:
> The lowly vineyard knows no weeding rakes,
> Nor ox with sloping share the furrow breaks:
> No pruner lops the tree's incumbering boughs,
> And rust grows thick on the neglected ploughs. (2:22)

The pattern of Keats's stanza is the same, moving from a processional—in his case the sacrifice rather than a wedding—to a description of a town "emptied" of its people. We might even imagine Keats arriving at the notion of the eternally empty city of the urn from Catullus's distortion and acceleration of time as almost instantaneously equipment begins to rust, oxen go soft, and vines grow wild. In both poems, these passages gesture towards a loss, an absence, that underwrites the poems' more apparent argument.

It is not, however, so much specific connections between the two poems that are important as it is Keats's use of a Catullan style and his pursuit of

9. Marjorie Levinson, Keats's *Life of Allegory: The Origin of a Style* (Oxford: Basil Blackwell, 1988), excerpted above, p. 547–55.

a Catullan argument against the epic and the heroic. The urn is identified as a "Sylvan historian," suggesting almost oxymoronically that it is engaged with history—the realm of epic—and that it is from a pastoral world, a world we do not normally think of as having a history. Such an identification makes sense, however, when the ode is linked to the epyllion, with its ability to engage within a small compass the subject matter of epic while rejecting its ethos. Within the even smaller, lyric compass of the ode, Keats turns from the possibility of epic legend to the pastoral world of the "happy melodist," the "bold lover" and the "happy, happy boughs." Stanzas two and three of the ode work a Catullan inversion upon the traditional economy of desire: if epic requires men to abandon women, Keats imagines a world in which the beloved woman "cannot fade . . . / For ever wilt thou love, and she be fair!" If Catullus's abandoned Ariadne is frozen by her grief and "looks out like a stone bacchanal," Keats will freeze not the moment of rupture and loss but that of rapture and lust, as he depicts the "Bold lover" as a stone figure who "never canst . . . kiss, / Though winning near the goal," and whose love is thus "For ever warm and still to be enjoyed, / For ever panting, and for ever young." Keats offers an image of eternal eros in order to offer a Catullan answer to the denigration of sexual love by an ethos of the heroic career.

After opposing this eternal erotic to destructive heroism in the first three stanzas, Keats in his fourth stanza replaces the epic's abandonment of women with an abandoned community. It is not a woman who is sacrificed here, as, say, Dido is sacrificed; it is the heifer "lowing at the skies" (l. 33). It is not Ariadne who is abandoned but the "little town by river or sea shore, / Or mountain-built with peaceful citadel" that is "emptied of this folk, this pious morn" (ll. 35–37). The epic ethos that embraces heroic warfare over erotic play, the nation and piety over lovers and their pleasure, is finally seen as destroying the community it would mold into a nation as the "folk" are led from its "peaceful citadel" or "little town" to be taken to the sacrifice that those who wish to build nations, religions, or empires always demand.

IV

Of course, such stories of love versus duty, of abandonment and sacrifice, were not played out only in classical myth. Keats's text leads us to another site where such issues were central. The final stanza of the ode evokes the urn's "Fair attitude," alluding to a real woman known for her fair attitudes and her ability to give shape to modern man's dreams of Attic art: Emma Hamilton, wife of Sir William Hamilton, the one-time owner of the Portland Vase, and mistress of Admiral Nelson, the Aeneas who did not want to leave his Dido to pursue heroic action. The art of her attitudes as she crossed class barriers to offer a new appreciation of classical culture provides an important context for Cockney classicism; the story of her loves suggests how the Theseus-Ariadne, Aeneas-Dido archetype was invested at the time with new cultural energy and why Keats would draw on it and on Catullus's version of it in particular.

When in 1784 Hamilton returned to Italy without the Portland Vase, he had already been approached by his nephew Charles Greville about acquiring a beauty more likely to tease him out of thought, Greville's mistress,

Emma Lyons, well known in artistic circles as a model of classical figures for Romney and others, and earlier a scantily glad "Goddess of Youth and Health" attending James Graham's "celestial bed" where she learned to use classical costumes and poses for erotic purposes.[1] She eventually became Hamilton's wife, calling forth such comments as that of Horace Walpole, who—knowing of Emma's representations of famous classical images—quipped, "Sir William has actually married his gallery of statues."[2]

Walpole refers to Emma Hamilton's attitudes, a kind of performance art in which she impersonated classical statues in the flesh, moving from one image to another with a fluidity and rapidity that was apparently astonishing. While Emma represented a great many figures and a wide range of emotions, she was particularly renowned for her figures of suffering, and one of her best-known attitudes was that of the abandoned Ariadne. These performances, which were slightly scandalous for it was rumored that they were enacted in a state of undress appropriate to the subjects represented, were admired by many visitors to Naples, including Goethe. Emma inaugurated another way of reproducing classical works of art, and she had her imitators who also offered "attitudes," from the great equestrian Andrew Ducrow who adopted the poses of various famous statues while riding horseback to Madame Wharton who at mid-century offered at her theater Walhalla representations of such images as Venus rising from the sea, Edwin Landseer's *Lady Godiva*, Canova's *Nymph*, and Raphael's *Bacchanalian Triumph*. While such performances were advertised as a way of improving art through a study of the human body and also as a means of bringing art to the people, their appeal seems to have largely been that of an arty strip show. Emma Hamilton had shown the way to generate an audience for the classics by making them sources of erotic titillation.

Emma Hamilton's erotic classicism was, however, turned against her: if Hamilton's beloved Portland Vase could be reduced to endless imitations, his beloved Emma could be traduced through repeated parodies. These caricatures arose in the wake of Emma's affair with Lord Nelson when England began to fear that Nelson cared more for Emma than for prosecuting the war, that he had become an Antony dallying in the bed of a Cleopatra. Rowlandson introduced the Hamilton-Nelson triangle into several of his pornographic images of aging husbands and young lovers. In "Modern Antiques," an aging Sir William prowls among ancient Egyptian artifacts—perhaps brought back after Nelson's successful Egyptian mission—while Emma and Nelson as the two young lovers meet inside a mummy case. In "Lady Hxxxxx Attitudes," Rowlandson has the elderly Sir William display the naked Emma (who interestingly rests her foot upon a Grecian urn) to a young artist; in this world of eroticized classicism—where there is a statue of a satyr seizing a woman while on the floor two classical statues kiss—Emma becomes the final art object and her husband becomes an art dealer as pimp displaying her to the young man.

Gillray's images were even harsher. In *A Cognoscenti contemplating ye Beauties of ye Antique*, the aging Sir William Hamilton—who had joined Richard Payne Knight in arguing for the centrality of priapic cults to

1. See Eric Jameson, *The Natural History of Quackery* (Springfield, Ill.: Charles C. Thomas, 1961), pp.112–32.
2. Walpole, *Correspondence*, vol. 9 (New Haven: Yale University Press, 1944): 349.

ancient theology—looks at various Dionysian and priapic objects (including a cracked Grecian urn), in the middle of which stands a bust of Emma, while on the walls Emma is portrayed as Cleopatra keeping Nelson, England's Antony, from battle. Gillray also depicted Emma at a moment of abandonment in his *Dido in Despair!* Nelson this time is Aeneas sailing off with his fleet, leaving Emma with the decrepit Sir William asleep in the bed, with his eroticized antiquities strewn about the floor and a book of "attitudes" open to a recumbent nude on the settee. In this etching, Gillray makes explicit the connection between Hamilton's classical collections, Emma's roles in her attitudes, and the part she played in life. Part of the power of Gillray's image is that it explores the confusion of the boundary between art and life in this romantic triangle: where does art end and life begin in this circle of role-playing attitudes developed from the classics but now apparently being played out in life? Of course, Gillray uses this power to try to reinforce the conventional economy of desire rejected by Catullus and Keats: women must be abandoned and real men must go to war if England is to be saved; the erotic world is left to dirty old men.

As Gillray's use of Emma's attitudes or Walpole's comment on the Hamilton marriage suggest, they fear that the confusion between duty and pleasure arises from a confusion between hard reality and the world of play that is art. It is because Emma Hamilton has made these classical images come alive in the flesh that they have become eroticized. It is because she is capable of playing Cleopatra or Dido in life that Nelson is in danger. Emma is the Pygmalion and Galatea myth become real, and these men find it frightening.

Rowlandson's *Pygmalion and Galatea* belongs with these other images, for it evokes Emma Hamilton's ability to provide her lovers with statues come alive, with idealized images made real. As in *Modern Antiques*, we seem to be in a museum, surrounded by classical art objects, in this case a series of libidinous female statues and a huge urn on the base of which we see the mad pursuit of a maiden loth. A man, presumably Pygmalion, lies back on a couch while the woman, presumably the awakened Galatea, mounts him, bending down to kiss him and grasping his sexual organ in order to couple with him. She is the bold lover who, frozen in Rowlandson's image, never can kiss or consummate her desire, though their genitals are winning near the goal. This coupling, as opposed to the rape of a woman occurring on the urn in the background, would seem a more happy love, forever warm and still to be enjoyed, even if it is a breeding in which the woman is actively overwrought and the male, overcome by desire, is turned to hard marble. Here is the world of the eroticized classicism rejected by Gillray and his audience, a celebration of female sexuality absolutely opposed to the abandonment of women.

It was exactly for offering such titillating scenes from the classics that works such as Keats's *Endymion* were attacked. From the early "I stood tiptoe upon a little hill" and its celebration of the "pure deliciousness" of the union of Cynthia and Endymion, through *Endymion*, *The Eve of St. Agnes*, and the "Ode to Psyche," and on to Keats's late poems to Fanny Brawne, we find Keats both using the erotic to grant his poetry power and reflecting through his poetry on the power of desire. His famous "negative capability" letter (above, p. 109), sometimes read as a defense of an art that rises above both the lived life of the passions and ideological argument, works to link art to both political and erotic power. Keats famously discusses Benjamin West's *Death on a Pale Horse*: "It is a wonderful picture, when West's age is considered; But there is nothing to be intense upon; no women one feels mad to kiss; no face swelling into reality. the excellence of every Art is its intensity, capable of making all disagreeables evaporate, from their being in close relationship with Beauty & Truth—Examine King Lear & you will find this examplified throughout." In the words of the "Ode on a Grecian Urn," art should "tease us out of thought." But how does art accomplish this? Not through the pursuit of a formal, abstract beauty that is often found to be the burden of this letter.

We can get a better sense of what Keats is arguing for here if we contrast his remarks with those of Joyce's Stephen Dedalus when, in the context of a discussion of classical nudes, he seeks to resolve a similar question of how tragic art treats the "disagreeables" of life while offering beauty: "The feelings excited by improper art are kinetic, desire or loathing. Desire urges us to possess, to go to something; loathing urges us to abandon, to go from something. These are kinetic emotions. The arts which excite them, pornographical or didactic, are therefore improper arts. The esthetic emotion (I use the general term) is therefore static. The mind is arrested and raised above desire and loathing."[3] Many readings of Keats's passage tend to conform it to the view expressed by Dedalus: art is seen as raising the mind above desire and loathing, above "disagreeables," in order to unite it with Truth and Beauty. However, we need to see that truth and beauty are for Keats didactic and pornographic, in the terms offered by Dedalus. For Keats, beauty in art offers women one is mad to kiss; that is, he asks for the painterly equivalent of a cheap thrill, pornographic titillation. And in a letter that begins with the trials of radical publishers Wooler and Hone and ends with the censorship of Shelley's *Laon and Cythna*, it is hard to believe that Keats's truth is somehow a nondidactic, apolitical abstraction.

Keats's beauty is not some Platonic abstraction; it finds its practical and paradigmatic embodiment in that which is erotically attractive, in that which provokes desire and which thus unites the desiring self with the provocative other. His truth is not some absolute sought by Coleridge— who would give up a "fine verisimilitude" through an "irritable reaching" after a totalizing truth—but the contingent ideological positions that one constructs as one seeks what Keats calls "a recourse somewhat human independant of the great Consolations of Religion and undepraved Sensations—of the Beautiful—the poetical in all things—O for a Remedy against such wrongs within the pale of the World" (letter to Benjamin Bailey, 3 November 1817, p. 100). The beauty that evokes desire is the consolation offered in a world denied the Truth; and in that this desire connects the self with an other beyond the self—in that it is the sign of a world beyond the self's illusions, a ground for the ideological—it also offers us all the truth we can know within "the pale of the world." In other words, " 'Beauty is truth, truth beauty'—that is all / Ye know on earth, and all ye need to know."

Emma Hamilton—who through her attitudes embodied the ideal, who offered an erotic moment that through her art seemed to touch eternity— lived out the reality of breathing human passion as her beauty gave way to

---

3. James Joyce, *A Portrait of the Artist as a Young Man* (New York: Viking, 1964), p. 205.

old age, drinking, and corpulence, as her role changed from Galatea coming alive for her lover to Dido abandoned by hers. The danger of an art less embodied than hers—and the danger posed by Keats's urn but not his ode—is that it can replace the beautifully contingent, fragile power of the lived and passing moment of human passion with a static and thus infinitely reproducible because not unique and passing aesthetic image. The images of the lovers in the second and third stanzas of Keats's ode, like the images in Rowlandson's etching of Pygmalion and Galatea or on many actual Grecian urns, move towards the infinitely reproducible world of pornographic sexuality—reproducible not only in the sense that pornographic images and texts endlessly repeat on another, providing the same acts, positions, variations over and over again, but also in the sense that one can always return to the pornographic text or image to discover the same sexual moment. Part of the appeal of pornography is that it is "All breathing human passion far above," that it offers forever the same arousal, it promises the same fulfillment free from the contingent complications of the disagreeables of lived life. While lived sexuality may be now satisfying, now frustrating, now full of love, now almost mechanical, now seemingly perfect, now frighteningly routine, a pornographic text offers the identical pleasure over and over again. Every time we turn to Rowlandson's print, we will see the same moment of foreplay; every time we read Keats's urn we will see the same love "ever warm and still to be enjoyed." If the mechanical reproduction of works of art threatens the aura of art, pornographic reproduction threatens the aura of sensual life itself. In refusing the status of the Classic, the True—which can be infinitely reproduced because it claims to be eternally the same independent of form or context—and in rejecting the appeal of the pornographic—with its endless reiteration of masculine satisfaction—Keats's ode, in its Cockney classicism of contextual contingency and of the embodied erotic of an Emma Hamilton, defends art and life against both reductions.

JAMES CHANDLER

An "1819 Temper": Keats and the History of Psyche[†]

Rehabilitating Psyche

Characteristically, Keats himself gives us reason to regard the *Ode to Psyche* as a new beginning in his poetic development. Enclosing a copy to George and Georgiana on April 30, Keats prefaces it by saying that it is "the last I have written" and "the first and the only one with which I have taken even moderate pains—I have for the most part dash'd of[f] my lines in a hurry. This I have done leisurely—I think it reads the more richly for it and will I hope encourage me to write other thing[s] in even a more peacable and healthy spirit" (p. 331). It seems fair to say that one reason for the special "pains" Keats took with this poem—"pains" becomes a loaded term in

† From *England in 1819: The Politics of Literary Culture and the Case of Romantic Historicism* (Chicago: University of Chicago Press, 1998), pp. 409–25. Reprinted by permission of the author and University of Chicago Press. The author's notes have been edited. Page numbers for letters refer to this Norton Critical Edition.

the context of a fable involving arduous tasks and trials—was that its subject matter, the fable of Psyche, had just come to *mean* so much to him. It allegorized what he took to be issues of moment. That Keats composed the *Ode to Psyche* to be a kind of manifesto poem is evident from the way in which it signals connection with other poems that had themselves been offered or regarded as poetic manifestos: Wordsworth's prospectus to *The Recluse* and several of his related lyrics, Shelley's response to the Wordsworthian program in *Alastor* and *Mont Blanc*, and less immediately, Milton's *Ode on the Morning of Christ's Nativity*. The fable of Psyche afforded Keats the opportunity to write his own psychic development large and to do so in terms most apposite to what he would call, later in 1819, the "present struggle" of his own historical situation (p. 366).

Though Keats, like Tighe, drew on Apuleius, and says as much, even the most cursory glance at the *Ode to Psyche* reveals that, unlike Tighe, and indeed unlike most earlier writers on Psyche, Keats does not actually retell the fable itself. * * * In lieu of retelling the fable, Keats offers an act of historiography in the unlikely form of a verse apostrophe, a form signaled at the outset: "O Goddess! hear these tuneless numbers, wrung / By sweet enforcement and remembrance dear, / And pardon that thy secrets should be sung / Even into thine own soft-conched ear" (ll. 1–4). How the poem moves from the present tense of the historical present (as opposed to a historical present tense) is crucial to understanding how the poem achieves its "history effect" within the severe constraints of the lyric form.

The question of history in this poem has been obscured, even vexed, because of a striking feature of its structure: the chiastic arrangement of its stanzas. The first and last of the four stanzas address Psyche while offering different set-piece descriptions of her and her situation; the middle two stanzas address Psyche while offering set-piece accounts of the rites, instruments, and institutions of her proper worship. * * *

On the reading I propose, the iterations function historiographically, though perhaps, as in Marx's notion of repetition, with generic variation in the repeated events. The catalogue is introduced in stanza two:

> O latest born and loveliest vision far
>   Of all Olympus' faded hierarchy!
> Fairer than Phœbe's sapphire-region'd star,
>   Or Vesper, amorous glow-worm of the sky;
> Fairer than these, though temple thou hast none,
>   Nor altar heap'd with flowers;
> Nor virgin-choir to make delicious moan
>   Upon the midnight hours;
> No voice, no lute, no pipe, no incense sweet
>   From chain-swung censer teeming;
> No shrine, no grove, no oracle, no heat
>   Of pale-mouth'd prophet dreaming. (ll. 24–35)

Without actually rehearsing anything that might count as a version of Apuleius's narrative, Keats has effected a key displacement of it in this catalogue of failed obeisance and subsequent compensation. For in Apuleius's account, the worship of Psyche as a mortal leaves Venus neglected, and it is because *Venus's* rituals are going unobserved and her fanes unattended that she calls in her son Cupid against Psyche in the first place.

The impression of the centrality of stanzas 2 and 3 in the poem is deepened by the conspicuous length of the catalogue that is repeated in detail in the poet's entreaty to the goddess Psyche that he be allowed to compensate her:

> . . . let me be thy choir, and make a moan
>   Upon the midnight hours;
> Thy voice, thy lute, thy pipe, thy incense sweet
>   From swinged censer teeming;
> Thy shrine, thy grove, thy oracle, thy heat
>   Of pale-mouth'd prophet dreaming. (ll. 44–49)

The substitution of the "no" by the "thy" (or by the "my"-*as*-"thy") is obviously foregrounded by the wholesale repetition of the other terms, but it is simply impossible to understand how the iteration functions in the poem without addressing the passage (i.e., the opening lines of stanza 3) that is itself given such emphasis by virtue of its bridging of the two catalogues.

The transition between the two appearances of the catalogue is effected by the following difficult and finely worked verses:

> O brightest! though too late for antique vows,
>   Too, too late for the fond believing lyre,
> When holy were the haunted forest boughs,
>   Holy the air, the water, and the fire;
> Yet even in these days so far retir'd
>   From happy pieties, thy lucent fans,
>   Fluttering among the faint Olympians,
> I see, and sing by my own eyes inspired.
> So let me be thy choir. . . . (ll. 36–44)

The difficulties here lie in part in the syntactical ambiguities created by Keats's use—throughout the poem but here particularly—of participle forms in different grammatical positions (e.g., "believing," "haunted," "retir'd," "fluttering"). The tense or time of these participles is not in every case clear. As with the crucial syntactical confusion of the speaker and the nightingale in Keats's next great Ode ("'Tis not through envy of thy happy lot, / But being too happy in thine happiness, / That *thou* . . ."), the indicators of reference here are hard to make out. "Fluttering," for example, itself flutters among a variety of possible times and cases in the syntax of these lines, as if replaying at large that most clichéd of Spoonerisms (but most apposite for Psyche): "butterfly" / "flutter by." But even as they make ambiguous the issues of time and circumstance in the poem, these lines already begin to recreate a narrative in which to reestablish intelligibility for the iterated elements in the two catalogues. This narrative is not itself being offered as a version of Apuleius's fable but instead as a developmental history of Western culture that can actually be laid out in a subtextual time line plotting the poem's crucial points of reference in the past, a line on which Apuleius's moment itself can be located. Thus, where in the final distancing moment of *The Eve of St. Agnes* the speaker withdraws to a perspective on the historical present tense of the action in which it all now appears as having happened "ages long ago," the *Ode to Psyche* gives historicist force to the old cliché by actually tracing out these ages over time.

It is not just that the *Ode* is an epochal history in which Apuleius's moment itself has a place. It is also that the stages of this history, indeed, are projected backward and forward from the post-Augustan moment of Psyche's mythologization in Apuleius, as if the mythical apotheosis of Psyche, instead of the mythical incarnation of Christ, were being offered as the pivot of western religious history. Keats acknowledges his reliance on Apuleius in the late-April journal-letter entry to George and Georgiana: "You must recollect that Psyche was not embodied as a goddess before the time of Apulieus the Platonist who lived after the Agustan age, and consequently the Goddess was never worshipped or sacrificed to with any of the ancient fervour—and perhaps never thought of in the old religion— I am more orthodox than to let a hethan Goddess be so neglected" (p. 331). The poem's first major historical shift is premised on the distinction between early and late antiquity, whereby the "old religion" of early antiquity is explicitly associated with "antique vows" and the "fond believing lyre." Later antiquity is marked by a skepticism that we may hold responsible for the faintness of the older Olympian gods and the fading of their hierarchy. This gradual disappearance or demotion coincides with the "appearance" of the beautiful Psyche and her promotion to divine status. Apuleius's fable, in other words, which dates to about the mid-second century A.D., is not only a *late story* of Psyche as a goddess but also, explicitly, an account of her *late apotheosis*. Psyche begins as a human being in a plot of the gods but is promoted to divinity and granted immortality at the end.

Further, if we stop to ask what, apart from her beauty, characterizes Psyche in Apuleius's fable, we find that it is not her faith or her piety toward the existing divinities. Psyche represents the apotheosis not of fideism but of skepticism, or at least of an empiricism that insists on the proof of the senses. The eighteenth-century connection of Psyche with empirical sense is clear from Voltaire's *Philosophical Dictionary*, which informs its readers that "the Greeks had invented the faculty *Psyche* for the sensations."[1] It is precisely Psyche's empirical curiosity about her invisible lover, her wish to see for herself, that sets her on the course to immortality. And this will-to-seeing remains unreformed in the course of her arduous travails, as evidenced in her inability to refrain from opening the box containing Proserpine's beauty in the final stage of the last quest. The Keatsian speaker alludes to this skeptical, show-me brand of empiricism in the *Ode to Psyche* and makes it part of the assimilation of Psyche to his own psyche. Just as she can be described as "too late for the fond believing lyre," so, when the speaker identifies the modernity of his own frame of reference, his fitness to make amends for centuries of neglect, he declares: "I see, and sing, by my own eyes inspired" (l. 43).

The late-antique period on the poem's underlying time line, then, is one implicitly characterized by a skeptical empiricism. The next period that follows it on that time line, though less explicit, is just as clearly built into the poem's historical frame of reference. We can bring its contours to light by asking why, given her deification, Psyche has neither temple nor any of the usual accouterments of divinity. * * * The skepticism that attended the

---

1. Voltaire, *Philosophical Dictionary*, trans. and ed. Peter Gay (New York: Harcourt, Brace & World, 1962), p. 470.

fading of the Olympians from popular consciousness presumably had something to do with this, but so too, surely, did the Christianization of Rome, which dates roughly to the era of Apuleius. Christianity took over the doctrine of the immortality of the soul, but removed it from the history in which, from Plato himself to the writer Keats refers to as "Apuleius the Platonist," it was developing. In orthodox Christianity, one might argue, the deification of the soul is not purchased at the expense of the Sky God's "fading"—at the expense of the many gods, but not of the One God.

This is where the echoes of Milton's *Nativity Ode*, astutely tallied in Vendler's account,[2] can be most helpful, for they strongly suggest that Keats is producing a late riposte to the Christian challenge to the authority of pagan mythologies. Milton, in terms that reappear all over Keats's poem, produced an ode on the birth of Christ in which that moment spells the end of polytheism and the fulfillment of the plan of the God of Scripture. One stanza from the Ode suffices to illustrate:

> The Oracles are dumb,
> No voice or hideous hum
>   Runs through the arched roof in words deceiving.
> *Apollo* from his shrine
> Can no more divine,
>   With hollow shriek the steep of *Delphus* leaving.
> No nightly trance, or breathed spell,
> Inspires the pale-ey'd Priest from the prophetic cell. (173–80)[3]

At the same time, however, as a poet of the English seventeenth century, Milton himself belongs to the historical moment when the Christian challenge to paganism and classicism was beginning to meet stronger and stronger resistance—Milton was staving off a perceived threat. And Keats, aware of Milton's historical position, implies an intellectual history, familiar enough to us, that was just in his time becoming conventional after more than a millennium and a half of the Christian epoch, a period notorious for the perversities of chivalry and romance of the sort "smoked" in *The Eve of St. Agnes*, the neoclassicism of the Renaissance and the New Science of the seventeenth and eighteenth centuries are understood to undermine the ecclesiastical hegemony, to systematize the powers of observation, awaken the senses, and liberate the peoples of Europe from the dark ages.* * *

Implicit in Keats's developmental history, then, is an epoch of "enlightenment," in which superstition is explained and the political uses of superstition exposed. The way was now open to recover the "prior orthodoxy" (as Keats wryly calls it) of heathenism, to return to the developing course of pagan mythological consciousness—to pick up so to speak where Apuleius left off, with the decline of the sky gods and the myth of the elevation of the human soul to divine immortality through the agency of love. But what it means to pick up where Apuleius left off is not so simple a matter, since the skepticism implicitly celebrated in his account led first, as it were, to the blind faith of Christianity and then to the sensational skepticism of an Enlightenment that, in certain moments, lost sight of the soul altogether. Thus, Voltaire, in the same *Dictionnaire philosophique* where he had defined

---

2. Vendler, *The Odes of John Keats* (Cambridge: Harvard University Press, 1987).
3. *On the Morning of Christ's Nativity*, in John Milton, *Complete Poems and Major Prose*, ed. Merritt Y. Hughes (Indianapolis: Bobbs-Merrill, 1957), p. 48.

"Psyche" in terms of mere sensation, included an entry on the soul (*âme*), in which he analytically dismantled all "fine systems about souls that your philosophy has fabricated" without offering another in their place.[4] The "neglect" of Psyche that Keats playfully describes himself as too "orthodox" a heathen to countenance is thus a double neglect: the neglect of the pagan-Platonic "Psyche" in favor of the Christian "soul" and the neglect of the Psyche/soul in any form by the mechanist strain in Enlightenment moral philosophy.

* * * [C]an we trace the historical logic of Psyche, the transformations in the concept and character of the soul, from the mythology of the ancients to the enlightened sensory empiricism of the moderns without suffering either the soul's superstitious and retrograde debasement by the Christian church or its complete elimination by a hyperanalytic enlightened mechanism? Putting the problem this way allows one to register the full force of those allusions to Milton's *Nativity Ode* as establishing the place of Renaissance Christianity in a scheme of development. It also allows one to see that "picking up where Apuleius left off" involves neither striving to recapture Apuleius's moment nor interpreting the discrepancies between the *ab* of stanzas one and two and the *ba* of stanzas three and four as failures to achieve this. Rather, it involves continuing a process that Apuleius had advanced and that a millennium and a half of Christianity had interrupted. That the process was already underway with Apuleius is clear from the way in which he is given credit for aiding in the promotion of the human Psyche to divinity as the Olympians fade.

* * *

* * * I suggested at the start that the present tense of the poet's initial address is historically indeterminate. The present tense implicit in the end of the poem, on the other hand, is a historically determinate one. We are led by this line of analysis to inquire into the contours of the present scene, the present "time" (as distinct from what Keats calls "the time of Apuleius") regarded as a scene or situation. . . .

The Politics of "Soul Making"

As a problem for the *Ode to Psyche* itself, the question of the present scene might redirect attention to the opening stanza to see if what is initially understood there as an ahistorical present must not be reread in the light of the poem's conclusion. Looking again at that opening stanza, we can now observe that after the salutation to Psyche we are given a brief description of the poet's recent vision. After asking the goddess Psyche to "hear these tuneless numbers, wrung / By sweet enforcement and remembrance dear," the speaker shifts into a past-tense report:

> Surely I dreamt to-day, or did I see
>   The winged Psyche with awaken'd eyes?
> I wander'd in a forest thoughtlessly,
>   And, on the sudden, fainting with surprise,
> Saw two fair creatures, couched side by side
>   In deepest grass, beneath the whisp'ring roof

---

4. Voltaire, *Philosophical Dictionary,* p. 66.

Of leaves and trembled blossoms, where there ran
A brooklet, scarce espied. (ll. 5–12)

Now, one way of seeing this first stanza as taking place in historical time would be to identify the historicity of this little lyric narrative: "I wandered. . . ." Is it possible to place this mode of utterance in a discursive history? The answer, I believe, is decidedly yes, in that Keats's lines so neatly mimic what was already a well-known lyric of his own time (as it has remained for ours). It is Wordsworth's stanzas on the daffodils from the 1807 *Poems*, which had been recently reprinted (in 1815) as part of his major round of publication in 1814–15: "I wandered lonely as a cloud / . . . When all at once I saw. . . ."[5] The echo of Wordsworth's lyric would count for less here, if it were not also a signal of Keats's appropriation of Wordsworth's characteristic structural device for these memory lyrics. A first stanza of "thoughtless" vision, followed by meditation, followed by a revisiting of the scene of the first stanza "in thought"—to use the phrase from the *Immortality Ode* ("We in thought will join your throng").

But what kind of sense does it make to think of the historically present "scene" of the *Ode to Psyche* as one somehow presided over by Wordsworth's poetry? We know from independent evidence that the contemporary poet whom Keats personally regarded as most influential in setting the scene for his (Keats's) own writing was almost certainly Wordsworth. He is also the poet whom Keats read as most promising in his impulses to urge this twofold modern challenge, i.e., to mount resistance at once to enlightenment and to Christianity. We know that Keats regarded *The Excursion* as one of the three great wonders of his age, but we also know precisely which part of it most attracted his interest: the Wanderer's account in book 4 of the appeal of ancient mythology to a deracinated modernity. * * * Wordsworth's writings about pagan mythology betray deep ambivalences in that one can find as much evidence of his renunciation of it as of his endorsement of it.[6] When, at Benjamin Haydon's insistence, Keats recited his *Hymn to Pan* to Wordsworth at their only meeting in 1817, a poem using some of the older poet's own material, Wordsworth responded with chilling curtness: "A Very pretty piece of Paganism."[7] Nonetheless, Keats clearly saw in Wordsworth's most programmatic work the signs of tendencies he took to be more "advanced" and less superstitiously Christian than such a comment would indicate.

Some of the evidence that Keats saw these tendencies lies in the way he deploys Wordsworthian terms, idioms, and structures in the *Ode to Psyche*, especially the echoes of the lines that Wordsworth appended to *The Excursion*. These lines, we recall, were meant to serve as a "prospectus to the design and scope" of the massive modernizing poetic project of which *The Excursion* and the yet-unpublished *Prelude* formed a part. The "remembrance dear" of line two of the *Ode*, for example, echoes the famous opening of this text:

5. Wordsworth, *Poems in Two Volumes, and Other Poems, 1800–1807* (Ithaca, N.Y.: Cornell University Press, 1983), p. 331.
6. See Alex Zwerdling, "Wordsworth and Greek Myth," *University of Toronto Quarterly* 33 (July 1964): 341–54.
7. Hyder E. Rollins, ed., *The Keats Circle*, 2 vols. (Cambridge, MA.: Harvard University Press, 1948), 2:143–44.

> On Man, on Nature, and on Human Life
> Musing in Solitude, I oft perceive
> Fair trains of imagery before me rise,
> Accompanied by feelings of delight
> Pure, or with no unpleasing sadness mixed;
> And I am conscious of affecting thoughts
> And dear remembrances, whose presence soothes
> Or elevates the Mind, intent to weigh
> The good and evil of our mortal state.[8]

We follow the echo to a textual site in which the *Ode to Psyche* seems to have been conceived. Here is Wordsworth defining his project as the attempt to make his poetry out of his own unconscious associations ("affecting thoughts" and "dear remembrances") and to make his subject the "individual mind" in its relation to the soul and to the world of outward circumstances. He goes on to explain:

> —To these emotions, whenceso'er they come,
> Whether from the breath of outward circumstance,
> Or from the Soul—an impulse to herself,
> I would give utterance in numerous Verse.
> . . .
> Of the individual Mind that keeps her own
> Inviolate retirement . . .
> I sing: "fit audience let me find though few!" (ll. 10–23)

Toward the end of the *Ode to Psyche* Keats will speak of building a fane for Psyche "in some untrodden region of my mind," a distinct echo of Wordsworth's later claim in the prospectus to look boldly into what he calls "the Mind of Man, / My haunt and the main region of my song." The added word, "untrodden," is itself a Wordsworthian importation, this time from "She dwelt among the untrodden ways."[9]

My point is not that Keats wishes to "smoke" Wordsworth with his *Ode to Psyche*. It is rather that Keats echoes Wordsworth in such a way as to mark the latter's most important work as already a kind of *Ode to Psyche*, a poetry with implications similar to those that Keats is arguing for. Both texts present themselves as modern acknowledgments of the notion that true divinity resides not with the sky gods, in the heaven of heavens, but, as Wordsworth puts it, in a world "to which the heaven of heavens is but a veil" (l. 30). More specifically, Wordsworth's emphasis on the soul—here and, just as famously, in the *Immortality Ode*—needs to be seen, as Keats intuitively understood, against the back-drop of enlightenment attempts to dissolve the soul into the mechanics of the body.

I have argued elsewhere that Wordsworth defined his great post-1797 literary project against the intellectual background of *Idéologie*.[1] This was the

---

8. Ernest de Selincourt and Helen Darbishire, eds., *The Poetical Works of William Wordsworth,* 5 vols. (Oxford: Clarendon, 1949), 5:3. And see, of course, M. H. Abrams's book-length commentary on the Prospectus in *Natural Supernaturalism* (New York: W. W. Norton, 1971), passim.
9. For a sensitive account of the orchestrating of these and other echoes in Keats's allusive text, see Donald C. Goellnicht, " 'In Some Untrodden Region of My Mind': Double Discourse in Keats's 'Ode to Psyche,' " *Mosaic* 21 (Spring 1988): 91–103. For a comprehensive tally of Keats echoes and recorded readings of Wordsworth, see Beth Lau, *Keats's Reading of the Romantic Poets* (Ann Arbor: University of Michigan Press, 1991), pp. 11–69.
1. See my *Wordsworth's Second Nature* (Chicago: University of Chicago Press, 1984), pp. 216–34.

program of the Directory, that hyper-Enlightenment phase of the French Revolution between the end of the Reign of Terror and the Napoleonic coup (1794–98). It was at that time that the Institut National was founded in Paris under the leadership of Destutt de Tracy for purposes of regrounding the work of the enlightened Girondist party on a purer scientific basis. The word itself, "idéologie," De Tracy's coinage, was supposed to name the core discipline of this new educational scheme in such a way as to keep it free from all ambiguity or superstition. One of the terms explicitly rejected by De Tracy's committee was "psychology," and it was ruled out precisely because it carried associations with the concept of the "soul."[2] A similar set of developments can be traced in late-eighteenth-century England, where debates about mind and body engaged by the likes of Richard Price and Joseph Priestley were repeatedly articulated in relation to the question of the soul's immortality and inevitably given a political cast. Addressing these debates on the reconception of the soul in this period, Simon Schaffer concludes that the "combination of a philosophical materialism and conjectural history implied a revised account of a future state."[3] And this "revised account" is the one I claim Keats takes as his point of departure in working out the meaning of the Psyche fable in 1819.

All this becomes reasonably evident in Keats's long meditation on a new theory of the soul in the journal-letter entry to George and Georgiana written a few days before the *Ode to Psyche* itself, on April 21:

> The common cognomen of this world among the misguided and superstitious is "a vale of tears" from which we are to be redeemed by a certain arbitrary interposition of God and taken to Heaven—What a little circumscribed straightened notion! Call the world if you Please "The vale of Soul-Making." Then you will find out the use of the world . . . I say "*Soul making.*" Soul as distinguished from an Intelligence. There may be intelligences or sparks of the divinity in millions—but they are not Souls till they acquire identities, till each one is personally itself. Intelligences are atoms of perception—they know and they see and they are pure, in short they are God—how then are Souls to be made? How then are these sparks which are God to have identity given them—so as ever to possess a bliss peculiar to each ones individual existence? How, but by the medium of a world like this? This point I sincerely wish to consider because I think it a grander system of salvation than the chrystian religion—or rather it is a system of Spirit-creation. (p. 330)

The posture of "enlightenment" is conspicuous here. Keats explicitly opposes his comments to the views of the "misguided and superstitious" at the start, and, in reviewing his speculations a few sentences on, he claims to have sketched "a system of Salvation which does not affront our reason and humanity" (p. 330). At the same time, this exercise is just as obviously an effort to recuperate the concept of the soul from those who would deny it outright. The sense of a historical present, defined by the tension between

---

2. See Emmet Kennedy, *A Philosophe in the Age of Revolution* (Philadelphia: American Philosophical Society, 1978), pp. 44–47, and Jan Goldstein, *Console and Classify: The French Psychiatric Profession in the Nineteenth Century* (Cambridge: Cambridge University Press, 1987), p. 246.
3. Simon Schaffer, "States of Mind: Enlightenment and Natural Philosophy," in *The Languages of Psyche*, ed. G. S. Rousseau (Berkeley: University of California Press, 1990), p. 285.

enlightenment analysis and Christian superstition, seems very much assumed in Keats's rhetoric here.

* * *

* * * When Wordsworth shifted attention from "ideology" to "psychology," from the brain to the soul, in poems such as the *Immortality Ode*, the occasion of the new poetic articulation is, famously, the lost sense of the "visionary gleam." And, as he explained in a later commentary on the poem, his default framework for writing his way through the difficult issues of the poem was the Platonic myth of the soul's preexistence. Wordsworth referred to his use of Plato in the *Ode* as a kind of convenience, an Archimedean point on which to stand—just as, in invoking the Platonizing cosmology for use in his prospectus, he calls his own poem a domain in terms of which the Heaven of Heavens is but a veil. In both poems by Wordsworth, as in Keats's account, the soul, Psyche, enjoys a kind of provisional, self-consciously post-Enlightenment rehabilitation. The relevant difference is that Wordsworth represses the historical dimension of his argument, resting content with making quantitative comparisons to Milton, claiming (for example) that he needs a "greater muse." Keats, by contrast, stresses the chronological dimension, suggesting a temporal development in which both he and Milton (and Wordsworth, for that matter) have their part. The emphasis on what is (necessarily) "greater" in Wordsworth shifts to what is (historically) "later" in Keats.

* * * [W]e might say that the historical "present" of the speaker's final utterance in the *Ode to Psyche*, its place on his time line, is 1819. This is the moment when the poet offers his individual mind as the site of a divinity, the principle of human life, newly reacknowledged and only now, in the history of Psyche, able to be celebrated as it ought to be, and married, as it ought to be, with the principle of love that enables it to reproduce itself. On this reading, I would argue, the conclusion of the poem is not so "private" as it is often thought. For the putative internality of poem's final vision appears at the end of a public history. The Psyche who will lodge in Keats's mind—become *Keats's* psyche—has a history, is indeed partly constituted by a history, which tells of how she has been conceived over time. She can be what Keats now claims she is by virtue of his way of following Wordsworth's lead in seeing her that way. The ways of soul-making in 1819, in other words, will assume a more highly developed form by virtue of the recognition that *that* is all we know on earth and all we need to know. Anything else is just what Keats calls superstition.

ALAN BEWELL

"To Autumn" and the Curing of Space[†]

The Quest for Autumn

In 1832, in the preface to his *Poetical Works*, Leigh Hunt argued that one reason recent criticism had been so critical of his writing was that it had

† From *Romanticism and Colonial Disease*, by Alan Bewell (Baltimore: The Johns Hopkins University Press, 1999), pp. 175–84. Reprinted by permission of the author and of the Johns Hopkins University Press. The author's notes have been edited. Page numbers for letters refer to this Norton Critical Edition. *L* refers to Rollins's edition.

understood its "tropicalisms" as a personal *affectation* rather than an expression of his cultural background, his father having been born in Barbados. "It was the mistake of the criticism of a northern climate," he writes, "to think that the occasional quaintnesses and neologisms, which formerly disfigured the *Story of Rimini*, arose out of affectation. . . . While I was writing them, I never imagined that they were not proper to be indulged in. I have tropical blood in my veins, inherited through many generations, and was too full of impulse and sincerity to pretend to anything I did not feel" (xv–xvi).[1] The production of the "cockney school of poetry" it seems, arose from a criticism that mistook authentic tropical excess for social mannerism. In distancing himself from this colonial style, suggesting that the "formerly disfiguring" aspects of his verse derived from cultural differences and from inexperience with the demands of a literature of a "northern climate," Hunt was following the lead of his previous protégé, for in "To Autumn" Keats also sought to write against the dangerous tropicalism of his earlier verse. The subject of the poem is deceptively simple. What could be more natural, one might think, than for an English poet walking through the Winchester countryside in September 1819 to write a poem on autumn? Only a month later, Shelley did the same thing in "Ode to the West Wind."

Yet at a time when colonialism had made apparent the connection between health and climate, the seasonal cycle of spring, summer, fall, and winter was not taken for granted. As James Thomson well knew when he wrote *The Seasons*, this cycle was what tropical regions lacked, and over the course of the eighteenth century it had become a basis for claims about the epidemiological superiority of England over other regions of the globe. "To Autumn" is a veritable catalog of national imagery—the vines, apples, gourds, and hazelnuts, and the "thatch-eves," "moss'd cottage-trees," "cyder press," "stubble-plains," and "garden-croft[s]'s" of English landscape painting. In what remains a classic analysis, Geoffrey Hartman suggests that "To Autumn" is "an ideological poem whose very form expresses a national idea." Delineating a geography of literary form, he points out that its ideological commitments are registered not in thematic, but in formal terms, as the "English or Hesperian" lyric, the product of a westering consciousness, "overcomes not only the traditional type of sublime poem but the 'Eastern' or epiphanic consciousness essential to it." He notes its unfevered quality: " 'To Autumn' seems to absorb rather than extrovert that questing imagination whose breeding fancies, feverish overidentifications, and ambitious projects motivate the other odes."[2] It is indeed a poem in which Keats sought to create a poetic space that would no longer bring on fever. Geography, medicine, and aesthetics are thus profoundly allied. Most treatments of the impersonality of the poem, which speak of its "transhistorical" subject and the complete absence of the poet from the poem, emphasize the universality of its climate and its landscape, thus ignoring its embodiment of the national ideal of "temperate space."[3] Climate and

---

1. In his *Autobiography*, Hunt is quite proud of his West Indian and Philadelphian origins. His father, a "true exotic" from Barbados, "ought not to have been transplanted" to America, he writes (10–11). In explaining both his family's and his own financial difficulties, he argues that the fault lay in "the West Indian blood of which we all partake, and which has disposed all of us, more or less, to a certain aversion from business" (17).
2. Hartman, *The Fate of Reading and Other Essays* (Chicago: University of Chicago Press, 1975), p. 126.
3. See, for instance, Bate, p. 581. For a valuable discussion of the importance of weather in the poem, see J. Bate, "Living with the Weather," *SiR* 35 (1996): 431–47.

landscape thus are not a repression of the political but are instrumental in articulating this ideal, for a primary assertion of the poem is that the best environments exhibit a balance of extremes. As the season between summer and winter, moderating both the cold "mists" of America and the hot "fruitfulness" of the tropics, autumn in England is portrayed as a space of "mellow" fruition, for both places and poets.

More successfully than *Hyperion*, "To Autumn" enacts a curing of space by tempering pathogenic extremes. These extreme geographical environments, linked imaginatively to colonial spaces, are not removed from the poem, however, but instead enter its almost classical balance as elements to be moderated. The poem does not simply represent and celebrate a detropicalized England; it enacts its coming into being as the clearing of the landscape in the harvest combines with the cooling weather to temper a space that would otherwise risk overabundance, disease, and decay. To understand the construction of this healthy landscape, therefore, one must also register the pathogenic geographies that not only inhabit the borders of the poem but enter into and are transformed within it, as the "cold" and the "hot" are remade as the "warm." By examining Keats's references to tropical environments, which constitute one pole of a geography of pathogenic extremes, I hope to show how the idea of a healthy, unfevered English environment during this period was always constructed in relational terms, as a hybrid tempering of the dangers of colonial environments. The landscape of "To Autumn" constitutes a kind of biomedical allegory of the coming into being of English climatic space out of its dangerous geographical alternatives.

The opening lines epitomize the differential patterning shaping the entire poem:

> Season of mists and mellow fruitfulness,
>   Close bosom-friend of the maturing sun;
> Conspiring with him how to load and bless
>   With fruit the vines that round the thatch-eves run . . .
>   (1–4)

Critics have justifiably seen this harmonic interaction of sun and soil in positive terms, as an emblem of the way the autumnal landscape "conspire[s]" that is, "breathes together" (*conspirare*), with the late-season sun "to load and bless" humankind with a harvest. But one should not ignore the possible darker breathings of landscape that this balance displaces, for medical topographers saw the combination of a rich landscape overloaded with vegetation and a hot sun as the primary cause of miasmas, the "misty pestilence" of *The Fall of Hyperion* (1.205). James Annesley argues, for instance, that "when the action of the sun upon the rich moist soil takes place, exhalations are formed of a more noxious description, and malignant remittents, continued fevers of a bad type, yellow fevers, and dysenteries, usurp the place of the milder forms of disease, which the same place, when differently circumstanced, will produce."[4] Conspiring can become conspiracy, just as "close" is the antithesis of those healthy spaces "open to the currents of air" that Keats celebrates in his letter to Taylor (*L*, 2:155).[5] As William

---

4. James Annesley, *Researches into the Causes, Nature, and Treatment of the More Prevalent Diseases of India, and of Warm Climates Generally* (2nd ed. London: Longman, Brown, Green, and Longmans, 1841), p. 22.

5. For a suggestive discussion of the political valences of "conspiring" in the context of the recent events at Manchester, see Roe, *John Keats and the Culture of Dissent*, pp. 253–57.

Babington and James Curry (who spent eight months in Bengal) noted in lectures similar to those Keats attended at Guy's Hospital, this dangerous combination of heat and decaying vegetation explained the greater incidence of fever during autumn: "Operation of heat shewn by the more noxious effects of marsh effluvia in warm, than in cold climates and seasons;—and especially in autumn, when heat is often greatest, and many vegetables spontaneously die and rot."[6] Under the influence of a less "mature" sun, such a "loading" of the earth, ripening fruit "to the core," would hardly be a blessing. Focusing on the conditions by which environmental pathogens were generated—the conspiracy of sun and soil that produces steams, mists, miasmas, effluvias, and "vegetable putrefactions"— Keats tempers the breath of autumn. There is a danger too in "continual summer," as life in the tropics (where "warm days . . . never cease") made abundantly clear. Too much honey makes the bees' hive uninhabitable: "For summer has o'er-brimm'd their clammy cells" (10–11). "Clammy" suggests "sticky," but it also conveys even more vividly the cold sweats, the "clammy perspirations" that accompany fever (Babington and Curry, p. 54), as in Glaucus's declaration that "a clammy dew is beading on my brow" (*Endymion* 3.568).

In constructing this temperate landscape, Keats drew substantially on Leigh Hunt's 15 September 1819 *Examiner* column, "The Calendar of Nature," which I quote in part:

> Autumn has now arrived. This is the month of the migration of birds, of the finished harvest, of nut-gathering, of cyder and perry-making, and, towards the conclusion, of the change of colour in trees. The swallows, and many other soft-billed birds that feed on insects, disappear for the warmer climates, leaving only a few stragglers behind, probably from weakness or sickness, who hide themselves in caverns and other sheltered places, and occasionally appear upon warm days. (574)

The three great themes of autumn—harvest, the coloring and defoliation of the landscape, and the southern migration—shape Hunt's naturalistic description. Despite his emphasis on the vitality of the season, he nevertheless notes that for the sick, and for the "few stragglers" who cannot migrate, it is a difficult time. Its "chill and foggy" mornings and evenings are "not wholesome to those who either do not or cannot guard against them." It is a season of abundance: "There is grain for men, birds, and horses, hay for the cattle, loads of fruit on the trees, and swarms of fish in the ocean." Nevertheless, for "the soft-billed birds which feed on insects," it is time for their departure to the "southern countries." For Hunt, England is structured not only by climatic, but also by dietary temperance: "Repasts apparently more harmless are alone offered to the creation upon our temperate soil."

Nicholas Roe has recently demonstrated that Hunt used his column to comment indirectly on recent political events and to call for political reform (pp. 257–63).[7] Roe's analysis recognizes how active a role constructions of nature played in the conceptualization of political life during

---

6. William Babington and James Curry, *Outlines of a Course of Lectures on the Practice of Medicine, as Delivered in the Medical School of Guy's Hospital* (London: Bensley, 1802–6), p. 15.
7. Roe, *Keats and the Culture of Dissent*. See also William Keach, "Cockney Couplets: Keats and the Politics of Style," *Studies in Romanticism* 25 (1986): 182–96.

this period.[8] This discourse drew much of its sustenance and vocabulary from a larger "politics of climate," grounded in the biomedical construction of national environments. In this regard the opening paragraph to Annesley's chapter "General View of the Causes Chiefly Productive of Disease in Warm Climates, Particularly in India" provides a useful counterpoint to the "Calendar of Nature." Annesley insists on the importance of medicine for any adequate "philosophical, civil, or political" view of societies. "When the obvious and intimate relations subsisting between the earth's surface and the human species—between man and the soil on which he moves, the productions of the earth which surround and feed him, and the air which he is constantly inhaling into his body are considered—the conditions of these agents, as far as they can be recognized by sensible properties, or inferred from their manifest effects, become matters of great interest in medical science, and of surpassing importance, in philosophical, civil, and political points of view." Conditions of the atmosphere not only are "the chief and immediate sources . . . of the strength and perfection of the mental and corporeal constitution of man . . . and . . . of the diseases which harass him, stunting his physical and moral growth, or sweeping him from amongst living animals, of which he is the head and master," but are "also the most productive, although the more remote causes of national character—of advancement in all the arts, sciences, and refinements of life in some countries, and of moral and physical debasement in others."

Following a logic similar to Keats's, Annesley argues that the differences between the physical environments of temperate and tropical regions shape their political institutions, "the freedom, prosperity, and greatness" of the inhabitants of the former, and "the degenerate and debased condition of the species" in the latter. Hunt's demand for a fairer and more balanced distribution of freedoms ("The poet still takes advantage of the exuberance of harvest and the sign of the Zodiac in this month, to read us a lesson on justice" [574]) is thus based on the belief that a liberal politics should be the natural produce of a temperate climate. As Annesley suggests:

> The constitutions of the atmosphere derived from soil and situation, according to their nature, are not only the productive sources of disease, but also the chief spring of the perfection of the human frame, and of its degeneracy—the influential causes of the various degrees of human science presented to us in the different kingdoms of the world—of the freedom and greatness of nations, and of their enslaved and degraded conditions—of the rise and downfall of empires. They should equally interest the scientific physician, the philosopher, the enlightened legislator, and the arbiters of the fates of nations. (8)

Read within the context of contemporary medical geography, the political, philosophical, and medical symbolics of atmosphere, Keats's attempt to create in "To Autumn" a poetic temperate space, which moderates the dangers of more extreme world environments, is not "transhistorical" but expressive of a larger geopolitics of environment that served as the ground of more specific political arguments.

---

8. McGann's "Keats and the Historical Method" has established the dominant view that politics is repressed or evaded in "To Autumn."

Keats's construction of the geography of Englishness through the active moderation of more extreme geographical environments, by cooling down and clearing away the tropical elements that enter the poem, can also be seen in the second stanza:

> Sometimes whoever seeks abroad may find
> Thee sitting careless on a granary floor,
>   Thy hair soft-lifted by the winnowing wind;
> Or on a half-reap'd furrow sound asleep,
>   Drows'd with the fume of poppies, while thy hook
> Spares the next swath and all its twined flowers. (13–18)

The phrase "whoever seeks abroad" has been reasonably glossed to mean "whoever seeks out of doors," especially since Autumn is portrayed in this stanza as an agricultural laborer. Yet more commonly, especially in medical literature, it refers to a journey outside one's own country, a "change of air." That Keats was considering going abroad at this point can hardly be doubted, yet the poem strives to produce conviction that a cure can be found at home. Recognizing this global positioning of Autumn helps explain Keats's extraordinary inclusion (oddly unremarked) of *opium*—"the fume of poppies"—in his catalog of the elements that compose an English autumn. Here Keats is recalling his letter to Taylor and his comments on the soporific and "enervating" effects of the fumes of the furrow which are now a drug. The stanza's concluding image of Autumn at a "cyder-press, with a patient look," watching "the last oozings hours by hours" suggests that time has almost come to a standstill even as it extracts the essence of summer from the landscape to the very last drop. Ooze, however, also conveys darker meanings, as it refers to marshland and to the muddy decaying sediment that was largely blamed for tropical miasmas.[9] And "patient look" provides a wonderful condensation of meaning, for Keats could hardly use these words without reference to their obvious medical meaning or to the Latin root of "patient" meaning "to suffer." In a poem that seeks to achieve a calm acceptance of time, change, and mortality, the "patient" is indeed an exemplary figure.* * *

In "To Autumn" Keats was as much intent on clearing his own poetic ground as on clearing physical space. In stanza 3, the formal features of this detropicalization are given their clearest expression. As others have noted, the opening question, "Where are the songs of spring?" recalls the feverish world of the odes, supplanted by English autumn. Here the floralism and "excess of greenth" of the earlier verse is replaced by "stubble-plains." Keatsian floralism nevertheless remains as a submerged element: the "*stubble-plains*" are more masculine, but they still have a "rosy hue" and the "barred clouds" still "bloom." The "soft-dying day" voices the deeper elegiac tones of impending mortality, yet even here the sunset, as it "touch[es] the stubble-plains with rosy hue," echoes and contrasts with the angry diseased morning of *Hyperion*: Hyperion's palace "touch'd with shade of bronzed obelisks, / Glar'd a blood-red" (1.178–79). Insect life is at a minimum (only

---

9. Annesley, for instance, argues that "the low grounds at the mouths of rivers, or along their course, are rendered thus particularly insalubrious by the deep, rich, and moist soil which form them; by the quantity of rich mud and slime deposited upon them, particularly after inundations, and by the luxuriant vegetation, part of which must necessarily in a warm climate be always undergoing decay, with which they abound" (13).

gnats and "hedge-crickets" remain), in contrast to the increasingly dominant idea of the tropics as dominated by insect life. Keats's reference to European willows, or "sallows," is another example of his extraordinary
capacity to draw health out of a context of pathogenic meanings, for a "sallow" complexion, the sickly yellowish hue caused by liver complaints, was
seen as a primary symptom of exposure to a tropical environment. Annesley remarks: "Not the least important of all the symptoms which ought to
be viewed as premonitory of intertropical diseases, are, the states of the surface of the body, and the appearance of the countenance. . . . When the
countenance is collapsed, sallow, and languid, then the powers of the system may be viewed as being deficient" (p. 143). Henry Marshall notes that
women were not exempted "from the exhausting effects of a tropical climate. They in general soon lose the plumpness of health, the countenance
becomes sallow, and the general complexion pale and colourless."[1] The
landscape of "To Autumn" presents an English face, yet it achieves this
quality differentially, by rewriting the fever-ridden features of the tropics.
   The landscape of the final stanza is still a breathing landscape, as the
"winnowing wind" of stanza 2 continues in the "light wind" of stanza 3,
upon whose soft breath the dirgelike song of the gnats rises or falls, "lives
or dies." Linda and Michael Hutcheon have noted the integral relation
between breath, song, and disease in the European discourse on tuberculosis, most notably in the dramatic figure of the consumptive operatic heroine.[2] "To Autumn" draws its song from similar sources as it rewrites dying
in English terms: the tropical environment with its sudden enteric and
hepatic fevers is rewritten in the tubercular language of a "soft-dying day."
Sallow, it is worth noting, was also used in regard to tubercular complex-
ions. In the early stages of pulmonary consumption, James Clark notes,
"the skin of such a patient will be found in an unhealthy condition: either
harsh and dry, or moist, clammy, and relaxed. Its color, too, is often
changed to a *sallow*, and, in some cases, to a dirty yellowish hue; and,
except on the cheeks, there is always a deficiency of red vessels."[3] In the
final image of the "gathering swallows" that "twitter in the skies," there is
certainly an oblique reference to the sore throat that Keats had been suffering for more than a year—"each swallow a triumph."[4] Perhaps Keats was
already considering leaving England, or maybe he was thinking of the "few
stragglers" that Hunt mentioned as being left "behind, probably from
weakness or sickness, who hide themselves in caverns and other sheltered
places, and occasionally appear on warm days?"
   In a letter to J. H. Reynolds, Keats confirms the ideal of temperateness
that shapes his view of autumn. Apparently sensing the strangeness of
applying moral categories to weather, he writes: "How beautiful the season
is now—How fine the air. A temperate sharpness about it. Really, without
joking, chaste weather—Diane skies" (p. 359). The ideal of temperance
also shapes his remarks on landscape. "I never lik'd stubble fields so much

---

1. Henry Marshall, *Notes on the Medical Topography of the Interior of Ceylon* (London: Burgess and
   Hill, 1821), p. 75.
2. *Opera: Desire, Disease, Death* (Lincoln: University of Nebraska Press, 1996).
3. James Clark, *Treatise on Pulmonary Consumption* (London: Sherwood, Gilbert and Piper, 1835),
   p. 44, emphasis added.
4. Paul Frye, "History, Existence, and 'To Autumn,'" *SiR* 25 (1986): 218.

as now," he declares. "Somehow a stubble plain looks warm—in the same way that some pictures look warm." For the first time, he seems able to appreciate the stubble fields of England over their geographical alternatives. Keats makes "warm" into a heavily value-laden term: such fields look warm, and they produce within the viewer an equally moderated response. The reference to English landscape paintings emphasizes that the environment he is celebrating in "To Autumn" is itself a unique fiction, something he first saw in paintings and then read into the country environs of Winchester.

Just as "To Autumn" constructs the myth of a national environment, it also claims that English poetry should mirror the healthy temperate zone it comes from. Critics have correctly seen the poem as the celebration of a new kind of poetic voice. "I always somehow associate Chatterton with autumn," Keats writes. "He is the purest writer in the English Language. He has no French idiom, or particles like Chaucer's—'tis genuine English Idiom in English words" (p. 359). This emphasis on a pure, native language can be seen in the poem's verbal indebtedness to Thomson, Chatterton, and Coleridge and its avoidance of words with Latin roots. At the same time, Keats announced his decision to abandon *Hyperion* because "there were too many Miltonic inversions in it—Miltonic verse cannot be written but in an artful or rather artist's humour. I wish to give myself up to other sensations. English ought to be kept up" (p. 359). In a related letter Keats expands on these comments, writing that "I shall never become attach'd to a foreign idiom so as to put it into my writings. The Paradise lost though so fine in itself is a curruption of our Language—it should be kept as it is unique—a curiosity, a beautiful and grand Curiosity. The most remarkable Production of the world—A northern dialect accommodating itself to greek and latin inversions and intonations" (p. 371). Milton is portrayed as a cultural monster, a hybrid, employing a "northern dialect" yet allowing too much of the south to enter his poetry "The purest english I think—or what ought to be the purest—is Chatterton's," Keats goes on to say. "Chatterton's language is entirely northern—I prefer the native music of it to Milton's cut by feet." Having identified with Chatterton's pure "uncorrupted" language of autumnal England, Keats speaks of his recent recognition of the need to stand "on my guard against Milton." In words that have less to do with poetic influence than with a whole range of environmental and medical assumptions about the link between poetry nationality, and climate, he asserts that "Life to [Milton] would be death to me." I doubt Keats intended this comment to be taken only metaphorically.

Following a chain of associations that link English landscapes and chaste skies to notions of linguistic purity, Keats concludes his letter to Reynolds with a reference to his sisters, now living in Devonshire. "Your sisters by this time must have got the Devonshire ees—short ees—you know 'em—they are the prettiest ees in the Language," he writes, punning on both the alphabetic letter and "ease" (p. 360). Where love—from *Endymion* to the "Ode on a Grecian Urn"—had produced fever, "A burning forehead, and a parching tongue" (30), Keats now seems to be seeking a less passionate, more "chaste" gendering of space. "O how I admire the middle siz'd delicate Devonshire girls of about 15," he declares. "There was one at an Inn door holding a quartern of brandy—the very thought of her kept me *warm* a whole stage—and a 16 miler too" (p. 360, emphasis added). Since *ease* is the root of "dis-ease," Keats's mythologizing of the "warmth" produced by Devonshire girls can be seen, like "To Autumn" itself, as a very personal expression of a desire for health. It is hardly surprising that Devonshire, during this period, was being promoted as a particularly equable climate, "a favorite resort of the invalid," a region particularly suitable for counteracting consumption because of its "atmosphere, soft, warm, and charged with aquaeous vapour."[5] Keats admits that "To night I am all in a mist; I scarcely know what's what;' and he points out that lately he has suffered from depression, the "blue-devils," yet he nevertheless hopes that the place has a prophylactic power; you "need not fear . . . while you remain in Devonshire" (p. 359).

In September 1819 Keats hoped he had finally found a poetic style that no longer depended on or produced fever, one that would allow him to "look / Upon his mortal days with temperate blood" ("On Fame," ll. 1–2). He claimed he was no longer the person he once was. "From the time you left me, our friends say I have altered completely—am not the same person. . . . Some think I have lost that poetic ardour and fire 'tis said I once had—the fact is perhaps I have." He echoes Wordsworth in seeking to "substitute a more thoughtful and quiet power. . . . Quieter in my pulse, improved in my digestion; exerting myself against vexing speculations—scarcely content to write the best verses for the fever they leave behind." He goes on to stress, "I want to compose without this fever. I hope I one day shall" (pp. 368–69). Keats obviously hoped he had found a native poetry that would no longer make him ill, that having sojourned too long in a poetic tropics he had finally come home, gaining control over the fever that had become a regular part of his life. "I have got rid of my haunting sore throat—and conduct myself in a manner not to catch another" (L, 2: 200).[6]

This hope was not fulfilled, and much of the pathos of "To Autumn" derives from the sad personal circumstances that motivated this extraordinary celebration of a nativist aesthetic. It is the only poem in which Keats was able to create an unfevered literary environment out of the fevered landscapes of his earlier poetry, an achievement based on the belief that a poetry modeled on the English countryside would be healthier than other literary spaces. Yet this ideal environment, drawn largely from English landscape paintings, was not a space Keats had much experience with. It was, indeed, largely a national fiction, which grew in importance as more and more people left Britain for the colonies.[7] Alongside Keats's claim that he had adopted a new self should be set his admission that London has itself become foreign. "I walk'd about the Streets," he writes, "as in a strange land" (L, 2: 187). In March 1820, in one of many letters obsessed with the dangers of English weather, Keats remarks to Fanny Brawne, "What a horrid climate this is" (L, 2: 278).

5. Thomas Shapter, *Climate of the South of Devon; and Its Influence upon Health* (London: Churchill, 1842), p. 122.
6. Less than a month later, Keats became a vegetarian, explaining that "I have left off animal food that my brains may never henceforth be in a greater mist than is their by nature" (L, 2: 225).
7. For a good assessment of this aspect of the poem, see also Newey, "Keats, History, and the Poets," in Roe (ed.), *Keats and History*, pp. 185–90.

ANDREW BENNETT

The "Hyperion" Poems†

Failure

"Hyperion" opens with a catalogue of negations—death, silence, stillness—
a catatonic opening to a poem which cannot move and which elaborates
the epic negation of Romantic writing, that is the negation, embedded
within the modern verse-epic, of the possibility of audience: "No stir of
air . . . Not so much life . . . not one light seed . . . the dead leaf fell . . . A
stream went voiceless by, still deadened more . . . No further . . . nerveless,
listless, dead / Unsceptred . . . realmless eyes were closed" (1.7–19).

* * * I shall follow through the logic of the proposition that the negations
which open "Hyperion" are related to Keats's earlier romance-epic,
Endymion and, in particular, to the public responses to that earlier poem.
The trope of negation which figures the opening to "Hyperion" will be read
as a negation of *Endymion* and, in turn, be read as a response to the critical reception of that poem. * * *

* * * Indeed, the conditions of publication for "Hyperion" themselves
announced the relationship between *Endymion*, "Hyperion," and Keats's
audience as once again a poem was presented to the public with a gesture
of a denial of audience: Keats's publishers added a notorious "Advertisement" to the 1820 volume stating not only that "Hyperion" was printed
"contrary to the wish of the author," but also that the fragmentary nature
of the poem was due to the reviews of *Endymion*: "The poem was intended
to have been of equal length with *Endymion*, but the reception given to that
work discouraged the author from proceeding." * * * [T]he Advertisement
does indicate a very important source of authorial anxiety which informs
the narrative shape of "Hyperion" and of its rewriting, "The Fall of Hyperion": rather than preventing Keats from continuing with "Hyperion" as the
publishers' Advertisement stated, the reviews might be said to have provided an important generating force for the writing of "Hyperion" in the
first place.

It is, therefore, worth considering the precise nature of the criticisms of
Endymion. These criticisms may be schematically enumerated as follows:
derivative language and style (especially from Leigh Hunt); irregular versification; "vicious" diction (neologisms, invented participles, compound
epithets, "cockney" slang); misuse of classical mythology; obscurity/mean-
inglessness; overuse of "conceits"; immorality/obscenity; (social/literary)
vulgarity; prurience; radical/Jacobinical politics; rambling narrative form.[1]
"Hyperion" can be read, in part, as a reaction to these criticisms: the way
in which the poem seeks to assert *Paradise Lost* as its linguistic model
implicitly acknowledges the force of (some of) the criticisms by attempting to adopt a more respectable model of poetic decorum than, for

---

† From *Keats, Narrative, and Audience: The Posthumous Life of Writing* (Cambridge: Cambridge University Press, 1994), pp. 144–58. Reprinted by permission of the author and Cambridge University Press. The author's notes have been edited. Page numbers for letters refer to this Norton
Critical Edition; *L* refers to Rollins's edition.
1. See a selection of the negative reviews above, pp. 272–80. For a discussion of these attacks, see
Kim Wheatley, "The *Blackwood's* Attacks on Leigh Hunt," *Nineteenth-Century Literature*, 47
(1992): 1–31.

example, Leigh Hunt's *The Story of Rimini*. Similarly, the potential for charges of political or ethical subversion in "Hyperion" is limited not only by a focus on epic rather than libidinal and even incestuous themes, but also by a certain repression of "sensuous" language and a reduced concentration on sensuous perception. Moreover, there is a significant alteration in narrative form, towards a far simpler, more direct, and less wandering narration.[2] All of these may be seen in terms of acquiescence to criticism (sympathetic or not) to *Endymion*. On the other hand, in once again taking classical mythology as his subject, Keats is defiantly asserting both his right and his ability to rewrite the classics against the sarcastic irony of reviewers who mocked both his education and his class position in this respect. Similarly, the politics of "Hyperion," which may be read as at least "liberal" or "progressive" (if not exactly revolutionary), also stand in defiance of the tone of the critical reviews. Simply by writing a plot of revolution, simply by asking political questions about the nature and effect of revolution, Keats might be seen to be reacting against the kinds of political limitations which certain reviewers of *Endymion* (and the attacks on the "Cockney School") attempted to impose. Thus, to read "Hyperion" as a "reaction" to the more hostile reviews of *Endymion*, is to recognize the tensions within such a reaction, to recognize the contradictions and duplicities within the relationship between a poem and its empirically determined audience.

The silence, the stillness, the lack of speech and inability to speak which structures the opening lines of "Hyperion," then, might be read as a negation of the fecund wordiness of *Endymion*—the fault of a poet who was, in J. R. Lowell's term, "overlanguaged" (*KCH*, p. 361)—a poem which was governed by the intricate arabesque of (micro)narrative line, and the abundance of embedded narratives. The silencing figured in the opening to "Hyperion"—represented by the Naiad who "'mid her reeds / Press'd her cold finger closer to her lips" (1.13–14)—also involves a repression of narrative form, a silencing, at least, of the extrinsic, decorative, surrogate encrustations of narrative in *Endymion*. Numerous critics have pointed out that Keats seems to have achieved what he said he would in "Hyperion," that is a poem written "in more naked and grecian manner," a poem in which "the march of passion and endeavour will be undeviating" (*L*, 1: 207). In fact, however, although this seems to be an adequate description of the projected narrative, the extant fragment is characterized most generally by a stunted narrative form, by narrative potential. * * * This impossible narrative trajectory or the impossibility of narrative trajectory itself, is asserted in Saturn's first speech with his agonized claim that "it must—it must / Be of ripe progress—Saturn must be King" (1.124–5), and his dilation on this sense of obligatory narrative progression:

> "Yes, there must be a golden victory;
> There must be Gods thrown down, and trumpets blown
> Of triumph calm, and hymns of festival

---

2. On the relationship between the narrative form of "Hyperion" and *Endymion*, see Martin Aske, *Keats and Hellenism: An Essay* (Cambridge: Cambridge University Press, 1985), pp. 73–4; Michael Ragussis, *The Subterfuge of Art: Language and the Romantic Tradition* (Baltimore: The Johns Hopkins University Press, 1978), pp. 39–41, also comments on the "implicit distinction' between the two poems.

Upon the gold clouds metropolitan,
Voices of soft proclaim, and silver stir
Of strings in hollow shells; and there shall be
Beautiful things made new, for the surprise
Of the sky-children; I will give command:
Thea! Thea! Thea! where is Saturn?" (1.126–34)

The sense that these potential narratives will remain potential is given by the "command" which appears as a question, "where is Saturn?" Similarly, the first description of "Hyperion" is marked by a comparable force of negation:

Not at dog's howl, or gloom-bird's hated screech,
Or the familiar visiting of one
Upon the first toll of his passing-bell,
Or prophesyings of the midnight lamp;
But horrors, portion'd to a giant nerve,
Oft made Hyperion ache.   (1.171–6)

* * * [I]t is precisely the resistance to stories in the traditional sense which provides the generative anxiety for Keatsian narrative—an anxiety over tellability which includes both the ontological possibility of their being told and the pragmatic possibility of their gaining an audience.

With this in mind, we might suggest that the narrative trope most characteristic of "Hyperion" is that which Gerald Prince has defined as the "disnarrated." Prince explains the "disnarrated" as "all the events that *do not* happen but, nonetheless, are referred to (in a negative or hypothetical mode) by the narrative text." Prince makes the important distinction between the "disnarrated," on the one hand, and on the other hand narrative ellipsis, in which events are left untold "because of some narrative call for rhythm, characterization, suspense, surprise, and so on."[3] Furthermore, Prince also emphasizes the significance of the disnarrated to the pragmatics of narration. Through the inclusion of the "disnarrated," the poet can assert the tellability of his story by comparing it favourably with other possible/potential tales: if the disnarrated includes narratives which do not deserve to be told or cannot be told, the narration which *is* told is, by implication, tellable. Bearing in mind that one of the most virulent attacks on *Endymion*, that by John Wilson Croker in the *Quarterly Review*, opens with an assertion that the reviewer was unable to read beyond the first book of the poem (*KCH*, pp. 110–11), the question of tellability, of enticing or seducing the reader into reading on, might be understood to have been a crucial consideration in "Hyperion."

We might elaborate Prince's concept of the "disnarrated" in terms of its being constituted by two related formal strategies: negation and alterity. The disnarrated produces negation by referring to what is not or cannot be narrated. At the same time, by asserting an alternative to its own narrative this negation produces what we might term "alterity" or the "other" of narrative.[4] A narrative is then defined in terms of narratives which are not itself. A few examples of strategies of alterity and negation in "Hyperion"

3. Gerald Prince, "The Disnarrated", *Style*, 22 (1988), p. 2.
4. Prince, *ibid.*, p. 8, n. 1, suggests, as an alternative to "disnarrated," the term "alternarrated," which would explicitly express this alterity.

will give some indication of the extent to which the poem is structured around the "disnarrated," and the extent to which it is produced by this (de-)construction—by the failure of "Hyperion."

In the first of the poem's overtly self-reflexive statements of poetic incompetence, when the narrator attempts to repeat or express Thea's speech, we find a narratorial sense of an alternative discourse:

> Some mourning words, which in our feeble tongue
> Would come in these like accents; O how frail
> To that large utterance of the early Gods! (1.49–51)

On one level this is a further assertion of the silence of the written text: the pathos of writing is suggested by the negative force of "tongue . . . accents . . . utterance" and by the previous line's fore-grounding of the materiality of voice, "solemn tenour and deep organ tone."[5] On another level, however, Keats is providing an example of the doubling of the disnarrated: "Hyperion" is structured as an other of narrative. Similarly, the very syntax of Saturn's speech, his assertion of power and of narrative possibility, are expressed in terms of negation:

> "But cannot I create?
> Cannot I form? Cannot I fashion forth
> Another world, another universe,
> To overbear and crumble this to nought?
> Where is another chaos? Where?" (1.141–5)

Here the repeated negative "cannot" works against the interrogative mode almost as if the phrase "cannot I . . ." was semantically identical with "I cannot." Saturn's sense of his own impotence conflicts with his understanding of "another universe": thematically, the "disnarrated" is represented by the fallen Titans' sense of their failure. Moreover, this pressure of negation deep within the language affects the narrative ordering of plot and subplot: moving from Saturn to the other Titans, Keats reproduces the alterity of Saturn's speech so as to assert the congruence of narrative worlds:

> Meanwhile in other realms big tears were shed,
> More sorrow like to this, and such like woe,
> Too huge for mortal tongue or pen of scribe. (1.158–60)

Negation and alterity are explicitly expressed in what might otherwise have been a conventional modulation from one scene to another; but here the lexicon of alterity—"other . . . like . . . such like too huge . . . or"—alerts us to the fact that in this articulation of poetic inadequacy a more crucial sense of potential narrative failure is indicated.

Paradoxically, perhaps, when the modulation is achieved, we find a disconcerting familiarity in the predicament of Hyperion, as if the alternative narrative line, which promised to rescue the threatened silence of the narration of the fallen Titans, is simply a repetition of the first, providing no possibility of development. The descriptions of Saturn and Hyperion overlap in their stillness: "Blazing Hyperion on his orbed fire / Still sat, still snuff 'd the incense" (1.166–7). The adverbial "still" of a continuing action also involves adjectival motionlessness and silence: indeed, there is a chias-

---

5. On the question of voice in "Hyperion," see Anya Taylor, "Superhuman Silence: Language in *Hyperion*," *SEL*, 19 (1979), pp. 673–87, and Aske, *Keats and Hellenism*, pp. 94–6.

tic reciprocity of grammar and meaning in the two senses, because although the word works grammatically as an adverb denoting continuation, this presupposes a former reference which is unavailable to the reader—an anterior disnarrated—so that the sense of stillness or silence is produced through narrative absence. The phrases also point to another kind of "disnarrated" in their syntactic echoing of Miltonic inversion. Indeed, this sense of an anterior disnarrated repeatedly disrupts reading with an overwhelming sense of an alternative narrative lying deep within the uncluttered syntax of the verse.* * * These local failures of narrative form, all of them failures of narrative transition (on the level of *discours*), seem to be symptoms of an underlying problem with the narrative form of "Hyperion," and seem to predict—even to predicate—the "failure" and abandonment of the poem: if these structural features—the internal mechanisms of narrative—alert the reader to narrative incompetence or solecism, then the superstructure of narrative telling seems unlikely to succeed.

* * * [T]he failure of "Hyperion" may be read in a number of different ways: the stilling of narrative may be understood to be generated by the fear or anxiety that there will be no audience for this poem and a consequent paralysis of narrative; it may be read in terms of a crucial and irreducible disjunction between the language of men and the language of gods by which the epic mode articulates the language of gods and in so doing excludes itself from audience (see 1.49; 2.101; 2.120); it may be read in terms of the mode of reading configured by the poem—perplexity and incomprehension (2.130f.; 3.48) and an impossible figure of reading as an access to immortality (3.111), a reading into which the reader dies.

This latter explanation for the stilling of narrative is, of course, related to our notion of Romantic posterity as the posthumous life of writing, and might be approached through the figure of the dead hand of Saturn with which "Hyperion" opens. There are two hands in the opening twenty lines of "Hyperion," both of which strongly figure negation: first there is the admonitory hand of the Naiad—"the Naiad 'mid her reeds / Press'd her cold finger closer to her lips" (1.13–14). This deadened hand at the start of the poem interdicts speech, language, poetry and prefigures the dead hand of Saturn four lines later:

> Upon the sodden ground
> His old right hand lay nerveless, listless, dead,
> Unsceptred. (1.17–19)

* * * Similarly, the opening to "The Fall of Hyperion" figures the hand as the still-life or living-death of poetry and of the relationship between text and audience:

> Whether the dream now purposed to rehearse
> Be Poet's or Fanatic's will be known
> When this warm scribe my hand is in the grave. (1.16–18)

The Induction to "The Fall" reads the dead hand of the opening to "Hyperion"—just as the whole of "The Fall" may be understood as a reading of the earlier poem[6]: the later poem explicitly refigures the relationship of

---

6. See James Kissane, "The Authorization of John Keats," *KSJ*, 37 (1988), p. 70: "The Fall" is "a parasitic engrafting upon the original, a kind of palimpsest."

poetic death to audience in "Hyperion." In the Induction to "The Fall," the death of the poet and his status as "poet" or "fanatic" is implicitly related to the "death" of the reader not only because of the way that the lines allow no reading other than that mediated by "This living hand," but also because there is already within these lines a question of the life or death of the audience: "Who alive can say / 'Thou art no poet; may'st not tell thy dreams?'" (1.11–12). If there is no one *alive* who can judge on the poetic merits of the poem, then the explicit request for such judgement and its deferral to a time after the death of the writer might also be read as a reading or "saying" deferred until after the death of the reader.

The crucial difference between "Hyperion" and "The Fall of Hyperion," then, is this: "Hyperion" figures death as a pre-condition for inspiration, it is a poem crucially concerned with the notion of dying into poetic creation, a mortal creativity; "The Fall," on the other hand, is crucially concerned to figure *reading* as an activity irreducibly bound up with death. And it is through "The Fall" that we can read the death of the audience in "Hyperion." In what follows, I shall attempt to elaborate the figured reader in "The Fall" and implicitly to read "Hyperion" through this figured reading.

Faulture

* * *

Unlike the minor alterations, the pragmatic and socially (in-)decorous revisions to "The Eve of St Agnes," Keats's rewriting of "Hyperion" amounts to a comprehensive doctoring of its earlier form.[7] The rewriting of "Hyperion" as "The Fall of Hyperion" results in a central inquiry into the nature of the poet-reader relationship. Although critics tend to insist on reading "The Fall" as an allegory of the birth of poetic creativity, such a birth is crucially mediated by the notion of reading: despite critics' attempts to elide or suppress this point, the narrator is primarily figured as a "dreamer"—and a dreamer who watches and reacts, who provides an audience for a "tragedy"—while the question of the narrator's status as a creator or poet is explicitly and repeatedly placed in suspense. And while "The Fall" seeks to assert the irreducible conflation of poetic reading with poetic writing, the extant narrative produces a dying into reading. * * * What are the narrative strategies brought into play here? To what extent are the concerns of the passage generated by their audience?

> Fanatics have their dreams, wherewith they weave
> A paradise for a sect; the savage, too,
> From forth the loftiest fashion of his sleep
> Guesses at Heaven: pity these have not
> Trac'd upon vellum or wild Indian leaf
> The shadows of melodious utterance.
> But bare of laurel they live, dream, and die;
> For Poesy alone can tell her dreams,
> With the fine spell of words alone can save

---

7. For studies of these alterations, see Jeffrey Baker, *John Keats and Symbolism*, p. 108; Paul D. Sheats, "Stylistic Discipline in *The Fall of Hyperion*," *KSJ*, 17 (1968), pp. 85–7; and Robert D. Wagner, "Keats's "'Ode to Psyche' and the Second 'Hyperion,'" *KSJ*, 13 (1964), pp. 35–6.

Imagination from the sable charm
And dumb enchantment. Who alive can say
"Thou art no poet: may'st not tell thy dreams?"
Since every man whose soul is not a clod
Hath visions, and would speak, if he had lov'd
And been well nurtured in his mother tongue.
Whether the dream now purposed to rehearse
Be Poet's or Fanatic's will be known
When this warm scribe, my hand, is in the grave.   (1.1–18)

The interpretive shift which is needed here is that which would move from hermeneutics to pragmatics. In fact, whatever the confusions of thought in the Induction, the lines have demonstrably produced a reception of "The Fall of Hyperion" which is defined within the terms presented by the Induction itself. The Induction offers the reader an explicit commentary on the poem to follow, a commentary which both directs readers' attention and provides evaluative comment. It asserts, most fundamentally (and logically prior to any thematic or analytical statement), a social function for poetry, an acknowledgement of the pragmatic, public nature of poetic discourse and, at the same time, a recognition of the fundamental importance of the relationship between poet and audience: if the audience judges well, then the poem exists as a poem, if they judge against it, the dream is a "fanatic's." This is a radical redescription not only of the poet's role, but of the very nature of poetic discourse and of the definition of "literature": the poem can only exist as poetry with the consent of its audience.[8] This may explain the significance of "rehearse": only when the audience receives and approves the poem will it be "performed." The last line of the Induction is an accurate metaphor for the nature of literary production in an age of mechanical reproduction, where the living hand of the poet, his handwriting, is "dead" as it is read in its printed form: the line lucidly marks the gap between writing and reception. Usually taken as an attempt to define the poet against the dreamer/fanatic, the Induction also vitally asserts the public nature of the poetry.

This assertion of the pragmatic basis of poetic expression is also implicitly asserted by the alterations in narrative form made in rewriting "Hyperion," the most notable of which is the alteration made in narratorial voice from third to first person. Through this alteration in voice, the narrator becomes the reader-surrogate, and the narrative of the Titans is mediated through his reactions to the story: Keats's rewriting of the poem recognizes the limitations of the earlier poem's attempt to isolate poetry from its audience. As many critics have recognized, "Hyperion" seems to be deeply ambivalent about its sympathy towards the Titans and the Olympians: the poem fractures and halts in its movement from the tragic to the Apollonian.[9] The disnarrated which characterizes the form of "Hyperion" is another expression of this ambivalence. The first-person narration of "The Fall," then, allows for an altered focus of narrative and an altered emphasis on the events: instead of the question of sympathy for the Titans or the Olympians, the emphasis falls on the

---

8. In fact, this is the kind of pragmatic definition of "literature" produced by, for example, Costanzo Di Girolamo, in *A Critical Theory of Literature* (Madison: University of Wisconsin Press, 1981), p. 65.
9. See William C. Stephenson, "The Performing Narrator in Keats's Poetry," *KSJ*, 26 (1977), p. 63, and Balachandra Rajan, *The Form of the Unfinished: English Poetics from Spenser to Pound* (New Jersey: Princeton University Press, 1985), p. 231.

narrator's reactions to events—a shift which organizes the narrative around the question of response. What this reader-narrator makes possible is, precisely, the alterity to which "Hyperion" continually alluded: the story which Keats writes now is the alternative, the supplementary story.

In "Hyperion," the crucial mechanics of the transition from one character to another, from one episode to another, is constituted by disjunction, resulting in a narrative form which seems to reflect the picture of the fallen Titans as broken statues strewn around the poem: thematic *disjecta membra* are actualized in narrative form. In "The Fall," by contrast, these limitations, these fault-lines in the narrative texture, become the transitions between levels of framing and are motivated by the subjective experience of the narrator (from consciousness to sleep, from solitude to dialogic exchange, from talk to vision, from *discours* to *histoire*, etc.). Thus, instead of breaking off from one line of narrative and moving to another, "The Fall" is crucially structured around the "faultures" of narration.[1] It is within the spaces formed by the disjointed articulations of narration, that "The Fall" is narrated, just as it is the *supplementary* narrative of response that becomes critical. This is a movement from immobility to movement, from the totalities of narrative or history to the dispersal of event or process, from continuity to disjunction, from place to space, and thus from failure to faulture.

The framing structure of "The Fall" is the most complex of all of Keats's narratives.[2] Eventually in "The Fall," the several layerings of frame look like this:

Induction > garden > dream > vision> "Hyperion"

The Induction (1.1–18) frames the whole poem; the first scene within the garden (1.19–57) is a vision which is interrupted by sleep and opens out into another embedding in the dream of the struggle of the narrator to become a poet or reader (1. 58–256); this leads to a greater visionary potential, represented in the vision of Moneta's face which I have classified as a further embedding, as "vision," because the narrator seems to be on a qualitatively different narratorial level (1.256–90); this visionary potential opens out into Moneta's narration of the immortal struggle which, referring to Keats's first attempt, I have labelled "Hyperion" (1.291–end). Such rigorously complex embedding provides an unstable, liminal quality to the poetry, which continually threatens to slide, through a "faulture," on to a different plane of narration, just as Moneta's narrations continually slide into the narrator's "vision." At the same time, such a technique radically distances the *histoire* from "the world" and from the reader, who must view the tale through the various implicit commentaries of embedded narrative level:[3] like the poet-narrator (the reader's surrogate), the reader must struggle through various thresholds before he or she is able to approach the story of "Hyperion." This is, on one level, a typically Romantic manoeuvre, asserting epistemological dislocation and authorial suspension and, in contrast to the first "Hyperion," suggests ways in which that poem's desire

1. "Faulture" is Keats's neologism in "The Fall" (1.70).
2. On Keats and framing, see Robert M Adams, "*Trompe l'Oeil* in Shakespeare and Keats," *Sewanee Review*, 61 (1953), pp. 245–6.
3. Through the use of the first-person narrator, there is, of course, a strong sense of narratorial intimacy: see F. K. Stanzel, *A Theory of Narrative*, 2nd edn., tr. Charlotte Goedsche (Cambridge: Cambridge University Press, 1984), pp. 79–110, on the choice of first- and third-person narrators. John Barnard, *John Keats* (Cambridge: Cambridge University Press, 1987), p. 129, comments on the way in which "The Fall" "paradoxically attain[s] a severe impersonality through intense subjectivity."

for coherence, for narrative form, and, by implication, for a negation of audience, has evolved into a poetics inhabiting the unstable interstice of text and audience.

The major episode of reading in "The Fall" is that in which the figured reader, the narrator-poet, reads Moneta's face. For Helen Vendler, Moneta's eyes figure the inspiration of the poet, asserting an aesthetic which explicitly denies audience:[4]

> Half closed, and visionless entire they seem'd
> Of all external things—they saw me not,
> But in blank splendour beam'd like the mild moon,
> Who comforts those she sees not, who knows not
> What eyes are upward cast.   (1. 267–71)

If we read Moneta's face with Vendler as a figure for poetic inspiration and a denial of audience, it becomes clear that Keats's text is itself a transgression of precisely this law of authorial ignorance or disdain: how would it be possible to read Moneta's face as a negation of audience in poetic creativity if "The Fall of Hyperion" does not itself engage with precisely this question? In as much as "The Fall" presents an implicit ideology of the poet detached from and ignorant of its audience, the poem itself must fall outside of this definition of poetry because of its explicit engagement at this point with the question of reading. But audience is not only figured by this "figural" ideology of authorial ignorance. We have already seen that the Induction presents the poem as constituted by its audience. At the same time the notion of the unbridgeable ontological gap between poet and reader apparently presented by the face of Moneta is also transgressed by the scene itself which, despite many critics' apparent blindness to the point, is constituted as a figure of reading. It is clearly the case that the narrator explicitly *reads* Moneta's face:

> As I had found
> A grain of gold upon a mountain's side,
> And twing'd with avarice strain'd out my eyes
> To search its sullen entrails rich with ore,
> So at the view of sad Moneta's brow,
> I ached to see what things the hollow brain
> Behind enwombed.   (1.271–7)

* * * Keats's letter to Shelley, which exhorts the older poet to "'load every rift' of your subject with ore" (p. 524) is an obvious counterpart to these rich entrails, and in "The Fall" the poet is exhorting his readers, by the use of a reader-surrogate, to "strain [their] eyes": if Keats's poetry is "loaded with ore," the task of the reader must be to extract the wealth embedded within it. Earlier, the voice of Moneta had declared that if the narrator cannot ascend the steps "thy bones / Will wither in few years, and vanish so / That not the quickest eye could find a grain / Of what thou now art" (1.110–13): the poet who is no poet will lack all reception, will be invisible to the public eye. Thus the "faultures" by which the narrative is organized, the liminal stratifications of narrative embedding, provide rich pickings for the eyes of avaricious readers.

---

4. Vendler, *The Odes of John Keats*, pp. 216, 222, 224.

ιat "The Fall" would seem to present, then, is a figure of poetry which
t self-identical: that is, the role of the reader is presented in "The Fall"
shattering of the self-identical, hermetic inspiration of poetry. The face
Moneta may, as Vendler and others have read it, produce an ideology of
ılipsistic, self-enclosed and self-referential poetic making, and we might
mis)read the word "disinterested" as Keats's word for this process (see *L*, 1:
205, 293; 2: 79, 129, 279). But at the same time this figure of poetry
demands to be read, demands to be read as a figure of reading, and as such
threatens to shatter the illusion of aesthetic isolation. As such, "The Fall"
figures the activity of reading as a transgression of the poetic text.

* * *

If reading in "The Fall" is transgressive, the poem also emphasizes its
difficulty—not only in terms of the hermeneutic difficulties of ignorance,
confusion, bewilderment of "Hyperion," but also in the way that reading is
strenuous and physically and emotionally draining. In particular, the narrator's struggle towards Moneta which I have been "reading" is figured as
a struggle *against* the condition of the fallen Saturn:

> I strove hard to escape
> The numbness; strove to gain the lowest step.
> Slow, heavy, deadly was my pace: the cold
> Grew stifling, suffocating, at the heart;
> And when I clasp'd my hands I felt them not. (1.127–31)

* * * Episodes such as the vision of Moneta must be understood to have been
phenomenally successful in controlling the audience through its figuration
of poetic inspiration, its presentation of a particular configuration of the ideology of poethood, while at the same time presenting a transgressive undermining of precisely that audience response. * * * [O]ne can make one's
dream real—as Moneta does—by making others dream it. The reality of the
imagination, the reality of Adam's dream, is constituted by the audience for
that dream: the reality of the dream is not constructed by the dreamer, who
knows that it is only a dream. Rather, the reality of the dream is constructed
by the transgressive reading of the dreamer's audience.

John Keats: A Chronology

JK = John Keats
GK = George Keats
TK = Tom Keats
FK = Fanny (Frances Mary) Keats
FB = Fanny Brawne

1795   JK born October 31 at the Swan and Hoop Livery Stables, 24 Moorfields Pavement Row, London. He was the eldest child of Frances Jennings Thomas and Thomas Keats, who was chief ostler of the Swan and Hoop, owned by Frances's father. 1795 is a bad year for crops, leading to high food prices. Napoleon's army has invaded Italy. George III's coach is stoned at the opening of Parliament in January; Pitt introduces the "Two Acts" to prevent mass protest meetings.

1797   GK born February 28.

1799   TK born November 18; the Keatses move to Craven Street, City Road.

1801   Edward Keats born; he dies before February 1, 1805.

1803   FK born June 3; in August JK and GK begin attending John Clarke's Enfield Academy, a school rooted in dissenting and radical traditions. JK meets Charles Cowden Clarke at Enfield. TK would later join his brothers there. War with France is resumed in May after the Peace of Amiens.

1804   Thomas Keats dies in a riding accident on April 16. Frances is remarried to William Rawlings on June 27. The Keats children move in with their maternal grandparents, John and Alice Jennings, at Ponders End near Enfield. Pitt starts his second ministry; Napoleon has himself declared emperor.

1805   Grandfather Jennings dies in March; the family moves to Edmonton. Admiral Nelson dies at the victory at Trafalgar; Napoleon scores a major victory over the Austrians and Russians at Austerlitz.

1806   JK's mother leaves her husband and severs contact with the children until 1809.

1810   JK's mother dies of tuberculosis and is buried on March 20. Grandmother Jennings appoints John Sandall, a merchant who later fled to Holland, and Richard Abbey, an old family friend and a tea broker, as guardians for the children; the Keats brothers would have disputes with Abbey over their inheritance.

1811   JK leaves Enfield Academy and is apprenticed by Abbey to Thomas Hammond, an Edmonton surgeon and apothecary. GK becomes a clerk for Abbey but later quits over a dispute with a junior partner,

Hodgkinson. Prince of Wales becomes Regent after the king falls ill. Luddites smash frames to protest working conditions, and there are bread riots around Nottingham.

1814   JK writes his first poems, including "Imitation of Spenser," "On Peace," after Napoleon's first exile to Elba, and a sonnet "To Byron." Grandmother Jennings dies in December and is buried on the 19th; FK goes to live with the Abbeys.

1815   On February 2, JK pens "Written on the Day that Mr. Leigh Hunt Left Prison" (Hunt was in prison for libeling the Prince Regent); "To Hope" and "Ode to Apollo" are also written in February. In October JK, having completed his apprenticeship with Hammond, enters Guy's Hospital; he lodges in St. Thomas's Street, where he meets Henry Stephens, among other students. JK becomes part of the circle around George Felton Mathew, to whom he writes a verse epistle in November; other Mathew circle poems, such as "To Some Ladies" and "On Receiving a Curious Shell," are written at this time. Napoleon returns for the Hundred Days (March–June) before being defeated at Waterloo on July 15. The victorious powers form the "Holy Alliance" to control post–Napoleonic Europe. The Corn Bill is passed; attempts to reform Parliament resume with the end of the Napoleonic wars.

1816   On March 3, JK is entered as a dresser to the surgeons at Guy's Hospital. JK meets Joseph Severn in the spring. JK publishes his first poem, "O Solitude," in the *Examiner*, May 5, 1816. On July 25 JK passes his examination at Apothecaries' Hall, making him eligible to practice as an apothecary, physician, or surgeon. From July–August, JK and TK vacation at Margate on the coast, where JK writes a verse epistle to GK. In September, JK writes a verse epistle to C. C. Clarke. By October, the Keats brothers are living at 8 Dean Street, Southwark; in November, they move to 76 Cheapside. In October, JK meets Robert Benjamin Haydon, John Hamilton Reynolds, and Leigh Hunt, becoming a key member of Hunt's circle. After an evening in October with C. C. Clarke, JK writes "On first looking into Chapman's Homer." After a visit to Haydon's studio on November 3, he writes, on November 20, a sonnet addressed to Haydon ("Great Spirits"). Hunt prints his "Young Poets" article in the December 1 *Examiner*, celebrating JK, Reynolds, and Percy Shelley, whom JK meets around this time. JK has abandoned medicine for poetry. JK writes "Sleep and Poetry" during October–December and completes "I stood tip-toe upon a little hill" by December 18. He joins Hunt in a sonnet contest on December 30, each penning a poem "On the Grasshopper and Cricket"; "Written in Disgust of Vulgar Superstition" was perhaps also from a sonnet contest on December 22. A year of economic woes and political dissent climaxes in the Spa Fields Riot in December.

1817   On January 20, JK dines at Horace Smith's house with Hunt, Haydon, and Shelley. JK participates in a circle that also includes Hazlitt, the Novellos, and Godwin. Hunt publishes a series of JK's poems in the *Examiner*; C. and J. Ollier publish *Poems* on March 3. On March 1 or 2, Haydon takes JK to see the Elgin Marbles, about which he writes two sonnets, published in the March 9 *Examiner* and *Champion*, which also prints Reynolds's laudatory review of *Poems*. By March, the Keats brothers have moved to Benjamin Bentley's house, 1 Well Walk, Hampstead. Around this time, JK meets John Taylor, his future publisher, and through him, Richard Woodhouse; Reynolds introduces JK to Charles Wentworth Dilke. He also meets Charles Armitage Brown and Benjamin Bailey. JK begins *Endymion* in April. He leaves London on April 14 and crosses to the Isle of Wight on the 15th and writes "On the Sea" from Carisbrooke on the 17th; TK joins him at Margate on April 24. TK and JK visit Canterbury. In late May or early June, JK visits Bo-Beep, a coastal town, and meets Isabella Jones, before returning to Hampstead by June 10. Meets Charles Brown during the summer on the Hampstead Road. Hunt reviews *Poems* in the *Examiner*, June 1, July 6, 13. JK finishes Book II of *Endymion* by late August. In September, JK visits Benjamin Bailey at Oxford, where he works on Book III. In October, he returns to Hampstead where he sees Reynolds, Hunt, Haydon, and Shelley; JK is ill and taking mercury. *Blackwood's* begins its "Cockney School" attacks. In late November, JK travels to Burford Bridge, where he completes the first draft of *Endymion* (November 28). On December 15, he attends *Richard III* starring Edmund Kean; on the 18th he sees Kean play Luke Traffic in *Riches*, and reviews the performance in the December 21 *Champion*. He sees the Drury Lane pantomime on the 26th and publishes a review on January 4, 1818. On the 20th he goes to the Royal Academy exhibition, where he sees Benjamin West's *Death on a Pale Horse*. He writes to his brothers (December 21, 27) about West, the drama, Hunt, Thomas Wooler, William Hone, and "negative capability." During this period, JK meets William Wordsworth and recites his "Hymn to Pan" from *Endymion*, with Wordsworth finding it a "pretty piece of paganism." Haydon hosts the "immortal dinner" (December 28), with JK, Lamb, and Wordsworth among others in attendance. While the year ends with Hone's acquittal, the year had seen the suspension of habeas corpus and the passage of the Seditious Meetings Act, among other measures against democratic societies and reformers. The Regent's only daughter, Princess Charlotte, dies.

1818   JK begins revising *Endymion*, as he attends the theater (two reviews published in the January 4 *Champion*), hears Hazlitt lecture on poetry, and visits with a range of friends and acquaintances, including Wordsworth. He writes a poem on a lock of Milton's hair owned by Hunt (January 21) and a sonnet on rereading *King Lear* (January 22). In February, he begins *Isabella*. He writes "To the Nile" in a sonnet competition with Hunt and Shelley (February 4) and two poems on Robin Hood in response to poems by Reynolds. At Hunt's with the Shelleys, he meets Thomas Love Peacock, Thomas Jefferson Hogg, and Claire Claremont (February 11). In March, JK leaves London for Teignmouth with TK, who is suffering from tuberculosis. JK completes his revisions to *Endymion* and writes a first preface (March 19), which is rejected by his publishers. He writes a verse epistle to Reynolds (March 25). In April, he pens a

new preface for *Endymion* (April 10), which is published around
the 27th by Taylor and Hessey; JK sees an advance copy on the
24th and sends his publishers an errata list. He completes *Isabella*
(April 27). JK's letter to Reynolds (May 3) compares life to "a large
Mansion of Many Apartments." JK and TK return to Hampstead by
May 11; he is "very much engaged with his Friends." "Hymn to
Pan" from *Endymion* appears in the May 9 *Yellow Dwarf*, a radical
journal. GK marries Georgiana Wylie (c. May 28). The *British
Critic* attacks *Poems* in June, while an unsigned review (by
Reynolds, Woodhouse, or John Scott?) praising *Endymion* appears
in the June 8 *Champion*. On June 22, JK departs with Brown and
the GKs for Liverpool, where the latter depart for the United
States. JK continues with Brown on a walking tour of the Lake District and Scotland. On June 27, JK leaves a note for Wordsworth at
Rydal. On June 29, JK and Brown climb Mount Skiddaw, on July 1
visit Burns's tomb, on July 6–8 visit Ireland, on July 11 visit Burns's
cottage, on July 24 travel by boat to Iona, Staffa, and on August 2
climb Ben Nevis. JK, feeling ill, returns to London by boat August
8; he reaches Well Walk on August 18 to find TK very ill. Around
this time, he meets FB. The fourth Cockney School attack, target-
ing JK, appears in *Blackwood's* for August 1818. In September,
John Wilson Croker joins in the assault in the *Quarterly Review*
(dated April 1818); defenses of *Endymion* appear in the *Morning
Chronicle*, *Alfred*, *West of England Journal*, and the *Examiner* in
October. Around September 19, JK meets Jane Cox at the Reynoldses. While TK grows weaker and JK continues to feel ill, JK visits
with various London friends, including Hazlitt, Hunt, and Haydon;
on October 24, he sees Isabella Jones. By November, JK is writing
Hyperion. In November, Hunt publishes "The Human Seasons"
and "To Ailsa Rock" in his *Literary Pocket Book*. On December 1,
TK dies, and JK accepts Brown's invitation to live with him at
Wentworth Place, now the "Keats House" in Hampstead. JK and
FB fall in love and have reached an "understanding" by December
25. Toward the end of the year, JK writes "Fancy" and "Bards of passion and of mirth."

1819   Around January 18, JK goes to Chichester (where he meets Brown
at the Dilkes) and Bedhampton, where he writes *The Eve of St.
Agnes*. He returns to London on February 1 or 2. JK is having financial problems and dealing with Abbey; Haydon is pestering him for
loans. On February 13–17, JK writes "The Eve of St. Mark." On
March 1, he visits the British Museum with Severn who decides (c.
March 29) to exhibit his miniature of JK at the Royal Academy. JK
is reading Hazlitt's attack on Gifford, editor of the *Quarterly
Review*, along with Thomas Moore and Beaumont and Fletcher.
On April 11, he walks with S. T. Coleridge; around this time he
dines with Hunt, with whom he visits Leicester's gallery (April 12),
and hosts a "claret feast" for Dilke, Reynolds, and others. On April
21, JK writes a review of Reynolds's parody, *Peter Bell*, which
appears in the April 25 *Examiner*; on April 21 or 28, he writes "La
Belle Dame Sans Merci." By the end of the month, he has abandoned *Hyperion* and written "Ode to Psyche." He writes "Ode to

a Nightingale" (published in the July *Annals of Fine Arts*), "Ode on a Grecian Urn," and perhaps "Ode to Melancholy" in May; "Ode on Indolence" may have been begun in March but is complete by June 9. He returns all borrowed books, burns old letters, and contemplates moving to Devonshire or becoming a ship's surgeon. On June 27, JK travels with Rice, reaching the Isle of Wight on the 28th; Brown arrives around July 22. On August 12, JK and Brown move to Winchester. In July and August, JK and Brown work on *Otho the Great*, while JK writes *Lamia* and reworks *Hyperion* as *Fall of Hyperion*. JK returns to London on September 11 in response to a letter from GK, and while there, he joins the large crowds watching Henry Hunt's entry into London. He returns to Winchester on the 15th, where he writes "To Autumn" (the 19th) and reads Burton's *Anatomy of Melancholy* and Ariosto. Announcing that he is giving up *The Fall of Hyperion* and that he will not publish *Isabella*, he contemplates becoming a journalist in Westminster. Around October 8, JK and Brown return to London; JK visits FB in Hampstead on the 10th. October 11–14, he lodges in Westminster; 18–20, he is with the Dilkes but returns to Wentworth Place around the 21st. In October–November, he works on "King Stephen" and "The Jealousies," and writes "The day is gone" and "I cry your mercy"; he decides not to publish what he has written and reads Holinshed's *Chronicles* as he contemplates writing on the Earl of Leicester. On December 20, JK hears that *Otho the Great* has been accepted by Drury Lane for the next season. As he continues to be unwell, he and FB become engaged. In August, the militia charges a demonstration in the "Peterloo Massacre"; the repressive "Six Acts" are passed in December.

1820　GK arrives from the U.S. to raise money and dines with JK on January 9; GK's money problems add to JK's. JK and GK spend a good deal of time with their old friends before GK leaves for Liverpool and the U.S. on January 28. JK sends *Otho the Great* to Covent Garden around January 13. "Ode on a Grecian Urn" is published in the January *Annals of the Fine Arts*. On February 3, JK has a severe hemorrhage in the lungs and is confined to his house until the middle of March. Barry Cornwall sends him two of his volumes of poetry toward the end of February. Feeling better in March, JK revises *Lamia* volume for publication; the 1820 volume will be delivered to Taylor and Hessey on April 27. On March 25, JK attends a private showing of Haydon's *Christ's Entry into Jerusalem*, which includes the face of JK in the crowd. In the April issue of Baldwin's *London Magazine*, a favorable review of *Endymion* (perhaps by P. G. Patmore) appears, an indication of a turn against the reactionary assault on JK's work. Brown rents Wentworth Place, as he prepares to depart for Scotland; JK sails with him as far as Gravesend on May 6. At Hunt's suggestion, JK moves to 2 Wesleyan Place, Kentish Town, in Hunt's neighborhood but still close to FB in Hampstead. Hunt publishes "La Belle Dame Sans Merci" in the May 10 *Indicator*. After another hemorrhage, JK moves in with the Hunts at Mortimer Terrace on June 23. Hunt publishes "As Hermes once" in the June 28 *Indicator*, also writing with JK a

"Now" on the hot summer weather. In early June, JK corrects the proofs of the 1820 volume; he receives advance copies on June 30 (one of which is given to Barry Cornwall). The volume is published by Taylor and Hessey on July 1 or 2. "Ode to a Nightingale," "To Autumn" (reprinted in the London *Chronicle*) and other poems are published in the July 1 *Literary Gazette*. Lamb praises the 1820 volume in the July 19 *New Times*; Hunt reprints the review in the July 30 *Examiner*. Hunt's own review appears in the August 2 and 9 *Indicators*. Francis Jeffrey offers a positive review of *Endymion* and the 1820 volume in the influential *Edinburgh Review* for August. By July 5, JK has been told by his doctors to travel to Italy for his health. On August 12, he receives an invitation from Shelley to stay with him in Italy. A dispute that same day with the Hunt family leads to JK's moving back to Hampstead to stay with the Brawnes. As his health worsens, his friends raise money for him to travel to Italy; he hopes Brown will go with him, but when he cannot, Joseph Severn agrees to accompany Keats. In September, positive reviews of the 1820 volume appear in the *Monthly Magazine,* the *New Monthly Magazine,* the *British Critic,* and Baldwin's *London Magazine* (perhaps by John Scott). JK writes his will and assigns the copyrights of *Endymion* and *Poems* for £100 each. On September 17, JK and Severn board the *Maria Crowther*. Hunt publishes a friendly farewell in the September 20 *Indicator*. After a long, unpleasant voyage, JK and Severn reach Naples on October 21 where they are held in quarantine for ten days; they are released on October 31, Keats's twenty-fifth birthday. They leave Naples by November 8 and arrive in Rome on the 15th, where they take lodgings at 26 Piazza di Spagna in the English district at the foot of the Spanish Steps. On November 30, he writes his last extant letter, to Brown. His health worsens in December.

1821   JK dies at 11 P.M. on February 23 and is buried in the Protestant Cemetery in Rome on the 26th. By March 17, the news of his death reaches his friends in London. George III dies and the Regent takes the throne as George IV; he seeks to discredit and to divorce his wife through a parliamentary trial. The Cato Street Conspiracy to assassinate the cabinet fails.

1822   On July 8, P. B. Shelley dies by drowning.

1824   On April 19, Byron dies in Greece where he had gone to join the fight for Greek independence.

1826   FK marries the novelist Valentin Llanos, who had visited JK during his last days in Rome.

1833   FB marries Louis Lindo.

1834   Woodhouse dies. Coleridge dies.

1841   GK dies December 24.

1842   Brown dies in New Zealand.

1843   Georgiana Keats marries John Jeffrey.

1846   Haydon kills himself.

1850   Wordsworth dies.

1851   Bailey dies.

1852   Reynolds dies.

1859   Hunt dies.
1865   FB dies.
1875   C. C. Clarke dies.
1879   Severn dies.
1889   FK dies.

Selected Bibliography

I. MANUSCRIPT FACSIMILES AND TRANSCRIPTIONS

"Hyperion": A Facsimile of Keats's Autograph Manuscript, with a Transliteration of the Manuscript of "The Fall of Hyperion: A Dream." Ed. Ernest de Selincourt. Oxford: Oxford University Press, 1905.
The Odes of Keats & Their Earliest Known Manuscripts in Facsimile. Ed. Robert Gittings. Ohio: Kent State University Press, 1970.
The Manuscripts of the Younger Romantics: John Keats (MYR JK). 7 vols. Gen. Ed., Donald H. Reiman. New York: Garland Press, 1985–88.
Volume 1: Poems (1817): A Facsimile of Richard Woodhouse's Annotated Copy in the Huntington Library. Ed. Jack Stillinger (1985).
Volume 2: Endymion: A Facsimile of the Revised Holograph Manuscript. Ed. Jack Stillinger (1985).
Volume 3: Endymion (1818): A Facsimile of Richard Woodhouse's Annotated Copy in the Berg Collection. Ed. Jack Stillinger (1985).
Volume 4: Poems, Transcripts, Letters, Etc. Facsimiles of Richard Woodhouse's Scrapbook Materials in the Pierpont Morgan Library. Ed. Jack Stillinger (1985).
Volume 5: Manuscript Poems in the British Library: Facsimiles of the "Hyperion" Holograph and George Keats's Notebook of Holographs and Transcripts. Ed. Jack Stillinger (1988).
Volume 6: The Woodhouse Poetry Transcripts at Harvard. A Facsimile of the W² Notebook, with Description and Contents of the W¹ Notebook. Ed. Jack Stillinger (1988).
Volume 7: The Charles Brown Poetry Transcripts at Harvard. Facsimiles including the Fair Copy of "Otho the Great." Ed. Jack Stillinger (1988).
John Keats: Poetry Manuscripts at Harvard: A Facsimile Edition (JKPMH). Ed. Jack Stillinger. Cambridge: Harvard University Press, 1990.

II. PUBLICATIONS AND EDITIONS OF KEATS'S POETRY AND LETTERS

Publications during Keats's lifetime:

Poems (1817). London: C. & J. Ollier, 1817. (Facsimile ed. Jonathan Wordsworth. Oxford: Woodstock Books, 1989).
Endymion (1818). London: Taylor and Hessey, 1818. (Facsimile ed. Jonathan Wordsworth. Oxford: Woodstock Books, 1991).
Lamia, Isabella, The Eve of St. Agnes, and Other Poems (1820). London: Taylor and Hessey, 1820. (Facsimile ed. Jonathan Wordsworth. Oxford: Woodstock Books, 1990).

Collected Editions, Critical Editions and Textual Studies:

The Poetical Works of Coleridge, Shelley, and Keats. Paris: G. and W. Galignani, 1829.
Life, Letters, and Literary Remains of John Keats. Ed. Richard Monckton Milnes. 2 vols. London: Edward Moxon, 1848.
Another Version of Keats's "Hyperion." Ed. Richard Monckton Milnes. Miscellanies of the Philobiblon Society 3 (1856–57).
The Poetical Works of John Keats. Ed. Lord Houghton (R. M. Milnes). London: Edward Moxon, 1876.
The Letters of John Keats to Fanny Brawne. Ed. Harry Buxton Froman. London: Reeves and Turner, 1878.
The Poetical Works and Other Writings of John Keats. Ed. Harry Buxton Forman. 4 vols. London: Reeves and Turner, 1883.
The Poetical Works of John Keats Given from His Own Editions and Other Authentic Sources and Collated with Many Manuscripts. Ed. Harry Buxton Forman. London: Reeves and Turner, 1884. 6th ed. 1898.
Letters of John Keats to his Family and Friends. Ed. Sidney Colvin. London and New York: Macmillan, 1891.
The Complete Works of John Keats. Ed. Harry Buxton Forman. 5 vols. Glasgow: Gowers & Gray, 1901.
The Poems of John Keats. Ed. Ernest de Selincourt. London: Methuen, 1905.
Poetical Works of John Keats. Oxford Standard Authors Edition. Ed. H. B. Forman. Oxford: Oxford University Press, 1906.
John Keats's Antomical and Physiological Note Book. Printed from the Holograph in the Keats Museum, Hamptead. Ed. Maurice Buxton Forman. Oxford: Oxford University Press, 1934.
The Poetical Works and Other Writings of John Keats. The Hampstead Keats. Ed. H. Buxton Forman; rev. Maurice Buxton Forman. 8 Volumes. New York: Charles Scribner's Sons, 1938–39. Rpt. New York: Phaeton Press, 1970.

The Keats Circle: Letters and Papers 1816–1878. Ed. Hyder Edward Rollins. 2 vols. Cambridge: Harvard University Press, 1948.
The Letters of John Keats. Ed. Maurice Buxton Forman. 4th ed. London, New York: Oxford University Press, 1952.
The Letters of John Keats, 1814–1821. Ed. Hyder E. Rollins. 2 vols. Cambridge: Harvard University Press, 1958.
Poetical Works of John Keats. Ed. H. W. Garrod. 2nd ed. Oxford: Oxford University Press, 1958.
"Richard Woodhouse's Interleaved and Annotated Copy of Keats's *Poems* (1817)." Stuart M. Sperry, Jr. *Literary Monographs* 1 (Madison, 1967): 101–64; 308–11.
John Keats. Poems of 1820 and The Fall of Hyperion. Ed. D. G. Gillham. London: Collins Publishers, 1969.
The Poems of Keats. Ed. Miriam Allott. London: Longman, 1970.
The Letters of John Keats.. Ed. Robert Gittings. Oxford: Oxford University Press, 1970.
John Keats: The Complete Poems. Ed. John Barnard. Harmondsworth: Penguin, 1973.
The Texts of Keats's Poems. Jack Stillinger. Cambridge: Harvard University Press, 1974.
The Poems of John Keats. Ed. Jack Stillinger. Cambridge: Harvard University Press, 1978.
Keats's Endymion: A Critical Edition. Ed. Stephen T. Steinhoff. Troy, NY: The Whitston Publishing Company, 1987.
John Keats. Ed. Elizabeth Cook. New York and Oxford: Oxford University Press, 1990.
Keats's Paradise Lost. Beth Lau. Gainesville: University of Florida Press, 1998.
Selected Letters of John Keats. Rev. ed.: based on the texts of Hyder Edward Rollins. Ed. Grant F. Scott. Cambridge: Harvard University Press, 2002.

III. BIBLIOGRAPHIES AND REFERENCE WORKS

Ford, George H. *Keats and the Victorians: A Study of His Influence and Rise to Fame 1821–1895.* New Haven: Yale University Press, 1944.
Keats-Shelley Journal Bibliography. The bibliography was begun in 1952 and covers back to July 1950. The bibliographies from July 1950 to June 1962 are reprinted in *Keats, Shelley, Byron, Hunt and their Circles.* Ed. D. B. Green and E. G. Wilson. Lincoln: University of Nebraska Press, 1964. The bibliographies covering July 1962 to December 1974 are reprinted in *Keats, Shelley, Byron, Hunt and their Circles.* Ed. R. A. Harley. Lincoln: University of Nebraska Press, 1978. See also the Romantic Circles Bibliography, edited by Kyle Grimes: www.rc.umd.edu/reference/bibliography/index.html.
MacGillivray, J. R. *Keats: A Bibliography and Reference Guide with an Essay on Keats's Reputation.* Toronto: University of Toronto Press, 1949.
Keats: The Critical Heritage. Ed. G. M. Matthews. New York: Barnes and Noble, 1971.
The Romantics Reviewed: Contemporary Reviews of British Romantic Writers. Ed. Donald Reiman. Part C: *Shelley, Keats, and London Radical Writers.* New York and London: Garland Press, 1972.
A Concordance to the Poems of John Keats. Ed. Michael G. Becker, Robert J. Dilligan, and Todd K. Bender. New York: Garland Publishing, 1981.
Stillinger, Jack. "John Keats." *The English Romantic Poets: A Review of Research and Criticism,* 4th ed. Ed. Frank Jordan. New York: Modern Language Association, 1985, 665–718.
Pollard, David, ed. *A KWIC Concordance to the Letters of John Keats.* East Sussex: Geraldson Imprints, 1989.
Evert, Walter H., and Jack W. Rhodes. *Approaches to Teaching Keats's Poetry.* New York: Modern Language Association, 1991.
Kucich, Greg. "John Keats" *Literature of the Romantic Period: A Bibliographic Guide.* Ed. Michael O'Neill. Oxford: Clarendon Press, 1998. pp. 143–66.

IV. BIOGRAPHICAL SOURCES AND BIOGRAPHIES

Hunt, Leigh. *Lord Byron and Some of His Contemporaries; with Recollections of the Author's Life, and of His Visit to Italy.* London: Henry Colburn, 1828.
Milnes, Richard Monckton. *Life, Letters, and Literary Remains of John Keats.* 2 vols. London: Edward Moxon, 1848.
Hunt, Leigh. *Autobiography.* London: Smith, Elder, 1850.
Clarke, Charles and Mary Cowden Clarke. *Recollections of Writers.* London: Low, Marston, Searle & Rivington; New York: Charles Scribner's Sons, 1878.
Life and Letters of Joseph Severn. Ed. William Sharp. London: Sampson Low, Marston & Co., 1892.
Colvin, Sidney. *John Keats: His Life and Poetry His Friends Critics and After-Fame.* London: Macmillan, 1917.
Lowell, Amy. *John Keats.* 2 vols. Boston: Houghton Mifflin, 1925.
The Keats Circle: Letters and Papers 1816–1878. Ed. Hyder Edward Rollins. Cambridge: Harvard University Press, 1948.
More Letters and Poems of The Keats Circle. Ed. Hyder Edward Rollins. Cambridge: Harvard University Press, 1955.
The Diary of Benjamin Robert Haydon. Ed. Willard Bissell Pope. 5 vols. Cambridge: Harvard University Press, 1960–63.
Bate, Walter Jackson. *John Keats.* Cambridge: Harvard University Press, 1963.
Ward, Aileen. *John Keats: The Making of a Poet.* New York: Viking, 1963.
The Letters of Charles Armitage Brown. Ed. Jack Stillinger. Cambridge: Harvard University Press, 1966.
Bush, Douglas. *John Keats: His Life and Writings.* New York: Collier, 1966.

Gittings, Robert. *John Keats*. London: Heinemann, 1968.
Marquess, William Henry. *Lives of the Poet: The First Century of Keats Biography*. University Park: Pennsylvania State University Press, 1985.
Coote, Stephen. *John Keats, A Life*. London: Hodder, 1995.
Motion, Andrew. *Keats*. New York: Farrar, Straus and Giroux, 1997.
Joseph Severn: Letters and Memoirs. Ed. Grant F. Scott. Burlington, VT: Ashgate, 2005.

V. CRITICAL STUDIES

• indicates works included or excerpted in this Norton Critical Edition

Aske, Martin. *Keats and Hellenism: An Essay*. Cambridge: Cambridge University Press, 1985.
Barnard, John. *John Keats*. Cambridge: Cambridge University Press, 1987.
———. "Keats, Reynolds and the 'Old Poets.'" *Proceedings of the British Academy* (1989): 181–200.
Bayley, John. "Keats and Reality." *Proceedings of the British Academy* (1962): 91–125.
• Bennett, Andrew. *Keats, Narrative and Audience: The Posthumous Life of Writing*. Cambridge: Cambridge University Press, 1994.
Bewell, Alan. "The Political Implication of Keats's Classicist Aesthetic." *Studies in Romanticism* 25 (1986): 221–30.
———. "Keats's 'Realm of Flora.'" *New Romanticisms: Theory and Critical Practice*. Ed. David L. Clark and Donald C. Goellnicht. Toronto: University of Toronto Press, 1995, pp. 71–100.
• ———. *Romanticism and Colonial Disease*. Baltimore: The Johns Hopkins University Press, 1999.
Bloom, Harold. "Keats and the Embarrassments of Poetic Tradition." *The Ringers in the Tower: Studies in Romantic Tradition*. Chicago: University of Chicago Press, 1971, pp. 71–98.
———. *The Visionary Company*. New York: Doubleday, 1961.
Bostetter, Edward E. "Keats." *The Romantic Ventriloquists*. 1963; rpt. Seattle: University of Washington Press, 1975, pp. 136–80.
Brooks, Cleanth. "Keats's Sylvan Historian: History Without Footnotes" (1944); *The Well Wrought Urn: Studies in the Structure of Poetry*. 1947; rpt. New York: Harcourt Brace Jovanovich, 1975, pp. 151–66.
Bromwich, David. "Keats." *Hazlitt: The Mind of a Critic*. New York: Oxford University Press, 1983, pp. 362–401.
———. "Keats's Radicalism." *Studies in Romanticism* 25 (1986): 197–210.
• Chandler, James. *England in 1819: The Politics of Literary Culture and the Case of Romantic Historicism*. Chicago: University of Chicago Press, 1998.
Clark, David L. and Donald C. Goellnicht (eds.). *New Romanticisms: Theory and Critical Practice*. Toronto: University of Toronto Press, 1995.
• Cox, Jeffrey N. *Poetry and Politics in the Cockney School: Keats, Shelley, Hunt and Their Circle*. Cambridge: Cambridge University Press, 1998.
———. "Lamia, Isabella and The Eve of St. Agnes." In *Cambridge Companion to Keats*. Ed. Susan Wolfson. Cambridge: Cambridge University Press, 2001, pp. 53–68.
Curran, Stuart. *Poetic Form and British Romanticism*. New York: Oxford University Press, 1986.
de Almeida, Hermione. *Romantic Medicine and John Keats*. New York: Oxford University Press, 1991.
———, ed. *Critical Essays on John Keats*. Boston: C. K. Hall, 1990.
• de Man, Paul. "Introduction: The Negative Road." *John Keats: Selected Poetry*. New York: New American Library, 1966, pp. ix–xxxvi.
Dickstein, Morris. *Keats and His Poetry: A Study in Development*. Chicago: University of Chicago Press, 1971.
———. "Keats and Politics," *Studies in Romanticism* 25 (1986): 175–81.
Ende, Stuart. *Keats and the Sublime*. New Haven: Yale University Press, 1976.
Evert, Walter. *Aesthetic and Myth in the Poetry of Keats*. Princeton: Princeton University Press, 1965.
Finney, Claude. *The Evolution of Keats's Poetry*. 2 Volumes. Cambridge: Harvard University Press, 1936.
• Fraistat, Neil. *The Poem and the Book*. Chapel Hill: University of North Carolina Press, 1985.
Fry, P. Paul. "History, Existence and 'To Autumn.'" *Studies in Romanticism* 25 (1986): 211–19.
Gallant, Christine. *Keats and Romantic Celticism*. Basingstoke: Palgrave Macmillan, 2005.
Gittings, Robert. *The Living Year*. London: Heineman, 1954.
———. *The Mask of Keats*. Cambridge: Harvard University Press, 1956.
Goellnicht, Donald C. *The Poet-Physician: Keats and Medical Science*. Pittsburgh: University of Pittsburgh Press, 1984.
Hartman, Geoffrey. "Poem and Ideology: A Study of Keats's 'To Autumn.'" *The Fate of Reading*. Chicago: University of Chicago Press, 1975, pp. 57–73.
———. "Spectral Symbolism and Authorial Self in Keats's *Hyperion*." *The Fate of Reading*. Chicago: University of Chicago Press, 1975, pp. 124–46.
Hirst, Wolf Z. *John Keats*. Boston: Twayne, 1981.
• Homans, Margaret. "Keats Reading Women, Women Reading Keats." *Studies in Romanticism* 29 (1990): 341–70.
Jack, Ian. *Keats and the Mirror of Art*. Oxford: Oxford University Press, 1967.
Jones, Elizabeth. "Keats in the Suburbs." *KSJ* 45 (1996): 23–43.
———. "Writing for the Market': Keats's Odes as Commodities." *Studies in Romanticism* 34 (Fall 1995): 343–64.
Jones, John. *John Keats's Dream of Truth*. London: Chatto and Windus, 1969.

Kandl, John. "Private Lyrics in the Public Sphere: Leigh Hunt's *Examiner* and the Construction of a Public 'John Keats.'" *KSJ* 44 (1995): 84–101.

Keach, William. "Cockney Couplets: Keats and the Politics of Style." *Studies in Romanticism* 24 (1986): 182–96.

Kelley, Theresa M. "Poetics and the Politics of Reception: Keats's 'La Belle Dame Sans Merci.'" *ELH* 54 (1987): 333–62.

Kucich, Greg. *Keats, Shelley, and Romantic Spenserianism.* University Park: Pennsylvania State University Press, 1991.

———. "The Poetry of Mind in Keats's Letters." *Style* 21 (1987): 76–94.

———. "Keats in Transition: The Bicentenary and Its Provocations." *Romanticism* 2 (1996): 1–8.

Lau, Beth. *Keats's Reading of the Romantic Poets.* Ann Arbor: University of Michigan Press, 1991.

———. "Protest, 'Nativism,' and Impersonation in the Works of Chatterton and Keats." *Studies in Romanticism* 42 (Winter 2003): 519–39.

Levinson, Marjorie. "The Dependent Fragment: 'Hyperion' and 'The Fall of Hyperion.'" *The Romantic Fragment Poem: A Critique of a Form.* Chapel Hill: University of North Carolina Press, 1986, pp. 167–87.

• ———. *Keats's Life of Allegory: The Origins of a Style.* New York: Basil Blackwell, 1988.

Luke, David. "Keats's Letters: Fragments of an Aesthetic of Fragments." *Genre* 2 (1978): 209–226.

McGann, Jerome J. "Keats and the Historical Method in Literary Criticism" (1979). *The Beauty of Inflections: Literary Investigations in Historical Method & Theory.* Oxford: Clarendon Press, 1985, pp. 9-65.

Mellor, Anne K. "Keats and the Vale of Soul-Making." *English Romantic Irony.* Cambridge: Harvard University Press, 1980, pp. 77–108.

———. *Romanticism & Gender.* New York: Routledge, 1992, pp. 171–86.

Mitchell, Thomas. "Keats's 'Outlawry' in 'Robin Hood.'" *SEL* 34 (1994): 753–69.

Morton, Timothy. *The Poetics of Spice: Romantic Consumerism and the Exotic.* Cambridge: Cambridge University Press, 2000, pp. 148–70.

Muir, Kenneth, ed. *John Keats. A Reassessment.* Liverpool: Liverpool University Press, 1958.

Murray, John Middleton. *Studies in Keats.* Oxford: Oxford University Press, 1930.

O'Rourke, James, ed. "'Ode on a Grecian Urn': Hypercanonicity and Pedagogy." Romantic Circles Praxis Series (October 2003). romantic.arhu.umd.edu/praxis/grecianurn/

Perkins, David. *The Quest for Permanence: The Symbolism of Wordsworth, Shelley, and Keats.* Cambridge: Harvard University Press, 1959.

Pettet, E. C. *On the Poetry of Keats.* Cambridge: Cambridge University Press, 1957.

Rajan, Tilottama. *Dark Interpreter: The Discourse of Romanticism.* Ithaca: Cornell University Press, 1980.

Richardson, Alan. *British Romanticism and the Science of the Mind.* Cambridge: Cambridge University Press, 2001.

Ricks, Christopher. *Keats and Embarrassment.* London: Oxford University Press, 1976.

Ridley, M. R. *Keats's Craftmanship.* Oxford: Oxford University Press, 1933.

Robinson, Jeffrey C. *Reception and Poetics in Keats: "My Ended Poet."* Basingstoke: Palgrave Macmillan, 1998.

• Roe, Nicholas. *John Keats and the Culture of Dissent.* Oxford: Clarendon Press, 1997.

——— ed. *Keats and History.* Cambridge: Cambridge University Press, 1994. Essays by Susan Wolfson, Martin Aske, John Barnard, Daniel Watkins, Kelvin Everest, Terence Hoagwood, Michael O'Neill, Vincent Newey, Nicholas Roe, Theresa Kelley, Greg Kucich, Nicola Trott, John Kerrigan.

Ryan, Robert. *Keats, the Religious Sense.* Princeton: Princeton University Press, 1976.

——— and Ronald Sharp, eds. *The Persistence of Poetry: Bicentennial Essays on Keats.* Amherst: University of Massachusetts Press, 1998. Essays by Jack Stillinger, M. H. Abrams, Walter Jackson Bate, Aileen Ward, Ronald Sharp, E. Boland, Susan Wolfson, Donald H. Reiman, Elizabeth Jones, Debbie Lee, Terence Hoagwood, Hermione de Almeida, David Bromwich, George Steiner, P. Levine.

Rzepka, Charles J. *The Self as Mind: Vision and Identity in Wordsworth, Coleridge, Keats.* Cambridge: Harvard University Press, 1986.

———. "'Cortez—or Balboa, or Somebody Like That': Form, Fact, and Forgetting in Keats's 'Chapman's Homer' Sonnet." *KSJ* 51 (2002): 35–75.

Scott, Grant F. *The Sculpted Word: Keats, Ekphrasis, and the Visual Arts.* Hanover: University Press of New Hampshire, 1994.

• ———. "Introduction." *Selected Letters of John Keats.* Ed. Grant F. Scott. Cambridge: Harvard University Press, 2002, pp. xxi–xxxiii.

Sharp, Ronald. *Keats, Skepticism, and the Religion of Beauty.* Athens: University of Georgia Press, 1979.

Slote, Bernice. *Keats and the Dramatic Principle.* Lincoln: University of Nebraska Press, 1958.

• Sperry, Stuart M. *Keats the Poet.* Princeton: Princeton University Press, 1973.

Spurgeon, Caroline. *Keats's Shakespeare.* Oxford: Oxford University Press, 1924.

Stewart, Garrett. "*Lamia* and the Language of Metamorphosis." *Studies in Romanticism* 15 (1976): 3–41.

• Stillinger, Jack. *"The Hoodwinking of Madeline" and Other Essays on Keats's Poems.* Urbana: University of Illinois Press, 1971.

———. "Keats and Coleridge." *Coleridge, Keats, and the Imagination: Romanticism and Adam's Dream.* Ed. Robert J. Darth and John Mahoney. Columbia: University of Missouri Press, 1990, pp. 7–28.

———. "Keats and His Helpers: The Multiple Authorship of *Isabella.*" *Multiple Authorship and the Myth of Solitary Genius.* New York: Oxford University Press, 1991, pp. 25–49.

———. "Multiple Readers, Multiple Texts, Multiple Keats." *Journal of English and Germanic Philology* 96 (1997): 545–66.

———. *Reading "The Eve of St. Agnes": The Multiples of Complex Literary Transaction.* New York: Oxford University Press, 1999.

———. *Romantic Complexity: Keats, Coleridge, and Wordsworth.* Chicago: University of Illinois Press, 2006.

Swann, Karen. "Harassing the Muse." *Romanticism and Feminism.* Ed. Anne K. Mellor. Bloomington: Indiana University Press, 1988, pp. 81–92.

———. "The Strange Time of Reading." *European Romantic Review* 9 (1998): 275–82.

Thorpe, Clarence Dewitt. *The Mind of John Keats.* Oxford: Oxford University Press, 1926.

Trilling, Lionel. "Introduction" to *The Selected Letters* (1951); rpt. "The Poet as Hero: Keats in His Letters," *The Opposing Self.* New York: Viking Press, 1955, pp. 3–49.

———. "The Fate of Pleasure." *Beyond Culture.* London: Secker and Warburg, 1955, pp. 65–89.

Vendler, Helen. *The Odes of John Keats.* Cambridge: Harvard University Press, 1983.

———. *Coming of Age as a Poet: Milton, Keats, Eliot, Plath.* Cambridge: Harvard University Press, 2003.

Waldoff, Leon. *Keats and the Silent Work of Imagination.* Urbana: University of Illinois Press, 1985.

Walker, Carol Kyros. *Walking North With Keats.* New Haven: Yale University Press, 1992.

Wang, Orrin. "Coming Attractions: 'Lamia' and Cinematic Sensation." *Studies in Romanticism* 42 (Winter 2003): 461–500.

Wasserman, Earl R. *The Finer Tone: Keats' Major Poems.* Baltimore: Johns Hopkins University Press, 1953.

Watkins, Daniel P. *Keats's Poetry and the Politics of the Imagination.* Madison: Fairleigh Dickinson University Press, 1989.

Whale, John. *John Keats.* Basingstoke: Palgrave Macmillan, 2005.

Wolfson, Susan J. *Formal Charges: The Shaping of Poetry in British Romanticism.* Stanford: Stanford University Press, 1997.

———. "Keats and the Manhood of the Poet." *European Romantic Review* 6 (1995): 1–37.

———. "Keats the Letter-Writer: Epistolary Poetics." *Romanticism Past and Present* 6 (1982): 43–61.

———. *The Questioning Presence: Wordsworth, Keats, and the Interrogative Mode in Romantic Poetry.* Ithaca: Cornell University Press, 1986.

———, ed. *Keats and Politics: A Forum. Studies in Romanticism* 25 (1986).

———, ed. *The Cambridge Companion to Keats.* Cambridge: Cambridge University Press, 2001.

Index

Keats's poems are listed by title and first line. Keats's letters are listed by recipient and date. Reviews are listed by author and/or journal in which they appeared. Other literary pieces are listed by author and title. The criticism is listed in the table of contents.